Created Equal

Created Equal

A History of the United States

THIRD EDITION

Jacqueline Jones
Brandeis University

Peter H. Wood
Duke University

Thomas Borstelmann
University of Nebraska

Elaine Tyler May
University of Minnesota

Vicki L. Ruiz
University of California, Irvine

PEARSON
Longman

New York San Francisco Boston
London Toronto Sydney Tokyo Singapore Madrid
Mexico City Munich Paris Cape Town Hong Kong Montreal

Executive Editor: Michael Boezi
Assistant Development Manager: David B. Kear
Senior Development Editor: Marion B. Castellucci
Executive Marketing Manager: Sue Westmoreland
Media Editor: Melissa Edwards
Supplements Editor: Brian Belardi
Editorial Assistant: Vanessa Gennarelli
Director of Market Research: Laura Coaty
Production Manager: Ellen MacElree
Project Coordination, Electronic Page Makeup, Interior Design and Cartography: Electronic Publishing Services Inc., NYC
Cover Designer/Manager: Wendy Ann Fredericks
Photo Researcher: Photosearch, Inc.
Senior Manufacturing Buyer: Alfred C. Dorsey
Printer and Binder: Quebecor World/Dubuque
Cover Printer: Coral Graphics
Cover/Frontispiece Photo: Mexicans at the U.S. immigration station, El Paso, Texas. Courtesy of the Library of Congress.

Credits for literary selections, selected maps and figures, and timeline photos appear on pages C-1–C-3.

Library of Congress Cataloging-in-Publication Data

Created equal : a history of the United States / Jacqueline Jones . . . [et al.]. — 3rd ed.
   v. cm.
  Includes bibliographical references and index.
  ISBN-13: 978-0-205-58581-6 (complete ed.)
  ISBN-10: 0-205-58581-7 (complete ed.)
  1. United States—History. 2. United States—Social conditions. 3. United States—Politics and government.
4. Pluralism (Social sciences)—United States—History. 5. Minorities—United States—History. 6. Pluralism
(Social sciences)—United States—History—Sources. 7. Minorities—United States—History—Sources.
  E178.C86 2009
  973—dc22

           2007045111

Please visit us at www.ablongman.com

ISBN 13: 978-0-205-58581-6 (Complete Edition)
ISBN 10:   0-205-58581-7 (Complete Edition)
ISBN 13: 978-0-205-58583-0 (Volume I)
ISBN 10:   0-205-58583-3 (Volume I)
ISBN 13: 978-0-205-58584-7 (Volume II)
ISBN 10:   0-205-58584-1 (Volume II)

1 2 3 4 5 6 7 8 9 10—QWD—11 10 09 08

To our own teachers, who helped set us on the historian's path, and to our students, who help keep us there. You have touched our intellects, our hearts, and our lives.

A nuestros propios maestros, quienes nos ayudaron a seguir en el sendero de historiador, y a nuestros estudiantes que ayudan a mantenernos allí. Usted han tocado nuestros intelectos, nuestros corazónes, y nuestras vidas.

Brief Contents

Detailed Contents

Maps

Tables

Interpreting History

The Wider World

Envisioning History

> *"I have a dream that one day this nation will rise up and live out the meaning of its creed: 'We hold these truths to be self-evident: That all men are created equal'. . . ."*
>
> —*Dr. Martin Luther King, Jr., Washington, DC, August 28, 1963*

Since the First Edition of *Created Equal* was published in 2002, we have been overwhelmed by the enthusiastic response to the book and its theme—that the United States is a country with a history of diverse racial, ethnic, regional, economic, and political groups made up of immigrants and their descendants, African Americans, native-born peoples, women and men, people of different ages and sexual orientation, and the powerful and the oppressed, all staking their claims on an American identity. We have gratefully listened when users of the book suggested ways to make improvements; this Third Edition is based on the cumulative suggestions of more than 170 reviewers who helped us find ways to make the book a better fit for their own classrooms.

We began the preface to the previous edition by noting that one of our teammates, Professor Vicki L. Ruiz, took office in 2005 as the President of the Organization of American Historians (OAH). She became the first Latino American scholar to hold that one-year, elected leadership position, and she did an impressive job. In this preface for the Third Edition, we are pleased to announce that another *Created Equal* author, Professor Elaine Tyler May, will become the President of the OAH in 2009. We celebrate this major honor bestowed upon two members of our team. These laurels are a tribute to their outstanding accomplishments as historians, and to the progress of the OAH in integrating women fully into all ranks of the historical profession. This progress reminds us why we wrote *Created Equal*, and why we chose to highlight the rich diversity of the American people.

Centuries ago, when the American Continental Congress approved the Declaration of Independence with its preamble's lofty claim that "all men are created equal," not everyone was impressed or inspired. The English philosopher Jeremy Bentham immediately made fun of the "contemptible and extravagant" document. The preamble, he protested, "would be too ridiculous to deserve any notice." The clever philosopher could hardly have been more wrong. Over the centuries since its publication, the powerful phrases of the Declaration have inspired people in the United States and around the world. After all, it was revolutionary for its authors to assert, as a "self-evident" and undeniable truth, that all humans are "created equal; that they are endowed by their Creator with certain unalienable rights; that among these are life, liberty, and the pursuit of happiness." Granted, the Founding Fathers conceived of the new nation as a political community for white men of property. But for generations, diverse racial and ethnic groups, as well as people of different ages, genders, or sexual orientation, have stressed that *all* Americans are endowed with basic individual rights that cannot be taken away. Repeatedly, they have cited the Declaration in their struggles to achieve a more inclusive definition of American citizenship.

Thus *Created Equal* illuminates the story of various groups of men and women, rich and poor, all "created equal" in their common humanity, claiming a social and political identity for themselves as Americans. In tracing their worlds, *Created Equal* also explores diverse forms of engagement—political, diplomatic, cultural, military, and economic—between the United States and other countries and cultures over time.

What's New in the Third Edition

Our aim, in crafting the Third Edition, is to provide students with a solid understanding of the individuals and forces that have shaped our history, both within the nation's changing borders and also through America's complex and crucial relations with the rest of the world. In doing so, we are mindful that history is never static, and that we must be responsive to shifting classroom needs. Therefore, we have drawn on almost a decade of creative feedback about the first and second editions from colleagues, instructors, and students who have used the book, as well as our own classroom experiences. Our primary goal is to improve each reader's experience and to deepen student understanding of the American journey. To that end, this edition introduces a number of significant additions and substantive changes.

Two Unifying Themes Focus the Narrative

In preparing the Third Edition, we have elected to focus on two particularly significant themes. Both themes are durable and many-sided. Emphasizing them has allowed us to bring continuity and clarity to the rich American story. Throughout the text, we have included new material related to both of these themes:

■ **Diversity and inclusion.** In considering the theme of diversity, we acknowledge the formation of social and political identity as a central element of the American story. We examine how individual Americans have understood and identified themselves by gender, religion, region, income, race, and ethnicity, among other factors, while using the ideal of "created equal" to push for inclusion in the American nation. American Indians, African Americans, Latinos, Asian immigrants, members of distinct religions and social classes, women of every background—all of these people have played major roles in defining what it means to be an American. At the same time, individuals' identities are by no means fixed or static. For example, Chapter 20 now opens with a brief profile of W. E. B. DuBois, who was born in Massachusetts in 1869. In 1895, DuBois became the first African American to receive a history doctoral degree from Harvard University. Over his long career, DuBois defied categorization, working as a sociologist, a journalist, an editor, a poet, and a fervent reformer. Known as a brilliant and productive scholar, he also embraced the role of activist on behalf of people of color, not only in the United States but also around the world. In his writings and speeches, DuBois repeatedly expressed the aspirations of all races "for equality, freedom and democracy."

■ **Globalization.** By heralding universal, unalienable rights, the Founding Fathers implied that the principles expressed in the Declaration possessed a global reach. For centuries, America has not existed in isolation from the rest of the world. Since the earliest days of colonial settlement, Americans have traded goods, cultural practices, and ideas with peoples outside their borders. As an immigrant nation, the United States has developed ties of human kinship with cultures in all parts of the world. In the twenty-first century, our linkage to the entire globe is more evident than ever. Today, many of the foods we eat, the clothes we wear, and the cars we drive originate abroad. Whether considering matters of commerce, migration, religion, security, health, or the environment, citizens of the United States regularly encounter broad forces that transcend national boundaries. The dilemmas of globalization are not new, but they now confront us in unprecedented ways. As Americans, we are now more than ever obliged to examine and discuss the role of our country—past, present, and future—in the wider world.

These themes serve as the lenses through which we view the traditional narrative framework of American history. Readers of *Created Equal* will learn about the major political developments that shaped the country's past, as well as the roles of diverse groups in initiating and reacting to those developments. Chapter 13, for example, which focuses on the 1850s, includes a detailed account of the effects of the slavery crisis on Congress and the political party system, as well as a discussion of shifting group identities affecting Indians, Latinos, northern women, and enslaved and free blacks. Chapter 18, on the 1890s, covers the rise of the Populist party and stirrings of American imperialism, as well as a discussion of barriers to a U.S. workers' political party and challenges to traditional gender roles. Thus, *Created Equal* builds on the basic history that forms the foundation of most major textbooks and offers a lively and comprehensive look at the past by including the stories of many different kinds of Americans and by emphasizing the nation's global connections.

New Features Support the Themes and Broaden the Use of Historical Sources

To provide students with pertinent, in-depth treatment of global issues and show them how objects and visuals can tell us about the past, we have introduced two new features:

■ **"The Wider World"** is a new feature that strengthens the globalization theme and keeps it in the foreground throughout the book. "The Wider World" appears in each chapter, introducing a person, a graph, a table, or an image that helps students to place that era of American history within its international context. "The Wider World" provides an informative and helpful exercise in expansive historical thinking. Repeatedly, the feature enables readers to compare specific aspects of American society, culture, politics, and economy with foreign counterparts. Among "The Wider World" features are charts and graphs juxtaposing American statistics on a variety of subjects with comparable data regarding other countries. Topics include equality in post-Revolutionary America (Chapter 9), when women got the right to vote in various countries (Chapter 15), the number of immigrants who later went back home (Chapter 19) and the use of the death penalty worldwide (Chapter 30). Chapters 7 and 8 introduce several remarkable and contrasting world travelers from the eighteenth century: an African American couple named Tom and Sally Peters, and the unique global hiker, John Ledyard. This feature reminds readers that the country's complex relationship with foreign places and cultures is not simply a recent development. It has been an enduring theme throughout American history, and at every stage we can learn more fully about our past by considering its international dimensions. Each "The Wider World" feature concludes with questions that ask students to think critically about the relationship of the local and the global.

■ **"Envisioning History"** is a new feature that draws upon the visual sophistication of today's students, alerting them to the many types of sources that historians rely upon, including engravings, maps, banners, pieces of fine art, public monuments and enduring material objects. With the growth of underwater archaeology, even sunken ships are yielding valuable evidence to historians. In Chapter 3, for example, we describe how archaeologists on the Texas coast recently salvaged the submerged remains of a small vessel used by the French explorer La Salle in the 1680s. Exploring paintings, photographs, and political cartoons can also allow us to "envision" American history in new ways. In Chapter 10, a painting depicts a federal agent greeting a group of Creek Indians in the early nineteenth century. The agent looks approvingly at signs of the Indians' willingness to adopt elements of European American agriculture, such as plowing fields and raising livestock. In Chapter 21, a photo of immigrants selling tamales and ice cream in a Los Angeles suburb illustrates the ways in which newcomers served, and altered, the changing tastes and desires of middle-class consumers; while in Chapter 25 a picture of a family fallout shelter suggests the impact of the atomic age on domestic life. A political cartoon satirizing the complicated American voting system is used in Chapter 29 to prompt consideration of the confusion and problems that surrounded the contested presidential election of 2000. Each "Envisioning History" feature concludes with questions that help students analyze the artifact or graphic.

Pedagogical Features Help Students Master American History

Several new features enhance the book's accessibility for students and provide aids to studying.

- A new **focus question at the beginning of each major section** helps students to anticipate and understand the major points of the section as they read it. Taken together, a chapter's focus questions provide guidance for reviewing the chapter's important content.

- A new **chronology** of the period's most important events appears at the end of each chapter, helping students put historical developments in the proper sequence, thus providing a framework for understanding the broader themes of the period.

- Each presidential election is summarized in a new **election table,** providing students with a framework for understanding political developments over the years.

- New **For Review** questions at the end of each chapter help students to grasp major ideas and enter into discussion about larger issues. They encourage students to make connections among the different sections of the chapter and to other periods in American history.

Substantive Changes, Rewriting, and a New Design Improve the Text

Our retooling did not stop with new features. In every chapter, we took the opportunity to make **adjustments, small and large, in content, organization, and presentation, making sure that the standard topics of American history are covered well**. For many of these improvements, we took our cue from suggestions made by the many historians who reviewed the text. For instance, Chapter 4, on the "terrible transformation" to race slavery in colonial America, now contains fresh material on slavery in the North, and in Chapter 9, the discussion of the crucial Supreme Court decision, *Marbury v. Madison*, has been expanded. The last ten chapters have been particularly reworked. Of course, as each year passes, there is more to incorporate. Chapter 30 now stretches through the second election of the second President Bush. It covers the devastation caused by Hurricane Katrina in 2005, plus the midterm elections of 2006 that altered the balance of power in Congress. It deals with the extended wars in Iraq and Afghanistan. We also **sharpened the chapter introductions, rewrote sections of the text, and improved transitions within chapters, tightening and condensing** where possible.

Furthermore, we **redesigned the text** and introduced **new illustrations and maps**. An added bonus from all this work has been to **reduce the book's overall length,** making it more convenient and accessible, but no less comprehensive. Textbooks, like people, can often afford to lose a little weight these days (and use less paper), so we have tried to do our part! *Created Equal* is still hefty—American history remains a rich and expansive saga—but we hope you will agree that a shorter book is a better book, especially given the new features that appear in this new edition.

Chronological Organization

One of the challenges in writing *Created Equal* has been to emphasize the way major developments affect specific generations of Americans. Thus, the text is organized into ten parts, most of these covering a generation. Many textbooks organize discussions of immigrants, cities, the West, and foreign diplomacy (to name a few topics) into separate chapters that cover large time periods. In contrast, *Created Equal* integrates material related to a variety of topics within individual chapters. Although the text adheres to a chronological organization, it stresses coherent discussions of specific topics within that framework.

This chronological approach provides students with a richer understanding of events. Chapter 15, for example, which covers the years immediately following the Civil War, deals with Reconstruction in the South, Indian wars on the High Plains, and the rise of the women's and labor movements, stressing the relationships among all these developments. To cite another example, many texts devote a single chapter exclusively to America's post-World War II rise to global power. But this complex process spans more than two generations, so *Created Equal* integrates material related to that development in a sequence of chapters that stretch from 1945 to the present. Each of these seven chapters illustrates the effects of dramatic world developments on American social relations and domestic policy on a decade-by-decade basis. This approach reflects the way in which we lead our lives—and the way our parents and grandparents led theirs. It allows readers to appreciate the rich complexity of any particular time period and to understand that all major events occur within a social and political context that is specific and unique.

Other Special Features

To assist students and teachers alike, this book retains a number of special features from the second edition that are suitable to a variety of classrooms. They will help readers connect more readily to the American past, and they will encourage students to engage with unfamiliar and surprising aspects of American history on their own. These features include:

- **Parts.** As in previous editions, *Created Equal* consists of ten parts covering three chapters each. A two-page opening section that lays out basic themes and sketches key developments of the period introduces each part.

- **Chapter introductory vignettes.** Every chapter begins with a story that introduces the reader to groups and individuals representative of the themes developed in the chapter. In the Third Edition, we have included eight new chapter vignettes. For example, Chapter 7, covering the American Revolution, starts by sketching the war experience of families from one small village in New Hampshire: Peterborough. Chapter 19 profiles Upton Sinclair, the writer whose exposure of the meat packing industry led to food inspection laws; while Chapter 23 introduces the story of Frank Steiner, a young Jew from Vienna whose family perished in the Holocaust. Steiner managed to escape from the Nazis, going first to Shanghai, China, and then ending up in San Francisco. Chapter 27, on the 1970s, now begins with the story of Emily Howell Warner, a Coloradoan who became the nation's first female commercial airline pilot. Chapter 29, on the 1990s, introduces the increasing gap between rich and poor with a brief profile of Jack Welch, whose annual compensation as CEO of General Electric reached 123 million dollars

- **"Interpreting History."** This feature consists of a primary document on a topic relevant to the chapter's themes. The "Interpreting History" feature takes many different forms—letters, sermons, court decisions, labor contracts, congressional hearings, interviews, poems, and songs. Students thus have an opportunity to analyze primary documents and to better appreciate the historian's task—reading materials critically and placing them in their larger socio-historical context. Questions at the end of each document point students toward major issues and encourage them to analyze both the rhetoric and the larger meaning of the document. The Third Edition includes four new documents through which we hear the voices of a variety of Americans. In Chapter 9, a farmer worries that the wealthy "few" will upend the legacy of the American Revolution, to the detriment of the common folk. In Chapter 11, a woman records in detail her many duties as a housekeeper of a Spanish mission in early nineteenth-century California. In Chapter 20, an individual goes to court during World War I in an effort to reestablish the U.S. citizenship that had been taken from her when she married a British citizen. And in Chapter 30, President George W. Bush lays out the principles behind the "war on terror" in a speech to West Point graduates in 2002.

- **Glossary.** Located at the back of the book, the glossary is a list of hundreds of historical terms and significant events culled from the text and defined in a sentence or two. These entries include everything from court cases (*Plessy v. Ferguson*) and pieces of legislation (Alien and Sedition Acts) to political groups (Democratic-Republicans) and cultural designations (Victorians). In addition, the glossary defines words and phrases familiar to historians but unlikely to be found in a conventional dictionary. Examples include: middle ground, "Republican Mother," yellow journalism. All the terms presented in the glossary are highlighted in **boldface type** in the chapter text.

- **Maps, charts, photos, and artifacts.** Illustrations—photographs, tables, pictures of objects from the time period, and figures—enhance the narrative. Large maps offer great geographical detail and invite students to understand and discuss the relationship between geography and history.

- **MyHistoryLab.** Icons in the margin throughout the pages of the book identify assets on the Pearson U.S. history Web site—MyHistoryLab—that relate to the chapter content and themes. The icons indicate the kind of asset—document, map, image, video, or audio—and the title of each asset. These Web asset icons are representative of the thousands of additional resources on MyHistoryLab, including an e-book version of the entire text, history-related Web sites and other sites to visit, bibliographies, source documents, interactive maps, videos, audio clips, and history-related Web sites designed to enrich students' study of U.S. history.

The Third Edition of *Created Equal* remains true to the vision that first inspired us to craft this book. Its basic framework focuses on the political events and economic structures discussed in most American history textbooks. But the work is distinctive in several ways. It demonstrates a broad geographical scope and environmental awareness, from the very beginning of the narrative. Also, the text is consistently attentive to matters of economic, social, and political power; it suggests vividly how power has been acquired, used, challenged and redistributed over time. *Created Equal* lays out and sharpens the chronology of American history, while integrating a rich variety of groups and individuals into that framework. This Third Edition tells the dramatic, evolving story of America in all its complexity—the story of a diverse people "created equal" yet struggling creatively to achieve equality.

—The Authors

Supplements for Instructors and Students

FOR QUALIFIED COLLEGE ADOPTERS

Name of Supplement	Available in Print	Available Online	Instructor or Student Supplement	Description
Instructor's Resource Center (IRC)		✓	Instructor Supplement	Web site for downloading relevant supplements. Password protected. Please contact your local Pearson representative for an access code. *www.ablongman.com/irc*
MyHistoryLab		✓	Both	With the best of Longman's multimedia solutions for history in one easy-to-use place, MyHistoryLab offers students and instructors a state-of-the art interactive instructional solution for your U.S. history survey course. Built around a complete e-book version of this text, MyHistoryLab provides numerous study aids, review materials, and activities to make the study of history an enjoyable learning experience. Icons in the e-book link directly to relevant materials in context, many of which are assignable. MyHistoryLab includes several hundred primary source documents, videos, images, and maps, all with accompanying analysis questions. It also includes a History Bookshelf with 50 of the most commonly assigned books in U.S. history courses and a History Toolkit with guided tutorials and helpful links. MyHistoryLab is flexible and easy-to-use as a supplement to a traditional lecture course or to administer as a completely online course. *www.myhistorylab.com*
MyHistoryKit for American History		✓	Both	Online package of study materials, gradable quizzes and over 1,000 primary sources organized generically by typical American history themes to support your U.S. history survey text. Access code required. *www.myhistorykit.com*
American History Study Site		✓	Both	Online package of practice tests, Web links, and flashcards organized generically by major history topics to support your U.S. history survey text. Open access. *www.longmanamericanhistory.com*
Instructor's Manual	✓	✓	Instructor Supplement	Each chapter includes a chapter overview, lecture supplements, and questions for class discussion. Text specific.
Test Bank	✓	✓	Instructor Supplement	Contains thousands of conceptual, objective, and essay questions. Text specific.

(Continued)

Name of Supplement	Available in Print	Available Online	Instructor or Student Supplement	Description
Computerized Test Bank	✓	✓	Instructor Supplement	Includes all items in the printed test bank. Questions can be edited, and tests can be printed in several different formats. Text specific.
PowerPoint Presentation		✓	Instructor Supplement	*Created Equal* contains an outline of each chapter of the text and full-color images of maps and figures. Text specific. *www.ablongman.com/irc*
Digital Transparency Masters		✓	Instructor Supplement	*Created Equal* contains full-color images from the text. Available exclusively on the Instructor's Resource Center. Text specific. *www.ablongman.com/irc*
Comprehensive American History Digital Transparency Masters		✓	Instructor Supplement	Vast collection of American history transparency masters. Available exclusively on the Instructor's Resource Center. *www.ablongman.com/irc*
Discovering American History Through Maps and Views Digital Transparency Masters		✓	Instructor Supplement	Set of 140 full-color digital transparency masters includes cartographic and pictorial maps, views, photos; urban plans and building diagrams; and works of art. Available exclusively on the Instructor's Resource Center. *www.ablongman.com/irc*
History Digital Media Archive	CD		Instructor Supplement	Contains electronic images, interactive and static maps, and video. Available on CD only.
Visual Archives of American History, Updated Edition	CD		Instructor Supplement	Contains dozens of narrated vignettes and videos as well as hundreds of photos and illustrations. Available on CD only.
Study Guide	✓		Student Supplement	Contains chapter overviews, learning objectives, identifications, mapping exercises, multiple-choice and essay questions, and critical thinking exercises. Available in two volumes. Text specific.
Vango Notes		✓	Student Supplement	Downloadable MP3 audio topic reviews. Includes major themes, key terms, practice tests, and rapid reviews. *www.vangonotes.com*
Study Card for American History	✓		Student Supplement	Distills course information down to the basics, helping students quickly master the fundamentals and prepare for exams.
Research Navigator Guide	✓	✓	Student Supplement	A book that contains an access code to EBSCO ContentSelect, *The New York Times,* and "Best of the Web."

Name of Supplement	Available in Print	Available Online	Instructor or Student Supplement	Description
Longman American History Atlas	✓		Both	100 full-color maps.
Mapping America: A Guide to Historical Geography	✓		Student Supplement	18 exercises explore the role of geography in history.
Voices of *Created Equal*	✓		Student Supplement	Two-volume collection of primary sources, organized to correspond to the table of contents of *Created Equal*.
America Through the Eyes of Its People	✓		Student Supplement	Two-volume comprehensive anthology of primary sources expertly balances social and political history and includes up-to-date narrative material.
American History Timeline	✓		Student Supplement	Gives students a chronological context to help them understand important political, social, economic, cultural, and technological events.
Sources of the African-American Past	✓		Student Supplement	This collection of primary sources covers key themes in the African-American experience.
Women and the National Experience	✓		Student Supplement	Primary source reader contains both classic and unusual documents describing the history of women in the United States.
Reading the American West	✓		Student Supplement	Primary sources in the history of the American West.
A Short Guide to Writing About History	✓		Student Supplement	Teaches students to write cogent history papers.
American History Firsthand: Working with Primary Sources	✓		Student Supplement	This two-volume collection of loose leaf reproduced primary sources exposes students to archival research.
Longman Penguin Putnam Inc. Value Packs	✓		Student Supplement	A variety of Penguin-Putnam texts are available at discounted prices when bundled with *Created Equal*. Complete list of available titles at *www.ablongman.com/penguin*.
Library of American Biography Series	✓		Student Supplement	Renowned series of biographies that focus on figures who had a significant impact on American history. Complete list at *www.ablongman.com/html/lab*.

Jacqueline Jones was born in Christiana, Delaware, a small town of 400 people in the northern part of the state. The local public school was desegregated in 1955, when she was a third grader. That event, combined with the peculiar social etiquette of relations between blacks and whites in the town, sparked her interest in American history. She attended the University of Delaware in nearby Newark and went on to graduate study at the University of Wisconsin, Madison, where she received her Ph.D. in history. Her scholarly interests have evolved over time, focusing on American labor and women's, African American, and southern history. She teaches American history at Brandeis University, where she is Harry S. Truman Professor. In 1999, she received a MacArthur Fellowship.

Dr. Jones is the author of several books, including *Soldiers of Light and Love: Northern Teachers and Georgia Blacks* (1980); *Labor of Love, Labor of Sorrow: Black Women, Work, and Family Since Slavery* (1985), which won the Bancroft Prize and was a finalist for a Pulitzer Prize; *The Dispossessed: America's Underclasses Since the Civil War* (1992); and *American Work: Four Centuries of Black and White Labor* (1998). In 2001, she published a memoir that recounts her childhood in Christiana: *Creek Walking: Growing Up in Delaware in the 1950s*. She recently completed a book titled *Savannah's Civil War*, which spans the period 1854 to 1872 and chronicles the strenuous but largely thwarted efforts of black people in lowcountry Georgia to achieve economic opportunity and full citizenship rights during and after the Civil War.

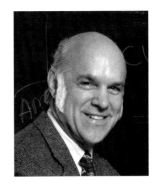

Peter H. Wood was born in St. Louis (before the famous arch was built). He recalls seeing Jackie Robinson play against the Cardinals, visiting the courthouse where the *Dred Scott* case originated, and traveling up the Mississippi to Hannibal, birthplace of Mark Twain. Summer work on the northern Great Lakes aroused his interest in Native American cultures, past and present. He studied at Harvard (B.A., 1964; Ph.D., 1972) and at Oxford, where he was a Rhodes Scholar (1964–1966). His pioneering book *Black Majority* (1974), concerning slavery in colonial South Carolina, won the Beveridge Prize of the American Historical Association. Since 1975, he has taught early American history and Native American history at Duke University. The topics of his articles range from the French explorer LaSalle to Gerald Ford's pardon of Richard Nixon. He has written a short overview of early African Americans, entitled *Strange New Land*, and he has appeared in several related films on PBS. He has published two books about the famous American painter Winslow Homer and coedited *Powhatan's Mantle: Indians in the Colonial Southeast* (revised, 2007). His demographic essay in that volume provided the first clear picture of population change in the eighteenth-century South.

Dr. Wood has served on the boards of the Highlander Center, Harvard University, Houston's Rothko Chapel, and the Institute of Early American History and Culture in Williamsburg. He is married to colonial historian Elizabeth Fenn. His varied interests include archaeology, documentary film, and growing gourds. He keeps a baseball bat used by Ted Williams beside his desk.

Thomas ("Tim") Borstelmann, the son of a university psychologist, grew up in North Carolina as the youngest child in a family deeply interested in history. His formal education came at Durham Academy, Phillips Exeter Academy in New Hampshire, Stanford University (A.B., 1980), and Duke University (Ph.D., 1990). Informally, he was educated on the basketball courts of the South, the rocky shores of New England, the streets of Dublin, Ireland, the museums of Florence, Italy, and the high-country trails of the Sierra Nevada and the Rocky Mountains. He taught history at Cornell University from 1991 to 2003, when he moved to the University of Nebraska–Lincoln to become the first E. N. and Katherine Thompson Distinguished Professor of Modern World History. Since 1988 he has been married to Lynn Borstelmann, a nurse and hospital administrator, and his highest priority for almost two decades has been serving as the primary parent for their two sons. He is an avid cyclist, runner, swimmer, and skier.

Dr. Borstelmann's first book, *Apartheid's Reluctant Uncle: The United States and Southern Africa in the Early Cold War* (1993), won the Stuart L. Bernath Book Prize of the Society for Historians of Foreign Relations. His second book, *The Cold War and the Color Line: American Race Relations in the Global Arena,* appeared in 2001. At Cornell he won a major teaching award, the Robert and Helen Appel Fellowship. He is currently working on a book about the United States and the world in the 1970s.

Elaine Tyler May grew up in the shadow of Hollywood, performing in neighborhood circuses with her friends. Her passion for American history developed in college when she spent her junior year in Japan. The year was 1968. The Vietnam War was raging, along with turmoil at home. As an American in Asia, often called on to explain her nation's actions, she yearned for a deeper understanding of America's past and its place in the world. She returned home to study history at UCLA, where she earned her B.A., M.A., and Ph.D. She has taught at Princeton and Harvard Universities and since 1978 at the University of Minnesota, where she was recently named Regents Professor. She has written four books examining the relationship between politics, public policy, and private life. Her widely acclaimed *Homeward Bound: American Families in the Cold War Era* was the first study to link the baby boom and suburbia to the politics of the Cold War. The *Chronicle of Higher Education* featured *Barren in the Promised Land: Childless Americans and the Pursuit of Happiness* as a pioneering study of the history of reproduction. *Lingua Franca* named her coedited volume *Here, There, and Everywhere: The Foreign Politics of American Popular Culture* a "Breakthrough Book."

Dr. May served as president of the American Studies Association in 1996 and as Distinguished Fulbright Professor of American History in Dublin, Ireland, in 1997. In 2007 she became president-elect of the Organization of American Historians. She is married to historian Lary May and has three children, who have inherited their parents' passion for history.

Vicki L. Ruiz is a professor of history and Chicano/Latino studies and interim Dean for the School of Humanities at the University of California, Irvine. For her, history remains a grand adventure, one that she began at the kitchen table, listening to the stories of her mother and grandmother, and continued with the help of the local bookmobile. She read constantly as she sat on the dock, catching small fish ("grunts") to be used as bait on her father's fishing boat. As she grew older, she was promoted to working with her mother, selling tickets for the *Blue Sea II.* The first in her family to receive an advanced degree, she graduated from Gulf Coast Community College and Florida State University, then went on to earn a Ph.D. in history at Stanford in 1982. She is the author of *Cannery Women, Cannery Lives* and *From Out of the Shadows: Mexican Women in 20th-Century America* (named a Choice Outstanding Academic Book of 1998 by the American Library Association). She and Virginia Sánchez Korrol have coedited *Latinas in the United States: A Historical Encyclopedia* (named a 2007 Best in Reference work by the New York Public Library). Active in student mentorship projects, summer institutes for teachers, and public humanities programs, Dr. Ruiz served as an appointee to the National Council of the Humanities. In 2006 she became an elected fellow of the Society of American Historians. She is the past president of the Organization of American Historians and currently serves as president of the American Studies Association.

Active in student mentorship projects, summer institutes for teachers, and public humanities programs, Dr. Ruiz served as an appointee to the National Council of the Humanities. In 2006, she became an elected fellow of the Society of American Historians. She is a past president of the Organization of American Historians and the Berkshire Conference on the History of Women. She currently serves as president of the American Studies Association. The mother of two grown sons, she is married to Victor Becerra, urban planner, community activist, and gourmet cook extraordinaire.

> *Created Equal tells stories across generations, regions, and cultures, integrating the lives of individuals within the economic, political, cultural, global, and environmental vectors shaping their lives. We cherish the telling of stories, for it is within these tales that we remember the ánimo y sueños (spirit and dreams) of the American people.*
>
> —*Vicki L. Ruiz*

How Did You First Come to Write This Book?

Elaine: The challenge came from fellow teachers. We had a chance to watch a video recording of a lively conversation with a dozen first-rate history instructors from all across the country. They loved teaching American history, but they felt that current textbooks held them back. Listening to them talk showed me there was a real need for a book that was broad and lively, combining social and political history. When Longman asked if we would undertake such a book, we all agreed that the timing was right.

Jacqueline: I thought that writing a new kind of text would be a real intellectual challenge. We have the opportunity to rethink and reconfigure the traditional American history narrative, and that's exciting.

Peter: At the time, I was teaching one of those special classes, a group of history majors that really clicked. Four of the best students had parents from other countries—South Africa, Mexico, Haiti, Vietnam—and all four were fascinated by American history. I remember thinking, "I'd love to be part of a team of historians who developed a text that would excite the whole broad spectrum of young Americans."

Thomas: Writing a textbook was attractive because it's so complementary to what I do in the classroom, particularly teaching the introductory American history survey. Having the chance to try to tell the entire story of the American past was exciting as a balance to the other work we do.

Tell Us About the Title—*Created Equal.*

Jacqueline: The title reflects our commitment to be inclusive in our coverage of different groups and the part they played in shaping American history. Of course, we are invoking the Declaration of Independence: "We hold these truths to be self-evident, that all men are created equal." That document, and those words, have inspired countless individuals, groups, and nations around the world.

Peter: We all recognize the phrase "created equal" from the Declaration of Independence, but we rarely ponder it. For me, it represents an affirmation of humanity, the family of mankind. But it also raises the deepest American theme: the endless struggles over defining whose equality will be recognized. I suppose you could say that there is equality in birth and death, but a great deal of inequality in between. Many of those inequities—and their partial removal—drive the story of American history.

Tom Paine understood this in 1776 when he published *Common Sense*. Months before the Declaration of Independence appeared, Paine put it this way: "Mankind being originally equal in the order of creation, the equality could only be destroyed by some subsequent circumstance."

How and Why Did You Choose the Themes That Structure the Text?

Thomas: We have chosen to highlight two important and overlapping themes in *Created Equal*. One is American diversity and social inclusion over time; the other is increasing globalization and its implications over centuries. Selecting these twin themes reflects what we see as the current and future state of the field of U.S. history, but our choice is also meant to address the vital needs of an emerging generation of students. The prominence of multiculturalism in recent decades made clear that identity remains a central piece of the American story. But too much attention to how individual Americans understand and identify themselves (by religion, class, region, sex, race, or ethnicity) has often led to a discounting of the political and economic structures of American society. In exploring American cultural diversity, it is important to remember that who has material wealth and power at any time, and how they use it, is also fundamental in shaping the American story. Second, the increasing globalization of the U.S. economy and American society in recent decades (through rising immigration, for example, and changing trade patterns) has reminded us of how deeply the United States has always been engaged with the rest of the world. Because America is an immigrant nation and the modern world's superpower, America's foreign and domestic affairs have always been intertwined. And the deepening awareness in recent decades of the fragility of the earth's environment has added to our global awareness. Indeed, for a new generation of students, the environment itself represents the clearest example of the interconnectedness of American and international history.

Jacqueline: It was time to integrate recent scholarship related to the many different groups that have been part of the American story, and to open up that story to include all geographical areas. For far too long, U.S. history seemed to be a tale told from, and about, the eastern seaboard. Giving special attention to the nation's significant social and environmental diversity has allowed us to explore in fresh ways how American cultural, political, and economic developments have been influenced by the nation's natural resources and landscape—and vice versa. This approach helps students to understand that differences in political and material resources, in access to power, have played a significant part in shaping the country's history. We balance this perspective by showing how America emerged as a uniquely open and middle-class nation. The United States has attracted immigrants from all over the world throughout its history, making us a strikingly global nation. No other society has so many roots stretching all around the world.

Elaine: *Created Equal* brings together aspects of the nation's story that are usually examined separately. It demonstrates that the people who make change are not only those in major positions of power; they are also ordinary Americans from all backgrounds. We illuminate ways that diverse Americans have seized opportunities to improve their lives and their nation. We also address the ongoing interaction between the United States and the rest of the world, examining the nation in a truly global context. We started with an understanding that the North American land itself is a major player in the story—the environment, the different regions, and the ways in which people, businesses, public policies, and the forces of nature have shaped it. Our emphasis on the process of globalization over time helps to broaden that perspective. As American citizens inhabiting a "shrinking" planet, we are all learning to think harder than ever about complex links between the local and the global—past, present, and future.

How Is the Book Organized?

Peter: History is the study of change over time, so chronology becomes extremely important. We wanted to emphasize central themes, but we wanted to explore and explain how they related to one another at any given moment. So we made a conscious decision to be more chronological in our presentation than many recent texts. It makes for less confusion, less jumping back and forth in time, than when broad themes are played out separately. After all, this is the way we lead our own lives—sequentially.

Jacqueline: Most of the ten separate parts in the book cover about a generation each. The parts give students a sense of the big picture over a longer period—the way our themes fit together and the impact of major developments on a particular generation of Americans. The chronological organization of the book forces us to understand the "wholeness" of any particular period—to consider links among political, social, economic, and cultural developments. By maintaining a strictly chronological focus, we hope to show students how the events and developments of any one period are intertwined with each other. For example, for coverage of the period after the end of the Civil War, it is important to show links between the Indian wars in the West and the process of Reconstruction in the South. In most texts, those regional perspectives are separated into different chapters, but in *Created Equal*, these connections are presented together in Chapter 15.

How Has Teaching the Text Influenced You?

Jacqueline: In teaching the text I've learned more about what interests and challenges my students. One day we had a long discussion about a particularly gruesome photograph of a black man who was the victim of a lynching. Is there a place for such graphic and disturbing pictures in a survey text? We discussed whether students needed to see those images, and what they might learn from them. So after writing the material, putting together the features, and choosing pictures, I find it gratifying to see all those elements actually generate a great discussion in the classroom.

Peter: Even when you have been teaching for decades, you learn new things every year. That was especially true for me recently, when I decided to teach an overview of U.S. history in one fifteen-week term. I called it "One Nation—One Semester," and we zipped through *Created Equal* at a pace of two chapters per week. You would think that on such a fast-moving train, everything would become a blur. But it didn't work that way. Instead, it was more like a plane ride, where we could look down from a high altitude, moving fast but watching things unfold below us. Sure, some details were lost in our rapid ride, but students were able to make broad connections that they would not have seen otherwise. "I liked the chance to learn about specific trees," one of them told me, "but we got to see the whole forest, too."

Thomas: I love connecting the big picture to the smallest details of daily life. *Created Equal* does this, and teaching it forces me to think constantly about these connections. In my classroom we spend a lot of time wrestling with broad themes of diplomacy, globalization, national politics, cultural diversity, and economics. But the text helps us link these themes directly to everyday choices, from grocery shopping and music styles to how we read newspapers and the size of houses.

Elaine: During each particular time period, I find myself more aware of the connections among diverse themes. That reflects the way we wrote the book. I teach in a more layered way now, forging links among cultural, political, social, and economic developments rather than carving out those topics separately.

What Were Your Goals in Tackling a Major Revision for the Third Edition?

Thomas: We love lively writing. The first two editions were well written, but we were especially eager to use this major revision to make the text still more engaging and accessible for students. We have also worked very hard to draw even greater attention to the global connections in the American past. In the years since the first two editions, globalization has accelerated, and the Third Edition reflects that reality. Older, more narrow national histories are a thing of the past.

Vicki: For me, the contextualization of stories was important—to explain more clearly why these voices mattered and what they tell us about the American past. I understood the historical context, but at times I forget that students appreciate additional background so they can place individuals within their historical moments. I want our readers to take away from the text the messiness of the past—to challenge a paradigm of an inevitable "march of progress." So many disparate groups and regions have shaped our national history.

Jacqueline: I hoped to streamline the previous edition and at the same time retain those elements that are most appealing—the stories of individuals, the unique blend of social and political history. I was also eager to expand our coverage of foreign relations, broadly defined; it makes the book fresh and timely.

Elaine: History is not just the telling of events from the past. It is an interpretive art. The way we interpret history—making links, weighing priorities—is naturally shaped by the times in which we live. The world of today changes quickly – it has altered dramatically since we wrote the first and even the second edition of Created Equal. I wanted to consider the American past again through the interpretive lens of the present, attentive to the stories, themes, and events that have shaped the nation and the world we all inhabit.

What Do You Hope Students Will Get Out of the Book?

Peter: I want readers to connect. In a good history class, or a strong history book, you start to care about, argue with, and connect to the persons you are studying. Pretty soon, their tough choices and surprising experiences in life start to resemble our own in ways we never expected, even though their worlds are dramatically different from ours.

Jacqueline: Many texts only pay lip service to diversity. Non-elite groups are tacked on, marginalized, or segregated from the "real" story of America. In *Created Equal*, by presenting a more inclusive view of the past, we want to give students a fuller and more accurate account of American history.

As authors, we could not have completed this project without the loving support of our families. We wish to thank Jeffrey Abramson, Lil Fenn, Lynn Borstelmann, Lary May, and Victor Becerra for their interest, forbearance, and encouragement over the course of many drafts and several editions. Our children of all ages have been a source of inspiration, as have our many students, past and present. We remain grateful to scores of colleagues and friends who have helped shape this book, both directly and indirectly, in more ways than they know.

Special thanks are due to Steve Fraser for his insightful suggestions at a crucial time. Along the way, Rob Heinrich, Matthew Becker, Scott Laderman, Matt Basso, Chad Cover, Eben Miller, Andrea Sachs, Mary Strunk, Melissa Williams, Louis Balizet and Jason Stahl provided useful assistance; their aid was invaluable. Two dedicated teachers, Jim Hijiya and Hannah Page, each read the entire manuscript and offered many helpful comments that have made the Third Edition stronger. We are grateful for their hard work.

We thank all of the creative people at Longman (and there are many) who have believed in our project and have had a hand in bringing this book to life. From the start, Priscilla McGeehon, Betty Slack, and Sue Westmoreland offered us their expertise and friendship. Michael Boezi has embraced *Created Equal* and given it his full and effective support, encouraging, pushing, and humoring us in all the right ways. We are especially grateful to Marion Castellucci, who has overseen this new edition with such care and understanding. She has sharpened our thoughts, clarified our prose, and kept us on schedule with wonderful grace and good spirits.

We also wish to express our deep gratitude to our consultants and reviewers whose candid and constructive comments about the Second Edition text and the Third Edition manuscript contributed greatly to this revision. Collectively, they pushed us hard with their high standards, tough questions, and shrewd advice. The thoughtful criticisms and generous suggestions from these colleagues have helped improve the book.

Terry Alford,
Northern Virginia Community College

Marynita Anderson,
Nassau Community College

Melissa Anyiwo,
University of Tennessee, Chattanooga

Emily Blanck,
Rowan University

Rebecca Borton,
Northwest State Community College

J. D. Bowers,
Northern Illinois University

Kimberley Breuer,
University of Texas, Arlington

Charlotte Brooks,
State University of New York, Albany

Vernon Burton,
University of Illinois at Urbana-Champaign

Eduardo Canedo,
Columbia University

Nancy Carnevale,
Montclair State University

James S. Day,
University of Montevallo

Christian R. Esh,
Northwest Nazarene University

Barbara C. Fertig,
Armstrong Atlantic State University

Colin Fisher,
University of San Diego

Jennifer Fronc,
Virginia Commonwealth University

Jessica Gerard,
Ozarks Technical Community College

Traci Hodgson,
Chemeketa Community College

Charlotte Haller,
Worcester State College

Rose Holz,
University of Nebraska, Lincoln

Creed Hyatt,
Lehigh Carbon Community College

Michael Jacobs,
University of Wisconsin, Baraboo

Jeff Janowick,
Lansing Community College

John S. Kemp,
Truckee Meadows Community College

Cynthia Kennedy,
Clarion University of Pennsylvania

Michael Lansing,
Augsburg College

Chana Kai Lee,
University of Georgia

Kyle Longley,
Arizona State University

Eric Mayer,
Victor Valley College

Beth Ruffin McIntyre,
Missouri State University

Jennifer McLaughlin,
Sacred Heart University

Eva Mo,
Modesto Junior College

Sandy Moats,
University of Wisconsin, Parkside

Carl H. Moneyhon,
University of Arkansas at Little Rock

Matthew Mooney,
Santa Barbara City College

Daniel S. Murphree,
University of Texas, Tyler

Peter C. Murray,
Methodist University

C. Samuel Nelson,
Ridgewater College

Jason C. Newman,
Cosumnes River College

Ting Ni,
Saint Mary's University

Steven Noll,
University of Florida

David R. Novak,
Purdue University, Calumet

Daniel Prosterman,
Syracuse University

Nannette Regua,
Evergreen Valley College

Thomas Rowland,
University of Wisconsin, Oshkosh

Leonard Sadosky,
Iowa State University

Carli Schiffner,
Yakima Valley Community College

Cornelia F. Sexauer,
University of Wisconsin

David J. Silverman,
George Washington University

Melissa Soto,
Cuyahoga Community College

Robert A. Taylor,
Florida Institute of Technology

David Tegeder,
Santa Fe Community College

Emily Teipe,
Fullerton College

Gary E. Thompson,
Tulsa Community College

Michael M. Topp,
University of Texas, El Paso

Sylvia Tyson,
Texas Lutheran University

Anne M. Valk,
John Nicholas Brown Center, Brown University

David Voelker,
University of Wisconsin, Green Bay

Randall Walton,
New Mexico Junior College

Charles Westmoreland,
University of Mississippi

Larry C. Wilson,
San Jacinto College

David Wolcott,
Miami University

Jason Young,
State University of New York, Buffalo

Finally, we also owe much to the many conscientious historians who reviewed the First and Second editions throughout many drafts and offered valuable suggestions. We acknowledge with gratitude the contributions of the following:

Ken Adderley,
Upper Iowa University

Leslie Alexander,
Ohio State University

John Andrew,
Franklin and Marshall College

Yvonne Baldwin,
Morehead State University

Abel Bartley,
University of Akron

Donald Scott Barton,
Central Carolina Technical College

Mia Bay,
Rutgers University

Marjorie Berman,
Red Rocks Community College

Chris Bierwith,
Treasure Valley Community College

Charles Bolton,
University of Arkansas, Little Rock

Susan Burch,
Gallaudet University

Tommy Bynum,
Georgia Perimeter College

Robert B. Carey,
Empire State College, SUNY

Todd Carney,
Southern Oregon University

JoAnn D. Carpenter,
Florida Community College, Jacksonville

Kathleen Carter,
Highpoint University

Jacqueline M. Cavalier,
Community College of Allegheny County

Jonathan Chu,
University of Massachusetts

Amy E. Davis,
University of California, Los Angeles

Judy DeMark,
Northern Michigan University

Ann Denkler,
Shenandoah University

James A. Denton,
University of Colorado

Joseph A. Devine,
Stephen F. Austin University

Paul E. Doutrich,
York College of Pennsylvania

Margaret Dwight,
North Carolina Agricultural and Technical University

Susan Edwards,
Cy-Fair College

Ronald B. Frankum,
Millersville University

Nancy Gabin,
Purdue University

Lori Ginzberg,
Pennsylvania State University

Gregory Goodwin,
Bakersfield College

Amy S. Greenberg,
Pennsylvania State University

Mike Haridopolos,
Brevard Community College

Nadine Isitani Hata,
El Camino College

James Hedtke,
Cabrini College

Andrew M. Honker,
Arizona State University

Adam Howard,
University of Florida

Fred Hoxie,
University of Illinois

Tera Hunter,
Carnegie Mellon University

David Jaffe,
City College of New York

Jeremy Johnson,
Northwest College

Yvonne Johnson,
Central Missouri State University

Kurt Keichtle,
University of Wisconsin

Anne Klejment,
University of St. Thomas

Dennis Kortheuer,
California State University, Long Beach

Rebecca A. Kosary,
Texas Lutheran University

Michael L. Krenn,
Appalachian State University

Joel Kunze,
Upper Iowa University

Joseph Laythe,
Edinboro College of Pennsylvania

Chana Kai Lee,
Indiana University

Kurt E. Leichtle,
University of Wisconsin, River Falls

Dan Letwin,
Pennsylvania State University

Gaylen Lewis,
Bakersfield College

Xiaobing Li,
University of Central Oklahoma

Mike Light,
Grand Rapids Community College

Kenneth Lipartito,
Florida International University

Kyle Longley,
Arizona State University

Edith L. Macdonald,
University of Central Florida

Michelle Espinosa Martinez,
St. Philip's College

Lorie Maltby,
Henderson Community College

Sandra Mathews-Lamb,
Nebraska Wesleyan University

Constance M. McGovern,
Frostburg State University

Henry McKiven,
University of South Alabama

James H. Merrell,
Vassar College

Earl Mulderink,
Southern Utah State University

Steven Noll,
University of Florida

Jim Norris,
North Dakota State University

Elsa Nystrom,
Kennesaw State University

Gaye T. M. Okoh,
University of Texas, San Antonio

Keith Pacholl,
California State University, Fullerton

William Pelz,
Elgin Community College

Melanie Perrault,
University of Central Arkansas

Delores D. Petersen,
Foothill College

Robert Pierce,
Foothill College

Louis Potts,
University of Missouri, Kansas City

Sarah Purcell,
Central Michigan University

Niler Pyeatt,
Wayland Baptist University

Steven Reschly,
Truman State University

Arthur Robinson,
Santa Rosa Junior College

Robert E. Rook,
Fort Hays State University

Thomas J. Rowland,
University of Wisconsin, Oshkosh

Steven Ruggles,
University of Minnesota

Christine Sears,
University of Delaware

Rebecca Shoemaker,
Indiana State University

Howard Shore,
Columbia River High School

James Sidbury,
University of Texas

Mike Sistrom,
Greensboro College

Arwin D. Smallwood,
Bradley University

Melissa Soto-Schwartz,
Cuyahoga Community College

Margaret Spratt,
California University of Pennsylvania

Rachel Standish,
Foothill College

Jon Stauff,
St. Ambrose University

David Steigerwald,
Ohio State University, Marion

Kay Stockbridge,
Central Carolina Technical College

Stephen Tallackson,
Purdue University, Calumet

Daniel Thorp,
Virginia Tech University

Michael M. Topp,
University of Texas, El Paso

Clifford Trafzer,
University of California, Riverside

Deborah Gray White,
Rutgers University

Scott Wong,
Williams College

Bill Woodward,
Seattle Pacific University

Nancy Zens,
Central Oregon Community College

David Zonderman,
North Carolina State University

Created
Equal

Part One

North American Founders

We sometimes call the framers of the U.S. Constitution America's Founding Fathers, using capital letters for emphasis. The men who met in Philadelphia in 1787 were indeed founders in a political sense, having drafted our enduring frame of government. But the 1780s seem recent in relation to most of North America's long human history. We must explore far back in time, long before the eighteenth century, to find the varied men and women who were the continent's first founders. As we study America's early past, two kinds of foundation builders emerge: the distant ancestors of today's Native Americans and newcomers from abroad who colonized North America in the sixteenth and seventeenth centuries.

Our earliest human ancestors evolved in Africa and then spread across the landmass of Eurasia. They entered Asia more than 60,000 years ago and reached Europe more than 40,000 years ago. Some even crossed to Australia roughly 40,000 years ago. But evidence suggests that humans reached the Americas from Asia much later, probably less than 20,000 years ago. These first arrivals took advantage of the land bridge that joined Siberia to Alaska when Ice Age glaciers caused a dramatic decline in sea levels. Roughly 14,000 years ago, these hunters apparently bypassed melting glaciers to reach the North American interior. They came on foot, but additional newcomers may have skirted the Pacific coast in small boats or even drifted across the South Pacific.

We still understand very little about these earliest Americans. What we do know is that they spread rapidly across North America over the next thousand years. They continued to hunt mammoths and other large animals until these ancient species became extinct. Later, their descendants adapted to a wide range of different environments, learning to fish, hunt for smaller game, and gather berries. It has been 10,000 years since the extinction of the mammoths and 3,000 years since the early signs of agriculture in the Americas. By 500 C.E., complex societies were beginning to appear in equatorial America, and a succession of diverse and rich societies had arisen in the Americas by the time a second set of founders appeared around 1500.

Although Vikings from Scandinavia had preceded Christopher Columbus by five centuries, their small outpost on the coast of Newfoundland lasted only a few years. In contrast, when Columbus reached the West Indies in October 1492 and then returned to Spain, his voyage launched a human and biological exchange between the Eastern and Western Hemispheres that has never ceased. Spanish and Portuguese ships initiated this exchange, but vessels from England, France, and Holland soon followed. Half a century after Columbus's first voyage, Spanish overland expeditions had already pushed from Florida to Arkansas and from Mexico to Kansas. French explorers in Canada had penetrated far up the St. Lawrence River, hoping to find a Northwest Passage to Asia.

Europeans brought new materials such as iron and new animals such as horses, cattle, and pigs. They also brought deadly diseases previously unknown in the Americas, such as measles and smallpox, which had a catastrophic impact on Native American societies. By 1565, Europeans had established their first lasting outpost in the North American continent, the town of St. Augustine in Spanish Florida. Two decades later the English tried, unsuccessfully, to plant a similar colony at Roanoke Island along the coast of what is now North Carolina.

In the first decades of the seventeenth century, permanent European settlements took hold at Quebec on the St. Lawrence River and at Santa Fe near the Rio Grande. A transatlantic outpost of English society appeared at Jamestown on Chesapeake Bay in 1607. Farther north, behind the sheltering hook of Cape Cod, other English settlers formed additional coastal outposts and renamed the region New England.

Numbers were small at first, but these communities and others endured and expanded, often with crucial help from Native Americans, who knew the keys to survival in their own domains. The gradual success of these European footholds prompted imitation and competition; colonizers clashed with each other and with longtime Indian inhabitants over control of the land and its resources. Disappointed in their early searches for easy mineral wealth, the new arrivals took advantage of other resources: cutting timber, catching fish, raising tobacco, or trading for furs. The French in particular, with aid once again from Native Americans, explored the interior of the continent. By 1700, they had laid claim to the entire Mississippi River valley and established a colony on the Gulf of Mexico.

Each new colonizing enterprise in the seventeenth century took on a distinctive life of its own—or, rather, numerous lives. First of all, there was the internal life of the community: who would be allowed to take part, how would participants govern themselves, and how would they subsist? In each instance, relations with the region's native inhabitants constituted a second unfolding story. Complicated ties to Europe—economic, religious, social, and political—made a third crucial narrative. Furthermore, relations between colonies and between the distant European powers that backed them had a determining influence, as when England took over the Dutch colony at New Netherland in the third quarter of the seventeenth century. Finally, there was the compelling drama of the newcomers' relationship to the environment itself. These founding generations labored to understand—or to subdue and exploit without fully understanding—the continent they had started to colonize.

Chapter 1

First Founders

Illustration by Andy Buttram courtesy of the Illinois State Museum

■ The skeleton of Kennewick Man revealed an enlarged right arm, strengthened by hurling spears with the ancient throwing device known as an atlatl.

"This is real old C.S.I.," Hugh Berryman told reporters. As a forensic anthropologist, Dr. Berryman knew all about "crime scene investigation." He had come to Seattle in July 2005 as part of an eleven-member team to examine the bones of a deceased human. "It's the type of skeleton that comes along once in a lifetime," commented another member of the team.

In 1996, two outdoorsmen near the Columbia River in Kennewick, Washington, had stumbled on the bones of a middle-aged man. At first, authorities guessed they had the corpse of an early white settler. But tests revealed it to be much older—9,400 years old, in fact. That touched off years of legal wrangling over control of one of the most ancient skeletons ever found in the Americas.

When the team of experts finally won the right to examine Kennewick Man, they found him to be five feet nine inches tall, roughly forty years old, with early arthritis in his knees. Healed injuries to his head and ribs suggested a tough life. Years before his death, an enemy attack had embedded a stone point in his right hipbone. "This is like an extraordinary rare book," Berryman observed, "and we are reading it one page at a time."

The discovery of Kennewick Man followed a century of mounting study into when and how human beings first came to inhabit North America. In 1907, on the three-hundredth anniversary of Jamestown, amazingly little was understood about who had lived in North America before the first successful English colonists arrived. Everyone knew that the Italian explorer Christopher Columbus had reached the Caribbean while attempting to sail to the

Indies for Spain in 1492. They had learned in school that Columbus, thinking he had reached the Asian islands close to India and China ("the Indies"), mistakenly lumped America's peoples together as "Indians." But most Americans still knew very little about who the earliest North Americans really were.

In the past century, that has changed dramatically, as scholars have steadily learned more about the continent's first inhabitants. An expanding American history now stretches back in time far before the Jamestown settlement and reaches broadly from coast to coast. Its earliest roots lie with the ancient Indians of the continent over many millennia. In addition, the foreigners who suddenly intruded into portions of the Native American world in the sixteenth century—speaking Spanish, French, and occasionally English—also represent a significant beginning. All these people now number among America's first founders.

Ancient America

▒ *What types of evidence are used to explain the arrival of humans in North America?*

Early in the twentieth century near Folsom, New Mexico, archaeologists found a man-made spear point resting between the rib bones of a type of ancient bison that had been extinct for 10,000 years. They named such thin projectile tips Folsom points, after the site. Their discovery proved that humans had lived and hunted on the continent far earlier than scientists had ever imagined. It sparked a revolution in North American archaeology. Soon after the Folsom find, amateurs at nearby Clovis, New Mexico, spotted some large, well-chipped spearheads. In 1932, collectors found more of these so-called Clovis points in the same vicinity, this time beside the tooth of an extinct mammoth. They lay underneath a soil layer containing Folsom points, so they were clearly even older.

Clovis Points

Since then, scientists have unearthed Clovis-like points throughout much of North America. According to the latest calculations, humans started creating these weapons roughly 13,900 years ago and ceased about 12,900 years ago. Between those early dates, therefore, people were hunting widely on the bountiful continent. Using scant remaining traces, such as spear tips, archaeologists continue to push back and refine the estimated date for the appearance of the first people in the Americas. Recently, they have unearthed evidence suggesting the possible presence of pre-Clovis inhabitants.

THE QUESTION OF ORIGINS

Like all other peoples, Native American societies retain rich and varied accounts of their own origins. No amount of scientific data can diminish or replace tribal creation stories that serve an important cultural purpose. In these powerful sagas, America's first human inhabitants emerge from the earth, are created by other animals, or receive life from the Great Spirit. At the same time, modern researchers continue to compile evidence about the origin and migrations of the diverse peoples who inhabited the Americas for thousands of years before the arrival of Christopher Columbus.

Iroquois Creation Story

Scientists have determined that the most recent ancestors of modern humans moved from Africa to spread across the Eurasian landmass, the area comprising Europe and Asia, scarcely 70,000 years ago. By 40,000 years ago some of these Stone Age hunter-gatherers had already reached Australia. Others lived on the steppes of central Asia and the frozen tundra of

Kenneth Garrett/National Geographic Image Collection

■ Archaeologists digging at Cactus Hill, Virginia, and several other sites have unearthed artifacts that suggest human habitation before the arrival of hunters using Clovis points. The foreground objects are laid out clockwise by apparent age, with the most recent at the top. Clovis-like spearheads appear in the second group. The third and fourth groups, taken from lower layers of soil, are thought to be older items, some reaching back well beyond 14,000 years. With the most primitive tools, it becomes difficult to separate implements made by humans from natural rock fragments.

Siberia. They had perfected the tools they needed to survive in a cold climate: flint spear points for killing mammoths, reindeer, and the woolly rhinoceros; and bone needles to sew warm, waterproof clothes out of animal skin.

Over thousands of years, bands of these northern hunters migrated east across Siberia in search of game. Eventually they arrived at the region where the Bering Strait now separates Russia from Alaska. The geography of this area has fluctuated over time because of dramatic changes in global climate. Between 25,000 and 11,000 years ago, cold conditions expanded arctic ice caps, trapping vast quantities of the earth's water in the form of huge glaciers. As a result, ocean levels sank by 300 feet—enough to expose a low bridge of land 600 miles wide between Asia and America.

The Bering land bridge formed part of a frigid, windswept region known as Beringia. Small groups of people could have subsisted in this cold landscape by hunting mammoths and musk oxen. As the climate warmed and the ocean rose again, some might have headed farther east onto higher ground in Alaska. If so, these newcomers would have been cut off permanently from Siberia as water once more submerged the land bridge. But the same warming process also eventually opened a pathway through the glaciers blanketing northern America.

This ice-free corridor along the eastern slope of the Rocky Mountains could account for the sudden appearance of Clovis hunters across much of North America nearly 14,000 years ago. Small bands of people, armed with razor-sharp Clovis points, spread rapidly across the continent, destroying successive herds of large animals that had never faced human predators before. According to this theory, generations of hunters known as **Paleo-Indians** moved swiftly south as local game supplies dwindled. They would have migrated as far as the tip of South America within several thousand years.

In recent decades, three new developments have complicated the picture. At Cactus Hill, Virginia, and other sites, archaeologists have uncovered artifacts suggesting the presence of immediate predecessors to the Clovis people. In addition, a provocative discovery in South America—a campsite at Monte Verde, Chile, dating back more than 14,000 years—suggests to some that small groups may have used simple boats on a coastal route around the North Pacific rim. Reaching the Northwest Coast, their descendants could have hugged the shoreline to reach South America by water in gradual stages. Finally, genetic comparisons of different peoples, present and past, are yielding increasingly specific, if controversial, details about

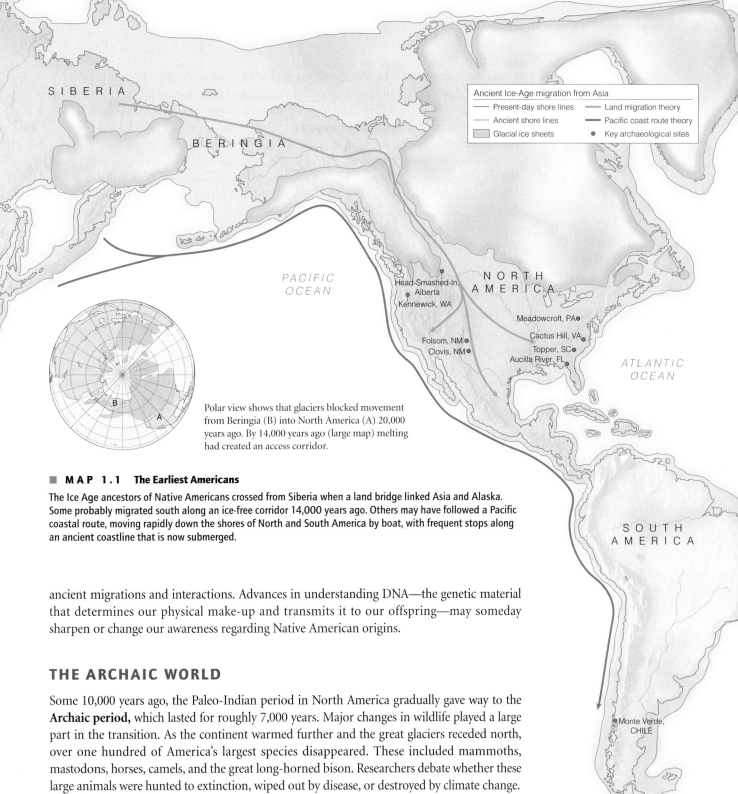

Polar view shows that glaciers blocked movement from Beringia (B) into North America (A) 20,000 years ago. By 14,000 years ago (large map) melting had created an access corridor.

■ **MAP 1.1** **The Earliest Americans**

The Ice Age ancestors of Native Americans crossed from Siberia when a land bridge linked Asia and Alaska. Some probably migrated south along an ice-free corridor 14,000 years ago. Others may have followed a Pacific coastal route, moving rapidly down the shores of North and South America by boat, with frequent stops along an ancient coastline that is now submerged.

ancient migrations and interactions. Advances in understanding DNA—the genetic material that determines our physical make-up and transmits it to our offspring—may someday sharpen or change our awareness regarding Native American origins.

THE ARCHAIC WORLD

Some 10,000 years ago, the Paleo-Indian period in North America gradually gave way to the **Archaic period,** which lasted for roughly 7,000 years. Major changes in wildlife played a large part in the transition. As the continent warmed further and the great glaciers receded north, over one hundred of America's largest species disappeared. These included mammoths, mastodons, horses, camels, and the great long-horned bison. Researchers debate whether these large animals were hunted to extinction, wiped out by disease, or destroyed by climate change.

Whatever the causes—and probably there were many—human groups had to adapt to the shifting conditions. They developed new methods of survival. Inhabitants turned to the smaller bison, similar to modern-day ones, that had managed to survive and flourish on the northern plains. Archaic-era hunters learned to drive herds over cliffs and use the remains for food, clothing, and tools. One such bison jump is located in eastern Colorado. Another mass kill location, known as Head-Smashed-In, is in western Alberta; native peoples used this Canadian site for 7,000 years. A weighted spear-throwing device, called an atlatl, let hunters such as the Kennewick Man bring down medium-sized game. Archaic peoples also devised nets, hooks, and snares for catching birds, fish, and small animals. By 4,000 years ago, they were even using duck decoys in the Great Basin of Utah and Nevada.

Though genetically similar, far-flung bands of Archaic Indians developed diverse cultures as they adapted to very different landscapes and environments. Nothing illustrates this diversity more clearly than speech. A few early languages branched into numerous language families, then divided further into hundreds of separate tongues. Similar cultural variations emerged in everything from diet and shelter to folklore and spiritual beliefs.

All of these variations reflected local conditions, and each represented an experiment that might potentially lead to more elaborate social arrangements. Eventually in the Americas, as elsewhere, the cultivation of domesticated plants led to settled **horticultural** societies. A more stable food supply allowed the creation of surpluses, prompting larger permanent villages, wider trade, and a greater accumulation of goods. With this settled lifestyle, daily subsistence no longer required everyone's labor. With specialized tasks came greater social hierarchy—stratification into distinct classes—and the emergence of hereditary chiefdoms where one powerful extended family wielded political control.

> *Bands of Archaic Indians developed diverse cultures as they adapted to very different landscapes and environments.*

Frequently, a class of priests appeared near the top of the expanding hierarchy, mediating between the people and a god or gods who were intimately involved in human affairs. Slaves, unknown in hunting and gathering societies, appeared at the bottom of the hierarchy, since captives could be put to work for their conquerors. An expanded labor force not only produced more food; it created public works that showed (and enhanced) the power of the chiefs and priests. As populations grew and social structures became more complex, greater specialization ensued. This allowed the development of more extensive communities with more elaborate political and religious activities and greater concentrations of power. But such developments were slow and uneven, depending on local conditions.

THE RISE OF MAIZE AGRICULTURE

One condition remained common to all the various Archaic American groups, despite their emerging regional differences: they all lacked domesticated animals. Diverse peoples living in Eurasia had managed to domesticate five important species—sheep, goats, pigs, cows, and horses—by 6,000 years ago, leading to the creation of stable pastoral societies. But none of these mammals existed in the Americas, nor did camels, donkeys, or water buffalo, the other large animals that lend themselves to domestication. Archaic Indians, like their Asian forebears, did possess dogs, and settlers in the Andes domesticated the llama over 5,000 years ago. Herds of buffalo and deer could be followed, and even managed and exploited in various ways. But no mammal remaining in the Americas could readily be tamed to provide humans with milk, meat, hides, and hauling power.

Although their prospects for domesticating animals were severely limited, early Americans had many more options when it came to the domestication of plants. Humans managed to domesticate plants independently in five different areas around the world, and three of those regions were located in the Americas. First, across parts of South America, inhabitants learned to cultivate root crops of potatoes and manioc (also known as cassava, which yields a nutritious starch). Second, in **Mesoamerica** (modern-day Mexico and Central America), people gradually brought squash, beans, and maize (corn) under cultivation—three foods that complement one another effectively in dietary terms.

Maize agriculture became a crucial ingredient for the growth of complex societies in the Americas, but its development and diffusion took time. Unlike wheat, the Eurasian cereal crop that offered a high yield from the start, maize took thousands of years of cultivation in the Americas to evolve into an extremely productive food source. The differences between Mesoamerica and North America proved substantial when it came to mastering maize agriculture. Southwestern Indians in North America began growing thumb-sized ears of maize only about 3,000 years ago (at a time of increasing rainfall), well after the crop had taken hold in Mesoamerica. More than a thousand years later, maize reached eastern North America, where it adapted slowly to the cooler climate and shorter growing season.

In the East, a different agriculture had already taken hold, centered on other once-wild plants. This was the third zone where the independent domestication of plants occurred in the Americas. As early as 4,000 years ago, eastern Indians at dozens of Archaic sites were cultivating domesticated squash and sunflowers. These domesticated plants provided supplemental food sources for eastern communities that continued to subsist primarily by hunting and gathering until the arrival of maize agriculture in the eastern woodlands during the first millennium C.E.

> *As early as 4,000 years ago, eastern Indians at dozens of Archaic sites were cultivating domesticated squash and sunflowers.*

About 3,000 years ago, as maize cultivation began in the Southwest and gardens of squash and sunflowers appeared in the Northeast, the first of several powerful Mesoamerican cultures—the Olmec—emerged in the lowlands along the southwestern edge of the Gulf of Mexico. Their name meant "those who live in the land of rubber," for they had learned how to turn the milky juice of several plants into an unusual elastic substance. The Olmec, considered the "mother culture" of Mesoamerica, grew maize and manioc in abundance, and their surplus of food supported a hierarchical society. They built large burial mounds and pyramids, revered the jaguar in their religion, developed a complex calendar, and played a distinctive game with a large ball of solid rubber. Since they traded widely with peoples across Mesoamerica, they passed on these cultural traits, which reappeared later in other societies in the region.

Olmec traders, traveling by coastal canoe, may even have encountered and influenced the culture that existed in northeast Louisiana 4,200 to 2,700 years ago. The Poverty Point culture (named for a key archaeological site) involved trade networks on the lower Mississippi River and its tributaries. It stands as a mysterious precursor to the mound-building societies of the Mississippi Valley that emerged much later. Remnants of these more extensive Mississippian cultures still existed when newcomers from Europe arrived to stay, around 1500. In many parts of North America, smaller and less stratified Archaic cultures remained intact well into the era of European colonization. To subsist, they combined hunting for a variety of animals with gathering and processing local plant foods.

A Thousand Years of Change: 500 to 1500

■ *How did complex cultures arise in the Americas in the millennium before Columbus?*

The millennium stretching from the fifth century to the explorations of Columbus in the fifteenth century witnessed dramatic and far-reaching changes in the separate world of the Americas. In the warm and temperate regions on both sides of the equator, empires rose and fell as maize agriculture and elaborate irrigation systems provided food surpluses, allowing the creation of cities and the emergence of hierarchical societies.

On the coast of Peru, between roughly 100 and 800, the Moche people created delicate gold work, intricate pottery, and huge pyramids to honor the sun. In the 1400s, centuries after the Moche and their neighbors disappeared, the expansive Inca empire emerged in their place. Inca emperors, ruling from the capital at Cuzco, prompted the construction of a vast road system throughout the Peruvian Andes. Stonemasons built large storage facilities at provincial centers to hold food for garrisons of soldiers and to store tribute items such as gold and feathers destined for the capital. Until the empire's fall in the 1530s, officials leading pack trains of llamas ferried goods to and from Cuzco along mountainous roadways.

MAP

Pre-Columbian Societies of the Americas

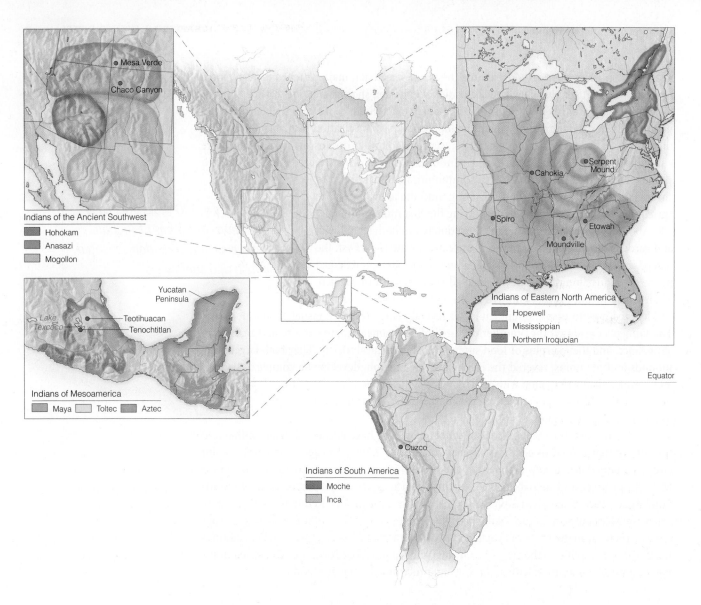

■ **MAP 1.2 America in the Millennium before Columbus, 500–1500**

A number of distinctive cultures emerged in the Americas during the ten centuries before 1500. Most learned from their predecessors—Mississippians from Hopewell, and Aztec from Maya, for example—but debate continues over the full extent of trade and travel networks at any given time.

Similarly, Mesoamerica also saw a series of impressive civilizations—from the Maya to the Aztec—in the millennium spanning 500 to 1500 in the western calendar. Developments in North America in the same millennium were very different, but they bear enough resemblance to patterns in Mesoamerica to raise difficult questions about early contacts. Did significant migrations northward from Mesoamerica ever take place? And if not, were there substantial trade links at times, allowing certain materials, techniques, ideas, and seeds to reach North American peoples? Or did the continent's distinctive societies, such as the Anasazi in the Southwest and the Cahokia mound builders on the Mississippi River, develop almost entirely independently?

VALLEYS OF THE SUN: THE MESOAMERICAN EMPIRES

In Mesoamerica, the Maya and the Aztec established rich empires where worship of the sun was central to their religious beliefs. Mayan culture flourished between 300 and 900. The Maya controlled a domain stretching from the lowlands of the Yucatan peninsula to the highlands of what is now southern Mexico, Guatemala, Honduras, and El Salvador—an area half the size of Texas. They derived their elaborate calendar—a fifty-two-year cycle, with each year made up of twenty-day months—and many other aspects of their culture from the earlier Olmec, but they devised their own distinctive civilization. The Maya built huge stone temples and held ritual bloodletting ceremonies to appease their gods. Recently, researchers have deciphered the complex pictographs, or glyphs, that appear throughout Mayan art. New discoveries are pushing back the earliest dates for Mayan culture.

The Maya, like the Moche in Peru, declined rapidly after 750, and dominance in Mesoamerica moved farther west, where great cities had arisen in the highlands of central Mexico. The people who constructed the metropolis of Teotihuacan in the Mexican highlands remain an enigma. They appear to have traded with the Maya and perhaps with the Olmec before that. They laid out their immense city in a grid, dominated by the 200-foot Pyramid of the Sun. By 500, the city held more than 100,000 inhabitants, making it one of the largest in the world. But Teotihuacan's society declined fast, for unknown reasons, succeeded first by the Toltec and then by the Aztec.

The Aztec (or Mexica) had migrated to the central Valley of Mexico from the north in the twelfth century. Looked down on at first by the local people, they swiftly rose to power through strategic alliances and military skill. According to legend, the Aztec war god instructed Aztec priests to look for the place where a great eagle perched on a cactus. They found such a spot, on a swampy island in Lake Texcoco. By the 1400s the Aztec had transformed the island into Tenochtitlán, an imposing urban center, located on the site of modern Mexico City.

> *Looked down on at first by the local people, the Aztec swiftly rose to power through strategic alliances and military skill.*

The impressive city of Tenochtitlán, surrounded by Lake Texcoco and linked to shore by causeways, became the Aztec capital. Its architecture imitated the ruined temple city of Teotihuacan, which lay thirty-five miles to the north. The Aztec also adopted many other features of the cultures they had displaced. They used the cyclical fifty-two-year Mesoamerican calendar, and they worshipped the great god Quetzalcoatl, the plumed serpent associated with wind and revered by the Toltec, their predecessors in the Valley of Mexico. Constant military readiness, clear gender roles, strict civic order, and a pessimistic worldview characterized Aztec society.

Eager to expand their empire, the Aztec launched fierce wars against neighboring lands. But their primary objective was not to kill enemies or gain more territory. Instead, Aztec warriors demanded tribute and took prisoners from the people they subdued. They then sacrificed numerous captives at pyramid temples to placate the gods. These deities, they believed, would in turn protect them as they conducted further wars of capture, leading to more tribute and sacrifices.

Like the Inca of Peru, the Aztec imposed harsh treatment on the peoples they conquered, extracting heavy annual taxes. This stern policy caused outlying provinces to resent Aztec authority and made the centralized empire vulnerable to external attack. When a foreign assault prompted the empire's downfall in the early sixteenth century, the challenge came from a direction that Aztec priests and generals could not predict.

THE ANASAZI: CHACO CANYON AND MESA VERDE

The great urban centers of Peru and Mesoamerica had no counterparts farther north. The peoples inhabiting North America in the millennium before Columbus never developed the levels of **social stratification**, urban dynamism, architectural grandeur, astronomical study, or intensive corn agriculture that characterized the Maya, Inca, or Aztec. Yet elements of all these traits appeared in North America, especially in the Southwest and the Mississippi Valley, with the emergence of increasingly settled societies and widening circles of exchange. Could north–south movements back and forth have occurred? Recently, researchers have identified a north–south traffic in turquoise, highly prized in both Mexico and the Southwest.

■ Cliff Palace, at Mesa Verde National Park in southwest Colorado, was created 900 years ago, when the Anasazi left the mesa tops and moved into more secure and inaccessible cliff dwellings. Facing southwest, the building gained heat from the rays of the low afternoon sun in winter. Overhanging rock protected the structure from rain, snow, and the hot midday summer sun. The numerous round kivas, each covered with a flat roof originally, suggest that Cliff Palace may have had a ceremonial importance.

David Muench

Three identifiably different cultures were already well established in the North American Southwest by 500. The Mogollon occupied the dry, mountainous regions of eastern Arizona and southern New Mexico. Mogollon women were expert potters who crafted delicate bowls from the clay of the Mimbres River. Families lived in sunken pit houses that were cool in summer and warm in winter. The Hohokam, their neighbors to the west in south-central Arizona, did the same. The Hohokam also constructed extensive canal and floodgate systems to irrigate their fields from the Gila and Salt rivers. According to their Native American successors, who still dwell in the Phoenix area, the name *Hohokam* means "those who have gone."

Farther north, where Utah and Colorado meet Arizona and New Mexico, lived the people remembered as the Anasazi, or "ancient ones." By 750 the Anasazi inhabited above-ground houses of masonry or adobe clustered around a central ceremonial room dug into the earth. They entered this sunken religious chamber, known as a kiva, by descending a ladder through the roof. The climb back up symbolized the initial ascent of humans into the Upper World from below. European explorers later used the Spanish word for town, *pueblo*, to describe the Anasazi's complex multistory dwellings of masonry or adobe.

Beginning in the 850s, Chaco Canyon in the San Juan River basin of northwest New Mexico emerged as the hub of the Anasazi world. Wide, straight roads radiating out from Chaco let builders haul hundreds of thousands of logs for use as roof beams in the nine great pueblos that still dot the canyon. The largest, Pueblo Bonito, rose five stories high in places and had 600 rooms arranged in a vast semicircle.

After 1130, a prolonged drought gripped the area, and the turquoise workshops of Chaco Canyon fell silent. Many of the inhabitants headed north, where dozens of Anasazi communities with access to better farming conditions dotted the landscape. Gradually—with populations growing, the climate worsening, and competition for resources stiffening—the Anasazi moved into sheltered cliff dwellings such as Cliff Palace at Mesa Verde in southwestern Colorado, with its 220 rooms and 23 kivas. Reached only by ladders and steep trails, these pueblos offered protection from enemies and shelter from the scorching summer sun. But the environmental crisis proved too great; warfare intensified

■ The most striking Mississippian earthwork to survive is the enigmatic Serpent Mound, built in the eleventh century by the Fort Ancient people in southern Ohio. The snake (holding an egg in its mouth) has links to astronomy because its curves are aligned toward key positions of the sun. The serpent may even represent Halley's Comet, which blazed in the heavens in 1066. Completely uncoiled, the earthwork would measure more than a quarter-mile in length.

over scant resources. When another prolonged drought (1276–1299) forced the Anasazi to move once again, survivors dispersed south into lands later occupied by the Hopi, Zuni, and Rio Grande peoples.

THE MISSISSIPPIANS: CAHOKIA AND MOUNDVILLE

Earlier, in the Mississippi Valley, the Hopewell people had prospered for half a millennium before 500 C.E. (in the era of the Roman Empire in Europe). The Hopewell lived mainly in Ohio and Illinois. But their network of trade extended over much of the continent. Hopewell burial sites have yielded pipestone and flint from the Missouri River valley, copper and silver from Lake Superior, mica and quartz from Appalachia, seashells and shark teeth from Florida, and artwork made from Rocky Mountain obsidian and grizzly-bear teeth.

Hopewell trading laid the groundwork for larger mound-building societies, known as the Mississippian cultures, which emerged in the Mississippi Valley and the Southeast in roughly the same centuries as the great Mesoamerican civilizations and the Anasazi in the Southwest. The Mississippian tradition developed gradually after 500. Then after 900, it flourished broadly for six centuries, as centralized societies combined thriving agricultural economies with long-distance trade in scarce goods.

Shifts in technology and agriculture facilitated the rise of the Mississippians. Bows and arrows, long employed in arctic regions of North America but little known elsewhere, became widespread in the eastern woodlands around 700. At the same time, maize underwent a transformation from a marginal oddity to a central staple crop. Across the East, food supplies expanded as Native American communities planted corn in the rich bottomland soil along the region's many rivers. With greater productivity, commercial and religious elites took advantage of farmers and asserted stronger control over the community's increasing resources.

Separate Mississippian mound-building centers have been found as far apart as Spiro, in eastern Oklahoma, and Etowah, in northern Georgia. The largest complex was at Cahokia on the American Bottom, the twenty-five-mile floodplain below where the Illinois and Missouri rivers flow into the Mississippi. On Cahokia Creek, near East St. Louis, Illinois, dozens of rectangular, flat-topped temple mounds still remain after almost a thousand years. The largest mound—indeed, the largest ancient earthwork in North America—rises 100 feet in four separate levels, covering 16 acres and using nearly 22 million cubic feet of earth. A log palisade with gates and watchtowers once enclosed this temple mound and its adjacent plaza in a 200-acre central compound. Nearby, residents used engineering and astronomy skills to erect 48 posts in a huge circle, 410 feet in diameter. This creation, now called Woodhenge after England's Stonehenge, functioned as a calendar to mark the daily progression of the sun throughout each year.

Reconstructed View of Cahokia

Cahokia's mounds rose quickly in the decades after 1050, as the local population expanded beyond 10,000. A succession of powerful leaders reorganized the vicinity's small, isolated villages into a strong regional chiefdom that controlled towns on both sides of the Mississippi River. These towns provided the chiefdom's centralized elite with food, labor, and goods for trading. The elaborate religious rituals and the wealth and power of the leaders are seen in a burial site opened by archaeologists in the 1970s. The body of one prominent figure, presumably a chief, was laid out on a surface of 20,000 shell beads. Near him lay six young adults who must have been relatives or servants sacrificed at the ruler's funeral. They were supplied with hundreds of stone arrowheads—finely chipped and neatly sorted—plus antler projectile points and numerous ceremonial objects. Around 1100, the population of Cahokia perhaps exceeded 15,000 people. It then waned steadily over the next two centuries as the unstable hierarchy lost its sway over nearby villages.

> *Mississippian mound-building centers have been found as far apart as Spiro, in eastern Oklahoma, and Etowah, in northern Georgia.*

As Cahokia declined, other regional chiefdoms rose along other rivers. The most notable appeared at Moundville in west-central Alabama, fifteen miles south of modern Tuscaloosa. The site, with more than twenty flat-topped mounds, became a dominant ceremonial center in the thirteenth century. But by 1400, Moundville's Mississippian elites had started to lose their power. Throughout the prior millennium, societies had grown by linking agriculture and trade, only to suffer when they reached their environmental limits. A river could dry up or change course; a key local resource, such as timber or game, could diminish sharply. Also, trade could be interrupted or curtailed. When the Europeans first appeared, they would be welcomed by many Native Americans as potential trading partners.

Linking the Continents

■ *Why is the first voyage of Columbus in 1492 still viewed as such an earth-changing event?*

Estimates vary widely, but probably around one-sixth of the world's population—as many as 60 to 70 million people—resided in the Americas when Columbus arrived in 1492. Most of them lived in the tropical zone near the equator, where their ancient ancestors had developed efficient forms of agriculture. But roughly one-tenth of the hemisphere's population (6 to 7 million) dwelt in North America, spread from coast to coast.

We cannot rule out the occasional appearance in America of ancient ocean travelers. Around 400, Polynesian mariners sailed their double-hulled canoes from the Marquesas Islands in the South Pacific to the Hawaiian **archipelago.** Conceivably, in the millennium before 1500, one or two boats from Africa, Ireland, Polynesia, China, or Japan sailed—or were blown—to the American mainland. But any survivors of such a journey would have had little genetic or cultural impact, for no sustained back-and-forth contact between the societies occurred. Even the seafaring Norse from Scandinavia, known as Vikings, never established a lasting colony. Their brief Vinland settlement a thousand years ago at L'Anse aux Meadows in northern Newfoundland is now well documented, but they remained only a few years at this coastal site. Native American societies, therefore, knew nothing of the people, plants, animals, and microbes of the Eastern Hemisphere.

America's near isolation ended dramatically, beginning in the late fifteenth century, after innovations in deep-sea sailing opened the world's oceans as a new frontier for human exploration. Chinese sailors in the North Pacific or Portuguese mariners in the South Atlantic could well have been the first outsiders to establish ongoing contact with the peoples of the Western Hemisphere. Instead, it was Christopher Columbus, an Italian navigator in the service of Spain, who became the agent of this sweeping change. He stumbled upon the Americas by accident and misinterpreted what he had found. But his chance encounter with a separate realm sparked new patterns of human migration, cultural transfer, and ecological exchange that would reshape the modern world.

OCEANIC TRAVEL: THE NORSE AND THE CHINESE

Scandinavian settlers had colonized Ireland in the 830s and Iceland in the 870s. These seafarers—led by Erik the Red—reached Greenland in the 980s. When Erik's son, Leif, learned that Norse mariners blown off course had sighted land farther west, he sailed from Greenland to the North American coast. Here he explored a region near the Gulf of St. Lawrence that he named Vinland.

Around 1000, Leif Eriksson's relatives directed several return voyages to Vinland, where the Norse Vikings built an outpost called Straumfjord. The tiny colony of 160 people, including women and children, lived and grazed livestock in Vinland for several years until native peoples drove them away. The Greenlanders returned occasionally to cut timber, and they traded with inhabitants of northeastern Canada for generations. But by 1450, Norse settlements in Greenland had died out completely and the trade with Native Americans had stopped.

Whether sailors in Europe knew much about Norse exploits in the North Atlantic remains shrouded in mystery. What Europeans did know, vaguely, was the existence of the distant Chinese empire. They called the realm Cathay, a term used by Italian merchant Marco Polo, who journeyed from Venice across Asia along the fabled Silk Road in the 1270s. Polo returned to Italy in 1292 to publish his *Travels,* an account of adventures in China during the reign of Kublai Khan.

> *Chinese strength in overseas exploration and trade reached its height in the early fifteenth century under Admiral Zheng He.*

Marco Polo told of many things unknown to Europeans, including rocks that burned like wood (coal) and spices that preserved meat. Lacking winter fodder for their herds, Europe's farmers regularly slaughtered numerous cattle in the fall and pickled or salted the beef to preserve it. Asian spices such as nutmeg, cinnamon, pepper, ginger, and cloves, if they could be obtained, would offer new preservatives. When renewed Islamic power in the Middle East cut off the Silk Road to Cathay, Europeans searched for other ways to reach that far-off region.

The desire to obtain oriental spices at their source fueled European oceanic exploration, leading eventually to the transformation of the Americas. Yet it was China, not Europe, that first mastered ocean sailing on a large scale. Chinese strength in overseas exploration and trade reached its height in the early fifteenth century under Admiral Zheng He (pronounced "Jung Huh"). Between 1405 and 1433, this brilliant officer led seven large fleets to the Indian Ocean, sailing as far as east Africa. His immense treasure ships, 400 feet long and equipped with cannon, carried strange items—even giraffes—home to Asia.

Then, abruptly, China turned away from the sea, passing up its chance to become the first global maritime power. The Chinese, once poised to play a leading role in early oceanic trade, therefore lost an opportunity to shape the destiny of North and South America. Within a century of Zheng He's accomplishments, the royal court grew dismissive of foreign trade and turned inward. Chinese officials destroyed the logbooks of earlier voyages and curtailed production of oceangoing vessels. Instead of powerful China facing the Pacific, it was tiny Portugal, overlooking the Atlantic, which emerged as the leader in maritime innovation and exploration in the fifteenth century.

PORTUGAL AND THE BEGINNINGS OF GLOBALIZATION

Geography and religious zeal helped spur Portugal's unlikely rise to world prominence. The tiny maritime country faced the sea at the crossroads between Mediterranean commerce and the coastal traffic of northern Europe. This strategic location on the **Iberian** peninsula also exposed Portugal to the ongoing conflict between Christianity and Islam. The religion founded by Muhammad (born at Mecca in 570) had spread rapidly across North Africa from Arabia. By the eighth century, followers of Islam (known as Muslims, Moslems, or Moors) had crossed the Strait of Gibraltar to establish a kingdom in southern Spain. Centuries later, Spanish and Portuguese Christians rallied to force the Muslims out of the Iberian peninsula—a campaign that concluded in 1492—and to join other militant Europeans in fighting against Islamic power in the Middle East.

When Christian crusades to the holy land failed to defeat the Muslims and reopen overland trade routes to China, European strategists dreamed of skirting Africa by sea to reach Asia. The Portuguese were well positioned to lead this flanking movement around the areas under Muslim control. And if no such oceanic route to Asia existed, some speculated that Portuguese exploration south beyond Africa's Sahara Desert still might provide links to a strong Christian ally. For generations, Europeans had fostered legends of a wealthy kingdom somewhere in Africa ruled by a black Christian known as Prester John. Even if Prester John's realm could not be found, probes south from the Iberian Peninsula by ship might explore the extent of Islamic influence and seek out African converts to Christianity.

Intellectual and economic motives also existed for Portuguese ventures along the coast of sub-Saharan Africa. Such journeys, presenting new challenges in shipbuilding and navigation, could boost European knowledge of the unknown and open new markets. The first step involved an investment of leadership and resources, before early efforts could bear fruit and give the exploration process a momentum of its own.

Prince Henry of Portugal (1394–1460) provided these initial ingredients. In 1415 the young prince—later honored as "Henry the Navigator"—had crossed the Straits of Gibraltar to fight Muslims at Ceuta in North Africa. Committed to the campaign against Islam, Henry then waged a religiously inspired crusade-at-sea, building his headquarters at Sagres in southwest Portugal. The center overlooked the ocean near Cape St. Vincent,

■ Prince Henry of Portugal rarely went to sea himself. Instead, he established a base at Sagres, overlooking the Atlantic Ocean. From here, beginning in 1418, he sent mariners south along the African coast. They quickly laid claim to the islands of the eastern Atlantic, and by the 1440s they had initiated trade along the west African coast, carrying gold and slaves back to Portugal.

Courtesy, Algarve Tourism Board

The Lateen Rig: A Triangular Sail That Helped to Conquer Oceans

Viking ships and other medieval European sailing vessels used square sails that were only effective when traveling "with the wind." On a journey facing *into* the wind, it was often necessary to use oars instead of sail power. But Arab sailors on the Red Sea and the Indian Ocean had devised a solution. For more than a thousand years, they had been employing a "lateen rig" for their feluccas and dhows. The long wooden "yard" (a flexible beam attached to the mast) can be cumbersome, but it holds a triangular sail that offers mariners more options in directing their ships. The angled leading edge of the lateen sail allows a vessel to sail into the wind, tacking back and forth on a zigzag course against a prevailing breeze, as well as to sail downwind like a square-rigged ship.

In late medieval times, European sailors on the Mediterranean Sea adopted this innovation. (Scholars call this process "cultural diffusion," in which a valuable innovation passes from one society to another, rather than being invented separately.) Lateen sails appeared on the early Iberian caravels sent into the Atlantic by Prince Henry of Portugal. Aided by this novel rigging, later European sailors, including Columbus, could follow prevailing winds on long voyages without fear that they would be unable to sail home in the opposite direction. In the age of oceanic exploration, each journey brought increased knowledge of deep-sea winds and currents. But it was the lateen sail that allowed mariners to explore the farthest reaches of the globe and still return safely, tacking steadily to make headway against opposing winds.

QUESTIONS

1. European acquisition of the lateen sail illustrates cultural diffusion. What are some other examples of one society borrowing a technological innovation from another?

2. Lateen rigs allowed ships to sail into the wind, so they no longer needed bulky oars and extra crewmen to row. What new advantages did this create for long ocean voyages?

The Wider World

the western tip of Europe. From there, his sailors launched a far-reaching revolution in human communication and trade, perhaps the most momentous single step in a **globalization** process that continues to the present day.

Henry's innovative ships, known as caravels, pushed south along the African coast. Their narrow hulls, deep keels, and high gunwales were well suited for ocean sailing. On the masts, their array of canvas usually included several lateen sails. These triangular sails, long used by Arab sailors on the Red Sea, helped mariners to maneuver against headwinds. Other innovations proved equally valuable. Henry's experts at Sagres drew on the work of Jewish cartographers from the island of Majorca to develop state-of-the-art charts, astronomical tables, and navigational instruments.

With these advantages, and years of experience, Henry's captains slowly mastered the winds and currents near West Africa. In the process, they located three island groups off northwest Africa: the Canaries, the Madeiras, and the Azores. Before midcentury, Portuguese settlers on the never-inhabited island of Madeira had burned off all the timber and started planting sugar for export. In the 1440s, Portuguese mariners began seizing people who lived on the coast of Africa and deporting them as slaves to the new Atlantic sugar island. In addition, Portuguese captains carried slaves back to Europe and sold them there to supplement the growing trade in ivory and gold from sub-Saharan Africa. Nevertheless, when Henry died in 1460, his mariners had still glimpsed only a small portion of the African coast, sailing as far as what is now Sierra Leone.

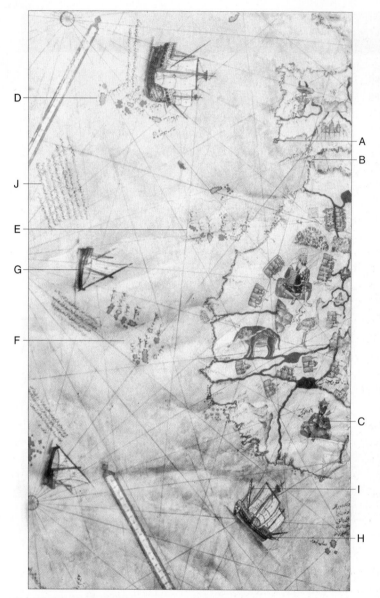

■ This Atlantic chart illustrates key aspects of Portuguese success in overseas exploration. Cape St. Vincent (A), where Prince Henry built his headquarters at Sagres, lies near the Strait of Gibraltar (B), the narrow entrance to the Mediterranean Sea. As Henry's mariners explored along the African coast for a sea passage to Asia, they also looked for possible allies such as Prester John, a mythical black king (C). They used the island groups of the eastern Atlantic to check their position: Azores (D), Madeiras (E), Canaries (F). Their small caravels (G) adopted the triangular lateen sail seen on traditional Arab boats in the Red Sea. Larger square-rigged ships that later sailed from Portugal to India (H) also incorporated lateen sails on a mast at the stern (I). A skilled Turkish navigator—who had never sailed on the Atlantic—made this unusual map in 1513. Piri Re'is used charts captured from a Christian ship in the Mediterranean; his inscriptions (J) are in Turkish.

LOOKING FOR THE INDIES: DA GAMA AND COLUMBUS

During the 1480s, following a war with Spain, the Portuguese renewed their African designs. In 1482 they erected a trading fort called Elmina Castle on the Gold Coast (modern Ghana) to guard against Spanish competition and to support exploration toward the east. Finally, in 1487, Bartolomeu Dias rounded the southernmost tip of Africa, the Cape of Good Hope, proving that a sea link existed between the Atlantic and Indian oceans. The Portuguese could now sail to India and tap into the rich spice trade flowing from the islands of Southeast Asia that Europeans vaguely called the Indies. Success came a decade later with the voyage of Vasco da Gama, who set out from Lisbon in 1497. After two years, his ship returned from India laden with pepper and cinnamon. The Portuguese had at last opened a southeastern sea route to the silk and spice markets of the East.

Meanwhile, the rulers of rival Spain gambled on finding a profitable *westward* route to the Indies. Ferdinand of Aragon had married Isabella of Castile in 1469, leading to the unification of Christian Spain under a single royal family. Pooling resources, they used force to reconquer portions of their realm still under Muslim control. In 1492, King Ferdinand and Queen Isabella finally succeeded in driving the Muslims from Spain by military means. The monarchs imposed Christian orthodoxy and forced Jews into exile. That same year, they agreed to sponsor an Atlantic voyage to the west by Christopher Columbus, a charismatic dreamer in his early forties whose arguments often relied on obscure passages in Christian scripture and conflicting ancient geography treatises.

It was the navigator's experience and knowledge that gained him the trust of Spain's king and queen, for he had practical familiarity with the Atlantic world. Born in Genoa, Italy, the son of a weaver, Columbus had gone to sea at age nineteen. He had visited the Madeiras, West Africa (Guinea), and perhaps even Iceland. His brother Bartholomew was a mapmaker, and both men had heard stories from sailors aboard English and Portuguese fishing vessels. They told of islands, real and imagined, which dotted the Atlantic. Columbus had tried unsuccessfully to convince various European monarchs, including Henry VII of England, that an alternative route to China could be found by sailing west.

On August 3, 1492, Columbus set out to test his audacious plan. Leaving Spain with ninety men aboard three small vessels, he headed for the Canary Islands, eluding

Portuguese caravels sent to stop him. From the Canaries, his ships sailed due west on September 6. After a voyage of three or four weeks, he expected to encounter the island of Cipangu (Japan), which Marco Polo had mentioned, or to reach the coast of Asia, where Polo had seen the court of the Great Khan. After weeks without sight of any land, his crew worried that they might not have enough supplies for the long return home. So Columbus gave out a false, reduced estimate of each day's headway, leading his sailors to believe they were still close to Europe. He recorded the much longer, more accurate distance in his own private log, but he harbored huge illusions regarding his actual whereabouts.

Why these misunderstandings? The mariner made several crucial mistakes. Like other Europeans, Columbus knew the world was round, not flat, and he accepted the idea of the ancient geographer Ptolemy that by using north–south lines, one could divide the globe into 360 degrees of longitude. But he questioned Ptolemy's estimate that each degree measures fifty nautical miles at the equator. (Each actually measures sixty miles.) Instead, Columbus accepted an alternative figure of forty-five miles, making the circumference of his theoretical globe 25 percent smaller than the real distance around the earth. Besides *under*estimating the world's circumference, he compounded his error by *over*estimating two other crucial distances: the breadth of the Eurasian landmass and the extent of Japan's separation from China. The first distance is actually 130 degrees of longitude, and the second is 20. Columbus used authorities who suggested 225 and 30 degrees, respectively. His estimates placed Japan 105 degrees closer to Europe, at the longitude that runs through eastern Lake Superior and western Cuba.

> *Early on October 12, the distressed sailors finally sighted a small island, naming it San Salvador after their Christian savior.*

Early on October 12, the distressed sailors finally sighted a small island, naming it San Salvador after their Christian savior. The inhabitants in the Bahamas proved welcoming, and Columbus recorded pleasure over the "gold which they wear hanging from their noses. But I wish to go and see if I can find the island of Cipangu." Within several weeks he located a large and beautiful island (Cuba, not Cipangu), and he estimated that the Asian mainland of the Great Khan was only "a 10 days' journey" farther west. He claimed a nearby island as La Isla Española, the Spanish island, or Hispaniola (current-day Haiti and the Dominican Republic). He noted stories of hostile islanders farther south called Caribs, or Caniba, who were said to devour their enemies. "I repeat," he asserted, "the Caniba are no other than the people of the Grand Khan." (Upon hearing of these fierce Caribs, Europeans soon fashioned the word *cannibal* and named the region the Caribbean.)

DOCUMENT

From the Journal of Christopher Columbus

Bolstered by these encounters, the explorers returned hastily across the Atlantic on a more northerly route. They weathered a horrendous winter storm to reach Spain in March 1493. Columbus told the Spanish court that he had reached the Indies off the Asian coast, and he displayed several natives he called "Indians" to prove it. His three later voyages did not shake this belief, which he clung to until his death in 1506. The captain, one observer wrote in 1493, "has sailed . . ., as he believes, to the very shores of India, . . . even though the size of the earth's sphere seems to indicate otherwise." Columbus had not reached the lands he sought, but his initial voyage of 1492 would have immediate and extraordinary consequences.

IN THE WAKE OF COLUMBUS: COMPETITION AND EXCHANGE

Within months of Columbus's return, the pope in Rome issued a papal bull, or decree. This pronouncement, titled *Inter Caetera,* claimed the entire world as the rightful inheritance of Christianity. It brashly divided the globe between two Christian powers, Spain and Portugal, by drawing a line through the western Atlantic Ocean from the North Pole to the South Pole. For 180 degrees of longitude west of the line, the Spanish alone could

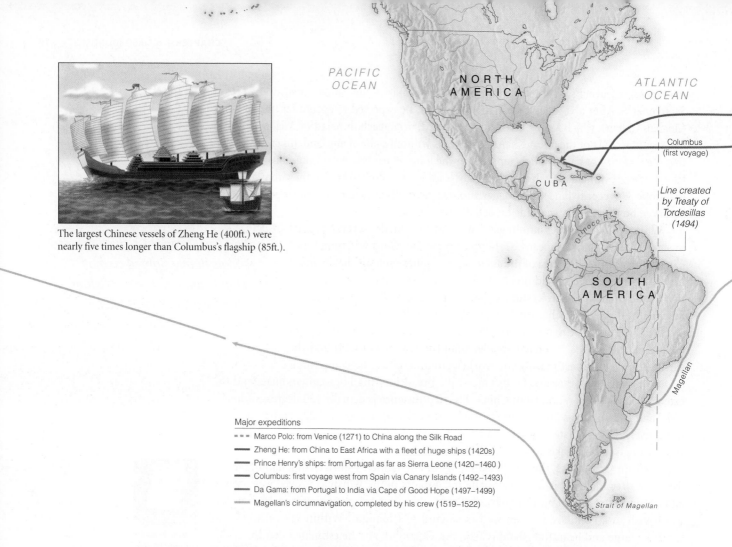

The largest Chinese vessels of Zheng He (400ft.) were nearly five times longer than Columbus's flagship (85ft.).

PACIFIC OCEAN

NORTH AMERICA

ATLANTIC OCEAN

Columbus (first voyage)

CUBA

Line created by Treaty of Tordesillas (1494)

Orinoco R.

SOUTH AMERICA

Magellan

Major expeditions

- - - Marco Polo: from Venice (1271) to China along the Silk Road
——— Zheng He: from China to East Africa with a fleet of huge ships (1420s)
——— Prince Henry's ships: from Portugal as far as Sierra Leone (1420–1460)
——— Columbus: first voyage west from Spain via Canary Islands (1492–1493)
——— Da Gama: from Portugal to India via Cape of Good Hope (1497–1499)
········ Magellan's circumnavigation, completed by his crew (1519–1522)

Strait of Magellan

■ **MAP 1.3   Opening New Ocean Pathways Around the Globe, 1420–1520**

In the 1420s, ships from Portugal and China explored opposite coasts of Africa. But China withdrew from oceanic trade, and European mariners competed to explore the earth by sea. Within a century, Magellan's ship had circled the globe for Spain. The colonization in North America is a chapter in this larger saga of exploration.

continue to seek access to Asia. The Portuguese king claimed that east of such a line, on the other half of the globe, Portugal would have a monopoly in developing the route that Dias had opened around the Cape of Good Hope. The two Iberian powers affirmed this division of the earth in the Treaty of Tordesillas (1494).

That same year Columbus led a huge fleet back to Hispaniola, taking 1,200 men aboard seventeen ships. By employing only men to launch Spain's overseas empire, the 1494 expedition initiated a pattern of warfare against native Caribbean men and intermarriage with indigenous women. A mestizo, or mixed-race (Spanish/Indian), population emerged swiftly in Spanish settlements there. On his third Atlantic crossing (1498), Columbus glimpsed the wide mouth of Venezuela's Orinoco River. Given the huge volume of fresh water entering the sea, he knew he had reached a large landmass, perhaps a part of Asia. When Amerigo Vespucci, another Italian in the service of Spain, saw the same continent in 1499, he described it as a *Mundus Novus,* or New World. European geographers wrote his name, *America,* across their maps.

Meanwhile, a third Italian navigator—John Cabot (or Caboto)—obtained a license from the English king, Henry VII, to probe the North Atlantic for access to Cathay. Cabot knew that English mariners from the port of Bristol had been fishing in the waters off Newfoundland for decades. In 1497, Cabot sailed west from Bristol across the Atlantic to

Newfoundland and perhaps Nova Scotia, thinking he was viewing the coast of Asia. When Cabot died at sea during a follow-up voyage the next year, Henry VII, the founder of England's new Tudor dynasty lacked the resources to pursue the explorer's claims. Nevertheless, the ventures of Columbus had sparked widespread excitement and curiosity in European ports. Within a generation, navigators and cartographers began to comprehend the geographic reality that Columbus had so thoroughly misunderstood. Their increasing knowledge fueled greater transatlantic contact.

After thousands of years, the long separation of the hemispheres had been broken. The destinies of the world's most divergent continents swiftly became linked. Those links fostered human migrations of an unprecedented scale. Moreover, with European ships came transfers of seeds and viruses, bugs and birds, plants and animals that forever reshaped the world. Scholars call this phenomenon the **Columbian Exchange.** The phrase acknowledges Columbus as the crucial initiator, but it also underscores the two-way nature of the flow.

Within a matter of decades, this dramatic Columbian Exchange saw the movement west across the Atlantic of cows, sheep, pigs, chickens, and honeybees—all unknown in the Western Hemisphere. Horses, which had disappeared from the Americas thousands of years earlier, arrived once again aboard Spanish ships. So did Old World foods such as

IMAGE

Early Botanical Illustration — New World Plants

NEW WORLD to OLD WORLD

Corn, Beans (kidney, lima, navy, pole), Turkey, Pumpkin, Peanut, Sunflower

Syphilis

Horses, absent from the Americas for nearly 10,000 years, returned aboard Spanish ships. They awed Native Americans at first and played a crucial role in European conquests. "After God," the Spanish wrote, "we owe victory to the horses."

■ **FIGURE 1.1   The Columbian Exchange**

The voyages of Columbus 500 years ago initiated a dramatic interchange between once-isolated continents. The so-called Columbian Exchange involved the movement of numerous plants and animals to and from the Americas, including those shown here. Seeds and microorganisms have been a crucial part of this process, which continues at an ever-increasing rate.

All photos from photos.com, except horses: Courtesy, Bancroft Library, University of California, Berkeley (SF309 G7 M25 1769 pl.20)

sugar cane, coffee, bananas, peaches, lemons, and oranges. But westbound European ships also carried devastating diseases unknown in the Americas, such as smallpox, measles, malaria, and whooping cough. Returning east across the Atlantic, ships also carried a great deal in the opposite direction. Gradually they transported to the Old World such New World novelties as corn, potatoes, pumpkins, chili peppers, tobacco, cacao, pineapples, sunflowers, and turkeys. Many Europeans suspected that syphilis, the sexually transmitted disease which spread across Europe during the wars of the 1490s, had been introduced from America by Columbus's returning sailors. The ongoing Columbian Exchange had dimensions and implications few could imagine; the planet and all its inhabitants would never be the same again.

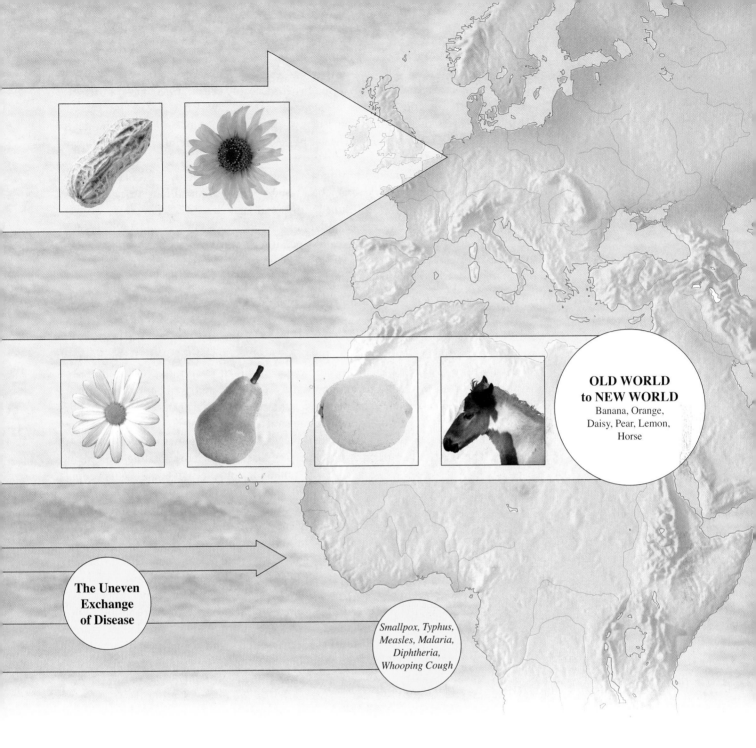

OLD WORLD to NEW WORLD
Banana, Orange, Daisy, Pear, Lemon, Horse

The Uneven Exchange of Disease

Smallpox, Typhus, Measles, Malaria, Diphtheria, Whooping Cough

Spain Enters the Americas

■ *What factors motivated and shaped Spain's rapid intrusion into sixteenth-century America?*

Throughout the sixteenth century, European mariners, inspired by the feats of Columbus and da Gama, risked ocean voyaging in hopes of scoring similar successes. Those who survived brought back novelties for consumers, information for geographers, and profits for ship owners. New wealth prompted further investment in exploration, and expanding knowledge awakened cultural changes for both explorers and the people they met.

The dynamic European era known as the Renaissance, or rebirth, owed much to overseas exploration. Returning mariners brought reports of surprising places and people. Their experiences challenged the inherited wisdom of traditional authorities and put a new premium on rational thought, scientific calculation, and careful observation of the natural world.

In turn, Europe's Renaissance stimulated ever wider exploration as breakthroughs in technology and navigation yielded practical results. Sailing south around Africa and then east, Portuguese caravels reached China by 1514 and Japan by 1543. Sailing west, Spanish vessels learned first that the Caribbean did not offer a passage to Asia and then in 1522—through Magellan's global voyage—that the ocean separating America and Asia was enormous. In the West Indies, and then elsewhere in the Western Hemisphere, Native Americans began to pay dearly for the exchange that ships from Spain had initiated.

THE DEVASTATION OF THE INDIES

Spanish arrival in the West Indies in 1492 triggered widespread ecological and human disaster within decades. Well armed and eager for quick wealth, the early colonizers wrought havoc on the Taino Indians and Caribs who inhabited the islands. The strange newcomers killed and enslaved native peoples and extracted tribute from the survivors in the form of gold panned from streams. Spanish livestock trampled or consumed native gardens, prompting severe food shortages. Worse, European diseases ravaged countless villages. The West Indian population plummeted. Island societies totaling more than 1 million lost nineteen of every twenty people within a generation.

This near-extinction had three consequences. First, devout Catholics back in Spain protested the loss of potential American converts. When Dominican friars reached Cuba in 1510, they denounced Spanish brutality as sinful. The Indians, they argued, possessed souls that only Christian baptism could save. A Spanish soldier named Bartholomé de Las Casas, who repented and joined the Dominican order, led the outcry for reform. In his scathing exposé titled *The Devastation of the Indies,* he opposed genocide and urged conversion.

Second, in response to the steep drop in population, Spanish colonizers began importing African slaves. The same Christians who bemoaned Native American enslavement justified this initiative to replace the decimated Indian workforce in mining for gold. A few enslaved Africans were brought from Seville to Hispaniola as early as 1502. After 1510, several dozen black workers were sent from Spain each year, mostly (in the words of Columbus's son) "to break the rocks in which the gold was found." But Spanish landowners in the West Indies soon saw the prospects for growing sugar cane with African labor, following the Portuguese precedent in Madeira and the

The Pierpont Morgan Library/Art Resource, NY

■ As the Indian population of the Caribbean plummeted in the face of new diseases and exploitation, the Spanish began importing Africans to the New World as slaves. Many were put to work mining precious metals. Here men are forced to dig for gold nuggets beside a mountain stream, then wash them in a tub and dry them over a fire, before handing them to their Spanish master to weigh in his hand-held scale.

Azores. By 1518, European investors had started to ship black slaves directly from Africa to the Caribbean.

Third, decimation in the islands prompted the Spanish to intensify their explorations. Captains looked for new sources of Indian labor, fresh lands to exploit, and easy passageways to the Pacific. They pushed out from the Caribbean in several directions. In 1510, they established a mainland outpost at Darien on the Atlantic coast of Panama. From there, Vasco Núñez de Balboa pressed south over the mountainous **isthmus** to glimpse the Pacific in 1513. That same year, Juan Ponce de León sailed northwest from Puerto Rico, where he had amassed a fortune as governor. Despite later tales that he sought a fountain of youth, he actually hoped the nearby land, which he named Florida, would yield new gold and slaves. But the peninsula's Indians were already familiar with Spanish raiders. They turned Ponce de León away after he claimed the region for Spain.

THE SPANISH CONQUEST OF THE AZTEC

By 1519, the Spanish had determined that the Gulf of Mexico offered no easy passage to Asia. They needed fresh alternatives. In Spain, crown officials sought someone to sail southwest, around the South American continent that Columbus and Vespucci had encountered. For this perilous task, they recruited a Portuguese navigator named Ferdinand Magellan, who had sailed in the Indian Ocean. On his epic voyage (1519–1522), Magellan located a difficult passage through the tip of South America—now called the Strait of Magellan. But the journey also revealed the vast width of the Pacific. The crew nearly starved crossing its enormous expanse, which covers one-third of the earth's surface. Warring factions in the Philippines killed Magellan and twenty-seven of his men shortly after they reached the islands. However, one of his ships, the *Victoria*,

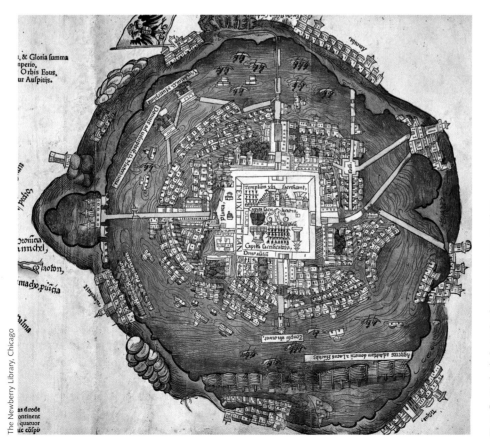

The Newberry Library, Chicago

■ Cortés enclosed this map of Tenochtitlán in a letter to King Charles V (the Holy Roman Emperor and grandson of Ferdinand and Isabella). The map remained secret in Spain, but it was published in a 1524 Nuremberg edition of the letter, giving many Europeans their first glimpse of the defeated Aztec capital that was later rebuilt as Mexico City. The city plan shows the causeways over Lake Texcoco and the central square, with high temples where Aztec priests conducted human sacrifices. The flag with the double-headed eagle of Charles V's Hapsburg dynasty may mark Cortés's headquarters.

"These Gods That We Worship Give Us Everything We Need"

Interpreting History

Three years after Cortés captured Tenochtitlán in central Mexico, twelve missionaries from the Franciscan order arrived in the city to preach Christianity to the conquered Aztec. In several meetings with principal elders and priests, they explained their beliefs and laid out their plans through a translator. Similar talks would take place throughout America in later generations.

No transcript of the 1524 conversations exists, but another Franciscan, the famous preserver of Aztec culture Bernardino de Sahagún, gathered recollections of the encounter from both sides and reconstructed the dialogue. He published his version in 1564, creating parallel texts in Spanish and Nahuatl, the Aztec language. "Having understood the reasoning and speech of the twelve," Sahagún reports, the city leaders "became greatly agitated and fell into a great sadness and fear, offering no response." The next morning, they requested a complete repetition of the unsettling message. "Having heard this, one of the

The Bibliothèque Nationale, Paris

principal lords arose, asked the indulgence of the twelve, . . . and made the following long speech."

Our lords, leading personages of much esteem, you are very welcome to our lands and towns. . . . We have heard the words that you have brought us of the One who gives us life and being. And we have heard with admiration the words of the Lord of the World which he has sent here for love of us, and also you have brought us the book of celestial and divine words.

You have told us that we do not know the One who gives us life and being, who is Lord of the heavens and of the earth. You also say that those we worship are not gods. This way of speaking is entirely new to us, and very scandalous. We are frightened by this way of speaking because our forebears who engendered and governed us never said anything like this.

made it back to Spain via Africa's Cape of Good Hope, becoming the first vessel to circumnavigate the globe.

As news of Magellan's voyage raced through Spain in 1522, word also arrived that a Spanish military leader, or *conquistador,* named Hernán Cortés had toppled the gold-rich empire of the Aztec in central Mexico. Like other ambitious conquistadores, Cortés had followed Columbus to the Caribbean. In 1519, hoping to march overland to the Pacific as Balboa had done, Cortés sailed along Mexico's east coast and established a base camp at Vera Cruz. He quickly realized he had reached the edge of a powerful empire.

At Tenochtitlán the Aztec emperor, Moctezuma, reacted with uncertainty to news that bearded strangers aboard "floating islands" had appeared off his coast. Ominous signs—shooting stars, fierce storms, unknown birds—had foretold an extraordinary arrival. If the newcomers' leader was the returning god Quetzalcoatl, the court had to welcome him with the utmost care. The emperor sent basketloads of precious objects encrusted with gold to Cortés's camp. But the elaborate gifts only alerted Cortés and his men to the Aztec's wealth.

Although the Spanish numbered scarcely 600, they had several key advantages over the Aztec. Their guns and horses, unknown in America, terrified the Indians. When Cortés found coastal peoples staggering under heavy Aztec taxes, he recruited them as willing allies. A young Indian woman (christened Doña Marina, or La Malinche) acted as Cortés's translator and companion. In an aggressive show of force, Cortés marched directly to the capital and seized Moctezuma as his hostage.

The Spanish still faced daunting obstacles. But sickness worked decisively to their advantage. Smallpox was a disease the Aztec had never encountered before, so they lacked any immunity. The European illness reached the mainland with the invading army, and

On the contrary, they left us this our custom of worshiping our gods. . . . They taught us how to honor them. And they taught us all the ceremonies and sacrifices that we make. They told us that . . . we were beholden to them, to be theirs and to serve countless centuries before the sun began to shine and before there was daytime. They said that these gods that we worship give us everything we need for our physical existence: maize, beans, chia seeds, etc. We appeal to them for the rain to make the things of the earth grow.

These our gods are the source of great riches and delights, all of which belong to them. . . . They live in very delightful places where there are always flowers, vegetation, and great freshness, a place . . . where there is never hunger, poverty, or illness. . . . There has never been a time remembered when they were not worshiped, honored, and esteemed. . . .

It would be a fickle, foolish thing for us to destroy the most ancient laws and customs left by the first inhabitants of this land. . . . We are accustomed to them and we have them impressed on our hearts. . . . How could you leave the poor elderly among us bereft of that in which they have been raised throughout their lives? Watch out that we do not incur the wrath of our gods. Watch out that the common people do not rise up

against us if we were to tell them that the gods they have always understood to be such are not gods at all.

It is best, our lords, to act on this matter very slowly, with great deliberation. We are not satisfied or convinced by what you have told us, nor do we understand or give credit to what has been said of our gods. . . . All of us together feel that it is enough to have lost, enough that the power and royal jurisdiction have been taken from us. As for our gods, we will die before giving up serving and worshiping them. This is our determination; do what you will.

QUESTIONS

1. *Why would the Aztec priests fear an uprising of the common people under these circumstances? How would you respond to a similar situation?*

2. *As suggested near the end of this chapter, a similar religious confrontation was taking place in Europe in 1524, during the early years of the Protestant Reformation. Contrast and compare these two situations.*

Source: Kenneth Mills and William B. Taylor, *Colonial Spanish America: A Documentary History* (Wilmington: Scholarly Resources, 1998), 21–22.

a crushing epidemic swept the Aztec capital in 1521. The disaster let Cortés conquer Tenochtitlán (which he renamed Mexico City) and claim the entire region as New Spain.

MAGELLAN AND CORTÉS PROMPT NEW SEARCHES

Cortés's conquest of Mexico raised Spain's hopes of additional windfalls in the Americas. In 1531, Spanish raiders under Francisco Pizarro set sail from Panama's Pacific coast for Peru, with plans to overthrow the Inca empire. Pizarro had limited resources (180 men and 37 horses), but smallpox assisted him, as it had helped Cortés, and his invaders accomplished their mission. Marching overland to Cuzco in 1533, they killed the emperor, Atahualpa, and sacked the mountain capital for the gold it contained.

Meanwhile, inspired by the explorations of Magellan, Spanish mariners pressed across the Pacific from the west coast of Mexico. Cortés dispatched three ships for the Philippines, and one actually reached its destination. Still, not until the 1560s did Spanish cargo ships, known as galleons, accomplish the arduous round trip across the Pacific from Acapulco to the Philippines and back.

Balboa and Cortés had failed to find a water passageway near the equator that could link the Atlantic directly to the Pacific. And while Magellan had located a navigable strait at the tip of South America, his new route appeared extremely long and dangerous. Therefore, fresh interest emerged in Europe for finding a shorter passage to Asia somewhere in the northern hemisphere. In 1524, Italian navigator Giovanni da Verrazzano, sailing for the French, renewed the search initiated by John Cabot. Verrazzano reached North America near the Outer Banks of North Carolina; he wondered if Pamlico Sound, visible beyond Carolina's barrier islands, might be the Pacific. He then cruised north, entering New York harbor and exploring further along the coast before returning to France without finding a strait. In 1526, Lucas Vásquez de Ayllón led 500 men and women from the Spanish Caribbean to the Santee River region (near present-day Georgetown, South Carolina) to settle and explore. But Ayllón fell sick and died, and the colony proved short-lived.

In 1528, a rival of Cortés and Ayllón named Pánfilo de Narváez launched another ill-fated expedition from Cuba. Narváez landed near Florida's Tampa Bay with 400 soldiers, hoping to travel overland to find riches or a Pacific passageway. But disease, hunger, and Indian hostilities plagued the party's journey along the Gulf Coast. Only four men—three Spanish and one North African black named Esteban—survived to make an extended trek on foot across the Southwest from Galveston Bay to Mexico City. The leader of this tiny band, Álvar Núñez Cabeza de Vaca, wrote about their odyssey after he returned to Spain in 1537. Scholars now recognize Cabeza de Vaca's *Relation* (1542) as an early classic in North American literature.

THREE NEW VIEWS OF NORTH AMERICA

Even before Cabeza de Vaca published his narrative, Europeans initiated three more expeditions into North America. Each probed a separate region of the continent, hoping to gauge the land's dimensions, assess its peoples, and claim its resources. Together, the three enterprises made 1534 to 1543 the most extraordinary decade in the early European exploration of North America, for Native Americans and newcomers alike.

DOCUMENT

Jacques Cartier: First Contact with the Indians

In the Northeast, Frenchman Jacques Cartier visited the Gulf of St. Lawrence in 1534 and bartered for furs with the Micmac Indians. He returned the next year and penetrated southwest up the St. Lawrence River into Canada. (The name comes from *kanata*, the Huron-Iroquois word for "village.") After a friendly reception at the large Indian town of Hochelaga near modern Montreal, the French returned downriver to camp at Stadacona, the future site of Quebec. Following a hard winter, in which he lost twenty-five men to scurvy, the explorer and his remaining crew sailed for France.

Cartier returned again in 1541, building a fort on high ground overlooking the St. Lawrence River. (In 2006 archaeologists located the exact site near Quebec, tipped off by

> *Cartier returned again in 1541, building a fort on high ground overlooking the St. Lawrence River.*

a single shard of European pottery dating from the 1540s.) From this base, the explorer hoped to find precious minerals and signs of a water passage farther west to the Pacific Ocean. He found neither. When he returned to France, Parisians ridiculed his rock crystals as "Canada diamonds." In Cartier's wake came a colonizing party of several hundred in 1542, led by a nobleman named Roberval. It contained several hundred French settlers, including women for the first time. But again, scurvy and cold took a heavy toll at the Quebec campsite, and the weakening colony withdrew after a single winter. Despite a decade of contacts with Indians of the St. Lawrence valley, the French still had not established a beachhead in the New World. Nevertheless, they had demonstrated their resolve to challenge Spain's exclusive claim to American lands.

The Spanish, meanwhile, launched two intrusions of their own—one in the Southeast and one in the Southwest. News of Pizarro's 1533 triumph over the Inca in Peru helped renew the search for wealthy kingdoms to conquer. In 1537, Emperor Charles V of Spain granted one hardened veteran of the Peruvian campaign—Hernando de Soto—the right to explore and conquer in and beyond Florida, establishing a personal domain for himself and his descendants. The conquistador spent most of his fortune assembling a force of more than 600 soldiers that reached Tampa Bay in 1539. The enterprise included several women and priests, along with scores of servants and African slaves, plus 200 horses. De Soto had also brought along a herd of 300 pigs that multiplied rapidly and provided food during the long march through the interior.

Over the next four years, de Soto's party traveled across parts of ten southern states. They hoped to find a city as wealthy as Cuzco in Peru or Tenochtitlán in Mexico. Instead,

Two decades after Verrazzano's explorations, this 1547 chart shows the early claims of France in North America. It depicts the men and women of Roberval's short-lived colonizing expedition as they disembarked in 1542, watched by Native Americans. Perhaps to feature the large St. Lawrence River, the European mapmaker put North at the bottom and South at the top. Hence, the Atlantic coast seems upside-down to our eyes, with Florida appearing in the upper right-hand corner.

they encountered only scattered villages. Towns that refused to provide the intruders with porters or guides met with brutal Spanish reprisals that made use of attack dogs. At Mabila near modern-day Selma, Alabama, de Soto's mounted army, brandishing swords and lances, killed several thousand Native Americans who had dared to attack them with bows and arrows. Still, Spanish frustrations grew due to difficult terrain, stiff Indian resistance, and failure to find riches. After exploring beyond the Mississippi River, de Soto died of a fever in 1542. His disheartened followers escaped downstream to the Gulf of Mexico the next year, leaving epidemic sickness in their wake.

At the same time, another encounter was unfolding in the Southwest. By 1539, Spanish sailors voyaging up Mexico's western coast had explored the Gulf of California and skirted the Baja Peninsula. Over the next four years, similar expeditions cruised the coast of California and southern Oregon. Once again, they found no signs of a passage linking the Pacific and Atlantic oceans. In Mexico, speculation about gold in the north had intensified after the appearance of Cabeza de Vaca. His African companion, Esteban, guided a reconnaissance party north in 1539. Esteban was killed by the Zuni Indians, but exaggerated accounts of the region's pueblos prompted rumors about the seven golden cities known as Cibola.

The next year, aspiring conquistador Francisco Vásquez de Coronado set out from northern Mexico to reach these wealthy towns before de Soto could. He left his post as a frontier governor and assembled a huge expedition with more than 300 Spanish adventurers and 1,000 Indian allies. However, his grandiose expectations were quickly dashed. The pueblos of the Zuni, he reported, "are very good houses, three and four and five stories high," but the fabled "Seven Cities are seven little villages." Hoping to gauge his distance from the Pacific, Coronado sent explorers northwest. When they reached the amazing but impassable Grand Canyon, they realized they could go no farther and returned.

> *Spanish newcomers imposed a heavy burden on the Pueblo Indians, demanding food and burning helpless towns.*

Spanish newcomers imposed a heavy burden on the Pueblo Indians, demanding food and burning helpless towns. Desperate to get rid of Coronado, the Pueblo told him stories of a far-off, wealthy land called Quivira. They secretly recruited a Plains Indian to lead the Spaniards to some place where men and horses "would starve to death." In the spring of 1541, he guided Coronado's party northeast onto the Great Plains, repeating tantalizing tales of gold and silver. Coronado's soldiers became the first Europeans to see this rolling ocean of grass and its endless herds of buffalo. But when Quivira proved to be a Wichita Indian village in what is now central Kansas, the Spanish strangled their deceitful guide and made their way back south to New Spain. At one point, as they crossed northern Texas, they even came within 300 miles of de Soto's ill-fated party in eastern Arkansas. But neither de Soto nor Coronado—nor Cartier in the north—ever discovered wealthy cities or a sea passage to the Far East.

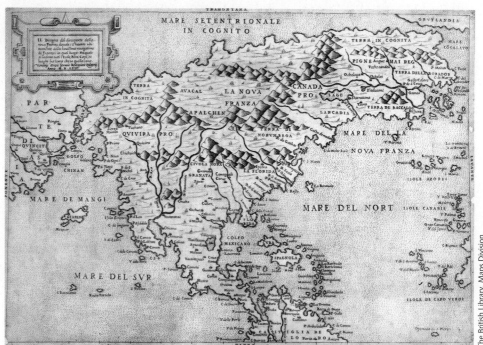

The British Library, Maps Division

■ European mapmakers learned quickly about the expeditions into the North American interior led by Cartier, de Soto, and Coronado. This 1566 Italian chart places New France, or Canada, in the North, and shows the Indian town of "Ochelaga" visited by Cartier. "La Florida," labeled twice, includes not only the crudely drawn peninsula but also all of the Southeast explored by de Soto. The imagined regions of Cibola and Quivira, sought by Coronado, appear in the Southwest. European hope of a Northwest Passage from the Atlantic to Asia continues, and the size of the North Pacific remains uncertain, so Japan (Giapan) is shown near the coast of California.

The Protestant Reformation Plays Out in America

▪ *How did Europe's sharp religious split influence the early colonization of North America?*

In 1520, while Cortés vied with the Aztec for control in Mexico and Magellan maneuvered around South America, the pope excommunicated a German monk named Martin Luther. Three years earlier, Luther had nailed a list of ninety-five theses to the church door at Wittenberg, challenging long-standing church practices and papal authority. Luther's followers questioned lavish church spending—construction of the ornate St. Peter's Basilica was under way in Rome at the time—and the practice of selling religious pardons to raise money. They also rejected the church's elaborate hierarchy and criticized its refusal to translate the Latin Bible into modern languages.

Luther's reform movement triggered the division of western Christianity into competing religious camps, bitterly at odds. For their written protestations against the papacy, Luther and his fellow insurgents received the enduring name *Protestants*. Their movement became known broadly as the Reformation. Those who opposed it, siding with Rome, launched a Counter-Reformation to defend and revitalize the Roman Catholic Church.

For the first time in history, a controversy in Europe made waves that washed onto American shores. Throughout the remainder of the sixteenth century, European national and religious conflict played out in part overseas, a pattern that repeated itself in future centuries. France and Spain, Catholic powers competing for dominance in Europe, wrestled to claim control of Florida. England, an upstart island nation with a rising population, an expanding navy, and a monarchy at odds with the pope in Rome, seized control of Ireland and launched its first attempt to plant a colony in North America.

REFORMATION AND COUNTER-REFORMATION IN EUROPE

As zeal for Luther's religious reforms spread across Europe, it split communities and even sparked armed conflict. In Switzerland, a priest named Ulrich Zwingli led the revolt. He abolished the practice of confession, condemned the church calendar full of fasts and saints' days, and defied the tradition of a celibate clergy by marrying. Zwingli was killed in battle in 1531, but the Swiss Reformation soon found a new leader in John Calvin. A French Protestant, Calvin settled in Geneva and for more than two decades (1541–1564) ruled the city as a church-centered state.

> *Kings and queens gradually expanded court bureaucracies and asserted greater control over their subjects and economies.*

Calvin imposed his own strict interpretation on Lutheranism and drew dedicated followers to his church. Offended by expensive vestments and elaborate rituals, he donned a simple black "Geneva" robe. He argued that faith alone, not "good works," would lead Christians to be saved. He preached that God alone determined salvation; it could not be bought by giving **tithes** to the church. Only a select few people, Calvin explained, were destined to be members of God's chosen elect. Moreover, only an informed clergy and the careful study of scripture could reveal signs of a person's status. Soon, Calvinist doctrine helped shape Protestant communities across northern Europe: Huguenots in France, Puritans in England, Presbyterians in Scotland, and the Dutch Reformed Church in the Netherlands.

The Protestant Reformation that Luther had ignited coincided roughly with another important change in Europe, the emergence of the modern nation-state. Kings and queens gradually expanded court bureaucracies and asserted greater control over their subjects and economies. They strengthened their armies, gaining a near monopoly on the use of force, and they took full advantage of the new medium of printing. As religious ferment spread and local allegiances gave way to a broader sense of national identity, strong sovereigns moved to distance themselves from papal authority in Rome.

The emergence of England as a nation-state under the Tudor dynasty (founded by Henry VII in 1485) illustrates this shift in power away from Rome. When Henry VIII succeeded his father in 1509, he married Catherine of Aragon, the youngest surviving daughter of Spain's royal couple, Ferdinand and Isabella. As queen, she suffered numerous miscarriages and was unable to produce a male heir, so in 1533 the restless monarch sought a divorce. When the pope refused to grant an annulment of the king's marriage, Henry VIII wrested control of the English church from papal hands and had Parliament approve his divorce and remarriage. The new Church of England, or Anglican Church, continued to follow much of the Catholic Church's doctrine. However, its "Protector and only Supreme Head" would now be the English monarch. During her long reign from 1558 to 1603, Henry VIII's daughter Queen Elizabeth I managed to steer the Church of England on a middle course between advocates of Catholicism and extreme Protestants.

Throughout Europe, as zealous believers on both sides of the debate staked out their positions, attempts to heal religious divisions gave way to confrontation. Reformation challenges to the pope in Rome, whether from local parishes or powerful monarchs, met with stiff resistance as Catholic leaders mobilized opposition. Their followers rallied to defend Roman Catholicism in a variety of ways. Taken together, these efforts are known as the Counter-Reformation.

A militant new Catholic religious order called the Society of Jesus, or the Jesuits, represented one dimension of the Counter-Reformation. Led by a Spanish soldier named Ignatius Loyola and willing to give their lives for their beliefs, these dedicated missionaries and teachers helped reenergize the Catholic faith and spread it to distant parts of the world. Another institution, the Inquisition, reflects a different side of the Counter-Reformation. In 1542, Catholic authorities established a new religious-judicial proceeding, known as the Inquisition, to help resist the spread of Protestantism. Heretics—individuals accused of denying or defying church doctrine—were brought before the Inquisition's strict religious courts. Those who refused to renounce their beliefs suffered severe punishment, including torture and execution. These heresy trials made clear to Inquisition leaders that the advent of printing was helping spread the works of Luther and his Protestant allies. In 1557, therefore, the pope issued an "Index" of prohibited books.

In Spain, King Philip II, who ruled from 1556 to 1598, led an Inquisition to root out Protestant heresy. The Spanish monarch came close to acquiring England as well. In 1588, he dispatched a fleet of warships—the Spanish Armada—in hopes of seizing control in London and restoring the Catholic faith as England's sanctioned religion. A sudden storm and hasty mobilization by the island nation foiled the Spanish king's invasion. But Philip II's confrontation with the navy of Queen Elizabeth I epitomized the sharp new division between Catholic and Protestant power in Europe. This deepening antagonism—religious, ideological, and economic—shaped events overseas in the second half of the sixteenth century. The struggle became especially clear in Florida, the vague region claimed by Spain that encompassed Indian lands from Chesapeake Bay to the Gulf of Mexico.

COMPETING POWERS LAY CLAIM TO FLORIDA

As Spain used force to obtain the dazzling wealth of New World societies, its European rivals looked on jealously. As early as 1523, French sea raiders had captured Spanish ships returning from Mexico with Cortés's bounty of Aztec gold, silver, and pearls. Ten years later, French pirates made a similar haul. To protect the flow of riches from America, the Spanish soon initiated a well-armed annual convoy to escort their wealth from Havana to Seville. Each year, Spain's huge West Indies treasure fleet made an enticing target as it followed the Gulf Stream along the Florida coast.

But France had its own designs on Florida, furthered by the special concerns of French Huguenots. Unsure of their future in a religiously divided country, these Protestants took a

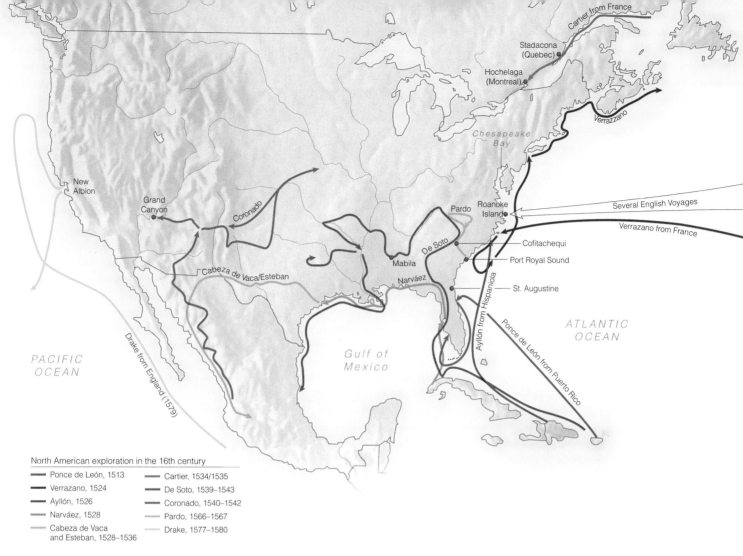

North American exploration in the 16th century

- Ponce de León, 1513
- Verrazano, 1524
- Ayllón, 1526
- Narváez, 1528
- Cabeza de Vaca and Esteban, 1528–1536
- Cartier, 1534/1535
- De Soto, 1539–1543
- Coronado, 1540–1542
- Pardo, 1566–1567
- Drake, 1577–1580

■ **MAP 1.4** **The Extent of North American Exploration by 1592**

By 1592, a century after Columbus's initial voyage, European explorers and colonists had touched the edges of North America, and a few had ventured far inland. But they had not found riches or a passageway to the Pacific, and only the Spanish had managed to establish a lasting foothold along the Florida Coast.

leading role in the colonization efforts of France. In 1562, French Huguenots established a settlement at Port Royal Sound (Parris Island, South Carolina), close to the route of Spain's annual treasure fleet. The effort lasted only two years and aroused Spanish suspicions of "Lutheran" intruders.

Undaunted, the French backed a larger colonizing effort to Florida in 1564. When French Protestants erected Fort Caroline on the St. John's River at present-day Jacksonville, the Spanish crown took swift action. In 1565, Philip II sent 300 soldiers and 700 colonists under Pedro Menéndez de Avilés to oust the French and secure Florida. Menéndez captured Fort Caroline and massacred hundreds of French settlers. The heretics, he feared, might attack the treasure fleet, forge alliances with Florida's Indians, or provoke revolt among slaves in the Spanish Caribbean. To prevent further French incursions on Florida's Atlantic coast, Menéndez established a new outpost at nearby St. Augustine. He also sent Juan Pardo north from Port Royal Sound to establish half a dozen forts in the interior.

With French threats defeated, the Spanish at St. Augustine attempted to plant strategic missions farther north to convert Native Americans to Christianity and secure Spain's land claims. In 1570, eight missionaries from Loyola's Society of Jesus sailed north from Florida to Chesapeake Bay. There, the Jesuits established a mission to convert local Indians and looked for "an entrance into the mountains and on to China." But the friars' rules and

■ In 1562, French Protestants established a short-lived colony at Port Royal Sound on the South Carolina coast. "The commander, on landing with some soldiers, found the country very beautiful, as it was well wooded with oak, cedar, and other trees. As they went through the woods, they saw Indian peacocks, or turkeys, flying past, and deer going by." Traveling upstream beyond Parris Island, they surprised an encampment of Indians, "who, on perceiving the boats, immediately took flight," leaving behind the meat "they were roasting."

beliefs antagonized the Native Americans. By the time Menéndez visited the region in 1572, all the missionaries had been killed. Spain's failure to secure a foothold on Chesapeake Bay soon proved costly, as a new European rival appeared on the scene. Almost overnight, Protestant England emerged as a contending force in the Atlantic world. Now English adventurers began challenging Spanish dominance in the Caribbean and along North America's southeastern coast.

THE BACKGROUND OF ENGLISH EXPANSION

The voyages of John Cabot and the visits of Bristol fishing vessels to Newfoundland's Grand Banks had stimulated an early English interest in the Atlantic. But for several reasons this curiosity intensified after 1550. Henry VIII had used his power, plus the wealth he had seized from the Catholic Church, to build a sizable navy before he died in 1547. The merchant fleet grew as well, carrying English wool and cloth to Antwerp and other European ports. In addition, the English population, which had declined in the previous 150 years, grew steadily after 1500. Overall numbers more than doubled during the sixteenth century.

England's rising population created new pressure on limited resources, especially land. Tenants needed access to agricultural plots in order to subsist, but the growing market in English woolens made property owners eager to enclose pastures for sheep grazing, even if it involved pushing tenants off the land. This gradual squeeze, known as "the enclosure movement," set countless rural people adrift to seek work in towns and cities. London's population soared from 50,000 in 1500 to 200,000 a century later.

Emphasis on wool production had additional unforeseen effects. At midcentury, Europe's market in textile goods became saturated with cheap woolens and collapsed suddenly. English cloth exports fell 35 percent in 1551, prompting merchants to search for new avenues of foreign commerce. Starting in the 1550s, therefore, England's overseas exploration pushed in all directions. Investors in the new Muscovy Company sent ships north around Scandinavia through the Arctic Ocean, but they failed to find a northeastern route above the Asian landmass to China. Other English vessels sailed south to Morocco and the Gold Coast, challenging the Portuguese monopoly of the African trade. English mariner John Hawkins conducted three voyages to West Africa during the 1560s. Horning in on the growing transatlantic slave traffic, he purchased Africans and then sold them in Caribbean ports to Spanish buyers.

Philip II, having driven the French out of Florida, had had enough of Protestant interlopers. A Spanish fleet forced Hawkins and his young kinsman Francis Drake out of Mexican waters in 1568. But thereafter, English sea rovers, with quiet support from Elizabeth, stepped up their challenges to Spain on the high seas. Drake proved the most wide-ranging and successful. On a voyage to the Pacific (1577–1580), he plundered Spanish ports in Peru and landed near San Francisco Bay. He claimed California for England as New Albion and then sailed around the globe. In the 1580s, Drake continued, in his words, "to singe the Spaniard's beard." He sacked ports in the West Indies, encouraged slave uprisings against the Spanish, and attacked the settlement at St. Augustine. He also captured numerous treasure ships, sank two dozen enemy vessels in their home port at Cadiz, and helped defeat Philip's Spanish Armada in 1588.

England's anti-Catholic propagandists made Drake a national hero. Moreover, they painted Spanish cruelties toward Indians in the New World in the worst possible terms. To bolster their case, they translated the vivid tracts of Las Casas into English. Writers loyal to the Counter-Reformation rejected this smear tactic as a "black legend," while Protestants in England countered that Las Casas was a firsthand witness and conscientious reformer, not a fabricator of lies. Whatever the later verdict on Spain's early conduct overseas, the English themselves proved far from innocent. In the Elizabethan years, they established their own pattern of violence during their brutal conquest of Ireland. Many who played leading roles in this bloody takeover came to view a colony in America as the next logical step in England's aggressive overseas expansion.

British Museum/Bridgeman Art Library, New York

■ Painter John White accompanied Martin Frobisher on a search for the Northwest Passage in 1577. When the English captured several inhabitants of Baffin Island, the young artist painted an Eskimo mother and her baby, with attention to her warm clothing and the way she carried the child. White later took part in several voyages to Roanoke Island. His striking pictures were widely copied in Europe, but the original watercolors only become known in the twentieth century.

"The World as a Clover": Mapping for Art, Religion, or Science

Envisioning History

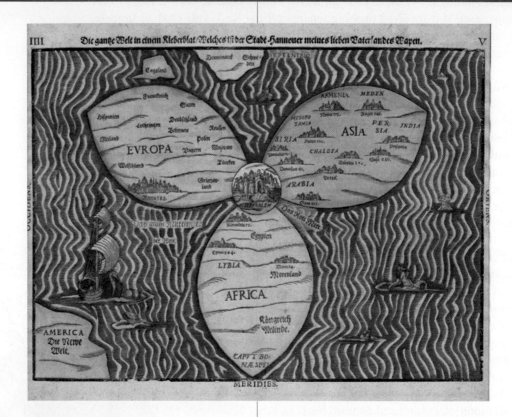

Every map is a work of art, reducing a three-dimensional world to two dimensions. In any age, some charts have a scientific or commercial purpose, while others offer symbolic or spiritual meaning. World maps drawn in medieval Europe had a religious origin and use, so they highlighted the holy city of Jerusalem at the center. As oceanic exploration increased, Europeans developed sophisticated navigational charts that emphasized practical information rather than artistic symbolism. But the older tradition of allegorical maps continued, as shown by this fanciful world diagram created in Germany in 1582.

This depiction was made later than the other sixteenth-century maps that appear in this chapter. The creator came from Hanover, a city that used a three-leafed clover on its crest, so he portrayed "The Whole World as a Clover Leaf." The Christian holy land is at the center, while England and the Red Sea are clearly visible. Scandinavia and America float at the edges of the chart, and strange sea creatures populate the oceans. Portraying a symmetrical clover enhances the map's aesthetic appeal, but it also vastly exaggerates the relative size of Europe in comparison to Africa and Asia.

QUESTIONS

1. Compare this 1582 map with the other sixteenth-century charts in this chapter. In each case, who might have commissioned such a map, and for what potential uses?

2. Specifically, how does this map reflect the slowness of Europeans to cope with new geographical knowledge provided by Marco Polo, Columbus, da Gama, and Magellan?

LOST COLONY: THE ROANOKE EXPERIENCE

Sir Humphrey Gilbert, who had served in Ireland, was one Elizabethan with an eye on America. In 1576, Gilbert published his *Discourse for a Discovery for a New Passage to Cathay.* In it, he speculated on a short northwestern route to China. Martin Frobisher, another veteran of the Irish campaign, undertook voyages to locate such a route. He mistakenly thought he had found the passage, or strait, to Asia. As evidence, he brought back members of an Eskimo family he believed to be Chinese, and English artist John White drew their pictures. The next year, writing an essay on "How Her Majesty May Annoy the King of Spain," Gilbert proposed a colony in Newfoundland. The queen granted him a patent—a license giving him exclusive rights—for such a project. But shipwrecks and desertions doomed the venture to failure. When Gilbert died at sea on the homeward voyage, his half-brother, Walter Raleigh, obtained a similar patent to plant a colony in North America.

In 1584, Raleigh sent explorers to the Outer Banks, the string of coastal barrier islands below Chesapeake Bay that Verrazzano had glimpsed sixty years earlier. They brought back two Indian informants and positive reports about the land near Roanoke Island. The next month, Richard Hakluyt, England's foremost advocate and chronicler of overseas expansion, handed Elizabeth an advisory paper entitled "Western Planting." The document called for the establishment of a strategic outpost on the North American coast, where the English could launch attacks against Spanish shipping, hunt for useful commodities, and convert Indians to Protestant Christianity.

Raleigh's three efforts to establish such an outpost failed in rapid succession. In 1585, he first sent Ralph Lane, a hardened veteran of the Irish campaigns, to build a fort at Roanoke Island. Like other Europeans who had preceded him to America, Lane anticipated "the discovery of a good mine, or a passage to the South Sea." But storms in mid-ocean scattered his ships, and most of Lane's initial force never arrived. Those who did, including artist John White, fared badly because of scarce food, bad discipline, and hostile relations

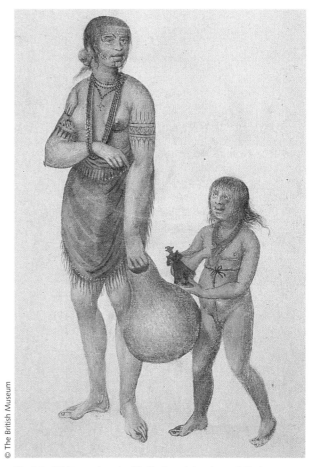

© The British Museum

■ John White made valuable firsthand drawings of Native Americans living in what is now coastal North Carolina, including the wife and daughter of a local leader. The woman kept her "haire trussed opp in a knott," had tattoos on her arms, wore "a chaine of great pearles," and often carried "a gourde full of some kinde of pleasant liquor." The girl holds an English doll, for Indian children "are greatly Deligted with puppetts . . . brought oute of England."

with the Indians. Francis Drake, arriving in 1586 after harassing the Spanish in the West Indies and Florida, expected to find a thriving enterprise. Instead, he carried the disheartened soldiers back to England. They had paid a price, Hakluyt commented, "for the cruelty and outrages committed by some of them against the native inhabitants of that country." A second expedition diverted to the Caribbean to prey on enemy shipping, after leaving a few men at Roanoke, who did not survive.

In May 1587, John White led a third English venture to America, with 110 people, including women and children. They planned to settle on Chesapeake Bay, but a contentious captain refused to carry them farther north after an initial stop at Roanoke Island. In August the settlers sent White back to England for more supplies; they would leave a message for him if they moved. When he finally returned in 1590—delayed by England's clash with the Spanish Armada—he found the site deserted. The word *Croatoan* carved on a post suggested that survivors had joined the nearby Croatan Indians, but the Lost Colony's fate remains a source of endless speculation. The Spanish, worried by the English foray, drew up plans for a fortification at Chesapeake Bay, but warfare between Spain and England kept both countries preoccupied elsewhere until Philip II and Elizabeth I died.

CHRONOLOGY: 14,000 YEARS AGO TO 1590 C.E.

14,000 years ago	Early Paleo-Indians in Florida and Pennsylvania regions, and also in Monte Verde, Chile.
13,900 to 12,900 years ago	Clovis hunters spread across North America.
10,000 to 3,000 years ago	Archaic Indians flourish in diverse settings.
4,200 to 2,700 years ago	Poverty Point culture exists in Louisiana.
300 to 900 C.E.	Mayan culture flourishes in Mesoamerica.
500 to 600	Teotihuacan in central Mexico becomes one of the world's largest cities.
900 to 1100	Anasazi culture centers in Chaco Canyon in Southwest.
1000	Norse explorers establish a Vinland colony in Newfoundland.
1100	Cahokia in Illinois becomes one focus of Mississippian culture.
1400	Aztec build capital at Tenochtitlán (site of modern Mexico City).
1405 to 1433	Chinese fleet of Admiral Zheng He reaches Indian Ocean and Africa's east coast.
1418 to 1460	Prince Henry of Portugal sends ships to explore Africa's west coast.
1492	First voyage of Columbus.
1494	Treaty of Tordesillas arranges division between overseas claims of Spain and Portugal.
1517	Martin Luther launches Protestant Reformation.
1519	Cortés invades Mexico.
1519 to 1522	Magellan's ship circumnavigates the globe and returns to Spain.
1534 to 1543	Expeditions of Cartier (Canada), de Soto (Southeast), and Coronado (Southwest) probe North America.
1565	Spanish establish St. Augustine.
1585 to 1590	English attempt to establish Roanoke colony fails.

Conclusion

For approximately 150 centuries, people descended from distant Asian ancestry had explored and settled the bountiful Western Hemisphere. In every region of North America, from the arctic north to the semitropical Florida Keys, they had adapted and multiplied, building distinctive and durable ways of life over countless generations. Then suddenly, in a single century, unprecedented intrusions brought newcomers from foreign lands to the coasts of the Americas, in wooden castles that floated on the sea. At first, local inhabitants retained the balance of power; the fate of a colonizing effort could hinge on Indian relations. But the number of foreigners only increased with time. In the next century, the contest for European control of the Atlantic seaboard began in earnest.

For Review

1. How has our awareness about the earliest human societies in the Western Hemisphere changed over the past century?

2. Why did complex societies develop in Mesoamerica and Peru, close to the equator?

3. Amerigo Vespucci called the Western Hemisphere a "New World" in 1499. What reasons can you offer for or against using this term today in discussing North and South America after 1500?

4. If you lived in Madrid, Spain, in 1525, how might your understanding of world geography differ from your grandparents' views fifty years earlier?

5. Discuss the paradox that English charges of Spanish cruelty in the Americas ("the black legend") may be both valid and exaggerated. Can you cite a similar paradox among other countries in modern times?

6. After reading this chapter, where would you mark the beginning of American history? How would you defend your choice in comparison to other options for an earlier or later starting point?

7. Describe at least three ways in which the Columbian Exchange dramatically altered history in North America and elsewhere by 1600.

Created Equal **Online**

For more *Created Equal* resources, including suggestions on sites to visit and books to read, go to **MyHistoryLab.com**.

Chapter 2

European Footholds in North America, 1600–1660

■ A *Mayflower* replica is now part of the restored Plymouth Colony site.

In the summer of 1621, an Englishman and an Indian left Plymouth Village on foot to visit a Native American leader named Massasoit and secure his support for the struggling English colony. During their forty-mile journey, Stephen Hopkins and Squanto saw numerous signs of a wave of disease that had swept the New England coast four years earlier, killing thousands of Indians. Skulls and bones still lay aboveground in many places. The two men who encountered these grim scenes had come together from strikingly different backgrounds.

Back in 1609, Hopkins had left England in a fleet heading for Jamestown in Virginia. When a storm wrecked his ship on the uncharted island of Bermuda, he and others rebelled against their official leader. Accused of mutiny and sentenced to hang, Hopkins pleaded his case and narrowly escaped the noose. Hopkins made it back to England and started a family, but in 1620 he decided to return to America. At the English port of Plymouth, Hopkins, his pregnant wife, Elizabeth, and several children and servants became paying passengers on a ship called the *Mayflower*. The vessel had been chartered to carry a group of English Protestants to America from their exile in Holland.

During the arduous passage, tensions mounted. Hopkins was among those who muttered "mutinous speeches" and argued that "when they came ashore, they should use their own libertie, for none had power to command them." But after Elizabeth gave birth, Hopkins joined the other forty men aboard in signing the Mayflower Compact. The agreement bound all the passengers together in a "Civil Body Politic" to be governed by laws "most meet and convenient for the general good." They reached New England in early winter, and Hopkins and others laid out the village of Plymouth in the snow. There, the newcomers met Squanto, a Native American with a command of English who helped them negotiate with local Indians.

Squanto had also endured Atlantic travel. He remembered the first French and English fishing vessels, which had appeared when he was a small boy. In 1614 Squanto was among twenty-seven Indians taken hostage aboard an English ship and sold into slavery in Spain. Escaping, he spent time in England and Newfoundland before returning home in 1619, only to find his entire village swept away by disease.

The *Mayflower* pilgrims, arriving a year after Squanto's return, also suffered heavy losses. Of the 102 settlers who had begun the voyage, half of them died in Plymouth Colony by the next spring. But in New England, as elsewhere in America, death seemed to play favorites in the following years. As colonization continued, recurrent epidemics took a particularly heavy toll on Native Americans, who lacked immunity when exposed to foreign diseases for the first time. In 1622, Squanto fell sick and died of a fever, leaving no relatives behind. In contrast, Stephen and Elizabeth Hopkins lived on to see numerous children and grandchildren thrive.

Near Cape Cod and Chesapeake Bay, local Indians had initially welcomed newcomers from England as potential military allies. But by the middle of the seventeenth century, arriving settlers had taken over Indian land in both Massachusetts and the Chesapeake region. The success of these English-speaking colonists would exert a lasting influence on the future direction of American society. But their stories unfolded as part of a far wider North American drama that included a diversity of European groups and embraced both the Atlantic and the Pacific shores. Whether confronting newcomers from Spain, France, Holland, or England, scores of Native American communities faced new challenges that altered traditional Indian ways of living and sometimes threatened their very survival.

Spain's Ocean-Spanning Reach

■ *What motivated Spain to extend the northern borders of its New World empire?*

In 1580, Spain's Philip II laid claim to the throne of Portugal, unifying Europe's two richest seaborne empires. But this consolidation, which endured until 1640, created problems. First, combining with Portugal put huge additional burdens on the overstretched Spanish bureaucracy. Second, the global success of the combined Iberian empires invited challenges from envious rivals in northern Europe. The new international competition came from France, Holland, and England, aspiring naval powers with imperial ambitions that touched the Pacific as well as the Atlantic.

In 1598, for example, ten ships from Amsterdam found their way to the Pacific, defying Spanish claims for control of that ocean. One of these Dutch vessels, piloted by Englishman Will Adams, ended up in Japan, where the new Tokugawa dynasty (1600–1868) was consolidating its control. Adams visited Edo—the rising military town that would grow into modern-day Tokyo—and even built a ship for the *shogun* (ruler). Adams's experiences (which inspired the 1975 bestseller *Shogun*) serve as a reminder that by 1600, competition for oceanic control had stretched far beyond the Atlantic. Who would dominate Pacific sea-lanes to America?

Freedom of the Seas: Grotius and Maritime Law

In our era, air travel has given rise to the growing field of air and space law. Similarly, in the sixteenth century, the expansion of oceanic travel led to legal conflicts and the growth of international maritime law.

In 1494, a treaty had divided the world equally between Spain and Portugal, and in 1580 those two kingdoms were combined under Philip II, creating a global monopoly. That same year, Spain's ambassador in England complained to Elizabeth I about the recent incursion of Francis Drake into Pacific waters. The queen replied that everyone had equal access to the sea and the air. Her clever retort would be given legal strength in the next generation by the great Dutch jurist and humanist Hugh de Groot, best known by his Latin name, Hugo Grotius (1583–1645).

Grotius grew up in the Netherlands at a time when Dutch, French, and English ships were challenging Spain's monopoly on the high seas. Seventeenth-century seafarers stood to make huge profits, but they faced intense competition and few rules. As a Dutch poet put it: "Wherever profit leads us, to every sea and shore, for love of gain the wide world's harbors we explore." After studying a case in which a Dutch vessel seized a Portuguese ship in Asian waters, Grotius, a gifted young lawyer, drafted a treatise putting such incidents in a broader context. In 1609, at age twenty-six, he published *Mare librum*, underscoring the freedom of the seas.

Grotius lived an eventful life, enduring prison and surviving a shipwreck. He was a pioneer in framing international law and exploring the rules of warfare. But his argument that the sea could not be the property of any country proved

■ This 1633 pamphlet is a reprint of an earlier essay on the freedom of the seas by Hugo Grotius, the Dutch legal expert who helped shape modern maritime law.

controversial, as rival maritime nations claimed control over neighboring waters. Eventually, however, Grotius's farsighted argument that the oceans should be free for all to use gained acceptance, paving the way for expanding networks of trade that continue to the present day.

QUESTIONS

1. How would Grotius's argument for freedom of the seas benefit rising European countries committed to overseas trade, such as England and the Netherlands?

2. If expanding oceanic trade gave rise to international maritime law, what developments might give birth to new areas of law in our own time?

The Wider World

VIZCAÍNO IN CALIFORNIA AND JAPAN

In April 1607, a letter from the king of Spain reached Mexico City. The king commanded his viceroy in charge of affairs in Mexico (New Spain) to create an outpost on California's Monterey Bay. Spanish galleons returning through the North Pacific from Manila (Spain's recently established port in the Philippines) desperately needed a coastal haven after crossing the immense ocean. Monterey Bay was well supplied with water, food, and timber. The sheltering harbor would provide a perfect way station, where ships could take on supplies and make repairs before heading south.

But the viceroy in Mexico City had other ideas. He diverted the necessary funds into a search for the fabled North Pacific isles of Rica de Oro (Rich in Gold) and Rica de Plata (Rich in Silver). To hunt for the mysterious islands, the viceroy chose a seasoned navigator who had already explored the California coast and taken part in the Pacific trade. Sebastián Vizcaíno had sailed to Manila from Acapulco on Mexico's west coast. His ships had carried Mexican chocolate to the Philippines and brought back silks and spices from Asia. Dispatched in 1611, Vizcaíno found no isles of gold and silver, but he did visit Japan. When he finally returned across the Pacific in 1613 aboard a vessel built in Japan, he brought

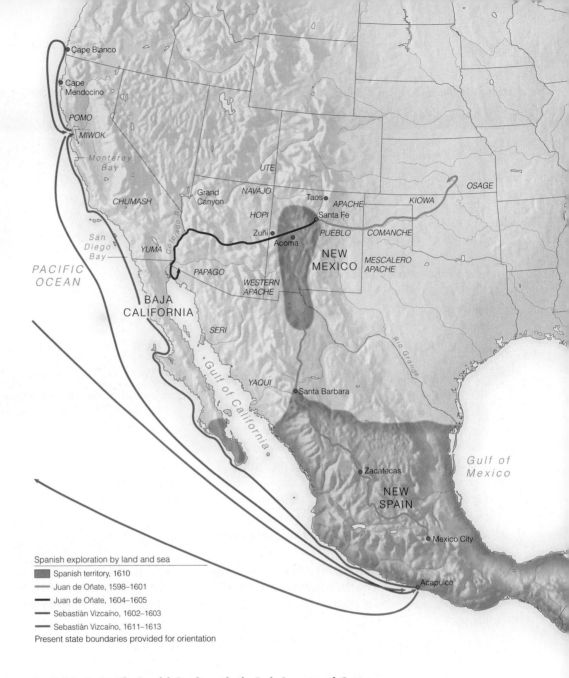

■ MAP 2.1   The Spanish Southwest in the Early Seventeenth Century

180 Japanese with him to Mexico. This unique delegation was bound for Spain and Italy to open doors between East and West. However, the Tokugawas soon began to persecute the European traders and Christian missionaries who had been allowed in the Japanese islands for a generation, so the frail link between Europe and Japan through Mexico never developed further.

Tokugawa officials, it seems, feared that tolerating foreigners in Japan's ports might "propagate the doctrine of the Catholics" and undermine their supremacy. Moreover, developing Japanese fleets might bring guns to warlords and disrupt hard-won peace. "No Japanese ship or boat whatever, nor any native of Japan, shall presume to go out of the country," a government edict declared in 1638. It added, "whoso acts contrary to this shall die, and the ship with the crew and goods aboard shall be sequestered till further order. All Japanese who return from abroad shall be put to death."

So Japan passed up an opportunity for naval expansion, just as Ming China had done two centuries earlier after the voyages of Zheng He. Instead, the new dynasty adopted a policy of commercial and cultural isolation that lasted for more than 200 years. Had Japanese society followed another route, co-opting Western technologies and aggressively exploring and colonizing the Pacific, the subsequent history of North America and the world would almost certainly have taken a very different path.

For the Spanish, Vizcaíno's Pacific adventure consumed crucial funds, and the possibility of a Spanish settlement at Monterey quickly disappeared. Concerned that their empire had already become overextended, Spanish officials postponed plans to colonize California's coast. In addition, Spain wondered whether to maintain its existing North American colony in Florida and its newest frontier province: New Mexico.

OÑATE CREATES A SPANISH FOOTHOLD IN THE SOUTHWEST

In 1598, Juan de Oñate renewed the northern efforts of Coronado's expedition several generations earlier. Setting out from New Spain, he led 500 men, women, and children north into the upper Rio Grande valley to create the province of New Mexico. Oñate was a wealthy man—his father had discovered a major silver mine at Zacatecas—and he had bold ambitions. Aided by Franciscan friars (organized followers of St. Francis loyal to the pope), Oñate and his mixed-race colonists expected to convert the Indians to Christianity. Expanding outward from the compact apartment-like native towns, or pueblos, the intruders hoped to open a vast new colonial realm. It would be a "new world," they proclaimed, "greater than New Spain."

DOCUMENT

Don Juan de Oñate, Letter from New Mexico to the Victory

But Oñate drastically underestimated the difficulties. When embittered Indians at Acoma pueblo killed eleven of his soldiers in 1599, he retaliated by bombarding the mesa-top citadel, killing 800 inhabitants and enslaving nearly 600 others. Hearing of the brutal repression of the residents of Acoma, neighboring pueblos reluctantly submitted to Spanish demands for labor and food. Colonial reinforcements arriving in 1600 were dismayed by the harsh conditions; Oñate needed new discoveries for the colony to prosper. In 1601, he launched an expedition east onto the Great Plains, but the venture proved as futile as Coronado's earlier march had been.

> Oñate's new "Mexico" remained isolated and impoverished, with the newcomers strapped for clothing and food.

To make matters worse, a drought gripped the Rio Grande valley, and many of the recent settlers departed, complaining that the region lacked woods, pastures, water, and suitable land. When Oñate returned from the plains, he found that two-thirds of his tiny colony had given up and returned to Mexico. Foiled on the east and weakened along the Rio Grande, Oñate next pressed west to seek a link to the Pacific. When he reached the Gulf of California in 1605, he mistook it for the great ocean and envisioned a possible link to the Pacific trade.

In fact, however, Oñate's new "Mexico" remained isolated and impoverished, with the newcomers strapped for clothing and food. The colonists, desperate to survive, pressed hard on the native peoples. They demanded tribute in the form of cotton blankets, buffalo hides, and baskets of scarce maize. In winter, ill-equipped Spanish-speaking soldiers stripped warm robes off the backs of shivering women and children; in summer, they scoured each pueblo for corn, torturing residents to find out where food was hidden.

Meanwhile, a few hundred Pueblo Indians—intimidated by the Spanish, desperate for a share of the food they had grown, and fearful of attacks by neighboring Apache— began to accept Christian baptism and seek Spanish protection. By 1608, when the crown threatened to withdraw support from the struggling province, the colony's Franciscan missionaries appealed that their converts had grown too numerous to resettle and too dependent to abandon. Their argument may have been exaggerated, but it caught the attention of authorities.

Besides, England and France were launching new colonies in Virginia and Canada. Since mapmakers still could not accurately calculate longitude (east-west position on the globe), no one was sure whether these bases created by international rivals posed

■ Acoma, often called Sky City, sits atop a high sandstone mesa west of Albuquerque, New Mexico. The name means "place that always was," and the pueblo has been continuously inhabited for roughly 1,000 years. Acoma's Native American community survived a devastating attack by Spanish colonizers in 1599.

a threat that was dangerously close at hand. Worried Spanish officials finally agreed with the Franciscan friars that New Mexico must carry on. They replaced Oñate with a new governor and asserted royal control over the few dozen settlers who remained in the colony.

NEW MEXICO SURVIVES: NEW FLOCKS AMONG OLD PUEBLOS

The Spanish decision to hold on in New Mexico reshaped life for everyone in the region. At least 60,000 Indians living in nearly sixty separate pueblos found their world transformed and their survival threatened over the next half-century. In 1610 the new governor, ruling over scarcely fifty colonists, created a capital at the village of Santa Fe. Within two decades, roughly 750 colonists inhabited the remote province, including Spanish, Mexican Indians, Africans, and mixed-race children.

The racial and ethnic diversity of New Mexico repeated the colonial pattern established in New Spain, where Iberians had been intermarrying with Indians and Africans for several generations. Similarly, labor practices and religious changes also followed models established after the conquest of the Aztec in Mexico. As in New Spain, certain privileged people in the new colony received **encomiendas;** such grants entitled the holders (known as an *encomenderos*) to the labor of a set number of Native American workers. With labor in short supply throughout the Spanish colonies, other settlers led occasional raids against nomadic Plains Indians, keeping some captives and shipping others south to toil as slaves in the Mexican silver mines.

Meanwhile, the number of Franciscan missionaries rose rapidly. They forbade traditional Pueblo celebrations, known as **kachina** dances, and destroyed sacred kachina masks. Their combination of intense zeal and harsh punishments prompted many Indians to learn Spanish and become obedient converts. However, it also drove the Indians' own religious practices underground—literally, into the hidden, circular kivas that had long been a focal point for Native American spiritual activities in the region. There, people kept their traditional faith alive in secret and passed sacred rituals along to the next generation.

The Spanish brought more than Christianity to New Mexico. The newcomers also transferred novel crops (wheat, onions, chilies, peas) and planted new fruits (peaches, plums, cherries). Settlers introduced metal hoes and axes, along with donkeys, chickens, and other domesticated animals previously unknown to the native inhabitants. Horses and cattle, led north from New Spain in small herds, eventually revolutionized life across the North American West. But the most immediate impact came from Spanish sheep, well suited to the semi-desert conditions. Each friar soon possessed a flock of several thousand, and Pueblo artisans wove wool into cloth.

The Spanish made Santa Fe the capital of their New Mexico colony in 1610 and built the church of San Miguel there in 1626. Though destroyed in the Pueblo Revolt of 1680, it was rebuilt and has remained in use. "The floor is bare earth," wrote an eighteenth-century observer, "the usual floor throughout these regions."

But the Pueblo world, like Squanto's world, was eroding under the onslaught of new European diseases. The large Pueblo population, cut in half in the sixty years since Coronado's appearance, still numbered more than 60,000 in 1600, after the arrival of Oñate's colonizing expedition. Yet sickness, along with warfare and famine, cut this number in half again by 1650 and in half once more by 1680.

CONVERSION AND REBELLION IN SPANISH FLORIDA

By 1600, Spanish Florida also disappointed imperial officials. Dreams of gold-filled kingdoms and a strategic passage from the Southeast to the Orient had never materialized. The Spanish government regarded the outpost at St. Augustine as an undue burden and planned to disband the colony. But Franciscan missionaries won the day, as in New Mexico. They argued that scores of Indian towns appeared ready to receive Christianity. By 1608, the crown had decided to let the colony continue.

A handful of missionaries fanned out among the Indians of northern Florida, erecting small churches and mission schools. They recruited Indian students aggressively, without regard to age or sex. In 1612, Francisco de Pareja published an illustrated, bilingual confessional in Castilian Spanish and Timucuan, the earliest text in any North American Indian language. The book enabled wary friars to ask villagers, "Have you said suggestive words?" and "Have you desired to do some lewd act with some man or woman or kin?"

Contact with Christian beliefs and books came at a steep price, for each inland village was expected to help feed the colonial garrison and settlement at St. Augustine. Native women neglected their own household crops to grow additional maize and grind it into meal. Annually, Spanish officials requisitioned Indian men from each village to transport the cornmeal overland to the Atlantic coast and return to the mission carrying supplies for the

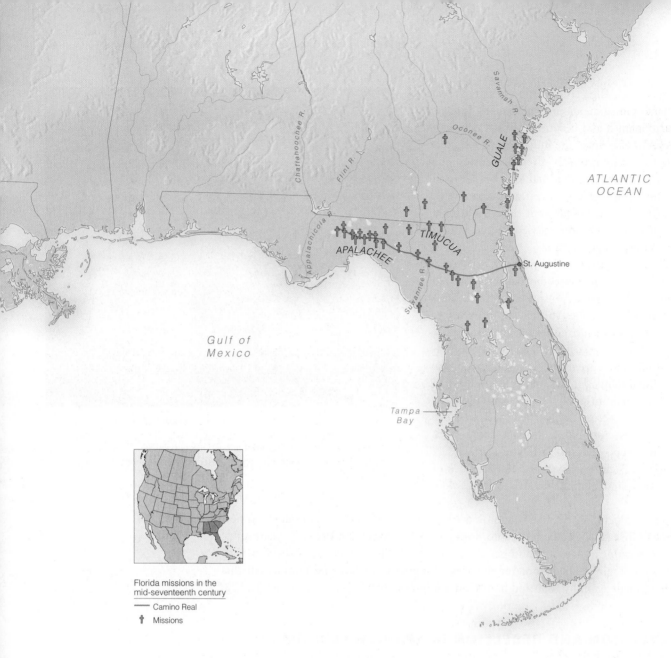

Florida missions in the
mid-seventeenth century
——— Camino Real
† Missions

■ MAP 2.2 Sites of Catholic Missions in Spanish Florida in the Mid-Seventeenth Century

MAP

**Native American
Population Loss,
1500–1700**

Franciscans. Imported candles, communion wine, and mission bells all had to be hauled inland. The trip to and from the coast lasted several weeks. After 1633, when missions appeared in the western province of Apalachee (near modern Tallahassee), the treks from the Atlantic Coast along the *camino real,* or "royal road," took even longer.

Friars and Indian bearers traveling to the interior also carried sickness from St. Augustine. Epidemics of foreign diseases—measles, bubonic plague, malaria, typhus, smallpox, and influenza—took a devastating toll on the Native Americans. Harsh work conditions and poor diets lowered people's resistance to illness. Indians expired more rapidly than the Spanish could convert them, and friars hastened to baptize the dying and claim their souls for Christ. In a letter to the Spanish king in 1617, a Franciscan reported that the local population had been cut in half in the five years since his arrival "on account of the great plagues and contagious diseases that the Indians have suffered." But he reassured his majesty that "a very rich harvest of souls for heaven has been made in the midst of great numbers of deaths."

As whole villages disappeared, Hispanic entrepreneurs began to expand cattle ranching across the newly vacated lands of northern Florida. Faced with encroaching farms, crushing labor demands, and frightful mortality, local native leaders saw their power reduced and their communities depleted. These conditions sparked a short-lived revolt by Indians at Apalachee in 1647. Nine years later, when the governor at St. Augustine feared a possible attack by English ships, a wider Native American uprising shook Timucua in north-central Florida.

In the end, the English threat to Spanish Florida did not materialize in 1656, but the rumor underscored how much had changed in the preceding half-century. Two generations earlier, in 1600, no European power besides Spain had possessed a solid foothold in any portion of the Americas. But over the next six decades, France, Holland, and England all asserted claims on the American mainland. These rivals challenged Spain not only in the Atlantic but in the Pacific as well.

■ The Spanish found that glass beads, colorful and easy to transport, made fine gifts and trade items in their contacts with Florida Indians. Chiefs often received special quartz crystal beads and pendants to retain their loyalty.

Mission San Luis, Florida Division of Historical Resources

France and Holland: Overseas Competition for Spain

■ *How did the expanding beaver trade shape the French and Dutch colonies before 1660?*

At the turn of the seventeenth century, interlopers from Holland challenged Spanish colonizers in the Philippines and Portuguese traders in Japan. These Dutch efforts illustrated the growing competition among European powers for control of the world's oceans. In London, commercial leaders received a royal charter to create the English East India Company in 1600, and merchants in Amsterdam took a similar step. Hoping to capture Portugal's lucrative Asian trade, they established the Dutch East India Company in 1602. Over the next half-century, Dutch sailors reached Australia, Tasmania, and New Zealand. They took Malacca (near Singapore) from the Portuguese in 1641 and charted the coast of northern Japan in 1643. By 1652, they had also founded a Dutch colony at Cape Town, on the southern tip of Africa.

The united powers of Spain and Portugal proved even more vulnerable in the Atlantic. To be sure, annual Spanish convoys continued to transport Mexican gold and silver to Europe, along with Asian silks and spices shipped to Mexico via the Pacific. Portuguese vessels carried Africans to the New World at a profit. But ships from rival European nations preyed on these seaborne cargoes with increasing success. Defiantly, these competitors also laid claim to numerous islands in the Caribbean.

By 1660, the English had taken control of Barbados, Providence Island, Antigua, and Jamaica; the Dutch had acquired St. Maarten, St. Eustacius, Saba, and Curaçao; and the French had claimed Guadeloupe, Martinique, Grenada, and St. Lucia. For France, however, the most promising Atlantic prospects lay farther north, in Canada. There, Spanish power was absent, hopes for a Northwest Passage persisted, and French imperial claims stretched back generations.

TABLE 2.1

North American Colonies by Nationality, 1560–1660

European Power (Catholic/Protestant)	North American Colony (date founded–ended)	Largest Town (date founded)
Spain (C)	Florida (1565)	St. Augustine (1565)
	New Mexico (1598)	Santa Fe (1610)
France (C)	Port Royal (SC) (1562–1653)	Charlesfort (1562)
	St. John's River (FL) (1564–1565)	Fort Caroline (1564)
	New France (1603)	Quebec (1608)
Holland (P) (The Netherlands)	New Netherland (1609)	New Amsterdam (1626) (now New York, NY)
Sweden (P)	New Sweden (1637–1655)	Fort Christina (1637) (now Wilmington, DE)
England (P)	Roanoke (NC) (1585–1590)	Roanoke (1585)
	Virginia (charter issued 1606)	Jamestown (1607)
	Maryland (charter issued 1632)	St. Mary's (1634)
	Popham (Sagadahoc) (on Kennebec River in ME) (1607–1608)	Fort St. George (1607)
	Plymouth (1620)	Plymouth (1620)
	Massachusetts Bay (charter issued 1629)	Boston (1630)
	Rhode Island (charter issued 1644)	Providence (1636)
	New Haven (1643–1664; then absorbed into CT)	New Haven (1637)
	Connecticut (Fundamental Orders 1639; charter granted in 1662)	Hartford (1636)

THE FOUNDING OF NEW FRANCE

Since the time of Jacques Cartier, fishing boats from the coast of France had crisscrossed Newfoundland's Grand Banks. One old French salt claimed to have made the voyage for forty-two consecutive years. The trade increased after 1580, as crews built seasonal stations for drying codfish along the American coast. These stations prompted greater contact with Indians; soon Europeans were exchanging metal goods for furs on terms that pleased all. A Native American could trade a worn-out robe made from beaver skins for a highly valued iron kettle. European artisans could remove the soft underlayer of fur from the pelts and mat the short hairs into felt for making fashionable and waterproof beaver hats. One robe yielded felt for six to eight expensive hats, so dealers could pocket a profit and still purchase scores of kettles and knives for the next year's exchange.

As North Atlantic fishing and trading expanded, the domestic situation in France improved. In 1598, King Henry IV issued the Edict of Nantes, a decree granting political rights and limited toleration to French Protestants, or Huguenots. With religious wars curtailed, the king could contemplate new colonization initiatives in America. An experienced French soldier and sailor named Samuel de Champlain emerged as a key leader in this effort. Between 1599 and 1601, Champlain scouted Spain's New World empire and brought back suggestions to Paris for overseas advancement of French interests. He even offered a proposal to create a canal across the Isthmus of Panama. But from 1602 until his death in 1635, Champlain devoted himself to the St. Lawrence River region, where Acadia on the Atlantic coast and Canada along the extensive river valley made up the anticipated realm of New France.

In 1608, Champlain and several dozen other men established the outpost of Quebec, where Cartier and Roberval had wintered generations earlier. In June 1609, Champlain joined a band of Algonquin and Huron Indians in a raid on the Iroquois in what is now upstate New York. When they engaged their Iroquois enemies in battle, Champlain fired his gun—a novelty in the region—killing several war chiefs and sparking a rout. For the powerful **Iroquois League** south of the St. Lawrence (the Five Nation confederation composed of the Seneca, Cayuga, Onondaga, Oneida, and Mohawk Indians), the defeat sparked decades of warfare against the French. For the newcomers from France, the victory sealed good relations with the Algonquin and Huron, ensuring the survival of Quebec and spurring unprecedented commerce. Within fifteen years, Native Americans were trading 12,000 to 15,000 beaver pelts annually via the St. Lawrence River valley.

In 1627, the powerful first minister in France, Cardinal Richelieu, pressed for greater French settlement in Canada through a new private company. He banned Huguenots from participating and pushed to make sure that only Roman Catholics were allowed to migrate to Canada. But his expansive policies alarmed rival England, which captured Quebec briefly in 1629. When restored to French control several years later, the tiny outpost contained fewer than 100 people. In an effort to expand the meager settlement and populate the fertile valley upriver from Quebec, French authorities began granting narrow strips of land with river frontage to any Catholic lord who would take up residence there and bring French tenants to his estate. By 1640, the small colony of 356 inhabitants, with 116 women, included 64 families, 29 Jesuits, and 53 soldiers.

Champlain's drawing of the battle on Lake Champlain, 1609.

COMPETING FOR THE BEAVER TRADE

Cardinal Richelieu's power in France epitomized the ongoing Counter-Reformation. This outpouring of Catholic zeal reached as far as North America. In 1635 Jesuits founded a college in Quebec, and in 1639 six nuns arrived to begin a hospital and a school for Indian girls. Other religious workers established a station farther west in 1641 in territory recently dominated by the Iroquois. This strategic outpost, where the Ottawa River joined the St. Lawrence, marked the beginnings of Montreal. From there, the French planned to control the beaver trade as it expanded west. They also hoped to prevent the Iroquois League from diverting furs south to Holland's new colony on the Hudson River.

But the desperate Iroquois nations, facing collapse, took a stand. Increasing contact with Europeans and their contagious diseases had brought catastrophic epidemics to the Iroquois homelands below Lake Ontario. Beginning in 1633, sicknesses that were new to the region swept away some 10,000 people and cut the Five Nations' population in half within a decade, emptying the distinctive longhouses that made up Iroquois villages. According to Iroquois tradition, survivors must swiftly replace deceased individuals with new captives to maintain the community's strength and continuity. Pressed by grieving families, Iroquois warriors initiated a generation of violent campaigns intended to capture and absorb neighboring groups. These so-called mourning wars are also remembered as the Beaver Wars because they included a clear economic as well as cultural motive. Besides captives, the Iroquois aggressors sought furs. If they could seize pelts before the valuable items reached the French, they could trade them to the Dutch for guns and powder. Well armed, they could then engage in further wars for captives and furs.

This spiral of aggression put the Iroquois on a collision course with the Huron and their allies, a small band of Jesuit missionaries willing to risk martyrdom in New France. Eager for Native American converts, the Jesuits focused their attention on Huronia, the region east of Lake Huron and Georgian Bay. There, 30,000 Huron Indians lived in large, settled villages. The Jesuits erected chapels at four of these towns and constructed a central base at St. Marie near Georgian Bay. Having volunteered for hardship, they witnessed far more of it than they ever imagined.

First came the same foreign epidemics that had wasted the Iroquois; smallpox cut down roughly two-thirds of the Huron population, or 20,000 people, between 1635 and 1640. Then came the Iroquois themselves, bent on capturing Huron women and children to revitalize their longhouses, swept empty by disease in the 1630s. Armed by Dutch traders eager for furs, 1,000 Iroquois warriors descended on the weakened Huron in March 1649. They burned villages, secured captives, tortured several priests to death, and seized large stocks of pelts. The Iroquois then launched raids on the St. Lawrence River valley, disrupting the fur trade and frightening the several thousand French inhabitants. By 1660, it seemed that New France—thinly settled, weakly defended, and poorly supplied—might face the same extinction that the much older and larger Huronia community had suffered. (See Map 2.3 on p. 53.)

A DUTCH COLONY ON THE HUDSON RIVER

The Dutch traders who supplied firearms to the Iroquois in exchange for furs owed their start to English-born navigator Henry Hudson. In 1609, sailing for the Dutch East India Company, Hudson crossed the Atlantic in search of a western passage to the Orient. He visited Chesapeake Bay and Delaware Bay, and in September he rediscovered modern-day New York harbor, the bay that Verrazano had entered in 1524. Flying the Dutch flag above his vessel, the *Half Moon*, Hudson sailed north up the broad river that now bears his name. Along the way, he obtained food and furs from Algonquin Indians in exchange for knives and beads. He noted that saltwater ocean tides pushed sixty miles upstream—Indians called the river "the water that flows two ways." But no channel to the Pacific materialized.

The Dutch moved quickly to gain a foothold in the area, calling it New Netherland. Ships from Amsterdam appeared far up the Hudson, exchanging metal goods for beaver

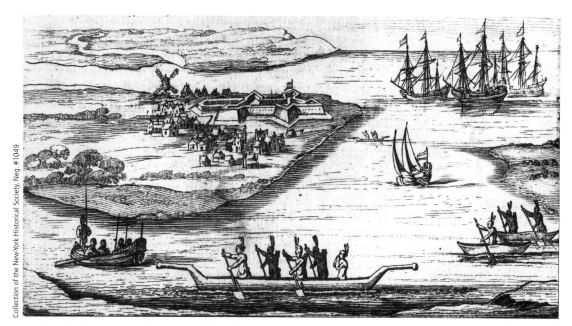

Collection of the New-York Historical Society, Neg. #1049

■ When the Dutch erected the village and fort of New Amsterdam beside the Hudson River in the late 1620s, a traditional windmill became a strange new part of Manhattan Island's skyline.

pelts and occasionally leaving men behind to trade with the Indians. Soon the Dutch had established a year-round trading post at Fort Orange, near present-day Albany. Mohawk traditions recall how the Indians "Planted the Tree of Good Understanding" with the Dutch newcomers, whom they called *Kristoni*, for "I am a metal maker."

In 1621, responsibility for New Netherland—the region claimed between the Delaware and Connecticut rivers—fell to the newly chartered Dutch West India Company (DWIC). Modeled on the Dutch East India Company, this enterprise made Holland a formidable force in the Atlantic, especially after the spectacular Dutch capture of the Spanish silver fleet off Cuba in 1628. The DWIC concentrated on piecing together an empire in the South Atlantic. Dutch ships seized part of sugar-rich Brazil (1632), the island of Curaçao near Venezuela (1634), and Portugal's African outpost at Elmina, on the coast of modern-day Ghana (1637). But the DWIC also laid plans for a North American colony.

To begin, the company transported a group of poor, would-be settlers to New Netherland in 1624, offering as an inducement "the profit that each can make for himself." To secure the boundaries of the province, officials sent colonists far up the Hudson to Fort Orange and deposited several farm families along the Connecticut and Delaware rivers. However, Peter Minuit, the colony's director from 1626 to 1631, saw danger in this dispersal. He worried that the widely scattered newcomers lacked defenses, trade, and community ties. To consolidate settlement, he purchased Manhattan Island—the eventual site of New York City—from the local Indians in 1626. The island's southern tip, where Minuit erected a small fort, overlooked a spacious harbor at the mouth of the Hudson. Like Amsterdam itself, the promising location—named New Amsterdam—combined shelter from the sea with easy access to interior settlements and to ocean trade.

By 1630, the village of New Amsterdam already boasted several windmills and 270 settlers, clustered in cottages near the fort. When the Dutch built a wall around their village to protect against Indian attacks, the road inside this palisade became known as Wall Street. Next, the DWIC granted huge estates along the Hudson to wealthy *patroons* (patrons), similar to the French land grants along the St. Lawrence. Hoping that private investment would strengthen their colony, the company gave a wilderness tract to any wealthy investor who could send fifty people to farm there as tenants. An Amsterdam diamond merchant named Kiliaen van

Rensselaer formed the first and most lucrative of these patroonships near Fort Orange. But this effort to promote migration faltered, and new conflicts began to appear on several fronts.

When the company threw open the Indian trade to others besides its own agents, the careless and greedy actions of unregulated traders sparked violence. The bloodshed known as Kieft's War (1643–1645) was sanctioned by the brash Indian policies of Willem Kieft, the colony's incompetent director general. In 1643, without public approval, Kieft ordered a midnight raid by company soldiers against tribute-paying Indians on both sides of the Hudson. Native retaliation for the massacre nearly destroyed New Netherland before Kieft's welcome removal in 1645.

The nearby colonies of rival powers also posed problems. The Dutch squabbled constantly with settlers from neighboring New England over fur-trading rights and other matters. To the south, the small colony of New Sweden materialized on the west side of the Delaware River in 1637. The several hundred Scandinavians who built Fort Christina (now Wilmington, Delaware) were Swedes and Finns hoping to establish their own trade with the Indians. The English too had designs on the region, as awareness grew that the river stretched far to the north and its owners could cut into New Netherland's western fur trade. But in 1655, these rivals were obliged to surrender the Delaware valley to a Dutch fleet.

"ALL SORTS OF NATIONALITIES": DIVERSE NEW AMSTERDAM

The symbol of Dutch power in the region, and the commander of the fleet that seized New Sweden, was Peter Stuyvesant. The son of a Calvinist minister, he had served as governor of Dutch Curaçao in the Caribbean, losing his right leg in a battle with the Spanish at age thirty-four. Recuperating in Holland, he married Judith Bayard, the Huguenot woman who nursed him back to health. In 1647, she was pregnant with their first child when the couple sailed from Amsterdam for New Netherland, in the service of the DWIC. There, Stuyvesant would rule aggressively for several decades, before England seized the colony in 1664.

Stuyvesant limited beer and rum sales, fined settlers for promiscuity and knife fighting, and established a nine-member night watch. When a group of English Quakers, members of the newly formed Society of Friends, arrived at New Amsterdam in 1657, Stuyvesant attempted to expel the radical Protestants and fine any who gave them shelter. However, Dutch residents of Flushing, on Long Island, defied his ban and signed a public letter of objection stressing religious toleration.

To address the colony's chronic labor shortage, Stuyvesant endorsed trade in African slaves and used his Caribbean connections to expand this traffic. When the Portuguese forced Holland out of Brazil in 1654 and closed that sugar colony to Dutch slave vessels, some of the ships brought their cargoes to New Amsterdam instead. Like the Dutch-speaking blacks already living in the colony, most of these newcomers were enslaved for life. But the DWIC, the largest importer and owner of slaves in New Netherland, granted "half-freedom" to some whom it could not employ year-round. These people, in return for an annual fee, could travel freely and marry, acquire property, and hire out their labor. By 1664, African arrivals made up more than 10 percent of New Netherland's population and 20 percent of New Amsterdam, the colony's capital.

> *New Amsterdam, home to fewer than 2,000 people, also had a small Jewish contingent, the first in mainland North America.*

New Amsterdam, home to fewer than 2,000 people, also had a small Jewish contingent, the first in mainland North America. In 1654, twenty-three Sephardic Jews reached Manhattan, forced out of Brazil by the Portuguese. Stuyvesant, strident in his anti-Semitism, claimed such "blasphemers of the name of Christ" would "infect and trouble this new colony." But the DWIC, which included Jewish stockholders and was eager for newcomers of all kinds, overruled the governor's request to expel the refugees. In the end, colony officials authorized a Jewish ghetto, or segregated neighborhood, where the newcomers could pray together freely in private. At first, however, they were not allowed to construct a synagogue for public worship.

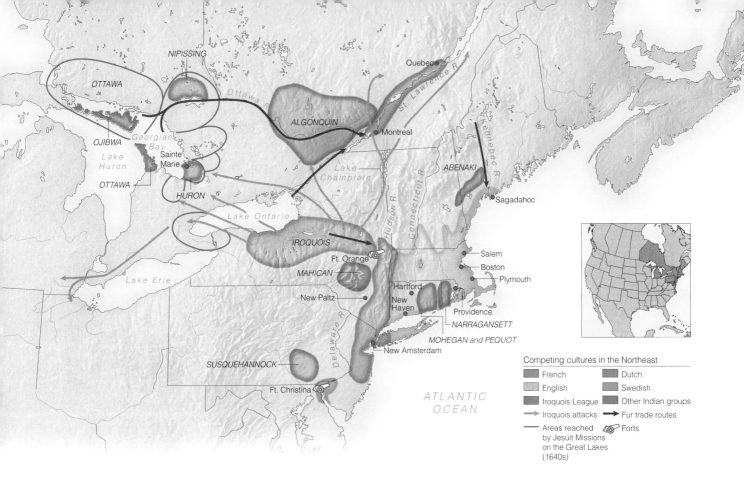

■ **MAP 2.3** **European and Native American Contact in the Northeast, 1600–1660**
French and English colonization efforts brought devastating diseases to the Five Nations of the Iroquois
League. Eager to take captives and profit from the growing trade in furs, the Iroquois ranged north and west
to make war on the French and their Huron Indian allies.

In the early 1660s, the colony continued to grow more diverse, "slowly peopled by the scrapings of all sorts of nationalities," as Stuyvesant complained. The accents of Danes, Bavarians, and Italians could already be heard on the streets of New Amsterdam. Huguenots occupied New Paltz near the Hudson; farther north, other newcomers founded Schenectady in 1661. Swedes and Finns continued to prosper along the Delaware, and numerous English had settled on Long Island. Compared with New France, New Netherland seemed far more populous, prosperous, and ethnically diverse. But while the French colony to the north endured for another century, the Dutch enterprise was soon absorbed by England. For despite a slow start, the English managed to outdistance all their European rivals and establish thriving North American colonies in the first half of the seventeenth century.

English Beginnings on the Atlantic Coast

■ *What factors worked for and against the early English colonization efforts in America?*

When Queen Elizabeth I passed away in 1603, several important elements were already in place to help England compete for colonial outposts. The trade in wool had prompted many large landholders to fence in their fields and turn to raising sheep. This "enclosure" movement pushed thousands of tenants off the land, and these uprooted people flocked to urban centers in search of work, forming a supply of potential colonists. Also, the country had an expanding fleet of English-built ships, sailed by experienced mariners. In addition, England had a group of seasoned and ambitious leaders. A generation of

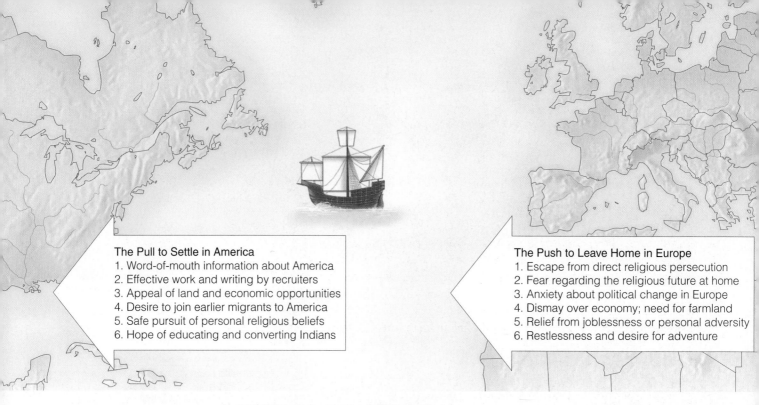

The Pull to Settle in America
1. Word-of-mouth information about America
2. Effective work and writing by recruiters
3. Appeal of land and economic opportunities
4. Desire to join earlier migrants to America
5. Safe pursuit of personal religious beliefs
6. Hope of educating and converting Indians

The Push to Leave Home in Europe
1. Escape from direct religious persecution
2. Fear regarding the religious future at home
3. Anxiety about political change in Europe
4. Dismay over economy; need for farmland
5. Relief from joblessness or personal adversity
6. Restlessness and desire for adventure

■ **FIGURE 2.1** **The Tough Choice to Start Over**

soldiers (many of them younger sons of the property-holding elite known as the gentry) had fought in Europe or participated in the brutal colonization of Ireland.

Because Elizabeth I died without heirs, the king of Scotland, James Stuart, succeeded her as ruler. During the reigns of James I (1603–1625) and his son Charles I (1625–1649), religious and economic forces in England prompted an increasing number of people to consider migrating overseas. With the expansion of the country's Protestant Reformation, religious strife escalated toward civil war, which erupted in 1642. During the tumultuous 1630s, English public officials were glad to transplant Puritans and Catholics alike to foreign shores. In turn, many ardent believers—weary of conflict or losing hope for their cause at home—welcomed the prospect of a safe haven abroad. Economically, the development of joint stock organizations enabled merchants to raise capital and spread the high risk of colonial ventures by selling numerous shares to small investors. At the same time, the fluctuating domestic economy threatened family stability and prompted many disadvantaged people to seek their fortunes elsewhere.

THE VIRGINIA COMPANY AND JAMESTOWN

For Richard Hakluyt, England's leading publicist for overseas expansion, the proper focus seemed clear: "There is under our noses," he wrote in 1599, "the great & ample country of Virginia." Great and ample, indeed, especially before the rival Dutch established New Netherland. On paper, the enormous zone that England claimed as Virginia stretched north to south from the top of modern-day Vermont to Cape Fear on Carolina's Outer Banks. From east to west, it spanned North America from the Atlantic to the Pacific, however narrow or wide the continent might prove to be.

In 1606, James I chartered the Virginia Company as a two-pronged operation to exploit the sweeping Virginia claim. Under the charter, a group of London-based merchants took responsibility for colonizing the Chesapeake Bay region. Meanwhile, merchants from England's West Country, based in the seaports of Plymouth, Exeter, and Bristol, took charge of developing the northern latitudes of the American coast. In 1607, two ships from Plymouth deposited roughly a hundred settlers, led by George Popham, at the Sagadahoc (Kennebec) River in Maine. The settlers built houses and erected a fortress (Fort St. George) at the mouth of the river. They even constructed a small sailing vessel called the *Virginia*, the first of hundreds of ships that the

English would build from American forests. But frostbite, scurvy, and dwindling supplies forced the Popham colony to retreat home in 1608, two decades after the Roanoke failures.

A parallel effort by the Londoners proved more enduring—but just barely. In April 1607, three ships bearing 105 men sailed into Chesapeake Bay. Their leaders carried instructions to hunt for Roanoke survivors (they found none) and to search for gold. They were also to look westward from high hills in search of the Pacific Ocean. (After all, longitude remained a mystery, and the width of the continent was unknown. In the previous century, Verrazano claimed to have spied an arm of the Pacific from the Atlantic, and Drake, sailing into San Francisco Bay at the same latitude as the Chesapeake, had claimed that region for the English as New Albion.) The new arrivals in Chesapeake Bay disembarked on what appeared to be a secluded island near a broad river. Within months, these subjects of James I had named the waterway the James River and established a fortified village beside it called Jamestown. In June, hoping for quick rewards, they shipped to London various stones that they thought contained precious gems and gold ore.

Mural of Jamestown Settlement

When the rocks proved worthless, the colonists' dreams of easy wealth evaporated. So did their fantasies about pushing west to the Pacific. During Jamestown's first winter, a fire destroyed the tiny settlement, and death from hunger, exposure, and sickness cut the garrison's population in half. The governor and council appointed by the Virginia Company bickered among themselves, providing poor leadership. Fully one-third of the early arrivals claimed to be gentlemen, from England's leisure class—a proportion six times higher than in England—and most proved unaccustomed to hard manual labor. Moreover, all the colonists were employees of the company, so any profits from their labor went to repay London investors.

> *During Jamestown's first winter, death from hunger, exposure, and sickness cut the garrison's population in half.*

Despite the unsuitable make-up of the garrison, conditions improved briefly with the emergence of John Smith as a vigorous leader. He dealt brazenly with the local Powhatan Indian confederation, numbering more than 13,000 people. Captain Smith soon reached a tenuous accommodation with the paramount chief, Powhatan, who had been steadily expanding his power across the Tidewater region. (Later, Smith claimed to have been assisted and protected by Powhatan's young daughter, Pocahontas.) Still, the Jamestown colony limped along with meager support, living in fear of Spanish attacks.

With hopes of a swift bonanza dashed, the London merchants decided to alter their strategy. They would salvage the venture by attracting fresh capital; then they would recoup their high initial costs by recruiting new settlers who could produce staple products suited for export—perhaps grapes, sugar, cotton, or tobacco. In 1609, amid much fanfare, the company began to sell seven-year joint stock options to the English public. Subscribers could invest money or they could sign on for service in Virginia. Company officials promised such adventurers at least a hundred acres of land when their investment matured in 1616. In June 1609, 500 men and 100 women departed for the Chesapeake aboard nine ships.

"STARVING TIME" AND SEEDS OF REPRESENTATIVE GOVERNMENT

When the battered fleet reached Jamestown, the new arrivals found insufficient supplies. Moreover, the first settlers had failed to discover a profitable staple crop. The colonists depended heavily on the Native Americans for food, and Powhatan's Confederacy proved increasingly unwilling and unable to share its harvest. In a grim "starving time," the ill-equipped newcomers scavenged for berries and bark. Extreme hunger drove a few to cannibalize the dead before dying themselves. By the spring of 1610, seven of every eight people had died; scarcely sixty remained alive.

John Smith, "The Starving Time"

In June, these survivors abandoned their ghost town altogether. But as they set sail for England, they encountered three long-overdue ships entering Chesapeake Bay with fresh

National Geographic Society. © 1998 Photo by Steve Rawls

■ Inexperience prompted initial English difficulties at Roanoke and Jamestown, but so did poor weather. Scientists studying the region's bald cypress trees have recently shown (from certain narrow rings) that terrible droughts struck the coastal area in the late 1580s and again from 1606 through 1612. These two sequences of narrow annual rings are visible under the magnifying glass.

supplies and 300 new settlers. Reluctantly, they agreed to try again. More years of harsh discipline, Indian warfare, and chronic mismanagement followed. Another force—a severe local drought—also conspired against the hapless newcomers. Indian and English crops alike shriveled from 1607 through 1612.

Relief came from an unexpected quarter: the "bewitching vegetable" known as Orinoco tobacco. This plant, grown in parts of the West Indies and South America, had captured English taste in the previous generation. Sales of this New World product in England sent profits to the Spanish crown, prompting James I to launch a vigorous antismoking campaign in 1604. In his tract titled *Counterblaste to Tobacco*, the king condemned inhaling the noxious weed as a dangerous, sinful, and enfeebling custom, "lothsome to the eye, hatefull to the Nose, harmefull to the braine, daungerous to the Lungs."

John Rolfe, reaching Jamestown in 1610, promptly joined in the colonists' search for a viable staple. He found that local Indians cultivated an indigenous tobacco plant, but it proved "poor and weake, and of a byting tast." Rolfe, a smoker himself, suspected that sweet-flavored Orinoco tobacco could prosper in Virginia soil. Within a year, Rolfe had somehow managed to obtain seeds, and by 1612 his patch of West Indian tobacco was flourishing. The next year, he grew a sample for export. Desperate settlers and impatient London investors were delighted by Rolfe's successful experiment. Soon production of the leaf soared at Jamestown, to the neglect of all other pursuits.

During Virginia's initial tobacco boom, recently starving settlers saw handsome profits within reach. Because land was plentiful at first (a novelty for the English), the only limitations to riches were the scarcity of workers and the related high cost of labor. Any farmer who could hire half a dozen field hands could increase his profits fivefold, quickly earning enough to obtain more land and import more workers. The company transported several shiploads of apprentices, servants, and London street children to the labor-hungry colony. When a Dutch captain delivered twenty enslaved blacks in 1619, settlers eagerly purchased these first Africans to arrive in English Virginia. They also bid on the 100 women who disembarked the same year, shipped from England by the company to be sold as wives and workers. Still, men continued to outnumber women more than three to one for decades to come.

To encourage English migration further, the Virginia Company offered transportation and fifty acres to tenants, promising them ownership of the land after seven years of work. Men who paid their own way received fifty acres, plus an additional **headright** of fifty acres for each household member or laborer they transported. The Virginia Company went out of its way to assure its colonists of access to such established English freedoms as the right to trial by jury and a representative form of government. The company established civil courts controlled by English common law, and it instructed Virginia's governor to summon an annual assembly of elected **burgesses**—the earliest representative legislature in North America. First convened in 1619, the House of Burgesses wasted no time in affirming its commitment to fundamental English rights. The governor, the house said, could no longer impose taxes without the assembly's consent.

LAUNCHING THE PLYMOUTH COLONY

To attract additional capital and people, the Virginia Company began awarding patents (legal charters) to private groups of adventurers to "build a town and settle . . . there for the advancement of the general plantation of the country." The newcomers would live independently on a large tract, with only minimal control from the governor and his council. Two such small colonies originated among English Protestants living in exile in Holland because their separatist beliefs did not allow them to profess loyalty to the Church of England. The first group of 180, based in Amsterdam, departed for America late in 1618 on a crowded ship. Winter storms, sickness, and a shortage of fresh water destroyed the venture; scarcely fifty survivors straggled ashore in Virginia.

A second group of English Separatists, residing in the smaller Dutch city of Leiden, fared better. Most had migrated to Holland from northeast England in 1608. This group openly opposed the hierarchy, pomp, and inclusiveness of the Church of England. Instead, they wanted to return to early Christianity, where small groups of worthy (and often persecuted) believers formed their own communities of worship. After a decade in Holland, many of them had wearied of the foreign culture. They were dismayed by the effect of worldly Leiden on their children, and they also sensed, correctly, that warfare would soon break out in Europe. A few families pushed for a further removal to America, despite the obvious dangers of such a journey.

Possible destinations ranged from South America to Canada. Dutch entrepreneurs suggested the Hudson River. But in the end, still loyal to England, the Separatists decided to use a patent granted by the Virginia Company to a group of English capitalists. On the negative side, the migrants had to work for these investors for seven years. They also had to take along paying passengers who did not share their beliefs. On the positive side, they received financial support from backers who paid to rent a ship. Moreover, instead of having their daily affairs controlled from London, they could elect their own leader and establish civil authority as they saw fit. In short, they had the power to govern themselves.

In September 1620, after costly delays, thirty-five members of the Leiden congregation and additional Separatists from England departed from Plymouth, along with other passengers. They were crowded aboard the *Mayflower*, a 160-ton vessel bound for Virginia. But a stormy two-month crossing brought them to Cape Cod (in modern-day Massachusetts), which was no longer considered part of the Virginia Company's jurisdiction. Sickly from their journey and with winter closing in, they decided to disembark at the spot they called Plymouth rather than push south to Chesapeake Bay. Earlier, they had signed a solemn compact aboard the *Mayflower* binding them together in a civil community.

> *"They had now no friends to welcome them . . . . Besides, what could they see but a hideous and desolate wilderness."*

William Bradford, the chronicler and longtime governor of Plymouth Colony, later recalled their plight: "They had now no friends to welcome them nor inns to entertain or refresh their weather-beaten bodies. . . . Besides, what could they see but a hideous and desolate wilderness." Bradford could scarcely exaggerate the challenge. His own wife drowned (an apparent suicide) shortly after the *Mayflower* dropped anchor. And by the time the ship departed in April, an illness had swept away half the colonists. Those remaining planted barley and peas, but the English seeds failed to take hold.

Still, settlers had abundant fish and wildlife, along with ample Indian corn, and soon reinforcements arrived from England, bringing needed supplies. The newcomers also brought a legal patent for the land of Plymouth Plantation. With Squanto's aid, the settlers secured peaceful relations with Massasoit's villages. When survival for another winter seemed assured, they invited Massasoit and his followers to join in a three-day celebration of thanksgiving so that, according to one account, all might "rejoice together after we had gathered the fruit of our labors."

LISTEN

"Plymouth Colony"

The Puritan Experiment

■ *How were the Puritans strengthened or weakened by seeing themselves as God's chosen people?*

After more than a generation of costly colonization attempts, England still had little to show for its efforts when Charles I inherited the throne in 1625. Then two forces prompted rapid change: positive publicity about America and negative developments at home. John Smith, long a key promoter of overseas settlement, drew inspiration from the early efforts at Jamestown and Plymouth. In 1624, he published a best-seller predicting future success for these regions. Smith's *Generall Historie* went through six printings in eight years. Ironically, the book's popularity depended in large part on the grim religious, political, and economic conditions in England that suddenly gave such literature a broad appeal.

FORMATION OF THE MASSACHUSETTS BAY COMPANY

European Christianity had taken a number of different forms since the religious upheaval sparked by Luther a century earlier. The first Protestants had demanded a reformation of the Roman Catholic Church and had questioned papal authority over Christians. Now many non-Catholic English worshippers doubted whether the Church of England (also known as the Anglican Church) had gone far enough toward rejecting the practices of Rome. They lamented what they saw as the church's bureaucratic hierarchy, ornate rituals, and failure to enforce strict observance of the Christian Sabbath each Sunday. Puritans scoffed at the gaudy vestments of Anglican bishops, elaborate church music, and other trappings of worship unjustified by biblical scripture. Instead, they praised the stark simplicity that John Calvin had brought to his church in Geneva.

As English Calvinists grew in number, their objections to the Church of England increased. They protested that the Anglican Church, like the Catholic Church, remained inclusive in membership rather than selective. They argued for limiting participation only to the devout, and they insisted that the Church of England should be independent and self-governing rather than tied to the monarchy. This keen desire for further cleansing and purity, so common to reformers, spurred the ongoing movement known as Puritanism.

> *Puritans scoffed at the gaudy vestments of Anglican bishops, elaborate church music, and other trappings of worship unjustified by biblical scripture.*

Some of the most radical members of this broad religious coalition became known as Separatists (including Bradford and the Plymouth pilgrims), because they were committed to an extreme position: complete separation from what they saw as the corrupt Church of England. But many more Puritans (including most of the reformers who migrated to Massachusetts Bay) resisted separation. They hoped to stay technically within the Anglican fold while taking increased control of their own congregations—a practice known as congregationalism. Unwilling to conform to practices that offended them, these nonseparating Congregationalists remained determined to save the Anglican Church through righteous example, even if it meant migrating abroad for a time to escape persecution and demonstrate the proper ways of a purified Protestant church.

An emphasis on instructive preaching by informed leaders lay at the heart of the Puritan movement. Translation of scripture from Latin and its publication into everyday languages the people spoke or read, using the newly invented printing press, had been a central theme of the Reformation. An improved English translation of the Bible in 1611, known as the King James Version, provided further access to scripture for all who could read or listen. But James and his bishops, realizing that a "priesthood of all believers" threatened their power, moved to control who could preach and what they could say. A 1626 law prohibited preaching or writing on controversial religious topics such as the conduct of the clergy, the nature of church hierarchy, and the interpretation of scripture. "There should be more praying and less preaching," wrote one royal supporter, "for much preaching breeds faction, but much praying causes devotion."

Puritans believed that the sermon should form the center of the Christian worship service. Their churches resembled lecture halls, emphasizing the pulpit more than the altar. In preaching, Puritans stressed a "plain style" that all listeners could understand. Moreover, they urged listeners to play an active role in their faith—to master reading and engage in regular study and discussion of scripture. In response to mounting public interest in these practices, Puritan ministers intensified their preaching and published their sermons. In effect, they dared authorities to silence them.

Reprisals came swiftly, led by William Laud, bishop of London, whom Charles I elevated to archbishop of Canterbury in 1633. Laud instructed all preachers to focus their remarks on biblical passages and avoid writing or speaking about controversial religious matters. The bishop's persecution of Puritan leaders who appeared to disobey these orders only broadened their movement at a time when the king himself was arousing Protestant suspicions. In 1625, Charles I had married Henrietta Maria, Catholic sister of the French king, and had granted freedom of worship to English Catholics, disturbing a wide array of Protestants in the realm. When the House of Commons refused to approve finances for his policies, he arrested its leaders and disbanded Parliament in 1629. He governed on his own for eleven years by levying taxes without parliamentary approval.

As England's church grew more rigid and its monarchy more controlling, the nation's economy took a turn for the worse. The cost of rent and food had risen more rapidly than wages, and workers paid dearly. Jobs became more scarce after 1625, and unemployed workers staged local revolts. In 1629, entrepreneurs who viewed New England as a potential opportunity teamed up with disaffected Puritans to obtain a charter for a new entity: the Massachusetts Bay Company. Through a generation of costly trial-and-error experiments, the English had amassed great expertise in colonization. Given the worsening conditions at home, especially among the Puritan faithful, proposals for overseas settlement attracted widespread attention.

"WE SHALL BE AS A CITY UPON A HILL"

During the next dozen years, more than 70,000 people left England for the New World. Two-thirds of them sailed to the West Indies, attracted by the prospect of a warmer climate and a longer growing season. But a large contingent of Puritans embarked from England for the new colony at Massachusetts Bay adjacent to the Plymouth settlement.

A loophole in the king's grant permitted them to take the actual charter with them and to hold their company meetings in America. This maneuver took them out from under the usual control of London investors and let them turn the familiar joint stock structure into the framework for a self-governing colony. By 1629 advance parties had established a post at Salem for people who "upon the account of religion would be willing to begin a foreign plantation."

In England, meanwhile, a Puritan squire named John Winthrop assumed leadership of the Massachusetts Bay Company. "God will bring some heavy Affliction upon this lande," he predicted to his wife, but the Lord "will provide a shelter & a hidinge place for us and others." In exchange, God would expect great things from these chosen people, as from the Old Testament Israelites. "We are entered into covenant with him for this work," Winthrop told his companions aboard the *Arbella* en route to America in 1630.

Winthrop laid out this higher Calvinist standard in a memorable shipboard sermon titled "A Model of Christian Charity." The values that others merely profess, he explained, "we must bring into familiar and constant practice," sharing burdens, extending aid, and demonstrating patience. "For this end, we must be knit together in this work as one," regardless of social rank. If we fail, he warned, "the Lord will surely break out in wrath against us, and make us know the price of the breach of such a covenant."

Worcester Art Museum, Worcester, Massachusetts. Gift of Mr. and Mrs. Albert W. Rice (1963.134)

■ Port records for 1635 show that groups leaving London varied markedly, depending on their colonial destination. Young children were common aboard ships heading for New England, as were women and girls. Among passengers for New England, eight of every twenty were female. In contrast, females made up only three in twenty of those going to Virginia and one in twenty among people heading for Barbados.

Anne Bradstreet: "The Tenth Muse, Lately Sprung Up in America"

Interpreting History

The Puritans who migrated to America stressed literacy and education as part of their faith. They left extensive court records, sermons, and diaries, but few of these surviving documents come from the pens of women. The poems and reflections of Anne Bradstreet provide a notable exception. "Here you may find," she told her children shortly before her death in 1672, "what was your living mother's mind."

The lifelong poet was born Anne Dudley in Lincolnshire, England, in 1612. She already "found much comfort in reading the Scriptures" by age seven. "But as I grew to be about 14 or 15," she recalled, "I found my heart more carnal, and . . . the follies of youth took hold of me. About 16, the Lord . . . smote me with the smallpox . . . and again restored me." That same year, she married Simon Bradstreet, the son of a minister. Two years later, despite a frail constitution, she sailed for Massachusetts Bay with her husband and her father (both future governors of the colony) aboard the *Arbella*.

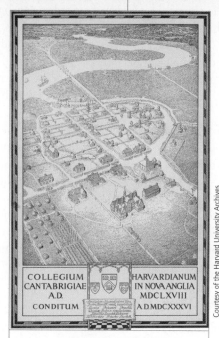

■ Cambridge looked something like this in the 1660s. The large building in the foreground is Harvard College, founded in 1636, and the smaller brick building beside it is the Indian College, built in 1655. The village was even smaller when Anne Bradstreet resided there briefly after her arrival in Massachusetts Bay.

Courtesy of the Harvard University Archives

COLLEGIUM CANTABRIGIAE A.D. CONDITUM   HARVARDIANUM IN NOVA ANGLIA MDCLXVIII A.D. MDCXXXVI

Anne Bradstreet was alert to all that seemed strange and different in America. When I "came into this country," she related, "I found a new world and new manners." The young couple set up housekeeping in the town of Cambridge, on the Charles River, but life was difficult at first. Anne suffered from "a lingering sickness like a consumption." Moreover, "It pleased God to keep me a long time without a child, which was a great grief to me and cost me many prayers and tears." Finally, she bore a son in 1633, and seven more children followed.

As the family grew and moved about, "Mistress Bradstreet" wrote poems and meditations, although detractors hinted that she should put down her quill pen and take up a sewing needle. "If what I do prove well, it won't advance," she lamented in rhyme; "They'l say it's stol'n, or else it was by chance." Nevertheless, a book of her poems was published in England in 1650, hailing her as "The Tenth **Muse**, Lately Sprung Up in America."

As a writer, Anne Bradstreet was more interested in spiritual improvement than literary grace. "Many speak well," she observed, "but few can do well." Throughout

Far from hiding in obscurity, dedicated Puritans must set a visible example for the rest of the world, Winthrop concluded. "We shall be as a city upon a hill."

The *Arbella* was one of seventeen ships that brought more than 1,000 people to New England in 1630. The English newcomers chose Winthrop as governor and established Boston as their port. They colonized Indian lands depopulated by recent epidemics. By the time civil war erupted in England in 1642, nearly 20,000 people had made the journey, eager to escape the religious persecution and governmental tyranny of Charles I. Whole congregations migrated with their ministers; other people (more than 20 percent) crossed as servants. But most came as independent families with young children. On average, of every 100 newcomers, roughly half were adults (thirty men to twenty women); the other half were all under age eighteen, divided about evenly between boys and girls.

Earlier settlers traded food, lodging, and building materials to fresh arrivals in exchange for textiles, tools, money, and labor. When new groups of church members wanted to establish a village, they applied for land to the General Court, a legislature made up of representatives elected from existing towns. Well before 1640, English settlements dotted the coast and had sprung up inland along the Connecticut River, where smallpox had decimated the Indians in 1633. There, English outposts rose at Hartford and Springfield; newcomers hoped to farm the fertile river valley and also attract part of the inland fur trade away from the French and Dutch. In 1639, some of the new towns along the navigable river agreed to a *life, she followed a simple creed: "There is no object that we see; no action that we do; no good that we enjoy; no evil that we feel or fear, but we may make some spiritual advantage" of it. Nothing epitomizes this belief more clearly than "some verses upon the burning of our house, July 10th, 1666." Bradstreet composed the lines on an unburned scrap of paper as she groped to make sense of the calamity. The poem helped her to mourn her loss, take stock of her blessings, and renew her faith. In part, it reads,*

> In silent night when rest I took,
> For sorrow neer I did not look,
> I waken'd was with thundring nois
> And Piteous shreiks of dreadfull voice . . . .

> I, starting up, the light did spye,
> And to my God my heart did cry . . . .
> Then coming out beheld a space
> The flame consume my dwelling place.

> And, when I could no longer look,
> I blest his Name that gave and took,
> That layd my goods now in the dust:
> Yea so it was, and so 'twas just . . . .

> When by the Ruines oft I past,
> My sorrowing eyes aside did cast,

> And here and there the places spye
> Where oft I sate, and long did lye.

> Here stood that Trunk, and there that chest;
> There lay that store I counted best:
> My pleasant things in ashes lye,
> And them behold no more shall I . . . .

> Then streight I gin my heart to chide,
> And did thy wealth on earth abide?
> Didst fix thy hope on mouldring dust,
> The arm of flesh didst make thy trust? . . . .

> Thou hast a house on high erect
> Fram'd by that mighty Architect . . . .
> The world no longer let me Love,
> My hope and Treasure lyes Above.

QUESTIONS

1. *How might Anne Bradstreet's eventful life before age twenty have shaped her into a poet?*

2. *Imagine losing your home and belongings in a storm, flood, or fire. Would it deepen or weaken your religious beliefs? How about your need for material possessions?*

rudimentary government, known as the Fundamental Orders (though Connecticut waited a generation before gaining its formal colonial charter in 1662).

The sheer number of land-hungry settlers drove the rapid expansion. So did friction among newcomers, who competed for scarce resources and complained about price controls and other economic constraints intended to impose civic order. In his initial call to "work as one," Winthrop had worried that migrants would neglect the duties of spiritual regeneration. However, the sharpest dissents came from zealous people who feared that the religious experiment had not gone far enough. Challenging authority lay at the heart of radical Protestantism, for its practitioners stressed inner conviction and personal belief over outward conformity and deference to wealth and status. The more seriously New England's believers took their "errand into the wilderness," the more contentious they became about the proper ways to fulfill their covenant with God.

DISSENTERS: ROGER WILLIAMS AND ANNE HUTCHINSON

Like the biblical Hebrews before them, the Puritans—self-appointed saints—believed that God had chosen them for a special mission in the world. The Almighty, they believed, would watch carefully, punish harshly, and reward mightily. Inevitably, some devout people, raised to question authority in England, continued to dissent in New England, and some were drawn to the more tolerant and open Dutch colony on the Hudson. Their stormy careers illustrate that not all Puritans accepted the idea that women should defer to men, or that the English should dominate the Indians.

Strong-willed Deborah Moody, for example, was an aristocratic Puritan who migrated to New England in her fifties. Offended by the "conceite" and "bickering" in her Massachusetts congregation, she joined other dissidents, known as Anabaptists, who protested that children too young to understand the faith should not receive baptism. When authorities denounced Lady Moody as a "dangerous" woman, she led a group to New Amsterdam. The Dutch governor, eager for settlers, gave the newcomers land south of Breukelen (Brooklyn) on eastern Long Island. There, near what is now Coney Island, they established the first North American settlement directed by a woman. Though Deborah Moody remains obscure, two other early dissenters—Roger Williams and Anne Hutchinson—are remembered as effective challengers to the leadership of the Massachusetts Bay colony.

When Williams arrived in Boston, his Separatist leanings angered Bay Colony authorities, who still hoped to reform the Anglican Church rather than renounce it. The recent graduate of Cambridge University had other ideas that proved equally distressing. The young minister argued that civil authorities, inevitably corrupt, had no right to judge religious matters. Williams even pushed for an unprecedented separation of church and state—to protect the church. He also contended that the colony's land patent from the king had no validity. The settlers, he said, had to purchase occupancy rights from the Native Americans. Unable to silence him, irate magistrates banished Williams from Massachusetts Bay in the winter of 1635. Moving south, he took up residence among the Narragansett Indians and built a refuge for other dissenters, which he named Providence. Still subject to arrest in Boston, he sailed home to England by way of tolerant New Amsterdam in 1643. Once back in London, he persuaded leaders of England's rising Puritan Revolution to grant a charter (1644) to his independent colony of Rhode Island.

A more explosive popular challenge centered on Anne Hutchinson. The talented eldest daughter of an English minister, she had grown up in England with a strong will, a solid theological education, and a thirst for spiritual perfection. She married a Lincolnshire textile merchant and took an active part in religious discussions while also bearing fifteen children. When her Puritan minister, John Cotton, departed for New England, Hutchinson claimed that God, in a private revelation, had instructed her to follow. In 1634, the family migrated to Boston, where Hutchinson attended Cotton's church and hosted religious discussions in her home. The popularity of these weekly meetings troubled authorities, as did her argument that the "Holy Spirit illumines the heart of every true believer." Hutchinson downplayed outward conformity—modest dress or regular church attendance—as a route to salvation. Instead, she stressed direct communication with God's inner presence as the key to individual forgiveness.

> Winthrop sentenced Hutchinson to banishment as "a woman not fit for our society."

Most Puritans sought a delicate balance in their lives between respected outer works and inner personal grace. Hutchinson tipped that balance dangerously toward the latter. To the colony's magistrates, especially Winthrop, such teaching pointed toward anarchy—more troublesome when it came from a woman. These officials labeled Hutchinson and her followers as Antinomians (from *anti*, "against," and *nomos*, "law"). But the vehement opposition faction grew, attracting merchants who chafed under economic restrictions, women who questioned men's domination of the church, and young adults who resented the strict authority of their elders. By 1636, this religious and political coalition had gained enough supporters to turn Winthrop out as governor.

Challenged by this Antinomian Crisis, members of the Puritan establishment fought back. They divided the opposition to win reelection for Winthrop, they established Harvard College to educate ministers who would not stray from the fold, they staged a flurry of trials for contempt and sedition (the crime of inciting resistance to lawful authority), and they made a special example of Hutchinson herself. After a two-day hearing in which she defended herself admirably, Winthrop sentenced Hutchinson to banishment as "a woman not fit for our society." Forced into exile, Hutchinson moved first to Rhode Island and later to New Netherland, living at Pelham Bay near the estate of Joseph Bronk (now called the Bronx). There, she and six of her children, plus nine of her followers, were killed in an Indian attack in 1643. A river and a parkway in New York still bear her name.

EXPANSION AND VIOLENCE: THE PEQUOT WAR

Immigration to New England slowed during the 1640s because of religious and political upheaval at home. In England, Puritans and supporters of Parliament formed an army and openly challenged royal authority during the English Civil War. After seizing power, these revolutionaries beheaded Charles I in 1649, abolished the monarchy, and proclaimed England a republican commonwealth. Settlers in Massachusetts Bay struggled to square such sweeping developments in England with Winthrop's earlier assurance that the eyes of God and humankind would be fixed on New England. Making matters worse, religious and economic controversies intensified as the next generation quickly came of age. Needing new farmland and intellectual breathing room, fresh congregations began to "hive off" from the original settlements like swarms of bees. By 1640, New Hampshire, Rhode Island, and Connecticut each had at least four new towns that would provide the beginnings for independent colonies.

But the northeastern forest was not an empty wilderness, any more than the Chesapeake tidewater, the Florida interior, or the mesas of New Mexico had been. As the Hutchinsons discovered, newcomers who pushed inland were co-opting the land of long-time residents. Pressure on New England's Native Americans erupted in armed conflict in the Pequot War of 1637, at the height of the Antinomian Crisis. The Pequot Indians, English allies recently weakened by smallpox, resided near the mouth of the Connecticut River. Unfortunately, Puritan settlers, led by John Winthrop's son, were attempting to launch a town at Old Saybrook in the same vicinity. From Boston, Governor Winthrop fanned fears that the Pequot "would cause all the Indians in the country to join to root out all the English."

Recruiting Narragansett and Mohegan Indians to the English side, the colonists unleashed all-out war against the Pequot. The campaign culminated in a dawn raid on a stockaded Pequot town that sheltered noncombatants. The invaders torched the village (at Mystic, Connecticut) and shot or put to the sword almost all who tried to escape. Some 400 Indian men, women, and children died. The Puritans' Indian allies were shocked by the wholesale carnage. English warfare, they protested, "is too furious, and slaies too many men." Chastened by this intimidating display of terror and weakened by recurrent epidemics, the tribes of southern New England negotiated away much of their land over the next generation, trading furs to the expanding colonists and seeking to understand their perplexing ways.

Having gained the upper hand, the Bible-reading English made gestures to convert their Native American neighbors. The Massachusetts General Court encouraged missionary work, forbade the worship of Indian gods, and set aside land for "praying towns" to encourage "the Indians to live in an orderly way amongst us." In Cambridge, the Reverend John Eliot labored to create and print a 1,200-page Indian Bible, using English words when terms such as "horse," "brass," "book," and "psalm" did not exist in the Massachusett language. At Harvard, officials committed by their charter to the "education of the English and Indian youth of this Country" erected a well-publicized Indian College.

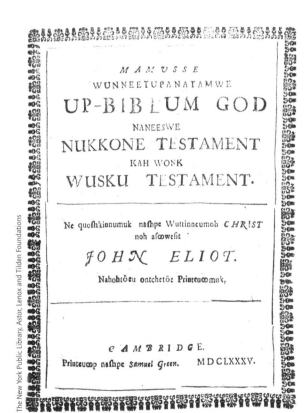

The New York Public Library, Astor, Lenox and Tilden Foundations

■ John Eliot and several Indian assistants translated the Old and New Testaments into the Massachusett language, printing 1,000 copies of their thick Indian Bible in 1663. This title page appeared on the second edition in 1685.

The Chesapeake Bay Colonies

■ *In what ways did the rapid spread of tobacco help or hurt the Chesapeake colonies?*

On Chesapeake Bay, settlers' relations with the Indians remained strained at best during the first half of the seventeenth century. In 1608, in an effort to secure the support of Indian leadership, the English performed an elaborate ceremony granting a scarlet cloak and a copper crown to Chief Powhatan. But two years later, suspicious that he was harboring runaway colonists, the English burned the nearest Indian villages and unthinkingly destroyed much-needed corn. A wife of one Indian leader, taken captive, watched English soldiers throwing her children in the river and shooting them in the head before she herself was stabbed to death.

For both sides, hopes of reconciliation rose briefly in 1614 with the match between Pocahontas, daughter of Powhatan, and John Rolfe, the prominent widower who had introduced tobacco. But the marriage proved brief; Pocahontas died in England three years later, after bearing one child. Leaders intended the wedding alliance as a diplomatic gesture toward peace. But it did little to curtail the settlers' bitterness over their lingering dependence on Indian supplies. For their part, the Native Americans resented the encroaching tobacco fields and belligerent tactics of the new settlers.

■ Captain John Smith boasted that in 1608 he intimidated Opechancanough with his pistol to disarm the Indians and obtain their corn. The insult was not forgotten; decades later, the Pamunkey leader launched two major attacks on the Jamestown colony. This image of the early incident appeared in Smith's popular *Generall Historie* of 1624.

Courtesy of the John Carter Brown Library at Brown University

THE DEMISE OF THE VIRGINIA COMPANY

Powhatan's death in 1618 brought to power his more militant younger brother, Opechancanough, the leader of the Pamunkey tribe. His encounters with the English had been frequent and unfriendly. John Smith had even taken him captive at gunpoint to extort food supplies. By 1618, the English were taking Indian land to grow tobacco, and more newcomers were arriving annually. Over the next three years, forty-two ships brought 3,500 people to the Chesapeake colony. The influx disheartened the Indians, and Opechancanough and his followers in the Powhatan Confederacy sought ways to end the mounting intrusion. Briefly, disease seemed to work in the Indians' favor. Immigrants who made the long sea voyage with poor provisions often fell ill in the swampy and unhealthy environment of Jamestown. By 1622, the colony's inhabitants were dying almost as rapidly as newcomers arrived. Sickness had carried off 3,000 residents in the course of only three years.

Opechancanough sensed a chance to deliver the finishing blow. He planned a sudden and coordinated offensive along the lower James River. On March 22, 1622, his forces attacked the English, surprising the outlying settlements and sparing no one. Of the 1,240 colonists, nearly 350 lost their lives. Warned by an Indian, Jamestown survived the uprising, but hope for peaceful relations ended. In London, word of the attack fueled opposition to the Virginia Company among disgruntled investors. In 1624, King James annulled the company's charter, making Virginia a royal colony controlled by the crown. In the colony's first seventeen years, more than 8,500 people, almost all of them young, had embarked for the Chesapeake. By 1624, only fifteen of every 100 remained alive.

The surviving colonists placed a bounty on Opechancanough's head, but attempts to ambush or poison him failed. The Indian leader lived on, nursing his distrust of the English. In 1644, he inaugurated a second uprising that killed some 500 colonists. But the English

The Chesapeake Region, 1600–1660

- Powhatan Confederacy in 1607
- English settlement by 1650
- New Sweden, 1637–1655
- Maryland boundary in 1632
- Current state boundaries

■ **MAP 2.4** **Cultures Meet on the Chesapeake**

When the English founded Jamestown in 1607, the numerous tribes of the Powhatan Confederacy controlled a wide region south of the Potomac River. In 1632, King Charles I granted all of Virginia north of the Potomac River to Lord Baltimore for his Maryland colony. This domain, with its capital at St. Mary's, stretched from the headwaters of the Potomac to the Delaware River. It reached north to 40 degrees (above the current boundary of Maryland), and it included the settlement of New Sweden on the Delaware (1637–1655). By midcentury, European settlement remained confined along main waterways.

settlement had grown too large to eradicate. By this time old age forced the "Great General" to be carried on a litter. When the English finally captured him and brought him to Jamestown in 1646, Opechancanough was too old to walk unassisted. Still, he remained defiant until shot in the back by one of the Englishmen guarding him.

After two years of brutal warfare, the Pamunkey and their allies in the Powhatan Confederacy conceded defeat and submitted to English authority. From then on, they would pay a token annual tribute for the privilege to remain on lands that had once belonged to them. With the way cleared for Chesapeake expansion, land-hungry English settlers appeared in ever-increasing numbers in Virginia and the smaller and younger Maryland colony.

MARYLAND: THE CATHOLIC REFUGE

Maryland owed its beginnings to George Calvert, a respected Catholic member of England's government. He was named the first Baron of Baltimore, in Ireland, in 1625. Calvert, now Lord Baltimore, had a keen interest in colonization, and in 1632 he petitioned Charles I for land in the Chesapeake. The king granted him 10 million acres adjacent to Virginia, to be named Maryland in honor of the Catholic queen, Henrietta Maria. The Maryland charter

DOCUMENT

The Charter of Maryland (1632)

gave the proprietor and his heirs unprecedented personal power, especially in the granting of lands to colonists without limitations based on religious belief.

Because Calvert died before the royal charter took effect, his eldest son, the second Lord Baltimore, took charge of the settlement effort. In 1634, the *Ark* and the *Dove* carried more than 200 settlers—both Protestants and Catholics—to the new colony. There, they established a capital at St. Mary's, near the mouth of the Potomac River. With the execution of the king in 1649 and the creation of an anti-Catholic commonwealth in England, the Calvert family provided a haven in Maryland for their coreligionists. However, Catholics never became a majority in the Chesapeake colony.

In 1649, Maryland's assembly passed an Act Concerning Religion, guaranteeing toleration for all settlers who professed a belief in Jesus Christ. This assertion of religious toleration, though limited, proved too broad for many to stomach. In the 1650s, supporters of the English Puritan cause seized power in Maryland, repealed the act, and briefly ended the Calverts' proprietorship. But by 1660, with the restoration of the Stuart monarchy in England, proprietary rule returned to the prosperous farming colony.

THE DWELLINGS OF ENGLISH NEWCOMERS

By 1660, Virginia and Maryland totaled roughly 35,000 settlers, scattered along the edges of the bay and its adjoining tidewater rivers. In New England, where far fewer immigrants had arrived, the overall numbers were still somewhat smaller—perhaps only 25,000. But in the northeast, early marriage and long life expectancy prompted a rapidly rising population. From the start, Puritans embarking for New England had generally set out as families. The presence of thousands of wives and daughters led to the swift formation of stable households, and the balance between the sexes soon proved almost even. New England women took on crucial aspects of domestic production, cooking, baking, weaving, sewing, and gardening. Their numerous children provided additional hands, hauling water, making candles, and churning butter where labor was in short supply. In contrast to New England, the Chesapeake still could not maintain its colonial population without steady infusions of newcomers. A sickly climate kept life expectancy low, and men continued to outnumber women by more than two to one.

> *In both New England and the Chesapeake, initial crude shelters gave way to small frame houses.*

In both regions, housing was a primary concern, and newcomers brought English building traditions with them. But contrasting climates and differing priorities prompted the evolution of different architectural styles. In both New England and the Chesapeake, initial crude shelters gave way to small frame houses, usually with clapboard walls, as arrivals took advantage of the ample wood supply. At first, roofs were made of thatch—bundles of grass and straw. But as nails became more abundant, thatch yielded to lighter and less flammable wooden shingles.

Large New England families, facing longer winters indoors, needed warmer dwellings with more interior space. Many added another room at the gable end of a frame house, surrounding the external stone chimney and turning the cooking hearth into a central fireplace. Digging a cellar, building thick walls, and adding a second story made efficient use of heat from the log fire. New Englanders often linked additional storage rooms and animal sheds to the house for warmth as well.

Early Chesapeake houses, in contrast, were less solid and substantial. Most structures remained one story high, a simple wooden frame set on posts, with mortise-and-tenon joints and a dirt or plank floor. Oiled paper or wooden shutters covered most windows, as glass was rare. Since skilled bricklayers were few, most chimneys used wattle-and-daub construction, a simple weave of sticks and vines, covered with clay daubing. Tidewater residents built chimneys outside the house to help dissipate heat, and additional spaces were spread out, rather than being centralized under one roof. "All their drudgeries of cookery, washing, dairies, etc.," reported one Virginian, are done in small buildings "detached from the dwelling houses which by this means are kept cool and sweet."

A Roof Overhead: Early Chesapeake Housing

Lumber was plentiful in the Tidewater region, but labor was scarce and tools were crude. As a result, most structures were small and insubstantial, and seventeenth-century Chesapeake settlers lived in cramped quarters. This cutaway drawing illustrates the construction and floor plan of a house for "ordinary beginners," described in a pamphlet for potential migrants. The entire frame rested on sunken posts above an earth floor and was held together with wooden pegs inserted into mortise-and-tenon joints. A livable cottage often took less than two months to build.

During this period, only a few fashionable homes used brick construction. Thomas Jefferson, a Virginian who had an eye and pocketbook suited for grander architecture, noted with dismay in the 1780s that "the private buildings are very rarely constructed of stone or brick, much the greatest portion being of scantling and boards, plastered with lime. It is impossible to devise things more ugly, uncomfortable, and happily more perishable." Not surprisingly, only half a dozen structures built before 1660 still survive in Virginia and Maryland.

QUESTIONS

1. Which factors had the largest effect on early Chesapeake housing design: materials, climate, labor, or cultural traditions?

2. Thomas Jefferson asserted that it would be impossible to devise anything more ugly or uncomfortable than an early Chesapeake cottage. How does your own notion of what is beautiful and comfortable in a house or apartment differ from the ideas of your grandparents, your friends, or Jefferson?

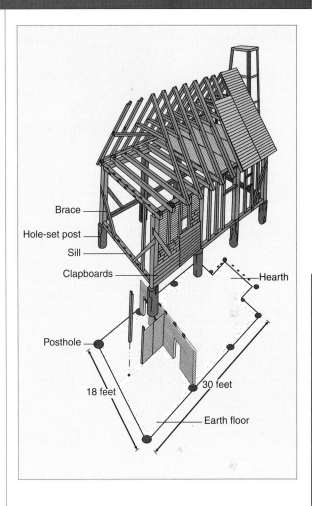

Brace
Hole-set post
Sill
Clapboards
Hearth
Posthole
18 feet
30 feet
Earth floor

THE LURE OF TOBACCO

Chesapeake residents spent most of their time out of doors, clearing land and tending fields. They readily adopted corn as a subsistence crop, and their imported livestock flourished. But early efforts to find a marketable export product met with disappointment. Hope for silk production disappeared when rats ate a supply of imported silkworms. Seeds of Mexican cotton, brought from southern Europe in 1621, failed to take hold. Experiments with oranges, pineapples, and grapes led nowhere. Chesapeake lumber sold well at first, but it was John Rolfe's tobacco plant that emerged as the tidewater's unlikely crop of choice.

Virginia's annual tobacco exports grew from a total weight of 2,000 pounds in 1615 to 500,000 in 1626. By 1630, saturated markets and stiff taxes led to slumping tobacco prices, so Virginians diversified their efforts. The beginning of the Massachusetts Bay colony created a demand for food that Chesapeake farmers met with well-timed coastal shipments. In 1634, they reported selling to "their zealous neighbours of New England tenne thousand bushels of corne for their releefe, besides good quantities of beeves, goats and hoggs, whereof this country hath great plentie." Such diversification proved brief, however. By 1640, London was receiving almost 1.4 million pounds of tobacco annually.

Tabacum latifolium.

CHRONOLOGY: 1598–1660

1598	Spanish colonize New Mexico.
1607	England's Virginia Company launches colony at Jamestown.
1608	Champlain establishes Quebec
1610	Santa Fe becomes capital of Spanish New Mexico.
1619	Virginia creates an elected assembly.
1620	*Mayflower* passengers establish Plymouth Colony.
1622	Opechancanough leads surprise attack on Jamestown colonists.
1626	Dutch establish New Amsterdam on Manhattan Island.
1630	English Puritans found Massachusetts Bay Colony.
1636	Antinomian Crisis stirred by Anne Hutchinson divides Massachusetts Bay.
1637	Pequot War in New England.
1641	Montreal established in New France.
1644	Roger Williams obtains charter for his Rhode Island colony.
1649	Parliament executes King Charles I and abolishes the monarchy during England's Civil War.
1660	Restoration of monarchy in England under Charles II.

Though tobacco prices remained low throughout much of the seventeenth century, newcomers to Virginia and Maryland still managed to eke out a profit. They could grow the plants amid stumps in partially cleared fields. They could learn the many necessary procedures—planting, weeding, worming, suckering, topping, cutting, stripping, and curing—as the crop progressed. In short, it took hard work, but little farming experience, to bring cured tobacco to waterfront docks. Since captains charged by volume rather than weight, planters reduced shipping costs by devising a uniform barrel size and developing ways to press more leaves into each cask.

Still, the problems were formidable. Tobacco depleted the soil rapidly, so crop yields dwindled after several years. Then farmers had to leave their plots fallow, allowing them to recover, while clearing new fields for planting. This time-consuming task forced them onto marginal land that was poorly drained and less fertile. It also moved them away from navigable rivers, raising transportation costs. Storms, droughts, and crop diseases posed constant threats, and dependence on a single product in a distant and uncertain overseas market created added risks. By midcentury, Chesapeake planters worried about market saturation and overproduction. But by then, for better or worse, growing the noxious weed had become a way of life. Virginia and Maryland farmers found themselves enmeshed in the high-risk world of tobacco production. Dependence on the troublesome crop would expand across the upper South for centuries to come.

Conclusion

During half a century, the French, Dutch, and English had all moved to challenge Spanish claims in North America. By 1660, all four of these maritime powers of western Europe had taken aggressive steps to establish permanent footholds on the fringes of the enormous continent. In each instance, the European colonizers benefited first from the presence of knowledgeable Native Americans and then from the sharp decline of those same people through warfare and the onslaught of new diseases.

Granted, warfare with foreign invaders and death from unfamiliar illnesses had become a part of Native American history in the preceding century. But the sixteenth century was an era of tentative European exploration. In contrast, the first half of the seventeenth century saw Europeans move beyond occasional forays to permanent colonization. Spain, France, Holland, and England each had formidable assets in Europe and on the high seas. By 1660 all had sponsored colonial settlements that had endured for several generations, and each had begun to taste the seductive fruits of empire in America and elsewhere.

The English, slowest to become involved in overseas colonization, had caught up with their competitors by 1660. Among European countries, England had proven the most aggressive in forming expansive family-based colonies rather than military garrisons or trading outposts. As a result, by 1660 the population of England's North American settlements had already outstripped those of its imperial rivals. Indeed, fledgling English communities were growing at an increasing pace, thanks in particular to the rapid expansion in New England. This emerging superiority in numbers would prove advantageous in the imperial clashes that lay ahead.

For Review

1. What relevance did Spain's access to the Pacific have to its ambitions for colonization in the New World?

2. Why was Dutch New Netherland more culturally diverse than French Canada?

3. Among the forces shaping early migration to America shown in Figure 2.1 on page 54, which proved most important in colonizing Virginia? New England?

4. Why did the differing ideas of Anne Hutchinson and Roger Williams pose such a challenge to Puritan authorities in New England?

5. For Chesapeake colonists who survived past 1620, what large forces (often beyond their control) shaped their settlement over the next four decades?

6. How did religious views, demographic factors, and geography shape the success of European empires in North America after 1600?

Created Equal Online

For more *Created Equal* resources, including suggestions on sites to visit and books to read, go to **MyHistoryLab.com**.

Chapter 3

Controlling the Edges of the Continent, 1660–1715

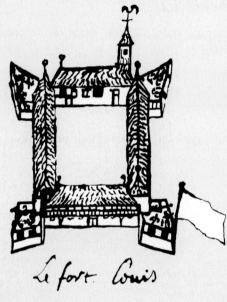

■ French fort at Mobile, 1705

In April 1704, Marguerite Messier Le Sueur, joined by her five children, loaded a large canoe on the Montreal waterfront. She worked with her brother, Jean-Michel Messier, and a guide to prepare for an immense inland journey to a new French outpost on the Gulf of Mexico. There she planned to meet her husband, explorer-trader Pierre-Charles Le Sueur. At age twenty-eight, Marguerite had already been married half her life, having wed Pierre-Charles in 1690 when he was thirty-four and she had just turned fourteen.

Marguerite was deeply involved, through family ties, in the dramatic changes taking place throughout the vast North American hinterland claimed by France. Her cousin, an adventurous Canadian named Pierre Le Moyne d'Iberville, had established the French colony of Louisiana near the mouth of the Mississippi River in 1699, and three years later Iberville and his younger brother Bienville had started the village of Mobile (near present-day Mobile, Alabama) to serve as the first capital. In 1702, Marguerite's husband, long active in Canada's far-flung western trade, had paddled down the Mississippi, taking furs to the new outpost at Mobile. After building a house for his family there, he accompanied Iberville back to France.

In 1704, confident about the future success of the Louisiana venture, Le Sueur sent word to his wife in Montreal to start the inland expedition of nearly 2,000 miles to Mobile. Pierre-Charles himself departed from France aboard the *Pelican* for the same destination, hoping to reunite with his family. With the ice gone from the St. Lawrence, Marguerite and her party set out from Montreal on April 30, 1704, making their way up river and passing through Lake Ontario and Lake Erie. After more than a year, they reached Kaskaskia in southern Illinois and began to descend the Mississippi River. Marguerite's brother and a daughter died before the travelers finally reached their destination. When the survivors arrived at Mobile in August 1705, more bad news awaited them: the voyage of the *Pelican* had met with disaster.

Marguerite's husband had boarded the ship in France, joining missionaries, soldiers, and potential brides recruited to go to Mobile. But during a stopover in Cuba, Pierre-Charles and others caught yellow fever and died before the immigrants reached Mobile. The town—home to just 160 men and a dozen women—hardly had enough food and shelter for the sickly newcomers, and yellow fever spread quickly. The epidemic swept away forty residents in two months and decimated nearby Indian villages.

Still, life at the outpost persisted. Townsmen welcomed the *Pelican*'s eligible young women, ages fourteen to eighteen, and priests celebrated thirteen marriages within the first three weeks. New children were being born to these couples by the late summer of 1705, when Marguerite arrived from Montreal. Though distraught by news of Pierre-Charles's death, the young widow moved her children into the house he had built for them. She resumed her maiden name, Marguerite Messier, and determined to begin a fresh chapter of her life in the new Louisiana colony.

The changes taking place in North America during Marguerite Messier's lifetime occurred within a broad international context. In the second half of the seventeenth century, European maritime powers were caught up in a global race to expand and protect their overseas empires, and the chessboard was constantly changing. For example, by the 1670s, Dutch authorities had been forced to withdraw entirely from North America. As the Dutch departed, the Spanish, French, and English intensified their competition, starting towns wherever possible in order to stake their claims.

In the East, England expanded the number and size of its coastal colonies. English port towns multiplied along the Atlantic seaboard. English newcomers also pressed inland along numerous rivers to found towns. Many of these towns (such as William Byrd's trading post that became Richmond, Virginia) appeared at the "fall line," the point where waterfalls blocked passage upstream and provided waterpower to run gristmills. Farther inland, conflicts with hard-pressed Native Americans became more intense.

Pushing up from the south, meanwhile, Spain struggled to retain its foothold in Florida and New Mexico and to lay claim to parts of Arizona and Texas as well. New Spanish towns appeared at Albuquerque, El Paso, and Pensacola. Of the three competing powers, only France, pressing west and south from the St. Lawrence Valley, managed to penetrate the interior of the continent extensively. Its government created a string of forts from the Great Lakes to the Gulf of Mexico: Detroit, Peoria, and Mobile all came into being under the French flag.

One fundamental question recurred in numerous places during the decades after 1660: who has the right to govern? Often, boundaries were vague and structures of control were weak; religious dissenters and political rebels who felt excluded or exploited could openly question the legitimacy of those in charge. In congregations, towns, and whole colonies, challenges to authority arose repeatedly. Disruptions and violence became familiar experiences for thousands of people inhabiting North America.

France and the American Interior

■ *Why did France gain access to North America's interior before other European powers?*

The potential wealth of the North American interior had long intrigued government ministers in France. If Canadian fur traders could explore this vast domain and befriend its Indian inhabitants, France might control some of the continent's most fertile farmland and keep its extensive natural assets out of the hands of European rivals. If the French could recruit enough Native Americans as loyal allies, they might even threaten the rich mines of the Spanish empire in Mexico and challenge the growing English colonies lying to the east of the Appalachian mountains. But for France to realize such wide ambitions, the French king, Louis XIV, would need to make North American colonization a national priority, and the extent of his commitment remained uncertain.

THE RISE OF THE SUN KING

King Louis XIV stood at the center of France's expanding imperial sphere. Indeed, so much seemed to revolve around him that he became known as the "Sun King." He had inherited the French throne in 1643, as a child of five, and in 1661, at age twenty-two, he assumed personal control of a realm of 20 million people. During most of his long rule—from 1661 to his death in 1715 at age seventy-seven—Louis dominated European affairs. Always a builder of monuments, he expanded the Louvre in Paris and then dazzled the French nobility and clergy with his opulent new palace at Versailles.

In religion, the Sun King challenged the authority of the Catholic pope on one hand and suppressed the dissent of French Protestants (known as Huguenots) on the other. In politics, he centralized the monarchy's power as never before. His administration consolidated the laws of France, strengthened the armed forces, and expanded commerce. His government ministries foreshadowed the power of modern nation-states by regulating industry, promoting road building, and imposing tariffs and taxes.

Throughout Louis XIV's reign, his officials followed a set of policies known as **mercantilism,** a system in which a government stressed economic self-sufficiency and a favorable balance of trade. By avoiding foreign debts and drawing in valuable resources from its competitors and its own colonies, a state could pay for wars abroad and costly projects at home. The French mercantilist strategy was to exploit labor efficiently and import raw materials cheaply, while exporting expensive manufactured products, such as glassware, wine, silk, and tapestries, in exchange for foreign gold and silver. France's colonists, like those of Spain and England, were expected to generate much-needed natural resources and to serve as eager consumers for the mother country's manufactured goods.

■ Louis XIV, the Sun King.

In Paris, finance minister Jean-Baptiste Colbert emerged as the chief architect of this strategy of aggressive mercantilism. At home he taxed foreign imports, removed domestic trade barriers, and improved internal transportation. Moreover, he reduced worker holidays and outlawed strikes. With an eye toward colonial expansion, Colbert improved France's ports and created a code to regulate maritime shipping. He expanded the naval fleet and pressed French sailors into its service. Pushing still harder, he organized overseas trading companies and provided insurance for their expensive ventures. In addition, he sanctioned France's involvement in the African slave trade. Colbert yearned to acquire new territory to increase the empire's self-sufficiency and keep overseas resources out of enemy hands. To that end, he and his successors encouraged French exploration of North America on an unprecedented scale.

Map labels (as they appear on the map):

Lake Superior · Sault-Ste-Marie · Ft. Michilimackinac · Montréal Lachine · Ft. Frontenac · L. Ontario · Ft. Conti · Lake Huron · Lake Michigan · Detroit · Lake Erie · Minnesota R. · Mississippi R. · Wisconsin R. · Fox R. · Ft. St. Joseph · Peoria (Ft. St. Louis) · Illinois R. · Ft. Crèvecoeur · Wabash R. · Ohio R. · Missouri R. · Kansas R. · Cahokia · Ft. de Chartres · Kaskaskia · Arkansas R. · Arkansas Post · Brazos R. · Colorado R. · Neches R. · Trinity R. · Red R. · Natchez (Ft. Rosalie) · Natchitoches · Ft. Toulouse · Mobile (Ft. St. Louis) · Biloxi (Ft. Maurepas) · Pensacola (1698) · San Antonio (1718) · San Juan Bautista (1700) · La Salle killed · New Orleans (1718) · English Turn · Ft. St.Louis · Gulf of Mexico · Matagorda Bay · Rio Grande · Mississippi R.

Routes of important French explorations

La Salle, 1670
Jolliet and Marquette, 1673
La Salle, 1679–1682
La Salle and colonists from France, 1685
La Salle's party, 1687
Iberville, 1699
St. Denis, 1714
La Harpe, 1719
French Fort
✝ Spanish Missions 1716–1717
▪ Spanish settlements

Present state boundaries provided for orientation

■ **M A P   3 . 1   France in the American Interior, 1670–1720**

The government of Louis XIV assumed direct control over New France (Canada and neighboring Acadia on the Atlantic coast) from a private company in 1663. Colbert hoped to diversify production away from the fur trade, so he shipped artisans to the colony, plus livestock and tools. To promote domestic life and population growth, the government also transported young single women and announced cash incentives for early marriages and large families. Many of the soldiers sent to protect New France from Iroquois and English threats stayed on to establish farms.

On balance, however, Colbert's plans for a prosperous, well-populated colony failed. The small population of New France—10,000 by 1680—never grew as rapidly as French imperial strategists desired. The harsh winters and short growing seasons hindered the expansion of agriculture. Also, Louis XIV imposed restrictions to make sure that any colonist

Avantures mal-heureuses du Sieur de la Salle.

■ When La Salle's expedition landed on the Texas coast in 1685, one ship ran aground and broke up (background); another departed quickly from Matagorda Bay. La Salle's colonists had only the *Belle* (foreground), and it sank in a storm the following year. In 1995, archaeologists found the vessel in shallow water and salvaged the remains.

sent overseas was a pious and loyal Catholic. "In the establishment of a country," Colbert declared, it was important "to plant good seed."

In 1685, Louis XIV revoked the Edict of Nantes, which for nearly a century had guaranteed French Protestants their legal rights. Faced with persecution, thousands of frightened Huguenots prepared to leave the country. But the king forbade the dissenters from traveling to France's colonies. In contrast to the English, the French did not use their overseas colonies as havens for outcasts, troublemakers, and religious dissidents.

EXPLORING THE MISSISSIPPI VALLEY

In New France, intrepid explorers had probed steadily across the Great Lakes, reaching the western shores of Lake Michigan in 1634. There, Winnebego Indians (today's Ho-Chunk Nation) told of a river called the "Messisipi," and rumors of this river circulated among French Canadians for a generation. Finally, in 1673, trader Louis Jolliet, joined by a Jesuit priest named Jacques Marquette, entered the upper Mississippi and descended to the mouth of the Arkansas River. If the Mississippi waterway flowed south into the Gulf of Mexico, instead of west to the Pacific as some explorers hoped, perhaps the river could give France a path to the wealth of New Spain and provide French settlers with access to a warm-water port. "The worst thing about Canada," Colbert observed, is that the St. Lawrence, "being so far to the north, allows ships to enter only during four, five or six months of the year."

Officials in Quebec moved to exploit these western prospects, making effective use of an experienced young adventurer: René-Robert Cavelier, Sieur de La Salle. In 1679, inspired by Jolliet's exploits, La Salle and his men pushed west through the Great Lakes to erect forts on the Illinois River, a tributary of the Mississippi. These outposts strengthened French trading ties with local Indians and provided a launching point for more exploration. In 1682, La Salle led a contingent of French and Indians south from the Illinois to explore the lower Mississippi. He returned to confirm that the great river indeed emptied into the Gulf of Mexico. He claimed the vast land drained by the river and its tributaries for Louis XIV, naming the entire river basin "Louisiana" after his king.

But La Salle, hindered by poor maps and crude navigational instruments, had mislocated the mouth of the Mississippi. Therefore, when he tried to return by sea, sailing from France with several hundred colonists, he mistakenly disembarked on the Texas coast early in 1685. At Matagorda Bay (southwest of modern Galveston), his large supply ship broke apart on a shoal before all the cargo had been removed, and a second vessel departed quickly, taking along 100 discouraged settlers. Those who remained had only a small worm-eaten frigate, the *Belle*, to provide any hope of gaining supplies or relocating. After a winter storm sank that ship near shore the following year, the colonization plan unraveled completely. Jealous lieutenants eventually killed the French commander before he could find the Mississippi River. Most of the people La Salle had brought perished in the Texas wilderness, lost like the English settlers at Roanoke a century before.

La Salle's Ship, the *Belle*, Is Raised from a Watery Grave

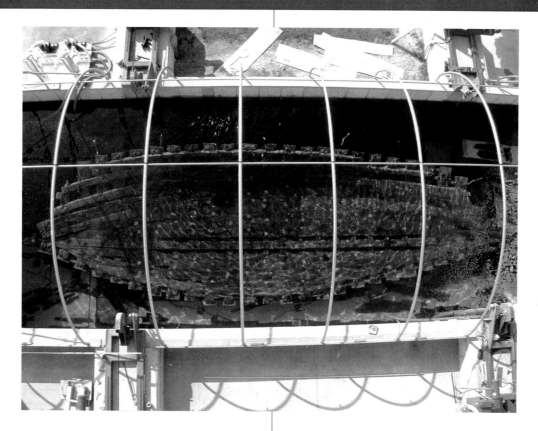

La Salle's ill-fated French colonists reached the Texas coast early in 1685. They struggled to gain a foothold and determine their whereabouts. The biggest setback came the following year when their remaining ship, the *Belle*, ran aground in shallow water during a February storm. "They went on board almost every day," recalled survivor Henri Joutel, "bringing what they could each time until a wind blew in from the sea that stirred up the waves and made the hull of the ship settle deep into the sand."

The small vessel—only fifty-one feet long, with a fourteen-foot beam—remained covered for more than 300 years. Then in 1995, marine archaeologists from the Texas Historical Commission located the mud-covered hull below shallow water in Matagorda Bay. They drove pilings to create a wall around the wreck and then pumped the water out of this cofferdam so they could excavate their prize discovery piece by piece. Amazingly, the mud had preserved most of the ship's contents, including dishes, cannons, muskets, and trade goods such as beads, axes, and knives—everything needed to begin a European colony in the New World.

The next step involved preserving the ship and its fragile artifacts at a research laboratory at Texas A&M University. At a remote site on a deserted airfield, workers built a huge vat (shown here) where the immersed hull could be reassembled and stabilized. Gradually, the remains of the *Belle* and its contents are being made ready for viewing at the new Texas State History Museum in Austin.

QUESTIONS

1. Why do most Americans know more about the English lost colony in North Carolina than the French lost colony in East Texas?

2. In what ways might a sunken vessel, such as the *Belle*, be a more valuable "time capsule" than an abandoned village site?

KING WILLIAM'S WAR IN THE NORTHEAST

The French colonizers had overreached themselves. They had failed to find a route to the Pacific, to challenge Spanish power in the Gulf of Mexico, or to establish a southern port. Spread thin by the widening fur trade, French Canadians were in a weak position to repel renewed Iroquois attacks along the St. Lawrence River in the 1680s. Moreover, a strengthened Protestant regime

"Marry or do not marry"

Interpreting History

F ather Jacques Gravier (1651–1708) visited French posts from Mackinac to Mobile. The Jesuit spent most of his time at Fort St. Louis (modern Peoria) among several thousand Illinois Indians, compiling a dictionary of their language and seeking to win converts. In 1691, he built a chapel outside the fort and erected a thirty-five-foot cross. He concentrated on teaching young people, offering prizes—colored beads, needles, rosaries, small knives—to those who learned the catechism. The daughter of powerful Chief Rouensa (Aramepinchone, whom Gravier called Marie) proved especially interested. But French traders and Indian leaders remained wary of his message.

I was surprised by the indifference to instruction, . . . notwithstanding the politeness with which the old men received me. One of them told me in confidence that his tribesmen had

An Illinois chief, holding a calumet (c. 1700). "They are tattooed behind from the shoulders to the heels, and as soon as they have reached the age of twenty-five, on the front of the stomach, the sides, and the upper arms."

Thaw Collection, Fenimore Art Museum, Cooperstown, NY

resolved to prevent the people from coming to the chapel to listen to me, because I spoke against their customs. Many children and young people were sick, and I had not as free access to all of them as I would have wished. . . . They cry out against me as if I were the cause of the disease. . . . I was looked upon in most of the cabins as the bird of death; and people sought to hold me responsible for the disease and the mortality.

[In 1694 Marie's] father and mother.. brought her to me in company with the Frenchman whom they wished to have for a son-in-law. [Michel Accault was a wealthy and experienced trader whom La Salle had sent to explore the Upper Mississippi in 1680. But Marie indicated] that she did not wish to marry; that she had already given her heart to God, and did not wish to share it. . . . I told [Accault and the parents] that God did not command her not to marry, but also that she could not be forced to do so. . . . The father . . . told me that

emerged in London with the ascent of William III to the English throne in 1689. This transition set in motion more than 100 years of bitter struggle between Protestant England and Catholic France. Their ideological and military struggle often included North America.

The American conflict began in the Northeast with the outbreak of King William's War in 1689. In that year the Iroquois, well supplied with English arms, launched raids on the French near Montreal. The French struck back, terrorizing the English frontier and setting fire to outposts in New York and New England. At Fort Loyal (modern Portland, Maine) raiders butchered 100 English men, women, and children who had surrendered, and they took others captive.

Leaving their dead unburied, survivors fled south toward Salem and Boston in Massachusetts. Many who experienced the attack viewed it as part of a wider design to undo the Reformation and expand the authority of the Catholic Church.

After eight years of bloodshed, King William's War ended in a stalemate in 1697. Hurt by the hostilities in their region, the Iroquois soon promised to remain neutral during any future colonial wars between France and England, a pledge they generally honored for more than half a century. The French, having strengthened their position in Canada, revived the "southern strategy" for a Gulf Coast colony that had so obsessed Colbert and La Salle.

A turn in European events opened the door for renewed French efforts in the American heartland. King Carlos II of Spain fell ill without an immediate heir, and the royal courts of Europe competed to determine his successor. Louis XIV, eager to acquire Spain's European realm and American dominions for France, proposed that his grandson, Philip of Anjou, receive the Spanish crown. But England supported an opposing candidate, so the War of Spanish Succession (1701–1714) broke out soon after Carlos died.

inasmuch as I was preventing his daughter from obeying him, he would also prevent her from going to the chapel. That very night her father gathered the chiefs of the four villages, and told them that, since I prevented the French from forming alliances with them...he earnestly begged them to stop the women and children from coming to the chapel.

I thought I should not remain silent after so great an insult had been offered to God. I went to the commandant of the fort, . . . who answered in an insulting manner that I had drawn all this upon myself, through my stubbornness in not allowing the girl to marry the Frenchman, who was then with him. [The Jesuit demanded that the commandant support him against the chiefs. The French leader] replied coldly that he would speak to the chiefs; but, instead of assembling them at once, he waited until the afternoon of the following day, and even then I had to return to him from the purpose. [Then Gravier advised Marie:] My daughter, God does not forbid you to marry; neither do I say to you: 'Marry or do not marry.' If you consent solely through love for God, and if you believe that by marrying you will win your family to God, the thought is a good one.

Marie, age sixteen, married Accault and bore two sons before he died. By 1704, she had married another French trader, Michel Philippe, and moved to the new town of Kaskaskia. There Philippe turned to farming and amassed a sizable estate, including an Indian servant and five black slaves. Marie raised six

more children before her death in 1725. Her will, dictated in French and then translated into the Illinois language, withheld property from one son who continued to live as an Indian. Her priest, Father Gravier, had been shot in the arm by an Indian in 1705. The arrowhead could not be removed, and he died three years later.

QUESTIONS

1. *Regarding the Rouensa-Accault marriage, can you explore the differing motives of Marie, her parents, Michel Accault, and Father Gravier?*

2. *Can you recreate an argument in 1720 at Kaskaskia between Catholic Marie and the son remaining loyal to the ways of Chief Rouensa?*

FOUNDING THE LOUISIANA COLONY

Even before new hostilities erupted in Europe in 1701, Louis XIV and his ministers took steps to secure French claims in the Gulf of Mexico, despite Spain's naval dominance in the area. By renewing La Salle's plan for a Louisiana colony, France could strengthen its hand in the impending war over succession to the Spanish throne. A colony on the Gulf of Mexico would provide a southern outlet for the French fur trade and a strategic outpost to counter Spain's new fort at Pensacola in western Florida.

England also saw advantages to establishing a base on the lower Mississippi. Such a post could challenge Spanish and French claims to the Gulf region and increase English trade with the Chickasaw and other southern Indians. In 1698, a London promoter quietly made plans to transport a group of Huguenot refugees to the mouth of the Mississippi. Catching wind of this scheme, the French naval minister, Comte de Pontchartrain, organized his own secret expedition to the Gulf of Mexico under an aspiring Canadian officer, Pierre Le Moyne d'Iberville.

Coming from a large and well-connected Montreal family, the Le Moynes, Iberville quickly drew several siblings into the gulf colonization plan, including his teenage brother, Bienville. Iberville and his party sailed for the Gulf of Mexico from the French port of Brest in 1699. Their ship entered the mouth of the Mississippi in time to repel the English expedition at a site on the river still known as English Turn. They also managed to build a fort at nearby Biloxi Bay before returning to France.

The two brothers were now well on their way to creating the Gulf Coast colony that La Salle and his followers had failed to establish. A second voyage let Iberville conduct further reconnaissance of the lower Mississippi. On a third trip, in 1702, he established Fort Louis, near Mobile Bay, giving French traders access to the Choctaw Indians. Young Bienville, placed in charge of Fort Louis, labored to sustain the tiny outpost at Mobile. Iberville himself left to pursue other schemes and died an early death in 1706.

Enmeshed in the War of Spanish Succession, France ignored its new Gulf colony. Epidemics reduced Louisiana's newcomers and took a far heavier toll on Indian neighbors. Settlers drawn from Canada, with prior wilderness experience, maintained close ties with local Native Americans and resented the incompetence and haughtiness of colonists sent from France. The latter complained about the poor living conditions and looked down on the uneducated Canadians. However, despite social friction and a chronic lack of supplies from France, the small community at Mobile survived, including the widow Marguerite Messier and her children.

Far to the north, additional posts reinforced French territorial claims, fostered the fur trade, and protected neighboring Indians against Iroquois raids. The village of Peoria sprang up on the Illinois River in 1691. Not far away, Catholic missions appeared nearby at Cahokia (1697) and Kaskaskia (1703). Fort de Chartres took shape in southern Illinois in 1719. Farther north, the French established two other strategic posts. In 1689, they laid out a garrison where Lake Huron joins Lake Michigan. In 1701, they created a lasting town, Detroit, on the strait (*le détroit* in French) connecting Lake Erie to Lake Huron. The founder of this village, Monsieur Cadillac, foresaw a prosperous future for the new trading post, since Detroit would be accessible "to the most distant tribes which surround these vast sweet water seas."

> Over two generations, the French had established a solid claim on the American interior.

In 1712 the French crown, its resources depleted by a decade of warfare in Europe, granted control over Louisiana to a powerful Paris merchant, Antoine Crozat. Drawing Cadillac from Detroit to serve as Louisiana's governor general, Crozat hoped to develop connections to mineral-rich Mexico and to discover precious metals in the Mississippi watershed. But probes on the upper Mississippi, the Missouri, and the Red rivers yielded no easy bonanza. Instead, explorers established three new trading posts among the Indians: Natchitoches on the Red River, Fort Rosalie on the Mississippi (at Natchez), and Fort Toulouse (near modern Montgomery, Alabama).

When Louis XIV died in 1715, the colonial population of Canada's St. Lawrence Valley had crept up to nearly 25,000, but fewer than 1,000 colonists lived in Lower Louisiana and the Illinois Country combined. Nevertheless, over two generations, the French had established a solid claim on the American interior. Their position was an ongoing challenge to English and Spanish competitors. The crescent of wilderness outposts arcing north and then east from the Gulf Coast offered a useful network for additional exploration, Indian trade, and military conquest. French control of the Mississippi Valley remained a real possibility until the era of Thomas Jefferson and Napoleon Bonaparte nearly a century later.

The Spanish Empire on the Defensive

■ *How did Indian experiences with the Spanish vary in Arizona, New Mexico, and Florida?*

Whereas France's power expanded during Louis XIV's reign, Spain's overextended empire continued to weaken. This decline opened the door for Louis to maneuver his own grandson onto the Spanish throne in 1700 as Philip V. Meanwhile, Spanish colonizers struggled to defend vast territorial claims in North America that spread—on paper—from the Gulf of California to the Florida peninsula.

In Spain's remote colonies of New Mexico and Florida, local administration often proved corrupt, and links to imperial officials at home remained weak and cumbersome.

For several generations, the Indian majority had resented the harsh treatment and strange diseases that came with colonial contact. Now, cultural disruptions and pressures from hostile Indian neighbors fanned the flames of discontent. In the late seventeenth century, a wave of Native American rebellions swept the northern frontier of New Spain.

THE PUEBLO REVOLT IN NEW MEXICO

The largest and most successful revolt took place in New Mexico, where soldiers, settlers, and priests, sent north by Spanish authorities at the beginning of the century, had staked out a remote colony along the upper Rio Grande. There, Pueblo Indians from dozens of separate communities (or pueblos) united in a major upheaval in August 1680. They murdered twenty-one of the forty friars serving in New Mexico, ransacked their churches, and killed more than 350 settlers. After laying siege to Santa Fe, the rebels drove the remaining Spanish colonists and their Christian Indian allies south out of the province and kept them away for more than a decade. Several thousand stunned survivors took refuge in what is now El Paso and soon began questioning Indian informants to find an explanation for the fearsome uprising.

DOCUMENT

Pedro Hidalgo, Legal Statement (1680)

Diverse factors, stretching back over decades, had combined to ignite the Pueblo Revolt of 1680. First, a five-year drought beginning in 1666 inflicted a famine with long-lasting effects on the peoples of New Mexico. Second, around the same time, neighboring Apache and Navajo stepped up their hostilities against the small colonial population and the numerous Pueblo Indians who had been linked with the Spanish for several generations. The attackers were embittered by colonial slave raids that took Indian captives to work in Mexican silver mines. In retaliation, these raiding parties, riding stolen Spanish horses, killed livestock and seized scarce food. When colonial soldiers proved unable to fend off the hit-and-run attacks, their credibility among the Pueblo Indians living alongside the colonists weakened.

Third, a smoldering controversy over religion flared during the 1670s. When an epidemic struck in 1671, Spanish missionaries could not stem the sickness through prayers. In response, traditionalist Indian priests revived age-old Pueblo religious customs. Horrified, the Spanish friars and government officials united to punish what they saw as backsliding within a Pueblo population that seemed to have accepted key elements of the Catholic faith. At Santa Fe in 1675, they hanged three Indian leaders for idolatry and whipped and imprisoned forty-three others—including a militant leader from San Juan pueblo named Popé. Before the captives could be sold into slavery, armed Indians successfully demanded the release of Popé and the other prisoners.

Popé withdrew to Taos, the northernmost pueblo in New Mexico. From there, he negotiated secretly with like-minded factions in other pueblos, unifying resistance to Spanish domination and forging an underground movement. In part, he built support around widespread resentment of the Spanish **encomienda** system (requiring Indian communities to supply labor or pay tribute) and toward the Catholic Church (which forbade traditional Indian religious ceremonies). Indian women whom Spanish priests or soldiers had abused took Popé's side in this cultural clash. The movement also received secret support from numerous **mestizos** and **mulattos,** mixed-race people whose dark skin and lack of "pure" Spanish blood cost them any chance for advancement. Popé sent runners to each conspiring pueblo to fix the date for the rebellion. When the time came, his Pueblo warriors swiftly overcame their adversaries. Unified in triumph, the zealous victors smeared excrement on Christian altars and bathed themselves to remove the stigma of baptism.

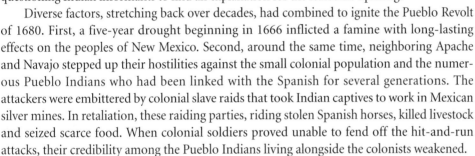

Pueblo Indians from dozens of separate communities (or pueblos) united in a major upheaval in August 1680.

But initial cohesion gave way to friction. The successful rebels soon quarreled over who should hold power and how best to return to ancient ways. Kivas would replace churches, and the cross would give way to the **kachina.** But what other parts of the imported culture should the Indians abandon? Various Pueblo groups could not agree on which Spanish words, tools, and customs to discard or which foreign crops and animals to retain.

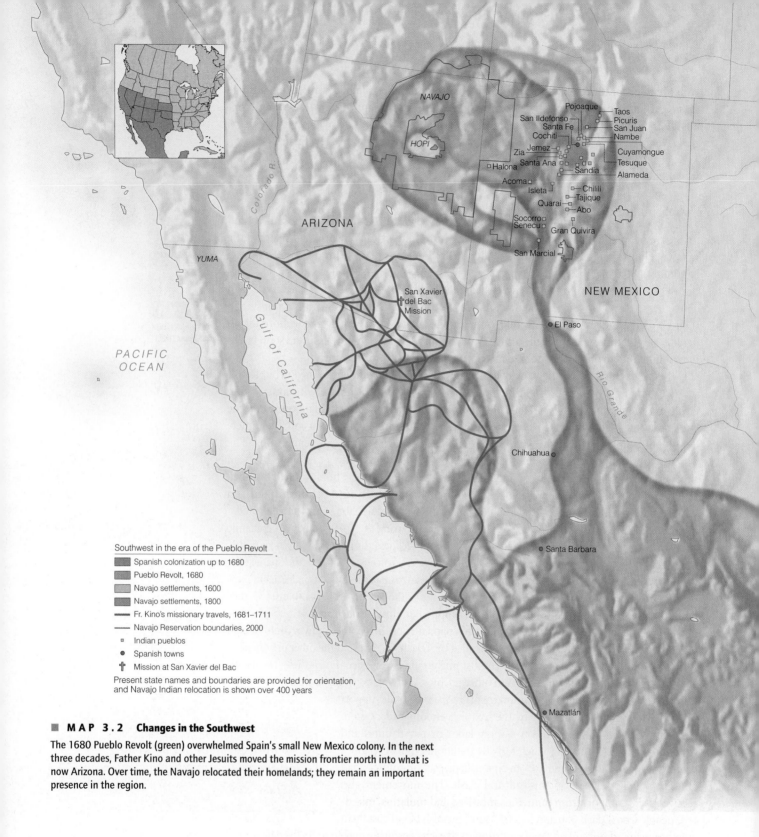

Southwest in the era of the Pueblo Revolt

- Spanish colonization up to 1680
- Pueblo Revolt, 1680
- Navajo settlements, 1600
- Navajo settlements, 1800
- —— Fr. Kino's missionary travels, 1681–1711
- —— Navajo Reservation boundaries, 2000
- ▫ Indian pueblos
- ● Spanish towns
- ✝ Mission at San Xavier del Bac

Present state names and boundaries are provided for orientation, and Navajo Indian relocation is shown over 400 years

■ **MAP 3.2   Changes in the Southwest**

The 1680 Pueblo Revolt (green) overwhelmed Spain's small New Mexico colony. In the next three decades, Father Kino and other Jesuits moved the mission frontier north into what is now Arizona. Over time, the Navajo relocated their homelands; they remain an important presence in the region.

In 1681, the Pueblo fended off a Spanish attempt at reconquest. But they remained divided among themselves and more vulnerable than ever to Apache raids. Within a decade, rival factions had deposed Popé, and another Spanish colonial army, under Governor Diego de Vargas, had entered New Mexico. It took the new governor several years to subdue the province, and the Pueblo managed another full-scale rebellion in 1696. But Vargas anticipated the revolt and crushed the opposition, just as Oñate had done a century earlier. In 1706, several soldiers and their families established the town of Albuquerque on its present site. Learning from prior mistakes, Spanish officials did not reimpose the hated *encomienda* system. A new generation of Franciscan missionaries tolerated indigenous Pueblo traditions as long as the Indians also attended Catholic mass.

NAVAJO AND SPANISH ON THE SOUTHWESTERN FRONTIER

The repercussions of rebellion and reconquest along the upper Rio Grande echoed throughout the Southwest. To the north, Pueblo refugees joined the Navajo and brought valuable experience as corn farmers. Corn, already known to the Navajo, now became an increasingly important food and sacred symbol for them. Moreover, the new arrivals had learned from the Spanish how to plant peach orchards and raise sheep. Navajo women—the weavers in their society—soon owned large flocks and wove wool blankets on their traditional portable looms. The Pueblo also brought more Spanish horses, a key asset that let the Navajo spread their domain west into fine grazing country in what is now northeast Arizona. Farther north, the Ute and Comanche also acquired horses after the Pueblo Revolt. Eventually, the Comanche pressed southeast onto the Texas plains.

After the Pueblo Revolt, officials in Mexico City worried about further upheavals along New Spain's wide northern frontier. Despite limited resources, authorities sent a few missionary-explorers north near the Gulf of California to spread Christianity and pacify hostile Indians. Year by year, these friar-explorers edged toward what is now southern Arizona, reaching the cactus-studded Sonoran Desert by the 1690s.

Eusebio Kino, a tireless Jesuit missionary born in Italy and educated in Germany, spearheaded the early exploration of the Arizona region. In 1701, he visited the large Indian village of Bak, located near the Santa Cruz River. There, among more than 800 inhabitants, he established the mission of San Xavier del Bac, near modern Tucson, Arizona. Kino's endless travels on horseback prompted additional missions farther south and west, but these outposts languished after his death in 1711. Warfare and sickness eroded the local population of Pima Indians, and attacks by Apache raiders destabilized the entire frontier region. Spain finally reinstalled priests at San Xavier del Bac and other missions along the Santa Cruz River in 1732. Four years later, a

Harald Sund/Getty Images

■ Horses and sheep arrived in the Southwest with the Spanish, and both became central to the Navajo (or Diné) culture in northern Arizona and New Mexico. Navajo women continue to herd sheep and weave their wool into rugs and blankets, as they have done for more than three centuries.

silver strike at "Arizonac," near present-day Nogales on the U.S.-Mexican border, provided a new name for the region, which would eventually become the state of Arizona.

BORDERLAND CONFLICT IN TEXAS AND FLORIDA

The encounters on Spain's other North American borderland frontiers took different forms, in part because European rivals appeared on the scene. Conflict with the French led the Spanish to found missions in Texas, a land they named after the local Tejas Indians. At first, responding to news about La Salle's ill-fated French colony, the Spanish made a brief attempt to establish a Texas mission in 1690, departing again in 1693. They renewed their effort two decades later, after Louisiana's Governor Cadillac (the founder of Detroit) sent explorers from Louisiana across eastern Texas to forge ties with Spanish communities south of the Rio Grande. Eager to open trade with the Spanish, the French visitors reached San Juan Bautista, below the modern U.S.-Mexican border, in 1714.

> The Indians of Florida, like the Pueblo in New Mexico, debated whether to reject generations of Spanish rule.

Spanish authorities, taken by surprise, dusted off plans for colonizing Texas. By 1717, they had established half a dozen small missions near the Sabine River, the boundary between modern Texas and Louisiana. The next year, to expand their missionary activities and secure the supply route from San Juan Bautista to these distant outposts in east Texas, the Spanish built a cluster of settlements beside the San Antonio River, at a midpoint on the trail from Mexico. Within two decades a string of missions stretched along the river. Indian converts tended herds of cattle and sheep and constructed aqueducts to irrigate new fields of wheat and corn. The earliest mission, San Antonio de Valero (1718), provided a nucleus for the town of San Antonio. Later known as the Alamo, the mission also strengthened Spanish claims to Texas against threats of French intrusion.

During the second half of the seventeenth century, the Indians of Florida, like the Pueblo in New Mexico, debated whether to reject generations of Spanish rule. The Columbian Exchange had altered their lives in dramatic ways. They ate new foods such as figs, oranges, peas, cabbages, and cucumbers. They used Spanish words—*azúcar* (sugar), *botija* (jar), *caballo* (horse)—and metal hoes from Europe allowed them to produce more corn. But expanded contact with colonizers created major problems as well. By 1660 devastating epidemics had whittled away at Florida's Native American towns. The Indians still outnumbered the newcomers more than ten to one, but they had to expend enormous energy raising, processing, and hauling food for the Spanish. When colonists grew fearful of French and English attacks after 1670, they forced hundreds of Indians to perform even more grueling labor: constructing the stone fortress of San Marcos at St. Augustine.

Nothing proved more troubling to Florida's Indians than the spread of livestock farming. St. Augustine's elite had established profitable cattle ranches on the depopulated savannas of Timucua, near present-day Gainesville in north-central Florida. These entrepreneurs ignored requirements to keep cows away from unfenced Indian gardens, and they enforced harsh laws to protect their stock. Any Florida Indian who killed cattle faced four months of servitude; people caught raiding Spanish herds had their ears cut off.

Resentment grew in Florida's scattered mission villages. Restless Indian converts wondered whether the English, who had founded their Carolina colony in 1670, might make viable allies. The English seemed eager to trade for deerskins, and they offered the Native Americans a steadier supply of desirable goods than the Spanish could provide. Several Indian communities moved closer to Carolina to test this new alternative for trade. But when France and Spain joined forces against the English after 1700, Florida's Indians suddenly found themselves caught up in a struggle far larger than they had bargained for.

Ever since the days of Francis Drake, the English had schemed to oust the Spanish from St. Augustine. In 1702, led by South Carolina governor James Moore, English raiders and their Indian allies rampaged through the Florida town. Yet the new stone fortress of

San Marcos held firm, protecting the inhabitants. Two years later, Moore invaded Apalachee (near modern Tallahassee), accompanied by 50 Englishmen and 1,000 Creek Indians. His troops crushed the mission towns, killing hundreds and carrying away more than 4,000 Indian captives. Most of them were women and children, whom the English sold as slaves in Carolina and the Caribbean. By 1706 the mission villages in Apalachee and Timucua lay in ruins. "In all these extensive dominions," lamented a Spanish official from St. Augustine, "the law of God and the preaching of the Holy Gospel have now ceased."

England's American Empire Takes Shape

■ *What are the varied origins of England's Restoration-Era American colonies?*

In 1660, as Louis XIV began his long reign in France and Spanish missionaries labored in New Mexico and Florida, England experienced a counterrevolutionary upheaval that dramatically influenced American colonial affairs. In the 1640s, amid violent civil war, rebels supporting Puritans and the Parliament had overthrown the ruling Stuart family, beheaded King Charles I, and abolished hereditary monarchy altogether.

For a brief period, England became a republican commonwealth without a king. But Oliver Cromwell, the movement's dictatorial leader and self-styled Lord Protector, died in 1658. Pressures quickly mounted to undo the radical Puritan Revolution and *restore* monarchical government. In May 1660, a strong coalition of conservative interests welcomed the late king's son back from exile and placed him on the throne as King Charles II. With monarchy restored in England, the renewed Stuart dynasty ruled from 1660 until 1688. The period is remembered in English politics and culture as the **Restoration Era.**

> *Many who had fought to end monarchy and strengthen Parliament sought refuge in the American colonies.*

The shift in London's political winds could hardly have been more sudden. Charles II moved quickly in 1660 to underscore the end of England's Puritan experiment. He ordered the execution of those who had beheaded his father in 1649. Many who had fought to end monarchy and strengthen Parliament sought refuge in the American colonies when their religious and political beliefs abruptly fell out of favor at home. Other elements of colonial demographics—early marriage, high birthrates, and a low level of mortality in most places— did even more to prompt expansion up and down the Atlantic coast.

MONARCHY RESTORED AND NAVIGATION CONTROLLED

Because most English colonists still lived within fifty miles of the Atlantic, an increase in people steadily broadened the opportunities for seaborne trade. Growing ship traffic, in turn, sparked government desires to regulate colonial navigation to bring mercantilist advantages to the restored monarchy. In 1660, Parliament passed a major new law designed to promote British shipping and trade.

The Navigation Act of 1660 laid out important conditions that shaped England's colonial commerce for generations. First, merchants could not conduct trade to or from the English colonies in foreign-owned ships. Second, key non-English products imported from foreign lands—salt, wine, oil, and naval stores (the tar, pitch, masts, and other materials used to build boats)—had to be carried in English ships or in ships with mostly English crews. Third, the law contained a list of "enumerated articles" produced overseas. The items listed—tobacco, cotton, sugar, ginger, indigo, and dyewoods—could no longer be sent directly from a colony to a foreign European port. Instead, merchants had to ship them to England first and then reexport them, a step that directly boosted England's domestic economy. Another Navigation Act, in 1663, required that goods moving from the European continent to England's colonies

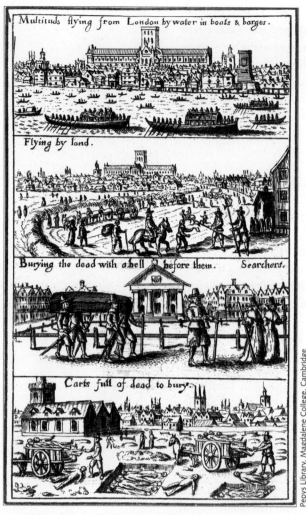

Multituds flying from London by water in boats & barges.

Flying by land.

Burying the dead with a bell before them.   Searchers.

Carts full of dead to bury.

■ **Images of the Great Plague in London, 1665.**

Pepys Library, Magdalene College, Cambridge

also needed to pass through the island. Moreover, they had to arrive and depart on English ships.

A later measure—the Plantation Duty Act of 1673—tried to close loopholes regarding enumerated articles. The new act required captains to pay a "plantation duty" before they sailed between colonial ports with enumerated goods. Otherwise, colonial vessels carrying such goods had to post bond before leaving harbor to ensure that they would sail directly to England. To enforce these rules, the government sent customs officers to the colonies for the first time. Backed by the Navigation Acts, England's fleets grew, and colonial trade became a major sector in England's economy.

Even the Great Plague, which swept England in 1665, could not blunt this mercantile growth. And when a catastrophic fire destroyed most of London the next year, the huge loss also provided an opportunity. Planners redesigned the city with the broad streets and impressive buildings that suited the prosperous hub of an expanding empire. The fashionable coffee shops that sprang up as a novelty in late-seventeenth-century London became common meeting places for exchanging news and views about England's increasingly profitable activities overseas. Much of what transpired in English North America was hashed out here, over pipes filled with Virginia tobacco.

DUTCH NEW NETHERLAND BECOMES NEW YORK

At the beginning of his reign, Charles II knew he had to build loyalty and strengthen an economy weakened by civil war. But the new monarch had expensive tastes and a depleted treasury. He soon found that he could reward loyal family members and supporters, at no cost to the crown, by granting them control over pieces of England's North American domain. With this prospect in hand, the king and his ministers sought to bolster foreign trade, expand the royal navy, and outstrip England's commercial rivals. They focused first on the Dutch.

As London stepped up its search for new profits, English officials moved to strengthen control over existing colonies and establish (or seize) new ones wherever possible. The Navigation Acts cut sharply into the Dutch carrying trade and spurred a decade of renewed warfare between England and Holland. For the most part, these intermittent Anglo-Dutch Wars ended in stalemate. But at the final Peace of Westminster in 1674, the English emerged with several gains in Africa and America that had lasting significance.

In West Africa, the English captured and held several key coastal outposts: an island at the mouth of the river Gambia (renamed James Fort for the Duke of York) and Cape Coast Castle on the Gold Coast (near Elmina, the African headquarters of the Dutch West India Company). This encroachment challenged Dutch dominance in the commerce for African gold and ivory. It also gave England the footholds it needed to force its way into the Atlantic slave trade. Charles II had already moved to take advantage of the situation. He granted a monopoly to the Royal Adventurers into Africa (1663) and then the Royal African Company (1672) to exploit the grim but highly profitable slave traffic. Within several generations, this ruthless initiative reshaped England's American colonies at enormous human cost.

Across the Atlantic, the English had seized the Dutch colony of New Netherland and its poorly defended port of New Amsterdam. Charles II claimed that the land had belonged to England from the time his grandfather endorsed the Virginia Company in 1606. The English king, eyeing the lucrative trade in beaver pelts that made New Netherland prosperous, used his royal prerogative to regain control of that domain. In 1664, he issued a charter putting the entire region between the Delaware and Connecticut rivers under the personal control of his brother James, Duke of York. That same year, James sent a fleet to claim his prize. When Governor Peter Stuyvesant surrendered the Dutch colony without a fight, the province and its capital on Manhattan Island each received the name *New York*. Fort Orange on the Hudson became Albany because England's traditional name was *Albion*. A Dutch fleet recaptured Manhattan briefly in 1673, but a treaty returned the colony to the English the following year.

> *Married women living in New Netherland lost ground in the transition to English rule.*

The Duke of York controlled an enormous domain (including the Dutch and English settlements on Long Island), and he wielded nearly absolute powers over his new dukedom. James never visited New York, but as proprietor, he chose the colony's governor. That official ruled with an appointed council and enforced "the Duke's Laws" without constraint by any assembly. English newcomers to the colony resented the absence of an elected legislature, and the governor finally authorized an elected body in 1683. But when the new assemblymen approved a Charter of Liberties endorsing government by consent of the governed, the Duke of York disallowed the legislature.

Married women living in New Netherland lost ground in the transition to English rule. Dutch law codes had ensured their full legal status, allowing them to hold property, make contracts, and conduct business. In contrast, English common law assigned wives to an inferior status known as **coverture.** They could not own property or keep control over money they earned, and they lacked any independent standing before the law.

As the English asserted political control over New York, the Dutch presence remained evident everywhere. Many English married into Dutch families and worshiped in the Dutch Reformed Church. The village of Harlem built a proper road to lower Manhattan in 1669, but an effort to change the town's Dutch name to Lancaster failed. English-speaking New Yorkers borrowed such Dutch words as *waffle, cookie, coleslaw,* and *baas* (boss). Anyone who was bilingual, such as Albany merchant Robert Livingston, had a special advantage. Livingston, an immigrant from Scotland, had learned to speak Dutch in Holland in his youth. His marriage in Albany to a prosperous young widow, Alida Schuyler Van Rensselaer, linked him to powerful Dutch families in the Hudson Valley, and much of his early wealth came from his ability to translate commercial documents between English and Dutch.

DOCUMENT

Church Record of a Marriage Conflict, Broaoklyn (1663)

THE NEW RESTORATION COLONIES

Charles II had spurred England's seizure of New Netherland by issuing a charter for control of the contested region to his brother, the Duke of York. To reward supporters, the king continued issuing royal charters granting American land, hoping to expand trade and colonization at no cost to the crown. In 1670, for example, he granted a charter to the Hudson's Bay Company. The deal gave the company's proprietors a monopoly on trade, minerals, and land across northern Canada. Farther south, Charles used charters to redistribute control along major portions of the Atlantic coast. His actions prompted an unprecedented scramble for colonial property and profits. Within decades, the English launched important settlement clusters in two regions: the Delaware River valley and the Carolina coast. Each depended upon lucrative royal charters offered to a small network of friends.

Most of these well-placed people belonged to the Councils for Trade and Plantations in London. Created in 1660, these advisory groups linked England's powerful merchants with crown officials. When Charles II issued a charter for Carolina in 1663, five of its eight initial proprietors served on those councils. In 1665, two of these same eight men became the proprietors of New Jersey. In addition, three of the eight played an active role in the Royal African Company, four became founders of the Hudson's Bay Company, and five became initial proprietors of the Bahamas. But Charles reached beyond this small group as well. In 1679, he made New Hampshire a proprietorship (an ill-fated experiment that lasted to 1708). In 1681, he paid off a debt to Quaker aristocrat William Penn by granting him a charter for Pennsylvania. (The generous arrangement included the "Lower Counties" that became Delaware in 1704.)

Penn's "holy experiment" to create a Quaker refuge benefited from earlier colonization south of New York. Dutch and Swedish settlers had inhabited the lower Delaware Valley for more than a generation. In 1665, the Duke of York carved off a portion of his vast proprietorship, granting the area between the Delaware and the Hudson to two friends: Lord John Berkeley and Sir George Carteret. They named the area New Jersey because Carteret had been born on the Isle of Jersey in the English Channel. Berkeley and Carteret promptly announced liberal "Concessions"—a representative assembly and freedom of worship—to attract rent-paying newcomers from England and the existing colonies. But their plans for profit made little headway.

In 1674, the proprietors divided these fertile lands into two separate provinces. East Jersey—where Newark was established in 1666—attracted Puritan families from New England, Dutch farmers from New York, and failed planters from Barbados. West Jersey was sold to members of the Society of Friends (including William Penn) who inaugurated a Quaker experiment along the Delaware River. Filled with egalitarian beliefs, the Quakers created a one-house **unicameral legislature,** used secret ballots, and gave more power to juries than to judges. West Jersey's "Concessions and Agreements" of 1677 barred taxation without the consent of the governed. This forward-looking document introduced a sunshine law, opening the doors of governmental meetings to all citizens. It also assured that no one could settle Native American land without consulting Indian leaders and obtaining their approval. The Quakers' idealistic effort foundered within decades, and by 1702 all New Jersey came under crown control as a royal colony. But by then, the Quakers had established a foothold in the neighboring colony of Pennsylvania.

> *West Jersey's "Concessions and Agreements" of 1677 barred taxation without the consent of the governed.*

THE CONTRASTING WORLDS OF PENNSYLVANIA AND CAROLINA

William Penn, Description of Pennsylvania (1681)

Proprietor William Penn laid out his capital for the Pennsylvania colony in 1682, naming it Philadelphia. Within two decades, this market center and "greene countrie towne" already had more than 2,000 inhabitants. An earnest Quaker, Penn professed pacifism and implemented many of the same policies tried in West Jersey. He emphasized religious toleration, and a growing stream of German Protestants and others facing persecution in Europe began to flow into Pennsylvania after 1700. Penn also made it a point to deal fairly with the Lenni-Lenape (Delaware) Indians. After purchasing their land, he resold it on generous terms to English, Dutch, and Welsh Quakers who agreed to pay him an annual premium, called a **quitrent.**

Penn drew inspiration from James Harrington, the English political philosopher. Harrington's book *Oceana* (1656) argued that the best way to create an enduring republic was for one person to draft and implement its constitution. After endless tinkering, Penn devised a progressive "Frame of Government" that allowed for trial by jury, limited terms of office, and no use of capital punishment except in cases of treason and murder. But he remained ambivalent about legislative democracy. Settlers resented his scheme for a lower house that could approve acts drafted by the governor but could not initiate laws. In a new Charter of Privileges in 1701, Penn agreed to the creation of a unicameral legislature with full lawmaking powers. Disillusioned, Penn then departed for England, writing, "The Lord forgive them their great ingratitude." Penn's expansive proprietorship belonged to his descendants until colonial rule ended in 1776.

In contrast to Pennsylvania, different development plans shaped the new Carolina colony—which split into North and South Carolina a generation later. Anthony Ashley-Cooper, leader of the Carolina proprietors, also drew inspiration from Harrington, but for a very different undertaking. *Oceana* had stressed that distribution of land determined the nature of any commonwealth, and Ashley-Cooper (later the first earl of Shaftesbury) was eager to establish a stable aristocratic system. With his young secretary, John Locke (later an influential political philosopher), he drew up a set of "Fundamental Constitutions" in 1669. They proposed a stratified society in which hereditary nobles controlled much of the land and wealthy manor lords employed a lowly servant class of "leetmen." Their unrealistic document tried to revive the elaborate feudal hierarchy of medieval times.

The new government framework also endorsed racial slavery, declaring that "Every Freeman of Carolina shall have absolute Power and Authority over his Negro Slaves." This endorsement was not surprising, given the proprietors' involvement with England's new slave-trading monopoly in Africa and their initial recruitment of settlers in 1670 from the sugar island of Barbados. When Carolina colonists founded Charlestown (later Charleston) between the Ashley and Cooper rivers in 1680, the proprietors had already modified aspects of their complicated scheme, setting aside feudalism to encourage greater immigration. Nevertheless, their endorsement of slavery shaped the region's society for hundreds of years.

Bloodshed in the English Colonies: 1670–1690

■ *To what degree was colonial violence after 1670 sparked by internal tensions or affairs in England?*

The appearance of isolated English settlements along the Atlantic coast did little, in most places, to alter traditional rhythms. Year after year, the daily challenges of subsistence dominated American life for Indians and colonists alike. The demanding seasonal tasks of clearing fields, planting seeds, and harvesting crops remained interwoven with the incessant chores of providing clothing, securing shelter, and sustaining community.

Over time, however, changing circumstances in America and Europe introduced new pressures up and down the Atlantic seaboard. On occasion after 1670, familiar routines gave way to episodes of bloodshed that threatened to tear whole colonies apart. Elsewhere in North America, Pueblo rebels were resisting the Spanish in New Mexico, and Iroquois warriors were challenging the French in Illinois Country. The English, with their larger numbers, posed an even greater cultural and economic problem for Native American inhabitants.

In 1675, embittered Wampanoag Indians and their allies rose up across southern New England in Metacom's War (or King Philip's War). The next year, frontier tensions in Virginia sparked the upheaval known as Bacon's Rebellion. A decade later, events in England prompted further tremors. Mounting opposition forced the unpopular King James II, who ruled from 1685 to 1688, to surrender the English throne to William of Orange. Parliament emerged from this transition (known in England as the "Glorious Revolution") with enhanced powers. In America, the end of rule by the Stuart dynasty was punctuated by controversy and violence in one colony after another.

> *After 1670, familiar routines gave way to episodes of bloodshed that threatened to tear whole colonies apart.*

METACOM'S WAR IN NEW ENGLAND

By 1675, the Native Americans of southern New England, like the Pueblo in New Mexico, had endured several generations of colonization. Yet they disagreed over how much English culture they should adopt. Many used English words for trading, English pots for cooking, and English weapons for hunting. Some had converted to Christianity, living in protected "praying towns." Several young men had enrolled in Harvard's Indian College, where they learned to write English, Latin, and Greek with an eye toward entering the ministry.

> *Colonists now outnumbered the remaining 20,000 Indians in southern New England by more than two to one.*

Massasoit, the Wampanoag **sachem** (leader) who had assisted the Pilgrims at Plymouth, made sure that his two sons, Wamsutta and Metacom, learned English ways. The two men raised pigs and fired guns, and the colonists called them Alexander and Philip, after the kings of ancient Macedon. But when Wamsutta died in the 1660s, shortly after succeeding his father, Metacom (now called King Philip) suspected foul play by the English. And Metacom had other grievances. Colonial traders made the Indians drunk and then cheated them. English livestock trampled Wampanoag corn, and if Indians shot the cattle, colonial courts imposed punishments. Land-hungry colonists now outnumbered the remaining 20,000 Indians in southern New England by more than two to one, and missionaries were drawing hundreds of Indians into Christian enclaves known as "praying towns."

One such convert was John Sassamon, who grew up among the colonists, learned to read and write English, and then taught school among other Indians. He became one of the first Native Americans to attend Harvard College and later preached the Gospel. Early in 1675, this respected go-between passed rumors of an impending Indian uprising to officials at Plymouth. When Sassamon died mysteriously days later, a jury of English and Indians blamed the revenge murder on three high-ranking Wampanoags. Their executions by the colonists in June outraged Metacom and triggered a long-expected conflict.

Metacom's warriors ravaged towns along the Connecticut River valley and near the coast, using the victories to recruit additional Indian allies. The colonists, unprepared after forty years of peace and unchallenged dominance, were caught off guard. Distrusting even the Christian Indians, Massachusetts officials relocated whole praying towns of Indian converts to windswept Deer Island in Boston Harbor.

By December, the Connecticut and Rhode Island colonies, terrified of being wiped out, united with Plymouth and Massachusetts Bay to create a force of more than 1,000 men. An Indian captive led them to a stronghold of the still-neutral Narragansett in a remote swamp a dozen miles west of Newport, Rhode Island. The colonists surprised and overwhelmed the fortified village, setting it ablaze during the fierce fighting. Indian survivors fled, leaving behind more than 600 dead. Many of the men, women, and children were "terribly Barbikew'd," minister Cotton Mather later recorded.

This "Great Swamp Fight," reminiscent of an earlier battle in the Pequot War, infuriated the Narragansett survivors, who joined Metacom's growing alliance. During the late winter of 1676, this loose confederacy continued to wreak havoc on New England villages. But as spring arrived, the coalition weakened and the tide turned. Sickness broke out among the fighters, who lacked food and gunpowder. The powerful Mohawk of the Iroquois Confederacy opposed Metacom from the west. Numerous Christian Indians joined the colonial forces, despite their painful internment at Boston's Deer Island.

With Metacom facing defeat, defections increased. In August, a former ally betrayed the resistance leader, shot him, and delivered his head to the English. As the struggle ground to a close, the colonists captured Metacom's wife and child, selling them into slavery in the West Indies along with hundreds of other prisoners of war. New England's remaining Indians became second-class inhabitants, confined to enclaves in the areas they had once dominated, while the colonists soon rebuilt and extended their domain.

■ **MAP 3.3   Metacom's War in New England, 1675–1676**

In fourteen months of war, New England Indians destroyed more than two dozen colonial towns and suffered their own heavy losses. The brutal conflict ended after the death of Metacom (the Wampanoag leader, also known as King Philip), near Mt. Hope, on August 12, 1676.

BACON'S REBELLION IN VIRGINIA

While smoke still billowed over New England, new flames broke out in Virginia. Social unrest had been growing under the stern governorship of Sir William Berkeley. England's wars with the Dutch cut into the tobacco trade and drew enemy ships into Chesapeake Bay. Unfree tobacco workers—more than 6,000 indentured Europeans and nearly 2,000 enslaved Africans—chafed against their harsh treatment. On the frontier, colonists resented the dependent Indians (Occaneechi, Pamunkey, and others) who traded furs in exchange for protection from other tribes. Settlers also feared the well-armed Susquehannock living near the Potomac River. "Consider us," Berkeley wrote to the king in 1667, "as a people press'd at our backes with Indians, in our Bowills with our Servants . . . and invaded from without by the Dutch."

By 1676, tensions in Virginia reached the breaking point. Officials had increased taxes to pay for fortifications, servant plots and mutinies abounded, and corruption ran rampant among Berkeley's close associates. The aging governor ruled from Green Spring, his huge estate near the capital, Jamestown. Fearing the hostile views of free men who did not own property, Berkeley had revoked their right to vote. He had not dared to call an election in fourteen years. He also dreaded outspoken preachers, free schools, and printing presses. "How miserable that man is," he wrote, "that Governes a People where six parts of seaven at least are Poore Endebted Discontented and Armed."

Benjamin Henry Latrobe, *View of Greenspring House*, 1796. Courtesy of The Maryland Historical Society, Baltimore, Maryland (1960.108.1.2.33).

■ Green Spring, the largest mansion in Virginia at the time of Bacon's Rebellion, symbolized the autocratic rule of Governor William Berkeley and his "Green Spring faction." The estate was seized by Bacon's forces in 1676 and later restored by Berkeley's widow.

DOCUMENT

Declaration against the Proceedings of Nathaniel Bacon (1676)

Even wealthy newcomers such as Nathaniel Bacon had trouble gaining access to Berkeley's inner circle. When Bacon arrived from England in 1674 at age twenty-seven, he received a council seat because of his connections and money. But rivals denied the ambitious gentleman a license to engage in the profitable fur trade. Impatient, Bacon soon condemned Berkeley's ruling Green Spring faction as sponges who "have sukt up the Publique Treasure." When frontier tensions erupted into racial violence, Bacon threw himself into the conflict, challenging Berkeley's leadership and launching aggressive campaigns. His frontier followers, eager for Indian land, killed friendly Occaneechi as well as hostile Susquehannock.

The governor, aware of the damage that Metacom's War had inflicted on New England, refused to sanction these raids. He feared "a Generall Combination of all the Indians against us." But Bacon's army continued to grow, as backcountry leaders joined landless poor and runaway workers—both black and white—to support his anti-Indian cause. When the desperate governor called for a rare election to assert his strength, Bacon's supporters dominated the new House of Burgesses. Berkeley retreated across Chesapeake Bay and hid on Virginia's eastern shore.

Throughout the summer of 1676, rumors swirled that Bacon might join with malcontents in Maryland and in the newly settled Albemarle region of northeastern North Carolina to carve out an independent enclave and seek aid from the Dutch or the French. The new assembly quickly restored the vote to propertyless men and forbade excessive fees. It limited sheriffs to one year in office and passed other measures to halt corruption and expand participation in government. As an incentive for enlistment in the frontier war, the assembly granted Bacon's recruits the right to sell into slavery any Indians they captured.

For their part, slaves and indentured servants took advantage of the breakdown in public controls to leave their masters and join Bacon. Networks of "news wives" (women who used facts and rumors to fan worker discontent) spread stories of oppressive conditions. In June rebel soldiers talked openly of sharing estates among themselves, and in August they took over Green Spring Plantation, where Berkeley kept sixty horses and 400 head of cattle. A month later, Bacon's army burned Jamestown to the ground.

But by October, the tide had turned. Bacon was dead, struck down by dysentery, and reinforcements for Berkeley were on the way from England. With armed vessels patrolling the rivers, Berkeley worked up enough nerve to return from the eastern shore. Soon propertied men who had joined with Bacon were changing sides again and receiving amnesty from the governor.

The revolt had been crushed, but the impact of the tumult proved huge. On the frontier, Bacon's violent campaign against the Indians had killed or enslaved hundreds and fostered bitter hatreds. In the Tidewater, the uprising had raised a frightening prospect for wealthy tobacco planters: a unified and defiant underclass of white and black workers. From then on, Virginia's gentry applied themselves to dividing the races and creating a labor force made up of African slaves. In London, the recently formed Royal Africa Company stood ready to further such a design.

THE "GLORIOUS REVOLUTION" IN ENGLAND

No sooner had peace returned to New England and Virginia than Stuart policies brought a new round of turmoil on both sides of the Atlantic. In England, debate revived over who would succeed Charles II on the throne. The irreligious Charles, an Anglican in name only, had no legitimate children. Therefore, his brother James, a convert to Catholicism, was first in line to inherit the crown.

In 1678, rumors spread regarding a "Popish Plot" by Catholics to kill the king so that James could take power. The House of Commons, fearful of rule by a Catholic king, urged that James be excluded from the line of succession. Instead of James, House members argued, why not consider James's Protestant daughters by his first marriage: either Mary (recently wedded to her Dutch cousin, William of Orange) or Anne? Angered by such interference, Charles II dissolved Parliament in 1681 and ruled on his own for the last four years of his life.

When Charles II died in 1685, the traditional rule of succession prevailed: James II took over the English throne. In France that same year, Louis XIV revoked the Edict of Nantes, which had protected French Protestants. Fear spread among England's Protestant majority that their country's new Catholic ruler, James II, might also sanction persecution of non-Catholics. These concerns mounted when James disbanded Parliament, raised a standing army, and placed a Catholic in command of the navy. Then in 1688, James's queen gave birth to a male heir. Protestant anxieties about a pending Catholic dynasty erupted into open resistance.

United by their fear of Catholicism, rival factions among England's political elite (known for the first time as "Whigs" and "Tories") temporarily papered over their differences. They invited the Protestant William of Orange, James's Dutch son-in-law, to lead an army from Holland and take the English crown. In November 1688, William crossed the English Channel with 15,000 men, prompting James to abdicate the throne and escape into exile. William and Mary were proclaimed joint sovereigns in 1689, accepting a Bill of Rights that limited royal power.

Jan Wyck, *William III Landing at Torbay*, 1688. National Maritime Museum Picture Library

■ Protestants in England and America opposed to King James II welcomed news that William of Orange (above) had arrived from Holland with his army in 1688 to take over the English throne.

Its position now enhanced, Parliament moved to grant toleration to Protestant dissenters, establish limited freedom of the press, and ensure regular parliamentary sessions. It also imposed limits on any permanent, paid military forces, known as standing armies, because they could accrue their own power and jeopardize civil authority. The English had thus preserved Protestantism and curtailed royal absolutism, all without bloodshed. Parliament hailed King William III as "our great Deliverer from Popery and Slavery." The propertied classes, who benefited most from the peaceful transition, hailed it as the "Glorious Revolution."

THE "GLORIOUS REVOLUTION" IN AMERICA

The succession of James II in 1685 did not bode well for England's American colonies. The new king not only professed the Catholic faith but also cherished absolute monarchy and distrusted elected assemblies. In colonial affairs, James favored revenue-generating reforms and direct obedience to the crown. He detested the powerful leaders in Massachusetts, for, as Congregationalists, they believed in a decentralized Protestant church. James also resented the fact that they disobeyed the Navigation Acts and asserted their right to self-rule, even after the crown revoked their charter in 1684. Moreover, he rejected the notion that colonists possessed the precious right claimed by the English at home: not to be taxed without giving their consent. The king envisioned an extensive reorganization of the American colonies.

> *The success of William and the demise of the Dominion of New England did not end royal efforts to tighten imperial control over New England.*

When James assumed the throne, his own colony of New York automatically became a royal province. Convinced of his divine right to set policy, the king nullified the charters of certain colonies in order to bring them under his control. As the cornerstone of his reorganization plan, James linked the New England colonies (plus New York and New Jersey in 1688) into one huge *Dominion of New England*. This consolidation, under an appointed governor general, would make it easier for England to suppress dissent, enforce shipping regulations, and defend the Dominion's frontiers—at least in theory.

In practice, the effort to forge a Dominion of New England proved a disaster. The move met such stiff resistance in America that a similar design for England's southern colonies never materialized. Control of the Dominion went to a military officer, Sir Edmund Andros. The heavy-handed Andros attempted to rule from Boston through a council he appointed, made up of loyal associates, without aid or interference from any elected legislature. He asserted the crown's right to question existing land patents, and he requisitioned a Congregational church for Anglican services. Worse, he offended local leaders by strictly enforcing the Navigation Acts to collect revenue. When participants in democratic town meetings raised objections, he jailed the leaders.

Colonists seethed with resentment toward this revival of Stuart absolutism, which claimed total obedience to the king and his officers as a divine right for the monarchy. Rumors of French invasions and Catholic plots swirled among staunch Protestants. In April 1689, welcome news that the Protestant William of Orange had invaded England inspired a revolt in Boston. Mobs showed public support for overthrowing the Stuart regime, and local leaders threw Governor Andros in jail.

The success of William and the demise of the Dominion of New England did not end royal efforts to tighten imperial control over New England. The new Massachusetts charter of 1691 consolidated neighboring Plymouth and Maine into the Massachusetts Bay colony. Moreover, it proclaimed that future governors would be appointed by the monarchy, as in other colonies. The men of Massachusetts, who had elected their own governor since the days of John Winthrop, would no longer have that right.

Emboldened by Boston's actions in 1689, New Yorkers ousted their own Dominion officials and set up a temporary government headed by Jacob Leisler. This German-born militia captain was a staunch Calvinist and hostile to the town's growing English elite. In Leisler's Rebellion, long-standing ethnic and religious rivalries merged with vague class hostilities: Leisler's supporters resented their treatment at the hands of the rich. They freed imprisoned debtors and attacked the houses of leading merchants. After a new governor arrived to take charge in 1691, the elite fought back. They lowered artisan wages and pressured the governor into hanging Leisler, on the grounds that his rebel followers were "growing dayly very high and Insolentt."

> *In Leisler's Rebellion, long-standing ethnic and religious rivalries merged with vague class hostilities.*

Similar tremors shook the Chesapeake region. In Maryland, where the Catholic proprietor ruled over a large and restive Protestant population, the governing Calvert family waited too long to proclaim its loyalty to King William. Fearing a "Popish" plot, assemblyman John Coode and a force of 250 armed Protestants marched on St. Mary's City and seized the government by force. The "happy Change in England" had replaced divine right rule with a more balanced constitutional monarchy, and Maryland settlers were determined to show their support.

Consequences of War and Growth: 1690–1715

■ *How did worldly success and wartime profits contribute to colonial unrest after 1690?*

The success of the Glorious Revolution hardly brought peace to England or its empire. On the contrary, warfare marked the reign of William and Mary and also that of Mary's sister, Queen Anne, who ruled from 1702 until her death in 1714. William immediately became involved in bloody campaigns to subdue highland clans in Scotland and overpower Catholic forces in Ireland. Moreover, English involvement against France in two protracted wars on the European continent had implications for colonists and Indians living in eastern North America. The War of the League of Augsburg in Europe became known to English colonists in America as King William's War (1689–1697), and the protracted War of Spanish Succession was experienced in America as Queen Anne's War (1702–1713).

Nowhere was the impact of these imperial wars more evident than in the rapidly growing colonies of the Northeast. Indeed, the earlier bloodshed of Metacom's (King Philip's) War, starting in 1675, had already aroused consternation and soul-searching. Bible-reading New Englanders viewed the violent decades that followed as a harsh test, or a deserved punishment, sent from the Almighty. They believed that God had watched closely over the initial Puritan "errand into the wilderness." Could it be, ministers now asked from the pulpit, that the Lord had some special controversy with the current generation? As communities grew more prosperous and became caught up in the pursuit of worldly success, were church members forgetting their religious roots and leading less pious lives? Invoking the Old Testament prophet Jeremiah, New England clerics interpreted most personal and collective troubles as God's punishment for the region's spiritual decline.

But such a sweeping explanation of misfortune only raised deeper questions. New Englanders could see clearly that the consequences of rapid change were not spread equally among all towns, congregations, and families. As in most war eras—and moments of economic and demographic growth—certain people and localities seemed to benefit while others fell behind. Some anxious believers saw the hand of Satan in the day-to-day

DOCUMENT

Benjamin Wadsworth, from *A Well-Ordered Family* (1712)

struggles of village life. Others argued that the worldly success and wartime profits of an expanding elite had undermined the community ideals of earlier generations. While flames engulfed isolated Massachusetts communities such as Deerfield and portions of the Maine frontier, fiery passions were also being aroused in older settlements, such as Salem and Boston.

SALEM'S WARTIME WITCH HUNT

One of the most memorable disruptions, the Salem witch hunt, occurred in Essex County, Massachusetts, a two-day ride on horseback from the embattled Maine frontier. In 1692, an outburst of witchcraft accusations engulfed the farm community of Salem Village. The strange episode remains one of the most troubling in American history.

Among European Christians, a belief in witches with a supernatural power to inflict harm stretched back for centuries. In the 1600s, witchcraft trials abounded in Europe, and in New England zealous believers had executed several dozen people in isolated cases. Three-fourths of those accused (and even more of those executed) were women. Most were beyond childbearing age, often poor or widowed, with limited power to protect themselves in the community. But the hysteria in Salem went far beyond other colonial witchcraft incidents, with more than 200 people accused and twenty put to death.

Early in 1692, more than half a dozen young women in Salem Village, ranging in age from nine to twenty, began to suffer violent convulsive fits. With reduced appetites and temporary loss of hearing, sight, and memory, they also experienced choking sensations that curtailed their speech. Vivid hallucinations followed. Elders noted that some of those stricken had spent time with Tituba, a slave woman brought from Barbados who lived in the local minister's household. By April, the adolescents had accused ten adults of being witches. Then some of the ten named others in their elaborate confessions, and the hysteria snowballed.

In a world where people considered satanic influence very real, frightened authorities seriously weighed the young women's stories of people appearing to them as devilish specters and apparitions. Overriding tradition, jurists allowed such "spectral evidence" in court, and convictions mounted. The court ordered public executions of the condemned on Gallows Hill, and the hangings (fourteen women and five men) continued through September. One poor and elderly farmer, Giles Cory, was pressed to death under heavy stones. Another man and three additional women died in jail. Only when accusations reached too high in the social hierarchy and when several accusers recanted their stories did the new governor finally intervene. He emptied the jails, forbade further imprisonments, and pardoned the surviving accused until the tremor could subside.

> *The hysteria in Salem went far beyond other colonial witch-craft incidents, with more than 200 people accused and twenty put to death.*

Why this terrible outburst? Some historians argue that strained relations between farm families and the more prosperous urban residents in the nearby port of Salem Town may have influenced the craze. Some emphasize the zeal and gullibility of those first assigned to investigate. Still others speculate that the absence of central authority, until Governor Phips arrived in the colony in May, allowed a troubled situation to spin out of control. Finally, commentators stress a perverse psychological dynamic that arises in any witch hunt, ancient or modern. In such cases, accused suspects often can save their own lives by supplying damaging and vivid confessions implicating others rather than by offering heartfelt denials of guilt. One or more of these factors surely came into play.

Yet devastation on the Maine frontier also contributed to what happened in Salem Village. The little Massachusetts town had numerous links to the war zone. A recent minister, George Burroughs, much disliked in the village, had come from Maine. He had returned there when the contentious parish refused to pay him. Traumatized survivors from King

William's War—the current conflict against the Abenaki and French—had trickled into the community. Significantly, more than half the young women who accused others of witchcraft had lost one or both parents in the brutal frontier wars. On February 5, just weeks before the first accusations, 150 Indian attackers had burned the Maine village of York 80 miles north of Salem, killing forty-eight people and taking seventy-three captives. Word of the raid no doubt triggered shocking memories among Salem's war refugees, especially the orphans who worked as servants in local households.

Fears deepened in April when one of the accused confessed that the Devil had tempted her while she had been living in Maine. Then it was reported that the specter of Reverend Burroughs "appeared" to an accuser. Charged with promoting witchcraft and encouraging the hostile Indians (whom the colonists saw as Satan's helpers), Burroughs was arrested in Maine and hanged on Gallows Hill. A servant named Mercy Short, who had been captured and orphaned by Indians, recalled disturbing dreams of the Devil. She told minister Cotton Mather that in her dreams Satan and his minions (who had "an Indian colour") had made "hideous assaults" upon her. Much of what Mather and others recorded as the work of Satan may actually have been posttraumatic stress in a frayed community during wartime.

DOCUMENT

Ann Putnam, Deposition (1692)

THE UNEVEN COSTS OF WAR

Throughout the 1690s and beyond, King William's War and Queen Anne's War made conflict a constant element of colonial life, but the burdens fell unevenly. For many colonial families, incessant warfare brought only death and dislocation. But for others, it offered new opportunities as the colonial economies expanded. Farmers with access to port towns shifted away from subsistence agriculture and grew crops for commercial sale. In doing so, they exposed themselves to greater financial risks, given transportation costs and market fluctuations. But they hoped to reap large profits.

Overseas trade and wartime smuggling offered investors even higher gains and larger risks. These activities, in turn, boosted demand for sailing vessels. Boston alone supported more than a dozen busy shipyards. They employed numerous shipwrights, caulkers, and other skilled workers who crafted hulls, ropes, masts, and sails. Military campaigns, such as the successful ones against the French at Port Royal in Acadia in 1690 and again in 1710, engaged hundreds of colonial soldiers and sailors. When an English fleet of sixty warships carrying 5,000 men docked at Boston in 1711, local provisioners (those who sold food and other provisions) reaped the rewards.

The crews of **privateers** (boats licensed to harass enemy shipping in wartime) made money if they captured a foreign vessel as a prize. But when peace returned, many refused to enter the ranks of the unemployed on land. Instead, hundreds became buccaneers, pirates who operated for their own gain while avoiding the arm of the law. After all, poor work conditions, brutal discipline, and low pay were the rule aboard merchant ships. Therefore many sailors, when stopped by pirates on the high seas, chose to join their ranks. During the brief heyday of piracy in the generation before 1725, the number of buccaneers reached several thousand—enough to create a crisis in Atlantic shipping—and many had colonial ties. Englishman Edward Teach (known as Blackbeard) won notoriety as a privateer-turned-pirate, haunting the Carolina coast until his death in 1718.

> *For many colonial families, incessant warfare brought only death and dislocation. But for others, it offered new opportunities.*

Everywhere, poorer families were most likely to sink under the burdens of war. Regressive taxes, requiring the same amount from a poor carpenter as from a rich merchant, obviously hurt impoverished people the most. So did high wartime prices for food and other necessities. Furthermore, many of the poor men recruited by the military became casualties of combat or disease, increasing the number of widows

■ For protection, the pirate Blackbeard often brought his ship into the shallow waters behind the barrier islands that form North Carolina's Atlantic coast. There, his crew bartered stolen goods at Ocracoke Island and reveled on the beach with local inhabitants.

living in poverty. As New England's port towns expanded, the growing distance between rich and poor struck local residents. The moral ties and community obligations—known as the social covenant—that Puritan elders had emphasized two generations earlier were loosening. In their place emerged a focus on secular priorities and a new, individualistic spirit.

In Boston, troubled ministers decried the hunger and poverty that they saw deepening in their parishes alongside unprecedented displays of wealth. Between 1685 and 1715, the share of all personal wealth in the town controlled by the poorest 60 percent of the population fell from 17 percent to 13 percent. At the same time, the portion controlled by the richest 5 percent climbed from 26 percent to 40 percent. Angry writers published irate pamphlets encouraging working people to take political action. They charged once-respected elites with studying "how to oppress, cheat, and overreach their neighbours."

No Bostonian wielded more economic power than Andrew Belcher, who first made money by supplying provisions to troops during Metacom's War. Each succeeding war brought Belcher larger contracts and greater profits. To the dismay of devout churchgoers and the working poor, he built a mansion on State Street and rode in an imported coach, attended by black slaves dressed in fancy livery. He owned twenty-two ships and invested in many more. He also repeatedly cornered the wartime grain market, spawning food shortages and raking in inflated profits as prices rose.

In 1710, Belcher asserted his right to ship 6,000 bushels of grain on the open market rather than sell flour at home, where people desperately needed bread. Indignant residents rebelled against Belcher's outright defiance of traditional community values. In the dark of night, they disabled his ship by sawing through the rudder. A grand jury declined to indict the protesters. Did ambitious and aggressive merchants such as Belcher cause the city's calamities, or did the townsfolk bring on their own troubles? Using a refrain that recurred in later generations, one godly conservative pointed a finger at the poor and implied they must be sinful if they could not subsist. "There was Corn to be had," he argued; "if they had not impoverished themselves by Rum, they might buy Corn." Only "the Devil's people" lacked food.

William Dampier: The World Became His University

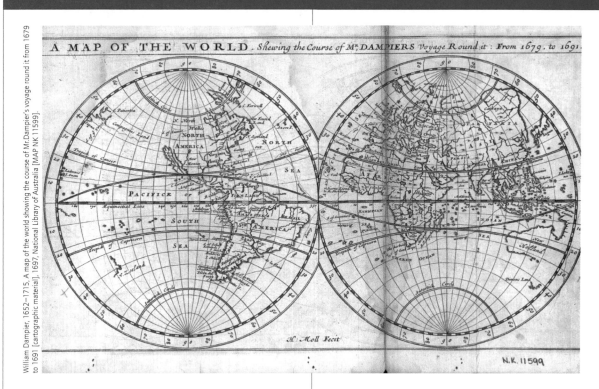

William Dampier, 1652–1715. A map of the world showing the course of Mr.Dampier's voyage round it from 1679 to 1691 [cartographic material], 1697, National Library of Australia [MAP NK 11599].

The Wider World

In July 1682, William Dampier sailed into Chesapeake Bay aboard a pirate ship. The remarkable naturalist, scarcely thirty-one, had already spent half of his life at sea. The son of an English tenant farmer, Dampier was apprenticed to a shipmaster after his mother died in the Great Plague of 1665. He first joined a pirate band in 1679, "more to indulge my curiosity than to get wealth."

The Chesapeake provided many safe havens for buccaneers, but it seemed too tame for the restless Dampier. He stayed in Virginia only thirteen months. "That country is so well known to our nation," he wrote, "that I shall say nothing of it." For Dampier, there was a wider world to be seen, and he eagerly renewed his travels.

Over the next nine years, Dampier sailed from ocean to ocean, taking copious notes on everything he saw. He dined on flamingo tongues in the Cape Verde Islands and cruised along Australia's remote north coast, where a bay now preserves his name. To assist English colonists "in our *American* Plantations," he recorded detailed notes on the various uses for coconuts that he encountered in the East Indies.

Dampier made his way back to England in 1691. Travel tales, both real and imagined, were flooding the European market. In 1697, therefore, the observant ex-pirate published his own best-seller: *A New Voyage Round the World*. He was one of the first to introduce such diverse words as *chopsticks* and *barbecue* into the English language.

Two years later, Dampier's gripping account was already in its fourth edition when the English Admiralty chose him to command its first South Seas voyage of exploration. Before he died in 1715 at age sixty-four, he had circumnavigated the world three times, and he had done more to inform English readers about the wider world than any writer of his generation.

QUESTIONS

1. In the late seventeenth century, why was it so difficult for European readers to distinguish between false travel tales and real accounts, such as Dampier's?

2. What are the advantages in gaining "knowledge and experience" by roaming the world rather than by seeking a formal education? What are the disadvantages?

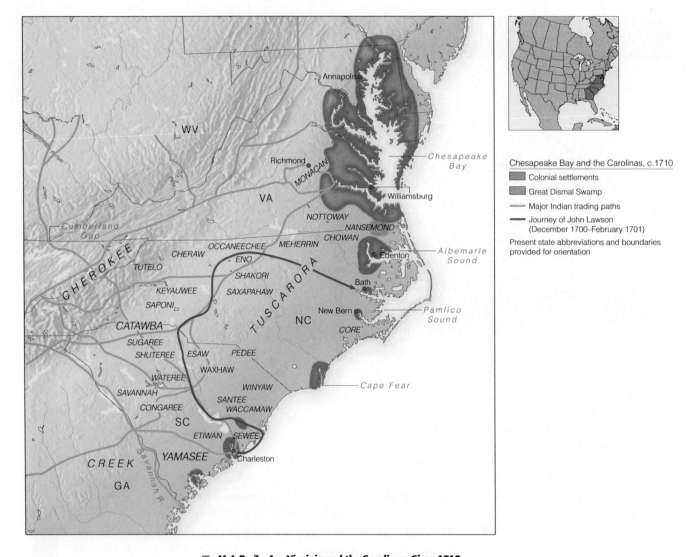

Chesapeake Bay and the Carolinas, c.1710
- Colonial settlements
- Great Dismal Swamp
- Major Indian trading paths
- Journey of John Lawson (December 1700–February 1701)

Present state abbreviations and boundaries provided for orientation

■ **M A P   3 . 4   Virginia and the Carolinas, Circa 1710**
After John Lawson made a 1,000-mile journey through the Carolina interior (1700–1701), he became an advocate for colonial growth. The expanding settlements of North Carolina and South Carolina pressed the Tuscarora and Yamasee Indians, who staged wars of resistance after 1710.

STORM CLOUDS IN THE SOUTH

Peace returned to New England's frontier villages and port towns in 1711, as negotiations began for ending Queen Anne's War in America and the related War of Spanish Succession in Europe. British diplomats gained favorable terms from France and Spain when they signed a treaty at Utrecht two years later. (The formal union of England and Scotland in 1707 under the name *Great Britain* had transformed the *English* empire into the *British* empire.) But London officials could not prevent fresh violence in North America, given the expansion of their British colonies. The Wampanoag, Narragansett, and Abenaki Indians had attempted to roll back the advancement of northeastern settlers in Connecticut, Massachusetts, and Maine. Now Native Americans in the Southeast sought to counter the encroachments of newcomers along the Carolina coast.

By the 1660s, settlers were drifting into the pine wilderness that would become the colony of North Carolina. Some were radicals fleeing the Restoration in England.

Others, such as John Culpeper, had moved north from the Carolina settlement on the Ashley River, where they disapproved of the hierarchical plans drawn up by Shaftesbury and Locke that gave the Carolina proprietors firm control over the new colony. Still others were runaway servants from Virginia and refugees escaping the aftermath of Bacon's uprising. In 1677, these newcomers, led by Culpeper, seized control in the Albemarle region just south of Virginia's Great Dismal Swamp. The proprietors suppressed "Culpeper's Rebellion," but in 1689 they agreed to name a separate governor for the portion of Carolina "That Lies north and east of Cape Feare." Another disturbance, "Cary's Rebellion" in 1710, led to official recognition of "North Carolina, independent of Carolina," the next year. (Surveyors marked off the dividing line with Virginia in 1728.)

In 1680, Native Americans still outnumbered newcomers in eastern North Carolina by two to one, but within thirty years that ratio had been reversed. The Naval Stores Act of 1705, passed by Parliament to promote colonial production of tar and pitch for shipbuilding, drew a stream of settlers to the pine forests of eastern North Carolina. By 1710, English communities existed on Albemarle Sound, at what is now Edenton, and on Pamlico Sound, at Bath (where Blackbeard and other pirates were frequent visitors). No one promoted the region more than John Lawson, who had made an extensive tour of Carolina in 1700, living among the Indians and assessing the land for colonization. The young explorer-naturalist returned to England in 1709 to publish an account of his travels, *A New Voyage to Carolina.*

THE BEASTES OF CAROLINA.

Courtesy, Dartmouth University Library

■ Frontispiece from John Lawson's *A New Voyage to Carolina* (London, 1709).

While in London, Lawson arranged to sell North Carolina land to a party of more than 600 Protestant immigrants from Bern, Switzerland. After a perilous Atlantic crossing—half the company died at sea—he led the survivors to the site of a Native American village at the mouth of the Neuse River. Lawson surveyed lots along the riverfront, and they "planted stakes to mark the houses and to make the principal streets." Within eighteen months, "sickness, want, and desperation" gave way to "a happy state of things," and Lawson headed inland from New Bern to eye more land for future settlement.

All this was too much for the Tuscarora Indians. Frustrated by corrupt traders and land encroachment, they launched a war in 1711 to drive out the intruders. They took Lawson prisoner, put him to death, and devastated the Swiss at New Bern. But they had waited too long. Within two years, the settlers—aided by a South Carolina force of several dozen whites and nearly 500 Yamasee Indians—had crushed Tuscarora resistance. Most of the Tuscarora survivors migrated north, where they became the sixth nation within the powerful Iroquois Confederacy.

Yamasee warriors from the Savannah River region helped British colonists quell the Tuscarora uprising. But in 1715, the Yamasee led their own rebellion. They too were troubled by encroaching settlers and aggressive traders, plus South Carolina's practice of exporting Native American captives to the West Indies as slaves. The Yamasee received support from

CHRONOLOGY: 1660–1715

1660	Restoration of monarchy in England under Charles II.
1664	Charles II grants a charter to his brother James, Duke of York, sanctioning the takeover of the Dutch New Netherland colony and the creation of New York.
1675 to 1676	Metacom's War in New England.
1676	Bacon's Rebellion in Virginia.
1680	Pueblo Revolt in New Mexico.
1681	Quaker William Penn receives charter for Pennsylvania.
1682	La Salle explores the Mississippi River and claims Louisiana for France.
1689	Dutch leader William of Orange and his wife Mary become joint English sovereigns in the Glorious Revolution, replacing King James II.
1692	Witchcraft trials in Salem, Massachusetts.
1699	Iberville begins colony in French Louisiana.
1711 to 1715	Tuscarora Indians in North Carolina, and then the Yamasee in South Carolina, resist English colonial expansion.

neighboring Creek Indians, Spanish-speaking colonists in Florida, and French traders at the new Alabama outpost of Fort Toulouse. The still-powerful Cherokee in southern Appalachia opted not to join in the Yamasee War. Otherwise, the Indians might have overwhelmed the South Carolina colony.

Conclusion

Inspired by the exploits of LaSalle and a generation of fur traders and missionaries, the French had made inroads into the heart of the continent, the huge Mississippi Valley. But most European intrusions remained confined to the fringes of the vast continent. The French established themselves in Louisiana, and small numbers of Spanish held onto footholds in New Mexico and Florida, while venturing into parts of Arizona and Texas.

The English newcomers, far more numerous, remained clustered along the Atlantic seaboard. When their rising numbers prompted expansion up local river valleys away from the coast, warfare with Native American inhabitants ensued. Along the length of eastern North America, from the Kennebec River to the Savannah, hundreds of settlers and Indians died violently during the half-century before 1715. Often the frontier struggles became entwined with wider conflicts between the rival European empires. These wilderness skirmishes seem minor compared with the battles raging in Europe at the same time. Despite the small scale of the conflicts in North America, however, Europe's imperial wars had started to influence developments in the English colonies.

Another element of Europe's expansion overseas—the transatlantic slave trade—had also begun to alter the shape of England's North American colonies. What had seemed only a small cloud on the horizon in the early seventeenth century had grown into an ominous force, with a momentum of its own, by the early eighteenth century. The storm hit hardest along the Southeast coast, where the arrival of thousands of Africans soon shaped a distinctive and repressive world of enslavement and exploitation that endured for generations. No sooner had the English gained control along the Atlantic edge of North America than they orchestrated a "terrible transformation" that placed thousands in bondage and altered the shape of American history.

For Review

1. What made the Pueblo Revolt of 1680 the most successful uprising against a colonizing power in the early history of North America?

2. How did Catholic missionaries aid, or hinder, the North American colonizing efforts of Spain and France?

3. How did the restoration of the monarchy in London in 1660 influence the evolution of England's American colonies over the next two generations?

4. Can you single out colonial incidents of ethnic, racial, political, religious, and class violence in this era? Or are these elements too thoroughly intertwined? Explain.

5. Carolina explorer John Lawson observed that by 1710 the Indians had been "better to us than we are to them." Do you agree?

6. Were developments during the half-century after 1660 as important to the future of North America as the earlier founding of Virginia and the New England colonies? Explain.

Created Equal Online

For more *Created Equal* resources, including suggestions on sites to visit and books to read, go to **MyHistoryLab.com.**

Part Two

A Century of Colonial Expansion to 1775

On April 19, 1775, New England farmers battled British soldiers at Concord Bridge. The confrontation marked the start of the American Revolution. (Each spring in Massachusetts, the date is still set aside as Patriots' Day and celebrated with the running of the Boston Marathon.) But how did colonies that were weak outposts before 1700 become strong enough to challenge the power of the British empire in the second half of the eighteenth century? The answer is not a simple one. Life changed in dramatic ways during the century before 1775, not only in New England but throughout much of North America.

The rapid spread of Spanish horses across the West allowed Native Americans, such as the Comanche and Sioux, to become mounted buffalo hunters on the Great Plains. The arrival of Russian fur traders disrupted traditional cultures on the Aleutian Islands and the coast of Alaska. At the same time, the gradual success of the new Louisiana colony gave France access to much of the Mississippi River valley. But the potential for a dominant French-speaking empire in America evaporated with the stunning defeat of French forces by the British in the Seven Years' War. As that global conflict ended in 1763, the Spanish also lost ground in North America. After claiming Florida for 200 years, they finally ceded the peninsula to the British, even as they began to extend Spanish missions up the coast of California.

Other changes were even more dramatic. In the eighteenth century, race-based slavery became an established aspect of colonial society in North America. The English had come late to the trans-atlantic slave trade, but by the 1660s they became aggressive participants in the lucrative traffic in human beings. English colonizers fashioned harsh slave-based societies in the Caribbean, then in the Chesapeake colonies of Virginia and Maryland, next in North and South Carolina, and finally, after 1750, in the recently established colony of Georgia.

Race slavery transformed the mainland colonies in terrible ways and had far-reaching results. Thousands of Africans arrived in North American ports in the eighteenth century. Strikingly, they were only a small fraction of the much greater transport of Africans to the Caribbean and Central and South America. Nevertheless, by 1750 there were nearly 250,000 African Americans living in North America. Most lived in the South, and most were enslaved, including several hundred in Spanish East Florida and several thousand in French Louisiana. By 1775, the number exceeded half a million. By then,

blacks made up more than 20 percent of the population of the British colonies, and the legal and social constraints that shackled their world remained tighter than ever.

Newcomers from Europe, as well as from Africa, altered the make-up of Atlantic colonies that had once been almost entirely English. Many of these newly arrived Europeans, unable to afford the cost of passage, had to pledge their labor for a period of years. But in contrast to the Africans, most European migrants came to America voluntarily and were free from obligations within a few years. The Atlantic crossing could be harrowing, of course, but for thousands the long-term advantages outweighed the short-term drawbacks. Artisans of all kinds were in high demand, and land was cheap. Colonial governments ruled with a light hand in comparison to the monarchies of Europe, and they competed with one another to attract newcomers. This competition for new arrivals bred relative religious and ethnic tolerance.

Pushed by events in Europe and drawn by opportunities in America, families flocked to Britain's North American colonies. This new flow from Europe and the British Isles, combined with the African slave trade, quickly generated a far more diverse colonial society on the foundations laid by earlier English immigrants. Prior generations of colonists had laid out towns, formed governments, and founded the rudimentary institutions of colonial social life. They had established an ambivalent pattern of interaction with Native Americans that involved warfare and displacement as well as trade and intermarriage. Also, they had located harbors, carved out roads, and started to build an economic infrastructure.

As numbers rose and diversity increased, a series of regional economies emerged along the eastern seaboard. Each sustained the local inhabitants while also serving the wider needs of the British empire. For much of the eighteenth century, the British crown promoted economic growth in the colonies through a workable combination of protectionist controls and benign neglect.

But the British victory over the French brought drastic new problems to eastern North America after 1763. Native Americans lost a valued trading partner and military ally when the French withdrew. Britain faced an enormous war debt and looked to its burgeoning colonies as a source of much-needed revenue. Within little more than a decade, Britain's North American colonists went from resentment and resistance to overt rebellion in the Atlantic world's first anti-colonial war of independence.

Chapter 4

African Enslavement: The Terrible Transformation

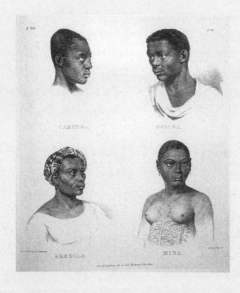

■ Africans arriving in America often had ornamental scarification (known as "country marks") on their bodies, as well as brands inflicted by slave traders and physical scars from the middle passage.

On a wintry day in January 1656, a mulatto servant named Elizabeth Key went before the local court in Northumberland County, Virginia. She was twenty-five years old. The late Colonel John Mottrom, a justice of the peace, had held Elizabeth as a slave, kept in perpetual bondage. She objected strongly, and she wanted to sue the executors of Mottrom's estate for her freedom and back pay. Bess, as she was known, presented a three-fold argument. First, as the daughter of a free man, she should inherit her father's legal status according to English law. Second, as a baptized Christian, she should not be enslaved. And third, she could produce a document showing that as a small child she had been "put out" to work until she was fourteen, following local custom. Such contracts for apprenticing a child for a fixed number of years were common in America, where labor was in short supply. But her term of work had expired long ago.

Key was accompanied in court by her white attorney and lover, William Greensted. They had had two children together and would marry six months later, when they finally won a favorable verdict. The executors of Mottrom's estate, eager to show that Bess's father was neither free nor Christian, implied that a Turkish crewman off a visiting ship was the woman's father. But the young couple produced witnesses who testified that Bess was the daughter of Thomas Key, a white man serving in the Virginia General Assembly, and his "Negro woman." One witness told the jury that Bess's mother had lived openly with Thomas Key and had said that the girl was Key's daughter.

Further testimony established that in 1636, not long before he died, Key had bound little Bess to Humphrey Higginson, a member of the Council of State. Higginson "promised to use her as well as if shee were his own Child"; that is, "more Respectfully than a Comon servant or slave." He even stood as her godfather when Bess was christened.

To be raised in a Christian church was no small matter at a time when Europeans viewed non-Christians captured in wars to be uniquely vulnerable to legal enslavement. For Bess, this circumstance helped her cause greatly, for she proved "able to give a very good account of her fayth." Furthermore, she produced clear evidence that her father had sold her to Higginson for nine years. Mr. Key had demanded that Higginson not dispose of her to any other person, such as to Colonel Mottrom. Rather, he was to give her the usual "freedom portion" of corn and clothes "and lett her shift for her selfe," either in England or Virginia, when her term expired.

The local jury accepted Elizabeth Key's three-part argument and pronounced her free. But the General Court overturned the verdict on appeal, only to be overruled in turn by a committee of the General Assembly. In the end, the committee determined that "Elizabeth ought to bee free." The assemblymen also argued that her last master owed her a "freedom portion," plus back pay "for the time shee hath served longer than Shee ought to have done." Still, the matter generated debate among settlers. In fact, several decades later, Elizabeth's case would have been decided differently. Moreover, the courts of Virginia might well have enslaved her children for life. And their offspring would have inherited slavery status as well.

A terrible transformation was under way in English colonial culture that would warp American society for centuries to come. It spread gradually, like a cancer, revealing a different pace and pattern in each mainland colony. During the 1620s and 1630s, a few black servants were working alongside white servants. But well before the end of the century, the grandchildren of those workers had been separated by skin color and physical appearance, according to emerging notions of "race." Free blacks persisted in the English colonies, but in most communities they became anomalies, for the tide was flowing against them. From now on, people of African ancestry were to be legally enslaved for life. Elizabeth Key and her children and grandchildren experienced the painful transition firsthand.

The Descent into Race Slavery

■ *How important was precedent in the English shift to hereditary enslavement of Africans?*

Some grim transitions in human affairs evolve slowly, even imperceptibly. Nothing shaped colonial cultures more forcefully than the European colonists' gradual commitment to the legalized enslavement of hundreds of thousands of people and their descendants. It is important to examine the slippery slope that led to perpetual servitude based on race.

THE CARIBBEAN PRECEDENT

The roots of race slavery in the Americas extend back to the era of Columbus, when warfare, sickness, and exploitation quickly decimated the native populations of the Caribbean after 1492. Hungry for human labor, the Spanish intruders began to import people from Africa to grow crops and dig for gold in the Caribbean islands. As the native population declined sharply through epidemics, the traffic in black newcomers expanded.

Spanish pressure for labor in the New World intensified further with the discovery of additional mines in Mexico and Peru. To meet the growing demand, Spain's king issued a contract (called the **asiento**) that allowed other European powers—such as Portugal, France, or the Netherlands—to import African slaves to the Spanish colonies. High profits drew eager participation. In the half-century between 1590 and 1640, more than 220,000 people arrived in chains from Africa at the Spanish empire's ports in Central and South America.

Meanwhile, the Portuguese purchased enslaved Africans to work their own expanding sugar plantations. They imported more than 75,000 slaves, mostly from the Congo River region of West Central Africa, to the Atlantic island of São Tomé in the sixteenth century. When Portuguese sugar production spread to coastal Brazil, so did the exploitation of African labor. By 1625, Brazil imported the majority of slaves crossing the Atlantic each year and exported most of the sugar consumed in Europe.

Long before the 1660s, therefore, Europeans had set a precedent for exploiting African workers in New World colonies. Religious and secular authorities frowned on actively enslaving people, especially if they were fellow Christians, but purchasing so-called infidels (those who followed other religions or opposed Christianity) could be tolerated, particularly if slavery had already been imposed on them by someone else. These West African victims were non-Christians, and most had already been enslaved by others, captured by fellow Africans in war.

Confident in this rationale, the Spanish and Portuguese adapted their laws to accept the enslavement of Africans. Moreover, the condition would be hereditary, with children inheriting at birth their mother's legal status. The Catholic Church backed the new labor system, though priests occasionally worked to alleviate suffering among Africans in the Americas. The pope did nothing to condemn the growing traffic, nor did the Protestant Reformation have a dampening effect. On the contrary, the rising Protestant sea powers of northern Europe proved willing to assist in the slave trade and take part in the dramatic "sugar revolution," growing sugar on a massive scale for expanding Atlantic markets.

The Dutch, for example, ruled Brazil for a generation in the first half of the seventeenth century, importing slaves to South America and exporting sugar. When the Portuguese regained control of Brazil at midcentury, they pushed out Dutch settlers. These outcasts took their knowledge about managing sugar plantations to the islands of the Caribbean. Some appeared in the new English possessions of Barbados and Jamaica, and soon they were directing African slaves in cutting, pressing, and boiling sugar cane to make molasses. The thick molasses could then be processed further to make rum and refined sugar for export. By the 1650s, slavery and sugar production were engulfing England's West Indian possessions, just as these twin features had already become central to the New World colonies controlled by Spain and Portugal. A looming precedent had been set. But as late as 1660, it was not at all clear that African slavery would gain a prominent place, or even a lasting foothold, in any of the North American colonies.

OMINOUS BEGINNINGS

As far back as the sixteenth century, African men had participated in Spanish explorers' forays into the Southeast, and some had remained, fathering children with Indian

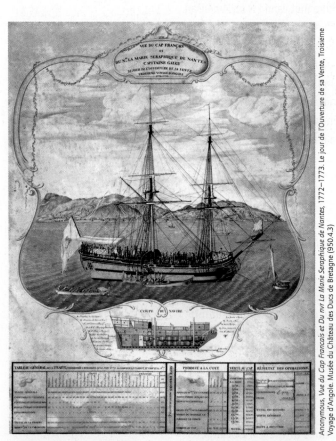

Anonymous, *Vue du Cap Francais et Du nvr La Marie Seraphique de Nantes*, 1772–1773. Le jour de l'Ouverture de sa Vente, Troisieme Voyage d'Angole. Musée du Château des Ducs de Bretagne (950.4.3)

■ This summary of an African slave-trading voyage shows wealthy planters boarding a French ship upon its arrival in the West Indies in order to buy slaves newly arrived from Angola. The crew has used an iron fence dividing the deck to protect against revolt during the voyage. The captain conducts business under an awning in the stern.

women. African slaves had helped establish the small Spanish outpost at St. Augustine in 1565, but a century later no additional coastal colonies had yet appeared on the mainland anywhere south of Chesapeake Bay.

Granted, Africans were present farther north in the fledgling settlements of the French, Dutch, and English. But their numbers remained small—several thousand at most—and few of these newcomers had come directly from Africa. Instead, most had lived for years in the Caribbean or on the mainland, absorbing colonial languages and beliefs. So they and their children, like Bess Key, were not viewed as complete outsiders by the European colonists. The legal and social standing of these early African Americans remained vague before the 1660s. Local statutes regarding labor were crude and contradictory; their interpretation and enforcement varied widely. Everywhere, workers were in demand, and most black newcomers found themselves laboring alongside European servants.

In the Massachusetts Bay colony, early Puritan settlers, casting about for sources of labor and for markets, exchanged goods for slaves in the Caribbean. In 1644, seafaring New Englanders even attempted direct trade with Africa. But the following year, Massachusetts authorities ordered a New Hampshire resident to surrender a black worker he had purchased in Boston. They argued that the man had been stolen from Africa, not captured in war, and should be returned to his home. For the earliest handful of black New Englanders, their standing proved uncertain in a region where religious status mattered far more than language, dress, or outward physical appearance. In 1652, Rhode Island passed a law limiting all involuntary service—whether for Europeans or Africans—to no more than ten years.

Nik Wheeler/CORBIS

■ West Africans still grow gourds and carve them into bowls, dippers, and musical instruments. Earlier Africans, deported as slaves, used American gourds to expand this tradition.

Along the Hudson River, the Dutch colonists had close ties with the sugar islands of the West Indies, where race slavery was already an accepted system. In New Netherland, therefore, the laws discriminated against black workers and limited their rights. But the statutes also provided loopholes that permitted social and economic advancement to the community's Africans, most of whom spoke Dutch. When an African woman named Anna van Angola obtained a tract of farmland on Manhattan in the 1640s, the governor made clear that there were no limitations on this "true and free ownership."

Chesapeake Bay lay even closer to the main routes of the Atlantic slave traffic. In 1619, a Dutch warship brought to Virginia more than twenty African men and women acquired as slaves in the Caribbean. Like people deported from England to the Chesapeake, they were put up for sale as servants. Terms of service varied, and some black newcomers earned their freedom quickly and kept it. But others saw their terms extended arbitrarily. In 1640, Virginia's General Court considered punishment for "a negro named John Punch" and two other servants who had escaped to Maryland. When apprehended, the Dutchman and the Scotsman each received four additional years of service, but the African was sentenced to unending servitude "for the time of his natural life." That same year, Virginia passed a law that prevented blacks from bearing arms. And a 1643 law taxing productive field hands included African American women but not white women.

These early efforts to separate Africans from Europeans by law set an ominous precedent in the use of skin color as a distinguishing marker. Still, rules governing the lives of people of color and their offspring remained ambiguous for several decades, and (as the case of Bess Key makes clear) efforts at exploitation could often be undone in court. But new forces would come into play in the mainland American colonies after 1660, consolidating the transition to hereditary African slavery.

ALTERNATIVE SOURCES OF LABOR

The legal status of African newcomers to English North America became distinctly clearer and less hopeful in the decades after 1660. The transatlantic slave trade, already more than a century old, provided certain English colonies with a ready source of African workers at a time when more obvious streams of inexpensive labor—captured Native Americans and impoverished Europeans—were dwindling.

For labor-hungry colonists, Native Americans were close at hand and knew the country well. They took captives when fighting one another, so colonists could buy Indian prisoners or seize them in frontier warfare. Europeans felt they could enslave such people in good conscience, since they were non-Christians who had been taken captive in war. But Native American numbers were declining steadily, owing to epidemics. And those who did become enslaved knew the countryside well enough to escape. Besides, traffic in Indian slaves disrupted the profitable deerskin trade, undermined wilderness diplomacy, and sparked conflict on the frontier.

Efforts to maintain a steady flow of cheap labor from Europe ran into different problems. The Great Plague of 1665 devastated the English population, and the London Fire the following year created a new need for workers of all kinds to rebuild the capital. England's labor surplus, which had been a boon to the first colonies half a century earlier, rapidly disappeared. Those who made their living in English ports by procuring labor for America were forced to nab youngsters off the streets. But even this practice (called by the new word *kidnapping*) was soon outlawed.

What persisted, however, was the widespread use of **indentures.** These contracts allowed poor individuals to pay for their Atlantic passage by selling their labor for a fixed

> England's labor surplus, which had been a boon to the first colonies half a century earlier, rapidly disappeared.

length of time. When these men and women reached America, they were obliged to work for several years in return for food and shelter. Still, the prospect of an independent future appealed to newcomers arriving without property. As an incentive to draw additional immigrants, colonial officials made clear that servants who completed their indenture could expect "freedom dues" (clothes, tools, and food from their former master) and their own land to farm. Established planters sensed three drawbacks: the indenture system created high labor turnover; it put added pressure on limited land resources; and it constantly created additional competing farmers.

Equally important, when indentured servants were mistreated, they had little difficulty in relaying their complaints home to other potential workers. The flow of ships back and forth between Europe and North America grew steadily in the century after 1660, so word of places where indentured servants were regularly abused or swindled quickly reached the other side of the Atlantic. As Europeans mulled over private letters, coffeehouse gossip, and sailors' reports, they could adjust their own plans for migration. Depending on what they heard or read, they might postpone a voyage or seek a more promising destination.

In contrast, the African slave trade lacked any similar "feedback loop." People swept up in the growing stream of unfree African labor had no access to information regarding New World conditions. A mere handful, among hundreds of thousands of enslaved Africans, ever managed to communicate with their homeland. As a result, the brutal treatment of black

represented—in modern terminology—the emergence of slave labor camps. These people received no wages for their labor, had no legal rights, and could be moved to some other location at any time. This deterioration in conditions occurred first, and most dramatically, in Virginia, where several thousand African Americans lived and labored by the 1670s.

BLACK INVOLVEMENT IN BACON'S REBELLION

Nothing did more to consolidate Virginia's slide toward race slavery than Bacon's Rebellion, the major uprising that shook the Chesapeake region in 1676 (see Chapter 3). The episode pitted aspiring gentry, led by Nathaniel Bacon, against hard-pressed Indian groups on the frontier and an entrenched elite in Jamestown. The rebellion underscored the dilemma created by Virginia's reliance on a steady flow of white indentured servants to cultivate tobacco. That labor supply was uneven at best, and large-scale planters constantly needed new recruits, since terms of service lasted only several years. Workers who earned their freedom—hundreds every year— were predominantly young, armed men who demanded property of their own. Whether they had to take it from rich landholders or neighboring Indians made little difference to them.

> A letter reaching London that fall suggested that at the height of the rebellion Bacon had "proclaimed liberty to all Servants and Negroes."

Free men, would-be farmers in search of land, made up part of Bacon's following, but diverse unfree workers also proved eager recruits. Such ill-treated people remained legally bound to large landholders for varying terms, and many of the Africans were undoubtedly bound for life. Together, they raised much of the colony's annual tobacco crop. The backbreaking labor prompted frequent unrest. These ragged workers, however long their term of service might be, had the most to gain and the least to lose from Bacon's revolt. According to the Virginia Assembly, "many evil disposed servants . . . taking advantage of the loosenes of the tymes . . . followed the rebells in rebellion." When Bacon fell ill and died in October 1676, many of his wealthier supporters reasserted their loyalty to the colonial government. But bound workers who had escaped from their masters continued the fight.

A letter reaching London that fall suggested that at the height of the rebellion Bacon had "proclaimed liberty to all Servants and Negroes." Clearly, the widespread unrest had given hope to the most downtrodden tobacco pickers, about a quarter of whom were black. As a Royal Commission put it, "sundry servants and other persons of desperate fortunes" had "deserted their masters and run into rebellion on the encouragement of liberty." When military reinforcements arrived in Chesapeake Bay from England in November, their commanding officer, Captain Thomas Grantham, found hundreds of laborers still in active revolt.

Impressed by their strength, Grantham chose to use deceit when he met with 800 heavily armed rebels, both white and black, at their headquarters near the York River. By distributing brandy and making vague promises regarding pardons and freedom, he persuaded most of the white men to surrender and return home. Only about "Eighty Negroes and Twenty English . . . would not deliver their Armes." According to Grantham, they threatened to kill him, asserting that they wanted "their hoped for liberty and would not quietly laye downe their armes." But when these last holdouts boarded a sloop to head downriver, Grantham disarmed the rebels and chained them below decks for return to their masters.

THE RISE OF A SLAVEHOLDING TIDEWATER ELITE

With Bacon's death and the arrival of British ships, propertied Virginians had narrowly averted a successful multiracial revolution, fueled from below by workers who resented their distressed condition. But clearly some future revolt might succeed, so the great planters of

■ A small minority of enslaved Africans became house servants to wealthy families in England and America. Though set apart from the black community and denied entry into white society, many traveled widely and described the outside world to fellow slaves confined to field labor.

the Chesapeake region moved to tighten their hold on political and economic power. After Bacon's Rebellion, a strategy of divide and conquer seemed in order. They moved to improve conditions for poor whites in ways that would reduce tension between classes and ensure deference and racial solidarity among Europeans. At the same time, they further reduced the legal status of blacks, solidifying their enslavement for life and increasing penalties for any show of opposition or dissent.

For precedent, the planters had the model provided by slavery-based colonial societies in the West Indies, including the English sugar island of Barbados. Their uneasiness continued over importing non-Christian strangers who spoke little, if any, English. But such doubts were more than offset by the prospect of laying claim to the children of slaves and to the lives and labor of all generations to come. Every child of every enslaved African woman became an additional worker, acquired by the master at no extra cost. These same women, moreover, were often more familiar with agricultural tasks than European servant women. Besides, planters could exploit black women and men more ruthlessly than they could whites, since there was no feedback to Africa affecting future labor supplies.

Increasing life expectancy in the Chesapeake region, resulting from sturdier dwellings and more stable living conditions, further motivated planters to move away from a workforce of indentured servants. For a self-interested planter, longer lives meant that a white indentured person, after serving only a few years, would become yet another long-term competitor in the crowded tobacco market. In contrast, Africans enslaved for life would yield profitable service for an increasingly long time. And they would be more likely than ever to produce healthy offspring. Boys and girls who survived childhood could then be forced to clear more land to grow additional crops.

Among a circle of wealthy investors, the enticement of such an economic bonanza overcame any cultural anxieties. The sudden lure of enormous gain outweighed any moral or religious scruples. Seizing the moment, these aggressive entrepreneurs established themselves as the leading families of Virginia. William Byrd was an apt example. The son of an English goldsmith, Byrd took over his uncle's trading post near the falls of the James River at age eighteen and soon married into a prominent family. As a frontier resident, he joined briefly in Bacon's uprising. But by the 1680s, he occupied a seat on Virginia's council and held several high financial posts. With his salary, he bought up his neighbors' tobacco and shipped it to England. He then used the proceeds to purchase cloth, kettles, muskets, and beads for the Indian trade. After exchanging these goods for deerskins, he exported the skins at a profit. In return, he imported trade goods from London and slaves and rum from the Caribbean, all of which he sold to small planters for more tobacco so the lucrative cycle could begin again.

In the 1690s, Byrd moved his operations closer to the seat of power, which remained at Jamestown until the capital shifted to nearby Williamsburg in 1699. He established a large estate at Westover, on the north bank of the James River, where he used scores of imported slaves to expand his assets and launch a family dynasty. By the 1730s, Byrd's son, like other wealthy slave owners, came to fear a "servile war" so violent that it would "tinge our rivers, as wide as they are, with blood."

For early merchant-planters such as the Byrds, the enormous profits offered by slavery outweighed the calculated risks. These ambitious men expected that the English-speaking Africans already present could assist in teaching newcomers to receive orders. They also assumed that slave laborers from diverse African societies could not communicate well enough with one another to cause dangerous disturbances. And of course, having now made skin color a determining feature of social order, they knew that black runaways could be spotted and apprehended readily in the free white community.

> *Wealthy slave owners came to fear a "servile war" so violent that it would "tinge our rivers, as wide as they are, with blood."*

CLOSING THE VICIOUS CIRCLE IN THE CHESAPEAKE

As the profitability of slavery increased, so did its appeal. By 1700, some 4,500 people were enslaved in Maryland in a total population of 35,000. And the colony's assembly was taking further measures to encourage the importation of slaves. Growing demand meant that merchants and sea captains who had only occasionally dabbled in the transportation of slaves now devoted more time and larger ships to the enterprise. Expansion of the slave-trading infrastructure made African workers readily available and affordable.

As the supply of enslaved black newcomers grew larger, planters eager to strengthen their position manipulated the established headright system. Traditionally, under this system, the colonial government granted to any arriving head of household fifty acres for every family member or hired hand he brought into the colony. The incentive was intended to spur migration from Europe, expand the free population, and develop the land through the establishment of family farms. But the wealthy planters who saw African slavery as a profitable labor source also controlled Virginia's legal system. For their own benefit, therefore, they extended the headright system so that a land bonus also went to anyone who purchased an African arrival as a lifelong slave. Thus, before the seventeenth century closed, a Virginia investor buying twenty slaves could also lay claim to headrights worth 1,000 acres of land.

To consolidate their new regime, planters worked through the church and the legislature to separate whites from blacks socially and legally. They undermined the position of free blacks and stigmatized interracial ties. A 1691 Virginia statute decried the "abominable mixture and spurious issue" that resulted from "Negroes, mulattoes and Indians intermarrying" with English or other white people. All such couples were "banished from this dominion forever." It also prohibited masters from freeing any black or mulatto unless they paid to transport that person out of the colony within six months.

Virginia's Negro Act of 1705 further underscored the stark new boundaries. It mandated that white servants who were mistreated had the right to sue their masters in county court. Slaves, in contrast, had no such right. Any enslaved person who tried to escape could be tortured and even dismembered in hopes of "terrifying others" from seeking freedom. When masters or overseers killed a slave while inflicting punishment, they were automatically free of any felony charge, "as if such accident had never happened." And if slaves were killed or put to death by law, the owners would be paid public funds for the loss of their "property." In scarcely forty years, prominent whites had used the law to transform the labor system of the Chesapeake, entrapping Africans and their descendants in perpetual slavery.

DOCUMENT

Of the Servants and
Slaves in Virginia
(1705)

England Enters the Atlantic Slave Trade

■ *Why did England, once suspicious of the trade, become a leader in transporting enslaved Africans?*

The Atlantic slave trade was the largest and longest-lasting deportation in human history. In nearly four centuries, more than 10 million people were torn from their homelands against their will and transported to the Caribbean and to Central, South, and North America. Several million more perished in transit. By 1700, more Africans than Europeans had already crossed the Atlantic to the Western Hemisphere. Their numbers grew over the following century as the commerce reached its height. As for the importation of Africans to *North* America, that part of the traffic expanded after 1700, but it remained a small portion of the overall Atlantic slave trade.

England took little part in the trade at first. However, the development of Barbados as a lucrative sugar colony and the expansion of English overseas ambitions changed matters quickly after 1640. In 1652, Prince Rupert, a nephew of the late Charles I, visited Gambia in sub-Saharan Africa and saw profits to be made. With the restoration of the English monarchy in 1660, Rupert's cousin Charles II immediately granted a monopoly on African trade to a small group of adventurers, and in 1672 he chartered the powerful new Royal African Company (RAC).

The RAC dispatched a steady flow of merchant ships along a triangular trade route. The first leg took captains to English outposts along the coast of West Africa, where they exchanged textiles, guns, and iron bars for gold, ivory, and enslaved Africans. After a transatlantic **middle passage** of one to three months, the captains sold slaves and took on sugar in the West Indies before returning to England on the final leg of the triangle.

> By 1700, more Africans than Europeans had already crossed the Atlantic to the Western Hemisphere.

The lure of profits prompted interlopers to horn in on the RAC traffic with increasing success. When the company's monopoly ended officially in 1698, English slave trading ballooned. In the mainland colonies, boat builders and ship owners from Boston to Charleston sought out a portion of the trade, concentrating first on links to the Caribbean. In 1713, England obtained the *asiento*, the lucrative contract to deliver Africans to Spain's colonies in America. By the 1730s, British ships controlled the largest share of the Atlantic slave trade. They continued to dominate the traffic for the next seventy years.

TRADE TIES BETWEEN EUROPE AND AFRICA

By the 1680s, it had been two centuries since Portuguese sailors had visited Africa's western shores and established a post at Elmina, in modern-day Ghana. Dozens of these depots, controlled by rival European powers and their local allies, dotted the sub-Saharan coastline. (They became known as *factories*—an early use of the word—since a factor, or manager, ran each imperial trading post.) This string of European outposts began at the mouth of the Senegal River, just above Cape Verde, the continent's westernmost point; it ended below the mouth of the Congo River, in present-day Angola. In between, the coastline curved some 5,000 miles. It embraced diverse geographic environments—from open savannas to thick forests—and scores of distinctive cultures. All along this coastline, villagers caught fish and gathered salt for trade with herders and farmers living farther inland.

Generations of contact with oceangoing ships brought new pressures and opportunities to African coastal communities. Local merchants formed alliances with European partners to trade gold and ivory to sea captains for imported textiles and alcohol. People with links to several cultures became crucial to this competitive commerce. Just as outsiders occupied posts on the African coast to learn local ways, an important African occasionally traveled north by ship to gain knowledge of European languages, ideas, and religion. For example, Aniaga, the brother of the king of Guinea, was sent to France around 1680.

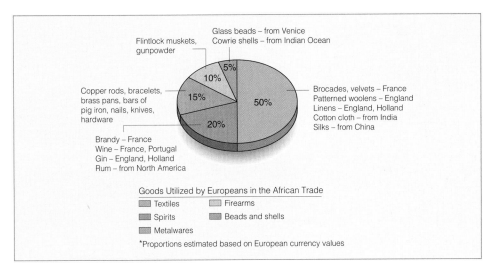

Goods Utilized by Europeans in the African Trade

- Textiles
- Spirits
- Metalwares
- Firearms
- Beads and shells

*Proportions estimated based on European currency values

■ **FIGURE 4.1**
Goods Traded in Africa

As European ship captains expanded trade along the African coast, they tailored their cargoes to suit the demands of local markets.

When the African prince reached Paris, Louis XIV "was pleas'd to have him Educated, Instructed and Baptiz'd." Aniaga eventually became a respected captain in the French military, but after several decades he expressed a desire to return home. He promised to promote the work of French traders and missionaries, so "his Majesty loaded him with Presents, and order'd a Ship to carry him back to Guinea." In later years, Europeans complained that Aniaga "no longer remember'd he had been baptiz'd." Still, the prince often "express'd much Gratitude for the Kindness that had been shewn him in France." As an important local figure, he became a courteous and influential visitor aboard French ships reaching the Guinea coast.

THE SLAVE TRADE ON THE AFRICAN COAST

As sugar production expanded across the Atlantic, well-connected African traders responded to the growing demand for human labor. They consolidated their positions near suitable harbors and navigable rivers. From there, they bartered local servants and war captives to white agents (factors). In return, they obtained linen, beads, metal wares, and muskets, items that enhanced their prestige and let them extend their inland trading networks.

■ Slaves were held as prisoners in the interior before being marched to the African coast in groups known as coffles.

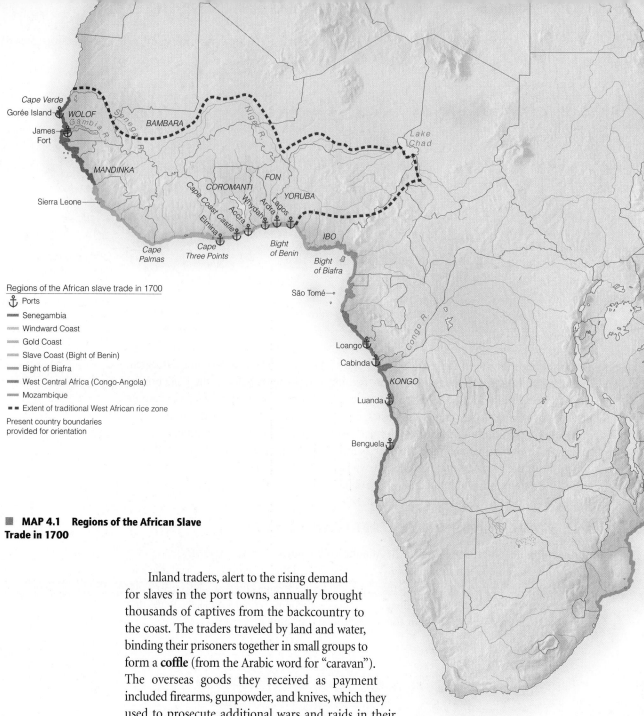

Regions of the African slave trade in 1700
⚓ Ports
━━ Senegambia
━━ Windward Coast
━━ Gold Coast
━━ Slave Coast (Bight of Benin)
━━ Bight of Biafra
━━ West Central Africa (Congo-Angola)
━━ Mozambique
■ ■ Extent of traditional West African rice zone
Present country boundaries
provided for orientation

■ **MAP 4.1   Regions of the African Slave
Trade in 1700**

Inland traders, alert to the rising demand
for slaves in the port towns, annually brought
thousands of captives from the backcountry to
the coast. The traders traveled by land and water,
binding their prisoners together in small groups to
form a **coffle** (from the Arabic word for "caravan").
The overseas goods they received as payment
included firearms, gunpowder, and knives, which they
used to prosecute additional wars and raids in their
homelands and to secure more captives.

By the 1660s and 1670s, the pace of deportation
across the Atlantic had reached an average rate of
nearly 15,000 people each year. It rose steadily to a high
of more than 65,000 people per year a century later. As the traffic grew, it became
increasingly organized, competitive, and routine. Shrewd African traders played one
European vessel against another for the best deals and hid illness among captives. When
they saw that a ship was eager to depart, they increased their prices. Hardened European
agents stockpiled the wares that African traders most wanted. They also learned to curry
favor with local officials and to quell unrest among captives, confined in the holding
pens known as **barracoons.** Experienced captains timed their ventures to avoid the
months when sickness was most rampant in the tropics. Through repeated voyages,
improved charts, and accumulated lore, they came to differentiate and exploit half a
dozen major slaving regions along Africa's Atlantic coast. Occasionally, they even ventured to Mozambique in southeast Africa and the nearby island of Madagascar.

The closest market where Europeans bargained for goods and slaves was Senegambia, or the northern parts of Guinea, between the Senegal River and the Gambia River. Gorée Island, off the coast of Senegal, and James Fort, located in the mouth of the Gambia, served as slave trading centers. The long Windward Coast extending to the southeast beyond Sierra Leone became known for its pepper and grain and for ivory in the south beyond Cape Palmas. To the east, from the area of Cape Three Points and Elmina to the factory at Accra, stretched the Gold Coast. There, the Portuguese had established Elmina to draw trade from the Asante gold fields in the interior. Farther east, the Slave Coast reached along the Bight of Benin to the huge delta of the Niger River. Trading depots at Whydah, Ardra, and Lagos drew captives from secondary ports in between. Beyond the Niger, where the African coast again turns south near Cameroon, lay the Bight of Biafra. English captains quickly learned the preferences for trade goods in each district, carrying textiles to the Gold Coast, cowrie shells to the Slave Coast, and metals to the Bight of Biafra.

The largest and most southerly slave-trading region along Africa's Atlantic coast was known as Congo-Angola or West Central Africa. Here, Catholic missionaries established footholds, and Portuguese traders exported slave labor for sugar production in Brazil and the Caribbean. Before 1700, more than half of all Atlantic slaves departed from West Central Africa. In the eighteenth century, the proportion remained over one-third, as French and English interests came to dominate the slave traffic out of Loango and Cabinda, north of the Congo River. South of the great waterway, the Portuguese continued to hold the upper hand at Luanda and Benguela. During the entire span of the slave trade, the Congo-Angola hinterland furnished roughly 40 percent of all African deportees to the Americas: more than 4.5 million men, women, and children.

THE MIDDLE PASSAGE EXPERIENCE

For every person the exodus was different. Harrowing individual stories depended on the particulars of how old the captives were, where they had lived, and how they were captured. Nevertheless, the long nightmare of deportation contained similar elements for all who fell victim to the transatlantic trade. The entire journey, from normal village life to enslavement beyond the ocean, could last a year or two. It unfolded in at least five stages, beginning with capture and transport to the African coast. The initial loss of freedom—the first experience of bound hands, harsh treatment, and forced marches—was made worse by the encounters with strange landscapes and unfamiliar languages. Hunger, fatigue, and anxiety took a steady toll as coffles of young and old were conveyed slowly toward the coast through a network of traders.

The next phase, sale and imprisonment, began when a contingent reached the sea. During this stage, which could last several months, African traders transferred "ownership" of the captives to Europeans. Many buyers subjected their new property to demeaning inspections and burned brands into their skin. Then they were put in irons alongside hundreds of other captives and guarded in a secure spot to prevent escape. For example, the underground dungeon at Cape Coast Castle on the Gold Coast had walls fourteen feet thick. A visitor in 1682 observed that the RAC's fortress provided "good security . . . against any insurrection."

Werner Forman Archive/Art Resource, NY

■ England's Royal African Company maintained more than a dozen small posts along the Gold Coast. Each outpost funneled slaves to this strong seventy-four-gun fortress known as Cape Coast Castle. Cut into rock beneath the parade ground, the vaulted dungeon inside could "conveniently contain a thousand Blacks...against any insurrection."

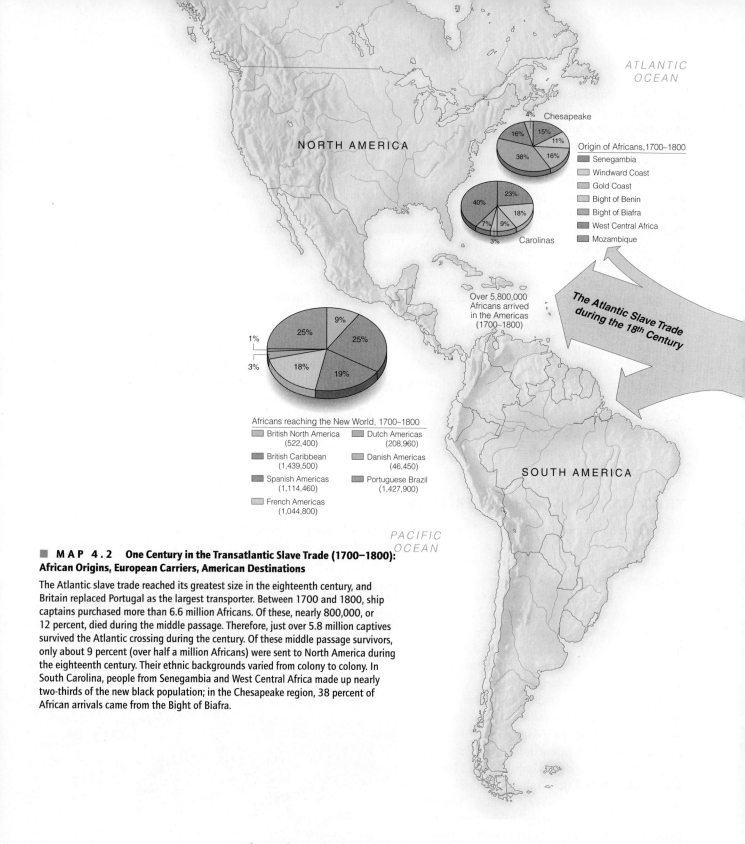

ATLANTIC OCEAN

NORTH AMERICA

Chesapeake

4%
16% 15%
      11%
38% 16%

Origin of Africans, 1700–1800
- Senegambia
- Windward Coast
- Gold Coast
- Bight of Benin
- Bight of Biafra
- West Central Africa
- Mozambique

23%
40% 18%
7% 9%
   3%
Carolinas

Over 5,800,000 Africans arrived in the Americas (1700–1800)

The Atlantic Slave Trade during the 18th Century

9%
25% 25%
1%
3% 18% 19%

Africans reaching the New World, 1700–1800
- British North America (522,400)
- British Caribbean (1,439,500)
- Spanish Americas (1,114,460)
- French Americas (1,044,800)
- Dutch Americas (208,960)
- Danish Americas (46,450)
- Portuguese Brazil (1,427,900)

SOUTH AMERICA

PACIFIC OCEAN

■ MAP 4.2 One Century in the Transatlantic Slave Trade (1700–1800): African Origins, European Carriers, American Destinations

The Atlantic slave trade reached its greatest size in the eighteenth century, and Britain replaced Portugal as the largest transporter. Between 1700 and 1800, ship captains purchased more than 6.6 million Africans. Of these, nearly 800,000, or 12 percent, died during the middle passage. Therefore, just over 5.8 million captives survived the Atlantic crossing during the century. Of these middle passage survivors, only about 9 percent (over half a million Africans) were sent to North America during the eighteenth century. Their ethnic backgrounds varied from colony to colony. In South Carolina, people from Senegambia and West Central Africa made up nearly two-thirds of the new black population; in the Chesapeake region, 38 percent of African arrivals came from the Bight of Biafra.

When a ship arrived, canoes transported the captives through the surf to the waiting vessel. Once aboard, prisoners might languish in the sweltering hold for weeks while the captain cruised the coast in search of additional human cargo. According to one English trader, "the negroes were so wilful and loth to leave their own country, that they often leap'd out of the canoes, boat and ship, into the sea, and kept under water till they were drowned." Crewmembers sometimes raised nets surrounding the deck to prevent attempts at escape or suicide.

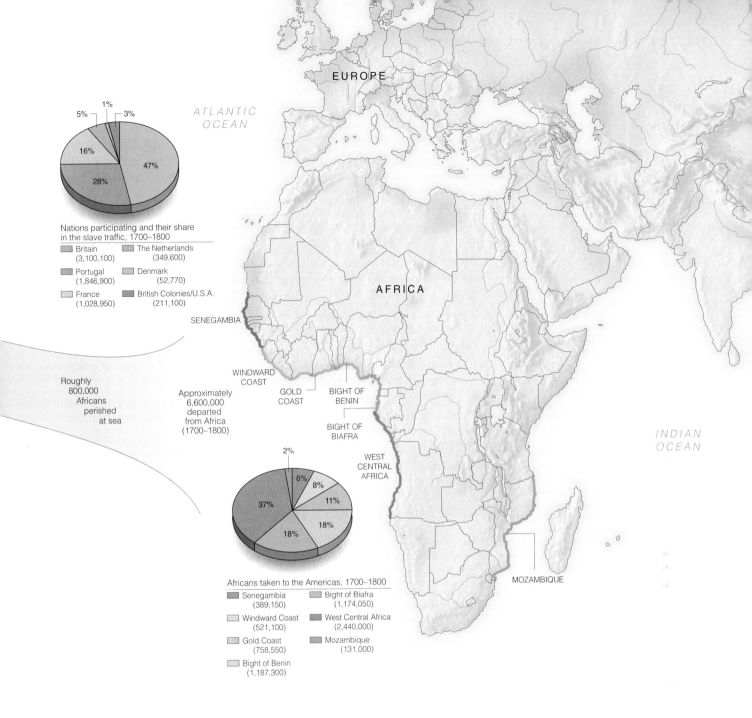

ATLANTIC
OCEAN

EUROPE

Nations participating and their share
in the slave traffic, 1700–1800

- Britain (3,100,100)
- Portugal (1,846,900)
- France (1,028,950)
- The Netherlands (349,600)
- Denmark (52,770)
- British Colonies/U.S.A. (211,100)

AFRICA

Roughly 800,000 Africans perished at sea

Approximately 6,600,000 departed from Africa (1700–1800)

SENEGAMBIA

WINDWARD COAST

GOLD COAST

BIGHT OF BENIN

BIGHT OF BIAFRA

WEST CENTRAL AFRICA

INDIAN OCEAN

MOZAMBIQUE

Africans taken to the Americas, 1700–1800

- Senegambia (389,150)
- Windward Coast (521,100)
- Gold Coast (758,550)
- Bight of Benin (1,187,300)
- Bight of Biafra (1,174,050)
- West Central Africa (2,440,000)
- Mozambique (131,000)

The ship's captain decided when to begin crossing the Atlantic, the harrowing third phase that constituted the actual middle passage. If he lingered too long to obtain more slaves at lower prices, he risked depleting his food supplies and raising the death toll among his crew and prisoners. If he departed too soon in an effort to shorten the voyage and preserve lives, including his own, he risked missing a drop in prices or a new contingent of slaves that could absorb his remaining stock of trade goods and bring more profits. He had to balance the danger of late summer hurricanes in the Caribbean against the need to arrive in America when harvests were complete—the time when planters had crops to send to Europe and money or credit to invest in African workers.

The Africans aboard each ship knew nothing of such calculations. Even those who had spent time serving as slaves among fellow Africans or fishing in coastal waters now faced an utterly alien plight, trapped in a strange wooden hull. When the crew finally raised anchor and unfurled the vessel's huge sails, the captives could only anticipate

IMAGE

Diagram of a Slave Ship
Filled for Middle
Passage

Alexander
Falconbridge, the
African Slave Trade
(1788)

the worst. Already the crowded hold of the ship had become foul, and the wooden buckets used as latrines had taken on a loathsome smell. The rolling of the ship on ocean swells brought seasickness and painful chafing from lying on the bare planks. Alexander Falconbridge, who sailed as a surgeon on several slave ships, recorded that "those who are emaciated frequently have their skin and even their flesh entirely rubbed off, by the motion of the ship, from the . . . shoulders, elbows and hips so as to render the bones quite bare."

Historians have documented more than 27,000 slave voyages, and an array of variables shaped each Atlantic crossing. Factors included the exact point of departure, the planned destination, the season of the year, the length of the journey, the supplies of food and fresh water, the navigational skills of the captain and crew, the condition of the vessel, the health and resolve of the prisoners, the vagaries of piracy and ocean warfare, and the ravages of disease. A change in weather conditions or in the captain's mood could mean the difference between life and death. The *Emperor*, crossing from Angola to South Carolina in 1755 with 390 Africans aboard, encountered a storm that lasted for a week. By the time the heavy seas subsided, 120 people had died in the hold.

Olauda Equiano, The
Middle Passage (1788)

While the grim details varied, the overall pattern remained the same. Ship after ship, year after year, the attrition continued. The constant rolling of the vessel; the sharp changes in temperature; the crowded, dark, and filthy conditions; and the relentless physical pain and mental anguish took a heavy toll. Pregnant mothers gave birth or miscarried; women were subjected to abuse and rape by the crew. Sailors threw the bodies of those who died to the sharks or, worse still, used them as bait to catch sharks, which they fed to the remaining captives.

SALTWATER SLAVES ARRIVE IN AMERICA

For the emaciated survivors of the Atlantic ordeal, two further stages remained in their descent into slavery: the selling process and the time called "seasoning." The selling process on American soil varied widely and could drag on for weeks or months after the ship dropped anchor. Prospective owners examined and prodded the newcomers in dockside holding pens. Those purchased were wrenched away from their compatriots and the shipmates with whom they had formed strong links during their shared miseries at sea. Slaves often were auctioned off in groups, or parcels, to ensure sale of the weak along with the strong. Then another journey brought them to the particular plantation where they were fated to work and probably to die.

Sale Notice

Most newcomers did not begin their forced labor immediately. Instead, they entered a final stage, known as seasoning, which lasted several months or longer. The strangers were distinguished as "saltwater slaves"—in contrast to "country-born slaves" who had

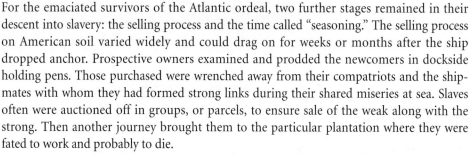

The strangers were distinguished as "saltwater slaves"—in contrast to "country-born slaves" who had grown up in America from birth.

grown up in America from birth. Seasoning gave them time to mend physically, regain their strength, and begin learning a new language. Inevitably, many suffered from what we now describe as posttraumatic stress syndrome.

As adults and children recovered from the trauma of the middle passage, they faced a series of additional shocks. Around them they found other Africans who had survived earlier voyages and still spoke their traditional languages. In conversation, they gradually learned where they were and what lay in store for them. They confronted strange foods, unfamiliar tasks, and even new names. They faced alien landscapes and unfamiliar diseases. Worst of all, they encountered a master or his overseer who made every effort to break the wills of these fresh arrivals and to turn them into compliant bondservants. Repeatedly, the powerful stranger used arbitrary force to demand the newcomers' obedience, destroy their hope, and crush any thoughts of resistance.

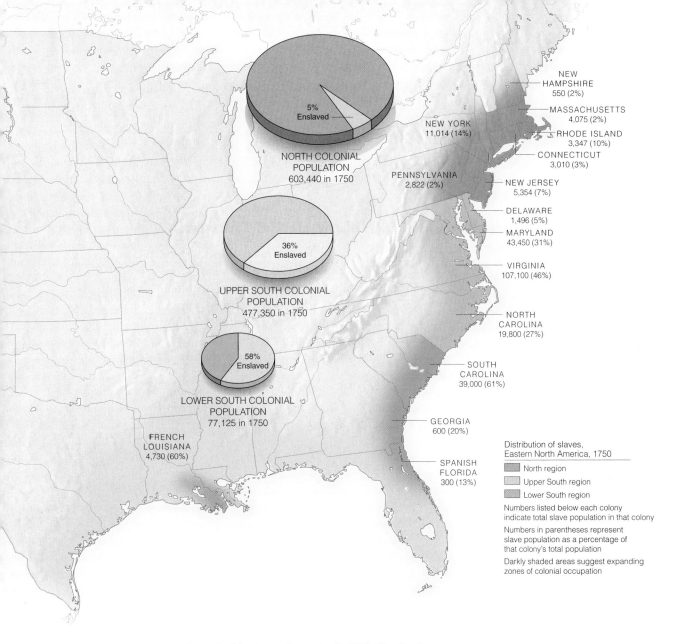

NEW
HAMPSHIRE
550 (2%)

MASSACHUSETTS
4,075 (2%)

RHODE ISLAND
3,347 (10%)

CONNECTICUT
3,010 (3%)

NEW JERSEY
5,354 (7%)

DELAWARE
1,496 (5%)

MARYLAND
43,450 (31%)

VIRGINIA
107,100 (46%)

NORTH
CAROLINA
19,800 (27%)

SOUTH
CAROLINA
39,000 (61%)

GEORGIA
600 (20%)

SPANISH
FLORIDA
300 (13%)

NEW YORK
11,014 (14%)

PENNSYLVANIA
2,822 (2%)

5%
Enslaved

NORTH COLONIAL
POPULATION
603,440 in 1750

36%
Enslaved

UPPER SOUTH COLONIAL
POPULATION
477,350 in 1750

58%
Enslaved

LOWER SOUTH COLONIAL
POPULATION
77,125 in 1750

FRENCH
LOUISIANA
4,730 (60%)

Distribution of slaves,
Eastern North America, 1750

North region

Upper South region

Lower South region

Numbers listed below each colony
indicate total slave population in that colony

Numbers in parentheses represent
slave population as a percentage of
that colony's total population

Darkly shaded areas suggest expanding
zones of colonial occupation

■ **MAP 4.3   Enslaved People Living in North America in 1750: Distribution
by Colony, Percentage of Total Population**

By 1750, nearly a quarter of a million people lived as slaves in eastern North America—more than 21 percent
of the colonial population. Almost all were Africans or the descendants of Africans, along with a few
thousand Native American and mixed-race slaves. In the North, slaves made up a small fraction of a large
population. By far the greatest number of slaves lived in the Chesapeake area, where they made up more
than a third of the total population. Enslaved people were less numerous but much more concentrated in the
lower South, making up a clear majority of the overall inhabitants. White settlers had already smuggled
several hundred slaves into the fledgling colony of Georgia, even though the exploitation of slave labor did
not become legal there until 1751.

Survival in a Strange New Land

■ *How did diverse Africans find common ground for resistance as slaves in America?*

By 1700, race slavery was accepted throughout the mainland colonies. Africans found
themselves scattered from northern New England to Gulf Coast Louisiana. But their
distribution was far from even. Among roughly 247,000 slaves in the colonies in 1750,
only 30,000 (or 12 percent) resided in the North, where they made up just 5 percent of the
overall population from Pennsylvania to New Hampshire. More than one-third of these

northerners (11,000) lived in the colony of New York, where they constituted 14 percent of the non-Indian inhabitants. All the rest of the people of African descent in North America—some 217,000 men, women, and children by the mid-eighteenth century—lived and worked in the Chesapeake region and the lower South. Fewer than 500 of these black southerners were in Spanish Florida, and fewer than 5,000 resided in French Louisiana.

AFRICAN RICE GROWERS IN SOUTH CAROLINA

Throughout the eighteenth century, by far the most North American slaves lived in Virginia or Maryland: 150,000 African Americans by 1750. But the highest *proportion* of enslaved workers lived in South Carolina, where Africans began outnumbering Europeans as early as 1708. By 1750, this black majority (40,000 people) constituted more than 60 percent of the colony's population. Almost all had arrived through the deepwater port of Charleston. Sullivan's Island, near the entrance to the harbor, with its **pest house** to quarantine incoming slaves and reduce the spread of shipborne disease, has been called the Ellis Island of black America.

What explains the emergence of South Carolina's slave concentration? For one thing, the colony was closer than Virginia to Africa and to the Caribbean. Moreover, it had been founded in 1670, just as the English were embracing plantation slavery and the African trade.

Alive Ravenel Huger Smith, *The Threshing Floor with a Winnowing-House (The Carolina Rice Plantation Series)*. Gibbes Museum of Art/California Art Association (37.09.22)

■ Rice plantations that emerged in coastal South Carolina around 1700 became labor camps where enslaved blacks were confined for generations, without wages or legal rights. In the 1850s, distant descendants of the region's first African workers were still being forced to plant, harvest, and process the huge rice crops that made their masters rich.

Indeed, some of the colony's original proprietors owned stakes in the Royal African Company. Also, some of Carolina's influential early settlers came directly from Barbados, bringing enslaved Africans and planter ambitions with them.

In the earliest days of colonization in South Carolina, newcomers lacked sufficient labor to clear coastal forests and plant crops. Instead, they let their cattle and pigs run wild. With easy foraging and warm winters, the animals reproduced rapidly. The settlers slaughtered them and shipped their meat to the Caribbean, along with firewood for boiling sugar cane and wooden barrels for transporting sugar. Ship captains also carried enslaved Native Americans to the West Indies and brought back African slaves.

The arriving Africans understood South Carolina's subtropical climate, with its alligators and palmetto trees, better than their European owners did. Many of these enslaved newcomers were already familiar with keeping cattle. Others, obliged to feed themselves, began growing rice in the fertile swamplands just as they had in West Africa. Half a century before, a brief experiment with rice in the Chesapeake region proved short lived. But a Virginia observer in 1648 had noted that the southern soil and climate seemed "very proper" for the cultivation of rice, "as our Negroes affirme," adding that rice "in their Country is most of their food."

South Carolina slave owners quickly realized that this plant, unfamiliar to much of northern Europe, held the answer to their search for a profitable staple crop. Soon, people who had tended their own irrigated rice crops near the Gambia River were obliged to clear cypress swamps along the Ashley and Cooper rivers to grow rice for someone else. Women who had prepared small portions of rice daily for their families in West Africa—pounding the grains with a wooden pestle to remove the husks, then tossing them in a broad, flat basket to winnow away the chaff—now had to process vast quantities of rice for export.

Before long, people in England had developed a taste for rice pudding, and London merchants were shipping tons of Carolina rice to other European countries, where it proved a cheap grain for feeding soldiers, orphans, and peasants. By the middle of the eighteenth century, South Carolina's white minority had the most favorable trade balance of any mainland colonists. Their fortunes improved even more when indigo, another African crop, joined rice as a profitable export commodity. Outnumbered by their enslaved workers, South Carolina's landowners passed strict Negro Acts patterned on those of the Caribbean. Legislation prohibited slaves from carrying guns, meeting in groups, raising livestock, or traveling without a pass. Statutes controlled everything from how they dressed to when they shoveled the dung off of Charleston streets. Everywhere, mounted patrols enforced the regulations with brutal severity.

> *The arriving Africans understood South Carolina's subtropical climate better than their European owners did.*

PATTERNS OF RESISTANCE

In South Carolina and elsewhere, enslaved African Americans pushed against the narrow boundaries of their lives. Like any other imprisoned population, they pressed to relieve their condition in any possible way. Time and again, they spread rumors, refused to work, broke tools, feigned illness, or threatened violence. In response, their owners tried to divide them in order to control them. Masters rewarded workers who acted obedient and diligent or who informed on fellow slaves. They imposed harsh punishments—whipping, mutilation, sale, or death—on those suspected of taking food, sowing dissent, or plotting revolt. And they encouraged the formation of black families, not only to gain another generation of laborers at no cost but also to create the emotional ties that they knew would hold individuals in check for fear of reprisals against loved ones.

Owners confined residents in the slave labor camps with curfews and pass systems and kept them from learning to read and from communicating freely with neighbors and

Drums and Banjos: African Sounds in English Colonies

■ Few African instruments survive from the colonial era. This Virginia slave drum resembles Ashanti drums in Ghana. African banjoes became common in the South.

In every area of life, the earliest African Americans blended remembered portions of diverse African cultures with strange new variations acquired from Europeans and Native Americans in the New World. Despite the harsh conditions of enslavement, this pattern of combining new and old applied to food and clothing, language and movement, housing and hairstyles. This mixing of worlds also appeared in the realm of music.

Once in America, Africans recreated cherished instruments they had left behind. Drums such as this slave drum from Virginia, which is similar to Ashanti drums in Ghana, reappeared quickly, and

Africans who had used drums to convey messages shared this skill with others. Conch shells and cow-horn trumpets could also send signals. In 1740, anxious South Carolina legislators outlawed slaves from "using or keeping drums, horns, or other loud instruments, which may call together, or give sign or notice to one another of their wicked designs and purposes." The Virginia militia, however, recruited free blacks "as Drummers and Trumpeters."

The most prominent African instrument was the banjo. "The instrument proper to them," Jefferson observed, "is the banjar, which they brought hither from Africa." A Maryland minister recalled, "the favorite and almost only instrument in use among the slaves there was a bandore; or, as they pronounced the word, banjer. Its body was a large hollow gourd, with a long handle attached to it, strung with catgut, and played on with the fingers."

Eventually, white musicians began making and playing their own banjos, just as black musicians soon took up the European violin. John Marrant, a young free black in colonial Charleston, remembered spending most evenings with older musicians. "My improvement was so rapid that in a twelve-month's time I became master of both the violin and the French horn." African American fiddlers became common in the South, playing African and English melodies, and much that lay in between.

QUESTIONS

1. How did musical traditions as different as spirituals, jazz, and blues eventually emerge from the African American experience?

2. How would music have assisted African Americans in resisting the most corrosive effects of generations of forced bondage?

relatives. They also refused to allow any impartial system for expressing grievances or appealing arbitrary punishments. Faced with such steep odds, many slaves submitted to the deadening routine of the prison camp to survive. But others resorted to diverse strategies to improve their situation or undermine their masters' dominance. Running away, even for a brief period, provided relief from forced work and deprived owners of the labor they depended on. Because arson created serious damage and was difficult to detect, some slaves burned down barns at harvest time. Others succeeded in killing their masters or overseers. Such acts of pent-up rage usually proved suicidal, but they also confirmed slave owners' worst fears. Realizing that many Africans could communicate using drums and could concoct poisons from herbs, white planters became even more fearful of blacks.

Above all, the prospect of open rebellion burned in the minds of prisoners and jailers alike. Often, therefore, it is hard to untangle episodes of white paranoia from incidents of actual revolt. Many innocent slaves were falsely accused. But countless others did discuss plans for resistance, and a few freedom fighters avoided detection or betrayal long enough to launch serious uprisings. Word of one upheaval, real or imagined, could spark others.

An early wave of slave unrest erupted in the dozen years after 1710, highlighted by violence in New York City in the spring of 1712. The leaders of the conspiracy were "Coromantee," or Akan people from Africa's Gold Coast region. Several dozen enslaved Africans and Indians, determined to obtain their freedom and kill all the whites in the town, set fire to a building. As citizens rushed to put out the blaze, the rebels attacked them with guns, clubs, pistols, staves, and axes, killing eight and wounding more. When the militia finally captured the insurgents, six of them committed suicide. Authorities executed eighteen, burning several at the stake, hanging others and leaving their bodies on display. Eager to curtail slavery following such unrest, the governor called for "the Importation of White Servants." New York's elected colonial assembly, expressing growing racial hatred, chastised free blacks and prohibited freed slaves from owning property.

A WAVE OF REBELLION

A second wave of black resistance swept the mainland colonies after 1730, fueled by the largest influx of Africans to date. In Louisiana, the French had moved their capital to the new town of New Orleans on the Mississippi River (1722) and had joined their Choctaw allies in a devastating war to crush the Natchez Indians and seize their lands (1729–1731). As French landowners staked out riverfront plantations, they also imported African slaves. The several thousand black workers soon outnumbered European settlers.

Fearful of attack, Louisiana's whites broke up two presumed slave plots in 1731. One involved a scheme to rebel while Catholic colonists attended a midnight mass on Christmas. Another apparent plot was revealed by the careless boast of a black servant woman in New Orleans. It included several hundred Bambara newcomers from Senegal who aspired to massacre whites, enslave other Africans, and take control of the region. The leader was a man known as Samba Bambara, a former interpreter at Galam on the Senegal River. Bambara had lost that post and been deported to Louisiana, where he became a trusted slave, supervising workers owned by the French Company of the Indies. When torture by fire failed to force confessions from the key suspects, officials hanged the servant woman. Then Bambara and half a dozen other men were "broken on the wheel" (put to death slowly by being tied to wagon wheels and having their bones broken).

The largest slave uprising in colonial North America broke out in 1739 near the Stono River, twenty miles southwest of Charleston. Several factors fueled the Stono Rebellion. By 1739, blacks exceeded whites nearly two to one among South Carolina's 56,000 people. The proportion of recently imported slaves had reached an all-time high. In addition, working conditions had worsened steadily as rice production expanded. Moreover, for several decades the Spanish in Florida had been luring slaves from South Carolina, knowing that the promise of freedom might destabilize Carolina's profitable slave regime. More than a hundred fugitives had escaped to Florida by 1738, when Florida's governor formed them into a free black militia company at St. Augustine. Hoping to win more defections, he allowed thirty-eight African American households to settle north of the city and build a small fortress—Fort Mose.

DOCUMENT

James Oglethorpe, The Stono Rebellion (1739)

■ Archaeologists have recently excavated the site of Fort Mose, near St. Augustine, Florida. Dozens of slaves who escaped from South Carolina received their freedom from the Spanish and established an outpost there in the 1730s.

Courtesy, Florida Museum of Natural History. Photo by James Quine

Meanwhile, the wider commercial rivalries of the British and Spanish continued elsewhere, leading to open warfare between the two Atlantic empires in 1739. The slave uprising at Stono erupted just after word reached Charleston that war had broken out between Spain and Britain. Other factors may also have influenced the rebels' timing. An epidemic in Charleston had disrupted public activities, and a new Security Act requiring all white men to carry arms to church was to take effect before the end of September.

Early on Sunday, September 9, 1739, twenty slaves from a work crew near the Stono River broke into a local store. There they seized weapons and executed the owners. Led by a man named Jemmy, they raised a banner and marched south, beating drums and shouting "Liberty!" The insurgents burned selected plantations, killed a score of whites, and gathered more than fifty new recruits. But armed colonists overtook them near the Edisto River and blocked their escape to St. Augustine. Dozens of rebels died in the ensuing battle. In the next two days, militia and hired Indians killed twenty more and captured an additional forty people, whom they immediately shot or hanged.

South Carolina officials displayed the heads of slain rebels on poles, stepped up night patrols, and passed a harsher Negro Law. Yet even these reprisals could not quell black hopes. In June 1740, several hundred slaves plotted to storm Charleston and take arms from a warehouse. However, a comrade revealed the plan. According to a report, "The next day 50 of them were seized, and these were hanged, ten a day, to intimidate the other negroes." In November, a great fire of suspicious origin consumed much of Charleston.

Fire also played a role in hysteria that broke out in New York City in 1741. Britain's ongoing conflict with Spain (1739–1743) fanned wild Protestant fears that Jesuit spies and Catholic slaves planned to burn the major towns in British North America. In March, a blaze consumed the residence of New York's governor and a local fort. Other fires soon focused suspicions on a white couple, John and Sarah Hughson, who had often entertained blacks at their alehouse. The Hughsons—thought to fence stolen goods for a black crime ring—were accused of inciting working-class unrest. In exchange for her freedom, a sixteen-year-old Irish indentured servant at the Hughsons' tavern testified that she had overheard the planning of an elaborate "popish plot."

In a gruesome spiral of arrests and executions, New York authorities put to death thirty-four people (including the Hughsons and two other whites) and banished seventy-two blacks. On one hand, the debacle recalled the Salem witch trials, as a fearful community engaged in judicial proceedings and killings on the basis of rumors and accusations. On the other hand, the New York Slave Plot recalled Bacon's Rebellion, for evidence emerged of cooperation between impoverished blacks and whites eager to see a redistribution of property. According to his accusers, a slave named Cuffee had often observed that "a great many people had too much, and others too little." He predicted that soon his master "should have less, and that he [Cuffee] should have more." Instead, he was burned at the stake.

The Transformation Completed

■ *What prevented antislavery ideas from gaining a stronger foothold in the American colonies?*

The mechanisms for extorting labor from tens of thousands of people were firmly in place. But to maintain the slave labor system, local governments had to be vigilant and repressive, prompting debates within the white population. At a time of growing humanitarian concerns in Enlightenment Europe, it took great effort to maintain the rationale for enslavement in America. Some colonists saw slavery as too morally degrading and physically dangerous to maintain. Powerful supporters of the institution, however, found it too rewarding to give up and suggested modifications instead. This was even true in the North, where the number of blacks, both enslaved and free, remained relatively small.

Stakes were highest in the South, where most African Americans lived. As race-based slavery came to shape the entire nature of early southern society, leaders argued over the troublesome presence of free blacks, including many with mixed racial ancestry. Increasingly, white southerners treated the continuing presence of free blacks as a contradiction and a threat. As early as 1691, the Virginia assembly passed an act restricting **manumissions** (grants of individual freedom by masters) because "great inconvenience may happen to this country by setting of negroes and mulattoes free." According to the act, such people fanned hopes of freedom among enslaved blacks by their mere presence. By 1723, additional Virginia statutes prevented free people of color from voting, taxed them unfairly, and banned them from owning or carrying firearms. Lawmakers went on to prohibit all manumissions, except when the governor rewarded "meritorious service," such as informing against other enslaved workers.

> *Increasingly, white southerners treated the continuing presence of free blacks as a contradiction and a threat.*

Farther south, the contrasting colonies of South Carolina and Georgia conducted their own debates. Following the Stono uprising, for example, legislators in Charleston imposed a heavy import duty on new African arrivals for several years, hoping to increase the ratio of whites to enslaved blacks in the South Carolina lowcountry. But free people who went further, challenging the existence of slavery, met stiff resistance from those with vested interests, as the experience of the new colony of Georgia demonstrates.

MAP

African Slave Trade, 1500–1870

SECOND-CLASS STATUS IN THE NORTH

While southern planters labored to intimidate their enslaved population and weaken or contain local free black communities, African Americans in the North faced related challenges. Northern slave populations, though very small in comparison to those in the southern colonies, were growing steadily. As the North's involvement in the Atlantic slave trade expanded, its economic and legal commitment to race slavery increased. Rhode Island's slave ranks jumped from 500 in 1720 to more than 3,000 in 1750. Everywhere, new laws made manumission more difficult and African American survival more precarious. Free blacks in northern colonies faced growing discrimination in their efforts to hold jobs, buy land, obtain credit, move freely, and take part in civic life. Only in the century after 1760 did northern free black communities gain the numerical and social strength to offer effective opposition to enslavement.

Whereas free blacks lacked the means to oppose slavery, prominent white Christians lacked the will. Even in Massachusetts, where religion remained a dominant force at the turn of the century and the number of slaves had scarcely reached 1,000 people, many leaders already owned black servants. They used them more to flaunt their prosperity than to expand their wealth. When Boston merchants purchased black attendants to serve as coachmen, few citizens objected.

"Releese us Out of This Cruell Bondegg"

Interpreting History

As researchers pay increasing attention to African bondage in the colonial era, new pieces of evidence continue to appear. This appeal, written in Virginia in 1723 by a mulatto Christian slave, was rediscovered in a London archive in the 1990s and transcribed by historian Thomas Ingersoll. It is addressed to Edward Gibson, the newly appointed bishop of London, whose position gave him religious oversight over all the Anglican parishes in England's American colonies, including Virginia. Gibson, through his pamphlets, had shown an interest in the Christianization of enslaved Africans, but like many contemporary church leaders, he had less interest in the liberation of slaves. This heartfelt document, prepared with great labor and at enormous risk, was simply filed away with the bishop's vast correspondence. It never received a response or prompted any further inquiry into conditions in Virginia.

George Morland, *Traite Des Negres*, 1790–1791. Colonial Williamsburg Foundation

■ When abolition of the slave trade finally became a public issue in England in the 1780s, British artists painted scenes criticizing the traffic. But two generations earlier, pleas from New World slaves aroused no response, even from the Bishop of London, who supervised the Church of England in the American colonies.

The protests that did appear were ambivalent at best, including the one offered in 1700 by Samuel Sewell of Massachusetts. He had taken part in the 1692 witchcraft trials at Salem (later apologizing for his role), and he would become the chief justice of the colony. In a tract titled *The Selling of Joseph*, Judge Sewell questioned African enslavement, suggesting that no one should carelessly part with liberty "or deprive others of it."

But even as Sewell questioned the institution of race slavery, he also revealed his sense of superiority. His pamphlet expressed skepticism that blacks could play a part in "the Peopling of the Land." African Americans, the judge commented, "can seldom use their freedom well; yet their continual aspiring after their forbidden Liberty, renders them unwilling servants." Reverend Cotton Mather, a slave owner who once berated Sewell as one who "pleaded much for Negroes," held a more adamant view. In *The Negro Christianized* (1706), the influential Puritan stressed that conversion and Christian instruction, far from earning African slaves their freedom, would make them into "better servants."

IS THIS "CONSISTENT WITH CHRISTIANITY OR COMMON JUSTICE"?

The conversion and instruction of slaves, rather than the abolition of slavery, became a mission for English philanthropist Thomas Bray, a pious, well-to-do Anglican committed to religious education and prison reform. In 1699, Bray founded the Society for Promoting Christian Knowledge to organize libraries in the fledgling colonies. The following year, the

August the forth 1723

to the Right Raverrand father in god my Lord arch Bishop of Lonnd . . . .

this coms to sattesfie your honour that there is in this Land of verJennia a Sort of people that is Calld molatters which are Baptised and brouaht up in the way of the Christian faith and followes the ways and Rulles of the Chrch of England and sum of them has white fathars and sum white mothers and there is in this Land a Law or act which keeps and makes them and there seed SLaves forever. . . .

wee your humbell and poore partishinners doo begg Sir your aid and assisttancce in this one thing...which is that your honour will by the help of our Sufvering [i.e., sovereign] Lord King George and the Rest of the Rullers will Releese us out of this Cruell Bondegg. . . ./ and here it is to bee notd that one brother is a SLave to another and one Sister to an othe which is quite out of the way and as for mee my selfe I am my brothers SLave but my name is Secrett/

wee are commandded to keep holey the Sabbath day and wee doo hardly know when it comes for our task mastrs are has hard with us as the Egypttions was with the Chilldann of Issarall. . . . wee are kept out of the Church and matrimony is deenied us and to be plain they doo Look no more upon us then if wee ware dogs which I hope when these Strange lines comes to your Lord Ships hands will be Looket in to. . . .

And Sir wee your humble perticners do humblly beg . . . that our childarn may be broatt up in the way of the Christtian faith and our desire is that they may be Larnd the Lords prayer the creed and the ten commandements and that they may appeare Every Lord's day att Church before the Curatt to bee Exammond for our desire is that godllines Shoulld abbound amongs us and wee desire that our Childarn be putt to Scool and Larnd to Reed through the Bybell

my Riting is vary bad. . . . I am but a poore SLave that writt itt and has no other time butt Sunday and hardly that att Sumtimes. . . . wee dare nott Subscribe any mans name to this for feare of our masters for if they knew that wee have Sent home to your honour wee Should goo neare to Swing upon the gallass tree.

QUESTIONS

1. *In 1723, do these mulatto petitioners identify more closely with their African and non-Christian relatives who are enslaved or with their European and Anglican relations who are free? Explain.*

2. *Using the same kind of phonetic spelling and good logic, draft a paragraph or two that might further strengthen this petition and prevent the bishop of London from setting it aside.*

Source: Thomas N. Ingersoll, "'Releese Us out of This Cruell Bondegg': An Appeal from Virginia in 1723," *William and Mary Quarterly*, 3rd Series, 51 (October 1994): 776–782.

bishop of London sent Bray to Maryland. He soon returned to England with a desire to train better ministers and to spread the Anglican faith in America among Europeans, Indians, and Africans. In 1701, Bray established the Society for the Propagation of the Gospel in Foreign Parts (SPG). The SPG strengthened the Church of England abroad in the eighteenth century by providing dozens of ministers to serve in the colonies.

But this Anglican foothold came at a steep price. Southern planters made SPG ministers agree that any promise they offered to slaves regarding heavenly salvation would not include hints of earthly freedom. With few exceptions, the Anglican clergy gave in, strengthening religious support of race slavery. In 1723, a heartfelt petition from a mulatto slave to the bishop of London, in which the author protested "Cruell Bondegg" in Virginia, went unanswered. That same year, Bray set up a trust of "Associates" to carry on his work. With limited success, they focused on converting blacks in the British plantation colonies.

By the 1730s, only a few whites in Europe or America dared to press publicly for an end to slavery. Christian Priber, who arrived in the South in 1735, was one such activist. The idealistic German hoped to start a utopian community in southern Appalachia. But his radical proposal for a multiracial "Paradise" uniting Indians, Africans, and Europeans posed a huge threat to South Carolina authorities. "He enumerates many whimsical Privileges and natural Rights, as he calls them, which his citizens are to be entitled to," wrote a scornful detractor, "particularly dissolving Marriages and allowing Community of Women and all kinds of Licentiousness." Worst of all, according to the coastal elite, this egalitarian haven at the "Foot of the Mountains among the Cherokees" was to be "a City of Refuge for all Criminals,

Debtors, and Slaves who would fly thither from [the] Justice of their Masters." Priber's brief career as a social agitator challenging the status quo ended in 1743, when he was arrested and brought to jail in Charleston. He died—or was killed—before his case could be heard in court.

At the same time, a New Jersey tailor and bookkeeper named John Woolman posed a less defiant but more enduring threat to race slavery. In 1743, at age twenty-three, this shy Quaker began to question his role in writing out bills of sale when his fellow Quakers purchased slaves. It struck him forcefully that "to live in ease and plenty by the toil of those whom violence and cruelty have put in our power" was clearly not "consistent with Christianity or common justice." Woolman traveled widely to Quaker meetings, north and south, pressing an issue that most Quakers preferred to ignore. "The Colour of a Man avails nothing," Woolman insisted, "in Matters of Right and Equity." When he drafted *Some Considerations on the Keeping of Negroes* (1754), members of the Quaker Yearly Meeting in Philadelphia published his booklet and circulated it widely in several editions. Four years later, led by Anthony Benezet, this group outlawed slaveholding among its local members. They set a precedent that many Quakers followed in the next generation, and they challenged other denominations to do the same.

OGLETHORPE'S ANTISLAVERY EXPERIMENT

The most sustained early challenge to the slavery system in the American South came in the Georgia colony, named after King George II. In 1732, a group of well-connected London proprietors (known as trustees) obtained a twenty-year charter for the region between English South Carolina and Spanish Florida. Ten of the twenty-one initial trustees were members of Parliament, and one, James Oglethorpe, had recently organized a "committee on jails" to investigate the condition of debtors in English prisons.

William Hogarth, *To Inquire into the State of the Gaols of This Kingdom.* © The National Portrait Gallery, London (NPG926)

■ In 1729, James Oglethorpe (seated, right front) chaired a parliamentary committee exposing the harsh conditions in English jails. When William Hogarth portrayed the committee's visit to Fleet Street Prison, the artist showed Oglethorpe's concern for a dark-skinned prisoner, a hint of Oglethorpe's future opposition to slavery in Georgia.

The trustees foresaw three related purposes—charitable, commercial, and military—for their experimental colony. Georgia would provide a haven for England's worthy poor, selected members of the neediest classes who could be transported across the Atlantic and settled on small farms. These grateful newcomers would produce warm-weather commodities—olives, grapes, silk—to support the empire, and their prosperity in turn would create a growing market for English goods. Finally, their presence would provide a military buffer to protect South Carolina from further warfare with the Yamasee and Creek Indians and from possible invasion by the Spanish in St. Augustine.

With Oglethorpe as their governor, an initial boatload of 114 settlers arrived in 1733 and began building a capital at Savannah. By 1741 the town, located on a bluff fifteen miles up the Savannah River, boasted more than 140 houses. It also had a wharf, a jail, a courthouse (which doubled as a church), and a building for receiving delegations of neighboring Indians. By then, more than a thousand needy English, plus 800 German, Swiss, and Austrian Protestants, had journeyed to Georgia at the trustees' expense. Another thousand immigrants had paid their own way. Like earlier colonizers, Georgia's first arrivals had trouble adjusting to a strange environment. Alligators, rattlesnakes, and hurricanes tested their resolve. Tension over governance only deepened their discouragement.

The idealistic trustees in London declined to accumulate property and profits for themselves in the colony, but they felt justified in controlling every aspect of Georgia's development. For example, they knew that gin was becoming a source of debt and disruption in Europe and that rum and brandy sold by traders was poisoning colonial relations with southeastern Indians. So in 1735 they outlawed the use of every "kind of Spirits or Strong Waters" while still allowing consumption of wine and beer. Georgia's early experiment with prohibition of hard liquor proved difficult to implement, and officials quietly stopped enforcing the law in 1742.

DOCUMENT

James Oglethorpe, Establishing the Colony of Georgia (1733)

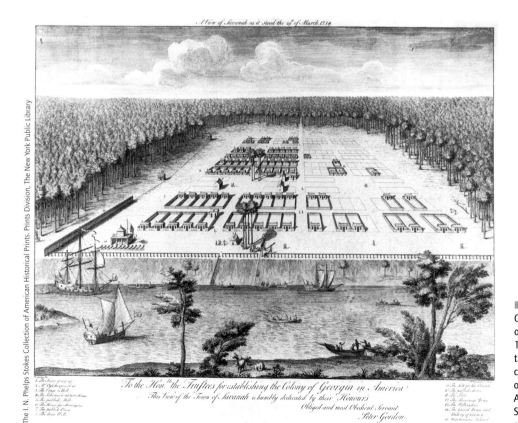

View of Savannah as it stood the 29th of March 1734.

To the Hon.ble the Trustees for establishing the Colony of Georgia in America
This View of the Town of Savanah is humbly dedicated by their Honours
Obliged and most Obedient Servant
Peter Gordon

■ Savannah, the capital of Oglethorpe's Georgia, was one year old when this view was sketched in 1734. The following year, Georgia's trustees officially outlawed slavery, creating a sharp contrast with the other British colonies in North America, especially neighboring South Carolina on the opposite bank of the Savannah River.

The I. N. Phelps Stokes Collection of American Historical Prints. Prints Division, The New York Public Library

Other efforts at control from above went further. The trustees refused to set up a legislature or to let settlers buy and sell land. Instead, they gave fifty acres of farm land to each family they sent over, plus a house lot in a local village, so all new towns could be well defended. But they parceled out land with little regard for variations in soil fertility. They also stipulated that owners could pass land on to sons only. Denying daughters the right to inherit, the trustees reasoned, would prevent men from creating large estates simply by marrying women who were likely to inherit big tracts of land. To prevent the concentrations of wealth that they saw developing in other colonies, the trustees said that no one could own more than 500 acres. Prohibiting massive estates would allow for thicker settlement and therefore greater manpower to defend the colony militarily.

But the most important prohibition, by far, involved slavery. Oglethorpe began his career as a deputy governor of the Royal African Company, but he died in 1785 opposing the slave trade. His sojourn in Georgia turned him against slavery. In neighboring South Carolina, he saw firsthand how the practice degraded African lives, undermined the morals of Europeans, and laid that colony open to threats of revolt and invasion. So Oglethorpe persuaded the trustees to create a free white colony, convincing them to enact a law in 1735 that prohibited slavery and also excluded free blacks. He believed that this mandate would protect Georgia from the corruptions of enslavement while also making it easier to apprehend black runaways heading to Florida from South Carolina.

In 1739, the Stono Rebellion and the outbreak of war between England and Spain strengthened Oglethorpe's belief that slavery undermined the security of the English colonies by creating internal enemies who would support any foreign attackers. He saw further evidence in 1740, when he failed in a wartime attempt to capture St. Augustine from Spain. Unable to take the Florida stronghold, the governor managed to seize neighboring Fort Mose, which had been erected by anti-English slaves who had escaped from Carolina.

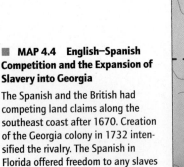

■ **MAP 4.4 English–Spanish Competition and the Expansion of Slavery into Georgia**

The Spanish and the British had competing land claims along the southeast coast after 1670. Creation of the Georgia colony in 1732 intensified the rivalry. The Spanish in Florida offered freedom to any slaves who escaped from South Carolina to St. Augustine, sparking the Stono Revolt in 1739. During the war between Britain and Spain (1739–1743), Georgians defeated the Spanish at Bloody Marsh and secured the disputed "Sea Island" region for the British. Within a decade, slavery became legal in Georgia, and scores of new labor camps appeared between the Savannah and the St. Mary's River, producing rice for export.

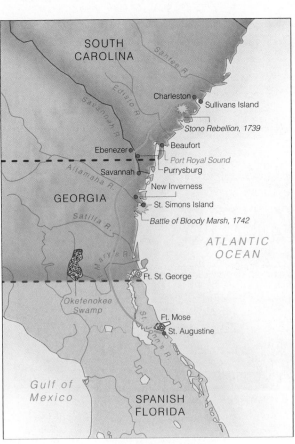

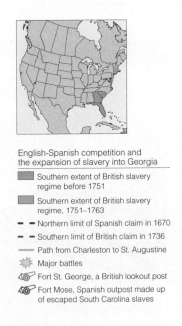

English-Spanish competition and the expansion of slavery into Georgia

■ Southern extent of British slavery regime before 1751

■ Southern extent of British slavery regime, 1751–1763

- - Northern limit of Spanish claim in 1670

- - Southern limit of British claim in 1736

— Path from Charleston to St. Augustine

✸ Major battles

Fort St. George, a British lookout post

Fort Mose, Spanish outpost made up of escaped South Carolina slaves

When a Spanish force retook Fort Mose, relying heavily on Indian and African American fighters, Oglethorpe saw the intensity with which ex-slaves would fight the English, their former masters.

The next year, fearing a counterattack, Oglethorpe issued a warning to imperial officials. He predicted that if Spanish soldiers captured Georgia, a colony inhabited by "white Protestants and no Negroes," they would then send agents to infiltrate the vulnerable colonies farther north and stir black rebellion. The Spanish, he argued, understood that the thousands of embittered slaves "would be either Recruits to an Enemy or Plunder for them." No sooner had he written his wartime prediction in 1741 than suspicious fires broke out in New York and Charleston.

THE END OF EQUALITY IN GEORGIA

As Britain's war with Spain continued, few whites could deny the Georgia governor's assertion that slavery elsewhere in British America was a source of internal weakness and strategic danger. In 1742, as the governor had predicted, Spain pushed from Florida into Georgia with an eye toward destabilizing the colonies farther north. Oglethorpe's troops repulsed the invading Spanish force in the crucial Battle at Bloody Marsh on St. Simons Island. The victory reduced the immediate threat to Britain's North American colonies, especially neighboring South Carolina, where Oglethorpe and his idealistic policies had numerous powerful opponents. These opponents now joined a group of so-called Malcontents in Savannah to question Georgia's continued prohibition against slavery. When this coalition challenged the trustees' antislavery stance, it prompted the first protracted North American debate about enslavement.

> Oglethorpe warned that the proslavery lobby seemed bent on "destroying the Agrarian Equality" envisioned in Georgia's initial plan.

In the face of numerous ills—including a sickly climate, poor soil, restrictive land policies, and lack of representative government—a well-organized Georgia faction argued that slavery was the one thing needed for the colony to prosper, since it would provide profits to slave owners regardless of Georgia's many drawbacks. Not everyone agreed. In 1739, Scottish Highlanders living at Darien on the Altamaha River had contacted Oglethorpe to lay out their practical arguments against importing Africans. Their petition expressed shock "that any Race of Mankind, and their Posterity, Should be sentenced to perpetual slavery." Immigrants from Salzburg, Germany, residing at Ebenezer on the Savannah River drafted a similar statement. But Georgia's Malcontents pushed back, demanding the right to import slaves. They drew encouragement and support from powerful merchant-planters in South Carolina. Eager to expand their trade in slaves from Africa and to open up new lands for profitable plantations, these well-to-do Carolinians dreamed of extending their successful rice operations into coastal Georgia.

Oglethorpe warned that the proslavery lobby, hungry to create large estates, seemed bent on "destroying the Agrarian Equality" envisioned in Georgia's initial plan. But the colony's trustees in London grew less unified, committed, and informed over time. Eventually, the persistent efforts of the proslavery pamphleteers bore fruit. In 1750, the trustees gave in on the matter of land titles. They allowed acreage to be bought and sold freely in any amount, which opened the door for the creation of large plantations. From there, it was just one more step to allowing slavery. The trustees finally gave in on the question of bondage, letting Georgians exploit slave labor after January 1, 1751. The 1750 law permitting slavery made futile gestures to ensure kind treatment and Christian education for slaves, but the dam had broken. Hundreds of slave-owning South Carolinians streamed across the Savannah River to invest in land. In 1752, the trustees disbanded, their patent expiring, their vision undone. By 1754, Georgia had become a royal colony.

Some argued that Georgia should simply be incorporated into South Carolina. In a sense it was: slave labor camps producing rice and indigo for export soon dotted the lowcountry on both sides of the Savannah River. Georgia's assembly passed a harsh slave code in

1755, based on South Carolina's. Two years later, it legislated a system of patrols to keep the brutal new regime in place. Georgia's effort to counter race slavery in North America had failed, a case of too little too late. After holding out for nearly two decades, the colony fell victim to the same divisive institution that had already taken root elsewhere.

Conclusion

From the outset, Africans in America offered determined resistance against slavery, and white colonists occasionally voiced dissent. But their efforts proved no match for soaring Atlantic commerce. Bit by bit, the slavery system gained a firm foothold in North America during the century after 1660. In southern colonies the system shaped the entire economy and social structure, creating a society based on race slavery. Farther north, where the institution never dominated, it still persisted as a disturbing element of colonial life.

These North American developments, involving thousands of lives, still represented only a small portion of the gigantic African slave traffic. Two final observations provide a broader Atlantic context. First, for the people swept up in the North American portion of the trade, their odyssey began comparatively late, for this dimension of the trade did not expand rapidly until after the 1670s. In the larger history of North American immigration, of course, their forced migration from Africa came relatively early. (Indeed, the proportion of blacks in the colonial population on the eve of the American Revolution—over 20 percent—was higher than it has ever been in the United States since then.) But in terms of the entire African slave **diaspora,** or dispersion, the influx to English North America occurred long after the traffic to Mexico, Brazil, and the Caribbean was well established.

Second, even at its height, the North American trade remained marginal in relation to the wider Atlantic commerce in African labor. For example, whereas roughly 50,000 enslaved men and women reached all the docks of North America between 1721 and 1740, the small West Indian islands of English Barbados and French Guadeloupe *each* received more than 53,000 Africans during the same period. In the next two decades, while Britain's mainland colonies purchased just over 100,000 Africans, Caribbean Islands such as English Jamaica (120,000) and French Saint Domingue (159,000) absorbed many more slaves.

During this single forty-year span (1721–1760), Brazil bought 667,000 African workers—more than would reach North America during the entire slave trade. All told, scholars currently estimate that some 650,000 Africans were brought to North America over several centuries. They represented roughly 6 percent of the total Atlantic commerce in enslaved people. Still, the number of North American slaves expanded from scarcely 7,000 in 1680 to nearly 29,000 in 1700 and to more than 70,000 in 1720. Half a century later, in 1770, because of importation and natural increase, 470,000 individuals were confined to enslavement from New Hampshire to Louisiana.

A century had passed since Elizabeth Key's generation saw the terrible transformation begin. Relative openness had given way to systematic oppression, and slavery's corrosive effects were felt at every level of society. An English visitor to the South in 1759 found provincial planters "vain and imperious," subject "to many errors and prejudices, especially in regard to Indians and Negroes, whom they scarcely consider as of the human species." It took another century before pressures developed that could unseat race slavery, sanctioned by law, as a dominant institution in the land.

CHRONOLOGY: 1672–1751

1672	Royal African Company (RAC) formed in London.
1676	Virginia and Maryland slaves join in Bacon's Rebellion.
1705	Virginia approves Negro Act.
1712	New York City slave revolt.
1713	British receive the contract (*asiento*) to supply African slaves to Spanish colonies.
1734	James Oglethorpe launches Georgia as a nonslave colony.
1739	Slave revolt in Stono, South Carolina.
1741	Alleged slave plot in New York City.
1751	Slavery is legalized in Georgia.

For Review

1. What role did the English Restoration of 1660 play in the establishment of African slavery in England's North American colonies?

2. What evidence exists that enslaved Africans, stripped of so much in the Middle Passage, still brought knowledge, skills, and cultural values with them to the New World?

3. If you had been an enslaved person, how would you have responded to harsh, arbitrary treatment? Why?

4. Though the evidence remains slim, how do you assess the idealistic multiracial experiment for a utopian southern community proposed by Christian Priber in 1735?

5. "In retrospect, the best time and place to halt and reverse the 'Terrible Transformation' would have been. . . . " How would you complete this thought?

6. In what ways can the destructive, uncontrollable African slave trade created by competing European powers be compared to the modern nuclear arms race?

Created Equal Online

For more *Created Equal* resources, including suggestions on sites to visit and books to read, go to **MyHistoryLab.com**.

Chapter 5

An American Babel, 1713–1763

Theodore Gentilz, *San Francisco del Espada en 1844*. Yanaguana Society Collection. Daughters of the Republic of Texas Library

■ Mission San Francisco del Espada, at San Antonio, had 1,100 cattle, 80 horses, and 16 pairs of oxen when this chapel was being constructed in the 1740s. By the time the United States annexed Texas a century later (1845), the church had fallen into disrepair.

In 1749, peace seemed a welcome prospect in the Spanish settlement of San Antonio in south-central Texas. On an August morning, hundreds of people gathered in the town plaza. Captain Turibio de Urrutia, the area's military commander, was there along with Father Santa Ana, who presided over the local missions. Across from them stood four Apache Indian chiefs with many of their people. Between the two groups, in the center of the plaza, Spanish and Indian workers began to dig a deep pit with steep sides. Those attending were about to witness one of the most important events in the town's brief history.

Three decades earlier, in the spring of 1718, a small Spanish expedition had established the town next to the San Antonio River. The newcomers built houses and excavated irrigation ditches to divert river water onto their fields. But they had occupied contested ground, on which the French and Indians also had designs. Undaunted by the failure of La Salle's Texas colony, the French had established Natchitoches on the Red River in 1716 and New Orleans on the lower Mississippi in 1718. French explorers began probing west along Louisiana's western frontier and trading with Indians in eastern Texas. Then in 1720, Apache bands, moving down from the north under pressure from the Comanche, attacked several settlers. The Spanish-speaking settlers responded with their own raids, capturing Apache women and children and selling them into Mexico as slaves.

Father Santa Ana protested such harsh tactics. The cleric hoped to make peace with the Apache and draw them into the expanding mission system, where they would accept Christianity, learn Spanish, and take up agriculture under the direction of missionaries. He called on Urrutia to stop selling slaves and provoking reprisals. At Santa Ana's urging, the captain modified his approach in 1749. After the spring raids, he ordered humane treatment of the 175 prisoners brought back to San Antonio. Rather than sell them as slaves, the Spanish locked up the men and dispersed the women and children among the missions and local households for "safekeeping." Urrutia and Santa Ana chose two women and a man from among the captives and sent them back to Apache country with a proposal for peace.

When the messengers returned with word that four important Apache chiefs were prepared to negotiate, the townsfolk welcomed the Apache delegation. Both sides were eager for peace, and the negotiations went smoothly. There was ceremonial feasting, important for such occasions, and the four chiefs attended a mass conducted by Father Santa Ana. After two days of discussion through translators, the Spanish released some of their Apache prisoners as a goodwill gesture, and both sides agreed to hold a formal peace ceremony in the plaza.

The next day all gathered to watch the workers digging the deep pit. Then the longtime adversaries buried their differences in an elaborate symbolic ritual. They lowered a live horse into the hole, along with other emblems of warfare: a lance, a hatchet, and a bundle of arrows. The four chiefs linked hands and walked solemnly around the pit, accompanied by the Spanish leaders. At a signal, all the onlookers suddenly grabbed up loose earth and tossed it into the hole. The horse was soon completely buried—a sacrifice for peace—and the ceremony broke up with shouts and celebration.

Though striking, the encounter between the Spanish and the Apache at San Antonio was not unique. During the same era, Europeans and Native Americans met to parley and trade in Detroit, Albany, Philadelphia, Charleston, St. Augustine, Mobile, New Orleans, and other colonial towns. Such formal occasions highlight a wider process of contact and interaction throughout the North American colonies in the half-century between 1713 and 1763. Everywhere, colonial expansion brought together Europeans, Africans, and Native Americans in surprising new contacts. Equally important, it forced different peoples *within* each of these three categories, despite contrasting backgrounds and customs, to rub shoulders with one another in unprecedented and unfamiliar ways.

These encounters had all been set in motion by the colonization process itself. Spanish missionaries lived among Tejas Indians in eastern Texas. French intruders laid claim to, and then lost control over, the Mississippi Valley. In Florida, English militia invading from Georgia fought escaped African slaves on the outskirts of Spanish St. Augustine. Some day-to-day meetings proved rewarding—a sound bargain, a helpful remedy, or a happy marriage. But other mixing was strained and uneasy at best—full of verbal misunderstandings, competing claims, harsh commands, or open violence. Everywhere, motives differed, accents jarred, and cultures clashed. In Philadelphia, Benjamin Franklin, a newcomer from Boston, protested the way in which Germans "swarm into our settlements, and by herding together establish their language and manner to the exclusion of ours."

For many Christians, the new confusions recalled the story of **Babel.** The people in that biblical city, despite their high ambitions, could not understand one another well enough to work together to build a tower. Eventually, they scattered abroad across the face of the earth. Bible-reading European Americans no doubt recalled that tale, especially during the great religious awakening that shook the English colonies in the 1740s, when the prospect of building something new and transcendent seemed close at hand. A German-born utopian named Christian Priber even attempted to establish an egalitarian realm in Appalachia where Europeans, Africans, and Native Americans could live peaceably together. Such dreams were not to be, however. Instead, the existing colonies continued to build up regional economies of their own, under British protection, and elements of a dominant Anglo-American culture began to emerge amid the Atlantic Babel's many voices.

New Cultures on the Western Plains

■ *How and why did life change dramatically for the Comanche and Sioux Indians after 1700?*

It makes sense that the Apache chose to bury a horse during their elaborate ceremony at the Spanish presidio in 1749. By this time the horse, recently introduced to the Indians, was transforming life on the Great Plains. It also makes sense that they buried arrows and hatchets rather than guns. Traditionally, the Spanish aspired to make the Indians into loyal subjects and Christian converts. From the time of Spain's arrival in the New World, therefore, Spanish officials had forbidden the sale of firearms to Native Americans.

In contrast, the French, Dutch, and English desired trade at almost any cost. They were less hesitant about supplying Indians with guns in exchange for furs, so firearms had become familiar to many eastern Indians during the seventeenth century. In the eighteenth century, guns began to spread west across the Mississippi River. Combined with the movement of horses from the southwest, this development had enormous consequences. New patterns of warfare altered Indian cultures. More powerful hunting techniques affected the regional economies and ecologies of the Native American West.

THE SPREAD OF THE HORSE

Although small horses once roamed the ancient West, they migrated into Asia thousands of years ago and became extinct in America. Horses returned with the early Spanish explorers. Around 1600, when New Mexico's early colonists brought mares north for breeding, horse herds developed in the Rio Grande valley. After the Pueblo Revolt in 1680, horses taken from the Spanish entered Indian trading networks and rapidly moved north from one culture to another.

By 1690, the Ute had obtained horses and traded them to the Shoshone. Before the mid-eighteenth century, horses had moved west of the Rocky Mountains to the Nez Perce and

Harrison Begay, *Night Chant Ceremonial Hunt*, 1947. Museum purchase, © The Philbrook Museum of Art, Inc., Tulsa, Oklahoma (1947.40)

The horse offered new mobility for hunting, as in this modern painting of Navajo riders. Tribes that had once tracked buffalo on foot at the edge of the Great Plains could now pursue herds across miles of open grassland. This was true for the Cheyenne, who were living in fixed villages in what is now South Dakota in the early eighteenth century. "After they got the first horses," recalled John Stands-in-Timber, "they learned there were more of them in the South and they went there after them." Cheyenne life would never be the same again.

north to the Blackfoot. The Apache brought horses east to the Caddoan cultures near the Red River and then north to the Pawnee, Arikara, and Hidatsa. Even tribes in the Southeast acquired Spanish horses from the West before they obtained English horses from the Atlantic coast. When La Salle descended the Mississippi in 1682, he met Indians who had heard rumors from the west about a mysterious animal. And when a Chickasaw leader drew a regional map on deerskin in 1723, he showed a Native American leading a horse east of the Mississippi River.

The first horses seemed utterly strange to the Indians. "The people did not know what they fed on. They would offer the animals pieces of dried meat," one elder recalled. "He put us in mind of a Stag that had lost his horns," another remembered, "and we did not know what name to give him. But as he was a slave to Man, like the dog, which carried our things, he was named the Big Dog." For generations, Native Americans had used dogs to pull provisions and bedding on a travois, an A-frame device made with tent poles. A larger animal could haul bigger loads, including longer tent poles. The long poles, in turn, allowed each family to live in a more spacious tipi.

Whether or not a tribe used tipis as dwellings, it could use the horse as a new source of food and as an aid in hunting. As the herds of horses expanded and Native Americans' riding skills improved, warriors rode into battle. On horses, they could conduct lightning raids over long distances. Soon raising, trading, and stealing horses became important activities, and a family's wealth and status depended partly on the number of horses at its command.

THE RISE OF THE COMANCHE

No Indian group felt the impact of the horse more dramatically than the Comanche. Their Shoshone-speaking ancestors had been hunter-gatherers on the high plains of Wyoming, living on small game, roots, and berries. The arrival of the horse around 1690 changed everything. It allowed family bands to migrate southeast from the Rockies to hunt the buffalo herds that grazed along the western edges of the Great Plains. From there, it was a short ride to the Spanish settlements of northern New Mexico, where they could trade buffalo hides for additional horses at Taos and Santa Fe. The Spanish noted the Shoshone-speaking arrivals in 1706, referring to them as Comanche in their records.

Officials in Santa Fe, fearful about their own defenses, looked for ways to halt Comanche aggression. They also hoped to convert the Apaches to Christianity and stop French traders from moving onto the Plains. In 1714, a French adventurer named Etienne Bourgmont had traveled up the Missouri River as far as the mouth of the Platte, near modern Omaha. In 1720, the Spanish sent soldiers northeast from Santa Fe to check the latest rumors of a French advance. But they pushed too far. An Indian war party, with French support, routed the force somewhere near present-day North Platte, Nebraska.

Seizing the advantage, Bourgmont pushed west onto the Nebraska Plains again in 1724, hoping to lure local tribes (such as the Pawnee and Padouca) away from their trade with the Spanish. "It is true that we go to the home of the Spaniards," a chief told him, "but they trade to us only some horses, a few knives, and some inferior axes; they do not trade in fusils [guns], or lead, or gunpowder, or kettles, or blankets, or any of the goods that the great French chief has given us. Thus the French are our true friends." But the French, far from their source of supply, were unable to sustain this trade advantage on the plains. Instead, the Comanche benefited most from the Spanish defeat in 1720, gaining greater access to markets in New Mexico. Comanche bands stepped up raids on Apache and carried captives to Santa Fe for sale as slaves at the annual *rescate,* or ransoming.

THE CREATION OF COMANCHERÍA ON THE SOUTHERN PLAINS

At first, New Mexico resisted the additional trade in slaves. The colony had not been able to protect Apache families or convert them; now it was being asked to buy them.

> Comanchería roughly equaled all the English settlements on the Atlantic coast in size.

But in the 1740s, officials in Santa Fe discovered that if they turned away Comanche traders, they faced the increasing power of Comanche war parties. So they granted the Comanche access to the *rescate* at Taos in exchange for assurances of peace. With a secure market for their hides, meat, and captives, the Comanche could now focus their raids on central Texas, where their hard-pressed Apache enemies had sealed a pact with the Spanish in 1749.

Not long after they buried the horse in the plaza at San Antonio, the Spanish began planning a mission and presidio (military post) among their new Apache allies. The outpost would lie 150 miles northwest of San Antonio on the San Saba River, near present-day Menard, Texas. But the post had been established for less than a year when an attack by 2,000 Indian warriors overwhelmed the little log mission in 1758. Comanche, many firing French-made guns, led the violent raid, and they returned the next year to capture 700 horses. "The heathen of the north are innumerable and rich," exclaimed a Spanish officer at San Saba. "They dress well, breed horses, [and] handle firearms with the greatest skill." A Spanish counterattack northward to the Red River did not stop the Comanche onslaught. Their continuing attacks finally forced the Spanish to withdraw from San Saba in 1767.

In less than two decades, the Comanche had overrun most of Texas. By the 1770s, mounted Comanche warriors commanded respect and fear across a vast domain. Their territory stretched south nearly 600 miles from western Kansas to central Texas, and it spanned 400 miles from eastern New Mexico to what is now eastern Oklahoma. This area, known as Comanchería, roughly equaled all the English settlements on the Atlantic coast in size. The Comanche continued to absorb smaller Native American groups and swell in numbers. By 1780, they had grown into a proud Indian nation of more than 20,000 people. Comanchería remained a powerful entity in the Southwest for decades.

THE EXPANSION OF THE SIOUX

Comanche strength depended not only on mounted warfare but also on trading horses to obtain guns. Because Spanish policy prohibited the sale of firearms to Native Americans, the Comanche looked east for weapons. They quickly discovered that by selling horses to their eastern allies, such as the Wichita Indians, they could receive French muskets from Louisiana in return. But the Comanche were not alone; the Sioux Indians also took advantage of the gun frontier as it inched steadily west.

By 1720, the French had established settlements at Peoria, Cahokia, and Kaskaskia in Illinois and at New Orleans, Natchez, and Natchitoches in Louisiana. French traders at these sites provided guns and other metal goods to Indians in exchange for salt, deerskins, beaver pelts, horses, and war captives. Native American groups that took advantage of this trade included the Tunica beside the lower Mississippi, the Caddo and Wichita along the Red and Arkansas rivers, and the Osage, Pawnee, and Omaha tribes near the Missouri.

By midcentury on the northern Great Plains, the horse frontier moving from the southwest had met the gun frontier moving from the east.

Farther north, muskets carried west from French posts on the Great Lakes and south from English bases in subarctic Canada proved especially important among the Sioux peoples, who trapped game and gathered wild rice by the lakes of their northern Minnesota homeland. The Comanche had mastered horses and then acquired guns; the Sioux, given their different location, first absorbed firearms and then adopted the horse. The results proved equally dramatic.

When the Sioux first encountered a gun from French voyageurs in the mid-seventeenth century, they called it *mazawakan*, meaning "mysterious or sacred iron." Initially, they used the few muskets they could obtain to fight their less well-armed Indian neighbors. By 1700 French traders, moving from the east, had established direct trade with the Sioux, offering a steady supply of guns and powder in exchange for furs.

For a generation, several Sioux bands (the Teton and Yanktonai) walked between two worlds. In the summers, they followed the buffalo onto the prairies, with dogs pulling travois and women carrying heavy burdens. As cold weather approached, they retreated to the edge of the woodlands to gather firewood and hunt beaver. In the spring, after trading meat and pelts to the French for guns and ammunition, they returned to the edge of the plains. They glimpsed their first horses not long after 1700. But it was several generations before the western Sioux had acquired enough mounts and developed sufficient confidence to drop their old customs and adopt a horse-centered way of life.

By midcentury on the northern Great Plains, the horse frontier moving from the southwest had met the gun frontier moving from the east. Saukamappee, a Cree Indian living with the Blackfoot, remembered vividly the surprise of the initial encounter. When he was a young man, his war party—well armed and on foot—had gone into battle against the Shoshone. "We had more guns and iron headed arrows than [ever] before," he recalled years later. "But our enemies . . . and their allies had Misstutim (Big Dogs, that is, Horses) on which they rode, swift as the Deer."

Indian women remembered the arrival of the horse and the gun with ambivalence. These new assets improved food supplies and made travel less burdensome, but the transition also brought disadvantages. Violent raids became more common. Young men who fought as warriors gained status in the community compared to older men and women. The

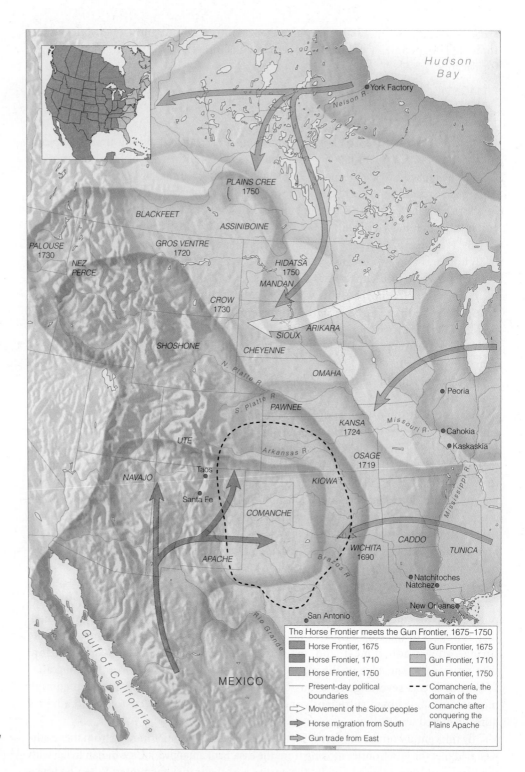

MAP 5.1   The Horse Frontier Meets the Gun Frontier, 1675–1750

The Horse Frontier meets the Gun Frontier, 1675–1750

- Horse Frontier, 1675
- Horse Frontier, 1710
- Horse Frontier, 1750
- Present-day political boundaries
- Movement of the Sioux peoples
- Horse migration from South
- Gun trade from East
- Gun Frontier, 1675
- Gun Frontier, 1710
- Gun Frontier, 1750
- Comanchería, the domain of the Comanche after conquering the Plains Apache

difficult task of processing slain buffalo increased, creating new work for women even as it provided fresh resources for the whole community.

As the overlap of horse and gun proceeded after 1750, Sioux men bearing muskets continued to acquire mounts and fight for control of the buffalo grounds. Their competitors, all of whom had recently acquired horses, now had guns as well. Within several decades, the Sioux had pushed their domain west to the Missouri River. Like the Comanche farther south, they had emerged as a dominant power on the Great Plains—a force to be reckoned with in the century ahead.

Britain's Mainland Colonies: A New Abundance of People

In what ways did Britain's North American colonies become "less English" after 1700?

West of the Mississippi, horses and guns brought dramatic shifts as the eighteenth century progressed. But east of the Appalachian Mountains, a different force prompted striking change: population growth. Several factors came together to push the demographic curve upward at an unprecedented rate after 1700. From our vantage point in the twenty-first century, the colonial seaports and villages appear tiny, and rural settlement seems sparse. But by the mid-eighteenth century, the coastal colonies represented the largest concentration of people that had ever occupied any portion of the continent.

Population growth characterized eighteenth-century life on both sides of the North Atlantic. In Europe, improvements in agriculture led to larger harvests and more fodder for keeping livestock alive through long winters. These changes prompted better diets. Improvements in food distribution and sanitation also stimulated population growth. But while European numbers rose at a gradual pace, the population of Atlantic North America surged. England in 1700 had 5.1 million people, a figure that increased a mere 14 percent to 5.8 million by 1750. In contrast, during the same half-century, the colonial population in British North America more than quadrupled, from 260,000 to nearly 1.2 million.

During these same decades, the Atlantic seaboard colonies made a permanent and dramatic shift away from a population that was almost entirely of English origin. Never before had North America seen such extensive ethnic and racial diversity. As the numerous cultures and languages indigenous to western Europe, western Africa, and eastern North America mixed and mingled, they gave rise to an American Babel.

POPULATION GROWTH ON THE HOME FRONT

Natural increase—more births than deaths—played an important role in colonial population growth. People married young, and the need for labor spurred couples to have large families. Benjamin Franklin, who became the best-known colonist of his generation, was born in Boston in 1706. He grew up in a household of seventeen children. Large families had long been commonplace, to compensate for frequent deaths among children. What made the Franklin family unusual was that all the children survived childhood and started families of their own.

A high birthrate typified most preindustrial cultures. It was the low death rate and long average life span that pushed up American population numbers. With no huge urban centers, colonial epidemics proved less devastating than in Europe. Food was plentiful, and housing improved steadily. Newborns who survived infancy could live a long life. (Franklin himself lived eighty-four years.) The 1720s and 1730s were peaceful, so soldiering did not endanger the lives of men of military age. For women, death related to pregnancy and childbirth still loomed as a constant threat. (Franklin's own mother was his father's second wife; the first wife died after bearing seven children.) Yet women still outnumbered men among people living into their sixties, seventies, and eighties.

Elderly grandparents were common, but the overall society was remarkably young, with well over half the population below the age of twenty. (See Figure 5.1.) The reasons seem clear. The ratio between men and women was becoming more even over time, the marriage rates for women remained extremely high, and there was no effective means of contraception. Women could only avoid pregnancy through sexual abstinence or by nursing their infants for a long period (since lactation reduces the chances of conception). Not surprisingly, children abounded.

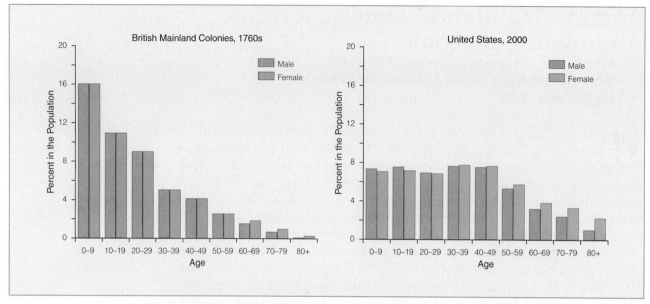

■ **FIGURE 5.1   Comparison of Overall Population Structure By Gender and Age: British Mainland Colonies, 1760s, and United States, 2000**

In the mid-eighteenth century, more than half of all people in the British mainland colonies were under age twenty, and fewer than two in ten were forty or older. In contrast, among all the living Americans at the start of the twenty-first century, fewer than three in ten are under twenty, and more than four in ten are age forty or older.

"PACKED LIKE HERRINGS": ARRIVALS FROM ABROAD

Frequent births and improving survival rates were only part of the population story. Immigration—both forced and free—also contributed mightily to the colonies' growth. The unfree arrivals came in two different streams from two separate continents and faced very different prospects. The largest flow of unfree arrivals came from Africa, and these forced migrants faced a bleak new life with few options for improvement. Well before the 1720s, the system of race-based slavery was sanctioned by law. By the 1730s, the expanding transatlantic slave trade brought at least 4,000 Africans to the colonies every year, and the rate increased steadily. In 1756, Charleston, South Carolina, received more than 2,200 slaves aboard fourteen ships (including vessels that bore grimly ironic names such as *Relief, Hope,* and *Success*).

A separate stream of unfree laborers came to the colonies from Europe. It included prisoners removed from crowded jails and indentured servants unable to pay their own way to America. Compared with enslaved Africans, these European migrants faced long-term prospects that were far more promising. Every year, hundreds of detainees in British jails were offered transportation to the colonies and a term of service laboring in America as an alternative to prison time or execution.

Deported felons joined the larger flow of unfree migrants from Europe: poor people, unable to pay their own passage, who accepted transportation to America as indentured servants. All were sold to employers to serve as workers, with scant legal rights, until their indenture expired, usually after three to six years. In the 1720s, Philadelphia shippers devised a variation on indentures known as the redemption contract. Under this **redemption system,** agents in Europe recruited migrants by contracting to loan them money for passage and provisions. On arrival in America, the recruits could then sign a pact with an employer of their own choosing. That person agreed to pay back the shipper, "redeeming" the original loan that had been made to the immigrant. In exchange, the newcomer (called a redemptioner) promised to work for the employer for several years,

Gottlieb Mittelberger, The Passage of Indentured Servants (1750)

receiving no more than room and board. After that, the redemptioners were on their own, and their prospects usually improved.

Besides Africans who remained unfree for life and Europeans who gained freedom after a period of service, a smaller stream of newcomers involved free families arriving from Europe who could pay their own way. Poor conditions at home pushed these risk-takers to try their luck in the New World. Glowing descriptions of abundant land at bargain rates caught their attention. American land speculators hoped to rent forest tracts to immigrant farmers who would improve the value of the land by clearing trees and building homes. In turn, Britain's imperial administrators sought to recruit non-English migrants from the European continent. Their immigrant settlements near the American frontier could bolster colonial defenses against foreign rivals and provide a buffer to ward off Indian attacks. In one of many pamphlets for German immigrants, Joshua von Kocherthal explained how South Carolina's proprietors would give a sixty-five-acre plot to each head of household, with the promise of more land if they needed it or if they came with a large group.

Even for those newcomers who paid for their own crossing, the Atlantic passage was a life-threatening ordeal. "The people are packed densely, like herrings," Lutheran minister Gottlieb Mittelberger recorded after a voyage to Pennsylvania. "During the journey the ship is full of pitiful signs of distress—smells, fumes, horrors, vomiting, various kinds of sea sickness, fever, dysentery, headaches, heat, constipation, boils, scurvy, cancer, mouth-rot, and similar afflictions." Despite such hardships, newcomers found economic opportunities awaiting them in America. They often wrote home glowing accounts of colonial life, and their letters helped boost the rising population further. In 1773, English customs officials quizzed twenty-nine-year-old Elizabeth McDonald about why she was departing for Wilmington, North Carolina. The unmarried Scottish servant replied that she was setting out "because several of her friends, having gone to Carolina before her, had assured her that she would get much better service and greater encouragement in Carolina than in her own country."

DOCUMENT

Elizabeth Sprigs, Letter to Her Father (1756)

NON-ENGLISH NEWCOMERS IN THE BRITISH COLONIES

Colonies that were thoroughly English at their origin became decidedly more varied after 1700. By far the largest and most striking change came from North America's increasing involvement in the Atlantic slave trade. By 1750, some 240,000 African Americans made up 20 percent of the population of the British colonies. Native Americans had been drawn into the mix in small numbers as slaves, servants, spouses, and Christian converts. But roughly four out of five colonists were of European descent. Among them, as among the Africans and Indians, many spoke English with a different accent, or as a second language, or not at all.

The New England colonies remained the most homogenous, but even there, 30 percent of the residents had non-English roots by 1760. The new diversity was most visible in New York because of the colony's non-English origins. A 1703 census of New York City shows that the town had no single ethnic majority. It remained 42 percent Dutch, with English (30 percent) and Africans (18 percent) together making up nearly half the population. The rest of the population included a small Jewish community (1 percent) and a growing number of French Protestants, or Huguenots (9 percent).

The French New Yorkers had fled to America after Louis XIV ended protection for the Protestant minority of France. When the king revoked the long-standing Edict of Nantes in 1685, he also prohibited Huguenot emigration, but

John Wollaston, Mary Spratt Provoost Alexander, undated. Museum of the City of New York, Gift of William Hamilton Russell (50.215.4)

■ Like many New Yorkers of her generation, shopkeeper Mary Spratt Provoost Alexander (1693–1760) spoke both Dutch and English. Her Dutch mother had married a Scottish immigrant, and Mary was the wife of a local attorney who also came from Scotland.

"Pastures Can Be Found Almost Everywhere": Joshua von Kocherthal Recruits Germans to Carolina

Joshua von Kocherthal grew up in southern Germany and trained to be a Lutheran minister. On a visit to London at the start of the eighteenth century, he learned of England's desire to recruit settlers to its American colonies. Because fellow Germans faced hard times at home, he led several groups to New York, where they established Neuberg (Newburgh) on the Hudson River. In 1706, Kocherthal published a German-language tract promoting migration to South Carolina. The popular booklet went through several editions in his homeland.

The winter of 1708–1709 was especially harsh east of the Rhine River. In the spring of 1709, a stream of German refugee families migrated north along the Rhine and then west to England. From there, they hoped to obtain passage across the Atlantic to South Carolina. Many carried Kocherthal's simple pamphlet, and they focused on the numerous advantages outlined in his brochure, especially the abundance of land. According to Kocherthal, the colonial government registered all land grants "to prevent errors or future arguments," and it exempted newcomers from taxes for several years. Best of all, food was plentiful, no feudal obligations or serfdom existed, and members of Protestant denominations had "freedom of religion and conscience."

South Carolina is one of the most fertile landscapes to be found . . . preferable in many respects to the terrain in Germany, as well as in England. . . . Game, fish, and birds, as well as waterfowl such as swans, geese, and ducks, occur there in such plentiful numbers that . . . newcomers can sustain themselves if necessary . . . until they have cleared a piece of land, sown seeds, and gathered in a harvest. . . . Among other things, there can be found in the wild so-called "Indian chickens" [turkeys], some of which weigh about 40 pounds or even more. These exist in incredible numbers. . . .

Hunting game, fishing, and bird-catching are free to anyone, but one shouldn't cross the borders of neighbors or of the Indians [who] live in complete peace and friendship with our families. In addition, their number decreases while the number of our people (namely the Europeans) increases. . . . Lumber can be found there in abundance, especially the most beautiful oaks, but also many of the nicest chestnuts and nut trees which are used by many for building and are considered better than oaks. One can also find beeches, spruces, cypresses, cedars, laurels, myrtle, and many other varieties.

Hogs can be raised very easily in great numbers at little cost, because there are huge forests everywhere and the ground is covered with acorns. . . . Above all, the breeding of horses, cows, sheep, hogs and many other kinds of domestic livestock proceeds excellently, because pastures can be found almost everywhere, and the livestock can remain in the fields the whole year, as it gets no colder in Carolina in the middle of winter than it does in Germany in April or October. . . . Because of the multiplication of livestock, almost no household in Carolina (after residing there a few years) can justifiably be called poor.

As far as vegetables and fruits are concerned, Indian corn predominates, thriving in such a way that one can harvest it twice a year and grow it wherever one wants to. Our local cereals such as wheat,

several thousand French Protestants escaped illegally and sought refuge in America. They established small communities such as those at New Rochelle in New York and along South Carolina's Santee River. South Carolina's governor protested against the Huguenots' early political activity: "Shall the Frenchmen, who cannot speak our language, make our laws?" But everywhere, they intermarried with the English and prospered in commerce. By the 1760s, several families with humble Huguenot origins—among them the Faneuils in Boston and the Laurenses, Manigaults, and Ravenels in Charleston—had amassed enormous fortunes.

At a time when France and Great Britain were at war, another infusion of French-speaking refugees, the Acadians, fared less well. In 1755, authorities evicted French colonials from Acadia in British Nova Scotia, fearing they might take up arms for France. Officials burned their homes and deported more than 6,000 of them to the various coastal colonies farther south. Mistreated for their Catholicism and feared as enemies during wartime, the Acadians struggled to get by. Resented in their new homes, many moved on to French Louisiana, where the Acadians, or **Cajuns,** became a lasting cultural force.

Scotland provided a much larger flow of migrants than France, stemming from two different sources. A growing stream of families, at least 30,000 people by 1770, came from Scotland itself. They were pushed by poverty, land scarcity, famines, and a failed political rebellion in 1745. In addition, a larger group known as the Scots-Irish came from Ulster in

Courtesy, Dartmouth University Library

■ In 1709, roughly 13,000 German immigrants seeking passage to America encamped for months at Blackheath, near London. The British government supplied them with tents, blankets, bread, and cheese, and churchgoers prayed for their welfare. But other Britons protested that the German strangers took "bread out of the mouths of our native handicraft men and laboring people, and increase the number of our poor which are too many and too great a burden to our nation already." Most of the refugees reached North America, serving as the vanguard for later German migration.

seeds. . . . There can already be found different kinds of our local apples. . . . As far as cabbage, beets, beans, peas, and other garden plants are concerned, not only do our local plants grow very well, but there are also many other varieties with excellent taste that are completely unknown to us. . . . Newcomers will do well to acquire all sorts of iron tools and bring these along. . . . If someone has lived in Carolina for a time and he wants to go to another country, he may do so freely at any time.

QUESTIONS

1. *Study the picture and caption regarding German refugees near London. Is that situation similar to, or different from, conditions in a modern refugee camp that you have read about or seen in the news? Be specific.*

2. *Do any of Kocherthal's observations about the natural world relate to the ongoing Columbian Exchange described in Chapter 1?*

Source: Translations by Dorothee Lehlbach from Joshua von Kocherthal, Ausfeuhrlicher und umstaendlicher Bericht von der beruehmten Landschaft Carolina, in dem engellaendischen American gelegen (Frankfurt: Georg Heinrich Oehrling, 2nd ed., 1709), in the Special Collections Library of Duke University.

rye, barley, and oats do well, but above all, rice thrives there as excellently as in any other part of the world, and it grows in such amounts that it can be loaded on ships and transported to other places. And as the inhabitants use rice so much and make much more profit from it than any other cereal, they are most keen on growing rice and there has been very little cultivation of other cereals.

All kinds of our fruits can be planted there, but . . . future arrivals would do well to bring along seedlings of any kind, or at least the

Northern Ireland. The British had encouraged these Scottish Presbyterians to settle in Ireland in the seventeenth century, displacing rebellious Irish Catholics. In Ulster the Scottish newcomers soon faced commercial and political restrictions from Parliament and the Anglican Church. By 1770, nearly 60,000 Scots-Irish had left Ireland for America.

Another stream, German-speaking immigrants, nearly equaled the combined flow of Scots and Scots-Irish settlers. They began to arrive shortly after 1700 as religious persecution, chronic land shortages, and generations of warfare pushed whole communities out of southern Germany and neighboring Switzerland. Roughly 30,000 migrated in the 1750s; by 1770 the total had reached 85,000. These refugees generally came as whole families, and they usually took up farmland on the fringes of the colonies. Germans occupied the Mohawk Valley in New York and Virginia's Shenandoah Valley, and they fanned out from Germantown across the rich farmland of Pennsylvania. Swiss founded New Bern, North Carolina, in 1710. Migrants from Salzburg established New Ebenezer near Savannah, Georgia, in 1734.

Almost all of the white, non-English newcomers, including several thousand migrants from Wales, were Protestant Christians. Many clung to their language and traditions. But most arrivals learned English, and their children intermarried with English settlers. A French visitor described a typical American "whose grandfather was an Englishman, whose wife is Dutch, whose son married a French woman, and whose present four sons have now four wives of different nations."

The Varied Economic Landscape

■ *What role did geography play in shaping the emerging regional colonial economies?*

Colonial Products

Population growth had consequences, and the changes began at the water's edge. Ships carrying newcomers docked most often at Boston, New York, Philadelphia, or Charleston. Each of these deepwater ports grew from a village to a bustling commercial hub, absorbing manufactured goods from Britain and shipping colonial produce abroad. All four towns spawned secondary ports located on neighboring rivers. In contrast, Chesapeake Bay had no single dominant port. There, Annapolis, Alexandria, and Norfolk all expanded, joined by the new town of Baltimore. But given the bay's many rivers, Atlantic ships often visited riverside plantations and villages to conduct separate business.

In Chesapeake Bay and elsewhere, inland commerce was conducted by boat wherever possible. Hartford and Springfield on the Connecticut River, Kingston and Albany on the Hudson, Wilmington and Trenton on the Delaware, and Savannah and Augusta on the Savannah all became active riverside trading centers. Richmond, Virginia, which began as a trading post at the falls of the James River, already had 250 inhabitants when it incorporated as a town in 1742. Trails and former Indian paths connected these river-based communities, easing the way for travelers in the hinterland. By the 1740s, a pathway known as the Great Wagon Road headed southwest from Philadelphia to Winchester in Virginia's Shenandoah Valley and then south through gaps in the Blue Ridge Mountains to the Piedmont region of Carolina.

Widening networks of contact, using boats and wagons, extended inland from the primary seaports. Expanding fleets of ships tied each major hub to distant Atlantic ports. As a result, farmsteads and villages that had been largely self-sufficient before 1710 gradually became linked to wider markets. Local production still met most needs.

But increasingly, the opportunity existed to obtain a new tool, a piece of cloth, or a printed almanac from far away. The new possibility of obtaining such goods lured farmers to grow crops for market rather than plant only for home consumption.

> *As local commercial systems gained coherence and strength, a string of regional economies developed along the Atlantic seaboard.*

As local commercial systems gained coherence and strength, a string of regional economies developed along the Atlantic seaboard. Coastal vessels and a few muddy roads linked them tenuously to one another. But geographical and human differences gave each a character of its own. Migration patterns reinforced this diversity, since arrivals from Europe often sought out areas where others already spoke their language or shared their form of worship. The influx of German farmers through Philadelphia, for example, gave unique traits to Pennsylvania. (Because the newcomers spoke German, or *Deutsch*, they became known as Pennsylvania Dutch.) The rising importation of Africans helped shape the economy and culture of Chesapeake Bay, and of coastal South Carolina. Besides the diversity among arriving peoples, American ecological differences also played a role. Variations in land and climate contributed to the emergence of five distinctive economic regions along the Atlantic coast.

SOURCES OF GAIN IN THE CAROLINAS AND GEORGIA

Two related but distinctive regions took shape along the southeastern coast, linked respectively to the two Carolina colonies. The larger one centered on the lowcountry of coastal South Carolina and Georgia. There, the warm current of the Gulf Stream moving north

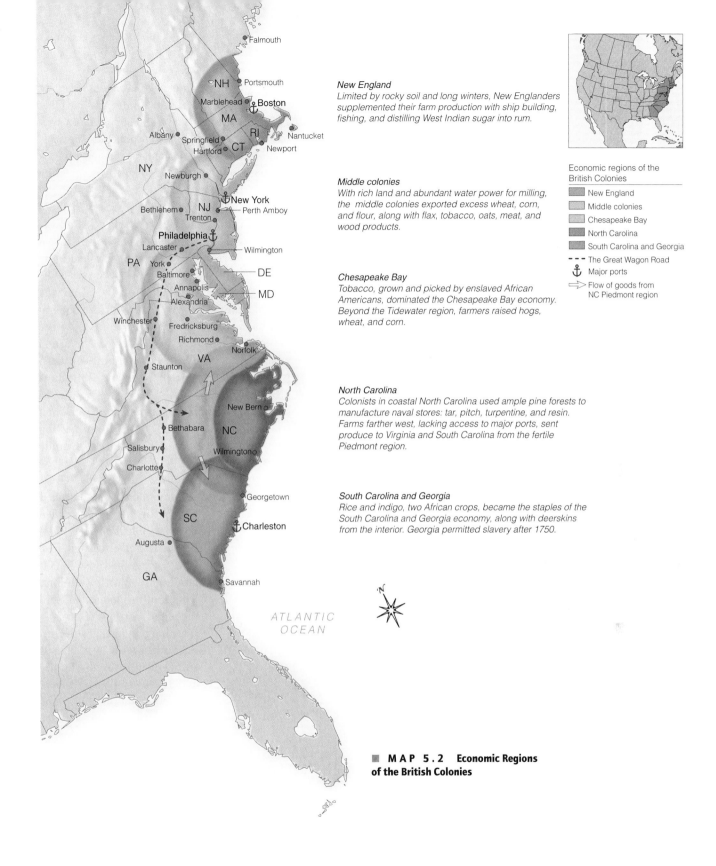

New England

Limited by rocky soil and long winters, New Englanders supplemented their farm production with ship building, fishing, and distilling West Indian sugar into rum.

Middle colonies

With rich land and abundant water power for milling, the middle colonies exported excess wheat, corn, and flour, along with flax, tobacco, oats, meat, and wood products.

Chesapeake Bay

Tobacco, grown and picked by enslaved African Americans, dominated the Chesapeake Bay economy. Beyond the Tidewater region, farmers raised hogs, wheat, and corn.

North Carolina

Colonists in coastal North Carolina used ample pine forests to manufacture naval stores: tar, pitch, turpentine, and resin. Farms farther west, lacking access to major ports, sent produce to Virginia and South Carolina from the fertile Piedmont region.

South Carolina and Georgia

Rice and indigo, two African crops, became the staples of the South Carolina and Georgia economy, along with deerskins from the interior. Georgia permitted slavery after 1750.

Economic regions of the British Colonies

- New England
- Middle colonies
- Chesapeake Bay
- North Carolina
- South Carolina and Georgia
- - - The Great Wagon Road
⚓ Major ports
⇨ Flow of goods from NC Piedmont region

ATLANTIC OCEAN

■ **M A P 5 . 2   Economic Regions of the British Colonies**

from Florida along the Sea Islands provided a long growing season. It also assured mild winters, in contrast to Europe, meaning that cattle and hogs could forage in the woods unattended for most of the year. As livestock multiplied, lowcountry settlers sold meat, barrel staves, and firewood to the sugar islands of the West Indies, purchasing African slave labor in return.

Some of the newcomers had grown rice in Africa before their enslavement. Planting rice for their own use, they soon showed that the crop could thrive in South Carolina. Once African know-how made clear the potential for rice cultivation, a system of plantation agriculture, imported from Barbados, took hold quickly after 1700. Rice production spread to Georgia after that colony legalized slavery in 1751. Another African plant, indigo, also took root as a money-making staple crop. For several generations after 1740, indigo from South Carolina provided the blue dye for England's rising textile industry.

On Charleston's busy docks, casks of deerskins piled up beside the barrels of rice and indigo. The extensive deerskin trade in South Carolina and Georgia depended on the Creek and Cherokee men who hunted the animals and the women who processed the hides. At the height of the trade in the 1730s, Indian and white hunters killed more than a million deer per year.

In North Carolina, a second regional economy evolved. North of Cape Fear, the sandy barrier islands known as the Outer Banks prevented easy access for oceangoing vessels and gave protection to pirates who harassed Atlantic shipping. Because the coastal geography hindered efforts to promote staple crop agriculture, colonists turned to the pine forest to make a living. A wide band of longleaf pine bordered the southern coastal plain from Virginia to Texas. In North Carolina it stretched inland for a hundred miles. With labor, this pine forest yielded an abundance of naval stores: the tar and pitch used by sailors to protect their ships and rigging. Workers hauled the finished products to Wilmington on the Cape Fear River, the colony's best outlet to the sea. By the 1770s, the port was well known for exporting naval stores, and a dozen sawmills dotted the river.

Farther inland, Scots-Irish and German families moved down the Great Wagon Road after 1740 to carve out farms across the Carolina Piedmont on lands controlled largely by several absentee owners in Britain. By 1763, Ben Franklin estimated that Pennsylvania had lost 10,000 families to North Carolina. Typical of this migration were the Moravians, a German-speaking religious group who established towns at Nazareth and Bethlehem, Pennsylvania, in the 1740s. In 1753, members of the expanding Moravian community bought a tract of 100,000 acres near modern-day Winston-Salem, North Carolina. They named it Wachovia, meaning "Peaceful Valley." Within several years they had developed prosperous farms, a pottery shop, and a tannery around their initial settlement, called Bethabara. The newcomers bartered seeds and tools with one another and shipped extra produce overland to South Carolina and Virginia.

Schomburg Center for Research in Black Culture, New York Public Library

■ In North Carolina, black workers cut pine trees and then burned the wood in closed ovens to turn pine resin into tar and pitch. These so-called naval stores were sealed into barrels and used by sailors to protect the ropes on ships.

John Moale, engraving, 1752. The I. N. Phelps Stokes Collection, The New York Public Library

■ In 1729, Maryland planters founded Baltimore to provide a port on Chesapeake Bay for shipping tobacco. The town had only 50 homes and 200 inhabitants when this 1752 sketch was made, but the seaport grew rapidly after that.

CHESAPEAKE BAY'S TOBACCO ECONOMY

North of the Carolinas, farmers in the colonies bordering Chesapeake Bay committed to tobacco production in the seventeenth century. They clung to that staple crop despite a long decline in its market price. After 1710, demand for tobacco revived and prices rose again, in part because snuff (pulverized tobacco inhaled through the nostrils) became popular among Europeans. Tobacco continued to dominate the Chesapeake economy.

However, local conditions in parts of Virginia and Maryland prompted crop diversification as the century progressed. Constant tobacco planting depleted the soil. Moreover, most farms lay far from any navigable river, and rolling huge casks of tobacco many miles to market proved expensive. Wheat and corn thus became important secondary staples. These new crops, along with flax, hemp, and apples for making cider, provided a buffer against poor tobacco harvests and spurred related activities such as building wagons, making barrels, and constructing mills. These trades, in turn, produced widening networks of local exchange and prosperity for white yeoman families, with or without slaves.

Before 1700, all the mainland colonies could be described as *societies with slaves.* After that, the northern colonies continued to allow enslavement, but they never relied on it. In contrast, the southern colonies, except for certain inland farmlands settled from the north, shifted early in the eighteenth century to become something different: full-fledged *slave societies,* tied economically and culturally to slavery. By midcentury, plantation owners remained less wealthy than their counterparts in the West Indies who lived off the profits of slave-grown sugar. But on average, members of the southern elite controlled far more wealth than their counterparts in the North. The profits of the plantation system spread widely through the rest of the European American community. By the 1770s, whites in the South averaged more than twice as much wealth per person as whites in the North. An estimate for 1774 puts the average white Southerner's net worth at £93, a sharp contrast to the comparable figure for counterparts in the middle colonies (£46) and New England (£38).

NEW ENGLAND TAKES TO THE SEA

North of Chesapeake Bay, two overlapping economic regions emerged: the long-established New England colonies and the somewhat newer and more prosperous middle colonies.

> *In timber-rich New England, shipbuilding prospered. Colonists established shipyards at the mouth of nearly every river.*

New England faced peculiar disadvantages, beginning with the rocky soil. Ancient glaciers had strewn stones across the landscape, and it was tedious work to haul them off the fields to build endless stone walls. As imports from London increased, New Englanders found no staple crop that could be sold directly to Britain to create a balance of trade. All the beaver had been hunted, and much of the best land had been occupied. The region's farm families had adapted well to the challenging environment and short growing seasons. Both men and women worked on handicrafts during the long, hard winters, and networks of community exchange yielded commercial prosperity in many towns. But with a rapidly growing population, successive generations had less land to divide among their children.

Increasingly, young men with little prospect of inheriting prime farmland turned to the sea for a living. In timber-rich New England, shipbuilding prospered. Colonists established shipyards at the mouth of nearly every river, drawing skilled carpenters and willing deckhands to the coast. By 1763, Marblehead, Massachusetts, with a fleet of a hundred ships, had grown to 5,000 people. That made it the sixth largest town in the thirteen colonies, behind only Philadelphia, New York, Boston, Charleston, and Newport, Rhode Island. Providence, at the top of Narragansett Bay, opened its first shipyard in 1711 and soon became a competing seaport.

By 1770, three out of every four ships sailing from New England to a British port were owned by colonial residents. In contrast, in the southern colonies from Maryland to Georgia, the proportion was only one in eight.

On Nantucket Island off Cape Cod, whaling became a new source of income. For generations, the islanders had cooked the blubber of beached whales to extract oil for lamps. In 1715, they outfitted several vessels to harpoon sperm whales at sea and then return with the whale blubber in casks to be rendered into oil. In the 1750s, they installed brick ovens on deck and began cooking the smelly blubber at sea in huge iron vats. This change turned the whaling vessel into a floating factory, and it prompted longer voyages in larger ships. By the 1760s, Nantucket whalers were cruising the Atlantic for four or five months at a time and returning loaded with barrels of whale oil.

"The Connecticut Peddler"

The fishing industry also prospered. All along the coast, villagers dispatched boats to the Grand Banks, the fishing grounds off Newfoundland. When the vessels returned, laden with fish, the townspeople graded, dried, and salted the catch. The colonists sent the best cod to Europe in exchange for wine and dry goods. Yankee captains carried the lowest grade to the Caribbean sugar islands, where planters bought "refuse fish" as food for their slaves. In return, skippers brought back kegs of molasses to be distilled into rum. By 1770, 140 American distilleries, most of them in New England, produced 5 million gallons of rum annually. Much of it went to colonial taverns and Indian trading posts. But some also went to Africa, aboard ships from Britain and New England. American rum, along with various wines and spirits from Europe, made up one-fifth of the total value of goods used to purchase African slaves.

As the New England economy stabilized, it became a mixed blessing for women. On the farm, their domestic labors aided the household economy and helped to offset bad

Solving the Problem of Longitude at Sea

■ English clockmaker John Harrison, the son of a carpenter, revolutionized global navigation in the 1760s with a reliable timepiece that allowed captains to calculate their longitude at sea.

Even before Columbus, sailors could determine their latitude, or north–south position, from the stars. But finding one's exact longitude, or east–west position, on the trackless ocean remained far more elusive. It depended on measuring time accurately, but pendulum clocks were no use on the rolling sea, and early pocket watches could be thrown off by changes of temperature and humidity. Again and again, mistakes in estimating longitude at sea proved disastrous. By the turn of the eighteenth century, Europeans considered this problem the greatest single barrier to the expansion of overseas trade.

Then in 1707, a dense autumn fog blanketed five British troop ships as they sailed north past the coast of France toward the west coast of England. The admiral was sure his course lay well to the west of the Scilly Isles, which protrude dangerously from the southwest tip of Britain. Indeed, when a sailor questioned the accuracy of their position, the commander ordered him hanged for insubordination. But hours later, on the night of October 22, the fleet foundered on the sharp rocks of the Scillies. Four huge ships broke up and sank; 2,000 men died in the pounding surf.

The scope of this disaster pushed British officials to redouble efforts to solve "the longitude problem." In 1714, Parliament passed the Longitude Act, establishing a Board of Longitude and offering £20,000 (roughly $12 million in today's money) to anyone who could devise a reliable way to determine longitude at sea. After four decades of experimentation, an English clockmaker named John Harrison (1693–1776) came up with a viable answer. Harrison devised a seaworthy and compact pocket watch that maintained accurate time over long periods, allowing navigators to determine longitude.

Using Harrison's chronometer, captains could set the time at the Royal Observatory in Greenwich, England, before departing. Then at sea months later, if the timepiece indicated midnight "Greenwich time" when the sun showed high noon locally, they knew they were halfway around the world, at a longitude of 180 degrees from Greenwich. Soon mariners everywhere on the globe computed their longitude east or west of Greenwich, which came to mark the prime meridian, or zero longitude, on later maps.

QUESTIONS

1. *Why was knowledge of exact longitude so important to sea captains who had no access to our modern global positioning system (GPS)?*

2. *What is the longitude of your own town? When it is noon at your home, what time is it in Greenwich, England?*

---

harvests. Mothers continued to teach their daughters to spin yarn, weave cloth, sew clothes, plant gardens, raise chickens, tend livestock, and churn butter. The products from these chores could be used at home or sold in a nearby village to buy consumer goods. While the husband held legal authority over the home, a good wife served as a "deputy husband," managing numerous household affairs, or perhaps earning money as a midwife to help make ends meet. She took charge entirely if her husband passed away or went to sea.

But for all their labors, women seemed to lose economic and legal standing to men as New England towns became larger and more orderly. Networks of local officials, consisting entirely of men, drafted statutes and legal codes that reinforced male privileges. Women found it difficult to obtain credit or receive a business license, and the law barred married women from making contracts, limiting their chance for activities outside the home. Gradually, male apothecaries and physicians with a smattering of formal training pushed traditional midwives away from the bedside. Even in the port towns, where women outnumbered men, their rights were limited, and poor women faced particular scrutiny. Selectmen and overseers of the poor had the power to remove children from a widowed mother and place them in the **almshouse.**

ECONOMIC EXPANSION IN THE MIDDLE COLONIES

The fifth regional economy, the one that flourished in the middle colonies between New England and Chesapeake Bay, improved upon these two neighboring worlds. The Europeans who resettled Indian lands in Delaware, Pennsylvania, New Jersey, and New York found a favorable climate, rich soil, and numerous millstreams. Unlike New Englanders, they developed a reliable staple by growing an abundance of grain. They exported excess wheat, flour, and bread as effectively as Southerners shipped tobacco and rice. But unlike the planters in Virginia and South Carolina, middle-colony farmers did not become locked in the vicious cycle of making large investments in enslaved workers and exporting a single agricultural staple. Instead, they developed a more balanced economy, using mostly free labor. Besides grain products, they also exported quantities of flaxseed, barrel staves, livestock, and pig iron. Large infusions of money from Britain during its long war against France in the 1750s further boosted this prosperous economy.

Whereas the Chesapeake had no dominant seaport, the middle colonies boasted two major ports of entry. Hundreds of Europeans, skilled in a craft and unwilling to compete with unpaid slave artisans in the South, flocked to the middle-colony seaports instead. Both Philadelphia and New York grew faster than rival ports in the mid-eighteenth century, passing Boston in size in the 1750s. Each city doubled its number of dwellings in the two decades after 1743, as brick structures with slate roofs replaced older wooden homes covered with inflammable cedar shingles. But new houses could not meet the ever increasing demand. By 1763, Philadelphia had more than 20,000 people, New York had nearly as many, and both cities faced a set of urban problems that had already hit Boston.

As the port towns grew, they became more impersonal, with a greater economic and social distance between rich and poor. Large homes and expensive imports characterized life among the urban elite. In contrast, the poorest city dwellers lacked property and the means to subsist. By the 1760s, Philadelphia's almshouse and the new Pennsylvania Hospital for the Sick Poor were overflowing. In response, Philadelphia's Quaker leaders established a voluntary Committee to Alleviate the Miseries of the Poor, handing out firewood and blankets to the needy. They also built a "Bettering House," patterned on Boston's workhouse, that provided poor Philadelphians with food and shelter in exchange for work.

In an effort to limit urban poverty, authorities in New York and Philadelphia moved newcomers to the countryside, where Dutch and German settlers had already established an efficient farming tradition. As immigration rose after 1730, the burgeoning region slowly expanded its economy far up the Hudson Valley, east into Connecticut and Long Island, and south toward Maryland.

The farm frontier pushed west as well. The acquisitive Thomas Penn had inherited control of Pennsylvania from his more idealistic father, founder William Penn. In 1737, the young proprietor defrauded the Delaware Indians out of land they occupied west of the Delaware River. In the infamous Walking Purchase, Penn claimed a boundary that could be walked in a day and half. Then Penn's men cleared a path through the woods and sent horsemen along to assist his runners, who covered more than fifty-five miles in thirty-six hours. In all, the fast-moving agents took title to 1,200 square miles of potential farmland near modern Easton and Allentown, Pennsylvania. Land-hungry settlers pressed the reluctant Delaware west toward the Allegheny Mountains and occupied the rich river valleys of eastern Pennsylvania. Land agents and immigrant farmers called the fertile region "the best poor man's country."

■ Soon after the Delaware chief Tishcohan posed for this 1735 portrait, his people lost valuable land due to Pennsylvania's notorious Walking Purchase.

Matters of Faith: The Great Awakening

■ *Why did economic and demographic growth go hand in hand with fresh religious intensity after 1730?*

Philadelphia epitomized the commercial dynamism of the eighteenth-century British colonies. The city was a hub in the fastest-growing economic region on the Atlantic seaboard. Ben Franklin, arriving there in 1723 at age seventeen, achieved particular success. Within seven years he owned a printing business. Within twenty-five years he was wealthy enough to retire, devoting himself to science, politics, and social improvement. He created a lending library, developed an efficient stove, promoted schools and hospitals, supported scientific and philosophical organizations, and won fame in Europe for his experiments with electricity.

The outburst of scientific inquiry and religious skepticism spreading through the Atlantic world at the time became known as the Enlightenment, and its spirit of rational questioning and reason was greatly aided by the printing press. In America, Franklin and his fellow printers personified the new Age of Enlightenment. By 1760, the British mainland colonies had twenty-nine printing establishments, more presses per capita than in any country in Europe. These presses squeezed out eighteen weekly newspapers and countless public notices, fostering political and business communication throughout the colonies. American printers also published an array of religious material, for the colonial spirit of worldly enterprise existed uneasily beside a longing for spiritual community and social perfection. The story of another Pennsylvania printer offers an apt example.

> *The colonial spirit of worldly enterprise existed uneasily beside a longing for spiritual community and social perfection.*

In 1720, three years before Franklin arrived in Pennsylvania, Conrad Beissel migrated to Philadelphia from Germany. He lived and preached in nearby Germantown; in 1738 he withdrew farther west to lead a life of unadorned simplicity. Soon other men and women joined him at his retreat near modern-day Lancaster, Pennsylvania. There they created Ephrata Community, the earliest of many wilderness utopias in North America. The communal experiment lasted for more than a generation, supporting itself by operating a printing press. Although Beissel pursued the same trade as Franklin, his experience as a dedicated seeker of spiritual truth represents a very different and important side of colonial life.

In the first half of the eighteenth century, colonists witnessed surprising breakthroughs in religious toleration but also bitter controversies within the ministry. In addition, they experienced a revivalist outpouring, with roots in Europe and America, that later became known as the **Great Awakening.** This stirring began in the 1730s, and it gained momentum through the visits from England of a charismatic preacher named George Whitefield (pronounced Whitfield). In most colonies, the aftershocks of the Awakening persisted for a full generation.

SEEDS OF RELIGIOUS TOLERATION

The same population shifts that made Britain's mainland colonies more diverse in the eighteenth century also created a new Babel of religious voices that included many non-Christians. Africans, the largest of all the new contingents, brought their own varied beliefs across the Atlantic. Some slaves from Portuguese Angola had had exposure to Catholicism in their homeland. But most Africans retained as much of their traditional religions and cultures as possible under the circumstances. At first, they were skeptical toward Christianity. An Anglican missionary recalled one black South Carolinian saying that he "preferred to live by what he could remember" from Africa. Christian efforts to convert Native Americans also had mixed results. A minister living near the Iroquois reported that Indians would beat a drum to disrupt his services and then "go away Laughing."

Paul Rocheleau Photography

■ Members of the Jewish community in Newport started Touro Synagogue in 1759, a century after the first arrival of their ancestors in the Rhode Island seaport. Completed in 1763, this gem of colonial architecture is the oldest existing synagogue in the United States.

Another non-Christian contingent, Jewish immigrants, remained few in number, with only several hundred families by 1770. Merchants rather than farmers, they established communities in several Atlantic ports, beginning in Dutch New Amsterdam (1654) and Newport (1658). Most were Sephardic Jews; that is, their ancestral roots were in Spain and Portugal. They came by way of the Caribbean, reaching Charleston in 1697, Philadelphia after 1706, and Savannah in 1733. A few of their children merged into the Protestant culture, but more than 80 percent of Jewish young people (including a handful of Ashkenazi Jews with ties to central Europe) found partners within their own small communities.

The majority of eighteenth-century newcomers to the British colonies were Christians. A few, such as the Acadians, were Catholics, but the rest had some Protestant affiliation. In the two centuries since the Reformation, numerous competing Protestant denominations had sprung up across Europe. Now this wide array made itself felt in America, as Presbyterians, Quakers, Lutherans, Baptists, Methodists, and smaller sects all increased in numbers. To attract immigrant families, most colonies abolished laws that favored a single "established" denomination. Nevertheless, New England remained firmly Congregational, and the southern gentry (plus merchant elite everywhere) concentrated increasingly within the Anglican Church.

Rhode Island had emphasized the separation of church and state from the start, and Pennsylvania had likewise favored toleration, both as a matter of principle and as a practical recruitment device to attract new settlers. Since migration from Europe was a demanding ordeal, those who took the risk were often people with strong religious convictions. Such newcomers looked for assurances that they could practice their religion freely, and colonies competed to accommodate them. In many places, religious tests still limited who could hold public office, but tolerance for competing beliefs was expanding.

Many felt that if any institution threatened the growing religious toleration in the colonies, it was, ironically, the British king's own denomination. The monarch headed the Anglican Church, and it had influential American members, including almost every colonial governor. Repeated talk by the Church of England about installing a resident bishop in America aroused suspicions among colonists who worshipped in other denominations. This was especially true in New England, where Congregationalists had long opposed ideas of religious hierarchy. In 1750, Boston, which had eighteen churches, rose up against a plan for an Anglican bishop. In a passionate sermon, Reverend Jonathan Mayhew preached that the town must keep "all imperious bishops, and other clergymen who love to lord it over God's heritage, from getting their feet into the stirrup."

THE ONSET OF THE GREAT AWAKENING: PIETISM AND GEORGE WHITEFIELD

As relative toleration became a hallmark of the British colonies, no one benefited more than German-speaking Protestant groups. Numerous religious sects, such as the Moravians, Mennonites, Schwenkfelders, and Dunkers, were fleeing persecution and poverty at home. As their numbers multiplied after 1730, hymns in German became a common sound on

Sabbath day. In 1743, before any American printer produced an English-language Bible, a press in Pennsylvania put out a complete German edition of Luther's Bible, using type brought from Frankfurt.

Collectively, these newcomers were part of a European reform movement to renew piety and spiritual vitality among Protestant churchgoers in an age of increasing rationalism and worldliness. Pietism, as this "Second Reformation" was called, had roots in eastern Germany and stressed the need to restore emotion and intensity to worship that had become too rational, detached, and impersonal. The German pietists reached out after 1700 to inspire Huguenots in France and Presbyterians in Scotland. They influenced reformers in the Church of England such as John Wesley, the founder of Methodism and a teacher at Oxford University. Through Wesley, pietist ideas touched George Whitefield during his time at Oxford in the class of 1736. Over the next decade, "the boy parson" became the first transatlantic celebrity. Hailed as a preaching prodigy, he sparked a widespread religious awakening in the American colonies.

As a boy growing up in England, George Whitefield left school at age twelve to work in the family tavern. But he still managed to attend college, and at Oxford he discovered Wesley and the pietists. He also discovered two other things: the lure of America and his calling to be a minister. His mentor, Wesley, had preached briefly in Georgia. So in 1738, at age twenty-three, Whitefield spent several months in the new colony, where he laid plans for an orphanage near Savannah.

Arriving back in England, Whitefield quickly achieved celebrity status. He drew large crowds with fiery sermons that criticized the Anglican Church. The evangelist's published *Journals,* priced at only sixpence, went through six editions in nine months. He also recruited an experienced publicist. In 1739, word of his popularity preceded him when he returned to America for an extended tour, the second of seven transatlantic journeys during his career. Building on religious stirrings already present in the colonies, Whitefield preached to huge and emotional crowds nearly 350 times in 15 months. He made appearances from Savannah to Boston, something no public figure had ever done.

The timing was perfect. Whitefield's brother was a wine merchant who understood the expanding networks of communication and consumption in the British Atlantic world. Whitefield realized that in America, as newspapers multiplied and roads increased, he could advertise widely and travel extensively. Other ministers from England had remarked in frustration that most colonists knew "little of the nature of religion, or of the constitution of the church." At times, each person seemed to hold to "some religious whim or scruple peculiar to himself." Whitefield thrived on this vitality and confusion. He had little taste for Protestant debates over church organization and sectarian differences. Instead, he believed that an evangelical minister should simply preach the Bible fervently to a wide array of avid listeners. Everywhere he went, Whitefield served as a catalyst for religious activity.

Courtesy, Winterthur Museum (63.639)

■ When George Whitefield visited America in 1739, his preaching spurred the Great Awakening. "God shews me," he wrote in his journal, "that America must be my place for action."

"THE DANGER OF AN UNCONVERTED MINISTRY"

The heightened commotion in American churches had local origins as well. The same tension felt in European parishes—between worldly, rational pursuits and an emotional quest for grace and salvation—also troubled colonial congregations. Occasional local revivals had taken place in America for decades. The most dramatic one occurred in Northampton, Massachusetts, in 1734–1735, spurred by a talented minister named Jonathan Edwards. As the colonies' most gifted theologian, Edwards anticipated Whitefield's argument that dry, rote "head-knowledge"

Jonathan Edwards

made a poor substitute for "a true living faith in Jesus Christ." "Our people do not so much need to have their heads stored," Edwards observed, "as to have their hearts touched."

In a fast-growing society, who would prepare suitable church leaders for the next generation? Candidates for the ministry could train at Harvard College (founded 1636), William and Mary (1693), Yale (1707), or one of several small academies. But these institutions could not instruct sufficient numbers. The shortage of educated ministers, combined with steady geographic expansion, meant that pulpit vacancies were common. A minister might oversee several parishes. Even if he tended only a single one, the great distances separating parishioners made it hard for any pastor to travel widely enough to address their needs. Feeling neglected, people voiced their dissatisfaction over the shortage of ministers.

Edwards, "Sinners in the Hands of an Angry God"

Problems in the pulpit included quality as well as quantity. Many college graduates had too much "head-knowledge" and too little common touch. Their fluency in Latin and Greek often earned them more disdain than respect from down-to-earth congregations. Most foreign-born ministers, such as Anglicans sent from England and Presbyterians from Scotland, had failed to find good positions at home. Too often, they showed limited appreciation for the local church members who paid their salaries, and they resented those who criticized their ministries.

One such critic was William Tennent, a Scots-Irish immigrant who arrived in Pennsylvania with his family in 1716. Dismayed by the cold, unemotional outlook of Presbyterian ministers, Tennent opened a one-room academy in a log house to train his four sons and other young men for the ministry. Local Presbyterian authorities challenged his credentials and disparaged the teachings of his "Log College." Eventually, the school moved and grew, becoming linked to the new College of New Jersey in 1746, which later evolved into Princeton University. But before this happened, Tennent's preacher sons allied themselves with Whitefield and managed to shake the colonial religious establishment to its roots.

One of Tennent's sons, Gilbert, eventually led a Presbyterian church in Philadelphia created by Whitefield's supporters. In 1740, at the time of Whitefield's triumphal tour, young

Gilbert Tennent delivered a blistering sermon entitled "The Danger of an Unconverted Ministry" that became a manifesto for the revival. Cutting to the heart of the matter, he condemned the "sad security" offered by incompetent, uncaring, and greedy ministers. "They are as blind as Moles, and as dead as Stones," he charged, "without any spiritual Taste and Relish." He argued that congregations should turn away from these "Orthodox, Letter-learned . . . Old Pharisee-Teachers" and listen to traveling preachers instead. It was "an unscriptural Infringment on Christian Liberty," Tennent proclaimed, "to bind men to a particular Minister, against their Judgement and Inclinations."

THE CONSEQUENCES OF THE GREAT AWAKENING

Whitefield hailed Gilbert Tennant and his brothers as "burning and shining lights" of a new kind. All the ministers and worshipers who joined in the movement began to call themselves "New Lights." Opponents, whom they dismissed as "Old Lights," continued to defend a learned clergy and emphasized head-knowledge on the difficult road to salvation. The Old Lights opposed the disruptions caused by so-called "itinerant ministers" who traveled freely from parish to parish without invitation. The New Light ministers, in contrast, appealed to people's emotions and stressed the prospect of a more democratic salvation open to all. They defended their wanderings, which made them more accessible to a broader public and less likely to become set in their ways. "Our Blessed Saviour was an Itinerant Preacher," they reminded their critics; "he Preach'd in no other Way."

Just as New Light preachers moved readily across traditional parish boundaries, they also transcended the lines between different Protestant sects. Their simple evangelical message reached across a wide social spectrum to diverse audiences of every denomination. Moreover, their stress on communal singing, expressive emotion, and the prospects for personal salvation drew special attention from those on the fringes of the culture, such as young people, women, and the poor. Not surprisingly, New Light ministers also made headway in spreading Christianity within various African American and Native American communities.

Members of the religious establishment, once secure as unchallenged leaders within their own church communities, now confronted a stark choice. Some powerful churchmen acknowledged their New Light critics and reluctantly welcomed the popular renegades into the local pulpits. Such a strategy might blunt the thrust of the revival, and it would surely raise church attendance. Other Old Lights, however, took the opposite approach: they clung to tradition and stability, challenging their new rivals openly. They condemned itinerancy and disputed the interlopers' right to preach. They mocked the faddish popularity of these overemotional zealots and even banned the New Light itinerants from local districts for the good of the parishioners.

Zealous New Light men and women tried to transcend the competing denominations and create a broad community of Protestant believers.

In the end, neither tactic stemmed the upheaval, which peaked in the North in the 1740s and in the South during the 1750s and 1760s. Its long-term consequences were mixed. Zealous New Light men and women tried to transcend the competing denominations and create a broad community of Protestant believers. But for all their open-air preaching, the reformers could never create such unity, and they left behind no new set of doctrines or institutional structures. Nevertheless, they created an important legacy. First, they infused a new spirit of piety and optimism into American Christianity that countered older and darker Calvinist traditions. Second, they established a manner of fiery evangelical preaching that found a permanent place in American life. Most importantly, they underscored democratic tendencies in the New Testament gospels that many invoked in later years when faced with other apparent infringements of their liberties.

The French Lose a North American Empire

What key factors undermined the French position in America in the decades after 1740?

In 1739, while George Whitefield launched his tour of the English colonies and the Stono slave rebellion erupted in South Carolina, the French dreamed of expanding their American empire. When Pierre and Paul Mallet set out up the Mississippi River from New Orleans that year, the two French Canadians suspected that the Missouri River, the Mississippi's mightiest tributary, stretched to New Mexico. If so, they hoped to claim a new trading route for France. Pausing in Illinois to gather seven French Canadian recruits, the Mallet brothers pushed up the Missouri, hoping it flowed from the southwest.

But the river flowed from the northwest instead. Disappointed, the party left the river in Nebraska, purchased horses at an Omaha Indian village, and set off across the plains, reaching Santa Fe in July. After a nine-month stay, most of them returned east across the southern plains the next year. When the Mallets completed their enormous circuit and returned to New Orleans, they brought word from the West of Indian and Spanish eagerness to engage in greater trade. From their perspective, the future of France in America looked bright indeed. But the promise disappeared entirely within their lifetimes.

Jean-Pierre Lassus, *Vue et Perspective de la Nouvelle-Orleans*, 1726. C.A.O.M. Aix-en-Provence (France) DFC Louisiane 71 (pf6B)

■ By 1726, New Orleans, with 100 cabins and nearly 1,000 inhabitants, was receiving shipments of trade goods from France and distributing them up the Mississippi River and its tributaries. Following a Louisiana hurricane in 1722, the levees along the waterfront were expanded, but flooding remains a threat to the low-lying city even today, as the huge devastation of Hurricane Katrina in 2005 made clear.

PROSPECTS AND PROBLEMS FACING FRENCH COLONISTS

In 1740, French colonists had grounds for cautious optimism. France already claimed a huge expanse of North America. Its wilderness empire ran strategically through the center of the continent. The potential for mineral resources and rich farmland seemed boundless, as French pioneers in the Illinois region already realized. No Europeans had shown greater skill in forging stable and respectful relations with Native Americans. A chain of isolated French forts stretched northward along the Mississippi River and then east to the lower Great Lakes and the St. Lawrence Valley. These posts facilitated trade with Native Americans and secured ties between Canada and Louisiana. With Indian support, more outposts could be built farther east near the Appalachian mountain chain to contain the English settlers and perhaps one day to conquer them.

At least three problems marred this scenario. First, the French population in America paled in comparison to the large number of English settlers. Canada still had fewer than 50,000 colonial inhabitants in 1740, whereas Britain's mainland colonies were rapidly approaching 1 million. Louisiana contained only 3,000 French people, living among nearly 4,000 enslaved Africans and 6,000 Native Americans. Second, French colonists lacked sufficient support from Paris to develop thriving communities and expand their Indian trade. The importation of goods from France was still meager and unpredictable. Finally, an ominous trickle of British hunters and settlers was beginning to cross the Appalachian chain. Carolina traders already had strong ties with the Chickasaw Indians living near the Mississippi River, and Virginia land speculators were eyeing lands in the Ohio Valley.

What seemed a promising situation for the French in 1740 was soon put to the test. Britain and France had long been on a collision course in North America. Colonial subjects of the two European superpowers had already clashed in a series of wars, with Indian allies playing crucial roles. After several decades of peace, warfare was about to resume. Two more contests, King George's War (1744–1748) and the French and Indian War (1754–1763) preoccupied colonists and Native Americans alike over the next two decades. In 1763, the Treaty of Paris ended the French and Indian War, part of a far broader conflict known in Europe as the Seven Years' War.

At that point, less than a quarter-century after the Mallet brothers' optimistic journey through the heartlands, the expansive French empire in North America suddenly vanished.

BRITISH SETTLERS CONFRONT THE THREAT FROM FRANCE

These colonial conflicts of the mid-eighteenth century, generally linked to wider warfare in Europe, had a significant impact on everyone living in the British mainland colonies. A few people took advantage of the disturbances to become rich. They provisioned troops, sold scarce wartime goods, sponsored profitable privateering ventures, or conducted forbidden trade with the enemy in the Caribbean. But many more people paid a heavy price because of war: a farm burned, a job lost, a limb amputated, a husband or father shot in battle or cut down by disease. From London's perspective, the Americans made ill-disciplined and reluctant soldiers. From the colonists' viewpoint, the British offered them too little respect and inadequate assistance.

Adding insult to injury, a hard-won victory on North American soil could be canceled out at the peace table in Europe. In 1745, during King William's War, Massachusetts called for an attack on Louisburg, the recently completed French fortress on Cape Breton Island that controlled access to the St. Lawrence River and nearby fishing grounds. After a long siege, the New England forces prevailed. But British diplomats rescinded the colonial victory, handing Louisburg back to France in 1748 in exchange for Madras in India.

Whatever their differences, the American colonists and the government in Britain saw potential in the land west of the Appalachian Mountains, and both were eager to challenge French claims there. In 1747, a group of colonial land speculators formed the Ohio Company of Virginia, seeking permission to develop western lands. Two years later the crown granted them rights to 200,000 acres south of the Ohio River if they would construct a fort in the area. Moving west and north, the Virginians hoped to occupy a valuable spot where the Monongahela and Allegheny rivers come together to form the Ohio River. The French had designs on the same strategic location (modern-day Pittsburgh, Pennsylvania) controlling the upper Ohio.

In 1753, the Virginia governor sent an untested young major in the colonial militia named George Washington—at age twenty-one already regarded as a promising officer—to warn the French to leave the area. The next spring, Virginia workers began erecting a fort at the Fork of the Ohio, but a larger French force drove them off and constructed Fort Duquesne on the coveted site. When Major Washington returned to the area with troops, he probed for enemy forces. In a skirmish on May 28, 1754, near modern Uniontown, Pennsylvania, his men killed ten French soldiers, the initial casualties in what eventually became history's first truly global war. With 450 men and meager supplies, Washington fortified his camp, calling it Fort Necessity, and dug in to prepare for a counterattack.

> *Throughout the British colonies in 1754, fears spread about the danger of French attacks and the loyalty of Native American allies.*

Throughout the British colonies in the early summer of 1754, fears spread about the danger of French attacks and the loyalty of Native American allies. Officials in London requested that all the colonies that had relations with the Iroquois send delegates to a special congress in Albany, New York, to improve that Indian alliance. Seven colonies sent twenty-three representatives, who hoped to strengthen friendship with the Iroquois nations and discuss a design for a union of the colonies.

With these goals in mind, the delegates to the Albany Congress adopted a proposal by Benjamin Franklin that called for a colonial confederation empowered to build forts and repel a French invasion. The colonies would be unified by an elected Grand Council and a president general appointed by the crown. The delegates hoped the design would be debated by colonial assemblies and implemented by an act of Parliament. But no colonial legislature ever ratified Franklin's far-sighted Albany Plan. "Everyone cries, a union is necessary," Franklin wrote, "but when they come to the manner and form of the union, their weak noodles are perfectly distracted."

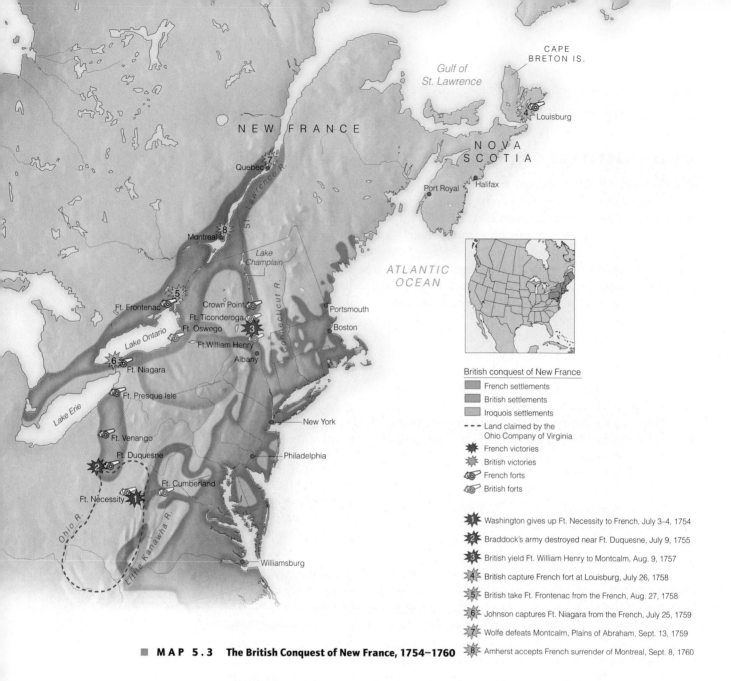

British conquest of New France

- □ French settlements
- □ British settlements
- □ Iroquois settlements
- - - - Land claimed by the Ohio Company of Virginia
- ✳ French victories
- ✳ British victories
- French forts
- British forts

1 Washington gives up Ft. Necessity to French, July 3–4, 1754

2 Braddock's army destroyed near Ft. Duquesne, July 9, 1755

3 British yield Ft. William Henry to Montcalm, Aug. 9, 1757

4 British capture French fort at Louisburg, July 26, 1758

5 British take Ft. Frontenac from the French, Aug. 27, 1758

6 Johnson captures Ft. Niagara from the French, July 25, 1759

7 Wolfe defeats Montcalm, Plains of Abraham, Sept. 13, 1759

8 Amherst accepts French surrender of Montreal, Sept. 8, 1760

■ **MAP 5.3 The British Conquest of New France, 1754–1760**

The main distraction came from Pennsylvania. On July 3, word arrived that the French had defeated Washington's small force at Fort Necessity. But the British were not willing to give up their claims to the Ohio Valley without a fight. Taking the lead, the Virginia government asked for help from Britain in conducting a war against the French and their Native American allies. The crown responded by dispatching General Edward Braddock and two regiments of Irish troops to America. Early in 1755, his force arrived in Virginia, where preparations were already under way for a campaign to conquer Fort Duquesne. Washington accepted an unpaid position as an aide to Braddock, and in June the combined British and colonial army of 2,500 began a laborious march west to face the French.

AN AMERICAN FIGHT BECOMES A GLOBAL CONFLICT

The early stages of the war in America could hardly have been more disastrous for Britain or more encouraging for France. According to his own secretary, the aging Braddock was poorly qualified for command "in almost every respect." A French and Indian force ambushed his column in the forest near Fort Duquesne, cutting it to pieces in the most

Putting Mary Jemison on a Pedestal

In 1910, near the Genesee River east of Buffalo, New York, a statue was erected to commemorate the unusual life of Mary Jemison (1743–1833). Like all historical statues, this one connects two stories: the actual life of the individual, plus the worldview of the benefactor erecting the monument and the artist creating the work.

In 1743, Mary Jemison was born at sea, aboard a ship bound for Philadelphia. She was the fourth child of immigrants from northern Ireland, Jane and Thomas Jemison. The Scots-Irish family carved out a frontier farm in central Pennsylvania. Thomas's brother died in George Washington's defeat at Fort Necessity when the French and Indian War erupted in 1754. Four years later, Shawnee and French raiders destroyed the

Jemison farm, killing and scalping most of their captives during a forced march to the Ohio River. They spared fifteen-year-old Mary, and she was adopted into the Seneca tribe of the powerful Iroquois Confederacy.

Jemison soon became the wife of a Delaware Indian in Ohio and the mother of a son named Thomas. But with the war ending and her husband dead, she trekked more than 600 miles on foot, carrying her infant in a cradle board on her back, to the Seneca homeland in western New York. Staying there by choice, she remarried and became a respected Iroquois parent, landowner, and negotiator. Her descendants remain members of the Seneca nation.

At age eighty, still speaking English fluently, Jemison recounted her personal history to a frontier doctor named James Seaver. He published *A Narrative of the Life of Mary Jemison* (1824), and her first-person account went through numerous editions, making her an American folk figure. Half a century later, the book inspired the Buffalo businessman and philanthropist William Letchworth. A friend and benefactor of the Seneca, Letchworth had Jemison's remains buried at his estate on the scenic Genesee River (now a state park), and he commissioned a statue to mark her grave. The sculptor, H. K. Bush-Brown, studied moccasins, buckskins, and cradle boards in Native American museums and then cast his bronze figure of "the white woman of the Genesee," striding through the wilderness with her child strapped to her back. The powerful but ambiguous monument was unveiled shortly before Letchworth's death in 1910.

QUESTIONS

1. *Why did Mary Jemison's* Narrative *have such lasting appeal? Is the 1910 bronze by Bush-Brown intended to be realistic or idealized—or a bit of both?*

2. *Think of a statue you have encountered portraying a famous person. Does it matter when it was created, or by whom? What ideas or values was it intended to convey?*

thorough defeat of the century for a British army unit. Elsewhere, Indian raids battered the frontiers, spreading panic throughout the colonies. With the local militia away at war, fears of possible slave uprisings swept through the South. The French commander, the Marquis de Montcalm, struck into New York's Mohawk Valley from Lake Ontario in 1756, then pushed south down Lake Champlain and Lake George in 1757. After a seven-day siege, he took 2,000 prisoners at Fort William Henry. In an episode made famous in *The Last of the Mohicans*, France's Huron Indian allies killed more than 150 men and women after their release from the fort.

The change in British fortunes came with the new ministry of William Pitt, a vain but talented member of the House of Commons. Pitt was an expansionist committed to the growth of the British Empire at the expense of France. He brought a daring new strategy to the war effort, and he had the determination and bureaucratic skill to carry it out. Stymied in Europe by the military might of the French army, the British would now concentrate their forces instead on France's vulnerable and sparsely populated overseas colonies. Under Pitt, the British broadened the war into a global conflict, taking advantage of their superior naval power to fight on the coasts of Asia and Africa and in North America as well. By 1758, Britain had undertaken a costly military buildup in America, with nearly 50,000 troops.

The Seven Years' War

To win colonial support for his plan, Pitt promised to reimburse the colonies generously for their expenses. In the South, guns, ammunition, and trade goods flowed freely to Britain's Native American allies. In the North, France lost Louisburg again in July 1758. Fort Frontenac on Lake Ontario fell in August. In November, the French destroyed and abandoned Fort Duquesne. The British seized the strategic site at the Fork of the Ohio, erecting a new post (aptly named Fort Pitt) and laying out the village of Pittsburgh beside it. In Canada, autumn brought a poor harvest, followed by the harshest winter in memory. Ice in the St. Lawrence, plus a British blockade, cut off overseas support from France. The Marquis de Montcalm huddled in the provincial capital at Quebec with his ill-equipped army.

In the spring of 1759, the British pressed their advantage, moving against Canada from the west and the south. As Britain's superintendent of Indian affairs in the region, Sir William Johnson had lived among the Iroquois nations for twenty years. His Mohawk Indian wife, Molly Brant, was the sister of Chief Joseph Brant. As British successes mounted, the Mohawks and other Iroquois became increasingly eager to support the winning side in the war. Sensing this, Johnson recruited 1,000 formerly neutral Iroquois to join 2,000 British regulars on the shores of Lake Ontario. With Johnson in command, they laid siege to Fort Niagara. The fort fell in July, a British victory that effectively isolated enemy posts farther west and obliged the French to abandon them. In August, a British force under Jeffery Amherst captured Ticonderoga and Crown Point on Lake Champlain. The stage was set for an assault on Quebec.

QUEBEC TAKEN AND NORTH AMERICA REFASHIONED

In London, William Pitt knew that capturing Quebec would conquer Canada. Months earlier, he had ordered James Wolfe "to make an attack upon Quebeck, by the River St. Lawrence." Wolfe's **flotilla,** with 8,500 troops, anchored near the walled city in late June. But the French held their citadel despite weeks of heavy shelling. Desperate and sick, Wolfe resorted to a ruthless campaign against the countryside that left 1,400 farms in ruins. Even this strategy failed to draw Montcalm's forces out to fight.

The future of the continent and its inhabitants hinged on a pitched battle between opposing European armies.

As a last resort, Wolfe adopted a risky plan to climb a steep bluff by the river and attack the vulnerable west side of the city. On the night of September 12, 1759, he dispatched troops in small boats to float quietly past French sentries and scale the formidable cliffs. At daybreak, twelve British battalions emerged on a level expanse known as the Plains of Abraham. The future of the continent and its inhabitants hinged on a pitched battle between opposing European armies. Montcalm and Wolfe staked everything in the clash, and both lost their lives in the encounter. By nightfall, the British had won a decisive victory, and four days later the surviving French garrison surrendered the city of Quebec.

Montreal fell to Britain the following year, and fighting subsided in America. But Pitt continued to pour public money into the global war, and one military triumph followed another. The British conquered French posts in India, took French Senegal on the West African coast, and seized the valuable sugar islands of Martinique and Guadeloupe in the French West Indies. When Spain came to France's aid in 1762, British forces captured the Philippines and the Cuban city of Havana. But British taxpayers resented the huge costs of

Thomas Johnson, engraving, 1759. The I. N. Phelps Stokes Collection of American Historical Prints, Prints Division, The New York Public Library

■ *Quebec, the Capital of New France,* by Thomas Johnson. A New England printer, eager to celebrate the fall of Quebec in 1759, copied an old image of the city from a French map. The sketch emphasizes the Catholic churches and seminaries that Louis XIV had promoted in the previous century. But in fact, British cannon fire during the siege of 1759 had devastated much of the town.

the war. Many also worried that the effort to humiliate France and Spain and undo their empires could spark retaliation in the years ahead. Rising criticism pushed Pitt from office, and peace negotiations began.

In a matter of months, the European powers redrew the imperial map of North America. Their complex swaps constituted the largest single rearrangement of territory in the history of the continent. First, France ceded to Spain the port of New Orleans and all of the Louisiana territory west of the Mississippi River. Then, in the 1763 Treaty of Paris, Spain turned over East Florida to Britain, receiving back Havana and the Philippines in return. France gave Britain its holdings between the Appalachians and the Mississippi River as well as the parts of Canada not already claimed by the Hudson's Bay Company. In exchange for this vast acquisition, the British returned the sugar islands of Martinique and Guadeloupe to the French, and they allowed France to retain fishing rights off Newfoundland.

In North America, this "first global war" had involved far more than the British versus the French. Diverse colonists drawn from Europe and Africa had a substantial part in the struggle, and for Indian societies caught between French and English forces, the stakes were particularly high. Ironically, the Paris peace treaty made no mention of the thousands of Native Americans whose homelands were being reassigned. The final results were striking. Britain emerged as the world's leading colonial power. After two centuries, France's North American empire disappeared abruptly, inviting further expansion by English colonists and making political independence from Britain a viable possibility.

Conclusion

For half a century, the complex currents of colonial life had recalled the ancient tale of Babel, as told in the Book of Genesis in the Bible. A confusion of voices, interests, and cultures competed and interacted over a wide expanse in North America. In the process, a string of related economic regions emerged along the eastern seaboard. The British colonies that composed these regions varied in ethnic make-up, but they were all expanding rapidly in population. This unprecedented demographic growth would alter the power and the place of the Atlantic colonies.

CHRONOLOGY: 1715–1763

1715	First whaling ventures from Nantucket.
1718	French lay out New Orleans; Spanish start San Antonio.
1734	Jonathan Edwards leads religious revival in Northampton, Massachusetts.
1737	Delaware Indians lose land to Pennsylvania through the Walking Purchase.
1739	George Whitefield's preaching tour sparks Great Awakening.
1741	British forces capture Louisburg.
1749	Spanish sign treaty with Apache at San Antonio.
1753	Moravians establish Bethabara in North Carolina.
1754	War breaks out in America between French and British. Franklin's Albany Plan.
1755	Braddock is defeated near Fort Duquesne.
1758	Comanche attack Spanish at San Saba Mission.
1759	Quebec falls to the British.
1760	George III becomes king of England. French surrender Montreal to British.
1763	Treaty of Paris ends the French and Indian War.

In 1763, Britain's mainland colonies contained more than 1.6 million people. The figure had quickly come to dwarf all the other population totals on the continent. Amazingly, in the thirteen years between 1750 and 1763, the British mainland colonies added more than 400,000 people. This number of new inhabitants—reflecting natural increase, European immigration, and the African slave trade combined—exceeded the entire population that had been living in British North America five decades earlier, in 1713.

The growth in numbers during the decades to come would be equally rapid, and the changes for the continent were even more dramatic and long lasting. In the dozen years after 1763, the same colonies that had failed to endorse Franklin's Albany Plan of 1754 proved increasingly willing to cooperate in their opposition to new and troubling British policies. As their shared identity grew, the colonists, for the first time, frequently referred to themselves—rather than to the Indians—as *Americans*. This shared identity contributed to the outbreak of the War of Independence in 1775.

For Review

1. How does the rapid appearance of horses on the Great Plains relate to the "Columbian Exchange" described in Chapter 1, page 21?

2. How did non-English newcomers—both European and African—help shape the regional cultures in Britain's Atlantic Coast colonies in this era?

3. In what ways does the biblical image of Babel fit, or not fit, the mainland British colonies in the first several generations of the eighteenth century? (To read the story of Babel, see Genesis Chapter 11.)

4. To what extent was North American history in the two generations before 1763 determined by distant events and decisions in Europe?

5. Do you agree with those experts who see the fall of Quebec in 1759 as one of the most important single events in early American history? Why?

6. Describe at least three major changes in this period that had a lasting impact on the future course of American history.

Created Equal **Online**

For more *Created Equal* resources, including suggestions on sites to visit and books to read, go to **MyHistoryLab.com**.

Chapter 6

The Limits of Imperial Control, 1763–1775

■ At age ninety-three, cobbler George Hewes still recalled his part in the "Boston Tea Party" of 1773.

By the 1760s, Boston had grown into a busy seaport of 16,000 people. The town remained tiny by modern urban standards, but it had become much larger and less intimate than John Winthrop's initial "city on a hill." With expansion, the gap between rich and poor had widened steadily, and the Seven Years' War (the French and Indian War) only worsened the inequality. During the war, wealthy Boston families such as the Hancocks multiplied their fortunes, building stately homes and importing elegant fashions. In 1764, young John Hancock, heir to his uncle's vast shipping business, inherited an immense fortune of £80,000 (nearly $50 million in today's money).

However, most Bostonians lived in a very different world, made worse by a terrible fire that swept the port in 1760 and the economic depression that gripped the region after the war ended in 1763. Half the townspeople had lifetime property and savings worth less than £40, and half of those possessed £20 or less. George Hewes, five years younger than Hancock, was born into this other Boston in 1742. At age seven, Hewes lost his father, a struggling butcher who also sold soap and candles. But unlike Hancock, George had no rich uncle; he became an apprentice shoemaker at age fourteen.

Despite the town's growth, rich and poor still encountered one another on occasion. If anything, those contacts increased during the tumultuous decade that gave rise to the American Revolution. Politics—both imperial and local—heated up in the 1760s, opening rifts in the ruling elite. Throughout the colonies, British officials and other people who supported the crown's policies became known as Loyalists, or Tories. The wealthy among them saw social and economic

Edward Savage, *John Hancock and His Wife*, n.d., (48.8). In the Collection of the Corcoran Gallery of Art, Bequest of Woodbury Blair (48.8)

■ Some wealthy colonists, like John and Dolly Hancock of Boston, joined the Patriot opposition during the 1760s and 1770s. Gradually, these merchants and planters forged a loose and convenient alliance with colonial artisans and workers who inhabited very different worlds.

dominance as their birthright and scorned their rivals for courting favor with the poor. In contrast, leaders of the emerging opposition (known as Whigs or Patriots) consisted of less conservative—often young and ambitious—members of the educated and professional classes. These people downplayed their rank and privilege to win popular support from those beneath them on the social scale.

In Boston, John Hancock was one such person. In 1763, after Hewes repaired an expensive shoe for Hancock, the merchant invited the young cobbler to a New Year's open house at his impressive mansion. In his old age, Hewes still recalled the occasion vividly. Intimidated by the wealth around him, he remembered being scared "almost to death" when the magnate toasted him and gave him a silver coin.

According to Hewes, the two men met again on very different terms a decade later. In December 1773, the shoemaker joined other activists, disguised as Indians, to empty chests of British tea into Boston Harbor. Hewes was one of the first to refer to the event as a "tea party." And he swore that in the darkness he rubbed elbows with Hancock himself and joined him in smashing a crate of tea. Symbolically, the two men were now working shoulder to shoulder. They came together across class lines in a coalition that would soon challenge Europe's strongest empire, Britain, and spark the Atlantic world's first successful anticolonial revolution.

America's implausible alliance between a portion of the colonial elite and a wide spectrum of working people developed gradually and imperfectly. During the decade before 1776, class and regional interests still divided British colonists on many occasions. Prosperous merchants, urban artisans, rural farmers, enslaved African Americans, and numerous wives and widows did not necessarily share common views and concerns. Indeed, they were frequently at odds. Nevertheless, within half a generation, enough of these diverse people—many as distant from one another socially as Hancock and Hewes—came together to stage a successful struggle for political independence.

What shared experiences and beliefs caused this unlikely and unstable partnership to emerge? What events shaped it and prompted it to gather momentum by July 1776, when John Hancock, as president of the Second Continental Congress, applied the first and largest signature to the American colonies' Declaration of Independence? In retrospect, we know that between 1763 and 1775 a significant change in identity took place. Little by little, for the first time, colonists from separate regions and backgrounds began to speak of themselves as Americans—a term that had previously applied only to Indians. (It may well be a sign of the increasing identification with North America that they occasionally wore symbolic Indian garb, as when Hewes and Hancock joined others in dumping tea in Boston Harbor.) At times this self-conscious new identification with North America went too far, as in the creation of a *Continental* Congress. In reality, of course, it did not represent the entire North American continent at all.

In fact, in the Midwest in 1763, thousands of Native Americans under the leadership of Pontiac were fighting to assert their own independence from European encroachment. On the Great Plains, the Comanche and Sioux contended for new territories. Still farther west, other peoples experienced the initial shocks of colonial contact. Suddenly, inhabitants of the Hawaiian Islands and the Alaskan coast were encountering European intruders for the first time. For rival

European empires, competing globally for mastery in the Atlantic, Pacific, and Indian Oceans, North America remained only one prize in a wider imperial contest.

Following the departure of the French, the push of rival powers to establish permanent control over the North American continent continued. But geographic ignorance, limited resources, weak bureaucracies, huge distances, strong-willed colonists, and resilient native inhabitants all posed limits for maintaining and expanding far-flung empires. Russia's foothold in Alaska, like Spain's presence in California, was new and tenuous at best. Spanish dominance at older outposts in Arizona, New Mexico, and Texas remained partial, as was Spain's grip on its newly acquired Louisiana territory. East of the Mississippi River, long-term British control finally seemed certain. But even Britain, secure after its decisive victory over France, would soon be fighting a losing battle to retain much of the American continent that it confidently claimed to control.

New Challenges to Spain's Expanded Empire

How did French, English, and Russian explorers in the Pacific threaten Spain's American empire?

With Spain's acquisition of Louisiana from France in 1763, the Spanish held nominal title to the entire West, from the Mississippi to the Pacific, populated by more than 1 million Native Americans. Whether Spain could explore and defend this vast domain, stretching north toward Alaska, remained an open question. Envious rivals were already probing North America's Pacific coast. French and British exploration voyages challenged Spain's dominance in the Pacific, and Russian colonization in Alaska spurred the Spanish to establish posts along the California coast. These rivalries, in turn, brought new pressures to bear on the West's diverse Indian peoples, even before the United States emerged as a separate entity with expansionist ambitions of its own.

PACIFIC EXPLORATION, HAWAIIAN CONTACT

Defeat in the Seven Years' War removed the French from North America in 1763. Burdened with heavy war debts, France sought fresh prospects in the unexplored South Pacific. As one Frenchman observed, the discovery of a new continent might furnish "opportunities for profit to equal all that has been produced in America." In 1766, a gifted French officer named Louis Antoine de Bougainville set out to search for "Terra Australis Incognita," the Pacific's fabled unknown southern land. Bougainville's voyage marked the first French circumnavigation of the world. Nevertheless, it revealed no continent—only small, lush islands such as Tahiti and Samoa. French hopes for immediate wealth from a new Pacific landmass went unfulfilled.

Not to be outdone, British captains pressed their own Pacific explorations. The most skilled and successful was James Cook, who ranged from the Arctic Circle to Antarctica during three momentous voyages beginning in 1768. In January 1778, during Cook's final voyage, his two vessels happened upon the Hawaiian Islands, eight major volcanic islands, plus 114 minor isles, stretching over 300 miles. More than thirteen centuries earlier (300–500 C.E.), seafaring Polynesians had migrated here in remarkable ocean-sailing canoes, arriving from the Marquesas Islands far to the south. Their descendants, perhaps as many as 300,000 people, lived in agricultural and fishing communities dominated by powerful chiefs.

"Farther than Any Other Man": Captain Cook's Second Voyage

The Wider World

The Ice Islands on the 9th January 1773, engraved by B. T. Pouney, 31st Feb 1777 (engraving) (b/w photo), Hodges, William (1744–97) (after)/Private Collection/The Bridgeman Art Library

■ In January 1773, Captain Cook's *Resolution* confronted the outer edge of an immense Antarctic ice field. Given the dangers, the explorer wrote, "we could not proceed one Inch farther South."

James Cook (1728–1779) had made a name for himself as a naval surveyor during the British siege of Quebec. In 1768, he commanded an expedition to explore the South Pacific and observe the transit of Venus between the planet Earth and the sun. Cook and his crew charted the isle of Tahiti, the South Island of New Zealand, and the east coast of Australia before returning around the globe to England in 1771.

Two more voyages followed. The third and final one—Cook was killed in the Pacific in 1779—is the best known, involving early exploration of Hawaii, careful observation of America's Northwest Coast, and the profitable sale of sea otter pelts in Canton, China. But some have called Cook's arduous second journey, a circumnavigation of the globe from 1772 to 1775, "the greatest single voyage in the history of the world." This memorable expedition from Britain is remarkable not only for its unprecedented three-year length, but also because of Cook's breakthroughs in navigation, geography, and healthy diets for sailors.

During the previous decade a fellow Yorkshireman, clockmaker John Harrison, had perfected a chronometer that allowed captains to determine longitude at sea (see page 153). Cook carried a replica of Harrison's timepiece and confirmed its accuracy. Armed with "our never failing guide, the Watch," he probed toward the South Pole in the Indian Ocean and again in the Pacific. His ship, the *Resolution*, sailed far into polar seas,

reaching 71 degrees south. Cook's Antarctic journey took him "farther than any other man has been before." The cold, lonely mission confirmed that no new nonpolar continent waited to be discovered in the southern hemisphere.

On long voyages, poorly nourished sailors often died of scurvy, a grim sickness caused by lack of vitamin C. But when the *Resolution* finally returned in 1775, the crew had lost only one man to disease, a remarkable achievement for the time. Cook's three-year journey proved that high mortality between decks could be prevented. The captain had stressed clean clothes, ventilated quarters, and a diet that included sauerkraut (preserved cabbage), lemon juice, and vegetables. He took special pride in "having discovered the possibility of preserving health amongst a numerous ship's company for such a length of time." Cook's discovery helped generations of sailors.

QUESTIONS

1. In what ways does Captain Cook epitomize the age of rational enlightenment associated with the second half of the eighteenth century?

2. Why would a long voyage at sea provide a suitable place to make important observations relating diet patterns to certain diseases?

John Webber, *A View of Kealakekua Bay*, c. 1781–1783. Dixson Library, State Library of New South Wales (3.293).

■ When Captain Cook anchored at Hawaii's Kealakekua Bay in 1779, he wrote in his journal that the islanders crowded aboard his two vessels and paddled around them in "a multitude of Canoes." Hundreds of others swam around the ships, along with "a number of men upon pieces of Plank." One such surfboarder is visible in the foreground.

The Hawaiians mistook Captain Cook for Lono, a deity they had expected to reappear, and treated him with hospitality and respect. "No people could trade with more honisty," the captain observed. During the next twelve months, Cook cruised up the west coast of North America. Two centuries after Francis Drake's visit, English mariners still hoped to find a sea passage through North America that might drastically shorten voyages from the Atlantic to Asia. But Cook encountered a solid coastline that stretched all the way to Alaska. Along the way, he traded with Northwest Coast Indians for sea otter pelts.

Cook's vessels returned south in 1779, and they were again greeted with fanfare on the big island of Hawaii. But admiration turned to resentment as the English outstayed their welcome, and an angry crowd of Hawaiians killed Cook and four of his mariners. After the captain's death, his two sloops stopped at Macao in China, where the crew sold their furs at a huge profit. Then they sailed back to England in 1780 with word of the money to be made selling North American sea otter pelts in China. The voyagers also confirmed a disturbing rumor: Russia already had a foothold in this lucrative Pacific traffic.

THE RUSSIANS LAY CLAIM TO ALASKA

In 1728, Vitus Bering, a Danish captain hired to serve in the Russian naval service, completed a three-year trek east across Siberia. Reaching the Kamchatka peninsula on the Pacific Ocean, he built a boat and sailed north between Asia and America through the strait that bears his name today. The journey ended European speculation that Asia was linked to North America. On a second expedition in 1741, Bering visited the Alaskan mainland and claimed it for Russia. He died on the return voyage, after a winter shipwreck on a frozen island.

Bering's crew finally returned to Kamchatka with valuable pelts. Their feat proved that round trips between Russia and America were both possible and profitable. Over the next generation, Russian merchants sent several expeditions to Alaska each year, bringing back furs that they traded with the powerful Chinese empire. One typical journey east along Alaska's Aleutian Island chain in 1752 brought back the pelts of 1,772 sea otters, 750 blue foxes, and 840 fur seals.

Dr. Douglas W. Veltre, Ph.D., Anchorage, AK

■ In 1991, 250 years after Vitus Bering's voyage to Alaska, Russians from Kamchatka sailed replicas of Bering's three small vessels across the North Pacific to Alaska. Aleksandr Maslov-Bering, a descendant of the explorer, poses beside the carved bow of one boat.

Before reaching Alaska, these rough Russian trappers had gathered furs in Siberia for generations using a cruel and effective system. They captured native women and children as hostages, then ransomed them back to their men in exchange for a fixed number of furs. In Alaskan waters, the trappers lacked the numbers, the boats, and the skill to collect large supplies of furs on their own. So they put their brutal hostage system into practice there as well. "They beach their vessels and try to take hostages, children and women from the island or nearby islands. If they cannot do this peacefully, they will use force," one Russian captain explained. "No matter where the Natives hunt, on shore or at sea, they must give everything" to the trappers. Native Alaskans resisted these intruders, but many eventually submitted in a desperate effort to survive.

In the quarter-century before 1780, thirty different companies sponsored expeditions to Alaskan waters. Harsh conditions and stiff competition between ships made the traffic risky for the Russians and far worse for the Aleutian Islanders. The newcomers, bringing diseases, firearms, and their brutal hostage-taking system, reduced the population of the islands. The remaining Aleuts were forced to overhunt their valuable wildlife, making their own survival even more precarious. As the human and animal population of the Aleutian Islands declined, the Russians pushed farther east in search of new hunters and hunting grounds.

The voyages from Kamchatka were growing longer and more expensive, so a Russian organizer, Grigorii Shelikov, planned an Alaskan base to facilitate operations. Shelikov and a partner formed a new company in 1781, and in 1784 they founded a permanent colonial settlement on Kodiak Island east of the Aleutians. The island's native residents offered fierce opposition, but soon Russian traders and Alaskan women were raising mixed-race families. By 1799, the firm had absorbed smaller competitors to become the Russian-American Company, with a monopoly from the czar.

In 1790, with the Kodiak base secure, Russians forced more than 7,000 island inhabitants to embark on vast fur hunts in their versatile two-seat kayaks. That same year, Shelikov hired Alexander Baranov to oversee the Kodiak post and expand operations down the Alaskan coast. In 1799, Baranov established an additional outpost at Sitka in southeast Alaska. When a raid by Tlingit Indians destroyed the fort in 1802, he rebuilt the post. Sitka, called New Archangel at the time, became the capital of Russian America in 1808. From here, Baranov eventually extended the company's reach south toward Spanish California, seeking new hunting grounds and a longer growing season.

SPAIN COLONIZES THE CALIFORNIA COAST

The Seven Years' War had left Spain's king, Carlos III, with vast new land claims in western North America. With only limited resources, the bureaucrats administering Spanish America struggled to oversee the huge domain, but they faced numerous obstacles. Many of the Native Americans across the Southwest resisted several decades of military suppression and slave raids. In addition, clerics offered their own resistance to government designs. The

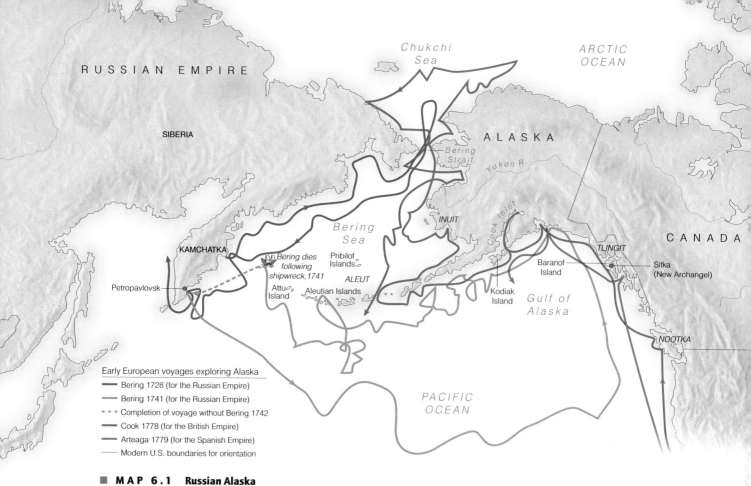

Early European voyages exploring Alaska
— Bering 1728 (for the Russian Empire)
— Bering 1741 (for the Russian Empire)
- - - Completion of voyage without Bering 1742
— Cook 1778 (for the British Empire)
— Arteaga 1779 (for the Spanish Empire)
— Modern U.S. boundaries for orientation

■ **MAP 6.1 Russian Alaska**

powerful Jesuits opposed administrative reform in the colonies, and in 1767 Carlos III expelled them from the Spanish realm. Unruly colonists posed a threat of their own. French inhabitants of New Orleans led a brief rebellion against Spanish rule in 1768. Finally, officials feared challenges in the Pacific from the British and the Russians. As early as 1759, a Spanish Franciscan had published *Muscovites in California,* warning of Russian settlements.

Mindful of the Russian threat, Spanish leaders in America concentrated on establishing a token presence along the Pacific coast. In 1769, they sent a small vanguard north from lower (Baja) California, led by Gaspar de Portolá and Franciscan friar Junípero Serra to establish an initial outpost at San Diego Bay. Portolá then pressed farther up the coast, building a **presidio** (or military garrison) at Monterey in 1770 to "defend us from attacks by the Russians, who," he believed, "were about to invade us."

After the removal of all Jesuits from Spanish America in 1767, numerous Franciscan missionaries, members of a competing Catholic order, expanded their work and took on new responsibilities. Following the lead of Father Serra, other Franciscans soon planted several missions between San Diego and Monterey. These included the San Gabriel mission in 1771, where colonists established the town of Los Angeles ten years later. In 1775, a Spanish captain sailed into spacious San Francisco Bay, and the next year a land expedition laid out the presidio and mission of San Francisco. A town sprang up at nearby San Jose the following year. As Franciscan fathers labored to convert the coast's diverse Indians, Spanish vessels pushed far up the Pacific shoreline. They established contact with the Northwest Coast Indians in 1774. Captain Ignacio de Arteaga reached the Gulf of Alaska in 1779, fourteen months after Captain Cook had been there.

Since Spanish ships traveling north from Mexico had difficulty supplying the few dozen settlers in California, authorities looked for an overland supply route to the coast from Santa Fe or Sonora. In 1774, Juan Bautista de Anza set out in search of a land route to California from the presidio he commanded at Tubac, south of Tucson. Accompanied by a Franciscan named Father

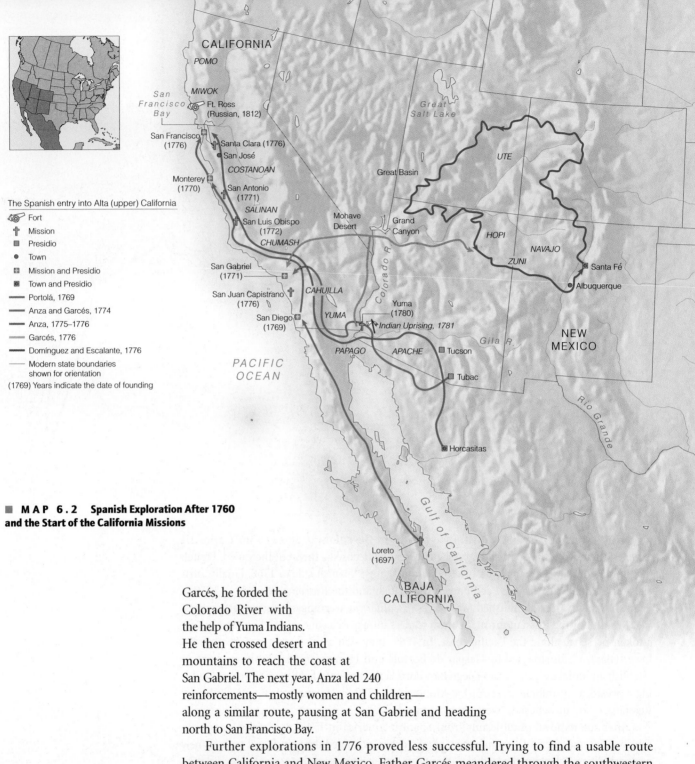

CALIFORNIA

POMO

San
Francisco
Bay

MIWOK

Ft. Ross
(Russian, 1812)

San Francisco
(1776)

Santa Clara (1776)

San José

COSTANOAN

Monterey
(1770)

San Antonio
(1771)

SALINAN

San Luis Obispo
(1772)

CHUMASH

San Gabriel
(1771)

San Juan Capistrano
(1776)

San Diego
(1769)

PACIFIC
OCEAN

CAHUILLA

YUMA

Mohave
Desert

Grand
Canyon

Great Basin

Great
Salt Lake

UTE

HOPI

NAVAJO

ZUNI

Santa Fé

Albuquerque

NEW
MEXICO

Colorado R.

Yuma
(1780)

Indian Uprising, 1781

Gila R.

PAPAGO

APACHE

Tucson

Tubac

Horcasitas

Gulf of California

Rio Grande

BAJA
CALIFORNIA

Loreto
(1697)

The Spanish entry into Alta (upper) California

- ⚜ Fort
- † Mission
- ▪ Presidio
- • Town
- ⊞ Mission and Presidio
- ▣ Town and Presidio
- —— Portolá, 1769
- —— Anza and Garcés, 1774
- —— Anza, 1775–1776
- —— Garcés, 1776
- —— Domínguez and Escalante, 1776
- —— Modern state boundaries
  shown for orientation
- (1769) Years indicate the date of founding

■ **MAP 6.2** **Spanish Exploration After 1760
and the Start of the California Missions**

Garcés, he forded the
Colorado River with
the help of Yuma Indians.
He then crossed desert and
mountains to reach the coast at
San Gabriel. The next year, Anza led 240
reinforcements—mostly women and children—
along a similar route, pausing at San Gabriel and heading
north to San Francisco Bay.

Further explorations in 1776 proved less successful. Trying to find a usable route
between California and New Mexico, Father Garcés meandered through the southwestern
deserts without success. Two other Franciscans, Fathers Domínguez and Escalante, left Santa
Fe on horseback in July 1776. They headed northwest across Colorado and Utah in search of
a more northern route to Monterey on the Pacific coast. But no such trail existed. Instead,
their five-month, 1,800-mile trek revealed the huge expanse of the Great Basin.

The Sonoran path to California that Anza had established proved short-lived. The Yuma
Indians, who had helped his party cross the Colorado River in 1774, soon began to resent
Spanish and mestizo trespassers. The last straw came in the summer of 1781, when a party of
colonial soldiers and settlers arrived at the river, heading for California with nearly a thousand head of livestock. When a sergeant demanded food from the Yuma, he reported that
"the Indians screamed out to me that the cows and horses destroyed their mesquite [trees]
and corn fields." The irate inhabitants asked him why the animals "were not fenced in," and
within weeks they retaliated. Father Garcés and more than 100 Spanish-speaking men,

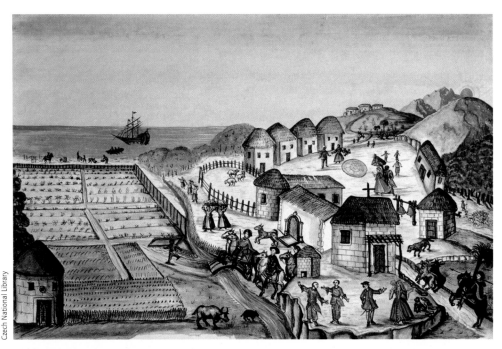

Czech National Library

■ Jesuit missionary Ignacio Tirsch drew this view of his mission at the southern tip of Baja California in the 1760s. A Spanish ship that has crossed the Pacific from the Philippines is anchored offshore. When the Jesuits were expelled from Spain's American empire in 1767, Tirsch returned to his home near Prague in eastern Europe.

women, and children died in the bloody Yuma Revolt, and hopes for a rapid expansion of the Spanish colony in California died with them.

Spain's limited naval strength in the Pacific could not prevent British contact with Hawaii or Russian exploration of Alaska. But the new Spanish settlements along the California coast endured, despite numerous problems. Far inland from these tiny Pacific outposts, the Spanish also managed to retain some control over their recently expanded North American empire. The same could not be said for the British regarding their own newly enlarged empire farther east. They had taken Canada from the French and Florida from Spain. Their military power dominated the Atlantic world. But their fortunes in North America were about to change.

New Challenges to Britain's Expanded Empire

■ *Why did the removal of French and Spanish interests pose new problems for Britain's North American empire?*

In September 1760, French forces at Montreal submitted to British commander Jeffery Amherst in the final surrender of the Seven Years' War. For Native Americans living east of the Mississippi, the French defeat had an immediate impact. General Amherst, who despised Indians as "treacherous" and "contemptible," intended to alter Native American relations in the interior to reflect the new balance of power. He promptly sent James Grant to South Carolina with instructions "to chastise the Cherokees," who had taken up arms against the growing number of English traders and settlers in western Carolina. With 2,800 soldiers—and more than eighty blacks to tend 700 packhorses and 400 beef cattle—Grant invaded Cherokee country in 1761. His men burned fifteen villages, without sparing women or children, and destroyed 1,500 acres of beans and corn.

William Hogarth's *The Times*, 1762

Envisioning History

The great English artist William Hogarth (1697–1764) became a founder of political cartooning. Born poor, the gifted painter and engraver showed a sharp eye for social satire. Hogarth's riotous street scenes used familiar images to offer political commentary and sway public opinion. His allegorical drawings inspired print satirists in the revolutionary era and later generations as well.

In 1762, as Britain maneuvered to end the costly war with France, Hogarth created *The Times,* a fanciful antiwar depiction of London in turmoil. At the center, beneath a dove of peace, King George III (or perhaps his minister, Lord Bute) attempts to put out a fire consuming half the globe, while William Pitt, the previous prime minister (on stilts), continues to fan the flames. London's mayor, who had made a fortune in American tobacco and supported Pitt's aggressive policies, appears at left, trumpet in hand.

Hogarth, ever alert to current events, shows the mayor advertising an Indian, "Alive from America." Several Cherokee chiefs were visiting London at the time, and officials were eager to have their cooperation following the recent frontier war in Carolina. The Native American dignitaries received royal treatment, touring Westminster Abbey, meeting with the king, and delighting thousands of curious

viewers at Vauxhall Garden. Hogarth sensed it would be hard to bring lasting peace to the tumultuous empire.

QUESTIONS

1. Study the clumsy way that workers are hoisting a sign marked "1762." How is Hogarth expressing his uncertainties about "the times"?

2. How would southern colonists react to news that their recent frontier enemies were being treated as dignitaries in London? How would Cherokees respond?

With the Cherokee chastened in the South, Amherst turned his attention to the Indians living north of the Ohio River. Here his harsh policies brought a swift response from the Native Americans. Their sudden retaliation took many lives and cost Amherst his command. And if Indians in the Midwest posed fresh challenges to Britain's expanded American empire, so did the colonists themselves.

MIDWESTERN LANDS AND PONTIAC'S WAR FOR INDIAN INDEPENDENCE

As soon as the British unseated their French competitors in the Ohio River valley, they prohibited traffic with Indians in such goods as knives, tomahawks, muskets, powder, and lead. They also cut back on the use of ceremonial gifts. When the French were still powerful, the British had been generous, but now, one Native American complained, "you Look on us as Nobody." As French traders withdrew, the British took over their strategic posts at Detroit and Michilimackinac. English settlers built new forts in the Ohio Valley and erected massive Fort Pitt over the ruins of Fort Duquesne. Indians at Niagara Falls commented in dismay at "so many Men and so much artillery passing by."

In 1761, wary Seneca proposed a preemptive strike against the British intruders. They failed to recruit their former enemies—the Ottawa, Potawatomie, and Huron—so the plan died. But the next year brought poor harvests, a harsh winter, and a deadly epidemic. Hard conditions, plus the lack of French trade, weakened these "three fires" of the Great Lakes region and made them more willing to take up arms. Early in 1763, word spread among Indians that France would cede Louisiana to Spain and give up Canada and the entire Midwest to Great Britain. For Native Americans, this shocking news undercut moderate leaders willing to accommodate the English.

Word that a treaty in far-off Paris might disrupt the entire region also drew attention to Neolin, a Delaware Indian prophet urging a return to ancient ways and a sharp separation from the corrupting Europeans. Neolin's vision of renewing independence by driving out the British appealed to many Native Americans in the Midwest, including Pontiac, a militant Ottawa warrior. In April, Pontiac addressed a great council of more than 400 Ottawa, Potawatomie, and Huron, meeting within ten miles of Fort Detroit. Invoking the Delaware Prophet's vision, he announced that the Master of Life resented the British and wanted them removed: "Send them back to the lands which I have created for them and let them stay there." By May, he had mobilized a coalition and laid siege to Detroit.

Soon Indians from eighteen nations had joined in Pontiac's widespread uprising. By mid-June 1763, both Detroit and Fort Pitt were under siege, and the British had lost every other Ohio Valley and Great Lakes outpost. As Indian raiding parties ravaged white communities in western Virginia and Pennsylvania, embittered settlers responded with indiscriminate racial killing. In December, white men from Paxton Creek descended on Christian families of Conestoga Indians near Lancaster, Pennsylvania, executing more than thirty peaceful converts. When eastern Pennsylvanians protested this outrage, the "Paxton Boys" marched on Philadelphia to demand increased protection on the frontier. General Amherst ordered his officers to spread smallpox if possible, and to take no Indian prisoners. The Indians deserved extermination, he ranted, "for the good of mankind."

The violence ended in a stalemate. Without French support, Native American munitions ran short, and Detroit and Fort Pitt endured. Indian militancy waned, and fighters deserted the coalition. Then in 1765, Pontiac was assassinated by a Peoria Indian in Illinois. Still, the uprising proved costly for the British and prompted a shift in policy. To avoid further warfare, officials moved to restore the Indian trade, keep squatters and debt evaders out of Indian country, and prevent colonial speculation in western lands. In October 1763, Major General Thomas Gage replaced Amherst in command of British forces.

In England, the crown went further. Late in 1763, it issued a proclamation forbidding colonial settlers from moving west across the Appalachian summit. Beyond that dividing line, all the land east of the Mississippi River would be reserved for Indians and a few authorized British soldiers and traders. While the Proclamation Line of 1763, drawn along the crest of the Appalachians, had only limited success, it frustrated Virginia's gentry. Such prominent men as George Washington and Thomas Jefferson were investors in land companies that speculated in large western tracts, hoping to obtain property cheaply from Native Americans and sell small parcels to eager settlers at a steady profit. But the British government, fearful of sparking unified Indian opposition and additional warfare, denied the Virginians' wishes and aroused their resentment.

GRENVILLE'S EFFORT AT REFORM

In 1763, the same year as the Proclamation Line, King George III appointed Robert Grenville to head a new government in London. Grenville's ministry immediately faced a series of intertwined problems. Britain's victory over the French in the Seven Years War had proved costly, nearly doubling the national debt to a staggering £146 million. As England's postwar depression deepened, returning soldiers swelled the ranks of the unemployed. Aggressive imperialists objected to what they saw as a timid peace settlement with France. In addition, rural mobs protested a new tax on domestic cider, imposed to help whittle away at the war debt.

No one promoted opposition to the government more than John Wilkes, a flamboyant member of Parliament (MP) who published the *North Briton*. In issue number 45 of this outspoken periodical, Wilkes attacked the king's peace settlement and the king himself. Grenville reacted quickly, issuing a general warrant to search the homes of all those connected to the paper. He also arrested the publisher, despite his status as an MP. Angered by the government's sweeping suppression of dissent, protesters made "Wilkes and Liberty!" and "45" into popular rallying cries.

Pressured at home, Grenville sought to impose order on Britain's growing American colonies through a series of reforms. The first step was to maintain a considerable military presence of nearly 7,000 troops in North America. Leaving them there could help enforce peace with the Indians, protect the newly acquired territories of Canada and Florida, and keep young British men employed overseas rather than jobless at home. Strapped for funds, Grenville hoped to pay for the transatlantic forces with money drawn from the very colonies the troops were defending.

> Grenville hoped to pay for the transatlantic forces with money drawn from the very colonies the troops were defending.

Raising money in this way would also remind the British colonies of their subordination to the sovereign power of Parliament. Colonists had grown wealthy by sidestepping the elaborate Navigation Acts and trading illegally with foreign powers, even during wartime. Sympathetic colonial juries had looked the other way. Worse, American legislatures had used their power of the purse to withhold money from any British governor who did not favor local interests. Finally, lax customs officers assigned to colonial ports often collected their salaries while remaining in England, without even occupying their posts.

As a preliminary step, Grenville ordered absentee customs officials to their colonial stations and dispatched forty-four navy ships to assist them. Next, he moved his first reform through Parliament: the American Duties Act of 1764, also known as the Revenue Act or the Sugar Act. The new law increased the duty on sugar and other products, such as wine, spirits, cloth, coffee, and indigo, entering the empire from non-British ports. But most importantly, it cut in half the long-standing import duty of sixpence per gallon on foreign molasses. Officials hoped that New England rum distillers, who had been secretly importing cheap molasses from the French West Indies without paying customs, would be willing to pay threepence per gallon. If enforced, the act would reduce smuggling and boost revenues while saving merchants from the heavy costs of bribing port officials and courtroom participants.

To ensure compliance, the Sugar Act strengthened the customs officers' authority to seize goods off arriving ships. It also established the first of several new vice-admiralty courts, intended to address maritime issues. The presiding judge was sent from England, not drawn from the local population. Moreover, the court sat at distant Halifax, Nova Scotia, so defendants had large travel expenses. Upon arrival, they faced a single appointed judge instead of a favorable hometown jury. Shockingly, a captain or shipowner accused of smuggling was presumed guilty until he could prove his innocence. If he failed to do so, he lost his seized property. "What has America done," protested critics, "to be stripped of so invaluable a privilege as the trial by jury?"

Additional statutes followed quickly. The Currency Act of 1764 prohibited colonial assemblies from issuing paper money or bills of credit to be used as legal tender to pay off debts. The move only worsened the money shortage in British America, where a lopsided trade balance was already draining gold and silver from the colonies to England. Colonial merchants had to pay Grenville's new duties using the same scarce hard money.

The next year, after resentful New Yorkers refused to provide firewood for General Gage's troops, Parliament passed a Quartering Act that obliged colonists to assist the army. Officers could requisition vacant barns and other buildings as temporary quarters when regular barracks and alehouses could not accommodate all their men. The local governor was to

DOCUMENT

Otis, "The Rights of the British Colonies Asserted and Proved" supply the soldiers, at colonial expense, with certain basic necessities they would expect at any inn: firewood, candles, bedding, salt, vinegar, utensils, and rations of beer and cider. Colonial assemblies had willingly voted such support during colonial wars. However, these peacetime requisitions, ordered by a distant Parliament, seemed to challenge their authority and smacked of indirect taxation.

THE STAMP ACT IMPOSED

There was nothing indirect about Grenville's most important reform: the Stamp Act. Early in 1765, Parliament approved the new statute "for raising a further revenue" to pay for "defending, protecting, and securing" the British colonies in America. The act was patterned on a law already in effect in England. It required stamps (rather like those on modern packs of cigarettes) to appear on a variety of articles in America after November 1, 1765. The list included legal contracts, land deeds, liquor licenses, indentures, newspapers, almanacs, and academic degrees. Even playing cards and dice had to bear a stamp.

Stamp Act Stamps

Colonial lawyers and printers were to purchase these stamps from designated agents, passing on the additional cost to their clients and customers. The official stamp distributor in each colony would receive a handsome fee equaling 7.5 percent of all stamp sales. The British Exchequer (Treasury) anticipated taking in £100,000 per year, to be held in a separate account and spent only for government operations in America.

Grenville's proposed stamp bill generated little debate in Parliament. William Pitt, the leader of the opposition party and a friend of the colonists, did not even attend the session. Only Isaac Barré, a veteran of the Quebec campaign, protested. Claiming to "know more of America than most of you," Barré challenged the assertion of Stamp Act supporters that England had nurtured and protected the colonies from earliest times. He defended the Americans as true "Sons of Liberty": loyal British subjects protective of their rights and quick to "vindicate them, if ever they should be violated."

Grenville countered Barré's claims. Americans, the minister argued, had nothing to fear from England. Granted, colonists had no actual representation in Parliament, but neither did the majority of subjects in England. Most of them did not have the right to vote for members of Parliament, yet all of them were said to be "virtually" (implicitly) represented. In other words, all British MPs supposedly had the best interests of the country's entire population at heart. If members of Parliament could look out for nonvoting subjects at home, surely they could provide the same sort of "virtual representation" for all British subjects throughout the realm.

Whether or not they spoke for colonists in America, most MPs viewed Grenville's stamp measure as appropriate and well conceived. They saw no legal distinction between external duties used to regulate trade and enforce the nation's navigation acts and internal taxes imposed by Parliament within the colonies themselves to raise revenue. Because the stamp tax applied to numerous daily articles used throughout the colonies, it would be widely and evenly distributed. Even better, revenues would grow steadily and automatically as colonial economic activity continued to expand.

So as not to cause alarm in the colonies, Parliament set initial stamp prices in America lower than those charged in England, although it could always raise the rates as colonists grew accustomed to the tax. Moreover, the tax was to be gathered quietly by Americans themselves in the course of doing business rather than extracted from citizens by tax collectors. In drafting the act, the ministry had consulted agents serving as lobbyists for the American colonies in London, including Benjamin Franklin. According to these public figures, prominent colonists were eager to accept the lucrative stamp distributorships. No one predicted an upheaval. But the Stamp Act soon unleashed a storm of organized resistance in ports where the stamps were to be sold.

> *The Stamp Act soon unleashed a storm of organized resistance in ports where the stamps were to be sold.*

THE STAMP ACT RESISTED

At first, colonial assemblies had mixed responses to the burdensome new tax. But in late May, the youngest member of the Virginia House of Burgesses—a rising country attorney named Patrick Henry—galvanized American resistance to the Stamp Act. Henry introduced a series of fiery resolves regarding the mandate. The House session was winding down, and many conservative members who endorsed Parliament's right to impose taxes had already departed from Williamsburg. With impressive oratory, the twenty-eight-year-old Henry managed to gain narrow passage of five separate resolutions. Young Thomas Jefferson recalled listening to the heated debate from a hallway, with other students from the College of William and Mary.

Henry's fifth and most provocative resolve asserted that Virginia's assembly had the "sole exclusive right and power to lay taxes" on the colony's inhabitants. The resolution passed by just one vote. In fact, opponents reintroduced it the next day, after Henry himself left town, and voted it down. But the spark had been struck. Within a month, distant newspapers were reprinting Henry's "Virginia Resolves." The papers included not only the resolution that had been voted down but also two ominous-sounding ones that had been drawn up but never introduced for a vote, since approval seemed unlikely. These provocative draft resolutions said that Virginians were "not bound to yield obedience" to such a tax, and anyone arguing otherwise must "be deemed an enemy" to the colony.

In Massachusetts, the assembly took a different approach. It issued a call for each colony to send delegates to a Stamp Act Congress in New York in October 1765 to "implore relief" from Parliament. Local citizens, inflamed by Virginia's resolutions and squeezed by an economic depression, prepared to take more direct action. In Boston, a small group of artisans and merchants known as the Loyal Nine mobilized to force the designated stamp distributor, Andrew Oliver, to resign before the stamps arrived from England. On August 16, a crowd of several thousand hanged an effigy of Oliver and tore down his newly erected Stamp Office. That night, the protesters ransacked Oliver's elegant house, drinking his wine and smashing his furniture. The next day, Oliver resigned his appointment.

As word of the protest spread, crowds took to the streets in scores of towns. Often the mobs were encouraged by local leaders who opposed the Stamp Act. These prominent citizens had started to organize in secret groups. Adopting the ringing phrase Isaac Barré had used before Parliament, they called themselves the **Sons of Liberty.** Their speeches and additional prompting helped to incite angry demonstrators. The crowds, in turn, forced the resignation of potential stamp distributors in ports from New Hampshire to the Carolinas. When a shipment of stamps finally arrived in New York City, nearly 5,000 people risked open warfare to confiscate the hated cargo.

Throughout the second half of 1765, the Sons of Liberty promoted street violence against specific targets. But they could not always control the demonstrations, since the debtors, sailors, blacks, and women drawn to such crowds all had separate grievances of their own. For example, on August 26 in Boston, just ten days after the raid on Oliver's house, a second mob launched a broader assault. Without sanction from the Loyal Nine or the Sons of Liberty, the crowd attacked the houses of several wealthy office holders, including the home of

The Library of Congress

■ Lawyers and artisans in the Sons of Liberty encouraged demonstrations against the Stamp Act. But they ran the risk, suggested here, that poor workers, black slaves, and women in the crowds might give their own meanings to the shouts of "Liberty!"

Hudson Bay Company

Nova Scotia

Quebec

Ft. Edward Augustus,
abandoned June 15, 1763

Ft. Michilimackinac,
June 2, 1763

Halifax

Quebec

Three Rivers

ME
(part of Mass.)

Annapolis
Royal

Montreal

Lake
Nipissing

St. Lawrence R.

NH

Portsmouth
Salem
Marblehead

Windham

Ft. Niagara

Albany

Lebanon
Hartford
Wethersfield

Boston
Pomfret
Plymouth

NY

MA

RI

Ft. Presque Isle,
June 14–17, 1763

Wallingford
New Haven
West Haven
Milford

CT

Norwich
Newport
New London

Ft. Detroit

PA

Ft. Venango,
June 13, 1763

Woodbridge

Lyme
Stratford
Fairfield
New York

Paxton

Piscataway

Ft. St. Joseph,
May 25, 1763

Ft. Sandusky,
May 16, 1763

Ft. Le Boeuf,
June 18, 1763

Amwell Twp.

Elizabeth Town
Perth Amboy
Brunswick

Ft. Pitt

Lancaster
Conestoga

NJ

Salem

Philadelphia

Baltimore

Ft. Miami,
May 27, 1763

Frederick Town

Elk Ridge Landing

Talbot
Annapolis

DE

Lewes

Ft. Ouiatenon,
May 31, 1763

Dumfries

MD

ATLANTIC
OCEAN

Leeds
Tappahannock

Ft. Chartres

Indian
reserve
(by proclamation 1763)

VA

Williamsburg

Norfolk

Spanish
Louisiana

NC

New Bern

Cross Creek

Duplin

Wilmington
Brunswick
Fort Johnson

SC

Proclamation Line 1763

Charleston

GA

Mississippi R.

Savannah

Boundary after 1764

West Florida

St. Mary's R.

Boundary in 1763

Mobile

Ft. Apalachee

St. Augustine

Pensacola

New Orleans

Gulf of
Mexico

East
Florida

British dominance in eastern North America

Acquired by Britain from France
Acquired by Britain from Spain
Prior British colonies, as of 1763
Reserved to Indians under British rule
Spanish Louisiana

Points of violence, 1763–1766

British forts seized during Pontiac's Rebellion in 1763
Towns demonstrating against the Stamp Act in 1765

Distribution of British troops

British posts 100–250 soldiers
British posts 250–600 soldiers
British posts over 600 soldiers

■ **MAP 6.3** **British North America, 1763–1766**

In 1763, the British worked to govern their new provinces in
Canada and Florida, while suppressing an Indian uprising in the
Midwest. With widely dispersed troops, they also tried to keep
colonists out of the Mississippi Valley and halt opposition to the
1765 Stamp Act.

Lieutenant Governor Thomas Hutchinson. Because he also served as chief justice of the Superior Court, Hutchinson had offended townspeople by issuing numerous warrants for debtors and collecting large fees for administering bankruptcies. He recounted how he fled when "the hellish crew fell upon my house with the Rage of devils and . . . with axes split down the doors," pillaging his entire estate.

In South Carolina several months later, the spirit of insurrection also went well beyond the careful boundaries intended by the Sons of Liberty. They were pleased when Charleston artisans hanged a stamp distributor in effigy, with a sign reading "Liberty and no Stamp Act." And they gave tacit approval when white workers harassed the wealthy slave trader and potential stamp distributor Henry Laurens with chants of "Liberty, Liberty!" Soon, however, enslaved African Americans also took to the streets, raising their own defiant cry of "Liberty, Liberty!" Fearing an insurrection by South Carolina's black majority, the same people who had sanctioned earlier street demonstrations quickly shifted their focus, believing that ideas of freedom had spread too far. The colonial assembly temporarily banned further importation of Africans. Local leaders expanded slave patrols and placed Charleston briefly under martial law.

Elsewhere, too, the colonial elites took steps to contain the turbulence. Many moved—often reluctantly—toward more radical positions, joining the Sons of Liberty and ridiculing the British concept of virtual representation. Colonial assemblies condemned Grenville's intrusive reforms. The Stamp Act Congress passed resolutions vehemently protesting both the Sugar and Stamp acts. But even as they challenged Parliament, these same local leaders counseled caution and restraint. They stressed their continuing loyalty to the crown and moved to control the violence, some of which was directed at them. Such moderation appealed to cautious merchants in Boston, New York, and Philadelphia. Reluctantly, they agreed to stop ordering British goods. They hoped that exporters in Britain, feeling the economic pinch of a colonial boycott, might use their political strength to force a repeal of the Stamp Act and defuse the tense situation.

DOCUMENT

Franklin, Testimony Against the Stamp Act

When politics in London prompted Grenville's sudden removal from office, hopes rose in America for a possible compromise resolving the Stamp Act crisis. In March 1766, these hopes were nearly fulfilled. The new ministry of Lord Rockingham, responding to merchant pressure as predicted, and also to the compelling rhetoric of William Pitt, persuaded Parliament to repeal the Stamp Act. But the colonial victory had a hollow ring to it, for the repeal bill was accompanied by a blunt Declaratory Act. In it, the members of Parliament declared clearly that they reaffirmed their power "to make Laws . . . to bind the Colonists and People of America . . . in all Cases whatsoever."

"The Unconquerable Rage of the People"

■ *How did events in America and Britain in the 1760s confirm the skeptical worldview of "Real Whigs"?*

As news of Stamp Act repeal spread, the Sons of Liberty organized elaborate celebrations in British America. In Charleston and Philadelphia, citizens staged public "illuminations," placing lighted candles in the windows of their homes. In Boston, fireworks lit up the town, and John Hancock treated the public to casks of Madeira wine. But word of the Declaratory Act had a sobering effect. Clearly, the problems surrounding colonial taxation and representation remained unresolved. The atmosphere of mutual suspicion and righteous indignation that had erupted during the Stamp Act crisis divided colonists further in the years ahead.

A flurry of pamphlets from colonial presses broadened awareness of the issues, sharpened arguments, and inspired new coalitions. For the first time, colonists from separate regions and different countries of origin began to identify themselves as Americans, gradually adopting a term their ancestors had applied only to Indians. Most importantly, as colonial leaders collaborated with one another, they discovered a shared viewpoint that gave heightened meaning and importance to each new event. This emerging ideology had deep roots stretching back into earlier periods in English history.

POWER CORRUPTS: AN ENGLISH FRAMEWORK FOR REVOLUTION

The radical ideas that had appeared during England's Civil War in the 1640s, when English subjects briefly overthrew their monarchy and proclaimed a Puritan Commonwealth, lived on long after the Restoration in 1660. Decades later, the English Whigs who led the Glorious Revolution in 1688 invoked some of these same principles when they limited the monarch's power and strengthened Parliament's authority. Succeeding generations of mainstream publicists hailed the rights of all freeborn English subjects and congratulated themselves that Great Britain (as England and Scotland became known in 1707) had achieved a truly balanced government. They drew on the ancient Greek philosopher Aristotle to explain their accomplishment.

Aristotle, his modern readers noted, had observed a cycle in politics. He believed that too much power vested in a king could eventually corrupt the monarchical form of government. Unbounded royal power led to a tyranny, misrule by a despot wielding absolute control. When nobles then asserted themselves against the tyrant (as English barons had done when they forced King John to sign the Magna Carta in 1215), the resulting aristocracy could easily turn corrupt as well. Abuse of power by such an oligarchy of self-serving nobles could then prompt the common people, known as the commons, to rise up. If the commons gained sway, they might build a democracy, but it too could degenerate, leaving only anarchy. Such a "mobocracy," therefore, could pave the way for an opportunistic leader to once more seize the scepter of royal power and start the cycle over again.

Confident English Whigs, the leaders of the country's dominant merchant elite, claimed that Britain had halted this vicious cycle by balancing the power of the nation's three estates. The king, they argued, epitomized the legitimate interests of monarchy; the House of Lords represented the aristocracy; and the House of Commons represented the commons—the rest of the population. However, a few of the more radical Whig theorists continued to oppose this consensus view long after 1700. Calling themselves the **Real Whigs,** these skeptics argued that the existing mixed government—which claimed an ideal and lasting balance between monarchy, the aristocracy, and the commons—was less perfect and more vulnerable than most people suspected.

A truly balanced government, the Real Whigs argued, is hard to achieve and difficult to maintain, for power inevitably corrupts. Schemers who obtain public office can readily disrupt such a fragile system, so its protection, these critics argued, demanded constant vigilance. They urged citizens to watch for the two surest signs of decay: the concentration of wealth in few hands and the resulting political and social corruption. Where others saw stability in England's exuberant growth, these Real Whigs perceived sure signs of danger in the powerful new Bank of England, the expanding stock market, and the rise in public debt.

No Real Whigs proved more vigilant than John Trenchard and Thomas Gordon. The two men sensed around them the same luxury and greed that had undermined the Roman Republic. They pored over the works of ancient writers such as the Roman statesman Cato, who described and challenged corrupt behavior. In 1721, they published *Cato's Letters: Essays on Liberty,* cautioning against "the Natural Encroachments of Power" and warning that "public corruptions and abuses have grown upon us."

> *A truly balanced government, the Real Whigs argued, is hard to achieve and difficult to maintain, for power inevitably corrupts.*

Trenchard and Gordon took particular offense at Britain's corrupt patronage system. Public positions were often used to reward loyal support. Many people appeared to gain a post (often in the colonies) through political ties rather than through skill or training. The authors of *Cato's Letters* saw each individual act of corruption, if unopposed, as representing a dangerous precedent. They reminded their readers that tyranny is usually imposed through small, subtle steps, for "if it is suffered once, it is apt to be repeated often; a few repetitions create a habit." Before the citizens realize that they are losing their liberties, the permanent "Yoke of Servitude" is in place, supported by military force. All hope of successful protest has disappeared. Equally insidious, would-be tyrants may actually "provoke the People to Disaffection; and then make that Disaffection an Argument for new Oppression . . . and for keeping up Troops." The encroachment of power over liberty, the authors concluded, is "much easier to prevent than to cure."

AMERICANS PRACTICE VIGILANCE AND RESTRAINT

Though Trenchard and Gordon attracted only limited attention in England, the two writers earned a wide American following. The popularity of *Cato's Letters* and related tracts continued to spread in the colonies during the 1760s, for colonists saw disturbing parallels between the warnings of Real Whig authors and current events in America. Now, as throughout history, a government tainted by corruption might deny adequate representation, initiate unjust taxes, or replace jury trials with arbitrary courts. Officials might curtail freedoms of press or religion to consolidate their power. Moreover, weak ministers might advise the king poorly or keep citizens' pleas from reaching his ears. If the people relaxed their guard, these ministers might even sanction a standing army in peacetime to impose arbitrary rule over their own population.

According to Real Whig doctrine, ordinary people must be alert but circumspect; a measured response to these threats was all-important. One stubborn or mistaken act by officials did not necessarily indicate a pattern of conspiracy. Also, it could be counterproductive to raise alarms too often. So prudent citizens should turn first to legal methods of redress. If the system was functioning properly, claims of real abuses would bring forth proper corrections. Even if forced to take to the streets as a last resort, crowds should be organized and purposeful, not uncontrolled. They should threaten property rather than people and hang effigies, not actual office holders.

For the most part, the Stamp Act demonstrations had followed this logic of restraint and had gained the desired effect. "In every Colony," wrote John Adams, "the Stamp Distributors and Inspectors have been compelled, by the unconquerable Rage of the People, to renounce their offices." But did individual demands for liberty have limits? If so, what were they? Could slaves seek liberty from their masters? What about wives from their husbands? Could tenants press for redress from rich landlords, or debtors from powerful creditors? Such questions generated widespread, heated debate in the turbulent quarter-century ahead.

Benjamin Blyth, *Abigail Adams*, c. 1766. Courtesy of the Massachusetts Historical Society, MHS #73

■ In 1766, at age twenty-two, Abigail Adams was already astute, practical, and well informed. Despite conventions of female deference, she shared political opinions and business decisions with her ambitious husband, Massachusetts lawyer John Adams.

RURAL UNREST: TENANT FARMERS AND REGULATORS

For colonists, certain events in Europe after 1765 seemed to confirm the views that the Real Whigs had passed down. When John Wilkes was repeatedly elected to Parliament but expelled from the Commons for his radical views, his American supporters rallied on his behalf. Similarly, British colonists embraced the short-lived cause of Pasquale Paoli, who fought to free the Mediterranean island of Corsica from domination by Genoa. Many colonists christened their sons after Wilkes or Paoli, and Pennsylvanians named new towns after these overseas heroes. The two men seemed to embody a broader struggle of liberty against tyranny—a contest that often flared up closer to home as well.

In local controversies, both large and small, the "Rage of the People" frequently boiled up from below. "The People, even to the lowest Ranks, have become more attentive to their Liberties," John Adams observed, "and more determined to defend them." While stamp protesters demonstrated in New York City, aggrieved tenant farmers staged a violent revolt against powerful landholders in the Hudson River valley. They chose an Irish immigrant as their leader, established a council, organized militia companies with elected captains, and broke open local jails to free debtors. They even set up their own people's courts to try captured Hudson Valley gentry, before British troops finally suppressed the revolt.

Unrest also shook the Carolinas in the interior region known to colonists as the backcountry, or the Piedmont. In South Carolina, the absence of civil government beyond the coastal parishes fostered lawlessness and disunity among white settlers until the governor extended circuit courts into the interior in 1769. In North Carolina, migrants seeking fertile land moved south from Virginia and Pennsylvania in a steady stream. When they arrived in the Piedmont, they found a local elite already appointed to county offices by the governor. The newcomers disliked these grasping office holders who possessed family and financial ties to powerful planters and merchants farther east. They seemed to epitomize, at the local level, the sorts of corruption that had long troubled Real Whig pamphleteers.

As backcountry settlers grew in numbers, they protested against their inadequate representation in North Carolina's assembly. They began organizing into local groups to better "regulate" their own affairs, and they soon became known as **Regulators**. These small farmers, many of them in debt after moving to a new region, protested loudly against **regressive taxes** that imposed the same burden on all colonists, regardless of their wealth or poverty. The Regulators' discontent turned into outrage when the coastal planters who dominated the assembly voted public funds to build a stately mansion in New Bern for William Tryon, the colonial governor. By this act, the slaveholding elite in eastern North Carolina hoped to establish the colony's permanent capitol building on the coast, and yet Piedmont farmers would bear most of the cost of constructing the mansion.

The decision to build "Tryon's Palace" at public expense confirmed the worst suspicions of backcountry settlers. The governor and his associates, they decided, were concerned primarily with their own wealth, at the expense of the public interest. Thousands of angry Piedmont farm families joined local alliances that swelled into the well-organized Regulator Movement. They filed petitions, withheld their taxes, closed courts, and harassed corrupt officials, protesting the "unequal chances the poor and weak have in contentions with the rich and powerful."

> *Thousands of angry Piedmont farm families joined local alliances that swelled into the well-organized Regulator Movement.*

Both sides dug in their heels. In 1771, Governor Tryon finally called out the militia and marched into the Piedmont. After defeating several thousand angry farmers at the battle of Alamance in May 1771, Tryon hanged six Regulator leaders in Hillsborough and forced backcountry residents to swear an oath of loyalty. Many refused, migrating farther south to backcountry Georgia or west to the Appalachian Mountains. Their leader, a Quaker named Herman Husband, barely escaped with his life. In North Carolina, just as in the Hudson Valley, well-to-do members of the Sons of Liberty dismissed the organized and militant farmers as misguided rabble.

"Squeez'd and Oppressed": A 1768 Petition by 30 Regulators

Interpreting History

In the 1760s, corruption prevailed among appointed officials in central North Carolina. Often holding numerous offices at once, these men managed elections, controlled courts, and gathered taxes. Apparently not all the tax money they collected made it to the public treasury. Nevertheless, any farmer who resisted paying might lose the plow horse or the milk cow that sustained the family. It could be "seized and sold" to cover a small tax payment or minor debt, with "no Part being ever Return'd" from the proceeds.

Banding together to better regulate their own affairs, angry farmers sought relief through every possible legal means. By 1768, these organized Regulators had exhausted most avenues of peaceful protest. The western counties where they resided were badly underrepresented in the colonial assembly. As a new session prepared to convene, they fired off a final round of petitions, assuring legislators that they were law-abiding citizens willing to pay their legal share of taxes. In this message of October 4, 1768, thirty Regulators begged for the appointment of honest public officials.

Photo courtesy of Tryon Palace Historic Sites and Gardens

■ Tryon's Palace, the governor's home in New Bern, North Carolina, built in 1768.

To the Worshipful House of Representatives of North Carolina

Your Poor Petitioners [have] been Continually Squez'd and oppressed by our Publick Officers both with Regard to their fees as also in the Laying on of Taxes as well as in Collecting. . . . Being Grieved thus to have our substance torn from us [by] . . . such Illegal practices, we applied to our public officers to give us some satisfaction . . . which they Repeatedly denied us.

With Regard to the Taxes, . . . we labour under Extreem hardships. . . . Money is very scarce . . . & we exceeding Poor & lie at a

A Conspiracy of Corrupt Ministers?

■ *Did the Boston Massacre highlight deep, justifiable colonial grievances, or was it a provoked attack, exploited by colonial dissidents?*

Numerous sharp divisions—some leading to armed conflict—continued to separate colonists of different classes and regions. But ill-timed steps by successive administrations in London attracted widening attention throughout British America, prompting uneasy new alliances. Colonists familiar with the dire warnings of Real Whig pamphleteers asked themselves a question: in the weak and short-lived ministries that succeeded Grenville's, were the leaders simply ill-informed, or were they corrupt? Colonists wondered whether there was some official conspiracy to chip away at American liberties. Even loyal defenders of the crown expressed frustration with new policies, fearing that they were too harsh to calm irate colonists, yet too weak to force them into line. "It's astonishing to me," wrote a beleaguered supporter from Boston, "after the Warning and Experience of the Stamp Act Times, that any new Impositions should be laid on the Colonies," especially "without even so much as a single Ship of Warr" to back up new measures.

Parliament's first new imposition after repealing the Stamp Act was the Revenue Act of 1766. This act further reduced the molasses duty, from threepence per gallon to a single great distance from Trade which renders it almost Impossible to gain sustenance by our utmost Endeavours. . . .

To Gentlemen Rowling in affluence, a few shillings per man may seem triffling. Yet to Poor People who must have their Bed and Bedclothes, yea their Wives Petticoats, taken and sold to Defray, how Tremenious [tremendous] . . . must be the Consequences. . . . Therefore, dear Gentlemen, to your selves, to your Country, and in Pity to your Poor Petitioners, do not let it stand any longer to Drink up the Blood and vitals of the Poor Distressed.

After seeking relief from existing taxes, the petitioners went on to question new burdens, such as the law imposing an additional tax "to Erect a Publick Edifice" for Governor Tryon in New Bern.

Good God, Gentlemen, what will become of us when these Demands come against us? Paper Money we have none & gold or silver we can Purchase none of. The Contingencies of Government Must be Paid, and . . . we are Willing to Pay, [even] if we [must] sell our Beds from under us. And [yet] in this Time of Distress, it is as much as we can support. . . . If, therefore, the Law for that Purpose can be happily Repealed, . . . May the God of Heaven Inspire you with sentiments to that Purpose.

We humble Begg you would . . . Use your Influence with our Worthy, Virtuous Governor to discontinue . . . such Officers as would be found to be ye Bane of Society, and [instead to] Put in the Common Wealth [officials willing] to Encourage the Poor

and . . . to stand [up] for them. This would Cause Joy and Gladness to Spring from every Heart. This would cause Labour and Industry to prevail over Murmuring Discontent. This would Raise your poor Petitioners . . . to a flourishing Opulent and Hoping People. Otherwise . . . disatisfaction and Melancholy must Prevail over such as Remain, and Numbers must Defect the Province and seek elsewhere an Asylum from Tyranny and Oppression. . . .

We leave it to you . . . in your great Wisdom . . . to pass such Act or Acts, as shall be Conducive to the welbeing of a whole People over Whose welfare ye are plac'd as Guardians. . . . For the Lords Sake, Gentlemen, Exert your selves this once in our favour.

QUESTIONS

1. *How, specifically, do the tone and content of this petition reflect the widespread political outlook, combining vigilance and restraint, described in* Cato's Letters?

2. *Pick some current issue that concerns you deeply and draft a brief, impassioned petition to your legislators. In compelling language, lay out your best arguments for action. Then, see if thirty people will sign your petition.*

Source: William S. Powell, James K. Huhta, and Thomas J. Farnham, eds., *The Regulators of North Carolina: A Documentary History, 1759–1776* (Raleigh: State Department of Archives and History, 1971), pp. 187–189. Some corrections have been made for readability.

penny, to discourage smuggling and raise revenue. Colonial merchants accepted this measure as an external tax designed to regulate imperial trade. Most paid the new duty, and customs revenues rose. But Real Whig warnings reminded them that compliance with seemingly innocuous legislation could set a dangerous precedent. The skeptics had a point, for Parliament soon imposed new hard-line measures.

THE TOWNSHEND DUTIES

The new statutes were set in motion by Charles Townshend, the chancellor of the Exchequer (or chief finance minister). He hoped Americans would accept "regulations of trade" intended to raise funds for colonial affairs. Townshend died suddenly in 1767, before his central measure took effect, but the bill carried his name. Passage of the Townshend Revenue Act sparked angry responses from colonists. The most telling came from John Dickinson, a moderate Philadelphia lawyer. He drafted a series of widely circulated "Letters from a Farmer in Pennsylvania," urging colonists to respond "peaceably—prudently—firmly—jointly." He dismissed any distinction between external and internal taxation, and he also rejected the idea that Americans had "virtual" or implicit representation in Parliament. "We are taxed without our own consent," Dickinson proclaimed to his readers. "We are therefore—SLAVES."

DOCUMENT

John Dickinson, Letters from a Farmer in Pennsylvania

The Revenue Act obliged colonists to pay duties for the importation of any glass, paint, lead, paper, and tea. Proceeds were to be spent in the colonies for "the administration of justice, and the support of civil government," a seemingly benevolent gesture. But Dickinson and other colonists pointed out what these two phrases actually meant. "The administration of justice" cloaked expanded searches of American homes and shops in which customs officers used hated "writs of assistance" to ferret out smuggled goods. "The support of civil government" ensured that governors and appointed office holders could draw their pay directly from the new duties instead of depending on an annual salary grant from the local assembly. In short, the new act removed from colonial legislatures one of their strongest bargaining tools in dealing with the crown: the power to pay or withhold the yearly salaries of key officials sent from Britain.

Similar acts and instructions followed. Asserting its sovereignty, Parliament disciplined the New York Assembly for its "direct disobedience" in refusing to comply with the Quartering Act of 1765. The crown instructed governors in America, now less dependent for their salaries on colonial lower houses, to disapprove any further measures from legislatures asserting their traditional control over how members were chosen, what their numbers should be, and when they would meet.

Equally galling, the Customs Act of 1767 established a separate Board of Customs for British North America. Ominously, the commissioners would live in Boston rather than London. To strengthen the board's hand, in 1768 Britain expanded the number of vice-admiralty courts in North America from one to four. It supplemented the court in Halifax (established by the Sugar Act of 1764) with new courts in Boston, Philadelphia, and Charleston. Furthermore, to look after its troublesome mainland colonies, the British government created a new American Department. It was to be overseen by the Earl of Hillsborough, a former president of the Board of Trade who became the first secretary of state for the American colonies. It also began to move British troops in America from remote frontier outposts to major Atlantic ports, both as a cost-cutting measure and as a show of force.

Americans found these measures threatening, especially when considered as a whole. In February 1768, the Massachusetts legislature, led by forty-six-year-old Samuel Adams, petitioned the king for redress. The legislators circulated a call to other colonial assemblies to voice similar protests. Condemning the Townshend Revenue Act as unconstitutional, they argued that it imposed taxation without representation. By removing control of the governors' salaries from colonial legislatures, they said, Parliament set the dangerous precedent of making royal officials "independent of the people." Lord Hillsborough demanded an immediate retraction of this provocative "Circular Letter" and ordered the dissolution of any other assembly that took up the matter.

VIRTUOUS RESISTANCE: BOYCOTTING BRITISH GOODS

In June, just as word arrived of the Wilkes Riot in London, events in Boston took a more radical turn. Defying Hillsborough, the Massachusetts assembly voted against rescinding its circular letter. On June 5, a dockside crowd faced down a "press-gang" from a British warship and protected local sailors from being forced (or "pressed") into naval service. Five days later, customs officials seized John Hancock's sloop, *Liberty*, and demanded that he pay import duties for a cargo of Madeira wine. This move sparked a huge demonstration, as citizens dragged a small customs boat through the streets and burned it on Boston Common. "Let us take up arms immediately and be free," Sam Adams was heard to say; "We shall have thirty thousand men to join us from the Country."

Emotions ran high. But most leaders sensed that any escalation of the violence would be premature and perhaps suicidal. They reined in demonstrations and instead initiated a massive boycott of British goods. Nonimportation plans called upon colonists to refrain from buying imported luxuries. Instead, they were to opt for virtuous self-sufficiency, buying locally and making more of what they needed. This strategy for resistance seemed broad-based, moderate, and nonviolent, so it held wide appeal. Since colonial women usually managed household affairs and family purchases, it drew them into the growing political debate.

LISTEN

"The Liberty Song"

As the nonimportation movement expanded, women of all ranks, self-proclaimed Daughters of Liberty, made, sold, and dressed in homespun garments. Anna Winslow (age eleven, of Boston) wrote proudly, "I chuse to wear as much of our own manufactory as pocible." Spinning moved from a tedious household chore to a patriotic act, and females of all ages took part in spinning bees to encourage household frugality. Newspaper editors urged them on, promising that women who were competing "with each other in their skill and industry" would also "vie with the men in contributing to the preservation and prosperity of their country and equally share in the honor of it."

Spinning moved from a tedious household chore to a patriotic act, and females of all ages took part in spinning bees.

Local associations sprang up, pledging to forgo imported tea and London fashions. A dozen colonial assemblies voted to halt importation of selected goods. In New York, the value of imports from Britain shrank from £491,000 to just £76,000 in a single year. The damage to English shipping proved substantial. Britain was losing far more revenue in colonial trade than it was gaining through the expanded customs duties.

Soon influential exporters in Britain were pressing their government for relief. When Baron Frederick North, who had succeeded Townshend, established a new ministry in January 1770, he received the king's consent to work toward a better arrangement with the colonies. On March 5, 1770, Lord North persuaded Parliament to repeal all the Townshend Duties except the one on tea. The move defused the colonial boycott, but it offered too little too late. Like the earlier Declaratory Act, this measure reaffirmed Parliament's disputed right to tax the colonists at will. Moreover, it came on the exact day that violence and bloodshed were escalating in Boston.

IMAGE

Women Signing an Anti-Tea Agreement

THE BOSTON MASSACRE

After the *Liberty* riot in June 1768, tensions had mounted in Boston, especially with the arrival in October of two regiments of British soldiers, well armed and dressed in their traditional red coats. Paul Revere, a local silversmith and member of the Sons of Liberty, crafted an ominous engraving entitled "British Ships of War Landing Their Troops." According to Real Whig beliefs, any appearance by a standing army in peacetime constituted danger. The issue of housing and feeding unwanted troops quickly became a political hot button. The soldiers pitched their tents on Boston Common, a central gathering place for boisterous crowds. Artisans in a sluggish economy welcomed the increased business that the men in uniform generated, but numerous unemployed workers resented the soldiers' "moonlighting," trying to earn extra pay by applying for local jobs.

With 4,000 armed men encamped in a seaport of scarcely 16,000, confrontation seemed inevitable. When rowdy American youths harassed the intruders as "redcoats" and "lobsterbacks," British officers ordered their men not to retaliate. Their refusal to fight only prompted more taunts. Affairs "cannot long remain in the state they are now in," wrote one observer late in 1769; "they are hastening to a crisis. What will be the event, God knows."

DOCUMENT

Boston Gazette, Description of the Boston Massacre

In March 1770, protesters took to the streets after a run-in between local workers and job-seeking soldiers. Rumors spread about a larger confrontation, and on March 5, around 9 p.m., a crowd gathered outside the customs house. When a harassed sentry

The Library of Congress

■ In Paul Revere's image of the 1770 Boston Massacre, soldiers defend the hated customs house by moonlight, while a sniper fires from a window clearly labeled "Butcher's Hall." The partisan engraving spread an anti-British view of the bloody event.

struck a boy with his rifle butt, angry witnesses pelted the guard with snowballs. As seven fellow soldiers pushed through the mob to assist him, firebells summoned more townspeople to the scene. The British loaded their rifles and aimed at the crowd, their bayonets fixed.

Into this tense standoff marched several dozen sailors, waving banners and brandishing clubs. Their leader was Crispus Attucks, an imposing ex-slave who stood six feet two inches. The son of a black man and an Indian woman, he had run away from his master two decades earlier and then taken up a life at sea. The scene was described later, at the trial resulting from the incident. John Adams, who assumed the unpopular task of defending the British soldiers, told the court: "Attucks appears to have undertaken to be the hero of this night." Damning the soldiers and daring them to fire, Attucks pressed his band of colonial sailors to the front, waving a long stick in the moonlight.

A slave witness named Andrew, who had climbed a post to get a better view, testified that Attucks "threw himself in, and made a blow at the officer," shouting, "kill the dogs, knock them over." Adams later showed the court how with one hand the sailor "took hold of a bayonet, and with the other knocked the man down." In the mayhem, a British gun went off, prompting a volley of fire from the other soldiers. The crowd recoiled in disbelief at the sight of their dead and wounded neighbors lying in the street, but they stayed past midnight to demand that the soldiers be jailed for murder. According to a printed report, Attucks and four others had been "killed on the Spot." The anti-British cause had its first martyrs.

By grim coincidence, the bloody episode in New England occurred only hours after Lord North addressed the House of Commons to urge removal of most Townshend Duties. His effort at reconciliation immediately became lost in a wave of hostile publicity. In Boston, Paul Revere captured the incident in an inflammatory engraving that circulated widely. The Sons of Liberty quickly named the evening violence of March 5 the Boston Massacre and compared its martyred victims to the Wilkes demonstrators who had perished in London during the Massacre at St. George's Field. "On that night," John Adams remarked, "the foundation of American independence was laid."

THE *GASPÉE* AFFAIR PROMPTS COMMITTEES OF CORRESPONDENCE

The overzealous conduct of customs officers gave colonists further cause for distrust. As traffic with Britain revived, after the repeal of most Townshend Duties and the end of the colonial boycott of English goods, so did the likelihood of conflict between merchants and customs inspectors. In the Delaware River region, local residents thrashed and jailed a customs collector in 1770. The next year, protesters stormed a customs schooner at night, beat up the crew, and stole their sails. Tensions ran especially high in Rhode Island. In 1769, Newport citizens seized the sloop *Liberty*—which crown agents had confiscated from John Hancock the year before and converted into a customs vessel—and scuttled it. In June 1772, the *Gaspée*, another customs boat said to harass local shipping, ran aground near Pawtuxet. In a midnight attack, more than sixty raiders descended on the stranded schooner in eight longboats, driving off its crew and setting fire to the vessel.

The destruction of the *Gaspée* renewed sharp antagonisms. The irate Lord Hillsborough sent a royal commission from London to investigate and to transport suspects to England for trial. But many of the attackers, such as John Brown of Providence, came from important Rhode Island families. Even a £500 reward could not induce local inhabitants to name participants. Besides, many viewed the order to deport accused citizens to England as a denial of their fundamental right to trial by a jury of their peers.

When the colonists took action, Virginia's House of Burgesses again led the way, as it had in the Stamp Act crisis. In March 1773, Patrick Henry, Thomas Jefferson, and Richard Henry Lee pushed through a resolution to set up a standing committee to look into the *Gaspée* affair and to keep up "Correspondence and Communication with our sister colonies" for the protection of rights. Following Virginia's example, ten other colonial legislatures promptly established their own Committees of Correspondence. In Massachusetts, people formed similar committees, linking individual towns. Within months a new act of Parliament, designed to rescue the powerful East India Company from bankruptcy, gave these emerging communication networks their first test.

Launching a Revolution

Could the British, through a more creative response to the Boston Tea Party, have averted the ensuing escalation toward violence?

In 1767, before Parliament imposed the Townshend Duties, Americans had imported nearly 870,000 pounds of tea from England. But the boycott movement cut that annual amount to less than 110,000 pounds by 1770, as colonists turned to smuggling Dutch blends and brewing homemade root teas. When nonimportation schemes lapsed in the early 1770s, purchase of English tea resumed, although a duty remained in effect.

Encouraged by this apparent acceptance of parliamentary taxation, Lord North addressed the problem facing the East India Company. The ancient trading monopoly owed a huge debt to the Bank of England and had 18 million pounds of unsold tea wasting in London warehouses. Many MPs held stock in the East India Company, so in May 1773 Parliament passed a law designed to assist the ailing establishment.

THE TEMPEST OVER TEA

The Tea Act of 1773 let the struggling East India Company bypass the expensive requirement that merchants ship Asian tea through England on its way to colonial ports. Now they could send the product directly to the colonies or to foreign ports, without paying to unload, store, auction, and reload the heavy chests. Any warehouse tea destined for the colonies would have its English duty refunded. These steps would reduce retail prices and expand the tea market. They would also quietly confirm the right of Parliament to collect a tea tax of threepence per pound.

The company promptly chose prominent colonial merchants to receive and distribute more than 600,000 pounds of tea. These consignees would earn a hefty 6 percent commission. But wary colonists in port towns, sensing a repetition of 1765, renewed the tactics that had succeeded against the Stamp Act. Sons of Liberty vowed to prevent tea-laden ships from docking, and crowds pressured local distributors to renounce participation in the scheme. "If they succeed in the sale of that tea," proclaimed New York's Sons of Liberty, "then we may bid adieu to American liberty."

"If they succeed in the sale of that tea," proclaimed New York's Sons of Liberty, "then we may bid adieu to American liberty."

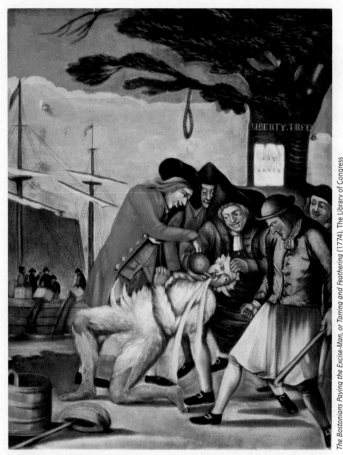

The Bostonians Paying the Excise-Man, or Tarring and Feathering (1774). The Library of Congress

■ A 1774 London cartoon expressed anger that Boston's Sons of Liberty, defying British authority, could overturn the Stamp Act, tar and feather revenue agents, dump East India Company tea, and use their "Liberty Tree" to hang officials in effigy.

In Boston, where tea worth nearly £10,000 arrived aboard three ships in late November, tension ran especially high. The credibility of Governor Thomas Hutchinson, who had taken a hard line toward colonial dissent, had suffered in June when Benjamin Franklin published private correspondence suggesting the governor's willingness to trim colonists' rights. When two of Hutchinson's sons were named tea consignees, the appointments reinforced townspeople's suspicions. The governor could have signed papers letting the three vessels depart. But instead he decided to unload and distribute the tea, by force if necessary. One could scarcely buy a pair of pistols in Boston, a resident observed on December 1, "as they are all bought up, with a full determination to repel force by force."

On December 16, the largest mass meeting of the decade took place at Boston's Old South Church. A crowd of 5,000, including many from other towns, waited in a cold rain to hear whether Hutchinson would relent. When word came in late afternoon that the governor had refused, the cry went up, "Boston Harbor a teapot tonight!" Following a prearranged plan, 150 men, disguised as Mohawk Indians and carrying hatchets, marched to the docks and boarded the ships.

As several thousand supporters looked on, this disciplined crew spent three hours methodically breaking open hundreds of chests of tea and dumping the contents overboard. The well-organized operation united participants representing all levels of society—from merchants such as John Hancock to artisans such as George Hewes. News of the event spurred similar acts of defiance in other ports. "This destruction of the Tea is so bold, so daring, so firm," John Adams wrote in his diary the next day, "it must have so important Consequences, and so lasting, that I can't but consider it as an Epocha in History." Sixty years later, as one of the oldest veterans of the Revolution, George Hewes still recalled with special pride his role in "the destruction of the tea."

THE INTOLERABLE ACTS

"The crisis is come," wrote British general Thomas Gage, responding to the costly Tea Party in Boston Harbor; "the provinces must be either British colonies, or independent and separate states." Underestimating the strength of American resolve, Parliament agreed with King George III that only stern measures would reestablish "the obedience which a colony owes to its mother country." Between March and June 1774, it passed four so-called Coercive Acts to isolate and punish Massachusetts.

The first of the Coercive Acts, the Boston Port Act, used British naval strength to cut off the offending town's sea commerce—except for shipments of food and firewood—until the colonists paid for the ruined tea. By the Administration of Justice Act, revenue officials or soldiers charged with murder in Massachusetts (as in the Boston Massacre) could have their trials moved to another colony or to Great Britain. The Quartering Act gave officers more power to requisition living quarters and supplies for their troops throughout the colonies. Most importantly, the Massachusetts Government Act removed democratic elements from the long-standing Massachusetts Charter of 1691. From now on, the assembly could no longer elect the colony's Upper House, or Council. Instead, the governor would appoint council members, and any town meetings would require his written permission.

Lord North's government went even further. It replaced Hutchinson with Gage, installing the general as the governor of Massachusetts and granting him special powers and three additional regiments. It also secured passage of the Quebec Act, new legislation to address nagging problems of governance in Canada after a decade of English rule. The act accommodated the Catholic faith and French legal traditions of Quebec's inhabitants. Moreover, it greatly expanded the size of the colony to draw scattered French settlers and traders under colonial government. Suddenly, Quebec took in the entire Great Lakes region and all the lands north of the Ohio River and east of the upper Mississippi River.

Expanding the province of Quebec to the Ohio River might extend British government to French wilderness outposts and help to regulate the Indian trade. But the move also challenged the western claims of other colonies. The Quebec Act appeared to favor Canada's French Catholics and Ohio Valley Indians—both recent enemies of the crown—over loyal English colonists. Resentment ran especially high in New England, where Protestants had long associated Catholicism with despotism. The Quebec Act, which denied the former French province a representative assembly and jury trials in civil cases, set an ominous precedent for neighboring colonies.

The Coercive Acts and the Quebec Act—lumped together by colonial propagandists as the Intolerable Acts—brought on open rebellion against crown rule. Competing pamphlets debated the proper limits of dissent. In *A Summary View of the Rights of British America,* Thomas Jefferson went beyond criticisms of Parliament to question the king's right to dispense land, control trade, and impose troops in America. Within months, Massachusetts had called for a congress of all the colonies. It also established its own Provincial Congress at Concord, a small village that lay seventeen miles west of Boston. Out of reach of British naval power, this de facto Massachusetts government reorganized the militia into units loyal to its own Committee of Public Safety. These farmer-soldiers became known as Minutemen for their quick response to Gage's repeated efforts to capture patriot gunpowder supplies.

FROM WORDS TO ACTION

While Massachusetts chafed under these new restrictions, shifting coalitions in each colony, ranging from conservative to radical, vied for local political control. Extralegal committees, existing outside the authorized structure of colonial government, took power in hundreds of hamlets. In Edenton, North Carolina, fifty-one women signed a pact to abstain from using imported products, including tea. London cartoonists mocked the action as the "Edenton Ladies' Tea Party," but women in other colonies made similar agreements to boycott British tea and textiles. During the summer, all colonies except Georgia selected representatives to the First Continental Congress.

> *During the summer, all colonies except Georgia selected representatives to the First Continental Congress.*

In September 1774, fifty-six delegates convened at Carpenters Hall in Philadelphia. Most had never met before, and they differed as much in their politics as in their regional manners. At first the delegates disagreed sharply over how best to respond to the Intolerable Acts. Joseph Galloway, a wealthy lawyer and commercial land speculator from Pennsylvania, urged a compromise with Britain modeled on the Albany Congress of 1754. His plan called for the creation of a separate American parliament, a grand council with

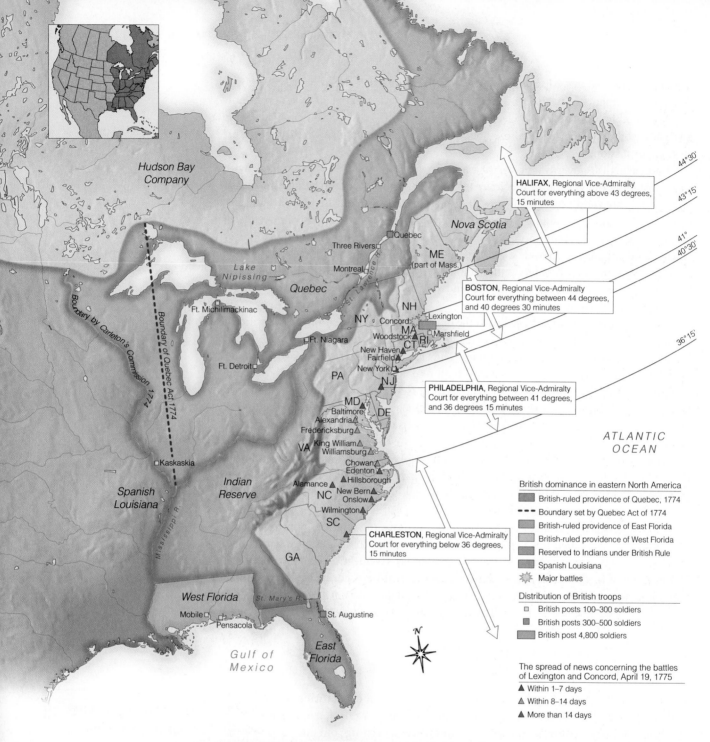

■ MAP 6.4 British North America, April 1775

Rising colonial unrest brought strong countermeasures. The British government organized regional vice-admiralty courts to punish smugglers; it greatly expanded Quebec in 1774; and it reallocated troops to the Boston area. When warfare erupted there in April 1775, the news spread throughout the colonies within weeks.

DOCUMENT

Henry, "Give Me Liberty or Give Me Death"

delegates elected by the colonial legislatures. The less conservative delegates opposed this idea for a colonial federation, under a president-general appointed by the king. Led by Patrick Henry of Virginia, they managed to table the Galloway Plan by a narrow vote.

When Paul Revere arrived from Boston on October 6, bearing a set of militant resolves passed in his own Suffolk County, further rifts appeared. Southern moderates, while expressing sympathy for Massachusetts, still resisted calls for a nonexportation scheme that would withhold American tobacco, rice, and indigo from Great Britain. But by the time the Congress adjourned in late October, it had issued a Declaration of Rights and passed a range of measures that seemed to balance competing views. On one hand, the Congress endorsed

194

the fiery Suffolk Resolves, which condemned the Coercive Acts as unconstitutional and spoke of preparation for war. On the other, it humbly petitioned the king for relief from the crisis and professed continued loyalty. But in practical terms, Galloway and the more conservative members had suffered defeat. Most importantly, the delegates signed an agreement to prohibit British imports and halt all exports to Britain except rice. They called for local committees to enforce this so-called Association, and they set a date—May 10, 1775—for a Second Congress.

Before delegates could meet again in Philadelphia, the controversy that had smoldered for more than a decade on both sides of the Atlantic erupted into open combat. Predictably, the explosion took place in Massachusetts. The spark came in the form of secret orders to General Gage, which he received April 14, 1775. The confidential letter from his superiors in London urged him to arrest the leaders of the Massachusetts Provincial Congress and regain the upper hand before the strained situation grew worse. He was to use force, even if it meant the outbreak of warfare.

On April 18, Gage ordered 700 elite troops from Boston to row across the Charles River at night, march ten miles to Lexington, and seize John Hancock and Sam Adams. Next, the soldiers were to proceed seven miles to Concord to capture a stockpile of military supplies. Alerted by signal lanterns, express riders Paul Revere and William Dawes eluded British patrols and spurred their horses toward Lexington along separate routes to warn Hancock and Adams. Bells and alarm guns spread the word that the British were coming. By the time the British soldiers reached Lexington, shortly before sunrise, some seventy militiamen had assembled on the town green. When the villagers refused to lay down their arms, the redcoats dispersed them in a brief skirmish that left eight militiamen dead.

From Lexington, the British column trudged west to Concord and searched the town for munitions. Four hundred Minutemen who had streamed in from neighboring communities advanced on the town in double file, with orders not to shoot unless the British fired first. At the small bridge over the Concord River, British regulars opened fire. "The shot heard

DOCUMENT

Warren, "Account of the Battle of Lexington"

Amos Doolittle, "The Battle of Lexington, Plate I," 1775. Connecticut Historical Society, Hartford, CT (Acc. #1844.10.1).

■ The shots fired at dawn by British troops, dispersing local militia from Lexington's town green, were the opening volley of the American Revolution. Amos Doolittle, a Connecticut soldier who responded to the alarm, later depicted the events of April 19, 1775. The date is still honored in New England as Patriots' Day.

'round the world" killed two men. The Americans loosed a volley in return, killing three. By noon, exhausted British forces were retreating in disarray. The redcoats made easy targets for the more than 1,000 Americans who shot at them from behind stone walls. A relief party prevented annihilation, but the British suffered severe losses: seventy-three killed and 200 wounded or missing. They encamped briefly at Bunker Hill, but lacking the foresight and strength to retain that strategic height, they soon returned to Boston. The Americans, with only forty-nine dead, had turned the tables on General Gage, transforming a punitive raid into a punishing defeat.

Conclusion

For the British, festering administrative problems in America had suddenly become a military emergency. A decade of assertive but inconsistent British policies had transformed the colonists' sense of good will toward London into angry feelings of persecution and betrayal. Britain's overseas empire, which had expanded steadily for two centuries, now seemed on the verge of splitting apart.

The years of incessant argument and misunderstanding reminded many, on both sides of the Atlantic, of watching a stable, prosperous household unravel into mutual recrimination. A once-healthy family was becoming increasingly dysfunctional and troubled. The assertive children grew steadily in strength and competence; the aging parents chafed at their diminished authority and respect. Predictably, authorities in London found the once-dependent colonists to be ungrateful, intemperate, and occasionally paranoid. With equal assurance, the American subjects saw Parliament, government ministers, and eventually the king himself as uninformed, selfish, and even deceitful.

As the limits of imperial control in North America had become more evident, colonists worked to overcome the regional and ethnic differences that had long been a fact of eighteenth-century life. Political independence no longer seemed implausible. With effort, class hostilities and urban-rural divisions could also be overcome. Redirecting old local resentments toward the distant and powerful British crown could increase the sense of unity among people with different personal backgrounds and resources.

Nor would British colonists be alone if they mounted a rebellion. On one hand, they could make the unlikely choice of liberating half a million slaves, empowering colonial women, and embracing the anti-British cause of Pontiac and numerous Native Americans. Such revolutionary moves would increase their strength dramatically in one direction. On the other hand, they could also take a more cautious and less democratic route. If men of substance could gain control of the forces that were being unleashed, they might curb potential idealism among slaves, women, tenant farmers, and the urban poor, giving precedence instead to policies that would win vital support from the continent of Europe in an American fight for independence. France, recently evicted from North America, and Spain, anxious about British designs in the Pacific, might both be willing allies, despite their commitment to monarchy. Such an alliance, if it ever came about, could push the limits of British imperial control to the breaking point.

For Review

1. Was the creation of Spanish missions in California a milestone, or a footnote, in early American history? Explain.

2. "By challenging the expansion of British military power in his homeland, Pontiac set an example for American colonists." Discuss.

3. Using Map 6.3, argue that the seeds of conflict in British America were already present by 1766.

4. How does the Regulator upheaval in North Carolina relate, if at all, to wider patterns of American resistance?

5. "By demanding 'obedience' in 1774, King George III treated his American colonies as unruly children, not as grown family members." Explain.

6. List (and prioritize) four main factors that explain how so many British colonists made the rapid shift from loyal subjects to irate rebels.

Created Equal Online

For more *Created Equal* resources, including suggestions on sites to visit and books to read, go to **MyHistoryLab.com.**

Part Three

The Unfinished Revolution, 1775–1803

Unidentified Artist, *Jonathan Knight*, c. 1797. Collection of American Folk Art Museum, New York, Promised gift of Ralph Esmerian (P1.2001.3). Photo Courtesy Sotheby's, New York

In 1775, Great Britain still possessed all of North America east of the Mississippi River, from Hudson Bay to the Gulf of Mexico. If the British could suppress the troublesome rebellion along the Atlantic seaboard, their prospects for expansion in America looked promising. Farther west, Spain had recently acquired the vast Louisiana Territory from France. The Spanish retained their dominance in the Southwest, and they were finally beginning to expand their claim to California by building a series of new missions and presidios.

By 1803, however, the broad picture had changed markedly. In the Pacific Ocean, Europeans had encountered the Hawaiian Islands for the first time, Russian fur traders had consolidated their hold in Alaska, and Spanish vessels along the Pacific coast faced increasing competition from the ships of rival nations. The British still held Canada and Florida, but the thirteen rebellious colonies had become an independent republic and had started to acquire new territories. The most spectacular acquisition was the Louisiana Territory, which the United States purchased in 1803, after Spain returned the region to France.

Few could have foreseen such an unlikely series of events in such a brief span of time. Thomas Jefferson drafted the Declaration of Independence in 1776 at age thirty-three. His generation had reluctantly become the effective leaders of a revolutionary movement by the mid-1770s. They contended ably with those who pushed for greater democratization, those who desired the stability of military rule, and even those who longed for the protection of the British monarchy.

These unlikely revolutionary leaders were by no means united in all their views and actions. They argued fervently over constitutional issues, domestic policies, and foreign alignments. Most reaped personal rewards from the new society's collective success. And they saw to it that these rewards reached far beyond their own households. Urban artisans, frontier farmers, and immigrant newcomers benefited from the removal of monarchy.

Such positive developments inspired optimism for many, both at home and abroad. Yet although the revolutionary era fulfilled the expectations of numerous citizens, it failed to meet the hopes and aspirations of other Americans. Many merchants and planters, indebted to British interests before 1776, gained by the separation from Great Britain and became creditors and investors in the new society. Many frontier farmers and army veterans, on the other hand, faced burdensome debts after the Revolutionary War.

Women worried that the numerous written constitutions of the period were unresponsive to their interests. In 1776, only New Jersey gave the vote among property holders to "all free inhabitants," including women. But this provision was undone a generation later,

in 1807, when New Jersey men objected to the idea of women having the right to vote. From New Hampshire to Georgia, committed "Daughters of Liberty" had made possible colonial boycotts through their industry and had managed families, farms, and businesses during the dislocations of war. Female access to education and the courts improved somewhat in the last quarter of the eighteenth century, but for most American women the advances were more symbolic than real.

For African Americans the disappointments were greater still. British offers of freedom prompted thousands of southern slaves to take up the Loyalist cause at great personal risk. Other free blacks and slaves, primarily in the North, shouldered arms for the Patriots, drawn by the rhetoric of liberty and the prospect of advancement. Even though they had chosen the winning side, they reaped few benefits. Although the number of free blacks increased after the Revolutionary War, the African slave trade to the United States resumed and received official protection. Slavery itself gained renewed significance with the transition to cotton production in the South and a federal constitution that sanctioned the power of slaveholders. Even in the North, where gradual emancipation became the norm by the end of the century, free blacks found their welcome into white churches and schools to be so half-hearted that many began organizing their own separate institutions.

Eastern Indians, like African Americans, had good reason to distrust the Revolution and its leaders. The majority, including most Iroquois and Cherokee warriors, sided with the British and paid a steep price in defeat. Throughout the Mississippi Valley, Native Americans who remembered the benefits of French trade and British military support faced relentless pressure as American speculators, soldiers, and settlers dissected their homelands. After 1803, government officials promised that the newly acquired lands beyond the Mississippi would become an Indian Territory, providing lasting refuge for displaced eastern tribes. If so, what was to become of the Native American nations that already inhabited these same western plains?

Like most political upheavals, the American Revolution left many questions unanswered and much business unfinished. Even the new federal government, in operation for little more than a decade by 1803, remained a work in progress. The specific roles and relative power of the government's three separate branches spurred endless debate, as did the proper place of the military and the most suitable direction for foreign policy. The Constitution ratified in 1789 seemed promising, but it remained an uncertain and largely untested framework.

Chapter 7

Revolutionaries at War, 1775–1783

North Carolina Museum of Art, Raleigh, Purchased with funds from the State of North Carolina (52.9.25).

■ In April 1775, riders spread word across New England that violence had erupted near Boston. William Ranney's history painting *First News of the Battle of Lexington* (1847) shows a small town preparing to send reinforcements. The ominous storm clouds suggest impending war.

The shots fired at Concord Bridge, Massachusetts, in April 1775 resounded immediately through all the villages of New England. In Peterborough, New Hampshire, a storekeeper promptly recruited a company of reinforcements to shoulder their rifles and march toward Boston. In his town of 549 people, not everyone was eager to join the risky fight. In fact, the Presbyterian chaplain deserted to the British as soon as the new company reached Massachusetts. However, before the long Revolutionary War ended in 1783, most of Peterborough's adult men had performed some sort of Patriot military service.

In Peterborough, as in countless other American towns, reasons for enlisting differed, and length of service varied greatly. At a moment of regional crisis, such as when General Burgoyne's British army threatened to isolate New England by thrusting down the Hudson Valley in 1777, most able-bodied men in Peterborough, young and old alike, entered the militia for several months, until the enemy had been stopped. But in Peterborough, as elsewhere, the most established merchants and farmers generally served least. They remained close to home and handled local affairs, while fewer than two dozen men, driven by poverty, ambition, or patriotic zeal, did most of the town's fighting.

No one in the community saw more action than William "Long Bill" Scott, a thirty-three-year-old husband and father when the war began. "I was a Shoemaker, & got my Living by my Labor." In April 1775, when Scott enlisted in the local militia company headed by his cousin, he refused to serve as a private. Convinced that his own "Ambition was too great for so low a Rank," he talked his relative into granting him a lieutenant's commission.

At Bunker Hill in June, Lieutenant Scott was severely wounded and left bleeding on the battlefield overnight. Taken captive the next morning, the prisoner hid his convictions from the British, claiming that he had no stake in the conflict except personal advancement. "If I was killed in Battle," he told a Tory interviewer, that would be "the end of me, but if my Captain was killed, I should rise in Rank, & should still have a Chance to rise higher." As to the "Dispute between Great Britain and the Colonies," Scott supposedly added, "I know nothing of it; neither am I capable of judging whether it is right or wrong."

If detached and skeptical at first, Long Bill Scott stayed the course, in contrast to many whose initial zeal for the cause faded quickly. Scott was deported to Halifax, Nova Scotia, when the British evacuated Boston, but he escaped and fought at New York the following year, only to be captured again. Newspapers told of his next dramatic escape: tying his sword around his neck and pinning his watch to his hat, he swam across the Hudson River at night. Scott returned to Peterborough in 1777 to recruit a company of his own, serving for several more years before old wounds made marching difficult. He finished the war as a volunteer on a navy frigate.

In all, a dozen Scott relatives from Peterborough gave forty years in wartime service to the army, the navy, and the state and local militias. In addition to Long Bill, his father and many of his cousins saw action, as did several of his sons, one of whom died of camp fever after six years of service. Long Bill himself sustained nine wounds and was captured twice, but his rewards proved slim. He sold his farm in 1777 to cover debts, but the notes he received in payment lost 98 percent of their worth within three years, and his military pay also depreciated sharply in value. He lost the down payment on another farm, and he was unable to care for his own children when his wife died. Destitute, he returned to army service in the mid-1790s. He died at Fort Stanwix in New York in 1796, at age fifty-four.

Despite his early disclaimers, Long Bill Scott's commitment to the Patriot cause proved unwavering. For most, the War of American Independence was not a clear, two-sided struggle in which colonists unified to oppose the English monarchy. Within each small community, and within the Atlantic theater as a whole, alliances often proved the old adage that "My enemy's enemy is my friend." Powerful merchants like John Hancock and Henry Laurens threw in their lot with the people in part because they had grown disillusioned with Parliament's political and commercial controls. Many enslaved blacks, eager for liberty from their masters, escaped to join the British. On the international scale, the monarchies of France and Spain swallowed their dislike for America's republican rhetoric, joining in a war that allowed them an opportunity to attack their long-standing rival, Britain. On the other hand, many Cherokee and Iroquois Indians, disillusioned by contact with land-hungry settlers, cast their lot with the British forces from overseas.

Not all Indian warriors or enslaved Africans sided with the British, and by no means all New England farmers or Virginia planters embraced the Patriot cause. In a landscape marked by uncertainty, large numbers of people at all levels of society opted for cautious neutrality as long as they could, while others shifted their allegiance as the winds changed. The final outcome of the conflict, therefore, remained a source of constant doubt. Looking back, Americans often view the results of the Revolutionary War as inevitable, perhaps even foreordained. In fact, the end result—and thus independence itself—hung in the balance for years.

Patriots and Slaves Toppling Statue of George III

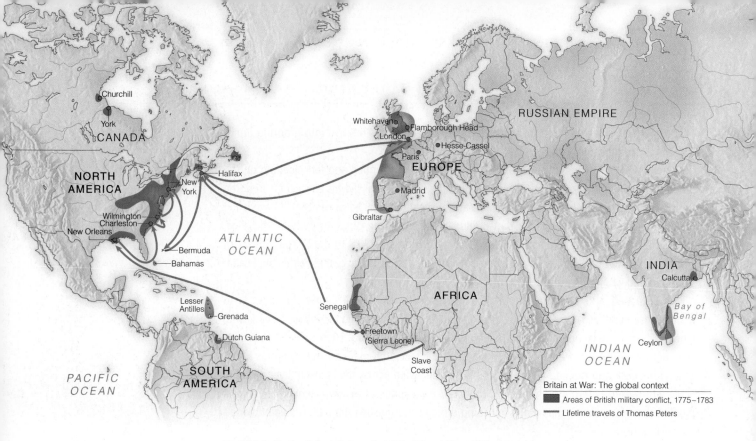

■ **M A P 7 . 1   Britain's American War Viewed in a Global Context**

War is always a source of rapid dislocation and movement, as in the remarkable case of African-born Thomas Peters, whose lifelong Atlantic journey is traced here (see The Wider World, page 203). For Britain, the colonial war that began in 1775 expanded within three years into a worldwide conflict against rival European powers. By 1783, the British lost American colonies while expanding their hold in India. General Cornwallis, for example, went on to serve the British in India after his defeat at Yorktown in 1781.

"Things Are Now Come to That Crisis"

■ *How were the Americans able to drive British forces out of Boston in March 1776, less than a year after the Battle of Lexington?*

DOCUMENT

Royal Proclamation of Rebellion (1775)

New England's Minutemen had rallied swiftly at Lexington and Concord. In the ensuing months, while George III prepared a proclamation declaring the colonists to be in open rebellion, Congress took the initial steps to form the Continental Army. It also launched efforts to force the British out of Boston and to pull Canada into the rebellion. If these predominantly Protestant rebels hoped to draw the French Catholics of Quebec into their revolt, would free whites also be eager to include the blacks of Boston, Williamsburg, and Charleston in the struggle for liberty? Or would it be the British who recruited more African Americans and furnished them with arms? The answers to such questions became clear in the fifteen months between the skirmish at Lexington and the decision of Congress to declare political independence from Britain in July 1776.

THE SECOND CONTINENTAL CONGRESS TAKES CONTROL

Enthusiasm ran high in Philadelphia in May 1775 as the Second Continental Congress assembled amid cheers and parades. Delegates moved quickly to put the beleaguered colonies on a wartime footing. They instructed New York to build fortifications. They also paid for a dozen new companies of riflemen—recruited in Pennsylvania, Maryland, and Virginia—to be sent north to aid the Minutemen surrounding Boston. They created

The Journey of Tom and Sally Peters

In 1760, a young Yoruba-speaking man, age twenty-two, had been taken from what is now Nigeria and shipped to Louisiana aboard the slave ship *Henri Quatre*. Forced to cut sugar cane, he rebelled so often that he was sold to a prosperous Scottish immigrant in Wilmington, North Carolina, and put to work operating a gristmill. The African took an English name, Thomas Peters, and started a family with a young woman named Sally.

During the fifteen years between Peters's abduction from Africa and the outbreak of hostilities between America and Britain in 1775, nearly 225,000 people had poured into the British mainland colonies. Of these, two in five (or 85,000 individuals) had been purchased in Africa and were enslaved in the coastal South. As open warfare erupted, Tom and Sally Peters, even more than most people in British North America, experienced hardships, opportunities, and enormous dislocations.

Late in 1775, word reached Wilmington that Virginia's governor, Lord Dunmore, had offered freedom to slaves who would take up arms for the British. So when ships of the Royal Navy arrived at the Cape Fear River in March, Tom and Sally Peters risked arrest to gain their personal liberty by bolting to the British vessels. Peters was with the British when General Clinton's forces tried to take Charleston, South Carolina, in June 1776.

Throughout the war, Peters served the British in a unit called the Black Pioneers. Wounded twice, he rose to the rank of sergeant and earned the promise of a farm in Canada. In 1783, as defeated Loyalists left New York City at the end of the war, he and his family joined other ex-slaves aboard the *Joseph James,* bound for Nova Scotia. Departing in November, the ship was blown off course by foul weather. Tom and Sally, with their twelve-year-old daughter Clairy and eighteen-month-old son John, spent the winter sheltered at Bermuda before finally joining 3,500 other black Loyalists in Nova Scotia in May 1784.

But the odyssey of the Peters family did not end in Nova Scotia. In 1790, after he and others had been denied the promised farmland, Thomas ventured to London as an advocate

■ Escaped slave Tom Peters was with the British fleet that attacked Charleston in June 1776. A South Carolina soldier sketched the American victory.

for these former slaves. He protested their treatment, petitioned for relief, and met with British abolitionists planning a colony of former slaves in West Africa. Eager for his family to join the effort, he returned to Canada and led 1,200 African Americans to Sierra Leone, where he died at Freetown in 1792. During a life that began and ended in Africa, Peters had seen New Orleans, Wilmington, Charleston, Philadelphia, New York, Bermuda, Halifax, and London. He had survived sixteen years of enslavement and fought his own war for the freedom and safety of family and friends.

QUESTIONS

1. Follow the journey of Tom Peters and his family on Map 7.1. In what ways does his life reflect the title for Part Three: "The Unfinished Revolution"?

2. If the Revolutionary War brought Tom and Sally Peters "hardships, opportunities, and enormous dislocations," how was their experience typical, or exceptional?

The Wider World

an Army Department under the command of a New York aristocrat, General Philip Schuyler, and approved an issue of $2 million in currency to fund the military buildup.

In late May, word arrived from Lake Champlain in New York of a victory for the Green Mountain Boys (farmers led by Ethan Allen, from the area that became Vermont) and soldiers under Benedict Arnold of Connecticut. They had captured Fort Ticonderoga, along with its cannons, and the new Army Department badly needed all such heavy arms. This initiative not only secured the Hudson Valley against a British attack from the north; it also allowed Schuyler to propose a strike against Montreal and Quebec via Lake Champlain and the Richelieu River. Congress approved the assault, to be led by General Richard Montgomery. It also approved a daring scheme submitted by Arnold. He planned to lead separate forces up the Kennebec River. They would assist Montgomery in seizing Quebec and winning Canada before the region could become a staging ground for British armies.

No single action by Congress had greater implications for coalition building among the colonies than the one taken on June 15, 1775. That day, members voted unanimously to appoint George Washington, a forty-three-year-old delegate from Virginia, "to command all the continental forces." Colonel Washington already headed a committee that was drawing up regulations to run the new army, and he had notable military experience. But among his strongest assets may have been his southern roots. Northern delegates—especially John Adams, who had nominated Washington—sensed the need to foster colonial unity by placing a non–New Englander in charge of the army outside Boston. For their part, Southerners sensed keen regional differences, particularly over slavery. They appeared jealous, as one delegate noted, "lest an enterprising New England general, proving successful, might with his victorious army" enforce control over "the southern gentry."

> *Putting a slaveholder in command signaled the beginning of an important alliance between the well-to-do regional leaders of the North and South.*

In military and political terms, the selection of Washington proved auspicious. The tall, imposing planter from Mount Vernon emerged as a durable and respected leader in both war and peace. But putting a slaveholder in command also closed certain radical options. It signaled the beginning of an important alliance between the well-to-do regional leaders of the North and South. Although no one could foresee it at the time, this alliance would contribute to the particular form of the federal Constitution a dozen years later. The bond endured, shaping the governing of the country until the middle of the next century.

"LIBERTY TO SLAVES"

The selection of Washington sent a strong message to half a million African Americans, increasing their skepticism about the Patriot cause and spurring many of them to risk siding with the British. For their part, the British sensed an opportunity to undermine rebellious planters. In June 1775, the British commander in America, Thomas Gage, wrote to London: "Things are now come to that crisis, that we must avail ourselves of every resource, even to raise the Negros, in our cause." One Lutheran minister who spoke to black house servants near Philadelphia the next year noted that they "secretly wished that the British Army might win, for then all Negro slaves will gain their freedom. It is said that this sentiment is almost universal among the Negroes in America."

In the South, rumors of liberation swept through the large African American community during 1775. Slaveholding rebel authorities countered with harsh measures to quell black unrest. In Charleston that spring, they deported an African-born minister, David Margate, for preaching a sermon that hinted at equality. Also, they focused their attention on a prominent free black man named Thomas Jeremiah, who had prospered as a skilled pilot guiding vessels between treacherous sandbars into the busy South Carolina port. In April, Jeremiah supposedly told an enslaved dockworker of a great war coming and urged slaves to prepare to seize the opportunity. Weeks later, nervous Patriot planters made the well-known free black into a scapegoat, accusing him of involvement in a plot to smuggle guns ashore from British ships to support a slave uprising. In August 1775, despite a lack of hard evidence against him, Jeremiah was publicly hanged and then burned.

That September, a Georgia delegate to Congress made a startling comment. He predicted that if British troops were to land on the Georgia and South Carolina coast with a supply of food and guns, offering freedom to slaves who would join them, then 20,000 blacks would swiftly materialize. In November, the beleaguered royal governor of Virginia, Lord Dunmore, attempted just such a scheme. Dunmore issued a proclamation granting freedom to the slaves of rebel masters who agreed to take up arms on behalf of the king. Hundreds responded to Dunmore's proclamation. They formed the Ethiopian Regiment and wore sashes proclaiming "Liberty to Slaves."

THE STRUGGLE TO CONTROL BOSTON

In the North, British forces had been confined in Boston ever since the Battle of Lexington. They would remain isolated on the town's main peninsula for nearly a year, supported by the Royal Navy. In early July 1775, Washington arrived at nearby Cambridge to take up his command and oversee the siege of Boston. He quickly set out to improve order among his men. He tightened discipline, enforced sanitation, calmed regional jealousies, and removed nearly a dozen incompetent officers.

Washington also wrote scores of letters to civilian political leaders and the president of Congress to muster support for his meager army. The Massachusetts legislature alone received thirty-four messages from the new commander. He made clear that nearly everything was in short supply, from tents and uniforms to gunpowder, muskets, and cannons. He dispatched twenty-five-year-old Henry Knox, a former bookseller and future general, to retrieve the cannons captured at Ticonderoga. The Patriots' siege, he informed Congress, could not succeed without heavy fieldpieces to bombard the city from the heights at Dorchester and Charlestown, across the water from Boston.

Even before Washington's arrival, the British and the Americans had vied for control of these strategic heights. Indeed, the British General Gage drew up plans to secure Charlestown peninsula by seizing its highest point, Bunker Hill. But the Patriots learned of the scheme. On the night of June 16, 1775, they fortified Breed's Hill, a smaller knoll 600 yards in front of Bunker Hill. The next afternoon, 1,500 well-entrenched but inexperienced Patriot volunteers confronted the full force of the British army as thousands watched from the rooftops of Boston.

Gage might easily have sealed off Charlestown peninsula with his naval power. Instead, he used 2,500 British infantry, weighed down by heavy packs, to launch three frontal attacks up Breed's Hill from the shoreline. The first two uphill charges fell back before withering volleys at close range. Finally, with adjoining Charlestown ablaze and rebel powder supplies exhausted, a third assault overran the hill and dislodged the Americans. Mistakenly, the engagement became known as the Battle of Bunker Hill. Although it was technically a British victory, success came at a terrible price. The encounter left 42 percent of British troops (1,054 men) wounded or dead—the worst casualty figures of the entire war. Gage lost his command and was replaced in October by General William Howe. The Royal Army no longer appeared invincible.

As Washington organized his rudimentary army near Boston during the second half of 1775, Henry Knox pursued his mission to retrieve the British ordnance captured at Ticonderoga. Using oxen, sledges, and local volunteers, he managed to haul forty-three heavy cannons east, across trails covered with snow and ice, from the Hudson Valley to the Massachusetts coast. His men delivered the guns in late winter, finally giving Washington the advantage he needed. If he could move the cannons to high ground and protect them, he knew they had enough range to bombard the enemy

Charles Willson Peale, George Washington in the Uniform of a British Colonial Colonel, c. 1772. Washington-Custis-Lee Collection, Washington and Lee University, Lexington, VA

■ In June 1775, Congress selected a wealthy Virginia planter to command its army. The choice of George Washington reassured southern slave owners and disappointed blacks and whites in the North who saw slavery as a contradiction in the struggle for freedom.

huddled in Boston. In March 1776, the general designed an operation to secure Dorchester Heights. The Americans made their surprise move at night, as they had at Breed's Hill. But that maneuver had occurred in warm June weather. This time, in contrast, the ground was frozen solid, and they knew they had no possibility of digging in to protect the exposed position.

Planning ahead, Washington had his men prepare thousands of bundles of sticks and saplings, known as fascines. They also constructed large timber frames, a dozen feet wide, called chandeliers. When moved into place and filled with fascines and bales of hay, these wooden frames created a redoubt that could withstand cannon fire or a ground assault. On the night of March 4, several thousand American soldiers, using 300 wagons and oxcarts, hauled these barriers into place on Dorchester Heights. Behind them, the troops placed the cannons Knox had hauled overland from Fort Ticonderoga. By morning, the Herculean task was complete. On the fifth anniversary of the Boston Massacre, the exhausted but jubilant troops took up their new position and prepared to combat an assault such as the one at Breed's Hill nine months earlier. This time, they were determined to hold their strategic height at all costs, and they agreed that anyone who retreated would be "fired down upon the spot."

> A British officer remarked that the Americans had done more in one night than most armies could do in months.

But the assault never came. Shocked by the transformation under cover of darkness, a British officer remarked that the Americans had done more in one night than most armies could do in months. Suddenly confronted with Washington's commanding guns, the forces in Boston could not stay put; they had to attack or withdraw. At first, General Howe prepared to advance by boat and storm the heights. But he lost his nerve, perhaps because he had commanded the charges at Breed's Hill and seen the devastation. Instead, he drew back from an assault on Dorchester Heights and began evacuating his army by sea. Officers hastily packed soldiers and supplies, along with goods plundered from Boston homes, aboard naval vessels in the harbor. They left behind numerous horses, too cumbersome to transport. By the end of March, the entire British force had retreated by ship to Halifax, Nova Scotia. There, Howe made plans to attack the rebels again at New York, where Loyalist support was stronger.

Declaring Independence

■ *In the context of the entire year 1776, why was Washington's successful crossing of the Delaware River on December 25 so significant?*

As Washington laid siege to Boston, other Americans had converged on British forces in Canada. General Montgomery's troops seized Montreal in November 1775. They then descended the St. Lawrence River to join Benedict Arnold's men near Quebec. Arnold's troops had struggled north through Maine's rugged Kennebec Valley and crossed into Canada under brutal winter conditions. Their combined force, under Montgomery, attacked the walled city of Quebec during a fierce snowstorm on the night of December 30. But the assault failed, and Montgomery perished in the fighting. Smallpox had already broken out in the American ranks, and it spread to new arrivals during the next five months. When British reinforcements reached Quebec in May, the Americans hastily retreated toward Lake Champlain. They left behind most of their baggage and hundreds of sick companions.

Hundreds more died of smallpox during the withdrawal of the shattered army. Others spread the deadly virus when they returned to their New England homes. "I got an account of my johns Death of the Small Pox at Canada," one New Hampshire father scrawled in his diary after learning that his twenty-four-year-old son had died while fighting against the King's forces. "He was shot through his left arm at Bunker Hill." Now, "in defending the just Rights of America," John had been taken "in the prime of life by means of that wicked Tyranical Brute (Nea worse than Brute) of Great Britan." In thousands of American households, strained loyalty was turning to explosive anger.

"TIME TO PART"

In January 1776, Thomas Paine's brilliant pamphlet *Common Sense* captured the shifting mood and helped propel Americans toward independence. Paine, a former corsetmaker, had endured a long series of personal and economic failures in England before sailing to Philadelphia in 1774 at age thirty-seven. To this passionate man, with his gift for powerful and accessible prose, America represented a fresh start. Arriving late in 1774, Paine poured his energy into bold newspaper essays. In one, he argued that African American slaves deserved freedom and ample land to become productive citizen-farmers.

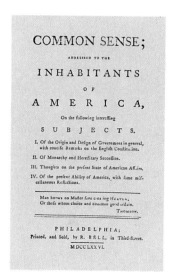

Paine's *Common Sense* sold an amazing 120,000 copies in three months, reaching all sorts of readers. The author promised to lay out "simple facts, plain arguments, and common sense" on the precarious American situation. He lambasted "the so much boasted constitution of England," and he went on to attack hereditary monarchy and the divine right of kings. "One honest man," Paine proclaimed, is worth more to society "than all the crowned ruffians that ever lived." He urged the creation of an independent constitutional republic that could become "an asylum for all mankind." "Reconciliation is now a fallacious dream," he argued: "'TIS TIME TO PART."

Paine's avid readers agreed. In the spring of 1776, one colony after another instructed its representatives to the Second Continental Congress to vote for independence. But many among the well-to-do had strong social and economic ties to London. They feared the loss of British imperial protection and the startling upsurge of democratic political activity among the lower orders. At first, Congress vacillated. Finally, with no sign of accommodation from England, most members agreed with Robert Livingston of New York that "they should yield to the torrent if they hoped to direct its course." In early June, Livingston, age thirty, joined the committee assigned to prepare a formal statement declaring independence from Great Britain. The Committee of Five also included Benjamin Franklin, John Adams, Roger Sherman, and the second youngest member of the Continental Congress, Thomas Jefferson.

John Adams to Abigail Adams (July 3, 1776)

The thirty-three-year-old Jefferson had recently returned to Philadelphia from Virginia, where his mother had died suddenly in March. Personally independent for the first time, he willingly took responsibility for crafting the document. He framed a stirring preamble, drawing on British philosopher John Locke's contract theory of government. Locke (1632–1702) believed that the sovereign power ultimately resided not in government but in the people themselves, who chose to submit voluntarily to civil law to protect property and preserve basic rights.

According to Locke, rulers possessed conditional, not absolute, authority over the people. Citizens therefore held the right to end their support and overthrow any government that did not fulfill its side of the contract. For any people facing "a long train of abuses," Jefferson wrote, "it is their right, it is their duty, to throw off such government and to provide new guards for their future security." He went on to catalogue the "repeated injuries and usurpations" committed by King George III. Meanwhile, on July 2, Congress voted on a statement affirming that "these United Colonies are, and of right, ought to be, Free and Independent States." Twelve colonies approved, with the New York delegation abstaining until it could receive further instructions from home. Having made the fundamental decision, the delegates then considered how to "declare the causes" behind their momentous choice to separate from Great Britain.

Over the next two days, all the Congress members edited the draft declaration submitted by the Committee of Five. They kept Jefferson's idealistic assertion that "all

Courtesy, American Antiquarian Society

■ John Trumbull spent years gathering portraits for his famous painting *The Declaration of Independence*. This engraving identifies individuals in the painting with their signatures. The artist placed the Drafting Committee in the center (31–35). He omitted signers for whom he had no likeness, and he included several nonsigners, such as John Dickinson.

men are created equal." But they removed any reference to slavery, except for the charge that the king had "excited domestic insurrections amongst us," a veiled reference to the Thomas Jeremiah debacle in Charleston and to Lord Dunmore's proclamation. With other changes in place, they finally voted to approve the revised Declaration of Independence on July 4, 1776.

John Hancock, the president of the Congress, signed the document with a flourish, and printers hastily turned it into a published broadside. The other signatures (contrary to folklore) came two weeks later, after New York had finally offered its approval. That last endorsement meant that fifty-six delegates could gather to sign their names to "The *unanimous* declaration of the thirteen United States of America." They did so at great risk. As they endorsed the document with their signatures, they knew that they were opening themselves to face charges of treason, punishable by death.

IMAGE

Signing of the
Declaration of
Independence

THE BRITISH ATTACK NEW YORK

While the Continental Congress debated whether to declare independence, the British maneuvered to suppress the rebellion. Strangling the revolt with a naval blockade appeared impossible, given the length of the American coastline. But two other strategies emerged—one southern and one northern—that shaped British planning throughout the conflict.

The southern design rested on the assumption that loyalty to the crown remained strongest in the South. If the British could land forces below Chesapeake Bay, support from white loyalists and enslaved blacks might enable them to gain the upper hand and push north to reimpose colonial rule elsewhere. In June 1776, troops under General Henry Clinton arrived off the Carolina coast with such a mission in mind. But Loyalists had already lost a battle to the Patriots at Moore's Creek Bridge near Wilmington, North Carolina, in February, and the British ships sailed to South Carolina instead. On June 28, they bombarded Sullivan's Island,

Labels on the map:

Quebec, 1775
Montreal, 1775
Ft. Ticonderoga, 1775
Saratoga, 1777
Bennington, 1777
Ft. Stanwix, 1777
Boston, 1775
Newtown, 1777
Princeton, 1777
New York, 1776
Monmouth, 1777
Trenton, 1777
Brandywine, 1777
Germantown, 1777
Vincennes, 1779
Charlottesville, 1781
Naval Battle, 1781
Yorktown, 1781
St. Louis, 1780
Kaskaskia, 1778
Guilford Courthouse, 1781
Moore's Creek Bridge, 1776
King's Mountain, 1780
Fishing Creek, 1780
Cowpens, 1781
Camden, 1780
Charleston, 1780
Savannah, 1779
Natchez, 1778
Mobile, 1780
Pensacola, 1781

ATLANTIC OCEAN

Mississippi R.

Overview of the Revolutionary War

☀ British victories
☀ Patriot victories

■ **M A P 7 . 2**   **Overview of the Revolutionary War**

at the mouth of Charleston harbor. But the Americans' cypress-log fortress withstood the cannon fire, and the attackers withdrew. The British did not renew their southern design for several years, concentrating instead on a separate northern strategy.

According to Britain's northern plan, troops would divide the rebellious colonies in two at the Hudson River valley, seizing New York City and advancing upriver while other forces pushed south from Canada. Then, having sealed off New England, they could finally crush the radicals in Massachusetts who had spearheaded the revolt and then restore the loyalties of inhabitants farther south. Lord George Germain, the aggressive new British cabinet minister in charge of American affairs, favored this plan. An overwhelming strike, he asserted, could "finish the rebellion in one campaign."

"Revoking Those Sacred Trusts Which Are Violated": Proclaiming Independence in South Carolina, May 1776

Interpreting History

Throughout the late spring of 1776, provincial assemblies, town meetings, and grand juries in the thirteen colonies began issuing their own pronouncements regarding a break with Great Britain. The authors drew on historical precedent, legal tradition, and emotional sentiment. They mixed lofty theory and Real Whig ideology with local concerns. They also incorporated rhetoric and ideas from current pamphlets, speeches, and newspaper essays.

At least ninety of these proclamations survive. Most are more impressive for their strong feelings than for their literary merit. But taken together, they suggest the sentiments, arguments, and words that were in the air when Jefferson drafted the Declaration of Independence. This document was drawn up and signed by fifteen members of the Cheraw District grand jury during their regular court session in Long Bluff, South Carolina, May 20, 1776.

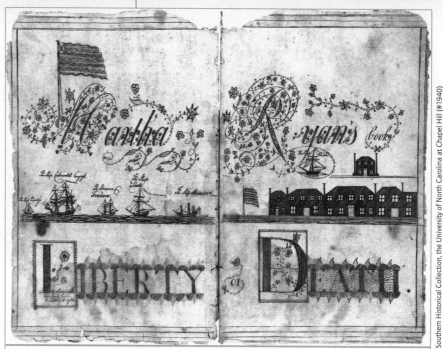

Southern Historical Collection, the University of North Carolina at Chapel Hill (#1940)

■ Young Martha Ryan used her cipher-book to do more than practice writing. She also drew American ships and flags and embellished the popular rallying cry "Liberty or Death."

The Presentments of the Grand Jury of and for the Said District

I. When a people, born and bred in a land of freedom and virtue . . . are convinced of the wicked schemes of their treacherous rulers to fetter them with the chains of servitude, and rob them of every noble and desirable privilege which distinguishes them as freemen,—justice, humanity, and the immutable laws of *God*, justify and support them in revoking those sacred trusts which are so impiously violated, and placing them in such hands as are most likely to execute them in the manner and for the important ends for which they were first given.

Early in 1776, Germain set out to generate a land and sea offensive of unprecedented scale. He prodded the sluggish admiralty for ships, and when he could not raise troops swiftly at home, he rented them from abroad. Russia declined a request for 20,000 soldiers, but the German states produced 18,000 mercenaries. Eventually, 30,000 German troops traveled to America, so many of them from the state of Hesse-Cassel that onlookers called all of them Hessians. Canada, having already repulsed Montgomery's American invasion, could provide a loyal staging ground in the north. "I have always thought Hudson's River the most proper part of the whole continent for opening vigorous operations," observed "Gentleman Johnny" Burgoyne, the dapper and worldly British general who arrived at Quebec with reinforcements in May 1776.

But plans for a strike south from Canada had to wait. Britain made its first thrust toward the mouth of the Hudson River by sea, using nearly 400 ships. In June, a convoy under General William Howe sailed from Halifax to Staten Island, New York, with 9,000 soldiers. By August, the general had received 20,000 reinforcements from across the Atlantic. His brother, Admiral Richard Howe, hovered nearby with 13,000 sailors aboard seventy naval vessels.

II. The good people of this Colony, with the rest of her sister Colonies, confiding in the justice and merited protection of the King and Parliament of *Great Britain,* ever . . . esteemed such a bond of union and harmony as the greatest happiness. But when that protection was wantonly withdrawn, and every mark of cruelty and oppression substituted; . . . self-preservation, and a regard to our own welfare and security, became a consideration both important and necessary. The Parliament and Ministry of *Great Britain,* by their wanton and undeserved persecutions, have reduced this Colony to a state of separation from her . . . as the only lasting means of future happiness and safety. . . . Cast off, persecuted, defamed, given up as a prey to every violence and injury, a righteous and much injured people have at length appealed to *God!* and, trusting to his divine justice and their own virtuous perseverance, taken the only and last means of securing their own honour, safety, and happiness.

III. We now feel every joyful and comfortable hope that a people could desire in the present Constitution and form of Government established in this Colony; a Constitution founded on the strictest principles of justice and humanity, where the rights and happiness of the whole, the poor and the rich, are equally secured; and to secure and defend which, it is the particular interest of every individual who regards his own safety and advantage.

IV. When we consider the publick officers of our present form of Government now appointed, as well as the method and duration of their appointment, we cannot but declare our entire satisfaction and comfort; as well in the characters of such men, who are justly esteemed for every virtue, as their well-known abilities to execute the important trusts which they now hold.

V. Under these convictions, . . . we . . . recommend it to every man . . . to secure and defend with his life and fortune a form of Government so just, so equitable, and promising; . . . that the latest posterity may enjoy the virtuous fruits of that work, which the integrity and fortitude of the present age had, at the expense of their blood and treasure, at length happily effected.

VI. We cannot but declare how great the pleasure, the harmony, and political union which now exists in this District affords; and having no grievances to complain of, only beg leave to recommend that a new Jury list be made for this District, the present being insufficient.

And lastly, we beg leave . . . that these our presentments be printed in the publick papers.—PHILIP PLEDGER, Foreman [and fourteen other signatures]

QUESTIONS

1. *While Thomas Jefferson was preparing the Declaration of Independence (see the text of the document in the Appendix), many local proclamations were in circulation. How does the South Carolina example compare in form, content, emotion, and clarity to Jefferson's document?*

2. *If many ideas and arguments present in the Declaration of Independence were indeed commonplace in the colonies early in 1776, how does this information enhance or alter your understanding of Thomas Jefferson's accomplishment?*

Source: Pauline Maier, American Scripture: Making the Declaration of Independence (New York: Knopf, 1997), 229–231.

On orders from Congress, General Washington moved south to defend New York City, a difficult task made harder by ardent Loyalist sentiment. Rumors swirled of a Loyalist plot to kidnap the general or even take his life. A bodyguard named Thomas Hickey, implicated in the Tory scheme, was hanged before a huge crowd of anxious onlookers in late June. Short on men and equipment, the general weakened his position further by dividing his troops between Manhattan and Brooklyn Heights on nearby Long Island.

A month after members of Congress signed the Declaration of Independence, the commander nearly lost his entire force—and the cause itself. General Howe moved his troops by water from Staten Island to the Brooklyn area and then outflanked and scattered the poorly trained Americans in the Battle of Long Island on August 27. Remarkably, the British leader called off a direct attack that almost certainly would have overrun the American batteries on Brooklyn Heights. When his equally cautious brother failed to seal off the East River with ships, rebel troops escaped disaster by slipping back to Manhattan in small boats under cover of night and fog.

"VICTORY OR DEATH": A DESPERATE GAMBLE PAYS OFF

New York Burning (1776)

Washington's narrow escape to Lower Manhattan from Long Island in August 1776 was only the first of numerous retreats. His army left New York City on September 15. The rebels withdrew from upper Manhattan and Westchester in October and from Fort Washington and Fort Lee on the Hudson—with heavy losses—in November. The Americans "fled like scared rabbits," one Englishman wrote. "They have left some poor pork, a few greasy proclamations, and some of that scoundrel Common Sense man's letters, which we can read at our leisure." With winter at hand, the Continental forces retreated southwest toward Philadelphia.

Desertions and low morale plagued the ragged American army as it withdrew from New York late in 1776. But General William Howe repeatedly failed to press his advantage. The British commander and his brother had received a commission from Lord North, who headed the government in London, permitting them to negotiate a peace settlement with the Americans whenever possible. They hoped that a strong show of force, without a vicious offensive that might alienate civilians, could bring the enemy to terms. Howe's troops offered pardons to repentant rebels and encouraged desertions from Washington's army. In early December, the dwindling American force hurried through Princeton, New Jersey, and slipped across the Delaware River into Pennsylvania. Confident of victory, the British again failed to pursue them, instead making camp at Trenton. Washington realized that unless circumstances changed quickly, "the game will be pretty well up."

■ This picture showing the noise and movement of the American victory at the Battle of Princeton was created by deaf painter William Mercer, whose father, Brigadier General Hugh Mercer, died in the battle.

William Mercer, *Battle of Princeton*, date unknown. Courtesy of the Historical Society of Pennsylvania (HSP) Collection, Atwater Kent Museum of Philadelphia

Distressed by civilian talk of surrender, Tom Paine again took up his pen. In the *Pennsylvania Journal* for December 19, he launched a new series of essays (*The American Crisis*) that began with the ringing words "These are the times that try men's souls." Paine mocked "the summer soldier and the sunshine patriot" who shrank from extreme trials. "Let it be told to the future world, that in the depth of winter, when nothing but hope and virtue could survive," vigilant citizens, "alarmed at one common danger, came forth to meet and to repulse it."

Action soon followed words. On Christmas Day 1776, Washington issued a new code phrase for sentinels: "Victory or Death." He ordered Paine's words read aloud to the troops. Then, after dark, his men recrossed the windswept Delaware River in a driving snowstorm and advanced on Trenton. Holiday festivities and foul weather had left the enemy unprepared for this desperate maneuver, and intelligence of the impending attack seems to have been ignored. The Americans inflicted a startling defeat, killing several dozen and capturing more than 900 Hessian soldiers.

Most American troops had signed up to serve for a brief term and return home, and many had joined the previous January for a one-year stint. Washington knew that numerous enlistments expired on December 31 and that men would leave if the brief offensive halted. So he advanced again on December 30. Howe sent fresh troops forward under Charles Cornwallis to confront the rebels, pinning them down at Trenton. But when the British paused before attacking, the Americans left their campfires burning and slipped out of reach. They then circled behind Cornwallis to surprise and defeat his reinforcements at Princeton on January 3. It was not the last time that Washington bested Cornwallis.

DOCUMENT

Letter from
a Revolutionary
War Soldier

The Struggle to Win French Support

▪ *Why did the French crown support the cause of the American Republic even though the new confederation had renounced the concept of hereditary monarchy?*

The successes at Trenton and Princeton restored a glimmer of hope for the tattered Continental Army and its supporters. As American forces took up winter quarters at Morristown, Howe withdrew his army from much of New Jersey to await the spring campaigns. As a result, anxious civilians in the region who had sworn their loyalty to the crown felt deserted. Public sentiment again swung toward the rebels. More importantly, news of the victories spurred support overseas for the American cause. French officials, eager to see their European rival bogged down in a colonial war, dispatched secret shipments of munitions to aid the revolutionaries.

One young aristocrat, the idealistic Marquis de Lafayette, was already on his way from France to volunteer his services to General Washington. But drawing forth an official French commitment to the American cause would take a larger show of success. That triumph finally came at the end of the next campaign season, with the Americans' stunning victory at Saratoga, deep in the Hudson Valley, 185 miles north of New York City.

BREAKDOWN IN BRITISH PLANNING

Among the Americans, two years of grim conflict had dampened the zeal that had first prompted citizens to enlist. Washington believed that the armed resistance could scarcely continue unless many more men made longer commitments to fight. He also insisted that his soldiers needed tighter discipline and better pay. In response, Congress expanded his disciplinary powers and offered a bonus to those who enlisted for a three-year term.

In a slumping economy, numerous recruits answered the call, including farmhands, immigrants, and unemployed artisans. All lacked training, supplies, and experience. Also, many of Washington's rural recruits had never been exposed to smallpox, so they lacked immunity to the devastating disease. When smallpox broke out among the American soldiers at Morristown, the commander promptly ordered mass inoculation. It proved to be one of General Washington's most shrewd decisions. Inoculation brings on a mild case of the disease, so the Virginian anxiously counted the days until his recuperating army could be ready to fight. "If Howe does not take advantage of our weak state," Washington commented in April 1777, "he is very unfit for his trust."

Despite American vulnerability, the British were slow to move. Lord North's ministry had fallen victim to its own contradictions. By seeking a decisive blow *and* a negotiated settlement in 1776, the British had achieved neither objective. They had also underestimated the persistence of Washington's army. During the 1777 campaigns, the British learned further hard lessons about the difficulty of their task and the need for coordinated plans.

General Burgoyne, returning to London for the winter, won government support for a major new offensive. He planned to lead a large force south from Canada via Lake Champlain, using the Hudson Valley to drive a wedge through the rebellious colonies. In support, a combined British and Indian force would strike east from Lake Ontario, capturing Fort Stanwix (east of modern-day Syracuse, New York) and descending eastward along the Mohawk River to meet Burgoyne at Albany. William Howe would push north from New York City to complete the design.

But General Howe had formed a different plan. Assuming Burgoyne would not need his help in the Hudson Valley, he intended to move south against Philadelphia. The two generals never integrated their separate operations, and the results were disastrous. In one six-month span, the British bungled their best chance for victory and handed their enemies an opening that permanently shifted the course of the war.

SARATOGA TIPS THE BALANCE

The isolated operations of Burgoyne and Howe got off to slow starts in late June 1777. Howe took two months to move his troops by sea from New York harbor to the headwaters of Chesapeake Bay. This delay gave the Americans time to march south, but an engagement at Brandywine Creek on September 11, 1777, failed to check Howe's advance north toward Philadelphia. The British finally entered the city in late September only to find that the rebel Congress had retreated to York, Pennsylvania.

At Germantown, just north of Philadelphia, Washington launched a surprise attack against the large Hessian garrison on October 4, but morning fog created so much confusion that the inexperienced Patriot troops allowed victory to slip away. Yet, as the battered army took up winter quarters at nearby Valley Forge, the defeats at Brandywine and Germantown seemed worth the price. The Americans had gained combat experience and had made Howe pay heavily for his hollow capture of Philadelphia. "Now," Washington wrote, "let all New England turn out and crush Burgoyne."

> *The Americans had gained combat experience and had made Howe pay heavily for his hollow capture of Philadelphia.*

Moving south from Canada in late June, "Gentleman Johnny" saw little likelihood of being crushed. His army consisted of 7,200 soldiers, with 1,500 horses to haul baggage and heavy equipment. British officers, foreseeing little danger, allowed nearly 2,000 women to accompany the huge force. General Burgoyne even brought his mistress along on the campaign. Weakened by tensions in their own command and knowing the British were on the march, the Americans fell back from Crown Point and Ticonderoga on Lake Champlain.

But as British supply lines lengthened, the crown's army grew less certain of victory. Burgoyne's soldiers expended valuable time cutting a roadway through the wilderness. Also, the reinforcements anticipated from the west had been turned back by Benedict Arnold

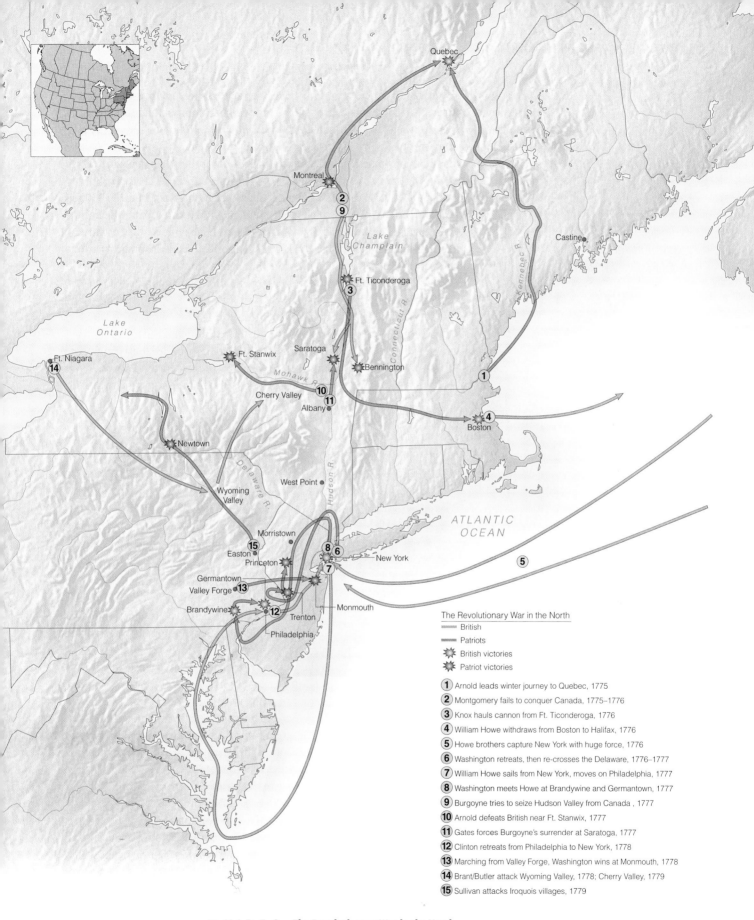

Quebec

Montreal

Castine

Lake
Champlain

② Ft. Ticonderoga
③

Lake
Ontario

Ft. Stanwix   Saratoga

Ft. Niagara   Bennington

Cherry Valley   ⑩
⑪
Albany   ①
Boston ④

Newtown

West Point

Wyoming
Valley

ATLANTIC
OCEAN

Morristown

⑮
Easton   ⑧ ⑥
Princeton   ⑦   New York
Germantown
Valley Forge ⑬
Brandywine   ⑫   Monmouth
Trenton   ⑤

Philadelphia

The Revolutionary War in the North

British

Patriots

British victories

Patriot victories

① Arnold leads winter journey to Quebec, 1775

② Montgomery fails to conquer Canada, 1775–1776

③ Knox hauls cannon from Ft. Ticonderoga, 1776

④ William Howe withdraws from Boston to Halifax, 1776

⑤ Howe brothers capture New York with huge force, 1776

⑥ Washington retreats, then re-crosses the Delaware, 1776–1777

⑦ William Howe sails from New York, moves on Philadelphia, 1777

⑧ Washington meets Howe at Brandywine and Germantown, 1777

⑨ Burgoyne tries to seize Hudson Valley from Canada , 1777

⑩ Arnold defeats British near Ft. Stanwix, 1777

⑪ Gates forces Burgoyne's surrender at Saratoga, 1777

⑫ Clinton retreats from Philadelphia to New York, 1778

⑬ Marching from Valley Forge, Washington wins at Monmouth, 1778

⑭ Brant/Butler attack Wyoming Valley, 1778; Cherry Valley, 1779

⑮ Sullivan attacks Iroquois villages, 1779

■ **M A P 7 . 3   The Revolutionary War in the North**

at Fort Stanwix. Even worse, American militia near Bennington badly mauled a British unit of 600 sent to forage for corn and cattle. With cold weather approaching and supplies dwindling, Burgoyne pushed toward Albany, unaware that Howe would not be sending help up the Hudson to meet him.

As Burgoyne's situation worsened, the American position improved. An arrogant British proclamation demanding submission from local residents only stiffened their resolve and drew out more rebel recruits. The Americans' strength grew to nearly 7,000 in September after Congress gave command in the Hudson Valley region to Horatio Gates. The new general was an ambitious English-born officer who harbored resentments toward his American superior, Washington, and toward the much-admired Benedict Arnold. While Burgoyne's army crossed to the Hudson River's west bank at Saratoga, Gates's American forces dug in on Bemis Heights, ten miles downstream.

> *An arrogant British proclamation demanding submission from local residents only stiffened their resolve and drew out more rebel recruits.*

On September 19, 1777, Patriot units under two aggressive officers, Benedict Arnold and Daniel Morgan, confronted the enemy at Freeman's Farm, not far from Saratoga. In the grueling battle, British forces suffered 556 dead or wounded, nearly twice the American losses. Gates's refusal to commit reinforcements prevented the Patriots from achieving total victory. Nevertheless, the American ranks swelled with new recruits who sensed a chance to inflict losses on Burgoyne's forces. On October 7, the beleaguered British tried once more to smash southward, only to suffer defeat in a second battle at Freeman's Farm. Morgan and Arnold once again played key roles, though Arnold suffered a crippling leg wound. When Burgoyne's entire army of 5,800 surrendered at nearby Saratoga ten days later, Gates took full credit for the stunning triumph.

FORGING AN ALLIANCE WITH FRANCE

Ever since declaring independence, Congress had maneuvered to win international recognition and aid for the new nation. Success came first with the Dutch. Although the Dutch Republic claimed neutrality, its colonial merchants supplied gunpowder for the rebellion through the West Indian island of St. Eustatius. When a ship flying the American flag approached the island in November 1776, Dutch officials fired cannons in salute—the first foreign acknowledgment of American sovereignty. Weeks later, Benjamin Franklin arrived in France as part of a commission sent to seek wider European support.

It was one thing for the Dutch Republic to recognize fellow republicans; it was quite another for the French king, Louis XVI, to endorse a revolution that opposed monarchy. Some in France, like the young Marquis de Lafayette, felt enthusiasm for the American cause as an expression of rational Enlightenment beliefs. But others, such as France's foreign minister, Comte de Vergennes, saw the colonists' revolt as an opportunity to avenge old grievances against Britain and undermine British power. Uncertain about the rebellion's chances for success, especially after the fall of Philadelphia, the government in Paris moved cautiously. It confined itself to substantial but covert assistance in the form of money and arms.

Word of the American victory at Saratoga suddenly gave Franklin greater leverage. When he hinted to the French that he might bargain directly with London for peace, Vergennes moved immediately to recognize American independence. France agreed to renounce forever any claim to British land in North America, and Franklin promised that the Americans would help defend French holdings in the Caribbean. Both parties pledged to defend the liberty of the new republic, and each agreed not to conclude a separate peace with Great Britain or to cease fighting until U.S. independence had been ensured by formal treaty. In May 1778, the Continental Congress approved this alliance. The next month, France entered the war, adding its enormous wealth and power to the American cause. A year later, Spain—unwilling to ally itself directly with the upstart republic but eager to protect its vast American assets from Great Britain—entered the war on the side of France.

For the British, what had been a colonial brushfire swiftly flared into a global conflict reminiscent of the Seven Years' War. These new hostilities with France meant possible invasions at home and inevitable attacks on outposts of Britain's empire. French ships seized Senegal in West Africa, took Grenada in the West Indies, and burned trading posts on Hudson Bay in Canada. London's annual war expenditures climbed from £4 million in 1775 to £20 million in 1782.

As war costs mounted in Britain, domestic opposition to the conflict in America intensified. Some members of Parliament pushed for a swift settlement. In 1778, a peace commission led by Lord Carlisle offered concessions to the Continental Congress, hoping to tear the French alliance apart. But the Carlisle Commission failed to win reconciliation. Other Britons went further in opposing the American war. Their diverse reasons included fear of French power, desire for American trade, disgust over war profiteering, ties to friends in America, and idealistic belief in the revolution's principles. Many drank toasts to General Washington and openly supported the American cause.

Faced with growing economic and political pressure, the king and his ministers briefly considered withdrawing all troops from the rebellious colonies and focusing on the French threat. Instead, when General Howe resigned as commander in chief in America, they instructed his successor, Sir Henry Clinton, to retreat from Philadelphia to New York and devote his main resources to attacking the French in the Caribbean. Over the next four years, discontent within Britain continued to escalate, and no strategy proved sufficient to pacify the Americans or to crush their rebellion.

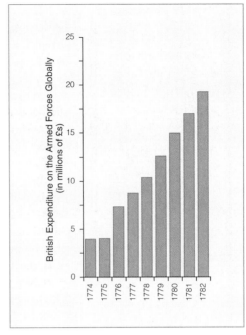

■ **FIGURE 7.1 British Government Expenses on Armed Forces Throughout the World, 1775–1782 (in Millions of Pounds)**

Britain's war budget soared after France entered the conflict in 1778, but major resources flowed toward India and the Caribbean, limiting the share available for North America.

Legitimate States, a Respectable Military

■ *If Americans were so fearful of centralized authority, how did they coordinate a successful political and military revolt against the powerful British Empire?*

Even with the new French alliance, the rebellious American states faced serious challenges on both the civilian and military fronts. They had thrown out their colonial governors and embarked on a dangerous war, but two fundamental questions still confronted them. First, how would the once-dependent colonies now be governed? And second, how could they shape a military force strong enough to defend themselves but not so powerful and unchecked as to seize control of their new civil governments?

THE ARTICLES OF CONFEDERATION

The Continental Congress had taken prompt initiative. Without clear authority, it had declared independence, raised an army, issued currency, borrowed money from abroad, and negotiated an alliance with France. Then it moved to bring greater stability and legitimacy to its work. In November 1777, one month after the victory at Saratoga, it approved the Articles of Confederation and presented this formal plan for a lasting and unifying government to the states for ratification. In every region, citizens were debating how much authority each new state government would have in relation to the larger federation. Who would have the power to levy taxes, for example, and who would control the distribution of land?

DOCUMENT

The Articles of Confederation (1777)

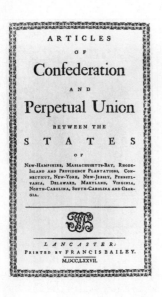

The Articles declared "The United States of America" to be a "firm league of friendship" between the thirteen former colonies. The final document proposed a weaker confederation than the one outlined in an earlier draft by John Dickinson. In the finished charter, each state would retain all independent rights and powers not "expressly delegated" to the Confederation Congress. Indeed, ties between the states seemed so loose that France considered sending thirteen separate ambassadors to America, and several European proposals to end the war suggested negotiating individually with each state.

According to the Articles, Congress could not collect taxes or regulate trade; it could only requisition funds from the states. Proportions would vary depending on each state's free population. Moreover, the Confederation had no separate executive branch; executive functions fell to various committees of the Confederation Congress. In addition, to the dismay of land speculators, the Congress would not control the western domains that several large states had claimed. Maryland, a small state without western claims, protested this arrangement and refused to ratify. To win the required approval from all thirteen states, drafters changed the plan and granted the Confederation control of western lands. After four years, the Articles finally won ratification in 1781.

Given the importance of the states, the task of designing new state governments seemed a higher priority to many than inventing a confederation structure. Some leaders in the Continental Congress returned home to help implement this state-level process. In May 1776, for example, two of Jefferson's friends in the Virginia delegation in Philadelphia departed for Williamsburg. They left their younger colleague behind, but they carried his written draft for a possible state constitution. Those already at work in Virginia accepted Jefferson's proposed preamble, and on June 29, 1776, Virginia led the way, adopting the first republican state constitution.

Virginia had already pioneered in another respect. Two weeks earlier, Virginia representatives approved a Declaration of Rights drawn up by George Mason. He affirmed the revolutionary concepts that all power derives from the people and that magistrates are their servants. He went on to endorse trial by jury, praise religious freedom, and condemn hereditary privilege. Over the next eight years, each state adopted a similar bill of rights to enumerate the fundamental limits of government power.

CREATING STATE CONSTITUTIONS

Though diverse, the thirteen states shared practical needs. Each had removed a functioning colonial government and needed to reestablish the rule of law under a new system. Britain possessed no written constitution, but the colonists had been ruled under published charters, and they shared a belief in the value of such clear and open arrangements. Thus they readily envisioned an explicit controlling document, or constitution, for each new state. Besides, the novel idea that government flowed from the people—as an agreement based on the consent of the governed—called for some all-encompassing, written legal contract.

A new written constitution, whether for a state or a union of states, represented something more fundamental and enduring than a regular law. It needed to be above day-to-day legal statutes and political whims. Somehow, the people, through chosen representatives, had to prepare a special document that citizens would affirm, or ratify, only one time. After the new government structure was in place, the constitution itself would be difficult, though not impossible, to change.

In 1779, Massachusetts legislators, under pressure from the public, fixed upon a method for providing the elevated status and popular endorsement for such a new document. Local voters in town meetings chose representatives for a specific constitution-drafting convention. These delegates, building on a model suggested by John Adams, crafted a suitable document, and their proposed constitution was then submitted to all the state's free men (regardless of race or property) for ratification. This widened constituency was intended to give special weight to the endorsement process.

Approval of the Massachusetts document was hotly debated. Many objected to the limits on popular power that were part of Adams's novel design. A reluctant revolutionary, Adams had dismissed Tom Paine as "ignorant, malicious, short-sighted." He had even composed a tract titled *Thoughts on Government* to counter the democratic enthusiasm of Paine's *Common Sense*. In his pamphlet, Adams argued that "interests" (like-minded groups), rather than people, should receive equal representation. In addition, he proposed sharing legislative responsibilities between a lower house, a senate, and a chief executive. Property requirements for these offices were steep, so wealthy interests would have power far beyond their numbers. The Massachusetts state constitution, ratified by a narrow margin, implemented these ideas. They signaled a turn away from the strongest popular radicalism of 1776 and foreshadowed the more conservative balance of interests that James Madison championed in the federal Constitution drafted in 1787.

DOCUMENT

John Adams, Thoughts on Government

This extended experiment in constitution writing was exhilarating and unprecedented. Never before in history, John Adams observed, had several million people had numerous opportunities "to form and establish the wisest and happiest government that human wisdom could contrive." Initial state efforts yielded varied results as the minority of white male citizens debated novel approaches to self-government. By 1780, the desire of prominent and well-established elites to rein in democratic power was evident. Yet, in comparison to the overseas monarchy they had rejected, even the most conservative of the new governmental designs seemed risky and bold.

At least three common threads ran through all the state constitutions. First, fearing executive might, drafters curtailed the rights of state governors to dismiss assemblies, raise armies, declare war, fill offices, or grant privileges. Colonial governors had been appointed from above, by proprietors or the crown, and they could serve terms of any length. In contrast, state governors would now be elected annually, usually by the assembly. Moreover, their service was subject to impeachment and controlled by term limits. In Pennsylvania, the most radical of the new constitutions did away with a single governor altogether, placing executive power in the hands of a twelve-member council elected by the people.

Second, drafters expanded the strength of legislatures and increased their responsiveness to the popular will. They made elections more frequent, and they enlarged the size of assemblies to allow greater local involvement. They also reduced property requirements for holding office and changed limits on the right to vote to allow wider participation.

Third, the constitution-makers feared the possible corruptions that came when people held more than one office at the same time. Having experienced these glaring conflicts of interest firsthand, they stressed the separation of executive, legislative, and judicial posts. The decision to prevent members of the executive branch from also holding a legislative seat removed any prospect for a cabinet-style government along the lines of the British model.

John Singleton Copley, *John Adams*, 1783. Courtesy of the Harvard University Portrait Collection, Bequest of Ward Nicholas Boylston to Harvard College, 1828. Photograph by Photographic Services. © President and Fellows of Harvard College (H74)

■ After independence, Americans had to create their own governments, and states experimented with new forms. John Adams of Massachusetts was part of a unique generation of lawyers who became skilled in the art of constitution-making.

TENSIONS IN THE MILITARY RANKS

A new republican order, whatever its nature, could not defend itself without a suitable fighting force. Just as defunct colonial administrations gave way to new state governments after much debate, colonial militia companies transformed into state militia amid serious arguments. In the state militias and in Washington's army, which was controlled and paid by the Continental Congress, tensions emerged from the start. Animated discussions erupted as to what constituted equitable pay, appropriate discipline, suitable tactics, and a proper distribution of limited supplies. Others argued over whether wealth, popularity, vision, military experience, political savvy, European training, or influential ties should play a role in determining who received, or retained, the cherished right to command.

> *Wealthy gentry assumed that they would command the state militias, while citizen soldiers demanded the right to choose their own leaders.*

One heated topic involved the election of officers. Wealthy gentry assumed that they would command the state militias, while citizen soldiers demanded the right to choose their own leaders. Another source of tension concerned the right of a prosperous individual to buy exemption from military service or to send a paid substitute. In 1776, as Washington's army retreated into Pennsylvania, militia in Philadelphia had chastised "Gentlemen who formerly Paraded in our Company and now in the time of greatest danger have turn'd their backs." They asked whether state authorities meant "to force the poorer kind into the field and suffer the Rich & the Great to remain at home?"

Three years later, some of these same Philadelphia militia, bitter that the burdens of the war always fell disproportionately on the poor, took part in what became known as the Fort Wilson Riot. Staging a demonstration in October 1779 spurred by soaring food prices, they intentionally marched past the stately home of James Wilson, where wealthy Patriots had gathered. "The time is now arrived," the demonstrators' handbill proclaimed, "to prove whether the suffering friends of this country, are to be enslaved, ruined and starved, by a few overbearing Merchants, . . . Monopolizers and Speculators." Shots were exchanged, and six died in the melee at "Fort Wilson." (Wilson himself went on to become a leader of the 1787 Constitutional Convention.)

Subtle class divisions also beset the Continental Army, where jealousies over rank plagued the status-conscious officer corps. Congressional power to grant military commissions, often on regional and political grounds, only intensified disputes. Also, Americans representing Congress abroad were empowered to promise high military posts to attract European officers. Some of these recruits served the American cause well, such as Johann de Kalb and Friedrich von Steuben (both born in Germany), and Thaddeus Kosciusko and Casimir Pulaski from Poland. In France, at age nineteen, the Marquis de Lafayette secured a commission to be a major general in America, and he assisted Washington impressively throughout the war.

In contrast, other foreign officers displayed arrogance and spread dissension. Irish-born Thomas Conway, for example, courted congressional opponents of Washington and encouraged the desires of General Horatio Gates to assume top command. Whether or not a concerted "Conway Cabal" ever existed, Washington managed to defuse tensions from Valley Forge during the hard winter of 1777–1778. His numerous letters helped consolidate his position with Congress and patch frayed relations with Gates.

Another rival for command of the army, English-born Charles Lee, met disfavor several months later, when Washington ordered him to attack the rear guard of Clinton's army as it withdrew from Philadelphia to New York. Lee mismanaged the encounter at Monmouth, New Jersey, on June 28, 1778, and only Washington's swift action stopped a premature retreat. The Battle of Monmouth ended in a draw, but American troops claimed victory and took pride in their swift recovery and hard fighting.

SHAPING A DIVERSE ARMY

The army's improved effectiveness came in large part from the efforts of Friedrich von Steuben, a European officer recruited by Benjamin Franklin after charges of homosexuality

Brian Hunt & Pennsylvania Capitol Preservation Committee

More than a century after the grim winter at Valley Forge, artist Edwin Abbey composed this mural of Steuben drilling Washington's soldiers in February 1778.

disrupted his German military career. He had arrived at Valley Forge in February 1778, offering to serve without pay. There he found soldiers with poor food, scant clothing, and limited training. Many Americans still wanted to see a more democratic citizen army, with elected officers and limited hierarchy. But Washington hoped to mold long-term soldiers into a more "Europeanized" force, and Steuben suited his needs. Shouting in several languages—he spoke no English—the newcomer worked energetically to drill soldiers. A written drill manual was drawn up, so that newly trained soldiers could drill others. Alexander Hamilton, who observed Steuben's strict training, gave him credit "for the introduction of discipline in the Army."

IMAGE

George Washington at Valley Forge

New discipline helped boost morale. Still, terms of service and wage levels remained sources of contention. So did the disparities in treatment and pay between officers and enlisted men. There were other grievances: inept congressional committees overseeing the war effort, incompetent officers filling political appointments, and a frustrating shortage of new recruits. Arguments also persisted over whether women or African Americans could serve in the army.

Women organized in diverse ways to assist the war effort, making uniforms and running farms and businesses for absent husbands. A few American women disguised themselves as men and fought. Deborah Sampson, for example, joined the Fourth Massachusetts Regiment, under the assumed name of Robert Shurtleff, and was wounded during her service. More commonly, women accompanied the troops to cook and wash in the camps. Earning scant pay, they carried water to the weary and wounded on the battlefield. Serving in these capacities, they formed a significant presence in both armies.

An estimated 20,000 women, many of them wives, may have accompanied the American army during the war. Washington reluctantly accepted the presence of women in camp, reasoning that they freed men for "the proper line of their duty." Mary Hays, the wife of a Pennsylvania soldier, endured the winter at Valley Forge, and later "Molly" Hays hauled pitchers of water on the battlefield and came to embody women's effort and commitment to the cause. When her husband was wounded at Monmouth, she is said to have set down her jug and joined his gun crew, earning folk-legend status as the cannon-firing "Molly Pitcher."

After petitioning to fight, free blacks were allowed to join the revolutionary army. Rhode Island even formed an African American regiment. In contrast, repeated proposals to arm southern slaves met with defeat. South Carolina and Virginia went so far as to move in the opposite direction, offering to give away slaves captured from Loyalist planters as a bonus to white recruits. Thus it is no surprise that thousands of enslaved people, especially in the South, risked their lives to escape to British lines.

THE WAR AT SEA

While Americans built their army into a respectable force, their lack of naval strength proved a constant disadvantage. As early as October 13, 1775, the Continental Congress had agreed to arm two vessels to prey on British supply ships on the Atlantic. The vote marked the birth of the American navy. Despite objections, Congress promptly appointed a committee to acquire sailing craft, and most of the thirteen states built up their own small navies for local purposes, adding to the confusion. The lack of central coordination proved deadly. When Massachusetts sent its ships "down east" along the Maine coast to challenge a Loyalist buildup at Castine in 1779, British vessels cornered the fleet at Penobscot Bay and crushed the enterprise.

Despite its strength, the British navy faced increasing challenges as more European powers joined the fray: France in 1778, Spain in 1779, and Holland in 1780. The English feared possible invasion, and French corsairs harassed Britain's coastline, joined by American captains. One such captain, a Scottish immigrant named John Paul Jones, arrived in European waters from America in early 1778, just as Franklin signed the pact

■ When British ships trapped an expedition from Massachusetts along the Maine coast in August 1779, the forty American vessels retreated up the Penobscot River. Before fleeing into the woods, the crews set fire to their boats, creating a spectacular blaze. "When they Blew up," one sailor wrote, "Shott and Timber flew verey thick up and Down the River."

with France. In April, Jones raided the port of Whitehaven in his native Scotland, and the propaganda triumph of an American success in British waters proved huge. The brazen young captain won an even greater victory the next year when his crew— including men of eleven nationalities—managed to board Britain's sleek new H.M.S. *Serapis* and capture the frigate before their own vessel sank.

In all, the Continental Navy equipped more than fifty vessels and captured nearly 200 British craft as prizes. But these numbers pale in comparison to the activities of American privateers. More than a thousand private shipowners obtained licenses from Congress to seize enemy ships and divide the proceeds among themselves and their crew. With international commerce curtailed, shipowners and sailors were eager to try their luck. Average pay aboard privateers was higher than on a government vessel, and discipline was less strict. In 1778, nearly 10,000 men were engaged in privateering aboard several hundred vessels. Their small, quick boats swarmed the Atlantic like troublesome gnats, frustrating England's mighty navy. According to one estimate, by war's end the British had surrendered 2,000 ships, 12,000 men, and goods valued at £18 million. And privateering drew merchant investors into the Patriot war effort, helping to bind the coastal elite more firmly to the American cause.

> *Privateering drew merchant investors into the Patriot war effort, helping to bind the coastal elite more firmly to the American cause.*

The Long Road to Yorktown

▪ *What conditions and events in America and Europe led to final American success in the War for Independence?*

By July 1778, Clinton's British forces had returned to New York City, and their situation had not improved. Frustrated in New England and the middle tier of states, Clinton revived the southern strategy discussed at the beginning of the war. Less thickly settled than the North, the South appeared more vulnerable. In addition, it supposedly contained a wide array of Loyalists who would offer support. Also, the South's lengthy growing season meant more fodder for wagon horses and cavalry mounts. The long southern coastline had little protection, and Washington's distant army would have trouble defending the region. Moreover, nearly 500,000 enslaved African Americans posed a threat to Patriot planters and represented potential support for British invaders. Finally, the same whites that dreaded slave rebellion also feared war with Native Americans, as Jefferson had explained in the Declaration of Independence. So the possible use of Indian allies also entered Britain's strategic calculation.

INDIAN WARFARE AND FRONTIER OUTPOSTS

Most Native Americans in eastern North America remained loyal to the British. Exceptions existed, such as the Oneida, Tuscarora, and Catawba, but Indians in many regions had long-standing grievances about the encroachments of colonial whites. In Appalachia, colonial land investors and frontier squatters had defied the king's Proclamation Line for more than a decade. When dissident Cherokee, led by a young war chief named Dragging Canoe, attacked intruders on the Watuaga River in July 1776, whites struck back. In all, 6,000 troops pushed into the mountains, laying waste to Cherokee villages.

Daniel Boone had already led migrants through Cumberland Gap in western Virginia to establish a fort on the Kentucky River at Boonesborough in 1775. By 1777, these pioneer families faced constant warfare against Indian adversaries fighting for their homelands. The

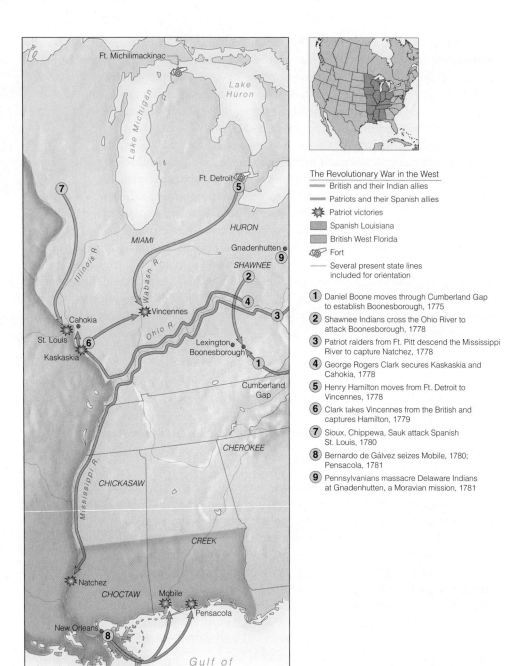

■ **MAP 7.4 The Revolutionary War in the West**

The Revolutionary War in the West

━━━ British and their Indian allies
━━━ Patriots and their Spanish allies
✸ Patriot victories
▨ Spanish Louisiana
▨ British West Florida
⚙ Fort
── Several present state lines included for orientation

① Daniel Boone moves through Cumberland Gap to establish Boonesborough, 1775
② Shawnee Indians cross the Ohio River to attack Boonesborough, 1778
③ Patriot raiders from Ft. Pitt descend the Mississippi River to capture Natchez, 1778
④ George Rogers Clark secures Kaskaskia and Cahokia, 1778
⑤ Henry Hamilton moves from Ft. Detroit to Vincennes, 1778
⑥ Clark takes Vincennes from the British and captures Hamilton, 1779
⑦ Sioux, Chippewa, Sauk attack Spanish St. Louis, 1780
⑧ Bernardo de Gálvez seizes Mobile, 1780; Pensacola, 1781
⑨ Pennsylvanians massacre Delaware Indians at Gnadenhutten, a Moravian mission, 1781

Native Americans were also being urged on by Henry Hamilton, the British commandant at far-off Detroit. In one six-month span, Hamilton, who became known as the Scalp Buyer, received 77 prisoners and 129 scalps from this frontier warfare.

Along the upper Ohio, violence escalated in 1777, when Americans killed Shawnee leader Cornstalk and his son during a truce. The next year, they murdered the neutral Delaware leader White Eyes, although they had recently hinted to him and other Native Americans in Ohio Country that the Indians might one day "form a state" and have "representation in Congress." Four years later, at the village of Gnadenhutten (south of modern-day Canton, Ohio), militia from Pennsylvania massacred 100 peaceful Delaware men, women, and children who had been converted to Christianity by Moravian missionaries.

By then, conflict involving Native Americans had also flared farther north. Joseph Brant, a mixed-race Mohawk leader educated in New England and loyal to the British, pushed south from Fort Niagara on Lake Ontario. Joined by a Loyalist band under John Butler, Brant and his men attacked poorly guarded frontier settlements. First in the Wyoming Valley of northeastern Pennsylvania and later in New York's Cherry Valley, the raiders killed hundreds of settlers. In the summer of 1779, American General John Sullivan led a campaign to annihilate Indian towns in reprisal.

Sullivan's revenge-minded troops, numbering more than 4,000, destroyed forty villages of the four tribes in the Iroquois Confederacy most linked to the British cause: the Mohawk, Onondaga, Cayuga, and Seneca. They avoided towns of the two Iroquois groups sympathetic to the Americans—the Oneida and Tuscarora—but elsewhere they chopped down orchards, torched crops, burned 160,000 bushels of corn, and sent several thousand Indian refugees streaming toward Fort Niagara. Hunger and retaliatory raids haunted the region until the end of the war.

While the British were passing arms and supplies to the divided Iroquois Confederacy through Fort Niagara, they also used several western posts to arm other Indian allies and seek an advantage in the interior. Soldiers at Fort Michilimackinac recruited Sioux, Chippewa, and Sauk warriors for an unsuccessful attack on Spanish-held St. Louis in 1780. At Fort Detroit, Hamilton continued to equip Ottawa, Fox, and Miami war parties to attack American newcomers migrating into the Ohio Valley.

In 1778, with support from his home state of Virginia, a young Patriot surveyor named George Rogers Clark organized a foray west to counter these raids and lend support to Spanish and French allies in the upper Mississippi Valley. He secured settlements on the Mississippi River, and in February 1779 he led a grueling winter march to the fort at

© 1992 Angel Art Ltd.

■ The British used Fort Niagara (on the southwest edge of Lake Ontario, at the mouth of the Niagara River) to launch attacks on American settlements and to shelter Indian allies. During the harsh winter of 1779–1780, 5,000 Iroquois refugees, made homeless by the scorched-earth campaign of General John Sullivan, camped near the fort in five feet of snow.

Vincennes in southern Indiana. In surprising that outpost on the Wabash River, the Americans managed to capture Henry Hamilton, but they failed to seize Detroit.

THE UNPREDICTABLE WAR IN THE SOUTH

The rebel war effort beyond the Appalachian Mountains expanded south in 1778, when Patriot raiders from Fort Pitt captured Natchez on the lower Mississippi and seized property in British West Florida. But it was the energetic governor of Spanish Louisiana, Bernardo de Gálvez, whose actions proved decisive. Living in New Orleans, Gálvez maintained a careful neutrality between the Americans and their British rivals through 1778. But when Spain allied with France and declared war on Britain the next year, the governor acted quickly to keep the British from gaining ground on the Gulf Coast.

> *Without additional guns, knives, and powder, Indian warriors could offer little assistance in Britain's ambitious plan to win back the South.*

Moving from west to east, Governor Gálvez drove the British from the Mississippi River in 1779, seized their fort at Mobile in 1780, and conquered Pensacola, the capital of British West Florida, in 1781. The fall of Mobile and Pensacola cut British supply lines to the southeastern interior, hurting Creek and Cherokee war efforts. Without additional guns, knives, and powder, Indian warriors could offer little assistance in Britain's ambitious plan to win back the South. It was support the British could ill afford to lose.

Still, the crown's forces regained control of most of Georgia from the rebels in 1778. The next year, they blocked American and French efforts to retake Savannah. Early in 1780, British generals Clinton and Cornwallis ferried troops by sea from New York to South Carolina. By May, this army had isolated Charleston and forced the surrender of 5,500 American troops—the largest loss of American men and weapons during the entire war. A confident Clinton returned to New York, leaving Cornwallis in command in South Carolina as fierce fighting erupted across the state. Banastre Tarleton's British cavalry, along with Loyalist supporters, went head to head against the guerrilla bands led by Thomas Sumter, Andrew Pickens, and Francis Marion.

In June 1780, Congress appointed Horatio Gates to take command of southern operations, and he hurried to the Carolinas with fresh troops. Gates's army confronted Cornwallis at Camden, South Carolina, 120 miles north of Charleston. The Americans, short on rest, food, and leadership, suffered another huge defeat. Two days after the Camden disaster, as Gates fled north ahead of his troops, Tarleton's cavalry landed another blow. They surprised Sumter's band of 800 partisans at Fishing Creek near the Catawba River and took 300 prisoners. Suffering almost no losses themselves, the cavalry inflicted 150 casualties and freed several hundred Loyalists and British regulars.

That September, as Washington absorbed word of the defeats at Camden and Fishing Creek, he received yet another rude shock. Benedict Arnold—in command of West Point, the key outpost controlling the Hudson River—had plotted to defect and yield the post to the British. An admired leader in battle, Arnold was also egotistical. Troubled by his war wounds and passed over by Congress for promotion, Arnold became increasingly alienated from the Patriot cause. The capture of General Arnold's British contact, Major John André, alerted Washington to the scheme. He hanged the major as an enemy spy, but Arnold escaped and received command of British troops.

Five years of war left Washington and Congress facing severe problems: soaring inflation, scarce resources, sinking citizen morale, and mounting disobedience among enlisted men. Early in 1780, soldiers from Massachusetts, New York, and Connecticut had mutinied in separate incidents. Members of the Pennsylvania and New Jersey Lines soon staged similar strikes over disputed terms of enlistment. The British had reason for optimism as Cornwallis pressed into North Carolina in the fall of 1780. But the next twelve months saw a dramatic reversal in their fortunes.

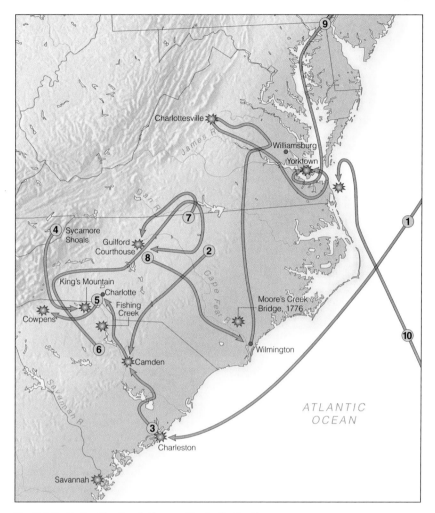

The Revolutionary War in the South
— British and their Loyalist allies
— Patriots and their French allies
✸ British victories
✸ Patriot victories

1 Clinton and Cornwallis force surrender of Charleston, May 1780
2 Gates moves the American army to Camden, August 1780
3 Cornwallis bests Gates at Camden and moves north, August 1780
4 Americans defeat Ferguson at Kings Mountain, October 1780
5 Morgan meets British at Cowpens, defeats Tarleton, January 1781
6 Cornwallis pursues Greene's army across the Dan River, February 1781
7 Greene confronts Cornwallis at Guilford Courthouse, March 1781
8 After a retreat to Wilmington, Cornwallis moves to Virginia, April 1781
9 Washington moves south, pins Cornwallis at Yorktown, August 1781
10 De Grasse from West Indies, defeats the British fleet, September 1781

■ **MAP 7.5   The Revolutionary War in the South**

That reversal began in October, when Patriots won a surprising victory at King's Mountain in the southern backcountry. Cornwallis had sent Major Patrick Ferguson and a troop of South Carolina Loyalists to guard his army's western flank and harry rebel supporters. But more than 800 frontiersmen rallied at Sycamore Shoals in the Watauga Valley and raced south to challenge the British. On October 6, just below North Carolina's southern border, these sharpshooters surrounded and decimated the Loyalist troops at King's Mountain. Ferguson died in the one-sided affair, and his force lost more than 1,000 men—killed, wounded, or captured.

THE FINAL CAMPAIGN

A shrewd change in American leadership followed the victory at King's Mountain. Congress, on Washington's advice, replaced Gates in the southern command with General Nathanael Greene, an experienced Rhode Islander who had served as the army's quartermaster general. Greene arrived in Charlotte, North Carolina, in December 1780, taking charge of a tattered army of only 1,600. Shocked by the violence of partisan warfare and conscious of the need to win public support, he urged restraint on such experienced guerrilla fighters as Sumter and Marion while weaving them into his overall plan to conduct an elusive "fugitive war." Greene decided to divide his small army and send half his men into South Carolina under the seasoned Daniel Morgan to harass the British flank. "It makes the most of my inferior force," he explained, "for it compels my adversary to divide his, and holds him in doubt as to his own line of conduct."

William Ranney, *The Battle of Cowpens.* Oil on canvas. Photo by Sam Holland. Courtesy South Carolina State House.

■ Though outnumbered, Daniel Morgan's inexperienced Patriot forces inflicted "a devil of a whipping" upon Banastre Tarleton and the British at Cowpens, South Carolina, in January 1781.

Cornwallis took the bait and dispatched Tarleton, who caught up with Morgan at Hannah's Cowpens, west of King's Mountain, on January 17, 1781. The outnumbered rebel militia lacked experience and discipline, but Morgan turned this weakness to an advantage at the Battle of Cowpens. He stationed the militia units in front of his Continental forces with orders to fire two rounds and fall back. Sensing an enemy retreat, the British force of 1,100 advanced too far too fast. Morgan's men promptly overwhelmed them. Tarleton managed to escape, but he left behind 100 dead, 800 prisoners, and most of his horses and ammunition. Morgan, whose force suffered only 148 casualties, rightly called the Battle of Cowpens "a devil of a whipping."

Though frustrated, Cornwallis clung to the belief that "a successful battle may give us America." He discarded all excess baggage and pursued the rebel army 200 miles across North Carolina. Greene directed a speedy retreat over swollen rivers to the Virginia border, then doubled back to confront the weary British in the Battle of Guilford Courthouse on March 15. Although the American forces eventually withdrew from the field, Cornwallis sustained such heavy losses that he was forced to alter his plans.

The British retreated to the coast at Wilmington, North Carolina, and then marched north in early summer 1781 to Yorktown, Virginia. There, Cornwallis hoped to obtain reinforcements by sea, rally Loyalists in the Chesapeake region, and divide the rebelling colonies once and for all. The design's success hinged upon naval superiority and timely support from General Clinton in New York. But Cornwallis could be assured of neither.

In August, the French fleet in the Caribbean set out for Chesapeake Bay. Admiral François de Grasse planned to spend eight weeks in North American waters. The move gave Washington brief access to impressive naval power, and he seized his chance. He sent word south to Lafayette in Virginia to keep Cornwallis contained at Yorktown. Then, to hold Clinton's forces in New York, he ordered his men to make a show as if preparing for a lengthy siege. But instead of besieging New York City, American soldiers and their French allies slipped away, secretly marching south to lay a trap for the British army.

Admiral de Grasse reached Chesapeake Bay with two-dozen ships at the end of August. On September 5, he repulsed a British fleet off the mouth of the bay, dashing Cornwallis's

■ The joint American–French victory at the siege of Yorktown, Virginia, in October 1781 ended British hopes for preventing American independence. As Cornwallis's troops marched out to lay down their arms, a band played "The World Turned Upside Down." "Finally," Lafayette wrote proudly, "everything came together at once, and we had a sensational turn of events. . . . The play is over."

hopes for relief by sea and allowing Washington to tighten the noose. When 9,000 Americans and 7,800 French converged on Yorktown in late September, they outnumbered their 8,000 opponents by more than two to one. The siege proved brief. Plagued by sickness and shortages of food and munitions, the British army surrendered on October 19, 1781. Sarah Osborn, who was present in the American camp, recalled how the defeated British "marched out beating and playing a melancholy tune, their drums covered with black handkerchiefs and their fifes with black ribbons tied around them." For Washington and his army, Yorktown was a stunning victory. Intermittent warfare continued for another year. But the Americans finally had powerful leverage to bargain for peace and to force Britain to recognize their independence.

MAP

The American Revolution

WINNING THE PEACE

After Yorktown, the final phase of the war played out in European courts. There, the diplomatic maneuvering proved complicated and risky, with Benjamin Franklin, John Adams, and John Jay as the key American players. Often at odds, the three men nevertheless managed to achieve a final triumph that proved as unlikely and momentous as Washington's victory in Virginia. They did it, wrote the immodest Adams, "in spite of the malice of enemies, the finesse of Allies, and the mistakes of Congress."

For the British, the road to the peace table had been long and unpleasant. Early attempts to negotiate a settlement—through the Howes in 1776 and the Carlisle Commission in 1778—had not mentioned independence. But conditions changed drastically after Yorktown. Domestic unrest in Britain had already boiled into riots, and the expanded war was going poorly in India and the West Indies. "O God, it is all over!" Lord North muttered when he received the news of Cornwallis's defeat in Virginia.

Benjamin Franklin: The Diplomat in a Beaver Hat

Why was Benjamin Franklin wearing a coarse beaver hat in the presence of French nobility? Had the diplomat grown careless and insensitive in old age? Probably not. Instead, the answer may lie in the fact that the creator of *Poor Richard's Almanac* had always possessed a remarkable awareness of *currents* and *movements*. He puzzled over how glass bent light rays, how wire conducted electricity, and how stoves circulated warm air. The talented inventor developed bifocals, devised the lightning rod, and designed the Franklin stove. He became the first scientist to identify the Gulf Stream.

Franklin also had a shrewd understanding of *social* currents. His gift for sensing, and shaping, public trends came into play once again after 1776, when Congress sent him to France to seek European support for the War of Independence. Settling in Paris, the seasoned politician became a major force

in winning the war and the peace that followed. He exploited his image as an Enlightenment scientist when he publicly embraced the great philosopher, Voltaire, at the French Academy of Sciences. At court, he charmed the ladies with his wit, while securing secret loans for the American cause.

Word of the British defeat at Saratoga strengthened Franklin's hand. Soon he had negotiated a formal alliance with France and been named America's minister to the French court. Gradually, the astute media master made himself the living emblem of America. European artists competed to paint his portrait, and sculptors captured his likeness in plaster, bronze, and marble. His sage image adorned vases, medallions like the one shown here, clocks, handkerchiefs and pocketknives. The balding American let his remaining hair grow long, and he made it fashionable for gentlemen to go without a powdered wig. Delighted by his own fame, he wrote in 1779 that his face had become "as well known as that of the moon."

Franklin's rustic cap provided the crowning touch. His beaver hat emphasized America's homespun style and reminded Europeans of the continent's natural riches. "Figure me in your mind," he wrote to a friend, "as very plainly dress'd, wearing my thin grey straight Hair, that peeps out under my only Coiffure, a fine Fur Cap, which comes down my Forehead almost to my Spectacles. Think how this must appear among the Powder'd Heads of Paris."

QUESTIONS

1. What elements of the American character did Franklin capture by wearing a fur cap "among the Powder'd Heads of Paris"?

2. How would Franklin's pose as a rustic philosopher have helped him in his earnest chores as a diplomat for a new country in need of aid?

Within months, Guy Carleton replaced Clinton in command of the remaining British forces in America, the hawkish Lord Germain stepped down from the cabinet, and North resigned after twelve years as prime minister. The king spoke briefly of abdicating, but instead, he approved a new ministry more suited to the rising antiwar sentiment in Parliament. The Earl of Shelburne became prime minister in July 1782. Even before he assumed office, he had authorized peace discussions with his old acquaintance, Benjamin Franklin.

Franklin was in a difficult position. The crucial alliance he had negotiated with France stated that the Americans would not sign a separate peace with Britain. Moreover, Congress, grateful for vital French military and financial support, had instructed the American negotiators to defer to the wishes of Vergennes. The Americans did not realize that the French foreign minister had already entertained thoughts of a truce that would leave London in control of all the territory it currently held in America. This consisted of Penobscot Bay in Maine (with its valuable supplies of naval timber), New York City, and parts of the lower South. Vergennes opposed the Americans' republican principles, and he refused to treat the American diplomats as equal partners.

Still, the American peace commissioners fared surprisingly well in the treacherous waters of European diplomacy, starting with Franklin's first informal talks with the British. He laid out four "necessary" points, leading with the recognition of American independence. To this he added the removal of British troops, the right to fish in Newfoundland waters, and the revision of the Canadian border, which the Quebec Act of 1774 had pushed south to the Ohio River. Franklin then noted some "desirable" items for later bargaining. The British, he suggested, should consider paying an indemnity for war damages, an act that would officially acknowledge their own blame for the war. Perhaps they should cede Canada to the United States as well.

For its part, Britain sought compensation for roughly 70,000 American Loyalists who had been driven from their homes, plus the right to collect old debts that colonists had owed to British merchants before 1776. Hoping to disrupt the American–French alliance and to reestablish trade with their former colonies, the British

Benjamin West, *Signing of the Peace Treaty*. Courtesy, Winterthur Museum (57.856)

■ The final American victory in the War of Independence came at the peace table, when negotiators John Jay, John Adams, and Benjamin Franklin won favorable terms in the 1783 Treaty of Paris. Benjamin West's unfinished painting also includes the absent Henry Laurens (rear) and Franklin's grandson (right), the delegation's secretary.

negotiated preliminary peace terms with the Americans in November 1782. In return for gaining independence, plus fishing rights and the withdrawal of British troops, the Americans agreed vaguely that their Congress would "recommend" that individual states approve compensation for confiscated Loyalist property.

On the Canadian boundary question, the Americans scored another success, but one that came at the expense of Indian nations. By giving up their bid for all of Canada, the negotiators persuaded Britain to relinquish the Ohio Valley and accept a northern boundary for the United States defined by the Great Lakes and the highlands marking the edge of the St. Lawrence River valley. In the west, the United States would reach to the Mississippi River. Americans would obtain free navigation on that waterway, despite Spanish opposition. In the South, the 31st parallel, above East and West Florida, would provide the American boundary.

The diplomats endorsed the final peace terms at Versailles, France, in September 1783. Amid all the other treaty terms, the British yielded East and West Florida to Spain. In the process, however, they made no mention of the Indians who had served as British allies in the American conflict. Abandoned, the Native Americans had to confront their new situation alone. To end up "betrayed to our Enemies & divided between the Spaniards and the Americans is Cruel & Ungenerous," protested the Creek leader, Alexander McGillivray. His people had been "most Shamefully deserted."

Conclusion

The War for Independence that began at Lexington lasted eight years. Like any lengthy armed struggle, it took a heavy toll on combatants and noncombatants alike. Personal survival itself was far from certain, as encounters with sickness and the enemy killed enlisted men. American

CHRONOLOGY, 1776–1783

1776	Thomas Paine, *Common Sense*.
	Declaration of Independence.
	Washington crosses the Delaware and wins victory at Trenton.
	New Jersey gives women the right to vote.
1777	Burgoyne surrenders at Saratoga.
	Washington defuses "Conway Cabal."
1778	U.S. forges an alliance with France.
1779	Sullivan's campaign against the Iroquois.
	"Fort Wilson" Riot, Philadelphia.
1780	Charleston falls to the British.
	British Major John André hanged as spy.
1781	Morgan defeats Tarleton at Cowpens, S.C.
	Cornwallis wins costly victory over Greene's American forces at Guilford Courthouse, N.C.
	Cornwallis surrenders at Yorktown.
	Articles of Confederation are ratified.
1782	Christian Delaware Indians massacred at village of Gnadenhutten in Ohio.
1783	Treaty of Paris ends the war.

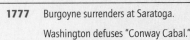

forces lost an estimated 25,000 soldiers, a huge number in proportion to the small overall population.

For those who avoided death, lesser dangers abounded. These included being uprooted from home, losing property, and going deeply into debt. Despite these constant personal uncertainties, a makeshift revolutionary army, learning as it marched, forced the British to concede American independence.

As in all wars, some of the most decisive action occurred far from the battlefield. In London, weakness and inconsistency in the chain of command combined with a lumbering bureaucracy and divided public sentiment to undermine the British war effort. Elsewhere in Europe, skillful American diplomats built the international alliances needed to secure victory, and they won peace terms that promised survival to the new confederation of states. At home, a flurry of constitution-writing unprecedented in history launched more than a dozen newly independent states, and the Articles of Confederation, approved after long delay, knit them together into a formal league with a common Congress.

Still, the new and complex art of republican self-government remained a work in progress, with some of the most difficult and contentious choices yet to come. The fragile unity built on fighting a common enemy would soon be strained to the limit, as new debates erupted over the meaning and direction of the unfinished revolution.

For Review

1. Was undermining or ending racial slavery a realistic strategic possibility for one or both sides in 1775–1776? Explain.

2. In July 1776, why did some Americans believe that the Declaration of Independence had been issued too soon, while others considered it too late?

3. To what extent did poor military planning by the British lead to the costly defeat of General Burgoyne's campaign at Saratoga in 1777?

4. How did the initial state constitutions, drafted soon after 1776, reflect the recent political experiences of wary former British colonists?

5. Along the entire length of the frontier, why did most Native American groups throw in their lot with the British during the Revolutionary War?

6. In what specific ways did French support make possible the American victory in the War of Independence?

Created Equal **Online**

For more *Created Equal* resources, including suggestions on sites to visit and books to read, go to **MyHistoryLab.com**.

Chapter 8

New Beginnings: The 1780s

■ Smallpox "spread like lightning through all the missions," causing "havoc which only those who have seen it can believe. The towns and missions were . . . deserted, and bodies were seen in the road." Some stricken Indians threw themselves into fires, "and still others set about burning the pustules with live coals." Time and again, "the poor little children, abandoned beside the dead, died without help." – Father Luis Sales, Baja California, 1781

During the Revolutionary War years, between 1775 and 1782, a huge smallpox epidemic ricocheted relentlessly across broad sections of North America. At times the epidemic entwined itself with the war, traveling on supply ships and moving with marching troops. In the Northeast, it struck during the siege of Boston and the attack on Quebec. In the South, it cut down hundreds of Virginia slaves who had escaped at the start of the war to join Governor Dunmore's "Ethiopian Regiment." The disease found additional victims during the British siege of Charleston in 1780.

Like the war itself, smallpox erupted first in Massachusetts. But the devastating contagion spread far more widely than the military destruction, proving truly continental in scope. It gained a foothold in New Orleans, Mexico City, and the trading posts that dotted the Canadian interior. In 1781, the disease ravaged Indian villages on the Northwest Coast, devastated missions on the Baja Peninsula, and erupted at California's San Gabriel Mission, where Spanish-speaking newcomers were building a village named El Pueblo de La Reina de Los Angeles (the start of modern-day Los Angeles). On the Atlantic coast, smallpox menaced Virginia as French and American troops surrounded the British at Yorktown. As the War of Independence ended, the transcontinental epidemic also drew to a close.

The contagion left a patchwork of destruction from the Atlantic to the Pacific. Smallpox losses were greatest among Native Americans; few groups or regions remained untouched. British sea captain George Vancouver, probing the Northwest Coast near the head of Puget Sound in 1792, observed numerous skulls, ribs, and other human remains "scattered about the beach." When Vancouver's pilot, Peter Puget, pressed farther into the sound that is now named for him, he found deserted villages that only a dozen years earlier had bustled with people. In its eight-year course, the fearsome virus took more than 130,000 North American lives, many times the total of 25,000 Americans lost in military service during the Revolution. In different ways, these two events exerted a drastic and lasting impact on the continent and its peoples.

As the dual scourges of epidemic and war subsided, fresh problems confronted North America's inhabitants. Great Britain's mainland colonies had won their independence, but questions remained as to which European powers would exert the most influence on the huge continent. In the North Pacific, Russians sent by Empress Catherine the Great intruded on the Alaskan coast. The British ruled Canada; the Spanish continued to claim much of the West; and in Paris, despite the approach of the French Revolution, some still dreamed of restoring the Mississippi Valley to the control of France.

In the fertile woodlands between the Appalachian Mountains and the Mississippi River, Indians whom Pontiac had sought to unify a generation earlier once again endured sudden trans-fers of their ancestral land between distant powers. Now the rapid incursion of American settlers added new urgency and desperation to their situation. Farther east, inhabitants of the Atlantic seaboard faced an array of problems after warfare and smallpox loosened their grip. Half a mil-lion people remained legally enslaved. During the Revolutionary War, they had seen that armed rebellion in the name of liberty could succeed, and they were potential allies for any European power seeking to disrupt the fragile new society.

In addition, members of the Confederation's Continental Congress in Philadelphia had a restless army to pay, a weak government to reform, and enormous war debts to confront. Acceptance of the Articles of Confederation in 1781 had not come easily, and all assumed that the basic structure of governance would demand further revision and adjustment. However, few could foresee that it would be set aside within eight years for a more centralized federal design.

Beating Swords into Plowshares

■ *Why did language matter so much to Americans in the years after the Revolutionary War?*

At first, in the wake of military victory over Britain, the short-term survival of the new United States of America seemed assured, thanks to years of intense fighting and skillful diplomacy. The former colonies had banded together under the Articles of Confederation, finally ratified in 1781, which placed specific governmental powers in the hands of an elected national legislature, or Continental Congress. But deeper questions persisted regarding the new republican experiment. Should power rest primarily with the victorious army, the wealthy merchants, or the artisans and farmers central to the revolutionary movement? Should author-ity be consolidated in the hands of a new and well-educated national elite, or should it be widely dispersed, with local communities and states empowered to manage their own affairs?

Equally important, what cultural patterns would take hold within the fledgling society? In these postwar years, scientific, educational, and humanitarian undertakings flourished. Literary endeavors also prospered, and lending libraries sprang up. "At no time did Literature make so rapid a progress in America, as since the peace," boasted a Massachusetts periodical in 1785. "It must afford real pleasure to every son of science, that our swords are beaten into ploughshares, and that the torch of Learning now shines

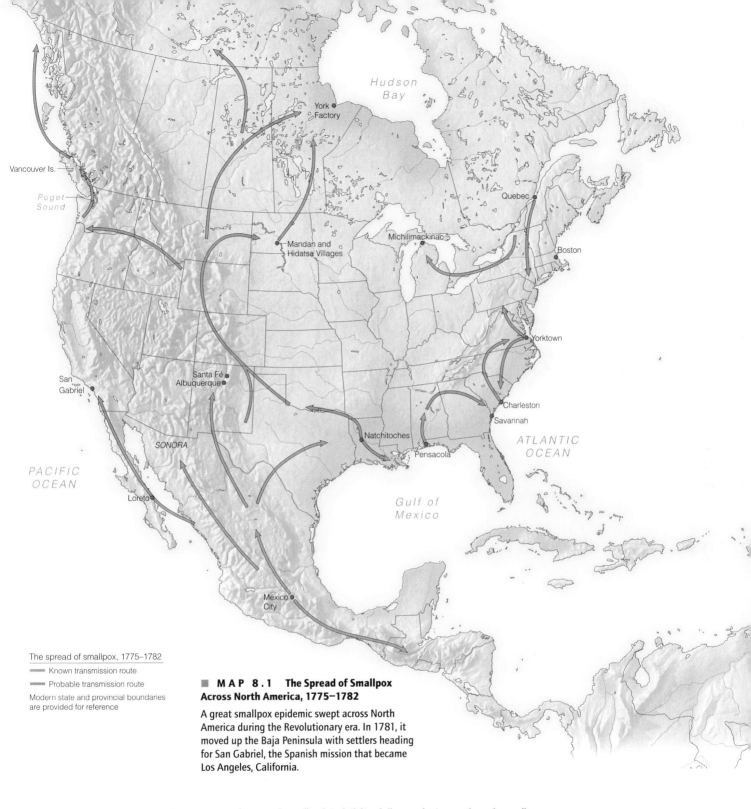

The spread of smallpox, 1775–1782

▬▬▬ Known transmission route

▬▬▬ Probable transmission route

Modern state and provincial boundaries
are provided for reference

■ **MAP 8.1 The Spread of Smallpox
Across North America, 1775–1782**

A great smallpox epidemic swept across North
America during the Revolutionary era. In 1781, it
moved up the Baja Peninsula with settlers heading
for San Gabriel, the Spanish mission that became
Los Angeles, California.

with such lustre in this western hemisphere." This biblical "swords into plowshares"
reference, evoking the prophet Isaiah, held deep meaning for a nation that had endured
nearly a decade of warfare, from Maine to Georgia.

WILL THE ARMY SEIZE CONTROL?

After their triumph at Yorktown, Washington's troops had moved north to press British
forces to evacuate New York City. More than 10,000 American troops and 500 officers
encamped at Newburgh, on the Hudson River. Exhausted soldiers were eager to receive
long-overdue pay and return home. Clearly, they could negotiate best for the promised

Demobilization: "Turned Adrift like Old Worn-Out Horses"

Interpreting History

Joseph Plumb Martin was born in western Massachusetts in 1760. He enlisted in the Continental Army before his sixteenth birthday and was encamped at West Point, New York, when peace finally arrived. Later, in a compelling narrative of his wartime experiences, he recalled the demobilization process from the perspective of a common soldier.

[On April 19, 1783,] we had general orders read which satisfied the most skeptical, that the war was over and the prize won [after] eight tedious years. But the soldiers said but little about it; their chief thoughts were closely fixed upon their situation. . . . Starved, ragged and meager, not a cent to help themselves with, and no means or method in view to remedy or alleviate their condition. This was appalling in the extreme. . . .

William Ranney painted this picture of homeward-bound Revolutionary War veterans in 1848, when the United States was at war with Mexico. The image offered a positive reminder of earlier American military success. But some soldiers leaving the Continental Army in 1783 had clearly fared better than others.

William Ranney, *Veterans of 1776 Returning from the War*, c. 1848. Dallas Museum of Art, Museum League Fund, Special Contributors and General Acquisitions Fund (Acc. 1981.40)

At length, the eleventh day of June 1783, arrived. "The old man," our captain, came into the room, with his hands full of papers. . . . He then handed us our discharges, or rather furloughs, . . . permission to

wages while they were still together and armed. Officers were especially reluctant to disband without clear assurances of money. In 1780, they had extracted from the Congress a promise of half pay for life, in imitation of the European model. In December 1782, with no sign of the money in sight, the disgruntled officers sent a delegation to Philadelphia to press their claims.

Within Congress, the men around financier Robert Morris, including James Wilson and Alexander Hamilton, wanted to bolster and centralize the Confederation's finances. To that end, they sought a new duty of 5 percent on imported goods to raise money from the states. Revenue from this "continental impost" could make the Confederation solvent and allow it to assume responsibility for paying off war debts. In turn, this commitment would tie the interests of wealthy citizens to the Confederation government's success. Morris even threatened to resign his post if the "nationalists" did not get their way. Rumblings from the officer corps would help these politicians push through the impost measure, crucial to their long-term goals. So they quietly encouraged the military dissidents in Newburgh.

In March 1783, anonymous petitions—penned by the staff of Washington's old rival, Horatio Gates—circulated among officers encamped at Newburgh. These inflammatory "addresses" contained a veiled threat of military takeover in order to impose stability after a turbulent revolution. They suggested that officers should sit tight, neither fighting nor laying down their arms, until Congress guaranteed their payment. If the government met their demands, they would be like "lambs," General Henry Knox wrote privately to a return home, but to return to the army again if required. This was policy in government; to discharge us absolutely in our present pitiful, forlorn condition, it was feared, might cause some difficulties. . . .

Some of the soldiers went off for home the same day that their fetters were knocked off; others stayed and got their final settlement certificates, which they sold to procure decent clothing and money. . . . I was among those. . . . I now bid a final farewell to the service. I had obtained my settlement certificates and sold some of them and purchased some decent clothing, and then set off from West Point. . . .

When those who engaged to serve during the war enlisted, they were promised a hundred acres of land, each. . . . When the country had drained the last drop of service it could screw out of the poor soldiers, they were turned adrift like old worn-out horses, and nothing said about land to pasture them upon. . . . Congress did, indeed, appropriate lands, . . . but no care was taken that the soldiers should get them. [Instead,] a pack of speculators . . . were driving about the country like so many evil spirits, endeavoring to pluck the last feather from the soldiers. The soldiers were ignorant of the ways and means to obtain their bounty lands. . . . It was, soldiers, look to yourselves; we want no more of you.

We were, also, promised six dollars and two thirds a month. . . . And what was six dollars and sixty-seven cents of this "Continental currency," as it was called, worth? It was scarcely enough to procure a man a dinner. . . . I received one month's

pay in specie while on the march to Virginia, in the year 1781, and except that, I never received any pay worth the name while I belonged to the army. . . .. It is provoking to think of it. The country was rigorous in exacting my compliance to *my* engagements . . . but equally careless in performing her contracts with me, and why so? One reason was that she had all the power in her own hands and I had none. Such things ought not to be.

After the war, Martin settled on the Maine frontier, and a speculator bought his right to 100 acres of bounty land in Ohio. In 1818, as a disabled laborer with a large family, he successfully petitioned Congress for a small pension to support the household. He died poor in 1850.

QUESTIONS

1. *Why did the government worry about discharging soldiers such as Martin in 1783, and why did many of them sell their final settlement certificates?*

2. *Are any of Martin's complaints still relevant for modern American combat veterans? Explain.*

Source: James Kirby Martin, ed., *Ordinary Courage: The Revolutionary War Adventures of Joseph Plumb Martin*, 2nd ed. (New York: Brandywine Press, 1999), 159–164.

---

fellow general. If not, they would become "tigers and wolves." Some American officers clearly envisioned the prospect of using military might to assert and retain political power. Without Washington's approval, the officers at Newburgh arranged a meeting to discuss their plight.

If the plotters hoped to draw Washington into the scheme, they were sorely disappointed. He attended the officers' meeting on March 15, but he used his commanding presence to discredit the ill-advised plan. His eyes weakened by endless wartime correspondence, he drew a pair of spectacles from his pocket, a surprising gesture that underscored his years of dedication and sacrifice. He then read aloud a letter from Congress containing assurances of support, and he urged his officers not to take any actions that would undermine the honor they had earned.

DOCUMENT

George Washington, The Newburgh Address

Within Congress, the frightening prospect of a coup weakened resistance to certain demands from the officers. Under extreme pressure, a representative from Connecticut finally altered his position and cast the deciding vote for a plan that responded to officer demands. The officers had gained the advantage, Samuel Adams was told, by playing up "the terror of a mutinying army" before reaching an accommodation. In late March, chastised by Washington, the officers disavowed the "infamous propositions" and accepted a congressional offer of full pay for the next five years. In April 1783, as Congress accepted a version of the 5 percent impost, momentous news arrived from Europe. Word spread quickly that preliminary articles of peace had been signed in Paris. By June, most soldiers were headed home.

IMAGE

Women Petition for War Compensation

THE SOCIETY OF THE CINCINNATI

Washington's strong stance against the suspected Newburgh conspiracy reminded his admirers of the familiar story of Cincinnatus, a general in Rome's early republic. The Roman Senate called Cincinnatus from his farm to command an army against invaders. After defeating the enemy, he put down his sword and took up his plow again rather than seize power as a military ruler. His selfless act earned Cincinnatus the lasting respect of the Roman people. Similarly, at a crucial moment for the American republic, Washington urged fellow officers to respect the fragile principle of civilian control over the military. His action, Thomas Jefferson told Washington, "probably prevented this revolution from being closed as most others have been by a subversion of that liberty it was intended to establish."

Still, Jefferson and others had grounds to fear that some military officers might meddle in politics while hiding behind the noble name of Cincinnatus. In May 1783, General Knox announced formation of the Society of the Cincinnati. The new organization invoked the name of the famous Roman, in a plural form, to put its members in the best light. But it was open only to officers in the Continental Army, certain male descendants, and invited honorary members.

Some onlookers believed that the "Cincinnati Club" was no more than a social fraternity for men united by their war experience. Benjamin Franklin assumed those joining the society had been drawn together simply by the lure of ceremony and recognition. Perhaps, he mused, these officers had "been too much struck with the Ribbands and Crosses they have seen . . . hanging to the buttonholes of Foreign Officers." But others sensed a more sinister purpose. After all, members contributed to a charitable fund that resembled a political war chest, and they maintained contact with each other through newsletters concerning "the general union of the states." Most ominously, participants endorsed hereditary membership, so that the eldest sons of Continental officers would join the society down through the generations.

For skeptics, the society appeared to plant the seeds of a self-perpetuating ruling class. In a scathing pamphlet titled *Considerations on the Society or Order of Cincinnati . . . with Remarks on Its Consequences to the Freedom and Happiness of the Republic,* Judge Aedanus Burke of South Carolina protested that the organization revealed a "thirst for power" and created a "race of hereditary patricians, or nobility." Critics such as Burke argued that the society would spawn a separate aristocracy of the very kind Americans had fought to erase.

Washington was automatically a member of the society, but Jefferson and other friends urged the general not to accept a leadership post. Struck by this "violent and formidable" opposition, Washington suggested changes in the society, including doing away with the hereditary and honorary memberships. However, he never played a central role in the organization, and his well-publicized alterations were never implemented. The Cincinnati exerted influence as an interest group before receding from politics in future generations.

RENAMING THE LANDSCAPE

The controversy over the Society of the Cincinnati represented part of a larger debate about the direction of postwar life. The victors in any revolutionary struggle must move quickly to solidify their success, heal internal differences, and fulfill bold promises. In the wake of the Revolutionary War, many Americans—despite continuing disagreements—set out to build a national culture and a shared identity. Those who had fought or had endured hardship because of the war wanted to create a country that would justify their sacrifices and uphold the ideals of the revolution. Like the Puritans before them, they aspired to provide new models for the Atlantic world.

They began with names. Everywhere, people christened new towns, counties, streets, and schools and renamed old ones. They replaced numerous British names, such as those of hated prewar governors, so Virginia's Dunmore County received the Indian name *Shanando* (later spelled *Shenandoah*). Because most people found references to royalty distasteful, King Street in Boston quickly became State Street. Still, royal figures who had aided the revolution received their due. Settlers on the Ohio River named their new town Louisville, honoring America's wartime alliance with King Louis XVI of France.

Political leaders popularized Christopher Columbus as well. For generations, the English had downplayed the explorer's importance as they contested Spanish claims in the Western Hemisphere. Now, American writers coined the ringing term *Columbia* for their land to stress its separation from Britain. In South Carolina, citizens named their new capital Columbia in 1786. Five years later, the proposed national capital was christened the District of Columbia. In New York City, when King's College reopened in 1784 under local governance, it was called Columbia College (later Columbia University).

Of all the new names, those honoring individual war heroes became the most popular. Citizens hailed foreign supporters of the revolution—such as Lafayette, Pulaski, and Steuben—by using their names on streets and towns. They saluted American officers the same way. Washington's name was used most often, but those of Montgomery, Wayne, Greene, Lincoln, Mercer, Marion, and others popped up as well. North Carolina named one of its trans-Appalachian forts on the Cumberland River Nashborough, after General Francis Nash, who had died at the battle of Germantown. Citizens changed the fort's name to Nashville in 1784. Two years later, inhabitants of a site on the Tennessee River named their new town Knoxville in honor of General Knox, who had become the Confederation's secretary of war the previous year.

> *Citizens hailed foreign supporters of the revolution—such as Lafayette, Pulaski, and Steuben—by using their names on streets and towns.*

AN INDEPENDENT CULTURE

New names were just part of the story. Many Americans felt that their whole language needed to be made more independent and accessible. Noah Webster, a schoolteacher who had fought against Burgoyne, believed that "as an independent nation, our honor requires us to have a system of our own, in language as well as government." In his *American Spelling Book* (1783), Webster championed a simple, uniform written language. He rejected conventions from England that appeared to be affections. Words such as *colour* and *labour* lost their silent *u*, *theatre* became *theater*, and *plough* was shortened to *plow*. The New Englander followed this success with an influential grammar book and a popular reader. Webster went on to produce *An American Dictionary of the English Language* (1828), which incorporated 5,000 new words, many of them reflecting Indian terms (*tomahawk*) and nature in America (*rattlesnake*).

Webster also joined other reformers in lobbying state legislatures for copyright laws that would protect the literary works that poured from the pens of ambitious writers. Philip Freneau, a classmate of James Madison at Princeton, drafted a poem titled "The British Prison Ship" (1781), about his war experiences. (He later planned, but never published, a biography celebrating the American traveler John Ledyard.) Authors living near Hartford, known as the Connecticut Wits, wrote similarly nationalistic poetry. Timothy Dwight, future president of Yale College, created "The Conquest of Canaan" (1785), and Joel Barlow composed an epic titled "The Vision of Columbus" (1787), heralding a bright future for the new nation.

Increasingly, the land itself captured the imagination of Americans. In 1784, a Connecticut silversmith engraved the first map of the new United States and a recent Yale graduate, Jedidiah Morse, published *Geography Made Easy*, which went through twenty-five editions. (Five years later, Morse wrote *The American Geography*, earning his reputation as the "Father of American Geography.") In Philadelphia, Quaker naturalist William Bartram drafted a pioneering nature book about his travels throughout the Southeast, and the versatile painter and patriot Charles Willson Peale launched a museum to promote interest in art and the natural world. From Monticello in Virginia, Thomas Jefferson corresponded with Peale and continued to pursue his own fascination with the

■ Exploring near the Altamaha River in Georgia, John Bartram and his botanist son William found "several curious shrubs, one bearing beautiful good fruit." They named it the Franklin tree after their scientist friend in Philadelphia, Benjamin Franklin. William painted a watercolor of the rare plant and saved seeds to protect the species.

American landscape. He promoted exploration, tested new crops, and tried his hand at archaeology by excavating ancient Indian mounds. In *Notes on the State of Virginia* (1785), Jefferson detailed his region's geography, society, and natural history.

In 1782, Hector St. John de Crèvecoeur, a Frenchman who lived in America, published *Letters from an American Farmer*. In the book's most famous essay, "What Is an American?" the author proclaimed that poor European immigrants became revitalized "in this great American asylum." According to Crèvecoeur, free people flourished in America not only because of "new laws" but also because of "a new mode of living, a new social system" that nurtured community growth. Societies for bettering jails, assisting debtors, and building libraries had existed before independence, but after the war Crèvecoeur watched a new generation creating voluntary associations at an unprecedented rate.

Earnest reformers launched more than thirty new benevolent organizations between 1783 and 1789. Some provided relief for the physically and mentally ill. Others aided strangers and immigrants. Still others granted charity to the poor and disabled or lobbied to reform harsh penal codes. In 1785, prominent New Yorkers John Jay and Alexander Hamilton joined like-minded citizens to form a Society for the Promotion of the Manumission of Slaves. Society members decried slavery as "disgraceful" and "shocking to humanity." In Connecticut, citizens banded together to stop the abuse of liquor. Members of this early **temperance** organization protested that the state's residents consumed 400,000 gallons of rum annually and that communities paid dearly in both financial and moral terms.

Similar efforts to reform and improve the new nation sprang up everywhere. The new Massachusetts Humane Society dedicated itself to assisting people in "suspended animation" between life and death, whether from drowning, drinking, heatstroke, or other causes. The society provided crude lifesaving equipment along waterfronts. It also constructed huts, stocked with food and firewood, to aid shipwreck survivors on isolated coastlines. Amid such general optimism, no sooner had the former colonists disentangled themselves from the British Empire than they began to speak of shaping an expansive empire of their own.

Competing for Control of the Mississippi Valley

■ *Why did control of the Mississippi Valley matter so much to Americans after the Revolution?*

It has ever been my hobby-horse," John Adams wrote in 1786, "to see rising in America an empire of liberty, and a prospect of two or three hundred millions of freemen, without one noble or one king among them. You say it is impossible. . . . I would still say, let us try the experiment." Westward expansion became a persistent American theme. During the postwar decade, interest and activity centered on the area between the eastern mountains and the Mississippi River. This huge region had been reserved for Indians in 1763, when King George III prohibited colonial settlement west of a line along the Appalachian crest. The domain beyond that "Proclamation Line" was divided in two at the Ohio River into a northern and a southern district, until the British ceded the entire region to the United States at the end of the Revolution.

Both north and south of the Ohio, Indians now faced a flood of newcomers. The area from the Ohio River to the Gulf of Mexico (which eventually became known as the Old Southwest) immediately became a magnet for southern pioneer families in search of land. Following an old buffalo trail and Indian trading path, they pushed west through Cumberland Gap, where southwest Virginia now touches Kentucky, and spread out across fertile portions of the lower Mississippi River valley. These aspiring homesteaders promptly faced resistance from Native American inhabitants and their Spanish supporters.

Looking first south, then north, from the banks of the Ohio, it is possible to see two distinctive stories unfold after 1783.

North of the Ohio River, other Americans flocked to claim rich woodland farms, pushing into the area between Ohio and Wisconsin often known as the Old Northwest. These migrants also met stiff opposition from Native Americans defending their homelands and from the Indians' British allies in neighboring Canada. By 1787, the Continental Congress had designated this region as the Northwest Territory and was busy revising an elaborate plan to establish a territorial government that could draw this domain into the union. Looking first south, then north, from the banks of the Ohio, it is possible to see two distinctive stories unfold after 1783.

DISPUTED TERRITORY: THE OLD SOUTHWEST

For a generation, Spain had been rebuilding its position north of the Gulf of Mexico and east of Texas in the Old Southwest, as part of wider reforms within its American empire. The Spanish had acquired Louisiana from France in 1763 and had conquered West Florida. In a 1783 treaty, Britain returned East Florida to the Spanish and agreed that Spain would retain West Florida. The Spanish occupied St. Augustine, Pensacola, New Orleans, and Natchez, as well as St. Louis farther north.

Because the Spanish controlled both banks of the lower Mississippi, they determined who could use the huge river for trade. Since 1763, they had let British subjects navigate freely on its waters, so trans-Appalachian fur traders had become accustomed to using this thoroughfare. Louisiana merchants paid for goods in Spanish silver, and settlers upriver needed such hard currency. During the Revolutionary War, Americans had retained access to the river, and the Spanish in New Orleans depended on produce from the north. Still, Spanish authorities feared American expansion into the Mississippi Valley. They debated whether to resist migrants pushing from the east, or to welcome such newcomers and profit from their trade.

In 1783, Spain was shocked when Britain, through its separate treaty with the United States, granted the Americans a generous southern boundary: the thirty-first parallel. The treaty terms also included the right of Americans to navigate on the Mississippi. The Spanish believed that they alone should decide whose boats had access to the river. Moreover, Spain had good reason to claim that its West Florida province stretched north *above* 31 degrees, at least to the mouth of the Yazoo River and perhaps as far as the Tennessee River.

For its part, the new Confederation had the force of numbers working to its advantage. The threat of Indian attacks had dammed up westward expansion since 1775. After the war, Americans migrated by the thousands to three existing centers of Anglo settlement in the Old Southwest. By 1785, 10,000 recent migrants clustered along the Holston, Watauga, and French Broad rivers above Knoxville. Nearly three times that many newcomers had already staked claims to the rich land south of the Ohio River between Lexington and Louisville. Another 4,000 were clearing farms along the Cumberland River around Nashville. Aggressive Americans talked about pushing even farther west. They imagined establishing a foothold on the Mississippi at Chickasaw Bluffs (modern Memphis) or perhaps seizing Natchez or New Orleans.

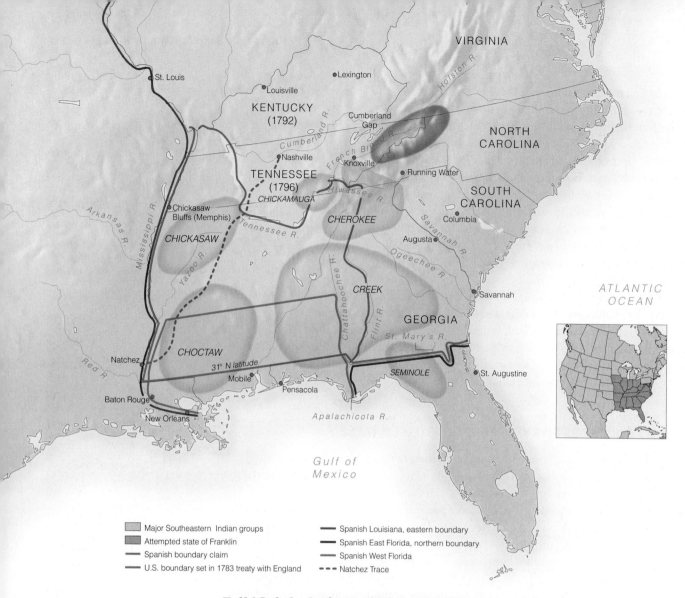

■ **MAP 8.2   Southern Land Debates After 1783**

Following the Revolution, competing forces collided in the trans-Appalachian South. The United States claimed land reaching the Mississippi River down to 31 degrees latitude. The Spanish claimed territory stretching north to the Tennessee River. Although major Indian tribes actually possessed much of the region, coastal states also claimed sweeping jurisdiction. In Georgia, for instance, settlement remained confined near the Savannah River, but the state sold speculators large tracts as far west as the Yazoo River.

SOUTHERN CLAIMS AND INDIAN RESISTANCE

In the southern states, powerful land speculators pressed their legislatures to support expansion. Georgia, unlike many other states, had not relinquished its western lands to the Confederation. The state's 35-million-acre Yazoo claim stretched west from the Chattahoochee River (Georgia's present boundary with Alabama) to the Mississippi River and from the lower border of modern-day Tennessee down to the thirty-first parallel (just above Mobile). "I look forward to a time, not very far distant," wrote Judge George Walton, when Georgia "will be settled and connected . . . from the shores of the Atlantic to the banks of the Mississippi." By 1789, Walton had been elected governor of the state, and the land business boomed. During his tenure, Walton signed warrants for huge tracts up to 50,000 acres, sometimes selling unusable or even nonexistent acreage.

Unlike Georgians, pioneers from Virginia and the Carolinas faced a rugged mountain barrier. But they still trekked west through Cumberland Gap. In the decade after the war, backwoodsman Daniel Boone worked as a surveyor for these migrants in the trans-Appalachian region of Virginia that became Kentucky in 1792. He accumulated more than 20,000 acres of his own, only to lose much of it in lawsuits with other claimants. During that same decade, North Carolina issued more land patents than it had created during the entire colonial era, most of them deeds for homesteads west of the mountains. Some of North Carolina's western landholders tried to create their own separate jurisdiction: the mountain state of Franklin. Without recognition from the Confederation government, their venture soon failed. Instead, all of North Carolina's western territory—from the Appalachians to the Mississippi—became the state of Tennessee in 1796.

Native American Southerners, living in all these lands, suddenly found themselves caught between the competing claims of Spain and the United States. The Cherokee, Creek, Choctaw, and Chickasaw—some 40,000 people—all debated which individuals and strategies to follow. Some responded to their new situation by selecting leaders with ties to European Americans. Among the Creek, for example, Alexander McGillivray rose to prominence. The son of a wealthy Scottish trader and a Creek woman, he had been raised on his father's Georgia plantation before becoming the Creek leader in 1782. The fact that he owned fifty slaves and kept a wine cellar may have boosted his bargaining power with Spanish and American officials. However, it also separated him from those he represented.

The renegade Cherokee warrior Dragging Canoe, who had split with tribal elders before the Revolution broke out, offered a different approach. Hundreds of militant Indians, discouraged by the compromises of their leaders, had joined his band of guerrilla fighters known as the Chickamauga living along the Tennessee River. From this well-protected location—near where Alabama, Georgia, and Tennessee now meet—the Chickamauga recruited allies and led forays to stop American encroachment. But Dragging Canoe died in 1792 before he could build a strong alliance with Indians north of the Ohio River.

John Trumbull, *Hopthle Mico*, 1790. Charles Allen Munn Collection, Fordham University Library, Bronx, New York (Catalog #3)

▪ In 1790, American artist John Trumbull paused from painting scenes commemorating the Revolution in order to sketch members of a Creek Indian delegation visiting New York City from Georgia. In this picture of an important Native American orator, a medal presented by the American government is visible amid the ruffles of his shirt.

"WE ARE NOW MASTERS": THE OLD NORTHWEST

Native Americans in the North also struggled to maintain their way of life and resist the newcomers. But white Americans lost no time in claiming Indian domains ceded by Britain in the 1783 Treaty of Paris. "We are now Masters of this Island," General Philip Schuyler boasted to the Iroquois, "and can dispose of the Lands as we think proper." Britain, however, refused to vacate western forts on the pretext that Americans still owed prewar debts to London merchants. Even so, the British could provide little material support to the region's Indians.

American delegations quickly drafted treaties with the Iroquois and the Ohio Valley tribes. Speaking bluntly, delegates asserted the right of the new United States government to Indian lands. They treated the Native Americans as dependents rather than equals, calling them "children" rather than "brothers." The negotiators even took hostages to force the Indians to accept their terms. Ordinary Americans sealed these claims with a surge of migration into western Pennsylvania and beyond. "The Americans . . . put us out of our lands," Indian leaders complained to the Spanish in 1784, "extending themselves like a plague of locusts in the territories of the Ohio River which we inhabit."

Americans initially remained divided among themselves over who would control the region. Connecticut retained a "western reserve" of 4 million acres south of Lake Erie that it used to satisfy claims from the state's war veterans. Similarly, Virginia held onto land rights

MAP

Western Land Claims
Ceded by the States,
1782–1803

for an even larger "military district" to repay soldiers and war victims. But one by one, the states of Massachusetts, New York, Connecticut, and Virginia ceded large territorial claims to the Confederation government.

These western acquisitions transformed the Confederation into something more than a league of states. With lands of its own to organize, the Confederation government took on attributes of a sovereign ruling body. As the number of cessions increased, Congress put Thomas Jefferson in charge of a committee to draft "a plan for the temporary Government of the Western territory." Before he departed for Europe to replace Benjamin Franklin as the American minister to France, Jefferson drew up a design for western land distribution.

After Jefferson sailed for France, his report became the basis for the Land Ordinance of 1785. Jefferson knew that in the South, where surveyors often staked out piecemeal claims on a first-come, first-served basis, the best property had gone to wealthy investors. Moreover, there had been endless boundary litigation over odd-shaped and overlapping lots. To avoid these complications, the 1785 ordinance called for surveyors to lay out a grid of adjoining townships, beginning at the point where the Ohio River flowed out of Pennsylvania. A township would include thirty-six numbered sections, each containing one square mile (640 acres). As its most far-reaching innovation, the ordinance reserved the income from one valuable section near the heart of every township to support public education.

Orderly surveying and public education were just parts of Jefferson's plan. Hoping to populate the region with a multitude of self-sufficient farm families, he proposed that the government give away land in small parcels. He envisioned self-government for these enterprising pioneers, not colonial status. For Jefferson, the more weight these independent farmers obtained in the American government the better, so he urged the rapid entry of numerous new territories into the union on an equal footing with the thirteen original states. He suggested creating up to fourteen small, rectangular districts in the west, with elaborate names such as Metropotamia. At least nine would be north of the Ohio River. Each could become a separate state with voting rights in Congress.

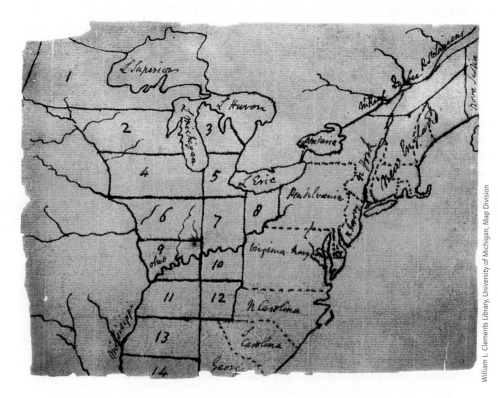

■ A sketch by Congressman Thomas Jefferson shows his proposal to divide the new interior territories into fourteen states (with Number 7 to be named Saratoga after the crucial Revolutionary War victory). By suggesting numerous compact states, Jefferson hoped to maximize the congressional voting power of western farmers. Others, eager to limit western power in Congress, pushed successfully for fewer, larger states.

William L. Clements Library, University of Michigan, Map Division

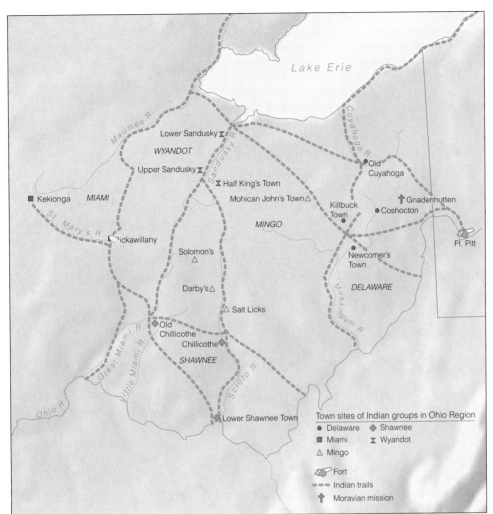

■ **MAP 8.3   Native American Ohio Before 1785**
For centuries, what is now Ohio was a land of Native American villages, located near rivers. Key eighteenth-century Indian towns and trails are shown here. (In 1781, whites massacred Christian Indians at the Moravian mission of Gnadenhutten.)

According to Jefferson's report, the first newcomers arriving in a district were to form a temporary government. When the local population reached 20,000, the residents could call a convention, frame a constitution, and send a delegate to Congress. When the district's population equaled the number of free inhabitants living in the smallest of the thirteen original states, that district could enter the union if certain conditions were met. Each new state must agree to support a republican form of government, remain part of the Confederation, and accept a share of the federal debt. It must also agree to exclude slavery after 1800. Congress accepted Jefferson's report, but then it modified the plan greatly. In its Land Ordinance of 1785, Congress ignored Jefferson's call for numerous districts, dismissed the notion of free land, and dropped the idea of ending slavery.

THE NORTHWEST ORDINANCE OF 1787

The huge task of surveying the wilderness north of the Ohio River into neat geometric squares would take years to complete. Almost immediately—and long before the initial ordinance could take hold—political shifts produced an entirely new law from Congress: the Northwest Ordinance of 1787. This law determining how territories north of the Ohio River would be

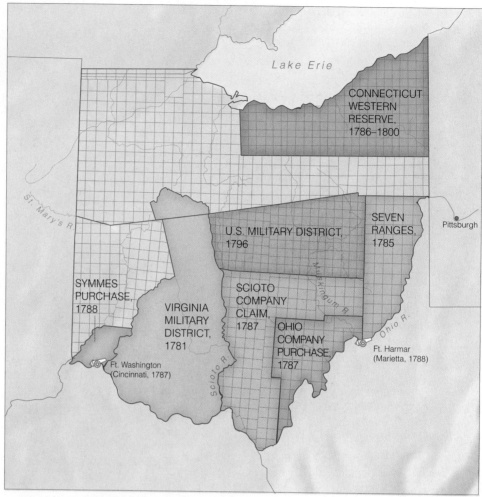

■ **MAP 8.4   Settlers' Ohio After 1785**

Starting in 1785, the American government imposed a novel grid system on the territory northwest of the Ohio River. Later, surveyors laid out similar straight geometric boundaries for states and counties across the natural landscape of the American West.

DOCUMENT

Northwest Ordinance (1787)

governed contained a number of changes to Jefferson's original plan. With regard to enslavement, it introduced an immediate prohibition of slavery north of the Ohio River. However, it made arrangements to deport fugitive slaves back to their owners in slaveholding states.

In various ways, the new ordinance was less democratic than the two earlier versions. Congress cut the possible number of new districts in the Northwest, specifying there could be only three to five new states. This move limited the potential political weight of the vast territory. In addition, the ordinance increased property requirements for citizens who wanted to vote or hold office. It also slowed the process by which new states could gain admission to the union. Eventually, Congress granted statehood to five new entities—Ohio (1803), Indiana (1816), Illinois (1818), Michigan (1837), and Wisconsin (1848)—but the process took more than half a century.

Most members of Congress feared democratic governance in the Old Northwest and the prospect of giving a strong voice to people with different regional interests. To retain control over the region, they provided for the appointment of territorial officials—a governor, a secretary, and three judges—instead of allowing elected governments. Even when territorial legislatures formed, the governor would have veto power over their actions. James Monroe, head of the committee that moved the bill through Congress, wrote candidly to Jefferson, "It is in effect to be a colonial government similar to what prevailed in these States previous to the revolution."

These changes benefited eastern land speculators—some of whom were members of Congress—who hoped to control the new lands for profit. They wanted to prevent the quick emergence of numerous western states that would play a powerful role in the national government. In 1786, former army officers in New England, joined by five surveyors who had seen the promising region firsthand, organized the Ohio Company to buy up western land. They dispatched a clever Massachusetts minister named Manasseh Cutler to lobby Congress to sell a huge tract to the company at bargain rates. Cutler joined forces with congressional insiders associated with another venture, the Scioto Company. Together, they engineered a deal providing 1.5 million acres to the Ohio Company and another 5 million acres for the Scioto investors.

Whatever suspicious bargains accompanied congressional passage of the Northwest Ordinance of 1787, the new law still granted basic rights to western residents. These guarantees—following state bills of rights—included religious freedom, trial by jury, and access to common-law judicial proceedings. Most important, the western territories were assured of full entry into the union as equal states rather than receiving dependent status as permanent colonies. This system established an orderly method for bringing new regions into the union, starting when Vermont became the fourteenth state in 1791.

Courtesy, Monroe County Historical Commission, Monroe, MI

■ Marie-Thérèse Lasselle (1735–1819) witnessed a generation of transitions in the Great Lakes region. She and her husband ran a trading post at Kekionga on the Maumee River (now Fort Wayne, Indiana). Long after the Revolutionary War drove them to Detroit, she created this self-portrait, using watercolor on embroidered silk.

Debtor and Creditor, Taxpayer and Bondholder

■ *Why did large bondholders care so deeply about what forces were in control of the state and national governments?*

The end of the Revolutionary War brought widespread economic depression. The money spent by foreign armies for goods and services dried up, and the split with Britain disrupted established patterns of commerce. When peace returned, merchants and artisans scrambled to find new markets and to locate new routes of profitable trade. Those who had preserved their holdings or made money during the war paid to get items from abroad that had been scarce during the fighting. These foreign purchases—whether for luxury goods or necessities—drained hard currency away from the states and increased the Confederation's debt.

Citizens everywhere felt the brunt of the postwar slump as prices dropped and the money supply shrank. As credit tightened, merchants called in their loans and unpaid bills. Families in debt, especially poor artisans and subsistence farmers, suddenly faced the threat of foreclosure and the loss of their property. They fought back in local elections, in state legislatures, and even in the streets. Violence broke out in state after state, from New Hampshire to Georgia, as hard-pressed people, many of them veterans, decried fiscal policies that favored wealthy bondholders. Heavy taxes were being used to pay annual interest on bonds held by members of the moneyed classes.

When armed conflict erupted in Massachusetts, wealthy merchants raised an army that suppressed the revolt, but they feared similar conflicts in the future. After all, in a number of states, democratic forces had shown that they had the strength to win control of the local legislatures. The Massachusetts rebellion therefore helped prompt a drastic effort to restructure and strengthen the national government through a special, closed-door convention in Philadelphia.

NEW SOURCES OF WEALTH

In 1783, the British government fired a parting shot at the former colonies. To nurture Britain's maritime trade and punish New England shippers, it restricted Americans from trading with the British West Indies. The move barred American ships from a key portion of Britain's imperial commerce, forcing merchants to seek out new avenues of trade. In 1784, an American vessel entered the Baltic Sea and established trade relations with Russia. Meanwhile, the New England whaling towns of Nantucket and New Bedford rebuilt their war-ravaged fleets and stepped up their search for whales to provide oil for American lamps. Captains had no trouble finding sailors in need of work, and ships sailed wherever they sensed possible profits.

Early in 1783, a Savannah merchant named Joseph Clay commented that a "vast number" of slaves had fled the South in wartime. As rice plantations renewed production, African workers were "exceeding scarce and in demand." Sensing a profit, foreign slave traders shipped 15,000 Africans to Georgia and South Carolina by 1785. New England captains soon joined in, sailing ships to Africa in hopes of renewing a trade that had been interrupted during the war. Antislavery sentiment had increased with the idealism of the Revolution, and several states, including Massachusetts, Rhode Island, and even Virginia, had outlawed slave imports. But these developments did not prevent American sea captains from transporting Africans to the Spanish West Indies, South Carolina, and Georgia. "The Negro business is a great object with us," Clay reported in 1784. "It is to the Trade of this Country, as the Soul to the body."

Financier Robert Morris took a global perspective, realizing that profits could be made by opening new trade routes to the Orient. The project would take an enormous investment—ten times the amount needed to send a ship to Europe—but the potential rewards were irresistible.

ATACKTED at JUAN, DE. FUCA. STRAITS.

■ This painting on glass shows Northwest Coast Indians menacing the American ship *Columbia* from their large war canoes. Captain Robert Gray was conducting trade for sea otter pelts to transport across the Pacific Ocean to China, where the soft fur was highly valued.

George Davidson, *Attacked at Juan de Fuca Straits*, c. 1792. Oregon Historical Society, OrHi 85076

"I am sending some Ships to China," Morris announced to John Jay, "in order to encourage others in the adventurous pursuits of Commerce." His first vessel left New York harbor for Canton by way of the Indian Ocean early in 1784. The *Empress of China* carried almost 30 tons of ginseng root—242 casks from the mountains in the "back part of Virginia"—highly prized by the Chinese. The ship's cargo also included 2,600 furs, which the Chinese used to line fashionable winter clothing, and $20,000 in hard currency, a huge drain on New York's economy.

In six months, the American vessel reached Canton, China's outlet for foreign commerce. "The Chinese had never heard of us," one sailor noted, "but we introduced ourselves as a new Nation, gave them our history, with a description of our Country," and stressed the mutual advantages of trade, "which they appear perfectly to understand and wish." The Chinese merchants welcomed trade with "the new people" and called their strange country "the flowery flag kingdom" because the stars on the American flag resembled blossoms. In May 1785, the *Empress of China* returned to New York loaded with tea, chinaware, and silk. Morris and his partners raked in a hefty 20 percent return on their investment.

> *Chinese merchants welcomed trade with "the new people" and called their strange country "the flowery flag kingdom."*

Other traders took notice. In 1787, the Browns, wealthy merchants in Providence, diverted a slave ship from the African trade to the China tea trade. That same year, six Boston investors sent two vessels—the *Columbia* and the *Lady Washington*—around Cape Horn at the tip of South America to trade for furs far up the Pacific coast. Within five years their captains, Robert Gray and William Kendrick, had pioneered new Pacific routes for American ships. Among the Nootka Indians on the American Northwest Coast, Captain Gray exchanged cloth and iron goods for sea otter pelts. Then he sailed the *Columbia* across the Pacific, pausing at Hawaii for supplies. Reaching Canton in 1789, Gray traded profitably and proceeded home through the Indian Ocean, making the *Columbia* the first American ship to circumnavigate the globe.

Because Gray's voyage confirmed the rewards of trade along the Northwest Coast, a diplomatic controversy flared the following year at Nootka Sound, on the west side of Vancouver Island. Although Spain protested British and American trading activities in the area, Gray was back on the Northwest Coast by 1792. He entered a powerful stream—where the states of Washington and Oregon now meet—and named it the Columbia River, after his ship. When he planted the American flag at the mouth of this major waterway, his action foreshadowed later territorial claims by the United States in the Oregon region. At the same time, Captain Kendrick, sailing in the *Lady Washington,* anchored off the Japanese island of Honshu, hoping to gain access for American trade. But Japan remained closed, and Kendrick's objective was not realized for another sixty-two years.

While American merchants probed for new markets abroad, they also moved to strengthen their economic and political position at home. Some wealthy investors bought up a variety of loan certificates, paper notes, and wartime securities issued by state governments and the Continental Congress, paying only a small fraction of the original value. Certificates issued to soldiers and officers at the end of the war rapidly became part of this speculative market when the original recipients sold their notes to prosperous speculators in return for needed cash.

As a result of such transactions, these paper holdings accumulated increasingly in the hands of the well-to-do. In Maryland, for example, the claims on $900,000 owed by the state became concentrated in the possession of only 318 people by 1790. Moreover, sixteen of these people controlled more than half of the total value, and the eight largest holders possessed 38 percent. As their speculative holdings increased, these few wealthy investors maneuvered to influence political events. They realized that whoever controlled the reins of power at the state and national levels would determine how the various notes of credit might be redeemed. Speculators who had purchased large quantities of these notes for a fraction of their face value stood to reap enormous profits in two ways. They hoped, and others feared, that the government would pay annual interest to the holders and then buy back ("redeem") all these paper arrangements at their original high face value.

John Ledyard's Wildly Ambitious Plan

■ Visiting Alaska with Captain Cook, Ledyard encountered Aleut seal hunters wearing elaborate visors and saw women who had joined the Russian Orthodox faith.

John Ledyard, now all but forgotten, was born in Connecticut in 1751. Almost from the start, he felt destined to "hop, skip, and jump about on this World of ours" in ways that others would find unimaginable. At Dartmouth, he ended his brief college career when he skipped classes to carve a dugout canoe and paddle it down the Connecticut River, wrapped in a bearskin. The young dropout then spent time at sea, touching Gibraltar, North Africa, and the West Indies, before entering the British military service. Glad to avoid the war erupting in America, he signed aboard Captain Cook's final Pacific expedition in July 1776 (see page 171).

During the four-year voyage, Ledyard climbed Table Mountain at Cape Town and obtained a tattoo in Tahiti. He also became the first American citizen to see North America's Pacific Coast from Oregon to Alaska. Like fellow crewmember George Vancouver, Ledyard aspired to return to the North Pacific, especially after pausing at Russia's Kamchatka Peninsula before the homeward voyage.

Back in England, Ledyard helped to encourage the new Pacific fur trade, but when he failed to book sea passage to the Northwest Coast, he conceived his most wildly ambitious plan. He intended to walk across Europe and Asia to Kamchatka. From there, as his friend Thomas Jefferson explained it, the New Englander would make his way "to the Western side of America, and penetrate through the Continent to our side of it."

After gathering funds from backers, Ledyard set out—with a wool cloak, two dogs, a hatchet, and a pipe. By September 1787, as the Constitutional Convention ended in Philadelphia, the intrepid hiker reached the Siberian outpost of Yakutsk, only 500 miles from the Pacific. But Russian fears that the American was a spy cut short his unlikely mission. Returning to Paris on foot in 1788, the unstoppable explorer dined with Jefferson and then embarked for Egypt.

Ledyard intended to travel across Africa from the Upper Nile to the Niger River, visiting Timbuktu and emerging at the Atlantic. "If he escapes through this journey," Jefferson wrote, "he will go to Kentuckey and endeavor to penetrate Westerly" all the way to the Pacific. But early in 1789, Jefferson received word that the thirty-seven-year-old wanderer had died mysteriously in Cairo. It would take the expedition of Lewis and Clark to complete the dream—shared by Jefferson and Ledyard—of a journey across North America.

QUESTIONS

1. Why would author Philip Freneau, known for glorifying the nationalist vision of his Revolutionary generation, have contemplated writing a biography of John Ledyard?

2. Ledyard's Russian adventure was sparked by the lure of the North Pacific region. What varied reasons drew some Americans of his generation to that remote area?

"TUMULTS IN NEW ENGLAND"

The few people who had acquired most of the paper securities wanted their holdings redeemed for hard currency. But the majority of citizens, faced with rising debts amid an economic downturn, resented the heavy taxes needed to pay interest on the debt to these wealthy speculators. Favoring easier credit, they urged their states to issue new paper money. This conflict was familiar from colonial times, when many merchants and planters, in debt to British firms, had chafed under Britain's tight fiscal policies. But the views of local elites had shifted, as they fought to gain control over their own state governments.

Wealthy merchants and planters now wanted to limit paper money to favor their new position as powerful creditors and holders of wartime certificates. Their opponents argued that issuing paper money could take the pressure off cash-strapped farmers and help retire enormous war debts. In seven states, these advocates of economic relief carried the day.

But as state governments put additional notes in circulation, rich creditors redoubled their efforts to control the levers of financial power. Confusion over currency made matters worse. While Congress resolved in 1785 that "the money unit of the United States of America [would] be one dollar," the transition was gradual. Since British pounds and Spanish dollars remained legal tender, control over the differing conversion rates in each state created opportunities for powerful speculators and savvy politicians.

Local battles over debt, credit, and currency issues hit hardest in the Northeast. In Massachusetts, a legislature sympathetic to creditors consolidated the state's huge war debts in a way that placed extreme tax burdens on ordinary citizens. Also, Britain's move to ban American ships from the British West Indies cut off the lucrative trade that New Englanders had created. For generations, American ship captains had sold fish, grain, and lumber to the islands in exchange for hard currency. Sudden exclusion from Britain's Caribbean colonies dried up the flow of much-needed cash into New England and undermined that region's economy.

> *Sudden exclusion from Britain's Caribbean colonies dried up the flow of much-needed cash into New England and undermined that region's economy.*

These changes had an immediate impact. In New Hampshire courts, debt cases rose sixfold from 1782 to 1785. Even if the debts themselves were not large, the heavy costs of traveling to court and paying high legal fees pushed thousands of families into insolvency. As long as the courts remained open, judges routinely ordered the seizure and sale of property. Embittered farmers watched as their horses, cows, wagons, and household goods were auctioned at low prices. Hard times often spark drastic responses, and New England's pot soon boiled over. Early in 1787, from his desk at Mount Vernon, Washington's secretary noted that the "tumults, insurrections, and *Rebellion* in New England have of late much engrossed the minds of the people here."

Newspaper accounts told of disturbing events in Rhode Island. Rural politicians seeking relief for indebted farmers swept into power during the April 1786 election, routing rich Providence merchants from their longtime dominance of the assembly. The newcomers quickly implemented their paper money platform. The Rhode Island region had a withered economy, and the state government carried a burdensome war debt. To address these matters, assemblymen approved a huge outlay of paper money. The assembly planned to distribute the new money among the towns and lend to citizens on equitable terms. As the economy rebounded, the revenue received back in taxes would then be used to pay off the state's debts, and the paper currency would be retired. To ensure the plan's success, legislators declared that all creditors must accept the money as legal tender.

Not surprisingly, creditors and speculators resented Rhode Island's currency law. They fumed at the new legislature's unwillingness to assume a share of the national debt and pay off wealthy bondholders, as other states had done. Without control over the legislature, these speculators feared they would be left holding all the continental securities they had acquired. They took swift action. Though heavily outnumbered, members of the moneyed class in Providence used their economic strength to fight back. Many merchants closed their stores rather than accept the new bills. Some even left the state to avoid being forced to accept debt payments in paper money. When judges who favored the merchants' cause finally declared the new statute unconstitutional, creditors everywhere sighed with relief. Their newspapers condemned the "Rogue Island" currency law as a dire example of the dangers of democracy.

SHAYS' REBELLION: THE MASSACHUSETTS REGULATION

In Massachusetts and New Hampshire, unlike Rhode Island, powerful merchants retained control over the new state assemblies. They resisted public pressure to generate more paper money. Instead, these creditors pushed to enforce debt collection by the courts, which would expand merchants' holdings and improve their standing in international trade. As in other states, a small contingent of wealthy speculators had bought up, at bargain rates, most of the public securities and certificates issued during the war. They anticipated enormous windfall profits if a government they controlled could redeem these notes, in gold and silver, at their full face value.

In New Hampshire, by 1785, securities valued at nearly £100,000 belonged to just 4.5 percent of the state's adult male population: 1,120 men among approximately 25,000. A mere 3 percent of this group—thirty-four men—controlled more than a third of this vast speculative investment. Most of these men had close ties to the current state government, situated in Exeter, near the coast. When farmers organized conventions to voice their economic grievances, merchants infiltrated and disrupted their meetings. In September 1786, 200 citizens, many of them armed war veterans, marched on Exeter to demand money reforms before conditions "drive us to a state of desperation." Officials organized cavalry units to confront the furious citizens, arresting their leaders from the crowd "as a butcher would seize sheep in a flock." As soon as the state's governor, General John Sullivan, had suppressed the dissenters, he issued a proclamation forbidding further conventions. He then wrote to the Massachusetts governor, James Bowdoin, offering to help crush similar unrest in the neighboring state.

DOCUMENT

Military Reports on Shays' Rebellion

Early in 1786, the Commonwealth of Massachusetts had imposed a heavy direct tax on its citizenry. Farmers in western Massachusetts lacked sufficient cash and already faced a wave of foreclosures for debt. They protested the tax law at town meetings and county conventions. When their complaints fell on deaf ears, they took actions into their own hands, "regulating" events as the North Carolina Regulators had done two decades earlier. The Massachusetts Regulation became known as Shays' Rebellion when Daniel Shays, a revolutionary officer who had served with distinction under Lafayette, emerged as one of its popular leaders. At first, these New England Regulators focused on closing the courts. In August 1786, 1,500 farmers marched against the Court of Common Pleas in Hampshire County and shut it down. The next month, another band closed the court in Worcester.

The confrontation escalated as winter set in. By January more than 1,000 Shaysites, knowing that their allies in New Hampshire had been defeated, moved to seize the federal arsenal in Springfield. But Governor Bowdoin had mobilized an army, financed largely by wealthy merchants in Boston. This private militia overpowered the westerners and forced all who did not flee to sign an oath of allegiance. Disarmed but not silenced, the dissidents succeeded in extracting some relief from the legislature. They also managed to defeat Bowdoin in the next election and replace him with a more popular governor, John Hancock.

The unrest in New England played into the hands of those advocating a stronger national government. (Rumors even circulated that nationalists had helped provoke the violence to rally support for their cause.) In a typical letter, Henry Knox expressed fear to his fellow general, John Sullivan, that "we are verging fast to anarchy." Writing in May 1787, he urged Sullivan to send delegates from New Hampshire to a crucial meeting that was about to begin in Philadelphia.

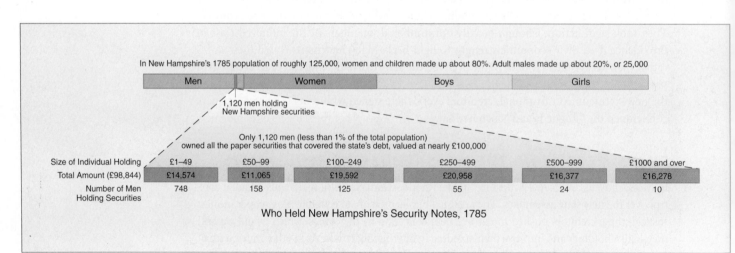

■ **FIGURE 8.1 Concentration of Security Notes in the Hands of a Few: The Example of New Hampshire in 1785**

Drafting a New Constitution

■ *How did nationalist leaders use their political skills to bring about the Constitutional Convention in Philadelphia?*

Even before Yorktown, Alexander Hamilton, Washington's youthful Caribbean-born aide-de-camp, had proposed a convention to restructure the national government. Now he worked with another young nationalist, James Madison, and their energetic supporters to bring it about. Congress had made earnest efforts toward reform, but any changes to the Confederation's governing articles required approval from all thirteen states. Thus, vital amendments—which would let Congress regulate commerce, raise revenue, and establish a judiciary, for example—proved nearly impossible. For some powerful leaders, especially merchants and creditors, a major political revision seemed in order.

Alexander Hamilton – Portrait

"Many Gentlemen both within & without Congress," wrote Madison, desire a "Convention for amending the Confederation." Still, it would take impressive leadership—Madison provided much of it—to seize the initiative and then generate enough momentum to change the rules of national government. Extensive compromise, both between elite factions and toward resistant popular forces, would be necessary at every stage along the path. After all, it would take an enormous push to engineer such a convention, to guide it to restructure the government along nationalist lines, and finally to persuade voting Americans to ratify the proposed changes and accept their legitimacy. To begin such a task, would-be reformers needed to convince the Confederation Congress to allow their revision plans to move forward. For that, they needed to recruit the enormous prestige of George Washington.

PHILADELPHIA: A GATHERING OF LIKE-MINDED MEN

The path began at Mount Vernon in 1785 when Washington hosted commissioners appointed by Maryland and Virginia to resolve state boundary disputes regarding the Potomac River. During the gathering, these men (including James Madison) scheduled a broader meeting on Chesapeake trade for the next year at Annapolis, Maryland. They invited all the states to send representatives. Only twelve delegates from five states showed up at Annapolis in September 1786, but news of the serious unrest in New England prompted talk of a more extended meeting.

Mount Vernon

Alexander Hamilton, as a representative from New York, persuaded the other delegates at the Annapolis meeting to call for a convention in Philadelphia the following May to discuss commerce and other matters. Madison won endorsement for the proposal from the Virginia legislature and then from Congress. Reform-minded congressmen, such as James Monroe, saw an opportunity to amend and improve the existing Confederation structure. But when the states sent delegates to Philadelphia the following spring, many of the appointees believed that amendments might not be enough. They were open to the more sweeping changes that Madison and other nationalists had in mind. The gathering that had been called to consider commercial matters and propose improvements to the Articles of Confederation soon became a full-fledged Constitutional Convention, a private meeting to design and propose an entirely new structure for governing the United States.

> *The gathering that had been called to propose improvements to the Articles of Confederation soon became a full-fledged Constitutional Convention.*

Madison reached Philadelphia in early May 1787. He immediately began drafting plans for drastic change and lobbying delegates, some of whom came early to attend a secret gathering of the Society of the Cincinnati. On May 25, when representatives from seven states had arrived, they launched the convention and unanimously chose Washington as the presiding officer. Participants agreed that they would operate behind closed doors and each state delegation would have one vote. There would be no public discussion or official record of the proceedings. Soon, delegates from twelve states had joined the gathering. Only Rhode Island did not send representatives.

The fifty-five delegates had much in common. All were white, male, and well educated, and many already knew one another. These members of the national elite included thirty-four lawyers, thirty public creditors who had bought up war securities, and twenty-seven members of the Society of the Cincinnati. More than a quarter of the participants owned slaves, and nearly a dozen had done personal business with financier Robert Morris of the Pennsylvania delegation. Not surprisingly, all seemed to agree that the contagion of liberty had spread too far. Elbridge Gerry of Massachusetts called the current situation "an excess of democracy."

> Most delegates agreed with this novel system of checks and balances, intended to add stability and remove corruption.

Specifically, these men feared recent legislation that state assemblies had adopted to assist hard-pressed citizens: laws that delayed tax collection, postponed debt payments, and issued paper money. Most delegates hoped to replace the existing Confederation structure with a national government capable of controlling finances and creating creditor-friendly fiscal policy. To be effective, they believed, a strengthened central government must have greater control over the states. Only Robert Yates and John Lansing of New York and Luther Martin of Maryland staunchly resisted expanding central power.

Many delegates, especially those from heavily populated states, thought the national legislature should be based on proportional representation according to population rather than each state receiving equal weight regardless of its numbers. Also, most wanted to see the single-house (unicameral) Congress of the Confederation replaced by upper and lower houses that would reflect the views and values of different social classes. John Adams had helped create such a two-house (bicameral) system in the Massachusetts constitution, thereby limiting pure democracy and giving more political power to propertied interests.

Besides calling for checks within the legislative branch itself, Adams had also laid out strong arguments for separating, and checking, the powers of each competing branch of government. For a sound and lasting government, Adams had argued, there should be **separation of powers;** the legislative branch should be balanced by separate executive and judicial branches that are equally independent. Most delegates agreed with this novel system of **checks and balances,** intended to add stability and remove corruption.

COMPROMISE AND CONSENSUS

The Philadelphia gathering, which lasted through the entire summer, would later be known as the Constitutional Convention of 1787. Even as a general consensus emerged within the small meeting, countless personal, practical, and philosophical differences persisted. Hamilton delivered a six-hour speech in which he staked out an extremely conservative position. He underscored "the imprudence of democracy" and stressed a natural separation between "the few and the many"—the "wealthy well born" and the "turbulent and changing" people. Hamilton's conservative oration called for the chief executive and the senators to be chosen indirectly, by elected representatives rather than by the people themselves, and he recommended that these high officials should serve for life. Such ideas undoubtedly appealed to many of his listeners, but all of the delegates knew that a majority of citizens would never accept such proposals. Pierce Butler of South Carolina, invoking ancient Greece, urged members to "follow the example of Solon, who gave the Athenians not the best government he could devise but the best they would receive."

This attentiveness of convention members to what the public would accept is illustrated by their approach to voting rights. Even delegates who wanted to limit the vote to property holders realized that various state constitutions, responding to popular pressure, had already distributed **suffrage** (the right to vote) more broadly. Property ownership was no longer a universal voting requirement, and states varied on whether religion, race, or gender could determine eligibility. James Wilson of Pennsylvania, second only to Madison in working to build a practical nationalist majority in the convention, pointed out that "it would be very hard and disagreeable" for any person, once enfranchised, to give up the right to vote. Accordingly, the delegates proposed that in each state all those allowed to vote for the "most numerous branch of the state legislature" would also be permitted to cast ballots for members of the House of Representatives. But they shied away from accepting direct election for the Senate or the president. Members deferred other difficult suffrage matters, saying that the rules for carrying out elections in each state should be worked out by the state legislature.

Time and again during the sixteen-week convention, these like-minded men showed their willingness to bargain and compromise. Lofty principles and rigid schemes often gave way to balancing and improvisation. For example, delegates who differed over the length for the chief executive's term of office and right to run for reelection also disagreed on the best method of presidential selection. Some of them suggested that ordinary voters should elect the president; others proposed that the state governors, or the national legislature, or even electors chosen by state legislators should choose the chief executive.

Finally, the aptly named Committee on Postponed Matters cobbled together an acceptable system: a gathering (or "college") of chosen electors from each state would cast votes for the presidency. This **electoral college** plan had little precedent, but it managed to balance competing interests. Under the scheme, state legislatures would set the manner for selecting electors. The least populous states would get a minimum of three electoral votes, and states with more people would choose more electors in proportion to their numbers, giving them added weight in the decision. The people could also participate in the voting process, though only if their state legislatures called for it. If no candidate won a majority in the electoral college, the House of Representatives would determine the president, with each state's delegation having one vote. The system was far from elegant or democratic, but it placated varied interests, and it won prompt approval.

QUESTIONS OF REPRESENTATION

As deliberations stretched across the long, hot summer of 1787, two central issues threatened to unravel the convention: political representation and slavery. Questions of representation pervaded almost every discussion, pitting large states such as Virginia, Pennsylvania, and Massachusetts against the less populated states. Madison's well-organized Virginians offered a comprehensive blueprint outlining a new national government that would have three separate branches. This design, called the "Virginia Plan," recommended a bicameral national legislature with proportional representation in each body. The House of Representatives would be chosen by popular election. Then members of the House would elect the Senate, choosing among persons nominated by the state legislatures.

Madison's system clearly favored populous states. Not surprisingly, a coalition of small-state delegates led by William Paterson of New Jersey submitted an alternative "New Jersey Plan." This less sweeping revision built on the existing Articles of Confederation. It called for a continuation of the current unicameral legislature, in which each state received an equal vote. A committee chaired by Benjamin Franklin broke the impasse. The idea of an upper house, or Senate, would be retained, and each state, whatever its size, would hold two senate seats. Seats in the House of Representatives would be determined proportionally, according to the relative population of each state. This lower house would initiate all bills dealing with finance and money matters.

> To implement proportional representation in a fast-growing society, the delegates provided for a national census every ten years.

To implement proportional representation in a fast-growing society, the delegates provided for a national census every ten years. No European country had attempted a regular periodic headcount, so the census represented a radical innovation at the time. This in turn raised a thorny question. Should slaves—people enumerated in the census yet denied the rights of citizens—be counted in determining a state's proportional representation in the national government? Slaveholding states wanted their human property to count because that would give those states more representation. The convention resolved this dilemma in mid-July with a "three-fifths" formula that Madison had proposed in earlier legislation. The odd recipe made every five enslaved people equivalent to three free people in apportionment matters.

In an ironic twist, the same week the Constitutional Convention delegates approved the notorious **three-fifths clause,** the existing government of the United States leaned in the opposite direction. Meeting in New York, members of the Confederation's Congress passed the Northwest Ordinance of 1787, which outlawed slavery in the new territory above the Ohio River. Because there was much contact between the two meetings, some scholars speculate that powerful Southerners agreed to give away the prospect of slavery north of the Ohio River in exchange for more support of slavery within the new plan taking shape in Philadelphia.

SLAVERY: THE DEEPEST DILEMMA

During the debate over the three-fifths clause, Madison commented that the greatest division in the United States "did not lie between the large & small States: it lay between the Northern & Southern," owing to "the effects of their having or not having slaves." This highly charged issue simmered beneath the surface for most of the summer.

In late August, with most other matters resolved, delegates could no longer postpone questions surrounding slavery. Yet again, a committee deliberated, and a bargain was struck. This time, hundreds of thousands of human lives were at stake. Planter delegates from Georgia and South Carolina refused to support any document that regulated the slave trade or curtailed slavery itself. They asserted that such a charter could never win acceptance at home. In part they were bluffing. In fact, constraints against slavery had wide popular appeal in the expanding backcountry of the Deep South, where independent farmers outnumbered planters, ministers questioned slavery, and pioneers wanted national support in confronting powerful Indians.

Yet few delegates challenged the proslavery posture, possibly because strong antislavery opinions could have prolonged or even deadlocked the convention. Weary participants were eager to complete their work and fearful of unraveling their hard-won consensus. Rather than force the matter, even those who disapproved of slavery rushed to compromise, heaping a huge burden on future generations. Southern delegates dropped their protests against giving Congress the power to regulate international shipping. In exchange, the framers approved a clause protecting the importation of slaves for at least twenty years. They also added a provision governing fugitive slaves that required the return of "any person held to service or labor." Through a calculated bargain, delegates had endorsed slavery and drawn the South into the union on terms that suited that region's leaders. The word *slave* never appeared in the finished document.

In early September, the convention members put the finishing touches on their proposal and wondered whether Americans would accept it. Winning state-by-state approval would involve an uphill battle, especially given the absence of a bill of rights. George Mason, who had drawn up Virginia's Declaration of Rights eleven years earlier, reminded members that such a set of guarantees "would give great quiet to the people." But in the convention's closing days, many delegates resisted the notion, and all were eager to adjourn. They overwhelmingly voted down Mason's suggestion.

Without a bill of rights, Mason, Elbridge Gerry of Massachusetts, and Edmund Randolph of Virginia refused to endorse the final document. Other delegates who dissented had already departed. Of the seventy-four delegates chosen at the convention's outset, fifty-five actually attended the proceedings, and only thirty-nine agreed to sign the finished plan. These small numbers made it more important than ever to end on a note of unanimity. By polling the state delegations instead of individual delegates, the document's authors shrewdly hid the three dissenting votes. This allowed them to assert, in Article VII, that their task—framing a new constitution for the United States—had been approved "by the unanimous consent of the States present" on September 17, 1787.

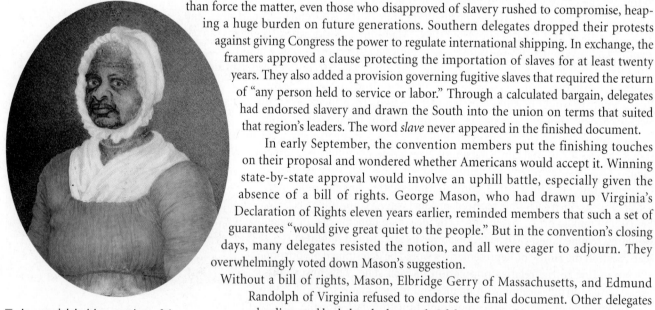

■ In a crucial decision, members of the Constitutional Convention chose to protect the slave trade and preserve slavery. One African American who had already taken matters in her own hands was Mumbet, a slave in Massachusetts and the widow of a Revolutionary War soldier. In 1781, she sued for her freedom on the grounds that "all were born free and equal." Her court victory proved a landmark in New England. Proudly, she took the name Elizabeth Freeman.

Ratification and the Bill of Rights

■ *Why was a bill of rights expected by citizens, omitted by the drafters of the Constitution, and later added?*

Committed nationalists now faced their most difficult task: winning public acceptance for an alternative structure that defied existing law. The proposed constitution ignored the fact that the Articles of Confederation—the document governing the United States at the time—could be amended only with the approval of all thirteen states. Instead, the text drafted in Philadelphia stated that ratification (acceptance through voting) by conventions in any nine states would make the new document take effect in those places. Moreover, the proposed ratification process left no room for partial approval or suggested revisions. Each state, if it wanted to enter the debate at all, had to accept or reject the entire proposed frame of government as offered.

THE CAMPAIGN FOR RATIFICATION

The Confederation Congress had acquiesced in allowing the convention to occur in the first place. Most congressional representatives had expected the meeting to produce proposals for amending the current government, not discarding it. But now that the Philadelphia conclave had ended, the Congress sitting in New York City balked at endorsing the revolutionary document. To avoid a lengthy and troublesome debate, proponents of the new constitution urged Congress simply to receive the frame of government as a possible proposal and then transmit it to the states without an endorsement. Congress did so on September 28, 1787, and the document's advocates portrayed the unanimous vote as an expression of approval.

Supporters had no time to lose because Pennsylvania's assembly was set to adjourn the next day. An early victory in that large and central state would be crucial for building momentum, so they rushed the congressional letter of transmittal from New York to Philadelphia. There, the assembly faction dominated by Robert Morris won a hasty vote to schedule a state ratifying convention. Over the next three months, Pennsylvania towns and counties elected delegates, a convention met, and the state voted to approve the new plan. Delaware had already approved it unanimously on December 7. New Jersey and Georgia promptly followed suit. By the end of January, Connecticut had also ratified. Other states called elections and scheduled conventions. Only Rhode Island, which had not sent delegates to the drafting convention, refused to convene a meeting to debate ratification.

By seizing the initiative early, the proponents of the new framework shaped the terms of debate. The drafters, anything but a cross-section of society, worked to portray themselves as such. They noted that their document began with the ringing phrase "We the people of the United States," a last-minute addition by Gouverneur Morris of New York. And Madison told the public that the text sprang from "*your* convention."

> *By seizing the initiative early, the proponents of the new framework shaped the terms of debate.*

Most important, in a reversal of logic and contemporary usage, the nationalists who supported the new constitution took for themselves the respected name of **Federalists.** They gave their opponents, a diverse assortment of doubters and critics, the negative-sounding term **Anti-Federalists.** The Federalists then used their ties to influential leaders to wage a media war for public support. They wrote letters, prepared pamphlets, and published essays praising the proposed constitution.

The strongest advocacy came from the pens of Alexander Hamilton and James Madison. The two men composed eighty essays for the New York press under the pen name *Publius.* John Jay added five more, and in the spring of 1788 the collection appeared as a book titled *The Federalist.* In the most famous piece, "Number 10," Madison challenged the widely accepted idea that a republic must be small and compact to survive. Turning the proposition

DOCUMENT

James Madison
Defends the
Constitution

around, he argued that minority opinions would fare better in a large nation, where diverse competing interests would prevent a unified majority from exerting control.

DIVIDING AND CONQUERING THE ANTI-FEDERALISTS

Opponents of the new plan were on the defensive from the start. Many had supported some government change, and most conceded the presence of economic difficulties. But the Federalists' dire predictions of impending chaos struck them as exaggerated. "I deny that we are in immediate danger of anarchy," one Anti-Federalist writer protested.

Patrick Henry, Against Ratification of the Constitution

Richard Henry Lee, president of the Confederation Congress, condemned the Federalists as a noisy "coalition of monarchy men, military men, aristocrats and drones." Other prominent figures joined him in opposition: George Clinton in New York; Luther Martin, Samuel Chase, and William Paca in Maryland; and Patrick Henry, George Mason, and Benjamin Harrison in Virginia. Though not always sufficiently forceful or committed, such notables became the spokespeople for a far wider array of skeptics.

Many opponents of the proposed constitution protested the plan's perceived threat to local political power. Despite Madison's reassurances in *Federalist* Number 10, they believed that local and state governments represented voters more fairly and responded to their needs and concerns more quickly than a distant national authority could. For some critics of the proposed constitution, this belief in local control expressed a radical democratic principle; for others it represented their provincial bias. In short, Anti-Federalists were too diverse to speak with a single voice. They included subsistence farmers living far from any navigable river or urban market, and war veterans who feared that their influence in republican government would be diminished by the

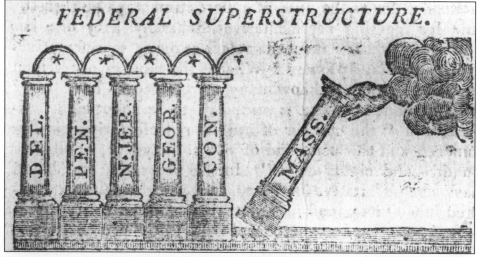

■ In 1788 newspapers tracked ratification of the new "federal superstructure" state by state. Massachusetts ratified the proposed Constitution in March—apparently aided by the Hand of God! New Hampshire provided the "ninth and sufficient pillar" in June, followed by Virginia four days later.

"Grand Federal Processions"

The essays contained in *The Federalist Papers* circulated widely and helped to build the case for ratification of the newly drafted Constitution, but well-organized parades provided the broadest demonstrations of support. These large and orderly public events were carefully planned, handsomely executed, and well publicized in the popular press. Predictably, two of the largest "Grand Federal Processions" were staged in Philadelphia and New York, where pro-ratification forces were strong.

Philadelphia's celebration on July 4, 1788, got underway with the ringing of church bells. A mounted trumpeter leading the vast procession proclaimed a "New Era," and judges carried a copy of the new Constitution. New York City's parade three weeks later was designed to help win ratification from a divided state convention meeting in Poughkeepsie. It featured diverse artisans, such as bakers who served cake to the crowd.

These events had the desired effect of conveying a message of Federalist patriotism and unity. "Rank for a while forgot all its claims," observed Philadelphia's Benjamin Rush, "and Agriculture, Commerce and Manufactures, together with the learned and mechanical professions, seemed to acknowledge, by their harmony and respect for each other, that they were all necessary to each other, and all useful in cultivated society."

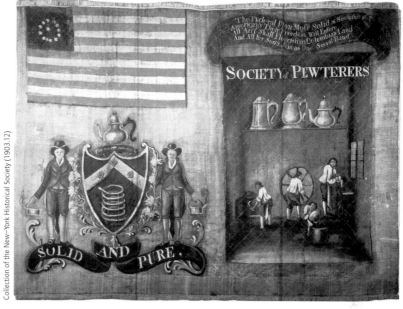

Collection of the New-York Historical Society (1903.12)

■ In New York City's parade urging ratification, on July 23, 1788, the Society of Pewterers carried this elaborate silk banner. A rhyme in one corner proclaims that under the proposed constitution, "All Arts Shall Flourish in Columbia's Land, And All Her Sons Join as One Social Band."

Envisioning History

QUESTIONS

1. Why would the involvement of diverse urban artisans such as butchers, tanners, sailmakers, and bakers have delighted Federalist organizers of pro-ratification parades?

2. Explain the patriotic double meanings behind these artisan slogans on parade banners: "Both Buildings and Rulers Are the Work of Our Hands" (Bricklayers); "With the Industry of the Beaver We Support Our Rights" (Hat Makers); "Solid and Pure" (Society of Pewterers).

proposed system. Many indebted people also opposed ratification, fearing that a strong national government would favor the interests of bondholders and foreign creditors ahead of the economic well-being of ordinary citizens.

If Anti-Federalists were numerous in the remote countryside, Federalists predominated in coastal commercial centers. Using a variety of tactics, they pressed their advantages in the fight to control state ratifying conventions. They lured prominent Anti-Federalist delegates with hints of high office, and they ridiculed vocal opponents as Shaysite extremists. In state after state, they forged coalitions linking commercial farmers living near towns and rivers with aspiring artisans and city-based entrepreneurs.

Through intensive politicking, the Federalists won approval in Massachusetts in February 1788, but only by a thin margin (187 votes to 168 in the ratifying convention). This commitment from "the Bay State" helped to sway Maryland in April, South Carolina in May, and New Hampshire in June. The Federalists could now claim the nine states needed to implement their plan, and in July they staged celebrations to hail the new Constitution of the

United States. In town after town, a "Grand Federal Procession" marched through the streets behind floats and banners, designed by groups of self-assured artisans, proud of their trades and of their prominent place in shaping the new republic.

The approved Constitution promptly became the law of the land. But in Massachusetts, advocates had triumphed only by promising to add an explicit bill of rights that gave written protection for valued civil liberties. The Federalists had to provide similar assurances during the summer to secure slim majorities in Virginia (89 to 79) and New York (30 to 27). North Carolinians had voted down the proposed frame of government at their first ratifying convention because it lacked a bill of rights. A second North Carolina convention, called in 1789, withheld approval until a bill of rights had actually been introduced into the first federal Congress as proposed amendments to the Constitution. In 1790, Rhode Island narrowly voted approval for the new framework (34 to 32) rather than risk being left in economic and political isolation.

ADDING A BILL OF RIGHTS

Abby Aldrich Rockefeller Folk Art Museum, Williamsburg, VA, Colonial Williamsberg Foundation (Acc. 1935.301.4 [slide 1989–1731])

In a society consisting of almost 3 million people, the franchise remained a limited privilege, open primarily to white men with property. All told, only about 160,000 voters throughout the country took part in choosing representatives to the state ratifying conventions. And only about 100,000 of these people—less than 7 percent of the entire adult population—cast votes for delegates who supported the Constitution. Federalists knew, therefore, that they would have to fulfill their pledge to incorporate a bill of rights. Madison, goaded by Jefferson from his post in Paris, promised Virginians that he would push to include the assurance of specific rights as amendments to the Constitution. In making this promise, he had two main motives. First, he hoped to ensure his own election to the nation's new House of Representatives. Second, he wanted to stave off the prospect that discontented states would call a second national convention "for a reconsideration of the whole structure of government."

In compiling a list of protections, or bill of rights, Madison drew from scores of proposals for explicit amendments put forward by the state ratifying conventions. He selected those, mostly dealing with individual rights, that could pass a Federalist-dominated Congress and would not dilute any of the proposed new government's powers. He set aside suggestions for limiting the government's right to impose taxes, raise a standing army, or control the time and place of elections. True to his word, Madison pushed twelve less controversial statements through the Congress as constitutional amendments, despite congressional apathy and opposition. Within two years, three-fourths of the states ratified ten of these short but weighty pronouncements. Hence, the first ten amendments—the **Bill of Rights**—quickly became a permanent part of the U.S. Constitution.

Many of the protections provided by the Bill of Rights harked back to lessons learned in earlier struggles with Parliament. The ten amendments guarded the right of the people to bear arms, limited government power to quarter troops in private homes, and banned unreasonable searches and seizures. They also guaranteed crucial legal safeguards by ensuring the right to trial by jury, outlawing excessive bail and fines, and prohibiting "cruel and unusual punishments." The First Amendment secured freedom of speech and of the press, protected people's right to assemble and petition, and prohibited Congress from meddling in the exercise of religion. By securing these freedoms, Madison engineered a final set of compromises that ensured the acceptance and longevity of the Constitution he had done so much to frame.

Conclusion

The long War for Independence had exhausted the new nation. Managing the difficult task of demobilization (disbanding the army) and reconstruction consumed American energy and resources in the 1780s. So did the new western domain, where Americans had to balance prospects for national expansion against the military threats posed by the European empires and Native American groups that claimed the region. Also, economic differences set aside during the war quickly reemerged; questions of wealth and property loomed large.

Therefore, when Confederation leaders imposed unprecedented taxes to pay off the war bonds gathered up by wealthy speculators, irate farmers and veterans protested that Congress was gouging "the Many" to enrich "the Few." These numerous dissenters pressured state governments to provide debt relief and issue paper money. But wealthy creditors reacted forcefully. These like-minded men maneuvered to create a new and stronger central government that could support their interests and override state-level economic measures favoring the common people. Sidestepping the existing government, they drafted a new constitution at a closed convention in Philadelphia in 1787.

By 1789, America's established leaders had campaigned successfully for ratification of the new constitution, in the face of bitter and varied opposition. Calling themselves Federalists, they had regained a secure grip on the reins of power, which had nearly slipped from their hands during the tumultuous 1770s. But the fierce debate over ratification of the Constitution raised fresh uncertainties about the long-term survival of the union. Much hinged on selection of the first president. Inevitably, George Washington emerged as the overwhelming favorite to become the first chief executive of the new republic.

CHRONOLOGY: 1783–1789

1783	Treaty of Paris.
	Newburgh Conspiracy is thwarted.
	Society of the Cincinnati is formed.
1785	Land Ordinance of 1785.
1786	Shays' Rebellion in Massachusetts.
1787	Constitutional Convention meets in Philadelphia.
	Constitution of the United States is drafted and signed.
	Northwest Ordinance creates Northwest Territory.
1788	Publication of *The Federalist*.
	Ratification of the Constitution.
	Madison agrees to draft Bill of Rights.
1789	George Washington is elected the first president of the United States.

For Review

1. Why did the prospect of a Newburgh Conspiracy and the creation of the Society of the Cincinnati upset many Americans?

2. How would Indians in the Mississippi Valley in the 1780s have viewed the "empire of liberty" envisioned by John Adams?

3. For the numerous debtors during the postwar economic depression of the 1780s, what factors worked for, and against, their interests?

4. To what extent is the genius of the American Constitution found in its unique, innovative structure of checks and balances?

5. If the Constitution's crucial "three-fifths clause" had been a "five-fifths clause" instead, who would have benefited?

6. Did leading nationalists exaggerate the difficulties of the 1780s to suit their agenda, or did they save the new union in a dire situation? Explain.

Created Equal Online

For more *Created Equal* resources, including suggestions on sites to visit and books to read, go to **MyHistoryLab.com**.

Revolutionary Legacies, 1789–1803

■ Actress Kameshia Duncan plays the runaway slave Ona Judge in the 2007 Florida Stage production of the play "A House with No Walls" by Thomas Gibbons.

Revolutionary ideals of freedom and equality were contagious. In the wake of the American Revolution, a young enslaved woman named Ona Judge acted on those ideals and escaped from bondage; she fled the household of her master and mistress, President George Washington and his wife, Martha Custis Washington.

In 1789, when the Washingtons moved from Virginia to New York, and later to Philadelphia (the nation's first capital), they took seven house slaves, including mulatto teenager Ona Judge, the first lady's personal attendant. By the mid-1790s, Ona Judge had made secret plans to escape from Philadelphia. Later, she said that she feared returning to the Washington's Mount Vernon estate, explaining: "I knew that if I went back to Virginia, I should never get my liberty." With help from other blacks in Philadelphia, the young woman found her way to Portsmouth, New Hampshire. There, she hoped, she would begin a new life of freedom.

The president's official duties and his personal interests clashed as he sought to locate the runaway. In 1793, Washington had signed into law the Fugitive Slave Act. This law provided that any owner of a fugitive must receive authorization from a local judge in order to retrieve his or her "property." However, the chief executive ignored this provision of the law and instead directly approached Josiah Whipple, the U.S. customs collector at Portsmouth. Washington claimed that his slave had been abducted by a mysterious Frenchman and directed Whipple to locate and return her.

Whipple managed to find Judge, but after talking to her, he doubted the president's claim that the young girl was the victim of a kidnapping. In a letter to Washington, Whipple noted that "she had not been decoyed away as had been apprehended, but that a thirst for compleat freedom . . . had been her only motive for absconding."

Whipple reported that Judge was willing to make a bargain with her master. Because she missed her family at home, she agreed to return to Virginia if Washington would promise to free her. The indignant president refused to negotiate, but at the same time, he did not want to risk causing a public uproar by ordering Whipple to forcibly return her. And so Ona Judge settled into life in New Hampshire, marrying John Staines, an African American sailor, in 1797 and starting a family. Two years later Washington sent his nephew to try to retrieve her once more. But this effort too failed when the new wife and mother told him, "I am free now and choose to remain so."

Ironically, by the mid-1790s Washington had made a provision in his will to free his own slaves after his death and the death of Martha. His decision was inspired at least in part by the patriotism and courage of black soldiers in the Revolutionary War. Yet despite Washington's growing personal opposition to slavery, he had felt duty-bound to try to retrieve the runaway. But the young woman's successful bid for freedom meant that the legacy of the Revolution had come home to the Washington household.

The story of Ona Judge reveals that revolutionary ideals reverberated throughout the new nation. After the war, many different groups sought to claim the freedom denied them by law or custom. In New England and the Upper South, increasing numbers of free people of color struggled to assert their rights. Throughout the states, some women had maintained a high degree of political engagement; New Jersey even granted propertied women the right to vote, if only for a brief period. Artisans also sought to wield new political clout. Western migrants, free blacks, women voters, artisan-politicians—they all revealed both the social tensions mounting in the new republic and the promise it offered to these same groups.

During the decade after the Revolution, the population of the new nation grew in size and diversity. The first census of the United States, conducted in 1790, tallied 3,929,214 people. Of this number, 757,208 were black. Throughout the states, people of various ethnicities clustered together in pockets. German-born people accounted for one-third of all Pennsylvanians, and almost one-fifth of New York residents were Dutch. Numbers of Northerners and Southerners were about equal. However, ethnic and regional differences proved less significant in shaping the emerging two-party system than the persistent split between urban-based merchants and rural interests such as southern planters. The Revolution also unleashed enormous creative energy as some people, freed of restrictions imposed by Great Britain, pursued new economic opportunities. In contrast, many artisans and small farmers continued to stagger under a burden of debt and new federal taxes. These groups considered the Revolution a betrayal of their vision for America.

The impulse for association so evident in the union of states helped to shape postwar society. In the Northwest, Ohio Indians created a confederacy among several groups in order to increase their collective power, much as the colonies had done before the war. And throughout the United States, ordinary people put into practice the grand theories of the Revolution by coming together to effect change. Exhorting their brothers and sisters to join in religious fellow-ship, revivalists formed new spiritual communities. Reform groups wrote constitutions for themselves in an effort to commit their principles to paper. Temperance advocates joined together and called on men and women to cast off the tyranny of drink.

Most dramatically, opponents of slavery kept alive the rhetoric and the ideals of the Revolution. In 1800, Gabriel, an enslaved blacksmith in Richmond, Virginia, plotted a rebellion to seize the city. His actions gave voice to the egalitarian principles articulated in Philadelphia in 1776 and again in Saint-Domingue in 1791, when slaves staged a bloody revolt against their French masters. (In 1804 they renamed the country Haiti.) Gabriel's rebels used the words of the nation's founders to justify their actions, rallying around the cry "Death or Liberty." One even compared himself to George Washington in his struggle to "obtain the liberty of [his] countrymen." Gabriel's vengeful plans to kill all whites except abolitionists failed when informants betrayed him to Richmond authorities. The foiled slave rebellion in Virginia gave expression to slaves' desire to share in the freedom of the new nation. More generally, in the 1790s, almost all Americans, regardless of creed or color, wrestled with the legacy of the Revolution.

Competing Political Visions in the New Nation

■ *What were the disagreements between the Federalists and the Democratic-Republicans in domestic policy? In foreign policy?*

In the first two decades of the new nation, domestic politics remained entwined in relations with the great European powers. For all their bold talk of freedom and liberty, the heirs of the Revolution continued to formulate public policies based on the models offered by Great Britain and France. Specifically, some Americans found much to admire in British traditions of social order and stability, traditions shaped by a strong central authority in the form of a monarchy. Other Americans derived inspiration from the French Revolution, which began in 1789. They believed that, for all its bloody excesses, the revolution represented an ideal of true democracy, an ideal at odds with the entrenched privilege inherent in monarchies and aristocracies. The British model appealed to Federalists, supporters of a strong central government. In contrast, the French model appealed to Anti-Federalists, soon to be called **Democratic-Republicans,** supporters of the rights of the states and of the active participation of ordinary citizens in politics. These divergent views shaped both foreign and domestic policy in the 1790s.

Within this contentious atmosphere, George Washington assumed the presidency in 1789, backed by the unanimous endorsement of the electoral college. Neither the ratification of the U.S. Constitution nor Washington's election silenced the debate over civil liberties and the nature of the national government. Responding to the concerns of the Anti-Federalists, Congress quickly passed ten amendments to the Constitution, collectively called the Bill of Rights. Ratified by the required number of states by 1791, the amendments were intended to protect white men from the power of government, whether local, state, or national. The Judiciary Act of 1789 established a national federal court system that included a five-member Supreme Court and the office of attorney general, charged with enforcing the nation's laws.

Like other public figures of the time, Washington believed that ideological differences between political leaders should never become institutionalized in the form of separate parties. These leaders believed politicians should debate issues freely among themselves, without being bound by partisan loyalty to one view or political candidate over another. However, by the late 1790s, the intense rivalry between Alexander Hamilton, Washington's secretary of the treasury, and Thomas Jefferson, his secretary of state, had produced a two-party system that proved remarkably durable. Representing two competing political visions, Hamilton and his supporters (known as Federalists) and Jefferson and his supporters (called Democratic-Republicans) disagreed on foreign diplomacy and domestic economic policies. Hamilton advocated a strong central government that would promote commerce and manufacturing. In contrast, Jefferson favored states' rights bolstered by independent small farmers who would serve as the nation's moral and political center.

In 1792, Washington ran for and won a second term. Four years later, he declined to run for a third term. His successor was his vice president, John Adams, an unabashed Federalist who rankled Jefferson and other more egalitarian-minded citizens. Between 1789 and 1800, the clash between the Federalists and the Democratic-Republicans reverberated in the halls of Congress, on the high seas, and in Indian country.

FEDERALISM AND DEMOCRATIC-REPUBLICANISM IN ACTION

An outspoken Federalist, Hamilton took bold steps to advance the commercial interests of the new nation. In 1789, as Washington's secretary of the treasury, he persuaded Congress to enact the first U.S. **tariff,** or tax, on imported goods. He argued this move would encourage home manufactures and raise money for the treasury. Hamilton also sought to strengthen the federal government through **monetary policy,** the way in which a nation meets its financial obligations, taxes its citizens, and regulates the money supply. At his prodding, in 1790 Congress agreed to fund the national debt—that is, to assume responsibility for repaying the government's creditors, including paying interest on the debt (a total of $54 million). Congress also assumed responsibility for debts that the individual states had incurred during the Revolution. To pay for all this, federal officials stepped up debt collection and imposed new taxes on individuals. In 1791, Congress also issued a twenty-year charter to the first Bank of the United States. Hamilton believed this institution, modeled after the Bank of England, would help stimulate the economy by circulating surplus funds held by the government.

An advocate of agricultural interests and the power of individual states, Jefferson disagreed with Hamilton on all these issues. Jefferson bitterly opposed the Bank of the United States, arguing that only the states could issue charters for financial institutions. He favored a lower tariff, urging that high-priced imports hurt farmers and other small consumers. The leader of the Democratic-Republicans believed that the government should not interfere in the lives of its citizens by imposing new taxes on individual households or on imported goods. According to Jefferson, governments, like individuals, should exercise restraint in their spending and should avoid accumulating debt.

Image Copyright © The Metropolitan Museum of Art/Art Resource, NY

■ Elijah Boardman of New Milford, Connecticut, poses at his desk in 1789. The portrait highlights Boardman's success as a merchant. His business prospered because wealthy Americans wanted to dress fashionably, as he did, with his ruffled sleeves, silk stockings, and fancy shoe buckles. In the background are some of the colorful, luxurious fabrics he sold. By the late eighteenth century, New England merchants were at the center of a thriving worldwide exchange of goods between Europe, the United States, and China. Their profits helped to finance the country's industrial revolution.

DOCUMENT

Alexander Hamilton, "Bank"

President-Elect Washington Is Greeted by the Women and Girls of Trenton, New Jersey

Envisioning History

J. I. Morton, *Washington's Reception by the Ladies on the Bridge at Trenton, N.J., April 1789: On His Way to New York to Be Inaugurated First President of the United States,* 1845. Museum of the City of New York, Harry T. Peters Collection (56.300.847)

In April 1789, President-elect George Washington traveled from his home in Virginia to his inauguration in New York City. Along the way, he was hailed by well-wishers who marked his election with parades and other kinds of celebrations. This scene shows the women and girls of Trenton, New Jersey, greeting Washington en route to New York. As he passed by, they sang, "Virgins fair and Matrons grave, / Those thy conquering Arms did save."

The women and girls whom Washington saved did not participate fully in the new nation. The founders identified citizenship with economic independence. By this definition, women, children, slaves, and other groups dependent on property owners could not become citizens. However, drawing on their relatively privileged status, elite white women sought to carve out a place for themselves as sustainers of the young Republic.

QUESTIONS

1. What is the significance of the wording on the banner ("The defenders of the mothers will be the protectors of the daughters")?

2. Describe some of the patriotic symbols and images adorning this picture.

3. What themes are the dress, posture, and activities of the women meant to convey?

4. What was the symbolic significance of Washington's appearance at Trenton?

5. During this period in American history, what were the cultural and class connotations of the word "ladies"?

Hamilton and Jefferson's opposing views of government shaped the American political party system for generations to come.

The different views epitomized by Hamilton and Jefferson found expression in American reactions to Europe's political turmoil surrounding the French Revolution. Since France had recently been a crucial wartime ally, most Americans at first supported the dramatic events unfolding there in 1789. By imposing constitutional constraints on their king, Louis XVI, the French seemed engaged in a heroic struggle much like that of the Patriots of 1776 who had challenged the enormous power of the British monarch. But when French radicals launched what became known as the Reign of Terror, American public opinion grew more critical.

In January 1793, leaders in Paris beheaded the French king and went on to execute aristocrats and presumed opponents of the revolution. In response, Federalist politicians argued that the bloody excesses in France should push American citizens toward a moderate and stable central government for the United States, more like that of Great Britain. Months later, when France and England went to war over territorial claims in Europe and the West Indies, American public opinion was divided. Fearing dangerous entanglements, President

Washington issued a Proclamation of Neutrality at the outbreak of the war, but few Americans could resist taking sides.

Tensions between France and the United States took a turn for the worse when France's first envoy to the United States, Citizen Edmond Genêt, ignored the Neutrality Proclamation and tried to enlist American support for French designs on Spanish Florida and British Canada. Nor did Britain endear itself to its former American subjects during these years. Pursuing French military forces in 1793, the British navy seized 300 American merchant ships plying the West Indian seas, forcing American sailors into service. In a practice known as impressment, British sea captains boarded American ships and captured sailors at gun-point. Meanwhile, along the United States' northwest border, British officials were supplying the Indians of the Ohio Confederacy with guns, alcohol, and encouragement in their fight against the Americans. Feeling squeezed by foreign powers in such ways, many Americans hoped that economic growth could assist the fledgling United States in resisting pressures from European rivals.

PLANTING THE SEEDS OF INDUSTRY

As debates swirled regarding American involvement in international affairs, questions arose over how to deal with the emerging industrial economy at home. During the late eighteenth century, most manufacturing still took place in individual households. Master artisans employed journeymen (skilled workers) and apprentices as well as their own wives and children. Throughout New England and the Mid-Atlantic, family businesses made everything from soap and candles to cloth and shoes.

In the 1790s, however, signs of an emerging manufacturing economy appeared, especially in the region stretching from New England to New York, New Jersey, and Pennsylvania. This area had all the ingredients for an American Industrial Revolution: water power from rushing rivers, a faltering agricultural economy that western producers would soon eclipse, capital from successful merchants, and a dense population offering both workers and consumers.

Key individuals helped spark the early changes, including Samuel Slater, a twenty-one-year-old English inventor who arrived in the United States in 1791. With financial support from Moses Brown, a wealthy merchant of Providence, Rhode Island, Slater constructed the first American machine for spinning cotton thread and launched his Steam Cotton Manufacturing Company in nearby Pawtucket. The nine boys and girls (ages seven to twelve) hired by Slater to operate the machinery were among America's first factory workers.

In 1793 another innovator, Massachusetts-born Eli Whitney, invented the cotton gin. This machine gave a tremendous boost to both the southern plantation economy and the fledgling northern industrial system. By quickly removing the seeds and other impurities from raw cotton, Whitney's cotton gin fostered the emergence of a new cotton economy. Southern planters expanded their holdings in land and slaves, rushing to meet the rising demand for cotton from mill owners in both England and New England.

By the mid-1790s, Hamilton and his supporters were praising the nation's economic growth and regional specialization. Traditional products of the Atlantic seaboard—tar and turpentine in North Carolina, tobacco in the Chesapeake region, wheat in the Mid-Atlantic states—flourished once again, as early canal and turnpike construction encouraged new markets. In New England, shipbuilding prospered, free from earlier British restrictions, and the fishing and whaling fleets expanded. The forests of Maine and New Hampshire produced wood for hulls, masts, planks, and barrels. In the Deep South, enslaved workers raised cotton, first in South Carolina and Georgia, later in the fertile lands of Alabama and Mississippi. Between 1792 and 1800, annual cotton production jumped from 3 million to 35 million pounds. The figure would soar to 93 million pounds by 1815.

ECHOES OF THE AMERICAN REVOLUTION: THE WHISKEY REBELLION

Washington, Proclamation Regarding the Whiskey Rebellion

Despite Hamilton's optimism about the growing economy, Washington's administration faced violent resistance to its policies from certain quarters. In 1794, farmers and grain distillers in southwestern Pennsylvania refused to pay their federal taxes. This **Whiskey Rebellion** was the culmination of a lengthy rural protest against Hamilton's "hard money" policy. By favoring hard currency (coinage) over the more plentiful paper money, the government constricted financial credit. With less money to lend, creditors charged high interest rates for loans. Courts forced debtors such as small farmers to repay loans even when money was extremely scarce. Those who could not pay their taxes or repay their loans faced foreclosure on their property.

Eager to strengthen the federal government and reduce the national debt, Hamilton devised a federal excise tax on whiskey. The plan aimed at distillers rather than consumers, and it imposed a higher rate on small producers. Therefore, the tax fell especially hard on backcountry farmers, who distilled their bulky grain harvest into whiskey for efficient shipment to eastern markets. Using the tactics of the Stamp Tax rioters a generation earlier, western Pennsylvania farmers attacked officials and tarred and feathered a man charged with collecting the whiskey tax. They set fire to the officials' offices, closed courts, blocked roads, and organized mass protests.

Hamilton, believing that a show of force would strengthen the federal government, urged the president to make western Pennsylvania a test case for enforcing the tax.

Frederick Kemmelmeyer, *General George Washington Reviewing the Western Army at Fort Cumberland the 18th of October, 1794, c. 1794.* Courtesy, Winterthur Museum (58.2780)

■ This 1794 painting seemingly evokes the American Revolution, when General Washington reviewed American troops. However, in this scene, President Washington is surveying some of the 13,000 state militiamen he commanded in an effort to suppress the Whiskey Rebellion in western Pennsylvania. Farmers objected to the new government excise tax on whiskey. In demonstrations that recalled the Stamp Act riots three decades earlier, protesters harassed federal tax collectors with cries of "Liberty and No Excise." The Whiskey Rebellion melted away quickly. Critics objected to Washington's willingness to use such a huge force against protesting American citizens.

In September, the government federalized 13,000 men from state militias to subdue the rebellion. To underscore the supremacy of the national government over the states, Washington personally led the troops into western Pennsylvania. However, when the soldiers arrived, they found that organized resistance had already collapsed.

Washington claimed that the Whiskey Rebellion had been incited by ignorant men who perverted the facts with their "suspicions, jealousies, and accusations of the whole government." Yet he failed to gauge the extent of country dwellers' economic distress. By defying federal authority so openly, the farmers expressed the general grievances of westerners who felt underrepresented in state legislatures and the halls of Congress. They also revealed the deep current of resentment against Federalist policies that was running through rural America.

SECURING PEACE ABROAD, SUPPRESSING DISSENT AT HOME

At the same time Washington was dealing with unruly farmers, he also had to address international concerns. In 1795, the president sent Chief Justice John Jay to England to negotiate a key treaty. The negotiations were intended to address several problems: British forts in the Northwest Territory, British seizure of American ships and sailors in the West Indies, and American debts owed to British creditors.

Jay obtained a treaty but failed to extract meaningful compromises from England. England grudgingly agreed to evacuate its northern forts and to stop seizing American ships. Jay, however, acquiesced to English demands that individual Americans pay the debts they owed to English creditors since before the Revolution. The Democratic-Republicans took alarm at Jay's concessions. The Americans believed that their victory in the war exempted them from long-standing financial obligations to their English creditors. In their view, the new agreement humiliated all Americans and threatened southern planters in particular.

Western agricultural interests did better with the1795 Treaty of San Lorenzo. Under this agreement, Spain allowed the United States to navigate the Mississippi River freely and to land goods at New Orleans free of taxes for three years.

DOCUMENT

The Treaty of San Lorenzo

With their eye on the next presidential election, the Democratic-Republicans began a vigorous campaign in favor of their own candidate, Virginia's Thomas Jefferson. They contrasted Jefferson, the friend of the small farmer, with the Federalists' choice, Vice President John Adams of Massachusetts, an advocate of strong central government run by the educated and wellborn. Jefferson's party expressed particular dismay over Washington's haste to crush the rebellious Pennsylvania farmers in 1794 and over Jay's treaty. Backed by the New England states, Adams won the election, though narrowly. Because Jefferson received the second largest number of electoral votes—68 to Adams's 71—the Virginian became the new vice president according to the terms of the Constitution then in effect (Article II, section 1).

In his farewell address, printed in newspapers but not delivered in person, Washington warned against the "insidious wiles of foreign influence" and against entangling alliances with foreign powers that could compromise America's independence and economic well-being. Nevertheless, upon assuming the presidency in 1797, Adams found that European powers still had a hold on American domestic and foreign relations. France began to seize American merchant vessels (300 of them by mid-1797)

TABLE 9.1		
The Election of 1796		
Candidate	**Political Party**	**Electoral Vote**
John Adams	Federalist	71
Thomas Jefferson	Democratic-Republican	68
Thomas Pinckney	Federalist	59
Aaron Burr	Democratic-Republican	30

PROPERTY PROTECTED. a la Françoise.

■ In 1798 Americans reacted indignantly to news that France had demanded a bribe and a large loan before its ambassadors would agree to meet with American envoys. In this political cartoon, America is portrayed as an innocent young woman assaulted by French diplomats. The incident precipitated an undeclared war on the high seas, called the Quasi War, between the two countries.

in retaliation for what it saw as favoritism toward England in Jay's treaty. In October of that year, President Adams sent John Marshall and Elbridge Gerry to join the U.S. ambassador to France, Charles Pinckney, to negotiate a new treaty with France. However, French intermediaries (referred to only as X, Y, and Z in the Americans' dispatches) demanded that the three U.S. commissioners arrange for a loan of $12 million to France and pay a $250,000 bribe. Only then would the envoys be allowed to speak to the foreign minister, Charles Talleyrand. The sentiments of the American public, outraged at the idea of paying a bribe and willing to defend their new nation against all aggressors, were captured in the cry "Millions for defense, but not one cent for tribute." Adams called the commissioners home, ending the "XYZ Affair."

Federalists throughout the country called for war against France, and the Adams administration sought to shore up the country's military forces by creating the Navy Department and the Marine Corps. Hoping to rid U.S. coastal waters of French ships that were preying on American vessels, in May 1798 Congress authorized American captains to seize such armed "pirates" sent from the Republic of France. Over the next two years, the undeclared so-called Quasi War pitted the American navy against its French counterpart until the two nations signed a treaty, called the Convention of 1800, in Paris.

Conflicts also continued to simmer on the domestic front. The Federalist-dominated Congress passed the **Alien and Sedition Acts** in 1798 to suppress the rising chorus of criticism from rural people, Democratic-Republican leaders, and newspaper editors. Such dissent, they charged, amounted to sedition—an act of insurrection against the government. These new laws made it more difficult for immigrants to become resident aliens, gave the president the power to deport or imprison aliens, and branded as traitors any people (U.S. citizens included) who "unlawfully combine or conspire together, with intent to oppose any measure or measures of the government of the United States."

Even though the Alien and Sedition Acts were unconstitutional—they violated the First Amendment's guarantee of freedom of speech—the Federalist-dominated Supreme Court upheld them. Consequently, Democratic-Republicans were by definition guilty of treason, for they advocated policies and supported candidates opposed by the Federalists, the party in power.

Ten newspaper editors were convicted, and many others charged and jailed, under the Sedition Act. Some Democratic-Republican lawmakers also spent time in jail because their speech offended their partisan rivals. Congressman Matthew Lyon of Vermont (founder of a

DOCUMENT
The Alien and Sedition Acts

newspaper called *Scourge of Aristocracy*) went to prison for suggesting that President Adams showed "unbounded thirst for ridiculous pomp, foolish adulation, and selfish avarice."

In 1798 and 1799, the state legislatures of Kentucky and Virginia issued a series of resolutions condemning the Alien and Sedition Acts. Outraged at what they saw as the Federalists' blatant power grab, the two legislatures proposed that individual states had the right to declare such measures "void and of no force." Thomas Jefferson (for Kentucky) and James Madison (for Virginia) wrote the actual resolutions, which declared that states could essentially ignore congressional authority. As authors of the **Kentucky and Virginia Resolutions,** the two Founding Fathers unwittingly laid the theoretical framework for Southerners to attempt to nullify federal laws in the future.

After the Revolution, unresolved questions related to foreign policy, economic development, and civil liberties shaped a larger national debate about the direction of the new nation. Another persistent question focused on the rights of minorities within a country founded on the principles of freedom and equality.

DOCUMENT

The Virginia and Kentucky Resolutions

People of Color: New Freedoms, New Struggles

■ *In what ways did the legacy of the Revolution shape the lives of African Americans in the North and South?*

Despite the differences between Federalists and Democratic-Republicans on certain fundamental issues, most American political leaders agreed that they had little interest in extending the legacy of the Revolution to people of color. Though some white Americans took to heart the ideals of liberty and freedom for all, most approved of laws that denied citizenship rights to black people, enslaved and free. In fact, a 1790 naturalization law limited naturalized U.S. citizenship to "free white persons," mocking the oft-heard claim that all people were equal under the law.

Despite the rhetoric of equality, other North American elites demonstrated an emerging preoccupation with matters of race as a means of categorizing people and distinguishing groups from each other. For example, Spanish officials in colonial New Mexico conducted a 1790 census that divided the population into a variety of groups based on ethnicity: Spanish, Indian, Mestizo (Spanish and Mexican Indian), *coyote* (Spanish and New Mexican Indian), mulatto (a person of African plus Spanish or Indian heritage), *genizaro* (children of acculturated Indians), and *color quebrado* and *lobo* (both designating some form of mixed-race parentage).

In the United States, the crosscurrents of the revolutionary legacy showed themselves most obviously in the status of African Americans. Most remained enslaved, and their numbers were increasing annually due to the continuation of the Atlantic slave trade. To some extent, however, people's fate depended on where they lived and labored. Soon after the United States won its independence from England, all the northern states lay the groundwork for the abolition of slavery. In the upper South, citing the egalitarian principles of the Revolution, some planters also freed their enslaved workers. But overall, economics rather than principles influenced these decisions, especially in the deep South, which relied heavily on enslaved labor for staple-crop production and thus discouraged individual and state plans for emancipation. In contrast, the North and upper South had been accustomed to using bound workers of all kinds, including white indentured servants and youthful apprentices, as well as slaves. With changes in the economy, owners of gristmills and other enterprises now wanted paid labor—a more flexible workforce that could be hired and fired at a moment's notice.

> In the United States, the crosscurrents of the revolutionary legacy showed themselves most obviously in the status of African Americans.

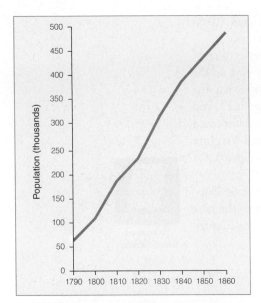

FIGURE 9.1 Growth in the American Free Black Population, 1790–1860

Source: The New York Public Library African American Desk Reference, (New York: Wiley, 1999) 38.

African Americans like Ona Judge showed extraordinary resourcefulness in escaping slavery and claiming freedom. But even free African Americans faced an uphill struggle in their efforts to achieve political rights and economic well-being. Free people of color found their employment options limited as whites competed with them for jobs and political representation. When they emerged from bondage, freed people created educational and religious institutions that affirmed their sense of community and shared heritage. But persistent white prejudice, sanctioned by law, limited their employment options and condemned many black men and women to poverty. Lacking full citizenship rights, they saw the Revolution as an unfulfilled promise rather than a glorious achievement.

BLACKS IN THE NORTH

For many northern blacks, the Revolution continued to resonate in their memories and their hopes. Gad Asher, seized from his home on the western coast of Africa around 1750, had been forced to work as a slave for a ship carpenter in East Guilford, New Jersey. During the Revolution, Asher had served as a soldier in his master's place. His owner promised him the money he would earn as a Continental soldier. Yet when Asher came home after the war, his master reneged on the promise. Eventually, Asher managed to earn enough money on his own to buy his freedom. In 1785, he and his wife had a son, Jeremiah. The youngster loved to hear his father and two other African American veterans talk of the "motives which had prompted them to 'endure hardness'" while fighting the British. Recalled Jeremiah many years later,

> I was so accustomed to hear these men talk, until I almost fancied to myself that I had more rights than any white man in the town. Such were the lessons taught me by the old black soldiers of the Revolution. Thus, my first ideas of the right of the colored man to life, liberty, and the pursuit of happiness, were received from these old veterans and champions for liberty.

Between 1790 and 1804, all the northern states abolished slavery. Some, such as New York and New Jersey, did so gradually, stipulating that the children of slaves must serve a period of time (as long as twenty-eight years) before they could gain their freedom. In 1800, over 36,500 blacks in the North were still enslaved, and some 47,000 were free. Pennsylvania did not liberate its last slave until 1847. Yet throughout the North, blacks—whether enslaved or free—were only a small percentage of the total population, ranging from less than 1 percent in Vermont to almost 8 percent in New Jersey.

At both the state and national levels, most free blacks lacked basic citizenship rights. In 1792, two years after Congress limited naturalization to "free white persons," it restricted the militia to white men. State legislatures in New England and the mid-Atlantic region imposed various other restrictions on free people of color. These measures limited blacks' right to vote, serve on juries, and move from place to place. Rectifying what some whites claimed was an "oversight" in their state constitutions, New Jersey and Connecticut later took special pains to disenfranchise African American men. Massachusetts offered free blacks the most rights, including the right to vote (for men) and the right of blacks and whites to intermarry.

As slaves, blacks had served in a variety of skilled capacities in the North. Yet as free people, they faced mounting pressures in trying to live independently. Certain jobs, such as those with the federal postal service, remained closed to them by law. And municipal authorities refused to grant them licenses to ply their trades, such as wagon driving. Lacking the means to buy tools and equipment and the ability to attract white customers,

New Bedford Whaling Museum (#803)

■ After the Revolution and well into the early nineteenth century, African Americans, both enslaved and free, served as sailors in disproportionate numbers. This picture suggests the dangers faced by all sailors who labored on whaling ships. By the 1790s, American whalers were searching for sperm whales as far away as the South Pacific. These whales were the source of several prized substances, including sperm oil (a fuel), spermaceti (used to make candles), and ambergris (an ingredient in expensive perfumes). During the heyday of the sperm whale industry, American fleets were killing 10,000 whales annually.

many black artisans had to take menial jobs. Increasingly, free black men took jobs as laborers, sailors, and domestic servants, and black women worked mostly as domestic servants and laundresses.

Still, free blacks in the North set about creating their own households and institutions. They moved out of the garrets and back rooms of houses owned by whites and set up housekeeping on their own. In Boston in 1790, one in three African Americans lived outside white households; thirty years later, eight in ten did so. In response to efforts of white Methodists to segregate church seating, Philadelphia black leaders formed the Free African Society in 1787. The first independent black church in the North, St. Thomas Protestant Episcopal Church, was founded in Philadelphia in the early 1790s. Black people also continued to celebrate their own festivals, typically featuring parades in which they dressed in their best clothes, played drums and other African musical instruments, and proclaimed their identity as a free people. In Massachusetts, blacks celebrated "Negro Election Day" by choosing their own "governors" and "judges," unofficial but influential community leaders (often African born). The celebrations gave men and women alike an opportunity to escape the confines of the workplace, even if only for a short time, and eat, drink, and dance with other people of color.

MANUMISSIONS IN THE SOUTH

Some southern slaves achieved freedom not by running away, but through legal means initiated by their owners. George Washington was not the only wealthy southerner to move to free his own slaves in his will. In 1782, the Virginia state legislature lifted a fifty-nine-year-old ban on manumission, a process by which owners released selected people from bondage. Over the next ten years, approximately 10,000 Virginia slaves gained their freedom through manumission, many as a result of provisions in the wills of their masters or mistresses. Some planters believed that the Revolution was the will of God, and they came to believe that slavery violated their religious principles. Some, taking to heart the rhetoric of the Revolution, objected to the glaring contradiction between the ideal of liberty and the reality of bondage. In 1802, a Maryland woman freed her slaves because, she said, the institution went against "the inalienable Rights of Mankind."

> *Some planters objected to the glaring contradiction between the ideal of liberty and the reality of bondage.*

In the upper South especially, private manumissions dramatically increased the free black population. There, the emergence of a more diversified economy, including craft shops and gristmills, had lowered slave prices and encouraged abolitionist sentiment among some lawmakers, clergy, and slave owners. In Baltimore alone, the free black population increased from around 325 to over 5,600 between 1790 and 1810.

Virginia planters George Washington and Robert Carter were unusual in terms of the numbers of slaves they manumitted (several hundred) and their efforts to ease the transition to freedom for people who possessed neither land nor financial resources. Washington arranged apprenticeships for younger freed blacks and pensions for aged ones. In 1792, Carter granted his older slaves small plots of land. In general, however, newly emancipated men and women had difficulty finding employment as free workers due to competition from both whites and enslaved workers. Nor was their freedom guaranteed: the 1782 Virginia manumission law provided that black debtors could be returned to slavery. The next year, Maryland went out of its way to stipulate that manumitted blacks were not "entitled to the rights of free men" except in their ability to own property.

Despite the growth in the free black population, the number of slaves actually increased in the upper South, from over 520,000 in 1790 to almost 650,000 in 1810. In the South, slavery proved to be an extraordinarily durable institution. At the same time, the institution of bondage spread west with the nation.

Continuity and Change in the West

■ *What were sources of conflict for people who lived in the Northwest Territory and the southern borderlands?*

Blacks may have derived inspiration from the struggle against Great Britain, but as the nation expanded west, so did the institution of slavery and notions of white supremacy. Western communities tended to duplicate their eastern counterparts. The sale of federal lands proved a boon for speculators, who extended credit to homesteaders and profited from the resale of the lands, now divided into small parcels. Charged high prices for their purchases and forced to buy expensive supplies transported across the Appalachians, some newcomers rapidly sank into debt. Nor did black Americans fare well, whether slave or free. Before 1800, many white families seeking a fresh start in the trans-Appalachian South took slaves with them into the new states of Kentucky and Tennessee. Even in the Northwest Territory (above the Ohio River), where slavery was prohibited by law, African American arrivals faced the same prejudices that shaped social relations in the East. Rather than extend the bounds of liberty, western settlement solidified ideas about white supremacy.

From the Canadian border to Georgia, the trans-Appalachian West had become a cultural battlefield. European Americans warred against Indians, but Indian leaders also disagreed bitterly with one another about how to respond. Should they defend their hunting

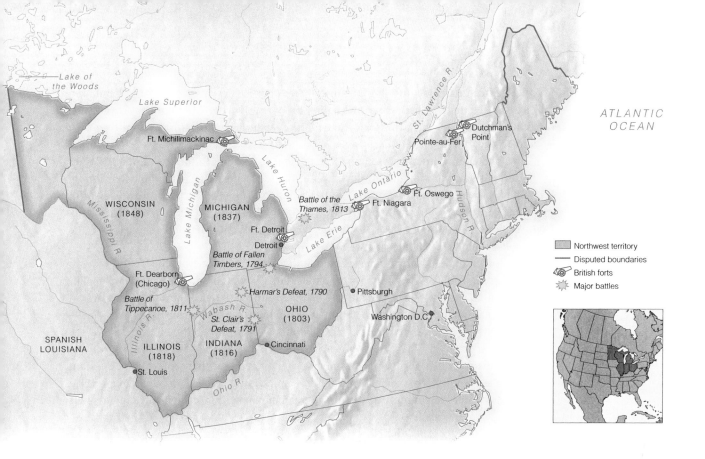

■ **MAP 9.1** **The Northwest Territory**

After the Revolution, the Northwest Territory became a battleground. Indians—both long-term residents and newcomers—as well as European American squatters and speculators vied for control of the land. The Northwest Ordinance of 1787 provided for territorial governments before an area could apply for statehood. The present-day states of Ohio, Indiana, Michigan, Illinois, and Wisconsin were carved out of the Northwest Territory. All had gained statehood by 1848, but only after almost sixty years of bloodshed between Indians and U.S. troops in the region.

grounds to the death or seek refuge elsewhere? For most, the answer was neither total resistance nor complete capitulation to an alien culture. Indeed, the history of the West during this period reveals the dangers of generalizing about "Americans," "Indians," and "foreigners." Yet one generalization holds true for all inhabitants: the abundance of land and natural resources, combined with the clash of cultures and the prevalence of armed men of different backgrounds, made life particularly dangerous in the borderlands.

INDIAN WARS IN THE GREAT LAKES REGION

The American Revolution destroyed one Indian confederation and led to the creation of another. The Iroquois Confederacy, including the Seneca, Cayuga, Onondaga, Oneida, Mohawk, Tuscarora, and the nations of present-day New York State, had suffered greatly during the war. Then, in the late 1780s, some members of the confederacy migrated westward and northward, away from their ruined fields and still-smoldering villages. Regrouping in Detroit, they sought to forge a new political alliance, this time with other Indians living along the Ohio River and in the Great Lakes region. Mohawk leader Joseph Brant (born Thayendanegea) urged the Algonquin, Shawnee, Delaware, Miami, and Wea, among others, to join in common purpose and resist U.S. territorial aggression, even as each group retained its separate identity. Together, he claimed, western Indians could "eat out of one bowl with one spoon."

The European Americans were determined to rid themselves of the persistent military threat posed by Indian and British forces in the Northwest Territory and so launched a

In 1786, artist Gilbert Stuart painted this portrait of Mohawk leader Joseph Brant, born Thayendanegea.

concerted campaign against Indians in the area that is present-day Ohio, Indiana, and Michigan. Under the leadership of Miami chief Little Turtle (Michikinikwa), and with support from the British, this Ohio Confederacy temporarily held off the advances of the American army.

The Ohio Confederacy offers some intriguing parallels to the coalition of colonies during the Revolution and to the union of the states afterward. Before the Revolution, Benjamin Franklin had marveled at the cohesion of the Six Nations (the precursor of the confederacy), drawing inspiration from the Indians' example. He noted, "If Six Nations of Ignorant savages" could create a union, then thirteen colonies led by white men should be able to do so also.

Joseph Brant pointed to the lesson that the Indians learned from the United States in creating the Ohio Confederacy: with political unity came military strength. Indians, like the colonists, sought to overcome regional and cultural differences among themselves. In both cases, disparate groups found common ground in their fight against a single enemy— Great Britain in the case of the thirteen colonies, the United States in the case of the Ohio Confederacy.

Members of the Ohio Confederacy soon discovered that their federation could not function as a completely independent political unit. In the early 1790s, the Indians relied heavily on the British for guns and artillery. And many Indians came to depend increasingly on trade with Europeans.

From 1775 to 1800, the Northwest Territory—the Great Lakes region west of the Appalachian Mountains and east of the Mississippi River—remained a vast **middle ground,** where Indian villagers coexisted with British traders and French trappers. The cultures of these groups intermingled. But the incursion of European American settlers into this middle ground disrupted Indian hunting practices. Violence escalated in an endless cycle of raids and retaliation. The U.S. citizens who settled in the area that is today Kentucky, Ohio, Indiana, and Michigan—the trans-Appalachian West—were the vanguard of the new, expanding republic. At the same time, they drew the army of the infant nation into a costly, bloody war.

Native Americans residing in the Northwest Territory in the 1790s included peoples who had long occupied the Great Lakes region and the upper Midwest, such as the Miami, Potawatomi, Menominee, Kickapoo, Illinois, Fox, Winnebago, Sauk, and Shawnee. Also present were refugees from the East: Ottawa, Ojibway, Wyandot, Algonquin, Delaware, and Iroquois displaced by the Revolutionary War. As they resettled in villages, they managed to retain some elements of their cultural identity, but in the seven years immediately after the Revolution, thousands died in Indian–white clashes in the region.

By encouraging European Americans to stake their claim to the area, the Northwest Ordinance inflamed passions on both sides.

What caused this violence? By encouraging European Americans to stake their claim to the area, the Northwest Ordinance inflamed passions on both sides: whites' determination to occupy and own the land and Indians' equal determination to resist this incursion. In 1790, under orders from President Washington, Brigadier General Josiah Harmar led a force of about 1,500 men into the Maumee River valley in the northwest corner of modern-day Ohio. Orchestrating two ambushes in September, Miami chief Little Turtle and his men killed 183 of Harmar's troops, driving the general back in disgrace. The next year, Washington chose General Arthur St. Clair to resume the fight. But when St. Clair's men met Little Turtle's warriors in November 1791 near the upper Wabash River, the Americans suffered an even greater defeat, losing over 600 men.

Washington tried once more to find a commander equal to Little Turtle. This time he chose General Anthony Wayne, a Revolutionary War hero dubbed "Mad Anthony" for his bold recklessness. Wayne mobilized a force of 3,000 men and constructed a string of new forts as well. At the battle of Fallen Timbers in August 1794, near present-day Toledo, hundreds of Indians perished before Wayne's forces. The withdrawal of British support helped doom the Ohio Confederacy. On August 3, 1795, 1,100 Indian leaders met at Fort Greenville (in western Ohio) and ceded to the United States a vast tract of Indian land: all of present-day Ohio and most of Indiana. Little Turtle helped negotiate the agreement.

PATTERNS OF INDIAN ACCULTURATION

White newcomers in the Northwest Territory swiftly made clear their belief that men should farm and herd sheep and cattle, while women should milk cows, raise chickens, tend the garden, spin thread, and weave cloth. However, Indian groups differed in their responses to the various attempts to persuade—or force—them to "accultur- ate" by adopting novel customs. At first, all learned from each other, as newly arrived settlers and indigenous peoples traded foodways, folk remedies, and styles of dress, adopting foreign habits while still retaining some old ways. Little Turtle himself chose among European American cultural traits; he drank tea and coffee, kept cows, and shunned leather breeches in favor of white men's clothing. The fact that his wife made butter suggested that she was skilled in the ways of European American homemakers.

> *The migration of whites into Indian hunting grounds rapidly depleted their game supply and devastated their crop fields.*

Adopting some habits of European Americans—for example, liquor consumption— amounted to self-destruction. Alcohol was a prized trade item. Moreover, European Americans and Indians often used it to lubricate political negotiations and cultural rituals. Yet conflicts over liquor, and tensions vented under the influence of liquor, became increasingly common—and deadly. Some Indian leaders, including Joseph Brant and Little Turtle, came to view the drinking of alcohol as a full-blown crisis among their people. Both believed that Indians must reject the white man's bottle if they were to survive.

But liquor was only one piece of a larger cultural puzzle, as the experience of the Cherokee, Chickasaw, Choctaw, Creek, and Seminole Indians in the southeastern United States revealed. The migration of whites into Indian hunting grounds rapidly depleted their game supply and devastated their crop fields. Unable to hunt efficiently for food, many in these groups took up new forms of agriculture after the Revolution, and they became known to whites as the Five Civilized Tribes. Women, who had tradi- tionally tended crops using hoes, gave way in the fields to men, who used plows provided by the federal government. Protestant missionaries encouraged Indian women to learn to spin thread and weave cloth. For more than a generation, the willingness of these southern tribes to accommodate themselves to European American law and divisions of labor allowed them to stay in their homeland and retain key elements of their cultural identity.

In southwest and far west borderland areas, Spanish officials met with mixed success in their attempts to convert Indians to Christianity and encourage them to engage in sedentary farming. The Spanish established missions, which served as economic outposts of Spain in California and the Southwest. These missions produced large amounts of wheat, corn, and beans, and they were also major stock-raisers of sheep and cattle. Without the missions, the Spanish *presidios* (forts) and *pueblos* (towns) would have perished. But the missions were also the means of converting and acculturating Indians.

For example, between 1772 and 1804, Spanish priests established nineteen missions among the Chumash, hunter-gatherers living in permanent villages along the California coast. When large numbers of the Indians moved to these settlements, they forfeited their traditional kin and trade networks, and their distinctive culture began to fade. Birth rates plummeted due to disruptions in family life (more women than men lived in the missions), and mortality rates increased dramatically as contact with the Spanish intro- duced new diseases.

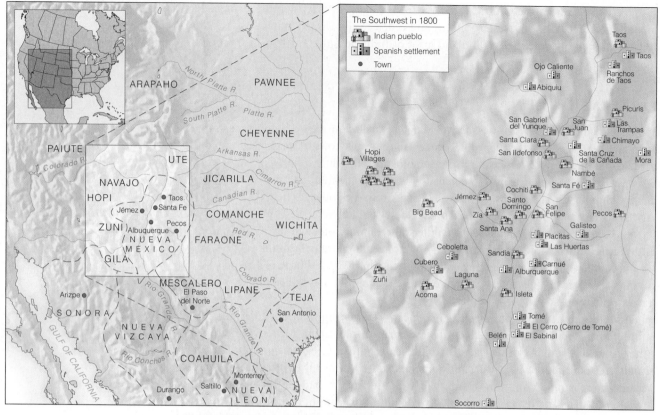

■ **MAP 9.2   The Southwest in 1800**

This map shows the pastoral and mountain borderlands (present-day north-central New Mexico) in 1800. Within this region, Spanish colonists and nomadic and pastoral Indian societies were often hostile to one another. But on an everyday local level, these groups engaged in a lively trade. Items of exchange included not only horses, guns, sheep, and buffalo hides, but also women and children captives. Men on both sides recognized the value of women captives in particular as symbols of male power.

In contrast, along the Texas Gulf Coast, the Spanish made little headway in their efforts to bring the Karankawa Indians into the missions. Members of this nomadic tribe arrived at the mission gates only when their own food reserves were low; in essence, the Karankawa simply included the missions in their seasonal migrations between the Gulf Coast and the coastal plain. The West represented a fluid, unsettled region where cultures collided and reconfigured themselves.

LAND SPECULATION AND SLAVERY

The West was not necessarily a place of boundless economic opportunity for all people who settled there. When European Americans poured into the trans-Appalachian West after the Revolution, they often carried alcohol and guns, staples of trade among all groups. These items proved a lethal mix, injecting violence into commercial and diplomatic relations among a variety of cultural groups. Land speculation and slavery helped the West come to resemble society on the eastern seaboard, with its hierarchies based on class, ethnicity, and race.

Eager investors and creditors thwarted many homesteaders' quest for cheap land. Schemes such as the Ohio Company of Associates foreshadowed the significance of land speculation in shaping patterns of settlement and property ownership further west in

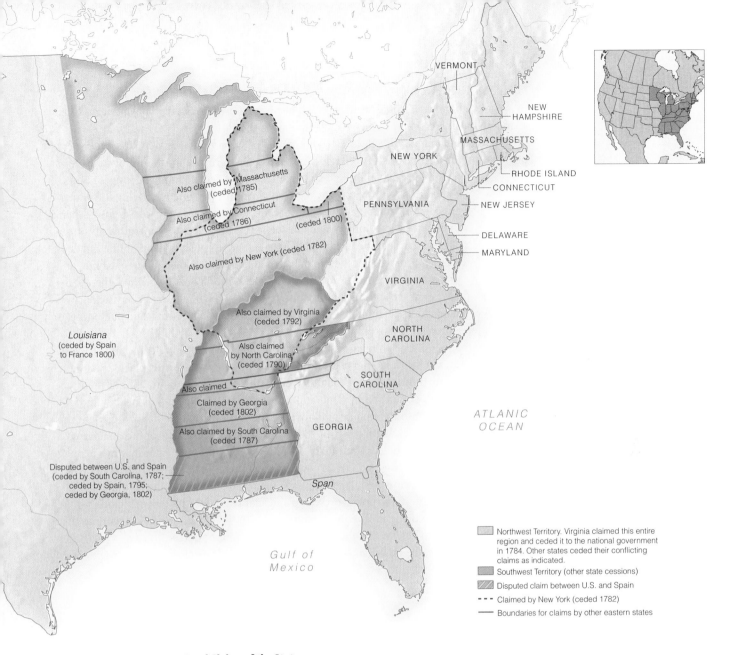

Labels on map:
VERMONT
NEW HAMPSHIRE
NEW YORK
MASSACHUSETTS
RHODE ISLAND
CONNECTICUT
PENNSYLVANIA
NEW JERSEY
DELAWARE
MARYLAND
VIRGINIA
NORTH CAROLINA
SOUTH CAROLINA
GEORGIA
ATLANTIC OCEAN

Also claimed by Massachusetts (ceded 1785)
Also claimed by Connecticut (ceded 1786)
(ceded 1800)
Also claimed by New York (ceded 1782)
Also claimed by Virginia (ceded 1792)
Also claimed by North Carolina (ceded 1790)
Also claimed
Claimed by Georgia (ceded 1802)
Also claimed by South Carolina (ceded 1787)

Louisiana (ceded by Spain to France 1800)

Disputed between U.S. and Spain (ceded by South Carolina, 1787; ceded by Spain, 1795; ceded by Georgia, 1802)

Span

Gulf of Mexico

Legend:
Northwest Territory. Virginia claimed this entire region and ceded it to the national government in 1784. Other states ceded their conflicting claims as indicated.
Southwest Territory (other state cessions)
Disputed claim between U.S. and Spain
Claimed by New York (ceded 1782)
Boundaries for claims by other eastern states

■ **M A P 9 . 3** **Western Land Claims of the States**

Several of the original thirteen colonies, including Massachusetts, Connecticut, New York, Virginia, South Carolina, North Carolina, and Georgia, claimed land west of the Appalachian Mountains. By 1802, these states had ceded their western lands to the federal government. The Land Ordinance of 1785 provided that this expanse be auctioned off in parcels no less than 640 acres each, with a minimum price of $1 per acre—too expensive for many family homesteaders, thus opening the way for investors to purchase and profit. Hoping to raise money through land sales, the federal government did not object to speculation.

later generations. With backing from wealthy investors, the Ohio Company quickly bought up tracts of land and then sold parcels to family farmers at inflated rates. A similar venture was initiated in Georgia in 1795, when speculators bribed state legislators for the right to resell huge tracts to the west of the state, land that the state did not even own. The state legislature passed the so-called Yazoo Act (named for a Georgia river) because of these bribes. The act resulted in the defrauding of thousands of buyers, whose land titles were worthless.

By protecting slavery and opening new territory to European American settlement, the new nation condemned southern blacks to a legal bondage that stood in stark contrast to revolutionary principles. Many settlers relied on slave labor. By the late eighteenth century,

Kentucky slaves numbered 40,000—more than 18 percent of the state's total population. In isolated settlements, where farmers owned just one or two slaves, African Americans faced a kind of loneliness unknown on large plantations in the East.

Patterns of land use directly affected the spread of slavery into the West. Despite eastern planters' use of European soil conservation techniques (crop rotation, use of manure as fertilizer), many of them had to contend with depleted soil in the upper South. Generations of tobacco growers had worn out the land, depriving it of nutrients. As a result, many growers were forced to abandon tobacco. Some of them moved west into Indian lands in the Mississippi Territory to cultivate cotton. The scarcity of labor motivated slave owners to push workers to the limits of their endurance. Slaves cleared potential farmland, rooted out tree stumps, and prepared the ground for cultivation. Once cotton could be planted, these same slaves worked in gangs under the sharp eye of a white overseer or black driver. Men, women, and children labored as human machines, planting, hoeing, and harvesting as much cotton as quickly as possible.

> *Whites in the western territories preserved and adapted slavery to extract financial profit from new areas of settlement.*

Many free people of color also found a less than hospitable welcome in the West. In 1802, delegates to the first Ohio territorial convention moved to restrict blacks' economic and political opportunities, even though fewer than 400 were living in Ohio at the time. Although slavery was outlawed in Ohio and other territories, blacks still lacked the right to vote. Soon after Ohio became a state in 1803, the legislature took steps to prevent the in-migration of free blacks altogether. In 1803, the territorial legislature of Indiana passed a "black law" prohibiting blacks or Indians from testifying in court against white people. Black families in the Northwest Territory were also vulnerable to kidnapping: some white men seized free blacks and sold them as slaves to plantation owners in the South.

Whites in the western territories preserved and adapted slavery to extract financial profit from new areas of settlement. The institution of slavery thrived in the West, revealing that few black people could claim that the West offered them new opportunities. For many other Americans, however, the post-Revolutionary period brought new challenges and opportunities in the realms of religion, work, and gender roles.

Shifting Social Identities in the Post-Revolutionary Era

■ *What kinds of traditional hierarchies were challenged by different groups of Americans in the wake of the Revolution? How successful were those challenges?*

The nation's founders had argued for an egalitarian society, one in which people prospered according to their talents and ambition. Of course, their definition of egalitarianism included only white men. Still, it was a revolutionary idea and led to challenges of social hierarchies after the Revolution. These hierarchies included the patriarchal (male-headed) family, established Protestant denominations, power systems based on social standing, and ideas about race and gender. Ordinary men and women penned letters to local newspapers, glorifying common laborers and questioning the claim to power of "the marchent, phesition [physician] the lawyer and divine [minister] and all the literary walkes of life, the Jutical & Executive oficeers & all the rich who live without bodily labour." This letter writer's creative spelling suggests that even people lacking in formal education felt free to voice their opinions on political issues of the day.

In the early nineteenth century, voluntary reform organizations multiplied across the nation, transforming the professions, the religious landscape, slavery, the rights of women, and a host of other American institutions. As these groups proliferated in the

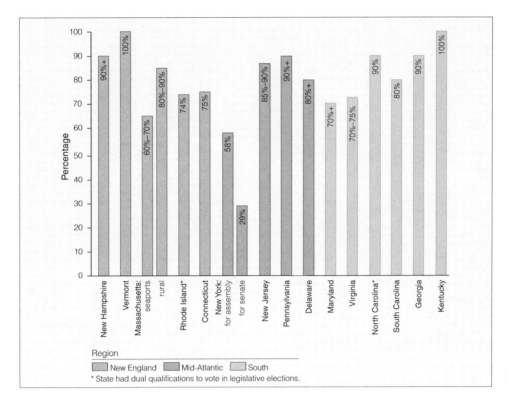

■ **FIGURE 9.2 Percentage of White Men Eligible to Vote in the United States, 1792**

Source: Robert J. Dinkin, *Voting in Revolutionary America: A Study of Elections in the Original Thirteen States, 1776–1789* (Westport, CT: Greenwood Press, 1982), 36–39.

years immediately after the Revolution, both the possibilities and limitations of reform became clear. Some groups—for example, white working men—sought to advance their own self-interest without showing much concern for the plight of African American laborers. In other cases, people banded together to target the behavior of a specific group: drunkards, slave owners, the irreligious, or prostitutes. These moral reform groups welcomed diversity among members, as long as new converts supported the cause.

THE SEARCH FOR COMMON GROUND

As people identified a common causes, a variety of groups emerged. Manumission and temperance societies had appeared during the Revolution. Other kinds of associations sprang up and multiplied after the war. For example, in southwestern Pennsylvania, tax resisters formed the Mingo Creek Society. The organization offered mediation services for citizens who felt "harassed with suits from justices and courts, and wished a less expensive tribunal." In New York, fifteen women formed the Society for the Relief of Poor Widows and Small Children. Often, free people of color in the North and South created new churches designated as "African," a testament to a shared heritage that predated their transportation to America and enslavement.

Americans redefined the family to accommodate new circumstances and ideas. Whites who chose to live in Indian villages felt they had found new families. Wrote Mary Jemison, a captive and then willing member of the Seneca, "It was my happy lot to be accepted for adoption." She described her initiation ceremony in these terms: "I was received by the two squaws to supply the place of their brother in the family; and I was ever considered and treated by them as a real sister, the same as though I had been born of their mother."

In some instances, the family metaphor extended to religious ties. Members of Baptist and Methodist congregations referred to themselves as brothers and sisters. They called their preachers "elder brother" or, in some places in the South, "Daddy." The Shakers,

Courtesy of Shaker Village of Pleasant Hill, Harrodsburg, KY

■ Men and women participate in a Shaker worship service in New Lebanon, New York. The formal name of the church was the United Society of Believers in Christ's Second Appearance. The group's more familiar name derived from their worship style, which involved trembling and shaking. They forbade marriage and sexual intercourse, relying on new converts to expand their ranks. Like several other Protestant denominations, the Shakers encouraged congregants to call each other brothers and sisters.

a sect founded by Englishwoman Ann Lee in the 1770s, forbade sexual intercourse between male and female members. In this group, the church itself replaced traditional family relationships.

One of the enduring legacies of the Revolution was an increase in the number of Protestant denominations (Table 9.2). All over the United States, people claimed the right to worship according to their own beliefs. The war against Great Britain had called into question many different kinds of authority, including the power of **established churches**— the Anglican (or English) church in the South and the Congregational church in New England. These churches had received financial support from colonial governments, and their members dominated the colonial political and economic elite. But more and more people resented the fact that their tax dollars went to support specific churches and ministers. For example, during the war, southern Baptists and Presbyterians refused to pay the salaries of Anglican clergymen, most of whom remained loyal to the King.

The new U.S. government furthered the cause of religious liberty. Article VI of the Constitution prohibited the use of any religious test as a qualification for holding office. The First Amendment guaranteed that the federal government would neither favor nor inhibit the expression of religious ideas. These provisions set in motion a gradual process by which the states disestablished churches. No longer would taxpayers' money

TABLE 9.2			
Religious Denominations in the United States, 1776 and 1850 (percentage of adherents)			
1776		**1850**	
Congregationalists	20.4	Methodists	34.2
Presbyterians	19.0	Baptists	20.5
Baptists	16.9	Roman Catholics	13.9
Episcopalians	15.7	Presbyterians	11.6
Methodists	2.5	Congregationalists	4.0
Roman Catholics	1.8	Episcopalians	3.5

Sources: Roger Finke and Rodney Stark, "How the Upstart Sects Won America: 1776–1850," *Journal for the Scientific Study of Religion* 28 (1989): 31, and the 1850 Census of the United States.

Courtesy, American Antiquarian Society

■ Published after the Revolution, this print ridicules the efforts of church-goers who sought to prevent the United States from transporting mail on Sundays.

be used to support the Anglican or Congregational—or any—denomination. Massachusetts managed to cling to the remnants of religious establishment until 1833. But by that time, Americans throughout the new nation had formed many new denominations and embraced the idea that religious faith was a matter of personal conviction. If Americans did not share the same religious beliefs, they could nevertheless embrace the common ground of religious freedom.

ARTISAN-POLITICIANS AND MENIAL LABORERS

Workers also found themselves searching for common ties that bound all laboring people together. In the decades after the Revolution, residents of port cities along the eastern seaboard grew accustomed to public parades marking special occasions: a visit from George Washington, the ratification of the Constitution, the Fourth of July. Most of these parades consisted of groups of artisans marching together, carrying the banners of their respective occupations. The bricklayers' flag declared: "Both Buildings and Rulers Are the Works of Our Hands."

Proud of their role in the Sons of Liberty and other revolutionary organizations, bricklayers—along with tanners, carpenters, glassblowers, weavers, and other groups of artisans—proclaimed themselves the proud citizens of the new nation. American labor organizations declared they shared a distinct revolutionary heritage that stressed the equality of all (white) freeborn men. Master artisans in several cities—including Boston, Albany, Providence, Portsmouth, Charleston, Savannah, and New York—created organizations called the General Society of Mechanics and Tradesmen that brought together skilled workers from a variety of fields. The proliferation of newspapers enabled these artisans to participate in a new, more open public forum. Such participation—as well as their high percentage of property ownership—in turn helped them gain influence within local politics. Indeed, artisans' organizations soon became quasi-political groups, extending their reach in ways that pre-Revolutionary trades-based associations had not.

But not all workers were so secure. As the country expanded and developed new systems of transport, the canal worker replaced the skilled artisan as the typical laborer. Moving around in search of work, canal diggers led an unsettled existence of backbreaking work that contrasted greatly with the more predictable life of urban artisans. For example, the Potomac Company sought to link the Potomac River near Washington, D.C., with its upriver tributaries through a series of short canals that bypassed waterfalls and walls of rock. Company owners (including George Washington, one of the original investors) first had to locate workers. Finding too few laborers willing to work on the project full-time, they

A Farmer Worries About the Power of "The Few," 1798

After the Revolution, many ordinary Americans debated the challenges faced by the new nation. For example, C. William Manning was a tavern keeper and farmer in Massachusetts. In 1798, he wrote an essay titled "The Key of Liberty." In his essay, Manning warns about the power of "the few"—the wealthy and influential—over the power of "the many"—ordinary people who must work hard for a living.

"In the sweat of thy face shalt thou get thy bread, until thou return to the ground,"* is the irreversible sentence of Heaven on man for his rebellion. To be sentenced to hard labor during life is very unpleasant to human nature. There is a great aversion to it perceivable in all men; yet it is absolutely necessary that a large majority of the world should labor, or we could not subsist. For labor is the sole parent of all property; the land yields nothing without it, and there is no . . . necessary of life but what costs labor and is generally esteemed valuable according to the labor it costs. Therefore, no person can possess property without laboring unless he gets it by force or craft, fraud or fortune, out of the earnings of others.

*Genesis 3:19

But from the great variety of capacities, strength, and abilities of men, there always was and always will be a very unequal distribution of property in the world. Many are so rich that they can live without labor—also the merchant, physician, lawyer, and divine, the philosopher and schoolmaster, the judicial and executive officers, and many others who could honestly get a living without bodily labors. As all these professions require a considerable expense of time and property to qualify themselves therefore, . . . so all these professions naturally unite in their schemes to make their callings as honorable and lucrative as possible.

Also, as ease and rest from labor are reasoned among the greatest pleasures of life, pursued by all with the greatest avidity, and when attained at once create a sense of superiority; and as pride and ostentation are natural to the human heart, these orders of men generally associate together and look down with too much contempt on those that labor.

As the interests and incomes of the few lie chiefly in money at interest, rents, salaries, and fees, that are fixed on the nominal value of money, they are interested in having money scarce and the price of labor and produce as low as possible. . . .

cobbled together a workforce from indentured servants, Irish immigrants, hired slaves, and farmers willing to earn wages on a part-time basis.

Organizing and disciplining such a large workforce caused supervisors endless headaches. Some of the men ran away. Others, provided with daily rations of rum, spent their evening hours quarrelling and brawling. They angrily confronted their bosses about the lateness and the size of their paychecks. Canal diggers represented a transition workforce of sorts, bridging the worlds of traditional, outdoor work with the more disciplined, regimented pace of the factory.

The plight of menial laborers (in the countryside and the cities) suggests the ironies that accompanied the decline of indentured servitude and the rise of the "free laborer." To be sure, master artisans attained a degree of economic independence. But for men and women who lacked skills, money, and wealthy patrons, freedom often meant financial insecurity and, in some cases, reliance on public or private charity. Those who did find work usually had the kinds of jobs that came with the booming economy of the late eighteenth century: moving goods from one place to another, building new structures, and providing personal services for the merchants who profited from all this commercial activity.

"REPUBLICAN MOTHERS" AND OTHER WELL-OFF WOMEN

The post-Revolution period was a time of flux for women as well as workers. Some well-educated women in the United States read English writer Mary Wollstonecraft's *A Vindication of the Rights of Woman* published in England and America in 1792. In that manifesto, Wollstonecraft argued that young men and women should receive the same kind of education. She objected to a special female curriculum that focused on skills such as needlepoint and musical accomplishments; this "false system of education," she charged, left women "in a state of perpetual childhood."

But the greatest danger the many are under in these money matters is from the judicial and executive officers, especially so as their incomes for a living are almost wholly gotten from the follies and distress of the many—they being governed by the same selfish principles as other men are. They are the most interested in the distresses of the many of any in the nation; the scarcer money is and the greater the distresses of the many are, the better for them. . . .

This is the reason why they ought to be kept entirely from the legislative body; . . . For in all these conceived differences of interests, it is the business and duty of the legislative body to determine what is justice, or what is right and wrong; and it is the duty of every individual in the nation to regulate his conduct according to their decisions. . . .

The reason why a free government has always failed is from the unreasonable demands and desires of the few. They cannot bear to be on a level with their fellow creatures, or submit to the determinations of a legislature where (as they call it) the swinish multitude is fairly represented, but sicken at the idea, and are ever hankering and striving after monarchy or aristocracy, where the people have nothing to do in matters of government but to support the few in luxury and idleness.

For these and many other reasons, a large majority of those that live without labor are ever opposed to the principles and operation of a free government; and though the whole of them do not amount to one-eighth part of the people, yet, by their combinations, arts, and schemes, have always made out to destroy it sooner or later.

QUESTIONS

1. *According to Manning, why have attempts at "free government" failed in the past?*

2. *How do you think Manning would view the institution of slavery?*

3. *What is the significance of the fact that Manning never published his views? What does this fact tell us about the nature of political debates during this time?*

4. *Do you think Manning is referring to Federalists when he condemns "the few"? Why or why not?*

Source: C. William Manning, "The Key of Libberty" (1798), in Major Problems in American History, Vol. 1: To 1877, Elizabeth Cobbs Hoffman and Jon Gjerde (Houghton Mifflin, 2002), 170–171.

In 1801, an anonymous "American Lady" published an essay titled "A Second Vindication of the Rights of Woman." In it, she claimed that "a good kitchen woman [that is, a household drudge] very seldom makes a desirable wife, to a man of any refinement." The anonymous "American Lady" and others who shared her opinion celebrated a new kind of woman—the **Republican mother**—who provided cultured companionship for her husband and reared her children to be virtuous, responsible members of society. This image of womanhood led to a new notion with patriotic overtones: that well-off women should dedicate themselves to tending the home fires rather than aspiring to a more public role in business or politics.

Prior to the Revolution, women tended to bear many children, since additional hands were needed to labor in the fields. But as the sons of farmers became store managers and bookkeepers, they had less need for the unpaid labor of their own children. The decline in white women's fertility rates after the Revolution suggests that the economy had shifted. And some women could now buy products their grandmothers had made at home. In particular, a small but influential group of well-to-do women in the cities were shedding their roles as producers of candles, soap, and textiles. Instead, they became consumers of these staples and of luxury goods, and they managed household servants. "Republican mothers" participated in the public life of the new nation as the guardians of the home and the socializers of children.

But the idea of the "Republican mother" also suggested a more radical notion. If such a woman wanted to earn the respect accorded all intelligent human beings, she must strive for an education equal to that of men's. In the 1790s, a number of academies for "young ladies" opened in New England, including Sarah Peirce's in Litchfield, Connecticut, and Susanna Rowson's in Medford, Massachusetts. Many female academies catered to boarders, students living away from home. These schools offered courses in such "womanly pursuits" as needlework, etiquette, and music. But many also offered a classical curriculum consisting of mathematics, foreign languages, and geography. This system of study encouraged young

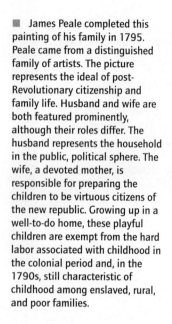

■ James Peale completed this painting of his family in 1795. Peale came from a distinguished family of artists. The picture represents the ideal of post-Revolutionary citizenship and family life. Husband and wife are both featured prominently, although their roles differ. The husband represents the household in the public, political sphere. The wife, a devoted mother, is responsible for preparing the children to be virtuous citizens of the new republic. Growing up in a well-to-do home, these playful children are exempt from the hard labor associated with childhood in the colonial period and, in the 1790s, still characteristic of childhood among enslaved, rural, and poor families.

women to think for themselves. In this respect, female academies challenged the view that women were intellectually inferior to and necessarily dependent on men.

Some elite women—like the anonymous "American Lady" and Alice Izard of Charleston, South Carolina—did not share this more radical viewpoint. In opposition to Wollstonecraft's argument in favor of equal education for young men and women, Izard expressed disgust with notions of female equality. "It is not by being educated with Boys, or imitating the manners of Men that we shall become more worthy beings," she proclaimed. Women need not attain public glory, she wrote, to gain "domestic honor and true praise."

Alice Izard was not alone in her beliefs. After the Revolution, many American women, even those of modest means, eagerly read advice manuals written by both native and foreign-born authors. These manuals stressed the importance of good manners over formal education. And even graduates of the new female academies often renounced aspirations to public life once they married and assumed household responsibilities.

Other women were more sympathetic to Wollstonecraft's arguments regarding women's equality with men. As the author of a series of essays on women's rights such as "On the Equality of the Sexes," published in *Massachusetts Magazine* in 1790, Judith Sargent Murray was the intellectual heir of Abigail Adams. With a notable lack of success, Adams had urged her husband, John, to secure married women's property rights in the Constitution. By arguing for the inherent equality of men and women, Murray echoed Wollstonecraft and Adams and laid the groundwork for the women's rights movement to come. The white women of means who came of age after the Revolution keenly felt the ties

Analectic Magazine, November 1802. Photo courtesy The New York Public Library

■ With the Revolution came a heightened awareness of the significance of women's education. Private academies offered instruction to elite young women. This engraving, titled *Return from a Boarding School*, appeared in the November 1802 issue of *Analectic Magazine*. The fashionably dressed student, on the right, sits at the piano and greets visitors while her father, on the left with her mother, agonizes over the tuition bill. The shovel, washtub, and broom indicate that the parents are hard-working, simple people. Yet the parlor, with its birdcage, furniture, and carpets, suggests that the household values both prosperity and sociability.

that bound them together, even as those ties limited their participation in the public sphere, especially after the wartime emergency had passed.

A LOSS OF POLITICAL INFLUENCE: THE FATE OF NONELITE WOMEN

The Revolution had given elite white women a rationale for speaking out in the realm of politics. Yet the war had a very different impact on other groups of women. Many Native American women, feeling the pressures of European American cultures, found their traditional roles had been weakened by the end of the eighteenth century. For example, among the Cherokee, the introduction of a European American division of labor lessened women's customary political influence as leaders and diplomats. Most European Americans believed that only men should serve in positions of authority, and so Cherokee women felt pressure to refrain from taking part in political negotiations and to subordinate themselves to men. By the end of the century, only men had the power to negotiate treaties and land transactions.

Ironically, women and children played a key role in the economy, diplomacy, and society of the southwest borderlands as captives. In 1800, this region encompassed present-day New Mexico, Arizona, and Texas (then territory belonging to Spain), as well as the Great Plains region stretching from modern-day Nebraska to Nevada, and north to Wyoming and South Dakota. A variety of Native American cultural groups, in addition to the Spanish-speaking colonists of New Mexico, created complex trading networks that depended on raiding each others' settlements and capturing women and children.

In 1791, an artist made this sketch of the wife of a Spanish soldier stationed at the presidio, or military garrison, in Monterey, California. Many elite Spaniards in the Americas went to great lengths to dress like their European counterparts. This woman is wearing the elegant dress, elaborate jewelry, and dainty shoes that befit her status. One eighteenth-century resident of New Mexico wrote that, despite the hot climate, European Americans "will go up to their ears in debt simply to satisfy their pride in putting on a grand appearance." However, most *nuevomexicanos* adopted some elements of Indian-style clothing, such as practical leather moccasins and garments made of buckskin and coarse woolens.

Courtesy, Museo de America, Madrid. Photo by Iris Engstrand

By the eighteenth century, this system had resulted in a vast regional market for female captives, Indians as well as Spanish-speaking Mexicans. Men of conquering groups prized the women of their enemies for several reasons. Female captives were valued as "honor wives," translators, and cultural mediators by their captors. Women had great exchange value; they could be bartered or traded for axes, hoes, bridles, horses, and livestock, and they could be used as pawns in diplomatic negotiations between warring parties. Captive women bore children who enlarged and strengthened the cultural groups that incorporated them. Finally, women and children captives were often forced to work for their new households, either as family members or as slaves. For example, in New Mexico, female Indian captives from Plains tribes (such as the Apache, Comanche, and Kiowa) became *genizaros* or servants, in Hispanic households. In some cases their masters set them to work tending sheep, an occupation that had been reserved for men in traditional native cultures.

When captive women bore children, they helped create new kinship networks that at times brought warring groups together. As workers, they contributed to economic development among many southwestern cultures. They were the link in a thick mesh of cultures that found themselves simultaneously "cousins" and combatants.

At the same time, within this regional exchange system, women of all groups, especially Indian and Hispanic women, bore the brunt of ongoing conflicts between American Indians and European Americans. Captive exchange depended on bloodshed and the labor exploitation of the most vulnerable members of society. Male warriors and soldiers ripped women from their families and villages and forced them to live in an alien culture and speak a foreign language. Even women who were later redeemed, or rescued, by their kin bore the stigma of enslavement and captivity for the rest of their lives.

These difficulties for Indian women were not restricted to the borderlands of the southwest. In the East, too, Indian women suffered greatly from conflicts with whites. Dispossessed of their land, they pieced together a meager existence. For example, in Natick, Massachusetts, Indian women turned to weaving and peddling baskets and brooms, while Indian men scrounged for wage labor.

For some Americans, the postwar years brought unprecedented opportunities to buy, sell, and trade. However, commercial development, combined with race and gender discrimination, offered only modest possibilities for many impoverished women, regardless of color. Like other free blacks, Chloe Spear of Boston "worked early and late" at a number of jobs, such as laundering and ironing clothes. Eventually, she managed to purchase her own home. In Rhode Island, Elleanor Eldrige started her work career at age ten in 1795. Thereafter, she worked as a domestic servant, spinner, weaver, dairymaid, and nurse. She finally went into business, first as a soapboiler and then as a wallpaperer and house painter. However, like many free blacks, Eldrige remained vulnerable to the machinations of white men who tried to defraud her of her hard-won earnings.

Some white women also felt the effects of fluctuations in the market economy. In Philadelphia in the mid-1790s, two former servants—Polly Nugent (married to a blacksmith who had just lost his job) and Grace Biddle (newly widowed)—had to plead for assistance from their former mistress, Elizabeth Drinker. The city's "Bettering House" for indigent people housed men and women, blacks and whites. In the late eighteenth-century, many women had neither the resources nor the opportunities to improve their lot. For nonelite women, even dramatic political developments—such as the ongoing debates between Federalists and Democratic-Republicans—offered little change to their way of life and their legal liabilities.

The Election of 1800

■ *In what ways did the election of the Democratic-Republican Thomas Jefferson signal a new direction for the new nation?*

The social turbulence of these years also played out in the political arena. The campaign of 1800 pitted Democratic-Republican Thomas Jefferson and his vice-presidential running mate, Aaron Burr, against the Federalist incumbent, John Adams, and his vice-presidential nominee, Charles Pinckney. Certain elements of the campaign were predictable. The Democratic-Republicans blasted treasury secretary Alexander Hamilton's economic policies and the Adams administration's military buildup. Jefferson's party also condemned the Alien and Sedition Acts, used to silence Adams's political opponents. For their part, the Federalists portrayed Jefferson as a godless supporter of the French Revolution. They also charged that he had fathered children by one of his slaves, Sally Hemings. (Two centuries later, DNA evidence, combined with African American oral traditions and testimony, suggested that this assertion was true.)

Jefferson prevailed in the 1800 election, but his victory did not come easily. The electoral college allowed delegates to vote separately for president and vice president, and as a result Jefferson tied with Burr. Each man received seventy-three votes. Then the decision went to the House of Representatives, which was dominated by Federalists. After a series of tied votes, Jefferson finally gained a majority. His selection in February 1801 marked the orderly transfer of power from the Federalists to the Democratic-Republicans, a peaceful revolution in American politics.

Yet the Federalists disagreed with Jefferson's claim that the presidential election of 1800 revealed a Democratic-Republican popular majority. Instead, the new president's opponents noted that he had benefited from the "three-fifths" clause of the Constitution. This provision allowed states to count each slave as three-fifths of a person for purposes of congressional representation. Thus congressional and electoral districts with large numbers of slaves gained a disproportionate number of representatives. In the electoral college, Jefferson received eight more votes than John Adams. Historians estimate that between twelve and fourteen electoral votes were cast by men holding so-called slave seats—that is, men who represented slave states that benefited from the extra representation the three-fifths clause provided them. These dozen or so electors came from districts with a total of half a million slaves.

Federalists in the North denounced Jefferson in no uncertain terms. In 1801, one Boston newspaper charged that the new president had made his "ride into the TEMPLE OF LIBERTY on the *shoulders of slaves*." Other Federalists charged that Jefferson was the "Negro President"—that, in the words of Senator William Plumer of New Hampshire, "the Negro votes made Mr. Jefferson president."

TABLE 9.3		
The Election of 1800		
Candidate	**Political Party**	**Electoral Vote**
Thomas Jefferson	Democratic-Republican	73
Aaron Burr	Democratic-Republican	73
John Adams	Federalist	65
Charles C. Pinckney	Federalist	64

The Old Plantation, c. 1790–1800. Abby Aldrich Rockefeller Folk Art Museum. Colonial Williamsburg Foundation, Williamsburg, Virginia

■ An anonymous artist captured this scene near the slave quarters of a South Carolina plantation, in 1800. It is unknown what kind of entertainment or celebration the musicians and dancers are engaged in. The two men on the right are playing musical instruments of West African origin: a banjo and a *quaqua*, or skin-covered gourd used as a drum. On large lowcountry plantations especially, Africans and their descendants preserved traditional musical forms and social rituals.

The three-fifths clause would continue to give southern slaveholders undue influence in presidential elections and in Congress. In 1793, the South's free population would have entitled that region to thirty-three seats; instead, forty-seven Southerners were elected and took office that year. This discrepancy would widen, with the South sending ninety-eight representatives (instead of the seventy-three that their white population would allow them) to Congress four decades later. The disproportionate representation of the southern states would preserve slaveholder dominance of the executive branch, the judiciary, and the Congress for the next sixty years.

As chief executive, Jefferson did little to change the direction of the country. Aware of his razor-thin victory, he retained many Federalist appointees. And his eagerness to expand the boundaries of the United States—which culminated in the Louisiana Purchase of 1803—solidified the Hamiltonian principles that favored commerce and trade over agrarian values.

THE ENIGMATIC THOMAS JEFFERSON

Who was Thomas Jefferson? In 1800, Jefferson, the presidential candidate, wrote, "I have sworn upon the altar of God eternal hostility against every form of tyranny over the mind of man." Yet Jefferson's own views on ordinary people were less heroic. Specifically, his deep skepticism about African American equality and the viability of Indian cultures helped to justify violent assaults on both groups in the early nineteenth century.

LISTEN

"Jefferson and Liberty"

Many Americans today know Jefferson as the author of the Declaration of Independence. But he also sought to defend slavery as a central institution in the new republic, and he regarded blacks as lacking in imagination and intelligence. Jefferson wrote much about the noble calling of the yeoman farmer. Yet he assigned the task of tilling the soil on his own estate (Monticello, near Charlottesville, Virginia) to his enslaved workers.

The president's views on Indians also did nothing to reverse the course of aggression in the West. He believed that land ownership created the stable institutions necessary for civilized behavior. Yet the system of private property, and the violent methods that whites used to enforce it, spelled the destruction of traditional Indian ways of life.

It is tempting to excuse Jefferson's racist beliefs by saying he merely reflected his time. But in fact, a significant number of Jefferson's contemporaries were voicing their

Comparative Measures of Equality in the Post-Revolutionary Period

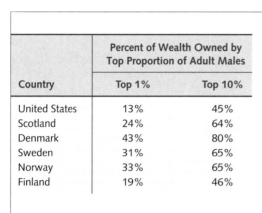

Country	Percent of Wealth Owned by Top Proportion of Adult Males	
	Top 1%	Top 10%
United States	13%	45%
Scotland	24%	64%
Denmark	43%	80%
Sweden	31%	65%
Norway	33%	65%
Finland	19%	46%

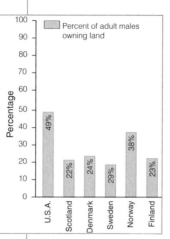

■ **Distribution of Wealth in the United States and Europe, 1798**

Source: Lee Soltow, *Distribution of Wealth and Income in the United States in 1798* (Pittsburgh: University of Pittsburgh Press, 1989), 238.

Many citizens of the early United States identified land ownership with political and economic independence. They believed that, unlike a tenant or a factory operative, the owner of real property (land) could not be pressured or swayed by a landlord or an employer to vote a certain way. In Europe at the time, a few households not only owned most of the land but also wielded a disproportionate amount of political and military power. In the United States, the availability of land, combined with the absence of a feudal system, allowed many white men the opportunity to own their own farms. The Democratic-Republicans believed that, by virtue of their hard work and their devotion to family, modest landowners would serve as the backbone of the new nation.

The chart and graph provide comparative data on two measures of economic equality in the United Sates in 1798. One measure, shown in the chart, is the percentage of wealth owned by the top 1 percent and 10 percent of adult males in the United Sates and other countries. In a completely egalitarian society, everyone would possess the same amount of

wealth and there would be no top or bottom group. The graph provides a related, but different, measure of equality by showing the percentage of adult males who owned land. The higher the percentage, the more equal the distribution of land in any society.

QUESTIONS

1. How do the chart and the graph measure equality in different ways? How do wealth and land ownership differ?

2. What are some of the characteristics of a society in which the top 1 percent of the population owns half or more of the country's total wealth?

3. What reasons for persistently high rates of immigration to the United States in the eighteenth and nineteenth centuries do these data suggest?

4. Given the egalitarian rhetoric of the Revolution, was the United States in 1798 living up to its ideals? Why or why not?

misgivings about slavery. While Jefferson acknowledged their arguments, he did not share their beliefs. A citizen of a transatlantic "republic of ideas," he corresponded with political thinkers—from John Adams to the Marquis de Lafayette—who understood the inherent tension between freedom for whites and slavery for blacks. Jefferson was aware that some of the northern states had written constitutions that incorporated the sentiments of the Declaration of Independence in ways that justified the abolition of slavery. Moreover, a notable number of Jefferson's wealthy Virginia compatriots (including George Washington) had chosen to free slaves, either by their own hand or through provisions of their wills, to practice in their own households what they preached to British tyrants.

Jefferson lived in an age when revolutionary enthusiasm was sweeping the western world. Challenges to slavery had rocked Europe; France outlawed slavery in 1794, although Napoleon later reinstated it. Abolition had also transformed the Western Hemisphere with the successful rebellion of the Saint-Domingue slaves in 1791. The United States provided the political theory and rhetoric to inspire abolitionists around the globe, but within the new nation, the debate over the institution of slavery continued to rage. The southern states, in particular, took decisive steps to solidify the institution within their own boundaries.

PROTECTING AND EXPANDING THE NATIONAL INTEREST

As president, Jefferson reconsidered his original vision of the United States: a compact country in which citizens freely pursued modest agrarian interests without interference from the national government or distractions from overseas conflicts. Indeed, during his years in office, the federal government moved toward increasing its power and the country grew in size.

Just before Jefferson assumed the presidency, the Federalist-dominated Congress had strengthened the national court system by passing the Judiciary Act of 1801. The act created sixteen circuit (regional) courts, with a judge for each, and increased support staff for the judicial branch in general. President Adams appointed these judges (called midnight judges because they were appointed right before Jefferson took office). Before stepping down, Adams had also appointed Secretary of State John Marshall as chief justice of the Supreme Court.

Adams's last-minute acts had long-term consequences. Marshall remained on the bench for thirty-four years. He presided over the court when it rendered its landmark ***Marbury v. Madison*** decision in 1803, which established the judiciary's right to declare acts of both the executive and legislative branches unconstitutional. This right, called judicial review, empowered the Supreme Court to decide whether an act of Congress was illegal. *Marbury v. Madison* established that Congress did not have the power to modify the Supreme Court's original jurisdiction as stated in the Constitution. Chief Justice Marshall wrote: "It is emphatically the province and duty of the judicial department to say what the law is."

> The European powers continued their operations in the territory west of the United States.

In the realm of international affairs, Jefferson asserted his own authority. Challenges from foreign powers prompted the Democratic-Republican president to take bold steps to protect U.S. economic and political interests abroad and along the country's borders. In 1801, Jefferson's administration launched a war against Barbary pirates in North Africa when Tripoli (modern-day Libya) demanded ransom money for kidnapped American sailors. (Together, the North African kingdoms of Tunis, Tripoli, Algeria, and Morocco were known as the "Barbary States.") The war against Tripoli, which spanned four years, revealed the extent of U.S. trade interests even at this early point in the nation's history. The United States signed a peace treaty with Tripoli in 1805 and paid $60,000 for the release of the American captives.

At the beginning of the nineteenth century, the European powers continued their operations in the territory west of the United States. In 1801, Napoleon persuaded the king of Spain to secretly cede the trans-Mississippi region called Louisiana to France. Retaining control of New Orleans, Spain denied the United States the right to use that city as a depository for goods awaiting shipment. In 1803, Jefferson sent his fellow Virginian, and prominent Anti-Federalist, James Monroe to Paris. Together with American ambassador Robert Livingston, Monroe set out to secure American trading rights in New Orleans. To the Americans' surprise, Napoleon agreed to sell the whole area to the United States. Frustrated by his inability to quell the Saint-Domingue revolt, Napoleon believed that the money would help fund future wars against England. At the time, Louisiana included most of the territory between the Mississippi and the Rocky Mountains—a total of 828,000 square miles. The United States agreed to pay $15 million for the Louisiana Purchase.

The Louisiana Purchase reversed the roles of Jefferson and his Federalist rivals. The president now advocated territorial expansion, but his opponents remained suspicious of the move. Devoted to a strict interpretation of the Constitution, Jefferson traditionally favored limiting federal authority. Yet he sought to justify the purchase by pointing out that it would finally rid the area of European influence. He proposed shifting Indians from the Mississippi Territory (part of present-day Alabama and Mississippi) to the West so that American newcomers could have the eastern part of the country to themselves. For their part, the Federalists feared that Louisiana would benefit mainly agrarian interests and eventually dilute New England's long-standing political influence and power. They suspected Jefferson of attempting to expand the influence of his own political party.

Neither the Democratic-Republicans nor the Federalists expressed much concern about the fate of the many Indian and Spanish-speaking inhabitants of Louisiana. All these peoples became residents, if not citizens, of the United States when the Senate approved the purchase in October 1803.

Conclusion

In the years immediately after the war, the American Revolution had far-reaching effects, both abroad and at home. In France in 1789, King Louis XVI's attempt to raise taxes provoked armed resistance among ordinary people, who claimed the right to create a new constitution for the country. Many French Revolutionaries were inspired by the American colonists' revolt against what they claimed were unfair policies of taxation. In the coming generations, emerging countries all over the world would echo the American revolutionary rhetoric of freedom in their own struggles against colonial oppression and government tyranny.

At home, Americans continued to challenge authority in many forms during the decade of the 1790s. In western Pennsylvania, debtors interfered with the work of federal tax collectors in the Whiskey Rebellion, just as Patriots had confronted British customs officials two decades earlier. Anglican clergy in the South and Congregational clergy in the North saw an erosion of their power, as Protestant denominations began to multiply and flourish. Throughout the country, African Americans sought to put into practice the ideals of the Revolution by arguing against slavery and in favor of universal emancipation. In the case of abolitionism, the Founders had unleashed a political movement that they neither approved nor anticipated.

By opening more western lands to European American migration, the Revolution had contrasting effects on different groups. In the West, Indian refugees from the East regrouped but found themselves vulnerable to federal troops bent on eliminating the American Indian

CHAPTER CHRONOLOGY: 1789–1803

1789	Judiciary Act of 1789 establishes national court system.
1790	Congress restricts citizenship to "free white persons." Northern states take steps to abolish slavery.
1791	Bill of Rights is ratified. Slaves revolt in Saint-Domingue (Haiti). Samuel Slater constructs first spinning machine on U.S. soil. Bank of the United States is chartered. 
1792	Washington is reelected president. Mary Wollstonecraft publishes *A Vindication of the Rights of Woman*.
1793	Washington issues Neutrality Proclamation. Eli Whitney invents the cotton gin.
1794	U.S. troops defeat forces of Ohio Confederacy. Whiskey Rebellion takes place in Pennsylvania.
1796	John Adams is elected president.
1797	XYZ Affair stirs anti-French sentiment.
1798	Quasi War waged with France (to 1800). Alien and Sedition Acts curb political dissent.
1800	Thomas Jefferson is elected president.
1801	War waged against Barbary pirates.
1803	Jefferson buys Louisiana Purchase. *Marbury v. Madison* asserts that judiciary can declare laws unconstitutional.

presence there. Soon, the region west of the Appalachian Mountains became a major battle-ground, as white farmers sought to own and cultivate the land that a multicultural mix of traders had occupied before.

During the last decade of the eighteenth century, the United States was not as independent of European influence as it hoped to be. Tensions between France and England continued to shape both the foreign and the domestic policy of the new nation. Some politicians admired the British system of hierarchy and order, while others believed that egalitarian, revolutionary France offered a model for the United States.

The election of Democratic-Republican Thomas Jefferson as president in 1800 provoked fear among Federalists. However, this peaceful transfer of power did not result in a radical challenge to the nation's goals. In fact, Jefferson supported the continuation of certain policies—such as federal support for the institution of slavery and for the displacement of Indians from their homelands. Moreover, the chief executive at times seemed to draw inspiration from the Federalists, who sought to centralize and expand federal authority. He presided over the creation of a national court system, and he expanded the boundaries of the new nation through the Louisiana Purchase in 1803. In the process, Jefferson implicitly acknowledged the Federalists' contention that the United States must develop a strong national government to meet the challenge of changing times.

By stating in his inaugural address, "We are all Republicans, we are all Federalists." Jefferson suggested that American political leaders of both parties shared essentially the same views about the role of government and the importance of economic opportunity for ordinary people. Most office holders also expressed suspicion of groups that professed religious beliefs that lay outside the mainstream of Protestantism. They considered slavery not a moral issue, but a political issue that individual states must address. They united behind the idea that Indians, blacks, and women should have no formal voice in governing the nation.

Despite these common principles, the post-Revolutionary era saw the rise of two opposing camps—those favoring local control and those supporting federal authority. Many people defined political interests in "either-or" terms: *either* the French system of political equality *or* the British monarchy; *either* the individual states *or* the federal government; *either* the farm *or* the factory. Such thinking promoted a narrow view of the United States, a society of great economic and ethnic diversity.

Despite this ideological split, the new nation gave white men opportunities practically unknown in the rest of the world. Regardless of their background, many white men could aspire to own property and to participate in the political process. The federal government supported economic growth by facilitating territorial expansion, technological innovation, and the protection of private property. As much for the prosperity it promoted as for the noble ideas it nourished, the Revolution continued to inspire liberation movements within the United States and throughout the world.

For Review

1. What were the limitations of the "either-or" clash of ideas between the Federalists and the Democratic-Republicans? How might an enslaved Southerner, or a member of one of the Five Civilized tribes, have perceived this political debate?

2. Choose three different groups and describe the ways the legacy of the Revolution affected their postwar experiences. Consider, for example, these issues: legal status, religious beliefs, labor, community life, and culture.

3. How did relations with European countries shape political debates in the United States between 1789 and 1803? In what ways had the new nation not fully achieved its independence?

4. Many of the Founding Fathers were suspicious of political parties. What developments in the decade following the war would have confirmed or dispelled those suspicions?

5. In political terms, at least, the United States emerged from the Revolution as a unified nation. In what ways did regional distinctions challenge the notion—or ideal—of unity among all Americans?

Created Equal Online

For more *Created Equal* resources, including suggestions on sites to visit and books to read, go to **MyHistoryLab.com.**

Part Four

Expanding the Boundaries of Freedom and Slavery, 1804–1848

In the first half of the nineteenth century, few if any nations could rival the United States' remarkable record of growth. At its founding, the country consisted of 4 million people living in thirteen states that hugged the eastern seaboard of North America. By the mid-nineteenth century, the nation's population had grown to 23 million people as a result of natural reproduction, foreign immigration, and the conquest of indigenous and Spanish-speaking peoples. Because of a mix of diplomatic pressure and military aggression, dramatic geographic expansion accompanied the burgeoning population growth. By 1850, the country sprawled across the continent to the Pacific Ocean.

Territorial expansion, economic growth, and increasing ethnic diversity profoundly shaped American politics in the first half of the nineteenth century. Innovations in transportation (the steamboat and railroads), communication (the telegraph), and the production of crops and textiles (reapers and mechanical looms) allowed Americans to move materials, people, and information more quickly and to produce food and goods more efficiently. Meanwhile, the immigration of large numbers of western Europeans, the rapid expansion of the free black population, and the conquest of Spanish-speaking peoples in the Southwest in 1848 challenged the United States' view of itself as an exclusively Anglo-Protestant nation.

Some citizens declared that the United States had a God-given duty and God-given right to expand its borders in opposition to the British and Russians in the Northwest and in opposition to Spain and later Mexico in the South and Southwest. Thus, territorial expansion brought the United States into conflict with other countries and groups that claimed the land. America's victory in the War of 1812 secured the nation's Great Lakes border and at the same time proved that American soldiers and sailors were the equal of England's seasoned fighting forces. In 1823, fearful that European powers would take advantage of independence movements in Latin America, the United States issued the Monroe Doctrine, stating that the era of colonization of the Americas was over.

Nevertheless, Indian tribes continued to resist the incursion of European Americans who believed that land was a commodity to be wrested from native peoples and then bought and sold. In the southern part of the country, the Five Civilized Tribes and other American Indian groups occupied territory coveted by both gold seekers and cotton growers. Many American voters demanded that their political leaders expand the nation's boundaries through a variety of means: treaty, negotiation, or military force.

Andrew Jackson, who assumed the presidency in 1829, was a fitting symbol and a representative politician of the age. Determined to enlarge the power of the executive branch of government, Jackson claimed to represent the interests of ordinary people in his political battles against the Second Bank of the United States and the Supreme Court, and in his forceful removal of Indian tribes from the Southeast to Indian Territory (present-day Oklahoma). Like other politicians of the time, Jackson conceived of citizenship as a system of rights and privileges for white men only.

Still, European Americans trumpeted the arrival of a new era of egalitarianism. Western settlers laid claim to political power, and suffrage restrictions based on property ownership crumbled in the wake of egalitarian legislation and rhetoric. Americans were restless, moving out west and back east again, around the countryside, and in and out of cities. Believing that people could and should work together to reform society, many created reform associations, embraced new religious beliefs, and joined political parties. New forms of association yielded new kinds of communities in an era characterized by great geographic mobility.

At the same time, two distinct power systems coalesced to ensure that certain groups would monopolize the political and economic life of the country. In the South, cotton planters launched an aggressive defense of the institution of slavery. In the North, an emerging socioeconomic class system deepened the differences between the political influence and material well-being of factory owners and machine operators.

For the country, therefore, growth brought great promise and great peril. Abolitionists, associations of working people, nativists (people hostile to immigrants), women's rights advocates, and a variety of other groups proclaimed their agendas for social change. Most significantly, by 1848 it was becoming more difficult for national lawmakers to resolve the question of whether to allow slavery in the territories. As passions rose, few could imagine a political compromise that would satisfy abolitionists and proslavery advocates alike. As mid-century approached, more and more Americans seemed prepared to express their convictions—or their prejudices and resentment—through violent means.

Chapter 10

Defending and Expanding the New Nation, 1804–1818

Charles B. J. F. Saint Memin, *Captain Meriwether Lewis*, 1807. Collection of the New-York Historical Society (Neg. 1971.125)

■ Captain Meriwether Lewis posed in Indian dress for this watercolor completed in 1807 by French artist C. B. J. Févret de Saint-Mémin.

In early November 1804, a group of soldiers worked feverishly to construct a rough military garrison on the north bank of the Missouri River, near several Mandan Indian villages and just west of modern Washburn, North Dakota. The soldiers knew they had to work quickly. Within a month, winter would descend on the northern Great Plains, and the temperature would plummet. In fact, not long after Fort Mandan was completed, the temperature registered 45 degrees below zero Fahrenheit.

The garrison provided shelter for the members of the **Lewis and Clark Expedition**, a party of exploration led by Meriwether Lewis and William Clark. Both captains in the U.S. Army, Lewis and Clark had been commissioned by President Thomas Jefferson to explore the upper reaches of the newly acquired Louisiana Territory, which had doubled the size of the country. With the ultimate goal of reaching what is today Oregon, their party spent the winter at Fort Mandan and joined the buffalo hunts and nightly dances sponsored by their hosts, the Mandan Indians. Between November 1804 and March 1805, Lewis and Clark also found time to record their observations on all manner of things natural and cultural. In their journals and their letters to President Jefferson, they described the language of the Hidatsa Indians and the beadwork of the Arikara, the medicinal properties of native plants, and the contours of the Missouri River. In a shipment prepared for the president, they included deer horns, pumice stones, and the pelt of a white weasel. Among an assortment of live animals, only a magpie and a prairie dog survived the journey to Washington, D.C.

Lewis and Clark's trek took 28 months to complete and covered 8,000 miles. Along the way, the two men assured the Indians they met that their expedition's purpose was purely scientific. However, Jefferson had also commissioned them to chart a waterway passage to the Northwest. The president hoped to divert the profitable fur trade of the far Northwest away from British Canada and into the hands of Americans by locating a river connecting the Northwest directly to eastern U.S. markets. Jefferson also instructed Lewis and Clark to initiate negotiations with various Indian groups, to pave the way for miners and ranchers to move into the area.

Throughout their journey, Lewis and Clark expressed awe of the magnificence of the land—its physical beauty and its commercial potential. While camped at Fort Mandan, Lewis described the Missouri: "This immence river so far as we have yet ascended waters one of the fairest portions of the globe, nor do I believe that there is in the universe a similar extent of country, equally fertile, well watered, and intersected by such a number of navigable streams." When the expedition's official report was published in 1814, it caused a sensation. Americans swelled with pride at the bounteous expanse called the upper Louisiana.

Lewis and Clark's party consisted of a diverse group of people, including British and Irish enlisted men, and Lewis's African American slave, York. At Fort Mandan, the group picked up Toussaint Charbonneau, a French Canadian, and his fifteen-year-old wife, Sacajawea, a Shoshone Indian. The explorers came to rely on Sacajawea's skills as an interpreter. And because women never traveled with Plains Indian war parties, Sacajawea's presence reassured suspicious Native Americans that the goal of the expedition was peaceful. White men were fond of boasting that "they were great warriors, and a powerful people, who, if exasperated, could crush all the nations of the earth." Indians heard these threats frequently and so were not inclined to look kindly upon an expedition of white men.

Lewis and Clark failed in their mission to locate a commercial route across the Rocky Mountains; the terrain proved too rugged. However, by sponsoring this and other major exploration parties, the federal government signaled its intention to help European Americans move west. The expedition also revealed that control of western waterways would be crucial to America's attempt to explore the interior of the continent and to establish trading relations with the Indians. The exploitation of waterways and water power proved a key component in the new nation's economic growth and development. In sum, the Lewis and Clark expedition yielded information that furthered westward migration, commercial development, and scientific knowledge about the western landscape.

During the first two decades of the nineteenth century, the United States faced a number of challenges from within and outside its borders, challenges that had long-lasting political and economic effects. Indians in general were a persistent threat to the new nation. Indeed, in the

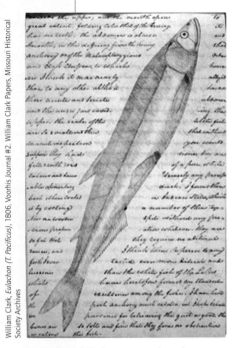

■ Lewis and Clark were not only explorers; they were also pioneering naturalists committed to gathering, recording, and studying plants and animal life in the West. William Clark drew this sketch of a eulachon, also called a candlefish, as part of his journal entry for February 25, 1806. Pacific Indians dried the oily fish and used it as a torch.

MAP

The Louusiana Purchase

Great Lakes region, various tribes maintained political and military alliances with the British in Canada. During this period, the United States faced its most severe test to date: a war with Great Britain that raged from 1812 to 1815. The war did not resolve all the disagreements between the two nations, and it revealed some unexpected vulnerabilities in the new nation's defenses. Yet overall, for the United States, the effects of this "Second American Revolution" were far reaching. The conflict eliminated the British from the Northwest once and for all. Its military heroes, including Andrew Jackson and William Henry Harrison, went on to illustrious political careers. The war also spurred industrialization and stimulated commerce. In the South, the cotton plantation system began to shape the political and economic life of the entire region.

Some Europeans who visited the United States during these years criticized Americans for their crudeness and their lack of accomplishment in literature, architecture, road building, and manners. Yet after the War of 1812, American patriotism soared. The country now stretched from New Orleans to the Canadian border—an enormous expanse blessed with rich natural resources. Its military leaders were the equal of, if not superior to, the finest European officers. However, some Americans began to see a threat to their sense of themselves as a unique people. That threat—the expansion of human bondage—would come not from the outside but from within their own borders.

British Aggression on Land and the High Seas

■ *What were the domestic and international consequences of Britain's persistent challenges to U.S. territorial sovereignty and trade relations with other nations?*

In the election of 1804, Democratic-Republican Thomas Jefferson and his vice-presidential running mate, George Clinton, a former governor of New York, easily bested their Federalist opponents, Charles C. Pinckney and Rufus King. Jefferson had gained widespread favor among the voters through the Louisiana Purchase, and his decision to repeal the federal excise tax on whiskey that had so angered farmers in the West secured his popularity. On the eve of his second term, he no doubt imagined himself examining the specimens and reading the reports that Lewis and Clark sent back from the West. Yet the ongoing squabbling between France and England and the increasing aggression of the British navy toward American sailors demanded his attention.

These developments overseas preoccupied Jefferson during his second term in office. England and France continued to challenge each other as the reigning powers of Europe. In 1805, the British navy, under the command of Lord Nelson, defeated the French and Spanish fleets in the Battle of Trafalgar off the coast of Spain. That same year, France reveled in its own triumph on land when Napoleon conquered the Austrian and Russian armies at the Battle of Austerlitz. Supreme on the seas, England in 1806 passed the Orders in Council, which specified that any country that wanted to ship goods to France must first send them to a British port and pay taxes on them. Many Americans believed that England's policies amounted to acts of military and economic aggression against the United States.

TABLE 10.1		
The Election of 1804		
Candidate	**Political Party**	**Electoral Vote**
Thomas Jefferson	Democratic-Republican	162
Charles C. Pinckney	Federalist	14

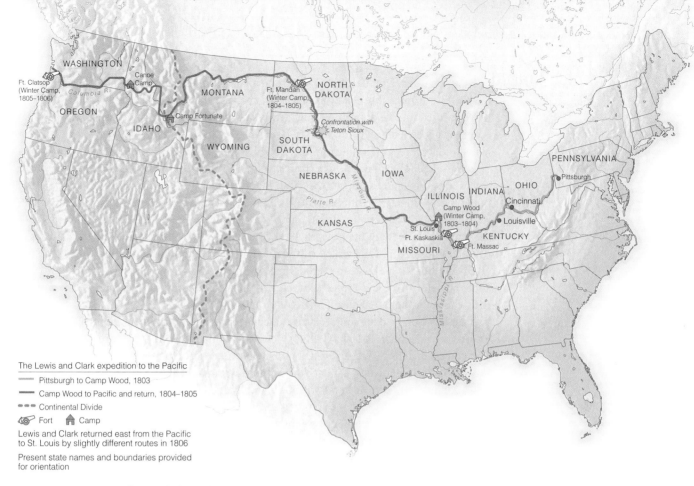

The Lewis and Clark expedition to the Pacific
— Pittsburgh to Camp Wood, 1803
— Camp Wood to Pacific and return, 1804–1805
••• Continental Divide
⚔ Fort 🏠 Camp

Lewis and Clark returned east from the Pacific to St. Louis by slightly different routes in 1806

Present state names and boundaries provided for orientation

■ **M A P 1 0 . 1** **Lewis and Clark Expedition, 1803–1806**

This map, showing the route of the Lewis and Clark Expedition, suggests the importance of interior waterways in facilitating travel and exploration in the West. Spain feared, rightly, that the Americans would use western rivers to establish trade links with the Indians and thereby challenge Spain's northern border with the United States.

Source: From Stephen Ambrose, *Undaunted Courage.*

THE EMBARGO OF 1807

Not content to control trade across the Atlantic as decreed by the 1806 Orders in Council, the British also seized sailors from American ships, claiming that these men were British seamen who had been lured away from their own vessels by American captains promising them higher wages. In some cases these claims were probably true. However, U.S. political leaders charged that an estimated 6,000 U.S. citizens had been seized by the British navy between 1808 and 1811, including an unknown number of African Americans, many of whom were working as mariners. Seafaring appealed to free men of color because it paid good wages; in the early nineteenth century, black mariners' pay equaled that of their white counterparts. In this line of work, a man's skill, not the color of his skin, determined the nature of his job. With limited economic opportunities on shore, black sailors accepted the danger and long absences from home. However, neither black nor white sailors had bargained for enforced service in His Majesty's Royal Navy.

Seizure, or impressment, reminded Americans of the period before the Revolution, when British "press gangs" prowled the docks of American port cities and seized colonial merchant sailors. In 1807, the tensions over impressment erupted into violence. Just ten miles off the shore of Virginia, the American ship *Chesapeake* came under attack from a British vessel. British naval officers claimed that the Americans were harboring four British deserters. In the ensuing exchange of cannon fire, three Americans were killed and eighteen wounded. Jefferson demanded that England leave American sailors and ships alone, but he was rebuffed.

President Jefferson decided to place an embargo on all exports to the European powers in an effort to force those nations to respect the rights of Americans on the high seas. The move aroused intense opposition in Federalist-dominated New England, where the regional economy depended heavily on foreign trade. The **Embargo Act of 1807** passed by Congress halted the shipment of goods from the United States to Europe. Because Europe—including England—relied heavily on American grain and timber, Jefferson hoped that the move would force England to respect American independence. The president saw this measure as preferable to either war with or capitulation to England, but the New England states, which were particularly hard hit by the embargo, saw the matter quite differently. As the effects of the embargo took hold, the New England grain growers saw the markets for their products dry up, and the timber industry suffered when local shipbuilding ground to a standstill. Southern tobacco and cotton planters faced similar hardship because of the embargo. By 1808, some of them had joined with Northerners to circumvent the embargo by moving their goods through Canada and then to Europe.

Yet Jefferson held his course. He prodded Congress to enforce the unpopular act, but his efforts provoked a backlash. Ordinary citizens compared him to George III, and New England politicians threatened to take their states out of the union. Despite all the uproar, the embargo did benefit Americans in some ways. Specifically, it encouraged New Englanders to rely more on goods produced locally and less on foreign imports. Jefferson had advocated a policy that had an unanticipated effect: it promoted industrialization at home. At the same time, the embargo seemed only to intensify, not lessen, tensions between England and the United States.

ON THE BRINK OF WAR

The Embargo of 1807 was one of many challenges American political leaders faced during the first decade of the nineteenth century. Both the Federalists and the Democratic-Republicans suffered a blow to their leadership in 1804. That year, the Federalist party lost Alexander Hamilton at the hand of his rival, Aaron Burr. Both successful New York attorneys, the two men had risen together through the political ranks in the 1780s and 1790s. Burr served as Jefferson's running mate in the election of 1800; four years later he ran for governor of New York. Incensed by a report that Hamilton had claimed he was "a dangerous man, and one who ought not to be trusted with the reins of government," as well as "still more despicable rumors," Burr challenged his antagonist to a pistol duel in Weehawken, New Jersey, in July 1804. (Many European American men, especially in the South, considered dueling a means to preserve their honor in response to a perceived insult leveled at them or at a family member.) Hamilton, mortally wounded in the affair, died the next day, and Burr's political career fell into ruins. In 1807 he stood trial for treason, charged with conspiring to create an empire for himself out of the territory Spain held west of the Mississippi. Acquitted of the charges, he nevertheless fled the United States for Europe.

Jefferson, declining to run for a third presidential term in 1808, left the stage as well soon after the inauguration of the new president, James Madison. Congress repealed Jefferson's embargo and replaced it with the Non-Intercourse Act, which eased the complete ban on exports to Europe. This measure permitted American exporters to ship their goods to all European countries except for France and England, still at war with one another. New Englanders opposed even this limited embargo.

Meanwhile, the Federalists' influence in Congress was waning. The partisan division within Congress—the Federalists, with their emphasis on a strong national government, against the localist Democratic-Republicans—gradually eased. That division had emerged in response to the ratification of the Constitution and debates over the direction of the new nation. By 1810, a new split had emerged—between young, hotheaded representatives from the West and their more conservative seniors from the eastern seaboard. The western group, or **war hawks,** called on the nation to revive its former glory, by force if necessary. Americans must uphold U.S. honor, they declared, by opposing European, especially British, claims to military dominance. The war hawks also yearned to vanquish the Indians who impeded settlement of the area west of the Mississippi.

TABLE 10.2		
The Election of 1808		
Candidate	**Political Party**	**Electoral Vote**
James Madison	Democratic-Republican	122
Charles C. Pinckney	Federalist	47
George Clinton	Democratic-Republican	6

Looking eastward, the war hawks saw an England determined to defile the honor of their young nation. In 1810, Congress passed legislation called Macon's Bill No. 2. Under its provisions, if either France or England agreed to resume trade with the United States, then the Americans would resume trade with that country and refuse to trade with the other. France's emperor Napoleon seized this offer to reestablish economic ties with the United States. Outraged, England began to contemplate war not only with its archenemy, France, but also with the upstart United States. The new nation had positioned itself directly in the middle of a conflict between the two major European powers.

Looking westward, the war hawks saw an equally threatening menace: the rise of an ominous Indian resistance movement that blended military strength with native spirituality. The movement was led by Shawnee brothers Tecumseh and Tenskwatawa. Tenskwatawa, also known as the Prophet, claimed that he had a vision in which he received a message from the world's creator. In the Prophet's words, the creator stated that European Americans "grew from the scum of the great water, when it was troubled by an evil spirit and the froth was driven into the woods by a strong east wind." The Prophet declared to other Indians, "They are numerous, but I hate them. They are unjust; they have taken away your lands, which were not made for them."

In 1808, the two brothers founded Prophet's Town in Indiana. They envisioned a sovereign Indian state and the preservation of Native American culture. Tenskwatawa spoke of a time and place where Indians would reject alcohol and scorn "the food of whites" as well as the "wealth and ornaments" of commercial trade. Tecumseh set out to deliver the message to as many Indian groups as possible, traveling the broad swath of territory from Florida to Canada.

In his journey south, Tecumseh found the Creek nation in Muskogee Territory particularly receptive to his message of Indian solidarity. By that time the Creek had lost millions of acres of land to the Americans. Tecumseh deputized a relative, Seekaboo, to remain with the Creek and instruct them in the religion of Tenskwatawa. He could not know that, within a few years, Tenskwatawa's message would spark armed conflict between the Creek and American troops.

Meanwhile, in 1809, the territorial governor of Indiana, William Henry Harrison, plied a group of Indian leaders with liquor, then got them to agree to sell 3 million acres to the U.S. government for just $7,600. Upon hearing of the deal, Tecumseh decried a new form of American aggression: "treaties" between U.S. officials and Indians who lacked the authority to sell their people's homeland. "All red men," Tecumseh proclaimed, must "unite in claiming a common and equal

The Library of Congress

■ This lithograph of the Prophet (Tenskwatawa) was based on an 1824 painting of the Shawnee mystic and holy man. Early in life, he suffered an accident with bows and arrows, losing his right eye. He and his older brother Tecumseh called on all Indians to resist the appropriation of their lands by whites and to renounce the way of life followed by whites, including the use of liquor. After the Indians' defeat at the Battle of Tippecanoe in 1811, the Prophet retreated to Canada. He returned to the United States in 1826. By that time he no longer wielded influence as a leader of the Shawnees.

The Public Domain in 1810

■ **MAP 10.2   The Public Domain in 1810**

This map indicates the expanse of western lands owned by the U.S. government in 1810, after the Louisiana Purchase. American war veterans received land warrants in return for military service in the Revolutionary War and the War of 1812. A warrant entitled the bearer to settle a specific number of acres of unoccupied land. Warrants could be transferred, sold, and traded like stocks and bonds. After the War of 1812, the government issued 29,186 land warrants for a total of 4.8 million acres.

Source: After Charles O. Paulin, *Atlas of Historical Geography,* Plate 57.

right in the land, as it was at first, and should be yet; for it never was divided, but belongs to all, for the use of each."

In November 1811, Harrison led 1,000 U.S. soldiers in an advance on Prophet's Town. But before they could reach the settlement, several hundred Shawnee under the command of Tenskwatawa attacked their camp on the Tippecanoe River. The Indians suffered a sound defeat, and Harrison burned Prophet's Town to the ground. A Potawatomi chief, Shabonee, who fought at the Battle of Tippecanoe, later recalled the false sense of superiority that had inspired the Indians' doomed attack on Harrison and his men. According to Shabonee, the Indians believed "the white soldiers are not warriors. Their hands are soft. Their faces are white. One half of them are calico [fabric] peddlers. The other half can only shoot squirrels." Warriors or not, the Americans had a distinct advantage over the Indians: better guns. Clearly, military technology, not just determination, would shape the western conflict. Yet in the ensuing war, the Americans faced not just Indian foes, but also one of the mightiest military forces in the world—the British army and navy.

The War of 1812

■ *What were the political and economic interests of the United States, the Indian tribes, and Great Britain and why did those divergent interests clash during the War of 1812?*

The defeat of the Shawnee at Tippecanoe only inflamed western war hawks' passions and stiffened their resolve to break the back of Indian resistance. But to achieve this goal, the United States would have to invade Canada and eliminate the British arms suppliers who had been trading with the Indians. Claiming the mantle of patriotism, western and southern members of the House of Representatives agitated for a war that would eliminate both the

British threat on the high seas and the Canada-based Indian–British alliance. These Americans wanted a war that would win for them a true independence once and for all. "On to Canada! On to Canada!" became the rallying cry of the war hawks.

In a secret message sent to Congress on June 1, 1812, President Madison listed Americans' many grievances against England: the British navy's seizure of American citizens, the blockades of American goods, and continued conflict "on one of our extensive frontiers," the result of "savages" who had the backing of British traders and military officials. Madison left it up to Congress whether the nation would continue to endure these indignities or would act "in defense of their natural rights." Seventeen days later, the House voted 79 to 49 and the Senate voted 19 to 13 to declare war on England and, by extension, the western Indians.

TABLE 10.3		
The Election of 1812		
Candidate	**Political Party**	**Electoral Vote**
James Madison	Democratic-Republican	128
De Witt Clinton	Federalist	89

Pennsylvania Gazette, "Indian Hostilities"

The **War of 1812** united Americans behind a banner of national expansion. But at the same time, it exposed dangerous divisions between regions of the country and between political viewpoints. Many New Englanders saw the conflict as a plot by Virginia Democratic-Republicans primarily to aid France in opposition to England and to add agrarian (that is, slave) states to the Union. In an ironic twist, the New England Federalists—usually staunch defenders of the national government—argued that states should control their own commerce and militias.

PUSHING NORTH

Although the Americans were better armed and organized than the western Indians, they were at a disadvantage when they took on the soldiers and sailors of the British Empire. The United States had not invested in the military and thus was ill-prepared for all-out war. The American navy consisted merely of a fleet of tiny gunboats constructed during the cost-conscious Jefferson administration. The charter for the Bank of the United States had expired in 1811, depriving the country of a vital source of financial credit. Suffering from a drop in tax revenues as a result of the embargo on foreign trade, the nation lacked the funds to train and equip the regular army and the state militias. Nevertheless, in the fall of 1812, the Americans launched an ambitious three-pronged attack against Canada, striking from Niagara, Detroit, and Lake Champlain. All three attempts failed miserably.

Lacking united, enthusiastic support on the home front, the U.S. offensive got off to a bad start. Yet some people, even in Federalist New England, believed that all Americans should support the war, regardless of the potential outcome. Writing from a Federalist stronghold in December 1812, Abigail Adams (the wife of former president John Adams) acknowledged to a correspondent that her home state of Massachusetts "had much to complain of" because the war had severely disrupted trade. However, she added, "that cannot justify [Massachusetts] in paralyzing the arm of Government [that is, opposing federal trade policies], when raised for her defense and that of the nation." She warned against "a house divided against itself," which she believed could be the nation's undoing.

In the West, the British moved to take advantage of divisions between Indians and Americans. In late 1812, Tecumseh (who had accepted a commission as a brigadier general in the British army) and British General Isaac Brock captured Detroit. Indians also participated in England's successful raid on Fort Dearborn (Chicago). In at least two cases, when U.S. soldiers marched into Canada, they lost their advantage when state militia members refused to cross the border. Leaders of these militias claimed that their sole purpose was to defend their states from attack, not invade foreign territory.

■ **MAP 10.3   The Northern Front, War of 1812**
Much of the fighting of the War of 1812 centered in the Great Lakes region. It was there, the war hawks charged, that the British were inciting Indians to attack American settlements. Conducted in 1812 and 1813, the campaign against Canada was supposed to eliminate the British threat and, some Americans hoped, win Canadian territory for the United States.

Yet the Americans scored some notable successes in 1813. That September, Commodore Oliver H. Perry defeated a British fleet at Put-in-Bay on Lake Erie. Exhilarated, he famously declared, "We have met the enemy and they are ours." But Perry's victory came at a steep price. Shortly before the engagement, about a third of all the officers and men in the American fleet had fallen victim to a typhus epidemic. And then at the end of the day's battle, of the 100 men who had reported for duty that morning, 21 were dead and more than 60 wounded.

Perry's hard-won victory forced the British back into Canada, over Tecumseh's objections. General William Henry Harrison followed in hot pursuit. British Colonel Henry Proctor marched his troops to eastern Ontario, leaving Tecumseh to try holding the Americans at bay. At the Battle of the Thames (that October), Harrison defeated the Indians. Many perished, Tecumseh among them. A group of Kentucky soldiers skinned what they mistakenly believed to be his corpse. His body was never found.

Later that autumn, an American campaign against Montreal failed. The Americans trudged back into New York State, the British close behind them. Flush with their victory in Montreal, the British captured Fort Niagara and set Buffalo and other nearby towns aflame.

By mid-1814, the English and their allies had also crushed Napoleon in Europe. This success freed up 15,000 British troops, who promptly sailed for North America. Still, in July 1814 the Americans, under the leadership of Major General Jacob Brown and Brigadier General Winfield Scott, managed to defeat the British at the Battle of Chippewa, across the Niagara River from Buffalo. But by the end of that year, the Americans had withdrawn to their own territory and relinquished their goal of invading and conquering Canada. The arrival of fresh British troops forced the Americans to defend their own soil.

FIGHTING ON MANY FRONTS

For the United States, the most humiliating episode of the war came with the British attack on the nation's capital. On August 24, 1814, the British army, backed by the Royal Navy, sailed into Chesapeake Bay. At the Battle of Bladensburg, Maryland, they scattered the American troops they encountered. The Redcoats then advanced to Washington, where they torched the Capitol building and the White House, causing extensive damage to both structures.

Residents of the capital city had received word that the British were advancing. On Sunday, August 21, public officials frantically packed up their books and papers. Private citizens gathered up their furniture and other belongings and left town. By Tuesday, the city stood nearly empty. As a ragtag American force succumbed to the British, President Madison "retired from the mortifying scene, and left the city on horseback." His aides and some military officers accompanied him. As it turned out, he escaped just in the nick of time: by Wednesday

The Library of Congress

■ The U.S. Capitol lies blackened and in ruins after British forces burned it in August 1814.

flames had engulfed not only the Capitol but also Madison's residence. Disorganized, hungry, and hot, the American troops had put up scant resistance. An eyewitness reported, "Our army may with truth be said to have been beaten by fatigue, before they saw the enemy."

DOCUMENT

Dolley Payne Madison to Lucy Payne Todd (1814)

Yet the Americans rallied, pursued the British, and bested them at the Battle of Baltimore. This victory inspired an observer, Francis Scott Key, to write "The Star Spangled Banner" as he watched "the bombs bursting in air" over Baltimore's Fort McHenry. The Americans scored another crucial victory in September, when U.S. naval commander Thomas McDonough crushed the British fleet on Lake Champlain near Plattsburgh, New York.

In the Southeast, Tecumseh's message of Indian unity had resonated with particular force among Native Americans once the war broke out. Some Cherokee and Choctaw cast their lot with the United States. A minority among the Creek was emboldened by Tenskwatawa's message, "War now. War forever. War upon the living. War upon the dead; dig up their corpses from the grave; our country must give no rest to a white man's bones." By 1813, a group of warriors called Red Sticks (for their scarlet-painted weapons) stood ready to do battle with U.S. forces. Yet they faced opposition from some of their own people, the White Sticks, who counseled peace. The Red Sticks finally decided to attack Fort Mims, north of Mobile.

In response, Andrew Jackson, leader of the Tennessee militia, received a commission as major general. His mission was to retaliate against the Indians. Jackson speculated in Indian lands in Mississippi Territory, and he called Native Americans "blood thirsty barbarians." Even in a country where anti-Indian sentiment ran high, his views were extreme. After the attack on Fort Mims, he vowed, "I must destroy those deluded victims doomed to destruction by their own restless and savage conduct." He often boasted about collecting the scalps of all his Indian victims, and he relished his new assignment.

Jackson's 3,500 troops laid waste to Creek territory. Regiments of Cherokee, Choctaw, and Chickasaw Indians, as well as White Sticks, helped the U.S. forces. During a monumental battle in March 1814, more than three-quarters of the 1,000 defending Red Sticks and a number of Indian women and children died at Horseshoe Bend (in modern-day Alabama). Jackson survived the battle thanks to the intervention of a Cherokee soldier. Some U.S. soldiers took their victory to a brutal extreme; they flayed the corpses of their victims and made horse bridles out of their skin.

The Library of Congress

■ This engraving, published in 1814, depicts the bombardment of Fort McHenry by British warships in September of that year. When he witnessed the battle, Francis Scott Key, a Washington lawyer, was aboard a prisoner exchange boat in Baltimore Harbor. He was seeking release of a friend captured by the British. After penning the poem "The Star Spangled Banner," Key set the words to music, using the tune of a popular English drinking song. Congress declared the song the national anthem in 1931.

Yet Jackson insisted on praising his soldiers as a civilizing force. They were only reclaiming the land from a band of savages, he maintained. In a post-battle speech to the men under his command, he declared, "In their places a new generation [of Indians] will arise who know their duties better. The weapons of warfare will be exchanged for the utensils of husbandry; and the wilderness which now withers in sterility . . . will blossom as the rose, and become the nursery of the arts."

In the Treaty of Horseshoe Bend that followed the massacre, the Americans forced the Creek Nation to give up 23 million acres. The remnants of the Red Sticks fled to the swamps of Florida, where they joined additional Creek, other Florida Indians, and numerous fugitive slaves in an emerging group known as the Seminoles (from the Spanish *cimarrones,* or runaway slaves).

Jackson next marched to New Orleans to confront the British. Knowing he would be facing some of Europe's finest soldiers, he assembled 7,000 men, U.S. soldiers and militia from the states of Louisiana, Kentucky, and Tennessee. Two Kentucky regiments consisted of free black volunteers, about 400 men in total. The Battle of New Orleans, fought on January 8, 1815, began with a ferocious assault by British soldiers. But within just half an hour, 2,000 of them lay dead or wounded. The Americans lost only 70. Jackson's backcountry shooters had vanquished the army of Europe's greatest military power.

Later, many Americans associated Andrew Jackson with the war's decisive battle and most glorious victory. But in fact, American and British negotiators had signed a peace agreement that ended the war two weeks before "Old Hickory" defeated the British in New Orleans. (Jackson received his nickname when one of his soldiers called him "tough as hickory.") The Battle of New Orleans might have been a glorious victory for the United States, but it was hardly the decisive battle of the war.

A Government Agent Greets a Group of Creek Indians

Benjamin Hawkins and the Creek Indians, c. 1805. Greenville County Museum of Art, South Carolina

Southeastern Indians varied widely in their willingness to adopt European American ways. Some Indians argued that the best way to preserve their community and remain on the land of their forebears was to accommodate themselves to white practices of trade and farming and to embrace European dress styles and Christian religious beliefs. Together the Creek, Cherokee, Chickasaw, Choctaw, and Seminole were called the Five Civilized Tribes as a result of their decision to give up hunting in favor of sedentary agriculture. This painting, completed by an unknown artist in 1805, shows a government Indian agent named Benjamin Hawkins meeting with a group of Creek Indians near Macon, Georgia. Hawkins expresses evident satisfaction with the Indians' neat cabins, well-tended fields, flocks of sheep, and bountiful harvest of vegetables.

QUESTIONS

1. In what ways have the Creek pictured here adopted European American ways? (Hint: The Indian men in the foreground are holding the handles of a plow.) In what ways have they retained elements of their traditional culture?

2. What is the significance of various means of conveyance pictured here—the carts and ships?

3. How does the artist seek to represent the role of Hawkins?

4. What elements in the painting suggest that this is a prosperous Creek settlement?

AN UNCERTAIN VICTORY

Before the Battle of New Orleans, in the fall of 1814, President Madison had decided to end the war. He dispatched John Quincy Adams, son of former president John Adams, to the Belgian city of Ghent to start negotiations. Representative Henry Clay and three other American envoys accompanied Adams. At first, British representatives to the meeting made two demands. The Americans, they said, must agree to the creation of an Indian territory in the upper Great Lakes region. They must also cede much of the state of Maine to England. The Americans refused, and the negotiations dragged on.

In the meantime, the New England states had grown increasingly impatient with what they called "Mr. Madison's war." As with the embargo, they saw the effort as a mistake and a threat to their regional commercial interests. In December 1814, Massachusetts, Connecticut, Rhode Island, New Hampshire, and Vermont sent delegates to a gathering in Hartford, Connecticut, to consider a course of action. The delegates demanded that the federal government give their states financial aid to compensate for the revenue they had lost as a result of disrupted trade. Some delegates even hinted that their states wanted to secede from the union. Although most delegates shied away from immediate action, the majority of them apparently wanted to leave open the possibility of secession.

> *American nationalism came at the expense of vast Indian homelands and thousands of lives on both sides.*

Back in Ghent, the British had reversed their initial position by late December. They had lost recent battles in upper New York and in Baltimore and, as always, were still worried about new threats from France. They dropped their demands for territory and for an Indian buffer state in the upper Midwest. They also agreed to an armistice that, in essence, represented a draw: both combatants would retain the same territory they had possessed when the war began. The British made no concessions to the Americans' demands that they stop impressing American sailors and supplying the western Indians with arms or that they revoke the Orders in Council. Still, most U.S. citizens considered the war a great victory for the United States. After Congress ratified the **Treaty of Ghent,** which ended hostilities between the two nations in 1815, the Americans and the British never again met each other across a battlefield as enemies.

DOCUMENT

The Treaty of Ghent (1814)

But some of the American soldiers and sailors who had survived the conflict paid a high price. For example, Benjamin F. Palmer was an American sailor imprisoned in an English jail from 1813 to 1815. There he subsisted on meager rations and witnessed unspeakable cruelties, including the murder of inmates by guards. In all probability, the Treaty of Ghent did not change Palmer's views of the British soldiers' "Brutal & Savage Barbarity." In total, 6,000 American combatants died or suffered wounds in the war. Yet survivors felt that they and their dead fellows had preserved the nation's honor.

Many Indians saw matters quite differently. For them, the War of 1812 had only stiffened white settlers' determination to take native peoples' land. Andrew Jackson would aggressively pursue a national political career. And so the Battle of Horseshoe Bend signaled not only a continuation of bloodshed but also a terrifying sign of things to come. American nationalism came at the expense of vast Indian homelands and thousands of lives on both sides. At the same time, in Washington, the end of the war softened partisan tensions, and lawmakers joined in celebrating the successful defense and the growing prosperity of the young nation.

The Era of "Good Feelings"?

■ *Did political and social realities justify the use of the term "the Era of 'Good Feelings'" to describe the period after the War of 1812?*

In 1816, the Democratic-Republicans nominated James Monroe for president, to run against Federalist candidate Rufus King. Although Monroe only narrowly won his party's endorsement, he soundly defeated King in the general election. Monroe benefited from several developments that had mortally wounded the Federalist party: the War of 1812 victory, presided over by a Democratic-Republican chief executive; the New England Federalists' flirtation with secession (and treason) during the war years; and the strong nationalist tendencies of both the Jefferson and Madison administrations, which had stolen the Federalists' thunder.

Addressing Congress in December 1817, Monroe expressed optimism about the state of the nation. The country's boundaries were secure, and the Indians had little choice but to retreat farther and farther west. The president predicted that, shortly, "Indian hostilities, if they do not altogether cease, will henceforth lose their terror." Equally inspiring, the Americans had once again defied the British

TABLE 10.4		
The Election of 1816		
Candidate	Political Party	Electoral Vote
James Monroe	Democratic-Republican	183
Rufus King	Federalist	34

Empire and won. Two treaties with Britain—the Rush-Bagot of 1817 and the Convention of 1818—set the U.S.-Canadian border at the 49th parallel and provided that the two countries would jointly occupy the Oregon Territory for ten years.

Monroe called on Congress to acknowledge "the vast extent of territory within the United States [and] the great amount and value of its productions" and to expand the construction of roads and canals. (In 1806, Congress had funded construction of a National Road.) It was this "happy situation of the United States," in Monroe's words, that ushered in what some historians call the **Era of Good Feelings,** a period relatively free of partisan political strife. By this time the Federalist party had dissolved, and Monroe faced no real party-based opposition to his administration. Voters continued to disagree over some issues of the day, such as the national bank and internal improvements. Some Northerners believed that slavery was wrong, a conviction that would soon give rise to **sectionalism** (intense political conflict between the North and South). Still, most Americans did not necessarily express their disagreements with each other in the form of bitter partisan wrangling. At the same time, the term "good feelings" may fully apply only to a narrow group of enfranchised citizens, men who shared common beliefs about territorial expansion and economic development.

The War of 1812 yielded little in the way of material gains for the United States or concessions from England. Yet it permanently reshaped American social, political, and economic life. The nation exploited the vulnerable southeastern Indians and hastened their removal from their homeland. Many veterans of the war gained land grants, military glory, and political influence in return for their sacrifices. Although the war had disrupted foreign trade, it also gave home manufacturers a tremendous boost. The textile industry spearheaded a revolution in industry. And a new class of workers—factory operatives (machine tenders)—emerged to symbolize both the promise and the hazards of machines.

PRAISE AND RESPECT FOR VETERANS AFTER THE WAR

American veterans of the War of 1812 won the praise of a grateful nation. Even the British expressed a grudging respect for Americans' fighting abilities. One British naval officer

Gilbert Stuart, *George Washington.* White House Historical Collection (White House Collection, Courtesy), (21)

■ Dolley Madison, wife of President James Madison, helped rescue this famous painting of George Washington by artist Gilbert Stuart when the British invaded Washington in August 1814. The full-length portrait hung in what was then called the President's House. She later wrote a friend that the British attack had rendered her "so unfeminine as to be free from fear." She had hoped to remain in the mansion "if I could have had a cannon through every window, but alas! Those who should have placed them there, fled."

Cherokee Women Petition against Further Land Sales to Whites in 1817

Interpreting History

*I*n traditional Cherokee society, men took responsibility for foreign affairs while women focused on domestic matters, leading to a roughly equal division of labor. However, European American diplomats, military officials, and traders dealt primarily with Indian men. As a result, beginning in the eighteenth century, Cherokee women's traditional influence was eroding within their own communities. In this new world, Indian warriors wielded significant power.

Nevertheless, Cherokee women insisted on presenting their views during the crisis of 1817–1819, when men of the group were deciding whether to cede land to U.S. authorities and move west. The following petition was supported by Nancy Ward, a Cherokee War Woman. This honorific title was bestowed on women who accompanied and attended to the needs of war parties. Ward had supported the colonists' cause during the American Revolution.

Peter Turnley/CORBIS

■ In 1987, Wilma Mankiller became the first woman to be elected principal chief of the Cherokee Nation of Oklahoma.

Amovey [Tennessee] in Council 2nd May 1817

The Cherokee Ladys now being present at the meeting of the Chiefs and warriors in council have thought it their duties as mothers to address their beloved Chiefs and warriors now assembled.

Our beloved children and head men of the Cherokee nation we address you warriors in council we have raised all of you on the land which we now have, which God gave to us to inhabit and raise provisions we know that our country has once been extensive but by repeated sales has become circumscribed to a small tract, and [we] never have thought it our duty to interfere in the disposition of it till now, if a father or mother was to sell all their lands which they had to depend on which their children had to raise their living on which would indeed be bad and to be removed to another country we do not wish to go to an unknown country [to] which we have understood some of our children wish to go over the Mississippi but this act of our children would be like destroying your

asserted, "I don't like Americans; I never did, and never shall." He had "no wish to eat with them, drink with them, or consort with them in any way." But, he added, he would rather not fight with "an enemy so brave, determined, and alert, and in every way so worthy of one's steel, as they have always proved." To reward U.S. veterans for their service, Congress offered them 160-acre plots of land in the territory between the Illinois and Mississippi Rivers. These grants did much to encourage families to emigrate west and establish homesteads.

Some military heroes of the war parlayed their success into impressive political careers. Andrew Jackson won election to the presidency in 1828 and 1832; William Henry Harrison was elected president in 1840. Countless others earned recognition within their own communities, and European American veterans were not the only ones to gain status and influence as a result of the conflict. For example, a Cherokee leader named the Ridge also earned the gratitude of American officials for his contributions to the war effort. He had accepted the government's attempts to press the Cherokee to adopt European American ways, settling in a log cabin (in northwest Georgia) rather than in a traditional Cherokee dwelling when he married a Cherokee woman named Susanna Wickett in the early 1790s. During the war against the Red Sticks, the Ridge served under Andrew Jackson and earned the title of major. For the rest of his life, the Cherokee leader was known as Major Ridge. His wife devoted herself to tending an orchard, keeping a garden, and sewing clothes, tasks traditionally performed by European American but not Native American women. Eventually, the family prospered and, like some other Cherokee, bought African American slaves. The Ridge family became Christians as well.

mothers. Your mothers your sisters ask and beg of you not to part with any more of our lands, we say ours. [Y]ou are our descendants and take pity on our request, but keep it for our growing children for it was the good will of our creator to place us here and you know our father the great president [James Monroe], will not allow his white children to take our country away for if it was not they would not ask you to put your hands to paper for it would be impossible to remove us all for as soon as one child is raised, we have others in our arms for such is our situation and will consider our circumstance.

Therefore children don't part with any more of our lands but continue on it and enlarge your farms and cultivate and raise corn and cotton and we your mothers and sisters will make clothing for you which our father the president has recommended to us all we don't charge anybody for selling our lands, but we have heard such intentions of our children but your talks become true at last and it was our desire to forewarn you all not to part with our lands.

Nancy Ward to her children[:] Warriors to take pity and listen to the talks of your sisters, although I am very old yet cannot but pity the situation in which you will hear of their minds. I have great many grand children which I wish they to do well on our land.

In addition to Nancy Ward, twelve Cherokee women signed the petition. Their names suggest the varying degrees of assimilation to white ways on the part of Cherokees in general. Petitioners included Cun, o, ah and Widow Woman Holder, as well as Jenny McIntosh and Mrs. Nancy Fields.

It is unclear what effect, if any, this petition had on Cherokee male leaders. The Cherokee nation did halt land cessions to whites between 1819 and 1835.

QUESTIONS

1. *How and why did motherhood confer authority on Cherokee women?*

2. *What is the significance and meaning of the land in Cherokee culture?*

3. *Does this petition provide evidence for the view that early nineteenth-century Cherokee men and women were adopting elements of European American culture? If so, what elements, and in what ways?*

Source: Cherokee Women to Cherokee Council, May 2, 1817, series 1, Andrew Jackson Presidential Papers, Library of Congress Manuscripts Division, Washington, D.C. Reprinted in Nancy F. Cott, Jeanne Boydston, Ann Braude, Lori Ginzberg, and Molly Ladd-Taylor, eds., *Root of Bitterness: Documents of the Social History of American Women* (Boston: Northeastern University Press, 1996), 177–178.

The Ridge's battlefield experiences earned him the respect of other Cherokee who embraced the "civilization" program that missionaries and government officials promoted. At the same time, the Ridge vehemently resisted U.S. officials' attempts to persuade the Cherokee to give up their lands to whites and move west. Emerging as a leader of the Cherokee nation after the War of 1812, he criticized members of his group who had abandoned their lands in favor of a new life in the West. He declared, "I scorn this movement of a few men to unsettle the nation, and trifle with our attachment to the land of our forefathers." The Ridge believed that his people should adopt some elements of white culture but should also hold fast to their native lands in opposition to white settlers and politicians.

A THRIVING ECONOMY

The War of 1812, along with the Embargo of 1807, stimulated home manufactures—especially the production of cloth and other goods in private households and factories. Home manufacturing resulted in a significant shift in the national economy—from reliance on imported goods to the production of those goods at home. The experiences of one rural Massachusetts family demonstrate the impact this shift had on individuals. Before the war, Lucy Kellogg and her sister worked at home, braiding straw hats to be sold at market. The war ruined their straw business, since economic hardship among New Englanders meant fewer people could afford to buy hats. In response, the sisters invested in cotton looms, which they used to make cloth. They secured cotton thread from the Massachusetts factories that had

Courtesy, American Antiquarian Society

■ This cartoon, c. 1810, reveals two sides to the western emigration question. On the right, a well-dressed Easterner sets out for Ohio. He encounters a dejected, ragged migrant returning home. The men's horses tell a larger story about the failed dreams and hardship endured by many western emigrants. In the caption the artist cautions travelers on "the impropriety and folly of emigrating" from New England to the "Western Wilderness."

sprung up during the war to compensate for the lack of English textile imports. The Kellogg sisters found a ready market for their shirts, gingham dresses, and bed tickings—products that were, in Kellogg's words, "good enough in time of war." Still, their family was restless, moving briefly to New Hampshire but then returning to Worcester, where they resumed farming.

The end of the war saw an upsurge in this kind of internal migration. New Englanders, especially, pushed west in search of new opportunities. Between 1800 and 1820, the population of Ohio grew from 45,000 to 581,000. New means of transportation—and new means to fund them—facilitated the movement of goods, people, and ideas from the East to the West (and, in some cases, back again). Indeed, traveling by stagecoach, wagon, boat, and horseback, Americans seemed to be on the move constantly. In 1807, an entrepreneur named Robert Fulton piloted the *Clermont*, his new kind of boat powered by steam, up the Hudson River from New York City. Steamboats traveled upriver, against the current, ten times faster than keelboats, which had to be pushed, pulled, or hauled by men or mules. Within a few years, such vessels were plying the Mississippi River and its major tributaries.

Improvements in land transportation also stimulated economic growth. The profits that the Philadelphia and Lancaster Turnpike earned by charging travelers tolls inspired other local private corporations to invest in roads. By 1810, several thousand such corporations were building roads up and down the East Coast. Funding came from a variety of sources, both public and private. Philadelphia textile mill owners financed transportation links with the city's hinterland (rural areas to the west) to carry their goods to the largest number of customers. Individual cities also invested in routes westward. The state of Virginia authorized a board of public works to expend funds for roads and other internal improvements. Western politicians flexed their political muscle in 1806 by securing congressional authorization for the building of the Cumberland (later National) Road, which snaked through the Allegheny Mountains and ended at the Ohio River.

The acceleration of commerce in the West, combined with the disruption in trade from Europe that had come with the embargo and war, stimulated manufacturing throughout the United States. Philadelphia's growth proved particularly dazzling. During the War of 1812, the city's craft producers did not have to worry about foreign competition. Local merchant-financiers, who otherwise might have been pouring their money into trade ventures, began to invest in manufacturing. As early as 1808, the city's new factories had compensated for the glass, chemicals, shot, soap, lead, and earthenware that no longer flooded in from England. Philadelphia soon took the lead in production of all kinds, whether carried out in factories, artisans' shops, or private homes. Metalworking, ale brewing, and leather production counted among the array of thriving industries that made Philadelphia the nation's top industrial city in 1815. Still, in 1820, about two-thirds of all Philadelphia workers labored in small shops employing fewer than six people.

TRANSFORMATIONS IN THE WORKPLACE

Even the earliest stages of the Industrial Revolution transformed the way people lived and worked. Some crafts—for example, the production of leather, barrels, soap, candles, and newspapers—expanded from small shops with skilled artisans into larger establishments with unskilled wage earners. In these cases, production was reorganized; now wage earners under the supervision of a boss replaced apprentices and journeymen who had formerly worked alongside a master artisan. These workers performed a single task many times a day instead of using their specialized skills to see a production process through to completion.

While skilled artisans were alarmed at the prospect of being reduced to mere "hands" tending machines, the sons and daughters of many New England farmers eagerly took new jobs in the mills. They appreciated the opportunity to escape close family supervision, to live on their own, and to earn cash wages. Some farm hands and manual laborers considered factory work, no matter how grueling and ill-paid, preferable to plowing fields, digging ditches, and hauling lumber. Chauncey Jerome, a young Connecticut man, lamented that few opportunities were open to him in rural areas: "There being no manufacturing of any account in the country, the poor boys were obliged to let [hire] themselves to the farmers, and it was extremely difficult to find a place where they would treat a poor boy like a human being."

New England rapidly became the center of mechanized textile production in the United States. By the late eighteenth century, Boston shippers were making handsome profits by supplying Alta California (the area from San Diego to present-day San Francisco). These merchants sent New-England-made goods such as cloth, shoes, and tools out west; they then sold Western otter pelts in China, and returned home laden with Chinese porcelains and silks. These profits helped finance New England's mechanized textile industry. By 1813, 76 cotton mills housing a total of over 51,000 spindles were operating within the vicinity of Providence, Rhode Island.

The Granger Collection, New York

■ This engraving, c. 1819, shows women working in an early textile mill. Women and children composed the work force of many early mills. This picture suggests the size of the intricate machinery, which dwarfs the women. For generations women had produced textiles at home, spinning thread and weaving cloth. For all factory operatives, these dark, cavernous places were new kinds of worksites—a striking contrast to the homes, shops, and fields where New Englanders traditionally had worked.

Courtesy, American Antiquarian Society

■ In the early nineteenth century, many skilled artisans worried that economic growth and development would erode their independence. They sought to portray themselves as upright and virtuous citizens and, by extension, superior to poor people who lacked either self-discipline or steady employment. These engravings feature sayings from Benjamin Franklin published in *Poor Richard Illustrated: Lessons for the Young and Old on Industry, Temperance, Frugality & c.*

Faced with a shortage of adult men (many were moving west), New England mill owners sought other local sources of labor. The Rhode Island system of production had relied on child spinners working in small mills. This system gave way to the Lowell model, based in Waltham and Lowell, Massachusetts, which brought young women from the surrounding countryside to work in gigantic mills. Many of the women were eager to earn cash wages and to escape the routine of farm life. Still, New England mill owners realized that they had to reassure Yankee parents that their daughters would find the factories safe, attractive places to work. Mill owners offered the young women housing in dormitory-like boardinghouses staffed by older women, called matrons, who looked after them.

These transformations in the workplace and in social relations disturbed some white male laborers in particular. They feared for their own status as freeborn, proud sons (and grandsons) of the Revolution. To them, the factory represented a loss of independence. In 1806, striking Philadelphia shoemakers charged, "The name of freedom is but a shadow." The court ruled that by joining together to withhold their labor from their employer, these workers were guilty of conspiring to raise their own wages. Some white laborers claimed that they were no longer in charge of their own work lives but instead were condemned to long hours and low pay.

Black men and women continued to suffer the stigma of slavery. Nearly all blacks in the United States were slaves or their descendants. This stigma determined the jobs for which blacks were hired and the pay they received. The 7,500 free blacks who lived in New York City in 1810 were only about 8 percent of the city's total population. But they made up fully 84 percent of all black people in the city (the rest were enslaved children who would not gain their freedom until they became adults). They struggled to earn a living, and they had limited employment options.

One job that was open to them was the dangerous, dirty work of cleaning chimneys. Black men served as master chimney sweeps and employed youths of their own race as assistants and apprentices. In an attempt to control the sweeps, the New York City Council tried to insist that they purchase expensive licenses to ply their trade. In response, a group of master chimney sweeps decried a double standard. Resenting what they considered unreasonably high licensing fees, they declared that they wanted to be treated "in the same manner as you have thought proper to do in respect to Cartmen, porter, measurer &c." To protect themselves, they established their own mutual aid society, the United Society of Chimney Sweeps. Some members asserted their equality with white men of the city by noting that they too had "served in the revolutionary war & some of them received wounds."

Industrialization was not confined to the Northeast; the southern states encouraged the development of textile mills as well. Yet in the South, industrialization had different social consequences. Many owners of southern industrial establishments sought to piece together their labor forces on the basis of the availability of different kinds of labor: enslaved and free, black and white, male and female, young and old. Thus, ironworks, gold and coal mines, brickworks, hemp factories, salt processing plants, and lumber, railroad, and canal camps often employed white men together with blacks, enslaved and free. In southern cities, white artisans concerned about losing their livelihood protested the use of skilled slave labor. But their complaints fell on deaf ears. Most members of city councils and regulatory boards owned slaves and had no intention of giving up their enslaved workers so that white artisans could find jobs.

Southern industry always reflected developments in the plantation economy. For example, when cotton prices rose, slave owners kept their slaves working in the fields. Thus, planters discouraged any kind of large-scale manufacturing that might disrupt the agrarian society they had built so carefully over so many years.

THE MARKET REVOLUTION

As new means of transportation facilitated the movement of ideas, goods, and people, natural barriers separating farms from towns and the West from the East began to crumble. Factory workers quickly and efficiently processed raw materials—leather into shoes, cotton into clothing. Wage earning replaced family labor and indentured servitude as the dominant labor system in the North. Together, all of these rapid economic transformations in the early nineteenth century fueled what some scholars have called the **market revolution.** Driven by improvements in transportation, increasing commercialization, and the rise of factories, powerful economic changes affected ordinary Americans and their everyday routines at home and on the job.

Historians disagree about whether these changes began to appear before the American Revolution or afterward, and whether these changes touched every segment of the population or only people living in or near cities. However, it is clear that, by the mid-nineteenth century, the United States had become a fundamentally different place compared to the colonies on the brink of revolt in 1776. Many people began to make a living and think about the world in ways we now consider "modern."

The gradual changes of the market revolution were driven by investment. Wealthy New England merchants led the way, but a wide variety of private individuals and public institutions were willing to invest their money and energy in new economic opportunities. Profits from foreign trade helped to build the textile factories that dotted the northeastern landscape. States and even towns used the money of taxpayers and private investors to build turnpikes and later to finance canals and railroads. Entrepreneurs pioneered the puttingout system, a form of production (of hats and other forms of clothing, for example) that enlisted the efforts of single women in the cities, as well as farm families during the winter season. These workers received raw materials from a merchant-capitalist and engaged in piecework in return for wages. Combined public–private investment in new forms of business organization and technology spurred American economic growth.

These changes spilled over into American social and religious life, encouraging some people to adopt an optimistic worldview about the possibilities inherent in American life—possibilities that included moving from one place to another, making money by selling new products, altering the natural landscape to make way for canals or factories, and aspiring to buy goods rather than produce goods at home. Foreign visitors often commented on the "restlessness" of Americans, their "acquisitiveness," and their impatience with tradition.

Not all Americans adopted this new way of looking at the world, but almost all groups felt its effects. Slave owners pushed black men, women, and children to work even harder in the fields of the South so that more cotton and rice could be exported to northern and European markets. Western Indians suffered the effects of European American conquest, as whites chopped down forests and cleared the land for farms, violently displacing native populations in the process. In New England textile mills, women and children operated the

D.B. Pawtucket Bridge and Falls, Pawtucket, RI, 1812. Watercolor and ink on paper. Painting. Museum Collection. Rhode Island Historical Society, RHx522

■ Early mills had four possible sources of energy—hands, animals, wind, and water. This water-powered paper mill on Brandywine Creek in northern Delaware, c. 1830, suggests the importance of waterfalls to the early Industrial Revolution. Other mills on the Brandywine manufactured cotton and woolen cloth and produced gunpowder.

machines that produced cloth. These operatives served as the vanguard of the Industrial Revolution in America.

By the second decade of the nineteenth century, America had clearly defined itself as a nation that embraced many different kinds of change in transportation and technology. Yet traditional forms of inequality and hierarchy endured, serving as distinguishing features of the market revolution. Furthermore, in the South, planters persisted in growing staples such as cotton and rice, in the process discouraging industrialization and strengthening the institution of slavery.

The Rise of the Cotton Plantation Economy

■ *How did staple-crop production shape the labor, culture, and family lives of slaves?*

The growth and spread of the cotton economy redefined the institution of slavery, the southern political system, and ultimately all of American history. With the invention of the cotton gin and the acquisition of the Louisiana Territory, cotton production boomed, and the enslaved population expanded. In 1790 plantations produced 3,000 bales (about 300 pounds each) of cotton; 20 years later, that number hit 178,000. Beginning in 1808, the United States outlawed the importation of new slaves. However, the astounding profitability of cotton heightened the demand for slave labor. Planters began to rely on the domestic slave trade—the forced migration of slaves from the upper South to the lower South.

The institution of slavery was marked by sharp regional variations, increasingly reflecting the impact of cotton cultivation on local economies. At the same time, the contours of an

Which Nations Transported African Slaves in the Early 1800s?

Article 1, section 9, of the U.S. Constitution stipulates: "The migration or Importation of such Persons as any of the States now existing shall think proper to admit, shall not be prohibited by the Congress prior to the Year one thousand eight hundred and eight." This provision meant that the United States could not outlaw the importation of African slaves until 1808. In 1807, Congress passed a law that officially ended the U.S. trade on January 1, 1808. Nevertheless, a number of European nations continued to transport enslaved Africans to the Western Hemisphere, as shown in this graph.

QUESTIONS

1. Overall, how does the United States compare to European nations in the number of Africans forcibly transported across the Atlantic in the period covered by the graph?

2. What accounts for Portugal's dominance in the trade? (Hint: Brazil was a Portuguese colony.)

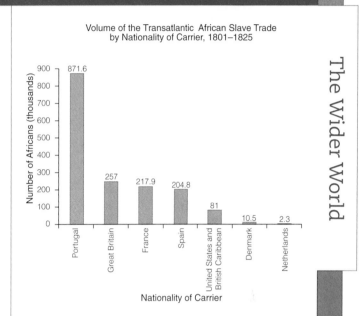

Volume of the Transatlantic African Slave Trade by Nationality of Carrier, 1801–1825

The Wider World

3. Why did the official end of the U.S. international slave trade stimulate domestic trafficking in slaves?

African American culture emerged. This culture had certain characteristics regardless of place, such as strong ties that bound nuclear and extended family members, rich oral and musical traditions heavily influenced by West African customs, and individual and collective resistance to slavery. White people as a group understood little of this culture; they viewed black people primarily as workers who would never become citizens. As U.S. military strength and nationalistic pride grew, southern planters imposed a harsher, more regimented system of slavery on the black population. The tension between the rhetoric of freedom and equality and the reality of slavery would continue to shape southern—and American—life for the next four decades.

REGIONAL ECONOMIES OF THE SOUTH

Throughout the South, shifts in production methods transformed the demographic and economic make-up of specific regions. For example, by the early nineteenth century, the Chesapeake tobacco economy had declined as a result of worn-out lands and falling prices. In its place arose a more diversified economy based on crafts, the cultivation of corn and wheat, and the milling of flour. Owners put enslaved men to work making barrels and horseshoes while forcing their wives, sisters, and daughters to labor as spinners, weavers, dairymaids, personal servants, and livestock tenders.

The lower South states of Georgia and South Carolina also saw their economies change during this period. The indigo export business never recovered from the Revolution, since colonial cultivators of the plant had relied heavily on British subsidies to shore up their profits. European customers now had to turn to Louisiana and Central America for indigo. In contrast, the lowcountry (coastal) South Carolina and Georgia rice economy recovered and flourished after the war. In a particularly rich rice district, All

**Plantation and
Southern Commerce**

Saints Parish, one out of two slaves lived on a plantation with more than a hundred slaves in 1790; thirty years later, four out of five lived on such large establishments. In these areas, the plantation owners often lived elsewhere, and black people constituted almost the entire population.

Adding to the wealth of South Carolina and Georgia was the rapid development of cotton cultivation, especially in the interior, away from the coast. There, prosperous cotton planters began to rival their lowcountry rice-growing counterparts in social status and political influence, and these slaveholders pushed steadily for western expansion. Cotton planters rushed into the Louisiana Territory after 1803. They accelerated an economic process that had begun in the late eighteenth century: the replacement of a frontier exchange economy with plantation agriculture. (Sugar dominated the New Orleans region; cotton, the rest of the lower Mississippi Valley.) By 1800, slaves in lower Louisiana were producing 4.5 million pounds of sugar annually.

The reaches of the lower Mississippi took on an increasingly multicultural flavor. A strong Spanish influence persisted as a vestige of colonial days. Families of French descent (called Acadians) expelled from Nova Scotia, a Canadian province, began to settle in southern Louisiana in 1765. French-speaking planter-refugees and their slaves from revolutionary Saint-Domingue came to New Orleans while the city was still in French hands (1800 to 1803). Between 1787 and 1803, nearly 3,000 slaves arrived from Africa, Spanish West Florida, and the Chesapeake to be sold in New Orleans, followed by even larger numbers of slaves from the North after 1803. Slave owners who settled in Natchez, on the banks of the Mississippi River, grew cotton—and grew rich.

BLACK FAMILY LIFE AND LABOR

The number of enslaved persons in the United States grew from about 717,000 in 1790 to more than 1.5 million in 1820 and continued to increase rapidly over the next four decades. Since importation of Africans ended officially in 1808, these numbers suggest a tremendous rate of natural increase. Some planters continued to buy slaves brought into the country illegally after 1808. But most of the increase stemmed from births. The preferences of both slave owners and slaves account for this development. Southern planters encouraged black women to bear many children. These white men gained new (future) workers when enslaved women gave birth. And many planters believed that slave populations bound together by family ties would be less likely to engage in resistance, such as violent rebellion or running away.

At the same time, enslaved African Americans valued the family as a social unit; family ties provided support and solace for a people deprived of fundamental human rights. Even under harsh conditions, black people fell in love, married (albeit informally, without the sanction of law), had children, and reared families. Despite the lack of protection from local, state, and national authorities, the slave family proved a remarkably resilient institution.

Despite the lack of protection from local, state, and national authorities, the slave family proved a remarkably resilient institution.

The stability of individual slave families depended on several factors, including the size and age of the plantation and the fortunes and life cycle of the slave owner's family. Very large or long-established plantations had more two-parent slave families than did the small or newer holdings, which tended to have more unrelated people. Slave families were broken up when whites died and their "property" was bequeathed to heirs. Slaves might also be sold or presented to other family members as gifts. Many slave families suffered disruption in response to the growing demand for slaves in the fresh cotton lands of Alabama and Mississippi. The forced migration from upper South to lower South necessarily severed kin ties, but slaves often reconstituted those ties in the form of symbolic kin relationships. Families adopted new, single members of the slave community, and the children called these newcomers "Aunt" or "Uncle."

Since plantations functioned as slave labor camps, owners generally showed little or no inclination to take family relationships into account when they parceled out work assignments to men, women, and children. Rather, those assignments, and the conditions under which slaves performed them, reflected the size and crops of a particular plantation. During the period 1790 to 1860, an estimated 75 percent of slaves worked primarily as field hands. On large plantations the division of labor could be quite specialized. Men served as skilled carpenters, blacksmiths, and barrel makers, and women worked as cooks, laundresses, nursemaids, and personal maids.

Rice slaves continued to work under the task system. Each day, after they completed a specific assigned task, they spent their time as they chose, within limits. The women washed clothes and cleaned the living quarters. The men hunted and fished. Both men and women visited friends and worked in their own gardens. Slaves jealously guarded their limited forms of freedom. One white man in Georgia described a slave who had completed his appointed task for the day: "His master feels no right to call on him," leaving him "the remainder of the day to work in his own corn field."

Even in the cotton-growing regions, where blacks labored under the regimented gang system, slaves tried to work for themselves in the little free time they had on Saturday afternoons and Sunday. In Louisiana, one white observer noted that the slave man returning to his living quarters after a long, hot day in the fields "does not lose his time. He goes to work at a bit of the land which he has planted with provisions for his own use, while his companion, if he has one, busies herself in preparing [meals] for him, herself, and their children." Family members who grew or accumulated a modest surplus—of corn, eggs, vegetables—in some cases could sell their wares in a nearby market or to slaves on another plantation.

Some slaves took goods from their master's storeroom and barn and sold or traded them to other slaves or to poor whites. These transactions often took place under the

Francis Guy, *Perry Hall Slave Quarters with Field Hands at Work*, c.1805. Maryland Historical Society, Baltimore Maryland (86.33)

■ This painting, c. 1805, by Francis Guy is titled *Perry Hall Slave Quarters with Field Hands at Work*. Enslaved workers, organized in a gang, cultivate tobacco on a Chesapeake plantation. After the turn of the century, the center of the plantation staple-crop economy moved south and west. The Chesapeake region of Maryland and Virginia developed a more diversified economy than that of the rich cotton lands of Alabama and Louisiana.

cover of darkness. Planters complained of slaves who stole their cattle, hogs, chickens, sacks full of cotton, farm equipment, and stores of ham and flour. In 1806, planters in lowcountry South Carolina, along the Combahee River, railed against a problem that would grow worse in the coming years: "pedling boats which frequent the river . . . for the purpose of trading with The Negroe Slaves, to the very great loss of the Owners, and Corruption of such slaves." Thus slaves' various forms of labor fell into at least three categories: work performed at the behest of and directly under the supervision of whites, labor performed by and for family members within the slaves' living quarters, and the sale (or sometimes clandestine exchange) of goods with masters, other slaves, and poor whites.

> *Taken together, the burdens of work, family, and community life were especially harsh for enslaved women.*

Taken together, the burdens of work, family, and community life were especially harsh for enslaved women. Later, the daughter of a slave remembered the labors of her mother with a mixture of pride and bitterness: the older woman "could do anything. She cooked, washed, spun, nursed, and labored in the field. She made as good a field hand as she did a cook." Recalled the daughter, their master said that her mother could "outwork" any slave, male or female, in the county.

At the same time, women were particularly vulnerable to the many and often violent demands of whites in the fields and in the "Big House," the residence of the master and mistress. Hoping to instill fear in their workers, overseers often punished the most vulnerable members of the slave community—elderly persons and pregnant women among them. Frederick Douglass, a Maryland slave who escaped to the North in the 1830s, explained that "the doctrine that submission to violence is the best cure for violence did not hold good as between slaves and overseers. He was whipped oftener who was whipped easiest."

After toiling in the fields, women and young girls would return to their quarters to prepare the evening meal, wash the family's clothes, and tend to the children. Because owners were more likely to separate fathers rather than mothers from their children, women shouldered the bulk of child-rearing responsibilities and dreaded the day when their offspring might be sold away from them.

Tight-knit slave families, which included extended kin relations as well as blood ties, shaped black women's preferences for work assignments. Although white Southerners later in the century would come to glorify the "spoiled" and "petted" house slave, in fact many black women considered manual labor in the fields preferable to domestic service in the Big House. House servants faced almost routine sexual exploitation from masters and masters' sons. In response to these forms of infidelity, a jealous mistress would often take out her frustration and rage not on the men of her own household but on the slave women who worked under her supervision in the parlor and kitchen.

House servants were on call twenty-four hours a day and held to exacting standards in washing and cooking for the white family. For all these reasons, an enslaved woman might prefer arduous field labor, and the opportunity to spend more time with her family, over service in the Big House. Yet whites persisted in viewing black women as workers first and foremost and as family members only incidentally, if at all.

RESISTANCE TO SLAVERY

Enslaved men and women did not always behave according to their masters' demands. In 1817, the New Orleans City Council decreed that slaves could sing and dance at a stipulated place—Congo Square—every Sunday afternoon. Thereafter, a variety of groups came together to make music. These groups included recent immigrants from Saint-Domingue and slaves newly imported from Africa; slaves from neighboring plantations, in town for the day; and free people of color (Creoles), who often blended Spanish and

French classical music traditions. One eyewitness observed that the Congo Square musicians "have their own national music, consisting for the most part of a long kind of narrow drum of various size." In towns and on plantations throughout the South, black people drew from West African musical styles, using drums as well as banjolike instruments, gourd rattles, and mandolins. Over the generations, several uniquely American musical styles flowed from Congo Square and other southern gathering places.

In their artistic expression, dress, hairstyles, and language, slaves sought to preserve their cultural uniqueness and create an existence that slaveholders could not touch. In the South Carolina lowcountry, slaves spoke Gullah. Originally a pidgin—a blend of words and grammatical structures from West African languages and English—Gullah later developed into a more formal Creole language. Slaves throughout the United States also mixed West African religious beliefs with Christianity. Many West African groups believed in a close relationship between the natural and supernatural worlds. In slave quarters, spiritual leaders not only preached a Christianity of equality but also told fortunes and warned away "haunts" (spirits of the dead).

In gatherings of many kinds, enslaved Americans affirmed their bonds with one another and their resistance to bondage. For example, funerals provided opportunities for music and expressions of group solidarity. Many slaves adhered to a view of the world that blended Christian and West African religious elements. This view held that funerals marked a rite of passage for the deceased person. In funeral services and other observances, the rich oral and musical traditions that characterized slave life preserved collective memories of Africa and the lore of individual families and kin networks.

Black resistance to slavery took many forms. Slaves might work carelessly in an effort to resist a master's or mistress's demands. During the course of their workday, some slaves

John Antrobus, *Plantation Burial*, c. 1860. Historic New Orleans Collection, accession no. 1960.46

■ British artist John Antrobus titled his 1860 painting *Plantation Burial*. Held at night, after the workday, slave funerals provided an opportunity for the community—including slaves from nearby plantations—to come together in mourning. Planters remained suspicious of such gatherings, which were marked by African musical forms and religious rituals. Whites feared that slaves would conspire under the cover of darkness.

broke hoes and other farm implements. A cook might burn the biscuits, thus spoiling a special dinner party for her mistress. Striking out more directly, the African-influenced "conjurer"—often a woman who had a knowledge of plants and herbs—could wreak havoc on a white family by concocting poisons or encouraging disruptive behavior among slaves.

Slaves also stole goods from their masters and at times stole themselves by running away. (This practice was more common among young, unmarried men than among those who had family obligations.) In plotting their escapes, many blacks took advantage of the ways the natural landscape shaped pathways away from the plantation and out of slavery. In the lowcountry region of South Carolina and Georgia, black men skilled as river pilots stole skiffs and made their way silently through mazes of creeks and inlets to seek freedom in the anonymity of Charleston or Savannah. The built environment of the city, with its narrow alleyways and bustling dock areas, could provide cover for the recent fugitive. In these port cities and in others along the South Atlantic seaboard, some blacks bided their time, hoping to stow away or use forged documents to pass for a free person of color on a steamship, in order to make their way north to Boston or New York. George Washington's slave Ona Judge took advantage of the refuge afforded her by two northern cities—Philadelphia, Pennsylvania, and Portsmouth, New Hampshire.

> *Slave masters and mistresses created a number of myths about the black people they exploited.*

Throughout the southern interior, blacks fled to the swamps, marshes, and forests in an effort to hide out for short or extended periods of time. They lived off the land: fishing, trapping small animals, or scavenging for berries or nuts. In their plans for escape, would-be fugitives had to take into consideration both the obstacles and the potential inherent in their natural environment.

Despite the extraordinary peril involved, some slaves revolted. In St. Charles and St. John the Baptist parishes in Louisiana, an 1811 revolt of 400 slaves cost two whites their lives and left several plantations in flames. The original participants, led by Charles Deslondes, a free man of color, acquired new members as they marched toward New Orleans. U.S. troops cut their advance short, killing 66 of them. In the Southeast in 1817 and 1818, 400 to 600 runaway slaves converged on the swamps of central Florida, uniting with Indian refugees from the Red Stick War. Together, they raided Georgia plantations until Andrew Jackson and his soldiers halted them in April 1818.

To justify their own behavior, slave masters and mistresses created a number of myths about the black people they exploited. Whites had a vested interest in believing that their slaves felt gratitude toward them. Skilled in the so-called deference ritual, some slaves hid their true feelings and acted submissively in the presence of white people. Owners and overseers alike interpreted this behavior as a sign of black contentment.

Yet most whites understood that danger could lurk beneath the surface of the most accommodating slave. Therefore, the prevailing stereotypes of black men and women encompassed two caricatures: "Sambo" and "Mammy" were childlike and grateful, and "Nat" and "Jezebel" were surly, cunning, dangerous, and unpredictable. One Kentucky slave, Susan, was described by a planter in 1822 as "the biggest devil that ever lived." Susan reportedly poisoned a stud horse and set a stable on fire, causing $1,500 worth of damage, after managing to escape from handcuffs.

Although some planters boasted of their fatherly solicitude for their slaves, in fact slave owners harbored deep fears about the men and women they held in bondage. These fears explain the barbaric punishments that some owners inflicted on men, women, and children. Whip-wielding overseers made pregnant women lie down in a trench in the fields, presumably so that the lash would not harm the fetus. Even in "respectable" southern families, slave owners branded, mutilated, and beat enslaved workers for resisting discipline or to deliver a warning to other potentially defiant slaves. In the slave South, American cries of freedom, equality, opportunity, and the blessings of citizenship rang hollow.

Conclusion

During the first two decades of the nineteenth century, the natural landscape shaped the political, military, and economic development of the new nation. Politicians known as "war hawks" believed that American national honor depended on the conquest of Indians in the West and England on the high seas. The War of 1812 represented not only the end of British interference within the continental United States but also the next chapter in the bloody saga of European Americans' acquiring Indian lands through purchase or, more often, forcible seizure. Without British support in the form of troops and guns, Indians in the Great Lakes region suffered devastating losses.

Many Americans owed their livelihoods to the shape of the land or to the riches embedded in it. Powered by water rushing from the hills to the sea, textile mills gave rise to a new class of factory workers. With the annexation of the Louisiana Territory in 1803, the rich lands of the South provided fertile ground for the spread of the slave system. As European Americans migrated west and to the Mississippi Valley, they replaced the trading economy with family farms and plantations, sawmills, and gristmills.

Though enslaved to the brutal demands of plantation economies, African Americans sought to turn the contours of the land to their own advantage. They used rivers, seaports, swamps, and marshes as hiding places and as refuges from slavery. Despite the differences in labor organization characteristic of cotton and rice cultivation, southern blacks developed strong family ties, a vibrant religious tradition, and multiple forms of everyday resistance to the system of slavery.

During this period, dramatic historical developments stirred the spirit of American nationalism. The Louisiana Purchase magnified the natural wealth of the young nation, and the federal government encouraged citizens to exploit that wealth through trade and settlement. The War of 1812 bolstered the American economy by stimulating technological innovation and the growth of manufacturing. Territorial expansion combined with economic development to create new jobs for a burgeoning population. Unlike the rigidly class-conscious nations of Europe, America seemed to offer limitless possibilities—at least for propertied white men, the only people entitled to the full rights of citizenship. Gradually, the two-party system of the Democratic-Republicans and the Federalists dissolved, as the nation secured its boundaries and met the challenge of British aggression. The old models of France and England, a legacy of the Revolution, gave way to new issues reflecting the challenges faced by an industrializing nation.

Southern cotton planters and northern factory owners derived their newfound prosperity from very different sources: staple-crop agriculture on one hand and the emerging industrial system on the other. At the same time, these two groups had much in common. As they expanded their operations, whether sprawling plantations or gigantic mill complexes, they displaced smaller landowners and

CHRONOLOGY: 1804–1818

1804	Lewis and Clark Expedition (1804–1806).
1805	British navy defeats French and Spanish fleets at Battle of Trafalgar.
1806	Congress authorizes funds for construction of National Road.
1807	Jefferson places embargo on all U.S. exports to Europe.
	U.S.S. *Chesapeake* attacked by British vessel.
	Robert Fulton pilots first steamboat up the Hudson River.
1808	Congressional ban on slave trade takes effect.
	Non-Intercourse Act prevents exports to France and England.
	Tecumseh and Tenskwatawa found Prophet Town in Indiana.
1811	Battle of Tippecanoe.
	Revolt of 400 slaves in Louisiana.
1812	War of 1812 begins.
1813	Red Sticks battle U.S. troops at Battle of Horseshoe Bend.
1814	British forces attack Washington, D.C.
1815	Treaty of Ghent ends War of 1812.
	Battle of New Orleans.
1816	Tariff of 1816.
1818	Andrew Jackson battles Seminole in Florida.

raised land prices. Members of both elite groups proved restless entrepreneurs, eager to move around to find the freshest lands and the cheapest labor. Their personal wealth and their political power set them apart from the people under them—the slaves and wage earners—who produced that wealth. And both the southern "lords of the lash" and the northern "lords of the loom" depended on large numbers of slaves to grow cotton. Thus, the fluffy white fiber of the cotton boll is perhaps a most fitting symbol of the emerging American economy. Producing and processing it yielded tangible benefits for a few and created a new, harsher world of work for many.

For Review

1. Who were the war hawks, and why did they emerge as such a potent political force in Congress? Why were most from the West?

2. In 1812, in what ways did the British and Indians see the United States as their common enemy? In what ways did the interests of the British and their Indian allies differ?

3. In the United States, what were the political, social, and economic consequences of the War of 1812?

4. What issues did the War of 1812 resolve? Leave unresolved? Is it accurate to call the war a victory for the United States?

5. Explain the market revolution and its effects on American society. Which groups benefited?

6. What elements of African American culture revealed the slaves' struggle to live life on their own terms, rather than on the terms dictated by white masters and mistresses? Within the plantation, in what ways was the power of slaveholders limited or restricted?

7. Did the United States change substantially between 1812 and 1818? Explain.

Created Equal Online

For more *Created Equal* resources, including suggestions on sites to visit and books to read, go to **MyHistoryLab.com**.

Chapter 11

Society and Politics in the "Age of the Common Man," 1819–1832

■ John Gadsby Chapman painted this portrait of David Crockett in 1834.

Campaigning for political office in Tennessee in the 1820s was not an activity for the faint of heart. Candidates competed against each other in squirrel hunts, the loser footing the bill for the barbecue that followed. A round of speechmaking often was capped by several rounds of whiskey enjoyed by candidates and supporters alike. Into this boisterous arena stepped a man unrivaled as a campaigner. David Crockett ran successfully for several offices, including local justice of the peace in 1818. He served in the state legislature from 1820 to 1824, and he was elected to the U.S. House of Representatives in 1826, 1828, and 1832. The plainspoken Crockett knew how to play to a crowd and rattle a rival. He bragged about his skill as a bear hunter and ridiculed the fancy dress of his opponents. He condemned closed-door political caucuses (small groups of party insiders who hand-picked candidates) and praised grassroots democracy. Crockett claimed he could out-shoot, out-drink, and out-debate anyone who opposed him. If his opponent lied about him, why, then, he would lie about himself: "Yes fellow citizens, I can run faster, walk longer, leap higher, speak better, and tell more and bigger lies than my competitor, and all his friends, any day of his life." Crockett's blend of political theater and folksy backwoods banter earned him the allegiance of voters like him—people who, though having little formal education, understood the challenges of carving a homestead out of the dense thickets of western Tennessee.

Crockett's raucous brand of campaigning appealed to Westerners—that is, European Americans living just west of the Appalachian Mountains. His social betters might sniff that he was a rough, ignorant man—in the words of one Tennessee political insider, "more in his proper place, when hunting a Bear in the cane Brake, than he will be in the Capital." But newspaper reporters and defeated opponents alike grew to respect his ability to champion ordinary farmers. As a politician, Crockett spoke for debtors, squatters, and militia veterans of the Revolutionary War. He scorned the wellborn in favor of those who could shoot down and skin a wolf.

In 1790, 100,000 Americans (not including Indians) lived west of the Appalachian Mountains; half a century later that number had increased to 7 million, or about four out of ten Americans. During the 1820s, European American settlers in the trans-Appalachian West transformed the style and substance of American politics. Beginning with Kentucky in 1792, western states began to relax or abolish property requirements for adult male voters. Even the English that Americans spoke changed. New terms introduced into the political vocabulary reflected the rough-hewn, woodsman quality of western electioneering: candidates hit the campaign trail, giving stump speeches along the way. They supported their party's platform with its planks (positions on the issues). As legislators, they voted for pork-barrel projects that would benefit their constituents at home. Emphasizing his modest origins, David Crockett became widely known as Davy Crockett. (It is hard to imagine anyone calling the Sage of Monticello Tommy Jefferson.)

Davy Crockett, Advice to Politicians (1833)

Western settlers attacked centralized, eastern-based institutions of wealth and privilege. They scorned a six-person Supreme Court that could overturn the laws of Congress and the individual states. They opposed the privately held Second Bank of the United States, which, its critics charged, enriched its own board of directors at the expense of indebted farmers. And they railed against federally sponsored internal improvements, such as turnpikes and canals, which, many western homesteaders believed, served the interests of well-connected merchants and financiers.

Western voters rejoiced with the 1828 election of Andrew Jackson of Tennessee to the presidency. Here, they claimed, was a person who would battle eastern financiers and at the same time support white settlers' claims to Indian lands in the West. Jackson held out the promise that ordinary people would have a political voice and access to expanding economic opportunities.

During his two terms in office (1828–1836), Andrew Jackson so dominated the American political landscape that historians have called him the symbol of an age and the representative man of his time. Born in humble circumstances, orphaned at age fourteen, Jackson achieved public acclaim as a lawyer, military officer (in the War of 1812), and finally president. In promoting a strong central government, and the authority of the chief executive in particular, he clashed with southern states' rights advocates. Jackson backed up his vision with the use of violence and, at times, contempt for the law, as evidenced in his removal of Indians from the Southeast. Nevertheless, Jackson's view appealed strongly to workers and small farmers who resented what they viewed as entrenched eastern privilege in politics and the economy.

Yet democracy had its limits during this period. White voter participation in presidential elections soared, from 25 percent of eligible voters in 1824 to 50 percent in 1828. Still, most people could not vote. Slaves and American Indians remained barred from even the rudiments of formal citizenship. White married women, who could neither own property nor vote, found themselves second-class citizens. Almost all free people of color, whether in the

North, South, or Midwest, likewise lacked basic rights—to vote, serve on juries, or send their children to public school.

Further complicating this age was the rise of distinct social classes. Acquiring great economic and political significance, the class system seemed to mock the idea of equality. The outlines of this system appeared in the 1820s in the Northeast, where business and factory managers received salaries, not hourly wages, and their wives were full-time homemakers and mothers. New forms of popular literature, such as the *Ladies Magazine,* published in Boston, glorified the middle-class family, especially the pious wife and mother who held moral sway over it.

The "Age of The Common Man" was thus rife with irony. Jackson himself embodied many apparent contradictions. An Indian-fighter, he adopted a young Indian boy as his ward. A foe of privilege, he was a slave owner. A self-professed champion of farmers and artisans, he expressed contempt for their representatives in Congress. He also took steps to expand the power of the executive branch. The 1820s in general revealed these larger contradictions as national leaders pursued a more democratic form of politics on one hand and supported a system based on class and racial differences on the other. The resulting tensions shaped American society and politics in the third decade of the nineteenth century.

The Politics Behind Western Migration

■ *How did western expansion affect the nation's politics and economy of the 1820s?*

As the United States gained new territory through negotiation and conquest and as people moved west, these changes were reflected in international and domestic political relations. At the highest levels of politics, President James Monroe warned Europe not to interfere any longer in the Western Hemisphere. Congressional debates over whether Missouri should be admitted to the Union as a slave or free state sent shock waves throughout the country. Of the political conflict over the fate of slavery in the territories, the elderly Thomas Jefferson wrote, "This momentous question, like a firebell in the night, awakened and filled me with terror. I considered it at once as the death knell of the Union."

This migration also led to fundamental changes in the everyday political lives of Americans. As new states were carved out of the West, gaining national influence in Congress, traditional methods of choosing candidates and the old political parties of Democratic-Republicans and Federalists came under fire. Parties began to choose their presidential nominees in conventions, not in caucuses of legislators, and more and more states abolished the requirement that would-be voters and office holders had to own property.

However, the opening of the West to European American settlement, which invigorated white men's democracy, also sowed seeds of economic and political conflict. The newcomers made their way not through empty territory but through Native American homelands. Western debtors' economic distress echoed in eastern centers of finance. Once in the West, most of these settlers faced the same kinds of conflicts that increasingly preoccupied Easterners, especially those between masters and slaves and debtors and creditors.

MAP

Expanding America
and Internal
Improvements

THE MISSOURI COMPROMISE

In 1819, the United States consisted of twenty-two states. Slavery was legal in half of them. Late that year, the territory of Missouri applied to Congress for statehood. This move set off panic in both the North and South because a twenty-third state was bound to upset the delicate balance

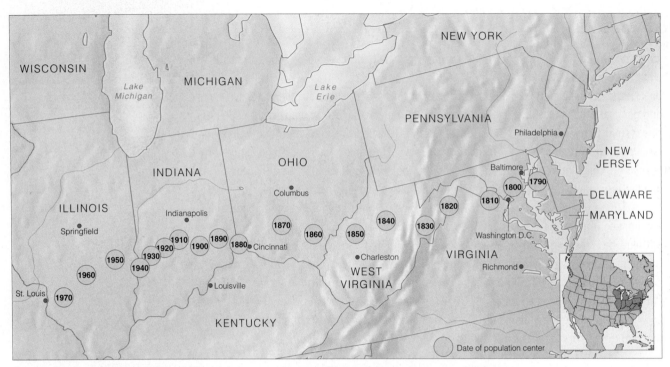

■ **M A P 1 1 . 1 The Center of Population Moves West, 1790–1970**

In 1830, most European and African Americans still lived along the eastern seaboard. Yet the statistical center of the country had shifted dramatically westward as settlers moved across the trans-Appalachian West. Migrants from the South sought out the fresh cotton lands of Alabama and Mississippi, while New Englanders created new communities in the upper Midwest. Migration to areas such as Wisconsin and Georgia was contingent on the removal of Indians from those areas, either by treaty or by military force.

of senators between slave and free states. Representative James Tallmadge of New York proposed a compromise: no slaves would be imported into Missouri in the future, and the new state would gradually emancipate the enslaved men and women living within its borders. The Tallmadge Amendment was defeated in the House as Southerners resisted this blatant attempt to limit the spread of slavery. The debate over the future of Missouri occupied Congress from December 1819 to March 1820.

In the Senate, Rufus King of New York claimed that Congress had the ultimate authority to set laws governing slavery. However, his colleague William Pinckney of Maryland retorted that new states possessed the same rights as the original thirteen; they could choose whether or not to allow slavery. Maine's application for admission to the Union suggested a way out of the impasse. Speaker of the House of Representatives Henry Clay of Kentucky proposed a plan calling for Missouri to join the Union as a slave state. At the same time, Maine, originally part of Massachusetts, would become the twenty-fourth state and be designated a free one. In the future, slavery would be prohibited from all Louisiana Purchase lands north of latitude 36°30', an area that included all territory north of present-day Missouri and Kansas. The House and the Senate finally approved the compromise, which maintained the balance between the number of slave and free states.

The day Congress sealed the compromise, Secretary of State John Quincy Adams of Massachusetts walked home from the Capitol with Senator John C. Calhoun of South Carolina. The two men engaged in a muted but intense debate over slavery. Calhoun claimed that the institution "was the best guarantee to equality among the whites." Slavery, he asserted, demonstrated that all white men were equal to one another and superior to all blacks. Unnerved by Calhoun's comments, Adams concluded that the debate over Missouri had "betrayed the secret of [slaveowners'] souls." By reserving backbreaking toil for blacks, wealthy planters fancied themselves aristocratic lords of the manor. Adams confided in his

Slave states
Free states and territories
Open to slavery by Missouri Compromise
Closed to slavery by Missouri Compromise

■ MAP 11.2 The Missouri Compromise

Missouri applied for statehood in 1819, threatening the balance between eleven free and eleven slave states. According to a compromise hammered out in Congress, Missouri was admitted as a slave state, and Maine, formerly part of Massachusetts, was admitted as a free state. Slavery was banned above the 36°30' parallel.

diary that night, "They look down upon the simplicity of a Yankee's manners, because he has no habits of overbearing like theirs and cannot treat negroes like dogs."

Adams acknowledged that the compromise had kept the number of slave and free states in balance. Still, he reflected, slavery "taints the very sources of moral principle." Would it not have been better to confront the issue squarely and amend the Constitution in favor of free labor in all new states admitted to the Union? Adams feared that the North-South conflicts over the issue might someday imperil the nation itself. He concluded ominously, "If the Union must be dissolved, slavery is precisely the question upon which it ought to break." Five years later, Adams won the presidency of the United States. Elected separately by the voters, his vice president was none other than John C. Calhoun. Over the next four years, the two men managed to maintain an uneasy political alliance.

WAYS WEST: THE ERIE CANAL

Missouri was just one of the territories west of the Mississippi River where the population had increased during this period. Through land grants and government financing of new methods of transportation, Congress encouraged European American migrants to push their way west and south. The Land Act of 1820 enabled Westerners to buy a minimum 80 acres at a price of $1.25 an acre in cash—even in those days, a bargain homestead. Built with the help of government legal and financial aid, new roads and canals, steamboats, and, after the early 1830s, railroads facilitated migration. Between 1820 and 1860, the number of steamboats plying the Mississippi River jumped from 60 to more than 1,000. Canals linked western producers to eastern consumers of grains and cattle and connected western

LISTEN
"The Erie Canal"

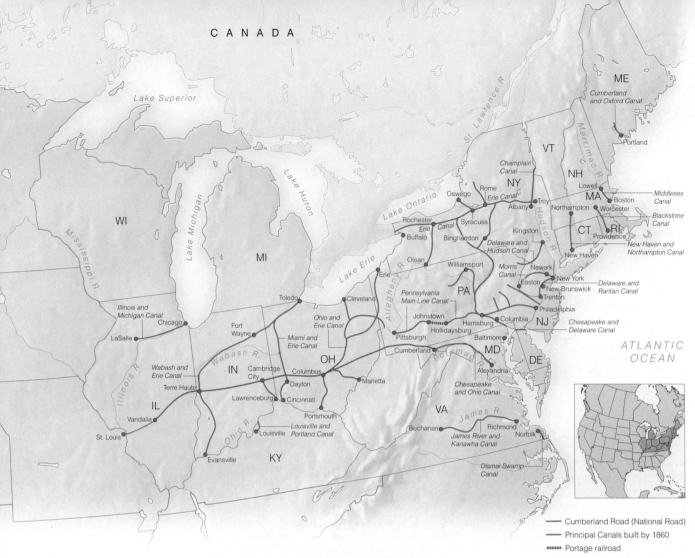

■ **MAP 11.3 Principal Canals Built by 1860**

Many canals were expensive ventures and, in some cases, engineering nightmares. The Erie Canal had a competitive advantage because it snaked through the Mohawk Valley, the only major level pass through the mountain chain that stretched from Canada to Georgia. In contrast, the Pennsylvania Main Line Canal, which ran from Harrisburg to Pittsburgh, used a combination of inclined planes and steam engines in ten separate locations to haul boats up and down the Allegheny Mountains.

consumers to eastern producers of manufactured goods. Shipping costs and times between Buffalo and New York shrank. Cities such as Rochester and Syracuse, New York, and Cincinnati, Ohio, flourished because of their geographic position along key waterways. Among the most significant of these waterways was the **Erie Canal.**

Begun in 1817, the canal was a marvel in engineering, financial, and social terms. Forty feet wide at the water's surface and 4 feet deep, the "artificial river" ascended 680 feet on its east-west rise and included 83 locks and 18 aqueducts along the way. The 363-mile canal linked the New York cities of Troy and Albany, on the Hudson River, with Buffalo, on the eastern tip of Lake Erie. The waterway allowed farmers throughout the Great Lakes system to send crops and livestock as far east as the Atlantic Ocean, and it allowed East Coast manufacturers to market their products throughout the Midwest.

Yet many people at the time believed that the canal promised more than an economic boon. In their eyes, the project had great political and religious significance as well. Today it is difficult for us to appreciate the excitement and enthusiasm that greeted its opening. The completion of the canal in 1825 was marked by an elaborate celebration called the "Wedding of the Waters." The vision, skill, and hard work that went into building the canal demonstrated "the *spirit and perseverance* of REPUBLICAN FREE MEN," read a capstone on the canal locks at Lockport. Politicians claimed that they had the responsibility to make use of the nation's abundant natural resources. An early supporter of the canal project,

■ This drawing of the Erie Canal at Lockport, New York, illustrates two of the ways internal improvements overcame natural barriers to trade and transportation—through canal locks (foreground) and a tall trestle bridge (background).

New York's prominent political leader Gouverneur Morris, promoted this view. He claimed that failing to build the canal would show "a want of wisdom, almost of piety, not to employ for public advantage those means which Divine Providence has placed so completely within our power." Marveling at the intricate lock system, one observer claimed that, aided by technology, humans could now hope to master nature itself: "It certainly strikes the beholder with astonishment, to perceive what vast difficulties can be overcome by the pigmy arms of little mortal men, aided by science and directed by superior skill." Human ingenuity, together with gunpowder and raw human and oxen muscle power, could literally level mountains.

By any measure the state of New York saw a spectacular return on its investment. Though the state had financed the project's whole cost of $7 million on its own, by 1882 it had taken in over $121 million in tolls charged to the users of the waterway. Factories, gristmills, taverns, and inns sprang up along the canal banks, stimulating local economies. Throughout the 1830s and 1840s, approximately 30,000 men, women, and children labored to maintain the canal, operate the locks, and load and pull barges (as many as 3,400 in operation at one time). The prosperity generated by the canal greatly benefited New York City, which emerged as the most important financial center in the country.

The canal also contributed to major social transformations. By making inexpensive manufactured goods accessible to large numbers of people in rural New York and the Midwest, the canal helped to raise the material standard of living of people outside large cities. In the late 1820s, a series of religious revivals swept through western New York, as some people embraced the idea that a new day was dawning, a day when men and women could control their own destiny—even the salvation of their own souls. If ordinary people could now move mountains, was not almost anything possible?

On the other hand, some people believed that prosperity exacted a high price from local communities. A new, unruly mix of boatmen, passengers, and longshoremen changed sleepy farm towns into bustling centers of trade. Not everyone welcomed the change. According to one critic, every settlement along the waterway now boasted "from 3 to 6 groggeries, and all those for the benefit for the traveling public . . . 'Rum, Gin, Brandy, Wine, Beer, Cider, Bread, Milk, and Groceries,' meet the eye every few miles." While some people saw the canal as a sign of progress of religious proportions, others lamented the passing of a traditional, tranquil way of life. Yet virtually everyone would have agreed with the Reverend F. H. Cuming, who spoke at a ceremony marking the completion of the canal in 1825 and proclaimed in awe: "the mountains have been leveled; the vallies have been filled; rivers and gulfs have been formed over them," and in the process, a new river, manmade, was born.

SPREADING AMERICAN CULTURE—AND SLAVERY

These debates did little to keep Americans from pressing west, and they took a variety of routes to get there. In the 1820s, desperate planters moved out of the exhausted lands of the upper South (the states of Virginia and Maryland), the Carolinas, and Georgia, westward into Alabama, Arkansas, Louisiana, and Mississippi. This migration across the Appalachian Mountains furthered the nationalist idea of the "expansion of liberty and freedom," a view held by many whites regardless of political affiliation. Yet it also spread slavery. The sight of slave coffles—groups of men, women, and children bound together in chains, hobbling down a city street or a country road—became increasingly common in this western region. The increase in slaves to the west is evidenced by the increased production of cash crops. In 1821, Virginia, North Carolina, South Carolina, and Georgia produced two-thirds of the nation's cotton crop; the rest came from recently settled areas. Just a dozen years later the proportions shifted: Tennessee, Louisiana, Alabama, Mississippi, and Florida together produced two-thirds of all cotton, and the remaining one-third came from older areas.

European Americans also migrated across the border into Mexican territory. In 1821, Spain approved the application of a U.S. citizen, Moses Austin, to settle 300 American families on 200,000 fertile acres along the Colorado and Brazos river bottoms in southeastern Texas. Austin died soon after, but his son Stephen carried on his legacy. Within two years, the younger Austin had received permission (now from the government of newly independent Mexico) to bring in another 100 families. These settlers, together with squatters, numbered about 1,500 people. Although the Mexican constitution prohibited slavery, some of the newcomers brought their slaves with them, and some free people of color came on their own. All

HAULING THE WHOLE WEEKS PICKING

William Henry Brown, *Hauling the Whole Weeks Picking,* 1842. Historic New Orleans Collection (1975.93.1 and 1975.93.2)

■ The rich bottomlands of the Mississippi Delta proved ideal for growing cotton. After the forced removal of the Five Civilized Tribes, slave owners established expansive plantations in the delta. This scene, painted in 1842 by artist William Henry Brown, shows a group of slaves bringing in "the whole weeks picking" of cotton on the Vick plantation near Vicksburg, Mississippi.

The Global Trade in Cotton

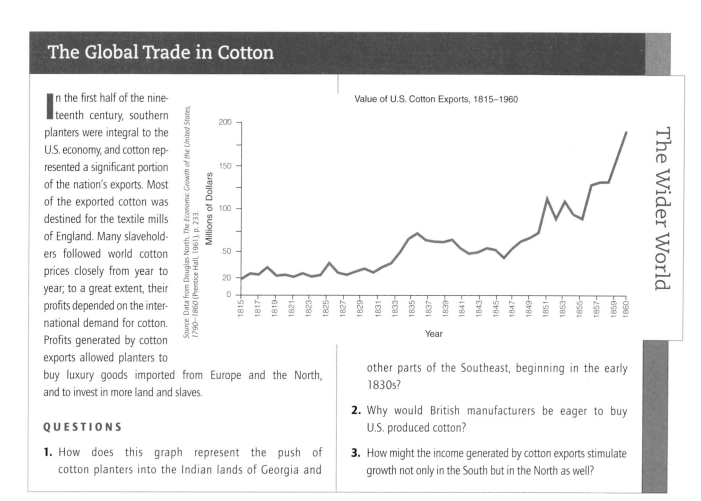

In the first half of the nineteenth century, southern planters were integral to the U.S. economy, and cotton represented a significant portion of the nation's exports. Most of the exported cotton was destined for the textile mills of England. Many slaveholders followed world cotton prices closely from year to year; to a great extent, their profits depended on the international demand for cotton. Profits generated by cotton exports allowed planters to buy luxury goods imported from Europe and the North, and to invest in more land and slaves.

Source: Data from Douglas North, The Economic Growth of the United States, 1790–1860 (Prentice Hall, 1961), p. 233.

Value of U.S. Cotton Exports, 1815–1960

QUESTIONS

1. How does this graph represent the push of cotton planters into the Indian lands of Georgia and other parts of the Southeast, beginning in the early 1830s?

2. Why would British manufacturers be eager to buy U.S. produced cotton?

3. How might the income generated by cotton exports stimulate growth not only in the South but in the North as well?

The Wider World

---

these migrants from the United States called themselves **Texians** to distinguish themselves from the *Tejanos,* or Spanish-speaking residents of the region. These newly arrived Texians agreed to adopt the Roman Catholic faith and become citizens of Mexico. During the rest of the decade, 900 additional families sponsored by Austin arrived in Texas. They were followed by 3,000 squatters. This mass migration raised well-founded fears among Mexican officials that they would lose authority over the American newcomers within their borders.

THE PANIC OF 1819 AND THE PLIGHT OF WESTERN DEBTORS

In 1819, a financial panic swept across the nation, followed by an economic depression that hit western states and territories particularly hard. The Second Bank of the United States played a major role in triggering this economic downturn, which came to be called the Panic of 1819. Granted a twenty-year charter by Congress in 1816, the bank resembled its predecessor, seeking to regulate the national economy through loans to state and local banks. In 1819, the national bank clamped down on small, local wildcat banks, which had extended credit to many people who could not repay their loans. Many homesteaders were not self-sufficient farmers but producers of staple crops or proprietors of small enterprises. They relied on credit from banks and local private lenders. As a result, the national bank's crackdown on wildcat banks had a devastating impact on western households. Debtors unable to meet their obligations had their mortgages foreclosed, their homes seized, and their crops and equipment confiscated. Ruined by the Panic of 1819, many western farmers developed an abiding hatred of the Bank of the United States and a deep resentment of eastern financiers.

MAP 11.4 Mexico's Far Northern Frontier in 1822

This map shows Mexico's far northern frontier in 1822. When Moses Austin died suddenly in 1821, the task of supervising the settlement of migrants from the United States fell to his son Stephen. The Mexican government authorized the younger Austin to act as empresario of the settlement. He was responsible for the legal and economic regulations governing the settlements clustered at the lower reaches of the Colorado and Brazos rivers.

Davy Crockett's own family history suggests the plight of families dependent on bank credit to create homesteads out of western territory. The son of a propertyless squatter, Crockett had an intense fear of debt. Although he campaigned as a hunter and a farmer, he had built several enterprises on land he leased or owned on Shoal Creek in south-central Tennessee: a water-powered gristmill, a gunpowder factory (worked by slaves), an iron ore mine, and a liquor distillery. For each venture, he had to borrow money from local creditors. Spending much of his time away from home, Crockett relied on his wife, Elizabeth, and his children to manage these businesses. (He had three children by his first wife, Polly, who died in 1815, and eventually would have three more with Elizabeth.)

The depression of 1819 cut off Crockett's sources of credit, and in 1822 a flash flood swept away his gristmill and powder factory. Without milled grain, the distillery could no longer operate. Creditors immediately set upon the family, demanding payment of their debts. The Crocketts were fortunate enough to own land they could sell, using the proceeds to repay their debts. Nevertheless, they decided to move farther west, to a remote area on the banks of the Obion River in northwest Tennessee. There they started over. Crockett described the area as a "complete wilderness" (although he noted that it was also "full of Indians who were hunting"). The region still showed the effects of an earthquake that had occurred in 1811. With its downed trees and thick brambles, the fissure-riddled landscape presented challenges to the farmers who ventured there. Once again, Crockett needed bank loans, this time to buy flour and seed for cotton.

Many western settlers engaged in the same sort of cycle: borrowing to improve their land, then selling out and moving on. Unable to pay their debts, the least fortunate among them were thrown in jail. In several states, politicians urged the abolition of debtors' prison. They pointed out that jailing people who owed money did little to ensure that the debt would be repaid. New York state legislators passed such a law in 1831 in response to a group of well-to-do petitioners who argued that debtors' prison was "useless to the creditor—oppressive to the debtor—injurious to both."

Crockett advocated a system that would allow local sheriffs to buy debtors' property at bankruptcy auctions and then sell it back to the former owners. He denounced the bankers and other creditors who "had gone up one side of a creek and down another, *like a [raccoon],* and pretended to grant the poor people great favors" in making them loans that the moneylenders knew they could not afford to repay. Then these creditors demanded their money and wiped out families, taking their land and livestock. Too often, according to Crockett, the backwoods farmer was burdened by debt and vulnerable to economic depressions and scheming creditors.

The Panic of 1819 caused widespread economic distress. Small farmers who lost their land through foreclosure could not produce crops for the eastern market, contributing to the rise in the price of food. Deprived of credit, small shopkeepers also felt the effects of the economic depression. With rising unemployment, consumers could not afford to buy cloth, and as the demand for cotton fell, southern plantation owners, too, felt the contraction. Within a few years Andrew Jackson would capitalize on the fears and resentments of workers, farmers, planters, and tradespeople as he championed the "common man" in opposition to what debtors called the "eastern monied interests." In doing so, he would transform the two-party system.

THE MONROE DOCTRINE

Despite the troubled economy, James Monroe won reelection easily in 1820. He benefited from the disorganization of his opponents and from the demise of the Federalist party. Congressman John Randolph of Virginia suggested that the voters were unanimous on only one issue: their indifference to Monroe. As it turned out, the president's 231–1 victory in the electoral college was the last chapter in the so-called Era of Good Feelings.

On the international front, Monroe's second term opened on a tense note. Foreign nations continued to claim land and promote their own interests near U.S. borders. The United States remained especially wary of the Spanish presence on its southern and western borders. In 1818, President Monroe authorized General Andrew Jackson to broaden his assault on the Seminole—a group composed of Native Americans and runaway slaves—in Florida. For the previous two years, U.S. troops had pursued fugitive slaves into Spanish-held Florida. Now Jackson and his forces seized the Spanish fort at Pensacola and claimed all of western Florida for the United States. The United States demanded that Spain either suppress the Seminole population or sell all of east Florida to the United States. With the Transcontinental Treaty of 1819, Spain gave up its right to both Florida and Oregon (although Britain and Russia still claimed land in Oregon). In 1822, General Jackson became the first governor of Florida Territory.

Farther north, in 1821 the emperor of Russia forbade non-Russians from entering the territory north of the 51st parallel and the open sea 100 miles off the coast of what is now Canada and Alaska. The Russians had established trading posts up and down that coast, some almost as far south as San Francisco Bay. Meanwhile, rumors circulated that European monarchs were planning new invasions of Latin America.

Fearful of an alliance among Russia, Prussia, Austria, Spain, and France, President Monroe and Secretary of State John Quincy Adams formulated a policy that became a landmark in American diplomatic history. Adams rejected a British proposal that Great Britain and the United States join forces to oppose further Spanish encroachment in Latin America. He convinced Monroe that the United States must

TABLE 11.1		
The Election of 1820		
Candidate	**Political Party**	**Electoral Vote**
James Monroe	Democratic-Republican	231
John Quincy Adams	Democratic-Republican	1

stand alone against the European powers—Spain in the south and Russia in the northwest—if it hoped to protect its own interests in the Western Hemisphere. In his annual message to Congress in December 1823, the president declared that the era of Europe's colonization of the Americas had ceased. Henceforth, Monroe said, foreign nations would not be allowed to intervene in the Western Hemisphere.

The United States conceived the **Monroe Doctrine** as a self-defense measure aimed specifically at Russia, Spain, and Britain. With the Russo-American Treaty of 1824, Russia agreed to pull back its claims to the area north of 54°40', the southern tip of the present-day Alaska panhandle. However, the United States did not have the naval power to back up the Monroe Doctrine with force. The doctrine was at first more a statement of principle than a blueprint for action, intended to discourage European powers from political or military meddling in the Western Hemisphere. The doctrine would have greater international significance in the late nineteenth century, when the United States developed the military might to enforce it.

DOCUMENT

The Monroe Doctrine
(1823)

ANDREW JACKSON'S RISE TO POWER

The election of 1824 provided a striking contrast to the bland affair four years earlier in which Monroe had been elected. In 1824, the field of presidential nominees was crowded, suggesting a party system in disarray. Most notably, all the candidates called themselves "Democratic-Republicans." The label meant little more than the fact that most politicians sought to distance themselves from the outmoded "Federalist" label, which hearkened back to the post-Revolutionary period, rather than pointing forward to the nation's new challenges. Nominees included Secretary of State John Quincy Adams, Representative Henry Clay of Kentucky, and Andrew Jackson, now a senator from Tennessee. Jackson received the highest number of electoral votes (99), but no candidate achieved a majority. As a result, the election went to the House of Representatives.

Clay withdrew from the race. He had promised Jackson his support but then endorsed Adams, whom the House subsequently elected. When Adams named Clay secretary of state, Jackson's supporters cried foul. The election, they charged, amounted to nothing more than a corrupt deal between two political insiders.

TABLE 11.2			
The Election of 1824			
Candidate	**Political Party**	**Popular Vote (%)**	**Electoral Vote**
John Quincy Adams	Democratic-Republican	30.5	84
Andrew Jackson	Democratic-Republican	43.1	99
William H. Crawford	Democratic-Republican	13.1	41
Henry Clay	Democratic-Republican	13.2	37

Haunted by these charges, Adams served his four-year term under a cloud of public distrust. A member of a respected New England family and the son of former president John Adams, the new chief executive had served with distinction in Monroe's cabinet. Still, Adams proved ill suited to the rough-and-tumble world of what came to be called the New Democracy. During his presidency, Adams advocated a greater federal role in internal improvements and public education, a variation on Henry Clay's "American System," a set of policies that promoted a national bank, public funding of canals and turnpikes, and a high tariff to protect domestic manufacturers.

Adams's party, now calling itself the **National Republicans,** faced a formidable challenge in the election of 1828. Having seethed for four long years, Andrew Jackson's supporters (the Democratic-Republicans) now urged "the people" to reclaim the White House. The campaign was a nasty one. Jackson's opponents attacked his personal morality and that of his wife and his mother. Jackson's supporters countered with the charge that Adams was corrupt and that he and his cronies must be swept from office. At campaign rallies, Jacksonians waved about brooms to signal their disgust with the current administration.

A Rowdy Presidential Inauguration

The presidential inauguration of Andrew Jackson in March 1829 was notable in several respects. Jackson was the first military leader since George Washington to be elected president. For the first time, the inaugural ceremony took place on the east front of the U.S. Capitol building, establishing a tradition that continues to this day. After the ceremony, Jackson and his supporters walked from the Capitol to the White House, where a large party was held.

The Library of Congress

Some commentators disapproved of what they considered the excessively lively inauguration gala for the president. One critic described the affair this way: "On their arrival at the White House, the motley crowd clamored for refreshments and soon drained the barrels of punch, which had been prepared, in drinking to the health of the new Chief Magistrate. A great deal of glassware was broken, and the East Room was filled with a noisy mob." The president, in danger of being crushed by the crowd, had to flee from the party.

QUESTIONS

1. Does this picture seem to support the critic who referred to inaugural guests as a "motley crowd" and a "mob"? Why or why not?

2. What is the significance of the fact that a wide range of age groups, and both men and women, attended the inaugural festivities?

3. The Jackson inaugural party was the first attended by large numbers of ordinary people. By opening the doors to the White House, do you think that Jackson was sending a signal about the nature of his presidency? If so, what was it?

4. Outgoing President John Quincy Adams attended neither this inauguration nor the party that followed. Why do you think that was so?

5. Modern inaugural festivities include a large number of parties held in various venues throughout the city of Washington, rather than one large gathering at the White House. What does this reveal about the presidency and American culture today?

By the time of the 1828 election, the Democratic-Republicans and their rivals had developed sophisticated national organizations. They sponsored local entertainments such as parades and barbecues. These gatherings brought out the vote and cultivated party loyalty. With the decline of state laws regulating voter qualifications, ordinary people in the South and the West cast ballots for the first time. The "Hero of the Battle of New Orleans" won a stunning victory, accumulating a record 647,292 popular votes. His supporters hailed the well-to-do slaveholder as the president of the "common" (meaning white) man.

DOCUMENT

Andrew Jackson, First Annual Message to Congress (1829)

TABLE 11.3			
The Election of 1828			
Candidate	**Political Party**	**Popular Vote (%)**	**Electoral Vote**
Andrew Jackson	Democratic	56.0	178
John Quincy Adams	National Republican	44.0	83

Jackson's inauguration trumpeted the triumph of a white man's democracy; at the same time, the raucous celebration that followed gave an indication of the tumult that would characterize his presidency. Inspired by the common-man rhetoric of the president-elect, over 20,000 of his supporters thronged the streets of Washington to celebrate the transfer of power. After taking the oath of office at the Capitol, Jackson walked to the White House, and the boisterous crowd followed. Thousands of people invited themselves inside the president's residence, and Jackson at one point found himself jostled by the celebrants, some of them well lubricated by too much alcohol. He soon escaped and decided to spend his inaugural night not in his new home, but in a nearby hotel. Outside his window, the revelry continued through the night. Back at the White House, large numbers of uninvited guests proceeded to wreck furnishings and cause general havoc. Presidential aides scurried to fill tubs with whiskey in order to lure the crowd outside. Some observers reacted with horror, alarmed that Jackson's appeal to the "common man" would bring disorder and dishonor to the nation.

In office, Jackson tightened his party's grip on power by introducing a national political spoils system, a process by which successful candidates rewarded their supporters with jobs and tossed their rivals out of appointed offices. The spoils system let the Democratic-Republicans—now called the **Democrats**—build a nationwide political machine. Not surprisingly, it also provided fertile ground for corruption and fueled the debate over the use and limits of federal authority.

Federal Authority and Its Opponents

■ *How did Jackson expand the power of the presidency? Who supported and who opposed Jackson's policies regarding federal authority?*

When Americans defeated the British in the War of 1812, they ensured the physical security of the new nation. However, the war's end left a crucial question unanswered: what role would the federal government play in a republic of states? During Andrew Jackson's tenure, Congress, the chief executive, and the Supreme Court all jockeyed for influence over one another and over the states. Jackson claimed a broad popular mandate to increase the power of the presidency. He used this power to force Georgia Indians off their land and to end the charter of the Second Bank of the United States.

At the same time, militant southern sectionalists regarded the growth of federal executive and judicial power with alarm. If the president could impose a high tariff on the states and if the Supreme Court could deny the states the authority to govern Indians within their own borders, might not high-handed federal officials someday also threaten the South's system of slavery?

JUDICIAL FEDERALISM AND THE LIMITS OF LAW

In a series of notable cases, the Supreme Court, under the leadership of Chief Justice John Marshall, sought to limit states' power to control people and resources within their own boundaries. In *McCulloch v. Maryland* (1819), the Court supported Congress's decision to grant the Second Bank of the United States a twenty-year charter. The state of Maryland had

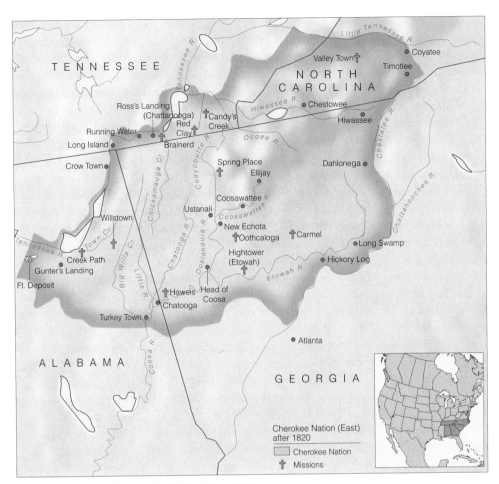

■ **MAP 11.5 The Cherokee Nation After 1820**

This map shows the Cherokee Nation on the eve of removal to Indian Territory (present-day Oklahoma). The discovery of gold in the region sparked a constitutional battle over control of Cherokee land. In 1832, the Supreme Court ruled that the federal government had ultimate authority over Indian nations. The state of Georgia ignored the ruling and sought to enforce its own laws in Cherokee territory.

imposed a high tax on notes issued by the bank. Declaring that "the power to tax involves the power to destroy," the Supreme Court ruled the state's action unconstitutional. The justices held that, although the original Constitution did not mention a national bank, Congress retained the authority to create such an institution. This fact implied that Congress also had the power to preserve it. This decision relied on what came to be called a "loose construction" of the Constitution to justify "implied powers" of the government, powers not explicitly stated in the Constitution.

In 1832, a case involving the rights of the Cherokee Nation brought the Court head to head with President Jackson's own brand of federal muscle-flexing. With the expansion of cotton cultivation into upland Georgia in the early nineteenth century, white residents of that state increasingly resented the presence of their Cherokee neighbors.

At the same time, some Cherokee worked and worshipped in ways similar to European Americans: they cultivated farmland, converted to Christianity, and established a formal legal code. On July 4, 1827, Cherokee leaders met in convention to devise a republican constitution. In the grand tradition of the Patriots of 1776, the group proclaimed the Cherokee a sovereign nation, responsible for its own affairs and free of the dictates of individual (U.S.) states.

By the late 1820s, however, many white people, including the president, were calling for the removal of the Cherokee from the Southeast. The 1829 discovery of gold in the

Georgia hills brought 10,000 white miners to Cherokee territory in a gold rush that the Indians called the "Great Intrusion." President Jackson saw the very existence of the Cherokee Nation as an affront to his authority and a hindrance to Georgia's economic well-being. He resented the fact that the Cherokee considered themselves a sovereign nation, independent of the U.S. president. Jackson, in fact, favored removing all Indians from the Southeast to make way for whites. He declared that Georgia should be rid of "a few thousand savages" so that "towns and prosperous farms" could develop there. In 1830, with the president's backing, Congress passed the Indian Removal Act. The act provided for "an exchange of lands with the Indians residing in any of the states or territories, and for their removal west of the river Mississippi."

DOCUMENT
Memorial of the
Cherokee Nation
(1830)

Outraged by this naked land grab, the Cherokee Nation refused to sign the removal treaties specified by Congress as part of the Indian Removal Act. In a petition to Congress in 1830, members of the group declared, "We wish to remain on the land of our fathers. We have a perfect and original right to claim this, without interruption or molestation." In an effort to protect their land titles, the Cherokee first tried to take the case to Georgia courts, but Georgia refused to allow them to press their claim. The Georgia legislature maintained that it had authority over all the Indians living within the state's borders, and that the Cherokee Nation lacked jurisdiction over its own people. The Cherokee Nation appealed to the Supreme Court.

The Cherokee hoped that the Supreme Court would support their position that they were an independent entity, not bound by the laws of Georgia. In a set of cases—*Cherokee Nation v. Georgia* (1831) and *Worcester v. Georgia* (1832)—the Court agreed that Georgia's authority did not extend to the Cherokee Nation. Governor Wilson Lumpkin of Georgia rejected these Supreme Court rulings. Jackson, too, ignored the Court's display of judicial authority. Of the *Worcester* decision, Jackson declared, "John Marshall has made his decision. Now let him enforce it."

> *The Georgia legislature maintained that it had authority over all the Indians living within the state's borders.*

Some of the president's own supporters protested his determination to deprive landowners—even Indian landowners—of their personal property. Davy Crockett announced that he was voting his conscience and opposing Jackson's Indian removal policy. Declared Crockett, "I believed it was a wicked, unjust measure, and that I should go against it, let the cost to myself be what it might." Nevertheless, in 1832 the president sent troops to Georgia to begin forcing the Indians out of their homeland.

THE "TARIFF OF ABOMINATIONS"

Besides engineering the removal of the Cherokee, Jacksonian Democrats continued the post–War of 1812 policy of high tariffs. In 1828, they pushed through Congress legislation that raised fees on imported manufactured products and raw materials such as wool. Facing a disastrous decline in cotton prices after the Panic of 1819, Southerners protested. To survive, they had to both sell their cotton on the open world market and buy high-priced supplies from New England or Europe. In their view, the higher the tariff on English goods, the less likely the English were to continue to purchase their cotton from southern planters. Southerners dubbed the 1828 legislation the "Tariff of Abominations."

A renewal of the tariff four years later moderated the 1828 rates. But by this time, South Carolina politicians were in no mood to sit back and accept what they saw as the arrogant wielding of federal power. They drew on past precedents in developing a theory called **nullification**—the idea that individual states had the authority to reject, or nullify, federal laws. The Virginia and Kentucky Resolutions of 1798 and 1799 and the Hartford Convention of New England states during the War of 1812 had previously raised this issue of state sovereignty.

The nullification crisis began when politicians led by Senator John C. Calhoun met in a convention in 1832 and declared the tariff "null and void" in South Carolina. But Jackson struck back swiftly. In his Nullification Proclamation of December 10, 1832, he argued that states' rights did not include nullification of federal laws or secession from the Union. The president then sent a token military and naval force to South Carolina to intimidate the nullifiers. Henry Clay, now senator from Kentucky, brokered a compromise agreement: a 10 percent reduction in the Tariff of 1832 over a period of eight years. This compromise finally eased tensions, and the South Carolina nullifiers retreated for the time being. However, they continued to maintain "that each state of the Union has the right, whenever it may deem such a course necessary . . . to secede peaceably from the Union."

THE "MONSTER BANK"

A similar struggle unfolded over the power of the federal government to control a central bank. The repository of federal funds ($10 million), the Second Bank of the United States in the 1830s had thirty branches and controlled the money supply by dictating how state banks should repay their loans: in paper notes or in currency. As a central (though privately held) institution, the bank also aided economic growth and development by extending loans to commercial enterprises.

In 1832, Jackson vetoed a bill that would have renewed the charter of the Second Bank of the United States, which was due to expire in 1836. Somewhat contradictorily, Jackson claimed to represent the interests of small borrowers such as farmers, but he also advocated hard money (currency in the form of gold or silver, not paper or credit extended by banks). Traditionally, small lenders objected to hard money policies, which kept the supply of currency low and interest rates for borrowers high. Jackson also objected to the bank's work as a large commercial institution. For example, he blamed the bank for precipitating the panic and depression of 1819 by withholding credit from small banks, causing them to recall their loans and, in some cases, fail.

Jackson condemned the bank as a "monster" intent on devouring hardworking people and enriching a few eastern financiers. In his veto message to Congress, he fumed, "The humble members of society—the farmers, mechanics, and laborers—who have neither the time nor the means of securing like favors to themselves, have a right to complain of the injustice of their Government." By vetoing the bank bill, Jackson angered members of Congress and his own cabinet. They had urged him to recharter the bank because they believed the credit system was necessary for economic progress and expansion. Convinced that Jackson had overextended his reach, his opponents seized on the issue as a sign of the chief executive's political vulnerability. Harboring presidential ambitions himself, Henry Clay was certain that the bank controversy would prove Jackson's downfall.

However, Clay, the "Great Compromiser," badly miscalculated. Congress upheld Jackson's veto of the national bank (the bank closed when its charter expired in 1836). Nominated for pres-

ident by the National Republicans in 1832, Clay drew support from merchants who had benefited from Bank of the United States loans and from the sizable contingent of Jackson-haters. Still, Jackson won in a landslide against Clay. The president carried not only his stronghold, the West, but also the South and substantial parts of New York, Pennsylvania, and New England.

TABLE 11.4			
The Election of 1832			
Candidate	**Political Party**	**Popular Vote (%)**	**Electoral Vote**
Andrew Jackson	Democratic	55.0	219
Henry Clay	National Republican	42.4	49
John Floyd	Independent	–	11
William Wirt	Anti-Masonic	2.6	7

While in office, Jackson used his veto power a total of twelve times. All his predecessors *combined* had used it just ten times. When his opponents finally formed a political party in 1834, they called themselves **Whigs,** after the English antimonarchist party. In choosing this name, their intention was to ridicule "King Andrew." In the words of the states' rights advocates, Jackson's high-handed manner was "rather an appeal to the loyalty of subjects, than to the patriotism of citizens." The Whigs opposed the man who had built up the power of the presidency in defiance of Congress and the Supreme Court.

> Andrew Jackson's expansion of federal power profoundly affected American society and politics.

Andrew Jackson's expansion of federal power profoundly affected American society and politics. The "age of the common man" produced mixed results for different groups of Americans. On the one hand, greater numbers of white men were able to vote and participate in the political process. The principle of universal manhood suffrage challenged traditional notions that only the wellborn and wealthy were deserving and capable of political leadership and elective office. On the other hand, Native Americans, slaves, free blacks, and women all continued to face inequality and exclusion from the polling place and the jury box. The experiences of these groups highlighted the contradictions in Jacksonian beliefs and policies.

Americans in the "Age of the Common Man"

■ *How did the work of Indians, free and enslaved African Americans, and women change during the "Age of the Common Man"?*

In the early 1830s, a wealthy Frenchman named Alexis de Tocqueville visited the United States and wrote about the contradictions he saw in Jacksonian America. In his book *Democracy in America* (published in 1835), Tocqueville noted that the United States lacked the rigid hierarchy of class privilege that characterized European nations. With universal white manhood suffrage, white men could vote and run for office regardless of their class or religion. However, Tocqueville also noted some sore spots in American democratic values and practices. He commented on the plight of groups deprived of the right to vote; their lack of freedom stood out starkly in the otherwise egalitarian society of the United States. He sympathized with the southeastern Indians uprooted from their homelands. He raised the possibility that conflicts between blacks and whites might eventually lead to bloodshed. He even contrasted the situation of young unmarried white women, who seemed so free-spirited, with that of wives, who appeared cautious and dull. He concluded, "In America a woman loses her independence forever in the bonds of matrimony." Tocqueville saw America for what it was: a blend of freedom and slavery, of independence and dependence.

WARDS, WORKERS, AND WARRIORS: NATIVE AMERICANS

Population growth in the United States—and on the borderlands between the United States and Mexican territory—put pressure on Indian societies. Yet different cultural groups responded in different ways to this pressure. Some, like the Cherokee, conformed to European American ways and became sedentary farmers, and, in some cases, owners of African American slaves. Other Indians were forced to work for whites. Still others either waged war on white settlements and military forces or retreated farther and farther from European American settlements in the hope of avoiding clashes with the intruders.

Nevertheless, prominent whites continued to denigrate the humanity of all Indians. In the 1820s, Henry Clay claimed that Indians were "essentially inferior to the Anglo-Saxon race . . . and their disappearance from the human family will be no great loss to the world." In 1828, the House of Representatives Committee on Indian Affairs surveyed the Indians of the South and concluded that "an Indian cannot work" and that all Indians were lazy and notable for their "thirst for spirituous liquours." According to the committee, when European American settlers depleted reserves of wildlife, Indians as a group would cease to exist.

Members of the Cherokee Nation bitterly denounced these assertions. "The Cherokees do not live upon the chase [for game]," they pointed out. Neither did the Creek, Choctaw, Chickasaw, and Seminole—the other members of the Five Civilized Tribes, so called for their varying degrees of conformity to white people's ways.

Charting a middle course between the Indian and European American worlds was Sequoyah, the son of a white Virginia trader-soldier and a Cherokee woman. A veteran of Andrew Jackson's campaign against the Creek in 1813–1814, Sequoyah moved to Arkansas in 1822, part of an early Cherokee migration west. In 1821, he had finished a Cherokee syllabary (a written language consisting of syllables and letters, in contrast to pictures, or pictographs). The product of a dozen years' work, the syllabary consisted of eighty-six characters. In 1828, the *Cherokee Phoenix*, a newspaper based on the new writing system, began publication in New Echota, Georgia.

Newberry Library, Chicago

■ Artist Charles Bird King painted this portrait of Sequoyah while the Indian leader was in Washington, D.C., in 1828. Government officials honored him for developing a written form of the Cherokee language. He is wearing a medal presented to him by the Cherokee Nation in 1825. He later settled permanently in Sallisaw, in what is today Sequoyah County, Oklahoma.

Sequoyah's written language enabled the increasingly dispersed Cherokee to remain in touch with each other on their own terms. At the same time, numerous Indian cultural groups lost their struggle to retain even modest control over their destinies. In some areas of the continent, smallpox continued to ravage native populations. In other regions, Indians became wards of, or dependent on, whites, living with and working for white families. Some groups who lived close to whites adopted their trading practices. In Spanish California, the Muquelmne Miwok in the San Joaquin delta made a living by stealing and then selling the horses of Mexican settlers.

In other parts of California, Spanish missionaries conquered Indian groups, converted them to Christianity, and then forced them to work in the missions. In missions up and down the California coast, Indians worked as weavers, tanners, shoemakers, bricklayers, carpenters, blacksmiths, and other artisans. Some herded cattle and raised horses. Indian women cooked for the mission, cleaned, and spun wool. They wove cloth and sewed garments.

But even Indians living in or near missions resisted the cultural change imposed by the intruders. Catholic missionaries complained that Indian women such as those of the Chumash refused to learn Spanish. The refusal among some Indians to assimilate completely signaled persistent, deep-seated conflicts between native groups and incoming settlers. In 1824, a revolt among hundreds of newly converted Indians at the mission *La Purisima Concepción* north of Santa Barbara revealed a rising militancy among native peoples.

After the War of 1812, the U.S. government had rewarded some military veterans with land grants in the Old Northwest. Federal agents tried to clear the way for these new settlers by ousting Indians from the area. Overwhelmed by the number of whites, some Indian groups such as the Peoria and Kaskaskia gave up their lands to the interlopers. Others took a stand against the white intrusion. In 1826 and 1827, the Winnebago attacked white families and boat pilots living near Prairie du Chien, Wisconsin. Two years later, the Sauk chief Black Hawk (known to Indians as Ma-ka-tai-me-she-kia-kiak) assembled a coalition of Fox, Winnebago, Kickapoo, and Potawatomi. Emboldened by the prospect of aid from British Canada, they clashed with federal troops and raided farmers' homesteads and miners' camps.

In August 1832, a force of 1,300 U.S. soldiers and volunteers struck back, killing 300 Indian men, women, and children encamped on the Bad Axe River in western Wisconsin. The massacre, the decisive point of what came to be called the Black Hawk War, marked the end of armed Indian resistance north of the Ohio River and east of the Mississippi.

SLAVES AND FREE PEOPLE OF COLOR

In the 1820s, the small proportion of free blacks within the southern population declined further. Southern whites perceived free blacks as an unwelcome and dangerous presence, especially given the possibility that they would conspire with slaves to spark a rebellion. For these reasons some states began to outlaw private manumissions (the practice of individual owners freeing their slaves) and to force free blacks to leave the state altogether.

One free black who inspired such fears was Denmark Vesey. Born on the Danish-controlled island of Saint Thomas in 1767, Vesey was a literate carpenter as well as a religious leader. In 1799, he won $1,500 in a Charleston, South Carolina, lottery and used some of the money to buy his freedom. In the summer of 1822, a Charleston court claimed to have unearthed evidence of a "diabolical plot" hatched by Vesey together with plantation slaves from the surrounding area.

> Some states began to outlaw private manumissions and to force free blacks to leave the state altogether.

Yet the historical record strongly suggests that no plot ever existed. Black "witnesses" who feared for their own lives provided inconsistent and contradictory testimony to a panel of judges. Authorities never located any material evidence of a plan, such as stockpiles of weapons. Under fire from other Charleston elites for rushing to judgment, the judges redoubled their efforts to embellish vague rumors of black discontent into a tale of a well-orchestrated uprising and to implicate growing numbers of black people. As a result of the testimony of several slaves, thirty-five black men were hanged and another eighteen exiled outside the United States. Of those executed, Vesey and twenty-three other men said nothing to support even the vaguest charges of the court. This incident was only the most dramatic manifestation of white southerners' constant fear of a slave uprising.

In the North, some blacks were granted the right to vote after emancipation in the late eighteenth century; however, many of those voting rights were lost in the early nineteenth century. New Jersey (in 1807), Connecticut (1818), New York (1821), and Pennsylvania (1838) all revoked the legislation that had let black men cast ballots. Free northern blacks continued to suffer under a number of legal restrictions. Most were not citizens and therefore perceived themselves as oppressed like the slaves in the South.

A new group of black leaders in the urban North began to link their fate to that of their enslaved brothers and sisters in the South. In Boston, North Carolina–born David Walker published his fiery *Walker's Appeal to the Coloured Citizens of the World* in 1829. Walker called for all blacks to integrate fully into American society, shunning racial segregation whether initiated by whites or by blacks themselves. Reminding his listeners of the horrors of the slave trade, he declared that black people were ready to die for freedom: "I give it as a fact, let twelve black men get well armed for battle, and they will kill and put to flight fifty whites."

Northern black leaders disagreed among themselves on the issues of integration and black separatism—for example, whether blacks should create their own schools or press for inclusion in the public educational system. A few leaders favored leaving the country altogether, believing that black people would never find peace and freedom in the United States. Founded by whites in New Jersey in 1817, the American Colonization Society (ACS) paid for black Americans to settle Monrovia (later named Liberia) on the west coast of Africa. The

ACS drew support from a variety of groups: whites in the upper South who wanted to free their slaves but believed that black and white people could not live in the same country, and some slaves and free people of color convinced that colonization would give them a fresh start. A small number of American-born blacks settled in Liberia. However, most black activists rejected colonization. They had been born on American soil, and their forebears had been buried there. Maria Stewart, an African American religious leader in Boston, declared, "Before I go [to Africa] the bayonet shall pierce me through."

Northern whites sought to control black people and their movements. Outspoken black men and women such as Walker and Stewart alarmed northern whites who feared that if blacks could claim decent jobs, white people would lose their own jobs. African Americans who worked outdoors as wagon drivers, peddlers, and street sweepers were taunted and in some cases attacked by whites who demanded deference from blacks in public. In October 1824, a white mob invaded a black neighborhood in Providence, Rhode Island. They terrorized its residents, destroyed buildings, and left the place "almost entirely in ruins." The catalyst for the riot had come the previous day, when a group of blacks had refused to yield the inside of the sidewalk—a cleaner place to walk—to white passersby.

In the South, whites in 1831 took steps to reinforce the institution of slavery, using both violent and legal means. That year Nat Turner, an enslaved preacher and mystic, led a slave revolt in Southampton, Virginia. In the 1820s, the young Turner had looked skyward and had seen visions of "white spirits and black spirits engaged in battle . . . and blood flowed in streams." Turner believed that he had received divine instructions to lead other slaves to freedom, to "arise and prepare myself, and slay my enemies with their own weapons." In August he and a group of followers that eventually numbered eighty moved through the countryside, killing whites wherever they could find them. Ultimately, nearly sixty whites died at the hands of Turner's rebels. Turner himself managed to evade capture for more than two months. After he was captured, he was tried, convicted, and sentenced to death. A white man named Thomas Gray interviewed Turner in his jail cell and recorded his "confessions" before he was hanged.

Published in 1832 by Gray, *The Confessions of Nat Turner* reached a large, horrified audience in the white South. According to Gray, Turner said that he had exhibited "uncommon intelligence" when he was a child. As a young man, he had received inspiration

Granger Collection, New York

■ This drawing shows the slave rebel Nat Turner preaching to, and plotting with, a group of followers. Some white Southerners feared that any blacks who met together at night were plotting a slave revolt.

DOCUMENT

**The Confessions of
Nat Turner (1831)**

from the Bible, especially the passage "Seek ye the kingdom of Heaven and all things shall be added unto you." Perhaps most disturbing of all, Turner reported that, since 1830, he had been a slave of "Mr. Joseph Travis, who was to me a kind master, and placed the greatest confidence in me; in fact, I had no cause to complain of his treatment to me." Turner's "confessions" suggested the subversive potential of slaves who were literate and Christian and those who were treated kindly by their masters and mistresses.

After the Turner revolt, a wave of white hysteria swept the South. In Virginia near where the killings had occurred, whites assaulted blacks with unbridled fury. The Virginia legislature seized the occasion to defeat various antislavery proposals. Thereafter, all the slave states moved to strengthen the institution of slavery. For all practical purposes, public debate over slavery ceased throughout the American South.

LEGAL AND ECONOMIC DEPENDENCE: THE STATUS OF WOMEN

Regardless of where they lived, enslaved women and Indian women had almost no rights under either U.S. or Spanish law. However, legal systems in the United States and the Spanish borderlands differed in their treatment of white women. In the United States, most of the constraints that white married women had experienced in the colonial period still applied in the 1820s. A husband controlled the property that his wife brought to the marriage, and he had legal authority over their children. Indeed, the wife was considered her husband's possession. She had no right to make a contract, keep money she earned, vote, run for office, or serve on a jury. In contrast, in the Spanish Southwest, married women (both European and native) could own land and conduct business on their own. At the same time, however, husbands, fathers, and local priests continued to exert much influence over the lives of these women.

Although few women earned cash wages in the 1820s, almost all adult women worked.

European American women's economic subordination served as a rationale for their political inferiority. The "common man" concept rested on the assumption that men had the largest stake in society because only they owned property. That stake made them responsible citizens.

Yet women contributed to the economy in myriad ways. Although few women earned cash wages in the 1820s, almost all adult women worked. In the colonial period, society had highly valued women's labor in the fields, the garden, and the kitchen. However, in the early nineteenth century, work was becoming increasingly identified as labor that earned cash wages. This attitude proved particularly common in the Northeast, where increasing numbers of workers labored under the supervision of a boss. As this belief took root, men began valuing women's contributions to the household economy less and less. If women did not earn money, many men asked, did they really work at all?

In these years, well-off women in the northeastern and mid-Atlantic states began to think of themselves as consumers and not producers of goods. They relied more and more on store-bought cloth and household supplies. Some could also afford to hire servants to perform housework for them. Privileged women gradually stopped thinking of their responsibilities as making goods or processing and preparing food. Rather, their main tasks were to manage servants and create a comfortable home for their husbands and children.

In contrast, women in other parts of the country continued to engage in the same forms of household industry that had characterized the colonial period. In Spanish settlements, women played a central role in household production. They made all of their family's clothes by carding, spinning, and weaving the wool from sheep. They tanned cowhides and ground blue corn to make tortillas, or *atole*. They produced their own candles and soap, and they plastered the walls of the home.

Like women's work in general, the labor of wives and mothers in Spanish-speaking regions had great cultural significance. In the Mexican territory of California, Native women servants engaged in backbreaking efforts so that elite wives and daughters could wear snow-white linen clothing. One community member recalled that "certainly to do so was one of the chief anxieties" of well-to-do households: "There was sometimes a great deal of linen to be washed for it was the pride of every Spanish family to own much linen, and the mothers and daughters almost always wore white."

In the Spanish mission of San Gabriel, California, the widow Eulalia Pérez cooked, sewed, ministered to the ill, and instructed children in reading and writing. As housekeeper, Pérez kept the keys to the mission storehouse. She also distributed supplies to the Indians and the *vaqueros* (cowboys) who lived in the mission. She supervised Indian servants as well as soap makers, wine pressers, and olive oil producers. In her spare time, she dipped chocolates and bottled lemonade to be sold in Spain.

At Mission San Diego, Apolonaria Lorenzana worked as a healer and cared for the church sacristy and priestly vestments. From the time she arrived in Monterey at age seven (in 1800) until her death in the late nineteenth century, Lorenzana devoted her life to such labors. Although the priests tried to restrict her to administering the mission hospital, she took pride in her nursing abilities. She also taught herself to read and write. She later recalled, "When I was a young woman in California, I learned alone to write, using the books I saw, imitating the letters on whatever white paper I found discarded."

Indian women also engaged in a variety of essential tasks. Sioux and Mandan women, though of a social rank inferior to men, performed a great deal of manual labor in their own villages. They dressed buffalo skins that the men later sold to traders. They collected water and wood, cooked, dried meat and fruit, and cultivated maize (corn), pumpkins, and squash with hoes made from the shoulder blades of elk. These women worked collectively within a network of households rather than individually within nuclear families.

Many women, regardless of ethnicity, were paid for their work with food and shelter but not money. Nevertheless, some women did work for cash wages during this era. New England women and children, for example, were the vanguard of factory wage-earners in the early manufacturing system. In Massachusetts in 1820, women and children constituted almost a third of all manufacturing workers. In the largest textile factories, they made up fully 80 percent of the workforce.

The business of textile manufacturing took the tasks of spinning thread and weaving cloth out of the home and relocated those tasks in factories. The famous "Lowell mill girls" are an apt example. Young, unmarried white women from New Hampshire, Vermont, and Massachusetts, these workers moved to the new company town of Lowell, Massachusetts, to take jobs as textile machine operatives. In New England, thousands of young men had migrated west, tipping the sex ratio in favor of women and creating a reserve of female laborers. But to attract young women to factory work, mill owners had to reassure them (and their parents) that they would be safe and well cared for away from home. To that end, they established boarding houses where employees could live together under the supervision of a matron—an older woman who served as their mother-away-from-home.

Company towns set rules shaping employees' living conditions as well as their working conditions. In the early 1830s, a posted list of "Rules and Regulations" covered many aspects of the lives of the young women living at the Poignaud and Plant boardinghouse at

■ Although textile production was moving to factories, sewing garments remained a labor-intensive task performed by women at home. The plight of needlewomen became representative of the hazards faced by female workers in the new urban commercial economy of the late eighteenth and early nineteenth centuries. Many women sewed garments that they returned to a "jobber" for payment. The labor, often performed by candlelight in ill-lighted tenements, was tedious and ill paid. Laundry work also took up much of women's time.

Eulalia Pérez Describes her Work in a California Mission, 1823

Interpreting History

Born to Spanish parents in Baja, California, Eulalia Pérez was a widow with five daughters when she became the chief housekeeper for the San Gabriel Mission in the early 1820s. She secured her position by winning a cooking competition between herself and two other Spanish women. Here she gives an account of her many duties in the mission.

I made several kinds of soup, a variety of meat dishes and whatever else happened to pop into my head that I knew how to prepare. . . .

Because of all this, employment was provided for me at the mission. At first they

Mission San Carlos Borromeo in Carmel, California. Beyond the fountain is the mission's central courtyard. On the left is the *ranchería*, where Indians lived. In this and other missions along the California coast, Indians maintained separate residences in traditional-style dwellings. Even Indians who worked and prayed at the missions attempted to preserve their own customs related to clothing, food, and kin and family relations.

David Muench/CORBIS

assigned me two Indians so that I could show them how to cook. . . .

The missionaries were very satisfied; this made them think more highly of me. I spent about a year teaching those two Indians. I did not have to do the work, only direct them, because they already had learned a few of the fundamentals.

Lancaster, Massachusetts. The list told the women how to enter the building (quietly, and then hang up "their bonnet, shawl, coat, etc. etc. in the entry") and where to sit at the dinner table (the two workers with greatest seniority were to take their places at the head of the table). Despite these rules, many young women valued the friendships they made with their coworkers and the money they made in the mills. Some of them sent their wages back home so that their fathers could pay off the mortgage or their brothers could attend school.

But not all women wage-earners labored in large mills. In New York City, single women, wives, and widows toiled as needleworkers in their homes. Impoverished, sewing in tiny attics by the dim light of candles, these women were at the mercy of jobbers—merchants who parceled out cuffs, collars, and shirt fronts that the women finished. Other urban women worked as street vendors, selling produce, or as cooks, nursemaids, or laundresses.

The new delineation between men's and women's work and workplaces intensified the drive for women's education begun after the Revolution. If well-to-do women were to assume domestic responsibilities while their husbands worked outside the home, then women must receive their own unique form of schooling, or so the reasoning went. Most

After this, the missionaries conferred among themselves and agreed to hand over the mission keys to me. This was in 1821, if I remember correctly. . . .

The duties of the housekeeper were many. In the first place, every day she handed out the rations for the mess hut. To do this she had to count the unmarried women, bachelors, day-laborers, *vaqueros*. . . . Besides that, she had to hand out daily rations to the heads of households. In short, she was responsible for the distribution of supplies to the Indian population and to the missionaries' kitchen. She was in charge of the key to the clothing storehouse where materials were given out for dresses for the unmarried and married women and children. Then she also had to take care of cutting and making clothes for the men.

Furthermore, she was in charge of cutting and making the vaqueros' outfits, from head to foot—that is, for the vaqueros who rode in saddles. Those who rode bareback received nothing more than their cotton blanket and loin-cloth, while those who rode in saddles were dressed the same way as the Spanish-speaking inhabitants; that is, they were given shirt, vest, jacket, trousers, hat, cowboy boots, shoes and spurs; and a saddle, bridle and lariat for the horse. Besides, each vaquero was given a big silk or cotton handkerchief, and a sash of Chinese silk or Canton crepe, or whatever there happened to be in the storehouse.

They put under my charge everything having to do with clothing. I cut and fitted, and my five daughters sewed up the pieces. When they could not handle everything, the father was told, and then women from the town of Los Angeles were employed, and the father paid them.

Besides this, I had to attend to the soap-house, . . . to the wine-presses, and to the olive-crushers that produced oil, which I worked in myself. . . .

I handled the distribution of leather, calf-skin, chamois, sheepskin, Morocco leather, fine scarlet cloth, nails, thread, silk, etc.—everything having to do with the making of saddles, shoes and what was needed for the belt- and shoe-making shops.

Every week I delivered supplies for the troops and Spanish-speaking servants. These consisted of beans, corn, garbanzos, lentils, candles, soap and lard. To carry out this distribution, they placed at my disposal an Indian servant named Lucio, who was trusted completely by the missionaries.

When it was necessary, some of my daughters did what I could not find the time to do.

QUESTIONS

1. *What were some of the things produced at the mission?*

2. *Why did the position of housekeeper confer such high status?*

3. *What other kinds of workers in the mission does Pérez mention?*

4. *How does this account reveal some of the larger purposes of Spanish missions? In what ways were these missions colonial as well as religious enterprises?*

Source: Eileen Boris and Nelson Lichtenstein, eds., *Major Problems in the History of American Workers,* 2nd ed. (New York: Houghton Mifflin, 2002), 93–95.

ordinary women received little in the way of formal education. Yet elite young women had expanded educational opportunities, beginning in the early nineteenth century. Emma Willard founded a female academy in Troy, New York, in 1821, and Catharine Beecher established the Hartford Female Seminary two years later in Connecticut. For the most part, these schools catered to the daughters of wealthy families, young women who would never have to work in a factory to survive. Hailed as a means to prepare young women to serve as wives and mothers, the schools taught geography, foreign languages, mathematics, science, and philosophy, as well as the "female" pursuits of embroidery and music.

Out of this curriculum designed especially for women emerged women's rights activists, women who keenly felt both the potential of their own intelligence and the degrading nature of their social situation. Elizabeth Cady, an 1832 graduate of the Troy Female Seminary, later went on to marry Henry B. Stanton and bear seven children. But by the 1840s, she strode onto the national stage as a tireless advocate of women's political and economic rights. Still, women of all cultures remained under the control of men even as they contributed to local and national economic development in numerous ways.

Ties That Bound a Growing Population

■ *In what ways did Americans maintain a sense of community in the face of unprecedented migration and population growth?*

Conflicts stemming from racial and gender distinctions proved stubborn throughout this period of territorial expansion. The country's founders had disagreed among themselves about whether democracy could thrive in a large nation, where news necessarily traveled slowly and people remained isolated from their neighbors. Still, by the 1820s few Americans doubted that the nation could grow while preserving its democratic character. In fact, westward expansion seemed to promote democracy, as more ordinary white men than ever participated in the political process.

At the same time, population growth and migration patterns disrupted old bonds of community. When people left their place of birth, they often severed ties with their family and original community. New forms of social cohesion arose to replace these traditional ties. New religions sought to make sense of the changing political and economic landscapes. High literacy rates among the population created a new community of readers, a far-flung audience for periodicals as well as for a new, uniquely American literature. Finally, opinion-makers used the printed word to spread new ideas and values across regional boundaries. These ideas, such as glorification of male ambition, helped knit together scattered segments of the population, men and women who began to speak of an "American character."

NEW VISIONS OF RELIGIOUS FAITH

New forms of religious faith arose in response to turbulent times. During the Indian Wars in the Old Northwest, a Winnebago prophet named White Cloud helped Black Hawk create a coalition of Winnebago, Potawatomi, Kickapoo, Sauk, and Fox Indians. A mystic and medicine man, White Cloud preached against the white man and exhorted his followers to defend their way of life, an Indian way that knew no tribal boundaries. White Cloud, the religious leader, and Black Hawk, the military leader, surrendered together to federal troops on August 27, 1832, signifying the spiritual component in the Indians' militant resistance to whites. Through the rest of the nineteenth century, a number of Indian groups found inspiration, and in some cases common ground, in the teachings of Indian religious leaders.

■ **FIGURE 11.1 Estimated Population of the United States, 1790–1860**
Colonial Times to 1967 (Washington, 1960)

Source: Historical Statistics of the United States, 7.

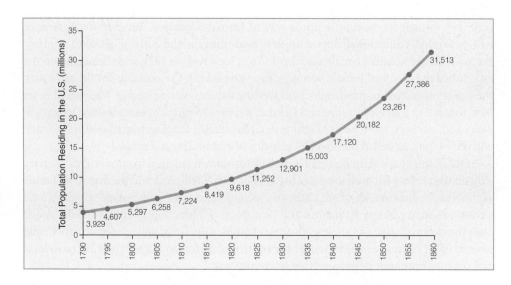

Laurie Platt Winfrey, Inc.

◼ The long-lived religious revival called the Second Great Awakening swept through the United States in the 1820s and 1830s. Charles Grandison Finney, an itinerant preacher, helped lead the movement. He urged listeners to consider themselves "moral free agents" with control over their own destinies. Services conducted outdoors, called "camp meetings," provided settings for mass audiences to engage in emotional release and personal testimonials of newly found faith.

New religious enthusiasms took hold in other parts of the country as well. In the late 1820s and early 1830s, the **Second Great Awakening** swept western New York. The fervor of religious revivals so heated the region that people began to call it "the Burned-Over District." Large numbers of people of various Protestant denominations attended week-long prayer meetings, sat together on the "anxious bench" for sinners, and listened, transfixed, as new converts told of their path to righteousness.

What explains this wave of religious enthusiasm? A major factor was a clergyman named Charles Grandison Finney, who managed to tap into the wellsprings of hope and anxiety of the time. A former lawyer, Finney preached that people were moral free agents, fully capable of deciding between right and wrong and doing good in the world. Finney's message had great appeal during this period of rapid social, economic, and technological change. In one sermon, he declared, "The church must take the right ground in regard to politics. . . . The time has come that Christians must vote for honest men." Of course, not all Christians agreed on what constituted the "right ground" in politics. But Finney sought to link the life of the spirit with political and reform efforts, and many men and women responded enthusiastically.

Throughout the country, religious institutions also grappled with questions about slavery. As the fear of possible black uprisings spread, white clergy in the South began to turn away from their former willingness to convert anyone. Instead, they began seeking respectability in the eyes of the well-to-do, slave-owning class. Incorporating masculine imagery into their sermons, they used the language of militant patriotism to distance themselves from the white women, slaves, and free people of color in their congregations. At a western revival in 1824, one itinerant Methodist minister described his military service in the War of 1812; he had helped to vanquish not only the British but also "the merciless savages of the forest, and to secure and perpetuate the liberties secured to us by our forefathers." These preachers strove to reinforce the power of husband over wife, parent over child, and master over slave, relations that defined the typical plantation household.

Elsewhere, some church leaders sought to purge Christianity of what they saw as its too-worldly nature and to revive the earlier, simpler church that Jesus and his disciples had established. On April 6, 1830, a young farmer named Joseph Smith Jr. founded the

Church of Jesus Christ of Latter-Day Saints—also called the Mormon Church—in Fayette, New York. Smith said that, in a vision, he had received the text of a holy book originally written by a Native American historian more than 1,400 years earlier. Transcribed from tablets Smith said were presented to him by an angel named Moroni, the text was called the *Book of Mormon*. Together with the Old and New Testaments, it formed the basis of a new faith. Over the next few years, the Mormon Church grew rapidly, claiming 8,000 members by the mid-1830s. However, the young church also aroused intense hostility among mainstream Protestant denominations that regarded the new group's theology with suspicion. It was almost impossible for religious institutions to escape the worldly realm of politics and social fragmentation.

LITERARY AND CULTURAL VALUES IN AMERICA

Around the same time, a young widow named Sarah Hale broke new ground for women. In 1828, she became the first woman to edit an American periodical when she accepted responsibility for editing the *Ladies Magazine*, published in Boston. Once a hatmaker but now a published poet and novelist, Hale aimed "to make females better acquainted with

This picture highlights an early Victorian ideal of domesticity. Here the Reverend John Atwood and his family, dressed in their Sunday best, gather in their well-appointed parlor to read the Bible. The piano, pictures on the wall, and rich fabrics all reveal the household's elite status.

their duties and privileges" through the articles in her magazine. Between 1825 and 1850, thousands of other magazines cropped up and then disappeared, the product of a growing audience of literate (and literary) city-dwellers. But the *Ladies Magazine*, later renamed *Godey's Lady's Book*, lived an uncommonly long life under Hale's editorial guidance.

The *Ladies Magazine* appealed primarily to well-off white wives and mothers in the Northeast, the South, and the West. They identified with its message promoting motherhood and the virtues of piety and self-sacrifice. The *Ladies Magazine* and other publications portrayed women as especially devout and thus powerful: men might claim as their domain "the government and the glory of the world," wrote Hale in 1832, "but nevertheless, what man shall become depends upon the secret, silent influence of women." That influence, Hale and other men and women like her believed, derived from women's roles as nurturers and caretakers.

Indeed, many of the poems and short stories published in the *Ladies Magazine* and other women's periodicals came under the category of sentimental literature. Such writing was calculated to appeal to readers' emotions, rather than their intellect, as their titles reveal: "Burial of a Motherless Infant," "The Blind Mother and Her Children," and "The Harp of the Maniac Maiden" (about a young girl's descent into insanity).

Just as sentimental fiction and poetry attracted a large readership among women, a number of male writers staked their claim to emerging American literature. Washington Irving, James Fenimore Cooper, and William Cullen Bryant all explored regional histories and landscapes in their works. In "Rip Van Winkle" (1819) and "The Legend of Sleepy Hollow" (1820), Irving wrote about the legends of upstate New York. Cooper explored the western New York region contested by the British, Americans, French, and Indians in the late eighteenth century in such works as *The Spy* (1821) and *The Last of the Mohicans* (1826).

Freed from the arduous household labor required of the colonial housewife, the idealized mother of the nineteenth-century emerging middle classes devoted herself to providing religious instruction to her children. This mother, portrayed in *Godey's Lady's Book*, teaches her daughter to pray. The bedroom furnishings suggest a life of physical comfort and ease.

Bryant, inspired by the sight of the Illinois plains in 1832, penned "The Prairies," a praise-song to the vast plains as beautiful and "quick with life." As the vanguard of a new generation of American authors, these writers began a literary "American Renaissance."

Along with this new American literary tradition, small towns across the nation began publishing newspapers to educate, inform, and entertain readers. News stories about national elections and legislation, about foreign monarchs and conflicts, reached log cabins in the West as well as elegant townhouses in Boston and Philadelphia. Wrote Washington Irving in 1820, "Over no nation does the press hold a more absolute control than over the people of America, for the universal education of the poorest classes makes every individual a reader."

Spreading new ideas was a crucial strategy for political activists, who appreciated the power of print media to change people's minds. During this period, intellectuals from the southern Americas came to see "*la famosa Filadelfia*" as an asylum for supporters of independence from Spain. Plugging into Philadelphia's vibrant print culture, writers from Cuba, Peru, Mexico, and other countries published political tracts in support of movements against colonial rule and post-independence monarchical structures. In addition, Philadelphia's numerous printers began publishing a variety of Spanish-language books for profit. As a result, Philadelphia became one of the major producers of Spanish-language materials in the hemisphere. Among dozens of books and pamphlets published in the city was Vincente Rocafuerte's 1821 *Ideas Necesarias a Todo Pueblo Americano Independiente, Que Quiera Ser Libre* (Essential Ideas for all Independent American Countries Seeking Freedom), a collection of translations of U.S. revolutionary documents such as Tom Paine's *Common Sense*.

More generally, widely distributed newspapers, books, and magazines promoted a set of values that writers claimed described an enduring American character. The ideal American supposedly was ambitious—ready to seize opportunity wherever it could be found—and at the same time devoted to home and family. In fact, these values strongly resembled those adopted by the British middle classes at the same time. Indeed, the United States spawned its own brand of middle-class sensibility called **Victorianism,** after the English queen who reigned from 1837 to 1901.

Five core values defined early American Victorianism. First, was a belief in the significance of the individual. People should be judged on the basis of their character, not on the circumstances of their birth. This belief, however, generally applied only to white men. Second, individuals should have the freedom to advance as far as their talents and ambition took them; no person should claim advantages over others by virtue of a noble title or aristocratic lineage. Third, work was intrinsically noble, whether performed by a canal digger wielding a pick-axe or a merchant using a quill pen. All people, regardless of their trade, deserved to reap the fruits of their labor. Fourth, everyone should exercise self-control and restraint in activities such as drinking and engaging in sexual relations. Finally, men and women occupied separate but complementary spheres. American society could be orderly and stable only if men could find a "haven from the heartless world" of work in their own homes. There, wives tended the hearth and infused the household with their love, self-sacrifice, and religious devotion.

Victorians often saw work as an individualistic endeavor, with men, women, and children earning wages for the number of hours they worked or for each task they performed. However, not all groups embraced Victorian attitudes. The Sioux and Mandan, among other Indian tribes, favored a way of life that valued community over the individual. Likewise, Spanish-speaking settlers of tight-knit adobe pueblos prized the close cooperation of men and women: *compadres* (godfathers) with *comadres* (godmothers). These settlers lived their lives according to the seasonal rhythms of agriculture and stock-raising.

In the South, slaveholders straddled both positions. They idealized both profit-seeking individualism and a traditional way of life based on community ties. These white men and women eagerly raked in the financial gains that flowed from their control over staple-crop agriculture. Yet in their public pronouncements, they scorned the exclusive pursuit of profit. They held their loyalties to family, kin, and community above the crass emphasis on cash that Yankees espoused. As conflicts between Indians and whites revealed, differences in values were far more than theoretical abstractions. Ultimately, they could wreak death and destruction, as Northerners and Southerners soon discovered.

Conclusion

Western settlement infused American politics with raw energy in the 1820s. Andrew Jackson was the first in a long line of presidents who boasted of their humble origins and furthered their careers by denouncing what they called the privileges enjoyed by wealthy Easterners. The western impulse for grassroots politicking shaped political reforms, such as those that abolished property requirements for white male suffrage. The challenges faced by western settlers in establishing homesteads and paying their debts emerged as national, not purely local, issues. Through the sheer force of his personality, Andrew Jackson exemplified these dramatic changes in the political landscape. Almost single-handedly, he extended the limits of executive power and remade the American party system in the process.

Many of the distinctive features of American society in the third decade of the nineteenth century can be traced to the "restlessness" of Americans who had the freedom and desire to move from one place to another. By seeking bank loans to build their family farms, western homesteaders relied on wildcat banks that collapsed in large numbers during the Panic of

1819, leading them to resent and distrust state banks and creditors in general. Believing that Americans had a "destiny" to occupy and control much of the Western Hemisphere, James Monroe's administration conceived the Monroe Doctrine as a way to discourage Russia, Spain, and Britain from blocking United States continental expansion. In the South, land-hungry European Americans used the courts to deprive the Cherokee and other American Indian tribes of their lands. Ironically, by this time the Cherokee had adopted many European American customs; some had converted to Christianity and engaged in farming.

As people moved out west and back again, they replaced traditional social ties with new ones. Religious revivals created new communities of Protestant believers. The increasing circulation of newspapers and magazines allowed even western migrants to subscribe to eastern periodicals and keep informed of the latest dress fashions and child-rearing techniques.

Westward migration had a profound effect on life in the East. The expanded western markets for eastern goods promoted manufacturing in New England and the Mid-Atlantic. When young men migrated west in search of opportunity, eastern textile mill owners turned to young women to serve as machine operatives. New forms of transportation, including canals and steamboats, provided new sources of employment for construction workers and craftsmen. Easterners eagerly read travel accounts, short stories, and novels that portrayed life in the western part of the country. Meanwhile, a new class of western debtors was giving its support to President Andrew Jackson. He denounced the Second Bank of the United States as a "monster" and refused to extend its charter. His bold sense of federal authority gave rise to a new national party, the Jacksonian Democrats; the party claimed support from debtors, workers, and small shopkeepers in all areas of the country.

At the same time, the contradictions in Jacksonian politics became ever more glaring. As the nation expanded its borders and diversified its economy, distinctions between social classes sharpened. Factory workers could not reliably afford to buy the cloth and shoes they produced with machines. Suffrage restrictions, especially those based on property ownership, crumbled under the weight of a Jacksonian ideology of equality. However, a majority of the population remained outside the body politic: women, slaves, and free people of color gained nothing in the way of formal political participation during the "Age of the Common Man."

Most significantly, western migration exposed the fragile political bargain that preserved the institution of slavery. By moving west, European Americans played unwitting roles in the great political drama that would take center stage over the next three decades. Meanwhile, the North and South eyed each other with increasing distrust. And the contrast between those who moved from place to place voluntarily and those who were forced to move became even more striking.

CHRONOLOGY: 1819–1832

1819 Spain cedes Florida to United States.
Tallmadge Amendment.
Panic of 1819 triggers economic depression.

1820 Missouri Compromise maintains North–South balance of power.
Washington Irving, "The Legend of Sleepy Hollow."

1821 Mexico gains independence from Spain.
Sequoyah completes Cherokee syllabary.

1822 Charleston officials convict and hang blacks in Vesey "plot."

1823 Monroe Doctrine declares Western Hemisphere off limits to Europe.
Catharine Beecher establishes Hartford Female Seminary.
Lowell textile mills open.

1824 Erie Canal opens.

1826 American Society for the Promotion of Temperance founded.

1827 Workingmen's party founded in Philadelphia.

1828 *Cherokee Phoenix* begins publication.

1829 Gold discovered on Cherokee lands in Georgia.

1831 Nat Turner leads slave rebellion in Virginia.
William Lloyd Garrison publishes *The Liberator*.

1832 Nullification crisis.
Worcester v. Georgia.
Jackson vetoes Second Bank of the United States.
Black Hawk War.

For Review

1. Some of Andrew Jackson's supporters declared that his experience as a military leader made him a good candidate for the presidency. In contrast, some of his opponents argued that Jackson's record as a general disqualified him for political leadership. How would you explain and evaluate this debate?

2. How did Jackson shape the role of the presidency and the federal government? What was the significance of the nullification crisis? The clash over the national bank?

3. What factors account for the rise of new political parties during this period?

4. Discuss the constitutional principles at stake in debates over the rights of the Cherokee.

5. Who benefited from and who was left out of the "Age of the Common Man"?

6. Victorianism was one among many cultures in the United States. What were some of the groups that adhered to cultural values distinct from those of the Victorians?

7. What was the larger political and social significance of a mass-produced print culture?

8. Is it appropriate to refer to this period as the Jacksonian Era? Why or why not?

Created Equal Online

For more *Created Equal* resources, including suggestions on sites to visit and books to read, go to **MyHistoryLab.com.**

Chapter 12

Peoples in Motion, 1832–1848

■ Norwegian immigrants to the United States, 1880s.

In the spring of 1847, Jannicke Saehle left her home in Bergen, a city on the western coast of Norway, and boarded a ship bound for New York City. From New York, the young woman traveled by steamship up the Hudson River to Albany. There she boarded a train to Milwaukee, Wisconsin. Although arduous, the journey had its pleasures. Piloted by a charming captain, the steamship resembled, in Saehle's words, "a complete house four stories high, and very elegantly furnished, with beautiful rugs everywhere." On the train, the passengers enjoyed each other's company as well as "the noteworthy sights that we rushed past." By the summer, Saehle was living with and working as a domestic servant for a Norwegian family, the Torjersens, in Koshkonong in southeastern Wisconsin. Founded in 1840, Koshkonong was a rapidly growing settlement of Norwegian immigrants farming the fertile prairie.

Jannicke Saehle was eager to make a new life for herself in the United States. For just a few months of service in the Torjersen household, she received the harvest of three acres of wheat for three years. In the fall, she found a job washing and ironing at a tavern in Madison. For the first five weeks, she earned a dollar a week. Then she received a raise of $.25 a week, with the promise of another raise, and relief from washing, at the end of the winter. Although she could not speak English, she was pleased to "enjoy the best treatment" from the tavern owners and patrons.

In September 1847, Jannicke Saehle wrote of her good fortune in America in a letter to her family back in Norway. She described "the superabundance of food" in the Torjersen home. On their forty-acre farm, the Torjersens kept swine and produced "tremendous amounts" of wheat, potatoes, beans, cabbages, cucumbers, onions, and many other kinds of vegetables. At the Madison tavern, she had "food and drink in abundance" and dined on the same fare served to the guests: for breakfast, "chicken, mutton [lamb], beef or pork, warm or cold wheat bread, butter, white cheese, eggs, or small pancakes, the best coffee, tea, cream and sugar." For supper she feasted on "warm biscuits, and several kinds of cold wheat bread, cold meats, bacon, cakes, preserved apples, plums, and berries, which are eaten with cream, and tea and coffee." Saehle felt heartbroken to see excess food thrown to the chickens and pigs, for, she wrote, "I think of my dear ones in Bergen, who like so many others must at this time lack the necessaries of life."

Jannicke Saehle was one of more than 13,000 immigrants from Norway, Sweden, and Denmark who arrived in the United States in the 1840s, a sixfold increase over the number of Scandinavians who had arrived the decade before. This migration continued to increase over the course of the nineteenth century. In the 1880s, more than 655,000 Scandinavians, fleeing poverty and military conflict, came to America. Many traveled to Wisconsin and Minnesota, where they farmed small homesteads and found the cold winter climate similar to that of their homeland.

In the rural upper Midwest, clashes between Indians and white settlers shaped the experiences of many immigrants. Newcomers to Minnesota especially did not fare well; there the great Sioux uprising of 1862 resulted in the deaths of hundreds of Indians and immigrant settlers, Swedes and Norwegians prominent among them. However, by the late 1840s, settlers in Wisconsin such as Jannicke Saehle had little reason to fear the Indians whose ancestral lands they occupied; the U.S. Army's destruction of a band of Sauk Indians under the leadership of Black Hawk in 1832 had opened up much of the area to whites.

In the 1830s and 1840s, patterns of settlement and employment among immigrant groups varied widely in the United States. For example, most Irish immigrants lacked the resources to move much farther west than the eastern seaboard ports where they landed. In contrast, many Germans arrived with enough money to buy farmland in the Midwest or take up a trade in east-ern cities. Nevertheless, Norwegian immigrants had much in common with other groups that came to the United States in these years. Many relied on compatriots who had already arrived for jobs and housing. The newcomers found employment in expanding regional economies. Communities of immigrants built their own religious institutions and mutual aid societies.

In the 1830s and 1840s, the United States was home to many peoples in motion. Groups of Indians in the Southeast and Midwest and slaves in the upper South were forced at gunpoint to move from one region of the country to another. From western Europe came poor and perse-cuted groups drawn to the United States by the demand for labor and the promise of religious and political freedom. Some Americans eagerly pulled up stakes and moved to nearby cities or towns in search of better jobs. Migrants with enough resources made the long journey across the Sonoran Desert in the Southwest to California, or to the Oregon Territory in the Northwest.

Population movements and economic change generated new forms of community and group identity. Some immigrants left behind old identities and created new ones for themselves in their new homes. In their native lands, many newcomers to the United States had lived and labored as peasants under the control of aristocratic landlords. Now in America, these immigrants worked as wage-earners or as small farmers. Urban workers founded the National Trades Union, an organization that tried to help laboring people wield political influence. Some women and men who believed in their power to change society banded together for any number of causes—including those that challenged basic institutions such as the nuclear family, slavery, and white supremacy. Some reformers established new communities based on alternative notions of marriage and child-rearing.

Partisan politics also entered a new era. By 1836, the "Second Party" system had emerged, as Jacksonian Democrats squared off against the Whigs on familiar issues, including tariffs and new systems of transportation. The Whigs, a coalition of anti-Jackson forces, sought to craft an economic program that would appeal to the largest number of voters. Less concerned with the purity of their ideas than with success at the ballot box, the Whigs saw their policies as a means to winning elections and not necessarily as ends in themselves.

The choices offered by the Whigs and Democrats failed to represent what many groups saw as their pressing political and economic interests. In response, many Americans turned to violence to advance or defend their causes. The deep-seated resentments or lofty aspirations among various ethnic and religious groups and social classes provoked bloodshed. Urban mobs vented their wrath against African Americans, abolitionists, and Irish immigrants and other Catholics. The government itself sponsored violence, which peaked in the late 1830s with the forced removal of southeastern Indians to the West, and again in the late 1840s, when the United States wrested a vast expanse of land from Mexico. Indeed, within the larger society, physical force seemed to be an acceptable means of resolving disputes; tellingly, politicians of all persuasions followed Andrew Jackson's lead and staked their claim to national leadership on the basis of their records as soldiers, military officers, and Indian-killers.

Although industrial machines such as locomotives and textile looms grew more sophisticated in these years, farming remained the primary occupation for many people. However, when the land refused to yield crops, millions of people had to move on—from the blighted potato fields of Ireland, the rocky soil of New England, or the worn-out cotton fields of the South. In search of new economic opportunities, some people moved into lands belonging to other people. In the territory occupied by native Spanish speakers in Texas or by Indians in the Southeast, people stood ready to fight—and die—for the land.

Mass Migrations

■ *What caused some groups to migrate voluntarily? Why were others forced to move against their will?*

When foreign visitors called Americans a "restless" people, they were referring to patterns of both immigration into and migration within the country. Between 1830 and 1850, 2.3 million immigrants entered the United States, up from a total of 152,000 during the two previous decades. In the 1840s, 1.7 million immigrants arrived. (In 1850 the country's total population stood at 23 million people). Most newcomers came from Ireland, Germany, England, Scotland, and Scandinavia.

Within the United States, individuals and families moved around the country with almost dizzying frequency in search of better jobs. They migrated from rural to urban areas, from one city to another, out west and then back to the east. In Boston, in any one year, about a third of the population left the city to find a new home elsewhere. In the late 1840s, almost half of all urban residents moved within a twelve-month period. For the country as a whole, an estimated one family in five moved every year, and on average every family moved once every five years. Many westward migrants had enough money to move overland and buy a homestead once they arrived in Wisconsin or Oregon. However, much of the population turnover in urban areas stemmed from landless people's relentless quest for higher wages and cheaper places to rent.

Population Change in Ireland, 1841–1851

Percentage of change
per county

+9   -20
0   -25
-13

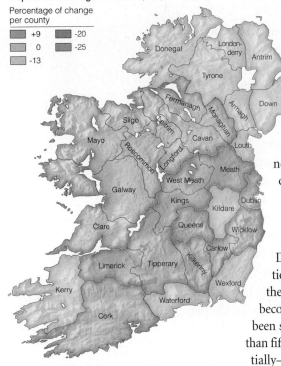

Pauperism in Ireland, 1847–1851

Over 50% of people
living in such poverty
as to be declared
paupers

■ **MAP 12.1   Population Change in Ireland, 1841–1851**

During the famine of the late 1840s, some counties in Ireland lost more than one-quarter of their population to out-migration. However, emigration rates in some of the very poorest counties were not always high. People there were too poor to pay for passage to the United States. The county of Kerry, in the country's southwestern corner, is an example.

Some people moved because other people forced them to—under the crack of a whip and in manacles. Slave traders in the upper South transported thousands of slaves to the lower South for sale "on the block." Indians underwent a kind of middle passage (the horrific slave-ship voyages between Africa and the Americas) when U.S. soldiers forced them to walk from their homelands in the Southeast to Indian Territory (now the state of Oklahoma). In the less settled West, however, older identities of race and ethnicity sometimes gave way to new identities forged from mixed cultures.

Europeans marveled at Americans' apparent willingness to search out new opportunities. But to some Americans, moving meant the death of dreams and the loss of hope for a better life.

NEWCOMERS FROM WESTERN EUROPE

During this period, hardships in western Europe led to increased immigration to the United States, especially from Ireland and the German states. For the long-suffering people of Ireland, by the early nineteenth century life had become more precarious than ever. Over the generations, small farm plots had been subdivided among heirs to the point that most holdings consisted of fewer than fifteen acres. At the same time, the population of Ireland had grown exponentially—to more than 4 million people in 1800. England treated Ireland like a colony that existed purely for the economic gain of the mother country (or, in the eyes of the Irish, an occupying power). A series of English laws and policies mandated that farmers export most of the island's grain and cattle, leaving the impoverished people to subsist mainly on a diet of potatoes. Then, beginning in 1845, a blight devastated the potato crop. In the next five years, a million people died and another million fled to the United States. The great Irish migration had begun.

Large numbers of poor Irish had settled in the United States even before the potato famine of the mid-1840s. In the 1820s, about 50,000 such immigrants arrived; the following decade saw a spike in numbers to more than 200,000. A more dramatic increase was yet to come. As the 1840s and 1850s unfolded, 1.7 million Irish men, women, and children emigrated to the United States. This exodus continued over the next century as more than 4.5 million Irish arrived. Many immigrants were single women who found work as servants and sent money back to Ireland.

By the 1870s, the Irish constituted fully 20 percent of the population of New York City, 14 percent of Philadelphia, and 22 percent of Boston (the "hub of Gaelic America"). Most Irish immigrants remained along the eastern seaboard, since they lacked the resources to move farther inland. The newcomers quickly formed mutual aid associations and other community organizations. In cities across America, the Sisters of Mercy, a Roman Catholic order founded in Dublin, established homes to provide lodging for single women and day nurseries for the children of working mothers.

The Irish newcomers soon realized that their struggle against poverty, discrimination, and religious persecution would not end in the United States. The large numbers of Irish immigrants who came to America in the 1830s threatened the jobs of native-born Protestants, who reacted with resentment and violence. Employers posted signs outside their doors reading "No Irish Need Apply." Despised for their Roman Catholicism and their supposed clannishness, the Irish competed with African Americans for the low-paying jobs at the bottom of the economic ladder. In 1834, a mob destroyed the Ursuline convent in Charlestown, near Boston, after terrifying the women and children residents and ransacking the building.

Nevertheless, by the 1850s, the Irish had gained a measure of influence in America. They filled many high positions in the Catholic Church and became active in the Democratic party. They maintained that their white skin entitled them to distance themselves from blacks and lay claim to full American citizenship. More than one hundred years later, the election of the first Catholic president of the United States—John Fitzgerald Kennedy of Boston, a descendant of famine-era immigrants on both his mother's and father's side of the family—became a milestone in the Irish American rise to political power.

The hardship endured by the Irish in the early nineteenth century mirrored the political and economic distress of many other people living in Europe at the time. In the revolutions of 1848 in the German states, France, the Austrian Empire, and parts of Italy, people struck out against monarchy and called for constitutional government. The Germans moved in especially dramatic numbers, with more than half a million arriving in the United States between 1831 and 1850. Those numbers exploded in the next few decades, as a failed uprising against the authoritarian Prussian state in 1848 led many German intellectuals, farmers, and workers to flee the region. Across western Europe, rising unemployment and unprecedented population increases made food scarce in both rural and urban areas, stimulating immigration across the Atlantic.

THE SLAVE TRADE

Forced migration of enslaved workers increased during this period as the slave trade became big business. Many wealthy traders made regular trips between the upper and lower South. Traders transported men, women, and children by boat down the eastern seaboard or down the Mississippi River, or chained and forced them to walk as much as twenty miles a day for seven or eight weeks at a time in the chill autumn air. Eventually, slaves stood on the block in the markets of New Orleans, Natchez, Charleston, and Savannah, where white men inspected them for health, strength, and compliance.

MAP

Slavery in the South

Between 1800 and 1860, the average price of slaves quadrupled, revealing a growing demand for bound labor. As many as one out of every ten slave children in the upper South was sold to the lower South (many to cotton planters) between 1820 and 1860. Slave households in Virginia bore the brunt of these forced separations. There, an estimated three-quarters of the people sold never saw their spouse, parents, or children again.

It was sometimes worse if they did. Moses Grandy, standing on a sidewalk one day, saw his wife in chains, in a coffle passing by. He recalled the scene in his 1844 autobiography:

> Mr. Rogerson was with them on his horse, armed with pistols. I said to him. "For God's sake, have you bought my wife?" He said he had; when I asked him what she had done, he said she had done nothing, but that her master wanted money. He drew out a pistol and said that if I went near the wagon where she was, he would shoot me. I asked for leave to shake hands with her which he refused, but said I might stand at a distance and talk with her. My heart was so full that I could say very little. . . . I have never seen or heard from her from that day to this. I loved her as I love my life.

Family members resented being separated from each other as well as the nature of the work itself.

Some cotton planters in the lower South found a new way to exploit their enslaved workforces when gold was discovered in northern Georgia in 1829. Many of the men who actually mined the gold were slaves. Some planters forced their slaves to toil in the gold mines after the cotton crop was harvested in the fall and before the new crop was planted in the spring. In the 1830s, Senator John C. Calhoun of South Carolina sent twenty of his slaves to work in his mine near Dahlonega in Georgia's Lumpkin County. Between 1833 and 1835, each of these black men dug out $500 worth of gold per year.

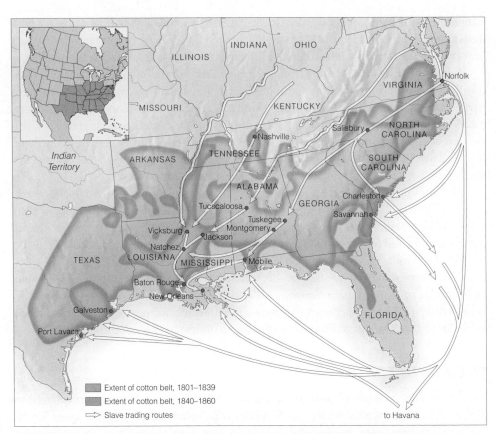

■ **MAP 12.2 Expansion of the Cotton Belt and Slave Trading Routes, 1801–1860**

This map shows the spread of cotton cultivation and routes followed by traders in transporting slaves from the upper South to the new plantations of the Southwest. After Texas won its independence from Mexico in 1836, the new republic legalized slavery. Many white landowners believed that they could not grow cotton without the use of slave labor.

Gold digging in northern Georgia was hard and dangerous; inexperienced miners built tunnels and flimsy shafts that were prone to cave-ins and other hazards. Mindful of the profits that white men derived from their labor, some enslaved men tried to hide nuggets of gold in their hair and clothing, planning to sell them later, but these efforts usually failed.

Voluntary migrations of African Americans formed the counterpoint of the slave trade as runaways and free people of color made their way out of the old slave states. An estimated 50,000 enslaved workers tried to escape each year, but few made it to the North and freedom. Some southern free people of color also headed to northern cities. By 1850, more than half of all Boston blacks had been born outside Massachusetts, with about one-third of those migrants hailing from the South. Slave runaways who lived in fear for their safety and their lives eluded census takers, but by mid-century as many as 600 fugitives lived in Boston.

Regardless of their place of origin, many migrants took up residence with other blacks, who helped ease the newcomers' transition to city life. These boarding arrangements strengthened ties between the enslaved and the free communities. For example, when authorities arrested the runaway George Latimer in Boston in 1842, free blacks in that city took immediate action. They posted signs condemning the police as "human kidnappers." Some tried to wrench Latimer physically from his captors. Still others sponsored protest meetings in the local African Baptist Church and made common cause with white lawyers sympathetic to abolition. Finally a group of blacks and whites raised enough money to buy Latimer from his owner and free him.

Meanwhile, throughout the urban North, whites began eyeing blacks' jobs. Irish immigrants in particular desperately sought work. Skilled black workers found it increasingly difficult to ply their trades as cooks, hotel and boat stewards, porters, brickmakers, and barbers.

An Owner Advertises for His Runaway Slave

Envisioning History

In September 1833, Nathan Cook, the owner of a gold mine in Auraria, Georgia, placed a notice for a runaway slave in a local newspaper, the *Western Herald*. This advertisement is typical for its time. It describes the physical characteristics of the young fugitive and offers a reward for his return. Many ads for runaway servants as well as slaves suggested they had a "down look"— they refrained from looking other people directly in the eye. This ad suggests that Henry ran away not of his own accord but at "the persuasion of some white person." Rather than acknowledge that their own slaves might want, and seize, their freedom, many masters blamed other unknown white people for encouraging enslaved men and women to run away.

Courtesy of Hargrett Rare Book & Manuscript Library/University of Georgia Library

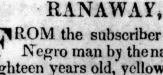

RANAWAY,

FROM the subscriber on the 12th inst. A Negro man by the name of Henry, about eighteen years old, yellow complected, slender made, 5 feet 8 or 10 inches high, has rather a down look, when spoken to, stutters, and materially changes his voice before ending a sentence. He belongs to a gentleman by the name of Eli H. Baxter of Hancock county, Geo. but was in my employ when he absconded in the neighborhood of Auraria, where I have been opperating on a gold mine, and was brought from North Carolina to this state, by a speculator. It is probable that he has been induced to leave, by the persuasion of some white person. Any person apprehending said Negro, and lodging, him in any safe Jail, will be suitably rewarded by dropping a line to E. H. Baxter, of Hancock county, or the subscriber in Auraria, Lumpkin county Geo.

NATHAN COOK.

Sept 28 —25—3t,

QUESTIONS

1. Although Henry is only eighteen years old, he has been uprooted multiple times. How does the description of him suggest the trauma he has suffered as a result of both his forced removal from North Carolina to Georgia and his work in the gold mines?

2. Cook had hired Henry's time from another man, Eli H. Baxter. What does Henry's running away suggest to us about the experiences of slaves who were hired out to work?

3. Why would Cook prefer to hire Henry, rather than buy a slave, to work in his gold mine?

4. What does Henry's story tell us about larger themes in the history of internal migration during the 1830s and 1840s?

In 1838, 656 black artisans in Philadelphia reported that they had to abandon their work because white customers would no longer patronize them. White factory owners in Philadelphia preferred white laborers. In that same city, a bustling site of machine shops and textile factories, almost no blacks did industrial labor of any kind.

TRAILS OF TEARS

Like enslaved blacks, many Indians were forced to migrate. Throughout the 1830s, the U.S. government pursued the policy of removing Indians from the Southeast by treaty or force. The 1832 Treaty of Payne's Landing, negotiated by the Seminole Indians and James Gadsden, a representative of Secretary of War Lewis Cass, aimed to force the Seminole out of Florida and into Indian Territory (present-day Oklahoma). The federal government promised to give individual Indians cash, plus blankets for the men and dresses for the women, in exchange for their lands. Government authorities also hoped to recapture the large number of runaway slaves who had sought refuge in Seminole villages deep in the swamps of central Florida.

Three years later, many of the Indians had departed for the West. But a small number withdrew deeper into the Everglades and held their ground. They were led by a young man

MAP

Native American Removal

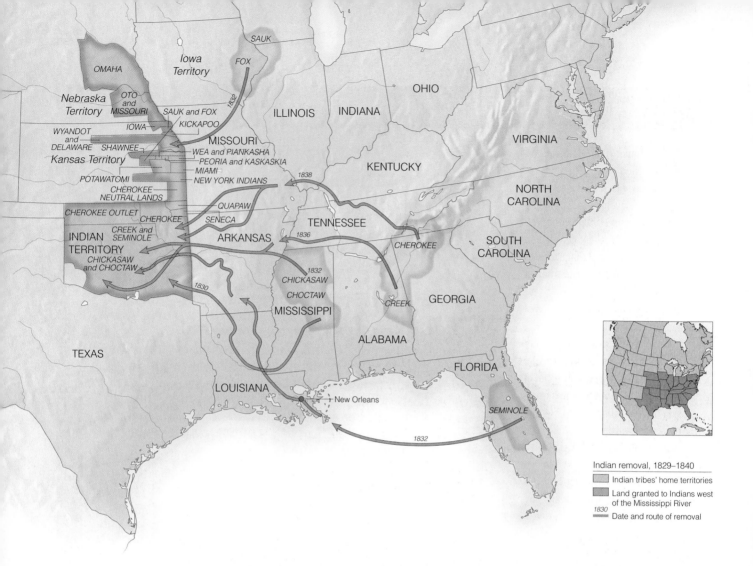

■ **MAP 12.3 Indian Removal**

Indian removal policies forced the Five Civilized Tribes to migrate from the southeast in the 1830s. Other groups from east of the Mississippi, such as the Sauk and Fox, were also obliged to move to the designated Indian Territory, where they crowded longtime Native American inhabitants. Later, many Plains Indians, including the Cheyenne and Comanche, were also forced to move to the region (present-day Oklahoma).

Courtesy American Heritage Center, University of Wyoming

named Osceola, who with his followers waged a **guerrilla war** (based on ambush tactics) against better-armed U.S. troops. Osceola's resistance, called the Second Seminole War, dragged on for seven years. Eventually, the government forced 3,000 Seminole to move west, but not until it had spent $20 million and 1,500 U.S. soldiers had lost their lives.

The Choctaw of the southern Alabama-Mississippi region, the Chickasaw directly to the north of them, the Creek in central Georgia and Alabama, and the Cherokee of North Georgia suffered the same fate in the 1830s. The Creek remained bitterly divided among themselves on the issue of removal, as did the Cherokee. Major Ridge, his son John Ridge, and Elias Boudinot, the leaders of the so-called Treaty Party of the Cherokee Nation, urged their people to give up their homeland and rebuild their nation in the West. The aging Major Ridge had reversed his earlier stance; now he favored migration from Georgia. John Ross and others like him opposed the Ridges and Boudinot. The Cherokee must remain in Georgia at all costs, Ross insisted. He claimed that he spoke for a majority of Cherokee. To silence him, the state of Georgia threw him in prison. Then it concluded negotiations with the Treaty Party, which agreed to sell Cherokee land to the federal government for $5 million. Elias Boudinot said, "We can die, but the great Cherokee Nation will be saved." Within a few years, the Ridges and Boudinot died at the hands of Cherokee assassins.

In 1838, General Winfield Scott, with 7,000 troops under his command, began rounding up the citizens of the Cherokee Nation. U.S. troops held men, women, and children in concentration camps before forcing them to march west. During the period from 1838 to 1839, nearly 16,000 Indians (and their African American slaves) were forced by federal authorities to make a journey from their homeland in the Southeast to western territory. The Indians called this journey the Trail on Which We Cried, also known as the **Trail of Tears.** Four thousand of them died of malnutrition and disease in the course of the 116-day forced march. U.S. troops confiscated or destroyed the material basis of Cherokee culture: sawmills, cotton gins, barns, homes, spinning wheels, meetinghouses, flocks, herds, and the printing press used to publish the *Cherokee Phoenix.* They often forcibly separated families. A soldier who participated in the operation saw children "separated from their parents and driven into the stockade with the sky for a blanket and the earth for a pillow."

U.S. officials claimed that troops had carried out the removal with "great judgment and humanity." However, an internal government report completed in 1841 revealed that the United States had reneged on even its most basic treaty promises. "Bribery, perjury, and forgery, short weights, issues of spoiled meat and grain, and every conceivable subterfuge was employed by designing white men." Many government agents seized goods such as blankets and food intended for Indians and sold these goods for profit. Military authorities suppressed the report, and the public never saw it.

MIGRANTS IN THE WEST

For many native-born migrants seeking a new life west of the Mississippi, the road proved neither smooth nor easy. For example, as the Mormon community moved west from New York, they met with religious persecution. The founder of the church, Joseph Smith, aroused

Courtesy American Heritage Center, University of Wyoming

■ One of the most dramatic western migrations was the Mormons' journey via the Overland Trail, beginning in the spring of 1847. Within five years, more than 10,000 members of the group had made the arduous trek to Utah. This group of Mormon emigrants poses for a group picture not far from their destination of Salt Lake City. Between 1840 and 1860, nearly 300,000 people journeyed overland to Oregon, California, and Utah.

the anger of his neighbors in Nauvoo, Illinois. They took alarm at the Nauvoo Legion, a military company formed to defend the Mormon community. They also heard rumors (for the most part true) that Smith and other Mormon leaders engaged in plural marriage, or polygamy, allowing men to marry more than one wife.

In 1844, this tension came to a head when the Nauvoo Legion destroyed the printing press owned by a group of rebellious church members who objected to what they considered Smith's authoritarian tactics. Civil authorities charged Smith and his brother Hyrum with the destruction of private property and arrested and jailed the two men in the nearby town of Carthage. In June 1844, an angry mob of non-Mormons broke into the jail and lynched the brothers.

By 1847, Brigham Young, who had inherited the mantle of leadership from Smith, determined that the Mormons could not remain in Illinois. Migrants, some of them pushing handcarts loaded with personal belongings, set out for the West. By 1852, 10,000 Mormons had settled in Salt Lake City in what is present-day Utah. With their large numbers and church-inspired discipline, the community prospered. They created an effective irrigation system and turned the desert into a thriving agricultural community.

But the Mormons had not settled an uninhabited wilderness. Around Salt Lake, Canadian trappers, Paiute Indians, and Spanish speakers from New Mexico crossed paths, some to hunt, others to gather roots and berries, herd sheep, or trade captives. A Christmas dinner celebrated near Great Salt Lake around this time revealed the multicultural mix of western life. The guests included Osborne Russell (a European American trader), a Frenchman married to a Flathead woman, and various other intermarried Cree, Snake, and Nez Perce Indians. The group feasted on the meat of elk and deer, a flour pudding, cakes, and strong coffee. After the meal, the women cleared the table. The men smoked pipes and then went outside and shot at targets with their guns.

GOVERNMENT-SPONSORED EXPLORATION

The Lewis and Clark expedition of 1803–1806 was the forerunner of many other U.S. government-sponsored efforts to map unknown territory and make scientific discoveries (see Chapter 10). One of these attempts was the South Seas Exploring Expedition of 1838, also known as the Wilkes Expedition, after its leader, Lt. Charles Wilkes. He commanded a squadron of 6 sailing vessels, 346 men, and 9 scientists and artists. They traveled nearly four years and over 87,000 miles, recording the landscape and wildlife of Antarctica, the South and Central Pacific islands, the California coast, the Pacific Northwest, and Southeast Asia. The expedition was the largest of its kind and also the last to use all-sail vessels.

Like his predecessors Lewis and Clark, Wilkes hoped to advance American diplomatic and economic interests through his explorations. He believed U.S. trade would benefit from the good harbors of the Northwest. He also aimed to provide maps and navigation charts for the U.S. whaling industry.

At the same time, Wilkes's expedition produced scientific discoveries of lasting value. One of the artists accompanying Wilkes was Titian Ramsey Peale, the son of the painter and amateur scientist Charles Willson Peale. A naturalist, painter, and photographer, the younger Peale had, at an early age, explored diverse regions such as Florida, the Rocky Mountains, and Central America. He understood how to study and preserve natural history specimens of animals, plants, and rocks. The samples he gathered on the Wilkes Expedition eventually formed the basis of the collections of the Smithsonian Institution, a museum of natural and social history in Washington, D.C., established by Congress in 1846.

Another expedition, this one overland and sponsored by the U.S. Topographical Corps of Engineers, surveyed the Northwest and aided migrants who eventually settled there. Led by John Charles Frémont, an engineer and mathematician, this 1843–1844 expedition included several Indians and fur trappers. They took precise measurements of the terrain using barometers and field telescopes.

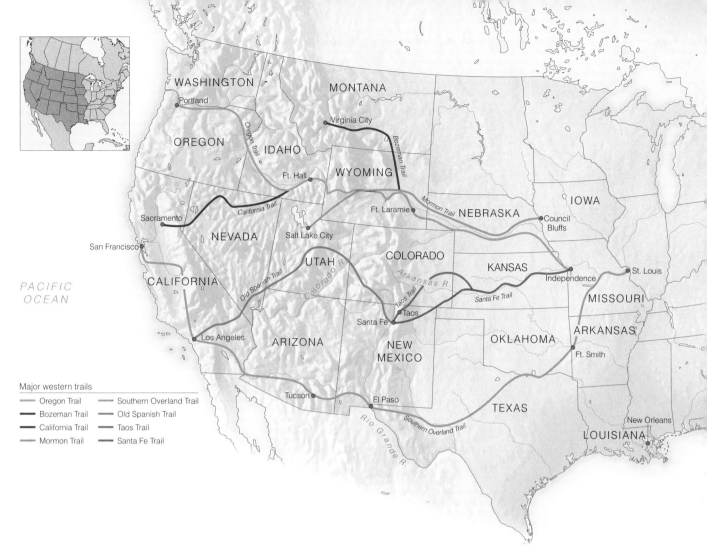

■ MAP 12.4 Western Trails

This map shows the major trails followed by western emigrants in the nineteenth century. Settlers endured long and dangerous journeys. For example, beginning at Independence, Missouri, and stretching to Portland, Oregon, the Oregon Trail was 2,000 miles long. Wagon trains had to traverse rocky terrain, scale mountains, and ford rivers. Along the way, outposts such as Fort Laramie and Fort Hall gave travelers a chance to refresh their supplies, rest their livestock, and repair their wagons. Though resentful of such incursions, Indians rarely attacked large wagon trains.

Frémont's final report had immense practical value for people migrating west, for it mapped the way and provided crucial information about pasture, sources of water, and climate. In addition to detailing plant and animal life, the *Report of Exploring Expeditions to the Rocky Mountains* described a middle ground where Indians spoke fluent Spanish, where whites employed Indian labor to grow their wheat and irrigate their fields, and where German immigrants followed a variety of agricultural pursuits. Like the Lewis and Clark party, the Frémont expedition mapped not an uninhabited "wilderness," but rather territory settled by diverse groups of people.

THE OREGON TRAIL

Protestant missionaries initially settled Oregon beginning in 1834. But in contrast to the Mormons, these northwestern colonists found themselves in the midst of hostile Native Americans. One young doctor and his wife from western New York, Marcus and Narcissa Whitman, established a mission near present-day Walla Walla, Washington. In 1843, the arrival of 1,000 emigrants in Oregon County signaled the beginning of what came to be called the Great Migration.

Missionaries and government officials helped spur the Great Migration of 1843 and spread "Oregon Fever" among economically depressed areas of the Midwest. That region of the country was still reeling from the effects of the Panic of 1837 and the subsequent economic downturn. Peter Burnett was captain of a group of people emigrating from western Missouri for Oregon in the spring of 1843. Burnett and others promised the group that in Oregon they would find not only a fertile land blessed with a mild climate, but also instant prosperity: "And they do say, gentlemen, they do say, that out in Oregon the pigs are running about under the great acorn trees, round and fat, and already cooked, with knives and forks sticking in them so that you can cut off a slice whenever you are hungry."

The **Oregon Trail** was 2,000 miles long. Covering from 12 to 15 miles a day, wagon trains took from four to six months to complete the journey. The natural landscape posed immense obstacles for the travelers. Treacherous river currents swept away whole wagons and their contents. Spring floods and summer droughts prevented the emigrants' livestock from feeding off the Plains grasses. After passing Fort Hall, northwest of Salt Lake City, the going got even rougher, through rocky terrain and uncharted mountains and forests. Emigrants had to rig systems of pulleys and ropes to move their wagons over the Blue Mountains of Oregon. At the end of the day, weary wives and mothers cooked dinner, bathed the children, and washed clothes, while the men plotted the next day's route. Caring for, and bearing, children on the trail was a particular burden borne by migrant women.

TABLE 12.1

Outfitting a Party of Four for the Overland Trail

Area	Item	Amount	Unit Cost ($)	Cost ($)	Weight (lbs.)
Transport	Wagon	1	90.00	90.00	
	Oxen	4 yoke	50.00/yoke	200.00	
	Gear		100.00	100.00	
Food	Flour	600 lb.	2.00/100 lb.	12.00	600
	Biscuit	120 lb.	3.00/100 lb.	3.60	120
	Bacon	400 lb.	5.00/100 lb.	20.00	400
	Coffee	60 lb.	7.00/100 lb.	4.20	60
	Tea	4 lb.	50.00/100 lb.	2.00	4
	Sugar	100 lb.	10.00/100 lb.	10.00	100
	Lard	200 lb.	6.00/100 lb.	12.00	200
	Beans	200 lb.	8.00/100 lb.	16.00	200
	Dried fruit	120 lb.	24.00/100 lb.	28.80	120
	Salt	40 lb.	4.00/100 lb.	1.60	40
	Pepper	8 lb.	4.00/100 lb.	.32	8
	Saleratus	8 lb.	4.00/100 lb.	.32	8
	Whiskey	1 keg	5.00/keg	5.00	25
Goods	Rifle	1	30.00	30.00	10
	Pistols	2	15.00	30.00	10
	Powder	5 lb.	.25/lb.	1.25	5
	Lead	15 lb.	.04/lb.	.60	15
	Shot	10 lb.	.10/lb.	1.00	10
	Matches			1.00	1
	Cooking utensils			20.00	25
	Candles and soap	65 lb.	From home	from home	65
	Bedding	60 lb.	From home	from home	60
	Sewing kit	10 lb.	From home	from home	10
	Essential tools			from home	20
	Clothing			from home	100
			Totals	$589.69	2216

Plains Indians resented the families traveling by wagon train. They believed these families were just one more group—like government scouts and military forces—determined to take their land. Small groups were particularly vulnerable to attacks by Indians. Some wagon trains used oxen because Indians had little interest in the animals, in contrast to horses. Despite the dangers and hardship, the Great Migration continued. In 1845, 3,000 people traveled the Oregon Trail. Two years later the number had increased to almost 5,000. Between the beginning of the Great Migration and 1869, an estimated 50,000 people took the trail to Oregon.

Some settlers established successful homesteads in Oregon, but the settlements founded by missionaries were fragile affairs. Discouraged and overwhelmed by homesickness, Narcissa Whitman eagerly awaited copies of the latest *Mothers' Magazine* sent to her by relatives in the East. After 1843, the influx of newcomers brought her some consolation, but it also brought outbreaks of measles, to which the Native Americans had no immunity. An ensuing epidemic among the Cayuse claimed many lives. In 1847, blaming the missionaries for the deaths of their people, several Indians attacked the Whitman mission, killing twelve whites, including Narcissa and Marcus Whitman.

Like Narcissa Whitman and Mormon women, some women went west with their families for religious reasons. But other women migrants made the journey only reluctantly. Despite hardship back east, they did not want to leave their female kin, who provided them with a network of support throughout their lives. For these reluctant migrants, the journey west and eventual settlement caused deep distress. However, some eventually found satisfaction in making new lives for themselves and their families.

NEW PLACES, NEW IDENTITIES

Like the West, the Midwest and the borderlands between U.S. and Spanish territories were meeting places for many different cultures. Leaving established communities behind, some migrants challenged rigid definitions of who was black, Indian, Hispanic, or European American. Moving from one place to another enabled—or forced—people to adopt new individual and group identities.

People who fell into one racial category in the East sometimes acquired new identities in the West. Some people classified as "black" in the South became "white" outside the region. For example, the commonwealth of Virginia classified the light-skinned George and Eliza Gilliam as black. Beginning their married life near Petersburg, they were well aware of Virginia's tightening restrictions on free people of color and their uncertain future where local officials knew who they were. In 1831, the couple decided to make a new life for themselves in western Pennsylvania. Eliza died in 1838, and George remarried nine years later. He prospered over the course of his lifetime. He worked as a doctor and druggist and invested in and sold real estate. George and his second wife, Frances, eventually moved to Illinois, then finally settled in Missouri.

Deutsches Ledermuseum

■ Plains Indians developed new art forms in response to the westward movement of European American trappers, missionaries, and settlers. Native artists used picture writing to describe violent encounters between Indians and intruders. They etched pictures on sandstone or painted them on cliffs or clothing. These battle pictographs, painted on a Cheyenne buffalo robe (c. 1845), bear similarities to other images produced by Flathead artists. Scholars believe that these drawings formed a language understood by a variety of Indian groups from Canada to the American Southwest.

In 1870, the census listed the value of Gilliam's estate at $95,000 (the equivalent of $2 million today). Public records in Pennsylvania, Illinois, and Missouri listed the family members as white. Outside the slave South, the Gilliams managed to reinvent themselves and embrace opportunities sought by many other Americans in this era of migration.

Throughout the West, migrants forged new identities as a matter of course. For example, many people straddled more than one culture in the western borderlands. In 1828, Mexican military officer José Maria Sanchez described the *Tejano* settlers, who were Spanish-speaking persons, some natives of Mexico and others born in provinces such as *Tejas* (Texas): "Accustomed to the continued trade with the North Americans, they have adopted their customs and habits, and one may say truly that they are not Mexican except by birth, for they even speak Spanish with a marked incorrectness." In other provinces of northern Mexico, European American Protestant traders and travelers mingled with Catholic native Spanish speakers.

Within borderlands, traditional power relationships came under attack as new Spanish-speaking elites emerged and Indian workers resisted oppression by the Spanish. In Alta California, the northern reaches of Mexico, diverse groups of people cohabited. Some landowners, including Indians, mestizos, and blacks, called themselves *gente de razon* (literally, "people of reason"), an ambiguous racial category. They sought to put to work gentiles (unbaptized Indians native to California) and *neofitos* (baptized Indians laboring for Roman Catholic missions). When the Mexican government ended its sponsorship of the mission system in the 1830s, many Indians found themselves in a condition akin to enslavement. For example, in New Mexico, an Indian woman might be considered not just a *crida* (servant), but also a *genizara* (a captive, a spoil of war).

In parts of the West, traditional social identities yielded to new ones, based less on a single language or ethnicity than on a blend of cultures and new ways of making a living from the land. The 1830s and 1840s marked the height of the Rocky Mountain fur trade. The trade could generate huge profits for the eastern merchants who controlled it. Individual trappers fared more modestly, ranging freely across national boundaries and cultures, going wherever the bison, bear, and beaver took them. These men demonstrated a legendary ability to navigate among Spanish, French, European American, and Native American communities.

Westerners coined new terms to describe the people representative of new kinds of cultural identity within trading communities. Some white men became "white Indians," and the children they had with Indian women were called "métis" (mixed bloods). William Sherley "Old Bill" Williams, a convert to the religion of the Osage Indians of the southeastern Plains, was not unusual in the ways he crossed cultural boundaries. He married an Osage woman, and when she died, he wed a New Mexican widow. His third wife was a Ute woman. Williams's life story suggests the ways that Indian and Hispanic women could serve as cultural mediators between native peoples and European American traders.

National Museum of American Art/Art Resource, NY

■ Among all Plains Indians, the Comanche were well known for their use of horses as items of trade and as a means of warfare. Here they show the artist George Catlin the way they use the bodies of their horses as shields in battle. This painting was completed in 1835.

CHANGES IN THE SOUTHERN PLAINS

For Plains Indians such as the Comanche and Kiowa, the horse represented a new way of life. Introduced into North America by Spanish conquistadors in the sixteenth century, the horse enabled Native American groups to hunt, move around, trade, and fight their enemies more effectively and efficiently (see Chapter 5). Horses were easy to feed—they foraged off the Plains grasses—and they became valuable objects of trade. By the early nineteenth century, the Comanche and Kiowa, together with the Cheyenne and Arapaho, had developed a far-flung trading empire that depended on horses for both travel and currency. Throughout the Arkansas basin (the present-day lower Midwest and Southwest), these groups traded horses and mules to European American traders, who in turn supplied people emigrating west along the Santa Fe trail.

Yet the Indians' trading successes came at a high price. The natural environment could not sustain the growing number of horses nor withstand dramatic changes caused by this new form of trade. The needs of their horses began to shape the migratory patterns of the Cheyenne; now they had to spend their winters in the mild river bottoms, where the horses found shelter and water. In the spring, bands were forced to move in search of the open grasslands their horse herds depended on. As the demand for horses grew, so did violence associated with raiding parties. New status distinctions emerged within Indian groups, as a small number of wealthy people—owners of large herds of horses—dominated trade and leadership positions.

As raiding parties traveled long distances to find horses, they relied on increasing numbers of bison to feed themselves. Yet bison and horses coexisted uneasily and competed for natural resources, including water and grasslands. Gradually the number of bison

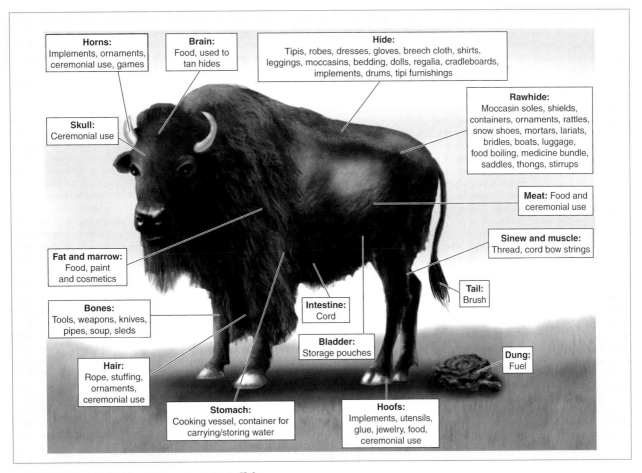

■ **FIGURE 12.1 How Indians Used the Buffalo**

The U.S. and Other Rail Networks Compared

The Wider World

Though a relatively young country, the United States early developed the most extensive railroad network in the world. Railroads contributed to the economy in several ways: They moved people, things, and information quickly and efficiently. They knit together the national economy by transporting manufactured goods from the East to the West and South, cotton from the South to the North, and cattle and grain from the West to the East. In the United States, the rail industry came to serve as a major employer, since it relied on so many people to design and manufacture engines and cars, lay and

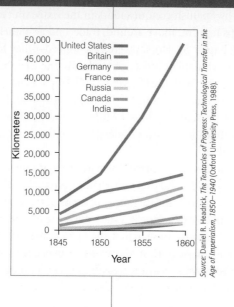

Source: Daniel R. Headrick, *The Tentacles of Progress: Technological Transfer in the Age of Imperialism, 1850–1940* (Oxford University Press, 1988).

maintain tracks, work as engineers, and cater to the needs of passengers.

QUESTIONS

1. What factors account for the rapid growth of U.S. railroads? Does the large size of the United States fully explain its development of an extensive rail system?

2. Why, by the 1840s, had railroads surpassed turnpikes and canals as the preferred means of moving large quantities of people and things over long distances?

dwindled, causing hardship among southern Plains Indians. More and more reliant on trade, Indians saw their food supplies—and with them their subsistence economy—gradually disappear. By the 1830s, the Indian horse-trading empire was undergoing a dramatic decline, the victim of its own success. The Comanche numbered 20,000 in the 1820s, and only a quarter of that number in the 1860s.

A Multitude of Voices in the National Political Arena

■ *Why did debates over the rights (or lack thereof) of workers, slaves, and immigrants lead to the rise of new political organizations?*

Streams of migration through Indian territory changed both the natural and the social landscape of the West, where diverse peoples forged new social identities—or had new social identities thrust upon them. As various groups moved and made new homes for themselves, they created new political interests. These new interests both enlivened the political life of the country and gave expression to ominous sounds of conflict. The increasing diversity of the American population, combined with specialized regional economies, heightened tensions within and between different groups and sections of the country. The Second Party system, which replaced the Federalist–Anti-Federalist rivalry of the early nineteenth century, was characterized by intense competition between the Jacksonian Democrats and anti-Jackson Whigs. But this new system could not accommodate the old or new conflicts based on race, religion, ethnicity, regional loyalties, and political beliefs. Social and cultural disputes between nativists and immigrants and between abolitionists and defenders of slavery spilled out of the courthouse and the legislative hall and into the streets. Public demonstrations ran the gamut from noisy parades to bloody clashes. During these displays, resentments between ethnic and religious groups, arguments over political issues, and opposition to reformers often blended together.

WHIGS, WORKERS, AND THE PANIC OF 1837

One polarizing force, President Andrew Jackson, did not run for a third term in 1836 due to a bout with tuberculosis. The Democrats nominated his vice president and friend Martin Van Buren of New York. The Whig party, led by Senator Henry Clay and other anti-Jackson congressmen, drew their support from several groups: advocates of Clay's American System (policies that supported a national bank, public funding of canals and turnpikes, and protective tariffs), states' rights Southerners opposed to Jackson's heavy-handed use of national power, and merchants and factory owners in favor of the Second Bank of the United States. **Evangelical Protestants** from the middle classes also joined the anti-Jackson forces; they objected to his rhetoric stressing class differences, because they believed that individual religious conviction, not a group's material status, should shape politics and society. Still somewhat disorganized, these allied groups fielded three candidates: Hugh White of Tennessee, Senator Daniel Webster of Massachusetts, and General William Henry Harrison of Indiana. Benefiting from the Whigs' disarray, Van Buren narrowly won the popular vote but swept the electoral college.

During this period, political candidates of all persuasions in northeastern cities began to court the allegiance of workers aligned with a new trade union movement. People worried about making a living tended to favor the Democratic party, which spoke against class privilege and the wealthy and upheld the tenets of white supremacy. In the late 1820s and early 1830s, a variety of trade organizations had formed to advance the interests of skilled workers (the "producing classes," they called themselves). These unions pressed for a ten-hour workday and the abolition of debtors' prisons. They also objected to paper money (so that workers would receive their wages in hard currency rather than bank notes), and higher wages.

The founding of the **National Trades Union** (NTU) in 1834 made workers more politically visible. The union represented workers as diverse as jewelers, butchers, bookbinders, and factory workers. In Philadelphia in the early 1830s, for example, the local NTU organization, called the General Trades Union, consisted of fifty trade societies and supported a number of successful strikes. Both Whigs and Democrats professed allegiance to the union, but neither party went out of its way to represent the interests of workers over other groups, such as farmers and bookkeepers.

A major economic depression, the **Panic of 1837,** created even larger troubles for the trade union movement. Brought on by overspeculation—in canals, turnpikes, railroads, and slaves—the panic deepened when large grain crops failed in the West. British creditors worsened matters when they recalled loans they had made to American

TABLE 12.2			
The Election of 1836			
Candidate	**Political Party**	**Popular Vote (%)**	**Electoral Vote**
Martin Van Buren	Democratic	50.9	170
William Henry Harrison	Whig		73
Hugh L. White	Whig	49.1	26
Daniel Webster	Whig		14
W. P. Magnum	Independent	—	11

DOCUMENT

Clay, "Defense of the American System"

Nicolino Calyo, *Street Cries: The Butcher,* 1840–1844. Museum of the City of New York. Gift of Mrs. Francis P. Garvan in memory of Mr. and Mrs. Francis P. Garvan (55.6.22)

◼ In the antebellum period, factory operatives represented only a small percentage of all U.S. workers. Many kinds of skilled craftsmen, such as the butcher pictured here, continued to ply their trades in time-honored ways. Some of these skilled workers formed labor unions affiliated with the National Trades Union.

customers. The depression lasted until the early 1840s and devastated the NTU and its constituent organizations. Up to one-third of all Americans lost their jobs when businesses failed. Those fortunate enough to keep their jobs were in no position to press for higher wages. Not until the Civil War era did members of the laboring classes recapture political momentum at the national level.

SUPPRESSION OF ANTISLAVERY SENTIMENT

Enslaved black workers were also at the center of contention in these years. In 1831, a Boston journalist named William Lloyd Garrison launched the *Liberator,* a newspaper dedicated to "immediate emancipation" of all slaves. Two years later, a group of sixty blacks and whites formed the American Anti-Slavery Society. That same year, Great Britain abolished slavery in the West Indies. This move encouraged like-minded Americans eager to cooperate with their British counterparts to abolish slavery everywhere. In the United States, the abolition movement enlisted the energies of a dedicated group of people who believed not only that slavery was immoral but also that the federal government must take immediate steps to destroy this "peculiar institution."

DOCUMENT

Garrison, First Issue of *The Liberator*

Both northern free people of color and white women and men provided financial support to the society. All the supporters showed a great deal of courage within a larger American society indifferent to the issue of slavery. Well-to-do black leaders, including Henry Highland Garnet, Charles Lenox Remond, and his sister Sarah Parker Remond, spoke out on behalf of southern blacks in chains. Fugitive slaves, including Frederick Douglass, Solomon Northup, and William and Ellen Craft, electrified northern abolitionist audiences with their firsthand accounts of the brutality of slavery and of their own daring escapes from bondage.

A few white women also became active in the abolitionist cause. Sarah and Angelina Grimké, for example, left the household of their slave-owning father in Charleston, South Carolina, and moved to Philadelphia. The Grimké sisters offended many other whites by speaking before mixed groups composed of men and women, blacks and whites. The Grimkés were struck by what they considered the similar legal constraints of slaves and white women. White men considered both groups unworthy of citizenship rights, childlike in their demeanor, well suited for domestic service, and inherently unintelligent.

Abolitionist activities provoked outrage not only from southern slave owners but also from anti-abolitionists and their allies in Congress—in other words, most northern whites. In Washington, D.C., the House of Representatives imposed a gag rule on antislavery petitions, forbidding them to be read aloud or entered into the public record. Supporters of slavery also resorted to violence. In 1834, a mob of whites attacked a school for young women of color operated by a white teacher, Prudence Crandall, near New Haven, Connecticut. A local paper charged that the school was fostering "levelling [egalitarian] principles, and intermarriage between whites and blacks." The next year in Boston, a mob attacked the *Liberator* founder, William Lloyd Garrison, tying a rope around him and parading him through the streets of that city while onlookers jeered. Antiblack riots broke out in New York City, Philadelphia, and Cincinnati in 1834, and again in Philadelphia in 1842. Indeed white workers attacked blacks so often in the 1830s and 1840s that bricks became known as "Irish confetti" because of the way immigrants used them as weapons.

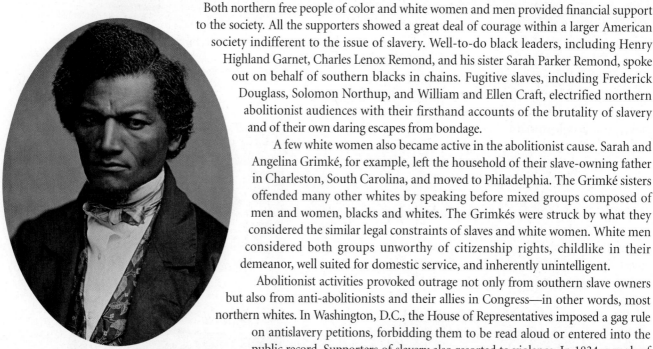

■ Born a slave in Maryland in 1818, Frederick Douglass became a leading abolitionist speaker, editor, and activist. Not content to condemn southern slaveholders exclusively, he also criticized northern employers for not hiring blacks. Trained as a ship caulker, Douglass faced job discrimination in the shipyards in New Bedford, Massachusetts, where he and his wife, Anna, settled soon after he escaped slavery and they moved north (in 1838).

Still, these dramatic episodes had little noticeable impact on the two major political parties. In 1840, the Democrats renominated Van Buren, although many people blamed him for the depression. Eager to find a candidate as popular as Andrew Jackson, the Whigs selected William Henry Harrison; his supporters called him "Old Tippecanoe" in recognition of his

Library Company of Philadelphia (1835–7 / P8658)

■ The artist titled this print *New Method of Assorting the Mail, as Practised by Southern Slave-Holders*. In July 1835, a proslavery mob broke into the U.S. post office in Charleston, South Carolina, and burned abolitionist literature. The sign on the side of the building offers a "Reward for Tappan." The brothers Arthur and Lewis Tappan were wealthy New York City merchants who funded abolitionist activities. Southern slaveholders hoped to stem the north–south flow of abolitionist literature, which took the form of sermons, pamphlets, periodicals, and resolutions.

defeat of Indians at the battle of the same name in 1811. As Harrison's running mate, the Whigs chose a Democratic politician, John Tyler, who had been both governor of and a senator from Virginia. To counter their reputation as well-heeled aristocrats, the Whigs promoted Harrison as a simple, humble man living in a log cabin and drinking hard cider. They rallied around the slogan "Tippecanoe and Tyler Too."

By this time, the Whigs had gained strong support among wealthy southern planters, who worried that Van Buren would not protect their interests in slavery. Harrison won the election, but he contracted pneumonia at his inauguration and died within one month of taking office. Ridiculed as "His Accidency," Tyler assumed the presidency and soon lost his core constituency, Whigs who favored a strong central government, by vetoing bills for both a national bank and higher tariffs. The new president found support among members of the Whig party who were ardent supporters of states' rights. As a result, he proved a poor standard-bearer for the numerous nationalist-minded Whigs. As a former Democrat himself, Tyler learned a hard lesson: that the Whig party was a loose coalition of groups with varying views on a range of issues, rather than a unified party bound to a single idea or principle.

Abolitionists could claim few victories, either real or symbolic, during these years. However, they did take heart from the *Amistad* case. In 1839, the Spanish-owned ship, *Amistad*, carried fifty-three illegally purchased Africans from Havana to another Cuban port. White sailing along the

TABLE 12.3			
The Election of 1840			
Candidate	**Political Party**	**Popular Vote (%)**	**Electoral Vote**
William Henry Harrison	Whig	53.1	234
Martin Van Buren	Democratic	46.9	60
James G. Birney	Liberty	<1	—

■ This picture shows the Spanish slave ship, *Amistad*, anchored off the eastern tip of Long Island, in 1839. The slaves, under the leadership of Cinqué, had commandeered the vessel near Cuba. The Africans, charged with murdering the ship's captain, were held in New Haven, Connecticut, until a U.S. Supreme Court ruling led to their release and return to Africa in 1842. Abolitionists hailed the eventual freeing of the *Amistad* captives as one of their few successes in the fight against slavery before the Civil War.

coast, the Africans, under the leadership of a young man named Cinqué, rebelled, killed the captain, and took over the ship. Soon after, U.S. authorities captured the ship off the coast of Long Island. President Van Buren wanted to send the blacks to Cuba. However, a federal district court judge in Hartford, Connecticut, ruled that because the African slave trade had been illegal since 1808, the Africans had been wrongfully enslaved. The U.S. government appealed the case to the Supreme Court.

To raise funds for the *Amistad* case, Philadelphia black leader Robert Purvis paid to have Cinqué's portrait painted; then antislavery activists sold copies for $1 each. In 1841, former president John Quincy Adams argued the Africans' case before the Supreme Court. The Court ruled in their favor. Of the original fifty-three men, women, and children, thirty-five had survived, and they returned to Africa. Slavery advocates and abolitionists alike pondered the question, could the law be used to dismantle slavery?

NATIVISTS AS A POLITICAL FORCE

Immigration, like slavery, aroused strong feelings. Among the active players on the political scene were the **nativists,** who opposed immigration and immigrants. The immigrants who came to the United States were a varied group in terms of their jobs, religion, and culture. Some farmed homesteads in Michigan, and others worked in northeastern factories. But to nativists, these distinctions made little difference: all immigrants were foreigners and thus unwelcome. Some nativists were also **temperance** advocates, calling for the prohibition of alcohol; they objected to the Irish drinking in taverns and the Germans drinking in their *Biergarten*. Protestants worried that large numbers of Catholic immigrants would be loyal to the pope in

■ Taken on May 9, 1844, this daguerreotype is one of the first American photographs to record an urban civil disturbance. A crowd gathers outside Philadelphia's Girard Bank, at the corner of Third and Dock streets. At the time, soldiers called in to quell the riot were occupying the bank. Called the Bible Riots, the clash between Protestant and Catholic workers revealed tensions arising from nativism, temperance activism, and the use of the Protestant version of the Bible in the public schools.

Rome, the head of the Catholic Church, and thus undermine American democracy. Members of the working classes, black and white, feared the loss of their jobs to desperate newcomers who would accept low, "starvation" wages. But nativists objected just as much when immigrants kept to themselves—in their Catholic schools or in their German *Turnverein* (gymnastics clubs). They also complained when immigrants participated in U.S. politics as individual voters and members of influential voting blocs.

Samuel F. B. Morse, the artist and inventor, was among the most vocal nativists. In the early 1840s, he ceased painting portraits and turned his creative energies to developing a form of long-distance electric communication. Congress financed construction of the first telegraph line, which ran from Washington to Baltimore. In May 1844, Morse sent a message in code, "What hath God wrought!" and the modern telegraph was born. The precursor of all later communication innovations, the telegraph revolutionized the spread of information and tied the country together.

Morse was convinced that Catholic immigrants in particular (mostly the Irish) were a grave threat to American democracy. In his book *Imminent Dangers to the Free Institutions of the United States* (1835), Morse charged that Catholics favored "monarchical power" over republican governments. Catholicism was like a cancer, he wrote: "We find it spreading itself into every nook and corner of the land; churches, chapels, colleges, nunneries and convents are springing up as if by magic every where." In his fears, Morse expressed nostalgia for a simpler past, even as his technical ingenuity paved the way for the modern world.

DOCUMENT

Morse, Foreign Immigration

In 1844, an openly nativist political organization, the American party, elected six of its candidates to Congress and dozens of others to local political offices. In 1849, nativists founded the Order of the Star-Spangled Banner. The nativist political groups was also called the Know-Nothing party because it cautioned its members to profess ignorance when asked about its existence.

In some cases, anti-Catholic prejudices in particular helped to justify territorial expansion. Many U.S. Protestants believed the government was justified in seizing the land of Spanish-speaking Catholics in the West. They claimed religious and cultural superiority over Hispanos.

As Protestant explorers, traders, and travelers reported on their experiences in the Southwest, their condemnation of Mexican Roman Catholics set the stage for the U.S. conquest of northern Mexico in the late 1840s. On the other hand, some Protestant nativists objected to U.S. expansion in the West, because they did not want to increase the number of Catholics in the nation.

During this period, nativists formed the short-lived American party to mobilize the native-born working classes against immigrants. Increasingly, Americans believed that the traditional two-party system was incapable of resolving the great social and political issues of the day. As a result, some people also formed new reform organizations to address the deficiencies of the major political parties and to right the perceived moral wrongs of America. Some reformers emphasized personal transformation as the key to lasting social change. Others attempted to agitate through legal channels. Regardless of their cause, all reformers believed they possessed the ability and the responsibility to make America a better place. Yet people continued to disagree about what that "better place" should and would look like.

Reform Impulses

■ *What were the major reform movements of the 1830s and 1840s? What were the various strategies used by reformers to effect social change?*

In August 1841, writer Lydia Maria Child recorded a striking scene in New York City: a march sponsored by the Washington Society, a temperance group, snaked its way through the streets. The procession stretched for two miles and consisted of representatives from "all classes and trades." The marchers carried banners depicting streams and rivers (the pure water favored over liquor) and poignant scenes of the grateful wives and children of reformed drunkards. Stirred by the martial sounds of trumpets and drums, Child wrote that the music was "the voice of resistance to evil." She added, "Glory to resistance! for through its agency men become angels."

Inspired by faith in the perfectibility of human beings and heartened by the rapid pace of technological progress, many Americans set about trying to "make angels out of men," in Child's words. In the process, various reform associations targeted personal habits such as dress and diet, conventional beliefs about sexuality and the status of women, and institutions such as schools, churches, and slavery. Their efforts often brought women out of the home and into public life. Yet not all Americans shared the reformers' zeal. Even those who did rarely agreed about the appropriate means to transform society.

PUBLIC EDUCATION

In the eyes of some Americans, a growing nation needed new forms of tax-supported schooling. As families moved from one area of the country to another, public education advocates pointed out, children should be able to pick up in one school where they had left off in another. Members of a growing middle class wanted to provide their children with schooling beyond basic literacy instruction (reading and writing skills) and had the resources to do so.

Horace Mann, a Massachusetts state legislator and lawyer, was one of the most prominent educational reformers. In 1837, Mann became secretary of the first state board of education. He stressed the notion of a **common school system** available to all boys and girls regardless of class or ethnicity. In an increasingly diverse nation, schooling promoted the acquisition of basic knowledge and skills. But it also provided instruction in what Mann and others called American values: hard work, punctuality, and sobriety.

By the 1840s, public school systems attended by white children had cropped up across the North and the Midwest. Local school boards eagerly tapped into the energies of women as teachers. School officials claimed that women were naturally nurturing and could serve as "mothers away from home" for small children. Furthermore, schools could pay women only a fraction of what men earned. Between the 1830s and 1840s, the number of female schoolteachers in Massachusetts jumped more than 150 percent. In 1846, writer and educator Catharine Beecher created a Board of National Popular Education, which sent unmarried female New England teachers to the Midwest.

Despite the lofty goals of Mann and other reformers, public schooling did not offer a "common" experience for all American children. Almost exclusively, northern white children benefited from public school systems. Slightly more than one-third of all white children attended school in 1830; twenty years later, the ratio had increased to more than one-half. In northern cities, these proportions were considerably higher; there reformers were able to provide elementary-school instruction for relatively large numbers of white children, both immigrant and native-born.

By contrast, few black children had the opportunity to attend public schools. In the South, slave children were forbidden by law to learn to read and write. Recalled one former slave many years later, "dey [owners] didn't teach 'em nothin' but wuk [work]." By the 1830s, schools for even the children of free people of color had to meet in secret. In the North, many black households needed the labor of children to survive, resulting in black school-attendance rates well below those of whites. Throughout the Northeast and Midwest, black children remained at the mercy of local officials, who decided whether they could attend the schools their parents' tax dollars helped support.

All over the country, education remained an intensely grassroots affair, belying the reformers' call for uniform systems. Local communities raised money for the teacher's salary, built the schoolhouse, and provided wood to heat the building. Southern states did not develop uniform public education systems until the late nineteenth century. Lacking local, popular support for tax-supported schooling, poor white children remained illiterate, while wealthy parents hired tutors for their own children or sent them to private academies.

An increase in the literate population resulted in an increased demand for higher education. The number of colleges more than doubled from 46 to 119 between 1830 and 1850.

Albertus del Orient Browere, *Mrs. McCormick's General Store*, 1844. Fenimore Art Museum, Cooperstown, New York (N-0387.55)

■ Artist Albertus Browere titled this 1844 painting *Mrs. McCormick's General Store*. These barefoot boys are getting into trouble. Reformers advocated universal, compulsory schooling as one way to rid street corners of young mischief makers. Had these youngsters lived in the country, they probably would have been working in the fields.

Oberlin College in Ohio (founded in 1833) accepted black men as well as women of both races in 1837. Oberlin and Mount Holyoke, a college for women in Massachusetts (founded in 1837), were unusual for their liberal admission policies. Other forms of education also multiplied. Lyceums—societies offering informal lectures by speakers who traveled from place to place—attracted hordes of adults regardless of their formal education. By the mid-1830s, approximately 3,000 local lecture associations, mostly in New England and the Midwest, were sponsoring such series. In addition, local agricultural fairs offered informal practical instruction to rural people.

In rural communities of black and white Southerners, Native Americans, and Mexicans, women continued to practice time-honored ways of midwifery and healing.

Formal training for professionals such as physicians and lawyers also changed during this period. By the 1830s, almost all states required that doctors be licensed. The only way to attain such a license was to attend medical school, and these schools excluded women. In regions of the country where medical schools appeared, the self-taught midwife gradually yielded to the formally educated male physician. In contrast, in rural communities of black and white Southerners, Native Americans, and Mexicans, women continued to practice time-honored ways of midwifery and healing.

ALTERNATIVE VISIONS OF SOCIAL LIFE

As in education, the crosscurrents of reform showed up clearly in debates about sexuality, the family, and the proper role of women. For example, reformer Sylvester Graham argued that even husbands and wives must monitor their sexual activity. Sexual excess between husband and wife, he claimed, caused ills ranging from headaches, chills, and impaired vision, to loss of memory, epilepsy, insanity, and "disorders of the liver and kidneys." Graham also promoted a diet of special crackers made of wheat flour (now called Graham crackers) and fruit (in place of alcohol and meat) in addition to a regimen of plain living reinforced with cold showers.

Other reformers disagreed with Graham's notion that people must repress their sexuality to lead a good and healthy life. Defying conventional standards of morality, sponsors of a number of experimental communities discouraged marriage-based monogamy (a legal commitment between a man and a woman to engage in sexual relations only with each other) and made child-rearing the responsibility of the entire community, rather than just the child's parents. These communities were communitarian—seeking to break down exclusive relations between husband and wife, parent and child, employer and employee—in an effort to advance the well-being of the whole group, not just individuals within it. These communities were also **utopian,** seeking to forge new kinds of social relationships that would, in the eyes of the reformers, serve as a model for the larger society.

Many of these communities explicitly challenged mainstream views related to property ownership and the system of wage labor as well as rules governing relations between the sexes. The Scottish industrialist and socialist Robert Owen founded New Harmony in Indiana in 1825, basing his experiment on principles of "cooperative labor." In 1826, Owen released his "Declaration of Mental Independence," which condemned private property, organized religion, and marriage. By this time, 900 persons had joined the New Harmony order.

Several other prominent communitarian experiments that challenged conventional marital relations were vehemently criticized, and participants were sometimes physically attacked by their neighbors. Salt Lake City Mormons, who practiced plural marriage, continued to meet intense hostility from outsiders. Another group, the Oneida Community, founded in upstate New York near Utica in 1848 by John Humphrey Noyes, went even further than the Mormons in advocating an alternative to monogamy. At its peak, Oneida consisted of 300 members who endorsed the founder's notion of "complex marriage," meaning communal sexual unions and community-regulated parent–child relations. Charges of adultery eventually forced Noyes to flee the country and seek refuge in Canada.

MAP

Utopian Communities
before the Civil War

NETWORKS OF REFORMERS

Many moral reforms overlapped with and reinforced each other. For example, women's rights advocates often supported temperance. Husbands who drank, they pointed out, were more likely to abuse their wives and children and to squander their paychecks. Angelina and Sarah Grimké gained prominence as both abolitionists and advocates for women's rights. They followed Sylvester Graham's program, and for a short time they sported "bloomers" (loose-fitting pants popularized by dress reformer Amelia Bloomer) in place of cumbersome dresses.

Dorothea Dix spearheaded a major reform effort that gained the support of a variety of politicians and activists. As a young woman, Dix had worked as a teacher and writer. In 1836, she visited England, where she met several prominent British reformers. Five years later she volunteered to teach a Sunday school class for women at an East Cambridge jail not far from Boston. Her first day there, in March 1841, changed her life—and the face of American antebellum reform—forever.

Dix found among the inmates not only women accused of prostitution and vagrancy, but also women who were clearly mentally ill. All of them were miserable, shivering in the cold. Dix was horrified that insane persons were imprisoned with criminals. She set out on a campaign to investigate the conditions under which the mentally ill were confined. Over the next eighteen months, she investigated every prison, almshouse, and asylum in Massachusetts. She kept careful notes, which later formed the basis of her petitions, or "memorials," demanding better treatment for all insane persons. At one place she found people "confined . . . in *cages, closets, cellars, stalls, pens! Chained, naked, beaten with rods,* and *lashed* into obedience." Dix presented her findings to the Massachusetts state legislature. Heartened by the public outcry she had inspired, she widened her investigation to include the states of Rhode Island and New York. In the late 1840s, she traveled to another dozen states in the South, Mid-Atlantic, and Midwest.

Dix found crucial support from several prominent reformers. Massachusetts Senator Charles Sumner, an outspoken abolitionist, and Horace Mann, the driving force behind the common school system, championed her cause. Though associated most famously with the plight of the mentally ill in antebellum America, Dix went on to play a pivotal role in the feminization of the nursing profession during the Civil War when she energetically promoted the use of women as nurses in Union hospitals.

Most striking is the overlap between abolitionism and women's rights. Some middle-class white women contemplated the chains of slaves and saw mirrored in those chains their own legal and social inferiority. They argued that free white women, like enslaved persons, were denied basic legal rights such as the right to own property. Women, like slaves, they suggested, could not aspire to a higher education or positions of religious or political authority; their main purpose in life was to serve (white) men. These reformers often underestimated their own privileges—for example, they never had to worry about their children being sold away from them. Yet the link between the two movements—in both ideas and personnel—was dramatic.

Treated as second-class citizens within the abolitionist movement, many women felt compelled to act. When Elizabeth Cady Stanton and other American women attended the 1840 World Anti-Slavery Convention in London, male leaders of the British and Foreign Anti-Slavery Society relegated the women delegates to a balcony and excluded them from the formal deliberations. Eight years later, Cady Stanton worked with Lucretia Mott,

■ Margaret Fuller was one of the foremost American intellectuals of the antebellum period. Throughout her life she remained conscious of an inner struggle between her passionate self, desiring an active life, and her intellectual self, wanting to engage in study and debate with other scholars. She explored Transcendentalism, feminism, social reform, and finally the revolutionary fervor of Italian nationalism.

a Quaker minister; Susan B. Anthony, a women's rights activist; and other similarly inclined women and men to organize the first women's rights convention in Seneca Falls, New York.

Women's rights advocates made some progress independent of the abolitionist movement. In 1838, both New York and Pennsylvania passed legislation giving married women control over any real property (land) or personal property they brought to marriage. In 1839, Mississippi passed the Married Women's Property Law, intended to protect the fortunes of the married daughters of wealthy planters.

> Transcendentalists believed in the primacy of the spirit and the essential harmony between people and the natural world.

Massachusetts resident Margaret Fuller explored many reform impulses of the day during her brief life (1810–1850). Educated in the classics by her father at home in Cambridge, in the 1830s she embraced a new intellectual sensibility called Transcendentalism. Fuller cultivated friendships with two other famous Transcendentalists living in the Boston area: Ralph Waldo Emerson and Henry David Thoreau. Transcendentalists believed in the primacy of the spirit and the essential harmony between people and the natural world. They took their inspiration from European Romantics, who celebrated the beauty of nature in art, music, and literature. In 1845, Fuller published *Woman in the Nineteenth Century*, one of the first feminist works written by an American. "I would have Woman lay aside all thought, such as she habitually cherishes, of being led and taught by men," wrote Fuller. She then embraced the role of investigative journalist, writing about the plight of slaves, Indians, and imprisoned women for the New York *Tribune*.

Some reformers and elected officials believed that the greatest reform movement of all was to expand the boundaries of the United States. They believed that the country should increase its territory and in the process bring more people under the American flag. Yet this "reform" impulse relied not on persuasion or education but on military force. The resulting armed conflict on the nation's borders produced new levels of tension within its borders. Americans could no longer ignore the increasingly divisive issue of slavery.

The United States Extends Its Reach

■ *Why was seizing the land that would become the state of Texas so important to so many Americans?*

Efforts to reform society at home went hand in hand with a determination to expand the nation's borders, especially in the Southwest. In the mid-1840s, the editor of the *New York Morning News* declared that the United States had a "manifest destiny" to "overspread the continent" and claim the "desert wastes." Those inhabiting the "desert wastes"—Mexican settlers and a variety of Indian groups—apparently would have little say in the matter. The term **manifest destiny** soon became a catchall phrase, justifying American efforts not only to conquer new territory but also to seek out new markets for American goods across the oceans.

THE LONE STAR REPUBLIC

In the early 1830s, the Mexican government became alarmed by the growing number of American emigrants to Texas. Worried that the settlers would refuse to pledge allegiance to Mexico, that country closed the Texas border to further in-migration. By 1835, only one out of every eight residents of Texas was a *Tejano* (a native Spanish speaker); the rest, numbering 30,000, hailed from the United States. The U.S.-born Texians, together with some prominent *Tejanos*, had become increasingly well armed and militant. They organized volunteer patrols to attack Indian settlements. These forces became the precursor of the Texas Rangers, a statewide organization of law enforcement officers.

In 1836, the Texians decided to press for independence from Mexico. Only by becoming a separate nation, they believed, could they trade freely with the United States, establish their own schools, and collect and spend their own taxes. The pro-independence Texians included Davy Crockett, who had moved there in 1835. A few months later, Crockett and other armed Texians retreated to a Spanish mission in San Antonio called the Alamo. They were joined by a small group of *Tejanos* who resented Mexico's heavy-handed control of Texas. In March 1836, a military force led by Antonio López de Santa Anna, president of the Republic of Mexico and a general in the army, battled them for thirteen days. All 187 defenders of the Alamo died at the hands of Santa Anna and his men; the Mexican leader lost 600 of his own troops. Historians disagree on whether all of the Alamo defenders died fighting or if some were executed by Mexican soldiers.

In April a force of Texians and their *Tejano* allies, including military leader Juan Seguin, surprised Santa Anna and his men at the San Jacinto River and killed another 600 of them. The victors captured Santa Anna and declared themselves a new nation. Sam Houston, former U.S. congressman from Tennessee and commander in chief of the Texian army, became president of the Republic of Texas (also called the Lone Star Republic) in 1837. Some *Tejanos* who objected to Mexican policies also supported the new republic; these included José Antonio Navarro, Francisco Ruiz, and Lorenzo de Zavala, who became its vice president.

In the northern territories of Mexico, many Spanish speakers had long felt abandoned by the Mexican government, which had made no provisions for their self-government and inhibited trade relations with the United States. Although other Mexican provinces protested the way they were treated by the government, Texas was the only Mexican state to launch a successful rebellion against Mexico.

Texas's independence raised the fears of U.S. abolitionists and imperiled blacks living in the new republic. In contrast to Mexico, which had abolished slavery in 1829, Texas approved a constitution that not only legalized slavery but also prohibited free blacks from living in the country. Greenbury Logan, a black man who owned a farm near Austin, petitioned to stay. He wrote, "Every privilege dear to a free man is taken away." But vigilantes forced him to leave. They also forced out many *Tejanos*. Among them was Juan Seguin, who had helped defeat Santa Anna at the Battle of San Jacinto and was now the mayor of San Antonio. Not until 1981 did another *Tejano*, Henry Cisneros, hold the office of mayor of the city of San Antonio.

THE ELECTION OF 1844

As an independent republic, Texas became a hotly contested political issue in the United States. During the election of 1844, politicians began to debate whether the United States should annex Texas. Van Buren was outspoken in his opposition to the idea. As a result, the frankly expansionist Democrats spurned the former president as a candidate and nominated James K. Polk of Tennessee. They called for "the reannexation" of Texas and the "reoccupation" of Oregon. Their rallying cry became "Fifty-Four Forty or Fight," a reference to their desire to own the area (expressed in terms of its longitude and latitude coordinates) claimed by the British in present-day Canada south of Alaska and west of the Continental Divide. Kentucky congressman Henry Clay received the Whig nomination after he announced he was against the annexation of Texas. But under pressure from Southerners, he later changed his mind, to the disgust of party leaders.

Neither the Democrats nor the Whigs had shown an interest in directly addressing the issue of slavery in the last presidential election. Yet in 1844, the controversy over the annexation of Texas made it impossible for the two parties to ignore the growing controversy over

Max Rosenthal, *Henry Clay*. National Portrait Gallery, Smithsonian Institution/Art Resource NY

■ Henry Clay had a distinguished career as statesman and politician for more than four decades. He was secretary of state under President John Quincy Adams, served as speaker of the House of Representatives for a longer term than anyone else in the nineteenth century, and represented Kentucky in the Senate. A prominent Whig leader, he promoted "the American System" of tariffs and federal subsidies for transportation projects. By 1840, members of both parties were boasting of their (supposed) humble origins. Here Clay is portrayed as the "Old Coon" because the Whigs had adopted the raccoon as their symbol.

TABLE 12.4			
The Election of 1844			
Candidate	**Political Party**	**Popular Vote (%)**	**Electoral Vote**
James K. Polk	Democratic	49.6	170
Henry Clay	Whig	48.1	105
James G. Birney	Liberty	2.3	—

bound labor. Under the banner of the young Liberty party, some abolitionists charged that territorial expansion would mean the continued growth and prosperity of the slave system; they pointed to the public pronouncements of southern planters, who were outspoken in their desire to expand their slaveholdings into the fertile lands of Texas.

For their part, Democrats and Whigs believed, correctly, that most voters would ignore slavery when they cast their ballots. Thus members of both parties tried to silence both sides of the slavery debate. They turned a deaf ear to the proslavery advocates on one hand and squelched northern abolitionist opinion by ignoring petitions to Congress on the other. In the end, Polk won the election. The expansionists had elected one of their most ardent champions to the highest office in the land.

Still, Polk was not interested in going to war with Great Britain over the vast territory of Oregon. In 1846, the two countries reached a compromise. Britain would accept the 49th parallel as the border between Canada and the United States and retain the disputed islands off the coast of Vancouver. The United States settled for one-half of its original claim to Oregon. Thereafter, it was free to turn its full attention to extending its southern and western borders.

WAR WITH MEXICO

Texian leaders wanted to become part of the United States. In 1845, as one of his last acts as president, Tyler invited Texas to become the twenty-eighth state. He also understood that

Joseph Vollmering, The U.S. Naval Expedition Under Comore. M. C. Perry, Ascending the Tuspan River, 1848. Amon Carter Museum, Forth Worth, Texas (1976.33.2)

■ This painting shows the U.S. Navy going up the Tuxpan River in Mexico during the U.S.-Mexican War. Located on the Gulf Coast halfway between Vera Cruz and Tampico, Tuxpan was the last significant Mexican port to be seized by U.S. forces by the spring of 1847. Commodore M. C. Perry assembled a formidable force of marines and infantry to take over the town.

Upper California
Oregon Territory
Unorganized Territory
IOWA
Fremont
Bear Flag Revolt, June 14, 1846
San Francisco, July 10, 1846
Ft. Leavenworth
MISSOURI
Monterey, July 7, 1846
NEW MEXICO
Kearny
Stockton
ARKANSAS
Gila R.
Santa Fe, Aug. 16, 1846
San Diego
Kearny
LOUISIANA
El Brazito, Dec. 25, 1846
PACIFIC OCEAN
Rio Grande R.
TEXAS
New Orleans
Sacramento River, Feb. 27, 1847
Chihuahua
Doniphan
Wool
Taylor
Corpus Christi
Gulf of Mexico
Scott
Buena Vista, Feb. 22–23, 1847
Monterrey, Sept. 21–24, 1846
Matamoros
Tampico, Nov. 14, 1846
Scott
Mexico City, Sept. 13–14, 1847
Veracruz, Mar. 29, 1847

U.S.–Mexican War
- U.S. territory
- Territory ceded by Mexico, 1848
- Disputed area
- Mexican territory
- ⇨ U.S. troop movements
- ✧ U.S. victory
- ✦ Mexican victory

■ **MAP 12.5** **The U.S.–Mexican War (1846–1848)**
During the U.S.–Mexican War, American troops marched deep into the interior of Mexico. General Winfield Scott raised the American flag over Mexico City on September 14, 1847. The treaty that concluded the war was named after the village of Guadalupe Hidalgo, a few miles north of the Mexican capital. The U.S. army withdrew the last of its troops from foreign soil in July 1848.

annexing Texas was a way to goad Mexico into open hostilities; Mexico had warned the United States that such a move would mean war. A joint resolution of both houses of Congress confirmed Texas statehood in December 1845.

The boundaries between Mexico and the new state of Texas remained in dispute. Mexico recognized the Nueces River as the boundary for Texas. In contrast, Texians and U.S. politicians envisioned the boundary a hundred miles to the south at the Rio Grande. Complicating matters further, the new president, James K. Polk, had sent an envoy, John Slidell, to purchase California and a disputed section of Texas from Mexico. Mexico refused the deal. Nevertheless, around this time, Polk wrote in his diary that if he could not acquire all of New Mexico and

Senator John C. Calhoun Warns Against Incorporating Mexico into the United States

Interpreting History

In January 1848, Senator John C. Calhoun delivered a speech, addressing his remarks to President Polk and to his fellow lawmakers. He urged them to resist calls to incorporate all of a conquered Mexico into the United States. Calhoun favored the spread of slavery into new territories. However, here he expresses the fear that residents of Mexico were incapable of becoming suitable U.S. citizens, for "racial" reasons.

It is without example or precedent, either to hold Mexico as a province, or to incorporate her into our union. No example of such a line of policy can be found. We have conquered many of the neighboring tribes of Indians, but we never thought of holding them in subjection—never of incorporating them into our Union. They have either been left as an independent people amongst us, or been driven into the forests.

I know further, sir, that we have never dreamt of incorporating into our Union any but the Caucasian race—the free white race. To incorporate Mexico, would be the first instance of the kind of incorporating an Indian race; for more than half of the Mexicans are Indians, and the other half is composed chiefly of mixed tribes. I protest such a union as that! . . .

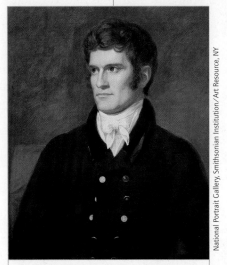

■ Portrait of John C. Calhoun by Charles Bird King, c. 1818–1825.

National Portrait Gallery, Smithsonian Institution/Art Resource, NY

Sir, it is a remarkable fact, that in the whole history of man, as far as my knowledge extends, there is no instance whatever of any civilized colored races being found equal to the establishment of free popular government, although by far the largest portion of the human family is composed of these races. . . . Are we to associate with ourselves as equals, companions, and fellow-citizens, the Indians and mixed race of Mexico? Sir, I should consider such a thing as fatal to our institutions.

Calhoun then moves on to another theme. He disputes the notion that Mexico can begin as a territory and then work its way up to statehood, following the standards Congress set for other western territories.

You can establish a Territorial Government for every State in Mexico, and there are some twenty of them. You can appoint governors, judges, and magistrates. You can give the people a subordinate government, allowing them to legislate for themselves, whilst you defray the cost. So far as the law goes, the thing is done. There is no analogy between this and our Territorial Governments. Our Territories are only an offset of our own people, or foreigners from the same regions from which we came. They are small in number. They are

---

California through diplomatic negotiation, he was determined to obtain them by force. The stage was set for war.

Armed conflict broke out in January 1846. U.S. troops, under the command of General Zachary Taylor (a veteran of wars against Tecumseh, the Seminole, and Black Hawk), clashed with a Mexican force near the mouth of the Rio Grande near Matamoros. Taylor had deliberately moved his troops across the Nueces River into disputed territory; his intention was to provoke an armed response from Mexico. A skirmish ensued, eleven Americans were killed, and Taylor pulled back. Polk used this military action as justification for a declaration of war against Mexico. The president declared, "American blood has been shed on American soil."

Not all Americans supported the war. Transcendentalists such as Henry David Thoreau objected to what they saw as a naked land grab. Refusing to pay taxes for what he considered a war to expand slavery, Thoreau went to jail. Nativists also objected to the war, fearing that the United States would have to assimilate thousands of Indians and Spanish-speaking Roman Catholics. Some members of Congress, including a newly elected U.S. Representative from Illinois named Abraham Lincoln, also condemned Polk's "act of aggression."

DOCUMENT

Corwin, "Against the Mexican War"

incapable of forming a government. It would be inconvenient for them to sustain a government, if it were formed; and they are very much obliged to the United States for undertaking the trouble, knowing that, on the attainment of their majority—when they come to manhood—at twenty-one—they will be introduced to an equality with all other members of the Union. It is entirely different with Mexico. You have no need of armies to keep your Territories in subjection. But when you incorporate Mexico, you must have powerful armies to keep them in subjection. You may call it annexation, but it is a forced annexation, which is a contradiction in terms, according to my conception. You will be involved, in one word, in all the evils which I attribute to holding Mexico as a province. In fact, it will be but a Provincial Government, under the name of a Territorial Government. How long will that last? How long will it be before Mexico will be capable of incorporation into our Union? Why, if we judge from the examples before us, it will be a very long time. Ireland has been held in subjection by England for seven or eight hundred years, and yet still remains hostile, although her people are of kindred race with the conquerors. A few French Canadians on this continent yet maintain the attitude of hostile people; and never will the time come, in my opinion, Mr. President, that these Mexicans will be reconciled to your authority. . . . Of all nations of the earth they are the most pertinacious—have the highest sense of nationality—hold out the longest, and often even with the least prospect of effecting their object. On this subject also I have conversed with officers of the army, and they all entertain the same opinion, that these people are now hostile, and will continue so. . . .

We make a great mistake, sir, when we suppose that all people are capable of self-government. We are anxious to force free government on all; and I see that it has been urged in a very respectable quarter, that it is the mission of this country to spread civil and religious liberty over all the world, and especially this continent. It is a great mistake. None but people advanced to a very high state of moral and intellectual improvement are capable, in a civilized state, of maintaining free government; and amongst those who are so purified, very few, indeed, have had the good fortune of forming a constitution capable of endurance.

Calhoun also warns that "these twenty-odd Mexican States" would eventually have power in Congress. He asks his listeners whether they would want their own states "governed by" these peoples.

QUESTIONS

1. *Why does Calhoun assume that, if the United States incorporates Mexico into its territory, the federal government "must have powerful armies to keep them [Mexicans] in subjection"?*

2. *How might Calhoun's more extreme expansionist colleagues—those in favor of seizing all of Mexico—have countered his arguments against such action?*

Source: Clyde A. Milner, ed., *Major Problems in the History of the American West: Documents and Essays* (Lexington, MA: D.C. Heath, 1989), 219–221.

Predictably, opponents of slavery were among Polk's most outspoken critics. Soon after the outbreak of war, Representative David Wilmot of Pennsylvania attached an amendment to a bill appropriating money for the war. Called the Wilmot Proviso, the measure declared that "neither slavery nor involuntary servitude shall ever exist" in territories the United States acquired from Mexico. Though a member of the Democratic party, Wilmot spoke primarily as a white Northerner; he wanted to preserve the West for "the sons of toil of my own race and color." Wilmot's views show how racial prejudice and antislavery sentiment coexisted in the minds of many white Northerners. The House approved the proviso, but the Senate did not. Southern Democrats claimed that Congress had no right to deprive slaveholders of their private property anywhere in the nation.

Meanwhile, Polk launched a three-pronged campaign against Mexico. He sent Taylor into northern Mexico and ordered General Stephen Watts Kearny into New Mexico and then into California. Following the third directive of the campaign, General in Chief of the U.S. Army Winfield Scott coordinated an amphibious landing of 10,000 soldiers at Vera Cruz, on the Gulf of Mexico. Mexican forces tried to defend their homeland using guerrilla tactics, but U.S. soldiers overcame them in part by terrorizing civilians. Scott acknowledged that the men under his command had "committed atrocities to make Heaven weep and every American of Christian morals blush for his country. . . . Murder, robbery and rape of mothers and daughters in the presence of tied-up males of the families." Some U.S. soldiers were among those sickened by the sight of atrocities. The San Patricio Soldiers, Irish immigrants who had signed up to fight in the U.S. Army, included 100 men who went over to the Mexican side, rather than engage in the killing and the pillaging of churches and convents.

In September 1847, Mexico City surrendered and the war ended. Mexico had been in no shape to resist superior U.S. firepower. The United States paid for Scott's victory with 13,000 lives and $100 million; the Mexicans lost 20,000 lives. In the Treaty of Guadalupe Hidalgo, approved by the Senate in 1848, Mexico agreed to give up its claims to Texas. The United States gained all of Texas as well as the area west of Texas, comprising present-day New Mexico, Arizona, Utah, Nevada, and California; in all, almost one-half of the territory of Mexico was ceded to the United States under the treaty. Male residents of areas formerly held by Mexico were given one year to decide whether to stay in the United States and become citizens or return to Mexico. They were also entitled to retain their titles to the land, a provision that proved difficult to enforce in the face of European American land hunger.

The U.S. government paid Mexico $18.25 million. Of that amount, $15 million was designated as payment for land lost; the rest was restitution to U.S. citizens who might bring claims against Mexico for damaged or destroyed property during the war. Americans had conflicting views of the treaty. Abolitionists saw it as a blood-drenched gift from American taxpayers to slaveholders. Others argued that Polk had squandered a rare opportunity to seize all of Mexico.

The conflict over Texas finally forced politicians to address the issue of slavery, a subject they had successfully avoided since the Missouri Compromise in 1820. Yet the possibility existed that the current two-party system would mean little in a larger battle that pitted the North against the South. The U.S. victory in the war against Mexico roused the passions of abolitionists and their enemies, and proved that the two-party system could not resolve, or even contain, the greatest political issue of the day.

Conclusion

In the 1830s and 1840s, mass population movements affected almost every aspect of American life. Immigrants from western Europe helped to swell the nation's labor force in Midwestern farming communities and eastern cities. The arrival of the Roman Catholic Irish provoked a backlash among native-born Protestants and spawned a nativist political movement. Groups of people bound together by a particular ethnic identity, religious faith, or set of principles found room to set up their own communities apart from other groups. In contrast, Native Americans such as the Cherokee, together with African American slaves, had little control over their own movements; these groups were forced to move so that white men—modest homesteaders as well as wealthy slaveholders—could prosper.

Reformers in the United States and Europe went back and forth across the Atlantic, exchanging ideas related to women's rights, the abolition of slavery, and utopian communities. More generally, as people, ideas, and things moved around the country at a rapid rate, more Americans believed they had the responsibility and the ability to change the nation. Different reform groups adopted different strategies and goals; in many cases, their causes reflected a growing and diverse population. Labor reformers argued that wage-earners must organize themselves into unions in order to protect themselves from economic downturns such as the Panic of 1837. Public school reformers believed that, regardless of where they lived, children should have access to a common form of education. Temperance reformers looked disapprovingly at immigrants who considered drinking alcohol a social pastime and not a moral vice. Despite this reform ferment, the Whigs and the Democrats remained aloof from many of the most pressing issues of the day; they sought to avoid large-scale disagreements that would serve to alienate large numbers of voters. As a result, the two parties became increasingly irrelevant as Americans debated among themselves the proper course for the country's future.

The optimism that fueled reform movements spilled over into a newly invigorated American nationalism that encouraged military conquest. As European Americans pushed the boundaries of the country west and south, they clashed with Indians and foreign powers who claimed those lands as their own. Yet some Americans believed the nation must follow a "manifest destiny" to expand its borders the length and breadth of the continent. The Mexican-American War highlighted the restlessness among land-hungry slave owners and antislavery forces alike. The clash over the Wilmot Proviso in particular opened a new chapter in the wider debate over slavery. In considering the proviso, members of Congress gave up their party loyalties as Democrats or Whigs and began to think of themselves as Northerners and Southerners. When Wilmot proclaimed that he wanted to preserve the West for his "own color," he revealed that even antislavery Northerners did not necessarily consider black people as their equals. When Southerners indicated that even the vast expanse of Texas would not satisfy their desire for land, they revealed that the conflict of slavery was about to enter and new and dangerous stage.

For Review

1. Give examples of the ways that migration or immigration led certain groups to change their social or legal identities.

2. Why did so many northerners oppose both slavery and racial equality? (Consider the conflict over the western territories.) What were the various forms of migration that influenced the debate over slavery?

3. What reasons did Americans have for staying in motion during the 1830s and 1840s?

4. Why did some women see their role as social reformers as an extension of their roles as wives and mothers in the home?

5. In what ways did certain reforms of this period overlap with and reinforce one another?

6. Did all opponents of the Mexican War agree with one another? Why or why not?

7. How was slavery intertwined with manifest destiny and the Mexican War?

8. In what ways did sectional tension between the North and South increase during this period? How were those tensions expressed?

CHRONOLOGY: 1832–1848

1833	Great Britain abolishes slavery.
1835	Texas revolts against Mexico.
1836	Congress passes gag rule on antislavery petitions.
	Republic of Texas founded.
1837	Panic of 1837.
1838	Cherokee removal begins; Trail of Tears.
1840	Liberty party founded.
1841	John Tyler assumes presidency after death of William Henry Harrison.
	Supreme Court rules in favor of *Amistad* Africans.
1844	Mormon leader Joseph Smith killed by mob in Nauvoo, Illinois.
1845	Irish potato famine.
	Frederick Douglass, *Narrative of the Life of Frederick Douglass.*
	Texas becomes twenty-eighth state.
1846	Great Britain cedes southern part of Oregon Country to United States.
	Mexican-American War begins.
1847	United States wins battles of Buena Vista, Vera Cruz, Mexico City.
1848	Treaty of Guadalupe Hidalgo ends Mexican-American War.
	Women's rights convention in Seneca Falls, New York.
	Popular revolutions sweep Europe.

Created Equal Online

For more *Created Equal* resources, including suggestions on sites to visit and books to read, go to **MyHistoryLab.com**.

Part **Five**

Disunion and Reunion

The Civil War was the country's greatest political and moral crisis. By 1860, the two-party system could no longer contain the dispute between proslavery and antislavery forces. That dispute centered on the fate of slavery in new territories in the west. In particular, California's admission to the Union as a free state in 1850 caused a crisis that profoundly shaped national politics during the following decade. The new state revealed the many conflicts that divided Americans during the 1850s—clashes not only over slavery, but also over economic development and the legal rights of immigrants and minorities generally.

Several dramatic developments—the secession of southern states from the Union, the formation of the Confederate States of America, and a Confederate attack on a federal fort in Charleston Harbor—precipitated all-out war. In the spring of 1861, few people could have anticipated that the conflict would drag on for four long years and claim almost 700,000 lives.

The Second Party system, based on divisions between Whigs and Democrats, unraveled in the 1850s. Both parties represented coalitions of groups that expressed cultural, not sectional, sensibilities. Yet a series of events led to a realignment of parties into northern and southern camps. Many Northerners chafed under the Fugitive Slave Act of 1850, which required that all citizens assist law enforcement agents in retrieving runaway slaves for their owners. The founding of the Republican party in 1854 gave a political voice to Northerners hoping to preserve the western territories for family farmers who would not have to compete for land and labor with large slaveholders. In 1857, the Supreme Court ruled that black people had no rights that any court was bound to respect. Violent conflicts between proslavery and antislavery forces in Kansas and, in 1859, a failed raid by abolitionists on Harpers Ferry, Virginia, revealed that legislators' resolutions and maneuverings were insufficient to stave off bloodshed.

In pursuing a militant nationalism, Confederates hoped to compensate for their relative weakness in terms of population and industrial capacity compared with the North. They believed that they could use a large, docile black labor force to grow food and serve as a support system for the army. They anticipated that European nations, dependent on southern cotton, would extend them diplomatic recognition, and that white civilians would rally to the defense of their homeland no matter what the price in money or blood. Confederates also believed that western Indians would gladly assist them in their cause against a hated U.S. Army, and that brilliant southern generals could indefinitely outstrategize a huge, lumbering invading army. On all these counts they miscalculated, but their miscalculations were revealed only gradually.

During the war, white Southerners had to contend with two major unanticipated consequences of the conflict. First, war mobilization efforts across the South necessitated the centralization of government and economic policymaking. Principled states' rights supporters opposed these efforts. Second, slaves and free blacks alike proved traitorous to the Confederate cause. In myriad ways—running away from their owners and spying for the enemy, slowing their work pace in the fields, and fighting for the Union army—black people served as combatants in the war. They fought for their families and their freedom and for a country that would grant them full citizenship rights. In the North, only in late 1862 did President Abraham Lincoln announce that the United States aimed to destroy slavery, but violent antidraft, antiblack riots in several cities showed that the northern population was deeply divided over **emancipation**.

Soon after the end of the war, in April 1865, congressional Republicans began to challenge President Andrew Johnson's plan for reconstructing the South; they considered it too lenient toward the former Confederate states. In 1867, these political leaders had enough votes to enact their own plan, calling for the enfranchisement of black men in the South, the reorganization of southern state governments under leadership loyal to the Union, and the enactment of a labor contract system between southern landowners and black laborers.

Members of the Republican party backed a strong Union, a federal system in which the central government would ensure that individuals could pursue their own self-interest in the marketplace of goods and ideas. Yet the Civil War era exposed the limits of the Republican vision. The Plains Indians sought not citizenship but freedom from federal interference altogether. Women and working people challenged various components of the Republican ideal, with its emphasis on unbridled individualism and federal subsidies of business. African Americans aspired to own property, vote, and send their children to school, just as other nineteenth-century Americans did. They wanted to farm their own land and care for their own families free from white intrusion. Yet congressional Republicans did not enact large-scale land redistribution programs; most felt that once the rebels were subdued and slavery abolished, their duty was done.

Civil strife persisted into the postwar period. Union generals turned from quelling the southern rebellion to putting down armed resistance among the Plains Indians. Former rebels formed vigilante groups to attack black voters and their allies in the South. By the early 1870s, most Northerners had lost interest in the welfare of the former slaves and acquiesced as former Confederates reclaimed state governments. The last occupying forces withdrew from the South in 1877. In welding the country together as a single economic and political unit, the Republicans had triumphed. However, white Southerners retained control over their local social and political affairs. The revolution to secure African American civil rights was stalled for nearly 100 years.

Chapter 13

The Crisis over Slavery, 1848–1860

■ Chinese and European American miners pan for gold in the Auburn Ravine in California in 1852.

On January 24, 1848, Henry William Bigler took a break from building a sawmill for John Sutter in California's Sacramento Valley and penned in his pocket diary, "This day some kind of mettle was found . . . that looks like goald."

GOLD! News of the discovery at Sutter's mill spread like wildfire. By late 1848, immigrants from all over the world and migrants from all over the United States had begun to pour into the foothills of the Sierra Nevada Mountains. Dubbed "the Forty-Niners," they had journeyed westward across the mountains, from the tenements of New York City and the great plantations of Mississippi; north from Mexico; and over the oceans, from western Europe, China, and South America. Equipping themselves with simple mining tools, the Forty-Niners began to dig for buried treasure, determined to stake a claim and make a fortune. And so they sang:

> I'll scrape the mountains clean, my boys,
> I'll drain the rivers dry,
> A pocket full of rocks bring home,
> So brothers, don't you cry!

During the Gold Rush years of 1848 to 1859, various cultural groups were thrown in close proximity to each other. People from Belgium, France, Germany, Scotland, Chile, and Long

Island learned to appreciate flour and corn tortillas (*tortillas de harina* and *tortillas de maiz*) and beef cooked in chile, staples of the Mexican diet. More generally, in the West, women played an integral role within emerging regional economies. A gold miner might take a break from washing his clothes, straighten his aching back, and watch a Mexican woman and her daughter, well mounted on their horses, rounding up a herd of near-wild cattle. Maria Rita Valdez operated Rancho Rodeo de las Aguas, a sprawling southern California spread. An-Choi, a Chinese immigrant woman, earned a tidy sum by opening a brothel that catered to gold miners. Biddy Mason, an enslaved woman, successfully sued for her freedom and became the first African American homesteader in Los Angeles.

California came to be part of the United States as a result of the U.S.–Mexican War. In the 1848 Treaty of Guadalupe Hidalgo, Mexico agreed to hand over territory stretching from Texas northwest to California. As a result, the United States obtained a vast expanse of land—almost 530,000 square miles—called the **Mexican Cession.**

In addition to the land, the nation added to its population large numbers of men, women, and children already living in the area—13,000 Spanish speakers and 100,000 Indians (all former Mexican citizens) in California alone. After 1848, many migrants streamed into California and then pressed for statehood, granted in 1850. By that year 90,000 non-Indian settlers lived in the state. Prominent among the Forty-Niners were Chinese immigrants—20,000 had arrived in California by 1852. Within two decades, their numbers would swell to 50,000. From the American South came both free and enslaved African Americans; between 1850 and 1852, the California black population more than tripled from almost 700 people to over 2,200.

California became a state in 1850, but only after a bitter debate in Congress over the extension of slavery. The resulting **Compromise of 1850** included several provisions bearing on this issue: California would be admitted as a free state; slave-trading would be outlawed in the District of Columbia; carved out of the Mexican Cession, the Utah and New Mexico territories could decide for themselves whether to legalize slavery. Finally, a new, harsh fugitive slave law provided for the capture and return of slaves who found their way to free states in the North or West, including California. Though called a compromise, in fact these provisions inflamed the passions on both sides of the slavery debate—abolitionists in the North and slave owners in the South.

Despite California's status as a free state, the principle of free labor was often violated. For example, in 1850 the state enacted a law with the misleading title "An Act for the Government and Protection of the Indians," which provided for the indenture or apprenticeship of Indian children to whites for indeterminate periods of time. The law also allowed for the hiring out, to the highest bidder, of adult Indians deemed guilty of vagrancy. California also enacted discriminatory legislation against African Americans. The state's Fugitive Slave Law of 1852 decreed that, regardless of his or her current status, a black person who entered the state as a slave and thereafter attempted to remain on free soil was a fugitive slave. That year, three African American gold miners, Robert Perkins, Carter Perkins, and Sandy Perkins, all former slaves who had been freed by their owner, were arrested under the law and ordered reenslaved in their native Mississippi.

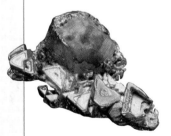

Other California labor systems revealed that the principle of free labor was not carried out in practice. Chinese immigrants to California entered the country organized in companies, or district associations, indebted to merchants for their transportation and bound to work for an employer until the debt was repaid. Fearing competition from cheap labor, alarmed European Americans labeled these Asian workers "coolies" (i.e., enslaved laborers). By 1852, the Chinese in California (almost all of them men) had been pushed out of mining as a result of the discriminatory Foreign Miners Tax, a measure leveled with special force against both Chinese and Mexican miners.

WHAT WE WANT IN CALIFORNIA.

FROM NEW-YORK DIRECT

FAMILY AND FIRE-SIDE

■ This pair of cartoons, titled "What We Want in California," suggests that migrants from the East hoped to reestablish a middle-class ideal in their new home. Above, an Indian family watches the arrival of a train from New York. Below, a European American family relaxes in a well-furnished parlor.

Although the Treaty of Guadalupe Hidalgo guaranteed U.S. citizenship rights to Mexicans, those rights were not enforced under the law. Many Mexicans found themselves vulnerable to violence and land dispossession perpetrated by the growing European American majority. They lacked political voice as well, as delegates to California's constitutional convention in 1849 stipulated that only white *Californios* (descendants of the original Spanish colonists) were entitled to vote, over the objections of the eight *Californios* among the forty-eight delegates in attendance. The majority of delegates also approved a measure prohibiting Indians and blacks from testifying against whites in court.

At midcentury the legal, economic, and cultural tensions among different groups in California mirrored tensions within the country as a whole. Migration into the Midwest accelerated. Slavery shaped life in the South, though most white southerners were not plantation owners. Rapid population growth, the coming together of many different cultures, and dramatic economic changes all fueled the conflict over slavery. The controversy surrounding California statehood revealed that awkward and unjust congressional "compromises" would satisfy neither side in a debate that was becoming increasingly strident and even violent. All over the nation, in the pages of the popular press, on the streets of Boston, in the cotton fields of Alabama, no less than in the courts of California, Americans gradually united around a radical proposition: there could be no compromise on the issue of whether human beings could be held as property.

Regional Economies and Conflicts

■ *To what extent, and in what ways, were U.S. regional economies interdependent by 1860? Were certain regions, or groups of people, outside the emerging national economy?*

It is tempting to view the decade of the 1850s with an eye toward the impending firestorm of 1861. However, in the early 1850s, few Americans could have anticipated the Civil War. At midcentury, the United States was going through a period of rapid transition. New developments such as railroads, the factory system, and more efficient farm equipment led to significant changes in regional economies and began to give shape to an emerging national economy. Continued European American migration into the Midwest, the Great Plains, and the Southwest intensified conflicts over land with Native Americans and Mexicans. Annexation of land in the Southwest and West and the conquest of Indians on the Plains produced wrenching social upheavals for Native Americans in those regions. Meanwhile, Americans continued to wrestle with the role of human bondage in this rapidly changing society. While the South continued to rely on slavery for staple-crop production, a free labor ideology grew stronger in the North.

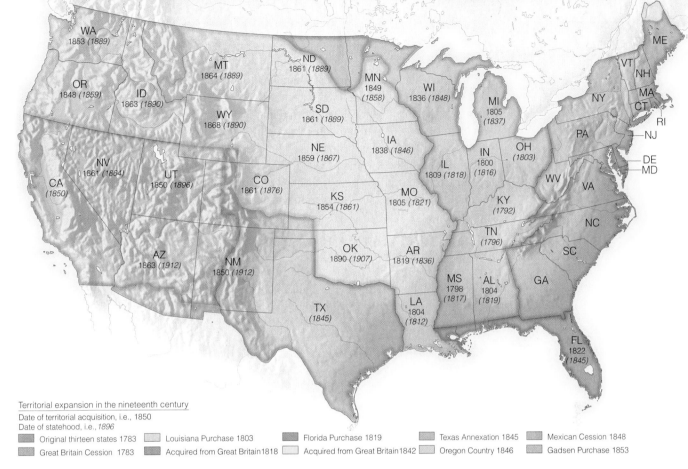

Territorial expansion in the nineteenth century

Date of territorial acquisition, i.e., 1850
Date of statehood, i.e., *1896*

- ▨ Original thirteen states 1783
- ▨ Great Britain Cession 1783
- ▨ Louisiana Purchase 1803
- ▨ Acquired from Great Britain 1818
- ▨ Florida Purchase 1819
- ▨ Acquired from Great Britain 1842
- ▨ Texas Annexation 1845
- ▨ Oregon Country 1846
- ▨ Mexican Cession 1848
- ▨ Gadsden Purchase 1853

■ **MAP 13.1 Territorial Expansion in the Nineteenth Century**

As a result of the Mexican War (1846–1848), the United States won the territory west of Texas by conquest. In 1853, James Gadsden, U.S. ambassador to Mexico, received congressional approval to pay Mexico $15 million for 55,000 square miles in present-day southern Arizona and New Mexico. That year marked the end of U.S. continental expansion.

NATIVE AMERICAN ECONOMIES TRANSFORMED

On the Plains, Indians confronted profound transformations in their way of life. Forced to relocate from the Southeast to Indian Territory (present-day Oklahoma), the Five Southern ("Civilized") Tribes—the Cherokee, Choctaw, Creek, Chickasaw, and Seminole—grappled with the task of rebuilding their political institutions. By the 1850s, the Cherokee had established a new capital at Tahlequah and set up public schools. They founded the Cherokee Female Seminary, with a curriculum modeled after that of an eastern women's college, Mount Holyoke in Massachusetts. They also published a Cherokee newspaper (the *Advocate*) and created a flourishing print culture in their own language.

In the 1850s, U.S. officials negotiated treaties with various Plains Indian groups to enable European Americans to move west without fear of attack. Most migrants were bent on heading straight for California or the Northwest, traversing the Plains, which they called the Great American Desert in the mistaken belief that the absence of trees there demonstrated the infertility of the soil. The Fort Laramie Treaty of 1851 and the Treaty of Fort Atkinson three years later provided that the government could build roads and establish forts along western trails and that, in return, Indians would be compensated with supplies and food for their loss of hunting rights in the region. A young Cheyenne woman, Iron Teeth, recalled "the government presents" to her people in these terms: "We were given beef, but we did not care for this kind of meat. Great piles of bacon were stacked upon the prairies and distributed to us, but we used it only to make fires or to grease robes for tanning." She and her family sought out other items from government trading posts: "brass kettles, coffee-pots, curve-bladed butcher knives, boxes of black and white thread."

United States Territorial Expansion in the 1850s

As whites moved west in large numbers to "scrape the mountains clean and drain the rivers dry," they disregarded U.S. treaties and tribal boundaries and overran the fragile settlements of Indians. Taking leave of the Fort Laramie conclave of 1851, Cut Nose of the Arapaho declared, "I will go home satisfied. I will sleep sound, and not have to watch my horses in the night, or be afraid for my women and children. We have to live on these streams and in the hills, and I would be glad if the whites would pick out a place for themselves and not come into our grounds." But within a generation, the Plains Indians were besieged by the technology, weaponry, and sheer numbers of newcomers heading west.

LAND CONFLICTS IN THE SOUTHWEST

To the southwest, the United States had gained control over a vast expanse of land, provoking legal and political conflicts over the rights and labor of the people who lived there, both natives and newcomers. Under the terms of the Treaty of Guadalupe Hidalgo, Mexico ceded not only California but also the province of New Mexico, territory that included the present-day states of New Mexico, Arizona, Utah, Nevada, and western Colorado. In 1853, the United States bought an additional tract of land from Mexico, 55,000 acres located in the area south of the Gila River (in present-day New Mexico and Arizona). Overseen by the U.S. secretary of war, a Mississippi planter named Jefferson Davis, the agreement was called the **Gadsden Purchase** (after James Gadsden, a railroad promoter and one of the American negotiators).

In Texas, newly arrived European Americans battled native *Tejanos* (people of Mexican origin or descent) for political and economic supremacy. White migrants from the southern United States brought their slaves with them to the region, claiming that the institution of slavery was crucial for commercial development. German immigrants came to central and east Texas, founding towns with German names such as Fredericksburg, Weimar, and Schulenburg. During the 1850s, commercial farming continued to replace subsistence homesteading as the cattle industry spread and the railroads penetrated the region. Although European Americans monopolized the courts and regional political institutions, *Tejanos* retained cultural influence throughout Texas, dominating the cuisine and styles of music and architecture.

The career of José Antonio Navarro reveals the complex political and cultural history of Texas during this period. Navarro was born in 1795 to a prominent family in San Antonio. Sympathetic to a *Tejano* uprising against Spain in 1813, his family had to flee the escalating violence and seek refuge in the United States. With other *Tejanos*, the Navarro family resented Spanish control of Texas, charging that Spain wanted only to extract as much wealth as possible from the region.

A childhood accident left Navarro lame, and because he could not join his friends in their outdoor activities—hunting, playing—he turned to reading and studying. He gained respect as a scholar and a leader. After his family returned to San Antonio, the young Navarro was

> *In Texas, newly arrived European Americans battled native Tejanos (people of Mexican origin or descent) for political and economic supremacy.*

elected mayor of the city (in 1822) at the age of twenty-six. He soon became a friend and supporter of Stephen Austin, believing that Americans would help bring prosperity to Texas. A firm believer in local rule, Navarro objected to Mexico's high-handed control of Texas. As a member of the joint state legislature (representing Texas and Coahuila) and later as a representative to the national Mexican Congress, Navarro tried to circumvent antislavery laws. He hoped to encourage U.S. slaveholders to move to Texas. In 1836, Navarro joined with a group of Texians (U.S.-born Texans) and signed Texas's Declaration of Independence from Mexico.

Austin and Navarro were committed to furthering harmonious relations between Texians and *Tejanos*. Yet Austin's death in 1836 left Navarro with few European American allies. When Texas joined the Union in 1846, Navarro embraced U.S. citizenship, but he deplored the newcomers' aggression in seizing *Tejanos'* land. The Americans' motto seemed to be, "If a *[Tejano]* man will not sell his land, his widow will." Navarro now saw the Americans as the enemies of his family and people. Over the next few years, he watched as *Tejanos* became a minority in San Antonio, and political and economic power shifted to the European Americans. During the course of his lifetime, he had remained loyal to his *Tejano* interests, opposing Spain, then Mexico, and now the United States for this disregard for the principle of local rule. He died in 1871, his dream of *Tejano* equality shattered.

Some Spanish-speaking residents in the Southwest reacted violently when U.S. courts disregarded the land titles held by *Californios* and *Tejanos*. In the early 1850s, California authorities battled Mexican social bandits such as Joaquin Murrieta, who, with his men, raided European American settlements. Murrieta and others argued that they were justified in stealing from privileged European Americans who, they claimed, disregarded the lives and property of Mexicans. In 1859, in the Rio Grande Valley of Texas, tensions between the *Tejano* majority and groups of European American law enforcement officers called the Texas Rangers erupted into full-scale warfare. Juan Cortina, who had fought on the side of Mexico during the Mexican War, orchestrated attacks on European Americans and their property in the vicinity of Brownsville. U.S. retaliation led to Cortina's War, pitting the Mexican leader against a young U.S. colonel, Robert E. Lee. Cortina became a hero to *Tejanos*. "You have been robbed of your property, incarcerated, chased, murdered, and hunted like wild beasts," he declared; "to me is entrusted the work of breaking the chains of your slavery."

The rich print culture developed by Hispanics in the Southwest helped to shape and galvanize public opinion against U.S. seizures of Hispanic lands. For example, in the 1850s, Spanish speakers in southern California published a newspaper dedicated to promoting social justice. Its name was *El Clamor Público* (the Public Clamor).

ETHNIC AND ECONOMIC DIVERSITY IN THE MIDWEST

Compared to the Southwest, the Midwest revealed a distinctive social make-up shaped by the European immigrants and the New Englanders who settled there. The Yankee Strip (named for the northeasterners who migrated there) ran through northern Ohio, Indiana, and Illinois and encompassed the states of Michigan, Wisconsin, and Minnesota. Here migrants from New England settled and established public schools and Congregational churches. Immigrants from western Europe also made a home in this region—the Germans, Belgians, and Swiss in Wisconsin, the Scandinavians in Minnesota. At times cultural conflict wracked even the smallest rural settlements. In some Wisconsin villages, equally matched numbers of Yankees and Germans contended for control over the local public schools, with the group in power posting notices for school board elections in its own language, hoping that its rivals would not show up at the polls.

> *The Midwest revealed a distinctive social make-up shaped by the European immigrants and the New Englanders who settled there.*

The lower Midwest, including the southern portions of Ohio, Indiana, and Illinois, retained strong cultural ties to the southern states, from which many settlers had migrated. Though residing in free states, they maintained broad support for the institution of slavery. In some cases they outnumbered their Yankee counterparts and managed to shape the legal system in a way that reflected a distinct antiblack bias. For example, Indiana's state constitution, approved in 1851, prohibited black people from voting, making contracts with whites, testifying in trials that involved whites, and even entering the state.

Most rural midwestern households followed the seasonal rhythms characteristic of traditional systems of agriculture. However, by the mid-nineteenth century, family farming had become dependent on expensive machinery and subject to the national and international grain markets. John Deere's steel plow (invented in 1837) and Cyrus McCormick's horse-drawn mechanical reaper (patented in 1854) boosted levels of grain production. Improved agricultural efficiency meant that the Midwest, both upper and lower, was fast becoming the breadbasket of the nation.

REGIONAL ECONOMIES OF THE SOUTH

Like the Midwest, the South at midcentury had its own diversity. The South Atlantic states encompassed a number of regional economies. Bolstered by the high price of cotton on the world market, slave plantations prospered in the Black Belt, a wide swath of fertile soil stretching west from Georgia. In many areas of the South, planters concentrated their money and energy on cotton, diverting slaves from nonagricultural labor to toil in the fields. During the 1850s, enslaved Virginia sawmill laborers, South Carolina skilled artisans, and Georgia textile mill operatives all found themselves reduced to the status of cotton hands. In some cases, white laborers took their places in mills and workshops. In other parts of the South, slaves combined field work with nonagricultural work. For example, on expansive low-country South Carolina rice plantations, slaves worked in the fields, but they also processed the raw material, preparing it for market.

Increasingly, northern critics described the South as a land of economic extremes, with wealthy planters enjoying their white-columned mansions while degraded blacks slaved obediently in the fields. The reality was more complicated. Even among whites, there were huge variations in material conditions and daily experiences. A large amount of wealth in land and slaves was concentrated among a small percentage of the white population, and many nonslaveholding whites were **tenant farmers,** leasing their land, mules, and implements from wealthy planters. In some areas as many as one of five farms was operated by tenant farmers; many of these were young men who aspired to become planters and slaveowners themselves some day.

At the same time, about half the total southern white population consisted of yeoman farmers, families that owned an average of fifty acres and produced most of what they consumed themselves (with the occasional help of a leased slave or a wage-earning white person). In upcountry Georgia and South Carolina, yeoman farmers maintained local economies that were little affected by the cotton culture of the great planters in the Black Belt. These families grew what they needed: corn for themselves and their livestock and small amounts of cotton that the women spun, wove, and then sewed into clothing. Men and women alike labored in neighborhood networks of exchange, trading farm produce such as milk and eggs for services such as shoemaking and blacksmithing. Nevertheless, even modest farmers shared with the great planters a southern way of life that prized the independence of white households and the supremacy of whites over blacks.

> About half the total southern white population consisted of yeoman farmers, families that owned an average of fifty acres.

The institution of slavery discouraged immigrants from moving to the rural South in large numbers. German artisans realized that slave labor would undercut their own wages, and Scandinavian farmers understood that they could not compete with large planters in terms of landowning or slave owning. However, the ethnic diversity of southern port cities offered a striking contrast to the countryside, where native-born Protestants predominated. In 1860, 54 percent of all skilled workers and 69 percent of unskilled workers in Mobile, Alabama, were immigrants. On assignment from the *New York Times* in the 1850s, journalist Frederick Law Olmsted noted that in New Orleans, German and Irish workers labored shoulder to shoulder with slave artisans, and although white immigrants "were rapidly displacing the slaves in all sorts of work," it was still possible to glimpse an "Irishman waiting on negro masons."

Throughout the slave states, black people continued to challenge the underpinnings of white supremacy. On the back roads of the plantation counties, late at night, poor workers of both races colluded against the planter elite: slaves swapped hams pilfered from smokehouses and bags of cotton lifted from storehouses for cash and goods offered by landless whites.

Southern blacks were a diverse group. In the cities, masters allowed highly skilled slaves to hire themselves out and keep part of the money they earned for themselves. In their pride of craft and in their relative freedom to come and go as they pleased, these people inhabited a world that was neither completely slave nor completely free. Located primarily in the upper South and in the largest towns, communities composed of free people of color supported churches and clandestine schools, mocking the white notion that all black people possessed a childlike temperament and were incapable of caring for themselves. During the 1850s, the population of free people of color increased from 54,333 to 58,042 in Virginia; in North Carolina the number increased from 27,463 to 30,463. The reality of southern society was not captured by the simple picture of white prosperity and black enslavement. Not all blacks were enslaved field hands, and not all whites were privileged landowners. The widespread mythology masked a more complicated social reality.

A FREE LABOR IDEOLOGY IN THE NORTH

In reaction to the southern slave system, the rural areas of the Northeast and Mid-Atlantic spawned a potent **free labor ideology,** which held that workers should reap what they sow, unfettered by legal systems of slavery and indentured servitude. Free labor advocates glorified the family farmer, the sturdy landowner of modest means who labored according to the dictates of the season and owed his soul—and his vote and the land he tilled—to no master. Nevertheless, the reality that sustained this ideal was eroding in the North during the 1850s.

More and more northerners were earning wages by working for bosses, rather than tilling their own land. Faced with competition from Midwestern farmers and burdened by unfavorable growing conditions imposed by rocky soil and a long winter, New Englanders were migrating to nearby towns and mill villages and to the West. By 1860, the region's textile and shoemaking industries were largely mechanized. From New Hampshire to Rhode Island, growing numbers of water-powered factories perched along the fall line, where rivers spilled swiftly out of the foothills and into the coastal plain. The all-white factory workforce included men and women, adults and children, Irish Catholics and native-born Protestants, failed farmers and young men and women eager to leave the uncertain, hardscrabble life of the countryside for the promise of the mill towns.

Yet the process of industrialization was an uneven one. For example, rural shoemaking workers labored at home, producing shoes for merchant capitalists who provided the raw materials and paid them by the piece. In contrast, in the huge new shoe factories of Lynn, Massachusetts, one worker at a Singer sewing machine achieved the same output as eleven people doing the same task by hand in their homes. In the seaport cities, wage earning had become the norm, although many men and women continued to toil in the hope that they might eventually work for themselves. Thus the seamstress aspired to own a dress shop, the hotel waiter a tavern, the journeyman carpenter a small business.

■ Maine textile workers, with their shuttles, pose for a formal portrait around 1860. Although women factory workers developed a collective identity distinct from that of middle-class wives, most young, native-born women eventually married and withdrew from the paid labor force. Many male factory workers were skeptical that women could or should play an effective role in labor organizations such as unions. Nevertheless, women workers in a number of industries, including textiles and shoes, formed labor organizations in the antebellum period.

In New York, Boston, Cincinnati, and elsewhere, large numbers of Irish newcomers successfully challenged small numbers of black workers for jobs at the lowest echelons of the labor force. In 1853, fugitive slave Frederick Douglass noted with dismay, "White men are becoming house-servants, cooks and stewards on vessels—at hotels. They are becoming porters, stevedores, hod-carriers, brickmakers, white-washers and barbers, so that blacks can scarcely find the means of subsistence." Stung by the contempt of Yankee Protestants, impoverished Irish Catholics sought to assert their equality through skin color. They distanced themselves from African Americans by claiming a white skin as a badge of privilege over the former slaves, a badge of equality with the native born.

Although northerners in general contrasted themselves to the "backward slave South," their region of the country retained elements of unfree labor systems. New Jersey did not officially emancipate the last of its slaves until 1846, and throughout the North, vestiges of slavery lingered through the mid-nineteenth century. As a group of disproportionately poor people, blacks in New England, the Mid-Atlantic, and the Midwest were vulnerable to labor exploitation, including indentured servitude and a system of "apprenticeship" whereby black children were taken from their parents and forced to work for whites. In Delaware, an African American charged with a petty crime could be "disposed as a servant" by court authorities to the highest bidder for a term of seven years.

Many nonslave workers did not receive pay for their labors. While the measure of a white man was rendered more and more in cash terms, wives and mothers throughout the country performed almost all of their work in the home without monetary compensation. On farms and in textile mills such as those of Pawtucket, Rhode Island, children played a key role in the livelihood of individual households but received little or nothing in cash wages. Some members of the white working classes began to condemn what they called wage slavery, a system that deprived them of what they considered a fair reward for their labors and left them at the mercy of merchant capitalists and factory bosses. These workers charged that they were paid so little by employers, their plight was similar to that of black slaves in the South.

> Which groups of people were entitled to American citizenship, with all the rights and privileges that the term implied?

Indeed, although Northerners did not often acknowledge the fact, their own region helped to sustain the institution of southern slavery in several ways: by purchasing raw cotton from planters, by tolerating the system of bondage as long as it was confined to the South, and by implementing their own discriminatory laws that in most states barred blacks from voting and sending their children to public schools.

While different regions developed specialized economies, these regions relied on each other for the production of staple crops and manufactured goods. The result was a national economy. Southern slaves produced the cotton processed in New England textile mills. Midwestern farmers grew the grain that fed eastern consumers. California Forty-Niners discovered the gold that expanded the national currency supply. Yet these patterns of economic interdependence were insufficient to resolve a persistent political question: which groups of people were entitled to American citizenship, with all the rights and privileges that the term implied?

Individualism Versus Group Identity

■ *In what ways did the American ideal of individualism create tensions with the group stereotypes and prejudices enshrined in 1850s laws and customs?*

In every region of the United States, discriminating ideas and practices began to exert greater force. People were defined ever more strongly on the basis of their nationality, language, religion, and skin color. They were more and more limited in their legal status and the jobs they could obtain. Degrading images of legally vulnerable groups—blacks, Chinese, Hispanics—became a part of popular culture, in the songs people sang and the pictures they saw in books and magazines. Through these means, native-born Americans of British stock sought to distance themselves from people of color and from immigrants.

Paradoxically, some writers also began to highlight the idea of American individualism during this time. Such authors extolled what they considered the universal qualities embedded in American nationhood. They believed that the United States consisted not of distinctive and competing groups, but of a collection of individuals, all bent on pursuing their own self-interest, variously defined. They believed that the "representative" American was ambitious and acquisitive, eager to make more money and buy new things.

Yet not everyone could afford to embrace this optimistic form of individualism. Many who were marginalized found emotional support, and in some cases even political power, in a strong group identity. For example, on the Plains, the Sioux Indians resisted the idea that U.S. officials could carve up territory and sell land to individual farmers at the expense of a people who pursued the buffalo across artificial political boundaries. During negotiations at

George Caleb Bingham, *Raftsmen Playing Cards*, 1847. Saint Louis Art Museum, Ezra H. Linley Fund by exchange (50.1934).

■ Just as American writers explored questions of national identity, American artists portrayed everyday scenes related to the vitality of American enterprise and democracy. This painting, *Raftsmen Playing Cards* (1847), was one from George Caleb Bingham's series of pictures of Missouri rivermen. A contemporary observer speculated that the youth on the right is "a mean and cunning scamp, probably the black sheep of a good family, and a sort of vagabond idler." Large rivers such as the Missouri and Mississippi remained powerful symbols of freedom in the American imagination.

Fort Laramie in 1851, Black Hawk, a leader of the Oglala Sioux, condemned the whites with his understatement, "You have split my land and I don't like it." In contrast to the Plains Indians, who wanted no role in American politics, African Americans and white women strove for full citizenship rights. These groups looked forward to the day when each person was accorded the same rights and was free to pursue his or her own talents and ambitions.

PUTTING INTO PRACTICE IDEAS OF SOCIAL INFERIORITY

Everywhere, European American men sought to achieve or preserve the most stable, well-paying, and appealing jobs for themselves. By promoting ideas related to the inferiority of African Americans, Hispanics, and immigrants, white men could justify barring these groups from the rights of citizenship and landownership as well as from nonmenial kinds of employment. In Texas, Mexican leader Juan Cortina condemned Anglo interlopers whose "brimful of laws" facilitated the seizure of *Tejanos'* land by U.S. law enforcement agents and the courts. In California, U.S. officials justified the exclusion of blacks, Indians, Chinese, and the poorest Mexicans from citizenship rights by claiming that members of these groups were nonwhite, or in the words of one state judge writing in 1854, "not of white blood." (Of course, the concept of "white blood" has no scientific basis; the different blood types—A, B, AB, and O—are found among all peoples.)

The precarious social status of various groups was revealed in patterns of their work. In California, white men pursued opportunities on farms and in factories while increasing numbers of Chinese men labored as laundrymen and domestic servants. Indians toiled as field hands under white supervision. In rural Texas, Anglos established plantations and ranches while more and more Mexicans worked as *vaqueros* (cowboys), shepherds, sidewalk vendors, and freighters. In Massachusetts mill towns, white men and women served as the forefront of

Professor George Howe on the Subordination of Women

Interpreting History

Antebellum southern elites prized what they called "natural" hierarchical social relations: the authority of fathers and husbands over daughters and wives, parents over children, rich over poor, and whites over blacks. According to slaveholders, clergy, and scholars, these relationships provided social stability and ensured that the weak and dependent would receive care from the rich and powerful. In July 1850, George Howe, professor of biblical literature at the Theological Seminary at Columbia, South Carolina, addressed the graduating class of a private women's academy. Howe suggested that the roles of women (elite white women) were enduring and never changing.

■ Louisa McCord was a member of an elite slaveholding family in South Carolina and an ardent supporter of slavery. Though an accomplished essayist, she believed that white women should remain subordinate to their fathers and husbands. In 1856 she wrote, "The positions of women and children are in truth as essentially states of bondage as any other, the differences being in degree, not kind." She added that the "true definition of slavery" thus "applies equally to the position of women in the most civilized and enlightened countries."

The Endowments, Position and Education of Woman. An Address Delivered Before the Hemans and Sigourney Societies of the Female High School at Limestone Springs

The duties of life to all human beings are arduous, its objects are noble—each stage of its progress is preparatory to some other stage, and the whole a preparation to an interminable existence, upon which, in one sense, we are hereafter to enter, and in another, have already entered. Others may slightly regard the employments, trials and joys of the school girl. I am

disposed to put on them a higher value. Our wives, sisters, and our mothers were in the same position yesterday. You will occupy a like [position] with them tomorrow. Whatever of virtue, of patient endurance, of poignant suffering, of useful labor, of noble impulse, of generous endeavor, of influence exerted on society for its good, has been exhibited in their example, in a few short years we shall see exhibited also in yours.

To woman, . . . there must be ascribed . . . acuteness in her powers of perception, . . . instincts . . . and emotions. When these are powerfully excited there is a wonderful vigor and determination of will, and a ready discovery of expedients to accomplish her wishes. She has readier sympathies, her fountain of tears is nearer the surface, but her emotions may not be so constant and

an industrial labor force while many African Americans of both sexes and all ages were confined to work in kitchens and outdoors as sweepers, cart drivers, and hawkers of goods.

Despite the divergent regional economies that shaped them, emerging ideologies of racial inferiority were strikingly similar. European Americans persisted in focusing on physical appearances, and they stereotyped all Chinese, Mexicans, and African Americans as promiscuous, crafty, "degraded," and intellectually inferior to whites. They characterized these groups as "cheap labor" who got by with little money: the Chinese supposedly could subsist on rice, Mexicans on beans and *tortillas*, blacks on the "fatback" of the pig. Such prejudices, in places as diverse as Boston, San Antonio, and San Francisco, prevented many people of color from reaching the limits of their own talents in mid-nineteenth-century America.

"A TEEMING NATION"—AMERICA IN LITERATURE

Ideas about ethnic and racial difference coexisted with notions of American individualism, which stressed forms of universal equality. The variety of voices that gave expression to the national ideals of personal striving and ambition suggested the growth, energy, and vitality of the United States in the 1850s. In the Northeast, the writers Ralph Waldo Emerson, Henry David Thoreau, Herman Melville, and Walt Whitman promoted a robust sensibility attuned to the challenges posed by the rigors of both the external world of natural beauty and the inner world of the spirit.

permanent as those of man. She has greater readiness and tact, purer and more noble and unselfish desires and impulses, and a higher degree of veneration for the virtuous and exalted, and when she has found the way of truth, a heart more constant and more susceptible to all those influences which come from above. To the gentleness and quiet of her nature, to its affection and sympathy, that religion which pronounces its benediction on the peace-makers and the merciful, which recommends to them the ornament of a meek and quiet spirit, which, in the sight of the Lord, is of a great price, addresses itself with more force and greater attraction than it addresses man. Born to lean upon others, rather than to stand independently by herself, and to confide in an arm stronger than hers, her mind turns more readily to the higher power which brought her into being. . . .

Providence, then, and her own endowments mark out the proper province of woman. In some cases she may strive for the mastery, but to rule with the hand of power was never designed for her. When she thus unsexes herself she is despised and detested by man and woman alike. England's Queen Victoria at the present moment, if not more feared, is far more beloved in the quiet of her domestic life, than Elizabeth was, the most feared of her female Sovereigns.

Howe ends his address by drawing an implicit comparison between the South and the North. Like many Southerners, he associated the North with labor radicalism, abolitionism, and challenges to the "natural" position of women.

When women go about haranguing promiscuous assemblies of men, lecturing in public, either on infidelity or religion, on slavery, on war or peace—when they meet together in conventions and pass resolutions on grave questions of State—when they set themselves up to manufacture a public opinion for their own advantage and exaltation—when they meet together in organized bodies and pass resolutions about the "rights of woman," and claim for her a voice and a vote in the appointment of civil rulers, and in the government, whether of Church or State, she is stepping forth from her rightful sphere and becomes disgusting and unlovely, just in proportion as she assumes to be a man.

QUESTIONS

1. *Professor Howe clearly believes that men and women are "naturally" different from one another. But do you think he would consider women "inferior" to men? Why or why not?*

2. *Is Howe suggesting here that husband-wife relations are similar to slaveholder-slave relations? Support your response.*

3. *What were the tensions implicit in white women's status, considering that they were neither full citizens like their husbands nor slaves like the workers who toiled on their behalf?*

Source: George Howe, The Endowments, Position and Education of Woman. An Address Delivered Before the Hemans and Sigourney Societies of the Female High School at Limestone Springs, July 23, 1850 (Columbia, SC: I. C. Morgan, 1850), 5, 9, 10–11.

Some forms of literature offered an explicit critique of American materialism. According to Emerson, people were too concerned about material possessions; as he put it, things were "in the saddle," riding everyone. During the 1850s, Thoreau's work became more explicitly focused on nature. In his book *Walden* (1854), he described swimming in the Massachusetts pond of the same name: "In such transparent and seemingly bottomless water, reflecting the clouds, I seemed to be floating through the air as in a balloon." An appreciation of the wonders of nature—wonders that could be felt and tasted, as well as seen—amounted to a powerful force of democratization; anyone and everyone could participate. In turn, Thoreau actively supported the abolition of slavery; his love of nature formed the foundation of his belief in the universal dignity of all people in general and the cause of freedom for black people in particular.

DOCUMENT

"Walden" by Henry David Thoreau

In contrast, other writers celebrated busy-ness, whether in the field or workshop. In the introduction to his book of poetry *Leaves of Grass* (1855), Walt Whitman captured the restlessness of a people on the move: "Here is not merely a nation but a teeming nation of nations. Here is action untied from strings necessarily blind to particulars and details magnificently moving in vast masses." To Whitman, the expansiveness of the American landscape mirrored the American soul, "the largeness and generosity of the spirit of the citizen." His sensuous "Song of Myself" constituted an anthem for all Americans poised, gloriously diverse in their individuality (and their sexuality), to exploit the infinite possibilities of both body and spirit: "I dote on myself, there is a lot of me and all so luscious."

CHALLENGES TO INDIVIDUALISM

Bettmann/CORBIS

■ Isabella Baumfree was born into slavery in New York State in 1797. Thirty years later she escaped from bondage and became a preacher. In 1843, she changed her name to Sojourner Truth. A powerful orator, she spoke on behalf of abolitionism and urged white women's rights activists to embrace the cause of enslaved women. Truth sold small cards, called *cartes de visite*, to support herself. On this card, a portrait taken in 1864, she notes that she must sell her image ("the Shadow") to make a living.

Many men and women remained skeptical of—and, in some cases, totally estranged from—the wondrous possibilities inherent in Whitman's phrase, "Me, Me going in for my chances." In northern cities, individualism spawned the kind of creative genius necessary for techno- logical innovation and dynamic economic change, but it had little meaning for Native Americans in the West, most of whom were desperately seeking a collective response to new threats posed by cattle ranchers and the U.S. cavalry. On the Great Plains, groups such as the Pawnee performed ceremonies and rituals that celebrated kinship and village life above the individual.

African Americans in the North forged a strong sense of group identity. Though they rejected notions of white people's "racial" superiority, blacks had little choice but to think of themselves as a group separate and dis- tinct from whites. Their sense of group solidarity was manifested in everyday life and in political rhetoric and action. In northern cities, blacks took in boarders and joined mutual-aid societies in order to affirm the collec- tive interests of the larger black community. In contrast, well-to-do whites were increasingly emphasizing the sanctity of the nuclear family, composed solely of parents and children. Black leaders criticized the racist laws and ideas that affected the lives of black men, women, and children. For example, the charismatic Boston preacher Maria Stewart denounced the twin evils of racial and gen- der prejudice for condemning all black women to a life of menial labor: "How long shall the fair daughters of Africa be compelled to bury their minds and talents beneath a load of iron pots and kettles? The [white] Americans have practised nothing but head-work these 200 years, and we have done their drudgery."

Northern blacks furthered a sense of group identity through their own literary societies and newspapers. The purpose of black literary societies, such as the Boston Afric-American Female Intelligence Society, was to educate its members and uphold standards of morality. These groups grew out of the same impulse that led to the founding of African American newspapers during this period. As the black reading public increased, papers such as *Freedom's Journal* and *Colored American* published news from around the world, as well as highlighting biographical sketches of figures such as the poet Phillis Wheatley and Haitian revolutionary Toussaint L'Overture. Frederick Douglass published a series of papers in the 1850s, including the *North Star* (1847–1851), *Frederick Douglass' Paper* (1851–1858), and *Douglass' Monthly* (1858–1860). These publications informed readers of the growing controversy over slavery and also featured book reviews and works of fiction by Charles Dickens, Herman Melville, and Nathaniel Hawthorne, among other writers. The papers promoted the idea that their readers had a special identity not only as black Americans, but also as citizens of a wider literary world.

Similarly, some groups of women embraced a collective identity of womanhood, although the definition of that identity took several forms. For example, in the North, writers such as Catharine Beecher articulated a vision of female self-sacrifice fueled by family obliga- tions and emotional relationships. Beecher declared that self-sacrifice formed the "grand law of the system" by which women should live their lives. Informed by religious devotion and sustained by labors of love in the home, this female world offered an alternative to the masculine individualism necessary to profit-seeking, whether on the family farm or in the bank or textile mill. Yet middle-class women believed they could take pride in rearing virtuous citizens and caring for overworked husbands. Sarah Willis Parton (Fanny Fern) cautioned her readers in a series of sketches published in 1853 (*Fern Leaves from Fanny's Portfolio*) that marriage is "the hardest way on earth of getting a living. You never know when your work is done."

Well-to-do white women in the Northeast yearned to be productive and useful although they stood outside the cash-based market economy. Nevertheless, other groups of women cherished different kinds of aspirations. Organizers of the country's first conference devoted to the status of women, the Seneca Falls Convention held in upstate New York in 1848, derived inspiration from the abolitionist movement and protested the efforts of white men to exclude women from formal participation in it. In their demands for women's rights, Elizabeth Cady Stanton and Lucretia Mott linked the plight of the slave with the plight of free women, arguing that white men exploited and denigrated members of both groups. Stanton, Mott, and others received crucial support from African American leaders such as Sojourner Truth and Frederick Douglass. Delegates to Seneca Falls (including Douglass) approved a document called the "Declaration of Sentiments," modeled after the Declaration of Independence: "We hold these truths to be self-evident: that all men and women are created equal." This group of women thus claimed for themselves a revolutionary heritage and all the rights and privileges of citizenship: to own property in their own names, to vote, to attend schools of higher learning, and to participate "in the various trades, professions, and commerce."

> *Critiques of the dominant culture could at times uphold its lofty ideals while condemning everyday reality.*

Many women, including enslaved workers throughout the South and hard-pressed needleworkers toiling in cramped New York City tenements, could not devote themselves full-time to the care of hearth and home, nor could they aspire to a career of public agitation. In her autobiographical novel *Our Nig; or, Sketches from the Life of a Free Black, in a Two-Story White House, North* (1859), Harriet Wilson wrote bitterly of the fate of women such as her mother, a woman "early deprived of parental guardianship, far removed from relatives . . . left to guide her tiny boat over life's surges alone and inexperienced." Like the book's main character, Alfrado, Wilson herself had suffered at the hands of tyrannical white women employers, but at the end of the story Alfrado achieves a measure of dignity and independence for herself by setting up a small business. She thus offered an explicit challenge to both the arrogance of propertied white men and the homebound sentimentality of wealthy white women.

In sum, there was no single, transcendent American identity in the mid-nineteenth century. Yet critiques of the dominant culture could at times uphold its lofty ideals while condemning everyday reality. In his 1852 speech "The Meaning of July Fourth for the Negro," delivered in Rochester, New York, Frederick Douglass took the country to task for failing to live up to the principles of equality embodied in the Declaration of Independence: "Stand by those principles," he exhorted his listeners, "at whatever cost." His words foreshadowed a great war.

The Paradox of Southern Political Power

■ *Why could white Southerners dominate all three branches of the national government and still perceive themselves on the defensive, under siege?*

At the center of debates about hierarchies and equality, the institution of slavery needed to expand to survive. Decades of intensive cultivation were exhausting the cotton fields in the South. The planter elite was counting on the admission of new territories as slave states to preserve their threatened power in Congress. To slave owners, northern-sponsored efforts to block their expansion amounted to a death sentence for all that the white South held dear. In defense of the slave system, the white South had to mount a strong offense or die.

In the early 1850s, proslavery forces maintained firm control over all branches of the federal government. The presidential election of 1800 showed that the "three-fifths clause" of the Constitution gave disproportionate representation to the slave states, where each slave was counted as three-fifths of a person. By the 1850s, this provision had helped to further slave owners' interests in dramatic ways. Without the clause in place, the Wilmot Proviso, which would have banned slavery in the new state of Texas, would have passed Congress. Conversely, the **Kansas-Nebraska Act** of 1854, which allowed residents of Kansas to decide for themselves whether their state would be slave or free, would have failed. By 1850, slaveholders had dominated the office of the presidency for half a century. Ever since George Washington, presidents elected to a second term had been slaveholders, including Jefferson, Madison, Monroe, and Jackson. From the founding of the nation, eighteen of the thirty-one men who had served as Supreme Court justices had owned slaves. During the 1850s, abolitionists pointed out that six slave states with a combined total population less than that of the free state of Pennsylvania sent a total of twelve senators to Congress. Pennsylvania sent two.

Nevertheless, southern planters felt increasingly defensive as the country expanded westward. They warned against "the abolition excitement," which would necessarily upset the delicate balance between slave and free states. Gradually, this tension between southern strength and southern fears led to the fraying and then unraveling of the Jacksonian

TABLE 13.1							
U.S. Population, 1830–1860, by Region, Showing Nativity, Race, and Enslavement							
		White			**Negro**		
Year	**Total**	**Total**	**Native Born**	**Foreign Born**	**Total**	**Enslaved**	**Other Races**
Northeast							
1860	10,594,268	10,438,028	8,419,243	2,018,785	156,001	18	239
1850	8,626,851	8,477,089	7,153,512	1,323,577	149,762	236	–
1840	6,761,082	6,618,758	–	–	142,324	765	–
1830	5,542,381	5,417,167	–	–	125,214	2,780	–
Midwest							
1860	9,096,716	8,899,969	7,357,376	1,542,593	184,239	114,948	12,508
1850	5,403,595	5,267,988	4,617,913	650,075	135,607	87,422	–
1840	3,351,542	3,262,195	–	–	89,347	58,604	–
1830	1,610,473	1,568,930	–	–	41,543	25,879	–
South							
1860	11,133,861	7,033,973	6,642,201	391,772	4,097,111	3,838,765	2,277
1850	8,982,612	5,630,414	5,390,314	240,100	3,352,198	3,116,629	–
1840	6,950,729	4,308,752	–	–	2,641,977	2,427,986	–
1830	5,707,848	3,545,963	–	–	2,161,885	1,980,384	–
West							
1860	618,976	550,567	406,964	143,603	4,479	29	63,930
1850	178,818	177,577	150,794	26,783	1,241	26	–
1840	–	–	–	–	–	–	–
1830	–	–	–	–	–	–	–

Source: Historical Statistics of the United States, Colonial Times to 1957 (Washington, DC: U.S. Government Printing Office, 1960), 11–12.

An Artist Renders County Election Day in the Early 1850s

Envisioning History

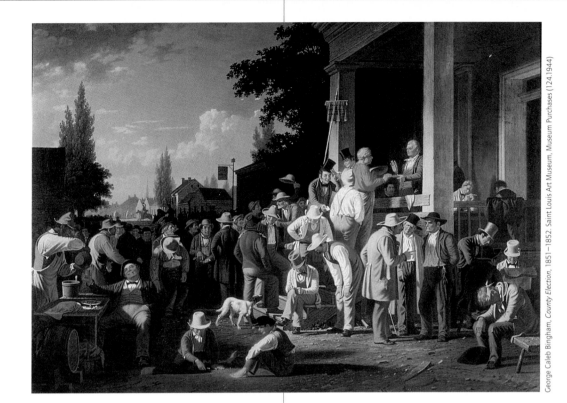

George Caleb Bingham, *County Election*, 1851–1852. Saint Louis Art Museum, Museum Purchase (124:1944)

George Caleb Bingham painted a series of pictures portraying local political customs. Titled *County Election*, this piece was completed in 1851–1852. In 1846, Bingham had lost a campaign to become a congressional representative from Missouri, so he had a political candidate's knowledge of the election process.

The voter expressing his choice before an election official (center right) is a reminder that most state and local elections had open balloting until the late nineteenth century. Throughout the nineteenth century, many voters were accustomed to announcing their choice of candidate in front of a large group of people at the polls. The first U.S. presidential election to require use of the secret ballot was the one held in 1892.

QUESTIONS

1. Besides voting, what other activities are the people in this scene engaged in?

2. What visual evidence suggests that election day brought together a cross-section of white males representing a range of classes and ages?

3. What social groups are conspicuous for their absence from this scene?

4. Do you think Bingham intended this painting to celebrate American democratic traditions? Why or why not?

5. What were some of the implications of the "popular sovereignty" method of deciding whether or not a state should outlaw slavery?

American party system. That system had relied on a truce maintained between Whigs and Democrats on the issue of slavery. A new party, the Republicans, fused the democratic idealism and economic self-interest of native-born Northerners in such a powerful way that white Southerners believed the institution of slavery was in danger of succumbing to the Yankee onslaught. A clash of ideas gradually slipped out of the confines of the polling place and into the realm of armed conflict.

TABLE 13.2			
The Election of 1848			
Candidate	**Political Party**	**Popular Vote (%)**	**Electoral Vote**
Zachary Taylor	Whig	47.4	163
Lewis Cass	Democratic	42.5	127
Martin Van Buren	Free-Soil	10.1	–

THE PARTY SYSTEM IN DISARRAY

In 1848, eight years after the appearance of the antislavery Liberty party, cracks in the two-party system of Whigs versus Democrats opened wider with the founding of the Free-Soil party. Free-Soilers challenged the prevailing notion that the Whigs and Democrats could continue to smooth over the question of slavery in the territories with a variety of patchwork policies and piecemeal compromises. The Free-Soil platform promoted a forthright no-slavery-in-the-territories policy and favored the Wilmot Proviso. In the presidential election of 1848, the Free-Soil party nominated former President Martin Van Buren, Democrat of New York. At the same time, Free-Soilers extended their appeal to the Whig party by supporting federal aid for internal improvements, free western homesteads for settlers, and protective tariffs for northern manufacturers.

Nevertheless, the two major parties persisted in avoidance politics. The Democrats chose General Lewis Cass as their standard-bearer, a man known as the "father of **popular sovereignty**," a doctrine allowing citizens of new states to decide for themselves whether to permit slavery within their borders. The Whigs put forth General Zachary Taylor, although the Louisiana slaveholder and Mexican War veteran had never held elected office. Taylor managed to parlay his military record into a close win in the fall of 1848. But Taylor died after a year and a half as president and was replaced by his vice president, Millard Fillmore.

In 1849, Southerners confronted a disturbing reality. Although slave owners controlled the presidency and the Supreme Court and outnumbered the North in the House of Representatives, California's application for statehood in 1849 raised the specter of an "unbalanced" federal system consisting of sixteen free states and fifteen slave states. The abolitionist threat appeared in other guises as well. The territories of Utah and New Mexico apparently were preparing to ban slavery once they became states. Abolitionists clamored for the immediate emancipation of all slaves. And black men and women worked with abolitionists in the upper South and the North to facilitate the escape of slaves through a network of safe stops called the **Underground Railroad**. The "railroad" consisted of Northerners, some white but most black, who served as "conductors" and "stationmasters" to shelter fugitives in their flight to the North or, in some instances, to Canada.

THE COMPROMISE OF 1850

Against this backdrop of sectional controversy, Congress debated the terms under which California would enter the Union in 1850. A young Democratic senator from Illinois, Stephen Douglas, helped cobble together the Compromise of 1850, under which California would enter the Union as a free state that year. New Mexico and Utah would eventually submit the slavery question to voters in those territories and thus put the idea of popular sovereignty to a practical test. The federal government would abolish the slave trade in Washington, D.C., a move that did not affect the status of slaves already living there, and shore up the Fugitive Slave Act of 1793 with a new, harsher measure.

The **Fugitive Slave Act of 1850** essentially did away with the notion of the North as free territory, for it required local and federal law enforcement agents to retrieve runaways

By the beginning of the Civil War in 1861, some 50,000 slaves had fled to Canada. After the war, 30,000 blacks returned to the U.S. with feelings of safety. Many slaves escaped to Canada, where they were protected from extradition by the British government that refused to accede to demands by the U.S. authorities.

Some slaves fled to Halifax, Nova Scotia.

In 1858, John Brown planned his attack on Harpers Ferry while in Canada.

Washington, D.C. 26.8% enslaved

It is estimated that the "Underground Railroad" consisted of 3,000 members who, by 1861, helped 75,000 slaves find freedom. Traveling by night and hiding by day, slaves moved generally by foot through swamps and streams to throw off the scent.

Some slaves fled to Andros Island in the Bahamas, where the British abolished slavery in 1833.

Blacks enslaved in 1850 as a percentage of state's black population

- 0%
- < 10%
- > 60%

⊙ In Cincinnati, Levi Coffin, President of "The Underground Railroad" helped more than 300 slaves escape.

■ MAP 13.2   The Underground Railroad

The Underground Railroad consisted of a network of people who helped fugitives in their escape from slavery. Many reached free territory in the northern United States or Canada, but others escaped to Mexico or nonslave Caribbean countries. Most "conductors" on the Underground Railroad were blacks, many of them free men and women living in the North.

no matter where they sought refuge in the United States. Blacks were denied a trial or the right to testify on their own behalf. Fugitive slave commissioners earned $10 for each runaway they returned to a claimant. By compelling ordinary citizens to aid in the capture of alleged fugitives, the law brought the issue of slavery to the doorstep of northern whites.

Despite these dramatic events, the presidential campaign of 1852 was a lackluster affair. The Democrats nominated an unknown lawyer, Franklin Pierce. Although he hailed from New Hampshire, Pierce supported slavery. The Whigs turned their back on the undistinguished President Fillmore and chose as their nominee General Winfield Scott, who had gained fame during the Mexican War. Pierce won the election, but the fate of the losing party was equally significant. The Whigs split into regional factions during the election, Northerners resenting Scott's support of the Fugitive Slave Act and Southerners doubting his

TABLE 13.3			
The Election of 1852			
Candidate	**Political Party**	**Popular Vote (%)**	**Electoral Vote**
Franklin Pierce	Democratic	50.9	254
Winfield Scott	Whig	44.1	42
John P. Hale	Free-Soil	5.0	—

devotion to slavery. This split foreshadowed the end of national political parties and the emergence of regional parties, an ominous development indeed.

EXPANSIONISM AND POLITICAL UPHEAVAL

The interests of southern planters affected not only domestic politics but debates and policies related to foreign affairs as well. Even as Congress was heatedly discussing the Compromise of 1850, Southerners were contemplating ways to extend their reach across and even beyond the continental United States. They wanted to find new, fresh, fertile lands for cotton cultivation, and they hoped to incorporate those lands into the United States. Such expansion would also bolster the political power of slave owners in Congress by someday adding new slave states to the Union.

In 1848, President Polk had made a gesture to buy Cuba from Spain, an offer that was rebuffed but one that did not discourage two privately financed expeditions of proslavery Americans from making forays into Cuba in an effort to seize the island by force on behalf of the United States. In 1854, the American ambassadors to Great Britain, France, and Spain met in Ostend, Belgium, and issued a statement declaring that, if Spain would not sell Cuba, the United States would be justified in taking control of the island. According to the Americans, the Monroe Doctrine gave license to the United States to rid the Western Hemisphere of European colonial powers. Noting that two of the three ambassadors hailed from slave states, abolitionists charged that the Ostend Manifesto was just one more ploy to extend the power of slaveholders throughout the Northern Hemisphere.

In 1855, a young proslavery American adventurer, Tennessee-born William Walker, gathered a band of fifty-eight mercenaries and managed to capture Granada, Nicaragua. Declaring himself president of Nicaragua, Walker encouraged the institution of slavery and won U.S. recognition for his regime in 1856. Walker was driven out of the country a year later.

The Gadsden Purchase of 1853 marked the end of westward land acquisition on the continent, but in a commercial sense, expansion continued past the edge of the continental United States. Americans saw the Pacific Ocean as a trade route and East Asia as a trading partner. Commodore Matthew Perry commanded a fleet of U.S. Navy ships that steamed into Tokyo harbor in 1853. The treaty Perry helped arrange with Japan in 1854 protected American whaling ships, sailors, and merchants in that part of the world and opened the door to an increase in trade later in the century.

By the mid-1850s, the uniting of the continent into what would eventually become the forty-eight contiguous states was a source of sectional tension as well as national pride. Fewer and fewer Northerners supported what they considered proslavery charades, so-called legislative compromises. And the territory of Nebraska, poised on the brink of statehood, forced national lawmakers to confront again the political problem of the expansion of slavery. Once more Senator Douglas from Illinois stepped in to fill the breach. Douglas believed that mutual accommodation between North and South demanded a constant process of negotiation and flexibility on both sides. Thus he argued that the gigantic territory be split into two new states, Kansas and Nebraska, whose respective voters would decide the issue of slavery for themselves. His proposal necessitated that part of the Missouri Compromise of 1820, the part that forbade slavery above the 36°30' line, would have to be repealed.

The Kansas-Nebraska Act became law in 1854, enraging northern Free-Soilers by dismantling the 1820 agreement. They became convinced that what they called the Slave Power Conspiracy would stop at nothing until slavery overran the entire nation. The measure also had a profound effect on the Plains Indians, for it deprived them of fully one-half

Free states and territories

Slave states

Indian Territory (unorganized)

Slave or free to be decided by popular sovereignty, Kansas–Nebraska Act

Slave or free to be decided by popular sovereignty, Compromise of 1850

■ **MAP 13.3   The Kansas–Nebraska Act, 1854**

Stephen A. Douglas, senator from Illinois, proposed the Kansas-Nebraska Act of 1854. (Douglas hoped to ensure that any transcontinental railroad route would run through Illinois and benefit his constituents.) To secure southern support for the measure, proponents of the bill repealed the Missouri Compromise of 1820. As a result of the act, settlers displaced many Plains Indians from their lands. In the mid-1850s, the territory of Kansas became engulfed in an internal civil war that pitted supporters of slavery against abolitionists.

the land they had been granted by treaty. Specifically, the act wrought havoc on the lives of Ponca, Pawnee, Arapahoe, and Cheyenne on the southern and central plains. European American settlers poured into the region, provoking Indian attacks. In September 1855, 600 American troops staged a retaliatory raid against an Indian village, Blue Water, in Nebraska, killing 85 Sioux and leading to an escalation in violence between Indians and settlers in the area.

The Compromise of 1850 and the Kansas–Nebraska Act

In their impatience with the two major parties, Free-Soilers were not alone in the early 1850s. The nativist American party, or Know-Nothings, condemned the growing political influence of immigrants, especially Roman Catholics. The American party, its ranks filled with former Whigs, tapped into a deep wellspring of resentment against immigrants on the part of urban, native-born workers as well as Protestant farmers anxious about retaining their influence in public affairs. The party wanted to limit the political participation of all foreign-born men by denying them the right to vote, whether or not they became U.S. citizens.

THE REPUBLICAN ALLIANCE

The rapid rise of the Know-Nothings further indicated that voters had grown disillusioned with the two-party system. Confirmation of that fact appeared on March 20, 1854, in the small town of Ripon, Wisconsin, when a group of disaffected Whigs created the **Republican party.** One core idea informed the party: that slavery must not be allowed to spread into the western territories. From this base, the Republicans built an organization so powerful that it would capture the presidency within six years.

The genius of the Republican party resided in its ability to create and maintain an alliance between groups with vastly different goals. Now forced by the Fugitive Slave Act of 1850 to serve slaveholders (by returning runaway slaves to them) and fearful of the potential of slaveholding Southerners to capture their party, some northern Democrats cast their lot with the Republicans. From the ranks of antislavery men—the long-suffering adherents of the Liberty and Free-Soil parties—came another wing of the Republicans. These party members openly proclaimed their belief in the power of the federal government to halt the relentless march of slavery and ensure that, throughout the land, free soil would be tilled by free labor, free men and women.

Yet antislavery Republicans were by no means unified on major issues apart from opposition to the extension of slavery. Many Northerners were willing to tolerate slavery as long as it could be confined to the southern states; they cared little or nothing for the rights of black people, slave or free. In fact, in the Midwest, Republicans saw no contradiction in calling for the end of slavery in one breath and for the end of black migration to the area in the next. They feared that as job competitors, blacks would force whites to work for less money than they were accustomed to, or would push whites out of jobs altogether.

From the ranks of the newly formed Illinois state Republican party emerged a formidable leader. Born in 1809 in Kentucky, Abraham Lincoln came from a modest background and followed a checkered path into Illinois Whig politics: from youthful plowhand and log-splitter, to local postmaster and county surveyor, and finally self-taught lawyer and member of the state legislature (1834–1842). Although his six-foot four-inch frame and humble background drew ridicule from wealthy people—a Philadelphia lawyer described him as "a tall rawly boned, ungainly back woodsman, with coarse, ill-fitting clothing"—Lincoln made good use of his oratorical gifts and political ambition in promoting the principles of free soil.

The presidential election of 1856 revealed the full dimension of the national political crisis. The Democrats nominated James Buchanan, a "dough-face" (i.e., proslavery Northerner) from Pennsylvania, with John Breckinridge of Tennessee as his running mate. In their platform they took pains to extol the virtue of sectional compromise on the slavery issue, by this time a very unpopular position. Meanwhile, the enfeebled Whigs could do little but stand by helplessly and declare as their "fundamental article of political faith, an absolute necessity for avoiding geographical parties," another plank decidedly out of favor with a growing number of voters. The Know-Nothings cast their lot with former President Millard Fillmore, offering voters little more than an anti-immigrant platform.

Drawing on former members of the Free-Soil and Whig parties, the Republicans nominated the expedition leader John C. Frémont of California for president. Their platform stated in no uncertain terms the party's opposition to the extension of slavery, as well as Republican support for a transcontinental railroad and other federally sponsored internal improvements such as rivers and harbors. The document also included the bold, noble rhetoric—in favor of "the blessings of liberty" and against "tyrannical and unconstitutional laws"—that would be the hallmark of the Republican party in the decade to come. Buchanan won the election, but Frémont's carrying eleven of the sixteen northern states bode well for the Republican party and ill for the slaveholders' union. In Illinois, Frémont had benefited from the tireless campaigning of Abraham Lincoln, who electrified ever growing crowds of people with the declaration that "the Union must be preserved in the purity of its principles as well as in the integrity of its territorial parts." The founding of the Republican party, with its unabashed pro-Union, antislavery stand, signalled that the days of political compromise on the issue of human bondage were rapidly coming to an end.

TABLE 13.4			
The Election of 1856			
Candidate	**Political Party**	**Popular Vote (%)**	**Electoral Vote**
James Buchanan	Democratic	45.3	174
John C. Frémont	Republican	33.1	114
Millard Fillmore	American	21.6	8

The Deepening Conflict over Slavery

■ *During the 1850s, what specific events and developments pushed the nation toward armed conflict?*

Only a small subset of Americans—adult white men—participated directly in the formation of new political parties that set the terms for congressional debates over territorial expansion and slavery. Nevertheless, during the 1850s, increasing numbers of ordinary people were drawn into the escalating conflict over the South's "peculiar institution" as some Northerners mounted concerted challenges, violent as well as peaceful, to the Fugitive Slave Act. The western territory of Kansas became a bloody battleground as abolitionists and proslavery forces fought for control of the new state government. Sites of struggle over the slavery issue included the streets of Boston, the Supreme Court of the United States, political rallies in Illinois, and a federal arsenal in Harpers Ferry, Virginia. No longer would the opposing sides confine their disagreements to congressional debates over the admission of new states. Nor would words be the only weapons. The country was rushing headlong into nationwide armed conflict.

THE RISING TIDE OF VIOLENCE

The Fugitive Slave Act of 1850 caused fear and alarm among many Northerners. In response to the measure, some African Americans, hiding in northern cities, fled to Canada, often with the aid of conductors on the Underground Railroad. Abolitionists, white and black, made dramatic rescue attempts on behalf of men and women sought by their self-proclaimed southern owners. In Boston in 1851, a waiter named Shadrach Minkins was seized at work and charged with running away from a Virginia slaveholder. During a court hearing to determine the merits of the case, a group of blacks stormed in, disarmed the startled authorities, and in the words of a sympathetic observer, "with a dexterity worthy of the Roman gladiators, snatched the trembling prey of the slave-hunters, and conveyed him in triumph to the streets of Boston." Shadrach Minkins found safety in Montreal, Canada, and a Boston jury refused to convict his lawyers, who had been accused of masterminding his escape.

DOCUMENT

Benjamin Drew,
Narratives of Fugitive
Slaves in Canada

The spectacular public rescue of Minkins, and other such attempts, both successful and unsuccessful, brought the issue of slavery into the realm of public performance in northern towns and cities. In 1851, in Christiana, Pennsylvania, a group of blacks violently resisted the attempt of a slaveowner to capture four fugitives. Two years earlier, four slaves had escaped from their master, Edward Gorsuch, who lived in Maryland. The four sought refuge with William Parker, himself a former slave, now living in Christiana, a small town in Lancaster County in the southeastern part of the state. When Gorsuch tracked the men to Christiana in September 1851, he brought with him a posse and a warrant for the fugitives' arrest. But a large group of blacks living in the area quickly armed themselves and converged on the Parker residence. In the ensuing melee, Gorsuch was killed. Federal prosecutors charged more than three dozen men (mostly black) with treason for protecting the fugitives, but a federal jury swiftly acquitted the defendants. The fugitives were never returned to slavery. White Southerners condemned the "Christiana Riot" as one more sign that the North aimed to destroy the institution of slavery, by force if necessary.

Gradually, the war of words over slavery cascaded out of small-circulation abolitionist periodicals and into the consciousness of a nation. In particular, author Harriet Beecher Stowe managed to wed politics and sentiment in a most compelling way. Her novel *Uncle Tom's Cabin* (1852) sold more than 300,000 copies within ten months and a million copies over the next seven years. The book, originally serialized in a magazine, the *National Era*, introduced large numbers of Northerners to the sufferings of an enslaved couple, Eliza and

When Was Slavery Abolished?

The Wider World

1335	Sweden (but not until 1847 in the colony of St. Barthelemy)
1761	Portugal
1791	Haiti, due to a revolt among nearly half a million slaves
1793	Canada, by the Act Against Slavery
1794–1802	France (first time), including all colonies (although abolition was never carried out in some colonies under British occupation)
1811	Spain (and its colonies, though this move was opposed in Cuba and Puerto Rico)
1813	Argentina
1821	Gran Colombia (Ecuador, Colombia, Panama, and Venezuela) through a gradual emancipation plan (Colombia in 1852, Venezuela in 1854)
1823	Chile
1829	Mexico
1833	Great Britain, including all colonies (in effect from 1 August 1834; in East Indies from 1 August 1838)
1835	Mauritius, under the British government.
1848	Denmark, including all colonies
1848	France (second time), including all colonies
1851	Peru
1861	Russia (abolished serfdom)
1863	The Netherlands, including all colonies
1865	United States (abolition occurred in some states before 1865)
1873	Puerto Rico (a colony of Spain)
1880	Cuba (a colony of Spain)
1888	Brazil
1897	Zanzibar (slave trade abolished in 1873)
1910	China
1929	Burma
1936	Ethiopia, by order of the Italian occupying forces
1959	Tibet, by order of the People's Republic of China
1962	Saudi Arabia
1980	Mauritania

This chronology shows when various countries abolished slavery on their own soil or in their colonies. American abolitionists watched foreign antislavery developments with great interest and felt keenly that their own country lagged behind others in outlawing human bondage. During the antebellum period, many U.S. activists maintained ties with their counterparts in Great Britain and other parts of Europe, meeting with them periodically in world antislavery conventions.

QUESTIONS

1. How do you account for the flurry of abolitionist legislation in Europe during the first six or seven decades of the nineteenth century?

2. How do you think slaveholders defended themselves against the abolitionists' charge that the South represented a backward way of life, one that other countries were in the process of rejecting?

3. How was the U.S. case different from that of empire-builders like Great Britain, France, Spain, the Netherlands, and other nations that had colonies?

4. Is it accurate to say that the United States did not outlaw slavery until 1865, considering that the northern states chose to do so in the years after the American Revolution?

George. Slavery's greatest crime, in Stowe's eyes, was the forced severance of family ties between husbands and wives, parents and children.

Southern slaveholders were outraged at Stowe's attempt to portray their way of life as an unmitigated evil. A South Carolina slaveholding woman, Louisa McCord, wrote: "We proclaim it [slavery], on the contrary, a Godlike dispensation, a providential caring for the weak, and a refuge for the portionless." Another Southerner, George Fitzhugh, took this argument to its logical conclusion. In his book *Cannibals All! Or, Slaves Without Masters* (1857), Fitzhugh claimed that civil society demanded the enslavement of the masses, whether white or black: "Some were born with saddles on their backs, and others booted and spurred to ride them—and the riding does them good." Fitzhugh also argued that slaves, who he claimed were cared for by benevolent planters, were better off than northern factory workers, who he asserted were exploited and neglected by indifferent employers.

Meanwhile, the territory of Kansas was becoming engulfed in a regional civil war. Proslavery settlers, aided and abetted by their compatriots (called Border Ruffians) from Missouri, installed their own territorial government at Shawnee Mission in 1855. Opposing these proslavery settlers were the Free-Soilers, some of whom had organized into abolitionist groups, such as the New England Emigrant Aid Company, and armed themselves with rifles.

This dangerous situation soon gave way to terrorism and insurrection on both sides. In 1856, in retaliation for a proslavery raid on the "Free-Soil" town of Lawrence, Kansas, an Ohio abolitionist named John Brown, together with his four sons and two other men, hacked to death five proslavery men at Pottawatomie Creek. The massacre only strengthened the resolve of proslavery advocates, who in the next year drew up a constitution for Kansas that effectively nullified the principle of popular sovereignty over the issue of slavery. Called the **Lecompton Constitution,** the document decreed that voters might approve or reject slavery, but even if they chose to reject it, any slaves already in the state would remain slaves under the force of law. By throwing his support behind the Lecompton Constitution, President Buchanan alienated northern members of his own party, and the Democrats followed the Whigs into North–South factionalism.

The spilling of blood over slavery was not confined to the Kansas frontier. In 1856, Senator Charles Sumner of Massachusetts, an outspoken abolitionist, delivered a speech on the floor of the U.S. Senate condemning "the Crime Against Kansas" (the Lecompton Constitution) and the men who perpetrated it, men he characterized as "hirelings picked from the drunken spew and vomit of an uneasy civilization," men who (like his own colleague Senator Butler of South Carolina) loved slavery the way that degenerates loved their prostitutes. Shortly after this speech, Congressman Preston S. Brooks of South Carolina, a relative of Senator Butler, leapt to the defense of the white South and attacked Sumner on the floor of the Senate, beating him into unconsciousness with a cane. Abolitionists contemplated the necessity of defending themselves and their interests, from the courtrooms of New England and the small towns of the West to the halls of Congress itself.

THE *DRED SCOTT* DECISION

Across the street from the Capitol, proceedings in the Supreme Court were more civil but no less explosive. In 1857, a former slave named Dred Scott sued in federal court, claiming that he was a citizen of Missouri and a free man. Scott maintained that he had become free once his master had taken him onto free soil (the state of Illinois and the territory of Wisconsin). In the case of **Dred Scott v. Sanford** (1857), the Court ruled that residence on free soil did not render a slave a free person, for regardless of their status, black people had "no rights which the white man was bound to respect." With this single decision, Chief Justice Roger B. Taney and the Court threw off the hard-won balance between slave and free states. In effect, the Court declared unconstitutional the Compromise of 1820, which had banned slavery in

Dred Scott

the region north of Missouri's southern boundary, because, the justices held, slave owners could not be deprived of their property without due process. This decision threatened the precarious freedom of the South's quarter million free people of color and extended the reach of slavery into the northern states.

Most white people residing outside the South never read the Court's ruling, but if they had, they probably would have agreed with the justices' claim that, since the earliest days of the Republic, blacks "had been regarded as beings of an inferior order, and altogether unfit to associate with the white race, either in social or political relations." At the same time, northern opinion makers warned that the decision made Northerners complicit in the slave system. Of the "slave power," the *Cincinnati Daily Commercial* thundered, "It has marched over and annihilated the boundaries of the states. We are now one great homogeneous slaveholding community." Even nonabolitionists had good reason to fear the long-term implications of the ruling, for it suggested that the institution of slavery was about to spill out of the confines of the southern states and into the rest of the country. Free white men and women feared competing with slaves in the workplace, whether in the West or East. These concerns increased with the onset of an economic depression in 1857 in the northeastern and midwestern states, as the mining of California gold produced inflation in the East.

THE LINCOLN–DOUGLAS DEBATES

Against this backdrop of economic turmoil and political conflict, the congressional elections of 1858 assumed great significance. In particular, the Senate contest in Illinois pitted the incumbent Democrat Stephen A. Douglas against Republican challenger Abraham Lincoln. In a series of seven public debates, the two men debated the political conflict over slavery as it had been shaped during the tumultuous decade after the Mexican War. Though no friend of the abolitionists, Douglas was quickly falling from favor within the Democratic party; the Supreme Court had nullified his proposal for popular sovereignty in the territories, and he had parted ways from his southern brethren when he denounced Kansas's Lecompton Constitution. Yet in the last debate between Lincoln and Douglas, held in Alton on October 15, 1858, Douglas declared, "I care more for the great principle of self-government, the right of the people to rule, than I do for all the negroes in Christendom."

Lincoln ridiculed the doctrine of popular sovereignty, which he maintained was as thin as the "soup that was made by boiling the shadow of a pigeon that had starved to death." He had no desire to root out slavery in the South, but "I have said, and I repeat, my wish is that the further spread of [slavery] may be arrested, and that it may be placed where the public mind shall rest in the belief that it is in the course of ultimate extinction." According to a reporter present, this last remark provoked great applause. And this was no minor confrontation between two candidates; it is estimated that in six of the seven debates, the two men spoke before crowds exceeding 10,000 people each. Lincoln lost the election (in which blacks were not allowed to vote as a matter of Illinois law), but more significantly, he won the loyalty of Republicans all over the North and put the white South on notice that the days of compromise were over. Meanwhile, with the admission as free states of Minnesota in 1858 and Oregon in 1859, Congress began to reflect a distinct antislavery bias.

HARPERS FERRY AND THE PRESIDENTIAL ELECTION OF 1860

On a Sunday night in October 1859, John Brown and nineteen other men (including at least five African Americans) launched a daring attack on the federal arsenal in Harpers

The Library of Congress

The Library of Congress

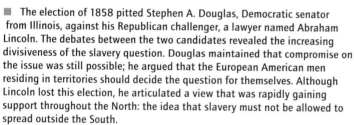

■ The election of 1858 pitted Stephen A. Douglas, Democratic senator from Illinois, against his Republican challenger, a lawyer named Abraham Lincoln. The debates between the two candidates revealed the increasing divisiveness of the slavery question. Douglas maintained that compromise on the issue was still possible; he argued that the European American men residing in territories should decide the question for themselves. Although Lincoln lost this election, he articulated a view that was rapidly gaining support throughout the North: the idea that slavery must not be allowed to spread outside the South.

Ferry, Virginia. They had received guns and moral support from some of the North's leading abolitionists, and their plan was to raid the arsenal and distribute arms to slaves in the surrounding area, thereby inciting a general rebellion that, they hoped, would engulf the rest of the South.

In planning this bold raid, Brown relied on funding from well-to-do Northerners who sympathized with his cause. But he had also turned for advice to a thirty-seven-year-old illiterate African American woman. Throughout northern abolitionist circles, Harriet Tubman became known as the "Moses" of her people for her role as one of the most productive "conductors" on the Underground Railroad. Born a slave in Dorchester County, Virginia, she suffered a blow to her head when she was a child. This injury caused her headaches and seizures throughout her life (she perhaps suffered from a form of epilepsy). Tubman herself escaped to Philadelphia in 1849. Over the next decade, she returned to Dorchester County a dozen times and guided as many as seventy friends and relatives to free territory in the North and Canada.

■ Augustus Washington, son of a former slave, took this picture of John Brown in 1846, thirteen years before the raid on Harpers Ferry, Virginia. A pioneer daguerreotypist, Washington operated a successful studio in Hartford, Connecticut. After the passage of the Fugitive Slave Act in 1850, Washington emigrated with his family to Liberia, an African settlement for American freeborn blacks and former slaves, founded as a republic in 1847.

The Ohio Historical Society (al00523)

Brown wanted to enlist Tubman's aid in recruiting former slaves to his small band of men. He also admired her ability to move about freely within slave territory, undetected by slave "patrollers," and he sought information about the informal slave communication network that Tubman knew and used so well. At a meeting with Tubman in St. Catherines, Canada, Brown called her "General Tubman," later claiming that she "was a better officer than most" men. He believed she had the ability to "command an army as successfully as she had led her small parties of fugitives."

Harriet Tubman would later serve as a spy and scout for the Union army during the Civil War. But John Brown's plan for an uprising of southern slaves came to an abrupt end. Soon after Brown initiated the raid, the Virginia militia cornered the band, but not before the insurrectionists had killed seven people (including a free man of color) and injured ten others. Within two days a U.S. Marine force, commanded by Lieutenant Colonel Robert E. Lee, had captured Brown and his surviving followers.

Two weeks later, Brown stood in a Virginia courtroom and declared that his intention indeed had been "to free the slaves." Brown was convicted of several charges: treason against the United States for his raid on the federal arsenal, murder, and inciting an insurrection. On December 2, 1859, before being led to the gallows, Brown handed a scrap of paper to one of his guards: "I John Brown am now quite *certain* that the crimes of this *guilty land: will* never be purged *away:* but with Blood." Brown failed as the instigator of a slave rebellion, but he succeeded as a prophet.

The raid on Harpers Ferry cast a shadow over the party conventions held in the summer of 1860. By then it was apparent that the national party system had all but disintegrated. Southerners in effect seceded from the Democratic party by walking out of their Charleston convention rather than supporting Stephen Douglas as candidate for president. Within a few weeks, representatives of both the northern and the southern wings of the party reconvened in separate conventions in Baltimore; Northerners gave the nod to Douglas and Southerners chose as their standard-bearer John C. Breckinridge, a proponent of extending slavery into the territories and annexing Cuba. Representing the thoroughly discredited strategy of compromise was the candidate of the Constitutional Union party, John Bell of Tennessee.

In Chicago, the Republicans lined up behind the moderate Abraham Lincoln and agreed on a platform that had something for everybody, including measures to boost economic growth (as promoted by Henry Clay's American System earlier in the century): a proposed protective tariff, a transcontinental railroad, internal improvements, and free homesteads for western farmers. The Republicans renounced the Know-Nothings. Lincoln had taken the lead in admonishing Republicans who sought to curtail the voting rights of European immigrants, such as the Germans and Scandinavians. Lecturing members of his own party in Massachusetts, he declared that, since he had denounced the oppression of black people, "I should be strangely inconsistent if I could favor any project for curtailing the existing rights of white men, even though born in different lands, and speaking different languages from myself."

Yet Republicans held out little hope for other groups demanding the rights and protection that flowed from American citizenship. Spanish-speaking residents of California, Chinese immigrants, free people of color throughout the North, Indian tribes from North Carolina to the northwestern states, the wives and daughters of men all over the country—these groups were not included in the Republicans' grand design for a country based on the principles of free labor.

Abraham Lincoln was elected president in 1860, although he received support from only 40 percent of the men who cast ballots. Lincoln won the electoral college, and he also received a plurality of the popular vote. However, ten southern states had refused to list him on the ballot; in that region of the country, he received almost no votes. Stephen Douglas won almost 30 percent of the popular vote; together, Douglas and Breckinridge outpolled Lincoln (2.2 million votes to 1.85 million). Nevertheless, the new president had swept New England, New York, Pennsylvania, and the upper Midwest. The regional interests of North and South took precedence over national political parties.

TABLE 13.5			
The Election of 1860			
Candidate	**Political Party**	**Popular Vote (%)**	**Electoral Vote**
Abraham Lincoln	Republican	39.8	180
Stephen A. Douglas	Democratic	29.5	12
John C. Breckinridge	Democratic	18.1	72
John Bell	Constitutional Union	12.6	39

Lincoln and his party represented the antislavery sentiments of northern family farmers. The South took heed of this dramatic shift in the national political landscape. By the end of 1860, South Carolina had seceded from the Union, and the nation headed toward war.

Conclusion

During his seventh debate with Stephen Douglas, Abraham Lincoln expressed his frustration with the inability and unwillingness of politicians to confront the issue of slavery squarely. Lincoln understood that slavery was the most significant and divisive topic of the day, yet the political system discouraged people from confronting it openly and honestly. Lincoln outlined the excuses used by people who wanted to avoid public discussion of slavery: "You must not say anything about it in the free States, *because it is not here.* You must not say anything about it in the slave States, *because it is there.* You must not say anything about it in the pulpit, because that is religion and has nothing to do with it. You must not say anything about it in politics *because that will disturb the security of 'my place.'* There is no place to talk about it as being wrong, although you say yourself it *is* a wrong." At the same time, Lincoln was speaking for large numbers of Northerners who believed that the national political system was not representing their interests.

In fact, people all over the country came to feel that the institution of slavery had relevance to their lives. In the slave states, black workers remained yoked to a system that denied their humanity and mocked the integrity of their families. In the nonslave states, free people of color understood that northern racial prejudice was but a variation of the slaveholders' theme of domination. New England farm families looking to move west were convinced that western homesteads would not improve their economic security if these homesteads were surrounded by plantations cultivated by large numbers of enslaved workers. Although they expressed little regard for the rights of blacks, enslaved or free, the northern laboring classes feared that the expansion of slavery into the western territories would limit their own economic opportunities; whether shoemakers, wagon drivers, or seamstresses, they could not possibly compete with bound workers in the labor market. The Republicans drew inspiration from the anxieties of all these groups, and the party's platform beckoned toward a future full of hope, a future that would fulfill the long-thwarted promise of the young country as a "republic of equal rights, where the title of manhood is the title to citizenship."

In contrast, southern whites of various classes agreed on a rallying cry that stressed independence from Yankee interlopers and freedom from federal interference. Yet this unifying

CHRONOLOGY: 1848–1860

1848	Gold is discovered in California.
	Women's Rights Convention, Seneca Falls, New York.
	Zachary Taylor elected president.
1849	"Forty-Niners" migrate to California.
1850	Compromise of 1850; Fugitive Slave Act.
1851	Fort Laramie Treaty.
1852	American (Nativist) party is founded.
	Harriet Beecher Stowe, *Uncle Tom's Cabin*.
1853	Gadsden Purchase.
	Matthew Perry's fleet enters Tokyo Harbor.
1854	Kansas–Nebraska Act.
	Republican party is founded.
1855	William Walker captures Granada, Nicaragua.
	Walt Whitman, *Leaves of Grass*.
1856	Lecompton (Kansas) Constitution.
	James Buchanan elected president.
1857	*Dred Scott* Supreme Court Case.
1858	Lincoln–Douglas debates.
1859	Harpers Ferry raid.
1860	Abraham Lincoln elected president.

rhetoric carried different meanings for different groups of Southerners. The owners of large plantations, desperate to preserve their enslaved labor forces and also hungry for fresh lands and renewed political power, scrambled to maintain their own privileges in the face of growing northern influence in Congress. Nonslaveholding farmers sought to produce all household necessities themselves and remain independent of the worldwide cotton market economy so crucial to the wealth of slave masters and mistresses. Yet almost all southern whites, rich and poor, stood allied, determined to take up arms to protect their households and their distinctive "southern way of life."

On the eve of the Civil War, complex forces roiled an ethnically diverse society. Ultimately the North and South marched into combat, each side united enough to mobilize huge armies. However, wartime strains would expose fault lines in the free labor coalition as well as in the slaveholders' republic.

For Review

1. How did free labor ideology further the notion of individualism?

2. Is it more accurate to describe the United States of the 1850s in terms of a national, unified economy, or in terms of a collection of regional economies? Explain.

3. When he delivered his 1852 speech "The Meaning of the Fourth for the Negro," was Frederick Douglass affirming American ideals and principles, or challenging them? Explain.

4. Discuss difficulties using the term "the American character" during this period.

5. What factors led to the demise of the two-party system that had been dominated by Whigs and Jacksonian Democrats? How would you evaluate the efforts of politicians who sought to "compromise" on the issue of slavery?

6. In what ways were the two antagonistic ideologies of free-labor and pro-slavery both aggressive in their territorial ambitions? Did either side constitute a "conspiracy" against the other?

7. Why was the pre-1854 national party system unable to contain or resolve the conflict over slavery?

8. What was the significance of the founding of the Republican party in the context of emerging sectional conflicts in the 1850s?

Created Equal Online

For more *Created Equal* resources, including suggestions on sites to visit and books to read, go to **MyHistoryLab.com**.

Chapter 14

"To Fight to Gain a Country": The Civil War

■ Sgt. F. L. Baldwin, a Union soldier, poses with an American flag as a backdrop.

Pensacola, Florida, was the site of a dramatic court-martial trial in April 1862, when five men were charged with treasonous acts against the Confederate States of America. "Possessed of information well calculated to aid the enemy," and thus capable of "giving intelligence" to the enemy, the defendants had endangered the security of Confederate troops stationed in the area, according to the chief prosecutor. At the conclusion of the three-day hearing, the court convicted the men and ordered that two of them, alleged ringleaders, be hanged. Later, the presiding officer claimed that "high Military Necessity" had mandated the swift trial and stern verdict: coastal communities were engulfed in a "general stampede" as planters tried to move slaves and livestock out of the way of the encroaching Union army. According to the officer, at stake in this trial was the very fate of the would-be new nation.

By 1862, Confederate leaders knew full well that the war for southern independence would be a hard and long one. Indeed, the Pensacola court-martial provided striking evidence of the political and military challenges faced by southern nationalists, for all of the defendants—George, Robert, Stephen, Peter, and William—were runaway slaves. The specific charges lodged against them read, "That the said slaves are intelligent beings possessing the faculties of Conveying information which would prove useful to the enemy and detrimental to the Confederate States." Clearly, these five men were combatants in the war, as threatening to the well-being of the Confederacy as any Yankee sharpshooter in a blue uniform. The charges also suggest that the Confederates were forced to repudiate elements of their own proslavery beliefs, which held that black people were childlike and servile, incapable of acting on their own, and grateful for the guidance and protection of southern whites.

The Pensacola slaves were assigned a defense lawyer, who attempted to show that they had not actually encountered any Union soldiers and so had had no opportunity to divulge information related to Confederate troop movement. Technically, then, they were not guilty of spying. In court, however, the accused men did admit that, ever since President Abraham Lincoln had taken office in early 1861, three white men in the vicinity (a whiskey seller, an employee of the slaves' master, and a shingle maker) had been encouraging them to seek their freedom behind Union lines.

Prosecuting officers believed that "strong measures" were needed to prevent the nefarious activities of "spys whether white or black." These officials therefore were unprepared for the firestorm of criticism that followed the announcement of the verdict. The owner of the slaves, General Jackson Morton, expressed outrage that two of his men were marked for summary execution. In a formal complaint to Confederate authorities, Morton denounced the hearing as "vulgar and improper." By the time the controversy faded, an impressive array of Confederate military officers (from sentinels to a lieutenant, a captain, a colonel, a major general, and a general) had had to justify their actions in convening the trial. The Confederate adjutant and inspector general took time out from more pressing matters to review the case for the secretary of war. In the words of one Confederate official, "The sacrosanctity of slave property in this war has operated most injuriously to the Confederacy." In the end, Peter and William were hanged, and George, Robert, and Stephen received, according to an army commander, "fifty lashes each, well laid on with a rawhide."

Though at a distinct disadvantage compared to the North in terms of troops, supplies, and industrial might, the white South managed to fight on for four long, bloody years. Early on, southern politicians hailed slaves as a tremendous asset, an immense, easily managed labor force that would grow food and dig trenches. Instead, African American men and women became freedom fighters, a source of subversion in the heart of the Confederacy. In October 1862, in response to the crisis of wartime slave management, the Confederate Congress passed a measure that exempted from military service one white man for every twenty slaves on a plantation. Many slave owners used this law to shield themselves or their sons from combat duty. In turn, the Twenty-Negro Law inflamed resentment among non-slave-owning small farmers, who charged that this rich man's war was actually a poor man's fight. Even within the ranks of the elite, conflicts over military strategy and national mobilization policies hobbled the Confederate effort. Many slaveholding women gradually came to see the sacrifice of their husbands, brothers, and sons as too high a price to pay for southern independence.

As defenders of slavery, the Confederates cast themselves as rebels in an age when the principle of individual rights was gaining ground. The citizens of France, Germany, and Italy were agitating on behalf of modern, democratic nation-states, and systems of serfdom and slavery throughout Europe and the Western Hemisphere were under siege. By early 1865, leading southern politicians and strategists had initiated a public debate over the possibility of offering slaves their liberty in return for military service. In acknowledging that African American men might serve as effective soldiers (as 179,000 of them had demonstrated in the Union army), the Confederates undermined their cause. White Southerners were fighting for their own nation, but African Americans were fighting to gain their own country as well.

The Republican conduct of the war on behalf of the North revealed the party's long-range, guiding principles. Yet several groups besides white southerners objected to a strong federal government, one that would weld the country together geographically as well as economically. The Lincoln administration met bitter resistance from Indian tribes as diverse as the Santee Sioux of Minnesota, the Cheyenne of Colorado, and the Navajo and Apache of the Southwest. In northeastern cities, Irish immigrants battled federal draft agents and attacked black women, men, and children, their supposed competitors in the workplace. The Civil War, then, was less a "brothers' war" between the white farmers of the North and South and more a conflict that pitted diverse groups against each other over the issues of slavery, territorial expansion, federal power, and local control. Yet by the end of the war in April 1865, for the time being at least, the Republican vision of a union forged in blood had prevailed, at the cost of nearly 700,000 lives.

Mobilization for War, 1861–1862

■ *How did the North and South prepare for war, and how did those preparations reflect each side's strategy for fighting—and winning—the war?*

On December 20, 1860, less than eight weeks after Abraham Lincoln was elected president of the United States, South Carolina seceded from the Union, determined, in the words of its own Declaration of Independence, to "resume her separate and equal place among nations." By February 1, 1861, Mississippi, Florida, Alabama, Georgia, Louisiana, and Texas (all states dependent on slave-based staple-crop agriculture) had also withdrawn from the United States of America. Three days later, representatives of the seven states met in Montgomery, Alabama, and formed the **Confederate States of America.** They also adopted a constitution for their new nation. Though modeled after that of the United States, this document invoked the power of "sovereign and independent states" instead of "we, the people."

DOCUMENT

Confederate
Constitution (1861)

Delegates to the Montgomery convention elected as their president Jefferson Davis, a wealthy Mississippi planter with an impressive record of public service. Davis was a graduate of West Point, a veteran of the Mexican-American War, and a former U.S. congressman and senator. He had also held the position of secretary of war in the Franklin Pierce administration. Chosen vice president was a former Whig from Georgia, Alexander H. Stephens. In devising a cabinet, Davis bypassed some well-known radical secessionists—"fire eaters" such as William Lowndes Yancey of Alabama and Robert Barnwell Rhett Jr. of South Carolina—on the assumption that the builders of a new nation would need skills different from those of the destroyers of an old one.

THE SECESSION IMPULSE

In some respects, the Civil War seems difficult to explain, for the two sides shared a great deal. In both the North and the South, most people were English-speaking Protestants with deep roots in the culture of the British Isles. Together they celebrated a revolutionary heritage, paying homage to George Washington and the other Founding Fathers.

Why, then, was the white South, especially the slave South, so fearful of Abraham Lincoln? Although Lincoln enjoyed a broad electoral college victory, he won only 40 percent of the popular vote in the election of 1860. Political support for Lincoln thus appeared slim, and he did not seem likely to use his authority to move against slavery. He had made it clear that, as president, he would possess neither the authority nor the desire to disturb slavery as it existed in the South. However, he summed up his philosophy before the secession crisis

Slave states that seceded before April 15, 1861
Slave states that seceded after April 15, 1861
Slave states that remained in the Union during the Civil War
Free states and territories allied with the Union
① Order of secession

■ **MAP 14.1 The Secession of Southern States, 1860–1861**

The southern states seceded from the Union in stages, beginning with South Carolina in December 1860. Founded on February 4, 1861, the Confederate States of America initially consisted of only that state and six Deep South states. The four upper South states of Virginia, Arkansas, Tennessee, and North Carolina did not leave the Union until mid-April, when Lincoln called for 75,000 troops to put down the civil rebellion. The slave states of Delaware, Maryland, Kentucky, and Missouri remained in the Union, but each of those states was bitterly divided between Unionists and Confederate sympathizers.

this way: "As I would not be a *slave*, so I would not be a *master*. This expresses my idea of democracy. Whatever differs from this . . . is not democracy."

Not surprisingly, then, southern elites felt threatened by Lincoln in particular and the Republicans in general, pointing to the new president's oft-repeated promise to halt the march of slavery into the western territories. Although he was in no position to achieve this goal by executive order, Lincoln did have the power to expand the Republican base in the South by dispensing patronage jobs to a small group of homegrown abolitionists. He could also make appointments to the Supreme Court as openings became available. The Republican party was not a majority party; it was a sectional party of the North and the upper Midwest. But this sectional party had managed to seize control of the executive branch of government, tipping the antebellum balance of power between slave and free states decisively in favor of the North. Slave owners feared that John Brown's 1859 raid on the federal arsenal at Harpers Ferry, Virginia, was just the first in a series of planned attacks on the slave South (see Chapter 13).

Two last-ditch efforts at compromise failed to avert a constitutional crisis. In December 1860, as South Carolina was seceding and other states were preparing to join it, neither northern Republicans nor lower South Democrats showed any interest in a series of proposed constitutional amendments that would have severely curtailed the federal government's ability to restrict the interstate slave trade or the spread of slavery. Called the Crittenden Compromise (after its sponsor, Senator John J. Crittenden, a Whig from Kentucky), this package of proposed amendments was defeated in the Senate on January 16, 1861. A peace conference, organized by the Virginia legislature and assembled in

February, revised the Crittenden Compromise, but key players were missing: the seven Confederate states and five of the northern states. Congress rejected the conference's recommendations at the end of February. By this time many Americans, radicals and moderates, Northerners and Southerners, were in no mood to compromise on the issue of slavery, especially its extension into the West.

In his inaugural address of March 4, Lincoln appealed to the South to refrain from any drastic action, invoking the historic bonds of nationhood, the "mystic chords of memory, stretching from every battle-field, and patriot grave, to every living heart and hearthstone." For the most part Lincoln's plea for unity fell on deaf ears. However, among the Southerners who initially resisted the secessionists' call to arms was the West Point graduate and Mexican-American War veteran Robert E. Lee of Virginia. Later, after Virginia seceded, Lee cast his lot with the Confederacy: "I cannot raise my hand against my birthplace, my home, my children," he declared. By his home, Lee meant the Commonwealth of Virginia, not the collection of disaffected states.

Indeed, in early April, the Confederacy was a rhetorical powerhouse, full of popular firebrands. But it was also a poor excuse for an independent nation, with only one-third of the U.S. population and almost no industrial capacity. Over the next few weeks, as the seven Confederate states attempted to coax the upper South to join their revolution, Lincoln emerged as an unwitting ally in their effort.

Located in Charleston Harbor, Fort Sumter was one of two Union forts in southern territory, and in the spring of 1861 it was badly in need of supplies. On April 12, Lincoln took the high moral ground by sending provisions but not troops to the fort. The Confederates found the move provocative nonetheless and began firing on the fort. After a thirty-three-hour Confederate bombardment, the heavily damaged fort surrendered without a fight. In response, many white Southerners, such as Mary Boykin Chesnut, the wife of a high-ranking Confederate official, cheered and embraced the "pomp and circumstance of glorious war."

Three days after the capture of Fort Sumter, Lincoln (anticipating a conflict no longer than ninety days) called for 75,000 northern volunteers to quell a civil uprising "too powerful to be suppressed by the ordinary course of judicial proceedings." By the end of the month, he had ordered a blockade of southern seaports. Condemning these moves as acts of "northern aggression," the upper South, including Virginia (deprived of its western part, which now formed a new state called West Virginia), Tennessee, Arkansas, and North Carolina all seceded from the Union by May 20. Grateful for the newfound loyalty of Virginia and eager to appropriate the Tredegar Iron Works in Richmond, the Confederacy moved its capital from the down-at-the-heels Montgomery to the elegant Richmond on May 11.

Certain segments of the southern population early demonstrated that they would withhold their support from the Confederacy. Yeoman farmers in the upcountry, Louisiana sugar planters dependent on world markets for their product, and people in the hill country of east Tennessee all voted for Unionist delegates to their respective state conventions that chose secession. Enslaved black workers, of course, could hardly be

Harper's Weekly, May 4, 1861

■ This drawing, titled *The House-Tops in Charleston During the Bombardment of Sumter*, appeared in the May 4, 1861, issue of *Harper's Weekly*, about three weeks after the event. Many Confederate women sent their husbands and sons into battle with great displays of patriotism. However, those parades and parties often masked deep fears. Noted one woman of her husband's departure, "It has always been my lot to be obliged to shut up my griefs in my own breast."

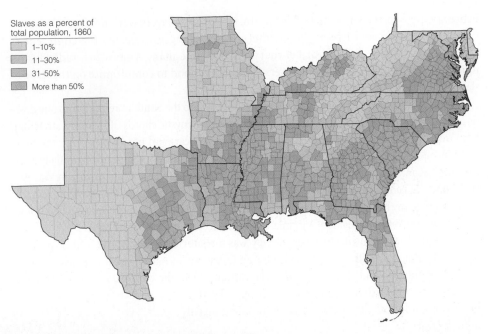

Slaves as a percent of
total population, 1860

■ 1–10%
■ 11–30%
■ 31–50%
■ More than 50%

■ **MAP 14.2   Slavery in the United States, 1860**

In the South, the areas of the greatest concentration of slaves were also the areas of greatest support for the Confederacy. During the war, the Appalachian mountain region and the upper Piedmont—the area between the mountains and the broad coastal plain—were home to people loyal to the Union and to people who became increasingly disaffected with Confederate policies as the war dragged on.

counted on to defend those who kept them in bondage. The Border States of Missouri, Kentucky, Maryland, and Delaware remained within the Union, although among their residents were many outspoken people who openly sympathized with the South.

■ General Robert E. Lee turned down President Abraham Lincoln's offer of the field command of the United States Army and chose instead to lead Confederate soldiers in battle.

PREPARING TO FIGHT

Poised to battle each other, the South and the North faced similar challenges. Both sides had to inspire—or force—large numbers of men to fight. Both had to produce massive amounts of cannon, ammunition, and food. And both had to devise military strategies that would, they hoped, ensure victory. In early 1861, white Southerners were boasting of the stockpiles of cotton that, if needed, would serve as leverage for military support, diplomatic recognition, and financial assistance from the great European powers. Plantations brimming with hogs and corn, it was expected, would sustain both masters and slaves, in contrast to the North, where cotton mills would lie idle and workers would soon descend to poverty and starvation.

From the beginning of the war, Confederates aimed for a strategy calculated to draw on their strengths. They would fight a purely defensive war with small units of troops deployed around the South's 6,000-mile border. Seasoned officers such as Robert E. Lee and Thomas J. Jackson would lead the charge to crush the Union armies that ventured into Confederate territory. Finally, the South could command 3 million black people (a third of its total population of 9 million), all of whom, it was assumed, would do the bidding of planters and the military. Whereas the North would have to conquer the South to preserve the Union, the Confederacy would only have to survive to win its independence.

A Civil War Encampment

The Library of Congress

Envisioning History

The Civil War was the first war in U.S. history after the advent of photography. Photographers captured not only the war's horrific cost in human lives, but also scenes of the immense military mobilization on both sides. This photo of Camp Northumberland, headquarters of the 96th Philadelphia Infantry, near Washington, D.C., shows Union soldiers in drill formation. Constructing and maintaining camps like this one required considerable time and energy. Soldiers were forced to wield shovels and axes as well as shoulder rifles. Wherever fighting occurred, the landscape was transformed, not only by the fierce battles, but also by the need on the part of Union and Confederate forces to feed and shelter vast armies and to transport them over large expanses of land.

QUESTIONS

1. How does this photograph suggest the different kinds of work needed to establish a large military encampment?

2. Many white men in the Civil War era considered military service a matter of honor. How might these men have reacted to military orders that demanded they perform "fatigue work"—manual labor in support of military operations?

3. What does the drill formation of these troops tell us about battlefield tactics during the Civil War?

4. Why were camps such as this one dangerous breeding grounds for disease?

At first, the North was inclined to think little past the numbers: in 1860, it possessed 90 percent of the manufacturing capacity and three-quarters of the 30,000 railroad miles in the United States. Its population, 22 million, dwarfed that of the South. The North retained control of the (admittedly less than formidable) U.S. Navy and all other resources of the federal government, including a bureaucratic infrastructure to facilitate troop deployment and communication. Its diversified economy yielded grain as well as textiles; it could mobilize a large army and feed it as well.

Early on, the North had a plan, but one that could hardly be dignified by the term *strategy*. It would defend its own territory from southern attack and target Confederate

■ **FIGURE 14.1**
Occupational Categories of Union and Confederate Soldiers

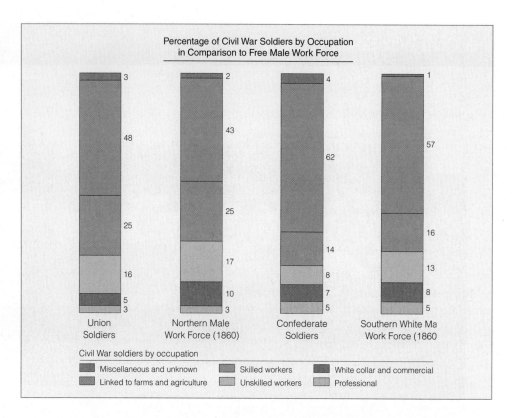

Percentage of Civil War Soldiers by Occupation
in Comparison to Free Male Work Force

Civil War soldiers by occupation

■ Miscellaneous and unknown   ■ Skilled workers   ■ White collar and commercial
■ Linked to farms and agriculture   ■ Unskilled workers   ■ Professional

leaders, under the assumption that latent Union sentiment in the South would arise to smash the rebellion before it went too far. Union gunboats positioned along the East Coast and up and down the Mississippi River would seal off the Confederacy from foreign supply lines. The North would also launch a political offensive calculated to undermine Confederate sympathizers by bolstering Unionist sentiment everywhere. Lincoln, for example, continued to appeal to slaveholders loyal to the Union, whether those slaveholders lived in the Border States or deep in the heart of the Confederacy.

Northerners also invoked a Revolutionary heritage to justify their cause. However, they downplayed the issue of unjust taxation and instead stressed the glories of the Union—in Lincoln's words, "the last, best hope of mankind" in an age of kings and emperors.

BARRIERS TO SOUTHERN MOBILIZATION

On July 21, 1861, at Manassas Junction (Bull Run), about thirty miles southwest of Washington, D.C., Union and Confederate forces encountered each other on the field of battle for the first time. This was the fight that earned Thomas "Stonewall" Jackson his nickname and bolstered his reputation, for Union troops skirmished briefly with the enemy and then turned and fled back to the capital, disgraced. In the coming weeks, Northerners gave up the idea that the effort to suppress the rebels would be an easy one, and Lincoln began to reorganize the country's officer corps and fortify its armies.

To win this initial victory, the Confederates had relied on the massing of several huge forces: those of Generals Joseph Johnston and P. G. T. Beauregard, as well as Stonewall Jackson. Consequently, southern military strategists decided they must continue to defend southern territory while going on the offensive against the Yankees (the "offensive-defensive" strategy was used for the duration of the conflict). In other matters, however, the South learned life-and-death lessons more slowly. Only gradually did the central paradox of the Confederate nation become abundantly clear: that a country founded on an agrarian ideal of "states' rights" needed to industrialize its economy and centralize its government operations to defeat the Union.

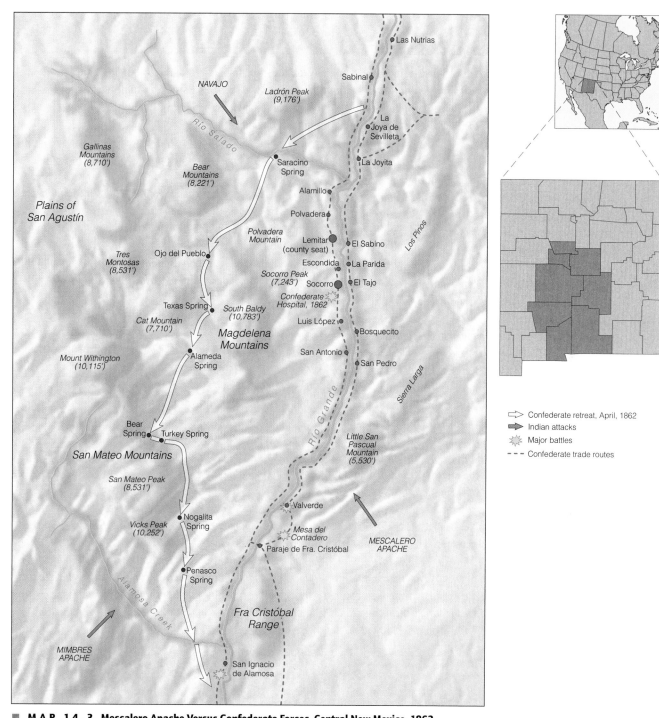

■ MAP 14.3 Mescalero Apache Versus Confederate Forces, Central New Mexico, 1862

The Confederates hoped to conquer the entire Southwest for slavery. In the summer of 1861, a force led by Colonel John R. Baylor invaded the Mesilla Valley in New Mexico Territory. The Southerners scored a series of notable successes until defeated at La Glorieta Pass, a battle called the Gettysburg of the West, in March 1862. This map shows how the Confederates, harried by the Apache and Navajo, retreated from New Mexico.

The first weeks of the war revealed that the South would pursue its antebellum aims of conquering western territory for slavery. An early victory of Texas forces over Union troops in New Mexico led to the formation of what slaveholders in that region called the Confederate Territory of Arizona. Over the next year, the Confederates launched successful assaults on the cities of Albuquerque and Santa Fe, in present-day New Mexico. However, southern troops

A Virginia Slaveholder Objects to the Impressment of Slaves

Interpreting History

During the Civil War, some southern slave owners bitterly resisted Confederate slave impressment policies. On December 4, 1861, John B. Spiece, an Albemarle County, Virginia, slaveholder and lawyer, wrote to the Confederate attorney general and protested government policy.

Dr Sir, Although a stranger to you, yet in consequence of the excitement and distress in this section of the country, in reference to a certain matter; I am constrained to address you, not merely on my own account; but on behalf of a large number of most respectable citizens. . . .

A practice has prevailed for some considerable time in *this* section of the country of impressing into service of the confederate army, the horses wagons and *slaves* belonging to the people.

The "Press masters" will go to their houses, and drag off their property to Just Such an extent as they choose; until it has not only created great excitement and distress; but bids fair to produce wide spread ruin. And I am told that these "Press masters" are paid by the Government the enormous price of *two dollars and fifty cents for each team which they impress*;—hence their anxiety and untiring exertions to increase the number;—thus making thirty or forty dollars pr day—

While I do not controvert the right of the Government to impress into its service *wagons and teams*; yet I do controvert the right to impress *Slaves*—It does seem to me that no one can be impress'd into military service of any kind, unless he is subject to military duty: because this whole business is relating to the Army, and is purely a military matter.—

The people in this section of the country are much attached to their slaves, and treat them in a humane manner—consequently they are exceedingly pained at having them dragged off at this inclement season of the year, and exposed to the severe weather in the mountains of north western Virginia. . . . Some have already died, and others have returned home afflicted with Typhoid fever, which has spread through the family to a most fatal and alarming extent.—

I am a practicing lawyer myself, but these "Press masters" will hear nothing from any one residing amongst the people.—

Therefore Sir, in consequence of the distress produced by the causes before mentioned, I am constrained to write to you; requesting you if you please, to give your opinion upon the questions involved.

To wit—If a man's wagon and team should be impress'd into Service, can his slave be impress'd to drive the said team—

Secondly—If a man has neither wagon or team can his slave be impress'd to drive some other team (*some* of the "Press masters" yield this *last* point, whilst others do not, and contend that they can impress just as many slaves as they choose from any plantation, taking all the negro men if they think proper.)—

Some few of the people have not been able to sow their grain this fall:—and there is deep dissatisfaction amongst the people—therefore I deem it proper and expedient that the authorities should know it—

Spiece goes on to cite the laws of the Commonwealth of Virginia, as amended in 1860, "by which it seems there is no power to impress Slaves." In the absence of Confederate congressional legislation to that effect, he argues, government authorities lack the legal right to take slaves from their owners. Spiece concludes his letter by suggesting that in taking slaves far from their homes, Confederate authorities were endangering the security of the would-be new nation.

amounted to little more than a band of plunderers; in Rio Abajo, for example, farmers and ranchers switched their allegiance to the Union after the rebels raided their homesteads.

Deprived of money raised from customs duties (the U.S. Navy blockade brought a halt to established patterns of overseas trade), the Confederacy relied on floating bonds ($400 million worth), raising taxes, and levying a 10 percent tax on farm produce. The Confederate treasury printed money at a furious rate ($1 billion over the course of the conflict), but its value declined precipitously; near the end of the war, one Confederate dollar was worth only 1.6 cents.

Raising a volunteer army and impressing slave labor (forcing slaves to labor for the military) met with stiff resistance from various quarters of southern society. For yeoman farm families, long defensive of the independence of their own households, Confederate mobilization efforts came as a rude shock. Antebellum Southerners believed that white fathers should protect and retain control over their dependents at all times. Planters expressed

■ These slaves are unloading ships at City Point, Virginia. Field hands impressed to work in Confederate factories, on wharves, and in mines experienced a new way of life off the plantation and out of the sight of their owners.

There is also a serious evil in impressing slaves for the service in North western Virginia:—whilst there they get to talking with *Union men* in disguise, and by that means learn the original cause of the difficulty between North & South: then return home and inform other negroes:—not long since one of my neighbors negro men went to his master, and desired to let him go again to the north western army—adding "I wish you to let me go further than I went before["]—I have the honor to be most respectfully your Obt Servt.

It is unknown whether Confederate officials responded to Spiece's letter.

QUESTIONS

1. *How does John Spiece demonstrate his talents as a lawyer in this letter?*

2. *In what ways does Spiece's reaction to slave impressment suggest changes in, or challenges to, southern planters' ideology of paternalism?*

Source: Ira Berlin, Barbara J. Fields, Thavolia Glymph, Joseph P. Reidy, and Leslie S. Rowland, eds., *Freedom: A Documentary History of Emancipation, 1861–1867*, Series 1, Vol. 1, *The Destruction of Slavery* (New York: Cambridge University Press, 1985), 782–783.

a well-founded fear that slaves impressed for a wide range of tasks, whether saltmaking or chopping trees or tending brick kilns, were difficult to control now that plantation discipline had been loosened. When the Confederate call for volunteers failed to produce the number of soldiers (and menial laborers) needed to fight the Union, the Richmond government in March 1862 implemented a military conscription law: all men between ages 18 and 35—later raised to 45—were called up for three years of service. The law exempted certain kinds of workers, such as railroad employees, schoolteachers, miners, and druggists, and allowed the buying of substitutes by draftees who could afford the $300 price for them. This last type of exemption allowed wealthy men to pay someone to fight in their place.

These provisions provoked anger not only among ordinary citizens but also among principled states' rights advocates such as governors Joseph Brown of Georgia and Zebulon Vance of North Carolina. Brown exempted large numbers of men from the draft, claiming that the Confederacy posed a greater threat to states' rights than did the Union. On January 1, 1862, 209,852 southern men were present for duty. Yet the northern force was more than twice as large, with 527,204.

Also complicating the Davis administration's attempts to mobilize for war was the refusal of the Confederates to form a political party system, on the assumption that unity among whites was the highest priority. However, the lack of parties meant that real differences over military and diplomatic strategy were reduced to infighting between shifting groups of elected officials and military men. Davis and members of his cabinet were quick to label dissent of any kind as treasonous, squelching legitimate debate on significant issues. In wartime Richmond, pro- and anti-Davis factions were made and unmade on the basis of rumor, innuendo, and the friendships and feuds among the wives of officers and politicians. In this respect, the white South clung to an outmoded identity as a collection of individuals bound to yield to no person, party, or government.

■ Stand Watie

INDIANS IN THE SERVICE OF THE CONFEDERACY

Just as the Confederates failed in their attempt to use fully the labor of enslaved workers, so they failed to reap much gain from the vaunted military prowess of Indians, especially those in Indian Territory (present-day Oklahoma). In 1861, southern military officials appealed to the Five Tribes for support, promising them arms and protection from Union forces in return. Only gradually and reluctantly did Cherokee leader John Ross commit his men to the Confederacy: "We are in the situation of a man standing alone upon a low naked spot of ground, with the water rising all around him."

More devoted to the Confederate cause was Stand Watie, the brother of one of the Cherokee leaders who signed the original removal treaty. Backed by many Cherokee slaveholders, Stand Watie mobilized young Indian men from several nations as a fighting force on behalf of the Confederacy. Among those responding to the call to arms were Choctaw and Chickasaw men, who formed Company E of the 21st Mississippi Regiment, "the Indian Brigade."

Although Indian Territory was considered of great strategic value to the Confederacy, southern military officials at times expressed frustration with the traditional battle tactics of Indian warriors, who were unused to military encounters that pitted long, straight rows of men on foot against each other. At the Battle of Elkhorn Tavern (Pea Ridge) in March 1862, Indian troops abandoned the battlefield in the face of cannon fire, leading their commander, Albert Pike, to demand that in the future they be "allowed to fight in their own fashion" rather than "face artillery and steady infantry on open ground." Yet most Confederate generals measured Indians by European American standards of what made a "proper" soldier on the battlefield. Many were labeled "undisciplined" and "not very reliable."

By the summer of 1862, the Confederacy had lost its advantage in Indian Territory. The Cherokee and Creek were divided in their loyalties, with some joining Union forces. By this time, the Comanche and Kiowa, resentful of the Confederacy's broken promises (guns and money diverted from them), had joined Union troops and were threatening to invade Texas.

THE ETHNIC CONFEDERACY

Throughout the Confederacy, whites expressed outrage at what they perceived was the North's unfair advantage. These Southerners claimed that their own army consisted overwhelmingly of native-born soldiers—in the words of Mary Boykin Chesnut, "those nearest and dearest [to us]—rank and file, common soldiers." In contrast, they claimed, Union ranks were composed of "crowds of Irish, Dutch, Scotch," and especially Germans. This view was misleading on both counts. Of the 2 million white soldiers and sailors who fought for the North, about 25 percent were immigrants. In contrast, the northern immigrant population amounted to almost a third of all white men of military age. Thus, the foreign-born were actually somewhat underrepresented in the northern army.

Moreover, the Confederacy was more of a multicultural endeavor than many white Southerners realized. Like Native Americans, immigrants and ethnic minorities in the South were divided in their loyalties. A Jewish lawyer and slaveholder, Judah P. Benjamin, served as a cabinet member and trusted adviser to Jefferson Davis. Prominent southern military officers included some from Ireland, Prussia, and France.

Immigrant workmen from southern cities—primarily Germans and Irish—filled the ranks of the Confederate army. Troops drawn from New Orleans included immigrants from Greece, Spain, Cuba, Scandinavia, Scotland, Belgium, and Poland. In that city, a German society founded to aid German immigrants began a monthly subscription series to aid the needy families of southern soldiers; the group sponsored theater performances, fairs, and a spring *Volkfest* (festival) to raise money. Some Louisiana ethnic groups formed their own home guards or volunteer corps. From the northeastern part of the state came the Madison Tips, composed of men who had hailed from County Tipperary, Ireland, and now labored on the Mississippi River levees. In Shreveport, Louisiana, Irish railroad workers formed the Landrum Guards and volunteered for service in the Confederate army.

On the other hand, ethnic loyalties did not rule out disloyalty and dissent within the Confederacy. In Texas, for example, some German immigrants supported abolition. Many of these were political refugees who had fled their native country after the failed revolutions of 1848. Throughout the war, Texas officials remained suspicious of Germans as a group; in 1863, reports that 800 German American men in Colorado, Fayette, and Austin counties were arming themselves to resist the draft law resulted in the jailing of their leaders. Nevertheless, the highest ranks of the Confederate military included immigrants from Germany or men of German heritage.

The *Tejano* community was also split in its loyalties. Some Hispanic men joined the Confederate army not out of conviction but out of fear that they would be sent out of the country if they refused. Others claimed that they were Mexican citizens and so not required to fight for the South. Yet a total of 2,500 Hispanic men joined the Confederate army. Colonel Santos Benavides, who commanded the 33rd Texas Cavalry, became the highest ranking *Tejano* to serve in the rebel army; on the battlefield he was joined by his brothers Refugio and Cristobal, both captains in the regiment.

Among those who fought for the South was the Cuban-born Loreta Janeta Velásquez. Velásquez's husband enlisted in the Confederate cause and was killed early in the war. The young widow then disguised herself as a man and, under the name of Lieutenant Harry T. Buford, fought under General Leonidas Polk during his Kentucky campaign in the early fall of 1861. She was wounded twice and left military service only to begin work as a Confederate spy. Like other women spies, Velásquez used gender stereotypes and expectations to her advantage. (Other women secret agents included Belle Boyd for the Confederates and Elizabeth Van Lew for the Union.) Women spies concealed messages under their skirts and inside elaborate hairdos. They moved back and forth between the North and South because officials on both sides of the conflict were reluctant to challenge a well-dressed woman. In the service of the southern cause, Velásquez carried military documents in her lady's satchel (a large purse) across enemy lines. Posing as a humanitarian, she visited Confederate prisoners in the North and interviewed them about military matters.

Velásquez traveled extensively and rarely missed an opportunity to engage Union officers in conversation. Of one young Union captain she encountered in Baltimore, she remarked: "I courted his friendship." Spinning a (tall) tale about her misfortunes in life, Velásquez gained the confidence of unsuspecting officers. These men were inevitably affected by her "pitiful narrative," Velásquez recalled later; their concern gave her an opportunity to pursue innocent-sounding questions about local troop movements and numbers.

■ This picture shows three Confederate surgeons, along with their African American servant, at a hospital in Lynchburg, Virginia. Confederate officials used enslaved men and women in a variety of capacities—as menial laborers, cooks, and laundresses in army camps, aides in hospitals, railroad hands, and industrial laborers.

■ A Hispanic woman, Janeta Velásquez (right) disguised herself as a soldier named Lt. Harry T. Buford (left) to serve the Confederacy. Later she operated as a spy for the South.

Determined to fight a defensive war, Confederates believed that they need not equal the North in terms of men or resources in order to prevail; they must only show fierce determination in holding their own territory against the onslaught of the invaders. But as the war dragged on, events would suggest that the South had badly miscalculated.

The Course of War, 1862–1864

■ *What obstacles did the South face in defending its territory against northern invaders?*

When the time came to marshal resources in the service of the national state, Northerners were at a distinct advantage over the states' rights men who dominated the Confederacy. Not only did the Union have more resources, but the Republicans' support for the centralization and consolidation of power also facilitated the war-mobilization process. In Congress, the Republicans took advantage of their new majority status and expanded federal programs in the realm of the economy, education, and land use. However, like Davis, Lincoln encountered vehement opposition to his wartime policies from some quarters. Meanwhile, on the battlefield, Union losses were mounting. The United States confronted an uncertain fate.

THE REPUBLICANS' WAR

Worried about disloyalty in the vicinity of the nation's capital, on April 27, 1861, Lincoln gave General Winfield Scott the power to suspend the writ of habeas corpus (a legal doctrine designed to protect the rights of people arrested) in Baltimore. By the end of the year, this policy, which allowed the incarceration of people not yet charged with a crime, was being applied in almost all of the loyal United States. Chief among those targeted were people suspected of interfering with war mobilization of men and supplies. Democrats stepped up their opposition to the president, denouncing him as a tyrant and a dictator. Meanwhile, from the other side of the political spectrum, abolitionists expressed their frustration with the administration's conciliatory policy toward the South in general and toward Unionist

TABLE 14.1				
Ohio Men Drafted for Military Service Who Reported for Duty or Hired Substitutes				
Occupation	Failed to Report	Exempted for Cause	Commuted or Hired Substitute	Held to Service
Unskilled Laborer	25%	45%	24%	6%
Skilled Laborer	25%	44%	22%	9%
Farmer and Farm Laborer	16%	34%	31%	19%
Merchant, Manufacturer, Banker, Broker	23%	46%	29%	2%
Clerk	26%	48%	24%	2%
Professional	16%	49%	29%	6%

slaveholders in particular. Lincoln insisted that his objective was "to save the Union, and . . . neither to save or destroy slavery."

Wartime manufacturing and commerce proved a boon to entrepreneurs. In Cleveland, a young commission-house operator named John D. Rockefeller was earning enough money to hire a substitute to serve in the army for him. In the middle of the war, he shifted his business from selling grain, fish, water, lime, plaster, and salt to refining the crude oil (used in kerosene lamps) recently discovered in western Pennsylvania. War profiteers seized opportunities in both the North and the South. In 1862, the *Southern Cultivator*, a magazine published in Augusta, Georgia, ran an article titled "Enemies at Home," denouncing the "vile crew of speculators" who were selling everything from corn to cloth at exorbitant prices.

The Republicans' willingness to centralize wartime operations led in 1861 to the formation of the U.S. Sanitary Commission. This agency recruited physicians, trained nurses, raised money, solicited donations, and conducted inspections of Union camps on the front. During the war, as many as 20,000 white and black women served as nurses, cooks, and laundresses in Union military hospitals. Black women worked primarily in the latter two categories. A long-time advocate of reform on behalf of the mentally ill during the antebellum period, Dorothea Dix served as superintendent of nurses.

The Republicans believed that the federal government should actively promote economic growth and educational opportunity, and they enacted measures previously thwarted by Democratic presidents and Congresses. In July 1862, the **Homestead Act** granted 160 acres of western land to each settler who lived on and made improvements to the land for five years. Congress also passed the **Morrill Act,** which created a system of land-grant colleges. (Many of these colleges eventually became major public universities, including Colorado State University, Kansas State University, and Utah State University.) Also approved in 1862, the **Pacific Railroad Act** appropriated to the Union Pacific and the Central Pacific Railroads a 400-foot right-of-way along the Platte River route of the Oregon Trail and lent them, depending on the terrain, $16,000 to $48,000 per mile.

During the first year and a half of war, Union military strategy reflected a prewar Republican indifference to the rights and welfare of both northern and southern blacks. In September 1861, Lincoln revoked a directive released by General John Frémont that would have authorized the seizure of property and the emancipation of slaves owned by Confederates in the state of Missouri. The president feared that such a policy would alienate slaveholders who were considering switching their allegiance to the Union. Later that fall, the capture of Port Royal, South Carolina, allowed Union soldiers to treat blacks as "contraband of war," denying slaveholders their human property but failing to recognize blacks as free people with rights.

As Union forces pushed deeper into Confederate territory, U.S. officers devised their own methods for dealing with the institution of slavery. By early 1862, the North had set

The Library of Congress

■ By 1862, Northerners were hailing General Ulysses S. Grant for his quick decisions and bold action, declaring that his initials stood for "Unconditional Surrender"—the demand he made upon defeated Confederate armies.

its sights on the Mississippi River valley, hoping to bisect the Confederacy and cut off supplies and men bound from Texas, Arkansas, and Louisiana to the eastern seaboard. In February, General Ulysses S. Grant captured Fort Henry and Fort Donelson on the Tennessee and Cumberland rivers, the Union's first major victory of the war; in April, New Orleans fell to Admiral David Farragut. In New Orleans, General Benjamin Butler attempted to retain the loyalty of Unionist slaveholders by returning runaway slaves to them. This policy was not always greeted with enthusiasm within Union ranks. A Massachusetts soldier, restless under the command of an officer sympathetic to "slave catching brutes," vowed, "I never will be instrumental in returning a slave to his master in any way shape or manner."

Butler also inflamed local Confederates with his "Woman Order" of May 15, 1862, which held that any woman caught insulting a Union soldier should be considered a prostitute and treated as such. As far away as the British House of Commons, members of Parliament condemned the "infamous" conduct of Butler toward what they considered respectable American ladies.

THE RAVAGES OF WAR

In the summer of 1862, the South suffered a hemorrhaging of its slave population, as the movement of Union troops up and down the eastern seaboard opened the floodgates to runaways. In August a group of Liberty County, Georgia, planters claimed that 20,000 slaves (worth $12 to $15 million) had absconded from coastal plantations, many of them holding "the position of Traitors, since they go over to the enemy & afford him aid and comfort" by providing information and erecting fortifications.

■ During the war, many slaves remained on the plantation, biding their time and waiting for an opportunity to escape. The arrival of the U.S. Army into an area prompted many to flee the slave quarters and seek refuge behind Union lines. These refugees are on their way to New Bern, North Carolina, in 1863.

Yet over the course of the summer, the Confederacy persevered on the battlefield, aided by the failure of Union armies to press their advantage. In June, General George McClellan was turned back on the outskirts of Richmond, convincing Lincoln not only of the incompetence of his chief general but also of the value of a less forgiving approach toward the South. In July, intending to pursue a more aggressive strategy against the massive southern military force, Lincoln brought back the boastful General John Pope from the western campaign ("where we have always seen the backs of our enemies") to command the 50,000 troops of the Army of the Potomac.

The second battle of Manassas in late August pitted Pope and the ridiculed "Tardy" George McClellan against Lee and Jackson. (Among Jackson's foot soldiers in that battle were New Orleans's Pelican Company F, a veritable "congress of nations" including native speakers of German, French, and Spanish.) Within five days, the Union had suffered 16,000 casualties out of a force of 65,000, whereas 10,000 in Lee's smaller force of 55,000 had been killed or wounded.

The Civil War Part I: 1861–1862

The summer of 1862 highlighted the difficulties faced by both sides in fighting a war during warm weather (when roads were passable) in the southern swamps and lowlands. More deadly than bullets and cannon to troops were diseases, especially diarrhea, dysentery, typhoid, pneumonia, and malaria. These killers affected major campaigns, including the failed Union attempt to capture Vicksburg in July. Languishing in the swamps near Richmond, one Union soldier wrote in his diary, "The Army is full of sick men."

In other parts of the country, the Union's war against the Confederates spilled over into savage campaigns against Indian tribes. An uprising among the Santee Sioux in Minnesota killed 500 whites before the state militia quashed the rebellion at Wood Lake in the fall of 1862. General James H. Carleton routed the Texas Confederates, who had been occupying New Mexico and Arizona, and then provided what he called a "wholesome lesson" to the Mescalero Apache and Navajo who had been menacing Hispanic villages in the area. Sending his troops out to locate the Mescalero, Carleton ordered, "The men are to be slain whenever and wherever they can be found. Their women and children are to be taken prisoner." Union soldiers captured Apache leader Mangas Colorado and later murdered him (although he had surrendered under a white flag). The Mescalero were forced to accept reservation status at Bosque Redondo in the Pecos River valley. Meanwhile, Colonel Kit Carson conducted a campaign of terrorism against the Navajo, burning *hogans* and seizing crops and livestock, claiming that "wild Indians could be tamed." Many of the survivors undertook the "Long Walk" to Bosque Redondo, a forced march reminiscent of the Cherokee Trail of Tears a generation before.

The bloodiest day of the war occurred on September 17, 1862, on the banks of Antietam Creek in northern Virginia. The Battle of Antietam claimed 20,000 lives and resulted in a Union victory, although it was a dubious victory indeed. Part of the battle took place in a thirty-acre cornfield, where Confederates had hidden themselves. Observing the tips of Southerners' bayonets glistening in the sunlight, General Joseph Hooker and his men mowed them down with firepower "as the grass falls before the scythe," in the words of a newspaper reporter present at the battle. The corpses mingled among the cornstalks presented a grisly sight. Nevertheless, Hooker recalled of the encounter, "The conduct of my troops was sublime, and the occasion almost lifted me to the skies, and its memories will ever remain near me."

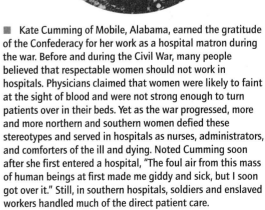

■ Kate Cumming of Mobile, Alabama, earned the gratitude of the Confederacy for her work as a hospital matron during the war. Before and during the Civil War, many people believed that respectable women should not work in hospitals. Physicians claimed that women were likely to faint at the sight of blood and were not strong enough to turn patients over in their beds. Yet as the war progressed, more and more northern and southern women defied these stereotypes and served in hospitals as nurses, administrators, and comforters of the ill and dying. Noted Cumming soon after she first entered a hospital, "The foul air from this mass of human beings at first made me giddy and sick, but I soon got over it." Still, in southern hospitals, soldiers and enslaved workers handled much of the direct patient care.

Minnesota Historical Society (Neg. #36339)

■ During August 1862, a bitter conflict between local Sioux Indians and rural homesteaders engulfed southern Minnesota. After U.S. troops suppressed the uprising, Lincoln pardoned many of the warriors, but thirty-eight were hanged at Mankato, Minnesota, on December 26, 1982. As shown here, a crowd gathered to watch the largest government execution in American history, and wagons waited to cart away the corpses. U.S. officials forced the surviving Sioux into reservations in present-day South Dakota.

DOCUMENT

Barton, Memoirs about Medical Life at the Battlefield (1865)

To journalists and soldiers alike, battles could offer stirring sights of long rows of uniformed men arrayed against each other, their arms at the ready, regimental flags unfurled in the wind. Yet for the women of Shepardstown, Maryland, left to clean up after the Antietam slaughter, there was no talk of the glory of war, only a frantic, round-the-clock effort to feed the Confederates and bind their wounds. Surveying the battlefield wreckage, one observer, Maria Blunt, lamented the carnage: the dead, but also men "without arms, with one leg, with bandaged sides and backs; men in ambulances, wagons, carts, wheelbarrows, men carried on stretchers or supported on the shoulder of some self-denying comrade." All over the South, white women established temporary hospitals in barns, private homes, and churches and mourned each human sacrifice to the cause: "A mother—a wife—a sister had loved him."

The extraordinarily high casualty rate in the war stemmed from several factors. Confederates and Federals alike fought with new kinds of weapons (rifles and sharpshooters accurate at up to 1,000 yards) while troops massed in old-style, close formation. Soft minié balls punctured and lodged in limbs, leading to high rates of amputation that in turn fostered deadly infections. One Alabama soldier observed in 1862: "I believe the Doctors kills more than they cour [cure]." In fact, twice as many Civil War soldiers died of disease and infection as were killed in combat.

The Library of Congress

■ This painting shows Union prisoners of war playing baseball at Salisbury, North Carolina. Baseball originated in northern working-class communities before the war. It was possible to put in a full day of work and then have time to play a game in the early evening. Southern elite white men scorned baseball, claiming that men of honor did not run—for any reason.

■ The bodies of soldiers lay where they fell on September 17, 1862, the single day that claimed the largest number of lives in the Civil War. Like many other battles of the war, Antietam was shaped by the physical features of the battlefield itself, with soldiers on both sides seeking cover in small groves of trees and behind rocks, road ruts, and fences made of stone and wood.

The Library of Congress

THE EMANCIPATION PROCLAMATION

Appalled by the loss of life but heartened by the immediate outcome of Antietam, Lincoln took a bold step. In September he announced that on January 1, 1863, he would proclaim all slaves in Confederate-controlled territory free. Lincoln used the Emancipation Proclamation not only to bolster northern morale by infusing the conflict with moral purpose but also to further the Union's interests on the battleground by encouraging southern blacks to join the U.S. Army. The measure left slavery intact in the loyal Border States and in all territory conquered by the Union. Consequently, nearly 1 million black people were excluded from its provisions. Skeptical of the ability of blacks and whites to live together, Lincoln remained committed to the colonization of freed blacks outside the United States (in Central America or the West Indies).

In the congressional elections of 1862, the Democrats had picked up strength in New York, Pennsylvania, and Ohio and carried Illinois. The lower Midwest in general harbored large numbers of Democrats who opposed the war (especially now that it was an "abolition war") and called for peace with the South; these so-called Copperheads disrupted Union enlistments and encouraged military desertions. The Emancipation Proclamation electrified abolitionists, but the war effort and the growing casualties were taking their toll among the laboring classes. Especially aggrieved were the working people who paid higher taxes (relative to those paid by the wealthy) to keep the war machine running, and the dockworkers and others who lost their livelihoods when trade with foreign countries ceased. Their resentment boiled over in the summer of 1863.

PERSISTENT OBSTACLES TO THE CONFEDERACY'S GRAND STRATEGY

From the beginning of the war, the North's effort to blockade 3,500 miles of southern coastline met with fierce resistance on the high seas. The South made up in resourcefulness what it lacked in a navy, relying for supplies on swift steamers manned by privateers. (British arms smuggled onto remote southern beaches could bring up to 700 percent in profits.) Seemingly invincible Confederate ships such as the ironclad *Merrimack* and the well-fortified British-built warships *Alabama* and *Florida* prowled the southeastern seaboard, sinking Union vessels and protecting the blockade runners. Nevertheless, by December 1861, Union forces had established beachheads in Confederate territory up and down the East Coast.

In November 1861, Union naval forces intercepted a British packet ship, the *Trent*, and seized two Confederate diplomats, James Mason and John Slidell, who were en route to London and Paris, where they planned to plead the South's case in a bid to gain diplomatic recognition. To avoid a rift with England, Lincoln and Secretary of State William H. Seward released the two men. In the process, Mason and Slidell lost whatever influence they might have had with European governments, and Lincoln enjoyed the praise of the British public for his moderation in handling the *Trent* affair.

> By December 1861, Union forces had established beachheads in Confederate territory up and down the East Coast.

More generally, Confederate hopes for diplomatic recognition foundered on the shoals of European politics and economics, in England and in the Western Hemisphere. English textile mills drew on their own immense prewar stockpiles of raw cotton and sought out new sources of the fiber in Egypt and elsewhere. Also, English workers flexed their political muscle in a successful effort to forestall recognition of the slaveholders' nation. Early in the war, the Confederates recognized the strategic importance of Mexico, both as a trade route for supplies and as a means of access to ports. In approaching Mexican President Benito Juárez for aid in late 1861, however, Confederate envoy John T. Pickett discovered that, although Mexicans still smarted from their defeat on their own land thirteen years before, the Juárez administration remained an ally of the United States.

By the summer of 1862, Britain and France were inclined to mediate peace in favor of Confederate independence, for the two powers assumed that the South's impressive victories in Virginia and Tennessee signaled a quick end to the war. Nevertheless, the Confederacy's autumn setbacks of Antietam and Perryville (in Kentucky), combined with the ennobling rhetoric of the proposed Emancipation Proclamation, proved that the Union was still very much alive. The diplomatic recognition the white South so desperately craved remained elusive.

The Other War: African American Struggles for Liberation

■ *In what ways did black people, northern and southern, enslaved and free, shape the course of the fighting?*

From the onset of military hostilities, African Americans, regardless of whether they lived in the North or the South, perceived the Civil War as a fight for freedom. Although they allied themselves with Union forces, they also recognized the limitations of Union policy in ending slavery. Therefore, blacks throughout the northern and southern states were forced to take action to free themselves as individuals, families, and communities. Twenty-year-old Charlie Reason recalled his daring escape from a Maryland slave master and his decision to join the famous 54th Massachusetts Infantry composed of black soldiers: "I came to fight *not* for my country, I never had any, but to gain one." Soon after the 54th's assault on Fort Wagner (outside Charleston Harbor) in July 1863, Reason died of an infection contracted when one of his legs had to be amputated. Wherever they lived, black people fought in countless ways to gain a country on their own terms.

THE UNFOLDING OF FREEDOM

Black people served as combatants in the war in ways that whites could neither anticipate nor fully appreciate. One noteworthy example is that of an enslaved woman named Nancy Johnson. For Johnson and her family, freedom unfolded only gradually, over the course of the war years. Later in life she would describe her own wartime journey out of slavery and into freedom as a series of novel, potent encounters with individual white people on the Liberty County, Georgia, rice plantation where she and her family lived.

One night, she and her husband, Boson Johnson, harbored an escaped Union prisoner of war, conveying him to safety the following day. Later she marveled that the Northerner had "sat in my room"—a remarkable occurrence, considering that, before the war, "white people didn't visit our house." Soon after, her master's grandson threatened to kill Boson Johnson if Nancy did not reveal the fugitive soldier's whereabouts. In a desperate bid to protect her family, she told the white man a boldfaced lie—"that I had seen nothing." In the course of the conflict, Nancy and Boson Johnson sheltered and fed others they considered their allies—deserters from the Confederate army, poor whites the couple "befriended . . . because they were on our side." These white men "were opposed to the war & didn't own slaves & said they would rather die than fight."

Other wartime confrontations with whites boded ill for the Johnsons and future generations of African Americans. As Union troops began to encroach on southeastern Georgia in December 1864, Nancy Johnson's master approached her and begged her to stay on the plantation—a slave owner pleading with a slave to work! But she "told him if the other colored people were going to be free that I wanted to be." She left the plantation, only to return a short time later. At that point her mistress accosted her, demanding to know "if I had come back to behave myself & do her work & I told her no that I came to do my own work." The white woman ordered Nancy to continue weaving cloth, "like a *'nigger,'*" prompting the black woman to retort "no[,] that I was free."

Nancy eventually agreed to weave forty yards of dress material, but only on the condition that she be paid for the work. When the cloth was woven and the white woman refused to pay, Nancy Johnson repeatedly demanded the money due her. Out of the crucible of war had emerged a new set of personal and public relationships. Here was a black woman demanding wages from her former mistress, and here was a former mistress shedding the veneer of paternalism and doing her best—cajoling, intimidating, making promises—to get a black woman back to the weaver's loom.

In January 1865, Union soldiers under the command of Brigadier General Judson Kilpatrick raided the plantation where the Johnsons lived. The soldiers made off with a huge stock of the family's belongings—dishes, tubs, kettles, bed linens, rice, lard, hogs, chickens, a horse, and even clothes. Years after the fact, Nancy Johnson could still vividly recall the chaotic scene: white men "starved & naked almost," shooting livestock, overturning corncribs, grabbing everything they could carry, including her young son who had been guarding wagons of provisions—"the soldiers took the wagons & the boy, & I never saw him any more." Among the raiding party Nancy Johnson recognized the soldier she and Boson had rescued earlier. When she approached him, he told her "he tried to keep them from burning my house but he couldn't keep them from taking everything we had." She protested to individual soldiers about the amount of food they were taking: "I told one of the officers we would starve." Of the white man who stole her children's clothes, she had a hard time believing that "a Yankee person would be so mean." Within a day and a half the troops were gone, leaving Nancy and Boson Johnson to pick up the pieces of their old life and begin a new one as best they could.

> *Black people served as combatants in the war in ways that whites could neither anticipate nor fully appreciate.*

We have no independent way to verify Nancy Johnson's dramatic story, which she recounted years later in an effort to prove her family's support for the Union Cause. But her story does confirm broad themes related to the experiences of African Americans during the Civil War. Many blacks sought to aid Union forces. The war disrupted labor relations on the plantation, as customary patterns of disciplining and controlling slaves dissolved in the chaos of war. When black people sought to work for themselves, they severed the bonds of slavery and seized freedom on their own terms. These transformations in the system of bondage helped to undermine the Confederacy.

ENEMIES WITHIN THE CONFEDERACY

DOCUMENT

Chesnut, A
Confederate Lady's
Diary (1861)

Slaveholding whites were shocked when they could not always count on the loyalty of "petted" domestics. Soon after the war began, South Carolina's Mary Boykin Chesnut expressed unease about the enigmatic behavior of one of her trusted house slaves, Laurence, asking herself of all her slaves, "Are they stolidly stupid or wiser than we are, silent and strong, biding their time?" A few months later, Chesnut's cousin was murdered while sleeping, bludgeoned by a candlestick; the cousin's slaves William and Rhody were charged with the crime. One of Chesnut's woman friends remarked of her own mulatto servant: "For the life of me, I cannot make up my mind. Does she mean to take care of me—or to murder me?" Now rising to the surface, such fears put whites on alert, guarding against enemies in their midst.

Yet no single white man or woman could halt the tide of freedom. Given the chance to steal away at night or walk away boldly in broad daylight, black men, women, and children left their masters and mistresses, seeking safety and paid labor behind Union lines. Throughout the South, black people waited and watched for an opportunity to flee from plantations, their actions depending on the movement of northern troops and the disarray of the plantations they lived on.

In July 1862, the Union's Second Confiscation Act provided that the slaves of rebel masters "shall be deemed captives of war and shall be forever free," prompting Union generals to begin employing runaway male slaves as manual laborers. Consequently, military authorities often turned away women, children, older adults, and the disabled, leaving them vulnerable to spiteful masters and mistresses. For black men pressed into Union military service and menial labor, and for their families still languishing on plantations, "freedom" came at a high price indeed.

■ Many southern black men experienced freedom as soldiers for the Union army. They embraced the era's rituals of manhood, including shouldering arms and participating in dress parades. Assembling in formation in Beaufort, South Carolina, in 1864, these soldiers belong to the 29th Regiment, U.S. Colored Troops.

The Library of Congress

THE ONGOING FIGHT AGAINST PREJUDICE

In the North, the Emancipation Proclamation spurred the enlistment of blacks in the Union army and navy. Eventually, about 33,000 northern blacks enlisted, following the lead of their brothers-in-arms from the South. For black soldiers, military service opened up a wider world. Some learned to read and write in camp, and almost all felt the satisfaction of contributing to a war that they defined in stark terms of freedom versus slavery. They wore their uniforms proudly.

Union wartime policies revealed, however, that African Americans would continue to fight prejudice on many fronts. Some northern whites approved recruiting blacks, reasoning that for each black man killed in battle, one white man would be spared. Until late in the war, black soldiers were systematically denied opportunities to advance through the ranks and were paid less than whites. Although they showed loyalty to the cause in disproportionate numbers compared with whites, most blacks found themselves barred from taking up arms at all, relegated to work deemed dangerous and degrading to whites. They intended to labor for the Union, but in the words of a black soldier from New York, "Instead of the musket it is the spade and the Whelbarrow and the Axe cuting in one of the horable swamps in Louisiana stinking and misery." For each white Union soldier killed or mortally wounded, two died of disease; the ratio for blacks was one to ten.

Many northern military strategists and ordinary enlisted men showed indifference at best, contempt at worst, for the desire of black fugitives to locate lost loved ones and begin to labor on their own behalf. In the course of the war, Union experiments with free black labor—on the South Carolina Sea Islands under the direction of northern missionaries, and in Louisiana under the direction of generals Nathaniel Banks and Benjamin Butler—emphasized converting the former slaves into staple-crop wage workers under the supervision of Yankees. Some of these whites, in their eagerness to establish "order" in former Confederate territory, saw blacks only as exploitable labor—if not cannon fodder, then hands to dig ditches and grow cotton.

Former slave Susie King Taylor recalled the heady, dangerous days of 1862, when she fled from Savannah and found refuge behind Union lines off the coast of Georgia. Despite receiving little pay for her labors for the First South Carolina Volunteers (later known as the 33rd United States Colored Cavalry), Taylor gained a great deal of satisfaction from her work on behalf of the Union cause and the black soldiers who fought for it. She conducted a school for black children on St. Simons Island and performed a whole host of tasks for the soldiers, from cleaning rifles to washing clothes and tending the ill. She understood that her own contributions to the war effort showed "what sacrifices we can make for our liberty and rights."

The Emancipation Proclamation did not materially change the day-to-day experiences of any slaves within southern territory, though many derived hope from the Union's new-found commitment to the abolition of bondage. That commitment changed the nature of the war from 1863 onward.

Harriet Beecher Stowe Center, Hartford, CT

■ Laura Towne and three of her pupils pose for a picture on Saint Helena Island, South Carolina, in 1866. A native of Pennsylvania, Towne traveled to the South Carolina Sea Islands in April 1862, soon after they were occupied by Union forces. She and her companion and fellow teacher Ellen Murray epitomized the hundreds of idealistic northern women who volunteered to teach southern black people of all ages during and after the Civil War. Declared Towne on her arrival in the South, "We've come to do antislavery work, and we think it noble work and mean to do it earnestly."

Battle Fronts and Home Fronts in 1863

■ *How did developments on the battlefield affect politics in both the North and South?*

In 1863, the North abandoned the strategy of conciliation in favor of an effort to destroy the large southern armies and deprive the Confederacy of its slave labor force. By this time the war was causing tremendous hardship among ordinary whites in the South. Meanwhile, Lincoln found himself caught between African American freedom fighters who resented the poor treatment they received from many white commanders, and white Northerners who took their opposition to the war in general and the military draft in particular into the streets. Deprivation at home and the mounting casualty rates on the battlefields were reshaping the fabric of American society, North and South.

DISAFFECTION IN THE CONFEDERACY

The Civil War assaulted Southerners' senses and their land. Before the war, slave owners and their allies often contrasted the supposed tranquility of their rural society with the rude, boisterous noisiness of the North. According to this view, the South was a peaceful place of contented slaves toiling in the fields, whereas the North was the site of workers striking, women clamoring for the vote, and eccentric reformers delivering street-corner harangues.

The war exploded on the southern landscape with ferocious force, and the rumble of huge armies on the march shook southern society to its foundations. For the first time, many Southerners smelled the acrid odor of gunpowder and the stench of rotting bodies. They heard the booms of near and distant cannon and the mournful sounds of church bells tolling for the dead. They saw giant encampments of soldiers cover what used to be cotton fields. Seemingly overnight, both armies constructed gorge-spanning train trestles and huge riverside docks and warehouses, all in preparation for conflict. As soldiers withdrew from the battlefield, they left behind a scarred and blood-spattered land, cornfields mowed down, fires raging in their wake.

> *Women from Virginia to Alabama protested a Confederate 10 percent "tax-in-kind" on produce grown by farmers.*

These sights and sounds were especially distressing to Southerners who objected to the war as a matter of principle or because of its disastrous effects on their own households. Scattered throughout the South were communities resistant to the policies of what many ordinary whites considered the Richmond elite—the leaders of the Confederacy. In western North Carolina, a group calling themselves Heroes of America declared their loyalty to the Union. In northern Mississippi, the "Free State of Jones [County]" raised troops for the Union army. Throughout the rural South, army deserters were welcomed home by their impoverished wives and children; it is estimated that during much of the war, as many as one-third of all Confederate soldiers were absent without leave at any particular time.

Groups of poor women resisted the dictates of the Davis administration, which was perceived as representing wealthy men and women who flaunted an extravagant wartime lifestyle of lavish dinners and parties. Women from Virginia to Alabama protested a Confederate 10 percent "tax-in-kind" on produce grown by farmers. Food shortages reached crisis proportions. In April 1863, several hundred Richmond women, many of them wives of Tredegar Iron Works employees, armed themselves with knives, hatchets, and pistols and ransacked stores in search of food: "Bread! Bread! Our children are starving while the rich roll in wealth."

Whereas some white women resisted the Confederacy, others leaped to the fore to provide essential goods and services to the beleaguered new nation. Virginia's Belle Boyd kept track of Union troop movements and served as a spy for Confederate armies. Poor women took jobs as textile factory workers, and their better-educated sisters found employment as clerks for the Confederate bureaucracy. Slaveholding women busied themselves running plantations, rolling bandages, and knitting socks for soldiers. Still, many women thought their labors were in vain. Of the Confederacy's stalled progress, Georgia's Gertrude Thomas noted, "Valuable lives lost and nothing accomplished."

THE TIDE TURNS AGAINST THE SOUTH

In the fall of 1862, Lincoln replaced General McClellan with General Ambrose E. Burnside and then General Joseph ("Fighting Joe") Hooker. In early May 1863, Lee and Jackson encountered Hooker at Chancellorsville, Virginia. The battle left Hooker reeling, but it also claimed the life of Jackson, mistakenly shot by his own men on May 2 in the early evening twilight. The South had lost one of its most ardent champions.

Lee decided to press his advantage by invading Pennsylvania and, it was hoped, encouraging northern Peace Democrats and impressing the foreign powers. The ensuing clash at Gettysburg was a turning point in the war. Drawn by reports of a cache of much-needed shoes, Confederate armies converged on the town, in the south-central part of the state, across the border from Maryland. Union forces pursued the southern troops. In a three-day

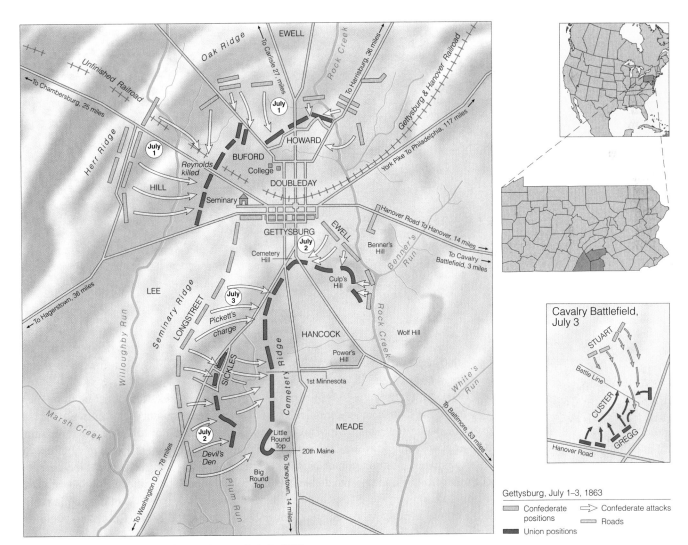

■ **MAP 14.4   The Battle of Gettysburg, July 1–3, 1863**

The three-day battle of Gettysburg was a turning point in the war. This map shows that Confederate soldiers made repeated assaults on Union lines. Lee's confidence in this strategy was misplaced, and some of his own staff recognized it. Recalled General James Longstreet of the third day of fighting: "My heart was heavy. I could see the desperate and hopeless nature of the charge and the hopeless slaughter it would cause. . . . That day at Gettysburg was one of the saddest of my life."

The Wider World

Deaths of Americans In Principal Wars, 1775–1991

War	Number Serving	Total Deaths	Battle Deaths	Other Deaths*	Wounded, Not Mortally
Revolutionary War 1775–1783	175,000–200,000	25,674	7,174	18,500	8,241
War of 1812 1812–1815	286,730	2,260	2,260	–	4,505
Mexican War 1846–1848	78,718	13,283	1,733	11,550	4,152
Civil War 1861–1865, Union	2,213,363	364,511	140,414	224,097	281,881
Civil War, Confederate	750,000–1,250,000	258,000	94,000	164,000	622,511
Spanish-American War 1898	306,760	2,446	385	2,061	1,662
World War I 1917–1918	4,734,991	116,516	53,402	63,114	204,002
World War II 1941–1945	16,112,566	405,399	291,557	113,842	671,846
Korean War 1950–1953	5,720,000	36,574	33,741	2,833	103,284
Vietnam War 1964–1973	8,744,000	58,209	47,424	10,785	153,303
Persian Gulf War 1990–1991	2,225,000	382	147	235	467

*Includes deaths from disease.

This table compares the number of American soldiers killed and wounded in the Civil War with figures for Americans killed and wounded fighting foreign foes in other wars. Note that these figures do not include the number of American foreign allies and enemies killed in combat during these wars.

QUESTIONS

1. How do you account for the tremendous difference in the number of American troops killed in the Revolutionary War as opposed to the Civil War?

2. Why are the rates of death from disease so high in many of these conflicts?

3. How do the figures for the Civil War compare to the figures for all other wars combined?

4. Given the tremendous loss of life during the Civil War, how would you characterize the significance of that conflict in American history?

5. Should the number of slaves who died of disease while working on Confederate fortifications be included in this table? If so, under what category?

DOCUMENT

Brewster, Three Letters from the Front (1862)

battle that began on July 1, the 92,000 men under the command of General George G. Meade were arrayed against the 76,000 troops of Robert E. Lee.

Gettysburg later came to represent the bloody consequences of a war fought by men with modern weapons under commanders with a premodern military sensibility. On the last day of the battle, the men under Major General George Pickett moved slowly into formation, passing hastily dug graves and the fragments of bodies blown to bits the day before. At 3 p.m., a mile-wide formation of 15,000 men gave the rebel yell and charged three-quarters of a mile across an open field to do battle with Union troops well fortified behind stone walls. Within half an hour, Pickett had lost two-thirds of his soldiers and all 13 of his colonels. The battle's three-day toll was equally staggering: 23,000 Union and 28,000 Confederate soldiers wounded or killed. Fully one-third of Lee's army was dead or wounded.

What made the soldiers of both sides fight on under these conditions? Some remained devoted to a cause. Others cared less about the Confederacy or the Union and more about proving their manhood and upholding their family's honor. Still others sought to avenge comrades slain in battle or to conform to standards of discipline drilled into them. Some prayed merely to survive.

The Union victory at Gettysburg on July 3, 1863, brought rejoicing in the North. The next day General Ulysses S. Grant captured Vicksburg on the Mississippi River, a move that earned him the rank of lieutenant general. Within a year Lincoln appointed him supreme commander of the Union armies.

CIVIL UNREST IN THE NORTH

Not all segments of northern society joined in the celebration of Union victories. Even principled supporters of the war effort were growing weary of high taxes and inflated consumer prices, not to mention the sacrifices of thousands of husbands, sons, and brothers. In May, federal soldiers had arrested the defiant and outspoken Copperhead Clement Vallandigham at his home in Dayton, Ohio. Subsequently convicted of treason (he had declared the conflict "a war for the freedom of blacks and the enslavement of whites"), Vallandigham was banished to the South.

Following a military draft imposed on July 1, 1863, the northern white working classes erupted. Enraged at the wealthy who could buy substitutes, resentful of the Lincoln administration's high-handed tactics, and determined not to fight on behalf of African Americans, white laborers in New York City, Hartford, Troy, Newark, and Boston (many of them Irish) went on a rampage. The New York City riot of July 11–15 was especially savage as white men directed their wrath against black men, women, and children. Members of the mob burned the Colored Orphan Asylum to the ground

> *Following a military draft imposed on July 1, 1863, the northern white working classes erupted.*

and then mutilated their victims before the federal government deployed 20,000 troops to New York to quell the violence and discourage other men from resisting the draft elsewhere. On August 19, the draft resumed.

THE DESPERATE SOUTH

Meanwhile, the South had to contend not only with dissent and disaffection at home but also with the stunning battle and territorial losses it suffered at Gettysburg and Vicksburg. On August 21, 1863, Jefferson Davis proclaimed a day of "fasting, humiliation and prayer." Even as Davis was invoking the name of the Almighty, 450 rebels under the command of William Clarke Quantrill were destroying the town of Lawrence, Kansas (long a hotbed of abolitionist sentiment), and killing 150 of its inhabitants. With the exception of Quantrill and John Singleton Mosby (whose squads of men roamed northern Virginia attacking Union posts and troops in 1863), Confederate military leaders shunned guerrilla warfare, preferring to meet the enemy on a field of honor. The desperate Quantrill raid on Lawrence demonstrated that the Confederate cause was, if not lost, then losing in the late summer of 1863.

Before the year was out, Davis faced other setbacks as well. Grant's successes at Missionary Ridge and Lookout Mountain, in Tennessee, caused both France and England to draw back from offering overt support to the Confederacy in the form of sales of navy warships or diplomatic recognition. The Confederate president had long counted on securing the support of the great European powers; now those hopes were dashed.

Dedicating the national cemetery at Gettysburg on November 19, 1863, Lincoln delivered a short address that affirmed the nation's "new birth of freedom" and its commitment that "the government of the people, by the people, for the people, shall not perish from the earth." Lincoln's speech is one of the great rhetorical masterpieces of American politics. In it he elevated the Civil War from a military conflict exclusively to a great moral struggle against slavery. In the South, more and more whites were flagging in their conviction that the system of bondage was worth the ultimate sacrifice in terms of their own lives and the welfare of their families.

■ **MAP 14.5** **African Americans in Civil War Battles, 1863–1865**

Confederates killed African American soldiers captured in battle at Fort Wagner in Charleston Harbor (1863), the Union garrison of Fort Pillow on the Mississippi River (1864), and Petersburg, Virginia (1864), among other battles. By the end of the war, black men had fought in more than 200 battles. Their performance in combat no doubt contributed to the Confederate proposal to arm slaves as soldiers in the last few weeks of the war.

The Prolonged Defeat of the Confederacy, 1864–1865

■ *During the last months of the war, what factors contributed to the defeat of the Confederacy?*

LISTEN

"When This Cruel War Is Over"

By 1864, northern generals, with Lincoln's blessing, had decided to fight a "hard war" against their tenacious enemy. Union troops were authorized to live off the land (denying southern civilians the necessities of life in the process), to seize livestock and other supplies indiscriminately, and to burn everything that the Confederates might find useful. The strategy was twofold: to harm irreparably what was left of Confederate morale and to facilitate the movement of northern troops through hostile territory. If northern troops could sever the area west of Georgia from the Confederacy and take Richmond and destroy its surrounding armies, the Union would be safe at last.

"HARD WAR" TOWARD AFRICAN AMERICANS AND INDIANS

The policy of "hard war" should not be confused with "total war," characterized by state-approved terrorism against civilians. However, Confederate policies toward black soldiers and Union policies toward Indian insurgents in the West did show elements of total war against particular segments of the population. In April 1864, Confederate General Nathan Bedford Forrest destroyed Fort Pillow, a Union garrison on the Mississippi River. After surrendering, black soldiers were systematically murdered. Wounded survivors were bayoneted or burned to death. Among southern generals, conventions of war (providing for the detention and exchange of prisoners of war) did not apply to African American soldiers.

Nor were Indians accorded even the minimal respect shown to most white combatants. In the early fall of 1864, a group of Cheyenne and Arapaho were camped along Sand Creek in the southeastern corner of Colorado. Black Kettle, a chief of the Cheyenne, had received promises from Union Colonel John M. Chivington and others stationed at Camp Weld in Denver that the two sides would remain at peace with each other. Therefore, on the morning of November 29, 1864, when Black Kettle saw Chivington leading a Colorado volunteer militia toward his settlement, he waved a white flag and stood his ground.

Colorado Historical Society (WPA-834; 10025492)

■ In September 1864, the Indian chiefs Black Kettle and White Antelope, with other Cheyenne and Arapaho leaders, met with Colonel John M. Chivington at Camp Weld, Colorado. The purpose of the meeting was to secure a truce between the Indians and European Americans in the area. Two months later, Chivington attacked an encampment of these Indians on the banks of Sand Creek, about 100 miles southeast of Denver.

Chivington did not come in peace. That day he and his men massacred 125 to 160 Indians, mostly women, children, and old people, returning later to mutilate the bodies. In response, Sioux, Arapaho, and Cheyenne launched their own campaigns against white migrants traveling the South and North Platte trails. Chivington declared that it was "right and honorable" to kill Indians, even Indian children, using any means.

"FATHER ABRAHAM"

The election of 1864 proceeded without major incident, although Lincoln faced some opposition within his own party. Together with his new running mate, a former slave owner from Tennessee named Andrew Johnson, Lincoln benefited from a string of Union victories won by Admiral David G. Farragut at Mobile, Alabama, and by General Philip Sheridan in Virginia's Shenandoah Valley. As a result, he defeated the Democratic nominee, his own former general, George McClellan, who managed to garner 45 percent of the popular vote. One of the keys to Lincoln's success was the "peace platform" that the Democrats had drafted at their convention the summer before.

TABLE 14.2			
The Election of 1864			
Candidate	**Political Party**	**Popular Vote (%)**	**Electoral Vote**
Abraham Lincoln	Republican	55.0	212*
George B. McClellan	Democratic	45.0	21

*Eleven secessionist states did not participate.

Support among Union soldiers for "Little Mac" dropped precipitously as a result, and Lincoln won three-quarters of the army's vote.

Despite his limited military experience, Lincoln possessed a strategic sense superior to that of many of his generals. He played down his own military experience, making light of his minor part in the Black Hawk War of 1832. In that conflict, he reminisced, he had engaged in "charges upon wild onions . . . [and] bloody struggles with the Musquetoes." However, he cared deeply about ordinary soldiers and talked with them whenever he had the opportunity. In return, Union troops gave "Father Abraham" their loyalty on the battlefield and, especially during the election of 1864, at the ballot box.

SHERMAN'S MARCH FROM ATLANTA TO THE SEA

The South's physical environment—its terrain, natural growth, and climate—shaped the course of the Civil War, and that environment was in turn transformed by the fighting. The Union army's famous march from Atlanta to the sea in the late fall of 1864 reveals the complex interplay of armies and the land.

Occupying the Piedmont city of Atlanta in the summer of 1864, General William Tecumseh Sherman believed that an assault on the Georgia coastline would have tremendous strategic and diplomatic benefits for the Union cause: "If we can march a well-appointed army right through [Confederate] territory, it is a demonstration to the whole world, foreign and domestic, that we have a power which [Confederate President Jefferson] Davis cannot resist. . . . I can make the march, and make Georgia howl!"

The Library of Congress

■ Like other officers in both the Union and Confederate armies, William Tecumseh Sherman had graduated from the United States Military Academy at West Point.

On November 15, Sherman's army left Atlanta, organized in four columns, 60,000 infantry and 5,550 cavalry strong. Along the 285-mile march, the army met only light resistance from a few thousand Georgia militia cavalry commanded by General Joseph Wheeler.

■ **M A P   1 4 . 6   Sherman's March to the Sea, 1864–1865**
General William T. Sherman's famous march to the sea marked the final phase of the Union effort to divide and
conquer the Confederacy. Sherman's men burned Atlanta to the ground in September 1864. In late December
they made their triumphant entry into the city of Savannah. Under a policy of "hard war," Sherman ordered his
troops to seize from civilians any food and livestock they could use and to destroy everything else, whether rail
lines, houses, or barns. White southerners expressed outrage over these tactics. Still, Sherman never systematically attacked civilians, a characteristic of the Union's "total war" against Native American peoples in the West.

The march itself was an engineering marvel. Confederate forces sought to block the enemy
advance by burning bridges, felling trees across roads, and planting land mines along the way.
Sherman responded to the challenge by encouraging able-bodied black men, now former slaves,
to join the army and work as part of its Corps of Engineers, who had the task of overcoming
natural obstacles. These workers, called "pioneers," constructed corduroy roads made with rails
or newly cut poles, allowing supply trains to traverse swampland and muddy ground. Sherman's
forces could repair bridges quickly, rebuilding a 1,000-foot-long span in as little as three days.
They became expert at using pontoons to cross rivers. Pontoons were structures consisting of
two boats with a trestle suspended between them. These temporary bridges could be dismantled
in as little time as thirty minutes and then reassembled as needed farther down the road.

The Union army also destroyed railroads, leaving the Georgia landscape littered with
smoldering, twisted iron ties. Observed John J. Hight, a Union chaplain from New York
State: "Our people are making a thorough wreck of them [the railroads]. The rails are torn
from the ties, which are then piled, and laid across them. The ties are then fired, and the rails,
while red hot in the center, are twisted. A rail, simply bent, can be used again, without being

CORBIS

■ This photo shows Confederate defenses on the eve of Union forces' assault on Petersburg, Virginia, in mid-summer 1864. The Confederates managed to hold the city until early April 1865. Wrote one Union soldier who survived the battle, "They had some awful and devilish devices and batteries fixed up. Around some of their batteries' earthworks, they drive thick beds of wooden stakes, sharpened to a point and slanting to the front, so that anyone who would charge them might as well charge a sword cane."

taken to the shop for repair, but a twisted bar cannot." These burned and twisted railroad ties became known as "Sherman's hairpins."

Sherman's army became famous for its foraging off the countryside. The general was convinced that large supply trains would slow his advance, and he was determined to impress upon Georgians the hopelessness of their situation. He therefore ordered raiding parties to seize food supplies and livestock from farms along the way. The raiders were indiscriminate in seizing animals, food, and goods from grand planters, modest yeoman farmers, and slaves, including Boson and Nancy Johnson.

If Sherman's march to Savannah depended on overcoming natural barriers, so too did the Confederates' escape from that city, on the night of December 19. Under the command of General William J. Hardee, Confederate soldiers worked feverishly for several days to construct a pontoon bridge leading from the city over the Savannah River and into South Carolina. Their efforts were delayed by fog and by ships running aground in the shallow Savannah River. Eventually engineers managed to fasten together thirty rice flats, each seventy to eighty feet long. Workers laid these flats end to end and then covered them with planks ripped from Savannah River wharves. Later contemplating his successful evacuation of the city, with his army intact and many civilians in tow, Hardee wrote: "Though compelled to evacuate the city, there is no part of my military life to which I look back with so much satisfaction." Hardee's pride in his pontoon bridge came at a high price; Sherman's capture of Savannah amounted to a death knell for the Confederacy.

THE LAST DAYS OF THE CONFEDERACY

The Civil War Part II: 1863–1865

After presenting Lincoln with the "Christmas gift" of Savannah in December, Sherman took his 60,000 troops north, slogging through swamps and rain-soaked terrain to confront the original secessionists. Later, he recalled with satisfaction, "My aim then was to whip the rebels, to humble their pride, to follow them to their inmost recesses, and make them fear and dread us." By mid-February, South Carolina's state capital, Columbia, was in flames. African American troops were among the triumphant occupiers of the charred city.

In the spring of 1865, Confederate leaders betrayed their desperation by initiating a debate over whether to arm slaves to fight for southern independence. At the beginning of the war, southern whites had believed that military service was an honor reserved for white men. But by early 1865, some political and military leaders, including Robert E. Lee, argued that the Confederacy should offer slave men the option of fighting in return for their freedom and the freedom of their families. However, the Confederate Congress never acted on this proposal.

By early April 1865, Grant had overpowered Lee's army in Petersburg, Virginia. Withdrawing, Lee sent a telegram to Davis, who was attending church in Richmond, warning him that the fall of the Confederate capital was imminent. Davis and almost all other whites fled the city. Arriving in Richmond on April 3, only hours after the city had been abandoned by Confederate officials and troops, was the commander in chief of the Union army, Abraham Lincoln. Flanked by a group of ten sailors, Lincoln calmly walked the streets of the smoldering city (set afire by departing Confederates). Throngs of black people greeted the president, exclaiming, "Glory to God! Glory! Glory! Glory!" When a black man kneeled to thank Lincoln, the president said, "Don't kneel to me. That is not right. You must kneel to God only, and thank Him for the liberty you will enjoy hereafter."

On April 9, Lee and his demoralized and depleted army of 35,000 found themselves outnumbered by Grant and Meade, and Lee surrendered his sword at Appomattox Courthouse in northern Virginia. Lee had rejected a plea by one of his men that the army disband and continue to fight a guerrilla war in the woods and hills. The general predicted that such a force "would become mere bands of marauders," destroying the countryside and with it what was left of the fabric of southern society.

The Library of Congress

■ The city of Charleston, South Carolina, lies in ruins after its defeat at the hands of Sherman's army in February 1865. This photo, taken in April, shows the shell of the city's famed Circular Church in the center.

Union officials assured rebel soldiers of protection from future prosecution (for treason) and allowed the cavalry to keep their horses for use in spring planting. When the ragtag members of the Stonewall Brigade—soldiers who had entered the war with Stonewall Jackson four years before—came forward to lay down their arms, the Union army gave them a salute of honor, acknowledging their bravery. However, this scene set the stage for the not-too-distant future, when the North and South reaffirmed their ties based on a shared "whiteness" in opposition to African Americans.

One of the last casualties of the war was Abraham Lincoln. Watching a comedy with his wife, Mary, at Ford's Theater in Washington on the night of April 14, 1865, Lincoln was assassinated by John Wilkes Booth, a Confederate loyalist fearful that the president was bent on advancing "nigger citizenship." Lincoln lingered through the night but died the next morning. Booth was caught and shot within a matter of days. Of the departed president, Secretary of War Edwin M. Stanton said: "Now he belongs to the ages."

Conclusion

Rather than asking why the South lost the Civil War, we might wonder why it took the North four years to win it. Despite all the political dissent and social conflict in the white South, despite the crumbling of the institution of slavery and the lack of support from the European powers, the Confederacy was able to mobilize huge armies under the command of brilliant tacticians such as Lee and Jackson. The war was fought on the battlefield by regiments of soldiers, not on the sea by navies or in the countryside by guerrillas. Therefore, as long as Confederate generals could deploy troops and outwit their foes during brief but monumental clashes, the Confederacy could survive to fight another day. The South had as its immediate goal the slaughter of as many Yankees as possible. Meanwhile, the North staggered under the

CHRONOLOGY: 1860–1865

1860	South Carolina secedes from Union.
1861	Confederate States of America is formed.
	Civil War begins.
1862	Minnesota (Santee) Sioux uprising.
	Congress passes Homestead, Morrill, and Pacific Railroad acts.
	Union victory at the Battle of Antietam.
1863	Emancipation Proclamation.
	Richmond Bread Riots.
	Union victory at Battle of Gettysburg with heavy losses on both sides.
	Northern antidraft riots.
	Lincoln delivers Gettysburg Address.
1864	Fort Pillow massacre of African American (Union) soldiers in western Tennessee.
	Sand Creek (Colorado) massacre of Cheyenne and Arapaho.
	Sherman's March to the Sea.
	Lincoln reelected president.
1865	Confederacy is defeated.
	Lincoln assassinated.

weight of mobilizing large numbers of soldiers in enemy territory and supplying them with the necessary resources far from home.

The South had entered the war armed with a states' rights ideology that held that all whites in the region were unified in support of slavery, and that black people were passive and childlike in their dependence on whites. The course of the war exposed the fallacy of this ideology. Even at the outset of the war, white Southerners differed in their support for the Confederacy, and as the conflict dragged, many poor whites believed they were sacrificing more for the cause than were their social betters. Blacks proved aggressive in fighting for their freedom, wreaking havoc on plantation discipline and on southern military strategy. And too, many Confederates were forced to accept the fact that in order to fight the war successfully, principled states' rights supporters must yield to those politicians advocating a more centralized effort in behalf of mobilizing for war and fighting the enemy.

In terms of soldiers' lives lost—620,000—the Civil War was by far the costliest in the nation's history. At the end of the war, the Union was preserved and slavery was destroyed. Yet, in their quest for true freedom, African Americans soon learned that military hostilities were but one phase of a wider war, a war to define the nature of American citizenship and its promise of liberty and equality. Thus April 1865 marked not so much a final judgment as a transition to new battlefields.

For Review

1. Despite the claims of white leaders, the South was not unified in fighting the Civil War. Identify three different social groups within the South and discuss why they either initially withheld their support for the Confederacy, or why their initial support for the cause gradually eroded over the course of the fighting.

2. What were the North's advantages over the South in terms of centralizing military, political, and economic operations during the war? Given those advantages, why did the Confederacy nevertheless believe it could win the war?

3. What were the effects, and limitations, of the Emancipation Proclamation in shaping the course of the war? In shaping southern and black communities during the war?

4. How did developments on the northern home front reflect the priorities of the Republican party?

5. In what ways did the war challenge white southerners' traditional beliefs about the role of slavery—and slaves—in southern society?

6. What accounts for the long duration of the Civil War and the very high mortality rates among military personnel during the conflict? Why did neither Jefferson Davis nor Abraham Lincoln seek a negotiated settlement to avoid further bloodshed?

Created Equal Online

For more *Created Equal* resources, including suggestions on sites to visit and books to read, go to **MyHistoryLab.com**.

Chapter 15

Consolidating a Triumphant Union, 1865–1877

■ In Savannah, African American Sunday School pupils pose for photographer William Wilson in 1890. After the Civil War, many southern black communities created, or enlarged and solidified, their own institutions, including schools and churches.

Courtesy of the Georgia Historical Society, William Wilson Collection

CHAPTER OUTLINE

- **The Struggle over the South**

- **Claiming Territory for the Union**

- **The Republican Vision and Its Limits**

The day of jubilee had come at last! In late December 1864, African American men, women, and children rejoiced when the troops of Union General William Tecumseh Sherman liberated Savannah, Georgia. The city's black community immediately formed its own school system under the sponsorship of a new group, the Savannah Education Association (SEA). The association owed its creation to the desire of freedpeople of all ages to learn to read and write. A committee of black clergy began by hiring fifteen black teachers and acquiring buildings (including the Old Bryan Slave Mart) for use as schools. By January 10, 1865, Savannah blacks had raised $800 to pay teachers' salaries, enabling several hundred black children to attend classes free of charge.

Following hard on the heels of the Union army, a group of northern white missionaries arrived in Savannah to seek black converts for two Protestant denominations, the Presbyterians and the Congregationalists. On the first day of school, in January 1865, these northern newcomers watched a grand procession of children wend its way through the streets of Savannah. The missionaries expressed amazement that the SEA was an entirely black-run organization. These whites had believed the former slaves incapable of creating such an impressive educational system.

In March 1865, the federal government, under the auspices of the newly formed Bureau of Refugees, Freedmen, and Abandoned Lands (Freedmen's Bureau), agreed to work with missionaries to open schools for black children throughout the former Confederate states. In Georgia, missionaries and government officials soon became alarmed that black leaders were willing to accept financial aid from them but not willing to relinquish control of SEA schools to the whites in return. The Northerners were also distressed by the militancy of certain local black leaders. One of these leaders was a former fugitive slave, Aaron A. Bradley, who arrived in Savannah from Boston in late 1865. Armed with a pistol and bowie knife, he began urging other blacks to free themselves from all forms of white power.

In an effort to wrest control of the SEA from Savannah blacks, northern missionaries and agents of the Freedmen's Bureau decided to withhold funds from the association. By March 1866, the city's black community, swollen by a refugee population, was no longer able to support its own schools. Northern whites took over SEA operations, and the association ceased to exist.

Almost a year earlier, on April 11, 1865, President Abraham Lincoln had appeared on the balcony of the White House to announce that the Union forces were victorious, the Confederate States of America defeated. Four years before, southern slaveholders had organized a rebellion against the federal government; their aim was to preserve slavery in the wake of the election of a Republican, antislavery president. The Civil War claimed nearly 700,000 American lives—more than all other conflicts (before or since) in American history combined. Yet the military defeat of the rebels did not resolve fundamental problems related to black people's status in the South or in the nation at large. Contemplating the difficult task ahead of the United States, Lincoln declared in that speech on April 11, just a few days before he was assassinated, "We must simply begin with, and mould from, disorganized and discordant elements."

During the months and years immediately after the war, a major conflict raged between supporters of African American rights and supporters of southern white privilege. Republican congressmen hoped to *reconstruct* the South by enabling African Americans to own their own land and to become full citizens. Southern freedpeople sought to free themselves from white employers, landlords, and clergy and to establish control over their own workplaces, families, and churches. In contrast, President Andrew Johnson appeared bent on *restoring* the antebellum power relations that made southern black field laborers dependent on white landowners. For their part, many southern whites were determined to prevent blacks from becoming truly free and equal citizens. Most former rebels remained embittered about the outcome of the war and vengeful toward the freedpeople.

The Civil War hardened the positions of the two major political parties. The Republicans remained in favor of a strong national government, one that promoted economic growth. The Democrats tended to support states' efforts to manage their own affairs, which included regulating relations between employers and employees, whites and blacks.

After the war, western economic development presented new challenges. In order to open the West to European American miners and homesteaders, the U.S. army clashed repeatedly with Native Americans. On the Plains and in the Northwest, Indians resisted white efforts to force them to abandon their nomadic way of life and take up sedentary farming. William Tecumseh Sherman, Philip H. Sheridan, and George Custer were among the U.S. military officers who had commanded troops in the Civil War and now attempted to subdue the Plains Indians and to promote white settlement. Sherman declared, "We must act with vindictive earnestness against the Sioux, even to their extermination, men, women and children." The former head of the Freedmen's Bureau, General Oliver O. Howard, oversaw the expulsion of Chief Joseph and his people, the Nez Perce, from their homeland in Southeast Washington's Walla Walla Valley in 1877.

U.S. soldiers also contributed to the building of the transcontinental railroad. A former Union military officer, Grenville Dodge, served as chief civil engineer for the Union Pacific Railroad, supervising huge workforces of immigrant laborers. The railroad industry was a potent symbol of postwar

U.S. nationalism. It also represented a robust, Republican-sponsored partnership between private enterprise and the federal government. Between 1862 and 1872, the government gave the industry subsidies that included millions of dollars in cash and more than 100 million acres of land. On the Plains, U.S. soldiers protected Union Pacific Railroad land surveyors against the retaliatory raids conducted by Indians who were enraged by this incursion into their territory and by the government's failure to abide by its treaties.

The Republicans' triumph prompted dissent from those people who feared that the victorious Union would serve the interests of specific groups such as men, employers, and white property owners. Some women's rights activists, for example, felt betrayed by the suggestion that this was "the hour of the Negro [man]." These women were not willing to wait indefinitely for their own voting rights. At the same time, in the bustling workshops of the nation's cities, many workers realized that they remained at the mercy of employers bent on using cheap labor. The founding of the **National Labor Union** in 1866 revealed that members of the laboring classes had a national vision of their own, one that valued the efforts of working people to earn a decent living for their families.

At great cost of human life, the Civil War decisively settled several immediate and long-standing political conflicts. The southern secessionists were defeated, and slavery as a legal institution was destroyed. Nevertheless, the relationship between federal power and group rights remained unresolved, leading to continued bloodshed between whites and Indians on the High Plains, as well as in the former Confederate states between Union supporters and diehard rebels. During the postwar period, now called the **Reconstruction era,** federal government officials attempted to complete the political process that the military defeat of the South had only begun: the consolidation of the Union, North and South, East and West. This process encompassed the nation as a whole.

The Struggle over the South

■ *How did various groups of northerners and southerners differ in their vision of the postwar South?*

The Civil War had a devastating impact on the South in physical, social, and economic terms. The region had lost an estimated $2 billion in investments in slaves; modest homesteads and grand plantations alike lay in ruins; and gardens, orchards, and cotton fields were barren. More than 3 million former slaves eagerly embraced freedom, but the vast majority lacked the land, cash, and credit necessary to build family homesteads for themselves. Hoping to achieve social and economic self-determination, African American men and women traveled great distances, usually on foot, in efforts to locate loved ones and reunite families that had been separated during slavery. At the same time, landowning whites considered black people primarily as a source of agricultural labor; these whites resisted the idea that the freedpeople should be granted citizenship rights.

In the North, Republican lawmakers disagreed among themselves how best to punish the defeated but defiant rebels. President Abraham Lincoln had indicated early that after the war the government should bring the South back into the Union quickly and painlessly. His successor wanted to see members of the southern planter elite humiliated but resisted the notion that freedpeople should become independent of white landowners. In Congress, moderate and radical Republicans argued about how far the government should go in ensuring the former slaves' freedom.

WARTIME PRELUDES TO POSTWAR POLICIES

Wartime experiments with African American free labor in Union-occupied areas foreshadowed these bitter postwar debates. As early as November 1861, Union forces had occupied the Sea Islands off Port Royal Sound in South Carolina. In response, wealthy cotton planters fled to the mainland. Over the next few months, three groups of northern civilians landed on the Sea Islands with the intention of guiding blacks in the transition from slave to free labor. Teachers arrived to create schools, and missionaries hoped to start churches. A third group, representing Boston investors, also settled on the Sea Islands to assess economic opportunities. By early 1862, they decided to institute a system of wage labor that would reestablish a staple crop economy and funnel cotton directly into northern textile mills. The freed slaves, however, preferred to grow crops for their families to eat rather than cotton to sell, relying on a system of barter and trade among networks of extended families. Their goal was to break free of white landlords, suppliers, and cotton merchants.

Meanwhile, in southern Louisiana, the Union capture of New Orleans in the spring of 1862 enabled northern military officials to implement their own free (nonslave) labor system. General Nathaniel Banks proclaimed that U.S. troops should forcibly relocate blacks to plantations "where they belong"; there they would continue to work for their former owners in the sugar and cotton fields, but now for wages supposedly negotiated annually. The Union army would compel blacks to work if they resisted doing so. In defiance of these orders, however, some blacks went on strike for higher wages, and others refused to work at all. Moreover, not all members of the Union military relished the prospect of forcing blacks to work on the plantations where they had been enslaved. Thus, federal policies returning blacks to plantations were contested even within the ranks of the army itself.

The Lincoln administration had no hard and fast reconstruction policy to guide congressional lawmakers looking toward the postwar period. In December 1863, the president outlined his Ten Percent Plan. This plan would allow former Confederate states to form new state governments once 10 percent of the men who had voted in the 1860 presidential election had pledged allegiance to the Union and renounced slavery. Congress instead passed the Wade-Davis Bill, which would have required a majority of southern voters in any state to take a loyalty oath affirming their allegiance to the United States. By refusing to sign the bill before Congress adjourned, Lincoln vetoed the measure (through a **pocket veto**). However, the president approved the creation of the Bureau of Refugees, Freedmen, and Abandoned Lands, or **Freedmen's Bureau,** in March 1865. The bureau was responsible for coordinating relief efforts on behalf of blacks and poor whites loyal to the Union, for sponsoring schools, and for implementing a labor contract system on southern plantations. At the time of his assassination, Lincoln seemed to be leaning toward giving the right to vote to southern black men.

PRESIDENTIAL RECONSTRUCTION, 1865–1867

When Andrew Johnson, the seventeenth president of the United States, assumed office in April 1865 after Lincoln's death, he brought his own agenda for the defeated South. Throughout his political career, Johnson had seen himself as a champion of poor white farmers in opposition to the wealthy planter class. A man of modest background, he had been elected U.S. senator from Tennessee in 1857. He alone among southern senators remained in Congress and loyal to the Union after 1861. Lincoln first appointed Johnson military governor of Tennessee when that state was captured by the Union in 1862 and then tapped him as his running mate for the election of 1864.

H. P. Moore/Collection of the New-York Historical Society, Neg. #37497

■ Residents of Edisto Island, one of the Sea Islands off the coast of South Carolina, pose with a U.S. government mule cart immediately after the Civil War. U.S. troops captured the island in November 1861. The following March, the government began to distribute to blacks the lands abandoned by their former masters. In October 1865, President Andrew Johnson halted the program. A group of angry and disappointed blacks appealed to the president, claiming, "This is our home, we have made these lands what they are." After meeting with the group, General Oliver O. Howard noted, "I am convinced that something must be done to give these people and others the prospect of homesteads."

Soon after he assumed the presidency, Johnson disappointed congressional Republicans who hoped that he would serve as a champion of the freedpeople. He welcomed back into the Union those states reorganized under Lincoln's Ten Percent Plan. He advocated denying the vote to wealthy Confederates, though he would allow individuals to come to the White House to beg the president for special pardons. Johnson also outlined a fairly lenient plan for readmitting the other rebel states into the Union. Poor whites would have the right to vote, but they must convene special state conventions that would renounce secession and accept the Thirteenth Amendment abolishing slavery. Further, they must repudiate all Confederate debts. The president opposed granting the vote to the former slaves; he believed that they should continue to toil as field workers for white landowners.

Initiated by presidential proclamation at the end of May 1865, the pardoning process revealed a great deal about Andrew Johnson as both a Southerner and a Republican politician.

462 PART 5 • DISUNION AND REUNION

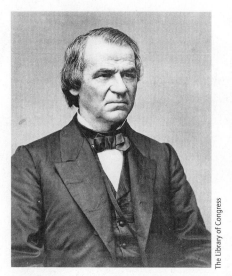

President Andrew Johnson.

He personally considered appeals from 15,000 men, all of whom were required to apply directly to the president for a pardon; these men included those who had served as high-ranking Confederate officials and who owned taxable property worth $20,000 or more. Of humble origins himself, Johnson relished the sight of the wealthiest Southerners nervously crowding his office and seeking his pardon—at times hundreds of men in a single day. With these pardons, Johnson aimed to humble a group of southern leaders he considered arrogant—he wanted to "punish and impoverish them," he said. He also hoped to win support for his own reelection from southern poor whites, men who approved of his effort to humiliate the planter elite. One former Tennessee politician who had known Johnson for many years believed that if "Johnson were a snake, he would lie in the grass to bite the heels of rich men's children."

While he was in office, Johnson sought to reassure Southerners that he believed blacks needed "the care and civilizing influence of dependence upon the white race." Indeed, many former rebels gradually came to see Johnson as their postwar political ally; they hoped that he would counter the power of what they called vengeful Yankee "fanatics." The former Confederate secretary of the treasury, Christopher Memminger, noted that Johnson "held up before us the hope of a 'white man's government' and it was natural that we should yield to our old prejudices."

Johnson also argued that individual states should make their own laws on black suffrage. Many Northerners agreed. Indeed, northern states seemed eager to impose upon the defeated South provisions that they themselves would not accept. In 1865, only five New England states (of all northern states) allowed blacks to vote. That year, three state referenda on the issue—in Minnesota, Wisconsin, and Connecticut—failed to win voter approval. Almost all northern Democrats opposed black suffrage, but many of their Republican neighbors shared the same views. During the summer of 1865, Pennsylvania Republicans proclaimed that any discussion of black voting rights was "heavy and premature."

Johnson failed to anticipate the speed and vigor with which former Confederate leaders would move to reassert their political authority. In addition, he did not gauge accurately the resentment of congressional Republicans, who thought his policies toward the defeated South were too forgiving. The southern states that took advantage of Johnson's reunification policies passed laws that instituted a system of near slavery. Referred to as **Black Codes,** they aimed to penalize "vagrant" blacks, defined as those who did not work in the fields for whites, and to deny blacks the right to vote, serve on juries, or in some cases even own land. The Black Code of Mississippi restricted the rights of a freedperson to "keep or carry fire-arms," ammunition, and knives and to "quit the service of his or her employer before the expiration of his or her term of service without good cause." The vagueness of this last provision threatened any blacks who happened not to be working under the supervision of whites at any given moment. People arrested under the Black Codes faced imprisonment or forced labor.

DOCUMENT

The Mississippi Black Code

At the end of the war, congressional Republicans were divided into two camps. Radicals wanted to use strong federal measures to advance black people's civil rights and economic independence. In contrast, moderates were more concerned with the free market and private property rights; they took a hands-off approach regarding former slaves. But members of both groups reacted with outrage to the Black Codes. Moreover, when the legislators returned to the Capitol in December 1865, they were in for a shock: among their new colleagues were four former Confederate generals, five colonels, and other high-ranking members of the Confederate elite, including former Vice President Alexander Stephens, now under indictment for treason. All of these rebels were duly elected senators and representatives from southern states. In a special session called for December 4, a joint committee of fifteen lawmakers (six senators and nine members of the House) voted to bar these men from Congress.

By January 1865, both houses of Congress had approved the Thirteenth Amendment to the Constitution, abolishing slavery. The necessary three-fourths of the states ratified the measure by the end of the year. However, President Johnson was becoming more openly defiant of his congressional foes who favored aggressive federal protection of black civil rights. He vetoed two crucial pieces of legislation: an extension and expansion of the Freedmen's Bureau and the Civil Rights Bill of 1866. This latter measure was an unprecedented piece of legislation. It called on the federal government—for the first time in history—to protect individual rights against the willful indifference of the states (as manifested, for example, in the Black Codes). Congress managed to override both vetoes by the summer of 1866.

In June of that year, Congress passed the Fourteenth Amendment. This amendment guaranteed the former slaves citizenship rights, punished states that denied citizens the right to vote, declared the former rebels ineligible for federal and state office, and voided Confederate debts. This amendment was the first to use gender-specific language, guarding against denying the vote "to any of the male inhabitants" of any state.

Even before the war ended, some northerners had moved south, and the flow increased in 1865. Black and white teachers volunteered to teach former slaves to read and write. Some white Northerners journeyed south to invest in land and become planters in the staple-crop economy. White southern critics called all these migrants **carpetbaggers.** This derisive term suggested that the Northerners hastily packed their belongings in rough bags made of carpet scraps—a popular form of luggage at the time—and then rushed south to take advantage of the region's devastation and confusion. To many freedpeople, whether they worked for a carpetbagger or a Southerner, laboring in the cotton fields was but a continuation of slavery.

Some former southern (white) Whigs, who had been reluctant secessionists, now found common ground with northern Republicans who supported government subsidies for railroads, banking institutions, and public improvements. This group consisted of some members of the humbled planter class as well as people of more modest means. Southern Democrats, who sneered at any alliances with the North, scornfully labeled these whites **scalawags** (the term referred to a scrawny, useless type of horse on the Scottish island of Scalloway).

Soon after the war's end, southern white vigilantes launched a campaign of violence and intimidation against freedpeople who dared to resist the demands of white planters and other employers. The Ku Klux Klan, begun by a group of Tennessee war veterans, soon became a white supremacist terrorist organization that spread to other states. In May 1866, violence initiated by white terrorists against blacks in Memphis, Tennessee, left forty-six freedpeople and two whites dead; in July, a riot in New Orleans claimed the lives of thirty-four blacks and three of their white allies. Vigilantes attacked blacks who tried to vote or to challenge planters who cheated their workers. Men in disguise broke into the homes of blacks at night, whipping and beating women as well as men. These bloody encounters demonstrated the lengths to which ex-Confederates would go to reassert their authority and defy the federal government.

Back in Washington, Johnson condemned the Fourteenth Amendment and traveled around the country, urging the states not to ratify it. He argued that policies related to black suffrage should be decided by the states. The president maintained that the time had come for reconciliation between the North and South. (The amendment would not be adopted until 1868.)

Congressional Republicans fought back. In the midterm election of November 1866, they won a two-thirds majority in both houses of Congress. These numbers allowed them to claim a mandate from their constituents and to override any future vetoes by the president. Moderates and radicals together prepared to bypass Johnson to shape their own reconstruction policies.

THE POSTBELLUM SOUTH'S LABOR PROBLEM

While policymakers maneuvered in Washington, black people throughout the postbellum (postwar) South aspired to labor for themselves and gain independence from white

A Southern Labor Contract

Interpreting History

The Library of Congress

■ After the Civil War, many rural southern blacks, such as those shown here, continued to toil in cotton fields owned by whites.

After the Civil War, many southern agricultural workers signed labor contracts. These contracts sought to control not only the output of laborers but also their lives outside the workplace.

On January 1, 1868, the planter John D. Williams assembled his workers for the coming year and presented them with a contract to sign. Williams owned a plantation in the lower Piedmont county of Laurens, South Carolina. He agreed to furnish "the said negroes" (that is, the three black men and two black women whose names were listed on the document) with mules and horses to be used for cultivating the land. The workers could receive their food, clothing, and medical care on credit. They were allowed to keep one-third of all the corn, sweet potatoes, wheat, cotton, oats, and molasses they produced.

overseers and landowners. Yet white landowners persisted in regarding blacks as field hands who must be coerced into working. With the creation of the Freedmen's Bureau in 1865, Congress aimed to form an agency that would mediate between these two groups. Bureau agents encouraged workers and employers to sign annual labor contracts designed to eliminate the last vestiges of the slave system. All over the South, freed men, women, and children would contract with an employer on January 1 of each year. They would agree to work for either a monthly wage, an annual share of the crop, or some combination of the two.

According to the Freedmen's Bureau, the benefits of the annual labor contract system were clear. Employers would have an incentive to treat their workers fairly—to offer a decent wage and refrain from physical punishment. Disgruntled workers could leave at the end of the year to work for a more reasonable landowner. In the postbellum South, however, labor relations were shaped not by federal decree but by a process of negotiation that pitted white landowners against blacks who possessed little but their own labor.

For instance, blacks along the Georgia and South Carolina coast were determined to cultivate the land on which their forebears had lived and died. They urged General Sherman to confiscate the land owned by rebels in the area. In response, in early 1865, Sherman issued Field Order Number 15, mandating that the Sea Islands and the coastal region south of

Presumably, they would pay their debts to Williams using proceeds from their share of the crop.

According to the contract, Williams's workers promised to

bind them Selves to be steady and attentive to there work at all times and to work at keeping in repair all the fences on Said plantation and assist in cuting and taking care of—all the grain crops on Said plantation and work by the direction of me [Williams] or my Agent. . . .

And should any of them depart from the farm or from any services at any time with out our approval they shall forfeit one dollar per day, for the first time and for the second time without good cause they shall forfeit all of their interest in the crop their to me the enjured person—they shall not be allowed to keep firearms or deadly wapons or ardent Spirits and they shall obey all lawful orders from me or my Agent and shall be honest—truthful—sober—civel—diligent in their business and for all wilful Disobedience of any lawful orders from me or my Agent drunkenness moral or legal misconduct want of respects or civility to me or my Agent or to my Family or any elce, I am permitted to discharge them forfeiting any claims upon me for any part of the crop. . . .

Moses Nathan	1 full hand
Jake Chappal	" "
Milly Williams	$\frac{1}{2}$ " "
Easter Williams	" "
Mack Williams	" "

At the end of the contract is this addition:

We the white labores now employed by John D. Williams on his white plains plantation have lisened and heard read the foregoing Contract on this sheet of paper assign equal for the black laborers employed by him on said place and we are perfectly Satisfied with it and heare by bind our selves to abide & be Governed & Controwed by it

Wm Wyatte	1 full hand
John Wyatte	1 full hand
Packingham Wyatte	$\frac{1}{2}$ " "
Franklin Wyatte	$\frac{1}{2}$ " "
R M Hughes	1 full hand
B G Pollard	1 full hand
George Washington Pollard	1 full hand

To sign the contract, all of the blacks and two of the whites "made their marks," signing with an "X" because they were illiterate.

QUESTIONS

1. *In what ways did sharecropping differ from wage labor?*

2. *Do you see evidence that family or kin members worked together on Williams's plantation?*

3. *What is the significance of the contract addendum signed by white laborers?*

Source: Rosser H. Taylor, "Postbellum Southern Rental Contracts" [from Furman University library, Greenville, South Carolina], *Agricultural History* 17 (1943): 122–123.

Charleston be divided into parcels of forty acres for individual freed families. He also decreed that the army might lend mules to these families to help them begin planting. Given the provisions of this order, many freed families came to expect that the federal government would grant them "forty acres and a mule."

As a result of Sherman's order, 20,000 former slaves proceeded to cultivate the property once owned by Confederates. Within a few months of the war's end, however, the War Department bowed to pressure from the white landowners and revoked the order. The War Department also provided military protection for whites to return and occupy their former lands. In response, a group of black men calling themselves Commissioners from Edisto Island (one of the Sea Islands) met in committee to protest to the Freedmen's Bureau what they considered a betrayal. Writing from the area in January 1866, one Freedmen's Bureau official noted that the new policy must be upheld but regretted that it had brought the freedpeople in "collision" with "U.S. forces."

In other cases, the Freedmen's Bureau opposed changes sought by African Americans, such as the ability of women to care for their children at home full-time. In April 1866, a white planter in Thomson, Georgia, wrote to a local Freedmen's Bureau official and complained that the black wives and mothers living on his land had refused to sign labor contracts. The planter explained, "Their husbands are at work, while they are nearly idle as it is possible for them to be, pretending to spin—knit or something that really amounts to nothing." These "idle" women posed a threat to plantation order, the white man asserted.

> Who should toil in the fields of the South? And under what conditions should they labor?

Women who stayed home to care for their families were hardly idle. Yet Freedmen's Bureau agents and white planters alike tended to define productive labor (among blacks) as work carried out under the supervision of a white man in the fields or a white woman in the kitchen. During the postwar period, a struggle ensued. Who should toil in the fields of the South? And under what conditions should they labor?

The physical devastation wrought by the war gave these questions heightened urgency. Most freedpeople understood that first and foremost they must find a way to provide for themselves. However, they thought of freedom in terms of welfare for their family rather than just for themselves as individuals. Men and women embraced the opportunity to live and work together as a unit; for many couples, their first act as free people was to legalize their marriage vows. Black women shunned the advice of Freedmen's Bureau agents and planters that they continue to pick cotton. These women withdrew from field labor whenever they could afford to do so. Enslaved women had been deprived of the opportunity to attend to family life. Now freedwomen sought to devote themselves to caring for their families.

During its brief life (1865 to 1868), the Freedmen's Bureau compiled a mixed record. The agency's most formidable challenge was its effort to usher in a new economic order in the South—one that relied on nonslave labor but also returned the region to prewar productivity levels in terms of planting and harvesting cotton. The Freedmen's Bureau established elementary schools and distributed rations to southerners who had remained loyal to the Union, blacks and whites alike. The Freedmen's Bureau's functions in the areas of education and labor represented a new and significant federal role in the realm of social welfare, yet the agency did not have the staff or money necessary to effect meaningful change. The individual agents represented a broad range of backgrounds, temperaments, and political ideas. Some were former abolitionists who considered northern-style free labor "the noblest principle on earth." These men tried to ensure safe and fair working arrangements for black men, women, and children. In contrast, some agents had little patience with the freedpeople's drive for self-sufficiency. While some bureau offices became havens for blacks seeking redress against abusive or fraudulent labor practices, others had little impact on the postwar political and economic landscape. For agents without means of transportation (a reliable horse), plantations scattered throughout the vast rural South remained outside their control. Because white landowners crafted the wording and specific provisions of labor contracts, the bureau agents who enforced such agreements often served the interests of employers rather than laborers.

DOCUMENT

Southern Skepticism of the Freedmen's Bureau (1866)

In fact, for the most part, postwar freedpeople pressed for their labor rights independently of the federal government. Their efforts took a dramatic form along the coastline of Georgia and South Carolina, where thousands of slaves had toiled in the muck-filled rice fields before the war. With the revocation of Sherman's Field Order Number 15, black laborers sought to negotiate with white landowners who wished to maintain rice cultivation in the region. Rice culture necessitated an intricate network of ditches, dams, and sluice gates; together these improvements amounted to a complicated hydraulic system. This system allowed for the periodic flooding of rice fields with fresh water from local canals and rivers. Resisting the heavy, hot, muddy work of conventional rice culture, and wishing to spend more time on their own crops, blacks forced landowners to institute labor-saving measures. These measures included the use of mules to pull rakes in order to clean out weed-choked ditches, and the use of wagons to carry rice from the fields to the barn. Some planters turned to other groups of workers—for example, Irish men who came out to the coast from the city of Savannah—whom they hired on a seasonal basis.

However, rice farming required year-round work to keep ditches, fences, and canals in good working order, jobs that seasonal workers could not or would not do. For their part, the freedpeople preferred to engage in subsistence farming and to fish and hunt to support their families. Gradually lowcountry planters realized they lacked the large, subordinate labor force that would make their rice competitive with the rice grown in other parts of the country and the world. In the low-country rice regions, then, black people's desire for economic autonomy, combined with the unhealthful and disagreeable nature of rice culture, transformed the local economy.

> *Freedpeople preferred to engage in subsistence farming and to fish and hunt to support their families.*

In the cotton regions of the South, freedpeople resisted the near-slavery system of gang labor that planters tried to enforce right after the war. Instead, extended families came together in groups called squads to negotiate collectively with landowners. Gradually, squads gave way to sharecropping families. The outlines of share-cropping, a system that defined southern cotton production until well into the twentieth century, were visible just a few years after the Civil War. Poor families, black and white, con-tracted annually with landlords, who advanced them supplies, such as crop seed, mules, plows, food, and clothing. Fathers directed the labor of their children in the fields. At the end of the year, many families remained indebted to their employer and, thus, entitled to nothing and obliged to work another year in the hope of repaying the debt. If a sharecropper's demeanor or work habits displeased the landlord, the family faced eviction.

DOCUMENT

A Sharecrop Contract

Single women with small children were especially vulnerable to the whims of landlords in the postbellum period. Near Greensboro, North Carolina, for example, when planter Presley George Sr. settled the year's accounts with his field worker Polly at the end of 1865, Polly was charged $69 for corn, cloth, thread, and board for a child who did not work. By George's calculations, Polly had earned exactly $69 for the labor she and her three children (two sons and a daughter) performed in the course of the year, leaving her no cash of her own. Under these harsh conditions, freedpeople looked to each other for support and strength.

BUILDING FREE COMMUNITIES

Independence in the workplace was not the only concern of freedpeople. Soon after the war's end, southern blacks set about organizing themselves as an effective political force and as free communities devoted to their own social and educational welfare. Differences among blacks based on income, jobs, culture, and skin color at times inhibited communal institution building. Some black communities found themselves divided by social status, with blacks who had been free before the war (including many literate and skilled light-skinned men) assuming leadership over illiterate field hands. In New Orleans, a combination of factors contributed to class divisions among people of African heritage. During the antebellum period, light-skinned freedpeople of color, many of whom spoke French, were much more likely to possess property and a formal education than were enslaved people, who were dark-skinned English speakers. After the Civil War, the more privileged group pressed for public accommodations laws, which would open the city's theaters, opera, and expensive restau-rants to all blacks for the first time. However, black churches and social organizations remained segregated according to class.

For the most part, postbellum black communities united around the principle that free-dom from slavery should also mean full citizenship rights: the ability to vote, own land, and educate their children. These rights must be enforced by federal firepower: "a military occupa-tion will be absolutely necessary," declared the blacks of Norfolk, "to protect the white Union men of the South, as well as ourselves." Freedpeople in some states allied themselves with white yeoman farmers who had long resented the political power of the great planters and now saw an opportunity to use state governments as agents of democratization and economic reform.

LISTEN

"Free at Last"

TABLE 15.1

Comparison of Black and White Household Structure in 27 Cotton-Belt Counties, 1870, 1880, 1900

1870 (N = 534)

Single Person %	Nuclear %	Ext. %	Aug. %	Ext./Aug. %	(Unrelated Adults %)	Total	
3.1	80.7	14.4	1.4	.3	.3	290	**Black**
2.1	71.3	7.4	17.6	1.2	.4	244	**White**
2.6	76.4	11.0	8.8	.7	.4	534	

1880 (N = 672)

Single Person %	Nuclear %	Ext. %	Aug. %	Ext./Aug. %	(Unrelated Adults %)	Total	
3.7	74.2	13.6	5.9	1.7	.8	353	**Black**
3.1	62.7	13.5	15.7	5.0	.0	319	**White**
3.4	68.8	13.5	10.6	3.3	.4	672	

1900 (N = 643)

Single Person %	Nuclear %	Ext. %	Aug. %	Ext./Aug. %	(Unrelated Adults %)	Total	
5.7	64.9	22.9	4.0	1.7	.8	353	**Black**
3.4	65.2	19.0	10.7	1.7	.0	290	**White**
4.7	65.0	21.2	7.0	1.7	.5	643	

Single person: one person living alone.
Nuclear: father, mother, and children.
Ext.: extended family consisting of parents, children, and kin.
Aug.: augmented household consisting of family and nonfamily members (boarders, servants, hired hands).
Ext./Aug.: combination of extended and augmented.
Unrelated adults: more than one unrelated adult living together.

Source: Jacqueline Jones, *Labor of Love, Labor of Sorrow: Black Women, Work and the Family from Slavery to the Present* (1985). Based on a sample of households (in selected cotton staple counties in Alabama, Florida, Georgia, Louisiana, Mississippi, North Carolina, South Carolina, and Texas) listed in the 1870, 1880, and 1900 federal population manuscript censuses.

Networks of freedpeople formed self-help organizations. Like the sponsors of the Savannah Education Association, blacks throughout the South formed committees to raise funds and hire teachers for neighborhood schools. Small Georgia towns, such as Cuthbert, Albany, Cave Spring, and Thomasville, with populations no greater than a few hundred, raised up to $70 per month and contributed as much as $350 each for the construction of school buildings. Funds came from the proceeds of fairs, bazaars, and bake sales; subscriptions raised by local school boards; and tuition fees. In the cash-starved postbellum South, these amounts represented a great personal and group sacrifice for the cause of education.

All over the South, black families charted their own course. They elected to take in orphans and elderly kin, pool resources with neighbors, and arrange for mothers to stay home with their children. These choices challenged the power of former slaveholders and the influence of Freedmen's Bureau agents and northern missionaries and teachers. At the same time, in seeking to attend to their families and to provide for themselves, southern blacks resembled members of other mid-nineteenth-century laboring classes who valued family ties over the demands of employers and landlords.

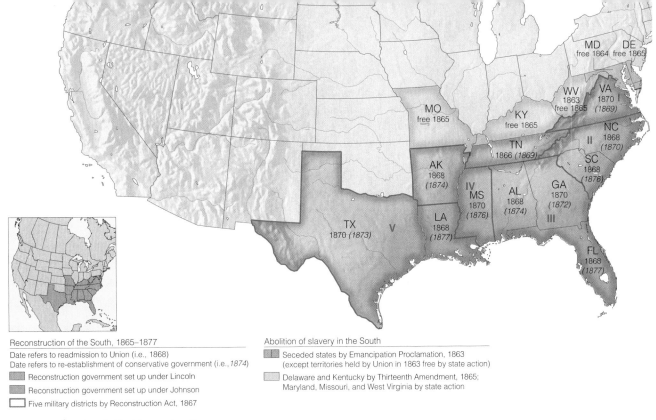

Reconstruction of the South, 1865–1877

Date refers to readmission to Union (i.e., 1868)
Date refers to re-establishment of conservative government (i.e., *1874*)

- Reconstruction government set up under Lincoln
- Reconstruction government set up under Johnson
- Five military districts by Reconstruction Act, 1867

Abolition of slavery in the South

- Seceded states by Emancipation Proclamation, 1863 (except territories held by Union in 1863 free by state action)
- Delaware and Kentucky by Thirteenth Amendment, 1865; Maryland, Missouri, and West Virginia by state action

■ **M A P 1 5 . 1   Radical Reconstruction**

Four of the former Confederate states—Louisiana, Arkansas, Tennessee, and Virginia—were reorganized under President Lincoln's Ten Percent Plan in 1864. Neither this plan nor the proposals of Lincoln's successor, Andrew Johnson, provided for the enfranchisement of the former slaves. In 1867, Congress established five military districts in the South and demanded that newly reconstituted state governments implement universal manhood suffrage. By 1870, all of the former Confederate states had rejoined the Union, and by 1877 all of those states had installed conservative (i.e., Democratic) governments.

Tangible signs of emerging black communities infuriated most southern whites. A schoolhouse run by blacks proved threatening in a society where most white children had little opportunity to receive an education. Black communities were also quick to form their own churches, rather than continue to occupy an inferior place in white churches. Other sights proved equally unsettling: on a main street in Charleston, an armed black soldier marching proudly or a black woman wearing a fashionable hat and veil, the kind favored by white women of the planter class. These developments help to account for the speed with which whites organized themselves in vigilante groups, aiming to preserve "the supremacy of the white race in this Republic."

CONGRESSIONAL RECONSTRUCTION: THE RADICALS' PLAN

The rise of armed white supremacist groups in the South helped spur congressional Republicans to action. On March 2, 1867, a coalition led by two radicals, Senator Charles Sumner of Massachusetts and Congressman Thaddeus Stevens of Pennsylvania, prodded Congress to pass the Reconstruction Act of 1867. The purpose of this measure was to purge the South of disloyalty once and for all. The act stripped thousands of former Confederates of voting rights. The former Confederate states would not be readmitted to the Union until they had ratified the Fourteenth Amendment and written new constitutions that guaranteed black men the right to vote. The South (with the exception of Tennessee, which had ratified the Fourteenth Amendment in 1866) was divided into five military districts. Federal troops were stationed throughout the region. These troops were charged with protecting Union personnel and supporters in the South and with restoring order in the midst of regional political and economic upheaval.

Reconstruction

Congress passed two additional acts specifically intended to secure congressional power over the president. The intent of the Tenure of Office Act was to prevent the president from dismissing Secretary of War Edwin Stanton, a supporter of the radicals. The other measure, the Command of the Army Act, required the president to seek approval for all military orders from General Ulysses S. Grant, the army's senior officer. Grant also was a supporter of the Republicans. Both of these acts probably violated the separation of powers doctrine as put forth in the Constitution. Together, they would soon precipitate a national crisis.

During the Reconstruction period, approximately 2,000 black men of the emerging southern Republican party served as local elected officials, sheriffs, justices of the peace, tax collectors, and city councilors. Many of these leaders were of mixed ancestry, and many had been free before the war. They came in disproportionate numbers from the ranks of literate men, such as clergy, teachers, and skilled artisans. In Alabama, Florida, Louisiana, Mississippi, and South Carolina, black men constituted a majority of the voting public.

Some states made substantial gains in terms of integrating blacks into local systems of law enforcement and justice. By 1872, Florida, Arkansas, Louisiana, and South Carolina had elected black judges. Black men served as city chiefs of police in Tallahassee, Florida, and Little Rock, Arkansas, and black men made up half the ranks of the police force in Montgomery, Alabama, and Vicksburg, Mississippi. Whites found these developments profoundly unsettling. One white attorney observed that calling black jurors "gentlemen of the jury" was "the severest blow I have felt."

Throughout the South, 600 black men won election to state legislatures. Still, nowhere did blacks control a state government, although they did predominate in South Carolina's lower house. Sixteen black Southerners were elected to the U.S. Congress during Reconstruction. Most of those elected to Congress in the years immediately after the war were freeborn. However, among the nine men elected for the first time after 1872, six were former slaves. All of these politicians exemplified the desire among southern blacks to become active, engaged citizens.

■ This drawing by famous political cartoonist Thomas Nast depicts the first black members of Congress. Left to right, front row: Senator Hiram Revels of Mississippi (the first African American to serve in the U.S. Senate), Representatives Benjamin S. Turner of Alabama, Josiah T. Walls of Florida, Joseph H. Rainey of South Carolina, Robert B. Elliott of South Carolina. Back row: Representatives Robert G. DeLarge of South Carolina, Jefferson Long of Georgia.

THE FIRST COLORED SENATOR AND REPRESENTATIVES.

In the 41st and 42nd Congress of the United States.

Newly reconstructed southern state legislatures provided for public school systems, fairer taxation methods, bargaining rights of plantation laborers, racially integrated public transportation and accommodations, and public works projects, especially railroads. All new state constitutions guaranteed black civil rights and most recognized the right of married women to hold property in their own names. With the exception of Louisiana, every new southern state constitution included a household exemption—from $1,500 to $5,000 worth of property that could not be seized by creditors. Many of these Republican-dominated legislatures were shaped by the drive to further economic development in the largely rural, agricultural South. Black and white Republicans agreed that tax breaks and subsidies to railroads would provide jobs and update the South's transportation system.

Nevertheless, the legislative coalitions forged between northerners and southerners, blacks and whites, were uneasy and, in many cases, less than productive. Southern Democrats (and later, historians sympathetic to them) claimed that Reconstruction governments were uniquely corrupt, with some carpetbaggers, scalawags, and freedpeople vying for kickbacks from railroad and construction magnates. In fact, whenever state legislatures sought to promote business interests, they opened the door to the bribery of public officials. In this respect, northern as well as southern politicians were vulnerable to charges of corruption. In the long run, southern Democrats cared less about charges of legislative corruption than about the growing political power of local black Republican party organizations.

In Washington in early 1868, President Johnson forced a final showdown with Congress. He replaced several high military officials with more conservative men. He also fired Secretary of War Stanton, in apparent violation of the Tenure of Office Act. Shortly thereafter, in February, a newly composed House Reconstruction Committee impeached Johnson for ignoring the act, and the Senate began his trial on March 30. The president and Congress were locked in an extraordinary battle for political power.

The final vote was thirty-five senators against Johnson, one vote short of the necessary two-thirds of all senators' votes needed for conviction. Nineteen senators voted to acquit Johnson of the charges. Nevertheless, to win acquittal, he had had to promise moderates that he would not stand in the way of congressional plans for Reconstruction. Johnson essentially withdrew from policymaking in the spring of 1868. That November, with Republicans urging Northerners to "vote as you shot" (that is, to cast ballots against the former Confederates), Ulysses S. Grant was elected president.

Political reunion was an uneven process, but one that gradually eroded the newly won rights of former slaves in many southern states. By the end of 1868, Arkansas, North Carolina, South Carolina, Louisiana, Tennessee, Alabama, and Florida had met congressional conditions for readmission to the Union, and two years later, Mississippi, Virginia, Georgia, and Texas followed. The Fifteenth Amendment, passed by Congress in 1869 and ratified by the necessary number of states a year later, granted all black men the right to vote. However, in some states, such as Louisiana and Georgia, reunification gave Democrats license to engage in wholesale election fraud and violence toward freed men and women. In 1870–1871, a congressional inquiry into the Klan exposed pervasive and grisly assaults on Republican schoolteachers, preachers, and prospective voters, black and white. The Klan also targeted men and women who refused to work like slaves in the fields.

In April 1871, Congress passed the Ku Klux Klan Act, which punished conspiracies intended to deny rights to citizens. But Klan violence and intimidation had already taken their toll on Republican voting strength.

Resenting the political power of both black and white Republicans, Louisiana Democrats unleashed a wave of violence during the 1875 elections. When the state's governor appealed to

TABLE 15.2			
The Election of 1868			
Candidate	**Political Party**	**Popular Vote (%)**	**Electoral Vote**
Ulysses S. Grant	Republican	52.7	214
Horatio Seymour	Democratic	47.3	80

President Grant for military troops to quell the bloodshed, Grant replied: "The whole public are tired out with these autumnal outbreaks in the South, and the great majority now are ready to condemn any interference on the part of the Government." In the absence of law enforcement, the Democrats swept to victory in 1875.

The library of Congress

■ This formal portrait of Blanche K. Bruce conveys his status as a wealthy and powerful politician.

THE REMARKABLE CAREER OF BLANCHE K. BRUCE

The career of Blanche K. Bruce reveals the opportunities and limitations faced by an emerging black leadership during Reconstruction. Born a slave in 1841, this light-skinned mulatto spent much of his childhood working on a tobacco farm in central Missouri. He learned to read at an early age and acquired an interest in plantation management. After the war began, Bruce managed to escape from slavery. He eventually settled in Hannibal, Missouri, where he established the first school for blacks and worked as a printer's helper. In 1866, he enrolled in Oberlin College in Ohio. Though he worked hard, sawing wood to pay tuition, he could not afford to continue his formal education.

In 1867, Bruce attended a political rally in Mississippi. He became convinced that the state, especially the Delta region, afforded both economic and political opportunity. He quickly rose up the local political ranks, starting as voter registrar in Tallahatchie County, serving as sergeant at arms of the state legislature, and then tax assessor, sheriff, and member of the board of levee commissioners for Bolivar County. Bruce soon earned a reputation for fairness and honesty in public service. In 1872, he served simultaneously as education superintendent, sheriff, and tax collector in Bolivar County. He had established himself as the most powerful black politician in the Delta. Meanwhile, Bruce began to buy houses and parcels of land in the county; by the 1880s, he was a wealthy man.

Blanche K. Bruce won support from the Republican-dominated state legislature in his bid to run for the U.S. Senate in 1874; a year later he was elected to that seat. As a U.S. senator, Bruce demonstrated an interest in navigation improvements and flood control of the Mississippi River. He was one of a few legislators to condemn discrimination against Chinese immigrants in California, expressing "a large confidence in the strength and assimilative power of [our] American institutions." When he lost his Senate seat in 1881, Bruce and his wife moved to Washington, D.C. There he held a series of federal patronage jobs and became a member of the city's African American elite. Ultimately, his rise to wealth and political power distanced him from poorer blacks. His four-decade odyssey from slavery to the fashionable salons of the nation's capital revealed the promise, as well as the limitations, of Radical Reconstruction.

During Reconstruction, the struggle over the South showed that different groups of Americans had different priorities for former Confederates and former slaves. Depending on their political leanings, people disagreed over the way the former Confederate states should eventually be readmitted to the Union. However, most Republicans saw the reconstruction of the South as only one step in a sweeping effort to weld the whole country into a single economic, political, and cultural unit.

Claiming Territory for the Union

■ *What human and environmental forces impeded the Republican goal of western expansion?*

While blacks and whites, northerners and southerners clashed over power in the South, poet Walt Whitman celebrated the "manly and courageous instincts" that propelled a brave, adventurous people west. Whitman hailed the march across the prairies and over the mountains as a cavalcade of progress. He and other Americans believed that the postbellum migration fulfilled a mission of national regeneration begun by the Civil War. Kansas's population grew by 240 percent in the 1860s, Nebraska's by 355 percent.

To unite the entire country was the Republican ideal. The railroads in particular served as vehicles of national integration. When the Central Pacific and Union Pacific Railroads met at Promontory Point, Utah, in 1869, the hammering of the spike that joined the two roads produced a telegraphic signal received simultaneously on both coasts, setting off a national celebration.

Meanwhile, regular units of United States cavalry, including two regiments of blacks, were launching attacks on Indians on the Plains, in the Northwest, and in the Southwest. Between 1865 and 1890, U.S. military forces conducted a dozen separate campaigns against western Indian peoples and met Indian warriors in battle or attacked Indian settlements in more than 1,000 engagements. In contrast to African Americans, who adamantly demanded their rights as American citizens, defiant western Indians battled a government to which, they steadfastly maintained, they owed no allegiance.

■ At Promontory Point near Ogden, Utah, workers joined the tracks linking the Central Pacific (its wood-burning locomotive, *Jupiter,* is on the left) with the Union Pacific (whose coal-burning engine No. 119 is on the right). This photo was taken during the May 10, 1869, celebration marking the completion of the transcontinental railroad. According to one eyewitness, the crowd included Indians, Chinese and Irish immigrants, European Americans, and Mexicans "grouped in picturesque confusion." Yet this official photo shows little evidence of the Chinese workers who helped engineer and build the Central Pacific line.

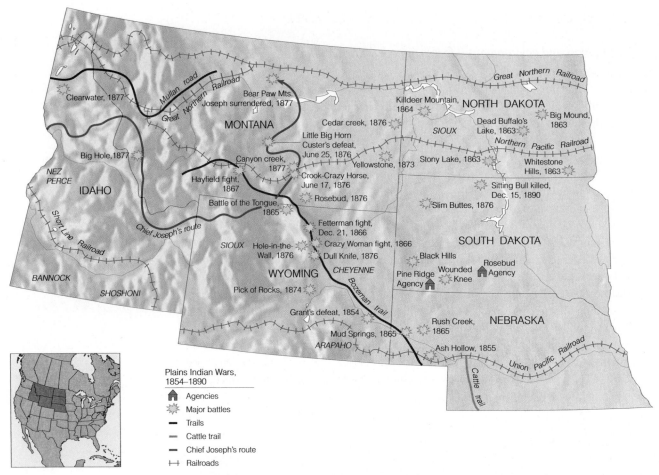

Plains Indian Wars,
1854–1890

🏠 Agencies
✸ Major battles
— Trails
— Cattle trail
— Chief Joseph's route
⊢⊣ Railroads

■ **MAP 15.2 Plains Indian Wars, 1854–1890**

Between 1854 and 1890, many of the conflicts between Indians and U.S. troops occurred along either railroad lines or trails used by European American settlers. For example, the Sioux, Cheyenne, and Arapaho fiercely resisted travelers along the Bozeman Trail running from Colorado to Montana.

FEDERAL MILITARY CAMPAIGNS AGAINST WESTERN INDIANS

In 1871, the U.S. government renounced the practice of seeking treaties with various Indian groups. This change in policy opened the way for a more aggressive effort to subdue native populations. In 1848, the United States had acquired a vast amount of western territory as a result of the Mexican-American War. As a result, the U.S. government abandoned its policy of pushing Indians ever farther westward. Instead, officials expanded the reservation system, an effort begun in the antebellum period to confine specific Indian groups to specific territories.

On the Plains, clashes between Indians and U.S. soldiers persisted after the Civil War. In 1867, at Medicine Lodge Creek in southern Kansas, the United States signed a treaty with an alliance of Comanche, Kiowa, Cheyenne, Arapaho, and Plains Apache. This treaty could not long withstand the provocation posed by wagon-train trails, such as the Bozeman, and the railroad. The year before, the Seventh U.S. Cavalry, under the command of Lieutenant Colonel George Custer, had been formed to ward off Indian attacks on the Union Pacific, snaking its way across the central Plains westward from Kansas and Nebraska. In November 1868, Custer destroyed a Cheyenne settlement on the Washita River, in present-day Oklahoma. The settlement's leader was Black Kettle, who had brought his people to reservation territory after the Sand Creek Massacre in Colorado in 1864. Custer's men murdered women and children, burned tipis, and destroyed 800 horses. Sickened by the scene, one

Two Artists Memorialize the Battle of Little Big Horn

Kicking Bear, *Battle of Little Big Horn*, c.1890. Courtesy of the Southwest Museum of the American Indian, Autry National Center, Los Angeles (1026.G.1)

Bettmann/CORBIS

Envisioning History

These pictures both portray the Battle of Little Big Horn in June 1876. In that clash, Lieutenant Colonel George Custer and his force of 264 U.S. soldiers attacked 2,500 Sioux and Cheyenne on the banks of the Little Big Horn River in Montana. During the battle, often referred to as "Custer's last stand," the Indians killed all of Custer's troops. The illustration below is from a book celebrating the life of Custer, which was published soon after the battle. At the time, the nation was in the midst of commemorating the centennial of its birth.

The picture above, a painting completed in 1890 by the Sioux artist Kicking Bear, also memorializes the battle. The figure in yellow buckskin at the left is Custer. In the upper-left corner are ghostlike figures, in the form of outlines of human shapes, meant to represent the spirits of the dead. At the center of the painting, Kicking Bear placed the figures of Sitting Bull, Rain-in-the-Face, Crazy Horse, and himself.

QUESTIONS

1. What are the differences in the composition of these two pictures? What are the similarities?

2. What is the significance of the term "Custer's last stand," and how is that term illustrated here?

3. What was the larger national context in which each of these artistic renderings was completed? How did that context shape the way each artist chose to portray the battle?

4. How do you account for the differences in the way horses are portrayed in each picture?

---

army officer later wrote sarcastically of the "daring dash" on the part of "heroes of a bloody day." The soldiers left piles of corpses scattered among the smoldering ruins of the village.

A series of peace delegations to Washington, several led by Red Cloud of the Sioux, produced much curiosity among whites but no end to the slaughter of people or animals in the West. Indians continued to attack the surveyors, supply caravans, and military escorts that preceded the railroad work crews. Lamenting the loss of his people's hunting grounds to the railroad, Red Cloud said, "The white children have surrounded me and have left me nothing but an island."

The Apache managed to elude General George Crook until 1875. Crook employed some of these Apache to track down the war chief Geronimo of the Chiricahua. Like many other

Geronimo and Natiche Surrender (1886)

Indian leaders, Geronimo offered both religious and military guidance to his people. He believed that a spirit would protect him from the white man's bullets and from the arrows of Indians in league with government troops. Yet Geronimo was tricked into an initial surrender in 1877, and he was held in irons for several months before gaining release and challenging authorities for another nine years.

In 1874, Custer took his cavalry into the Black Hills of the Dakotas. Supposedly, the 1868 Treaty of Fort Laramie had rendered this land off-limits to whites. Custer's mission was to offer protection for the surveyors of the Northern Pacific Railroad and to force Indians onto reservations as stipulated in the 1868 treaty. However, the officer lost no time trumpeting the fact that Indian lands were filled with gold. This report prompted a rush to the Black Hills, lands sacred to the Sioux. Within two years, 15,000 gold miners had illegally descended on Indian lands to seek their fortunes. The federal government proposed to buy the land, but leaders of the Sioux, including Red Cloud, Spotted Tail, and Sitting Bull, spurned the offer. "The Black Hills belong to me," declared Sitting Bull. "If the whites try to take them, I will fight."

During the morning of June 25, 1876, Custer and his force of 264 soldiers attacked a Sun Dance gathering of 2,500 Sioux and Cheyenne on the banks of the Little Big Horn River in Montana. Custer foolishly launched his attack without adequate backup, and he and all his men were easily overwhelmed and killed by Indian warriors, led by the Oglala Sioux Crazy Horse and others. Reacting to this defeat, U.S. military officials reduced the Lakota Sioux and Cheyenne to wardship status, ending their autonomy.

"The Black Hills belong to me," declared Sitting Bull. "If the whites try to take them, I will fight."

Indians throughout the West maintained their distinctive ways of life during these turbulent times. Horse holdings, so crucial for hunting, trading, and fighting, varied from group to group, with the Crow wealthy in relation to their Central Plains neighbors the Oglala and the Arikara. Plains and Plateau peoples engaged in a lively trading system. They exchanged horses and their trappings (bridles and blankets) for eastern goods such as kettles, guns, and ammunition. Despite their differences in economy, these groups held similar religious beliefs about an all-powerful life force that governed the natural world. People, plants, and animals were all part of the same order.

Even in the midst of brutal repression, Indian cultural traditions survived and in some cases flourished. On the West Central Plains and the Plateau, among the Crow, Shoshone, Nez Perce, and other tribes, women developed a new, distinctive style of seed beadwork characterized by variations of triangular patterns. These designs, made of beads selected for their quality and consistency, adorned leggings, gauntlets, and belt pouches. In these ways, the decorative arts were endowed with great symbolic meaning. When a wife embellished moccasins with patterns signifying her husband's military achievements, handicrafts assumed political as well as artistic significance.

THE POSTWAR WESTERN LABOR PROBLEM

In 1865, the owners of the Central Pacific Railroad seemed poised for one of the great engineering feats of the nineteenth century. In the race eastward from California, they constructed trestles spanning vast chasms, and roadbeds traversing mountains and deserts. Government officials in Washington were eager to subsidize the railroad. What the owners lacked was a dependable labor force. The Irish workers who began the line in California struck for higher wages in compensation for brutal, dangerous work. These immigrants dropped their shovels and hammers at the first word of a gold strike nearby—or far away. As a result, in 1866 the Central Pacific decided to tap into a vast labor source by importing thousands of Chinese men from their native Guandong province.

The Chinese toiled to extend the railroad tracks eastward from Sacramento, California, up to ten miles a day in the desert, only a few feet a day in the rugged Sierra Nevada Mountains. In nerve-wracking feats of skill, they lowered themselves in woven baskets to implant nitroglycerine explosives in canyon walls. Chinese laborers toiled through snowstorms and blistering heat

■ Chinese construction workers labor on the Central Pacific Railroad, c. 1868. Many Chinese immigrants toiled as indentured laborers, indebted to Chinese merchant creditors who paid for their passage to California. Isolated in all-male work camps, crews of railroad workers retained their traditional dress, language, and diet. After the completion of the transcontinental railroad in 1869, some immigrants returned to China and others dispersed to small towns and cities throughout the West.

Carleton Watkins/Union Pacific Museum

to blast tunnels and cut passes through granite mountains. With the final linking of the railroad in Utah in 1869, many Chinese sought work elsewhere in the West.

Signed in 1868, the Burlingame Treaty, named for Anson Burlingame, an American envoy to China, had supposedly guaranteed government protection for Chinese immigrants (most of whom were men) as visitors, traders, or permanent residents within the United States. Yet the treaty did not stop U.S. employers, landlords, and government officials from discriminating against the Chinese.

By 1870, 40,000 Chinese lived in California and represented one-quarter of the state's wage-earners. They found work in the cigar, woolen-goods, and boot and shoe factories of San Francisco; in the gold mining towns, now as laundry operators rather than as miners as they had before the Civil War; and in the fields as agricultural laborers. White workers complained of unfair competition from this Asian group that was becoming increasingly integrated into the region's economy.

Responding to these complaints, in 1870 Congress passed the Page Act. The act was intended to determine whether immigration from "China, Japan, or any Oriental country, is free and voluntary." Besides prohibiting Chinese forced laborers from entering the country, the Page Act prohibited the entry of any women who were prostitutes. This law placed the burden on Chinese women immigrants to prove that they were not prostitutes, slowing the immigration of single women as well as those married to Chinese men already in the country.

By this time, Hispanic workers had become the primary unskilled labor force in Los Angeles and surrounding areas. These workers were employed in the developing urban and service economies of southern California. Another labor group, California Indians, remained trapped in the traditional agricultural economy of unskilled labor. Whites appropriated Indian land and forced many men, women, and children to work as wage-earners for large landowners. Deprived of their familiar hunting and gathering lands, and wracked by disease and starvation, California Indians suffered a drastic decline in their numbers by 1870, from 100,000 to 30,000 in twenty years.

By the early 1870s, western manufacturers were faltering under the pressure of cheaper goods imported from the East by rail. At the same time, the growth of fledgling gigantic agricultural businesses opened new avenues of trade and commerce. Located in an arc surrounding the San Francisco Bay, large ("bonanza") wheat farmers produced huge crops and exported the grain to the East Coast and to England. These enterprises stimulated the building of wharves and railroad trunk lines and encouraged technological innovation in threshing and harvesting. Western enterprises had a growing demand for labor, whatever its skin color or nationality.

LAND USE IN AN EXPANDING NATION

The Union's triumph in 1865 prompted new conflicts and deepened long-standing ones over the use of the land in a rich, sprawling country. In the South, staple-crop planters began to share political power with an emerging elite, men who owned railroads and textile mills. Despairing of ever achieving antebellum levels of labor efficiency, some landowners turned to mining the earth and the forests for saleable commodities. These products, obtained through extraction, included phosphate (used in producing fertilizer), timber, coal, and turpentine. Labor in extractive industries complemented labor in the plantation economy. Sharecroppers alternated between tilling cotton fields in the spring and harvesting the crop in the fall, while seeking employment in sawmills and coal mines in the winter and summer.

As European Americans settled in the West and Southwest, they displaced natives who had been living there for generations. For example, the U.S. court system determined who could legally claim property. Western courts also decided whether natural resources such as water, land, timber, and fish and game constituted property that could be owned by private interests. In the Southwest, European American settlers, including soldiers who had come to fight Indians and then stayed, continued to place Mexican land titles at risk. Citing prewar precedents, American courts favored the claims of recent squatters over those of long-standing residents. In 1869, with the death of her husband (who had served as a general in the Union army), Maria Amparo Ruiz de Burton saw the large ranch they had worked together near San Diego slip out of her control. The first Spanish-speaking woman to be published in English in the United States, Ruiz de Burton was a member of the Hispanic elite. Nevertheless, she had little political power. California judges backed the squatters who occupied the ranch.

As they controlled more land and assumed public office, some European Americans in the Southwest exploited their political connections and economic power. In the process, they managed to wield great influence over people and vast amounts of natural resources. In the 1870s, the so-called Santa Fe Ring wrested more than 80 percent of the original Spanish grants of land from

■ With this 1870 photograph, the Kansas Pacific Railroad advertised the opportunity for western travelers to shoot buffalo from the comfort and safety of their railroad car. The company's official taxidermist shows off his handiwork. Railroad expansion facilitated the exploitation of natural resources while promoting tourism.

Robert Benecke, photographer. DeGolyer Library, Southern Methodist University, Dallas, Texas, Ag 1982.86.60

Spanish-speaking landholders in New Mexico. An alliance of European American lawyers, businesspeople, and politicians, the Santa Fe Ring defrauded families and kin groups of their land titles and speculated in property to make a profit. Whereas many ordinary Hispanic settlers saw land—with its crops, pasture, fuel, building materials, and game—as a source of livelihood, the Santa Fe Ring saw land primarily as a commodity to be bought and sold.

Seemingly overnight, boom towns sprang up wherever minerals or timber beckoned: southern Arizona and the Rocky Mountains west of Denver, Virginia City in western Nevada, the Idaho-Montana region, and the Black Hills of South Dakota. In all these places, increasing numbers of workers operated sophisticated kinds of machinery, such as rock crushers, and labored for wages. When the vein of ore was exhausted or the forests depleted, the towns went bust.

Railroads facilitated not only the mining of minerals but also the growth of the cattle-ranching industry. By 1869, a quarter of a million cattle were grazing in Colorado Territory. Rail connections between the Midwest and East made it profitable for Texas ranchers to pay cowboys to drive their herds of long-horned steers to Abilene, Ellsworth, Wichita, or Dodge City, Kansas, for shipment to stockyards in Chicago or St. Louis. Large meatpackers, such as Swift and Armour, prepared the carcasses for the eastern market.

Cattle drives were huge; an estimated 10 million animals were herded north from Texas alone between 1865 and 1890. They offered employment to all kinds of men with sufficient skills and endurance. Among the cowhands were African American horsebreakers and gunmen and Mexicans skilled in the use of the *reata* (lasso). Blacks made up about 25 percent and Hispanics about 15 percent of all cowboy outfits. Tracing the evolution of the Chisholm Trail, which linked southern Texas to Abilene, from Indian path to commercial route, one observer wrote in 1874, "So many cattle have been driven over the trail in the last few years that a broad highway is tread out, looking much like a national highway." Yet this new "national highway" traversed Indian Territory (present-day Oklahoma), lands supposedly promised to Indians forever.

WATCH

Cowboys and Cattle

In knitting regional economies together, federal land policies were crucial to the Republican vision of a developing nation. Yet a series of land use acts had a mixed legacy. The Mineral Act of 1866 granted title to millions of acres of mineral-rich land to mining companies, a gift from the federal government to private interests. In 1866, Congress passed the Southern Homestead Act to help blacks acquire land, but the measure accomplished little and was repealed in 1876. The Timber Culture Act of 1873 allotted 160 acres to individuals in selected western states if they agreed to plant one-fourth of the acreage with trees. Four years later, the Desert Land Act provided cheap land if buyers irrigated at least part of their parcels.

The exploitation of western resources raised many legal questions: Must ranchers pay for the prairies their cattle grazed on and the trails they followed to market? How could one "own" a stampeding buffalo herd or a flowing river? What was the point of holding title to a piece of property if only the timber, oil, water, or minerals (but not the soil) were of value? The Apex Mining Act of 1872 sought to address at least some of these issues. This law legalized traditional mining practices in the West by validating titles approved by local courts. According to the law, a person who could locate the apex of a vein (its point closest to the surface) could lay claim to the entire vein beneath the surface. The measure contributed to the wholesale destruction of certain parts of the western landscape as mining companies blasted their way through mountains and left piles of rocks in their wake. It also spurred thousands of lawsuits as claimants argued over what constituted an apex or a vein.

> *The Mineral Act of 1866 granted title to millions of acres of mineral-rich land to mining companies.*

It was during this period that a young Scottish-born naturalist named John Muir began to explore the magnificent canyons and mountains of California. Viewing nature as a means for regenerating the human spirit, Muir emphasized a deep appreciation of the natural world. He contrasted nature's majesty with the artificial landscape created by and for humans. In the wilderness, there is nothing "truly dead or dull, or any trace of what in manufactories is called

Colorado Historical Society (CHS.J 2067)

■ Chicago photographer Thomas J. Hine titled this stereograph "Old Faithful in Action, Fire Hole Basin." It is the first photograph of the eruption of the famous Yellowstone geyser. Costing 15–25 cents each, stereographs were a popular form of entertainment in middle-class households beginning in the 1860s. The stereoscope merged two identical photos to form a single three-dimensional image. Widely distributed stereographs of scenic natural wonders boosted western tourism.

rubbish or waste," he wrote; "everything is perfectly clean and pure and full of divine lessons."

Muir believed that the need to protect breathtaking vistas and magnificent stands of giant redwoods compelled the federal government to act as land-policy regulator, and he was gratified by the creation of the National Park system during the postwar period. By this time, pressure had been building on the federal government to protect vast tracts of undeveloped lands. Painters and geologists were among the first Easterners to appreciate the spectacular vistas of the western landscape. In 1864, Congress set aside a small area within California's Yosemite Valley for public recreation and enjoyment. Soon after the war, railroad promoters forged an alliance with government officials in an effort to block commercial development of particularly beautiful pockets of land. In the late 1860s, the invention of the Pullman sleeping car—a luxurious hotel room on wheels—helped spur tourism, and thus the drive to protect areas of natural beauty from farming, lumbering, stock raising, and mining. Northern Pacific railroad financier Jay Cooke lobbied hard for the government to create a 2-million-acre park in what is today the northwest corner of Wyoming. As a result, in March 1872, Congress created Yellowstone National Park. Tourism would continue to serve as a key component of the western economy.

Muir and others portrayed the Yosemite and Yellowstone valleys as wildernesses, empty of human activity. In fact, both areas had long provided hunting and foraging grounds for native peoples. Since the fifteenth century, Yellowstone had been occupied by the people now called the Shoshone. This group, together with the Bannock, Crow, and Blackfoot, tried to retain access to Yellowstone's meadows, rivers, and forests after it became a national park. However, U.S. policymakers and military officials persisted in their efforts to mark off territory for specific commercial purposes, while Indians were confined to reservations.

BUYING TERRITORY FOR THE UNION

Before the Civil War, Republicans had opposed any federal expansionist schemes that they feared might benefit slaveholders. However, after 1865 and the outlawing of slavery, some Republican lawmakers and administration officials advocated the acquisition of additional territory. Secretary of State William Seward led the way in 1867 by purchasing Alaska from Russia. For $7.2 million (about 2 cents an acre), the United States gained Alaska—and 591,004 square miles of land. Within the territory were diverse indigenous groups—Eskimo, Aleut, Tlingit, Tsimshian, Athabaskan, and Haida—and a small number of native Russians. Though derided at the time as "Seward's icebox," Alaska yielded enough fish, timber, minerals, oil, and water power in the years to come to prove that the original purchase price was a tremendous bargain.

> *For $7.2 million (about 2 cents an acre), the United States gained Alaska—and 591,004 square miles of land.*

The impulse that prompted Johnson administration support for the Alaska purchase also spawned other plans for territorial acquisitions. In 1870, some Republicans joined with Democrats in calling for the annexation of the Dominican Republic. These members of Congress argued that the tiny Caribbean country would make a fine naval base, provide investment opportunities for American businesspeople, and offer a refuge for southern freedpeople.

However, influential Senator Charles Sumner warned against a takeover without considering the will of Dominicans, who were currently involved in their own civil war. Some members of Congress, in a prelude to foreign policy debates of the 1890s, suggested that the dark-skinned Dominican people were incapable of appreciating the blessings of American citizenship. In 1871, an annexation treaty failed to win Senate approval.

In facilitating western expansion, Republicans upheld the ideal that prosperity would come to all people who worked hard. Indians were not part of the Republican vision of western prosperity. But other groups also questioned the Republican vision as it affected their own interests.

The Republican Vision and Its Limits

■ *What were some of the inconsistencies in, and unanticipated consequences of, Republican notions of equality and federal power?*

After the Civil War, victorious Republicans envisioned a nation united in the pursuit of prosperity. All citizens would be free to follow their individual economic self-interest and enjoy the fruits of honest toil. In contrast, some increasingly vocal and well-organized groups saw the expansion of legal rights, in particular giving black men the right to vote, as only initial, tentative steps on the path to an all-inclusive citizenship. Women, industrial workers, farmers, and African Americans made up overlapping constituencies pressing for equal political rights and economic opportunity. Together they challenged the mainstream Republican view that defeat of the rebels and destruction of slavery were sufficient to guarantee prosperity for everyone.

Partnerships between government and business also produced unanticipated consequences for Republicans committed to what they believed was the collective good. Some politicians and business leaders saw these partnerships as opportunities for private gain. Consequently, private greed and public corruption accompanied postwar economic growth. Thus, Republican leaders faced challenges from two very different sources: people agitating for civil rights and people hoping to reap personal gain from political activities.

POSTBELLUM ORIGINS OF THE WOMAN SUFFRAGE MOVEMENT

After the Civil War, the nation's middle class, which had its origins in the antebellum period, continued to grow. Dedicated to self-improvement and filled with a sense of moral authority, many middle-class Americans (especially Protestants) felt a deep cultural connection to their counterparts in England. Indeed, the United States produced its own "Victorians," the term for the self-conscious middle class that emerged in the England of Queen Victoria during her reign from 1837 to 1901.

At the heart of the Victorian sensibility was the ideal of domesticity: a harmonious family living in a well-appointed home, guided by a pious mother and supported by a father successful in business. Famous Protestant clergyman Henry Ward Beecher and his wife were outspoken proponents of this domestic ideal. According to Eunice Beecher, women had no "higher, nobler, more divine mission than in the conscientious endeavor to create a *true home.*"

Yet the traumatic events of the Civil War only intensified the desire among a growing group of American women to participate fully in the nation's political life. They wanted to extend their moral influence outside the narrow and exclusive sphere of the home. Many women believed they deserved the vote and that the time was right to demand it.

In 1866, veteran reformers Elizabeth Cady Stanton, Susan B. Anthony, and Lucy Stone founded the Equal Rights Association to link the rights of white women and African Americans. Nevertheless, in 1867, Kansas voters defeated a referendum proposing suffrage for both blacks and white women. This disappointment convinced some former abolitionists that the two causes should be separated—that women should wait patiently until the rights of African American men were firmly secured. Frederick Douglass declined an invitation to a women's suffrage convention in Washington, D.C., in 1868. He explained, "I am now devoting myself to a cause [if] not more sacred, certainly more urgent, because it is one of life and death to the long enslaved people of this country, and that is: negro suffrage." But African American activist and former slave Sojourner Truth warned: "There is a great stir about colored men getting their rights, but not a word about the colored women; and if colored men get their rights, and not colored women get theirs, there will be a bad time about it."

In 1869, two factions of women parted ways and formed separate organizations devoted to women's rights. The more radical wing, including Cady Stanton and Anthony, bitterly denounced the Fifteenth Amendment because it gave the vote to black men only. They helped to found the National Woman Suffrage Association (NWSA), which argued for a renewed commitment to the original Declaration of Sentiments passed in Seneca Falls, New York, two decades earlier. They favored married women's property rights, liberalization of divorce laws, opening colleges and trade schools to women, and a new federal amendment to allow women to vote. Lucy Stone and her husband, Henry Blackwell, founded the rival American Woman Suffrage Association (AWSA). This group downplayed the larger struggle for women's rights and focused on the suffrage question exclusively. Its members supported the Fifteenth Amendment and retained ties to the Republican party. The AWSA focused on state-by-state campaigns for women's suffrage.

In 1871, the NWSA welcomed the daring, flamboyant Victoria Woodhull as a vocal supporter, only to renounce her a few years later. Woodhull's political agenda ranged from free love and dietary reform to legalized prostitution, working men's rights, and women's suffrage. (In the nineteenth century, free love advocates denounced what they called a sexual double

■ The *Daily Graphic*, a New York City newspaper, carried this caricature of Susan B. Anthony on its June 5, 1873, cover. The artist suggests that the drive for women's suffrage has resulted in a reversal of gender roles. Titled "The Woman Who Dared," the cartoon portrays Anthony as a masculine figure. One of her male supporters, on the right, holds a baby, while women activists march and give speeches. On the left, a female police officer keeps watch over the scene.

When Did Women Get the Vote?

1893	New Zealand
1906	Finland
1913	Norway
1915	Denmark
1917	Canada
1918	Austria, Estonia, Germany, Hungary, Poland, Latvia, Russian Federation
1919	Belarus, Luxembourg, Netherlands, Ukraine
1920	Albania, Czech Republic, Slovakia, United States
1921	Armenia, Sweden
1928	Ireland, United Kingdom
1929	Romania
1930	Turkey, South Africa (whites)
1931	Spain, Sri Lanka
1932	Brazil, Thailand, Uruguay
1934	Cuba
1937	Philippines
1945	Croatia, Indonesia, Italy, Japan, Slovenia, Togo
1946	Cameroon, Guatemala, Liberia, Panama, Venezuela, Viet Nam, Yugoslavia
1947	Argentina, Mexico, Pakistan, Singapore
1948	Belgium, Israel, Niger, Republic of Korea, Suriname
1949	Chile, China, Costa Rica
1950	Barbados, Haiti, India
1955	Cambodia, Ethiopia, Honduras, Nicaragua, Peru
1962	Algeria, Australia, Monaco, Uganda, Zambia
1971	Switzerland
1972	Bangladesh
1974	Jordan
1980	Iraq
1984	South Africa (coloureds and Indians)
1990	Samoa
1994	South Africa (blacks)
2005	Kuwait

This chronology shows the year in which certain countries granted women the same voting rights as men. In the United States, women first pressed for suffrage in an organized way at the women's rights convention in Seneca Falls, New York, in 1848. At that time, many people (including many women) considered women's suffrage to be a radical idea. After the Civil War and the enfranchisement of African American men in 1867, more American women began to agitate for the right to vote.

This chronology does not reveal key themes in the global history of women's suffrage. First, many countries divided citizenship rights into a number of different components. For example, women in Norway won the right to run for election (the British would say "stand for election") in 1907, but not the right to vote until six years later. Second, some countries legally enfranchised women but did not enforce that right. In theory, all U.S. women had the right to vote in 1920, but in fact, the federal government did not guarantee that right to African American men or women until 1965. Third, a number of countries initially put literacy or other conditions on women's right to vote. The dates above indicate when, in those cases, restrictions were lifted. And finally, some local entities allowed women the right to vote before the national government sanctioned that right. For example, in the United States, some localities and some western states enfranchised women before 1920.

QUESTIONS

1. Which country enshrined in law "racial" differences among women for the purposes of suffrage?

2. What do you think accounts for the relatively large numbers of countries to enact women's suffrage during and after the two world wars of the twentieth century—1918–1919, and 1945–1946?

3. What assumptions about women account for the fact that some countries allowed women the right to run for office before granting them the right to vote?

---

standard, one that glorified female chastity while tolerating male promiscuity.) In 1872, Woodhull spent a month in jail as a result of zealous prosecution by vice reformer Anthony Comstock, a clergyman who objected to her public discussions and writings on sexuality. Comstock assumed the role of an outspoken crusader against vice. A federal law passed in 1873, and named after him, equated information related to birth control with pornography, banning this and other "obscene material" from the mails.

Susan B. Anthony used the 1872 presidential election as a test case for women's suffrage. She attempted to vote and was arrested, tried, and convicted. By this time, most women suffragists, and most members of the NWSA for that matter, had become convinced that they should focus on the vote exclusively; they therefore accepted the AWSA's policy on this issue. In the coming years, they would avoid other causes with which they might have allied themselves, including black civil rights and labor reform.

WORKERS' ORGANIZATIONS

Many Americans benefited from economic changes of the postwar era. Railroads, mines, and heavy industry helped fuel the national economy and in the process boosted the growth of the urban managerial class. In the Midwest, many landowning farmers prospered when they responded to an expanding demand for grain and other staple crops. In Wisconsin, wheat farmers cleared forests, drained swamps, diverted rivers, and profited from the booming world market in grain. Yet the economic developments that allowed factory managers and owners of large wheat farms to make a comfortable living for themselves did not necessarily benefit agricultural and manufacturing wage-workers.

■ A Norwegian immigrant extended family in the town of Norway Grove, Wisconsin, poses in front of their imposing home and up-to-date carriage in this photograph taken in the mid-1870s. Linking their fortunes to the world wheat market, these newcomers to the United States prospered. Wrote one woman to her brother back home in Norway, "We all have cattle, driving oxen, and wagons. We also have children in abundance."

Indeed, during this period, growing numbers of working people, in the countryside and in the cities, became caught up in a cycle of indebtedness. In the upcountry South (above the fall line, or Piedmont), formerly self-sufficient family farmers sought loans from banks to repair their war-damaged homesteads. To qualify for these loans, a farmer had to plant cotton as a staple crop, to the neglect of corn and other foodstuffs. Many sharecroppers, black and white, received payment in the form of credit only; for these families, the end-of-the-year reckoning yielded little more than rapidly accumulating debts. Midwestern farmers increasingly relied on bank loans to purchase expensive threshing and harvesting machinery.

Several organizations founded within five years of the war's end offered laborers an alternative vision to the Republicans' brand of individualism and nationalism. In 1867, Oliver H. Kelly, a former Minnesota farmer now working in a Washington office, organized the National Grange of the Patrons of Husbandry, popularly known as the **Grange**. This movement sought to address a new, complex marketplace increasingly dominated by railroads, banks, and grain elevator operators. The Grange encouraged farmers to form cooperatives that would market their crops and to challenge discriminatory railroad rates that favored big business.

Founded in Baltimore in 1866, the National Labor Union (NLU) consisted of a collection of craft unions and claimed as many as 600,000 members at its peak in the early 1870s. The group welcomed farmers as well as factory workers and promoted legislation for an eight-hour workday and the arbitration of industrial disputes. William Sylvis, a leader of the Iron Molders' International Union in Philadelphia and the second president of the NLU, sounded twin themes that would mark national labor union organizing efforts for generations to come. He called for an alliance of black and white workers. Yet at the same time, Sylvis defended the practice of excluding blacks from positions of leadership on the job and in the union. Impatient with such pronouncements, Isaac Myers, a black ship caulker from Baltimore, helped found the short-lived and small Colored National Labor Union in Washington, D.C., in 1868. Myers offered a view of citizenship that differed from white Republicans' exclusive emphasis on the franchise: "If citizenship means anything at all," the black labor leader declared, "it means the freedom of labor, as broad and universal as freedom of the ballot."

> In 1873, a nationwide economic depression threw thousands out of work and worsened the plight of debtors.

In 1873, a nationwide economic depression threw thousands out of work and worsened the plight of debtors. Businesspeople in agriculture, mining, the railroad industry, and manufacturing had overexpanded their operations. The freewheeling loan practices of major banks had contributed to this situation. The inability of these businesspeople to repay their loans led to the failure of major banks. With the contraction of credit, thousands of small businesses went bankrupt. The NLU did not survive the crisis.

However, by this time, a new organization had appeared to champion the cause of the laboring classes in opposition to lords of finance. Founded in 1869 by Uriah Stephens and other Philadelphia tailors, the Knights of Labor eventually aimed to unite industrial and rural workers, the self-employed and the wage earner, blacks and whites, and men and women. The Knights were committed to private property and to the independence of the farmer, the entrepreneur, and the industrial worker. The group banned from its ranks "nonproducers," such as liquor sellers, bankers, professional gamblers, stockbrokers, and lawyers.

This period of depression also laid the foundation for the Greenback Labor party, organized in 1878. Within three years after the end of the Civil War, the Treasury had withdrawn from circulation $100 million in wartime paper currency ("greenbacks"). The government also ceased coining silver dollars in 1873, despite the discovery of rich silver lodes in the West. With less money in circulation, debtors found it more difficult to repay their loans. To add insult to injury, the Resumption Act (1875) called for the government to continue to withdraw paper "greenbacks." Thus, hard money became dearer, and debtors became more desperate. In 1878, the new Greenback Labor party managed to win 1 million

PLATE 17

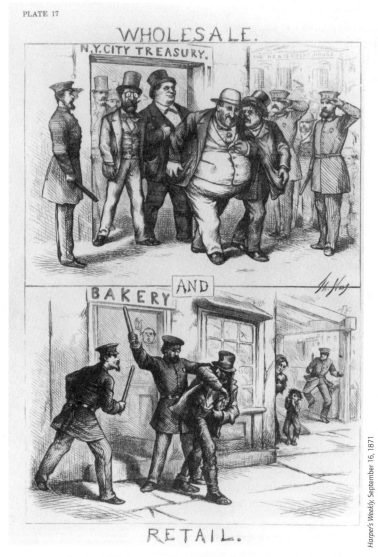

Harper's Weekly, September 16, 1871

▪ In 1871, Thomas Nast drew a series of cartoons exposing the corruption of New York City Democratic boss William M. Tweed and his political organization, Tammany Hall. In this drawing, published in *Harper's Weekly*, Nast depicts Tweed and his cronies engaging in a "wholesale" looting of the New York City treasury with the assistance of compliant police officers. Those same officers stand ready to crack down on the impoverished father who robs a bakery to feed his family. By portraying Tweed as an enemy of the poor, Nast ignored the fact that the political boss gained a large following among immigrant voters.

votes and elect fourteen candidates to Congress. The party laid the foundation for the Populist party that emerged in the 1890s.

Several factors made coalition building among American workers difficult. One was the nation's increasingly multicultural workforce. Unions, such as the typographers, were notorious for excluding women and African Americans, a fact publicized by both Frederick Douglass and Susan B. Anthony, to no avail. In 1869, shoe factory workers (members of the Knights of St. Crispin) went on strike in North Adams, Massachusetts. They were soon shocked to see seventy-five Chinese strikebreakers arrive by train from California. Their employer praised the new arrivals for their "rare industry." The shoemakers' strike collapsed quickly after the appearance of what the Massachusetts workers called this "Mongolian battery." Employers would continue to manipulate and divide the laboring classes through the use of ethnic, religious, and racial prejudices.

POLITICAL CORRUPTION AND THE DECLINE OF REPUBLICAN IDEALISM

Out of the new partnership between politics and business emerged an extensive system of bribes and kickbacks. Greedy politicians of both parties challenged the Republicans' high-minded idealism.

In the early 1870s, the *New York Times* exposed the schemes of William M. "Boss" Tweed. Tweed headed Tammany Hall, a New York City political organization that courted labor unions and contributed liberally to Catholic schools and charities. Tammany Hall politicians routinely used bribery and extortion to fix elections and bilk taxpayers of millions of dollars. One plasterer employed on a city project received $138,000 for two days' work. After the *Times* exposé, Tweed was prosecuted and convicted. His downfall attested to the growing influence of newspaper reporters.

Another piece of investigative journalism rocked the political world in 1872. In 1867, major stockholders of the Union Pacific Railroad had formed a new corporation, called the Crédit Mobilier, to build railroads. Heads of powerful congressional committees received shares of stock in the new company. These gifts of stock were bribes to secure the legislators' support for public land grants favorable

TABLE 15.3			
The Election of 1872			
Candidate	**Political Party**	**Popular Vote (%)**	**Electoral Vote**
Ulysses S. Grant	Republican	55.6	286
Horace Greeley	Democratic, Liberal Republican	43.9	66

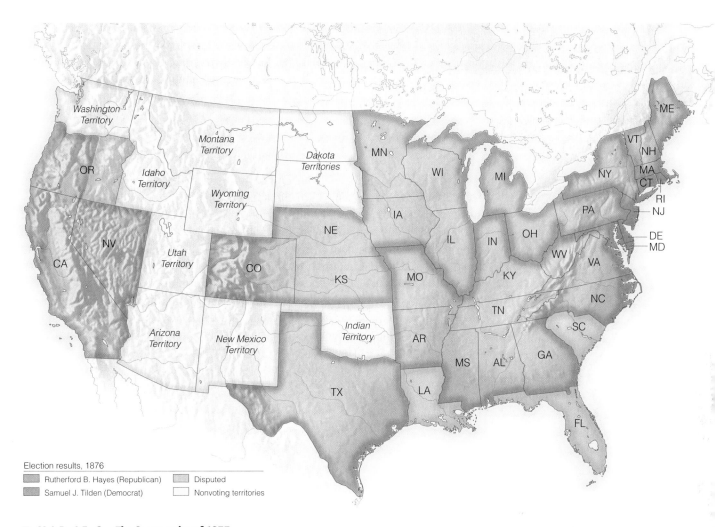

Election results, 1876

- ▨ Rutherford B. Hayes (Republican)
- ▨ Samuel J. Tilden (Democrat)
- ▨ Disputed
- ☐ Nonvoting territories

■ **MAP 15.3 The Compromise of 1877**

During the presidential election of 1876, returns from South Carolina, Florida, and Louisiana (the only states that remained under Republican control) were disputed. Under a compromise reached by Republicans and Democrats in Congress, Republican Rutherford B. Hayes became president and Congress removed all federal troops from the South.

to the new corporation. The *New York Sun* exposed a number of the chief beneficiaries in the fall of 1872, findings confirmed by congressional investigation. Among the disgraced politicians was Grant's vice president, Schuyler Colfax.

The 1872 presidential election pitted incumbent Grant against the Democratic challenger, *New York Tribune* editor Horace Greeley. Many Republicans, disillusioned with congressional corruption and eager to press forward with civil service reform, endorsed the Democratic candidate. Greeley and his Republican allies decried the patronage (or "spoils") system by which politicians rewarded their supporters with government jobs. Nevertheless, Grant won the election.

By 1872, after four bloody years of war and seven squandered years of postwar opportunity, the federal government seemed prepared to hand the South back to unrepentant rebels. The North showed what one House Republican called "a general apathy among the people concerning the war and the negro." The **Civil Rights Act of 1875** guaranteed blacks equal access to public accommodations and transportation. Yet this act represented the final, half-hearted gesture of radical Republicanism. The Supreme Court declared the measure unconstitutional in 1883 on the grounds that the government could protect only political and not social rights. White Southerners reasserted their control over the region's political economy.

TABLE 15.4			
The Election of 1876			
Candidate	**Political Party**	**Popular Vote (%)**	**Electoral Vote**
Rutherford B. Hayes	Republican	48.0	185
Samuel J. Tilden	Democratic	51.0	184

The presidential election of 1876 intensified public cynicism about deal making in high places. A dispute over election returns led to what came to be known as the Compromise of 1877. In the popular vote, Democrat Samuel J. Tilden outpolled Republican Rutherford B. Hayes, a former Ohio governor. However, when the electoral votes were counted, the Democrat had only 184, one short of the necessary number. Nineteen of the 20 votes in dispute came from Louisiana, South Carolina, and Florida, and these three states submitted two new sets of returns, one from each of the two main parties. A specially appointed congressional electoral commission, the Committee of Fifteen, was charged with resolving the dispute. It divided along partisan lines. The eight Republicans outvoted the seven Democrats to accept the Republican set of returns from Florida.

To break the logjam, the Democrats agreed that Hayes could assume office in return for the withdrawal of all remaining federal troops from the South. The Republicans tacitly agreed that their work there was finished and that blacks in the region should fend for themselves. Hayes declined to enforce the Civil Rights Act of 1875. White Southerners were free to uphold the principle of states' rights that had been traditionally invoked to deny blacks their rights in the region. Thus the Civil War failed to solve one of the most pressing issues of the day—the relation between federal and state power in protecting the rights of individuals.

Conclusion

During the dozen or so years after the Civil War, both northern Republicans and southern Democrats registered a series of spectacular wins and crushing losses. Though humiliated by the Union victory, southern whites eventually won the freedom to control their own local and state governments. As landlords, sheriffs, and merchants, they defied the postwar federal amendments to the Constitution and deprived African Americans of basic citizenship rights. By the end of Reconstruction, northern Republicans had conceded local power to their former enemies. Even an aggressive nationalism, it turned out, could accept traditional southern hierarchies: white over nonwhite, rich over poor.

Yet the Civil War was not only a fight between whites. During the conflict, black people had served as combatants in the struggle for freedom. They saw the war in different terms than did northern white Republicans and southern white Democrats. After the war, blacks pursued full citizenship rights while attempting to maintain institutional and cultural autonomy from white people regardless of political affiliation. In their quest, freed men and women met with mixed success. They gained the status of citizens under federal amendments to the Constitution, and black men gained the (formal) right to vote. Yet white Republicans, both in Congress and in southern state legislatures, proved to be disappointing allies to blacks who found themselves, increasingly, at the mercy of white vigilantes and other terrorist groups. During the Reconstruction period, blacks consolidated their families, established their own churches, and sought to work on their own terms in the fields. Yet lacking money and credit, they found it difficult to buy land and in the process achieve true independence from white landowners, bankers, and politicians.

At the end of Reconstruction, Republicans remained in firm control of national economic policy. The white South had secured its right to conduct its own political affairs, but the Republican vision of economic growth and development had become the law of the land. This vision was a guiding principle of historic national and, increasingly, international significance. Economic innovation in particular proved to be a force of great unifying power, stronger even than all the federal military forces deployed during and after the Civil War.

For Review

1. In what ways did African Americans and western Indians differ in their view of the federal government? How were those differences revealed in the military and political arenas after the war?

2. Was the Civil War a turning point in women's history? Why or why not?

3. Andrew Johnson was a Republican, and yet he and congressional Republicans engaged in a bitter fight during Reconstruction. Why?

4. In what ways did the outcome of the Civil War challenge the power of states' authority over their own economy and people? Was the war a clear victory for federal authority? Why or why not?

5. Did all workers share the same interests after the war? Choose three groups of workers and describe the challenges they faced during Reconstruction.

6. What did freedom mean to southern black people after the war? What were the limits on their freedom?

7. In what ways was or was not the effort to subdue the Plains Indians after 1865 an extension of the Civil War?

Created Equal Online

For more *Created Equal* resources, including suggestions on sites to visit and books to read, go to **MyHistoryLab.com.**

CHRONOLOGY: 1865–1877

1865	Freedmen's Bureau is formed.
	Lincoln is assassinated; Andrew Johnson becomes president.
	Thirteenth Amendment abolishing slavery is ratified.
1866	Civil Rights Act of 1866.
	Ku Klux Klan is organized.
1867	U.S. purchases Alaska from Russia.
	Reconstruction Act of 1867.
	Ratification of Fourteenth Amendment protecting civil rights.
1868	Johnson is impeached and acquitted.
	Fourteenth Amendment is ratified.
1869	Transcontinental Railroad is completed.
	National Woman Suffrage Association and American Woman Suffrage Association are formed.
	Knights of Labor is founded.
1870	Fifteenth Amendment enfranchising black men is ratified.
1871	Ku Klux Klan Act.
1873	Onset of economic depression.
1874	Congress passes Civil Rights Act.
1876	Battle of Little Big Horn.
	Contested presidential election between Rutherford B. Hayes and Samuel J. Tilden.
1877	Compromise of 1877.

The United States became a modern nation during the last quarter of the nineteenth century. Vast reserves of coal, timber, and water helped fuel a growing industrial economy. Railroad lines criss-crossed the nation and knit regional economies together. Large numbers of immigrants, many from eastern Europe, arrived in the United States, drawn by America's rising standard of living, high demand for labor, and religious and political freedom.

To raise the money needed to purchase expensive equipment and machinery, coal and oil producers and railroad owners formed modern corporations, businesses that were owned by stockholders rather than individuals. The largest businesses sought to dominate the marketplace by eliminating their competitors. Managers could cut production and operating costs by slashing the wages of workers or by installing labor-saving machinery. Either way, workers paid the price.

The generation that came of age after the Civil War witnessed a series of violent confrontations between workers and employers. Standards of industrial work discipline required workers to labor for long hours at dangerous, disagreeable jobs. Some workers formed new kinds of labor unions to combat the power of big business. Some organizations, such as the Knights of Labor, were national in scope and inclusive in their membership; others represented the interests of specific groups of workers. Employers, law enforcement officials, and judges used a variety of means to suppress strikes and other forms of collective action among workers. Nevertheless, local communities often supported the strikers, who were their friends and neighbors.

During the late nineteenth century, the national economy began to shift to the production of consumer goods. New products gave Americans new ways to spend their money. Manufacturers of everything from toothpaste to bathtubs advertised their goods to a mass market. In cities, department stores offered a dazzling array of goods.

Even as the country was becoming more ethnically diverse, advertisers promoted a single standard of physical beauty and material well-being. At the same time, some scholars and politicians seized on a revolutionary new theory of natural history to argue for the superiority of white, middle-class Americans. Social Darwinism served as the intellectual justification for unfettered economic growth and for the subjugation of darker-skinned peoples, at home and abroad.

Many Americans rejected the trends toward economic standardization and cultural homogeneity. Native Americans in the West continued to resist the railroad and its profound threat to their way of life. By 1890, the U.S. military had forcefully subdued most of these Indians, relegating many to reservations. Together with industrial workers throughout the nation, Hispanic villagers in the Southwest and African American sharecroppers in the South disputed the notion that progress could be defined exclusively in terms of economic growth and development.

Middle-class reformers sought to mediate between what they perceived to be two dangerous groups: arrogant industrialists and discontented workers. These reformers feared that rapid urban and industrial growth would cause rifts in the social fabric. Middle-class women pioneered in the founding of social settlements and other urban institutions to ease the transition of immigrants into modern American society.

The lines between national standards and local cultural interests often blurred. For example, for a short time Sioux chief Sitting Bull (Tatanka Iyotake) appeared with William ("Buffalo Bill") Cody's "Wild West" show, which played to enthusiastic audiences in the United States and Europe. Yet this Indian leader also led the Plains Indians as they attempted to resist U.S. military authorities. Some groups of Americans who sought to preserve their own cultural traditions nonetheless aspired to a middle-class way of life and its material comforts. Elite Hispanic families in the Southwest remained devoted to their Roman Catholic faith and at the same time followed up-to-date clothing fashions marketed by East Coast department stores.

The promise and the conflicts inherent in the emerging modern social order met head on in the 1890s. A new political party, the Populist party, mounted a brief but potent challenge to entrenched economic and political power. The Populists failed in their attempt to capture the presidency in 1896, but they offered a vision of a new kind of political party, one that would bring black and white farmers and industrial workers together in opposition to landlords, employers, and bankers.

In 1898, in an effort to protect its interests in the Western Hemisphere and to extend those interests into the Pacific, the United States went to war with Spain. This imperialist venture suggested the links among several impulses, including missionary outreach, commercial expansion, and white supremacist ideologies. By 1900, the United States was fast becoming a world leader in terms of manufacturing, technological innovation, and the rapid growth of its prosperous middle class.

Chapter 16

Standardizing the Nation, 1877–1900

Hulton Archive/Getty Images

■ When Andrew Carnegie retired in 1901, he sold the Carnegie Steel Company to American banker and financier J. P. Morgan for $480 million. Carnegie's personal fortune was about $500 million.

Andrew Carnegie lived a life full of contrasts and contradictions. Born into an immigrant family of modest means, he made a fortune in the steel industry; eventually he became the richest man in the world. At one point a strong supporter of labor unions, he nevertheless yielded day-to-day control of his steel mills to his business partner, who oversaw the brutal suppression of striking workers in 1892. A savvy manager and innovator, he remained dependent on his mother and waited until she died (when he was forty-three years old) before he felt free to marry. Possessed of an immense fortune, he tried mightily to give almost all of it away.

In 1835, when Andrew Carnegie was born, his parents Will and Margaret Carnegie were living in the village of Dunfermline, Scotland, where Will was a skilled weaver. The couple had two sons—Andrew and Tom, born eight years later. When steam-powered textile looms threw Will Carnegie and other handweavers out of work, the family emigrated to the United States and settled in Pittsburgh, Pennsylvania. Eager to work hard, Andrew took a series of jobs to help support the family: bobbin boy in a textile mill, tender of a steam boiler in a factory, clerk and then messenger in a telegraph office. By the time he was eighteen, he was personal assistant to Thomas Scott, superintendent of the Western Division of the Pennsylvania Railroad. Three years later, after the death of his father, Andrew assumed the role of family breadwinner; he also took over the job of Thomas Scott, who became president of the railroad.

Working for the railroad, Andrew Carnegie learned a great deal about running a gigantic business efficiently and profitably. He also invested in oil and railroads. In 1872, he visited England and gained firsthand information about the production of steel, a lighter, stronger material than iron. Three years later, he opened his own steel plant, the Edgar Thomson works in Pittsburgh. Carnegie named the plant for the current president of the Pennsylvania Railroad. He then proceeded to buy rival steel mills. In 1892, Carnegie's business partner, Henry Clay Frick, took extraordinary steps to end a strike among 10,000 workers at Homestead, another of Carnegie's plants in Pittsburgh. Frick relied on a private security force, the Pinkertons, and 8,000 state militia to put down the strike. Nine strikers and seven Pinkertons died in the ensuing violence, and the steelworkers' union, the Amalgamated Association of Steel and Iron Workers, was virtually crushed.

In his business life, Andrew Carnegie was a man of strong principles. In 1868, he had promised himself that he would not hoard the money he made; instead he would promote the "education and improvement of the poorer classes." During the course of his career, Carnegie gave away 90 percent of his fortune, founding the Carnegie Endowment for International Peace, as well as many public libraries around the country.

It was significant that Carnegie spent his formative years in business learning about railroads. These lessons paved the way for his own success in the steel industry. By 1877, the emergence of a national rail system signaled the rise of big business. The railroad industry produced America's first business bureaucracies, employing gigantic workforces to maintain, schedule, operate, and staff trains that traversed 93,000 miles of track. By 1890, the Pennsylvania Railroad had become the nation's largest employer, with 110,000 workers on its payroll. About one out of seven people worked in the rail industry. The people in charge of coordinating these vast operations were among the country's first professional, salaried managers.

The railroad industry was both a great centralizer and a great standardizer. Trains ran on schedules that were set by a central office, and those schedules relied on definitions of actual time that were standard throughout the nation. Moreover, trains broke down regional boundaries by transporting goods to all areas of the country. For the first time, trains carried brand-name goods and commodities to a national market. Levi-Strauss, a small clothier in San Francisco, shipped its famous denim pants to cowboys in Texas. Pillsbury Flour of Minnesota distributed its products to bakeries throughout the Midwest. Armour Meatpacking of Chicago sent its sausages to the East Coast. With the introduction of the refrigerated railroad car, trains also began carrying larger loads of fruits and vegetables over longer distances. The new traffic in produce stimulated commercial agriculture in the South and on the West Coast.

Few Americans amassed the fabulous fortunes of rich industrialists like Carnegie, yet most people aspired to a better life, even in modest terms. Proprietors, managers, and office workers filled the ranks of the comfortable middle class, men and women freed of the danger and drudgery of manual labor. Between 1880 and 1900, clerical workers tripled in number, and business managers increased from 68,000 to more than 318,000. Enjoying steady work and cash salaries, middle-class employees began to move their families out of the city. Urban areas were becoming increasingly befouled by smokestacks and congested with new factories and workshops.

Providers of goods and services celebrated a "standard" American viewed as white, native-born, middle-class, heterosexual, and Protestant. This image assumed special significance in the marketing of consumer products and in the appeal of new forms of leisure activities. Mass advertising techniques heightened distinctions that European Americans drew between themselves and people they considered inferior, exotic, or foreign.

Yet the energy and vitality associated with American popular culture served as a magnet for people all over the world. Beginning in the 1880s, eastern European immigrants streamed to the United States. They were also eager to partake of the country's plentiful jobs, material prosperity, and democratic openness. Well into the twentieth century, the nation still showed the ethnic and cultural diversity that was shaped by patterns of immigration during the late nineteenth century.

Industry expanded as a result of an incredible increase in population during this period. Between 1880 and 1890, the U.S. population grew from 50 million people to almost 63 million, and six new states entered the Union: North Dakota, South Dakota, Montana, and Washington in 1889; Idaho and Wyoming in 1890. This population and economic growth had contradictory effects. Blessed with abundant and diverse natural resources, American industries became competitive in the world marketplace. However, miners and loggers tended to "cut and run," despoiling streams and forests in the process. Economic growth and development transformed natural landscapes throughout the United States. In general, citizens benefited from the proliferation of new technological marvels, but consumers bore the brunt when big business raised prices and eliminated competition within an industry. Certain workers suffered when new machines displaced them from their jobs. These workers, and others who toiled for long hours under dangerous conditions for low pay, resisted the new order by joining unions or engaging in other kinds of protests against employers.

During the last third of the nineteenth century, the rise of big business, the mass production of consumer goods, and innovations in transportation produced national standards that shaped the economic and social life of the nation. Placing advertisements in newspapers and popular magazines, large companies sought to market their products to all parts of the country. These products, from household furnishings to new fashions in dress, helped to set the standard for middle-class life. In addition, advertising conveyed to the buying public an image of "American" beauty; this standard was narrow by definition but supposedly universal in its appeal. New kinds of commercialized leisure activities, such as shows, athletic competitions, and amusement parks, promoted the idea that all Americans, regardless of where they lived or what they did for a living, valued spectacles and thrilling forms of entertainment. At the same time, not all people embraced these standards or the assumption that underlay them—the notion that new kinds of goods and entertainment represented progress in American life.

The New Shape of Business

■ *What were the challenges faced by large business owners and managers who sought to mass produce and mass market their goods?*

In 1882, prospectors discovered gold in the creeks of Idaho's Coeur d'Alene region (in Indian territory, about ninety miles east of Spokane, Washington). Multiethnic boomtowns mushroomed in the surrounding area. The Northern Pacific Railway promoted settlement, and the primitive techniques that had been used in surface mining soon yielded to far more efficient hydraulic methods of extraction (a process in which powerful water hoses wash the soil away to expose gold deposits).

The mining industry in the region soon emerged as a big business. In 1885, an unemployed carpenter named Noah S. Kellogg set in motion a dramatic chain of events. Kellogg discovered a lode containing not only gold but also zinc and lead. In short order, he sold his

Some Major Inventions of the Late Nineteenth Century

INVENTIONS IN POWER:

1876	Four-stroke coal-gas engine, N. A. Otto, Germany
1880s	Steam turbine, Charles Parsons, U.K.; Gustaf de Laval, Sweden
1892	Diesel engine, Rudolf Diesel, Germany

METALLURGY AND MACHINE TOOLS:

1870–1916	Alloy steel, Robert Hatsfield, U.K.; F. W. Taylor, U.S.
1880–1910	Regenerative electric steel furnace, P. L. T. Herault, France; William Siemens and others, U.K.
1886–1887	Electrolytic method of producing aluminum, P. L. T. Herault, France; Charles Martin Hall, U.S.; Karl J. Bayer, Germany
1887	Cyanide process for extracting gold and silver, J. S. McArthur, R. W. and W. Forrest, and others, U.K.

AGRICULTURE:

1868	Refrigerated meat-packing, P. D. Armour, U.S.
1870s	Combination harvester, Numerous sources, U.S.
1874–1875	Barbed wire, Joseph Glidden, U.S.
1876	Stump-jump plow, R. B. Smith, J. W. Scott, and Charles Branson, Australia
1877	Automatic twine-binder, J. F. Appleby, Jacob Behel, and others, U.S.
1877–1879	Cream separator, Gustaf de Laval, Sweden
1890	Babcock centrifuge, S. M. Babcock, U.S.

TEXTILES:

1866	Knitting frame, Isaac W. Lamb, U.S.
1867	Knitting machine, William Cotton, U.K.
1880s	Development of knitting machine, Benjamin Shaw and Charles Fletcher, U.S.
1890s	Completely automatic loom, J. H Northrop, U.S.

INDUSTRIAL CHEMICALS:

1866	Nitroglycerine used in dynamite, Alfred Nobel, Sweden

MINING:

1863	Coal cutter, T. Harrison, U.K.
1880s	Field investigation for petroleum deposits, I. C. White, U.S.

TRANSPORTATION AND COMMUNICATION:

1876	Telephone, Alexander Graham Bell, U.S.
1885	Automobile, Karl Benz, Germany
1886	First high-speed car, Gottlieb Daimler, Germany
1887	Steam tricycle, Leon Serpollet, France
1903	First flight in airplane, Orville and Wilbur Wright, U.S.

The "economic revolution" of the last quarter of the nineteenth century transformed the United States and western Europe. Innovations in power, machines, transportation, and communication revolutionized the way people made things, traveled, and communicated with one other. Inventions and innovations reduced the amount of labor needed to produce certain goods and grow crops, and rendered industrial processes more efficient. These developments helped to shape consumer society in the late nineteenth century, and beyond.

QUESTIONS

1. Several innovations bear the names of their inventors. Which ones are familiar to you?

2. Some historians have suggested that inventions were a product of urbanization. Why might that be the case?

3. For a relatively young country, the United States produced a remarkable number of inventions and innovations. What accounts for this record?

4. What is the link between inventions and a rising standard of living?

Source: Elias H. Tuma, European Economic History: Tenth Century to the Present; Theory and History of Economic Change (New York: Harper and Row, 1971)

The Wider World

mines to a Portland businessman, who paid a whopping $650,000 for them. A group of eastern and California investors, and finally several large corporations, soon controlled major interests in the mines. By the mid-twentieth century, mining companies had dug more than a billion dollars' worth of metal out of Noah Kellogg's original stake.

Crucial to the process of mining and other innovations were engineers, who mastered the technical aspects of design and construction. Many American engineers were trained in Germany, but others attended such schools as the Massachusetts Institute of Technology (MIT) or Cornell University in New York State, both of which introduced electrical engineering into their curricula in 1882. American engineers, such as those who worked in Mexico under the auspices of mining companies and the railroads, served as the vanguard of American capitalism throughout the world.

> *American engineers served as the vanguard of American capitalism throughout the world.*

No matter what industry they were in, advocates of standardized industrial processes and mass marketing hoped to break down regional barriers and create an integrated national economy. Whether they specialized in railroads or shoes, wheat or steel, entrepreneurial business owners and managers pursued similar goals: to mine, grow, manufacture, or process large quantities of goods and then market them as widely, cheaply, and quickly as possible. Business put a premium on technological innovation, on the efficient use of workers, and on the reduction of uncertainties that accompanied a competitive marketplace. These guiding principles, formulated during the late 1870s and 1880s, laid the foundation for economic progress in late-nineteenth-century America.

NEW SYSTEMS AND MACHINES—AND THEIR PRICE

DOCUMENT

Edison, "The Success of the Electric Light"

The free enterprise system thrived on innovation. Indeed, during the 1880s, new machines, new technical processes, new engineering feats, and new forms of factory organization fueled the growth and efficiency of U.S. businesses. Many devices that became staples of American life appeared during this period. Alexander Graham Bell invented the telephone in 1876. Thomas A. Edison developed the phonograph in 1877 and the electric light in 1879. Cash registers and stock tickers soon became indispensable tools for American businesses. Beginning in the 1880s, railroad cars installed steam heat and electric lights, improving the comfort of passengers.

Some new forms of technology shaped the social division of labor. For example, the typewriter enabled businesses to produce standardized paperwork quickly and efficiently. Many employers believed that women had the nimble fingers necessary to operate this new kind of machine. In the late nineteenth century, clerical work and bookkeeping in general gradually became dominated by women, who were considered particularly well suited for these forms of labor.

During these years, more and more businesses perfected the so-called American system of manufacturing, which dated back half a century and relied on the mass production of interchangeable parts. Factory workers made large numbers of a particular part, each part exactly the same size and shape. This system enabled manufacturers to assemble products more cheaply and efficiently, to repair products easily with new parts, and to redesign products quickly. The engineers who designed the modern bicycle (which has wheels of equal size) used the American system to make their creation affordable to almost anyone who wanted one. The bicycle craze of the late nineteenth century resulted from the novelty and cheapness of this new form of transportation and recreation, one enjoyed by males and females of all ages. Production techniques used to make bicycles were later adapted to the manufacture of automobiles.

New technical processes also facilitated the manufacture and marketing of foods and other consumer goods. Distributors developed pressure-sealed cans, which enabled them to

■ **MAP 16.1** **Agricultural Regions of the Midwest and Northeast**

By 1890, several midwestern cities served as shipping centers, getting wheat and corn to the growing metropolitan areas of the Northeast and Mid-Atlantic. Farmers complained that the railroads gave discounts to large shippers, such as Standard Oil, and discriminated against small producers.

market agricultural products in far-flung parts of the country. Innovative techniques for sheet metal stamping and electric resistance welding transformed a variety of industries. By 1880, 90 percent of American steel was made by the Bessemer process, which injected air into molten iron to yield steel.

The agriculture business profited from engineering innovations as well, which often reached across national boundaries. As just one example, the first modern irrigation systems in the Southwest were constructed by Native Americans and Hispanics. And in the 1870s, Japan began importing American farm implements and inviting U.S. engineers to construct dams and canals for new steam- and water-powered gristmills and sawmills. Technology was a universal language, one that many peoples around the globe sought to master.

Long active in territorial exploration and land surveying, the federal government continued to assume a leading role in applied science. In 1879, the U.S. Geological Survey (USGS) was formed, charged with compiling and centralizing data describing the natural landscape, an effort that had originated in 1804 with the Lewis and Clark Expedition. In the 1880s, the federal government also began to systematize and disseminate information useful to farmers through the U.S. Department of Agriculture. In 1881, for example, the department's Entomology Bureau began to combine current research on insects with practical techniques for pest control.

Like factory machines, new agricultural machinery benefited consumers, but the need for hired hands evaporated. Early in the nineteenth century, harvesting an acre of wheat took fifty-six hours of labor; in 1880, that number dropped to twenty hours. One agricultural worker in Ohio observed, "Of one thing we are convinced, that while improved machinery is gathering our large crops, making our boots and shoes, doing the work of our carpenters, stone sawyers, and builders, thousands of able, willing men are going from place to place seeking employment, and finding none. The question naturally arises, is improved machinery a blessing or a curse?"

ALTERATIONS IN THE NATURAL ENVIRONMENT

**Resources and
Conflict in the West**

Innovation altered the natural landscape and hastened the depletion of certain natural resources. By the mid-1870s, Texas had new steam-powered lumber mills equipped with saw rigs that could produce up to 30,000 board feet a day. This capacity made Texas lumbering a big business, especially when it was combined with infusions of capital and the expansion of railroad lines into the piney woods region, along the eastern edge of the state. Texas lumber mills were poised to benefit from the exhaustion of the great forests of the eastern and Great Lakes states.

In the Chesapeake Bay, dredge boats were becoming more efficient in harvesting oysters, and shellfish reserves began to decline. In the mid-1880s, oyster harvesters took a record 15 million bushels from the bay; the shellfish simply could not replenish themselves. New means of commercial fishing also reduced supplies of salmon in the Northwest.

In 1884 in California, a federal court issued a permanent injunction against hydraulic mining, because it contributed to soil erosion and water pollution. Hydraulic mining had washed an estimated 12 billion tons of earth into San Francisco Bay, raising the floor of the bay several feet. At the same time, mercury flowing into nearby streams from gold mines in the San Jose hills was poisoning fish in the bay, creating pollution that would be felt well into the twentieth century. Similar cases of industrial pollution despoiled other parts of the country. In the absence of any laws to restrain them, Chicago meatpackers befouled the Chicago River with the byproducts of sausage, glue, and fertilizer.

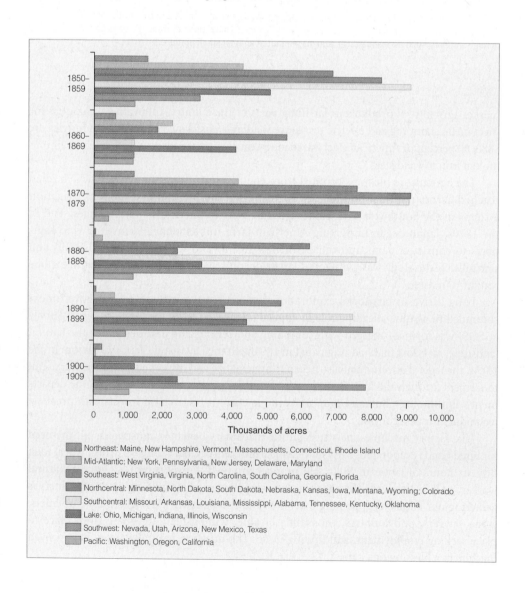

**■ FIGURE 16.1 Amount
of Forest Clearing Each Decade,
by Major Region, 1850–1909
(In Thousands of Acres)**

By stimulating manufacturing and extractive enterprises alike, the railroads powered these great environmental transformations, for better or worse. Trains enabled entrepreneurs to develop large-scale copper mines in Arizona, gigantic herds of longhorn cattle in Kansas, and vast steel mills in western Pennsylvania. Every western town clamored for a railroad station; they knew that places bypassed by the rails withered and died. The railroads enabled tourists to enjoy the beauty of western wilderness areas. Yet the railroads had an insatiable demand for lumber. Between the late 1870s and 1890, U.S. railroads accounted for 20 to 25 percent of all lumber consumed in the nation. They used wood for fuel, fences, trestles, and stations, along with countless railroad ties. In 1890, scientists estimated that the railroads would need 73 million board feet each year to make new ties to lay beneath expanding lines and to replace ties eaten by pests and decayed with age.

Animals also felt the effects of the railroad. Since buffalo herds impeded rail travel, railroads promoted the shooting of buffalo from trains, a "sport" that almost eradicated the species. By the mid-1880s, the great herds had disappeared, victims of ecological change (the incursion of horses into grazing areas), disease (spread by domestic livestock), and commercial enterprise. Eastern consumers prized buffalo-hide coats, and eastern factories used the hides to make steam-engine drive belts. Sioux leader Black Elk decried the slaughter and the "heaps of bones" left to rot in the sun.

INNOVATIONS IN FINANCING AND ORGANIZING BUSINESS

As agents of economic development and cultural change, the railroads knew no peer. As private enterprises, however, they faced the same challenges that all big businesses ultimately must address. The proliferation of independent lines and the high fixed costs associated with the industry made profits slim and competition intense. As a result, railroad companies began to come together in informal pools to share equipment and set prices industrywide. In the 1880s, these pools gave way to consolidation, a process by which several companies merged into one large company. Moreover, like other large

Courtesy of the Burton Historical Collection, Detroit Public Library

■ Following the wholesale slaughter of buffalo on the Great Plains, settlers earned money by gathering the skeletons. "The bones are shipped East by the carloads," reported the Dodge City *Times*, "where they are ground and used for fertilizing and manufactured into numerous useful articles." This mound of buffalo bones at the Michigan Carlson Works in Detroit, c. 1880, suggests the extent of the devastation.

buinesses, including oil and steel, the railroads sought to slash wages in order to decrease their cost of doing business. This decision had profound consequences for workers, who in some cases reacted violently.

In these years U.S. businesses grew larger and more quickly compared with their western European counterparts. This difference stemmed in large part from America's astonishing population growth and its rich natural resources. Equally significant, the United States possessed a social and legal culture favorable to big business. The absence of an entrenched, conservative elite, along with the spread of state and national laws that protected private property, stimulated the entrepreneurial spirit. The U.S. government refrained from owning industries, although it heavily subsidized the railroad industry. It taxed business lightly and did not tax individual incomes until 1913. Finally, American bankers such as J. P. Morgan aggressively promoted growth through their lending practices and bond sales.

Several large enterprises began to conquer not just local but also national markets. Examples include Bell Telephone (founded in Boston), the Kroger grocery business (Cincinnati), Marshall Field department store (Chicago), and Boston Fruit Company. In the South, Midwest, and West, investors rushed to finance gigantic mining operations and agribusinesses, such as the 1.5 million acres devoted to rice cultivation in southeastern Louisiana and bonanza wheat farms (as large as 38,000 acres) in the Red River Valley of North Dakota.

Owners of these enterprises devised new forms of business organization that helped them grow and survive in a dynamic economy. By combining, or integrating, their operations, manufacturers created large businesses called **trusts** to cut costs and monopolize an entire industry in the process. Unable to withstand the ruthless competition that favored larger enterprises, smaller companies folded. The two icons of American big business in the 1880s—Andrew Carnegie in steel and John D. Rockefeller in petroleum—proved master innovators in both the managerial and technical aspects of business.

Within a year of opening the Edgar Thomson Steelworks, Carnegie was producing steel at half the prevailing market price. He excelled at vertical integration, in which a single firm controls all aspects of production and distribution. Carnegie employed laborers in the Lake Superior region to mine the raw material, and he owned the ships and

■ Bonanza farms were huge agricultural enterprises, ranging in size from 15,000 to 50,000 acres. This photo shows a bonanza wheat farm in Oregon, c. 1890. Many of these farms relied not only on sophisticated machinery, but also on transient labor forces (up to 1,000 workers at a time) to help plow, plant, harvest, and thresh the crop. Some of the largest landowners abandoned farming when they had an opportunity to sell their vast holdings for a profit.

Oregon Historical Society, OrHi 92918

railroads that brought the ore to his mills in Pittsburgh and then transported the manufactured steel to customers.

Another form of business consolidation was horizontal integration, in which a number of companies producing the same product merge to reduce competition and control prices. In 1882, John D. Rockefeller, a former bookkeeper, horizontally integrated the petroleum industry by forming Standard Oil Trust. Stockholders in small companies turned over their shares to Standard Oil, which then coordinated operations and eliminated competition from other smaller firms. Standard Oil also practiced vertical integration. Like Carnegie, Rockefeller controlled not only a raw material (in this case, crude oil) but also processing plants, or refineries. He managed to keep transportation costs low by negotiating discount rates from rail shippers. Soon he had positioned himself to buy out his rivals—or ruin them.

Trusts placed a premium on efficient production, but they also worked to the disadvantage of consumers, who were hostage to high prices within industries that lacked competition. For the growing managerial class, trusts helped to eliminate some of the uncertainty associated with an unstable marketplace. They ensured industries' access to raw materials, cheap transportation, expansive markets, and reliable credit institutions.

IMMIGRANTS: NEW LABOR FOR A NEW ECONOMY

To operate efficiently, expanding industries needed expanding supplies of workers to grow crops, extract raw materials, and produce manufactured goods. Many of these workers came from abroad. The year 1880 marked the leading edge of a new wave of immigration to the United States. Over the next ten years, 5.2 million newcomers entered the country, almost twice the previous decade's level of 2.8 million.

> The year 1880 marked the leading edge of a new wave of immigration to the United States.

In the mid-nineteenth century, most immigrants hailed from western Europe and the British Isles—from Germany, Scandinavia, England, and Ireland. Between 1880 and 1890, they were joined by numerous Italians, Russians, and Poles. In fact, these last three groups predominated among newcomers for the next thirty-five years, their arrival rates peaking between 1890 and 1910. At the same time, immigrants from Asia, especially from China, were making their way to the kingdom of Hawaii, which was acquired by the United States in 1898. Between 1852 and 1887, 26,000 Chinese arrived on the islands. Almost 40 percent of all immigrants to the United States during this period were known as "birds of passage," men who were recruited by American employers and who, after earning some money, returned to their native land.

In some cases, domestic politics affected patterns of foreign immigration to the continental United States. For example, on the West Coast, the Chinese faced intense hostility from native-born white men who feared that "coolies" (Chinese immigrants) would depress their wages and take their jobs. Passed in 1882, the **Chinese Exclusion Act** aimed to stem the flow of Chinese immigration to the United States.

Many of the new European immigrants sought to escape oppressive economic and political conditions in Europe, even as they hoped to make a new life for themselves and their families in the United States. Russian Jews fled discrimination and violent **anti-Semitism** in the form of pogroms, organized massacres conducted by their Christian neighbors and Russian authorities. Southern Italians, mostly landless farmers, suffered from a combination of declining agricultural prices and high birthrates. Impoverished Poles chafed under cultural restrictions imposed by Germany and Russia. Hungarians, Greeks, Portuguese, and Armenians, among other groups, also participated in this great migration; members of these groups too were seeking political freedom and economic opportunity. More generally, beginning in Western Europe, the Industrial Revolution spread eastward and in the process displaced skilled workers in favor of factory hands. These dramatic economic transformations impelled many families to seek a better life in the United States.

Immigrants replenished America's sense of itself as a haven for the downtrodden, a place where opportunity beckoned to hard-working and ambitious people. "The New Colossus," written by American poet Emma Lazarus in 1883, pays tribute to the "huddled masses yearning to breathe free"—people from all over the world who sought refuge in the United States. The words of her poem are inscribed on the Statue of Liberty at the entrance to New York Harbor. (The people of France presented the statue, called "Liberty Enlightening the World," to America in 1884.)

Most of the newcomers found work in the factories, mills, and sweatshops of New York, Philadelphia, and Chicago. At the same time, large numbers of these fresh arrivals dispersed to other areas of the country to work in a wide variety of enterprises. Scandinavians populated the prairies of Iowa and Minnesota and the High Plains of the Dakotas. Immigrants from Mexico found work in the mines and beet fields of Colorado.

In the South, some planters began to recruit immigrants—especially western Europeans of "hardy peasant stock"—to take the place of blacks who resisted working for whites. Nevertheless, planters' experiments with recruiting immigrants amounted to little. Given the opportunity, many immigrants sought to flee from the back-breaking labor and meager wages of the cotton staple-crop economy. A group of Germans brought over to toil in the Louisiana swamps soon after the Civil War quickly slipped away from their employers; they had agreed to the arrangement only to gain free passage to America. Thirty Swedes who arrived in Alabama also deserted at an opportune moment, declaring that they were not slaves. South Carolina planters who sponsored colonies of Germans and Italians gave up in exasperation. The few Chinese who began work in the Louisiana sugar fields soon abandoned the plodding work of the plantations in favor of employment in the trades and shops of New Orleans. Still, in 1890, immigrant worker enclaves were scattered throughout the South. Irish, Polish, and Italian men were swinging pickaxes in Florida railroad camps. Italian men, women, and children were picking cotton on Louisiana plantations. Hungarian men were digging coal out of mines in West Virginia.

The story of Rosa Cassettari, a young woman who emigrated from northern Italy to the United States in 1884, suggests the challenges that faced many newcomers during this period. Rosa's husband, Santino, had preceded her to America. He had settled in an iron mining camp in Missouri. Leaving her son with relatives, Rosa received the assurances of friends and family: "You will get smart in America. And in America you will not be so poor."

In the steerage section of a steamship bound for the United States, Rosa found herself surrounded not only by *paesani* (fellow Italians) but also by Germans, Swedes, Poles, and French—"every kind," she remembered later. After arriving at Castle Garden (an immigration processing center at the tip of Manhattan and a predecessor of Ellis Island), Rosa and her *paesani* were approached by a smooth-talking, well-dressed, Italian-speaking man. Overcharging them for the train trip to Missouri, he left them with no money for food.

Life in the Missouri iron camp proved harsh—nothing like what Rosa had expected. Her husband, who was much older than she, neglected her; he preferred the company of prostitutes in the town. The iron was almost depleted, and some workers and their wives had moved on to a new mine in Michigan. Rosa's days centered on caring for her new baby and cooking for thirteen of the miners.

William E. Wilson Photographic Collection/Historic Mobile Preservation Society

■ A burst of technological innovation characterized many American businesses during the last quarter of the nineteenth century. Nevertheless, some, like southern cotton plantations, remained largely unmechanized. Commanding large numbers of (sometimes resistant) black and white workers, southern planters refrained from investing in labor-saving technology. This woman, working at the Savannah Cotton Exchange in 1880, carries a basket of cotton on her head, just as her enslaved foremothers did.

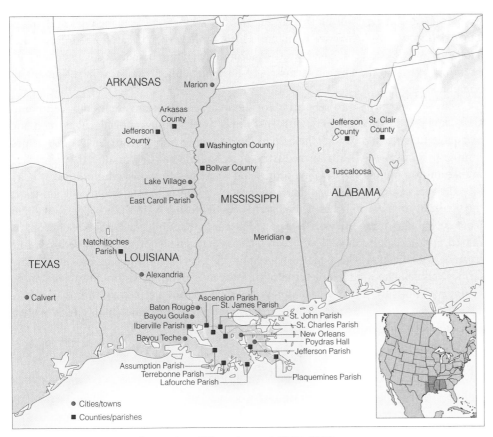

■ **MAP 16.2   Some Places Where Chinese Located, 1865–1880**

Immediately after the Civil War, some southern whites believed that immigrants would be more reliable and efficient workers than the freedpeople. Planters in Mississippi and Louisiana imported a small number of Chinese from California and others directly from Hong Kong. However, by the early 1870s, most of these workers had deserted the fields and moved to nearby towns and cities to work as artisans, grocers, and laundry operators.

Despite these realities, within a couple of years, Rosa grew used to America and considered herself an American. She returned briefly to her hometown in Italy but expressed impatience with the rigid social etiquette that separated the rich from the poor. She also yearned for the hearty meals that had become her staple in the iron camp. Back in Missouri, she mustered enough courage to leave Santino, traveling to Chicago and making a new life for herself in the Italian *colonia* (community) there. She eventually married another Italian man (the two had fallen in love in Missouri) and found work as a cleaning woman at Chicago Commons, a social settlement house. Her new husband alternated between working in construction and peddling bananas and cranberries. Rosa herself gained a reputation as a storyteller; later she said, "Me, I was always crazy for a good story."

The influx of so many foreign-born workers transformed the American labor market. Native-born Protestant men moved up the employment ladder to become members of the white-collar (professional) middle class, while recent immigrants filled the ranks in construction and manufacturing. By 1890, Italian immigrants accounted for 90 percent of New York's public works employees and 99 percent of Chicago's street construction and maintenance crews. Women and children, both native and foreign born, predominated in the textile, garment-making, and food-processing industries.

Specific groups of immigrants often gravitated toward particular kinds of jobs. For example, many Poles found work in the vast steel plants of Pittsburgh, and Russian Jews went into the garment industry and street-peddling trade in New York City. California fruit orchards and vegetable farms employed numerous Japanese immigrants. Cuban and Italian immigrants rolled cigars in Florida. In Hawaii, the Chinese and Japanese labored in the sugar fields; after they had accumulated a little money, they became rice farmers and shopkeepers. In Boston and New York City, second-generation Irish took advantage of their prominent place in the Democratic party to become public school teachers, firefighters, and police officers.

These ethnic niches proved crucial for the well-being of many immigrant communities. They provided newcomers with entry into the economy; indeed, many men and women got their first jobs with the help of kin and other compatriots. Niches also helped immigrants advance within an industry or economic sector. Finally, they enriched immigrant communities by keeping profits and wages within those communities.

The experience of Kinji Ushijima, later known as George Shima, graphically illustrates the power of immigrant niches. Shima arrived in California in 1887 and, like many other Japanese immigrants, found work as a potato picker in the San Joaquin Valley. Soon, Shima moved up to become a labor contractor, securing Japanese laborers for the valley's white farmers. With the money he made, he bought fifteen acres of land and began his own potato farm. Eventually he built a large potato business by expanding his holdings, reclaiming swampland, and investing in a fleet of boats to ship his crops up the coast to San Francisco. Taking advantage of a Japanese niche, Shima had prospered through a combination of good luck and hard work.

EFFICIENT MACHINES, EFFICIENT PEOPLE

Unlike George Shima, most immigrant workers did not become business owners. By the late nineteenth century, the typical industrial employee labored within an immense, multistory brick structure and operated a machine powered by water or steam. Smoky, smelly kerosene lamps gave way to early forms of electric lighting, first arc and then incandescent light bulbs. Long-standing industries, such as textiles and shoes, were now fully mechanized. The new products flooding the economy—locomotives and bicycles, cash registers and typewriters—streamed from factories designed to ensure maximum efficiency from both machines *and* the people who tended them.

In the 1880s, a few factory managers hired efficiency experts. The experts' goal was to cut labor costs in the same way that industry barons had shaved the costs of extracting raw materials or distributing final products. With huge quantities of goods flowing from factories, even modest savings in an employer's payroll could mean significant profits in the long run. Frederick Winslow Taylor,

TABLE 16.1								
Number of Firms by Number of Employees per Firm, 1850 and 1880								
	Number of Firms							
	1850				**1880**			
	No. of Employees				**No. of Employees**			
Industry	**0–5**	**6–50**	**50+**	**Total**	**0–5**	**6–50**	**50+**	**Total**
Iron and steel	6	13	3	22	6	20	17	43
Hardware	76	42	7	125	114	122	27	263
Machines and tools	42	44	6	92	96	113	19	228
Printing	36	60	10	106	105	148	36	289
Building construction	83	59	3	145	588	227	18	833
Clothing	165	294	43	502	301	255	93	649
Furniture	84	66	3	153	185	105	20	310
Metal	83	11	1	95	166	47	5	8
Meat	81	3	0	84	458	23	2	483
Harness	32	15	3	50	96	21	2	119
Baking	384	29	0	413	910	73	8	991
Shoes	339	224	20	583	441	139	34	614
Blacksmith	141	18	1	160	187	12	0	199

Note: Because the census recorded only firms producing more than $500 per year, there may be serious undercounting of firms with one or no employees.

Source: Census of the United States, 1850 and 1880.

chief engineer for the Midvale Steel Plant outside Philadelphia, pioneered in the techniques of efficient "scientific management."

Southern textile mill owners in the Piedmont region of South Carolina and Georgia devised their own strategies for shaping a compliant workforce. They employed only white men, women, and children as machine operators but threatened to hire blacks if the whites protested low wages and poor working conditions. Poor whites lived in company housing, their children attended company schools, and they received cash wages. In contrast, blacks remained in the countryside, impoverished and without the right to vote. In the cities of the North as well as the textile villages of the South, factory workers remained exclusively white until well into the twentieth century.

Regardless of where they lived, many workers aspired to better jobs and higher wages, not only to support their own families, but also to partake of a new culture of consumption that stressed the purchase of new kinds of mass-produced goods and commercialized entertainment and leisure activities. Cities were the primary site of this new culture.

The Birth of a National Urban Culture

■ *What technological and managerial innovations shaped the nation's largest cities in the late nineteenth century?*

In the 1880s, visitors to the territory of Utah marveled at the capital, Salt Lake City, where Mormon pioneers had made the desert bloom. Situated at the foot of the magnificent snow-covered Wasach Range, this oasis in the Great Salt Basin boasted a built landscape almost as impressive as the natural beauty that surrounded it. In the heart of Salt Lake City lay Temple Square. This broad plaza contained the Mormon Tabernacle, a huge domed structure. Next to it stood the Mormon Temple, a soaring six-spired granite cathedral still under construction. The new city had the advantage of rail service (Promontory Point, where the transcontinental railroad was joined, was not far away). Mines in nearby Bingham Canyon yielded rich lodes of silver, and large local smelters refined copper ores. Irrigation systems made the city self-sufficient in the production of foodstuffs. A settlement inspired by religious faith, Salt Lake City was at the same time thoroughly modern.

From 1875 to 1900, American cities developed increasingly sophisticated systems of communications and transportation.

Not just Salt Lake City, but other cities around the country began to assume monumental proportions. In New York, the 1880s marked the completion of Central Park and the Brooklyn Bridge and the arrival of the Statue of Liberty from France. Chicago, rebuilding after a disastrous fire in 1871, became a sprawling rail hub dotted with yards for western cattle, northern timber, and the trains that hauled them. In 1885, Chicago also became the location for a major architectural breakthrough by engineer William LeBaron Jenney. He designed the ten-story Home Insurance Building, the world's first metal frame skyscraper. The steel skeleton weighed only one-third as much as the thick stone walls needed to support a similar masonry building, and the design left room for numerous windows. Urban architecture would never be the same again.

Cities represented American notions of progress and prosperity; they were places where innovation, consumer culture, and new forms of entertainment grew and flourished. From 1875 to 1900, American cities developed increasingly sophisticated systems of communications and transportation. Streetlights, transportation networks, and sewer lines provided basic services to swelling populations of immigrants and rural in-migrants. Experts in the fields of urban design and architecture and ambitious entrepreneurs in the fields of entertainment and professional sports all left their mark on cities. In a country fascinated with

Museum of the City of New York/CORBIS

■ Admirers hailed New York City's Brooklyn Bridge as the eighth wonder of the world when it was completed in 1883. With a central span of 1,595 feet, it became the largest suspension bridge in the world. Built over 14 years, the bridge linked Brooklyn to Manhattan across the East River, using steel suspension cables nearly 16 inches thick. Its total cost was about $18 million.

new and bigger and better things, cities set the standard by defining a desirable way of life for a "typical" middle-class American.

Cities also represented a new cultural diversity in American life. At times uneasily, they accommodated immigrants from around the world. San Francisco's Chinatown formed a "city within a city" as hostile European Americans sought to circumscribe its residents. These growing cities required larger local governments to manage the services necessary for daily life. Politics, prejudice, and technology came together to shape the urban landscape.

ECONOMIC SOURCES OF URBAN GROWTH

Northeastern and mid-Atlantic cities emerged as centers of concentrated manufacturing activity. Yet, with the aid of eastern capital, western cities also flourished. New York's Wall Street and Boston's State Street, home to the nation's largest investment bankers, financed the Main Streets of the Midwest and West. Some urban areas prospered through milling, mining, or other enterprises, such as lumber and flour milling in Minneapolis and ore smelting in Denver. Others focused on manufacturing to serve a growing western population. Chicago was rivaled only by New York in terms of its industrial economy and the vast territory that it supplied with raw materials, processed food, and manufactured goods. Salt Lake City

Percentage of foreign-born population

- 30% and over
- 20%–29%
- 10%–19%
- 1%–9%
- No foreign-born population, under 1%, or unsettled

■ **MAP 16.3**   **Population of Foreign Born, by Region, 1880**

After the Civil War, large numbers of immigrants settled in northeastern cities. In addition, the upper Midwest and parts of the western mining frontier drew many newcomers from western Europe. The area along the country's southwestern border was home to immigrants from Mexico. Cuban cigar makers established thriving communities in Florida.

produced goods for the so-called Mormon Corridor of settlements that stretched west from the city to southern California. By the 1880s, San Francisco had a commercial reach that encompassed much of the West as well as Hawaii and Alaska. Writer Henry George noted, "Not a settler in all the Pacific States and Territories but must pay San Francisco tribute. Not an ounce of gold dug, a pound of ore melted, a field gleaned, or a tree felled in all their thousands of square miles, but must add to her wealth."

Throughout the country, new towns emerged as industrialists and factory owners sought to lure and retain workers. George M. Pullman, who manufactured railroad sleeping cars, built a town outside Chicago and named it after himself. In the South, company towns dotted the Piedmont region (textiles), the steep slopes of the Appalachian Mountains (coal and lumber), the piney woods of Texas (lumber), and the coast of Florida (phosphates). In the West, towns grew up around copper, coal, iron ore, and silver mines. These communities shared a unique characteristic: they directly linked housing, education, and commerce to a particular company.

No trend supported urban growth more than the arrival of newcomers from abroad. To stoke its furnaces, mill its lumber, and slaughter its cattle, Chicago relied on immigrants from Ireland, Slovakia, Germany, Poland, and Bohemia. Of the three cities with the highest percentage of foreign-born residents in 1880, San Francisco (45 percent) ranked higher than both Chicago (42 percent) and New York (40 percent). Yet all large cities also attracted migrants from America's own countryside, as native-born men and women fled the hardship of life on the farm. The use of increasingly efficient agricultural machines meant that rural workers had fewer job opportunities. Most of the migrants from rural areas to the cities were young women; they included Yankee girls from the hardscrabble homesteads of New England, daughters of Swedish immigrants in Minnesota, and native-born farm tenants in Indiana.

Rural folk sought the steady work and wages afforded by jobs in the city, but they were also drawn to the excitement that had become the hallmark of the urban scene. In the early nineteenth century, Thomas Jefferson had located the heart of America in its sturdy yeoman farmers. By the late nineteenth century, that heart had shifted to the city.

BUILDING THE CITIES

In 1886, the Reverend Josiah Strong, a proponent of Protestant missionary efforts abroad, condemned the American city as a "menace" to civilization. However, in decrying what he considered the evils of urban life, Strong described its appeal to people of all ages and both sexes: "It is the city where wealth is massed; and here are the tangible evidences of it piled many stories high. . . . Here are luxuries gathered—everything that dazzles the eye or tempts the appetite; here is the most extravagant expenditure." Strong was right that this conspicuous display of wealth would have profound implications for American politics and culture.

In these years, the American city was emerging as a technological marvel. Through a combination of money and engineering skill, cities managed to provide an adequate water

PROCESSION OF GAME

Soup
Venison (Hunter Style) Game Broth

Fish
Broiled Trout, Shrimp Sauce
Baked Black Bass, Claret Sauce

Boiled
Leg of Mountain Sheep, Ham of Bear
Venison Tongue, Buffalo Tongue

Roast
Loin of Buffalo, Mountain Sheep, Wild Goose, Quail, Redhead Duck, Jack Rabbit,
Blacktail Deer, Coon, Canvasback Duck, English Hare, Bluewing Teal, Partridge,
Widgeon, Brant, Saddle of Venison, Pheasants, Mallard Duck, Prairie Chicken,
Wild Turkey, Spotted Grouse, Black Bear, Opossum, Leg of Elk, Wood Duck,
Sandhill Crane, Ruffed Grouse, Cinnamon Bear

Broiled
Bluewing Teal, Jacksnipe, Blackbirds, Reed Birds, Partridges, Pheasants, Quails,
Butterballs, Ducks, English Snipe, Rice Birds, Red-Wing Starling, Marsh Birds,
Plover, Gray Squirrel, Buffalo Steak, Rabbits, Venison Steak

Entrees
Antelope Steak, Mushroom Sauce; Rabbit Braise, Cream Sauce; Fillet of Grouse
with Truffles; Venison Cutlet, Jelly Sauce; Ragout of Bear, Hunter Style; Oyster Pie

Salads
Shrimp, Prairie Chicken, Celery

Ornamental Dishes
Pyramid of Game en Bellevue, Boned Duck au Naturel, Pyramid of Wild-Goose
Liver in Jelly, The Coon out at Night, Boned Quail in Plumage, Red-Wing Starling
on Tree, Partridge in Nest, Prairie Chicken en Socle

■ **FIGURE 16.2 Menu from the Drake Hotel in Chicago, Illinois, for Thanksgiving, 1886**

Center for Southwest Research, University of New Mexico (Neg. 000-119-0569)

■ Many southwestern cities, such as Albuquerque, New Mexico, were laid out on an Old Town–New Town plan. The original center of settlement, Old Town was characterized by flat-roofed adobe buildings clustered on narrow streets. This photo shows Albuquerque's New Town in the 1880s. Located a mile and a half from Old Town plaza, it consists of Victorian-style buildings. The plan of New Town followed straight lines and right angles, "adapted to the railroad, the regenerator," in the words of one observer.

supply for private and commercial purposes, move large numbers of people and goods efficiently, get rid of waste materials, and illuminate thoroughfares at night. Professionals, such as landscape contractors, construction architects, and civil engineers, designed the parks, bridges, public libraries, and museums that made cities so attractive.

Cities grew upward and outward as a result of developments in mass production and technology. The availability of factory-assembled building materials accelerated the construction of private dwellings and office buildings. Elevators extended living and office spaces upward (in the Reverend Strong's words, "wealth is massed . . . piled many stories high"). The invention of the electric streetcar in 1888 permitted cities to spread out.

One of the greatest challenges for modern cities was to devise means to transport numbers of people over long distances and rough terrain in an efficient and inexpensive way. For most of the nineteenth century, cities relied on carriages pulled by horses. In 1885, approximately 100,000 horses pulled urban passengers through the United States. For many reasons, horsecars were not a satisfactory method of conveyance. In order to scale a hill, drivers had to add extra teams, causing passengers to wait at the bottom of the hill while fresh animals were harnessed to the car. The cost of maintaining a full complement of horses—the feed to sustain them and the stables to shelter them—taxed the budgets of many cities.

Horsecars also threatened the health of urban residents. Each animal deposited on city streets an estimated ten pounds of waste per day, forcing pedestrians to hold their noses while they picked their way through piles of manure. In 1900, health officials in Rochester,

New York, reported that the city's 15,000 horses produced an expanse of waste that would fill an acre of land 175 feet deep—a smelly pile, home to 16 billion flies.

The first successful electric trolley was developed by Julian Sprague, an engineer who founded the Sprague Electric Railway and Motor Company in 1884. The earliest electric streetcar consisted of a small four-wheel carriage connected to an overhead electric cable. Charging passengers a nickel or a dime, and averaging 10–15 miles an hour, these electric trolleys were cheaper, faster, and more versatile than horsecars. Unlike horses, trolleys did not become ill, or die, or balk at ascending a steep grade.

Because of the streetcar, residential suburbs began to crop up many miles from urban commercial cores in the 1880s. Wealthy and middle-class urban residents followed the street-car lines out of the city, hoping to find a green refuge from the grime and noise of downtown while maintaining a manageable commute to work.

As cities expanded, the challenges associated with providing services also grew more complex and expensive. A polluted water supply, for example, meant epidemics of diphtheria and cholera, so city taxpayers demanded waterworks that delivered drinkable water through intricate systems of dams, pumps, reservoirs, and pipes. Chicago had long pumped its sewage into Lake Michigan, the source of its drinking water. In the 1880s, the city financed the building of a canal and the reversal of the flow of the Chicago River. These changes sent the city's sewage away from Lake Michigan and into the Mississippi River instead. Begun in 1889, the 28-mile Chicago Sanitary and Ship Canal was completed seven years later. One awed observer marveled at the "powerful machinery for digging and hoisting, steam shovels, excavators, inclines, conveyors, derricks, cantilevers, cableways, channelers, steam drills, pumps, etc." The cost: $54 million.

> *As cities expanded, the challenges associated with providing services also grew more complex and expensive.*

LOCAL GOVERNMENT GETS BIGGER

These new systems of services, combined with the mushrooming immigrant neighborhoods, changed both the quality and quantity of urban problems. Zoning issues—who could build what, where, and when—became flashpoints for conflict as the interests of homeowners, developers, and municipal engineers collided. These controversies called for new forms of local government. Specifically, urban political leaders struggled to improve the city's public works while meeting the needs of multiple ethnic groups, private businesses, and expanding municipal bureaucracies.

Rising tax rates and ballooning municipal debts told an even larger story. In 1845, the city of Boston spent $8.29 per resident and owed its creditors $748,000. Thirty years later, per capita annual expenditures had risen fivefold, and the city's debt had multiplied to more than $27 million. Clearly, governing a city was an expensive, full-time enterprise and one that had the potential to be very lucrative to businesspeople and politicians.

Although New York's "Boss" Tweed had been convicted on charges of corruption in the early 1870s, the infamous Tammany Hall club carried on his legacy. The Democratic officials associated with this social and political organization perfected a system of kickbacks linked to municipal construction projects. Under this system, contractors paid politicians for city construction contracts. For example, a New York City courthouse that was supposed to cost a quarter of a million dollars ended up costing taxpayers 52 times that amount, or twice as much as the United States paid Russia for Alaska! In the 1880s, secretive networks of corruption that linked political parties, law enforcement personnel, city officials, and construction contractors flourished in many cities. These webs, or "machines," characterized urban life for decades to come.

Urban machines existed to secure jobs for their loyal supporters and line the pockets of those at the highest levels of power. Deal-making blurred the lines between private enterprise and public service as everyone from mayors to local ward organizers benefited from the modernization of the American city. In the process, urban bosses ensured that the streets were paved, tenement buildings erected, sewer lines laid, and trolley tracks extended. But taxpayers footed the bill, which included outrageous amounts of money used for bribes and kickbacks.

Local officials went out of their way to support the provision of illegal services, such as prostitution and gambling, demanded by their constituents. Money-grubbing politicians and police extorted "hush money" from brothels, gambling parlors, and unlicensed taverns. In turn, these places became absorbed into the bosses' local empires. Extorted fees greased the palms of the cop on the beat and the judge on the take.

Urban bosses had a vested interest in sponsoring new money-making venues for professional sports and supporting other forms of commercialized leisure activity. Baseball parks, boxing rings, and racetracks yielded huge sums in the form of kickbacks from contractors. Once built, stadiums and boxing rings generated profits indefinitely as fans filled the stands. Sporting events themselves also gave a city's political, legal, and judicial leaders a chance to meet each other and seal business deals. These events were also one part of a new culture of spectacle and entertainment that appealed to many groups of Americans.

Despite the outcry of reformers, who condemned corrupt urban bosses, these local politicians gained favor among their constituents when they provided needed goods and services, especially among the poor. The boss who provoked the wrath of "good government" men and women also won the loyalty of immigrants whom he helped by providing jobs, food, clothing, loans, and proper burials for their loved ones. For the boss, charity was good politics.

Thrills, Chills, and Bathtubs: The Emergence of Consumer Culture

■ *What were the social and economic consequences of the new consumer culture?*

On a hot summer day in 1890, a young mother named Emily Scanlon, with her three-year-old daughter in tow, paid the five-cent admission fee to a popular ride called the Toboggan Slide at the Brandywine Springs Amusement Park near Wilmington, Delaware. The two of them ascended a stairwell to the top of the three-story-high structure and then stepped into a car that ran on a wooden trough. When the attendant released the brakes, the car descended, pulled by gravity. It moved slowly at first, then picked up speed around a curve. Suddenly, Emily Scanlon stood up in the car (perhaps to retrieve her hat, which had blown off), and she and her daughter were thrown from the car. Mrs. Scanlon died instantly of a broken neck, but the youngster survived. Significantly, the tragedy did not provoke a shutdown of the ride or the installation of safety measures. Instead, park managers simply posted a sign that read, "Passengers must keep their seats." Patrons continued to enjoy the thrills of the toboggan.

> *Americans of all kinds began to sample a new realm of sensual experience either as participants or as observers.*

Brandywine Springs boasted an ornate gateway that proclaimed "Let All Who Enter Here Leave Care Behind." In cities around the country, amusement parks brought men and women, girls and boys together to enjoy merry-go-rounds, prizefights, and circus sideshows. By 1880, railroads and ferries were transporting crowds out of Manhattan to Coney Island, where working-class people mingled with the self-proclaimed "respectable" middle classes.

Late in the century, Americans of all kinds began to sample a new realm of sensual experience—one of physical daring, material luxury, and visual fantasy—either as participants or as observers. The ride at Brandywine Springs was an early prototype of the modern roller coaster. The park afforded patrons not only the thrill of riding the Toboggan Slide but also the sights and sounds of a carnival. The calliope (pipe organ) music and the brightly colored signs beckoned visitors to an exciting world apart from the humdrum routine of everyday life.

Ticket holders at Brandywine Springs were participating in an emerging consumer culture. With economic growth and high rates of productivity came the two ingredients necessary to a culture of consumption: industries that catered to the demand for novel experiences or ready-made goods, and people with enough money to buy them. Central to this culture was mass advertising, a form of appeal that sought to instill in consumers the desire for things that were new and visually attractive. Colorful spectacles of all kinds—whether in the form of a department store window or a well-publicized athletic event—became an integral part of American life.

SHOWS AND SPORTS AS SPECTACLES

Public officials, college administrators, and ambitious entrepreneurs alike discovered that Americans craved new and stimulating forms of entertainment and were willing to pay for them. Athletic events began to draw large crowds, revealing their potential as big business. Traveling road shows promoted new products and services by charming their audiences with exotic performances. Though modest by today's standards, such spectacles found a ready market in the United States and other countries.

In the quarter-century after Reconstruction, three major sports began to attract large national audiences. Organized baseball had existed since 1846, when the Knickerbocker Base Ball Club of New York met the New York Nine in Hoboken, New Jersey. (The score was 23 to 1, in favor of the Nine.) The National Baseball League, consisting of eight professional teams, was founded in 1876, the American League in 1900. In the 1880s, several new regulations—governing the overhand pitch, foul balls, and swingless strikes—helped to standardize the game.

■ Baseball cards, like this one featuring New York Giants player Tim Keefe, were sold at department stores. On the back of the card are listed other national athletes featured in the series. One "Wild West Hunter" is included: "Buffalo Bill" Cody. This card was also a cigarette advertisement.

(Both images) Courtesy, Transcendental Graphics

Also in the 1880s, Walter Camp, a former Yale University football player, introduced rules—for instance, the system of downs and the center snap to the quarterback—that made that sport quicker and more competitive. Camp was also behind the selection of the first "All America" team (1889) to stimulate fan interest. By this time towns, high schools, and colleges were fielding football teams.

Likewise, boxing emerged as a national, regulated sport. John L. Sullivan, an American, won renown as "the world's bare-knuckled champion" in 1882, even as more and more fighters had started wearing gloves. Sullivan then joined a traveling theatrical group and demonstrated gloved boxing to enthusiastic crowds all over the country. These exhibitions revealed the fine line between displays of physical prowess and theatrical performances. In 1889, Sullivan defeated an opponent in a 75-round match, the last heavyweight, bare-knuckled championship.

Performances based on skills of all kinds gained national audiences, as the career of William "Buffalo Bill" Cody reveals. Born in Iowa in 1846, Cody parlayed his early years as a Pony Express postal rider, cavalry scout, Indian fighter, and buffalo hunter into a form of mass entertainment. In his "Buffalo Bill Combination" show, cowboy and Indian actors performed skits depicting dramatic events in western history (from a European American point of view, at least). In 1876, Cody briefly left the stage to join a U.S. cavalry skirmish against the Sioux and Cheyenne. Soon he returned to the show to exhibit the dried scalp of the Cheyenne warrior Yellow Hand, whom he claimed he had killed in battle. Cody thus presented the subjugation of the Indians as a form of high drama, a scripted performance that audiences applauded from the comfort of their seats.

In 1882, Cody produced "Buffalo Bill's Wild West," a traveling road show that featured sharpshooter Annie Oakley, cowboy musicians, and Sioux warriors performing authentic Native American dances. Sioux leader Sitting Bull (Tatanka Iyotake), long an admirer of Annie Oakley (he called her "Little Sure Shot"), joined the show in 1885. Like other Indians who worked for Cody, Sitting Bull took advantage of the opportunity to escape the confines of the reservation (in his case, Standing Rock in North Dakota). As a member of the "Wild West" troupe, he also enjoyed decent food and accommodations. At a time when whites were denigrating Indian culture, Sitting Bull affirmed that culture by demonstrating his shooting and riding skills. However, white audiences jeered him—they saw him as less an entertainer and more an enemy warrior—and he left after just a year. By the 1890s, Cody was playing to audiences in Europe as well as the United States, dramatizing a West that was fast disappearing. Still, the sight of Annie Oakley shooting glass balls and clay pigeons out of the air, as well as mounted cowboys leading "Custer's last charge," gave customers their money's worth.

Denver Public Library/Western History/Genealogy Department (Neg. #B-133)

■ "Buffalo Bill" Cody and Sitting Bull pose for a promotional photo for the 1885 season of the "Wild West." Cody refrained from calling the production a "show," maintaining that it demonstrated frontier skills and recreated historical encounters (such as Custer's Last Stand and stagecoach robberies). The "Wild West" toured Canada and Europe and inspired many imitators.

ENTERTAINMENT COLLIDES WITH TRADITION

After the Civil War, various forms of mass entertainment gained huge, enthusiastic followings all over the country. The traveling circus provides a case in point. By the 1870s, such shows were erecting their tents in small towns and big cities alike. The largest shows employed hundreds of people as performers, cooks, carpenters, and wagon drivers. Circus owners provided their customers with exciting sights and sounds—death-defying lion-tamers, gravity-defying gymnasts and tightrope walkers, exhibits of wild animals such as elephants and tigers, rollicking brass bands, and the hilarious antics of clowns. Even people who could not afford to attend the main show enjoyed the elaborate parade that marked the circus's arrival in town. Sideshows featured people with unusual physical characteristics related to height, body weight, facial hair, and limb flexibility. On the circus grounds, people sold a variety of exotic foods, and performers provided previews of the afternoon or evening show. These early circuses foreshadowed several forms of popular twentieth-century entertainment, including movie spectacles, magic shows, and daredevil stunts.

Not everyone cheered when the circus wagons rolled into town. Men and women with conservative religious views often disapproved of circuses. They found much that offended them under the "Big Top"—the bawdy humor of clowns; the displays of young female acrobats and other performers clad only in tights or, even worse, appearing in various states of undress; the rowdy audiences that cheered wildly for each act. Outside, on the circus grounds, gamblers and other tricksters were intent on cheating children and other naive persons out of their money. Frequently, fistfights and gunfights broke out among circus employees and local youths, fights often fueled by an excess of alcohol all around. Moreover, the arrival of the circus caused schoolchildren to drop their books, field workers their hoes, and domestic servants their dish towels in their rush to the ticket office. Some people also charged that the circus encouraged the poor to squander what little money they had on frivolous pursuits.

> *Men and women with conservative religious views found much that offended them under the "Big Top."*

These concerns were especially prominent in the rural South. In 1876, a newspaper editor in southern Georgia warned his readers, "Of all the demoralizing things ever permitted to run at large through any town, a circus takes the lead. It completely unjoints every particle of social, moral, and religious machinery in any small town." Circus owners reacted to these warnings in creative ways. Many of them stressed the wild-animal exhibits as proof of God's power, worthy of the patronage of the most devout church member. Promoters of the John Robinson Circus claimed that its show possessed "the Largest and most Complete Menagerie, Aviary, and Aquarium in the World, Containing Living Specimens of our CREATOR'S GREAT HANDIWORK, of which 'They went in two and two, and Noah into the Ark, the male and female as God had commanded Noah.'" The Great Eastern Circus beckoned customers to view its wild animals "just as God made them, in his infinite wisdom." However, many people, circus-goers of all ages, needed no encouragement to spend an afternoon or an evening in a world apart from their everyday routines.

"PALACES OF CONSUMPTION"

In the cities of the late nineteenth century, the act of shopping for goods, especially luxury goods, became an adventure in itself. A new piece of the cityscape, the department store, welcomed customers into a world of luxury and abundance, a place of color, light, and glamour. These "palaces of consumption" showcased a variety of technological innovations. In Marshall Field's "Grand Emporium" (Chicago), Wanamaker's (Philadelphia), and Lord and Taylor (New York), shoppers glided from floor to floor on escalators and in elevators. Warmed by central heating, they browsed display cases, racks, and tables laden with enticing goods illuminated by arc lighting. Their money streamed into cash registers or to a central clerk through cash conveyors.

Thus, department stores not only offered a dazzling array of goods but also made shopping an exciting experience. This type of adventure appealed particularly to middle-class women, who had the leisure time and the cash to indulge in day-long shopping excursions. In 1880, a New Yorker could arrive at Macy's by taking the Sixth Avenue elevated train and spend the morning exploring any number of specialized departments: ribbons, women's and children's muslin underwear, toys, candy, books, men's furnishings, china and glassware, and so on. Fatigued at noon, she might visit the lunchroom to partake of a modest meal and then devote the rest of her day to examining the colored dress silks in a new department established the year before.

The department store clerk played a key role in marketing a new array of goods. The ideal clerk was a young, attractive woman who dressed well and showed inifinite patience in dealing with demanding shoppers. But life behind the counter was not always ideal for the women who worked there. They were caught between their male supervisors (who at times engaged in sexual harrassment) and the middle-class women they served. Though expected to dress fashionably, women clerks received low wages and faced long hours on their feet on the job. Like the workers who toiled to produce the goods stocked in department stores, the clerks were not in a position to buy many of the items arrayed in these new palaces of consumption.

The department store was an exclusively urban phenomenon, but mass merchandising reached far beyond cities. The material riches of American society became accessible to rural people through the mail-order catalogue. This marketing device was pioneered in 1872 by the Chicago company Montgomery Ward, the official supply house for the Farmers' Grange. On homesteads throughout the Midwest, family members gathered to pore over the thousands of items displayed in "The Great Wish Book." The company's motto? "Satisfaction guaranteed or your money back." Farm wives delighted in the latest Parisian

Refugio Amador and her five daughters, Emilia, Maria, Clotilde, Julieta, and Corina, were members of an elite Hispanic family in Las Cruces, New Mexico. Her husband, Martin Amador, was a prominent politician, merchant, hotel owner, and freighter. A subcontractor for the U.S. government, he supplied military troops in the area. The family shopped by mail-order catalogue from Bloomingdale's Department Store in New York City.

fashions, their husbands pondered the intricacies of McCormick threshing machinery, and the children studied the newest toys and fishing rods.

Late in the decade, a competitor appeared on the scene in the form of the Sears, Roebuck Catalogue. A former mail-order watch salesman, Richard Sears soon gained a reputation as a man who could "sell a breath of fresh air." Sears helped pioneer the field of modern advertising hyperbole, claiming, for example, that the sewing machine he offered was the "Best on Earth." Selling was fast becoming a circus sideshow.

"Rural Free Delivery Mail"

The mass production needed to satisfy eager customers depended on mass advertising, an enterprise still in its infancy in the 1880s. Yet some of the principles that would shape the future of this business were in place even at this early date. For instance, soon after the Civil War, the makers of Sozodont dentifrice (toothpaste) plastered the name of their product all over weekly religious magazines and more mainstream publications, such as *Harper's* and *Scribner's*. They labeled the natural landscape as well. Indeed, the word *Sozodont* on Maiden's Rock in Red Wing, Minnesota, was so large that steamboat passengers on the Mississippi River three miles away could plainly read it.

The career of L. Frank Baum illustrates the convergence of modern ideas about theatrical performances and sales spectacles. Born to a wealthy German American family in 1856, Baum grew up in upstate New York. His father had made a great deal of money from the oil industry, particularly Pennsylvania gushers that yielded a distinctive emerald green oil. The younger Baum was drawn to what he called the "dream life," with its guilt-free indulgence in pleasure. Together with his wife, he founded a theater troupe that toured the Midwest in the 1880s. He then made a brief foray into merchandising. He marketed Baum's Castorine (axle grease) and opened his own department store, Baum's Bazaar, in Aberdeen, South Dakota, in the northeast corner of the state. There, he also became editor of the town newspaper, the *Aberdeen Saturday Pioneer*.

Baum eventually moved his family to Chicago, where he embarked on a career as a department store window designer. He founded the National Association of Window Trimmers in 1898 and started a trade magazine, *The Show Window*. The magazine

What Every Woman Needs: An Ad for a Bathtub

PIONEER BATHTUB ADVERTISING
(From the Century Magazine for May, 1890.)

This advertisement for a bathtub appeared in the May 1890 issue of *Century Magazine*. In the 1880s, businesses tried to convince people that a wide array of products, formerly considered luxuries, were now necessities. This ad suggests that a Standard bathtub "is a luxury you can afford." Advertisers also began to use sophisticated psychological techniques to appeal to the desires of potential consumers. The ad asks the reader to "imagine how delicious a bath can be made by using one of our bath tubs."

QUESTIONS

1. To whom in particular does this ad seek to appeal, and why?

2. What are the assumptions the advertiser makes about the consuming public during this period?

3. What is the significance of the name of the company selling the bathtub?

4. How might a middle-class man or woman have reacted to this ad in 1890?

5. What basic advertising principles still evident in today's print, online, and television ads are incorporated in this ad?

encouraged designers to strive for a "sumptuous display" of goods and to highlight their rich textures and colors. Baum went on to become a popular writer of children's fiction. His famous book *The Wizard of Oz* (1900), an allegory of late nineteenth-century life, covered themes as diverse as women's rights and rural poverty. An accomplished and successful showman, Baum understood that Americans were eager to buy fantasy wherever they could find it: in a theater, department store, or children's book.

Whether the products were featured in a department store display case, show window, magazine advertisement, or mail-order catalogue, the face of modern merchandising was bound to be young, white, and well-to-do, brimming with health and material well-being. The new consumer culture was marked by a glaring double standard: although advertisers marketed to the millions, they established a very narrow standard of the "normal" American. In the quest to define and defend this narrow standard, influential politicians and intellectuals shared with advertisers certain assumptions about "normal" Americans, their physical appearance and cultural characteristics.

Defending the New Industrial Order

■ *What arguments were offered by defenders of the new industrial order, including politicians, business owners, and influential writers and thinkers?*

By the late 1870s, as consumer culture expanded, intense conflict over fundamental issues all but evaporated from national party politics. Although ethnic and cultural loyalties continued to inflame local and state elections, Republicans and Democrats at the national level disagreed about little except the tariff. Adhering to tradition, Republicans favored a higher tariff that would benefit domestic businesses by making imported goods more expensive. In contrast, Democrats argued that a higher tariff, and resulting higher prices for goods produced in the United States, would harm consumers. Members of the Republican Party called themselves the Grand Army of the Republic and "waved the **bloody shirt**"—that is, they reminded voters that many of their Democratic opponents, especially those in the South, had supported secession a generation before. Still, the two major parties openly shared a similar goal: to win as many jobs as possible for their respective supporters. Politics served as a vehicle for patronage and favors rather than as a conduit for ideas and alternative visions of the nation's future.

Many politicians also shared a belief in the idea of **laissez-faire** (a French phrase meaning to leave alone, referring to the absence of government interference in economic

Carnegie Library of Pittsburgh (#P-1987)

■ The Great Labor Uprising of July 1877 was the first national strike in U.S. history. As railroad lines proliferated, owners slashed wages in a bid to remain competitive. Railroad workers in some cities destroyed trains, tracks, and other equipment. Spreading eventually to 14 states, the conflict claimed the lives of more than 100 people and resulted in the loss of millions of dollars worth of private property.

Andrew Carnegie and the "Gospel of Wealth"

In an article titled "Wealth," published in the North American Review in 1889, steel manufacturer Andrew Carnegie defended the amassing of large fortunes on the part of a few. He hailed this trend as a sign of progress.

The conditions of human life have not only been changed, but revolutionized, within the past few hundred years. In the former days there was little difference between the dwelling, dress, food, and environment of the chief and those of his retainers. The Indians are to-day where civilized man then was. When visiting the Sioux, I was led to the wigwam of the chief. It was just like the others in external appearance, and even within the difference was trifling between it and those of the poorest of his braves. The contrast between the palace of the millionaire and the cottage of the laborer with us to-day measures the change which has come with civilization.

This change, however, is not to be deplored, but welcomed as highly beneficial. It is well, nay, essential for the progress of the race, that the houses of some should be homes for all that is highest and best in literature and the arts, and for all the refinements of civilization, rather than that none should be so. Much better this great irregularity than universal squalor. . . . Whether the change be for good or ill, it is upon us, beyond our power to alter, and therefore to be accepted and made the best of. It is a waste of time to criticise the inevitable.

Judge, July 25, 1903

■ This *Judge* cartoon depicts Andrew Carnegie dispersing his fortune. Many of his donations were used for the establishment of public libraries, a worthy cause according to Carnegie's "gospel of wealth."

or social affairs). Laissez-faire was actually a flexible concept, invoked to justify government indifference in some areas but government intervention in others. Indeed, politicians tended to favor laissez-faire in social matters more than in the economy. Thus, support for manufacturers and railroads in the form of tariff protection and land grants, for example, was justified. At the same time, however, Congress, the president, and the Supreme Court were reluctant to enact bold measures to redress the growing gap between rich and poor. In fact, certain clergy, businesspeople, and university professors sought to explain and defend the inequality between the captains of industry and the masses of ill-paid laborers. They argued that the system of industrial capitalism was desirable because it was "natural."

Nevertheless, many advocates of laissez-faire in social welfare policy supported government intervention in the economy. These observers argued that the government was justified in providing tariff protection to manufacturers and in using federal power to quell strikes of railroad workers. For example, in the summer of 1877, the president of the Pennsylvania Railroad, Thomas Scott, and other railroad officials were forced to contend with a workers' strike that spread throughout the country. Trying to cut costs in what had become a bitterly competitive business, many of the railroads had demanded that workers labor for longer hours for 10 percent less pay. Managers instituted the practice of "double-heading"—adding more cars to a train but not hiring more workers to tend them, placing added burdens on engineers and other workers. In response, beleaguered rail workers walked off the job. Men and women in other struggling industries—from

Carnegie believed that wealthy people had the responsibility to give away their money before they died, although he had distinct ideas about to whom—or to what—such money should be given. He elaborated on what came to be called the "gospel of wealth":

There remains, then, only one mode of using great fortunes; but in this we have the true antidote for the temporary unequal distribution of wealth, the reconciliation of the rich and the poor—a reign of harmony—another ideal, differing indeed, from that of the Communist in requiring only the further evolution of existing conditions, not the total overthrow of our civilization. . . . Under its sway we shall have an ideal state, in which the surplus wealth of the few will become, in the best sense, the property of the many, because it is administered for the common good, and this wealth, passing through the hands of the few, can be made a much more potent force for the elevation of our race than if it had been distributed in small sums to the people themselves. Even the poorest can be made to see this, and to agree that the great sums gathered by some of their fellow-citizens and spent for public purposes, from which the masses reap the principal benefit, are more valuable to them than if scattered through the course of many years in trifling amounts.

In 1901, Carnegie sold his steel company to banker J. P. Morgan for $480 million. By the time of his death, Carnegie had given away an estimated $350 million to a variety of causes and institutions.

QUESTIONS

1. *How does Carnegie link extremes of wealth and poverty with progress?*

2. *Why did Carnegie focus his philanthropic energies on building public libraries?*

3. *Why would Carnegie have rejected as impractical and unreasonable the argument that he should have paid his workers higher wages rather than distributing his profits to charity?*

Source: Andrew Carnegie, "Wealth," *North American Review* (1889).

laundresses and longshoremen in Galveston, Texas, to coal miners in Scranton, Pennsylvania, to packinghouse laborers in Chicago—also went on strike during what came to be known as the Great Labor Uprising of 1877. That July, the federal government deployed army troops as a strike-breaking force in Chicago, East St. Louis, Illinois, and Terre Haute, Indiana, among other cities.

In a letter to the *North American Review* magazine in August 1877, Thomas Scott justified his railroad's wage cuts and charged that the strikers were under the sway of vicious criminals. Scott hailed the railroads as truly national enterprises, "closely interwoven with the interests not only of our own but other countries." During the Civil War, Union forces had commandeered private rail lines, Scott pointed out. Now it was appropriate that the federal government protect the railroads in this time of crisis. Indeed, according to Scott, "this insurrection," the strike, presented a national emergency "almost as serious as that which prevailed at the outset of the Civil War."

One view of this period was provided by Mark Twain (Samuel Clemens) and Charles Dudley Warner in *The Gilded Age* (1873). Their book satirized the trend toward corruption in public affairs and the wild financial speculation that produced both poverty and great wealth. The growth of large businesses that received economic and political support from government officials served to enrich employers, investors, and politicians at the expense of workers and farmers. The term Gilded Age became synonymous with the excess and extravagance on the part of politicians and businesspeople alike during the last quarter of the nineteenth century.

TABLE 16.2			
The Election of 1880			
Candidate	**Political Party**	**Popular Vote (%)**	**Electoral Vote**
James A. Garfield	Republican	48.5	214
Winfield S. Hancock	Democratic	48.1	155
James B. Weaver	Greenback-Labor	3.4	–

THE CONTRADICTORY POLITICS OF LAISSEZ-FAIRE

In 1880, the undistinguished President Rutherford B. Hayes chose not to run for office again. That summer, the Republicans nominated James A. Garfield of Ohio, a former mule driver who had become a Civil War general. To counter the "bloody-shirt" effect, Democrats put forth their own former Union general: Winfield S. Hancock, who had been wounded at Gettysburg. Garfield won the popular vote by a narrow margin but easily defeated Hancock in the electoral college.

Garfield's arrival in the White House set off a race for patronage jobs among loyal Republicans. Indeed, overwhelmed by office-seekers, the new president remarked, "My God! What is there in this place that a man should ever want to get into it?" Then on July 2, 1881, Charles J. Guiteau, who had unsuccessfully sought the position of U.S. consul in Paris, shot Garfield in a Washington, D.C., train station. Garfield languished for a few months, finally dying on September 19.

Vice President Chester A. Arthur, a former New York politician, assumed the reins of government. Arthur's administration supported certain forms of government intervention in society, or "social engineering." Arthur and others believed that laissez-faire policies had their limits; strong measures were needed to counter what they and other conservatives considered immoral personal behavior. In 1882, Congress passed the **Edmunds Act.** Targeting Mormons, the act outlawed polygamy (the practice of having more than one wife at a time), took the right to vote away from the law's offenders, and sent a five-member commission to Utah to oversee local elections.

That same year, the Chinese Exclusion Act became the first piece of legislation to bar a particular group from entering the United States. Most Chinese immigrants took jobs that native-born whites shunned. Moreover, unemployment among California's white manufacturing workers in the 1870s was caused not by Chinese competitors but by the flood of cheap eastern-made goods carried into the state by the transcontinental railroad. As eastern goods entered California, manufacturers in the West laid off workers and closed factories. The Chinese thus became scapegoats for groups hit hard by larger economic changes.

The Alien Contract Law of 1885 outlawed indentured servitude, a highly exploitative labor system that had characterized early settlement of the Chesapeake in the seventeenth century. This law intended to bar Chinese immigrants who received no pay until they worked off the costs of their passage to the United States. However, the law carried no enforcement mechanism. Thus it proved ineffective in stopping labor practices that forced various immigrant groups—not just the Chinese—to labor in isolated worksites for years against their will.

In 1883, the Supreme Court hurt the cause of civil rights by declaring the Civil Rights Act of 1875 unconstitutional. The five cases involved in the Court's decision focused on exclusions of blacks from hotels, railroad cars, and theaters. The Court held that state governments could not discriminate on the basis of race but that private individuals could do so. This decision put an official stamp of approval on racist practices of employers, hotels, restaurants, and other providers of jobs and services.

Arthur surprised his critics by embracing the cause of **civil service reform.** This movement sought to inject professional standards into public service and rid the country of the worst excesses of the corrupt "spoils system," where political victors put loyal supporters into public jobs regardless of their qualifications. In response to Garfield's assassination by Guiteau, the disappointed patronage-seeker, Congress passed the **Pendleton Act** (1883). This measure established a merit system for federal job applicants and created the Civil Service Commission, which administered competitive examinations to candidates in certain classifications.

In 1884, Arthur fell ill (he would die shortly), and the Republicans nominated James G. Blaine of Maine as their candidate for the presidency. Blaine, who had benefited from corrupt deals in the past, offended the sensibilities of a group of reform-minded Republicans, who called themselves Mugwumps. (The term reportedly had its roots in an Indian

TABLE 16.3			
The Election of 1884			
Candidate	**Political Party**	**Popular Vote (%)**	**Electoral Vote**
Grover Cleveland	Democratic	48.5	219
James G. Blaine	Republican	48.2	182

word that meant "holier than thou.") As a result, Blaine was bested in the national election by the former mayor of Buffalo, Grover Cleveland, who became the first Democratic president in twenty eight years.

Throughout the 1880s, Congress and the chief executive ignored the laissez-faire principle selectively—for example, regarding Indian status. Like other critics of federal Indian policy, writer Helen Hunt Jackson in her 1881 book *A Century of Dishonor* called for applying the "protection of the law to the Indian's rights of property." Moved to act, Congress passed the **Dawes Act.** The new act was intended to improve the economic condition of Indians by eliminating common ownership of tribal lands in favor of a system of private property. The law distributed plots of land to individual Indians who renounced traditional customs. The law also encouraged these landowners to become sedentary farmers and to adopt "other habits of civilized life." In the end, however, the act amounted to little more than a land-grab on the part of whites; between 1887 and 1900, Indian-held lands decreased from 138 million acres to 78 million acres.

DOCUMENT
The Dawes Act

By the 1880s, local citizens, through the Grange and their elected public officials, were calling for the states to restrict the monopolistic practices of the railroads. Nevertheless, in *Wabash v. Illinois* (1886), the Supreme Court invalidated a state law regulating railroads, ruling that only Congress, and not the states, could control interstate transportation. The next year Congress took the initiative and passed the **Interstate Commerce Act** of 1887. This

DOCUMENT
Interstate
Commerce Act

The National Archives

■ Dakota Indians gather at the Standing Rock Reservation to receive government rations, c. 1880. To counter the Indians' increased dependence on the government for food, Congress passed the Dawes Severalty Act of 1887. U.S. agents cited the act in their efforts to ban crucial aspects of Indian culture, including native practices related to religion, education, language, and even dress and hairstyles.

TABLE 16.4			
The Election of 1888			
Candidate	**Political Party**	**Popular Vote (%)**	**Electoral Vote**
Benjamin Harrison	Republican	42.9	233
Grover Cleveland	Democratic	48.6	168
Clinton B. Fisk	Prohibition	2.2	–
Anson J. Streeter	Union Labor	1.3	–

legislation mandated that the railroads charge all shippers the same rates and refrain from giving rebates to their largest customers. The act also established the Interstate Commerce Commission to oversee and stabilize the railroad industry. Congress thus acknowledged that the public interest demanded some form of business regulation, although enforcement of the act was less than vigorous.

Cleveland invoked laissez-faire principles in 1887 when he vetoed legislation that would have provided seeds for hard-pressed farmers in Texas. As the president put it, "Though the people support the government, the government should not support the people." Cleveland also favored lower tariff rates, but most Americans favored government protection of domestic manufacturing in the form of higher tariffs. The Republicans exploited Cleveland's unpopular views on this issue, nominating Benjamin Harrison, grandson of President William Henry ("Tippecanoe") Harrison. The younger Harrison defeated his rival in the electoral college but not in the popular vote.

The principle of government laissez-faire was of little use in addressing a central paradox of the late nineteenth century: the free enterprise system was being undermined by the very forms of business organization it had spawned and nourished. Trusts and combinations were inherently hostile to competition. In 1890, Congress passed a piece of landmark legislation, the **Sherman Anti-Trust Act,** designed to outlaw trusts and large business combinations of all kinds.

SOCIAL DARWINISM AND THE "NATURAL" STATE OF SOCIETY

In the late nineteenth century, manufactured devices and engineering feats helped create a new social order, one marked by a few very wealthy industrialists, a growing middle class, and an increasingly diverse workforce of ill-paid field and factory hands. Brazenly borrowing from the theories of Charles Darwin, a British naturalist who had pioneered the study of evolution, some prominent clergy, businesspeople, journalists, and university professors sought to defend this new order as God-ordained, or "natural." These observers drew parallels between Darwin's theory of "survival of the fittest" and the workings of modern society. (In his book *The Origin of Species,* Darwin had discussed changes in animals, not people or societies.) In the United States, Social Darwinists warned that "unnatural" forms of intervention—specifically, labor unions or social welfare legislation—were misguided, dangerous, and ultimately doomed to failure. In essence, Social Darwinists distorted a sound scientific theory, misusing it to justify exploitation of the poor and laboring classes.

The ideology of **Social Darwinism** evolved in response to class conflict and other forms of social turbulence in the 1870s and 1880s. Famed Brooklyn minister Henry Ward Beecher cited what he called "the great laws of political economy" to preach the virtues of poverty ("it was fit that man should eat the bread of affliction") and the evils of labor unions. Beecher and like-minded thinkers agreed that the government had the right and the obligation to come to the rescue of private companies threatened by angry workers or consumers. These observers also made a distinction between public subsidies to railroads and tariff protection for domestic manufacturers on one hand, and public intervention on behalf of workers on the other.

Yale sociologist William Graham Sumner declared that society was like a living organism. For the species to remain healthy, individuals must prosper or decline according to their inherent characteristics. "Society, therefore, does not need any care or supervision," Sumner wrote in his 1883 treatise *What the Social Classes Owe to Each Other*. These views rationalized not only the hierarchies of the workplace but also the triumph of "Anglo-Saxons" on the North American continent and beyond. Editors of the *New York Times* interpreted Darwin's ideas as suggesting that "the red man will be driven out, and the white man will take possession. This is not justice, but it is destiny." In his book *Our Country* (1885), the Reverend Josiah Strong also drew on the ideas of Social Darwinism to claim that just as the fittest plants and animals endure in the natural kingdom, so "civilized" whites would eventually displace "barbarous," dark-skinned peoples, whether on the High Plains of South Dakota or on the savannas of Africa.

Not all Americans studied or debated the theories of Charles Darwin, of course. Nevertheless, middle-class opinion-makers, many of them Victorian Protestants, believed that their own religious and cultural values remained superior to those of other groups of people, at home and abroad. The United States was becoming increasingly diverse in both economic and ethnic terms. At the same time, white, prosperous, native-born Protestants contended that they set the standards for the rest of the nation. These standards revolved around the middle-class domestic ideal, with its rigidly proscribed gender roles, devotion to personal achievement (for men at least), and commitment to moral suasion (that is, regulating a person's behavior by appealing to his or her conscience). Agents of the Victorian middle class included schoolteachers, clergy, magazine editors, business leaders, and other well-educated people able and willing to influence the beliefs and behavior of others.

CHRONOLOGY: 1877–1889

1877	All federal troops withdrawn from the South, ending Reconstruction.
	"Great Uprising" of railroad employees and other workers.
1878	Thomas Edison patents the phonograph.
	San Francisco Workingmen's party stages anti-Chinese protests.
1879	First telephone line connects two American cities (Boston and Lowell, Massachusetts).
1880	New York City streets lit by electricity.
	James A. Garfield elected president.
1881	Charles Guiteau assassinates President Garfield.
1882	Standard Oil Trust is created.
	Chinese Exclusion Act.
1883	Pendleton Act (civil service reform).
1884	Grover Cleveland elected president.
1887	Interstate Commerce Act creates Interstate Commerce Commission.
	Dawes Act.
1889	First All-American football team, consisting of players from Yale, Harvard, and Princeton.

Conclusion

Some historians suggest that the great captains of industry were the chief representatives of widely held values in late nineteenth-century America. Men such as Carnegie and Rockefeller had the vision and personal ambition necessary to build large corporate enterprises. They became fabulously wealthy by providing the United States with the ingredients necessary to an economic revolution: steel, oil, and other materials. Their ideology of unbridled individualism encouraged many people to aspire to entrepreneurial independence: the tailor hoped someday to own a store, the cook dreamed of opening a restaurant. The explosion of economic activity during this period—a second American industrial revolution—widened the middle class and lent credence to the notion of widespread upward mobility, modest though it was in most cases.

Nevertheless, a case can be made that engineers were the true representatives of the age. As designers of railroads, mines, gravity-defying skyscrapers, and new systems of factory management, they oversaw the technical aspects of economic growth and development. Engineers melded science with mass production to yield a form of capitalism that thrived on consumers' deepest desires and anxieties. In the process, a new, complex national culture emerged.

This culture valued innovation, newness, fashion, change, and sensory stimulation. Advertisers sought to convince consumers that they should buy products that were up to date. Customers all over the country desired to experience thrilling and novel theatrical spectacles and athletic contests. "Desires" replaced more traditional "needs" when Americans of all ages contemplated buying clothes and household furnishings. Yet this culture also embraced impulses that were conservative, promoting the idea that white, Protestant, native-born

Americans set the standard against which other Americans were judged, and often found wanting. Still, many native-born Americans and immigrants to the United States found this vital, new consumer culture enormously appealing.

At the same time, the effort to homogenize and standardize American cultural impulses was not without complications. Throughout the nation, various groups rejected standardization in favor of local tradition or new forms of collective action. Thus, politicians and the Social Darwinists were forced to defend their outlook on life. Some of their critics advanced the idea that society was not a living organism at all. Rather, it was like a machine, a creation of people who had the ability—and the duty—to repair or adjust it. Around the country, in fact, the standardizers met with stiff resistance.

For Review

1. What were the effects of mechanical and technological innovations on midwestern agricultural laborers and steel workers? For these laborers, what was the price of "progress"?

2. In assembling large industrial workforces, what were the priorities of business managers? How did the drive for "efficiency" shape certain workplaces?

3. Many employers argued that they and their employers shared a "harmony of interests." How and why might workers have disputed this claim?

4. Contrast life on a western farm or a southern plantation to life in Chicago, New York, or San Francisco in 1890. Why did so many rural people, especially young people, move to the city?

5. What did circuses, baseball games, department stores, and amusement parks have in common in the late 1800s?

6. Why do some historians argue that consumer culture is inherently democratic? And why do others argue that consumer culture is an engine that produces economic and social inequality? Which view do you favor?

Created Equal Online

For more *Created Equal* resources, including suggestions on sites to visit and books to read, go to **MyHistoryLab.com**.

Chapter 17

Challenges to Government and Corporate Power, 1877–1890

■ By 1889, Santa Fe, New Mexico, had seen several centuries of cultural conflict.

In the spring of 1889, men in San Miguel County, northern New Mexico territory, armed themselves and donned masks. Mounting their horses, they rode out to attack their enemies. As members of a secret organization called *las Gorras Blancas* (the Whitecaps), they banded together in the dead of night and destroyed the fences of local cattle ranchers, chopping the wooden posts to pieces and scattering the barbed wire. In some of their raids, the rebels shot and wounded ranchers. Over the next year and a half, *las Gorras Blancas* broadened their targets. They burned bridges, haystacks, and piles of lumber; they cut telegraph wires and took axes to electric light poles and railroad ties belonging to the Atcheson, Topeka, and Santa Fe Railroad. The membership of the group overlapped with that of the **Knights of Labor,** a national labor union that boasted twenty local assemblies in San Miguel County, east of Santa Fe. On the night of March 11, 1890, *las Gorras Blancas* nailed pieces of paper to the buildings of East Las Vegas, the largest town in the county. These pages, copies of the insurgents' "platform," declared: "Our purpose is to protect the rights and interests of the people in general; especially those of the helpless classes."

Who were these determined nightriders? They were Hispanos (Spanish-speaking natives of the area). Their movement began when Juan José Herrera, together with his two brothers, Pablo and Nicanor, organized their neighbors in an effort to block European American ranchers from fencing their land. Labeled *las masas de los hombres pobres* (the masses of the poor people) by a local newspaper, *las Gorras Blancas* were desperately struggling to preserve a traditional way of life that was rapidly disappearing. Fenced lands prevented the area's Hispanic settlers from grazing their stock herds in the customary, open-range manner. The fence-cutters believed they were upholding American principles of justice and fair play.

Many Hispanos lived in adobe (baked-clay) dwellings in small river-valley villages surrounded by breathtaking mesas, ponderosa pine forests, and high dry plains. In addition to raising chickens and grazing sheep, families grew chiles, pinto beans, squash, and wheat. Together, villagers relied on the common lands that had come down to them from their ancestors—land originally bestowed through grants from Spain and then Mexico. After the Civil War, European American interlopers—sheep and cattle ranchers, lawyers, speculators, commercial lumberers, and the railroads—began to encroach on these common lands. Through local courts, the newcomers installed a system of private property that granted exclusive ownership to single individuals. It was these groups, with their fences and their laws governing land ownership, that *las Gorras Blancas* targeted.

Northern New Mexico had long witnessed battles between successive waves of settlers; for example, Spanish-speaking migrants had fought Comanche and Jicarilla Apache for the land in earlier generations. Yet the upheaval in San Miguel County in 1889 and 1890 did not simply pit Hispanic subsistence farmers against European American "land grabbers." The Spanish-speaking population itself was divided between poor villagers and elite *ricos* (merchants and landowners). Members of *las Gorras Blancas* quarreled among themselves over whose fences to cut and whose barns to burn. They also broke with European American members of the Knights of Labor, insisting that, as Hispanos, they had the right and the obligation to protect their common lands, by force if necessary. The insurgents even renounced some of their own Hispanic political leaders. These men, they charged, had become corrupted by greed and were willing to do the bidding of European American interlopers.

Las Gorras Blancas had only mixed success. They managed to discourage new European Americans from settling in the area, and they prevented the railroads from buying more rail ties in northern New Mexico. Yet the nightriders could not stem the tide of common land loss throughout the Southwest. The Court of Private Land Claims, established in 1891 by the U.S. government, resolved land disputes between Hispanic and European American claimants. Of the more than 35 million acres of land in dispute in the early 1890s, Hispanic claimants received title to little more than 2 million acres—barely one-twentieth of the land they had held in common.

Las Gorras Blancas represented a unique response to local conditions. But the group was also part of a growing, nationwide movement against the standards imposed by industrialization and capitalism. Around the country, a wide variety of individuals and organizations emerged in the late 1870s and the 1880s to challenge employers, landlords, and military and government officials. Members of these latter groups responded with a challenge of their own. Business, they proclaimed, must be allowed to develop fully and freely without "unnatural" intervention in the form of regulatory legislation or grassroots rebellions such as that of *las Gorras Blancas*.

It is difficult to generalize about those who contested the emerging order. Even their own names could be misleading. In the early 1890s, another group called "White Caps," this one in Mississippi, consisted of whites who terrorized black landowners. And although the Knights of Labor was a national union, it shaped its program in accordance with local issues. In San Miguel County, for instance, the issue was land—who controlled it and under what conditions. In Washington, D.C., the Knights' concern was the welfare of workers in the building trades. The Richmond, Virginia, Knights pioneered interracial organizing, living up to the group's motto, "An injury to one is an injury to all." In contrast, the San Francisco Knights spearheaded the move to bar Chinese laborers from the United States and to limit job opportunities for those who remained. Indeed, groups that challenged the authority of government and large business interests often disagreed among themselves about goals and strategies for change.

Rejecting new business principles that favored aggressive profit-seeking above all else, nightriders, union organizers, antimachine activists, visionary prophets, investigative journalists, and settlement house workers all offered alternative visions for America. Members of these groups debated among themselves the changes overtaking American society and the means to control them. Some wielded pens or used typewriters to effect change; others took photographs, collected data, or conducted interviews. Still others shouldered arms or torched haystacks. In some cases they sought to preserve local religious and social customs; in others they promoted the health and welfare of factory workers.

Some proponents of change advocated radical action that challenged the very foundations of American society. Others stressed the need to reform, but not change radically, certain elements of society and politics. Radicals and reformers alike derived ideas and inspiration from their European counterparts, for the issues confronting a rapidly industrializing society were not unique to the United States during this period. Nevertheless, Americans remained divided in their vision of the good and just society—a vision that would require the commitment of more than any one political party, labor union, reform association, or band of rebels to become reality.

Resistance to Legal and Military Authority

■ *What were the various protest strategies used by different groups of people who faced discrimination, and at times violence, from employers, government officials, vigilantes, and the U.S. military?*

America's march toward national economic centralization and integration was not steady. On the battlefield and in the courts, European Americans pressed their advantage, but these efforts met with stiff resistance from a variety of aggrieved groups. Members of these groups rightly believed they had much to lose from so-called progress. European Americans repeatedly used the notion of "racial" difference as a justification for depriving darker-skinned peoples of their claims to land, jobs, and even life itself. For example, California lawmakers at both the state and local levels approved legislation that discriminated against the Chinese as workers and as parents of school-age children. In an effort to seek redress, some Chinese took their claims to court.

In a similar vein, prejudice against African Americans assumed the form of discriminatory legislation and random violence. Blacks chafed under restrictions intended to bar them from good jobs and from associating with white people on an equal basis. Varieties of black resistance to white authority included migration out of the South to the West, creation of community institutions, and violent retaliation.

For their part, during the late 1880s, the Plains Indians responded to encroaching railroads, settlers, and military regiments by embracing a movement of spiritual regeneration. On the Plains, whites, and especially U.S. military officers, perceived this movement as more dangerous than an armed uprising, and they reacted accordingly.

CHINESE LAWSUITS IN CALIFORNIA

In San Francisco in 1878, Irish-born Denis Kearney founded the Workingmen's Party of California, composed primarily of unemployed whites. Kearney and others agitated for the violent expulsion of Chinese from jobs. They blamed Chinese shoemakers, tailors, and cigarmakers for the distress that native-born factory workers and tradespeople were suffering. One critic remarked that, although Kearney "practiced and preached" temperance when it came to the use of alcohol or tobacco, the labor leader favored expressing his own extreme opinions in an inflammatory way.

Opposition to the Chinese hardened in the 1880s. In San Francisco, the Knights of Labor and the Workingmen's Party of California helped to engineer the passage of the Chinese Exclusion Act, approved by Congress in 1882. This measure denied any additional Chinese laborers entry into the country while allowing some Chinese merchants and students to immigrate. (Put to the voters of California in 1879, the possibility of *total* exclusion of Chinese had garnered 150,000 votes for and only 900 against.) In railroad towns and mining camps, vigilantes looted and burned Chinese communities, in some cases murdering or expelling their inhabitants. In 1885, in Rock Springs, Wyoming, white workers massacred twenty-eight Chinese and drove hundreds out of town in the wake of an announcement by Union Pacific officials that the railroad would begin hiring the lower-paid immigrants. Cheered on by others, a mob burned the Chinese section of town to the ground. Such attacks erupted more and more frequently throughout the West in the late 1880s and into the 1890s. Whites contended that they must present a united front against all Chinese, who, they claimed, threatened the economic well-being of white working-class communities.

These whites also held that the Chinese, with their distinctive customs, would never fit into American life. Nevertheless, early on the Chinese demonstrated an understanding and appreciation of American political and legal processes. Beginning in Gold Rush days, Chinese immigrants had taken their grievances to court. In 1862, Ling Sing protested the $2.50 personal tax levied on Chinese exclusively. The California Supreme Court agreed (in *Ling Sing v. Washburn*)

■ In the West, Chinese mining companies used water management techniques based on traditional Chinese machinery such as the waterwheel. This photo shows a Chinese river-mining operation in Siskiyou, California, c. 1890. Chinese workers also constructed flumes, dams, canals, tunnels, and pumps to drain areas efficiently.

that the group could not be singled out for special taxes. In the 1870s, Chinese merchants used the provisions of the Civil Rights Act to challenge state and local laws that forbade them from holding certain jobs, living in white neighborhoods, and testifying in court. In the fall of 1885, Chinese residents of Rock Springs wrote a lengthy appeal to the Chinese consul in San Francisco, relating their story of the massacre and appealing for justice; 559 people signed the document.

In San Francisco in 1885, laundry operator Yick Wo was convicted under an 1880 municipal law prohibiting the construction of wooden laundries without a license. A native of China, Yick Wo had arrived in the United States in 1861. By the time of his arrest, he had operated a legal laundry for twenty-two years. When he applied for a license, the board of supervisors turned him down. His prominent European American lawyers soon learned that the board had denied licenses to all Chinese laundry operators who applied. In 1885, the lawyers petitioned the California Supreme Court, which upheld Yick Wo's arrest. The lawyers continued their appeal to the U.S. Supreme Court, maintaining that the board of supervisors intended to bar Chinese from independent laundry work altogether.

In *Yick Wo v. Hopkins* (1886), the Supreme Court reversed the state court's decision. The higher court held that the San Francisco laundry-licensing board had engaged in the discriminatory *application* of a law that on the surface was nondiscriminatory. (The local board had admitted favoritism toward white license applicants but offered no justification for its actions.) The majority opinion noted, "The very idea that one may be compelled to hold his life, or the means of living, or any material right essential to the enjoyment of life, at the mere will of another" has been considered "intolerable in any country where freedom prevails, as being the essence of slavery itself."

DOCUMENT

Yick Wo v. Hopkins

San Diego Historical Society Photograph Collection (3512-1)

■ Some Chinese made a prosperous life for themselves in the United States. This photo shows Ah Sue, her husband, Ah Quin, and their twelve children. Ah Sue found refuge in the San Francisco Chinese Mission Home in 1879. Two years later she and Ah Quin celebrated their Christian wedding in the Mission Home. Ah Quin rose from the position of cook to become a successful railroad contractor and merchant in San Diego.

Still, many cases challenging discriminatory laws never made it to the nation's highest court. And state and local courts in general often refused to acknowledge that Chinese immigrants had any civil rights at all. (Chinese immigrants were not granted citizenship until World War II, although their children born in this country qualified as citizens.) In 1885, the California Supreme Court heard the case *Tape v. Hurley,* brought by Joseph and Mary Tape on behalf of their daughter Mamie. Joseph Tape was a Chinese immigrant with some standing in the San Francisco Chinese community. Mary Tape had been raised in a Shanghai orphanage and had come to the United States with missionaries when she was eleven years old. She grew up to speak English fluently and dress as a European American. Their daughter Mamie was quite westernized as well.

Even so, Mamie Tape was barred from the city's public school system. The school board claimed that Mamie's presence in the classroom would be "very mentally and morally detrimental" to her classmates. The Tapes sued the city and won, but the school board retaliated by creating a separate school for children of Asian descent within Chinatown. Mary Tape wrote an angry letter to the board: "Dear Sirs, Will you please to tell me! Is it a disgrace to be Born a Chinese? Didn't God make us all!!! What right! have you to bar my children out of the school?" In the end, the Tapes decided to enroll their two children in the segregated school. Yet their legal protest kept alive the ideal of equality under the law.

> *Local white prejudice overwhelmed even Chinese who sought legal redress from violence and discrimination.*

In other instances, local white prejudice overwhelmed even Chinese who sought legal redress from violence and discrimination. In 1886, the Chinese living in the Wood River mining district in southern Idaho faced down a group of whites who had met and announced that all Chinese had three months to leave town. Members of the Chinese community promptly hired lawyers and took out an advertisement in the local paper stating their intention to hold their ground. As a community, they managed to survive. Still, their numbers dropped precipitously throughout Idaho as whites hounded many of them out of the state.

BLACKS IN THE "NEW SOUTH"

Similar problems plagued African Americans in what Atlanta journalist Henry Grady hailed as the "New South." The former Confederate states, he claimed, were now forward looking, prepared to embrace industrialization and promote the reconciliation of blacks and whites. According to Grady, it was time for the South to look to the future and join with a larger, modernizing America.

Grady's speech about the "New South" provided a label that stuck. Yet he doubtless spoke too soon and in terms too grandiose. True, he could point with pride to some dramatic industrial developments in the South. The eastern Piedmont (foothills region), for example, was undergoing a fledgling industrial revolution in the 1880s. Soon after James Bonsack invented a cigarette-rolling machine in 1880, James Buchanan Duke pioneered the production of machine-made cigarettes. In 1884, Duke's Durham, North Carolina, company was selling 400,000 of them each day. The southern textile labor force more than doubled between 1880 and 1890, from 17,000 men, women, and children to 36,000, many of them concentrated in the Carolinas and Georgia.

During this same period, with the backing of the Tennessee Coal, Iron, and Railway Company, the city of Birmingham, Alabama, specialized in pig iron production. Local manufacturers remained at the mercy of high shipping rates imposed by northern-owned railroads, which provided discounts only to raw materials going north and manufactured goods coming south. However, in 1889 even Andrew Carnegie acknowledged the formidable challenge posed by Birmingham blast furnaces to iron and steel producers in the North and abroad.

Factory and professional work in towns and cities offered new opportunities in the South as industry developed. However, these jobs were dominated by white men. Low-paid

George François Mugnier, the John N. Teunisson Photograph Collection, Louisiana Division, New Orleans Public Library

■ This bustling New Orleans waterfront scene, c. 1885, suggests the commercial vitality often associated with the "New South." However, a closer look reveals that all of the activity revolves around loading and unloading bales of cotton. In fact, the New South remained locked in a low-wage, staple-crop economy based on the production of cotton.

heavy labor, primarily in rural areas, continued to be the primary source of work for black men. After they finished harvesting cotton in the fall, many blacks worked at sawmills or in railroad construction camps during the winter.

The hardest and lowest-paid tasks, such as digging ore out of a hill in northern Alabama or constructing a railroad through the swamps of Florida, often went to convicts whom private employers had leased from the state. Most of these "convict lease" workers were black men who had been arrested on minor charges and then bound out when they could not pay their fines or court costs. In Mississippi a black man could be picked up for "some trifling misdemeanor," in the words of one observer, fined $500, and compelled to work off the fine (at a rate of five cents a day) for a local planter. With an almost unlimited supply of such workers, employers had little incentive to ease the brutal living and working conditions endured by these convicts.

Patterns of migration within and outside the South reveal blacks' efforts to resist discrimination. Some blacks fled the countryside and settled in southern cities where good jobs were limited but personal freedom was greater. In 1890, 15 percent of the southern black population lived in towns and cities; they represented a third of the South's total urban population. Gradually, a new black elite arose. These physicians, lawyers, insurance agents, and undertakers reached out to an exclusively black clientele and nourished a sense of community. Black men and women continued to sustain their own institutions, such as schools, lodges, benevolent societies, burial organizations, and churches.

In a variety of ways, black workers resisted the demands made upon them by white employers. Domestic servants and laundresses gathered in their off-hours to enjoy each other's company, and to dance and listen to music. To the extent that they were able, workers of all kinds abandoned particularly exploitative or abusive workplaces, leaving emloyers to contend with the disruption caused by high rates of labor turnover. Community celebrations honoring black veterans of the Civil War, or commemorating the Emancipation Proclamation, allowed black men and women to affirm their identities apart from the jobs they did. These informal strategies of resistance help to explain why white landlords and housewives were forever bemoaning the lack of "good help"—that is, subordinate workers who did not complain about the low wages or poor working conditions they endured.

Percentage of farms operated
by tenants or sharecroppers

70% and over   30%–39%
60%–69%   20%–29%
50%–59%   10%–19%
40%–49%   Less than 10%

■ **MAP 17.1** **Southern Tenancy and Sharecropping, 1880**

Tenants and sharecroppers were landless families who worked for a landowner. Tenant families usually owned a mule (to pull a plow); sharecropping families depended on their employers for food and farm supplies. This map tracks labor data in ten southern states, showing that rates of tenancy and sharecropping were highest in the areas dominated by the cotton staple-crop economy, the same areas where slavery prevailed in the antebellum period.

Despite Henry Grady's pronouncements, clearly the South had not abandoned its historical legacy of white supremacist ideologies. In fact, in the late 1880s, white Democrats feared the assertiveness of the new black elite. According to whites, this generation of men and women born as free persons and not as slaves must be "put in their place," quite literally. As a result, new state and local laws mandated separate water fountains for blacks and whites, restricted blacks to separate railroad cars and other forms of public transportation, and excluded them altogether from city parks and other public spaces. Long-standing customs barring black people from white-owned theaters, restaurants, and hotels now carried the weight of law. Taxpayers' money went into state school funds, which were then sent back to local districts. There the money was used to support two separate school systems, one white and well funded, one black and starved of cash. Legal discrimination against blacks came to be called the **Jim Crow** system. (The term, a reference to a minstrel show character named Jim Crow, had originated during the antebellum period.)

Black leaders throughout the country tried to keep a national spotlight on the legal and violent manifestations of the Jim Crow system. A rising tide of lynching engulfed the South, cresting in the 1890s, but white officials did little or nothing to halt it. Black men, women, and children were all vulnerable to the fury of the white lynch mob—on the most flimsy pretext. Perpetrators of these atrocities were rarely if ever apprehended and punished. Other blacks throughout the segregated South rightly feared that they too would be targeted if they spoke out against lynching. Yet northern blacks did not hesitate to highlight the hypocrisy of the federal government, which turned a blind eye toward this practice. Frances Ellen Watkins Harper, an educator and writer living in Philadelphia, issued the following challenge to an audience of white club women: "A government which has the power to tax a man in peace, draft him in war, should have the power to defend his life in the hour of peril." Harper condemned "the government which can protect and defend its citizens from wrong and outrage and does not."

"JIM CROW" IN THE WEST

Racial segregation was not limited to the South. The U.S. military enforced its own set of Jim Crow regulations. In 1869, Congress created the 24th and 25th Infantries (Colored) composed of African American soldiers. White officers were appointed to lead these segregated units; consequently, black men who aspired to positions of military leadership found their way blocked. (Before 1900, only three black men received commissions from West Point, and they faced systematic harassment at the academy and after graduation.) Some white officers, such as George Custer, refused to command black troops at all.

Military officials assigned black soldiers to the West, where they became known as buffalo soldiers. (The origins of the term are unclear. It may refer to the buffalo robes worn by many of the soldiers, or to Plains Indians' respect for the black men's skills on horseback.) Many of these men were proud to wear a U.S. soldier's uniform, an emblem of their newly won citizenship rights. Organized in two cavalry and two infantry regiments, the soldiers stationed in western outposts found that military duty entailed a combination of new opportunities and old forms of humiliation.

Within their garrisons, the buffalo soldiers performed a variety of tasks related to everyday military drills and maintenance. Black soldiers helped to construct new roads and forts, protect wagon trains of settlers, and patrol the porous border between the United States and Mexico. They were an integral part of campaigns to subdue the Cheyenne, Comanche, Sioux, Ute, Kiowa, and Apache Indians. They were among the soldiers deployed to quash strikes among workers (silver miners in Idaho, for example) and to fight forest fires in the Northwest. And, as members of an all-black regimental musical band, one group played for white audiences from Montana to Texas.

Often the buffalo soldiers encountered hostility from local townspeople, who resented their patronage of local establishments. In 1881, Tenth Cavalry troops stationed at Fort Concho near San Angelo, Texas, reacted angrily when a local white man killed a black soldier in a saloon. Another soldier had died at the hands of a local white within the previous two weeks. In the absence of justice for the murderers, the soldiers blanketed San Angelo with handbills. Signed "U.S. soldiers," the message read, "If we do not receive justice and fair play . . . someone will suffer, if not the guilty, the innocent. It has gone far enough." When some of the black soldiers attacked one of the men they believed guilty, the Texas Rangers entered the town to restore order. The army transferred the black companies out of the area and disciplined the leaders of the protest.

Once they were mustered out of the army, some black soldiers decided to settle permanently in the West. There they joined thousands of black migrants who were fleeing the Jim Crow South. In the late 1870s, 20,000 blacks from Tennessee, Mississippi, and Louisiana,

William Katz Collection

■ Among the "buffalo soldiers" who served with the U.S. military were these Seminole scouts. The Seminole traced their history to the eighteenth century, when Creek Indians and runaway slaves of African descent established communities together in Florida. During the lengthy Seminole Wars (1818–1858), many Seminole were relocated to Indian Territory (present-day Oklahoma). Some fled to Mexico before the Civil War. In 1870, they were recruited by the U.S. Army as scouts. Their unit was disbanded eleven years later. Racist policies of the military caused some to return to Mexico.

The Buffalo Soldiers and the Indian Wars of the West

- Lands where black soldiers fought and served during the Indian Wars
- The South–major source of black troops in the Indian Wars
- Soldiers policed Oklahoma before the Land Rush began in 1889
- Forts that housed black troops during the Indian Wars
- Major battles

38th and 41st Colored Infantry combined to form the 24th Buffalo Soldiers

39th and 40th Colored Infantry combined to form the 25th Buffalo Soldiers

■ **MAP 17.2 Buffalo Soldiers**

In 1866, Congress authorized the creation of four permanent military units consisting of black War veterans, who became known as the "Buffalo Soldiers." These army units played a prominent role in the Indian wars of the West from 1866 to 1890. They were stationed in federal forts scattered throughout the western states.

called "Exodusters," migrated into western Kansas. The migrants cited the South's convict lease system, poor schools, and pervasive violence and intimidation as reasons for their flight. Henry Adams, a native of Shreveport, Louisiana, and a U.S. army veteran, expanded on the migrants' grievances when he pointed to the failed promise of Reconstruction as the root cause of migration: "The whole South—every State in the South—had got into the hands of the very men that held us as slaves." Some of these migrants established all-black towns in Kansas, Colorado, Nebraska, and New Mexico. Though generally small and poor, such towns were at least free of the trappings of Jim Crow. They provided places for blacks to live on their own terms.

THE GHOST DANCE ON THE HIGH PLAINS

WATCH

Sioux Ghost Dance

Their lands and way of life threatened by whites, western Indians sought desperately to revitalize their culture and protect themselves. In 1889, an Indian named Wovoka offered the Plains Indians a mystical vision of the future, a vision that promised a return to the beloved past. A leader of the Paiute in Nevada, Wovoka preached what came to be called the Ghost Dance, part religion and part resistance movement. In 1889, a solar eclipse occurred while Wovoka was wracked by fever, and he claimed that the conjunction of the two events enabled him to glimpse the afterworld. The Indians could usher in a new day of peace, Wovoka proclaimed, and this new day would be a time free of disease and armed conflict. The buffalo would return, he promised, and the Indian men and women who had died would come back to replenish depleted villages.

Wovoka's call found its warmest reception among the Plains Indians. In 1890, an anthropologist recorded an exhortation that Wovoka delivered to the Cheyenne and Arapaho: "When you get home you must make a dance to continue five days. Dance four successive nights, and the last night keep up the dance until the morning of the fifth day, when all must bathe in the river and then disperse to their homes. You must all do in the same way." Some Indians donned "ghost shirts" made of white muslin and adorned with images of the sun, moon, stars, and various animals. They believed these garments would provide them with magical powers and protect them from the white men's bullets.

Many of the Indians who performed the Ghost Dance fell into a trance-like state, bringing inspiration to impoverished and disheartened reservation communities. However, as the ritual spread across the Plains, U.S. military officials grew anxious. In November 1890, E. B. Reynolds, a Special U.S. Indian Agent, described to his superiors in Washington the strange, seemingly dangerous behavior that had gripped the Indians on Pine Ridge Reservation in South Dakota: "The religious excitement aggravated by almost starvation is bearing fruits in this state of insubordination; Indians say they had better die fighting than to die a slow death of starvation, and as the new religion promises their return to earth, at the coming of the millennium, they have no fear of death."

As tensions between whites and Indians mounted, the Sioux leader Sitting Bull came to the fore. Born in the early 1830s, he had gained respect among his people as a Wichasa Wakan ("holy man"). At the Battle of the Little Big Horn, he helped protect Indian women and children from Custer's soldiers. Wooden Leg, a Northern Cheyenne, later described Sitting Bull as "altogether brave, but peaceable. He was strong in religion—the Indian religion." After leading his followers into Canada, Sitting Bull returned to the United States in 1881. He surrendered at Fort Buford, Dakota Territory, where he was held prisoner for two years. His brief stint as a performer in Buffalo Bill Cody's "Wild West" show left him disgusted with the ways of white people.

■ A popular artist whose work was featured in leading magazines of his time, Frederic Remington drew a scene from the Oglala Sioux Ghost Dance of 1890.

Indian cessions 1850–1890

- ▨ Indian lands ceded before 1850
- ▦ Indian lands ceded 1850–1890 with dates of "Treaties"
- ▨ Indian lands siezed without any formal "Treaty" cession
- — The Western States by 1890

■ **MAP 17.3   Indian Lands Lost, 1850–1890**

Between 1850 and 1890, many "treaties" signed by Indian groups and the U.S. government provided that Indians turn over land in exchange for cash payments. Yet U.S. military forces seized a large portion of western Indian lands by force, without signing any treaty agreements at all. By 1890, many Indians lived on reservations, apart from European American society.

Sitting Bull offered a pointed critique of the sedentary, materialistic way of life promoted by whites:

> White men like to dig in the ground for their food. My people prefer to hunt buffalo as their fathers did. White men like to stay in one place. My people want to move their tepees here and there to different hunting grounds. The life of white men is slavery. They are prisoners in towns or farms. The life my people want is a life of freedom. I have seen nothing that a white man has, houses or railways or clothing or food, that is as good as the right to move in open country, and live in our own fashion.

Sitting Bull rejected white notions of "progress" in favor of his people's traditions.

In mid-December 1890, military officials ordered Indian police to arrest Sitting Bull at his cabin on the Standing Rock Reservation in South Dakota. Alarmed by what they perceived as rising Indian militancy, white settlers in Nebraska and South Dakota pressured the government to rid the area of the "savages . . . armed to the teeth," men who were "traitors, anarchists, and assassins." While arresting Sitting Bull, his Indian captors killed him.

A week later, on December 28 and 29, soldiers of the Seventh Cavalry under Colonel James Forsyth, agitated by the tensions over Sitting Bull's death, attacked Indians at Wounded Knee Creek, South Dakota. Estimates of the number of Indians killed range from 150 to 250. More than 60 women and children were among those slain as they fled the oncoming troops. Of the 25 U.S. soldiers who perished, most apparently died from shots fired by their own comrades; according to a government eyewitness, the Indian men were unarmed when the cavalry attacked.

The massacre at Wounded Knee proved the last major violent encounter between Plains Indians and U.S. cavalry forces. By this time, many Indians throughout the Midwest lived on reservations and engaged in farming. In Oklahoma, for example, the Cheyenne learned how to grow cotton and watermelons. Government agents, eager to create independent farmers, instructed Indian men in the use of the plow. But John Stands-in-Timber, a Cheyenne, later recalled how plowing became a collective effort. It engaged the energies of Indian men from Oklahoma to Montana, he noted, as bands would work together until their task was done. Thus some Indian groups attempted to maintain communal work customs in opposition to the European Americans' glorification of ambition and individualism.

Nevertheless, Chinese immigrants, southern African Americans, and Plains Indians were not the only groups to feel aggrieved at the hands of private and public interests. In some cases, native-born white American men and women also protested against what they perceived to be unfair policies and practices on the part of businesses and the federal government.

DOCUMENT

Accounts of the Wounded Knee Massacre

Revolt in the Workplace

■ *What technological and structural changes in the workplace prompted farmers and workers to organize between 1877 and 1890?*

During the late nineteenth century, workers challenged employers and the new industrial order for many reasons. Factory operatives objected to long hours and to low pay in return for tending dangerous machines. Miners labored daily under hazardous conditions, often without necessary safety equipment or precautions. Field hands worried that they would soon be displaced by machines such as the giant threshers that were far more efficient—quicker and cheaper—than human labor. Small farmers resented their dependence on bankers and owners of grain elevators and railroads. Throughout the country, many different kinds of workers feared that the large influx of immigrants would provide a vast reserve of cheap labor that would depress the wages, and threaten the job security, of everyone.

> *During the late nineteenth century, workers challenged employers and the new industrial order.*

Workers launched different kinds of challenges against the system of industrial capitalism, which, many charged, enriched a few industrialists and bankers at the expense of the vast majority of laboring people. Workers joined together in unions, and in many cases they fought the violence of security forces with violence of their own. Some men and women destroyed the machinery that threatened to replace them in the workplace.

By the early 1890s, critics of the new industrial and agribusiness order had come together in the form of a new political group, the People's party, or **Populists.** This organization aimed to bring together urban and rural, male and female, agricultural and industrial workers to protest the hardships suffered by laborers of all kinds and to demand that the federal government take strong action in rectifying social ills.

Nevertheless, in workplace conflicts, the lines were not always strictly drawn between employees and employers. For example, the late nineteenth-century laboring classes never achieved the level of unity called for by the Populists. White workers often expressed intense hostility toward their African American and Chinese counterparts. Within small towns, shopkeepers and landlords at times showed solidarity with striking workers; in these cases community ties were stronger than class differences. Also, despite their critique of big business, workers often embraced the emerging consumer culture. In fact, many of them fought for shorter workdays and higher wages so that they could enjoy their share of the material blessings of American life—in department stores, movie theaters, and amusement parks. In the end, Populism was primarily a rural movement composed of small farmers, sharecroppers, and wage hands.

TROUBLE ON THE FARM

In the late summer of 1878, the combined effects of the recent national economic depression and the loss of jobs to labor-saving technology catalyzed a rash of machine breaking by farm hands throughout rural Ohio. The tactics of the machine-breakers bore some resemblance to those of *las Gorras Blancas* in northern New Mexico. In the Midwest, displaced farm hands burned the reapers, mowers, and threshers of their former employers. By autumn, the violence had spread to Michigan and Indiana. Scattered reports of torched reapers, mowers, barns, and crops emanated from Illinois, Iowa, Wisconsin, and Minnesota. Some wealthy farmers responded by abandoning their machinery and rehiring their farm hands. Technology, one noted, "ought to be dispensed with in times like these." By contrast, critics charged the machine-breakers with "short-sighted madness." True, seasonal farm hands were fast losing their usefulness in the new machine age. However, the protests revealed that even family farming had become a business. Now farmers needed to secure bank loans, invest in new machinery, and worry about the price of crops in the world market. These changes had profoundly altered labor relations between farm workers and farmers and between farmers and their creditors.

On the Northern Plains, farmers endured extremes of weather and the anxiety of uncertain harvests. In the mid-1880s, the plight of these Plains farmers worsened when a series of natural disasters highlighted their vulnerability to the elements. No form of modern technology could prevent the drought of 1886, which dragged on for a decade. Combined with declining wheat prices, the prolonged dry weather drove half the population of western Kansas and Nebraska back east to Iowa and Illinois between 1888 and 1892. Meanwhile, the bitterly cold winter of 1886–1887 decimated cattle herds throughout the region. The resulting "great die up" ended the days of the huge herds that ranged the Plains. Thereafter, ranchers would concentrate on smaller stock holdings and selective breeding.

Some American writers captured the bleakness of prairie life, highlighting the condition of farmers dependent on predatory institutions and machines, such as banks and railroads. Writing from firsthand experience of his native Wisconsin, Hamlin Garland portrayed the harsh life endured by men and women who toiled "under the lion's paw" of scheming creditors, speculators, and landlords. Other chroniclers of life on the Plains portrayed nature as a pitiless adversary that promised bountiful harvests one day but rained plagues of locusts the next.

These problems contributed to a radical turn in farmers' politics. In the 1880s, a national movement

■ Though their lives were later romanticized in novels, movies, and television programs, nineteenth-century cowboys engaged in hard, dangerous labor on the range. Against a backdrop of a large herd of cattle, these men pose for the photographer.

emerged and tapped into this wellspring of anger and discontent in farming regions throughout the nation. Men and women from the Plains states organized in the **National Farmers' Alliance,** or Northern Alliance, joined with their Louisiana, Texas, and Arkansas counterparts in the National Farmers' Alliance and Industrial Union, or Southern Alliance. The Colored Farmers' Alliance was formed in 1886.

The Southern Alliance pressed for an expanded currency, taxation reform, and government ownership of transportation and communication lines. Its members tended to ally with the Democratic party. The Northern Alliance also focused on the expansion of the currency supply—specifically, the coinage of silver—but advocated the formation of a third political party to advance its interests. Both of these large regional groups found adherents in the mountain West. There, miners and farmers joined together to protest the monopolistic powers of the railroads, privately owned water companies, and silver mining interests. These monopolies drove up consumer prices and depressed workers' wages.

TABLE 17.1					
Percentage of Farms Operated by Tenants or Sharecroppers					
	1880	**1890**	**1900**	**1910**	**1920**
North	19.2	22.1	26.2	26.5	28.2
New England	8.5	9.3	9.4	8.0	7.4
Middle Atlantic	19.2	22.1	25.3	22.3	20.7
East North Central	20.5	22.8	26.3	27.0	28.1
West North Central	20.5	24.0	29.6	30.9	34.2
South	36.2	38.5	47.0	49.6	46.9
South Atlantic	36.1	38.5	44.2	45.9	46.8
East South Central	36.8	38.3	48.1	50.7	49.7
West South Central	35.2	38.6	49.1	52.8	52.9
West	14.0	12.1	16.6	14.0	17.7
Mountain	7.4	7.1	12.2	10.7	15.4
Pacific	16.8	14.7	19.7	17.2	20.1
U.S.	25.6	28.4	35.3	37.0	38.1

Source: U.S. Special Committee on Farm Tenancy, *Farm Tenancy* (1937), 39, 36.

Most Alliance men and women farmed modest parcels of land. As small producers, they felt powerless to influence the businesspeople and politicians who affected their livelihoods and their life possibilities. Alliance members also presented themselves as the last line of

Nebraska State Historical Society, Solomon D. Butcher Collection

■ A Nebraska farm family poses proudly with their new windmill, c. 1890. Such devices powered water pumps that reached deep into the earth. Though expensive, windmills were necessities for drought-stricken farmers on the Plains, especially during the harsh years of the mid-1880s to the mid-1890s.

defense for the noble yeoman in the face of the corrupting influences of modern corporate capitalism. In rural Alabama, where the Farmers' Alliance had links with local schools and churches, the group's newspapers railed against the "filthy city," a "wicked place" of vice, crime, and dissipation. Farm folk thus distanced themselves from the "New South Creed," which promoted materialism and industrialization.

In many local groups, or suballiances, women stepped forward to claim their due as wives, mothers, and workers. Women argued that they were more than their husbands' helpmeets; they were partners in a family enterprise. As such, they demanded respect and a political voice. Wrote one woman to the *Weekly Toiler,* the paper of Tennessee's Alliance, "It would be better, methinks, if the men would say, 'come join us in the fight against your enemy' with as bold a front as he says, 'come Betsy, help me hang the meat, and drop the [seeds for] corn and potatoes.' "

Although the Farmers' Alliance identified itself primarily with agricultural interests, it made some notable forays into coalition-building as well. In 1889, the northern and southern groups attempted to combine with the Colored Farmers' Alliance. Together, these groups claimed more than 4 million members. They also sought to join with the Knights of Labor and thus bring all members of the "producing classes" together. By representing the financial interests of all farmers and highlighting the vulnerabilities of debtors, the organization foreshadowed the wider national appeal of the Populist party in the 1890s.

MILITANCY IN THE FACTORIES AND MINES

The new economy wrought profound hardship on members of the urban laboring classes as well as on small farmers. Many industrial workers faced layoffs and wage cuts during the economic depressions of the 1870s and 1880s. The great railroad strikes of 1877 (see Chapter 16) foreshadowed an era of bitter industrial conflict. Because no laws regulated private industry, employers could impose ten- to fifteen-hour workdays, six days a week. Industrial accidents were all too common, and some industries lacked safety precautions. Steelworkers labored in excessive heat; miners and textile mill employees contracted respiratory diseases. With windows closed and machines speeded up, new forms of technology created new risks for workers. Chicago meatpackers, who wielded gigantic cleavers in subfreezing lockers, and California wheat harvesters, who operated complex mechanical binders and threshers, were among those confronting danger on the job.

In 1884, the Massachusetts Bureau of Statistics of Labor issued a report outlining the occupational hazards for working women in the city of Boston. In button-making establishments, female workers often got their fingers caught under punch and die machines. Employers provided a surgeon to dress an employee's wounds the first three times she was injured; thereafter, she had to pay for her own medical care. Women operated heavy power machinery in the garment industry and exposed themselves to dangerous chemicals and other substances in paper-box making, canning, and confectionery manufacturing.

Organizing American Labor in the Late Nineteenth Century

Some women workers, especially those who monopolized certain kinds of jobs, organized and struck for higher wages. Three thousand Atlanta washerwomen launched such an effort in 1881 but failed to get their demands met. Most women found it difficult to win the respect not only of employers but also of male unionists. Leonora Barry, an organizer for the Knights of Labor, sought to change that. Barry visited mills and factories around the country. At each stop, she highlighted women's unique difficulties and condemned the "selfishness of their brothers in toil" who resented women's intrusion into the workplace. Barry was reacting to men such as Edward O'Donnell, a prominent union official who claimed that wage-earning women threatened the role of men as family breadwinners.

For both men and women workers, the influx of 5.25 million new immigrants in the 1880s stiffened job competition at worksites throughout the country. To make matters worse,

Yale collection of Western Americana, Beinecke Rare Book and Manuscript Library

■ Mining was one of the most hazardous occupations in the United States. Below-surface miners worked with explosives and sophisticated kinds of machinery. As a result, the chances of explosions, cave-ins, rockslides, and fires increased. These conditions help to account for the labor militancy of miners throughout the country. This photo shows a mining operation at Marysville, near Helena, Montana, c. 1885.

vast outlays of capital needed to mechanize and organize manufacturing plants placed pressure on employers to economize. Many of them did so by cutting wages. Like the family farmer who could no longer claim the status of the independent yeoman, industrial workers depended on employers and consumers for their physical well-being and very survival.

Not until 1935 would American workers have the right to organize and bargain collectively with their employers. Until then, laborers who saw strength in numbers and expressed an interest in a union could be summarily fired, blacklisted (their names circulated to other employers), and harassed by private security forces. The Pinkerton National Detective Agency, started in 1850 by Scottish immigrant Allan Pinkerton, initially found eager clients among the railroads. The Pinkertons, as they were called, served as industrial spies and police during some of the most bitter and violent strikes of the late nineteenth century.

For example, in 1876 a Pinkerton detective, James McParlan, was hired by railroad operators to infiltrate a local union of Irish immigrant miners in Schuylkill County, Pennsylvania. The miners, members of a secret society called the Molly Maguires, were determined to do battle against the mine owners, who not only suppressed union activity but also controlled local courts and law enforcement agencies. In 1875, the Mollies had called a strike, but their leaders were arrested and charged with waging a guerrilla war against the mines (and their Welsh and English superintendents). In court, McParlan offered testimony against the men, evidence that led to the conviction and execution (by hanging) of twenty of them. In the coming years, employers in a number of industries justified their repressive tactics by claiming that all unions represented a threat to law and order.

In small towns where one or two large industries predominated, workers often could count on their middle-class neighbors as allies. As members of churches and voluntary associations, middle-class and working-class people together upheld community values of family welfare in opposition to large industrialists concerned only with profits and worker productivity. In many cases, shopkeepers, tradespeople, clergy, and landlords objected to the arrival of out-of-town strikebreakers, Pinkerton detectives, or federal troops during labor disputes. During a boycott of anti-union hat factories in Orange, New Jersey, in

AGE & BEAUTY.

■ A card extols the Knights of Labor by suggesting that all people, regardless of age or gender, can labor in harmony together without the intrusion of bosses or supervisors. Terence V. Powderly became the group's leader, called Grand Master Workman, in 1879.

DOCUMENT

Bellamy, from *Looking Backward*

1885, the community rallied around the workers. Brewers and bakers refused to supply establishments that opposed the boycott. Service providers of all kinds, from owners of roller-skating rinks to "knights of the razor" (barbers), closed their doors to patrons who expressed sympathy with what was generally called "the foul." In Orange and other towns, then, coalitions of middle-class and working-class residents severely curtailed the industrialists' power.

The Knights of Labor, a secret fraternal order founded in 1869, came under the leadership of Terence V. Powderly a decade later. With this Irish American at the helm (he was called Grand Master Workman), the labor union made impressive gains in the 1880s. Under Powderly, the Knights launched a concerted effort to organize European American, African American, and Hispanic men and women workers.

In the late 1880s, the Knights attempted to organize the laboring classes of San Miguel County, New Mexico, and the other parts of the Southwest. The Knights welcomed cowboys into their organization at the same time they were urging railroad workers to join their ranks. One cowhand said, "No class is harder worked, none so poor paid for their services." A cattle drive north from Texas could last for three months and cover more than a thousand miles. On such drives, a single cowboy would be responsible for keeping 250 to 300 head of cattle in line. Wages remained miserable, and unrest spread.

In the spring of 1883, an extensive strike among cowboys enraged the owners of large ranches in the Texas panhandle. To quell the uprising, ranchers paid gunmen to intimidate the strikers and enlisted the support of the state's law enforcement agency, the Texas Rangers. It was a year before the strikers gave up.

In appealing to many different kinds of workers around the country, the Knights blended a critique of the late nineteenth-century wage system with a belief in the dignity of labor and a call for collective action. According to the Knights, business monopolies and corrupt politicians everywhere shared a common interest in exploiting the labor of ordinary men and women. The Knights advocated a return to the time when workers controlled their own labor and received a just price for the products they made. "We declare an inevitable and irresistible conflict between the wage system of labor and republican system of government," the Knights proclaimed.

In condemning the concentration of wealth in the hands of a few, the Knights drew on the ideas of popular social critics of the day. In New York City, Henry George, an economist and land reformer, gained the Knights' support when he ran for mayor on the United Labor party ticket in 1886. (He came in second, with 31 percent of the vote, ahead of a young, up-and-coming Republican named Theodore Roosevelt.) George had achieved national prominence with his book *Progress and Poverty* (1879), in which he advocated a single tax on property as a means of distributing wealth more equally.

Some critics and writers went further and advocated state **socialism,** the idea that the state rather than private individuals should own and control all forms of property. Journalist-turned-novelist Edward Bellamy echoed these themes. In his popular novel *Looking Backward* (1888), Bellamy envisioned a "cooperative commonwealth" in the year 2000, a socialist paradise in which poverty and greed had disappeared and men and women of all classes enjoyed material comfort and harmonious relations with their neighbors. This utopia was within reach, the author argued, if Americans could simply share in the nation's abundance.

The Nationalist movement, a network of clubs inspired by Bellamy's book, included Terence Powderly as a member. Powderly declared, "We work not selfishly for ourselves

The Jewish Diaspora

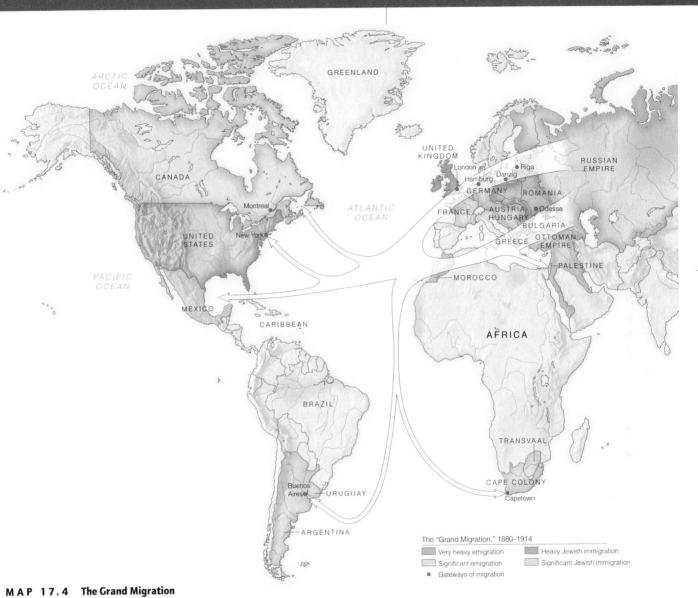

The "Grand Migration," 1880–1914

- Very heavy emigration
- Significant emigration
- ● Gateways of migration
- Heavy Jewish immigration
- Significant Jewish immigration

MAP 17.4   The Grand Migration

The Grand Migration of Jews out of Europe lasted from 1880 to 1914. This map shows that, while significant numbers of Jewish emigrants came to the United States, others went to different countries in the Northern and Western Hemispheres.

QUESTIONS

1. Why do you think large numbers of Jews decided to settle in countries other than the United States, including those in eastern Europe, the Middle East, Latin America, and South Africa?

2. Historians often highlight "push" and "pull" factors that shape patterns of immigration out of one country and into another (see Figure 2.1 on page 54 for an example). What "pushed" Jews out of the Russian empire and "pulled" them to the United States?

3. What factors might have influenced where a Jewish immigrant family would have ultimately decided to settle?

alone, but extend the hand of fellowship to all mankind." Between 1885 and 1886, the Knights undertook the difficult task of organizing black workers. Many blacks remained suspicious of white-led unions, and for good reason. Historically, the white labor movement had conceived itself as a way to exclude black men and women from stable, well-paying jobs.

In the city of Richmond, Virginia, where workplaces were strictly segregated by race, the Knights made great gains. African American women there found their job opportunities limited to domestic service, laundry work, and unskilled jobs in tobacco factories. Black men were almost entirely excluded from the artisan crafts. By the mid-1880s, the Richmond Knights boasted a total membership of 7,000, with a ratio of four blacks to three whites. Yet members were organized into two district assemblies, one for blacks, the other for whites.

> *In the city of Richmond, Virginia, where workplaces were strictly segregated by race, the Knights made great gains.*

In early 1886, a wave of strikes hit Richmond as painters, coopers (barrel makers), typographers, cotton press workers, and foundry workers, among others, all protested their low wages. A coalition between the Knights and black Republicans posed a formidable threat to the entrenched Democratic leadership. That spring, labor Republican candidates won a majority of seats on the Richmond city council and gained half the board of aldermen slots. Yet the issue of racial equality proved the undoing of the Knights' fragile biracial coalition. Throughout the South, a generation of blacks and whites had allied themselves with different political parties (the Republicans and Democrats, respectively). Moreover, white workers widely perceived blacks as potential strikebreakers. In Richmond, mutual distrust, combined with pressure from white groups such as the local Law and Order League, fragmented the Knights.

Throughout the South, segregation was the norm within biracial unionism. Whites—whether New Orleans dockworkers, Birmingham district coal miners, or lumber workers in East Texas and Louisiana—insisted on separate locals for blacks. Yet African Americans did not necessarily acquiesce to this arrangement. In 1886, Jere A. Brown, a member of the Carpenter and Joiners' Union of Cleveland, wrote to the *New York Freeman*, declaring to readers of the black newspaper, "For years I have been importuned to enter into the formation of an assembly to be composed exclusively of colored men, but have persistently refused, believing as I do in mixing and not in isolating and ostracizing ourselves, thereby fostering and perpetuating the prejudice as existing today."

In 1886, workers around the country began to mobilize on behalf of the eight-hour day. "Eight hours to constitute a day's work" was their slogan. The issue had broad appeal, but the growing diversity of the labor force made unity difficult. For example, among the white workers of the Richmond Knights were leaders with names such as Kaufman, Kaufeldt, Kelly, and Molloy, suggesting the ethnic variety of late nineteenth-century union leadership. This diversity paralleled the composition of the general population. In 1880, between 78 and 87 percent of all workers in San Francisco, St. Louis, Cleveland, New York, Detroit, Milwaukee, and Chicago were either immigrants or the children of immigrants. Most hailed from England, Germany, or Ireland, although the Chinese made up a significant part of the laboring classes on the West Coast. By 1890, Poles and Slavs were organizing in steel mills, and New York Jews were providing leadership in the garment industry. Italians were prominent in construction and the building trades. In many places, the laboring classes remained vulnerable to divisive social and cultural animosities. The diversity of ethnic groups, coupled with the fact that many newcomers from Europe adopted racist ideas to become "Americans," drove wedges between workers.

THE HAYMARKET BOMBING

The year 1886 marked the end of an era dominated by the Knights of Labor, as the organization experienced firsthand the difficulties of overcoming members' diverse crafts, racial prejudices, and political allegiances. In 1886, the Knights suffered serious setbacks in their efforts to organize railroad workers. Industrialists dug in their heels and, with the aid of hired detectives, took union leaders to court on charges of sabotage, assault, conspiracy, and murder.

On May 1, 1886, 350,000 workers in 11,562 business establishments went out on a one-day strike as part of the eight-hour-workday movement. In Chicago, home to militant labor anarchists, 40,000 workers participated in the strike. Among the Chicago leaders was Albert Parsons. A descendant of New England Puritans and a printer by trade, Parsons had lived in Waco, Texas, where he met his future wife, Lucia González, an Afro-Latina (probably born a slave). In 1873, the Parsonses had moved to Chicago to avoid Texas laws against "race mixing," which prohibited interracial marriage. There Albert joined the International Typographical Union, and Lucia took up dressmaking. They were counted among the most famous and feared radicals in the city. Chicago police described Lucia as "more dangerous than a thousand rioters."

On May 4, 1886, things took a bloody turn. Strikers called a rally in Chicago's Haymarket Square to protest the murder of two McCormick Reaper strikers the day before. During the rally, a bomb went off, killing a police officer and wounding seven others, who later died. Although the identity of the culprit was never discovered, eight **anarchists** (persons who denounce authority in all its forms), including Albert Parsons, were arrested. All eight (several of whom were German immigrants) were tried and sentenced to death for conspiring to provoke violence in what came to be called the **Haymarket bombing.** Though Parsons and several of the others had not been present when the bomb exploded, he and three other detainees were hanged in November 1887.

DOCUMENT

Engel, Address by a Haymarket Anarchist

■ Contemporary drawings such as this one convinced many Americans that labor activists, and anarchists in particular, were committed to violence, murder, and mayhem. The trials of the eight men arrested for the Haymarket bombing in Chicago were carried out in an atmosphere of public fear and hysteria. In 1893, Illinois Governor John P. Altgeld pardoned the three surviving defendants, declaring that they had not received fair trials.

Albert Parsons's Plea for Anarchy

On August 10, 1886, the New York Herald *published an essay by convicted Haymarket defendant Albert R. Parsons. In it, Parsons defends his views on anarchism. His theories on the inevitable clash between workers and capitalists echo the arguments of Karl Marx, the German political theorist. Marx predicted that the capitalist system would inevitably self-destruct and that the working classes would rise to rule the world.*

So much is written and said nowadays about socialism or anarchism, that a few words on the subject from one who holds to these doctrines may be of interest to the readers of your great newspaper.

Anarchy is the perfection of personal liberty or self-government. It is the free

The Library of Congress

■ Albert Parsons

play of nature's law. . . . It is the negation of force or the domination of man by man. In the place of the law maker it puts the law discoverer and for the driver, or dictator, or ruler, it gives free play to the natural leader. It leaves man free to be happy or miserable, to be rich or poor, to be mean or good. The natural law is self-operating, self-enacting, and cannot be repealed, amended or evaded without incurring a self-imposed penalty. . . .

The capitalist system originated in the forcible seizure of natural opportunities and rights by a few, and converting these things into special privileges, which have since become vested rights formally entrenched behind the bulwarks of statute law and government. . . .

Another committed suicide in his cell, and the rest received pardons years later. After her husband's death, Lucia ("Lucy") Parsons remained active in Chicago anarchist circles. In 1905, she became a founding member of a new, radical labor union called the Industrial Workers of the World.

The Haymarket hangings demoralized the labor movement nationwide. Now associated in the minds of the middle class with wild-eyed bomb throwers, the Knights suffered repercussions from employers and local police forces. After reaching a membership high of 700,000 in 1886, the Knights saw their ranks plummet to 100,000 by the end of the decade. Still, the execution of the Haymarket anarchists inspired young radicals—among them a recent Russian immigrant named Emma Goldman—to devote their lives to the cause of working people.

With the demise of the Knights of Labor, the **American Federation of Labor** (AFL) emerged to become the most powerful national labor movement. Samuel Gompers, an English immigrant cigarmaker, had founded the new group in 1886 partly in response to the Knights' attempts to usurp the Cigar Makers' International Union with a socialist-dominated local. The AFL garnered the allegiance of skilled trade workers and promoted basic goals such as better wages and working conditions. The AFL emphasized the walkout and boycott as strategies of labor protest. By the mid-1890s, the AFL had embraced a narrow base: skilled trades dominated by white men.

Yet the radical labor tradition persisted. Meeting in Paris in 1889, a congress of world socialist parties voted to commemorate the American workers who had marched in support of the eight-hour day during the turbulent year of 1886. The congress voted to set aside May 1, 1890, as a day of worldwide celebrations in support of labor and demonstrations in favor of the eight-hour workday. (May 1 became an international labor day, celebrated annually.) In the United States, the United Mine Workers (founded in 1890) and the American Railway Union (1893) followed the radical labor-organizing principles of the Knights of Labor long after the AFL attained its ascendancy.

And what of the laborer who for twelve or more hours weaves, spins, bores, turns, builds, shovels, breaks stones, carries loads, and so on? Does his twelve hours weaving, spinning, boring, turning, building, shoveling, etc. represent the active expression or energy of his life? On the contrary, life begins for him exactly where this activity, this labor of his ceases—viz: at his meals, in his tenement house, in his bed. His twelve hours work represents for him as a weaver, builder, spinner, etc., only so much earnings as will furnish him his meals, clothes, and rent. . . . The wage slaves are "free" to compete with each other for the opportunity to serve capital and capitalists to compete with each other in monopolizing the laborer's products.

Parsons argues that it is only a matter of time before the capitalist system "will collapse, will fall of its own weight, and fall because of its own weakness." He asserts that the fall of capitalism will usher in a new era of socialism, a system in which all property is held in common and workers can govern themselves. He concludes:

To quarrel with socialism is silly and vain. To do so is to quarrel with history; to denounce the logic of events; to smother the aspirations of liberty. Mental freedom, political freedom, industrial freedom—do not these follow in the line of progress? Are they not the association of the inevitable?

Ten days after this essay was published, Albert Parsons and the other Haymarket defendants were found guilty and sentenced to be hanged. Four of them, including Parsons, were executed on November 11, 1887. The true identity of the bomb-thrower remains a mystery to this day.

QUESTIONS

1. *What is the significance of Parsons's claim that the triumph of socialism is "inevitable" and "natural"?*

2. *Why did many Americans identify anarchists with violence?*

The rise of the labor-union movement and a third political party, the Populists, prompted some middle-class Americans as well to agitate for change in the industrial system. These reformers stressed education and legislation, and not labor radicalism, as means of change.

Crosscurrents of Reform

■ *How did social reformers differ from labor radicals in their assumptions about the need for, and the means of, social change?*

In the 1880s, a young Danish-born journalist named Jacob Riis prowled New York's East Side slum district in search of stories for the New York *Tribune* and the Associated Press bureau. In this part of the city, more than 37,000 tenement buildings housed more than 1 million people—newcomers from the far reaches of Europe and Asia. As a result of Riis's stories documenting the inhuman living conditions endured by so many men, women, and children, the city formed the Tenement House Commission in 1884. Riis persisted in his exposés. In 1890, he published a collection of his own photographs, along with explanatory notes. *How the Other Half Lives* is a powerful indictment of greedy landlords, indifferent city officials, and rapacious sweatshop owners. The photos of sleeping street urchins huddled around sidewalk heating grates, of impoverished English coal heavers and Indian needleworkers, are powerful even today. In the 1890s, his book galvanized the public in support of slum clearance and housing codes.

During the last decades of the nineteenth century, reformers adopted a range of causes. Some, like Riis, focused on the plight of the urban poor. Others challenged the Indian reservation system, which, they charged, left Indians poor and dependent on the federal government. Settlement house workers aimed to improve the lives of immigrant families. Middle-class women sought to protect and empower women by aiding abused or vulnerable wives and

Jacob Riis Photographs Immigrants on the Lower East Side of New York City

Envisioning History

Jacob Riis, "Street Arabs at Night," c. 1890. Museum of the City of New York, The Jacob A. Riis Collection, #123

Jacob Riis entitled this photograph "Street Arabs in Sleeping Quarters (Areaway, Mulberry Street)" and included it in his book *How the Other Half Lives*, published in 1890. A pioneer documentary photographer, Riis aimed to expose the poverty and wretched living conditions endured by many immigrants in New York's Lower East Side. In certain cases, Riis carefully positioned his subjects before photographing them. Thus, the boys shown here may have been pretending to sleep at his request.

QUESTIONS

1. If the boys were carefully posed by Riis before he took this picture, would that fact influence the way you perceive this image? Why or why not?

2. Why would homeless adults or children choose this type of place to sleep?

3. How are the children clothed?

4. What options did youngsters like these have when it came to making a living on the streets?

5. How might industrialist Andrew Carnegie have interpreted this photograph? Union leader Samuel Gompers?

6. Can you think of any recent photographs that have helped to shape debates on social reform or foreign policy?

mothers, promoting temperance in alcohol use, and supporting women's suffrage. Many reformers participated in a transatlantic community of ideas, learning about reform strategies and institutions from their European counterparts. They stressed legislation, education, and moral rewards over coercion in their efforts to change society.

Although reformers professed to favor the full integration of various ethnic groups into American life, at times they could hardly help but look down on the people they aimed to help. (*How the Other Half Lives*, for all its sympathetic portrayals of the poor, reinforces negative stereotypes of many immigrants.) Some of the people whom reformers hoped to help rejected part of their benefactors' package of values—Protestantism, for example—while accepting forms of concrete aid, such as shelter from abusive husbands. Thus the history of late nineteenth-century reform reveals the values and goals of not just middle-class Americans but of a wide variety of other social groups as well.

THE GOAL OF INDIAN ASSIMILATION

In the mid-nineteenth century, many European Americans, including government officials, had believed that the reservation system was a much-needed reform to protect western Indians. Whites reasoned that reservation Indians would remain separate from the rest of American society, to the benefit of everyone. Indians could preserve their own culture, and they would remain safe from the attacks of both homesteaders and U.S. troops. By segregating this group, European Americans were free to settle on rich farmlands, mine for gold and silver, and take advantage of timber resources in the West.

By the 1870s, the harsh reality of the reservation system prompted a group composed of both Native Americans and European Americans to call for reform. The reformers pointed out that many western Indians had previously roamed the Plains in search of buffalo and other sources of food, clothing, and shelter. Confining whole tribes to reservations meant that they lost not only their traditional means of feeding and housing themselves but their entire way of life. Reservation lands were often unsuitable for farming, leaving the residents on them without jobs or any other means to make a living. They depended on supplies of food, blankets, and clothing provided by the federal government. Kept apart from the rest of American society, denied the rights of citizenship such as education and the vote, many Indians fell victim to self-destructive behavior, including alcoholism and suicide.

> *By the 1870s, the harsh reality of the reservation system prompted a group composed of both Native Americans and European Americans to call for reform.*

Convinced that the reservation system was a failure, reformers began to call for the assimilation of Native Americans into mainstream American life. In 1879, Ponca chief Standing Bear toured the East Coast, speaking before large, receptive audiences in Chicago, Boston, New York, Philadelphia, and Washington. The chief had already received national attention for his role in the case *Standing Bear v. Crook* (1879). When Standing Bear's son and daughter died, the chief and thirty warriors attempted to leave Indian Territory and return to his homeland in Dakota Territory to bury them. On their way, they were captured by a U.S. cavalry force commanded by General George Crook. The Indians were imprisoned in Omaha, Nebraska. In their defense, two European American lawyers argued, "In time of peace, no authority, civil or military, exists for transporting Indians from one section of the country to another . . . nor to confine them in any particular reservation against their will." In his decision, the judge ruled that Indians were indeed persons under the law, with inalienable rights. The decision called into question the government's attempts to force Indians onto reservations and to keep them there.

Omaha Funeral Song

On tour, addressing well-to-do listeners, Standing Bear criticized the federal Indian Bureau and demanded that Indians be granted full citizenship rights. When he spoke, he was accompanied by two young Omaha Indians who seemed to represent the promise of assimilation. Susette LaFlesche, of French and Indian heritage, assumed the name Bright Eyes for the purpose of the tour. She announced that her people "ask you for their liberty." Her brother Joseph, attired in European American clothing, served as translator for Standing Bear, who appealed to crowds saying, "We are bound; we ask you to set us free."

Standing Bear's appeal helped to galvanize eastern reformers. The campaign for Indian assimilation bore a marked resemblance to the antislavery crusade before the Civil War. Both movements focused on the wrongs perpetrated by the U.S. government (slavery and the Indian reservation system). Both argued that the group in question deserved full citizenship rights. And both promoted the ideal of group self-sufficiency: blacks and Indians tilling the soil, embracing mainstream Christianity, and learning trades. Beginning in 1883, advocates of Indian

Courtesy, Hampton University Archives

■ Susan LaFlesche was the first Indian woman to become a physician in the United States. Together with her sisters Marguerite and Lucy, Susan attended Hampton Institute in Virginia, a vocational school for African Americans and Indians. This photo, c. 1885, shows Hampton students performing in a pageant at the school. Susan, center, and the woman on the right represented "Indians of the Past." The other students represented "Indians of the Present." Hampton's mission was to prepare its students for farming and the skilled trades.

assimilation sponsored annual conferences at Lake Mohonk, New York, to plot strategy for the coming year. These conferences brought together scholars, clergy, reformers, and politicians, all of whom considered their cause as part of the tradition of Protestant missionary outreach work.

The reformers believed that the values of white middle-class Protestants provided the best guide for Indians seeking to rid themselves of the hated reservation system. The Women's National Indian Association promoted "civilized home-life" on Indian reservations throughout the West. The Connecticut Branch organized a medical mission to the Omaha tribe in the 1880s. Branch members also paid for the education of another LaFlesche sibling, Susan (a graduate of Hampton Institute), at the Woman's Medical College of Philadelphia. Although LaFlesche's sponsors believed that Indian women could serve as effective agents of civilization, they had less faith in the capacity of Indian men to abandon their traditions and embrace the ways of whites.

Advocates of assimilation also received support from people who simply wanted the Plains Indians removed from their land to make way for European American settlers. The *New Orleans Times-Picayune* agreed that the reservation system was flawed, but not because Indians had suffered hardships under the system. The editorialist charged that Indians should not "any longer be permitted to usurp for the purpose of barbarism, the fertile lands, the products of mines, the broad valleys and wooded mountain slopes," which the dominant white society needed.

Out of these conflicting impulses—one on behalf of the Indians' welfare, the other in support of the destruction of Indians' claims to large tracts of land—came two major initiatives that would shape federal Indian policy in the years to come. The first was the Indian boarding school movement, begun in 1879 with the founding of a school in Carlisle, Pennsylvania. The purpose of the movement was to convert Indian children to Christianity, and to force them to abandon their native culture and learn literacy skills. The second was the Dawes Act, passed by Congress in 1887 with the intention of encouraging Indians to farm and apply for citizenship. By allowing reservation land to be divided into separate farms for individual Native American families, the federal act attacked the Indian tribal way of life directly. Moreover, ambitious land speculators and corrupt government officials sought to enrich themselves from the provisions of the act that allowed the sell-off of Indian lands to white buyers.

TRANSATLANTIC NETWORKS OF REFORM

During this period, American reformers derived ideas and inspiration from their European counterparts. This transatlantic exchange of ideas was greatly facilitated by improvements in sea transportation. During the 1870s and 1880s, ocean travel became cheaper and safer as well as more efficient and comfortable. The great shipping lines, such as Cunard, began to offer intermediate fares for middle-class passengers who did not want to travel in steerage but could not afford first-class compartments. In 1890, a tourist embarking from New York could cross the Atlantic in just ten days for about $30 (the price of a bicycle) on a well-appointed steamship. Writer Henry James traveled extensively in Europe before making his home in London in the mid-1870s. In his 1881 novel *Portrait of a Lady,* the main character, Isabel Archer, replies to an English gentleman who says he finds her motives for touring Europe "mysterious": "Is there anything mysterious in a purpose entertained and executed every year, in the most public manner, by fifty thousand of my fellow countrymen—the purpose of improving one's mind by foreign travel?"

> During this period, American reformers derived ideas and inspiration from their European counterparts.

Contacts between European and American scholars, students, artists, clergy, writers, and reformers enriched the intellectual life of the United States and bolstered the reform impulse. American women's rights supporters conferred with their counterparts in London. American college students attended classes at German universities. There American scholars absorbed ideas related to "reform Darwinism," the notion that state and private charitable intervention could improve modern social relations. Out of these ideas came the **Social Gospel,** a moral reform movement that stressed the responsibility of Americans to address the ills of modern urban life. Furthering this exchange of ideas, municipal and federal commissions studied labor unions and prisons on both sides of the Atlantic. Popular journals such as the *Nation* and *New Republic* reported on social policy initiatives of European governments.

An idealistic graduate of Rockford (Illinois) Female Seminary, Jane Addams journeyed to Europe for the first time in 1883. The sight of large numbers of poor people in London's East End made a lasting impression on her. She returned home, searching for a way to be useful and for "an outward symbol of fellowship…some blessed spot where unity of spirit might claim right of way over all differences." In 1888, she went again to England and visited Toynbee Hall, a social settlement founded to alleviate the problems of the laboring classes. Back in Chicago, she and her friend and former classmate Ellen Gates Starr decided to open a settlement house of their own. Called Hull House, it was located in the Nineteenth Ward, home to 5,000 Greek, Russian, Italian, and German immigrants.

Social settlement houses—so called because their goal was to help immigrants with the transition of settling in the United States—provided a variety of services for immigrants, including English language classes, neighborhood health clinics, after-school programs for children, and instruction in personal hygiene and infant care. Settlement houses lobbied and petitioned muncipal and state governments to enact laws that would improve the housing and working conditions of urban residents, especially immigrants. Settlements also sponsored dances and other social activities so that young people could enjoy a more wholesome form of recreation than the dirty commercial dance halls many patronized. In 1891, six settlements were in operation, including the Neighborhood Guild of New York City (1886) as well as Addams's Hull House in Chicago (1889). By 1900, the number stood at 200.

Later, Addams recalled that, with the opening of Hull House, she hoped to counter the anarchists and strikers. Like other reformers, Addams believed that social welfare activities would improve the lot of the poor and thus diffuse their radical, violent impulses. Moreover, she hoped to offer a sphere of useful work for young, well-educated women, who had few alternatives when it came to finding meaningful professional employment, such as university teaching or government service. Within the settlement house, she believed, these women reformers "might restore a balance of activity along traditional lines and learn of life from life itself." This was a place "where they might try out some of the things they had been taught."

WOMEN REFORMERS: "BEGINNING TO BURST THE BONDS"

Like the Indian assimilation movement, women's reform work in general during this period had a strong missionary strain. In San Francisco, the Occidental Branch of the Women's Foreign Missionary Society enlisted the aid of well-to-do women in sponsoring a rescue home for Chinese prostitutes. Without the protection of traditional kin ties, these immigrants remained vulnerable to sexual and physical abuse. The rescue home enabled the young women to escape the men who exploited them and, in some cases, to reenter society as married women, factory wage-earners, or small merchants.

In Salt Lake City, a group of women challenged the Mormon practice of plural marriage. In 1886, their Industrial Christian Home Association received a subsidy from Congress to provide shelter for "women who renounce polygamy and their children of a tender age." That same year some Denver women founded the Colorado Cottage Home, a rescue home for pregnant girls and women. Many women sought out by these reformers welcomed services such as job training and shelter from abusive men. However, some women declined to embrace other aspects of these charitable organizations, such as religious lessons.

The Women's Christian Temperance Union (WCTU) is an apt example of the missionary impulse behind late nineteenth-century reform. Though best known for its antialcohol crusade, the WCTU also sponsored homes for unwed mothers and day and night nurseries for the children of working women. It also stressed the need for women's "purity," claiming that women and children were the chief victims of men's alcohol consumption. But the group went further to denounce women's victimization at the hands of men in general.

Like national labor unions at the time, the WCTU organized African American women into local chapters separate from those of whites. Frances Ellen Watkins Harper served as head of the black division of the organization between 1883 and 1890. Harper, much in demand as a lecturer, also organized Sunday schools for black children and enlisted the aid of black clergy in her campaign against juvenile delinquency in Philadelphia.

Frances Willard, a white woman, also proved a popular national speaker from the time she founded the WCTU in 1879 until her death in 1898. She served as the organization's first president during those years and in 1883 formed a world temperance union. Willard believed

in the power of direct action. She exhorted groups of women to descend on taverns and rum shops and to shame customers into taking the "cold water pledge," which required its adherents to quench their thirst with cold water, not alcohol. An enthusiastic advocate of women's suffrage, Willard was instrumental in bringing women's issues into the political realm. In her speeches, she quoted women such as "a Presbyterian lady" who declared, "For my part, I never wanted to vote until our gentlemen passed a prohibition ordinance, and a month later chose a saloon keeper for mayor."

By the 1870s, the issue of women's suffrage had captured the attention of men and women throughout the country. In fact, the issue had special resonance in the West for several reasons. When European American women overcame the hardships associated with the challenge of settling the trans-Mississippi West, they considered themselves worthy of having an equal voice in the polling booth. Reflecting on her hard life as a settler in Circle Valley, Utah, Mrs. L. L. Dalton wrote in 1876 that she was "proud and thankful" to see women "beginning to burst the bonds of iron handed custom" and asserting their "co-heirship" with fathers, brothers, and husbands. Abigail Scott Duniway, who sympathized with the plight of overworked and often lonely farm wives, published a women's rights journal, *New Northwest,* in Portland, Oregon, from 1871 to 1887. In 1873, she had helped found the Oregon Equal Suffrage Association and served as its president.

Western politics pitted cattle ranchers against farmers, and religious and cultural groups against each other. These conflicts prompted the men of various groups to seek allies wherever they could find them—within their own households if necessary. The territorial legislature of Wyoming granted women the right to vote in 1869. Utah Territory followed suit in 1870, and Washington Territory in 1883. Territorial governments facilitated the enactment of women's suffrage, for they required only that the measure win the approval of a majority of the legislature and the approval of the governor. In contrast, states had to approve a constitutional amendment, which required support of two-thirds of the legislators and a majority of the voters. The states of Wyoming (in 1890), Colorado (in 1893), and Utah and Idaho (both in 1896) approved suffrage for women. Colorado's victory was the only one resulting from a successful statewide referendum.

In 1884, a group of women calling themselves the National Equal Rights Party convened in California. Delegates to the convention nominated Belva Lockwood for president of the United States. Born in Royalton, New York, in 1830, Lockwood was the first woman admitted to practice law before the Supreme Court (in 1879). She was a staunch proponent of women's suffrage and equal pay for equal work. Lockwood believed that her presidential candidacy would bring much-needed publicity to the cause of women's rights. In her acceptance speech, she called for "a fair distribution of the public offices to women as well as to men." She promised that, if elected, she would recommend in her inaugural speech "a uniform system of laws" that would reform marriage and divorce statutes in order to "make the wife equal with the husband in authority and right, and an equal partner in the common business." She also advocated breaking up the Indian reservation system and granting all Indians full citizenship rights. In the 1884 election, Lockwood received 4,149 votes cast in six states. From the late 1880s until her death in 1917, she devoted her energies to the cause of world peace.

The nature of the western suffrage movement points to the need to view women's rights, and women's activism in general, in their historical and regional contexts. For example, African American women also pressed for the right to vote, and their demands assumed special urgency amid violence and terrorism. Ida B. Wells would later lead an African American women's suffrage club in Chicago and play a pivotal role in the national suffrage movement. She began her public career as a crusading journalist in Memphis in the 1880s. In the early 1890s, she clashed with Frances Willard over the issue of lynching,

May Wright Sewall Collection/The Library of Congress

Frances Willard (1839–1898) grew up on a farm in Wisconsin Territory. She served as the first dean of women at Northwestern University in Illinois. In the mid-1870s, she decided to devote her life to the cause of temperance. From 1879 until her death, she was president of the Woman's Christian Temperance Union. Willard developed what she called a "Do-Everything policy." Under her leadership, the WCTU addressed a range of issues, including women's suffrage and workers' rights.

charging that the WCTU president refused to condemn the barbaric practice. Although Willard had been an active abolitionist and a steadfast campaigner for women's suffrage, according to Wells she was "no better or worse than the great bulk of white Americans on the Negro question." Thus women's political issues reflected tensions between blacks and whites as well as between women and men.

Conclusion

In the 1870s and 1880s, the Americans who challenged the power of government and big business represented a wide spectrum of ideologies, tactics, and goals. Some resisted violently, smashing the machines, trains, and telegraph poles that were transforming American society. The Ohio machine-breakers and southwestern *Las Gorras Blancas* destroyed property in an effort to assert their claims to a traditional way of life. Others formed new institutions such as settlement houses, reform associations, or political parties to advance their agenda on the national scene. Some people hoping to effect social change used the language of evangelical Protestantism, echoing the abolitionists who had called for the eradication of slavery before the Civil War. Others collected data and interviewed specific groups of workers, women, or immigrants in an effort, first, to expose the conditions under which these groups lived and labored, and second, to propose specific legislation to remedy those conditions. Plains Indians embraced religious mysticism in a failed attempt to halt the incursion of European Americans into their ancient hunting grounds. Thus, powerful groups encountered much resistance from people opposed to their narrow idea of progress—the idea that bigger factories, more efficient farm machinery, and a nationwide network of railroad lines would bring prosperity to all Americans.

At the same time, some groups agitated for full inclusion into American society, as citizens and as consumers. Some blacks resisted Jim Crow by voting with their feet and fleeing the oppressive system of southern sharecropping. They claimed citizenship rights in defiance of the white lawmakers and employers who aimed to keep all blacks in a state of near slavery. Too, mainstream women suffragists aspired to the rights and privileges of male voters; they hoped to achieve full integration into the American political system, rather than overhauling that system. In contrast to their radical counterparts in the Knights of Labor, members of the emerging American Federation of Labor refrained from criticizing the capitalist system; instead, AFL members argued that they deserved their fair share of American prosperity in the form of better wages and working conditions. None of these groups—black activists, women suffragists, or union members—found a welcoming home in either of the two main political parties. For evidence of lively critiques of American society and economy during this period, we must look beyond the Republicans and Democrats to those groups that offered innovative ideas and novel tactics to transform political discussions throughout the nation.

As Americans began to think more broadly about their own society, they began to think more broadly about their place in the world. Some men and women hoped to apply the principles of moral and civic reform to other countries west of the United States. The 1880s thus laid the foundations not only for a transatlantic republic of cultural exchange, but also for a transpacific empire of missionary work and trade. In the process, a new ideology of expansionism emerged, one that blended elements of economic gain, national security, and Christian missionary outreach to peoples in far-off lands.

CHRONOLOGY: 1877–1890

1877	"Great Uprising" of railroad employees and other workers.
1878	San Francisco Workingmen's party stages anti-Chinese protests.
1882	Chinese Exclusion Act.
1886	Accused Haymarket bombers tried and convicted.
1888	Edward Bellamy, *Looking Backward*. National Farmers' Alliance is founded.
1890	Wyoming admitted to the Union, first state to enfranchise women. National American Woman Suffrage Association is formed. Wounded Knee Massacre.

For Review

1. Discuss the role of law as both a facilitator of, and barrier to, economic and political equality among all Americans during this period

2. What were the arguments and counterarguments of the supporters and opponents of the Indian reservation system? Did all Indians share a particular point of view on this issue? Why or why not?

3. Why were so many labor unions, political organizations, and reform associations segregated by race?

4. Why did increasing numbers of middle-class Americans find transatlantic travel, and visits to Europe, so appealing? In what ways did patterns of foreign travel affect domestic life in the United States?

5. Between 1877 and 1890, which challenges to economic and military authority were successful? How do you account for their success? Why did other challenges fail?

6. What were the unique vulnerabilities of various groups of women to the forces of industrial and political change?

Created Equal Online

For more *Created Equal* resources, including suggestions on sites to visit and books to read, go to **MyHistoryLab.com.**

Chapter 18

Political and Cultural Conflict in a Decade of Depression and War: The 1890s

■ This group of Chiricahua Apache students arrived at the Carlisle Indian boarding school in 1890. Government-sponsored Indian education included dressing them in European American clothing and cutting their hair.

I n the early 1890s, Luther Standing Bear, a young man of Lakota Sioux origin, found himself suspended between two worlds. Born in 1868 in South Dakota, he had learned to hunt buffalo in the traditional manner of the Western Sioux. In 1879, he bowed to the wishes of his father, who insisted that he learn the ways of "Long Knives," or whites. The youth was among the first pupils to attend the new federal Indian boarding school in Carlisle, Pennsylvania. En route to Carlisle, the eleven-year-old regarded his journey—by boat and train—as an ordeal that he must endure with honor. Once at the school, he discovered that he was to become an "imitation of a white man"—and quickly.

Called Ota Kte (Plenty Kill) at home, he was now required to pick a new first name from among those listed on a classroom blackboard. He chose Luther. His teachers took away his blanket and moccasins and gave him a coat, pants, and vest to wear. They forbade him to speak his native language, and they cut his long hair. One of his classmates protested, "If I am to learn the ways of the white people, I can do it just as well with my hair on." Like most other youths at Carlisle, Luther Standing Bear learned to read and write English and to practice a craft (in his case, tinsmithing). His teachers encouraged him to embrace Christianity.

In 1884, as part of his government-sponsored training, Luther Standing Bear traveled to Philadelphia to work at the Wanamaker department store. The head of the Carlisle school, Captain Richard Henry Pratt, had sent the youth on his way with the words, "You are to be an example of what this school can turn out. Go, my boy, and do your best. Die there if necessary, but do not fail." After spending a year stocking shelves and performing other tasks at the famous store, the young man returned to South Dakota. There he taught Sioux children in a school near the place of his birth, now the Rosebud Indian Reservation.

In December 1890, U.S. military officials attacked and killed 150 to 200 Indians at Wounded Knee, South Dakota, near Luther Standing Bear's home. The young man subsequently moved with his family to the nearby Pine Ridge Reservation, where he began work as a shopkeeper and postal clerk. In the late 1890s, Luther Standing Bear served as an interpreter for Buffalo Bill's "Wild West" show during its tour in London. By 1912, he had become an American citizen and settled in southern California, where he began his acting career in the new motion picture industry. He appeared in some of the first movie westerns and became an Indian activist, speaking out against the "government prison" known as the reservation.

In the 1890s, Luther Standing Bear's journey took place amid economic depression, civil strife, and war. Throughout the decade, workers challenged the idea that the United States was immune to the bloody class conflict that had long plagued Europe. Some scholars lamented the closing of the western frontier, prompting fears that America's unique dynamic of growth and social improvement had come to an end.

Domestic developments had a profound effect on American foreign policy. Native-born whites began to seize upon new categories of racial difference to draw distinctions between various groups in the United States and around the world. Faced with declining consumer demand at home, politicians and businesspeople joined forces to expand American markets and American influence abroad. Economic and humanitarian interests often went hand in hand. Reformers claimed that the blessings of American consumer society would "civilize" darker peoples everywhere. In 1896, Merrill Gates, a philanthropist and advocate of Indian boarding-school education, described the goal of such education: "We need to *awaken in him* [the Indian] *wants*. . . . Discontent with the tepee and the starving rations of the Indian camp in winter is needed to get the Indian out of the blanket and into trousers—and trousers with a pocket in them, and with a *pocket that aches to be filled with dollars!*" America's imperialistic ventures would reveal a similar blend of economic interests and missionary outreach.

Thus, the 1890s were a time of stark contrasts. The same year the depression hit, the Chicago World's Fair, called the Columbian Exposition, celebrated American architectural and

technological progress. Among the exhibits was an early motion picture camera. This was a decade when bicycling became a craze, and the syncopated rhythms of a new form of music called ragtime were all the rage. But during the same decade, southern lynch mobs burned alive black men and women, and American military forces pursued a brutal war in Cuba and the Philippines.

Whereas some Americans tried to define rigid racial and nationalistic boundaries, others sought avenues of connection. A new political party, the Populist, or People's, party, aimed to bring together men and women of all backgrounds and regions. By advocating grassroots democracy as well as government action to regulate the economy, the party paved the way for the Progressive reforms of the early twentieth century.

Relying on a variety of means, from new legal and educational systems to commercial expansion and the deployment of military might, American elites attempted to consolidate their political power and cultural influence. In the process, the United States confronted not only the domestic challenges of sustaining a modern industrial society but also the world-wide challenges that pitted the enduring ideal of democracy against the emerging reality of **imperialism,** the notion that stronger powers had the right and even the obligation to assume control over the politics and natural resources of weaker peoples.

Frontiers at Home, Lost and Found

■ *How did fears about a closing western frontier affect American political, social, and cultural life in the 1890s?*

In 1893, historian Frederick Jackson Turner wrote an essay titled "The Significance of the Frontier in American History." Delivered as an address to a group of historians at the Columbian Exposition in Chicago, the essay presented a new way of thinking about American history. According to Turner, the process of settling the West had shaped all of American history. He argued that during the colonial period, the rigors of taming the land had transformed English colonists into more resourceful, more democratic people—in other words, into Americans. With each successive wave of western settlement, American society renewed itself. In his view, the West served as a safety valve, a place of opportunity that beckoned people out of crowded eastern cities. However, Turner noted, an 1890 Census Report had concluded that the frontier—a vague, receding zone at the edge of white settlement—had finally disappeared. The historian sounded an ominous note at the end of his address: "And now, four centuries from the discovery of America, at the end of a hundred years of life under the Constitution, the frontier has gone, and with its going has closed the first period in American history."

Turner's thesis promoted the idea of American "exceptionalism": the idea that its individualism and democratic values made the United States unique among the nations of the world. Yet his association of geography with an "American character" was simplistic at best. In his celebration of the sturdy settlers of the frontier, Turner ignored the bloody legacy of western settlement and its devastating effects on native and Spanish-speaking peoples.

Nevertheless, at the end of the nineteenth century, Turner and others were asking whether America needed to conquer new lands and "tame" certain peoples to preserve its distinctive character. Now that the frontier had disappeared, what was to prevent the United

Population density, 1890 (inhabitants per square mile)

90 and over	6–17
45–89	2–5
18–44	Less than 2

■ **MAP 18.1 Population Density, 1890**

In 1890, the United States contained vast tracts of wilderness. Some Americans worried that the Northeast was overpopulated and that, as a result, the country would face the same problems as Europe—class conflict, poverty, and urban ills.

States from becoming more like Europe? These concerns led to efforts to assimilate and "Americanize" Native Americans and European immigrants and to tighten systems of legal discrimination against others. In addition, some Americans turned their attention to "interior" frontiers of psychology, art, and spirituality. These issues also inspired some Americans to advocate extending the nation's military might and political authority beyond U.S. territorial boundaries. In the view of imperialists, if the American frontier at home was closing, the American frontier abroad should expand.

■ Frederick Jackson Turner's 1893 announcement that the western frontier had disappeared was premature. Here, homesteaders in Washington State cut down trees to carve a farm out of the forest, c. 1900. Felling gigantic hardwoods in the Northwest was a formidable challenge to family farmers.

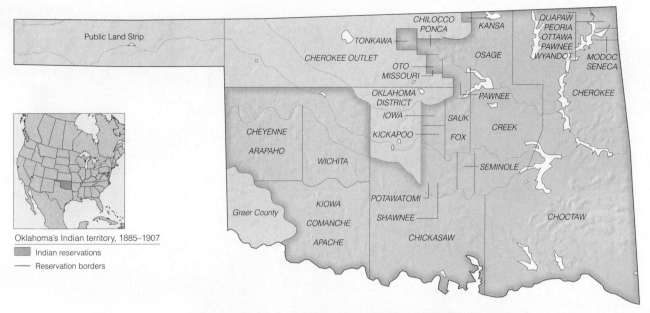

Oklahoma's Indian territory, 1885–1907

◼ Indian reservations

— Reservation borders

■ **MAP 18.2 Indian Territory and the State of Oklahoma, 1885–1907**

In the early 1890s, the federal government began to purchase land from the Five Civilized Tribes and other Indian groups to open Indian Territory to European American settlement. The lands of the Potawatomi, Shawnee, Iowa, Sauk, and Fox were opened in 1891; Cheyenne and Arapaho in 1892; the Cherokee Outlet in 1893; Kickapoo in 1895; and Kiowa, Comanche, Apache, and Wichita between 1901 and 1906. In 1907, Indian Territory and Oklahoma Territory merged to become the state of Oklahoma.

CLAIMING AND MANAGING THE LAND

As less and less land was available for cultivation, grazing, and mining, the politics of rural development entered a new phase. In the early 1890s, the last great parcel of Indian land was opened to European American farmers. Congress established the Territory of Oklahoma in 1890, and three years later, the Cherokee Outlet in the north-central part of the territory, combined with Tonkawa and Pawnee reservations, were thrown open to settlers and oil developers. On September 16, 1893, 100,000 people claimed 6.5 million newly opened acres in a single day. The "sooners," people who rushed to claim the land, gave the state of Oklahoma its nickname. The "Sooner State" was admitted to the Union in 1907.

Congress took other steps to manage western lands during the 1890s. The Court of Private Land Claims (1891) oversaw land disputes in New Mexico, Colorado, and Arizona. This court favored recent European American claimants over the Hispanic settlers who had received title to the lands from either Spain or Mexico generations earlier.

Land courts were only one example of an expanded federal role in the settlement of the West and management of the land. During the 1890s, the federal government continued to provide information and services for farmers through the U.S. Department of Agriculture. Policymakers argued over the proper balance between conserving natural resources for use by farmers, loggers, and oilmen and preserving the beauty of unspoiled panoramas for the enjoyment of all. In 1890, Congress established a national park in California's spectacular Yosemite Valley, where the Yosemite Indians had lived for hundreds of years. The 1891 Forest Reserve Act set aside forest reserves in the public domain (the vast tracts of land owned by the federal government). Logging companies were allowed to exploit these areas for their timber.

With his appointment as chief of the Division of Forestry in 1898, Gifford Pinchot sought to bring the issue of natural resource conservation to national attention. He believed that a managed forest could provide lumber and then renew itself. By contrast, John Muir and others argued that uninhabited regions should be preserved in their natural state, unmarred by dams, mines, or logging operations. In 1892, Muir founded the Sierra Club,

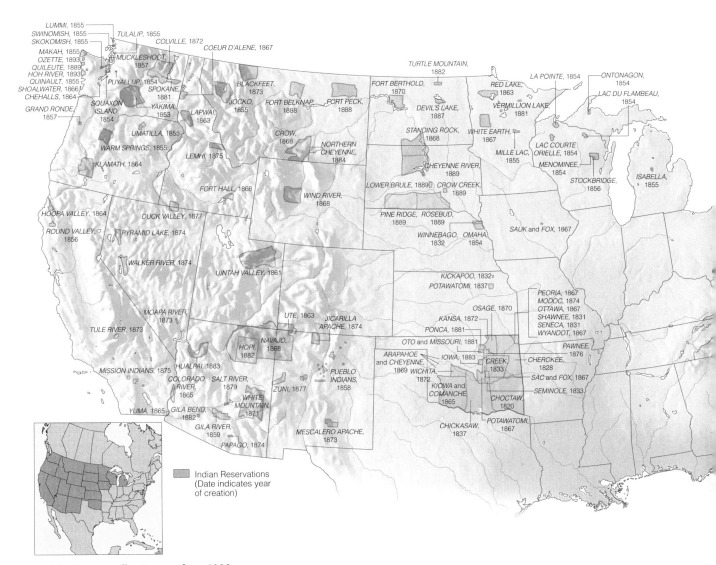

■ **MAP 18.3 Indian Reservations, 1900**

The Dawes Act, passed by Congress in 1887, intended to abandon the reservation system and integrate Indians into mainstream American society. Nevertheless, many reservations remained intact. As a group, Indians remained apart from European Americans. By the early twentieth century, the Indian as a "vanishing race" had become a familiar theme in novels and films. Yet Indian activists continued to press the cause of their people: to preserve native cultures and, at the same time, protest persistent poverty.

a group devoted to preserving wilderness. In 1899, both Muir and the Northern Pacific Railroad lobbied successfully for two new national parks, Mount Rainier in Washington and Glacier in Montana, highlighting the ongoing significance of railroad tourism. The philosophical disagreements between Pinchot and the conservationists on one hand and Muir and the preservationists on the other shaped a wider debate between conservationists and preservationists in the early twentieth century.

"Rusticating," or hiking and enjoying the beauty of nature, became a popular pastime for many Americans in the 1890s. By 1890, tourists from Boston could board a train and, eight hours later, reach the rocky coast of Maine's Frenchman's Bay, where large hotels provided comfortable accommodations and breathtaking views. Although the frontier of the cattle rancher and farmer was receding, the frontier of recreational tourism was growing by leaps and bounds, as excursion trains provided greater access to beach resorts and mountain retreats.

The National Archives

■ A middle-class Powhatan Indian family in Virginia poses for the camera, c. 1900. Since the seventeenth century, the Powhatan had intermarried with the Nanticoke of Delaware as well as African Americans of the Mid-Atlantic region. Communities such as these defied the efforts of scientists and others to rigidly categorize people according to race.

THE TYRANNY OF RACIAL CATEGORIES

The supposed closing of the western frontier, and with it the disappearance of the "safety valve" for restless Easterners, highlighted urban America's increasing class and cultural diversity. In an effort to categorize social groups, many national opinionmakers—scholars, journalists, and politicians—claimed that people should be distinguished from one another by their inborn, "natural" characteristics, ranging from skin color to facial bone structure and intelligence. Supposedly, these differences defined specific racial categories, such as Caucasoid, Mongoloid, and Negroid. In fact, so-called racial differences between groups were cultural differences. Pre–Civil War nativists had opposed foreign immigration because they considered native-born Protestants superior to people born in other countries. In contrast, late nineteenth-century scientific racists ranked "superior" and "inferior" races on an elaborate hierarchy encompassing all groups, native and foreign born.

Several factors account for this renewed obsession with race in the 1890s. European and American efforts to colonize and explore the far reaches of the globe brought whites face to face with darker-skinned peoples, whom scholars in the new discipline of anthropology studied and classified. The "New Immigration" from eastern Europe raised concerns about conferring citizenship on recent immigrants, such as Russian Jews, Poles, and Italians. Persistent violence along the U.S.-Mexican border, combined with the resistance of Indians and African Americans to the authority of white people, alarmed local and federal officials. Theories of "racial difference" were used to justify attempts to subordinate these groups, by violence if necessary.

Identification of racial categories pervaded the nation's popular, political, and legal cultures. Scientists filled scholarly journals and books with "evidence" of the superiority of the "white race," citing the size and weight of bones of various groups and comparing blacks and Jews in the United States with each other and with Eskimos in Greenland and Tapuyan Indians in Brazil. First published in 1895, the *Encyclopedia Britannica* listed the physical characteristics that allegedly distinguished the races from each other, including jaw projection and facial angles. Most people did not read these highly technical reports, but images in advertising and other forms of popular culture portrayed blacks and Asians as inferior, servile people.

In the South, the doctrine of white supremacy had disastrous consequences for African Americans. Beginning with Mississippi in 1890, over the next twenty years, white Democrats in all the southern states met in state constitutional conventions and imposed restrictions on the voting rights of African American men, using a variety of means: literacy requirements, poll taxes (fees that people had to pay to vote), and "grandfather clauses." These last measures stipulated that only men whose grandfathers had been eligible to vote before ratification of the Fifteenth Amendment could vote themselves. In some instances, the literacy requirements and poll taxes disenfranchised poor white men as well.

In 1896, the Supreme Court put its stamp of approval on segregated schools, trains, and streetcars in its *Plessy v. Ferguson* opinion. Four years earlier in New Orleans, a black man named Homer Plessy had refused to sit in a segregated railroad car. By a 7–1 majority, the Supreme Court ruled that states could exercise "reasonable" authority by segregating public accommodations. Such Jim Crow laws, according to the Court, did "not necessarily imply the inferiority of either race." Justice John Marshall Harlan dissented from the majority view, pointing out the obvious: "The white race deems itself to be the dominant race," a view that conflicted with the "colorblind" U.S. Constitution.

Between 1882 and 1901, more than 100 people, most of them black men, were lynched every year in the United States; the year 1892 set a record of 230 deaths. In the South, lynch mobs targeted black men and women who refused to subordinate themselves to whites. In 1892, a black woman born in slavery, newspaper editor Ida B. Wells, incurred the wrath of whites in her native Memphis when she condemned the killings of three black men. They had operated a Memphis store, the People's Cooperative Grocery Store, which competed for black customers with a nearby white-owned establishment. While defending their store from a mob of whites, the three men were lynched, their bodies mutilated. In the words of a friend, "They were succeeding too well. They were guilty of no crime but that."

Many black men victimized by lynch mobs were falsely accused of raping white women. In her newspaper *Free Speech,* Wells charged that accusations of rape were merely a pretext for the murder of black men. The southern white man, wrote Wells, "had never gotten over his resentment that the Negro was no longer his plaything, his servant, and his source of income." Death threats forced the editor to move north.

Whites targeted assertive black men and women, those "out of their place," especially professionals and property owners. In Wilmington, North Carolina, in November 1898, whites attacked Alex Manly, an African American newspaper editor who had labeled white men "a lot of carping hypocrites." He charged that white men who exploited black women sexually felt free to call for the murder of alleged black rapists. In retaliation, a mob destroyed Manly's offices and then turned on the city's black residents, driving them into the swamps and chasing them out of town at gunpoint. At least ten blacks were killed in the violence.

Yet even in the South, racial definitions were never as clear-cut or self-evident as racists, scientific or otherwise, claimed. For example, Italians and Jews occupied a middle ground between black and white, as class issues intermingled with racial categories. In 1891 in New Orleans, the lynching of a group of eleven Italian prisoners accused of conspiring to murder the city's chief of police met with no public outcry. Instead, a local newspaper condemned the "lawless passions" and "cutthroat practices" that it claimed were characteristic of all Italian immigrants. However, the Italian government protested loudly against the incident. Armed conflict between the two nations was averted only when the United States agreed to compensate the victims' families.

At the same time, Jewish shopkeepers and merchants in the South gained a conditional entry into the ranks of "whites." In Natchez, Mississippi, the small but prosperous Jewish community owned forty-five businesses, about a third of all in the town. Merchant Simon Moses and others like him built grand, Victorian-style houses and worshipped in an imposing synagogue, Temple B'Nai Israel. However, anti-Jewish feeling manifested itself in subtle ways. Living in an overwhelmingly Protestant region of the country, many southern Jews found themselves barred from local social organizations.

NEW ROLES FOR SCHOOLS

Between 1890 and 1899, nearly 3.7 million immigrants entered the United States; fewer than 1.4 million were English speakers from the United Kingdom and Ireland, while nearly 2.3 million were non-English speakers from Germany, Italy, Austria-Hungary, and Russia. The federal government assumed control of strictly monitoring and processing the men, women, and children who entered the United States. Ellis Island, in New York harbor, was opened in 1892. The West Coast immigration station and detention center, Angel Island,

Kenan Research Center at the Atlanta History Center

■ As a region, the South lacked the ethnic diversity characteristic of the rest of the country. However, small numbers of Jewish immigrants did settle in the South, and some managed to turn modest dry goods establishments into major urban department stores. Atlanta's Rich and Brothers Dry Goods store, shown here in the 1880s, was founded and owned by Jews.

Compulsory school attendance

▨ Compulsory school attendance pre-1880 law

☐ Compulsory school attendance by 1890

▨ Compulsory school attendance by 1900

Dates represent the year school attendance became compulsory

▪ **MAP 18.4 Compulsory School Attendance Laws, by State**

Several northeastern, midwestern, and West Coast states enacted compulsory school attendance laws before 1880. A large number of states joined this trend in the 1880s and 1890s. By 1900, the former Confederate and border states, plus Iowa, were the only states not to have laws requiring young children to attend school for part of the year.

in San Francisco Bay, was opened eighteen years later. During this period, public displays of patriotism became increasingly characteristic of American life. The recitation of the Pledge of Allegiance was introduced into public classrooms and courtrooms in the 1890s.

Many Americans saw formal education as a great equalizer of social groups, and many younger immigrants and the children of immigrants eagerly embraced American schooling as a means of upward mobility. However, schools did not always fulfill their promise as agents of equal opportunity for all. Increasingly, schools separated and grouped children according to their culture, religion, and class as well as race.

Reformers, missionaries, philanthropists, and government officials alike extolled the virtues of schooling tailor-made for particular groups. Presbyterian missionary women founded the Presbyterian College of the Southwest to instruct Spanish-speaking girls in both English and Protestantism. European American teachers taught young Indian women at the Cherokee Female Seminary near the Cherokee Nation capital at Tahlequah, Oklahoma. The teachers based the seminary's curriculum on that of Mount Holyoke, a college for women in Massachusetts.

However, many of the schools established by reformers and missionaries focused not on classical education but on teaching practical trades to students. These schools were designed to enable the pupils to become self-supporting upon graduation. For example, the school as a vehicle for vocational instruction found enthusiastic support among northern philanthropists concerned about education for southern black children and young people. A generation after the Civil War, the persistent poverty of many rural southern blacks convinced northern reformers that this group of Americans should be educated for a distinct form of second-class citizenship. Philanthropists, such as Julius Rosenwald of Chicago, upheld the notion of segregated public education. They created new institutions, or modified existing ones, to stress the trades and "domestic arts" at the expense of such subjects as philosophy, mathematics, and foreign languages. Embracing the "industrial education movement," the white trustees of the state-sponsored North Carolina Agricultural and Mechanical College (a segregated black college) voted to exclude women from the school altogether. They reasoned that "neither the girls or boys wanted to engage in the harder kinds of manual labor in the presence of the other sex, but would strive to dress up in fine clothes to impress the other."

This emphasis on vocational training provoked varied reactions from African American leaders. Born a slave in 1858, Booker T. Washington had labored in a West Virginia coal mine before attending Hampton Normal (teacher-training) and Agricultural Institute in Virginia. In 1881, he assumed the leadership of Tuskegee Institute, an Alabama school for blacks founded on the Hampton model. Speaking at the Cotton States Exposition, a fair held in Atlanta in 1895, Washington urged southern blacks to "Cast down your buckets where you are"—in other words, to remain in the South and to concentrate on acquiring manual skills that would bring a measure of self-sufficiency to black families and communities. In the same address, Washington proposed that blacks refrain from agitating for civil rights, such as the vote. In return, whites should refrain from attacking innocent men, women, and children. Ignoring this last part of the speech, whites hailed Washington's "Atlanta Compromise" proposal as one that endorsed racial segregation and second-class citizenship for blacks. Nevertheless, in the coming years, Washington worked secretly to undermine the legal foundations of some of the white South's most cherished institutions, including segregated railroad cars and rural forced labor.

DOCUMENT

Booker T. Washington, Atlanta Exposition Address

Challenging Washington's message, scholar-activist W. E. B. Du Bois ridiculed the notion that blacks should be content to become maids, carpenters, and sharecroppers. Similarly, in 1896, John Hope, a young professor at Roger Williams University in Nashville, Tennessee, and future president of Morehouse College and later Atlanta University, renounced Washington's apparent accommodationist stance: "If we are not striving for equality, in heaven's name for what are we living?" he demanded. "Rise, Brothers! Come let us possess this land. Never say, 'Leave well enough alone.' "

Some immigrant groups, responding specifically to the Protestant agenda of most public school systems, preferred to sponsor their own schools. In many urban areas, Roman Catholic nuns founded and staffed parochial (parish) schools that appealed to certain immigrant communities. By 1900, Catholics constituted the largest single denomination in the country, with 9 million members from diverse backgrounds. Catholic newcomers from southern and eastern Europe opposed what they claimed was the attempt by the Irish-dominated church hierarchy to "Americanize" Catholicism. One Chicago Catholic communicant, writing in the Polish-language paper *Zgodat*, charged that the effort to force Polish churchgoers to listen to and speak English was "an insult to all Polish parishes in Chicago as well as in the United States." Catholic churches and schools "built with the hard-earned money of us Polish people" should be kept under community control, he argued.

> *By 1900, Catholics constituted the largest single denomination in the country, with 9 million members from diverse backgrounds.*

New forms of schooling reinforced class and cultural distinctions. No longer dependent on the income their children might earn in the workplace, late nineteenth-century urban middle-class families could allow their sons and daughters to prolong their schooling. High school came to be considered a logical extension of public schooling. Between 1890 and 1900, the number of students graduating from high school doubled, from 43,731 to 94,883.

The spread of private institutions of higher education reflected the wealth of a new elite and new forms of socialization for young people of privilege. In 1891, Central Pacific Railroad builder Leland Stanford founded Stanford University in California in honor of his recently deceased son. The previous year, Standard Oil's John D. Rockefeller had established the University of Chicago.

College life was becoming associated with a particular stage of personal development, a stage marked not only by academic endeavors but also by uniquely American group activities, such as playing on or cheering for the school football team. College football games had become spectacles, drawing thousands of paying spectators but also costing a great deal of money to produce and staff. The 1892 Yale University athletic budget included funds to pay for transporting the football team and its retinue of doctors, trainers, cooks, and coaches from one game to the next. The game of basketball was invented in 1891, and soon many colleges formed teams that played the new sport. But not everyone viewed these developments as positive. An 1893 editorial in the *Nation* decried "the inordinate attention given to athletics in college" and suggested that "debt, drink, and debauchery" were the natural consequence.

CONNECTIONS BETWEEN MIND AND BEHAVIOR

In the 1890s, some scholars and writers proposed that, although America's geographic frontier was closed, the "interior" frontier (of the human will and imagination) still attracted the curious. In Vienna, professor-physician Sigmund Freud pioneered the study of the human unconscious, the mysterious realm of thought and feeling that lies hidden beneath the mundane activities of everyday life. Freud's *The Interpretation of Dreams* (1900) suggested that dreams reveal the dreamer's unconscious desires and that these desires shape routine behavior.

In the United States, the new discipline of psychology owed much to the work of Harvard University professor William James. In his *Principles of Psychology* (1890), James described the human brain as an organism constantly adjusting itself to its environment; people's surroundings profoundly influence their behavior, he argued. In *The Will to Believe* (1897), he explored the psychology of religious faith. According to James, religion, science, and philosophy all have immediate relevance to the way people live their lives, and these ways of thinking and believing can cast light on social problems and their possible solutions.

> *In the United States, the new discipline of psychology owed much to the work of Harvard University professor William James.*

Henry James, William's brother, explored the psychological dimensions of class, gender, and national identities in his works of fiction and literary criticism. In much of his fiction, Henry James probed the consciousness of his subjects and experimented with methods of controlling points of view. Such works as *Daisy Miller* (1878), *The Wings of the Dove* (1902), *The Ambassadors* (1903), and *The Golden Bowl* (1904) reveal his intense interest in encounters between European and American elites and the clash of cultures between the two groups.

Novelist Stephen Crane combined an unflinching look at reality—a blood-soaked Civil War battlefield or the slums of New York City—with a sensitive probing of human psychology. In *The Red Badge of Courage* (1894), Crane explores the fears and self-delusions of a Union soldier, basing his account on firsthand descriptions of the fighting a generation before. By stripping the story of all ideology—northern soldiers are hardly distinguishable from southern soldiers, and political issues are never mentioned—Crane suggests that the real war was that of the combatants battling their own private demons.

Kate Chopin wrote about gender roles in New Orleans Creole, or French-influenced, society. Her novel *The Awakening* (1899) prompted outrage among critics. They objected to the sympathetic portrayal of the wealthy married heroine, Edna Pontellier, who anguishes over her inability to reconcile her artistic, free-spirited temperament with her roles of wife and mother. At the end of the story, she chooses to commit suicide rather than submit to a life of convention. The novel focuses on Edna's reaction to the expectations other people have of her and on her gradual awakening to the idea that she must live life—or die—on her own terms.

Psychologists and novelists were not the only people to explore the uncharted territory of the mind. Some religious leaders saw human consciousness as the key to understanding spiritual growth and development. In the late nineteenth century, the Church of Christ, Scientist, founded by Mary Baker Eddy in 1879, prospered and grew. Eddy held that physical illness was a sign of sin and that such illness could be healed by Christian faith and prayer. By linking religious life to physical health, Eddy affirmed a crucial link between belief and personal well-being. In 1892, she reorganized her Christian Science faith around a mother church in Boston. Through branch churches, the American-born sect spread to more than sixty countries throughout the world.

As the United States seemed to be fragmenting into numerous classes, races, ethnic groups, and religious denominations, some Americans began to seek common ground with one another. For many of these Americans, the political process represented just one of several opportunities to bring together persons of diverse backgrounds to pursue common goals.

The Search for Domestic Political Alliances

■ *What were the coalitions and institutions that were created and strengthened in an effort to unite diverse groups in common purpose?*

In the 1890s, groups of Americans seemed to be estranged from each other as they rarely had been before. A few were enjoying the fruits of astonishing wealth, building for themselves magnificent, multimillion-dollar "summer cottages" reminiscent of glittering European palaces. In 1899, University of Chicago sociologist Thorstein Veblen coined the term conspicuous consumption to describe the expensive tastes of the ostentatious rich. Meanwhile, working men and women toiled long hours under dangerous conditions—when they had jobs. In 1895, the average worker was unemployed for three months of the year. Various ethnic and racial groups, native born and immigrant, were pitted against one another. Self-styled sophisticated city folk derided the "hayseeds" (unsophisticated rural people) on the farm.

> *The prosperous middle class hoped that certain unifying forces would connect different classes and ethnic groups.*

Still, the prosperous middle class hoped that certain unifying forces would connect different classes and ethnic groups. Businesspeople, lawyers, and other professionals placed their faith in public schools, cultural institutions such as public museums and libraries, and the desire for a more comfortable life to instill "American" values in newcomers and the poor. The 1890s also witnessed some remarkable alliances between groups of people who had never before found common ground. The Populist party had a profound impact on the nation's political landscape in the 1890s. And women, through their local and national organizations, helped to blend domestic concerns with politics, offering a new model of civic involvement.

CLASS CONFLICT

Congress passed the Pension Act of 1890 to provide pensions for all disabled men who had served in the Union army during the Civil War. To pay for the pensions, Congress imposed a high tariff (named the McKinley Tariff after Representative William McKinley of Ohio) on a wide variety of imported goods. The northeastern states, dependent on domestic manufacturing, traditionally supported a high tariff. Western states supported the McKinley Tariff in return for the Sherman Silver Purchase Act of 1890, under which the federal government promised to buy a total of 4.5 million ounces of silver each month and to issue banknotes for that amount redeemable in gold or silver. As a result, Westerners benefited from the infusion of federal cash used to purchase silver mined in the West.

But the pairing of a high tariff with the purchase of silver produced explosive political and economic results. The tax on imported manufactured goods hurt consumers, and when wages did not keep pace with prices, workers revolted. In 1892, steel magnate Andrew Carnegie and his company chairman Henry Clay Frick drastically cut wages at the Carnegie Steel Company's Homestead plant, near Pittsburgh. Workers went on strike in June. They armed themselves with rifles and dynamite and engaged in a pitched battle with some 300 detectives from the Pinkerton agency, men hired by Frick to break the strike. (Homestead town officials had refused Frick's request to subdue the strikers.) Ten people died, and sixty were wounded. In response to the violence, the governor of Pennsylvania mobilized the state's National Guard. The troops escorted strikebreakers to work. The company cut its workforce by 25 percent and reduced the wages of the strikebreakers. In the aftermath of the Homestead strike, the steelworkers' union lay in ruins. Gloated Frick, "Our victory is now complete and most gratifying."

> *The tax on imported manufactured goods hurt consumers, and when wages did not keep pace with prices, workers revolted.*

Around the same time, gold, copper, and silver miners in the West faced daunting barriers to labor organization from within and outside their ranks. Protestants harbored suspicions of Roman Catholics. Ancient animosities prevented the Irish from cooperating with the English. European Americans disdained Mexicans and the Chinese. However, the workers in Idaho's Coeur d'Alene mines managed to overcome these antagonisms and strike for union recognition. In March 1892, mine owners in the region formed a "protective association" and slashed wages. When workers walked off the job, the owners imported strikebreakers from other areas of the West. The strikers retaliated by blowing up a mine with dynamite. Fifteen hundred state and federal troops arrived on the scene, and the resulting clash left seven miners dead. The troops confined 300 striking miners in bullpens, where they remained for several weeks before their trials. Like the Homestead steel workers, the striking miners met with defeat. However, out of this conflict came a new organization, founded in Butte, Montana, in 1893: the Western Federation of Miners.

Widespread discontent over the tariff and simmering resentment on the part of debtors clamoring for unlimited coinage of silver helped unseat President Harrison in the election of 1892. The victorious Democratic candidate, Grover Cleveland, who had held the presidency before Harrison, took office once more in 1893 (the only defeated president to be reelected). A new and noteworthy player in the election of 1892 was the People's (Populist) party, whose candidate James B. Weaver polled more than 1 million votes. This strong showing put both the Republicans and Democrats on notice that the Populists had the potential to swing future national elections.

The first national convention of the Populist party took place in Omaha, Nebraska, in the summer of 1892. The party had emerged from the Farmers' Alliances that had so effectively organized black and white midwestern and southern farmers in the 1880s. In the 1890s the plight of western farmers reflected the state of American agriculture in general. On the Plains, farmers incurred ever deeper debts as they bought more land and invested in expensive machinery to raise pigs, cattle, wheat, and fruit for market. But to put food on their own tables, they had to pay cash for bacon, beef, bread, and canned peaches at the store. The price of wheat had been a dollar a bushel in 1870, but it was only 35 cents 20 years later. Dakota farmers lost 15 cents on every bushel of wheat they sent to market.

The Populist party platform endorsed at the Omaha convention supported "free and unlimited coinage of silver and gold at the present legal ratio of sixteen to one"; a graduated income tax; government ownership of railroad, telegraph, and telephone companies; and an end to land

TABLE 18.1			
The Election of 1892			
Candidate	**Political Party**	**Popular Vote (%)**	**Electoral Vote**
Grover Cleveland	Democratic	46.1	277
Benjamin Harrison	Republican	43.0	145
James B. Weaver	Populist	8.5	22
John Bidwell	Prohibition	2.2	–

speculation. The delegates also condemned government subsidies to private corporations (for example, land grants to railroads) and called for the direct election of U.S. senators. Populists supported other measures designed to make the political process more open and democratic, such as provisions for voters to recall corrupt elected officials and public referenda on pressing policy issues of the day.

The Populists sought to extend their reach beyond the cotton fields of the South and the plains of the Midwest to working men and women in the nation's cities. Though separated by geography and history, farmers and wage earners could lay claim to certain common interests. The Populists' 1892 platform included resolutions sympathizing "with the efforts of organized workmen to shorten the hours of labor" to an eight-hour workday (many workers were forced to toil twelve to fourteen hours daily) and expressing solidarity with the Knights of Labor in their struggles against "tyrannical" employers.

The Populists gained strength when a national economic depression hit in 1893. This dramatic downturn stemmed from several causes. As debtors clamored for "free silver," foreign investors in the United States became nervous, and European bankers began to call in their loans. A bubble of overbuilding and land speculation burst.

The effects of the depression were widespread. Within six months, 8,000 businesses failed, and as many as 20 percent of all workers lost their jobs. Some took to the road as tramps or hoboes to seek employment; others begged for charity. In 1894, Jacob S. Coxey, an Ohio quarry owner, dubbed himself a "general" and mobilized his own "army" of 5,000 men to march to Washington, D.C. There, the marchers protested the failure of the federal government to provide financial aid to its neediest citizens, now that the country was in the midst of the worst depression ever. "Coxey's Army" petitioned Congress to create extensive public works projects at the federal and local levels. However, the "army" met with an abrupt end when Coxey and his men were arrested for trampling the grass on Capitol Hill.

Also in 1894, Eugene V. Debs, head of the American Railway Union (ARU), inspired the union's 150,000 members to protest conditions at the Pullman Palace Car Company. Employees in the company town of Pullman near Chicago felt squeezed when the Pullman company cut their wages by one-third but left intact the rents on their company-owned houses. The resulting strike crippled railroads from Chicago to California. President Cleveland declared that he could not stand by while the strikers interfered with the delivery of the U.S. mail. The president sent troops to quell the uprising, crushing the strike. For the first time, a federal court issued an injunction to force workers to go back to their jobs. Debs and other ARU leaders defied the order and went to jail.

To workers all over the country, the response to the Pullman strike signaled a troublesome alliance between government and big business, two powerful forces that the poor and the unemployed could not hope to

TABLE 18.2		
Work Hours Needed to Produce Specified Amounts of Wheat, Corn, and Cotton, 1880 and 1900		
	1880	**1900**
Wheat		
Work hours per acre	20	15
Yield per acre (bu)	13.2	13.9
Work hours per 100 bushels	152	108
Corn		
Work hours per acre	46	38
Yield per acre (bu)	25.6	25.9
Work hours per 100 bushels	180	147
Cotton		
Work hours per acre	119	112
Yield of lint per acre (bl)	179	191
Work hours per bale[a]	318	280

[a] Yields are five-year averages, centered on year shown. For statistical purposes, a bale of cotton is 500 pounds gross weight or 480 pounds net weight of lint. Actual bale weights vary widely.

Source: *Historical Statistics of the United States, Colonial Times to 1957* (Washington, D.C.: U.S. Government Printing Office, 1960), 281.

■ Police and soldiers rout Jacob S. Coxey's "Army" in 1894. Coxey led a group of unemployed men in a march on Washington, D.C. They were seeking government relief—in the form of a public works program—to alleviate economic distress caused by the depression of 1893. As they marched, they sang a song that exaggerated their numbers one-hundred-fold: "We're coming, Grover Cleveland, 500,000 strong."

TABLE 18.3			
The Election of 1896			
Candidate	**Political Party**	**Popular Vote (%)**	**Electoral Vote**
William McKinley	Republican	51.1	271
William J. Bryan	Democratic	45.5	176

counter. That alliance seemed to be solidified in 1895 when federal gold reserves fell to a dangerous low of $41 million (it was widely believed that a minimum of $100 million in gold was necessary to sustain the paper currency in circulation). Cleveland authorized the sale of government bonds for gold, but he also turned to J. P. Morgan, a Wall Street banker, for a loan. Morgan and a group of bankers agreed to lend the government $65 million, earning a $7 million commission for themselves in the process.

Judicial decisions confirmed the belief of many farmers and workers that all branches of the federal government were conspiring to favor the rich at the expense of the poor. In 1895, the Supreme Court rendered two opinions that favored big business and the wealthiest Americans. In *United States v. E. C. Knight*, the Court ruled that the Sherman Anti-Trust Act of 1890 applied only to interstate commerce and not to manufacturers. The Court had decided in favor of the subject of the suit, the sugar trust that controlled 98 percent of the industry. In *Pollock v. Farmers' Loan and Trust Company,* the court struck down a modest federal income tax (2 percent on incomes over $4,000 per year). These decisions helped set the stage for the showdown between the Populists and the two major parties in 1896.

RISE AND DEMISE OF THE POPULISTS

In 1896, the Republicans nominated Congressman William McKinley of Ohio, whose name had graced the widely unpopular tariff bill of 1890. The Democrats turned their back on Cleveland, regarded as a pariah by members of his own party for his deal with Morgan and his high-handed tactics against the Pullman strikers. Without an obvious presidential candidate at their convention in Chicago in July, the Democrats seemed at loose ends. Then, out of the audience, a man rose to address the 15,000 delegates. William Jennings Bryan, a thirty-six-year-old Populist from Nebraska, electrified the assembly with his passionate denunciation of arrogant industrialists and indifferent politicians. The country must abandon the gold standard once and for all, he thundered: "You shall not press down upon the brow of labor this crown of thorns, you shall not crucify mankind upon a cross of gold." One awestruck listener, an alternate member of the Nebraska delegation, later said of Bryan's "Cross of Gold" speech, "There are no words in our language to picture the effect it produced upon the vast multitude which heard it." The next day, the Democrats chose Bryan as their candidate for president.

> *By nominating William Jennings Bryan, the Democrats took on the Populist cause of free silver.*

By nominating this eloquent upstart, the Democrats took on the Populist cause of free silver. Conservative Democrats bolted the party or sat out the election. Meanwhile, some Populists were appalled that the Democrats had picked conservative Maine banker Arthur Sewall as Bryan's vice-presidential running mate. Meeting in their own convention later in the summer, the Populists also chose Bryan as their candidate for president, but they instead ran Thomas E. Watson of Georgia for vice president. Thus, during his presidential campaign in the fall, Bryan had to contend with two different running mates from two different parties.

In the general election, McKinley received much support from his friend and political supporter Marcus (Mark) Hanna. A wealthy iron magnate and chair of the Republican National Committee, Hanna coordinated an effort to raise large sums of money for the Republicans ($16 million in total, far more than the Democrats' $1 million). He also fueled a nationwide hysteria over the possibility that Bryan would become president, blanketing the country with leaflets declaring "In God we trust, in Bryan we bust." Hanna charged that Bryan as president would mean disaster for businesspeople, bankers, and other creditors, who would now be at the mercy of working people, small farmers, and other debtors. Benefiting from Hanna's strategy and from divisions between the Populists and Democrats, McKinley triumphed in November. As a national force, the People's party rapidly disintegrated after the election of 1896.

Yet as a political movement encompassing disparate elements, the Populists left a mixed legacy. In some areas of the country, the party yielded some remarkable, if short-lived, biracial coalitions. In Grimes County, Texas, in the cotton-growing eastern part of the state, the Populist spirit survived for a few years beyond 1896. Some whites had split from the Democratic party, and some blacks had renounced their traditional allegiance to the Republican party. The alliance brought together blacks, such as school principal Morris Carrington, and whites, such as Garrett Scott, a Populist sheriff.

In the fall of 1899, the White Man's Union (WMU) emerged to oppose this noteworthy coalition. A member of the WMU tried to express its aims in poetry:

Twas nature's laws that drew the lines
Between the Anglo-Saxon and African races,
And we, the Anglo-Saxons of Grand Old Grimes,
Must force the African to keep his place.

The WMU made good on its vow to rid the county of "Negro rule." A November 1900 shootout at Anderson, the county seat, left Garrett Scott wounded and his brother Emmett and two other men dead. The gun battle effectively ended the Populist presence in Grimes County.

The Populists were unable to sustain a regionwide biracial coalition in the South. This failure suggests the power of white supremacist beliefs. The threat of cooperation between Republican and Populist voters was powerful, especially in such states as North Carolina. In that state, Republican-Populist fusion had captured the state legislature in 1894 and the governorship in 1896. Throughout the South, the black population was growing—a total of 10 million people in 1890, more than double the 4.5 million on the eve of the Civil War. Frightened by this development, white southern Democrats campaigned to disfranchise black men, beginning in the 1890s. Landless blacks and whites would find no common political ground again until the 1930s.

BARRIERS TO A U.S. WORKERS' POLITICAL MOVEMENT

In the 1890s, workers in Europe were forging new political parties to represent their interests, and in some cases to press a bold socialist agenda, in the forum of national politics. Although late nineteenth-century America showed dramatic evidence of bitter class conflict, it produced no viable workers' party or socialist movement. Why? The answer is not simple. Farmers and members of the industrial laboring classes all aspired to self-sufficiency, a life free of debt that released their wives and children from unremitting toil and provided some measure of material comfort. Nevertheless, both groups found it difficult to ally with each other.

The large influx of immigrants meant that competition for even low-paying jobs remained fierce among wage-earning men and women. Employers manipulated racial, ethnic, and religious prejudices among workers to keep them estranged. Between 1890 and 1900, at least twenty-nine major strikes—primarily in the iron, steel, coal-mining, meatpacking, railroad, and longshore industries—prompted management to employ African American strikebreakers.

The large influx of immigrants meant that competition for even low-paying jobs remained fierce among wage-earning men and women.

White Protestant workers seized on ethnic and religious distinctions to win advantages for themselves in the workplace. Their unions excluded certain racial and ethnic groups altogether. Even somewhat egalitarian unions fell prey to racial prejudice. For example, the United Mine Workers (UMW) professed to welcome both black and white workers into its ranks. However, an 1892 report from an African American organizer in Jellico, Tennessee, stated that "the whites declare that they won't work" under an African American boss. At best, whites relegated their black and female coworkers to segregated unions and enforced a discriminatory division of labor within the workplace.

Moreover, the pace and processes of mechanization and technological development varied from job to job, making it difficult for workers in one industry to form alliances with workers in

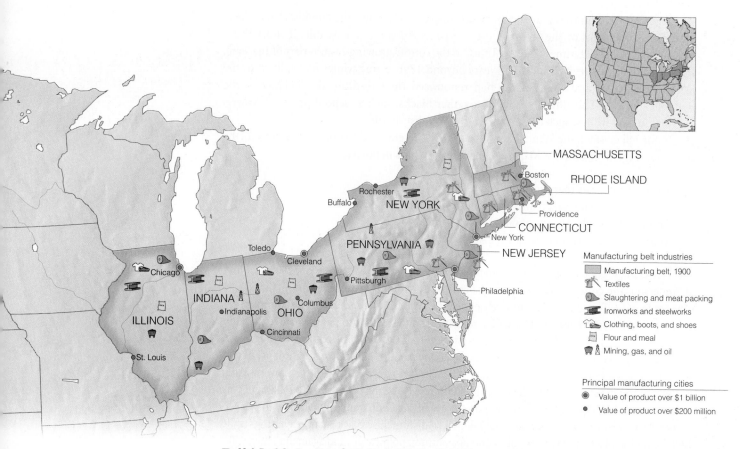

■ MAP 18.5   Manufacturing Belt in the United States, 1900

During the late nineteenth century, most manufacturing took place in the northeastern United States. Exceptions included flour milling in Minneapolis, meatpacking in Chicago, the growing textile industry in the southern Piedmont, and the emergence of steel production in Birmingham, Alabama, due to rich local deposits of iron and coal ore.

another. By 1900, the steel, shoe, and textile industries were fully mechanized. In contrast, skilled craft workers dominated the cigar, garment, and glass-blowing industries, although women machine operatives were beginning to challenge male cigarmakers. Taking pride in their craft and its traditions, skilled workers distanced themselves from those who tended machines.

Many American workers, regardless of ethnicity, religion, or industry, continued to believe that they could eventually own their own businesses; thus, they resisted casting their lot permanently with unions or other working-class organizations. High rates of geographic mobility also prevented workers from committing themselves to a particular union in a particular place. And the power of antistrike forces proved daunting. Private security agencies, such as the Pinkertons, as well as state-deployed National Guard troops, backed up the authority of employers, judges, mayors, and governors. Finally, unlike European parliamentary systems, U.S. politics was based on a "winner take all" principle. In America, the two major parties tried to capture the political center, discouraging coalition-building among smaller parties. Such alliances might have pushed the country farther to the left or right.

These factors help to account for the success of the American Federation of Labor (AFL) in attracting and retaining members. By the end of the nineteenth century, the AFL had rejected the rhetoric of radical labor leaders in favor of organizing a select group of workers, mostly skilled white men. Leaders of AFL union affiliates denounced "cheap labor" competitors, whether women workers or Japanese or Chinese immigrants. In the coming years, the AFL would prove that it had staying power, although it represented primarily the interests of white male craftsmen.

TABLE 18.4

Categories of Employment, 1880–1910

Occupation	1880	Percentage	1890	Percentage	1900	Percentage	1910	Percentage
Agriculture, forestry, and fishing	8,705	50.1	10,170	42.8	10,920	37.6	11,590	31.6
Extractive industries	310	1.8	480	2.0	760	2.6	1,050	2.9
Manufacturing	3,170	18.2	4,750	20.0	6,340	21.8	8,230	22.4
Construction	830	4.8	1,440	6.1	1,660	5.7	2,300	6.3
Commerce and finance	1,220	7.0	1,990	8.4	2,760	9.5	3,890	10.6
Transportation and communications	860	4.9	1,530	6.4	2,100	7.2	3,190	8.7
Services	2,100	12.1	3,210	13.5	4,160	14.3	5,880	16.0
Other	195	1.1	170	0.7	370	1.3	600	1.6
Total	17,390	100	23,740	100	29,070	100	36,730	100

Numbers given in thousands.

Source: International Historical Statistics (New York: Palgrave McMillan, 2003) 154.

CHALLENGES TO TRADITIONAL GENDER ROLES

In the 1890s, the women's suffrage, club, missionary, and social settlement movements emerged as significant political forces. Nevertheless, many white women in these movements remained steadfast in their refusal to embrace their nonwhite counterparts.

In 1890, the two major national women's suffrage associations, the National Woman Suffrage Association and the American Woman Suffrage Association, merged to form the National-American Woman Suffrage Association (NAWSA). Elizabeth Cady Stanton served as the new group's first president for two years. The suffrage movement exhibited contradictory impulses. On one hand, it brought together supporters from around the country and yielded striking examples of international cooperation. Beginning in 1890 and every year thereafter until 1920, members of NAWSA branches scattered throughout the United States met in convention to debate strategy. American women consulted with their counterparts in England and western Europe to advance their cause.

On the other hand, in an effort to be perceived as "respectable," many white native-born Protestant American suffragists sought to distance themselves from the poor, immigrants, African Americans, and the laboring classes. When NAWSA leaders called for a literacy requirement for voting, they implicitly left out immigrant and poor women. They also refused to admit black women's suffrage clubs into their umbrella organization. In the process, the white women turned their backs on some of the most committed supporters of their own cause.

Identifying themselves primarily as wives and mothers, some women entered the political realm through local women's clubs. They believed that personal intellectual development and group political activity would benefit both their own families and society in general. In the 1880s, the typical club focused on self-improvement through reading history and literature. By the 1890s, many clubs had embraced political activism. They lobbied local politicians for improvements in education and social welfare and raised money for hospitals and playgrounds. The General Federation of Women's Clubs (GFWC), founded in 1892, united 100,000 women in 500 affiliate clubs throughout the nation.

Yet the GFWC specifically excluded African American clubs. Black women formed their own national federation, the National Association of Colored Women (NACW), in 1896. Through club work, they spoke out against lynch mobs and segregationists and worked to improve their local communities. In 1899, the first president of the NACW, Mary Church Terrell, appeared

MAP

Women's Suffrage before the Nineteenth Century

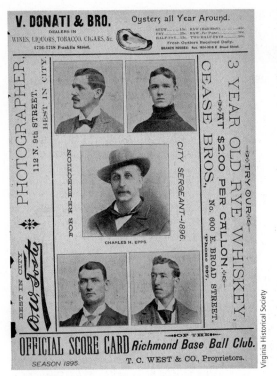

■ In 1896, Charles H. Epps, the city sergeant of Richmond, Virginia, ran for reelection. He distributed these cards to prospective voters. The cards suggest the masculine nature of politics at this time. This one doubled as a scorecard for the city's professional baseball team and carried advertisements for a local whiskey manufacturer and liquor and tobacco store.

before a mostly white organization, the National Congress of Mothers. She minced no words in contrasting the resources available to white mothers and children with the inferior medical care afforded African Americans. Declared Terrell, "So rough does the way of her infant appear to many a poor black mother that instead of thrilling with the joy which you feel, as you clasp your little ones to your breast, she trembles with apprehension and despair."

In some areas of the country, black and white women did make common cause—to further the goals of temperance, for example—although white women embraced these alliances uneasily. At the end of the century, black women in North Carolina sought to circumvent the sometimes violent political realm dominated by white men. They worked with middle-class white women through voluntary organizations, such as the Young Women's Christian Association and the Women's Christian Temperance Union.

In the West, Protestant-sponsored "mission homes" ministered to women in need. The San Francisco Presbyterian Chinese Mission Home offered a safe haven for Chinese women fleeing abuse and exploitation. Eastern women opened their pocketbooks to support not only the San Francisco mission but also shelters for unwed mothers and abused girls in other cities, in the name of virtuous womanhood.

Social settlements were unique institutions, founded and staffed by well-educated women, many of whom had attended elite women's colleges. The daily operations of the settlement house reflected the priorities of its founders, who often brought activists, public health officials, journalists, and laboring men and women together around the dinner table to discuss problems of the poor. Settlement house workers hoped to instill in poor women the values of domesticity and pride in American citizenship. By 1900, more than 200 social settlement houses were helping to acculturate immigrants by offering classes in a variety of subjects, including English, health, and personal hygiene. But their work was political as well. In 1893, the women social workers of Hull House successfully lobbied Illinois state legislators for the passage of antisweatshop legislation that would protect female employees and prohibit child labor.

Although often associated with immigrants in the largest cities, settlement houses reached diverse populations. In the late 1890s, a coalition of the Kentucky Federation of Women's Clubs and other organizations sponsored several teachers who organized a summer settlement called Camp Cedar Grove in the eastern part of the state. This venture provided the foundation for the Hindman Settlement School. The school, still in existence, initially aimed to acculturate mountain people to middle-class ways in dress, eating habits, and manners and to preserve traditional mountain music and crafts.

> *Although often associated with immigrants in the largest cities, settlement houses reached diverse populations.*

Sensitive to the racial prejudices of their clients and their neighbors, most early settlements failed to reach out to African Americans. This policy stimulated the development of black-led settlements, such as the Phyllis Wheatley Settlement in Minneapolis and the Neighborhood Union in Atlanta. Founded by Lugenia Burns Hope in 1908, the Neighborhood Union aimed, among other goals, "to bring about a better understanding between the races."

In the tradition of Frances Wright (an antebellum abolitionist) and Victoria Woodhull, some women challenged traditional gender relations that relegated women to dependence on men. Emma Goldman, a Russian immigrant and self-proclaimed anarchist, paired the sexual liberation of women with the rights of workers to live a decent life. A radical by any measure, Goldman was, nevertheless, not alone in rejecting the idea that marriage should always be permanent. Between 1890 and 1900, the divorce rate increased from 1 out of every 17 new marriages to 1 out of 12. More and more couples, middle class and working class, native born and immigrant, were seeking means to dissolve marriages that had failed.

Housing Interiors and the Display of Wealth

Yale collection of Western Americana, Beinecke Rare Book and Manuscript Library

Envisioning History

Culver Pictures

These photographs show the interiors of two kinds of dwellings at the end of the nineteenth century. The lower photo shows a Victorian parlor, home to wealthy European Americans. The Victorians used their parlors to display possessions that testified to their values and way of life. Books, family photographs, and musical instruments had great symbolic value. Families gathered to read aloud, pore over photo albums, and sing old favorites.

Yet the Victorians were not the only group of people to arrange elaborate displays of art and other cultural artifacts in central living spaces. The upper photo shows the inside of a Tlingit Indian chief's home in Chilkat, Alaska. Indians of the Northwest enjoyed an abundance of marine foods. They had time to devote to making intricate wood carvings in the form of masks and totem poles.

QUESTIONS

1. What kinds of objects are on display in these two photographs? How do these objects testify to the well-being of their owners?

2. Some Victorian men were worried that their opportunities for "manly" activity were vanishing with the western frontier. Why did these men consider parlors "female" spaces?

3. To the modern eye, these spaces look cluttered. How and why might the owners of these two homes see things differently?

Charlotte Perkins Gilman was among the most prolific and well-known critics of the conventional division of labor in the home. Through fiction, nonfiction, and poetry, she claimed that humankind had progressed beyond the point where brute strength was the determinant of social status. Gilman proclaimed that women, no longer content to remain dependent on men, must take their rightful place within the economy, working as equals with their brothers and husbands.

In *Women and Economics: A Study of the Economic Relations Between Men and Woman as a Factor in Social Evolution* (1898), she proposed that housework be divided into its specialized tasks to be performed by professionals. This system would free women from the unpaid, mind-numbing task of combined "cook-nurse-laundress-chambermaid-housekeeper-waitress-governor." In her critique of gender conventions, Gilman anticipated the feminist movement of the 1960s.

Men also pondered the effects of industrializing society on their own roles. Some elite men revolted against the trappings of Victorian culture. These men worked every day in business offices, not out of doors. Some yearned for "manly" activities such as courageous exploits against nature or other men. They believed that overstuffed parlors represented "feminine" interiors, and that life indoors—singing religious hymns around the piano or reading aloud to family members—stifled men's "natural" instincts for bravery and adventure. They yearned to embrace the outdoors and prove their masculinity in the process. As assistant secretary of the U.S. Navy in the late 1890s, Theodore Roosevelt worried that, in this age of machines, young men lacked the opportunities for "the strenuous life" their grandfathers had enjoyed. He argued that unapologetic masculine bravado provided the key to American strength and rejuvenation on both a national and personal level. In his multivolume history *The Winning of the West* (1889–1896), Roosevelt extolled America's relentless march to the Pacific: "The rude, fierce settler who drives the savage from the land lays all civilized mankind under a debt to him." Imperialism at home and abroad, he declared, was a "race-important work," one that should claim the energies of men as politicians and soldiers. These views helped to propel the United States into the realms of inperialism and international conflict.

American Imperialism

◼ *How did different groups define, and in some cases further, American interests abroad?*

In the 1890s, the United States began to extend its political reach and its economic dominance to other parts of the world. Americans looked beyond their borders and saw exotic peoples who represented a variety of opportunities—as consumers of American goods, producers of goods Americans wanted to buy, and objects of American benevolence. This view represented an extension of the reform impulse at home. Indeed, broader thinking about the United States' place in the world reflected a new desire among those who benefited from prosperity to spread American standards—in behavior, productivity, and quality of life—to other peoples.

The country's mighty industrial manufacturing sector demanded new markets and a wider consumer base. The economic depression of 1893, in particular, raised fears that manufacturers would have to contend with surpluses of goods that Americans could not afford to buy. American businesspeople and State Department officials established a partnership that combined private economic self-interest with national military considerations. Some molders of public opinion used the new languages of race and masculine virility to justify an "Anglo-Saxon" mission of conquest of "childlike" peoples. Meanwhile, European countries were carving up Africa and making economic inroads into China. Many Americans believed their own country should join the "race" for riches and "march" to glory as part of the international competition to exploit the natural resources and trade potential of weaker countries.

CULTURAL ENCOUNTERS WITH THE EXOTIC

In early October 1897, 30,000 spectators paid their 25-cent fee to enter New York's Excursion Wharf and observe the strange cargo of the recently arrived steamship *Hope*. Arctic explorer Robert Peary had returned from Greenland, bringing with him six Greenland Eskimos and a

37.5-ton meteorite dislodged from the Cape York region. Among the native Greenlanders were Qisuk and his seven-year old son, Minik. The American public hailed the intrepid explorer Peary as a hero. The American Museum of Natural History put the Eskimos on display, and New Yorkers regarded their odd clothing, language, and eating habits with intense curiosity. But their curiosity was only superficial and did not extend to protection for the young Minik.

Over the next year, four of the Eskimos (including Qisuk) died, and one other returned to his native land. The orphaned Minik survived and remained in the United States. Within a few years, he was abandoned by Peary and museum officials who had initially touted him as a significant scientific discovery. Minik returned to Greenland when he was a young man, but he was restless and unhappy there. He returned to the United States in 1916, eventually finding some peace with a New Hampshire farm family. He died in 1918, a victim of a worldwide flu epidemic.

Minik's short, tragic life reveals certain aspects of Americans' encounter with "exotic" peoples in the late nineteenth century. The Museum of Natural History subjected him and the other members of his group to close study. When Qisuk died, the museum conducted a mock burial for the benefit of his son but then created a public exhibit of Qisuk's bones. (Nearly 100 years later, the passage of the Native American Grave and Burial Protection Act provided an incentive for museum authorities to send the remains of the four Eskimos back to Greenland for burial.)

During the late nineteenth century, Americans were fascinated by artifacts and images dealing with faraway places, especially Africa, the Middle East, and Asia. This impulse, revealed in high art as well as popular culture, stereotyped darker-skinned, non-Christian peoples as primitive, sensual, and inscrutable. Chicago's Columbian Exposition of 1893 featured exhibits depicting harems, spice merchants, and turbaned warriors and performances of "hootchy kootchy dancers," scantily clothed young women grinding to the music of exotic instruments.

Throughout the late nineteenth century, photographers took pictures of Middle Eastern nomads and African villagers. American artists, such as Frederic Edwin Church and John Singer Sargent, traveled abroad to render romantic scenes of deserts, ancient ruins, and mysterious peoples in oils and in watercolors. Painter Eric Pape arranged to have himself tied to a pyramid so that he could partake of an "Egyptian experience"; he produced a painting called *Site of Ancient Memphis* in 1891.

These cultural tendencies could be used to sell products and entertainment. The glassmaker-jeweler Tiffany and Co. evoked Islamic art in its tea services and silver patterns. Tobacco companies marketed mass-produced cigarettes with "Oriental" brand names: Fatima, Omar, and Camel. Thus, a fascination with the exotic encompassed a wide range of impulses in American life and letters, bringing together explorers, scientists, artists, and advertising agents.

Image No. 220545 Courtesy the Library, American Museum of Natural History

■ The Greenland Eskimo Minik is shown here soon after his arrival in New York City in 1897. Minik was devastated by the death of his widowed father, Qisuk; the two were among six Eskimos brought to New York by Arctic explorer Robert E. Peary. Later in his life, Minik spoke of his father to a newspaper reporter, saying, "He was dearer to me than anything else in the world, especially when we were brought to New York, strangers in a strange land."

INITIAL IMPERIALIST VENTURES

The opening of Asia to American trade, combined with the military challenges posed by the major European imperial powers, stimulated the growth of the U.S. Navy in the 1880s. In 1883, Congress appropriated funds to build ninety small ships, one-third made of wood, the rest out of steel. Seven years later, Captain Alfred Thayer Mahan argued for a modern force of large seagoing battleships. In his book *The Influence of Sea-Power in History, 1660–1763* (1890), Mahan contended that if the United States aspired to be a world power, it must control the seas.

Seeking way stations for its ships, the United States negotiated control over both Pearl Harbor in Hawaii and the harbor at Pago Pago in Samoa in 1887. The State Department even achieved a voice in Samoan foreign relations to stave off rivals Great Britain and Germany, which also coveted Pago Pago. In 1889, warships of these three powers gathered in the Samoan harbor. Fortunately, a hurricane thwarted a showdown. The powers, unnerved by their near brush with war, agreed to establish joint control over the islands for the next ten years.

CHINESE FRUIT STORE. HONOLULU.

In October 1890, Secretary of State James G. Blaine hosted the first Pan-American Conference in Washington, D.C., a gathering of representatives from nineteen independent Latin American republics. Topics included the adoption of standardized weights and measures and a possible intercontinental railroad. These developments suggested the blurring of military, diplomatic, strategic, and economic interests—a mix that characterized American foreign policy for decades to come.

In 1895, the United States signaled to Great Britain that it was prepared to go to war to bar Europeans from colonizing or intervening in the Americas, a policy outlined in the Monroe Doctrine more than seventy years before. Britain had persisted in its long-standing claims to the jungle boundary between its colony of British Guiana and the country of Venezuela on the north-central coast of South America. President Cleveland made clear his intention to enforce the Monroe Doctrine. Britain, sensitive to other threats posed by European imperial powers to the far-flung British empire, backed down. Thereafter, Britain began to concentrate on strengthening its diplomatic ties with the United States.

Meanwhile, in the Pacific, the Hawaiian Islands seemed to pose both a threat and an opportunity for American interests. Located 2,000 miles from the California coast, Hawaii had a population of 150,000 in 1890. When English explorer James Cook landed there in 1778, the islands were inhabited exclusively by the descendants of ancient seafaring Polynesians. Protestant missionaries began to arrive in 1820, and the first sugar plantation appeared fifteen years later. In 1875, sugar planters and merchants, many of whom were related to missionaries, negotiated a treaty with the United States that let them ship the crop to the United States duty free. Production of Hawaiian sugar increased from less than 10,000 tons in 1870 to 300,000 tons by 1900.

By this time, Chinese, Koreans, Filipinos, Puerto Ricans, Japanese, and Portuguese had made their way to the Hawaiian Islands. These groups formed the bulk of the plantation labor force, for disease had decimated the native population. In the fields and in their barracks, immigrant contract workers followed a disciplined regimen under the supervision of mounted, whip-wielding overseers called *lunas*. Indeed, these laborers' workday bore a marked resemblance to that of sharecroppers on the largest cotton plantations of the U.S. South.

Not surprisingly, then, both clergy and growers were alarmed by the laborers' resistance to regimentation in the fields and in the quarters. Some men and women workers drank on Saturday night, smoked opium, and gambled. Worse, in the eyes of their employers, many grabbed any opportunity to flee the plantation in search of jobs as wage-earners or shopkeepers in the city of Honolulu. Some even became rice farmers on their own. Planters were forced to suspend operations to accommodate traditional festivals, such as the Chinese New Year, when workers decorated their barracks and cottages with colorful flags and lanterns. Missionaries and sugar planters alike hoped to transform the workers into more stable, compliant employees.

The McKinley Tariff of 1890 raised duties on imports of the islands' sugar. This served to overturn the 1875 pro-planter treaty, causing planters

The Granger Collection, New York

■ Born in 1838, Lydia Kamekeha became Queen Liliuokalani of Hawaii in 1891, after the death of her brother, King David Kalakaua. She reigned just two years before planters, backed by American marines, deposed her. She died in 1917.

(mostly Americans) to panic about their livelihood. They received no support from the islands' native leader, Queen Liliuokalani, who believed foreigners should be barred from running the country. In 1893, the planters, backed by American marines, launched a successful revolt that deposed the queen. They then called for the United States to annex the islands as a territory. Upon investigation, President Cleveland discovered that native Hawaiians opposed annexation and so refused to agree to the move. His refusal incurred the wrath of American imperialists, who claimed that the "Hawaiian pear" had been "ripe for the plucking."

THE WAR OF 1898

Those seeking to expand American influence also looked just south of Florida. In the Caribbean, Cuban nationalists staged an uprising against the Spanish in 1895. The leader of the insurrection was José Julian Martí. He had lived in exile in the United States from 1881 to 1895. In 1892, he established the Cuban Revolutionary Party (*Partido Revolucionario Cubano*) and soon over forty branches had appeared in New York, New Orleans, and Key West and Ybor City in Florida.

Rebelling against the repressive Spanish colonialists who had ruled the island for more than 400 years, native *insurrectos* under the leadership of Martí burned sugar cane and attacked passenger trains. American companies with large investments in the Cuban sugar industry (a total of about $50 million) were outraged at the destruction of their property; they had no sympathy for the *insurrectos*. Yet the arrival of Spanish military officials, who waged war against the rebels and confined prisoners in concentration camps, inflamed public opinion in the United States. Martí was killed in a battle with Spanish forces in 1895. By 1897, both businesspeople and humanitarians urged President McKinley to intervene in Cuba.

Two major American newspaper publishers, William Randolph Hearst and Joseph Pulitzer, seized the chance to boost their respective circulations by highlighting Spanish atrocities against Cubans. Pulitzer owned the St. Louis *Post Dispatch* and the *New York World*, and Hearst challenged him with the *San Francisco Examiner* and the *New York Journal*. The Hearst and Pulitzer newspapers engaged in **yellow journalism,** sensational news reporting that blurred the line between fact and fiction, spontaneous reality and staged theater.

Granger Collection, New York

■ The battleship *Maine* exploded and sank in Havana harbor on February 15, 1898.

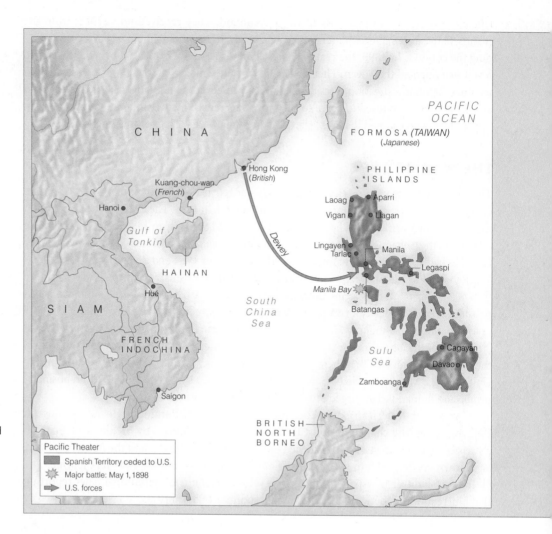

■ **MAP 18.6 The Spanish-American-Cuban-Filipino War of 1898**

In Cuba, the United States combined a blockade of the island with an army invasion to defeat Spanish forces. In the Philippines, the U.S. triumph over the Spanish opened a wider war between American occupying forces and native Filipinos.

On February 9, 1898, Hearst published a letter written by the Spanish minister in Washington, D.C., Dupuy de Lôme, in which de Lôme denounced President McKinley as a spineless politician. Six days later, the American battleship *Maine*, which had been sent to Havana harbor to evacuate Americans should the need arise, exploded and sank. Two hundred sixty officers and men were killed. Subsequent investigations concluded that the heat from one of the coal bins had ignited an adjacent powder magazine. But the Hearst papers implied that the Spanish were responsible for the blast. During the crisis in Cuba, the *Journal* was selling a million copies a day.

But the story of the *Maine* had broader implications. McKinley responded to American businesspeople who feared for their interests in Cuba and to other Americans who decried Spain's brutality toward the *insurrectos*. On April 11, 1898, McKinley called on Congress to declare a U.S. war against Spain. His own assistant secretary of the navy, Theodore Roosevelt, had reportedly called the president a "white-livered" poor excuse for a man. To Roosevelt and other supporters of war, much was at stake: the large American sugar investment, trade with the island, and American power and influence in the Western Hemisphere. Congress responded to McKinley's message by adopting the Teller Amendment, which declared that the United States would guarantee Cuba its independence once the Spanish were driven from the island. America went to war on April 29.

McKinley hoped to hobble the Spanish navy by making a preemptive attack on the fleet in the Spanish colony of the Philippines. Commodore George Dewey, stationed with the American Asiatic Squadron in Hong Kong, was dispatched with his ships to Manila Bay, where on May 1, 1898, his force of four battleships sank all ten rickety Spanish vessels, killing 400, with only a few

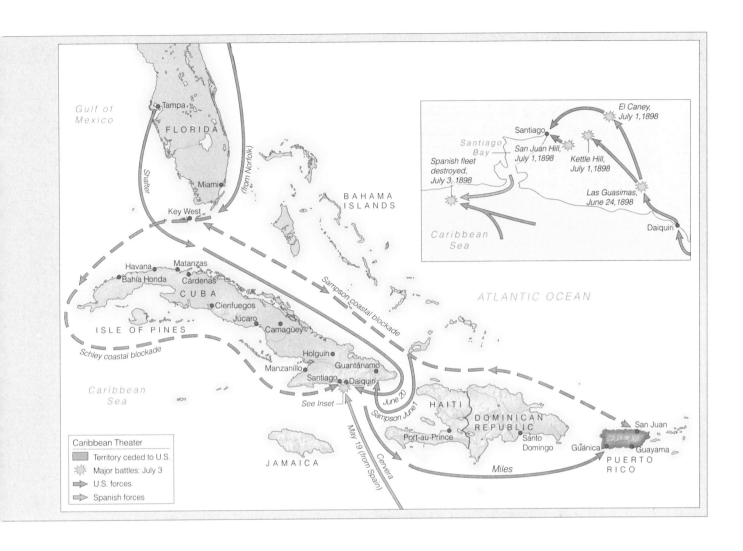

minor American casualties. Dewey waited in the harbor until American reinforcements arrived in August. Then, with the help of Filipino nationalists led by Emilio Aguinaldo, U.S. forces overran Manila on August 13. In 1895, the twenty-six-year old Agunialdo had joined a resistance movement battling Spanish forces in the Philippines. By 1896, he had risen to the rank of general. However, he went into exile in Hong Kong the following year, only to return in May of 1898 to assist U.S. troops in defeating the Spanish occupiers.

Meanwhile, congressional Republicans had found the necessary votes to annex Hawaii. They claimed that the United States needed the Pacific islands to secure a refueling way station for Dewey's troops. McKinley signed the congressional resolution on July 7, 1898. Hawaiian residents were granted citizenship rights, and the islands became an official U.S. territory in 1900.

Earlier in the summer of 1898, halfway around the globe, 17,000 American troops had traveled to Tampa, Florida, in preparation for their incursion into Cuba. Among them were the Rough Riders, a crew of volunteers organized by Lieutenant Colonel Theodore Roosevelt, who had resigned his post as assistant secretary of the navy to serve as an officer. The troops, woefully unprepared for combat in the tropical heat, landed near Santiago, Cuba, in late June.

On July 1, the Rough Riders engaged an unprepared Spanish force of about 2,000 at El Caney and San Juan Hill. The Rough Riders charged up nearby Kettle Hill (they were on foot, not on horses) and into American legend. Later in speeches, Roosevelt boasted of shooting a Spanish soldier at point-blank range. But Roosevelt neglected to mention that he and his men had received crucial support from two African American regiments that day. Blacks had formed a skirmish line at the bottom of the hill, and, according to an eyewitness, "with an

Roosevelt's Rough Riders

Proceedings of the Congressional Committee on the Philippines

Interpreting History

In January 1900, Congress established the Committee on the Philippines. Senator Henry Cabot Lodge of Massachusetts was appointed chair. The committee's task was to review the American conduct of the war. The testimony of two U.S. officers, which follows, foreshadows the difficulties faced by the United States in fighting a guerrilla war in Vietnam six decades later.

Brigadier General Robert P. Hughes testified in response to questions posed by committee members:

Q: In burning towns, what would you do? Would the entire town be destroyed by fire or would only offending portions of the town be burned?

GEN. HUGHES: I do not know that we ever had a case of burning what you would call a town in this country; but probably a *barrio* or a *sitio*; probably a half dozen houses, native shacks, where the *insurrectos* [rebels] would go in and be concealed, and if they caught a detachment passing they would kill some of them.

Q: What did I understand you to say would be the consequence of that?

GEN. HUGHES: They usually burned the village.

Q: All of the houses in the village?

GEN. HUGHES: Yes, every one of them.

Q: What would become of the inhabitants?

GEN. HUGHES: That was their lookout. . . . The destruction was as a punishment.

■ This photograph of a United States soldier during the War of 1898 is titled *The Church Saint Sat On by a Washington "Johnnie" [soldier]*. During the war, photographers produced vivid images that conveyed the dramatic effects of the U.S. invasion on the society and culture of the Philippines. Led by Emilio Aguinaldo, insurrectionists fought for Philippine independence, beginning in January 1899. Two years later, American forces captured Aguinaldo and established a colonial government in the country.

unearthly yell, charged up it" in company with the white soldiers. Federal military authorities had assigned African American men prominent combat roles in Cuba and the Philippines, believing that blacks were better able than whites to withstand the withering heat of the tropics.

By late July, American warships had destroyed the Spanish fleet in Santiago Bay. Again, Spanish losses were high (500 men killed) and American losses slight (1 man killed). According to Secretary of State John Hay, it had been "a splendid little war," just 113 days long. Battles claimed 385 American lives (although many times that number died from disease—malaria, typhoid, dysentery, and yellow fever—and from the rotten meat the soldiers ate). On August 12, 1898, Spain signed an armistice and later in the year ceded its claim to remnants of its empire, including Cuba and Puerto Rico in the Caribbean and the island of Guam in the Pacific. The United States forced Cuba to incorporate into its constitution (written in 1901) the Platt Amendment, which guaranteed continuing U.S. influence over the country, including the stationing of American troops at a naval station on Guantanamo Bay.

Meeting with Spanish negotiators in Paris, the United States agreed to pay $20 million for the Philippines. McKinley's motives in acquiring the islands stemmed from both commercial interests (the Philippines as a gateway to China) and religious concerns (the opportunity for Protestants to convert Spanish-speaking Roman Catholics). But Filipino rebels were not about to bow to a new colonial power. Over the next two years, the United States committed 100,000 troops to subdue the rebels and their leaders. Among the latter group was Aguinaldo, now resisting American forces the way he had resisted the Spanish five years

Q: The punishment in that case would fall, not upon the men, who would go elsewhere, but mainly upon the women and little children.

GEN. HUGHES: The women and children are part of the family, and where you wish to inflict a punishment you can punish the man probably worse in that way than in any other.

Q: But is that within the ordinary rules of civilized warfare? Of course you could exterminate the family, which would be still worse punishment.

GEN. HUGHES: These people are not civilized.

Sergeant Charles S. Riley also testified in response to the committee's questions:

Q: During your service there [in the Philippine Islands] did you witness what is generally known as the water cure?

A: I did.

Q: When and where?

A: On November 27, 1900, in the town of Igbaras, Iloilo Province, Panay Island.

Riley described to the committee a Filipino man, 40–45 years of age, stripped to the waist, with his hands tied behind him.

Q: Do you remember who had charge of him?

A: Captain Glenn stood there beside him and one or two men were tying him.... He was then taken and placed under the tank, and the faucet

was opened and a stream of water was forced down or allowed to run down his throat; his throat was held so he could not prevent swallowing the water, so that he had to allow the water to run into his stomach.... When he was filled with water it was forced out of him by pressing a foot on his stomach or else with their hands....

Q: What had been his crime?

A: Information had been obtained from a native source as to his being an insurgent officer. After the treatment he admitted that he held the rank of captain in the insurgent army—an active captain....

Q: His offense was treachery to the American cause?

A: Yes, sir.

QUESTIONS

1. *In what ways did the Filipino insurrection challenge the conventions of what congressional committee members called "civilized warfare"?*

2. *How did General Hughes justify the destruction of whole villages as part of the U.S. effort to suppress the insurrectionists?*

3. *What are the arguments for and against the practice of torture as a means of extracting information from enemy combatants?*

Source: Proceedings of the Congressional Committee on the Philippines, in Harvey Graff, ed., *American Imperialism and the Philippine Insurrection* (Boston: Little Brown, 1969), 64–79.

earlier. In 1901, he was captured by American troops and declared that he now recognized U.S. sovereignty over the Philippines.

In their fight against Filipino nationalists, U.S. troops used tactics that foreshadowed the U.S. war in Vietnam seventy years later. Hunting down guerrillas hiding in the jungle, American soldiers torched villages and crops. Using a form of torture known as the "water cure," they forced water down the throats of suspected rebel leaders in an effort to extract information. Four thousand Americans and 20,000 Filipinos died in combat. As many as 600,000 Filipino civilians succumbed to disease and starvation. Not until 1901 could the Americans claim victory over their "little brown brothers," as future president William Howard Taft referred to the Filipino people.

Ownership of the Philippine Islands gave the United States a foothold in Asia. In 1894–1895, Japan had waged a successful war against China, and European traders rushed into China to monopolize local markets and establish their own spheres of influence. Secretary of State John Hay issued a communication called the Open Door note in the summer of 1899; in it, he urged the imperial powers to respect the trading interests of all nations. The Europeans were reluctant to cede anything to their international competitors, and only Italy agreed to the terms of Hay's policy. But in 1900, the Boxer uprising in China prompted cooperation among the western powers. The Boxers, radical Chinese nationalists, killed 200 foreign missionaries and other whites in an effort to purge China of outsiders. Together, the Germans, Japanese, British, French, and Americans sent 18,000 troops to quell the revolt. The United States and European nations continued to compete for the China market well into the twentieth century.

MAP

World Colonial Empires, 1900

■ This contemporary Chinese drawing shows two of the country's mythic creatures—a dragon and a large serpent—vanquishing interlopers from western Europe and the United States during the Boxer Rebellion of 1900.

CRITICS OF IMPERIALISM

Theodore Roosevelt seemed to personify the nineteenth-century idea of American manifest destiny: the notion that the core of the nation's history was a militant mission to expand its territorial reach. However, not all Americans agreed with Roosevelt. New York financier Mark Hanna called him a "madman" and "that damned cowboy." Writer Mark Twain believed him "clearly insane" and "insanest upon war and its supreme glories." Twain and other prominent people founded the Anti-Imperialist League in 1898 in an attempt to stem the rising tide of militarism.

It is difficult to generalize about the politics of anti-imperialists during this period. AFL president Samuel Gompers and industrialist Andrew Carnegie both considered themselves members of the anti-imperialist camp, but clearly that stance did not mean they agreed on much, or even on anti-imperialism. Some critics of imperialism advocated a hands-off policy toward other nations in the belief that all peoples were entitled to self-determination.

The scholar-activist W. E. B. Du Bois predicted that the "color line" would constitute a fundamental division between the earth's peoples in the twentieth century. Du Bois warned that the aggressive political and military leaders of industrialized nations would continue to colonize and exploit people of color, whether in Africa, Asia, or Latin America. He argued that this divide, between white and black, rich and poor, industrialized and agricultural societies would be a decisive factor in shaping foreign relations in the century to come.

In contrast, other anti-imperialists used arguments about racial hierarchies to justify their opposition to expansion. Yale sociology professor William Graham Sumner, a proponent of Social Darwinism, argued that "uncivilized and half-civilized peoples" were hostile to democratic self-government and unprepared for its rigors. Thus, Sumner believed that American efforts to "civilize" and colonize foreign peoples would inevitably fail because those peoples were incapable of embracing American values.

Recent newcomers to the United States resented the idea that the "march of the flag" was an enterprise to be led by Anglo-Saxons (that is, people of English descent), as some imperialists claimed. German immigrants invoked their heritage of conquest, and the Irish juxtaposed their native culture with what they called the historic "brutal savagery" of

DOCUMENT

Sumner, "On Empire and the Philippines"

The Age of Imperialism, 1870–1914

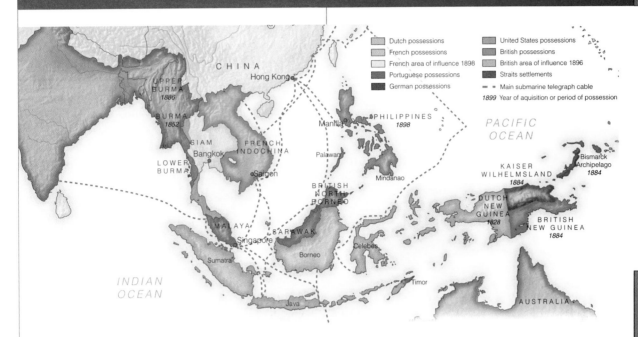

Dutch possessions
French possessions
French area of influence 1898
Portuguese possessions
German possessions

United States possessions
British possessions
British area of influence 1896
Straits settlements
– – – Main submarine telegraph cable
1899 Year of aquisition or period of possession

The Wider World

■ **MAP 18.7 Southeast Asia in the Age of Imperialism, 1870–1914**

Western nations expanded their colonial empires in the late nineteenth and early twentieth centuries. This map shows southeast Asia as a collection of possessions claimed by the United States and western European nations. These colonial powers introduced various western institutions into these areas, such as public schools, government bureaucracies, and factories. These institutions, in addition to innovations in communication and transportation—especially the telegraph, railroad, and steamship—produced dramatic changes in societies that had been governed by monarchies for centuries. Many colonizing nations sought to exploit the natural resources, trade, and labor of the lands they claimed. In the twentieth century, some of these colonial possessions developed radical nationalist movements in response to the legacy of colonialism.

QUESTIONS

1. What are the countries claimed by the United States in this part of the world during this period?

2. How do you explain the colonial ambitions of relatively small European countries such as Holland?

3. What were U.S. strategic interests in this part of the world?

4. How did U.S. interests differ from those of the European nations?

5. Why did the United States eventually seek to wield influence over the area known in this era as French Indochina?

the English. Nevertheless, supporting imperialism was one way for immigrants to proclaim their own Americanness and distance themselves from allegedly inferior peoples.

In the summer of 1900, the Democrats and Republicans prepared for the upcoming presidential election. Receiving the Democratic nomination once again, William Jennings Bryan was eager to press the outdated cause of free silver. He also condemned the American presence in the Philippines, although this issue, too, was rapidly losing the attention of the electorate. At the Republican convention, Roosevelt's supporters managed to win for him the slot as McKinley's running mate. That fall, the former Rough

CHRONOLOGY: 1890–1900

1890	National American Woman Suffrage Association is formed.
	Wounded Knee Massacre.
1891	Populist party formed.
1892	Ellis Island opens as screening site for immigrants.
	Miners strike in Coeur d'Alene, Idaho.
	Steelworkers strike at Carnegie's Homestead plant near Pittsburgh.
1893	Columbian Exposition opens in Chicago.
	Pro-American interests stage a successful coup against Queen Liliuokalani of Hawaii.
	Worst nationwide economic depression to date.
1894	Coxey's Army marches on Washington, D.C.
	Pullman workers strike.
1896	Supreme Court decides *Plessy v. Ferguson*, upholds segregation.
	W. E. B. Du Bois is first black person to receive a Ph.D. from Harvard.
1898	United States annexes Hawaii.
	Maine blows up in Havana Harbor.
	United States defeats Spain in Spanish-American-Cuban-Filipino War.
	Spain cedes Guam and Puerto Rico to United States, turns over Philippines in return for $20 million.
1899	Emilio Aguinaldo leads Filipino revolt against 70,000 U.S. occupying forces.
1900	U.S. troops sent to China to crush Boxer Rebellion.

Rider waged an exuberant campaign, accompanied by a retinue of gun-toting cowboys. When McKinley swept back into office in the fall, few Americans could have anticipated how central Roosevelt's vision would become to the country over the next two decades.

Conclusion

As Americans greeted the twentieth century, they might have marveled at the dramatic changes that had occurred in their country over the last 100 years. In 1800, the United States was home to 5.3 million people who lived in 16 states. One hundred years later, the country included 45 states and boasted a population of 76 million people. Many workplaces, fields as well as factories, were dominated by machines and the people who tended them. The economy was shifting from agriculture toward the mass production of consumer goods.

In the United States, the 1890s were a decade of great contrasts, a time of coalition-building among some political and social groups, but also a time of often violent conflict based on ethnic, religious, and racial ideologies of social difference. Some Americans embraced common ground through the public education system; they suggested that universal schooling was the best way to prepare children, regardless of their cultural or class backgrounds, to live together in a growing, diverse nation. The People's party attempted to overcome historic divisions between Republicans and Democrats, farmers and factory workers, especially in the South; the Populists aimed to forge new alliances that would be responsive to a rapidly changing society. On the other hand, deep and bitter divisions emerged among Americans. Some whites invoked what they called scientific research to classify and categorize various groups and thus "prove" that all whites were superior to all people of color. Other Americans pointed to changing gender relations as proof that women and men would, and should, follow different destinies in terms of their contributions to society. These divisions and debates had a profound effect not only on domestic policy at the end of the nineteenth century but on foreign relations as well.

In 1900, the United States exerted control over the land and peoples of Alaska, the Hawaiian and Samoan islands, the Philippines, Guam, Puerto Rico, and Cuba. These holdings, notable for their strategic significance, illustrated the growing willingness of the United States to extend its influence and economic reach—by armed force if necessary—to the far corners of the earth. The 1890s foreshadowed many of the major themes of the twentieth century. The Populists looked to the federal government to address social ills, paving the way for Progressives in the early twentieth century and New Dealers in the 1930s. Conservationists provided the foundation for the environmentalist movement of the 1970s. And suffragists were the foremothers of the modern women's movement. Yet for Americans, a generations-old contradiction lingered between prosperity and political equality for some groups, and poverty and political subordination for others. On the international stage, the United States was quick to take advantage of other nations if such action was deemed crucial to the "national interest." The new drive for worldwide economic and political power ran contradictory to America's revolutionary heritage, with its values of democracy and self-determination.

For Review   ■

1. Why is it difficult for historians to define the terms "race," "imperialism," and "frontier"?

2. What were the regional and class dimensions in conflicts over U.S. monetary policy?

3. What were the barriers to union organizing in the 1890s? How do these factors account for the lack of a viable socialist workers' party in the United States?

4. How successful were the Populists in welding together a coalition among farmers and factory workers and blacks and whites throughout the country? What are some of the problems faced by third parties in American politics more generally?

5. Describe the significance of these men and women for nineteenth-century American history: Ida B. Wells, William Jennings Bryan, Eugene V. Debs, Charlotte Perkins Gilman.

6. Describe three different kinds of encounters between the United States and foreign countries in the 1890s. What were the commercial implications of Americans' fascination with "the exotic"?

7. In what ways were economic and missionary interests linked in American foreign policy in the late nineteenth century?

Created Equal Online

For more *Created Equal* resources, including suggestions on sites to visit and books to read, go to **MyHistoryLab.com.**

Part Seven

Reform at Home, Revolution Abroad, 1900–1929

Lois Mailou Jones, American, 1906–1998, *The Ascent of Ethiopia*, 1932, Oil on canvas, 23 ½ × 17 ¼ in, Milwaukee Art Museum, Purchase, African American Art Acquisition Fund, matching funds from Suzanne and Richard Pieper, with additional support from Arthur and Dorothy Nelle Sanders [M 1993.191]. Photography by John Glembin.

Many Americans greeted the first years of the twentieth century with optimism. Developments at home and abroad seemed to promise a new era of prosperity and progress. The mass manufacturing of automobiles proved a boon to the economy and transformed patterns of travel, leisure, and consumption. The beginning of commercial air flights heralded a revolution in communication and transportation. Moving pictures and new musical forms such as jazz delighted millions.

Focused on the new challenges of urbanization and industrialization, Progressive reformers sought to use science to solve a wide range of problems related to public health and welfare. Some advocated overhauling the system of public education; others pressed for legislation banning the sale and distribution of alcohol. Some lobbied for worker health and safety legislation, and still others sought to exercise social control through eugenics and state-mandated sterilization.

A variety of groups challenged white men's exclusive claim to civil rights. African Americans took the national stage to argue for equality under the law and for freedom from state-sanctioned violence in the form of lynching and debt peonage. Beginning with the Great Migration of World War I, southern blacks abandoned the cotton fields to seek jobs in northern cities.

The changing roles of women bolstered the women's suffrage movement. Growing numbers of women were becoming labor organizers, reformers, and college professors. Rising divorce rates and the emergence of birth control as a political as well as a medical issue signaled challenges to the traditional patriarchal family. At the same time, conflicts among reformers emerged. For example, white middle-class suffragists hoped to maintain their "respectability" in an effort to win the support of reluctant male leaders; in the process, these women distanced themselves from working-class and African American women active in the suffrage movement. Suffragists' efforts paid off in 1920, with the ratification of the Nineteenth Amendment to the Constitution giving women the right to vote.

With its lively consumer culture and rising standard of living, the United States continued to attract newcomers from abroad. Immigrants from Mexico and eastern Europe sought refuge from poverty, oppression, and civil strife at home. In 1914, 1.2 million immigrants came to America, the largest number in a single year before or since that date. Between 1900 and 1930, more than 1 million Mexicans migrated north, most settling in existing Mexican American communities in the Southwest or creating new communities there or in the Midwest.

World War I shattered the belief among many Progressives that conflicts could be solved in a rational, peaceful way. The end of the war permanently entangled U.S. interests in European affairs. Moreover, revolutions in Mexico (1910) and Russia (1917) affected the United States directly, the former by spurring immigration across the country's southwest border, the latter by challenging the nation's system of industrial capitalism. Nevertheless, many Americans remained convinced that the country could and should isolate itself from world affairs.

Natural forces also remained beyond the control of reformers and government officials. The San Francisco earthquake of 1906, the great Mississippi flood of 1927, and the Florida hurricane of 1928 exacted devastating tolls in terms of human life and property damage. The local communities that were directly affected struggled for years to recover from these disasters.

But for many Americans, the 1920s were a time of peace and prosperity. New household appliances and conveniences lightened the burdens of housework. Radios and movies proved to be popular forms of entertainment. Traditional social mores gave way to expressions of sexual freedom. Progressive impulses waned as business values rose to take their place.

The decade after the end of World War I revealed both the persistence of old conflicts and the emergence of new ones within American society. Conservatives branded labor union organizers and socialists as unpatriotic and subversive. Mexicans and Asians on the West Coast and blacks in the rural South and urban North faced continued violence, brutality, and segregation, as well as legal discrimination in the workplace and in the courts. Protestant fundamentalists challenged the move toward secularism and rationalism, claiming that religious faith, not science, set the standard for morality in modern life. Responding to those who feared that foreign immigration represented a threat to American society, Congress imposed immigration restrictions in 1924. Put into effect in 1920, the Eighteenth Amendment to the Constitution prohibited the sale and distribution of alcoholic beverages. The three Republican presidents who served during the 1920s—Harding, Coolidge, and Hoover—retreated from the activist stance favored by their predecessors, including Theodore Roosevelt and Woodrow Wilson.

The stock market crash of 1929 revealed fundamental weaknesses in the American economy. A tide of bank failures engulfed individual American families even as it threatened businesses abroad. As the depression deepened, Americans lost faith in the private sector and unfettered capitalism and looked to the federal government to address the crisis.

Chapter 19

Visions of the Modern Nation: The Progressive Era, 1900–1912

■ A poster advertising the movie version of Upton Sinclair's *The Jungle*.

Upton Sinclair, a writer and political activist with a vision of a more equitable society, joined the expanding Socialist party in 1902. Four years later, at the age of twenty-eight, Sinclair published *The Jungle*, an exposé of the brutal exploitation of immigrant workers in the meat packing industry. The novel tells the story of Jurgis Rudkus, a Lithuanian immigrant who works in one of Chicago's meat packing plants. The book describes the squalid working conditions Jurgis endured in the plant, where filth, rats, and even workers' body parts ended up in the packages of ground meat. Sinclair hoped to win sympathy for the plight of immigrant workers with his vivid descriptions of the appalling conditions, and to turn the nation toward socialism.

The Jungle had a powerful impact, but the effect was not what Sinclair had hoped. Rather than spark interest in socialism, or even improved wages and working conditions, the novel aroused consumer indignation and led to the passage of the Pure Food and Drug Act (1906) and the Meat Inspection Act, which prohibited adulterated or fraudulently labeled food and drugs from interstate commerce. Sinclair later wrote with regret, "I aimed at the public's heart and by accident hit the stomach."

Sinclair's novel and its ultimate impact illustrate the many strains of reform in the early 1900s. As a socialist, Sinclair had a vision of a nation where unionized workers labored in dignity with good wages and working conditions, in industries kept in check by government ownership. Most of his readers, however, had a different vision: of an affluent nation where consumers could count on the quality of the products they purchased.

Even the leaders of industry had a vision, of a government that would provide a seal of approval to reassure citizens who would purchase their products, so they could reap the rewards of the free enterprise system. The Pure Food and Drug Act and Meat Inspection Act satisfied consumers and industry leaders but left Sinclair's primary concern, working conditions in the plants, largely unchanged.

Upton Sinclair was one of the many reformers whose responses to the rapid changes taking place in the nation were fueled by a faith in progress and a belief in the possibility for social improvement. During the first years of the twentieth century, the nation began to emerge as something profoundly different from what it had been in the past. The dramatic changes taking place, from industry and technology down to the most intimate levels of life, sparked equally dramatic efforts to control, tame, and regulate them. Because of the flurry of reform activity during this period, historians call it the Progressive Era. People from all parties participated in the wide range of reform efforts known as **Progressivism**.

Progressive Era reformers did not always agree, and sometimes their visions were in conflict. Some Americans pushed vigorously for greater equality; others worked just as hard to maintain prevailing hierarchies. Reform-minded politicians like Theodore Roosevelt led the nation into an era of strong national government with a global reach. Millions of immigrants came to the United States with hopes for a better future; many joined efforts to bring the democratic ideals of their adopted country into reality. Activists for gender and racial equality, labor leaders, and local reformers had a vision of the nation that rested on equal rights, decent wages and working conditions, and vibrant cities.

A wide range of reform activities sprang up to foster, tame, control, or resist the changes taking place. Social and cultural radicals pushed for a freer society liberated from sexual constraints, government controls, and industrial tyranny. Some reformers looked to science as a tool for social improvement. Innovative artists fused their creative energy to new technologies and media to generate and reflect the vibrant urban culture in film, music, literature, and the visual arts.

In all their variety and at all levels, reform movements reshaped the relationship between citizens and government. Despite their differences, those who promoted these reform efforts called themselves Progressives. The tensions among all these visions of the nation shaped the politics of the era.

Expanding National Power

In what ways did Theodore Roosevelt promote Progressive reform?

The person who most fully embodied the national Progressive movement was Theodore Roosevelt, president from 1901 to 1908. Roosevelt rose to prominence in the Republican party in the 1880s and held a number of important political posts, including assistant secretary of the navy (1897–1898) and governor of New York (1899–1900). In 1900, Roosevelt became vice president. But in September 1901, President McKinley was assassinated, and at age forty-two Roosevelt became the youngest person ever to occupy the Oval Office. As president, Roosevelt defined a Progressive reform agenda, using his power to regulate big business, intervene in labor disputes, extend the reach of the nation across the world, and control the uses of the natural environment.

TABLE 19.1			
The Election of 1900			
Candidate	**Political Party**	**Popular Vote (%)**	**Electoral Vote**
William McKinley	Republican	51.7	292
William Jennings Bryan	Democratic-Populist	45.5	155

THEODORE ROOSEVELT: THE "ROUGH RIDER" AS PRESIDENT

Roosevelt's particular brand of Progressivism expanded the power of the federal government both at home and abroad. A strong proponent of reform at home and American military and commercial presence abroad, he used the "bully pulpit" of the presidency to exert moral leadership and articulate the nation's international role.

One of Roosevelt's major reforms was to use the power of the federal government to regulate big business. Using the Sherman Anti-Trust Act of 1890, which gave the federal government the power to break up monopolies, Roosevelt in 1902 ordered the Justice Department to prosecute the Northern Securities Company, a $400 million monopoly that controlled all railroad lines and traffic in the Northwest. Within a year, the company was dissolved. Although this bold act earned Roosevelt the title of "trust-buster," it was not his intention to weaken big business. In fact, he believed that a strong country needed large, powerful industries, and he hoped to regulate them to keep big business strong.

The same year that Roosevelt took on the Northern Securities Company, he also used the powers of the federal government to intervene in a labor dispute. Striking coal miners in eastern Pennsylvania wanted recognition of their union, a 10 to 20 percent increase in wages, and an eight-hour day. But the mine owners refused to negotiate. Roosevelt summoned the mine owners and John Mitchell, president of the United Mine Workers union, to the White House for a meeting. He threatened to send in troops if the mine owners did not agree to the union's request for arbitration. The mine owners backed down, and the arbitrators negotiated a compromise that awarded the miners a 10 percent wage increase and a nine-hour day.

Roosevelt's efforts to foster American nationalism extended to his attitudes toward immigrants. He believed that discrimination against loyal newcomers harmed democracy: "It is a base outrage to oppose a man because of his religion or birthplace. . . . A Scandinavian, a German, or an Irishman who has really become an American has the right to stand on exactly the same footing as any native-born citizen in the land, and is just as much entitled to the

■ Born to a wealthy family in New York City, Theodore Roosevelt was a frail, asthmatic child. By the time he reached adulthood, he had transformed himself into a vigorous outdoorsman, embodying the "strenuous life" he promoted. Later presidents—most notably John F. Kennedy and George W. Bush—also transformed themselves from scions of East Coast privilege into icons of rugged masculinity—the sickly Kennedy into a war hero and sportsman, the wayward Bush into a folksy cowboy.

The Library of Congress

friendship and support, social and political, of his neighbor." He was proud of appointing a cabinet in which "Catholic and Protestant and Jew sat side by side." But to Roosevelt, becoming an American meant renouncing any loyalties to one's original homeland or culture.

> We must Americanize them in every way . . . [the immigrant] must not bring in his Old-World religious[,] race[,] and national antipathies, but must merge them into love for our common country, and must take pride in the things which we can all take pride in. He must revere our flag; not only must it come first, but no other flag should ever come second. He must learn to celebrate Washington's birthday rather than that of the Queen or Kaiser, and the Fourth of July instead of St. Patrick's Day. . . . Above all, the immigrant must learn to talk and think and be United States.

Roosevelt did not believe in cultural pluralism, the idea that the United States could include citizens who retained their ethnic heritage. Rather, he promoted the idea of a melting pot that would blend all diverse cultures into a unique American "race."

Although Roosevelt was a firm believer in Anglo-Saxon superiority, he was the first president to invite an African American leader, Booker T. Washington, to dine at the White House. Roosevelt's meeting with Washington demonstrated his willingness to stand up to southern politicians, but he did not follow that gesture with any meaningful policy initiatives such as antilynching or civil rights laws. His hospitality to a black leader sparked such a torrent of criticism that he never again invited Washington or any other African American to the White House.

In the 1904 presidential election, the popular and energetic Roosevelt won 57 percent of the popular vote against his Democratic rival, Alton B. Parker. This victory allowed Roosevelt to promote his vision of the nation for another four years.

TABLE 19.2			
The Election of 1904			
Candidate	**Political Party**	**Popular Vote (%)**	**Electoral Vote**
Theodore Roosevelt	Republican	57.9	336
Alton B. Parker	Democratic	37.6	155
Eugene V. Debs	Socialist	3.0	–

REACHING ACROSS THE GLOBE

Famous for quoting the adage "speak softly and carry a big stick," Roosevelt used an approach to foreign policy known as "Big Stick Diplomacy." He was a vigorous proponent of extending the reach of the nation across the globe. The United States was not alone in this effort. European and American imperial expansion reached a peak in the decades surrounding the turn of the twentieth century, bringing 75 percent of the world's land under the control of Europeans or their descendants.

Roosevelt built up the nation's military and commercial might to extend American power abroad. In one such effort, he proposed the construction of a canal across the Isthmus of Panama, which Congress approved in 1902. But Panama was still a province of Colombia, and Roosevelt was unhappy with the Colombian government's negotiating position regarding an American canal project. So he encouraged and aided Panamanian nationalists who seceded from Colombia in 1903. In return, the U.S. president got his canal deal with a newly independent Panama.

In 1904, Roosevelt further increased the authority of the United States to intervene in the affairs of nations in the Western Hemisphere through what came to be known as the Roosevelt Corollary to the Monroe Doctrine. While the Monroe Doctrine had told Europeans to stay out of the hemisphere, the Roosevelt Corollary declared that the United States would intervene wherever it wanted. Fearing political uprisings that might threaten American commercial interests, Roosevelt asserted that "chronic wrongdoing" might require that "some civilized nation" intervene in the affairs of another. "In the Western Hemisphere," he concluded, "this may force the United States . . . to the exercise of an international police power." The Roosevelt Corollary justified

> *Famous for quoting the adage "speak softly and carry a big stick," Roosevelt used an approach to foreign policy known as "Big Stick Diplomacy."*

later interventions in the Dominican Republic, Cuba, Nicaragua, Mexico, and Haiti—whether or not those countries wanted American interference.

In the Pacific, the bloody U.S. war against Filipino nationalists that began in 1899 lasted four years and killed more than 200,000 Filipinos, most of them civilians. The Americans crushed the revolt and established firm colonial rule in the Philippines. William Howard Taft became the colony's first governor-general in 1901. Taft developed a program of public works that included an infrastructure of roads, bridges, and schools. He also transferred government functions to those Filipinos who cooperated with American colonial powers, which increased tensions with nationalist rebels and led to continued brutality. Although the United States promised to grant Philippine independence, that promise was deferred until 1946.

PROTECTING AND PRESERVING THE NATURAL WORLD

While spreading American power abroad, Roosevelt also extended the reach of the government into the nation's natural environment. More than any previous president, he used the federal government to manage the natural world. Although his actions did not please everyone on all sides of the debate, Roosevelt's environmental efforts were among his most enduring legacies.

Roosevelt advocated both preservation and conservation. His preservation policies doubled the number of national parks, created sixteen national monuments, and established fifty-one

■ Lumberjacks pause while cutting down a giant spruce tree. President Theodore Roosevelt believed that the federal government should manage timberlands and other natural resources to prevent depletion while allowing their use. Roosevelt preserved some Pacific Northwest forests in national parks and refuges but allowed others to be cultivated for timber.

wildlife refuges. At the same time, he shared the view of conservationists that timberlands, areas for livestock grazing, water, and minerals needed federal government management of their use. Roosevelt transferred 125 million acres of public land into the forest reserves to prevent the depletion of timber, and he set aside land for dam sites, oil and coal reserves, and grazing lands. Some of these efforts faced strong opposition from preservationists, because of their negative impact on the natural environment.

Conservationists and preservationists battled frequently, and no issue was more divisive than water. Dams, reservoirs, and aqueducts brought water and electricity to arid regions, allowing such cities as Las Vegas and Los Angeles to flourish in areas that would otherwise be unable to support large populations. Conservationists favored such projects, but environmentalists opposed the flooding of river valleys. One of the most heated of these debates surrounded the damming of the Toulumne River flowing through the secluded and pristine Hetch Hetchy Valley in Yosemite National Park. The resulting reservoir was to supply San Francisco with fresh water, and the dam was to provide the city residents with cheap hydroelectric power.

The idea of damming and flooding Hetch Hetchy Valley met with considerable resistance, especially from the recently formed Sierra Club. Its founder, John Muir, railed against the city officials: "These temple destroyers, devotees of ravaging commercialism, seem to have a perfect contempt for Nature and, instead of lifting their eyes to the God of the mountains, lift them to the Almighty Dollar. . . . Dam Hetch Hetchy! As well dam for water-tanks the people's cathedrals and churches, for no holier temple has ever been consecrated by the heart of man." In spite of such protests, in 1913 Congress passed the Raker Act, authorizing the construction of the dam and reservoir.

The Library of Congress

■ An earthquake devastated San Francisco on April 18, 1906. Here a Chinese immigrant watches as the city goes up in flames. Chinatown was destroyed, along with much of the downtown.

Efforts to control the natural world were meager in the face of nature's own power. On April 18, 1906, an earthquake virtually leveled San Francisco. The nation saw in one deadly instant that human technological genius paled in the face of nature's fury. After the quake, fire devoured the city. In the words of the writer Jack London, "All the cunning adjustments of a twentieth century city had been smashed by the earthquake. The streets were humped into ridges and depressions, and piled with the debris of fallen walls. The steel rails were twisted into perpendicular and horizontal angles. The telephone and telegraph systems were disrupted. And the great water mains had burst. All the shrewd contrivances and safeguards of man had been thrown out of gear by thirty seconds' twitching of the earth-crust." The crumbled buildings of San Francisco offered a lesson in humility. "Never, in all of San Francisco's history, were her people so kind and courteous as on this night of terror," noted Jack London. Railroads carried thousands of refugees out of the city, free of charge. And the national government stepped in immediately, as it would countless times throughout the twentieth century in the face of disaster.

WILLIAM HOWARD TAFT: THE ONE-TERM PROGRESSIVE

The economy proved as unpredictable and difficult to control as the natural world. A financial panic in 1907 prompted Theodore Roosevelt to increase his efforts to overhaul the banking system and the stock market. But critics among Republican conservatives and the business elite blamed Roosevelt's reform policies for the economic downturn. Honoring his earlier pledge to step down—a pledge he came to regret—Roosevelt declined to run for reelection in 1908. The Republicans chose as their candidate William Howard Taft. Prior to his service in the Philippines, Taft had been a federal circuit judge. In 1904, Roosevelt appointed him secretary of war. Taft was a loyal ally who worked closely with Roosevelt on foreign and domestic

TABLE 19.3			
The Election of 1908			
Candidate	Political Party	Popular Vote (%)	Electoral Vote
William H. Taft	Republican	51.6	321
William Jennings Bryan	Democratic-Populist	43.1	162
Eugene V. Debs	Socialist	2.8	–

policies. Roosevelt assumed that Taft, after his victory in the general election, would fulfill Roosevelt's reform agenda.

Taft's respect for the separation of powers spelled out in the U.S. Constitution made him dubious about some of Roosevelt's extensions of the powers of the presidency. Nevertheless, Taft initiated far more antitrust suits than Roosevelt had during his presidency. Despite their similar political inclinations, Roosevelt's support for his protégé cooled. Although Roosevelt counted major business leaders among his own advisers, he was displeased when Taft appointed corporate lawyers rather than activist reformers to his cabinet. His displeasure increased when Taft abandoned the fight for an inheritance tax and a reduction in tariffs.

Taft departed from Roosevelt's foreign policy as well. In contrast to Roosevelt, who emphasized military might, Taft claimed that "Dollar Diplomacy" was the best way for the United States to exert influence in the world:

> This policy has been characterized as substituting dollars for bullets. It is one that appeals alike to idealistic humanitarian sentiments, to the dictates of sound policy and strategy, and to legitimate commercial aims. It is an effort frankly directed to the increase of American trade upon the axiomatic principle that the government of the United States shall extend all proper support to every legitimate and beneficial American enterprise abroad.

Taft's relationship with the Philippines illustrates both his policy of Dollar Diplomacy and his reinforcement of American imperialism abroad. Taft took Roosevelt's military rule of the Philippines a step further by promoting U.S. business interests there. As *El Renacimiento,* a Filipino newspaper, put it at the beginning of Taft's administration:

> For [Taft] the present generation is a generation of children, incapable of assuming the responsibilities of self-government; and this point of view we can never accept. Yet we recognize the power that lies in his hands. . . . President Taft, with the avowed purpose of helping the Filipinos, will encourage the introduction into this country of large capital which will buy up and exploit everything here worth having; and the inevitable result will be the complete domination of American commercial interests. When that day comes, of what benefit will be all this policy of education, this long preparation for self-government, except to make servitude more intolerable?

When Taft signed the higher Payne-Aldrich Tariff in 1909, he disappointed Republican Progressives and aligned himself with the conservative old guard of the party, those who had been most critical of Roosevelt.

Roosevelt returned from big-game hunting in Africa to enter the political spotlight once again. He toured the country in 1910, describing his plan for a "New Nationalism," a far-reaching expansion of the federal government to stabilize the economy and institute social reforms. The election of reformers of both parties to Congress in 1910 encouraged Roosevelt to challenge Taft for leadership of the Republican party. Although Roosevelt had wide public support and easily defeated Taft and the other challenger, Robert La Follette, in the thirteen states that held preferential primaries, the old guard still dominated the national party, and they nominated Taft at the Republican National Convention.

> Taft took Roosevelt's military rule of the Philippines a step further by promoting U.S. business interests there.

The day after Taft's nomination, Roosevelt and his supporters withdrew from the Republican party and formed the Progressive party. They nominated Roosevelt for president and California governor Hiram W. Johnson for vice president. Roosevelt boasted, "I am as strong as a bull moose," inspiring his followers to call themselves the **Bull Moosers.** Their reformist platform called for extensive controls on corporations, minimum wage laws, child labor laws, a graduated income tax, and women's suffrage. The Democrats nominated Woodrow

Wilson, former president of Princeton University and governor of New Jersey. Wilson also ran on a strong reform platform. Eugene V. Debs, the Socialist party candidate, vowed reform as well.

Wilson, Debs, and Roosevelt all agreed that Taft was too friendly to big business and that large corporations had too much power. But they disagreed as to what to do about it. Debs argued that the national government should take over the trusts. Roosevelt argued for a "New Nationalism,"

TABLE 19.4			
The Election of 1912			
Candidate	**Political Party**	**Popular Vote (%)**	**Electoral Vote**
Woodrow Wilson	Democratic	41.9	435
Theodore Roosevelt	Progressive	27.4	88
William H. Taft	Republican	23.2	8
Eugene V. Debs	Socialist	6.0	—

in which a strong federal government would regulate the trusts and, if necessary, curb their power. Wilson, reluctant to vest so much power in the government, called his approach the "New Freedom," believing that the government should dismantle the trusts and then revert to limited powers. The Republican vote split between Taft and Roosevelt, and the victory went to the Democratic candidate, Woodrow Wilson. After resounding Democratic defeats in the three previous presidential elections, the split among the Republicans delivered the White House to the Democrats, along with the first election of a southern president since 1848. Wilson took office amid an overwhelming popular mandate for reform.

The 1912 election had long-term implications for the realignment of the major political parties. Although during the election all three parties supported reform, the election established the Democrats as promoting big government, and the Republicans as the party of small government. While there remained regional differences, especially in the South where the Democrats stood for states' rights, this pattern prevailed throughout the twentieth century.

Immigration: Visions of a Better Life

■ *Where did immigrants settle, and what conditions did they encounter?*

By the time Woodrow Wilson became president in 1913, millions of immigrants had streamed into the United States. They came particularly from southern and eastern Europe, as well as Mexico and Asia. Bringing their hopes and dreams of a better future, many immigrants

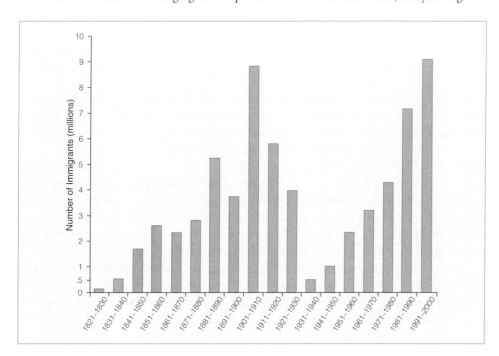

■ **FIGURE 19.1 Number of Immigrants Entering the United States, 1821–2000**

The number of immigrants entering the United States spiked in the first decade of the twentieth century and then dropped drastically as a result of the immigration restriction laws passed by Congress in the 1920s. Immigration increased again as laws changed after World War II, allowing new immigrant groups to enter.

The Immigrants Who Went Back Home

The Wider World

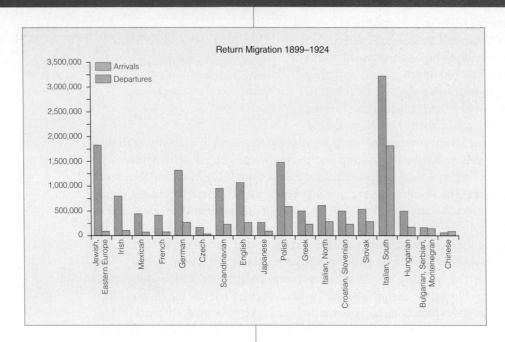

Return Migration 1899–1924

Althought the United States is widely known as a "nation of immigrants," not all of the immigrants stayed. This graph illustrates the wide variation in numbers of immigrants from different places who came to the United States between 1899 and 1924 and the numbers who returned to their home countries. Those most likely to stay, such as the Jews, faced severe persecution in eastern Europe and had little reason to return. In contrast, more than half of the southern Italians—the most numerous immigrant group—eventually returned to their homeland. The highest rate of return migration was among the Chinese, who with very few exceptions were excluded from entering the country during these years. As a result of the intense hostility they faced in America, as well as the scarcity of Chinese women for Chinese men to marry, more Chinese returned home during these years than entered the United States.

QUESTIONS

1. What explains the differences in rates of return for various immigrant groups?

2. In what ways did conditions in the immigrants' home countries affect their decision to stay or leave the United States?

WATCH

Ellis Island
Immigrants, 1903

sought to improve not only their own lives but also the conditions they found in their adopted country. The migration, which began in the latter decades of the nineteenth century, resulted largely from international economic and political upheavals. Facing severe hardships in their home countries, many people took the desperate action of departing for foreign lands. In the first decade of the century, nearly 9 million immigrants entered the United States, by far the largest number for any single decade until the end of the twentieth century. The United States was one of several potential destinations for these courageous and hopeful sojourners. America was particularly appealing because of its often exaggerated, but nonetheless real, opportunities for jobs and economic advancement, its official commitment to the freedom of religion and political thought, and its reputation as a nation that welcomed newcomers from abroad.

On arrival, many found that the "promised land" was not the paradise they expected. They faced crowded living conditions in urban tenements, jobs in sweatshops and factories with long hours, low wages, and miserable working conditions, and a hostile reception. Many Americans—including some whose own parents or grandparents had come to the United States as immigrants—looked down on the newcomers as "racially inferior" and

Pecentage of foreign-born population in 1900

- ▨ More than 30%
- ▨ 10–30%
- ▨ 1–10%
- ☐ Less than 1%, or no foreign-born population

■ MAP 19.1   Foreign-Born Population, 1900

The most famous points of entry for immigrants during the turn-of-the-century decades were New York's Ellis Island for people from Europe, and Angel Island off San Francisco for people from Asia. Most immigrants actually settled in the upper Midwest and the southwestern region bordering Mexico.

morally suspect, feared competition for jobs, and worried that the masses of poor foreigners in their midst would become a burden on taxpayers and public institutions. The Statue of Liberty may have held up the torch of welcome, but many citizens, from union halls to legislative chambers, wanted the newcomers to leave.

Many did leave. One-third of immigrants to the United States returned to their home countries. Others, especially those who faced severe hardships in the lands of their birth, were more likely to make the United States their permanent home, settling with their families and building communities.

Immigrants settled all over the country. Although some of the newcomers moved to rural areas and worked in agriculture, most settled in the cities, where they were joined by rural Americans leaving farms for new opportunities in the rapidly growing urban centers. In the first decade of the twentieth century, more than 4.5 million Americans moved from east to west, and nearly 80,000 migrated from south to north. All those on the move—from abroad and within the country—brought hopes and anxieties to their adopted homes. Over time, these newcomers would transform virtually every aspect of American life: political, economic, cultural, and social.

LAND OF NEWCOMERS

At the dawn of the twentieth century, the places with the highest percentages of foreign-born residents were not the coastal cities, with their visible immigrant ghettos, but the settlements of the upper Midwest and lower Southwest. In the growing towns and cities of the Midwest, newcomers from central Europe and Italy joined the earlier settlers from Germany and Scandinavia to form farming and mining communities on the rich soil and abundant iron deposits of the region.

Defining Whiteness

Naturalization laws pertaining to immigrants in the early twentieth century were based on racial categories. Asian immigrants, classified racially as "Mongolians," were not allowed to apply for U.S. citizenship. Naturalization was available only "to aliens being free white persons and to aliens of African nativity and to persons of African descent." Because racial theories were imprecise and fluid, and racial identities were not linked to nationality, immigrants occasionally challenged their racial classification to claim that they were "white." In 1908, John Svan, who was Finnish, petitioned in federal court to contest the labeling of Finns as Mongolians, claiming that he was white and, therefore, allowed to apply for U.S. citizenship. The petition demonstrates the acceptance of racial definitions based on phenotype—particularly skin color—as well as the imprecise nature of those

Minnesota Historical Society, Negative #93125. Photo by Maki of Virginia, Minnesota

■ These Finnish men living in Minnesota were among those whose racial classification was changed from "Mongolian" to "white" as the result of one Finnish immigrant's petition. Along with the Jews, Italians, Irish, and other immigrant groups now considered "white," Finns were classified as nonwhite until the laws and customs changed. Racial categories were fluid and imprecise, but whiteness conferred status and privileges.

definitions. In the case of John Svan v. the United States Government, the U.S. District Court in Duluth granted Svan's petition, legally changing his racial identity from Mongolian to white and reclassifying Finns as white people. Here is the court's memorandum, which allowed Svan to become a citizen:

John Svan was born in Finland and calls himself a Finn. . . . According to ethnologists, the Finns in very remote times were of Mongol origin; but the various groupings of the human race into families is arbitrary and, as respects any particular people, is not permanent but is subject to change and modification through the influences of climate, employment, intermarriage and other causes. There are indications that central and western Europe was at one time overrun by the Finns; some of their stock remained, but their racial characteristics were entirely lost in their remote descendants, who

In the 1890s, the upper Midwest was sparsely settled. As a result of the Dawes Act of 1887, which allocated tribal lands into individual parcels, much of the land originally held by Indians had been divided and sold. Most of the Indians who were native to that region were removed to reservations. The iron-rich areas near Lake Superior, previously the hunting, fishing, and gathering areas of local Native Americans, were now inhabited by lumberjacks who cut the forests. Mining companies discovered the iron deposits and began recruiting workers, first from northern Europe and then, after 1900, from southern and eastern Europe. By 1910, the iron range was home to thirty-five European immigrant groups. Gradually, these cohesive working-class communities, like others elsewhere, developed their own brand of ethnic Americanism, complete with elaborate Fourth of July celebrations and other festivities that expressed both their distinctive ethnic identities and their allegiance to their adopted country.

THE SOUTHWEST: MEXICAN BORDERLANDS

In spite of common expressions of patriotism, responses to the newcomers were not always friendly—especially for those with darker skins. Along the nation's border with Mexico, racial as well as class tensions permeated small towns. One dramatic incident highlights the depths of these hostilities. In 1904, a train carrying Irish orphans from a Roman Catholic foundling home in New York City chugged westward to deliver its small passengers to waiting Catholic families in Clifton and Morenci in the Arizona territory. Church officials at the New York orphanage had screened the families carefully and gained approval from the local parish priest to be certain that the couples hoping to adopt these children were devout now are in no danger of being classed as Mongols. The Osmanlis, said to be of Mongol extraction, are now among the purest and best types of the Caucasian race. Changes are constantly going on and those occurring in the lapse of a few hundred years with any people may be very great.

The chief physical characteristics of the Mongolians are as follows: They are short of stature, with little hair on their body or face; they have yellow-brown skins, black eyes, black hair, short, flat noses, and oblique eyes. In actual experience we sometimes, though rarely, see natives of Finland whose eyes are slightly oblique. We sometimes see them with sparse beards and sometimes with flat noses; but Finns with a yellow or brown or yellow-brown skin or with black eyes or black hair would be an unusual sight. They are almost universally of light skin, blue or gray eyes, and light hair. No people of foreign births applying in this section of the country for the full rights of citizenship are lighter-skinned than those born in Finland. In stature they are quite up to the average. Confessedly, Finland has often been overrun with Teutons and by other branches of the human family, who, with their descendants, have remained within her borders and are now called Finns. They are in the main indistinguishable in their physical characteristics from those of purer Finnish blood. Intermarriages have been frequent over a very long period of time. If the Finns were originally Mongols, modifying influences have continued until they are

now among the whitest people in Europe. It would, therefore, require a most exhaustive tracing of family history to determine whether any particular individual born in Finland had or had not a remote Mongol ancestry. This, of course, cannot be done and was not intended. The question is not whether a person had or had not such ancestry, but whether he is now a "white person" within the meaning of that term as usually understood. This is the practical construction which has uniformly been placed upon the law. . . . Under such law Finns have always been admitted to citizenship, and there is no occasion now to change the construction.

The applicant is without doubt a white person within the true intent and meaning of such law.

The objections, therefore, in my opinion should be overruled and it will be so ordered.

QUESTIONS

1. *According to the court, what might cause changes in the "groupings of the human race into families" over time? How does the court's opinion reflect prevailing attitudes toward race during the Progressive Era?*

2. *How did the court explain the transformation of Finns from the classification as "Mongols" to becoming "among the whitest people in Europe"?*

churchgoing Catholics, industrious workers, and respectable members of the community. On the appointed day, the hopeful parents waited eagerly as the orphans, dressed in their best clothes with their pink cheeks scrubbed clean, got off the train. But when the Anglo-Protestant residents of the town discovered that Mexican Catholic foster parents claimed these fair-skinned children, they were outraged.

That night, the Anglo women gathered to mobilize their husbands into a vigilante posse. In the middle of the night, during a driving rainstorm, the men went to the homes of the Mexican couples and kidnapped the children at gunpoint. The next day, the children were distributed among the vigilantes' families and other Anglo foster parents. Although the Catholic foundling home that had placed the children with the Mexican couples fought a lengthy legal battle to regain custody of the children, the Euro-Americans managed to keep the orphans. The Arizona Supreme Court validated the kidnapping in the name of the "best interests of the children," and the U.S. Supreme Court let the ruling stand.

The struggle over the orphans reflected tensions and divisions in the region along lines of class as well as race. The year before the arrival of the orphans, Mexican mine workers had struck for better wages and working conditions against the Anglo owners of the Arizona Copper Company. The owners put down the strike, and the conflict left bitter feelings on both sides. The vigilante kidnapping of the orphans was, in part, retaliation against the Mexican workers who had organized the strike the previous year.

Mexicans were a large presence in the Southwest; in 1900 there were 500,000 Mexicans living in the region. Most of the migrants to the Southwest found work in mining, railroads, and agriculture, usually as unskilled workers earning meager wages. Men, women, and

■ Mexican miners in Arizona struck against their Anglo employers in 1903. The mining company paid Mexican workers less than their Anglo counterparts. In addition to the human toll of death and disease caused by the dangerous conditions in the mines, copper mining also caused permanent damage to the environment.

Courtesy, Arizona Historical Society/Tucson (#58785)

children migrated in families or alone. Some estimates suggest that half were under the age of eighteen. Mexican migrant women as well as Hispanics born in the Southwest had to be particularly resourceful. According to one New Mexico native, "They were their own doctors, dressmakers, tailors and advisers."

Excluded from most labor unions until the 1920s, Mexican workers across the Southwest nevertheless organized strikes from time to time to improve wages and working conditions. During the first decade of the century, and especially after the Mexican Revolution, which increased migration across the border, nativist hostility to Mexicans in the Southwest intensified.

ASIAN IMMIGRATION AND THE IMPACT OF EXCLUSION

Along with Mexicans, Asians who settled in the West faced harsh conditions and discrimination. The Chinese Exclusion Act of 1882, which prohibited most Chinese from immigrating to the United States, was renewed and extended in 1902. As a result, the mostly bachelor Chinese community in the United States declined by nearly half between 1890 and 1920. Many died or returned to China, reducing the numbers from more than 107,000 to about 61,000. The sex ratio remained severely unbalanced, with about fourteen men for every woman.

During the exclusion era, certain categories of Chinese immigrants were allowed entry. Wives of Chinese men already in the United States could enter, as could teachers, students, and merchants. More than 20,000 Chinese arrived during the first decade of the new century. One such emigrant was Sieh King King, an eighteen-year-old student. In 1902, at a meeting of the Protect the Emperor Society, a reform party that advocated restoring the deposed emperor and establishing a constitutional monarchy in China, she addressed a packed hall in San Francisco's Chinatown. The *San Francisco Chronicle* reported that she "boldly condemned the slave girl system, raged at the horrors of foot-binding [a traditional Chinese practice in which girls' feet were tightly bound to keep them small] and, with all the vehemence of aroused youth, declared that men and women were equal and should enjoy

PACIFIC OCEAN

JAPAN

CHINA

INDIA

Arabian Sea

Bay of Bengal

South China Sea

PHILIPPINES

INDONESIA

Asian immigration exclusion

- Immigration restricted by Chinese Exclusion Acts (1882–1943)
- Asiatic barred zone (1917–1952)
- Japanese and Koreans restricted by "Gentleman's Agreement" (1907) and barred in 1924

■ **MAP 19.2** **Areas Excluded from Immigration to the United States, 1882–1952**

In 1882, the United States barred Chinese immigrants from entering the country; Japanese and Koreans were barred in 1924. In 1917, the exclusion was extended to people from India, Indonesia, and the Arabian Peninsula. Those laws remained in effect until 1943 and 1952, respectively.

the privileges of equals." Sieh King King expressed ideas that were emerging among urban radicals in the United States but also reflected political movements in their home countries.

Individual Chinese could also immigrate if they had family members in the United States. But sometimes it was extremely difficult to prove that the relationship existed. Immigration officials were particularly suspicious of women entering the country as wives. They had to prove that they were truly married and not prostitutes or concubines. If they were married in China, that proof was often difficult to establish. For example, Lau Dai Moy applied for admission as the wife of a U.S. citizen. She and her husband, Fong Dai Sing, were separately brought before authorities for questioning. They were interrogated for hours about the details of their wedding, and their answers were expected to match exactly, even though the wedding had taken place more than a year earlier. The young wife was asked about gifts or ornaments given to her by her husband, how long she wore a beaded headdress at her wedding, and the names of guests for whom she poured tea. If her description of details of the ceremony did not exactly match her husband's account, she would not be able to enter the country, regardless of the documentation she carried. Often the process could take several weeks or even months. Hopeful immigrants were detained as virtual prisoners in wretched conditions on Angel Island, the immigrant gateway in San Francisco Bay.

Many immigrants slipped into the country illegally, over the borders from Canada or Mexico. But entry for the Chinese at Angel Island was particularly difficult during the period of exclusion. To make it possible for others to emigrate, American-born Chinese frequently traveled back and forth, claiming on their return that they left a child in China and requesting permission for their offspring to emigrate. In this way they created space holders for imaginary kin, allowing other Chinese to enter the country. U.S. authorities knew of this system of "paper sons" and "paper fathers" and tried to stop the practice with elaborate and lengthy investigations that could last a year or more. But the hopeful new arrivals were not easily thwarted. Chinese Americans on the mainland smuggled information to their fictional relatives, cleverly providing details of their families and communities back home so that their stories would match. Since it was illegal to transmit such information and letters were read and confiscated, these messages often arrived concealed in walnut shells or other camouflages.

Lee Chi Yet was one such "paper son." As a poor farmer in China, he was not among those who could enter the country legally, so he purchased papers and posed as the son of another immigrant. After a humiliating physical examination, he faced intensive questioning. Fortunately, he had memorized all the details that went with his new name, identity, and family history, and he was allowed to enter. Eight years later he returned to China and married Wong Lan Fong. When his wife followed him to the United States the next year, she had a photo of their wedding as proof of her eligibility to enter. Like thousands of others, Lee Chi Yet and Wong Lan Fong overcame enormous odds to enter the country during the era of exclusion.

Although most Chinese were prohibited, Japanese immigrants could still enter the country, and nearly 300,000 did so between 1890 and 1920, when opportunities for relatively well-paying jobs in Hawaii and California offered an alternative to the economic crisis they faced in Japan. As one Japanese immigrant wrote in traditional *haiku* form,

> Huge dreams of fortune
> Go with me to foreign lands
> Across the ocean.

■ Wong Lan Fong and Lee Chi Yet on their wedding day in China. When she came to the United States to join her husband, Wong Lan Fong submitted this photograph as proof that she was married to Lee Chi Yet. The Immigration and Naturalization Service confiscated the photo to use as evidence in her case for admission to the country. The photo was later discovered by the couple's granddaughter, Erika Lee, while working on her Ph.D. in history and doing research on Chinese immigration during the exclusion era.

Courtesy of Dr. Erika Lee

As in China, marriages in Japan generally were arranged by families, and some men returned to Japan to meet and marry their brides. But cost and distance often prevented those meetings. Some women came to the United States as "picture brides" after an exchange of photographs. Although some women were disappointed with their often much older husbands, most accepted their fate as they would have accepted an arranged marriage in Japan. Others were delighted with the opportunity for adventure and life in the new land. As one picture bride explained, many of the people from her village had already gone to the United States, and she wanted to go, too: "I didn't care what the man looked like."

Although the Japanese formed less than 1 percent of California's population, they faced intense nativist hostility. The Japanese in California protested against the discrimination they faced, and in one case they successfully turned a local case of school segregation into an international incident. The Japanese government expressed its extreme displeasure at the segregation in San Francisco's schools. Hoping to avoid a confrontation with Japan—a significant military power that had just won a war with Russia—President Theodore Roosevelt interceded and convinced the San Francisco school board to rescind its segregation order. This incident led to the "Gentlemen's Agreement" of 1907, in which the Japanese government agreed to limit the number of immigrants to the United States. The numbers of new arrivals from Japan dwindled, and Japanese migrants instead began to settle in Brazil.

NEWCOMERS FROM SOUTHERN AND EASTERN EUROPE

Jews were among the most numerous immigrants in the early twentieth century. In 1880, there were about 250,000 Jews in America; by 1920, there were 4 million, the vast majority from eastern Europe. During those forty years, a number of factors motivated Jews to leave their small towns, or *shtetls*. Economic turmoil and restrictions on Jewish land ownership, trade, and business left many Jews impoverished. Anti-Semitic policies in Russia and eastern Europe confined many Jews to live in restricted areas. Even more devastating was the increase

International Museum of Photography at George Eastman House, Rochester, New York

■ At Ellis Island, this immigrant family received identification tags indicating that they had been examined and declared healthy. Those who were ill, or youngsters without relatives to meet them, were sent to quarantine houses. Some were refused entry and sent back to their home countries.

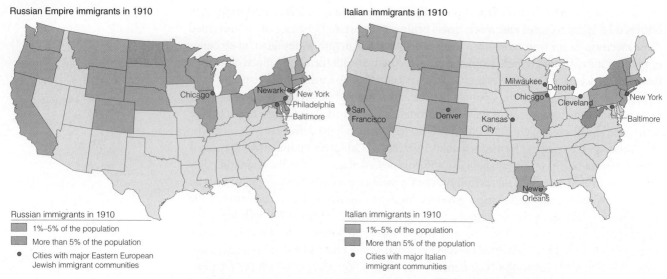

Russian Empire immigrants in 1910

Italian immigrants in 1910

Russian immigrants in 1910
- 1%–5% of the population
- More than 5% of the population
- ● Cities with major Eastern European Jewish immigrant communities

Italian immigrants in 1910
- 1%–5% of the population
- More than 5% of the population
- ● Cities with major Italian immigrant communities

■ **MAP 19.3 Russian and Italian Immigrants in the United States, 1910**

Immigrants from Russia and Italy settled across the Northeast, Midwest, and West, with concentrations in large cities. Louisiana was the only southern state with a large concentration of immigrants from eastern or southern Europe.

in anti-Semitic violence in the form of riots, or *pogroms*, in which Jewish towns were attacked and many Jews were beaten and killed. Although Jews faced intense persecution, they were nevertheless subject to the draft. Many young Russian Jews emigrated to avoid being conscripted into the czar's army.

Morris Bass was a typical young immigrant. At the age of twelve, he left his family and ventured alone across the Atlantic. The uncle who was to meet him forgot about his arrival, leaving Morris stranded in the quarantine building on Ellis Island. Although he was among the lucky ones who passed the medical exam and was declared healthy enough to enter the country, he could not be released until a relative came to claim him and guarantee that the boy would be provided with support. After two weeks, just as immigration officials were preparing to send him back to Russia, his uncle appeared. He brought Morris home and showed him where to sleep. But as soon as the boy heard his uncle snoring, Morris ran away, furious at this relative who had left him to suffer two miserable weeks in detention. He did not wander long in the crowded Jewish neighborhood of New York's Lower East Side before a butcher offered him a job, along with a place to sleep on a straw mat behind the shop.

Like many others, Morris prospered modestly. After a few years, he was able to strike out on his own as a pushcart peddler. Eventually, he sent home enough money to bring his parents and siblings to America. Some Jewish immigrants struggled to retain the faith and practices of Jewish orthodoxy that had defined their lives in the *shtetl*. But Morris was among those who wanted to assimilate into American life. He retained Jewish cultural practices but abandoned many religious rituals, such as refraining from work on Saturdays (the Jewish Sabbath) and wearing distinctive clothes. Nevertheless, he lived his life as a Jew among Jews, speaking Yiddish, celebrating the religious holidays, and maintaining a kosher home according to Jewish dietary laws, even though he rarely set foot in a synagogue.

Italian immigration also reached its peak between 1900 and 1914. While 90 percent of the Jews who migrated from Russia came to the United States, Italians ventured to many countries around the world. Turmoil in their home country resulting from the political and economic consequences of unification of the Italian peninsula prompted 27 million Italians—a third of Italy's population—to emigrate between 1870 and 1920. The majority of Italians who came to the United States arrived with their families and settled permanently, establishing strong communities and mutual aid societies. Most Italians were committed

MAP

Foreign-Born
Population, 1890

Roman Catholics, and they preserved their rituals, festivals, and faith in the new country. Like most immigrants, they worked hard for the well-being of their families. With their diverse traditions, customs, and skills, newcomers contributed to the tremendous cultural, social, and political vitality that was shaping the nation at the dawn of the new century.

Reformers and Radicals

■ *Who were the reformers and radicals, and what strategies did they use to promote their vision of society?*

The presence of large numbers of immigrants fueled much of the reform activity of the early 1900s. Their often impoverished and visibly squalid living conditions prompted calls for improved urban housing; their low wages and working conditions spurred labor activism. Immigrants themselves joined and often led efforts to improve American life through their active participation in socialist and labor movements as well as other reform and radical activities. Some native-born Americans opposed their increasing influence and their impact on American society.

Whether led by immigrants or native-born Americans, the vast array of reform movements transformed American life and reshaped the relationship between citizens and their government. Particularly in the western states, Progressive reformers adopted measures that would foster direct democracy. Oregon was the first state to adopt three reform procedures designed to allow voters more direct control over the political process. In 1902, Oregon approved the *initiative*, which allowed voters to bypass the state legislature and petition the state directly to submit specific measures to popular vote. The *referendum*, approved in the same year, permitted state legislatures to refer bills directly to the voters for approval or rejection. In 1908, Oregon adopted the *recall*, which gave citizens the right to call a special election to remove elected officials from office before the end of their term. These procedures have enabled voters to initiate measures at the grass roots. A century later, in 2003, California voters used the recall to unseat a governor for the first time. They voted to oust unpopular governor Gray Davis and elected Hollywood film star Arnold Schwarzenegger to replace him.

MUCKRAKING, MORAL REFORM, AND VICE CRUSADES

Upton Sinclair, whose influential novel *The Jungle* led to national legislation to regulate the food industry, was one of a group of investigative journalists who began to expose the ills of industrial life. President Theodore Roosevelt dubbed them "muckrakers" in 1906, to signal their tendency to unearth the dirtiest aspects of the nation's political and economic institutions. Although Roosevelt intended the term as an insult, the muckrakers embraced their label. Their best-known works illuminated corruption in business and politics. Ida Tarbell wrote a powerful exposé of the ruthless business practices of John D. Rockefeller, who transformed the Standard Oil Company into a monopoly. The nineteen-part series ran in

■ An immigrant family manages the daily routines of life in a tenement flat in 1910. Crowded conditions, poor ventilation, and inadequate plumbing made it impossible for impoverished residents such as these to maintain a clean and healthy environment.

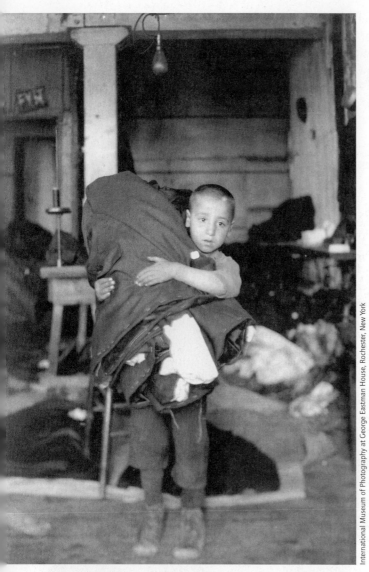

In the early twentieth century, many children, such as this young boy hauling material in the garment industry, worked long hours doing hard labor. Photographer Lewis Hine, who took this picture, worked for the National Child Labor Committee. His photographs documented the exploitation of child workers and helped generate support for child labor laws.

International Museum of Photography at George Eastman House, Rochester, New York

DOCUMENT

Steffens, from *The Shame of the Cities*

DOCUMENT

Mother Jones, "The March of the Mill Children"

McClure's magazine from 1902 to 1904. Her contemporary Lincoln Steffens unearthed scandals in city and state politics. By 1912, more than 1,000 muckraking articles appeared in widely read and popular magazines such as *McClure's*, *Everybody's*, and *Colliers*. Many of them exposed the exploitative practices of American industry.

Child labor was another concern of reformers. Children worked in fields and factories across the country, picking cotton in Texas, mining coal in West Virginia, working in the textile mills of North Carolina, and sewing buttons in urban sweatshops. Children of immigrants and rural migrants often assisted parents on farms or in shops, their labor an accepted part of the household economy. Many parents believed that work also offered children opportunities to learn discipline as well as a trade, and to gain a sense of pride and satisfaction as contributors to the family's needs. But the sorts of jobs available to children in the urban industrial world often were dangerous and unhealthy, characterized by long hours, low pay, and miserable working conditions. Reformers attempted to improve the conditions under which children worked and to establish age limits so that children could attend school and spend time in healthful recreation rather than in grim sweatshops and factories. Ultimately, child labor activists succeeded in passing legislation at the state level that restricted child labor, although these efforts were more successful in northern states than in the South.

Protective legislation for women was also controversial. Reformers campaigned for laws that would establish minimum wages, maximum hours, regulations against night work, and restrictions on heavy lifting. When they were unable to secure such safety measures for all workers, they argued that women needed special protections because of their physical frailty and their role as future mothers. Women's rights activists disagreed over these measures. Some argued that they were necessary to protect women from exploitation and dangerous working conditions. Others claimed that women should be treated the same as men, arguing that protective legislation implied that women needed special care and were not suited for particular kinds of work. These debates continued throughout the century.

Women were prominent among Progressive reformers. Jane Addams, founder of Hull House, the immigrant neighborhood center in Chicago, became one of the most admired women of her day. Many other influential women also left their stamp on the culture and public policies of the era. Florence Kelley, daughter of a prominent Philadelphia Quaker family, joined Addams's Hull House community and later headed the National Consumers' League (NCL) from 1898 until her death in 1932. Under her leadership, the NCL became the most effective lobbying agency for protective labor legislation for women and children. Kelley was instrumental in the successful defense of the ten-hour working day for women— and the principle of protective legislation—which was affirmed by the Supreme Court in its landmark 1908 *Muller v. Oregon* decision.

Another noted reformer was Helen Keller, whose work on behalf of the blind called attention to the needs of the disabled. Keller lost her sight and hearing from an illness at the age of nineteen months and learned to communicate through Braille and sign language, which she mastered through touch, with the help of her extraordinary teacher, Anne Sullivan. Keller went on to study at schools for the deaf and graduated with honors from Radcliffe College in 1904. A passionate socialist and advocate of women's rights along with other radical causes, Keller wrote several books, and she lectured worldwide with the assistance of interpreters.

Many Progressive reformers were prosperous American-born Anglo-Saxon Protestants. Along with their efforts to improve living and working conditions and alleviate the suffering of the poor, they also hoped to eradicate vice from their society. At the level of local government, many reformers promoted zoning laws that would keep commercial entertainments out of residential neighborhoods. Vice crusaders in most of the nation's large cities tried to eliminate prostitution and to patrol dance halls, movie theaters, and saloons. Gay men and lesbians risked arrest for socializing in public places. At the national level, vice crusading culminated in the passage of the Mann Act in 1910, which made it illegal to transport women across state lines for "immoral purposes." The Mann Act resulted in 1,537 convictions by 1916. Over the years, authorities used the Mann Act not only to police prostitution but also to regulate interracial sex.

> *Another noted reformer was Helen Keller, whose work on behalf of the blind called attention to the needs of the disabled.*

One such case garnered national attention. African American boxer Jack Johnson had defeated white fighters in the ring to become the world heavyweight champion in 1910. He was a hero to black Americans but a villain to many whites, who resented not only his athletic success but also his relationships with white women. In 1912, Lucille Cameron, a young white woman from Minnesota, visited Johnson's Chicago nightclub and the two began an affair. Cameron's mother brought charges of abduction against Johnson, but the young woman refused to testify, so the case was dismissed. The couple later married. Authorities continued their efforts to punish Johnson for his racial and sexual transgressions. When federal agents persuaded one of Johnson's former lovers, a white prostitute, to testify that Johnson had paid for her travel from Pittsburgh to Chicago, he was convicted under the Mann Act and sentenced to one year in prison.

WOMEN'S SUFFRAGE

The crusade for women's rights, including the effort to gain the vote, was already more than half a century old by 1900. But the movement gained momentum at the dawn of the twentieth century. A new generation of women's rights leaders came together in the suffrage movement. They included working-class women and young college-educated women, some of them with experience in the settlement houses. They initiated new grassroots strategies such as door-to-door campaigns to gather support for women's suffrage. The militancy of the suffrage movement in England inspired American activists to develop new tactics and international alliances. These activists achieved legislative success when several western states granted women the right to vote: Washington in 1910, California in 1911, and three more states in 1912. Eventually the movement united around the goal of enacting a federal amendment. In the nation's capital, women demonstrating peacefully for the right to vote faced violence from hostile crowds and officials. Many were arrested and jailed, where they met with physical abuse. When they protested with a hunger strike, they were brutally force-fed. Finally, after many years of activism, the required three-quarters majority of the states ratified the Nineteenth Amendment in 1920, granting women the vote.

Women's suffrage was achieved with a sometimes uneasy coalition. Some white suffrage leaders feared that any alliance with women of color would alienate southern voters whose support they needed to ensure ratification of the Nineteenth Amendment. They also hoped to win over to their cause racist and nativist critics in the North who feared that granting the vote to women would enfranchise "undesirable" voters, specifically immigrant and minority women. Some women's rights leaders, such as Belle Kearney, a southern suffragist, saw the ballot for women as a means of keeping African Americans in their place: "The enfranchisement of women would insure immediate and durable white supremacy, honestly attained." The suffrage movement also gained the support of conservatives who believed that women would vote for conservative causes such as prohibition and immigration restriction.

> Many minority women participated fully in the suffrage movement and became powerful allies of leading white suffragists.

Many minority women, such as Hispanic activist Adelina Otero Warren, participated fully in the suffrage movement and became powerful allies of leading white suffragists. As Otero Warren wrote to Alice Paul, who became leader of the National Women's Party, "I will take a stand and a firm one whenever necessary for I am with you now and always." Otero Warren's efforts helped secure New Mexico's ratification of the Nineteenth Amendment. These sorts of alliances built a strong multiracial reform movement, but the leaders did not always agree on priorities. The African American antilynching activist Ida B. Wells (also known by her married name as Ida B. Wells-Barnett) supported women's suffrage but was unable to convince the white women's rights leaders to denounce lynching. Ultimately, passage of the Nineteenth Amendment resulted from a combination of factors, including radical politics, civil rights and labor activism, strong support from a wide range of reformers, and an alliance with some conservative, racist, and anti-immigrant forces.

RADICAL POLITICS AND THE LABOR MOVEMENT

Progressive reformers believed that American capitalist democracy was basically a sound system that simply needed to be fixed to achieve its full promise. Radicals of the era, however, believed that the system was flawed and needed to be fundamentally transformed.

Socialism gained strength in America at the turn of the century, although it was never as strong in the United States as it was in Europe. Socialists promoted labor unions and the rights of women and formed their own political party. Socialist leader Eugene V. Debs, who had gained national fame for his role in the 1894 Pullman strike, became the spokesperson and leader of the Socialist party. Between 1900 and 1920, he was the party's candidate for president, gaining nearly a million votes, or 6 percent of the electorate, in the 1912 election. Although the socialists never gathered a large enough following to win national elections, they elected hundreds of candidates to local office.

Anarchism—the belief that all government is oppressive and should be abolished—also gained followers during these years. Emma Goldman, a Russian Jewish immigrant, was one anarchist who gained both fame and notoriety for her outspoken support of radical causes such as free love and birth control. Goldman was among the growing numbers of women who were leaders in the labor struggles of the day, although women were excluded from most unions. Only 3.3 percent of the 4 million women engaged in nonagricultural jobs in 1900 were members of trade unions. In 1903, the Women's Trade Union League (WTUL) brought together elite reformers and female laborers to help working women in their efforts to unionize. The number of women in unions doubled in the wake of the successful wave of strikes by young immigrant garment workers in 1909–1910.

Clara Lemlich was a Jewish immigrant who arrived in America filled with a passion for the rights of workers, much like her Chinese peer in San Francisco, Sieh King King. Lemlich's passion was also shared by many in her native land of eastern Europe. "I am a working girl," she declared in her native Yiddish, "one of those striking against intolerable conditions." Still in her teens, the petite young woman took the podium on the night of November 22, 1909, in front of thousands of striking workers in New York and roused them with her stirring, direct call for action: "I offer a resolution that a general strike be declared—now." The next morning, 15,000 garment workers went on strike, demanding that the workweek be reduced to 52 hours, with overtime pay and union recognition. Soon, the strikers swelled to number more than 20,000. Observers at the time were astonished to see lively, fashionably dressed young women filling the picket lines. Ninety percent of the striking workers were Jewish and Italian immigrants. The strikers drew a wide coalition of support that included labor unions, middle-class reformers, and activists for women's suffrage.

Ultimately, the strike ended when the striking workers overwhelmingly rejected an offer of better wages and working conditions that did not include recognition of their union. Calling the strikers "socialists," their more moderate allies broke from the union and left the young female workers vulnerable to the power of the company owners. The coalition of support fell apart, and most of the strikers eventually went back to work.

Less than two years later, a fire broke out in the top floors of the Triangle Shirtwaist Company, one of the centers of the 1919 strike. Scraps of material piled everywhere created a fire trap, quickly spreading the flames into a raging inferno. Rose Rosenfeld Freedman, a sixteen-year-old Jewish immigrant, was sewing buttons—at a wage of $3 for a six-day week—when the fire alarm sounded. Finding the exit doors locked, she followed the bosses to the roof, where firefighters hoisted her to safety. But she was among the lucky ones. Eight hundred workers, most of them young Jewish and Italian women, were trapped in the conflagration because company officials had locked interior doors to prevent the women from taking breaks outside.

■ Victims of the Triangle Shirtwaist Company fire.

The flames tore through the building in less than half an hour, leaving 146 young women dead. Those who did not succumb to flames and smoke jumped to their deaths. "One girl after another fell, like shot birds, from above, from the burning floors," remembered one witness. "They hit the pavement just like hail," recalled a firefighter. One reporter wrote, "I looked upon the dead bodies and I remembered these girls were the shirtwaist makers. I remembered their great strike of last year in which the same girls had demanded more sanitary conditions and more safety precautions in the shops. Their dead bodies were the answer."

The factory owners were charged with manslaughter, but their attorney argued that the building was in full compliance with safety laws, so they were acquitted of all wrongdoing. But compliance with the laws did not ensure safety for the workers. No laws at the time required adequate fire escapes or fire drills. Just a few months before the fire, the building had been inspected and declared "fireproof." The owners, in fact, profited from the tragedy.

Rather than investing in safety measures, they had purchased a huge fire insurance policy. Three years after the fire, they settled a small number of individual civil suits by paying $75 for each of 23 lives lost—a pittance compared to the $60,000 they gained from their insurance settlement.

The brutal working conditions that led to the Triangle Shirtwaist fire prevailed all over the country and mobilized workers in a wide range of industries. The Industrial Workers of the World (IWW), also known as the **Wobblies,** offered another possibility for labor radicalism. Organized in 1905 by socialists and labor militants, the IWW included women, blacks,

(Both photos) Courtesy Bud Freedman

■ Rose Rosenfeld Freedman, a worker at the Triangle Shirtwaist Factory, as a young immigrant, and decades later as a labor activist. The fire inspired her to lifelong activism. In 2000, at age 106, she lectured on sweatshops to enthralled students at Occidental College in Los Angeles. She died in 2001 at age 107, the last survivor of the Triangle Shirtwaist Company fire.

Brown Brothers

■ Elizabeth Gurley Flynn of the Industrial Workers of the World (IWW) addresses a crowd of women in 1913. Flynn was one of the organizers of the IWW, known as the Wobblies, an organization of workers from diverse backgrounds that enrolled nearly 3 million members.

immigrants, and unskilled and migratory laborers, workers generally shunned by the American Federation of Labor (AFL). The Wobblies organized about 3 million workers in the mines of the Rocky Mountain states, in the lumber camps of the Pacific Northwest and the South, and in the eastern textile and steel mills.

In 1912, the IWW supported a huge walkout of textile workers in Lawrence, Massachusetts. In response to a new state law shortening the workweek, one textile mill owner lowered the pay of the workers. Within days, ten thousand women and men went on strike. IWW organizers William Haywood and Elizabeth Gurley Flynn joined the local leaders of the strike. Daughter of radical Irish immigrants, and known as "the Rebel Girl," Flynn participated in numerous strikes, including the one in Lawrence. The strike was violent and bloody. One young woman was killed, and when Flynn organized an exodus of strikers' children for their safety, media coverage of the police beating women and children at the train station evoked considerable public sympathy for the strikers. Eventually, the owners granted a 5 percent pay raise and gave in to all of the strikers' demands. Although most of their gains eroded within a year, the strike stands as a triumph of solidarity among an ethnically diverse group of unskilled workers.

Although the Socialist party and the IWW were open to black members, they had no particular interest in combating racism or addressing the unique needs of African American workers. They assumed that labor activism would improve the lives of all workers. To address their unique concerns, black Americans organized on their own behalf.

RESISTANCE TO RACISM

Although there were notable exceptions, such as antiracist reformer Jane Addams, many white Protestant reformers were either indifferent to racial minorities or actively hostile to them. Moreover, most blacks lived in the rural South, where racial violence was most frequent and generally ignored or condoned by law enforcement officials, while most Progressive reform and civil rights activism was centered in northern and western cities.

Lynching was a brutal form of vigilante murder that prevailed mostly in the South after the Civil War, continuing well into the twentieth century. Although accurate statistics on lynching are difficult to confirm, nearly 100 lynchings per year were reported between 1900 and 1910. African American men and a small number of women were the primary targets of lynch mobs, although other minorities were also lynched. Between 1850 and 1930, 597 Mexicans died at the hands of vigilante mobs, half of them in Texas. Civil rights leaders spoke out against lynching and other forms of racial injustice. In a notorious 1915 case, Leo Frank was falsely accused of murdering thirteen-year-old Mary Phagan in the basement of a pencil factory in Atlanta. Although innocent of the crime, Frank was lynched by a mob yelling "hang him, hang him, hang the Jew!"

In a number of cities, white mobs assaulted entire black communities. Large numbers of African Americans were beaten and killed, their property destroyed. Although blacks fought back to defend their families and neighborhoods, many more blacks than whites died in these race riots. In Atlanta, Georgia, in 1906, a movement to disfranchise black voters culminated in false rumors of black men raping white women, which touched off a riot. As the city police looked on, four days of rioting led to a dozen deaths and hundreds of injuries. Two years later, in Springfield, Illinois, sensational newspaper accounts of a white woman's claim of sexual assault by a black man sparked an attack by a white mob on a black neighborhood. In the ensuing riot, two African American men were lynched, others were dragged from their houses and beaten, and six people died, including four whites. The violence shocked white liberal residents of Springfield, Abraham Lincoln's home town. Several of them joined African American leaders the following year in New York City to form the National Association for the Advancement of Colored People (NAACP).

Civil rights and antilynching activism had a long history by this time. Ida B. Wells-Barnett, who had launched an international crusade against lynching in the 1890s, worked to establish local and national networks of black women's clubs in the early twentieth century. In 1905, scholar and civil rights leader W. E. B. Du Bois joined with other black leaders to form the Niagara Movement, which called for an end to lynching, segregation, and discrimination in unions, the courts, and public accommodations, as well as for equal economic and educational opportunity. When black civil rights leaders joined with white Progressive allies to form the NAACP in 1909, they adopted the platform of the Niagara Movement and established a journal, *The Crisis*, with Du Bois as editor.

> *With a monthly circulation of 100,000,* The Crisis *alerted readers to the violence against black people and promoted the NAACP's campaigns against lynching.*

With a monthly circulation of 100,000, *The Crisis* alerted readers to the violence against black people and promoted the NAACP's campaigns against lynching and all forms of discrimination. While advocating peaceful and political civil rights activism, Du Bois also urged African Americans to defend themselves against racial violence. "If we are to die," he wrote in *The Crisis* after a black man was lynched in Pennsylvania in 1911, "in God's name let us not perish like bales of hay."

Work, Science, and Leisure

■ *How did new technologies and entertainments alter the aspirations and daily lives of Americans?*

Reformers, radicals, and activists of all varieties attempted to shape the nation in accord with their various visions. There was practically no area of life that was unaffected by change. Even the landscape changed as cities continued to grow not only outward but also upward, with the construction of towering skyscrapers, and downward, with the creation of subway systems. Brothers Orville and Wilbur Wright seemed to defy nature itself when they designed and flew the first airplane at Kitty Hawk, North Carolina, in 1903.

The nature of work changed as well. Women and men increasingly labored in industry rather than on farms, in large organizations rather than in small shops, and in enterprises that relied more on efficiency than on skilled craftswork. Science and technology reigned, changing the process of work as well as the fruits of production. Professional organizations of educators, social workers, physicians, and scientists emerged, while experts with academic credentials became leaders of many public institutions. It seemed as though science could solve virtually any problem. Advances in medical science contributed to improved public health. But in some cases, experts relied on scientific principles to solve social problems rather than confronting the underlying structural causes, such as widespread poverty.

Technological advances also contributed to new forms of leisure and entertainment in the rapidly growing cities. Building upon Thomas Edison's invention of the motion picture camera, Jewish entrepreneurs created the film industry in Hollywood, a suburb of Los Angeles. Amusement parks and nightclubs provided new venues for greater intimacy between unmarried men and women. Art, literature, and the music of black Americans emphasized the vitality and diversity of life in the nation's cities.

THE USES AND ABUSES OF SCIENCE

Reformers in a wide range of professions sought to improve society through scientific means. Public health was high on the reform agenda. Breakthroughs in science and medicine led reformers to expose the dangers of potions and remedies sold by street vendors. But crowding and lack of medical care still fostered the spread of disease, especially among the poor. Improved public sanitation alleviated the problem considerably in the early years of the twentieth century, reducing the incidence of typhoid fever by 70 percent. Among those who contributed to better conditions were community nurses. In 1900, the New York Charity Organization Society hired Jessie Sleet Scales, the first African American public health nurse, to address problems related to tuberculosis. Scales and other public health professionals implemented sanitation standards and provided care for poor communities, helping to control the spread of disease.

Public sanitation remained a problem, however, especially in crowded cities. An outbreak of typhoid among well-to-do New Yorkers led to Mary Mallon, an Irish immigrant, who had worked as a cook for a number of prominent families. When six members of a household where she worked developed typhoid, she was identified as a carrier of the disease. Authorities later discovered that typhoid outbreaks occurred in seven of eight households that had employed her. Although Mallon had no symptoms, she was forced to remain in a hospital for people with contagious diseases until she sued for her release in 1909; she was released in 1910. Mallon was instructed not to cook for a living, but as she had no other means to support herself, she went back to work as a cook. In 1915, she was arrested again after more typhoid cases were traced to her, and this time she was placed in isolation on an island, virtually as a prisoner, for twenty-six years, until her death in 1939.

The local press vilified Mallon, whom they dubbed "Typhoid Mary," and blamed her for the spread of the illness. As a carrier of the disease, she did indeed infect several people. But she was not the only source of contagion in the city. Typhoid, like many other diseases, was a public health problem. Although Mallon was an otherwise healthy person and had never been accused of a crime, she was imprisoned for what amounted to a life sentence. Quarantine was one of the few public health measures available prior to the development of antibiotics. It did not occur to city officials to pursue other alternatives, such as helping Mallon find a job in which she would not endanger others and developing a broad-based public health approach to the disease that would have improved sanitation in the city.

Reflecting an impulse to blame social problems on allegedly flawed individuals or groups was the eugenics movement, which advocated scientific breeding to improve the nation's racial stock. Drawing on theories of white racial superiority and unscientific notions of genetic inheritance, eugenicists believed that character traits were inherited, including tendencies toward criminality, sexual immorality, and lack of discipline leading to poverty. Eugenicists claimed that social problems resulted from the high birthrate of immigrants and others they considered racially inferior to educated middle-class Anglo-Saxon Americans with their low birthrate.

President Theodore Roosevelt was an outspoken advocate of eugenic reform. One of his major concerns was that Americans were shirking their duty to create a robust citizenry for the future. Alarmed by the dramatic decline in the birthrate of native-born Americans and the tendency of some college-educated women to remain single and childless, he feared that the immigrants, with their much higher birthrate, would overrun the nation. Roosevelt called upon Anglo-Saxon women to prevent what he called

New York American, June 20, 1909, 6.

■ "Typhoid Mary" unwittingly mixes death into an omelet in this 1909 poster warning against bad hygiene.

Resisting Eugenics: A Political Cartoon

Taminent Institute Library, NYU

■ "Breed!" by Arthur Young: A radical protest against the eugenics campaign, from *The Masses*, December 1915.

Some radicals resisted President Roosevelt's calls for native-born Americans to boost their birthrate. In this political cartoon published in *The Masses* in 1914, a young woman refuses the command to "breed," while in the background, hundreds of workers and soldiers march off to industry and war. The cartoon echoed the sentiments of a childless working woman who wrote in the *Independent* in 1907, "Now Gentlemen, You Who Rule Us, we are your 'wage slaves,' my husband and I. . . . You can refuse us any certainty of work, wages or provision for old age. We cannot help ourselves. But there is one thing you cannot do. You cannot use me to breed food for your factories."

QUESTIONS

1. Who or what does the male figure in the cartoon represent? What characteristics does he embody? Would he be a familiar figure to readers at the time?

2. What are the characteristics of the female figure? Why would readers of *The Masses* identify with her?

race suicide, much as male citizens had an obligation to defend the country if called to military duty. In his annual Message to Congress in 1903, Roosevelt warned:

> When home ties are loosened, when men and women cease to regard a worthy family life . . . as the life best worth living, then evil days of the commonwealth are at hand. There are regions in our own land, and classes of our population, where the birth rate has sunk below the death rate. Surely it should need no demonstration to show that willful sterility is, from the standpoint of the nation . . . the one sin for which the penalty is national death, race death. . . . No man, no woman, can shirk the primary duties of life, whether for love of ease and pleasure, or for any other reason, and retain his or her self-respect.

Some eugenics crusaders proposed compulsory sterilization of those they deemed unfit for parenthood. Indiana enacted a eugenic sterilization law in 1907, and other states soon followed. These laws gave legal sanction to the surgical sterilization of thousands of men and even greater numbers of women whom government and medical officials deemed "feeble-minded." Approximately one-third of these sterilizations occurred in California. The criteria for determining "feeblemindedness" were vague at best; often sexual impropriety or out-of-wedlock pregnancy landed young women—generally poor and often foreign born—in institutions for the feebleminded, where the operations took place. The Supreme Court upheld compulsory sterilization laws in the 1920s.

Not everyone with reformist impulses supported eugenic sterilization. Organized opposition came from the Roman Catholic Church, which saw sterilization not only as a violation of bodily integrity and human dignity, but also as unfairly targeting poor people and immigrants. As the field of genetics developed, scientists became increasingly uncomfortable with eugenics and eventually distanced themselves from the movement. Nevertheless, eugenic sterilization continued. Increasingly, women of color were targeted, and the practice continued well into the 1980s.

SCIENTIFIC MANAGEMENT AND MASS PRODUCTION

DOCUMENT

Taylor, Scientific
Management

In 1911, Frederick Winslow Taylor wrote *The Principles of Scientific Management*, a guide to increased efficiency in the nation's industries. He began his career as a laborer in the Midvale Steel Works near Philadelphia in 1878 and rose through the ranks to become the plant's chief engineer. Taylor developed a system to improve mass production in factories in order to make more goods more quickly. His principles included analysis of each job to determine the precise motions and tools needed to maximize each worker's productivity, detailed instructions for workers and guidelines for their supervisors, and wage scales with incentives to motivate workers to achieve high production goals. Over the next decades, industrial managers all over the country drew on Taylor's studies. Business leaders rushed to embrace Taylor's principles, and Taylor became a pioneering management consultant.

Henry Ford was among the most successful industrialists to employ Taylor's techniques. Born in 1863 on a farm near Dearborn, Michigan, the mechanically inclined Ford became an apprentice in a Detroit machine shop in 1879. Although he did not invent the automobile—the first motorcars were manufactured in Germany—he developed design and production methods that brought the cost of an automobile within the reach of the average worker. Ford experimented with the new internal combustion engine in the 1890s and built his first automobile in 1896. In 1903, he established the Ford Motor Company and began a profitable business. He introduced the popular and relatively inexpensive, mass-produced Model T automobile in 1908, which sold for $850. In 1913, Ford introduced the **assembly line** production system in which each worker performed one task repeatedly as each automobile in the process of construction moved along a conveyor. Assembly line manufacturing increased production while cutting costs. In 1914, Ford increased his workers' wages to $5 per day at a time when industrial laborers averaged only $11 per week. By 1916, the price of the Model T dropped to $360. In this sense Ford was a pioneer not only in production but also in consumption.

Although an industrial genius, Ford was narrow-minded and bigoted. A ferocious anti-Semite, he later became an active supporter of Adolf Hitler. He fought unionization fiercely with a private police force. But his production methods, as well as the Ford motorcar, became fixtures of twentieth-century business and consumer culture. Ford embodied many contradictions: he helped create modern life, but he was also repulsed by it. He built a nostalgic theme park in Deerfield Village, Michigan, where he brought together old houses and artifacts to replicate a small town of the nineteenth century, where there were no cars or factories. Yet Ford's own life's work had contributed to the disappearance of the way of life idealized in Deerfield Village.

NEW AMUSEMENTS

As Americans increasingly moved from rural to urban areas, and from farms to factories, new institutions of leisure emerged in the growing cities. Consumer culture was the flipside of business culture. One of the great ironies of American history in the twentieth century is that its popular culture—which more than anything else identifies the United States to the rest of the world—was largely a creation of immigrants and people of color. During the very years when these groups faced intense discrimination, they developed the cultural products that came to define America itself.

The motion picture industry is a case in point. In 1888, Thomas Edison invented the kinetoscope, the early motion picture camera. The pragmatic Edison thought that his new device might be used in education and industry. But he did not see much commercial potential for the gadget. Not until the early twentieth century did the moving picture begin to reach a wide audience. Moviemakers left the East Coast and moved to the West, taking advantage of the warm climate, cheap land, and nonunion labor. Within a few years, the moviemakers, mostly Jewish immigrants from Europe, established the film industry. By the late 1910s and 1920s, Paramount, Metro Goldwyn Mayer, and Fox Studios—all founded by Jews—had become leaders in movie making. Hollywood emerged as a major center of American popular culture, sending its products across the nation and abroad.

WATCH

Luna Park at Coney Island

The first audiences for the motion pictures were in the working-class neighborhoods of the growing cities. In New York alone, by 1910, there were 1,000 small storefront theaters and fun houses known as penny arcades where there had been none 20 years earlier. The number of saloons also increased, from 7,000 to 9,000, while the Coney Island amusement park drew thousands to its shimmering lights and thrilling rides. During these same years, the sounds of African American music began to attract audiences among immigrants as well as native-born whites. Youths from all ethnic groups flocked to dance halls, where they danced to the lively tunes often played by black musicians who "ragged" the beat with new jazz rhythms.

Working-class youth were not the only ones drawn to the new urban amusements. Glamorous nightclubs, known as cabarets, also began to appear, offering dining, dancing, music, and entertainment to the wealthy. Jesse Lasky opened the Follies Bergeres in New York in 1911. Lasky filled his cabaret with lavish furnishings, hired black musicians to play ragtime music, and charged high prices. "Everything about the Follies," Lasky wrote, "was unheard of in New York, including the prices." In an effort to render these upper-class cabarets respectable and distinguish them from the rowdy working-class dance halls, owners tamed the bawdy dances to express a more moderate sensuality.

> *Hollywood emerged as a major center of American popular culture, sending its products across the nation and abroad.*

"SEX O' CLOCK IN AMERICA"

The sexual mores and behavior of Americans seemed to be changing so dramatically that one observer announced "sex o'clock" had struck. Indeed, the codes of the past were challenged at every turn. Among the middle class, unchaperoned dating began to replace the previous system of a man "coming to call" at the home of a woman he hoped to court. Automobiles gave young couples more freedom and privacy. Physical intimacy became more acceptable.

In spite of efforts by their elders, native-born as well as immigrant youth challenged the sexual codes of the past. Young working women looked forward to fun in their leisure hours and sometimes exchanged physical intimacies for "treats" from men who took them out to a meal or a dance. These women were known as "charity girls," to distinguish them from prostitutes. Increasing sexual intimacy among unmarried men and women reflected heightened expectations for sexual satisfaction—for women as well as men. These years also witnessed a rise in the proportion of brides who were pregnant at marriage, from a low of 10 percent of nonslave brides in the mid-nineteenth century to 23 percent by 1910.

Marriage increasingly held the promise not only of love, intimacy, and mutual obligation, as it had in the nineteenth century, but also of sexual fulfillment and shared leisure pursuits. As expectations for marital happiness rose, so did the divorce rate. Liberal divorce laws, combined with expanding opportunities for women to support themselves, prompted increasing numbers of men and women to end unhappy marriages and try again. The rising divorce rate did not signal a decline in the popularity of marriage, however; a greater proportion of Americans married, and at increasingly younger ages. Those who divorced were likely to remarry, a pattern that continued through the twentieth century.

Some women did not marry but instead formed lifelong attachments to other women. Rarely identified as lesbian but often described as **Boston marriages**, these unions signified long-term emotional bonds between women who lived together. The widely admired reformer Jane Addams shared her life with Mary Rozet Smith for more than thirty years. Meanwhile, lesbians as well as gay men gained greater visibility in the cities. They frequented bars and clubs in such places as Greenwich Village and Harlem, hoping to avoid the attention of police, who were likely to arrest them for indecent conduct.

ARTISTS RESPOND TO THE NEW ERA

The break from tradition evident in social norms also infused the arts. Modern art burst upon the cultural landscape, defying conventions of artistic expression that had characterized the realistic landscapes and portraits of the nineteenth century. The city, technology, and the lives of ordinary people at work and at play formed core motifs for modern artists. Among the most controversial was a group of painters who used sensual forms and colors to depict urban amusements and diverse working-class subjects. Although these artists did not pioneer new styles of painting, their content was revolutionary. Robert Henri painted scenes of the city including ethnic minorities, George Luks depicted cabarets and nightlife, Everett Shinn portrayed prostitutes and other "low life" characters, John Sloan evoked New York's Lower East Side, immigrants, and theaters. Treating their subjects with dignity and humanity, these artists created works that exuded the vitality of urban life and conveyed a gritty reality free of moral condemnation. Contemptuous critics referred to the artists as the "Ashcan School," a label they embraced.

The city, technology, and the lives of ordinary people at work and at play formed core motifs for modern artists.

Modernism in the United States drew on artistic trends emerging in Europe, such as Art Nouveau, which involved a fusion of technological and organic forms drawn from the natural world. Theodore Roosevelt praised the new artistic impulse, which he saw as fitting the vibrancy of the new century. In 1913, the Association of American Painters and Sculptors held a major exhibition known as the Armory Show, which brought together the work of modern artists from Europe and the United States. The controversial exhibition shocked the traditional art world but established modern art as the experimental new style for the twentieth century.

Experimentation emerged in the folk arts as well. Maria Martinez, from San Ildefonso Pueblo in New Mexico, developed a form of black-on-black pottery that revived ancient forms and fused them with modern designs. She demonstrated her pottery making at the St. Louis World's Fair in 1904 and at Worlds Fairs over the next several decades. Collaborating with her husband, Julian, who engraved graceful designs onto her shiny black pottery, Martinez became one of the most famous American Indian artists of the century.

Photography also began to exhibit a new realism in the work of such documentary photographers as Lewis Hine, who photographed immigrants, industrial work, and urban street life, and such avant-garde artists as Alfred Stieglitz and Edward Steichen, who drew inspiration from artistic innovations in Europe.

The artistic movement known as realism also infused the writing of fiction. Theodore Dreiser's 1900 novel *Sister Carrie* narrates the story of an independent young woman who

George Luks, *The Café Francis*, c. 1909. Butler Institute of American Art, Youngstown, Ohio

■ *The Café Francis*, by George Luks, c. 1909. Luks was one of the "Ashcan school" artists who celebrated urban street life and popular culture. Their raw and sensual depictions of city entertainments stirred controversy among art critics at the time.

moves to Chicago and uses her sexuality to advance her ambition. Contrary to the morality tales popular at the time, Carrie does not suffer for her sins. Rather, she prospers, while her male lovers are destroyed by their infatuation with her. Because of the novel's scandalous content, Dreiser's publisher did not promote the book, although it was revived and republished in later years.

Popular music flourished in the first decade of the century, especially jazz. From its roots in slave songs, spirituals, and ragtime, jazz brought together the various strains of African American music and developed new forms, centered in New Orleans. Artists such as pianist Ferdinand "Jelly Roll" Morton and cornet player Charles "Buddy" Bolden were among the musicians who played the new syncopated rhythms.

Conclusion

Theodore Roosevelt at his "bully pulpit," Upton Sinclair with the power of his pen, Clara Lemlich speaking before thousands of immigrant workers, and Charles "Buddy" Bolden belting out new jazz sounds from his cornet—all promoted new and different visions of the modern nation. Nearly every aspect of life, from boardrooms to bedrooms, was affected by the flurry of activism that characterized the Progressive Era.

By the time Woodrow Wilson entered the White House in 1913, the nation looked different from what it had seemed at the turn of the century, and its people behaved differently too. Millions of immigrants from Europe, Asia, and Mexico had arrived in the United States and settled in towns and cities across the nation. Growing urban areas with new amusements and increasingly diverse populations emerged as centers of a national mass culture. New developments in science and technology brought the automobile and the motion picture to American consumers. At the same time, industrial production contributed to environmental damage, pollution, and dangerous working conditions.

Progressive reformers and labor activists mounted efforts to curb the ill effects of urban industrial society. Faith in science and expertise gave rise to pervasive optimism that social problems could be solved. Technological changes converged with the widespread belief that society is the sum of interdependent parts that can work together to mitigate the harmful effects of industrial life. At the local level as well as through state and national institutions, reformers sought to solve society's ills. Muckrakers exposed corruption, women's rights activists pushed for the vote, and African American leaders organized for civil rights and against lynching. In the West and Southwest, Mexicans and Asians challenged discriminatory laws and labor practices. At the same time, moralists and vice crusaders sought to tame what they considered dangerous challenges to the social order.

These years also witnessed a major expansion of national power. Presidents Roosevelt and Taft strengthened the role of the federal government through new efforts to regulate big business and by extending America's military and economic presence abroad. By 1912, most Americans supported a strong reform agenda. But within a few years, the nation became embroiled in a major world war that would challenge the inherent optimism of the Progressive Era.

For Review

1. Who were the Progressives, and why is this time period known as the Progressive Era?

2. What were the different visions of the nation's future that inspired reformers at the time? In what ways were they in conflict with each other?

3. How did Theodore Roosevelt and William Howard Taft use their presidential power? On which issues did they agree and disagree?

4. How did immigrants respond to their adopted country, and how did their American-born neighbors respond to them?

5. What issues did reformers and radicals address, and what changes did they help to achieve?

6. How did scientific and technological discoveries foster reform efforts?

7. How did new leisure institutions and artistic creativity alter urban life?

Created Equal Online

For more *Created Equal* resources, including suggestions for sites to visit and further reading, go to **MyHistoryLab.com**.

Chapter 20

War and Revolution, 1912–1920

■ The son of a Haitian immigrant, W.E.B. Du Bois (1868–1963) was the first African American to earn a Ph.D. at Harvard University. Du Bois became a distinguished historian and sociologist, as well as one of the nation's most influential voices on racial issues.

"This is the crisis of the world," wrote prominent African American scholar and activist W. E. B. Du Bois in his July 1918 editorial in *The Crisis*, as desperate armies struggled on the battlefields of Europe and the outcome of World War I hung in the balance. Du Bois served as editor of this influential NAACP journal, whose circulation soared from 1,000 in its first year of publication in 1910 to over 100,000 by 1918. Arguing that the threat of imperial German power "spells death to the aspirations of Negroes and all darker races for equality, freedom and democracy," Du Bois concluded, "Let us, while this war lasts, forget our special grievances and close our ranks with our own white fellow citizens and the allied nations that are fighting for democracy." World War I, as Du Bois understood, would touch every continent abroad and would reshape American life and politics at home.

At first, from 1910 to 1914, optimism about solving the nation's social problems rose as Progressive reformers attempted to ameliorate some of the worst aspects of modern industrial life. International developments then turned American attentions abroad. Traumatic revolutions swept through Mexico, China, and Russia, and the conflagration of the Great War—World War I, as it became known later—consumed all of Europe from 1914 to 1918 and eventually drew in the United States. What President Woodrow Wilson called the war "to make the world safe for democracy" encouraged people of color, both in the vast European-ruled colonies of Asia and Africa and in the segregated United States, to claim a place of greater equality. But at home the war also created pressures for conformity and intolerance for dissent. The United States emerged from the war with great prestige and power, but the Versailles Treaty of 1919 failed to create a lasting structure for world peace.

A World and a Nation in Upheaval

■ *What were the greatest challenges to the existing international and domestic order in the 1910s?*

American politics in the 1910s and the U.S. involvement in World War I must be understood within the context of change and uncertainty in the international system. While world affairs were still dominated by the wealthy nations of western Europe and North America, the first wave of the great revolutions of the twentieth century was beginning to wash away much of the old order. Tensions also sharpened within the United States over traditional hierarchies of color, gender, and class. The struggle between Progressive reform and conservative reaction pervaded public life in the United States and much of the rest of the world.

THE APEX OF EUROPEAN CONQUEST

On the eve of World War I, three-quarters of the world's population lived under the rule of Europeans or their descendants. Exploration of the most remote parts of the globe filled in the last blank spaces on world maps, including the North (1909) and South (1911) Poles. A 1913 expedition led by Episcopalian missionary Hudson Stuck reached the top of Alaska's Mt. McKinley, at 20,320 feet the highest peak in North America. The granting of statehood to Arizona and New Mexico in 1912 filled out the forty-eight mainland states, and the country's native inhabitants began to seem to white Americans less a current threat than a piece of the past to be preserved. The U.S. Treasury issued the first Indian head nickel the following year.

Technological innovations in transportation and communication tied the world more closely together. Just as the Suez Canal (1870) and the trans-Siberian railroad (1904) linked Europe more directly to Asia, the Panama Canal (1914) cut in half the travel time by water

between the East and West Coasts of the United States. Cables laid on the floor of the Atlantic Ocean in 1914 inaugurated telephone service between Europe and the United States. The first motorized flight by Orville and Wilbur Wright along the Outer Banks of North Carolina in 1903 led to transcontinental airmail service by 1920.

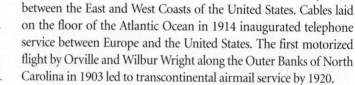

The competition that arose from the expansion of European power sowed the seeds of World War I. Germany, France, Britain, Italy, and Russia raced each other for new colonies and greater influence across Africa and Asia. The great powers of Europe, along with the United States and Japan, competed for world markets and raw materials. Conflicts within Europe over disputed borders (Alsace-Lorraine) and nationalist movements (the Balkans) further heightened tensions. The central rivalry emerged between a newly unified Germany (1871) and traditionally dominant Britain. Anticipating trouble, each of the major European powers sought allies to bolster its position. Britain, France, and Russia formed an alliance that became known as the **Entente** or sometimes the Allies. Germany, Austria-Hungary, and

Italy established their own alliance as the **Central Powers.** These unprecedented peacetime alliances between global empires meant that a single spark could ignite a worldwide war.

The United States emerged as a global power in this same period around the turn of the century. Fifteen years after it seized an overseas empire in 1898, the country's economic growth was stunning. In 1913, U.S. consumption of energy from coal and oil equaled that of Britain, Germany, France, Russia, and Austria-Hungary combined. The United States also brought a different history to the world stage. It had been born in 1776 in the first successful revolution by colonies against a European empire. Americans had long understood themselves as a people who opposed empires and supported self-government. The events of 1898 contradicted this legacy, and Americans remained ambivalent about their country's imperial venture. The U.S. Congress in 1916 promised eventual independence to the Philippines and granted U.S. citizenship to residents of Puerto Rico in 1917.

CONFRONTING REVOLUTIONS IN ASIA AND EUROPE

As president, Woodrow Wilson feared social upheaval. Born in 1856, he had grown up in Augusta, Georgia, amid the destruction of the Civil War, and he made his career as a political scientist and as governor of New Jersey (1910–1912) during a period of labor strife. Whatever Wilson's hopes for a stable social order at home and abroad, the global process of western capitalist expansion into decentralized, preindustrial societies was producing a widespread backlash by 1910. The first signs of a broad rejection of the world order dominated by the white nations of Europe and North America had already appeared. Ethiopia crushed an invading Italian army in 1896 in the first victory of an African state over a modern European one. In 1905, Japan destroyed the Russian army and naval fleet, putting Europeans on notice that their days of having their way in Asia were over. Harassed across eastern Europe in brutal pogroms, Jews under the leadership of Theodor Herzl founded the Zionist movement for a national homeland in Palestine in 1897. In 1912, blacks organized the African National Congress to struggle against racial oppression in South Africa, just as African Americans formed the National Association for the Advancement of Colored People (NAACP) in 1909.

The global process of western capitalist expansion into decentralized, preindustrial societies was producing a widespread backlash by 1910.

As nationalist movements in China, Russia, and Mexico overturned weak central governments controlled by foreign investors, American economic and security interests seemed to be at stake on three continents. In Asia, the Chinese deeply resented exclusive foreign enclaves that dominated their nation's coastal regions and exempted foreigners from the constraints of Chinese laws. Signs in Shanghai reading "No dogs or Chinese" suggested the attitudes that accompanied European and American control of the bulk of China's wealth. In 1911, nationalist revolutionaries inspired by Sun Yat-sen, a Hawaiian-educated Christian democratic reformer, overthrew the corrupt Qing dynasty that had proven unable to resist Western and Japanese incursions.

The American desire for an open door into China's trade—a door that no other powerful nation could close at will—conflicted with the rising imperial power of the region: Japan. The Tokyo government, which had annexed Korea in 1910, responded to the outbreak of World War I by seizing the valuable German-held Shantung Peninsula in northeastern China. In its 21 Demands to China, issued in January 1915, Japan made clear its plans to dominate the development of the Chinese economy. The American relationship with both China and Japan was undercut at home by continued discrimination and violence against immigrants from Asia, who remained ineligible for naturalization as U.S. citizens. In 1913, the California legislature passed the Alien Land Act to prevent ownership of land in the state by people "ineligible to citizenship"—people born in Asia, particularly those from Japan.

People of Asian descent on the West Coast of the United States did their best under conditions of enforced inequality. Unable to own land, Chinese immigrants eked out a daily living as migrant farm laborers or worked in laundries or restaurants. Cooks adapted their food to local tastes, creating dishes that looked Chinese but appealed to American tastes. One cook apparently created chow mein ("fried noodles") by accidentally dropping some Chinese pasta into a pot of simmering oil. The crisp, golden-brown result was a hit with his customers. David Jung opened a noodle company in Los Angeles in 1916 and is credited with inventing the fortune cookie—not a traditional Chinese dessert. Other Chinese immigrants worked as herbalists, tapping traditional Chinese medicines for a growing white clientele.

Beyond Asia, revolutionary struggles with implications for America also threatened the monarchs who ruled eastern Europe. For Russians, defeat at the hands of Japan in 1905 helped precipitate a thwarted democratic revolution in 1905 followed by two years of political turmoil. The **czar** survived to rule another decade, and thousands of political reformers—unionists, anarchists, and socialists—joined a growing wave of immigration from Russia to the United States. The wave crested in 1914 at 1.2 million people, most of them from east or south of the Alps. In June of that year, the assassination of the heir to the Austro-Hungarian throne by a Serbian nationalist in Sarajevo provided the spark that ignited the Great War. Russia's defense of the Serbs put the alliance system into action, and the Entente went to war with the Central Powers.

INFLUENCING THE POLITICAL ORDER IN LATIN AMERICA

Before World War I, the most important region of the world for the United States was Latin America, especially Central America, Mexico, and the Caribbean islands. This area guarded the nation's strategic southern flank, and American citizens and corporations invested more money in Latin America than in any other region of the world. President Wilson spoke of the ability of Latin Americans to govern themselves "when properly directed" and proceeded to provide that direction. U.S. marines occupied Haiti (1915), the Dominican Republic (1916), and Cuba (1917) and maintained their earlier presence in Nicaragua to defend American property and ensure that local debts were paid to American creditors. The Bryan-Chamorro Treaty of 1916 guaranteed that no other nation would build a competitor to the Panama Canal through Nicaragua. The United States purchased the Danish Virgin Islands in 1917 to keep them out of German hands.

American anxieties about stability to the south centered on Mexico. "Land for the landless and Mexico for the Mexicans" became the slogan of revolutionaries there between 1910 and 1920. They overthrew the thirty-five year pro-U.S. dictatorship of Porfirio Díaz, who modernized parts of the Mexican economy but left most Mexican families landless. U.S. stakes in the Mexican revolution were high. American investors owned 43 percent of all Mexico's wealth (other foreigners owned another 25 percent), and more than half of the country's trade flowed north to the United States. Moreover, by 1921 Mexico was the world's second largest exporter of oil. Washington feared the spread of radical political ideas northward as almost a million Mexicans crossed their northern

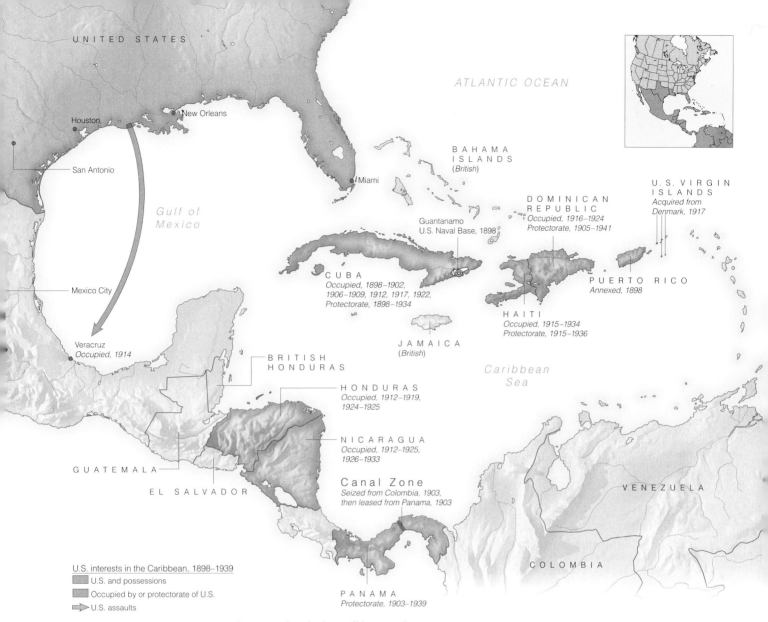

UNITED STATES

ATLANTIC OCEAN

Houston

New Orleans

San Antonio

*Gulf of
Mexico*

Miami

BAHAMA
ISLANDS
(British)

U.S. VIRGIN
ISLANDS
*Acquired from
Denmark, 1917*

DOMINICAN
REPUBLIC
*Occupied, 1916–1924
Protectorate, 1905–1941*

Guantanamo
U.S. Naval Base, 1898

Mexico City

CUBA
*Occupied, 1898–1902,
1906–1909, 1912, 1917, 1922,
Protectorate, 1898–1934*

PUERTO RICO
Annexed, 1898

HAITI
*Occupied, 1915–1934
Protectorate, 1915–1936*

Veracruz
Occupied, 1914

JAMAICA
(British)

*Caribbean
Sea*

BRITISH
HONDURAS

HONDURAS
*Occupied, 1912–1919,
1924–1925*

GUATEMALA

NICARAGUA
*Occupied, 1912–1925,
1926–1933*

VENEZUELA

EL SALVADOR

Canal Zone
*Seized from Colombia, 1903,
then leased from Panama, 1903*

COLOMBIA

U.S. interests in the Caribbean, 1898–1939

U.S. and possessions

Occupied by or protectorate of U.S.

U.S. assaults

PANAMA
Protectorate, 1903–1939

■ **MAP 20.1 U.S. Interests and Interventions in the Caribbean Region, 1898–1939**
By its size, wealth, and military power, the United States dominated the Caribbean region to its
south. American capitalists invested heavily in Mexico, Central America, and the Caribbean islands,
and U.S. troops often intervened to protect those investments. Puerto Rico (by acquisition from Spain)
and the Panama Canal Zone (by lease from Panama) became particularly important territories ruled by the
United States.

border during the revolutionary decade, tripling the number of Americans with recent
roots south of the Rio Grande.

Many came through El Paso, the "Ellis Island" for immigrants from the south. Fleeing
poverty and violence, they found both discrimination and employment. Since the Newlands Act
of 1902, dam building and irrigation in the Southwest had created a boom in commercial agriculture across California and Arizona and a desperate need for farm workers. Employers often
recruited south of the border. "I believe that the Mexican laborers are the solution to our common labor problem in this country," one cotton company executive told President Wilson. It was
not an easy life, especially for women who had to balance paid employment with taking care of
families. Grace Luna remembered picking cotton in Madera, California, where women scaled
ladders with up to 100 pounds of cotton on their backs and "some carried their kids on top of
their picking sacks." Most immigrants sought unskilled positions, but members of Mexico's
professional class—teachers, architects, and lawyers—also came north, for political asylum. The
new arrivals joined Mexican Americans who had lived in the region since it was part of Mexico.
They had not crossed the border; in 1848, the border had crossed them.

Robert D. Farber University Archives & Special Collections, Brandeis University

■ Louis Brandeis was an extraordinary figure in early twentieth-century American life. Born in a Jewish family in Louisville, Kentucky, in 1856—when race slavery still prevailed—he excelled at Harvard Law School and became a prominent attorney in Boston, known for his sympathy for working people. He was one of the nation's leading Progressive reformers when Woodrow Wilson named him to the U.S. Supreme Court in 1916, where he served until 1939 and developed a reputation as a principled defender of free speech. Brandeis was also a strong supporter of **Zionism,** the international movement to create a Jewish state in the British-controlled territory of Palestine. Brandeis University in Waltham, Massachusetts, founded in 1948, was named in his honor.

Wilson sought unsuccessfully to reestablish in Mexico a political order respectful of the rights of foreign property owners. Victoriano Huerta's use of assassination to seize power in Mexico City led Wilson to reverse the traditional U.S. policy of recognizing new governments once they were in power. Wilson twice sent U.S. troops into Mexico, at Veracruz in April 1914 to block a German arms shipment and then in pursuit of Francisco ("Pancho") Villa and his army after their 1916 assault on Columbus, New Mexico. The American forces under General John J. Pershing withdrew in early 1917 as the president prepared to enter the much larger war in Europe. Land redistribution and national control of the country's abundant mineral wealth, particularly oil, were written into Mexico's new constitution passed a few days later, and the revolutionary upheaval ended by 1920.

CONFLICTS OVER RACE AND ETHNICITY AT HOME

Just as social upheaval threatened monarchies and international investors abroad, less privileged Americans challenged traditional lines of hierarchy and control in the United States. Americans of all colors applauded the spectacular successes of Native American athlete Jim Thorpe at the 1912 Olympic Games in Sweden. In 1916, Wilson appointed Louis Brandeis as the first Jewish justice of the Supreme Court, but that same year anxieties about the future of white supremacy found a voice in the popular new book of a reactionary New York intellectual named Madison Grant. *The Passing of the Great Race*, a bigoted sociology tract, identified Jesus as "Nordic" to distance the central figure of the Christian faith from the many new Jewish immigrants in America.

The Wilson administration's "New Freedom" slogan did not apply to African Americans, who faced continuing discrimination in employment and housing. Many Progressive reformers, including the president, did not believe in racial equality. The president filled his cabinet with white Southerners who segregated the few federal agencies that had employed blacks. When Wilson took office, African Americans continued to be murdered publicly by vigilante mobs across the South at a rate of more than one person per week. But the president ignored requests from the recently formed NAACP for an antilynching law. The president endorsed D. W. Griffith's 1915 film *Birth of a Nation* as "history written with lightning." Griffith, a Kentucky-born champion of the "Lost Cause" of slavery in the South, had created a racist blockbuster that celebrated the Ku Klux Klan of the 1860s and helped inspire the Klan's rebirth that fall at Stone Mountain, Georgia.

WOMEN'S CHALLENGES

Women of all colors lived under particular burdens of discrimination. Their uniquely intimate relationships—as daughters, wives, mothers—with those who did not treat them as equals complicated their efforts at reform. So did their dilemma about women's roles in society: some sought full legal equality with men, and others wanted special

■ In February 1917, as the United States broke relations with Germany and began to prepare to enter World War I, supporters of women's suffrage continued to picket on the sidewalk outside the White House. College women joined the effort to ensure that winning liberty at home would go hand in hand with fighting for democracy abroad.

protections for women on the grounds that they were fundamentally different. At issue was the nature of women's political identity. Was their primary identification in their attachment to individual men or to the nation? American women lost their U.S. citizenship by marrying a foreigner, whereas American men did not. A growing chorus of female activists rejected this kind of double standard and focused on the key issue of suffrage.

American women's long struggle to vote came to a head in this decade. By 1912, a rising number of European nations and nine American states, all in the West, had granted the franchise to citizens of both sexes. Jeannette Rankin, a Republican feminist and pacifist from Montana, won election in 1916 as the nation's first female member of Congress. But suffragists varied in the tactics they believed most effective for winning the vote. The moderate National American Women Suffrage Association under the leadership of Carrie Chapman Catt worked within the political system, building an alliance with President Wilson after he endorsed women's suffrage in 1916 and supporting the U.S. entry into World War I the next year. Alice Paul and other militants formed the National Women's Party and opposed the war effort as inherently undemocratic because half the adult population could not vote. In 1917, five picketers were imprisoned for seven months for obstructing traffic in front of the White House; despite brutal force-feedings, Paul and Rose Winslow persisted in a hunger strike so "that women fighting for liberty may be considered political prisoners." In 1918, suffragist organizers helped elect a more sympathetic Congress that passed the Nineteenth Amendment, ending sex discrimination in voting two years later.

Contention over women's social roles also divided Americans. Traditionalists promoted the declaration of the first Mother's Day in 1913. The desire to provide special

Sex and Citizenship

According to common law and early American practice, white women were American citizens if they were born in the United States or chose to be naturalized. However, during the nineteenth century, U.S. law gradually came to reflect the principle of marital unity: that women should have the same citizenship status as their husbands. After 1855, foreign women who married male U.S. citizens automatically became U.S. citizens. Conversely, with the Citizenship Act of 1907, American women who married foreign men lost their U.S. citizenship. Ethel Mackenzie, born in California, had married a British subject in 1909. The couple lived in San Francisco, and Mackenzie—a woman's suffrage activist—decided to challenge the 1907 law. The U.S. Supreme Court eventually ruled against her, upholding the existing law in a 1915 decision, Mackenzie v. Hare. Not until the 1922 Cable Act did Congress permit American women who married foreign men (at least those from countries whose subjects were eligible for U.S. citizenship) to retain their own U.S. citizenship. Here is an excerpt from the Mackenzie v. Hare decision:

The question is, Did [Ethel Mackenzie] cease to be a citizen by her marriage? . . . [Mackenzie contends] that it was not the intention [of Congress] to deprive an American-born woman, remaining within the jurisdiction of the United States, of her citizenship by reason of her marriage to a resident foreigner. . . . [She is trying to persuade the Court that the citizenship statute was] beyond the authority of Congress. . . . [She offered the] earnest argument . . . that . . . under the Constitution and laws of the United States, [citizenship] became a right, privilege and immunity which could not be taken away from her except as a punishment for crime or by her voluntary expatriation. . . .

protections for women resulted in the Sheppard-Towner Act of 1921, which expanded the role of the new federal Children's Bureau in providing infant and maternal health services. The struggle over contraception reflected the large size of American families and how pregnancy dominated women's lives. Socialist Margaret Sanger campaigned for women's access to contraception, opening the nation's first birth control clinic in Brooklyn in 1916. Sanger's experiences as a public health nurse with working-class New Yorkers convinced her that controlling pregnancy was the central issue for helping women gain greater autonomy. Unable to separate sexual experience from reproduction and facing poverty and unsanitary living conditions, married women in the lower classes suffered frequent pregnancies and the often debilitating and sometimes fatal consequences of abortion, an illegal but common operation. Sanger reached a turning point after hearing the joking response of a physician to the desperate plea of one frail twenty-eight-year-old mother of three for help in preventing another pregnancy: "Tell Jake to sleep on the roof!" Sanger was appalled, and the young woman's subsequent death as a result of a botched abortion pushed Sanger to begin her crusade for contraception. Although Sanger's later support for eugenics troubled many of her supporters, she is credited with founding the modern birth control movement.

WORKERS AND OWNERS CLASH

Most adult Americans—workers—continued to find themselves in frequent conflict with their bosses and employers. Industrial capitalism's efficiency produced great material wealth, but 60 percent of it belonged to 2 percent of the population, whereas two-thirds of Americans owned only 2 percent of the wealth. The anticapitalist aspirations of the Socialist party and the Industrial Workers of the World (IWW) frightened both industrialists and the more conservative labor leaders of the American Federation of Labor (AFL), especially when the western-based IWW led two major strikes in the East, one a success in Lawrence, Massachusetts, in 1912 and the other a failure in Paterson, New Jersey, in 1913. The campaign against a wage cut at the vast Lawrence

[But the Court concludes:] . . . The identity of husband and wife is an ancient principle of our jurisprudence. It was neither accidental nor arbitrary and worked in many instances for her protection. There has been, it is true, much relaxation of it but in its retention as in its origin it is determined by their intimate relation and unity of interests, and this relation and unity may make it of public concern in many instances to merge their identity, and give dominance to the husband. It has purpose, if not necessity, in purely domestic policy; it has greater purpose and, it may be, necessity, in international policy. . . .

. . . The law in controversy deals with a condition voluntarily entered into. . . . The marriage of an American woman with a foreigner has consequences . . . [similar to] her physical expatriation. . . . Therefore, as long as the relation lasts it is made tantamount to expatriation. This is no arbitrary exercise of government. . . . It is the conception of the legislation under review that such an act [marriage to a foreign man] may bring the Government into embarrassments and, it may be, into controversies. . . . [Marriage to a foreign man] is as voluntary and distinctive as expatriation and its consequence must be considered as elected.

QUESTIONS

1. *According to the Supreme Court, how were a woman's national identity and marital identity related?*

2. *What assumptions did the Court make about women and marriage?*

Source: Ethel C. Mackenzie v. John P. Hare et al., 239 U.S. 299 (1915).

textile factory was especially impressive in uniting 20,000 workers of 40 different national backgrounds.

Some owners sought to undercut union campaigns by providing better working conditions and even company-run "unions." These carrots of concession were accompanied by the stick of force. Bolstered by sympathetic federal courts and state governors, companies usually refused to negotiate with workers who went on strike. This pattern reached a violent climax on Easter night in 1914 outside Ludlow, Colorado, in a mining camp owned by John D. Rockefeller Jr.'s Colorado Fuel and Iron Company. State militia and company guards broke a strike there with torches and machine guns, burning the miners' tent colony and killing two women and eleven children. A total of sixty-six strikers and strike supporters died in the conflict before federal troops eventually restored order. Ludlow recalled the actions of the Colorado militia exactly fifty years earlier, when it had destroyed the Cheyenne Indian camp at Sand Creek. Immigrant coal miners and their families—Slavs, Greeks, and Mexicans—had replaced Native Americans as the apparent threat to Colorado's social order.

Such brutality by owners against workers appalled most Americans. The Wilson administration slowly began supporting the right of laborers to organize for collective bargaining with their employers. Wilson's strong backing from Samuel Gompers and the AFL in the 1912 election initiated the modern alliance between labor and the Democratic party. The president named William B. Wilson, a U.S. congressman from Pennsylvania and a former labor activist with the Knights of Labor and the United Mine Workers, to head the new U.S. Department of Labor, the permanent agency established "to foster, promote and develop the welfare of working people" by improving their working conditions and mediating labor disputes. The president appointed labor lawyer Frank Walsh to chair the separate short-term U.S. Committee on Industrial Relations, which for two years explored the causes of industrial violence in public hearings. Walsh even grilled Rockefeller himself about the events at Ludlow, embarrassing the corporate titan by revealing his close involvement and clear responsibility for what had happened.

Denver Public Library, Western History Collection

■ Children of the striking coal miners gather in their tent colony outside Ludlow on the high plains of south-central Colorado, at the base of the mountains of the Front Range. Winter snows and cold temperatures made for a difficult life, as did the grueling and dangerous work of mining coal that was common across the state. Miners' children died with their mothers and fathers in the Ludlow massacre on April 20, 1914.

American Neutrality and Domestic Reform

■ *What were Americans' priorities from 1914 to 1917?*

Most Americans had roots of some kind in Europe and had long defined themselves in relation to life on "the continent." But they also considered themselves part of the New World that was separate from the Old World of kings, castles, and rigid social classes. When Europe stepped off the precipice in August 1914 into a war larger than any previously fought or imagined, few Americans wanted any part of it. Make "no entangling alliances," George Washington had urged his fellow citizens. Europeans must stay out of our hemisphere, the Monroe Doctrine had declared. Faithful to this tradition, Americans focused on domestic political reforms and on an economy revived by European demands for war-related goods, which created new jobs that lured many black southerners north. But international ties ultimately proved too important to the well-being of Americans for the country to remain indefinitely on the sidelines of World War I.

"THE ONE GREAT NATION AT PEACE"

When war came in 1914, Italy switched sides, joining Britain, France, and Russia in the Entente, or Allies. The Ottoman Empire—modern Turkey—joined Germany and Austria-Hungary, forming the Central Powers. Americans were stunned as "civilized" Europe slid into savage conflict. "The lamps are going out all over Europe," British Foreign Secretary Edward Grey observed. "We shall not see them lit again in our lifetime." Following traditional U.S. policy, Wilson urged Americans to remain neutral "in fact as well as in name" to promote an eventual "peace without victory."

Neutrality was profitable. Wilson stoutly defended the rights of neutrals to trade with belligerents, the same principle that had led the United States into the War of 1812

Casualties of the Great War, 1914–1918

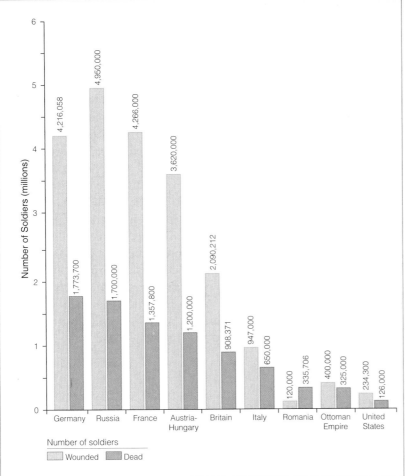

Number of soldiers
Wounded Dead

The large casualty numbers during World War I reflected the length of the war and the ineffectiveness of older tactics such as infantry charges against newer weapons such as machine guns and poison gas. The German and Austro-Hungarian armies fought on two fronts: in the east primarily against the Russians and in the west primarily against the French and British. Compared to the European combatants who fought for several years, the United States suffered far fewer casualties in its eighteen months of combat in the war. The figures in this graph do not include the additional 8 million civilian deaths caused by warfare and famine.

QUESTIONS

1. How might the scale of the human destruction in World War I, unprecedented before 1914, have affected the societies with the largest losses?

2. How might these casualty statistics help explain some of Wilson's difficulties in the postwar peace negotiations at Versailles in 1919?

against England. American industries depended on overseas trade, he believed, and "they will burst their jackets if they cannot find a free outlet to the markets of the world." After the recession of 1913–1914, war-related foreign demand from abroad for American farm and factory products jump-started the economy. In the course of World War I, American bankers extended $10 billion in loans to the Allies (primarily Britain and France), and the United States changed from a debtor nation to the world's largest creditor.

The nature of the fighting in Europe further bolstered the American determination to avoid being drawn into the conflict. Industrialized warfare brought fiendish new ways to kill human beings, including machine guns and poison gas. Gone were the days of bold maneuvers and dashing cavalry charges; now was the time of trench warfare, with its unrelenting misery, terror, and helplessness. Eight and a half million young men lost their lives and another 21 million were wounded, devastating an entire generation of European society. Eight million civilians also died as a result of the fighting, and an international outbreak of influenza in 1918 killed another 20 million around the world. Continuous shelling rendered whole sections of northern France a wasteland. Prewar optimism about human progress disappeared.

In the United States, neutrality also made political sense. Immigrants from every part of Europe lived and voted in the United States, so Americans had blood ties to all the

■ American women supported the war effort in many ways, including working in munitions factories, buying war bonds, single-parenting while husbands were away in the military, and volunteering as nurses for the armed forces in France. Here, African American women entertain black soldiers with music in a service club in Newark, New Jersey, in 1918.

belligerents. Commercial and political elites tended to identify with Britain and France, as did many other Americans. But among two of the largest groups of Americans, those with roots in Germany and Ireland, many took a different view. Few Irish Americans equated England with the cause of democracy after centuries of British rule in Ireland, and London's severe repression of the 1916 Easter Rising in Dublin bolstered their case. Jewish Americans who had fled from violent discrimination in the Russian empire opposed aid to the czar's government. The sheer scale of the immigrant stream to the United States between 1900 and 1914 reinforced the need to avoid Europe's conflicts. Native-born white Americans were already concerned with preserving unity in their increasingly varied and urban society. Allowing in the hatreds from Europe's battlefields would further exacerbate the ethnic and class tensions that worried social reformers and many politicians, including President Wilson.

REFORM PRIORITIES AT HOME

While the war unfolded abroad, most Americans remained focused on issues at home. Americans traditionally considered powerful government the primary threat to individual liberty, but the rise of mammoth corporations at the start of the twentieth century altered that calculation. Competition was disappearing, particularly in critical sectors of the economy such as oil production and railroads. Laissez-faire policies, by which federal agencies encouraged economic expansion, were no longer adequate. Only government, argued Progressive reformers, could balance the new might of the largest companies. This meant modest regulation of some aspects of the marketplace. Wilson's first term also encouraged such democratic reforms as the ratification of the Seventeenth Amendment for the direct popular election of U.S. senators (1913), previously chosen by state legislatures. Until American entry into the Great War in 1917 turned the nation to a very different task, this period marked the climax of the first chapter of twentieth-century liberalism.

Three areas topped the Wilson administration's reform agenda: taxes, the money system, and monopolies. The Underwood-Simmons Tariff of 1913 cut duties—taxes—on imported goods by almost one-half, helping American consumers and promoting freer trade. The Sixteenth Amendment (1913) allowed a federal income tax, which the 1916 Revenue Act put into effect. This was a progressive tax, one that took a larger percentage of the income of the rich than of the poor. The legislation also levied higher taxes on corporate profits and created the first federal estate tax on inheritances. Though small, a tax on inheritances supported the principle of equality of opportunity. It implied that children of the wealthy should not receive an unlimited head start in life and that Americans growing up without an inheritance should not be handicapped by the large inequalities among past generations.

Congress moved to regulate money in another new way as well. The absence of a centrally managed money system had long contributed to the exaggerated boom-and-bust cycles in the

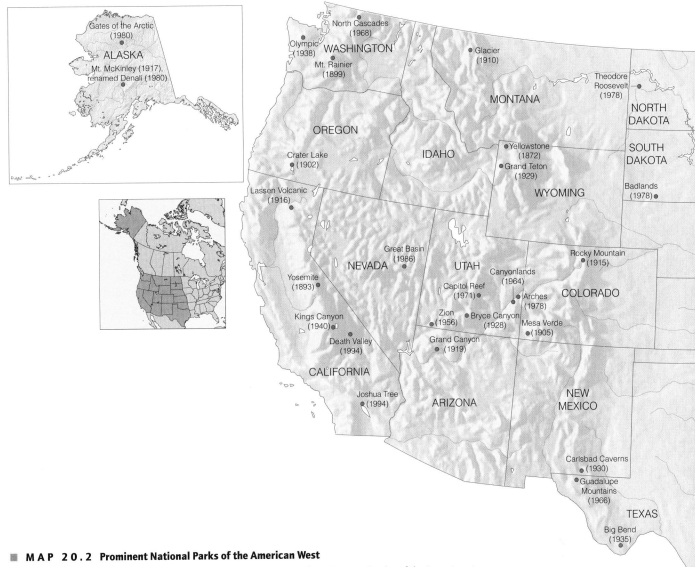

MAP 20.2 Prominent National Parks of the American West
The federal government owns much of the land in the American West. The U.S. Forest Service of the Department of Agriculture manages the forests that cover the region's mountains. The Bureau of Land Management (BLM) of the Department of the Interior oversees the more arid range lands at lower altitudes. The National Park Service cares for the parks established to protect and display some of the nation's most spectacular natural scenery.

American economy. The Federal Reserve Act of 1913 created a system of twelve Federal Reserve Banks to control the amount of currency in circulation, increasing it in deflationary times and decreasing it when inflation threatened. The system aimed to abolish economic depressions and prevent bank closures. It did not fully succeed, as the years after 1929 showed, but the Federal Reserve System did stabilize the American banking industry and helped position the dollar to become the dominant global currency.

No issue so dominated American politics between 1913 and 1915 as the tension between huge new corporations and the nation's antimonopoly tradition. The size and market share of companies such as U.S. Steel, American Tobacco, and Du Pont (chemicals) inhibited competition, just as Microsoft dominated computer software at the end of the twentieth century. Investigations by a congressional committee chaired by Arsene Pujo in 1913 revealed the concentration of financial power in the hands of J. P. Morgan and a few other New York bankers, dubbed the Money Trust. Congress created the Federal Trade Commission (1914) to investigate business practices that unfairly prevented competition. The Clayton Anti-Trust Act of 1914 supplemented the 1890 Sherman Anti-Trust Act by outlawing specific unfair business practices such as local price cutting and granting rebates to undermine competitors. The Clayton Act also delighted the AFL by declaring that unions should not be "construed to be illegal combinations in restraint of trade." Most federal judges remained unsympathetic to unions, but they could no longer wield the Sherman Act against striking workers rather than against the corporate trusts it had originally intended to target.

The early years after 1910 witnessed the rise of Progressive legislation to protect particular groups of citizens, especially women, children, and certain workers. States led the way, with half by 1913 passing workers' compensation laws to provide assistance to workers injured on the job and their families. Many states passed laws limiting or banning child labor. The Adamson Act (1916), providing for an eight-hour day for railroad workers, was the first case of the federal government regulating the hours of workers in the private sector.

Another kind of legislation focused on preserving natural landscapes. An increasingly urban, industrial society looked to its most beautiful rural places for solace. Local and state governments set aside parklands throughout the Progressive Era. Wilson followed in Theodore Roosevelt's conservationist footsteps by creating the National Park Service in 1916 to provide unified management of such new national treasures as Glacier National Park in Montana (1910), Rocky Mountain National Park in Colorado (1915), Lassen Volcanic National Park in California (1916), and Acadia National Park in Maine (1919).

THE GREAT MIGRATION

The Progressive Era of roughly 1900–1920 was anything but progressive from the viewpoint of many African Americans. White mob violence reached its apex in these years, with hundreds of lynchings and dozens of race riots. Most African Americans lived in the South, where segregation and discrimination trapped the majority in poverty. Many therefore

■ A migrant family from the South arriving in Chicago, c. 1916. Southerners of all colors, like Europeans, were drawn by the lure of better jobs to the industrial cities of the American Northeast and Midwest. With immigration from Europe slowed to a trickle by the onset of World War I, industry's demand for southern migrants increased sharply.

Historical Pictures/Stock Montage, Inc.

seized the unprecedented opportunity offered by the outbreak of the Great War. War-related orders created huge needs for workers in northern factories, and the war also closed the spigot of European immigration, drying up the standard source of new labor. Along with other cities, Chicago and Detroit became destinations for the **Great Migration** of more than half a million African Americans out of Dixie during the war years.

Encouraged by black newspapers such as the *Chicago Defender* and sometimes assisted by northern labor recruiters, black Southerners wanted to go "where a man is a man" regardless of his color. They still found plenty of discrimination in the urban North. But the large black communities of Philadelphia, Cleveland, and New York offered far greater independence than the rural South they left behind. Here "I don't have to humble to no one," one former Southerner wrote home. African Americans could vote, earn higher wages, send their children to better schools, and even sit where they wanted on streetcars. One woman newly arrived in Chicago was stunned the first time she boarded a trolley and saw black people sitting next to whites. "I just held my breath, for I thought any minute they would start something. Then I saw nobody notices it, and I just thought this is a real place for Negroes."

The Great Migration fit in a broader pattern of oppressed peoples seeking greater freedom and opportunity in the industrial workplaces of the American North. African Americans could not change their color and escape from discrimination, as could ethnic Europeans such as Irish, Italians, and Jews who struggled successfully against widespread prejudice to be identified as "white" (while still enduring elements of discrimination). But black Southerners moving to northern cities in pursuit of work and liberty acted much as European immigrants had, and they joined other newcomers—including Puerto Ricans—seeking urban work. The 1920 U.S. Census showed for the first time a majority of Americans living in towns and cities of at least 2,500 people.

MAP

African American
Population, 1910
and 1950

When war in Europe shut off most transatlantic immigration after 1914, it opened the door to newcomers who did not have to cross the submarine-infested ocean. Blacks who boarded trains for the North were joined by a similar number of white Southerners leaving rural poverty to look for jobs. A small stream of French Canadians found work in New England factories. A much larger stream of Mexicans and Mexican Americans flowed to jobs across the American Southwest and Midwest. Like African Americans, who had been leaving the South since the Civil War, people of Mexican descent had been moving across the American West for economic reasons since the mid-nineteenth century. World War I and the Mexican Revolution increased their numbers sharply, with the growing cities of Los Angeles, San Antonio, and El Paso remaining particular magnets for new immigrants. The number of Mexican Americans in Los Angeles soared from 6,000 in 1910 to nearly 100,000 in 1930.

LIMITS TO AMERICAN NEUTRALITY

Meanwhile, the fighting in Europe was not diminishing, and a steady undertow of interests and inclinations pulled against American neutrality. Most Americans who paid attention to events abroad favored the Allies over the Central Powers. The diversity of Americans' ethnic roots across Europe, Africa, Asia, and Latin America could not mask fundamental cultural and linguistic connections to England, the one-time "mother country." President Wilson deeply admired British political values and institutions, and most influential newspaper editors supported the British cause. Even Americans critical of the British Empire did not want to see the European continent under the autocratic rule of German Kaiser Wilhelm II.

A steady undertow of interests and inclinations pulled against American neutrality.

Concrete economic interests also tied the United States to the Allied side. During the three years of neutrality (1914–1917), American bankers lent 85 times as much to the Allied nations as to the Central Powers ($2.3 billion versus $27 million). Opponents

TABLE 20.1			
The Election of 1916			
Candidate	**Political Party**	**Popular Vote (%)**	**Electoral Vote**
Woodrow Wilson	Democratic	49.4	277
Charles E. Hughes	Republican	46.2	254
A. L. Benson	Socialist	3.2	–

of American entry into the war later pointed out that bankers and weapon makers had lobbied for joining the British cause, which fattened their wallets. But millions of other Americans also benefited from the nation's trade with Britain and France. Large corporations reaped the bulk of the profits, and agricultural and industrial workers earned decent wages in filling Allied war orders.

Certain powerful Americans, concentrated on the East Coast, tried from the start to prepare the country for entering the war. They emphasized that the U.S. military was much smaller than the forces of European states because of Americans' traditional aversion to large standing armies. Republicans such as Theodore Roosevelt and former Secretary of State Elihu Root led the war preparedness movement, which sought to pressure new immigrants into "100 percent Americanism" and to establish universal military training.

Debs, Critique of World War I

Progressives split over the war. More radical reformers opposed joining it as a matter of principle. "Let the capitalists do their own fighting and furnish their own corpses," socialist Eugene Debs wrote in 1914, "and there will never be another war on the face of the earth." Settlement house leader Jane Addams and black labor organizer A. Philip Randolph likewise opposed the war throughout, as did writer Randolph Bourne. They feared, presciently, that going to war would take the wind out of the sails of domestic reform.

Most Progressives followed President Wilson's leadership, opposing U.S. involvement in Europe at first but gradually shifting to support it. Roosevelt's return to mainstream Republicanism and his enthusiasm for war left Wilson the standard-bearer of Progressivism in the 1916 election. This allowed the president to squeak by conservative Republican nominee Charles Evans Hughes, winning a second term in the White House. "He kept us out of war," his supporters declared, but Wilson himself was less optimistic. He knew where German submarine warfare might lead: "Any little German lieutenant can put us into the war at any time by some calculated outrage."

The United States Goes to War

■ *How did fighting in World War I change the United States?*

Like Lyndon Johnson in 1964 regarding Vietnam, Wilson won reelection as a liberal reformer and a man of peace, only to go to war within six months. On April 2, 1917, Wilson asked Congress for a declaration of war against Germany "to make the world safe for democracy." Congress agreed by a large majority, and four days later the United States entered the Great War. The government limited antiwar criticism in an effort to ensure unity. Mobilization went slowly; it took almost a year before American soldiers in large numbers saw combat in the trenches of northern France. But troops of the Allied nations took heart from the knowledge that the Yanks were finally coming. American foodstuffs and munitions arrived more quickly, as did American naval ships protecting cargo vessels bound for England. The U.S. entry into the war ultimately provided the narrow margin of victory against the Central Powers.

THE LOGIC OF BELLIGERENCY

Wilson's insistence on the traditional rights of neutral nations to trade with belligerents clashed with German and British efforts to prevent trade destined for their enemy. The German use of the new submarines, or U-boats (from the German *Unterseeboote*), against

■ The body of a soldier lies caught in barbed wire in the "no man's land" between opposing trenches on the western front. Technological advances in weaponry helped make the fighting vastly more destructive in World War I than in previous wars. The sheer scale of the slaughter stunned combatants and observers, both in Europe and America, and helped turn many in the postwar generation to deep skepticism regarding the use of military force.

DOCUMENT

Wilson's War Message
to Congress

superior British surface forces pulled Americans into the war. Submarines were extremely vulnerable when not submerged. Before firing on a merchant or passenger ship that might be armed or carrying contraband (war materials), they refused to surface and warn civilian passengers—as required under international law—to evacuate on lifeboats. With Britain arming merchant ships and stowing munitions in the holds of passenger ships, U-boats were the key element in the German campaign to weaken the enemy. The British navy, in turn, seized American goods bound for Germany. But Britain's blockade of the German coastline and neutral ports nearby did not endanger civilians in the same way. "One deals with life; the other with property," Secretary of State Robert Lansing explained.

The deaths of civilians without warning on the high seas shocked and angered the American public, especially the sinking of the magnificent British ocean liner *Lusitania* in May 1915, which killed 128 U.S. citizens and a thousand others. However, some Americans believed Wilson to be less than neutral in negotiating with the British over their offenses while giving ultimatums to Germany. Lansing's predecessor as secretary of state, William Jennings Bryan, resigned in June 1915 to protest the president's manner of defending American trading rights. Bryan found both sides—stalemated and unable to gain victory in the trenches—reprehensible for trying to win by killing "noncombatant men, women, and children." Only their methods differed: Germany drowned innocent civilians; England starved them with its blockade. Hoping to keep the United States out of the war, the German government twice put its unrestricted submarine warfare on hold (the *Arabic* pledge of September 1915 and the *Sussex* pledge of May 1916). By January 1917, the British blockade had reduced German food rations per person to less than half the prewar level. Facing imminent starvation, Germany decided to take one last chance with unrestricted submarine warfare. The German government calculated that it could force a British and French surrender before enough American assistance arrived.

Preparing for war with the Americans, German Foreign Minister Arthur Zimmermann secretly offered German aid to the revolutionary Mexican government "to reconquer the lost

■ European demand for war-related goods brought the U.S. economy out of the deep recession of 1913–1914 and created hundreds of thousands of new jobs. U.S. entry into the war in April 1917 took several million men into the armed forces, opening better-paying opportunities in manufacturing to many women. Four workers at the Westinghouse Electric Company pause from their labors in 1918.

territory in Texas, New Mexico, and Arizona" if it joined the Central Powers. Mexico declined, but the Zimmermann telegram leaked to the press on March 1 and outraged Americans. The German threat seemed finally to have reached American soil. One last hindrance to joining the Allies disappeared with the revolution that same month in Russia, which replaced the monarchy with a social democratic government, one Wilson called "a fit partner for a league of honor." The president could now more genuinely call for a war to make the world "safe for democracy."

Still guarding American autonomy and wary of close identification with the French, British, and Russian empires, Wilson took the nation into war as an "Associated" power rather than a full-blown member of the Entente. The president believed that the United States, unique among the belligerents, sought only to defend principles rather than to acquire territory, assuring it of distinctive moral leadership at an eventual postwar peace conference. "We have no quarrel with the German people" but only with the "Prussian autocracy" whose U-boats were engaged in "a warfare against mankind," Wilson declared in calling Americans to a great crusade in Europe. "We desire no conquest, no dominion," but merely to be "one of the champions of the rights of mankind."

MOBILIZING THE HOME FRONT

Going to war entailed a complete reorientation of the American economy. For the U.S. Army and Navy to succeed abroad, mass production of war materials had to be centrally planned, and only the federal government could fulfill this role. Such an expansion of government regulation fit with the broader agenda of Progressive reform. Federal agencies could mediate some of the tensions between capital and labor as they focused on ensuring adequate food, clothing, and weapons for the troops at the front.

The Wilson administration created several new agencies to manage the war effort at home. The Selective Service Act established local boards to draft young men into the military. The U.S. Railroad Administration took control of the nation's primary transportation system to solve railroad tie-ups caused by heavy demands for war materials. The War Industries Board supervised all war-related production, allowing large manufacturers to coordinate their schedules without fear of antitrust action. The War Labor Board resolved disputes between workers and employers. The Committee on Public Information (CPI), run by Progressive journalist George Creel, who had served as director of publicity in Wilson's 1916 campaign, provided the government's version of information about the war. The CPI had the crucial task of inspiring and maintaining public support for Wilson's war policies.

The close cooperation between industry and government, combined with strong demand for American goods from the Allied governments, caused corporate earnings to soar. Cost-plus contracts guaranteed profits by eliminating competition and risk. "We are all making more money out of this war than the average human being ought to," one steel company official admitted privately. And some of the war gains were spread around, for a collaborative effort entailed keeping workers productive and content. Taking a position unprecedented in the U.S. government, the War Labor Board promoted an 8-hour workday and the right of workers to form unions. But even as the economy bustled, social unity proved elusive, especially when word of American casualties arrived from Europe.

ENSURING UNITY AT HOME

The deaths of U.S. soldiers and sailors made support for the war an emotional issue, and a pattern of repressing dissent took hold that outlasted the war itself. Everything German was particularly suspect. Several states banned teaching the German language (Nebraska briefly banned teaching any foreign language, even Latin). Sauerkraut became "liberty cabbage," frankfurters became hot dogs, and many German Americans anglicized their names. Temperance reformers cited German beer drinking in their successful campaign for a constitutional prohibition of alcohol production. Congress approved the controversial Eighteenth Amendment in December 1917 as a way to save grain for the war effort, and the states ratified it in 1919. Anti-German sentiment led to sometimes deadly violence against Americans of German descent. Congress passed sharply restrictive immigration legislation in 1917 as anti-German feeling fed broader prewar fears of new immigrants.

DOCUMENT

Buffington, "Friendly Words to the Foreign Born"

A wave of discontent among working Americans redoubled anxieties about national unity. The draft and reduced immigration thinned the ranks of labor as the war created a greater need for workers. For the first time in memory, laborers could choose between jobs, and corporations were dismayed by rising employee turnover rates. Workers worried about inflation, which doubled between 1914 and 1920. Seeking better wages and more control over the workplace, they joined unions and went out on 6,000 strikes during the year and a half in which the United States was in the war. Working-class women and men identified their own struggles with the war for democracy abroad by calling for the "de-Kaisering of industry" at home.

Industrialists saw the strikers differently. "All they seem to think of is money," one complained, mirroring what workers often said of employers. Anti-unionists tried to tar all of organized labor with the brush of disloyalty. The government passed the Espionage Act (1917) and Sedition Act (1918) to ban written and oral organizing against the war. Socialists who encouraged draft resistance, such as Eugene Debs and Wisconsin Congressman Victor Berger, went to prison. In *Schenck v. United States* (1919), the Supreme Court upheld restrictions on free speech in the case of a "clear and present danger" to the nation's

Political Cartoons and Wartime Dissent

Envisioning History

Once the United States joined the Allies in World War I, dissent against the war became associated for many Americans, including this cartoonist, with aiding the enemy: Germany. Here the antiwar Industrial Workers of the World (IWW) are depicted as allies of the German monarch, Kaiser Wilhelm—note the prominence of the "W." This is a particularly misleading and ironic portrayal because of the IWW's radical left-wing politics and fervent opposition to colonialism, capitalism, and monarchy, all features of the German state.

QUESTIONS

1. Regardless of their opposite ideologies, how much did the IWW's stance on the war help the German government?

2. In what situations today have governments tried to wound the reputations of dissidents by associating them with enemies of the nation?

LISTEN

The Speech That Sent Debs to Jail

security. The Justice Department worked closely with private "patriotic" organizations such as the National Security League, which helped spy on potential dissidents.

Hostility to unions mixed with fervent prowar sentiment to produce a forceful campaign against labor activists in the West. Along the Rocky Mountains from Montana to the Mexican border, striking copper miners under IWW leadership found federal, state, and local police forces as well as vigilantes lined up against them. Sheriff Harry Wheeler of Bisbee, Arizona, arrested more than a thousand strikers, many of them Mexican Americans suspected of sympathies with Pancho Villa. Wheeler, a former Rough Rider with Theodore Roosevelt in Cuba, locked the strikers into boxcars in the July heat of 1917 and towed them into the southern New Mexico desert before releasing them. Federal agents eviscerated the antiwar IWW by raiding its offices two months later and putting 166 of its leaders on trial. A visiting British coal-mining executive found "hostility to a quite unbelievable extent against organized labor."

Most African Americans agreed with W. E. B. Du Bois's call to "close our ranks shoulder to shoulder" with white fellow citizens in support of the war effort, although antiblack violence escalated. The arrival of 300,000 to 500,000 black Southerners in northern cities increased competition for jobs and housing, causing resentment among many whites. Employers contributed to tensions by recruiting African Americans as strikebreakers and pitting them against white workers. Whites rioted in East St. Louis on July 1, 1917, causing at least 47 fatalities, most of them black. Black soldiers from the North rebelled against the Jim Crow restrictions they found on southern military bases. On August 23, 1917, African American troops from Camp Logan near Houston intervened to protect a black woman being beaten by police on a downtown street. The resulting gunfire killed 16 whites and 4 African Americans. Swift Army court-martials resulted in executions of 19 of the black soldiers and life imprisonment of 63 others.

MAP 20.3 World War I in Europe and the Western Front, 1918

By the time U.S. troops arrived in force in northern France, the new Bolshevik (Communist) government of Russia had made peace with the Germans and withdrawn from the war. Germany now faced enemies only on one front—the western front—and moved all its troops there. In this dire situation for the French and British, American soldiers helped fill the gap in 1918.

JOINING THE WAR IN EUROPE

When the United States entered the war in Europe in 1917, crisis gripped the Allies. In the east, much of the war effort collapsed in the confusion of Russia's revolution against the czar. In the west, 49 divisions of the French army mutinied, refusing orders to make further suicidal advances. In the south, at Caporetto, Austro-Hungarian forces inflicted a disastrous defeat on the Italian army. It was not clear whether the Americans had joined soon enough to prevent Allied defeat.

No battle-ready American army waited at ports for immediate shipment to the trenches of northern France. U.S. commanders instead had to conscript and train nearly 5 million young men for an American Expeditionary Force (AEF) under General Pershing, and 16,000 young women volunteered for service overseas as nurses and Red Cross workers. U.S. troops participated in their first offensive operations in February 1918, although the veteran French and British lines had to stand largely on their own against the final German

■ Members of the 369th Infantry Regiment wear the Croix de Guerre (Cross of War) awarded to them for bravery by the French government. Like their white fellow soldiers, African American troops often fought bravely and with distinction on the fields of northern France. But they were segregated and given the hardest, most demeaning work by U.S. commanders, following the same pattern at home in the United States.

spring offensive. American soldiers later engaged in fierce combat at Belleau Wood, Château-Thierry, and St. Mihiel, ultimately losing 114,000 men. German General Erich Ludendorff attributed the sense of "looming defeat" among his troops to "the sheer number of Americans arriving daily at the front." As the only army growing stronger in 1918, the AEF contributed crucially to the fall offensive that convinced Germany to surrender on November 11.

Fighting with French and British allies gave many American troops an appreciation for Europeans that balanced the anti-immigrant sentiments common back home. White U.S. soldiers also bonded with each other across ethnic and religious lines while engaged in the supremely dangerous task of deadly combat. One young captain from Missouri, Harry Truman, returned from the war with a stronger appreciation for Europe that would help alter America's role in the world when he became president in 1945. Truman wrote home to his fiancée, Bess Wallace, from Nice on the south coast of France, "There is no blue like the Mediterranean blue." Almost 400,000 African American soldiers served with particular determination to prove their loyalty and courage, despite being segregated and given the hardest and least inspiring work. The French, delighted to have all who would help defend them, treated black GIs with a respect they had rarely known from whites in America. When acceptance led to growing pride among black troops abroad, U.S. commanders reacted with consternation. "It has gone to their heads," President Wilson worried.

THE RUSSIAN REVOLUTION AND THE WAR IN THE EAST

Events in Russia provoked the greatest long-term concerns. On April 8, 1917, just two days after the United States entered the war, Vladimir Lenin and 32 fellow **Bolshevik** refugees from czarism left their asylum in Zurich, Switzerland, on a train ride into history. They arrived in the Russian capital of St. Petersburg and in October seized control of the government, building a dictatorship of the Communist party in the name of the working class. The Bolsheviks opposed the Great War, condemning the battle for greater wealth and power as a demonstration of pure greed among rival capitalists. In the czar's archives, they found and published the secret treaties of the Entente for dividing up their prospective conquests after the war, both in Europe and in the colonies overseas. The defeat of the Ottoman Empire, for example, would open the Middle East—including what would become modern Iraq—to Western penetration. So while Wilson spoke of a war for democracy, the Bolsheviks asked Russians, "Are you willing to fight for this, that the English capitalists should rob Mesopotamia and Palestine?"

The answer, as Wilson feared, was no. In January 1918, the president gave the famous "Fourteen Points" speech to the U.S. Congress, outlining his aims of a postwar world built not on expansion and revenge but on national self-determination, open diplomacy, and freedom of commerce and travel, to be guaranteed by a new League of Nations. He hoped to dissuade the Bolsheviks from making a separate peace with Germany that would allow Germany to move all its troops to the western front. But Lenin, facing civil war at home, conceded huge swaths of the old czarist empire in eastern Europe to the Germans to gain peace with the Brest-Litovsk Treaty of March 3, 1918.

The competing visions of Wilson and Lenin for world order contained the roots of the Cold War that would dominate American life after 1945. Both leaders agreed that the old diplomacy of imperialist states competing for pieces of property around the globe would no longer work and that only the creation of democratic states would prevent further wars. But they understood democracy very differently. For Wilson, it meant self-governing nations with capitalist economies and republican political practices (at least in Europe and North America, and eventually elsewhere). For Lenin, it meant workers in every land overthrowing the owners of capital and setting up Soviet governments. Whereas Wilson viewed the world as a collection of nations, Lenin saw it as a battleground between two classes.

The Struggle to Win the Peace

■ *What kind of new world order did Wilson want, and to what extent did he achieve it?*

World War I killed more than 16 million people and wrought immeasurable physical, social, and psychological damage. Was it worth it? Citizens of the belligerent nations emerged from 1918 convinced that only a guarantee of a future free of war could redeem such suffering. Some put their hopes in the radical solution unfolding in Russia. Some in the Entente states believed that severe measures against Germany would ensure peace. Most looked to Woodrow Wilson in the winter and spring of 1919 as the world leader whose vision for a more peaceful, democratic postwar order was "all that had made the war tolerable to many of us," as one admirer put it. The president sailed for Europe in January to lead the conference that would shape the peace. Vast crowds greeted him enthusiastically as he toured England, Italy, and France.

PEACEMAKING AND THE VERSAILLES TREATY

War and revolution destroyed the four great empires of Russia, Germany, Austria-Hungary, and the Ottomans (based in modern Turkey). Meeting in Paris from January to June 1919, the "Big Three" of Wilson, French President Georges Clemenceau, and British

Changes in European boundaries after World War I

- Areas lost by Russian Empire
- Areas lost by Austro-Hungarian Empire
- Areas lost by German Empire
- Areas lost by Bulgaria

Names of the newly independent nations created at the Versailles Conference of 1919 are in bold

■ **MAP 20.4 Europe After World War I**

The outcome of World War I led to significant changes in the boundaries of Europe, particularly its eastern parts. Four great empires in the region—Russia, Germany, Austria-Hungary, and the Ottomans—collapsed. Negotiations at Versailles created a band of new nations, providing both self-determination and a bulwark against Russian communism.

Prime Minister David Lloyd George took on two major tasks to shape the postwar order. First, the three leaders redrew the map of eastern and central Europe and the Middle East to create nation-states out of the vanished empires. Second, they had to decide what to do about a defeated Germany. The possible spread of revolution gave the negotiations a particular urgency. Anticolonial revolts broke out in India and China, and pro-Soviet workers' councils seized power briefly in Hungary and southern Germany. "We are running a race with Bolshevism," Wilson warned, "and the world is on fire."

To put out the fire, the Big Three created a string of new nations running from Finland in the north to Yugoslavia in the south. Eastern Europeans were to be self-governing within

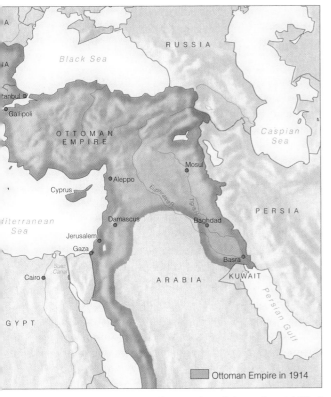
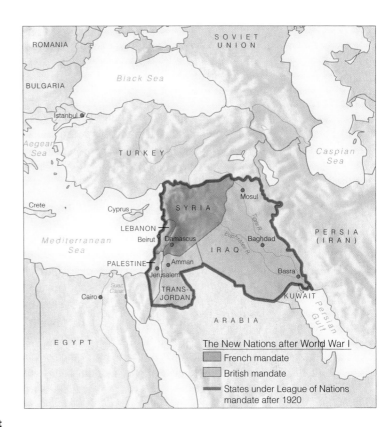

The New Nations after World War I
French mandate
British mandate
States under League of Nations mandate after 1920

Ottoman Empire in 1914

■ **MAP 20.5 The Creation of the Modern Middle East**

Allied with the British and French during World War I, Arab nationalists fought for independence from their Ottoman rulers. The heart of the old Ottoman Empire became the new nation of Turkey. The new League of Nations changed former Ottoman provinces into new nations: Syria and Lebanon under temporary mandate (protectorate) status with France, and Palestine, Transjordan, and Iraq under mandate status with Great Britain. Iraq itself was an entirely new creation, formed from the three former Ottoman provinces of Mosul (in the north), Baghdad (in the center), and Basra (in the south).

the new political boundaries. Ultimately, some of the new states—Czechoslovakia and especially Yugoslavia—lacked the sense of nationhood necessary for success and broke apart into smaller ethnic components in the 1990s. But a major purpose of these new nations for the negotiators in Paris was to establish an anticommunist belt keeping Russian communism out of Europe while satisfying their residents' desire for greater self-determination.

How far would "self-determination" go? Secretary of State Lansing worried that the president's language of democracy was "loaded with dynamite." The world's nonwhite majority wondered whether it applied to them. "Security of Life for Poles and Serbs—Why Not for Colored Nations?" asked one black newspaper in New York. A young nationalist from Vietnam named Ho Chi Minh tried but failed to get an audience with Wilson to ask for the Fourteen Points to apply to his French-ruled country; a generation later, Ho led the Vietnamese people's armed struggle against France and then the United States. The Big Three instead created the mandate system to provide for eventual self-determination for colonies after a period of tutelage under an established power. New states emerged out of the old Ottoman Empire: Syria and Lebanon under French control and Iraq, Palestine, and Transjordan under British rule. The Big Three also rejected Japan's proposal to include racial equality as a principle of the new **League of Nations.**

The German question predominated at the Paris conference. To create a long-term peaceful order in Europe, Wilson wanted lenient terms for Germany. But the French and British had lost much more in the war than the Americans, and they believed Germany must pay for that. French security seemed to depend on keeping its powerful

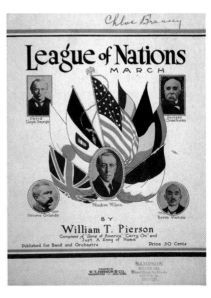

DOCUMENT

Henry Cabot Lodge's Objections to Treaty of Versailles

and aggressive neighbor down. The Versailles Treaty (named for the famous estate of King Louis XIV outside Paris, where it was signed) reflected compromises that gave each of the allies what it most wanted. To satisfy France and England, Germany had to admit guilt for causing the war and pay $33 billion in reparations, while losing much of its eastern territory to the new Polish and Czechoslovakian states. For Wilson, the League of Nations was the key: this new and unprecedented global organization would keep the peace by ensuring collective security for all nations. Disputes between nations would be mediated before they escalated to armed conflict, and potential aggressors would be deterred by the promise of collective action in defense of any threatened League member.

The absence of certain crucial players from the Paris negotiations undermined the resulting international order. The Soviets and the Germans did not participate. Wilson took in his entourage no representatives of the Republican party. This proved important, for Republicans had won the congressional elections two months earlier, giving them control of the process for ratifying any treaties. Most Republicans objected on principle to one key aspect of the Versailles Treaty: Article 10 of the League of Nations charter, guaranteeing ahead of time a collective response to defend any member's territory from attack. Treaty opponents were determined to preserve complete American autonomy, including freedom of action in Latin America. Henry Cabot Lodge Jr. of Massachusetts, the powerful Republican chair of the Senate Foreign Relations Committee, organized the two Senate votes rejecting American membership in the League. Hoping to stave off defeat for his idealistic plan, Wilson undertook a national speaking tour to promote the international organization. His strenuous effort failed to win American participation in the League, and it ultimately broke his fragile health. Wilson suffered a stroke on October 2, 1919, that left him incapacitated for the rest of his presidency.

WAGING COUNTERREVOLUTION ABROAD

Soon after Russia withdrew from the war, Britain, France, and the United States intervened in the civil war there between the Bolsheviks (the "Reds") and the various counterrevolutionary forces (the "Whites"). The initial military rationale in the summer of 1918 was to reopen the eastern front against Germany. The United States landed 7,000 troops in Vladivostock, on Russia's far Pacific coast, to help rescue a large group of former Czech prisoners of war from the Austro-Hungarian army who now wanted to join the Allied side, as well as to deter Japanese expansion into Siberia. In conjunction with the British, 5,000 U.S. soldiers went ashore at Archangel in northern Russia to prevent Allied supplies from falling into German hands. They quickly became involved in fighting the Red Army. The Wilson administration meanwhile funneled money and military intelligence to leaders of the White forces.

The Bolsheviks rejected certain values cherished by most Americans: the sanctity of private property and contracts, political liberty, and religious freedom. They liberalized divorce laws and legalized abortion, challenging conservative American attitudes about the relationships between women and men. And they established the Comintern in 1919 to promote similar revolutions around the world. Allied intervention in the Russian civil war failed to overthrow Lenin's government, however, and American troops pulled out in 1920. They left behind a powerful legacy of anti-American sentiment in Russia, exacerbated by Washington's refusal for the next thirteen years to recognize the Soviet government.

Anticommunists used the metaphor of infection to describe Bolshevism. The Kaiser, they said, had allowed Lenin to pass through

ТОВ. Ленин ОЧИЩАЕТ землю от нечисти.

■ "Comrade Lenin Sweeps the Globe Clean." This Bolshevik (Communist) drawing shows Vladimir I. Lenin (1870–1924), the leader of the Russian Revolution and founder of the world's first communist government, ridding the world of capitalists and monarchs. But Lenin also sought western trade and investment, especially from the United States, as a stimulus to reconstructing the devastated postwar economy of the new Union of Soviet Socialist Republics (USSR).

From Art of the October Revolution, Leningrad, Aurora Art Publishers, 1979

Germany on a "sealed train," lest the bacillus of revolution leak out and spread through the German population. This image had unusual power in 1918–1919 because of the spread of one of the twentieth century's worst killers. The "Spanish influenza" (named for one of its early victims, the king of Spain) hit the United States much harder than the Great War had, killing six times as many people (675,000). In an era before effective vaccines and drugs, little could be done for the 20 million stricken Americans besides comforting them, so nurses were in much greater demand than doctors.

Warning of Influenza
Epidemic, 1918

The wave of revolutionary upheaval that had begun in Mexico in 1910 and washed over Russia in 1917 continued to challenge imperial authorities around the globe. During World War I and the postwar negotiations at Versailles, Indians protested British rule of their land, Arab states rebelled against their Ottoman rulers, and Chinese students demonstrated against Japanese control of the Shantung peninsula. Nor was Western Europe immune to the forces of revolution. Americans of Irish descent cheered for the Irish Republican forces whose guerrilla warfare from 1919 to 1921 helped persuade Great Britain finally to grant independence to the Catholic majority of the island. Irish Americans also contributed money to the Irish Republican effort. Eamon de Valera, the leading political figure in the Irish struggle for independence, had been born in the United States. De Valera was imprisoned for his part in the unsuccessful Easter Rising of 1916, but after he escaped (with a key smuggled to him inside a cake), he spent most of 1919–1920 in America raising political support and $5 million for the Irish cause. Enthusiastic crowds greeted him from Boston to San Francisco. In 1922, the Irish Free State (later the Republic of Ireland) became Europe's newest independent nation, although the northern six counties remained under British rule.

THE RED AND BLACK SCARES AT HOME

In the United States, industrial unrest provoked fears of a Soviet-style revolution. Four million American workers, one out of every five, went out on strike in 1919—the highest proportion of the workforce ever. They sought improved wages and working conditions as well as recognition of the right to collective bargaining. In Seattle, a walkout by shipyard workers mushroomed into a general strike that shut down most of the city for a week. In Pittsburgh, the AFL led a bitter strike against U.S. Steel in pursuit of union recognition. The United Mine Workers led walkouts by hundreds of thousands of coal miners, which evolved into open warfare between miners and coal companies in West Virginia over the next two years. In Boston, three-quarters of the police force went on strike to protest wages lower than those of common laborers. Between April and June, anarchists mailed or delivered bombs to thirty-six prominent public figures, including Attorney General A. Mitchell Palmer in Washington. All were defused except two, one wounding the wife and maid of a U.S. senator from Georgia, the other destroying the front of Palmer's house and dismembering its anarchist deliverer.

Whereas many Americans sympathized with struggles for unionization, others viewed them as dangerous to private property and social order. They associated strikes with radical immigrants and anarchists and considered them

■ The Seattle General Strike Committee took on the responsibility of keeping essential services running in the city. Here its members issue groceries to union families, in January 1919. The cooperation necessary among organized workers to keep a strike going offered a different model of community interaction than did the individualism often touted by wealthier Americans.

"un-American." The **Red Scare** of 1919 associated reform and social justice of any kind with subversion. To break strikes, employers hired private armies from "detective" agencies such as the Pinkertons and the Baldwin-Felts, often staffed by World War I veterans. Private organizations promoting "100 percent Americanism," such as the Ku Klux Klan and the new American Legion, monitored and harassed potential subversives and the foreign born. Attorney General Palmer directed the deportation to Russia of 249 foreign-born radicals in December 1919, including anarchist and feminist Emma Goldman. "Palmer raids" led to the arrest of thousands more within a month. U.S. Army troops and state militias brought the ultimate force to bear against union organizers, most notably at the Battle of Blair Mountain on August 31, 1921, against several thousand striking West Virginia miners.

Violence against workers extended to African Americans after World War I. An upsurge in lynching included at least ten black veterans still in uniform and was not limited to the South. In Nebraska, white residents of Omaha butchered William Brown with such frenzy that thousands of federal troops had to be called in to restore calm. White mobs burned entire black communities to the ground, including Tulsa's Greenwood neighborhood in 1921 and the all-black town of Rosewood, Florida, in 1923. The Red Scare and the "Black Scare" merged in Phillips County, Arkansas, where black sharecroppers, many of them veterans, formed a union in 1919 to pursue equitable crop settlements from landlords. Fearing insurrection, local white leaders used 2,500 federal troops and white vigilantes to massacre more than 200 sharecroppers. But any inclination toward deference in the face of brutality was gone, and African Americans fought back fiercely against white marauders in deadly riots in Washington and Chicago in the summer of 1919. One black woman recalled that when she heard "our men had stood like men" in Washington, she cried for joy: "Oh, I thank God, thank God!"

Where was the president during this turmoil? Incapacitated by his stroke, Wilson lay resting in his bed in Washington, the administration managed largely by his wife, Edith, and his secretary, Joseph Tumulty. In any case, Wilson's segregationist policies suggested that he would have been unlikely to provide effective leadership in bridging the nation's racial divides. The only Republican of similar stature, Theodore Roosevelt, had died a few months earlier. "There is no leadership worthy of the name," a veteran reporter lamented. Wilson's breakdown came in the middle of the 1919 baseball World Series, which the heavily favored but poorly paid Chicago White Sox intentionally lost to the Cincinnati Reds, in an arrangement with gamblers. Eight "Black Sox" were banned from the sport. With its president out of action and its national pastime corrupted, the nation seemed adrift as the lights began to dim on the Progressive Era.

Conclusion

Within the United States, how much success could a varied generation of Progressive reformers claim by 1920? Women had won the vote with the Nineteenth Amendment, in an expansion of democracy second only to the combination of the Emancipation Proclamation of 1863 and the Thirteenth Amendment, outlawing slavery. African Americans who moved to the North usually could vote as well, unlike those who stayed in Dixie. On either side of the Mason-Dixon line, however, daily life for Americans of darker hue entailed picking one's way through a maze of discrimination. Most union campaigns stalled by 1920, beaten back by the physical force and cleverness of corporate employers and their government sympathizers. And when the Red Scare dissipated, most Americans did not return to the reform spirit of

CHRONOLOGY: 1912–1920

1912	Woodrow Wilson elected president.
1913	Federal Reserve Act.
1914	U.S. troops block German arms shipment to Mexico.
	World War I breaks out in Europe.
1915	U.S. marines occupy Haiti.
	Germans sink *Lusitania*.
	Film *Birth of a Nation* released.
1916	Jeannette Rankin elected first female member of Congress.
	U.S. marines occupy Dominican Republic.
	Woodrow Wilson reelected president.
1917	United States enters World War I.
	Russian Revolution.
	Residents of Puerto Rico granted U.S. citizenship.
1918	Spanish influenza epidemic kills 20 million worldwide.
	Sedition Act.
	Wilson's "Fourteen Points" speech to Congress.
1919	Versailles Treaty ends World War I.
	U.S. Senate rejects League of Nations.
	Eighteenth Amendment (prohibition)ratified.
1920	Nineteenth Amendment (women's suffrage) ratified.

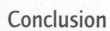

Progressivism. Many turned away from politics. Voter turnout in 1920 dipped below 50 percent for the first time in a century. Those who did vote that year gave the Republican party a sweeping victory. Promising "not revolution, but restoration," Ohio Senator Warren G. Harding took the White House. His speeches may have been, as one rival said, "an army of pompous phrases moving over the landscape in search of an idea," but most of the nation sought calm after the upheavals of the previous decade.

American contributions to democracy abroad were similarly ambivalent. U.S. troops provided a crucial push to victory for the Allies in World War I against the autocratic government of Germany. Whereas eastern Europeans named streets in their newly independent nations for President Wilson, few Latin Americans believed that U.S. invasions of Caribbean and Central American countries promoted self-government. Russians admired much about American society and the U.S. economy while resenting American troops in their land. Above all hung the problem of Germany, still the most powerful single nation in Europe. The Versailles Treaty imposed harsh terms and embittered a generation of German people. "If I were a German, I think I should not sign it," Wilson admitted privately. The Weimar Republic that replaced the abdicated German kaiser lasted through the 1920s. But the storms of the Great Depression swamped Germany's republican experiment and gave rise to Adolf Hitler.

For Review

1. How did Americans' own colonial and revolutionary past affect their responses to the Mexican Revolution and the Russian Revolution of 1917?

2. Why did the United States stay out of World War I for three years?

3. How did American neutrality fit with previous U.S. policies toward Europe and its conflicts?

4. Which were the most important Progressive reforms of the 1910s and why?

5. How true did Wilson's description of World War I as a war "to make the world safe for democracy" turn out to be?

6. How did the Wilson administration respond to the 1917 Bolshevik (Communist) Revolution in Russia?

7. How did workers benefit from World War I? How did the war affect African Americans?

Created Equal Online

For more *Created Equal* resources, including suggestions on sites to visit and books to read, go to **MyHistoryLab.com.**

Chapter 21

All That Jazz: The 1920s

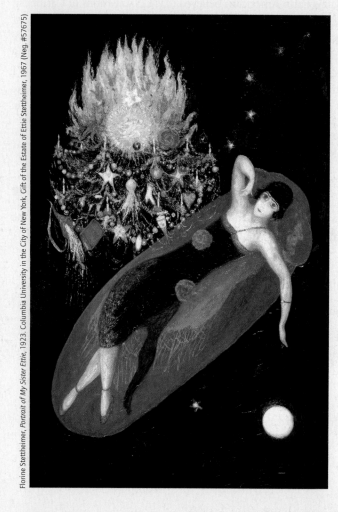

Florine Stettheimer, *Portrait of My Sister Ettie*, 1923. Columbia University in the City of New York, Gift of the Estate of Ettie Stettheimer, 1967 (Neg. #57675)

■ Florine Stettheimer's *Portrait of My Sister Ettie* (1923) conveys the glamour and sensuality of "flappers" like Marsha Linganfield.

In the Superior Court of Los Angeles in 1920, Lorimer Linganfield, a respectable barber, filed for divorce. Although his wife, Marsha, held him in "high regard and esteem as her husband," there were "evidences of indiscretion" in her conduct. She wore a new bathing suit, "designed especially for the purpose of exhibiting to the public the shape and form of her body." To his further humiliation, she was "beset with a desire to sing and dance at cafes and restaurants for the entertainment of the public." When Lorimer complained about her "appetite for beer and whisky" and extravagant tastes for luxury, she replied that he was "not the only pebble on the beach, she had a millionaire 'guy' who would buy her all the clothes, automobiles, diamonds and booze that she wanted." The ultimate insult was her refusal to have sexual intercourse, claiming that she did not want any "dirty little brats around her." The judge was sympathetic. Lorimer Linganfield won his suit—and Marsha won her freedom.

The Linganfields' difficulties represent a larger struggle as Americans shifted from the **producer economy** of the nineteenth century, complete with clearly defined gender roles and sexual mores, to the **consumer economy** of the twentieth century, with its new amusements, changing sexual behavior, and flamboyant "new women." Marsha Linganfield was a **flapper,** one of the young women of the 1910s and 1920s who broke from time-honored conventions. With short, "bobbed" hair, knee-length dresses, and boyish styles unencumbered by layers of petticoats, flappers flirted, petted, and danced "wild" dances like the Charleston, an African American dance brought north from South Carolina **juke joints.** Flappers blurred the line between "good girls" and "bad girls" that had previously defined proper female behavior.

The concerns of the Linganfields also reflect new middle-class preoccupations with private life and leisure as the political activism of the Progressives waned. Conservative politics at the national level prevailed throughout the decade. Disenchantment after World War I prompted national leaders to promote a foreign policy based on economic ties and trade, rather than military entanglements. Public policies of the era favored big business, as citizens engaged in moral revolutions rather than political ones. Anti-immigrant sentiment found expression in immigration restriction laws, which cut the flow of immigrants to a mere trickle. Prohibition also targeted immigrants and ethnic minorities by outlawing the bars and taverns that had served as sites of local political gatherings.

New forms of popular entertainment that developed in the 1920s, especially Hollywood movies and jazz music, became defining features of the nation itself. At a time when white, Anglo-Saxon, Protestant (WASP) men had control of nearly all government and business institutions, Jewish moviemakers and African American musicians were creating the culture that would soon represent the nation. As Congress closed off nearly all European and Asian immigration, Jewish immigrants built Hollywood into the most American of all industries, and as Jim Crow segregation continued, African Americans created the music that gave the 1920s its identity as "the Jazz Age."

The great heroes of the 1920s were celebrities admired for their individual achievements in sports and adventure. In 1927, the same year that baseball's Babe Ruth hit a record sixty home runs, Charles Lindbergh flew his small airplane, *The Spirit of St. Louis*, nonstop from New York to Paris in thirty-three and one-half hours, a feat that electrified the world and made him an instant hero. Professional sports came of age in the 1920s, giving rise to star athletes such as Babe Ruth, football's Red Grange, and boxing's Jack Dempsey. It was also a decade of tremendous visibility in women's sports, with such stars as tennis sensation Helen Wills and swimmer Sybil Bauer. In 1926, nineteen-year-old Olympic gold medalist Gertrude Ederle became the first woman to swim the English Channel. She broke the world record with her time of fourteen hours and thirty-one minutes, two hours faster than the times of the six men who had preceded her. On her return to the United States, 2 million cheering fans lined the streets of New York City to welcome her home. The nation idolized this new generation of heroes, who dominated headlines and drew admiring crowds wherever they went.

Often characterized as the "roaring twenties" of giddy prosperity and reckless good times, the era was noted for its youth culture, urban amusements, and consumer spending. By the end of the decade, almost half of all households owned a car or a radio; almost a third owned a washing machine or a vacuum cleaner. The purchasing power of wages rose steadily.

But these were also years of widespread poverty, especially in rural areas and urban ghettos. Many Americans were unable to afford the new consumer goods that were being mass produced. The expansion of consumer credit weakened the traditions of saving and frugality, while the disparity between rich and poor left the country vulnerable to the downturn of the economy. For those with money to invest, Wall Street beckoned. The stock market rose to perilous heights, only to collapse at the end of the decade.

The Decline of Progressive Reform and the Business of Politics

■ *What major developments signaled the end of the Progressive Era?*

Reformers who had championed the causes of the marginalized and disadvantaged lost influence in the 1920s, and the voices of workers, sharecroppers, and other poor people were muffled. After achieving the vote, the women's rights movement splintered as younger women sought new freedoms not through politics but through a social and sexual revolution. Widespread hostility toward immigrants and various ethnic groups was at the root of the outlawing of liquor, new laws restricting immigration, and the rise of the Ku Klux Klan. But Progressive political impulses did not entirely disappear, especially among African Americans, who continued to mobilize and organize for civil rights.

While most Americans turned their attention toward private life, politicians in Washington turned their attention toward business. Despite its many critics, business reigned with the support of national political leaders. After a brief recession following World War I, the economy grew steadily during the 1920s. The gross national product (GNP) increased 5.5 percent per year, from $149 billion in 1922 to $227 billion in 1929. Official unemployment remained below 5 percent throughout the decade, and real wages rose 15 percent. These trends fueled the popularity of the conservative, business-friendly presidents of the 1920s. Economic interests also drove foreign policy during the decade. After World War I, with much of Europe in shambles, the United States made loans to foreign countries, becoming the world's leading creditor nation. International markets opened up for American-made products, leading to a tremendous expansion in foreign trade. No wonder President Calvin Coolidge declared with pride in 1924, "The business of America is business."

> *While most Americans turned their attention toward private life, politicians in Washington turned their attention toward business.*

WOMEN'S RIGHTS AFTER THE STRUGGLE FOR SUFFRAGE

After the 1920 ratification of the Nineteenth Amendment giving women the right to vote, women's rights activism, like the rest of the Progressive reform movement, began to fragment. In 1923, the more radical wing of the suffrage movement, the National Women's Party (NWP), launched a campaign for the Equal Rights Amendment (ERA). If successful, this controversial proposal would have added these words to the Constitution: "Equality of rights under the law shall not be denied or abridged by the United States or by any state on account of sex."

The debate over the ERA in the 1920s reflected the fundamental question that would permeate women's rights activism throughout the rest of the twentieth century. On one side were those who believed that women were fundamentally the same as men and deserved equal rights; on the other side were those who argued that women were different and deserved special privileges and protections. Many women's rights activists opposed the ERA because it would undercut efforts to gain special legislative protections for women based on their presumed physical weakness and their potential for childbearing, such as maximum hours, regulations against night work, and limitations on the weight they could lift. These women disapproved of the goals and tactics of the NWP and formed their own nonpartisan organization, the League of Women Voters, which promoted a less radical agenda of social and political reform.

Despite the failure of the ERA, women did make some legislative gains in the 1920s. In 1921, Congress passed the Sheppard-Towner Act, which provided for public health nurses to educate mothers in prenatal and infant health care to reduce infant mortality. Physicians opposed the legislation because they did not want nurses providing medical care even though the nurses offered only preventive health care and advice. Doctors also worried that government-sponsored programs would compete with their private practices. Nevertheless, Sheppard-Towner remained in force until the end of the decade, when its budget was cut—a casualty of the conservative temperament in Congress that saw such forms of government support as socialistic.

> *As job opportunities for women increased, more wives had the means to abandon unhappy marriages.*

In the larger political arena, women continued to expand their influence by voting as well as by seeking elective office. But they often faced intense public scrutiny for entering the political fray. In 1922, for example, Adelina Otero Warren ran as a Republican candidate for the U.S. House of Representatives, the first New Mexican woman and the first Hispanic woman to run for national office. During the campaign, a cousin publicly revealed that Warren had lied about her marital status, claiming to be widowed when she was really divorced. That revelation dashed her political ambitions. But neither her divorce nor her attempt to pass as a widow was unusual at a time when marital breakdown still carried a heavy stigma, especially for women. The divorce rate doubled between 1900 and 1920 and continued to rise throughout the 1920s, in part the result of women's increasing independence. As job opportunities for women increased, more wives had the means to abandon unhappy marriages.

PROHIBITION: THE EXPERIMENT THAT FAILED

In 1920, the same year that women achieved the vote, female temperance crusaders also achieved success with the passage of the Eighteenth Amendment, which prohibited the manufacture and sale of alcohol. Several diverse interests came together to promote the ban on liquor. Leaders of the Anti-Saloon League and the Women's Christian Temperance Union had argued since the late nineteenth century that women and children suffered when men spent their paychecks at the saloon and returned home drunk and violent. Carrie Nation joined the temperance movement after her first marriage to an abusive drunkard. Nearly six feet tall and weighing 175 pounds, the imposing activist was arrested thirty times for smashing saloons with her trademark hatchet. World War I prompted others to support a ban on the manufacture of liquor to save grain for the war effort. Anti-immigrant "drys" had political motives for promoting Prohibition. They hoped to undercut the power bases of immigrant and ethnic politicians who used local saloons to forge their constituencies and **political machines.** The "wets" included alienated intellectuals, Jazz Age rebels, and many city dwellers whose social lives revolved around neighborhood pubs, especially in Irish and German communities.

The 1919 Volstead Act established a Prohibition Bureau within the Treasury Department. Federal agents had responsibility for enforcing the law, but their numbers were inadequate. In order to be effective, federal agents had to work closely with local law enforcement officials, but in some urban areas, local officials refused to cooperate. For example, New York repealed its Prohibition enforcement law in 1923, leaving small numbers of federal agents with the daunting task of shutting down the **speakeasies,** illegal clubs where liquor was sold. In sporadic raids, the beleaguered agents closed down some of the speakeasies, only to have them pop up again in new locations. Americans who wanted to drink liquor found many ways to acquire it. Illegal speakeasies abounded where customers could buy drinks delivered by rumrunners who smuggled in liquor from Canada, Mexico, and the West Indies. Many people concocted their own "bathtub gin" or "moonshine whiskey," homemade brews using readily available ingredients and household equipment.

LISTEN

"Prohibition is a Failure"

Prohibition was intended to cure society's ills. Instead, it provided vast opportunities for crime and profit, both among criminals and law enforcement agents. Without the profits from liquor, many nightclubs and restaurants went out of business, opening the way for gangsters and petty criminals to cater to the nightlife crowd. Organized crime received a major boost in the scramble to profit from illegal liquor. By 1929, Chicago mob king Al Capone controlled a massive network of speakeasies that raked in $60 million annually. Violence also increased. Chicago witnessed 550 gangland killings in the 1920s, with few arrests or convictions.

Prohibition also led to corruption. Authorities in St. Paul, Minnesota, for example, struck a bargain with gangsters who smuggled in liquor from Canada through the wilderness in northern Minnesota. After bribing the local police, the smugglers hid their stash in St. Paul's chalk caves along the banks of the Mississippi until they were able to transport it down the river.

Prohibition failed to live up to its promise. The first year after the passage of the amendment, alcohol consumption declined by two-thirds. But by 1929, the consumption of alcohol had climbed back up to 70 percent of its pre-Prohibition level. Expenditures for alcoholic beverages actually increased by 50 percent during the Prohibition era, no doubt in part because of higher black-market prices. In 1933, Congress repealed Prohibition.

REACTIONARY IMPULSES

The Red Scare after World War I (see Chapter 20) targeted ethnic minorities and inaugurated a decade of hostility to political radicals and foreigners. Shoemaker Nicola Sacco and fish peddler Bartolomeo Vanzetti were both: Italian immigrants and self-proclaimed anarchists. In May 1920, the paymaster and guard of a South Braintree, Massachusetts, shoe company was robbed and murdered, and Sacco and Vanzetti were arrested and charged with the crime. Sacco testified that he was in Boston at the time, applying for a passport, and his alibi was corroborated. Both men proclaimed their innocence and insisted that they were on trial for their political beliefs rather than the crime itself. Their Italian accents and advocacy of anarchism in the courtroom did not help their case with many Americans suspicious of foreign radicals, including the judge presiding at their trial. Despite a weak case against them, Sacco and Vanzetti were convicted of first-degree murder and sentenced to death.

Lawyers for the anarchists appealed the verdict several times to no avail. The convictions sparked outrage among Italian Americans, political radicals, labor activists, and liberal intellectuals who believed the two men were falsely

Bettmann/CORBIS

■ Speakeasy hostess Mary Louise Guinan appears unrepentant as she is arrested for selling alcohol during the Prohibition era. Law enforcement was futile because speakeasies that were raided and closed simply reopened in new locations.

Bettmann/CORBIS

■ Nicola Sacco and Bartolomeo Vanzetti, Italian self-proclaimed anarchists, were accused of murder in May 1920. The men and their supporters claimed they were on trial not for the crime but for their political beliefs and their immigrant status. After all appeals failed, the two were executed in 1927.

convicted. The case soon generated mass demonstrations, appeals for clemency, and petitions from around the world. In response, the governor of Massachusetts appointed a commission to review the case, but the commission concluded that there were no grounds for a new trial. Finally, on August 23, 1927, Sacco and Vanzetti were executed by electric chair at Charlestown State Prison.

The case of Sacco and Vanzetti underscored the anti-immigrant sentiment that prevailed in the 1920s. Although efforts to curtail immigration since the late nineteenth century had resulted in numerous federal laws, none were as harsh as those passed in the 1920s, which cut the flow of immigrants down to a tiny trickle. In 1921, Congress set temporary quotas that limited the number of European immigrants allowed into the United States. The number permitted to enter was set as a percentage of immigrants from each country who had lived in the United States in 1910. In that year, large numbers of immigrants from southern and eastern European countries lived in the United States, so the quota still allowed newcomers from those countries to enter. Then, in 1924, Congress passed the National Origins Act, also knows as the Johnson-Reid Act, imposing a limit of 165,000 immigrants from countries outside the Western Hemisphere and pushing back the quota basis to 1890, a time when British, German, and Scandinavian immigrants dominated the foreign-born population. The Johnson-Reid Act limited entry every year to 2 percent of the total number of immigrants from each country who were present in 1890. This measure effectively barred Jews, Slavs, Greeks, Italians, and Poles because their numbers were so small in 1890. In addition, the 1924 law reaffirmed the exclusion of Chinese immigrants and added Japanese and other Asians to the list, effectively closing the door to all migrants from Asia.

Agricultural interests in California and Texas lobbied hard to keep the door open to Mexicans because of the low-wage labor they provided. In the aftermath of the Mexican Revolution, many Mexicans hoped to find stability and jobs in the United States. Between 1910 and 1930, more than 1 million Mexicans, nearly one-tenth of Mexico's population, migrated to the United States, where they found work in the farms, railroads, and mines. Recruiters often stood along the border, waiting to sign up laborers. In 1930,

The Impact of Immigration Restriction

The Wider World

In the period before U.S. immigration restriction laws were passed in the 1920s, most immigrants to the United States were Jews and Roman Catholics from Russia and southern and eastern Europe. After immigration restriction, most immigrants came from western Europe and Canada and were more likely to be Anglo-Saxon Protestants. The global impact of these U.S. laws was significant. Before the 1920s, the United States had been one among many destination countries for immigrants. After these laws came into effect, many people who left their native countries went to countries other than the United States, altering the demographic and cultural mix of other nations.

QUESTIONS

1. Which countries of origin disappeared from the graph after 1921, indicating that their numbers of immigrants were too small to be included?

2. Which countries remained in relatively the same proportion after immigration restriction, even though their numbers were reduced?

3. What do the data in this graph suggest about the motives that prompted the 1920s immigration laws?

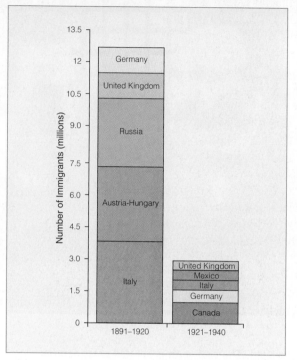

■ **Number of Immigrants and Countries of Origin, 1891–1920 and 1921–1940**

Mexican agricultural workers picked more than 80 percent of the perishable crops produced in the Southwest.

In spite of their many economic contributions, Mexicans, along with other racial minorities, faced harsh discrimination, especially from the Ku Klux Klan (KKK), which became the most powerful white supremacy group in the nation. The Klan revival remained relatively small in the North until 1920, when its leaders mounted a national membership drive. Klan membership included laborers, businesspeople, physicians, judges, social workers, and women who felt that their homogeneous small-town Protestant culture was threatened by the evils of modern life, brought on by the presence and influence of morally suspect outsiders.

The Klan used vigilante violence as well as political mobilizations not only to attack African Americans, their primary targets in the South following the Civil War, but also immigrants, Mexicans, Jews, Catholics, communists, feminists, and other radicals, as well as divorced or allegedly promiscuous women. Growing to 3 million members by the early 1920s, the Klan wielded considerable power, especially in Texas, Oklahoma, Oregon, and Indiana. In addition to vigilante violence, Klan members held elaborate rallies and parades, burned crosses to intimidate and threaten their foes, and endorsed political candidates. Klan efforts in Oregon persuaded the state's lawmakers to pass a compulsory public schooling bill in 1922 that would have closed private and parochial schools, but the U.S. Supreme Court overturned the law. The Klan-controlled legislature in Oklahoma impeached and removed an anti-Klan governor. The power of the Klan persisted through the twentieth century. As late as the 1990s, the Klan still held considerable influence in some localities, running candidates for office, holding rallies and parades, and seeking legitimacy through civic volunteer projects.

MARCUS GARVEY AND BLACK NATIONALISM

In the midst of a decade of reactionary policies toward outsiders and political activists, African Americans continued their struggle. Jamaican-born black nationalist Marcus Garvey moved to New York City's Harlem in 1916 and opened a branch of his Universal Negro Improvement Association (UNIA). Garvey urged black people to establish their own nation-state in Africa: "Africa was peopled with a race of cultured black men, who were masters in art, science, and literature. . . . Africa shall be for the black peoples of the world." The UNIA staged colorful parades, which Garvey led in military uniform. His followers proudly wore the UNIA uniform to express their support for the movement and joined the parades in large numbers. Garvey published a journal, the *Negro World,* and encouraged the establishment of black-owned businesses. By the 1920s, the UNIA had nearly 1 million followers and called for political justice and labor rights for black Americans.

In keeping with his belief in black-owned businesses, Garvey established the Black Star Line and encouraged his followers to invest in the shipping company. Nearly 40,000 African Americans invested three-quarters of a million dollars to purchase shares of Black Star stock. But the business ran into problems. Managers purchased ships that needed extensive and costly repairs, and the company ran up huge debts. In 1922, Garvey was arrested and charged with mail fraud for allegedly advertising and selling stock for a ship that did not exist. Although the government lacked any concrete evidence to prove the case against him, Garvey was convicted and sentenced to five years in prison.

Garvey kept up his political activities from prison, sending a message to his followers: "My work is just begun. Be assured that I planted well the seed of Negro or black nationalism which cannot be destroyed even by the foul play that has been meted out to me." Garvey was released after two years and deported to Jamaica as an undesirable alien. Nevertheless, the momentum he sparked continued. The black publication *The Spokesman* declared, "Garvey made thousands think, who had never thought before. Thousands who merely dreamed dreams, now see visions."

Hulton Archive/Getty Images

■ Marcus Garvey, founder of the Universal Negro Improvement Association (UNIA), c. 1920. Born in Jamaica, the African American nationalist leader encouraged black people to move to Africa and establish their own nation.

WARREN G. HARDING: THE POLITICS OF SCANDAL

With the exception of the continuing struggle of African Americans, political activism diminished as the spirit of reform declined. Presidential politics reflected the turn toward private concerns and political conservatism. Warren G. Harding, a former newspaper editor and U.S. senator from Ohio, won the 1920 presidential election by the biggest landslide since 1820. Harding established a conservative agenda that would last throughout the decade. He supported immigration restriction, opposed labor unions, and favored tariff protection, which placed a tax on goods entering the United States from abroad. In the wake of World War I, Harding distanced himself from Woodrow Wilson's peace settlement but promoted international treaties. In 1921 and 1922, his secretary of state, Charles Evans Hughes, achieved the first major disarmament accord, the Five-Power Naval Treaty, signed by Japan, Britain, France, Italy, and the United States. The five nations agreed to scrap more than 2 million tons of warships. Hughes extended the power of the United States abroad through economic ties and by encouraging banks to provide loans to war-ravaged Europe.

TABLE 21.1			
The Election of 1920			
Candidate	**Political Party**	**Popular Vote (%)**	**Electoral Vote**
Warren G. Harding	Republican	60.4	404
James M. Cox	Democratic	34.2	127
Eugene V. Debs	Socialist	3.4	—

Bettman/CORBIS

■ A cartoonist's view of the Teapot Dome scandal that plagued the Harding administration depicts the scandal blowing the lid off the Capitol building.

These successes notwithstanding, Harding's presidency was marred by scandal. He had built his political base by handing out favors and deals to his friends, and he continued to do so as president. His buddies used their offices and influence for personal gain, while Harding caroused with them, drinking, despite Prohibition, and engaging in notorious extramarital affairs. At first, the press ignored these obvious abuses, but by 1923, the many scandals finally broke. Harding's cronies were exposed for selling government appointments and providing judicial pardons and police protection for bootleggers.

The most serious scandal of Harding's presidency involved the large government oil reserves at Teapot Dome, Wyoming, and Elk Hills, California. At the urging of Secretary of the Interior Albert Fall, Harding transferred control over the reserves from the U.S. Navy to the Department of the Interior. After accepting a bribe of nearly $400,000 from two oil tycoons, Harry F. Sinclair and Edward L. Doheny, Fall secretly issued leases to them without opening up the competition to other oil companies, thereby allowing Sinclair and Doheny to pump oil from the wells in exchange for providing fuel reserves to the navy. Fall went to jail for a year as a result. In another scandal, Charles R. Forbes, head of the Veteran's Bureau, went to prison for swindling the government out of $200 million worth of hospital supplies. When Harding learned of the scandals that occurred in his close circle, he grew deeply worried. The stress probably contributed to the illness that killed him in 1923.

Warren G. Harding

CALVIN COOLIDGE: THE HANDS-OFF PRESIDENT

Harding's vice president, Calvin Coolidge, took over the presidency when Harding died in 1923. Sober and serious, this aloof New Englander was not vulnerable to scandal as his predecessor had been. Coolidge believed that the government should meddle as little as possible in the affairs of the nation. He took long naps every day and exerted very little presidential leadership. Known mostly for his hostility to labor unions and his laissez-faire attitude toward business, he was a popular president during the complacent mid-1920s.

Not everyone was pleased with Coolidge's probusiness politics, and opposition mobilized for the 1924 election. Progressive Republicans formed a new Progressive party and nominated Robert M. La Follette for president. The Progressive platform promoted conservation measures, higher taxes on the wealthy, doing away with the electoral college in favor of direct election of the president, and the abolition of child labor. The Democrats deadlocked between Catholic candidate Alfred E. Smith, an urban politician from New York, and Protestant William G. McAdoo, who had a base of support in the South and West. On the 103rd ballot, the delegates finally chose a compromise candidate, John W. Davis, a corporation lawyer. Coolidge claimed responsibility for the nation's prosperity and won easily, receiving more votes than the other two candidates combined.

TABLE 21.2			
The Election of 1924			
Candidate	**Political Party**	**Popular Vote (%)**	**Electoral Vote**
Calvin Coolidge	Republican	54.0	382
John W. Davis	Democratic	28.8	136
Robert M. La Follette	Progressive	16.6	13

Coolidge took pride in measures that prevented the government from interfering in the economy, such as his vetoes of the 1926 and 1928 McNary-Haugen bills, which would have provided government subsidies to farmers if farm prices dropped. The passage of the Revenue Act of 1926, a form of **trickle-down economics** intended to boost the economy, reduced the high income and estate taxes that Progressive reformers had put into place during World War I. Coolidge also continued Harding's efforts to sustain world peace. In 1928, under the leadership of Secretary of State Frank Kellogg and French Foreign Minister Aristide Briand, delegates from the United States, France, and thirteen other nations gathered in Paris to sign the Kellogg-Briand Pact, in which they agreed to resolve conflicts through peaceful solutions rather than war. Unfortunately, with no means to enforce the agreement, the pact did nothing to alleviate the international hostilities that later erupted into World War II.

HERBERT HOOVER: THE SELF-MADE PRESIDENT

The year 1928 also marked a turning point in domestic politics. In the presidential election that year, the Democrats broke tradition by selecting an Irish Catholic, Governor Alfred E. Smith of New York, as their candidate. It was the first time a major party had nominated a Catholic for president. Coolidge decided not to run for reelection in 1928, and the Republican party selected Secretary of Commerce Herbert Hoover as its nominee.

TABLE 21.3			
The Election of 1928			
Candidate	**Political Party**	**Popular Vote (%)**	**Electoral Vote**
Herbert Hoover	Republican	58.2	444
Alfred E. Smith	Democratic	40.9	87
Norman Thomas	Socialist	0.7	—

Prohibition figured prominently in the 1928 presidential campaign. Although the Democratic platform gave lukewarm support to the continuation of Prohibition, Smith made no secret of his support for the repeal of the Eighteenth Amendment. By contrast, Republican Herbert Hoover praised Prohibition as "a great social and economic experiment." The other major issue of the campaign was religion. Anti-Catholic sentiment was strong throughout the country, especially in the South, where Democrats either sat out the election or voted Republican. Smith's opponents attacked his Catholicism, charging that he was more loyal to the Vatican in Rome than he was to the United States. Although Hoover won by a substantial majority, Smith carried the nation's twelve largest cities. Smith's candidacy also laid the groundwork for another Irish Catholic, John F. Kennedy, who ran successfully on the Democratic ticket thirty-two years later.

Herbert Hoover epitomized the values of the self-made man. He was orphaned as a child and raised by relatives of modest means. After graduating from Stanford University, he went into mining and rose through the ranks to become a wealthy corporate leader. By age forty, he was already a millionaire. Hoover began his career in government during World War I, when he earned widespread admiration for handling the distribution of food relief to European war refugees. He then served ably as secretary of commerce in the Harding and Coolidge administrations. Shortly after winning the 1928 election, he predicted, "We in America today are nearer to the final triumph over poverty than ever before in the history of any land." But less than a year into his presidency, his optimism, along with the nation's economy, came crashing down.

Hollywood and Harlem: National Cultures in Black and White

■ *What developments in the arts and technology helped forge a national popular culture in the 1920s?*

While national politics turned conservative, cultural life exploded, especially in the nation's cities. In 1920, for the first time, the majority of Americans lived in towns and cities with populations greater than 2,500. Although this shift often is considered a watershed in the transformation from rural to urban America, it is worth noting that because the census defined any town with more than 2,500 inhabitants as urban, the majority of Americans still lived in small and ethnically homogeneous towns. Many small-town Americans still viewed big-city life with suspicion. They feared the decline of traditional American values of hard work, thrift, and discipline. Yet, at the same time, they were drawn to the new urban life. Jewish filmmakers, African American jazz artists, Irish and Italian club owners, and other "outsiders" created new leisure institutions where mainstream Americans shed their daytime routines for nightlife pleasures.

Hollywood on the West Coast and Harlem on the East Coast became centers of cultural innovation that spanned the nation. Eventually, the artistic productions of both centers attracted audiences of all racial, class, and regional backgrounds. Increasingly, as Americans moved from place to place, they encountered similar entertainments, music, arts, and consumer products. Movies, automobiles, radios, and advertising all fostered this emerging national culture.

■ Rudolph Valentino dances the tango in this famous scene from the 1920 film *The Four Horsemen of the Apocalypse*. Films in the 1920s featured exotic locales with foreign stars such as the Italian-born Valentino. In keeping with the public's taste for grandeur, lavish movie palaces emerged in cities across the country.

HOLLYWOOD COMES OF AGE

As movie theaters spread into towns and cities across the country, the messages of Hollywood began to reach a mass audience and forge a nationwide popular culture. Movie stars and their films provided models for new patterns of consumerism, leisure, city life, manhood and womanhood. Douglas Fairbanks showed middle-class men how to break free from the humdrum of white-collar work into the world of leisure. His attire of sports clothes changed the way men dressed in their off-work hours. Female stars, such as Clara Bow, epitomized the flapper and taught women how to be "naughty but nice."

Clara Bow, the "It" Girl

The most successful film director of the era, Cecil B. DeMille, made several films in which modern couples seek the right balance between fun and virtue in marriage. The popular DeMille formula offered a blueprint for couples like the Linganfields, whose divorce is described at the beginning of this chapter. In the typical DeMille plot, either the husband or the wife becomes bored with a spouse who, unable to shed drab old-fashioned virtue, refuses to take part in the leisure-oriented, sexually charged life of the 1920s.

Ironically, as the nation closed its doors to immigrants, foreigners on screen captivated the imagination of a native-born population drawn to the allure of the outsider. Movie stars like Greta Garbo from Sweden, Dolores del Rio, Lupe Vélez, and Ramón Novarro from Mexico, and Rudolph Valentino from Italy drew audiences with their foreignness. And yet, because movies were silent, their accented voices were not heard. Sound arrived in the late 1920s, bringing the voices and dialects of ethnic performers into the movies. In the first talking movie, *The Jazz Singer*, Al Jolson plays a young man drawn to urban nightlife and jazz, against the wishes of his Jewish immigrant parents. For native-born Americans watching films in small towns and cities, sound movies brought the diverse voices of the cities into their communities. For immigrants, sound movies carried their own familiar accents and allowed for a greater sense of identification with the stars on the screen.

THE HARLEM RENAISSANCE

While Hollywood developed on the West Coast, a flourishing center of African American culture emerged on the East Coast. The black arts movement known as the Harlem Renaissance drew on European as well as African and African American artistic traditions and gathered white as well as black intellectuals and artists. The young black poet Arna Bontemps was among the many artists drawn to Harlem. In 1924, he described Harlem as "a foretaste of paradise. A blue haze descended at night and with it strings of fairy lights on the broad avenues. From the window of a small room in an apartment on Fifth and 129th Street, I looked over the rooftops of Negrodom and tried to believe my eyes. What a city! What a world!"

Like many other Americans in the 1920s, Bontemps had moved around the country. Born in Louisiana, at age four he moved to Los Angeles with his parents, who left the South in the hope of raising their children in an atmosphere less hostile to African Americans. The family settled in Watts, at the time a white neighborhood, in the center of Los Angeles. He recalled, "We moved into a house in a neighborhood where we were the only colored family. . . . The people next door and up and down the block were friendly and talkative, the weather was perfect, there wasn't a mud puddle anywhere, and my mother seemed to float about on the clean air."

When Bontemps's Uncle Buddy arrived from Louisiana bringing stories of black life in the South, filled with "signs and charms and mumbo-jumbo," the boy was entranced. His father thoroughly disapproved of these stories, but Bontemps was drawn to the earthy sensuality of Uncle Buddy. He did not realize then that life in Jim Crow Louisiana had crushed Buddy's Creole pride and left him ruined and penniless.

When he was twenty-one, Bontemps moved to Harlem. There he looked for the "Negro-ness" he felt his upbringing in California had lacked. In Harlem he found a thriving black community unlike anything he had known before. He landed a teaching job, married, and settled with his family, becoming one of the most prolific writers of the Harlem Renaissance.

Renaissance writers laid claim to their identity as Americans while articulating the culture, aesthetics, and experiences of African Americans. The poet Langston Hughes challenged white America to accept African Americans in his 1925 poem "I, too, sing America":

I, too, sing America.

I am the darker brother.
They send me to eat in the kitchen
When company comes,
But I laugh,
And eat well,
And grow strong.

Tomorrow,
I'll be at the table
When company comes.
Nobody'll dare
Say to me,
"Eat in the kitchen,"
Then.

■ Poet Langston Hughes as a student at Lincoln University, Pennsylvania, in 1927. One of the major literary figures of the Harlem Renaissance, Hughes expressed the hopes, dreams, and sorrows of black Americans.

Schomburg Center for Research in Black Culture, Portrait Collection

Besides,
They'll see how beautiful I am
And be ashamed—

I, too, am America.

Although portraying the "exotic" and sensual in black culture was controversial among Harlem Renaissance critics, some of its greatest artists attracted huge followings among black as well as white audiences with unabashed and uninhibited celebrations of sexuality. Josephine Baker, scantily clad in her trademark "banana skirt," attracted large audiences by dancing to jazz rhythms. She also used her visibility to criticize American racism and to crusade against lynching. Moving to Paris in 1925, Baker opened her own Paris nightclub, Chez Josephine, where she danced every night. Later, during the Cold War era, she defied anticommunist censors by performing all over the world and speaking out against American racial discrimination.

The music of black America was such an important marker of the era that it provided the decade with its most lasting moniker, *the Jazz Age*. Emanating not from Harlem but from New Orleans, Chicago, and St. Louis, jazz was, nevertheless, central to the black arts movement and the emerging national culture. With the help of the recording industry and radio, jazz and the blues began to reach a wide audience, primarily among blacks but increasingly among whites as well. Blues lyrics expressed themes of working-class protest and resistance to racism. Women who sang the blues, including Bessie Smith, Ma Rainey, and Ethel Waters, asserted their sexuality, their passion for men or for women, their resistance to male domination, their sorrows, and their strength. In "I'm No Man's Mamma Now," Waters sang about divorce not in lament but in celebration:

You may wonder what's the reason for this crazy smile,

Say I haven't been so happy in a long while
Got a big load off my mind, here's the paper sealed and signed,
And the judge was nice and kind all through the trial.
This ends a five-year war, I'm sweet Miss Was once more.

I can come when I please, I can go when I please.

I can flit, fly and flutter like the birds in the trees.
Because I'm no man's mamma now. Hey, hey.

I can smile, I can wink, I can go take a drink,

And I don't have to worry what my hubby will think.
Because I'm no man's mamma now.

Black filmmaking also flourished during the Harlem Renaissance. During a period spanning three decades, pioneer filmmaker Oscar Micheaux made dozens of films, including *Within Our Gates* (1919) and *Body and Soul* (1924). His films addressed complex themes of class and racial conflict. Known for his style as well as his talent, the six-foot-tall Micheaux wore long Russian coats and wide-brimmed hats and used his charm to raise the necessary funding for his films. As one of his leading actors recalled, he entered meeting halls as if "he were God about to deliver a sermon. . . . Why, he was so impressive and so charming that he could talk the shirt off your back." Micheaux managed to persuade white theater owners in the South to show his films because of the revenues they promised. Southern theater owners showed Micheaux's films during all-black matinees and at special midnight screenings to white audiences drawn to the allegedly sensual and exotic black experience.

Few people outside the black community took the Harlem Renaissance seriously as a major artistic movement until the civil rights era decades later. Nevertheless, the cultural vitality of the black community in the 1920s contributed to the forging of a national mass culture. White patrons who went "slumming" in Harlem or danced to jazz music in clubs across the country incorporated the creativity and vitality of black America into their understanding and experience of modern American life. Still, African Americans continued to face segregation and lynching as well as limited political and economic opportunities.

RADIOS AND AUTOS: TRANSFORMING LEISURE AT HOME

Radio played a major role in disseminating the music of black America and linking people across regions through shared information, advertising, and entertainment. Portable radios became available in 1924. By the end of the decade, more than 6 million radios were in use nationwide. Radios brought jazz and other forms of popular music to the airwaves, transforming the way music was enjoyed in American homes. Americans became more inclined to listen to music on their Victrolas and radios than to make music themselves. By the mid-1920s, sales of records surpassed those of sheet music; production and sales of pianos also dropped precipitously.

The number of radio stations soared from 30 in 1922 to 556 the following year, and national broadcasts began to supersede local ones. Airwaves became so cluttered that by the mid-1920s, the federal government, through the leadership of then Secretary of Commerce Herbert Hoover, created the Federal Radio Commission to regulate and organize access. Meanwhile, American Telephone and Telegraph (AT&T) and the National Broadcasting Company (NBC) combined to form the first national network, which gave programs and advertisers access to audiences across the country.

As radios entered millions of American homes, automobiles began to extend the mobility of Americans. The automobile offered the possibility of commuting to work without relying on public transportation, encouraging the expansion of suburban communities. The number of passenger cars in the nation more than tripled during the 1920s. The Federal Highways Act of 1916 had produced a network of roads all over the country, providing construction jobs and a slew of new roadside businesses, from restaurants to garages. Automobiles also stimulated the tourist industry; Florida, California, and Arizona became vacation destinations in this period. At the same time, tourism disrupted Native American communities in the Southwest, and offered new sources of revenue, as curious motorists intruded into previously isolated reservations.

■ Views of Broadway in Fargo, North Dakota, the first taken in 1881, the second in the 1920s. By 1920, Fargo had developed into a bustling town with retail shops, paved roads, automobiles, and a streetcar line.

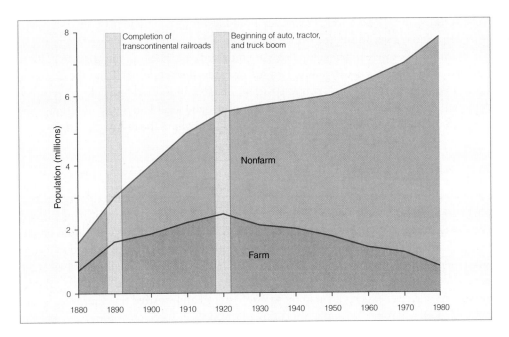

■ FIGURE 21.1

Transformation of the Upper Midwest, 1880–1980

With the completion of the transcontinental railroad, the population of the upper Midwest increased in both farm and nonfarm areas. When automobiles, tractors, and trucks became available, the farm population of the nation's "heartland" began to decline as the population of towns and cities increased.

Automobile production also revolutionized the consumer industry. The pragmatic Henry Ford built inexpensive, functional automobiles that he expected his workers to be able to purchase and keep. But Ford faced serious competition from General Motors' Alfred P. Sloan Jr., who developed the concept of **planned obsolescence** and put a new emphasis on auto styling to encourage customers to trade in their old cars for newer and more expensive models.

More than style, however, automobiles offered Americans mobility. Many people mortgaged their homes or did without indoor plumbing in order to purchase a car. In the late 1920s, writer Ernesto Galarza noted that the Mexican migrant laborer knew "the Ford is not a perennial flower . . . far too much of his meager income is left in the tills of gasoline stations and tire shops in his long treks along the Pacific Coast." Cherokee humorist Will Rogers quipped that "America is the only nation in the world that is going to the poor house in an automobile."

The automobile was part of a consumer society increasingly focused on leisure, pleasure, and intimacy. Courtship patterns changed, and sexual activity increased as young couples abandoned the front porch for the back seat. Women gained new freedom and autonomy when they, too, took the wheel. Moralists worried that the automobile would provide youth with too much independence and privacy. One juvenile court judge announced that "the automobile has become a house of prostitution on wheels."

DOCUMENT

Wembridge, "Petting and the Campus"

Science on Trial

■ *What did science contribute to American life in the 1920s, and where did scientific ideas fall short?*

Technological advances brought forth much of the new era of leisure and consumption: the motion picture camera, the automobile, household appliances, radios. Advances in medicine also improved the quality of life for many Americans. But scientific efforts to alter the natural world did not always lead to expected social benefits. One case in point was the engineering project to build levees along the Mississippi River to prevent flooding. These structures were expected to protect the settlements and agricultural developments in the fertile floodplains where the river would normally expand. As it turned out, the engineers were no match for the river. The levees were unable to hold the river back, leading to a tragic flood. The levees would again prove inadequate in 2005 when Hurricane Katrina swept into the Mississippi Delta, flooding the city of New Orleans.

Scientific ideas were tested in the 1920s not only along the banks of the Mississippi River but also in the nation's courtrooms. Two major cases, the Scopes trial and the Supreme Court's decision in *Buck v. Bell*, subjected scientific ideas to judicial and cultural scrutiny. Although decisions in both cases resolved the immediate legal issues, the questions they raised continued to generate controversy and debate throughout the rest of the century.

THE GREAT FLOOD OF 1927

For half a century, the engineers of the Mississippi River Commission had adhered to a policy of building levees, assuming that strong barricades along the river's banks would prevent flooding. With levees, the rich soil of the floodplains along the river could be settled and farmed rather than left empty to provide places for the river to expand and contract. But the levee policy proved to be a disastrous example of human failure to master the natural contours of the land. In March 1927, the rains came and the river rose. Public authorities and river experts assured those who watched and worried that the levees would hold. They were wrong. Torrential rains caused the river to rage across the levees and the land beyond. The flood caused more than $100 million in crop losses and $23 million in livestock deaths. Journalists at the time called it "America's greatest peacetime disaster."

With the help of the Department of Commerce and the National Guard, the Red Cross set up 154 relief camps for flood victims. The camps were racially segregated. Refugees in the white camps were free to come and go and had more comfortable and generous accommodations and rations than those in the black camps. Armed guards patrolled the camps for black evacuees and restricted people attempting to enter or leave. Black laborers had to register and give the names of their employers to receive any shelter or assistance. Only those employers were allowed to enter the camps and reclaim their workers. Relations between plantation owners and sharecroppers had been strained across the South before the flood, and many black laborers hoped to leave the plantations and find work elsewhere. But when labor agents came to the camps looking for workers to fill northern jobs, those patrolling the camps denied them entry. Federal authorities,

■ The Mississippi River flood of 1927 devastated 26,000 square miles of prime farmland and homes across seven states. Levees built along the river's banks proved inadequate, despite engineers' assurances that the structures would prevent flooding. More than 900,000 people lost their homes, and crops and livestock worth more than $120 million were destroyed.

Bettmann/CORBIS

■ **MAP 21.1** **The Mississippi River Flood of 1927**

The Mississippi River flood in 1927 sent water across a huge area of the South, extending as far west as Texas, covering most of Louisiana, Arkansas, and Mississippi, and reaching north into Kansas, Illinois, and Indiana.

including Secretary of Commerce Herbert Hoover, refused to intervene in local camp management. As a result, southern whites were able to force black sharecroppers back to work on their plantations. Despite the prisonlike conditions, many African American evacuees managed to escape and make their way north.

THE TRIUMPH OF EUGENICS: *BUCK V. BELL*

Race intersected with scientific theory in attempts to control not only nature but also the human world. In 1924, racial theorist Lothrop Stoddard wrote a best-selling book, *The Rising Tide of Color Against White World Supremacy*. In this polemic, Stoddard predicted a war among the "primary" races of the world and warned of the "weakening" of the white race through immigration and "mongrelization." Stoddard wrote, "The melting pot may mix, but does not melt. Each race type, formed ages ago . . . is a stubbornly persistent entity. Each type possesses a special set of characters: not merely the physical characters visible to the naked eye, but moral, intellectual, and spiritual characters as well."

Stoddard's theories had no scientific merit and were later thoroughly discredited. But in the 1920s, these dubious theories of racial superiority supported measures such as immigration restriction and eugenic sterilization laws. Eugenics was a pseudo-science based on notions of racial superiority. Eugenicists claimed that the Anglo-Saxon Protestant "race" was superior to all others, including Jews, southern Europeans, and Catholics as well as nonwhites. Racial superiority, according to eugenic reformers, might be compromised not only by mixing with inferior groups but also by the propagation of individuals whose mental or moral condition rendered them inferior, and whose offspring would diminish the quality of the Anglo-Saxon "stock."

These ideas were consistent with the theories of Social Darwinists, who claimed that Darwin's evolutionary theories were relevant to human society, arguing that only the "fittest" ought to survive (see Chapter 16). They opposed government aid to the poor and infirm, claiming that such assistance interfered with "natural selection" of the "fittest." Social Darwinists also supported eugenic theories that provided the rationale for sterilization of the "unfit."

Beginning in 1907, several states enacted eugenic laws that allowed the state to sterilize "inferior" individuals without their knowledge or consent. These laws authorized government and medical officials to determine whether or not an individual was inferior, or "feebleminded," and to order that the person be sterilized. Opponents of eugenic sterilization, mostly Catholic activists, challenged these laws in several states. In an effort to put an end to such challenges, eugenic advocates decided to test the constitutionality of the Virginia compulsory sterilization law. Their plan was to bring the case all the way to the U.S. Supreme Court, which they expected to uphold the law.

> *Beginning in 1907, several states enacted eugenic laws that allowed the state to sterilize "inferior" individuals without their knowledge or consent.*

The proponents of the law selected the case of Carrie Buck, in part because she was white. Eugenic advocates did not want race to be at the center of the case, especially because eugenic sterilization laws did not target particular races; they simply targeted the "feebleminded"—a term often used to describe people with mental retardation as well as poor, immigrant, or minority women who were sexually active. At the age of seventeen, Carrie Buck, the daughter of an unmarried woman, was raped and became pregnant; as a result she was sent to a state institution for the feebleminded. Buck was labeled feebleminded because she had borne a child out of wedlock and was therefore deemed morally unfit for parenthood. The noted eugenicist Harry Laughlin pointed out that Buck herself was born out of wedlock, as was her daughter, and described them as part of the "shiftless, ignorant and worthless class of anti-social whites of the South."

Carrie Buck was sterilized in 1927. No evidence established that Buck, her mother, or her daughter was below normal intelligence. Buck's daughter died as a child, but her teachers described the girl as bright. In writing the majority opinion for the Supreme Court that upheld the law, Justice Oliver Wendell Holmes wrote, "Three generations of imbeciles are enough." Within the next few years, thirty states had compulsory sterilization laws, and the number of operations rose dramatically. In the 1930s, the Nazis in Germany modeled their sterilization policies on the California law. By the 1960s, more than 60,000 involuntary sterilizations had been performed across the country; one-third were performed in California. Finally, in the 1980s, a rare alliance of traditional Catholics and feminist activists on an issue of reproductive rights succeeded in repealing compulsory sterilization laws.

SCIENCE, RELIGION, AND THE SCOPES TRIAL

Many Americans were troubled by eugenics and its corollary, Social Darwinism. The populist leader William Jennings Bryan was among them. Bryan, three times the Democratic candidate for president and Woodrow Wilson's secretary of state, had been a powerful voice for reform and social justice for thirty years. Bryan believed that Social Darwinism was an ill-founded misapplication of scientific theory used to support the subjugation of women, the second-class status of ethnic and racial minorities, the neglect of the poor, and the practice of eugenic sterilization.

In Bryan's last public crusade, he defended his principles in a courtroom in Dayton, Tennessee, in July 1925. Tennessee had recently enacted the Butler Act, which made it illegal to teach the theory of evolution in the schools. The American Civil Liberties Union (ACLU) announced that it would defend any teacher charged with violating the Butler Act. A twenty-four-year-old science teacher from the local high school, John Thomas Scopes, agreed to test the law. Using a state-approved textbook, Scopes taught a lesson on evolutionary theory on April 24 to his Rhea County High School science class. He was arrested on May 7 and quickly indicted by a grand jury. Bryan agreed to represent the prosecution; famed Chicago criminal lawyer Clarence Darrow headed the ACLU's team of defense lawyers.

The Rise and Fall of Man

Primate   **Neanderthal Man**   **Socrates**   **W. J. Bryan**

■ This satiric political cartoon, published during the Scopes trial, depicts the theory of evolution as the development of humans from their origins as apes to the "survival of the fittest," portrayed as William Jennings Bryan. Bryan argued the case against evolution in the famous courtroom drama.

Bryan did not oppose science, but he objected to its misapplication. Darrow did not oppose religion, but he argued that religious fundamentalists—"creationists" who believed in the literal interpretation of the Bible—should not determine the way science was taught in the schools. Reporters at the time, and since, cast the trial as a struggle between religion and science, with rural and small-town Americans on the side of creationism and secular urbanites supporting evolution. But the divide was not so clear-cut. Almost all advocates on both sides of the Scopes trial were Christians who disagreed over how to interpret the Bible. Both sides also accepted science; those opposed to the teaching of evolution considered it an unscientific theory.

The Scopes trial was one of the first national media events and contained elements of popular entertainment. It was quickly dubbed "the Monkey trial" because Darwin's theory of evolution demonstrated that humans and other primates, such as monkeys and chimpanzees, evolved separately from a common early primate form. The Scopes trial was the first jury trial broadcast on live radio. More than 900 spectators packed the courtroom, and hundreds more gathered in the streets, where a carnival atmosphere prevailed, complete with souvenir stands, food vendors, itinerant preachers, hucksters, and numerous chimpanzees accompanied by their trainers.

The trial did not deal with the question of the First Amendment, which guaranteed freedom of speech, nor the matter of who should decide the content of classroom education. Rather, religious fundamentalism was on trial. Although rules of evidence cannot apply to matters of faith, Darrow forced Bryan to defend his religious beliefs in a court of law. Darrow fully expected to lose the case so he could appeal it to the U.S. Supreme Court, and the jury obliged, reaching a guilty verdict in just nine minutes. Exhausted by the trial and ill with diabetes, Bryan died a week later.

Bryan technically won the case, but most reporters deemed the spectacle a victory for Darrow and the teaching of evolution. That assessment was premature. The Tennessee Supreme Court overturned the verdict on a technicality, robbing Darrow of his chance to take the case to the U.S. Supreme Court. Before the trial, most science textbooks included discussion of evolution; after the trial, material on evolution began to disappear. Laws against the teaching of evolution remained on the books until the U.S. Supreme Court overturned an Arkansas law in 1968.

The Scopes trial did not resolve the debate between creationists and evolutionists, and the controversy continued. In 2000, the Board of Education in Kansas ruled that creationism and evolution were both unproven theories and that both could be taught in the public schools. Debates over the teaching of evolution remained heated well into the twenty-first century. The Scopes trial may not have resolved anything, but it did have one significant unintended consequence. The trial generated tremendous interest in nonhuman primates.

After the trial, attendance at the nation's zoos skyrocketed, boosting their funding and prestige and improving the environment for animals in zoos. So in the end, the real winners in the "Monkey trial" were the monkeys.

Consumer Dreams and Nightmares

■ *What were the positive and negative effects of the 1920s consumer culture?*

The festive atmosphere at the "Monkey trial" reflected the American appetite for fun and entertainment. During the 1920s, spending on leisure and recreation nearly doubled. Faith in continuing prosperity promoted the extension of consumer credit to unprecedented heights. Previously, the only major item routinely purchased on credit was a house. But in the 1920s, installment buying became the rage for a wide range of consumer goods, from autos and radios to household appliances. Consumer debt rose from $2.6 billion in 1919 to $7.1 billion in 1929. As one official in a midwestern loan company remarked, "People don't think anything nowadays of borrowing sums they'd never have thought of borrowing in the old days. They will assume an obligation for $2,000 today as calmly as they would have borrowed $300 or $400 in 1890." This habit of buying on credit boosted the standard of living for many but also left families in a precarious situation and vulnerable to changes in the broader economy.

MARKETING THE GOOD LIFE

Advertising fueled much of the new spending. As one contemporary reporter noted, "Advertising is to business what fertilizer is to a farm." According to advertisers, consumer goods promised health, beauty, success, and the means to eliminate personal and embarrassing flaws, such as bad breath or dandruff. Cigarette companies used advertising to promote smoking as a symbol of independence for women and as a means to achieve beauty. Clever advertising campaigns promised women that if they would "reach for a Lucky Strike" instead of a sweet they would remain slim, healthy, and sexually appealing.

Advertising also fostered a vision of big business as a benevolent force, promoting individual happiness. In his 1925 best-seller *The Man That Nobody Knows*, advertising executive Bruce Barton portrayed Jesus as a businessman who gathered a group of twelve followers who believed in his enterprise and, through effective public relations and advertising, sold his product to the world. The consumer culture had its temples: movie palaces, department stores, and the 1920s innovation, the shopping center. Kansas City's Country Club Plaza, the nation's first suburban shopping district, was the brainchild of Jesse Clyde (J. C.) Nichols, who purchased fifty-five acres of swampland for the project. Like the architects of the movie palaces, Nichols looked to European aristocratic styles for inspiration. He chose a

JUST GOING ALONG
FOR THE RIDE

Many a General spare tire is never put to service during the single ownership of a car—they just go along for the ride. It is this year round freedom from tire worry that has spoiled General Tire users for any other tire. But more important is the factor of safety at today's high speeds. Generals are blowout proof and skid-safe and the exclusive low pressure feature makes comfort a luxurious reality. All of these advantages cost so little when you total up General's almost unheard of big mileage. The General Tire & Rubber Co., Akron, O.

The New
GENERAL
DUAL BALLOON
—*goes a long way to make friends*

The Advertising Archive Ltd.

■ In the 1920s, advertisers used sexualized images to sell all sorts of products. This advertisement for automobile tires provides very little information about the product but evokes images of fun and romance to capture consumers' attention.

Selling Treats in the Los Angeles Suburbs

Envisioning History

Two immigrants posing proudly in front of their tamale and ice cream wagon convey the spirit of modern American life in the 1920s. The wagon, an elaborate version of the recently mass-marketed motor car, drove along the streets of Glendale, a suburb of Los Angeles, offering hot and cold treats to the neighborhood.

QUESTIONS

1. In what ways does the photograph convey the consumer culture of the 1920s?

2. What do the details in the photograph tell you about the people who live in the neighborhood?

3. What does the photograph suggest about small business opportunities and entrepreneurship at the time?

Spanish-Moorish theme for the plaza that included courtyards and stucco buildings with red tile roofs and ornate towers. He adorned the plaza's streets and sidewalks with works of art, columns, wrought iron, and fountains. Most significantly, he designed his shopping center with the car in mind. The shopping center originally boasted eight filling stations and numerous garages and parking lots. Skeptical city leaders called it "Nichols' Folly," but the Country Club Plaza was a commercial success.

DOCUMENT

Advertisements from 1925 and 1927

F. Scott Fitzgerald, The Great Gatsby

Interpreting History

F. Scott Fitzgerald's 1925 novel The Great Gatsby *expressed the long-ings of many Americans of the 1920s to partake of the glamorous life of the wealthy and live out their vision of the American dream. The story revolves around the desires of the newly wealthy Jay Gatsby to be accepted into the ranks of New York's elite. He is infatuated with Daisy Buchanan, who lives across the Sound from him in Long Island, a green light from her dock beckoning to him. In this passage from the final paragraphs of the book, the narrator, Nick Carraway, comments on the elusiveness of Gatsby's dream— the American dream. The poignant ending of the novel foreshadows the collapse of the overextended leisure and consumer culture of the 1920s that led to the Great Depression of the 1930s.*

F. Scott Fitzgerald Papers, Manuscript Division, Department of Rare Books and Special Collections, Princeton University Library

■ Writer F. Scott Fitzgerald and his flapper wife, Zelda, personified the glamorous literati of the Jazz Age. In his writing, Fitzgerald both romanticized and criticized the decadent consumerism of the aspiring and upwardly mobile middle class. In this page from a scrapbook, their photos are adorned with autographs of other famous literary figures.

I spent my Saturday nights in New York because those gleaming, daz-zling parties of his were with me so vividly that I could still hear the music and the laughter, faint and incessant, from his garden, and the cars going up and down his drive. One night I did hear a material car there, and saw its lights stop at his front steps. But I didn't investigate. Probably it was some final guest who had been away at the ends of the earth and didn't know that the party was over.

On the last night, with my trunk packed and my car sold to the grocer, I went over and looked at that huge incoherent failure of a house once more. On the white steps an obscene word, scrawled by some boy with a piece of brick, stood out clearly in the moonlight,

A much less successful venture was the Florida land boom, based on fantasies of a consumer paradise. When World War I closed off routes to the European playgrounds of the American elites, shrewd developers began to lure people to buy property in Florida with visions of "the graceful palm, latticed against the fading gold of the sun kissed sky." These promotional efforts sparked a frenzy of investment in Florida real estate. To create "earthly paradises" and resorts, developers rushed to construct roads and find new land on which to build. Forging the Tamiami Trail across ninety miles of Everglades swamp entailed dredging a canal, blowing up the submerged limestone layer with dynamite, piling the broken limestone beside the canal, and then crushing it into a road surface. The dan-gerous work claimed the lives of many laborers and severely damaged the sensitive ecology of the vast Everglades wetland. When the road was finally completed in 1928, the land boom had collapsed, claiming the fortunes of many hopeful but misguided investors.

Human folly and nature's fury contributed to the Florida land boom and bust. Devastating hurricanes hit Florida in 1926 and again in 1928, killing thousands of people and destroying several towns. The destruction wrought by the hurricanes, and the expo-sure of exaggerated promotional advertisements and inflated prices, temporarily put an end to land speculation in Florida.

WRITERS, CRITICS, AND THE "LOST GENERATION"

Some social critics claimed that the infatuation with consumerism fostered not only economic disasters such as the Florida land boom but also a stifling conformity. Sinclair Lewis was one of several novelists of the 1920s whose books expressed biting criticism of the frantic pursuit of material gain and status. George Babbitt, the protagonist of Lewis's novel and I erased it, drawing my shoe raspingly along the stone. Then I wandered down to the beach and sprawled out on the sand.

Most of the big shore places were closed now and there were hardly any lights except the shadowy, moving glow of a ferry-boat across the Sound. And as the moon rose higher the inessential houses began to melt away until gradually I became aware of the old island here that flowered once for Dutch sailors' eyes—a fresh, green breast of the new world. Its vanished trees, the trees that had made way for Gatsby's house, had once pandered in whispers to the last and greatest of all human dreams; for a transitory enchanted moment man must have held his breath in the presence of this continent, compelled into an aesthetic contemplation he neither understood nor desired, face to face for the last time in history with something commensurate to his capacity for wonder.

And as I sat there brooding on the old, unknown world, I thought of Gatsby's wonder when he first picked out the green light at the end of Daisy's dock. He had come a long way to this blue lawn, and his dream must have seemed so close that he could hardly fail to grasp it. He did not know that it was already behind him, somewhere back in that vast obscurity beyond the city, where the dark fields of the republic rolled on under the night.

Gatsby believed in the green light, the orgiastic future that year by year recedes before us. It eluded us then, but that's no matter—tomorrow we will run faster, stretch out our arms farther. . . . And one fine morning—

So we beat on, boats against the current, borne back ceaselessly into the past.

QUESTIONS

1. *Why would Fitzgerald use the Dutch sailors of the colonial period as a point of reference in this passage?*

2. *Critics have often pointed to Fitzgerald's ambivalence about modern urban life as expressed in* The Great Gatsby. *Do you see any ambivalence in this passage?*

3. *In this passage, is Fitzgerald optimistic or pessimistic about the American dream?*

Babbitt (1922), struggles to become accepted and successful in his small town by conforming to the empty materialism and standardized opinions accepted and prized by his neighbors.

F. Scott Fitzgerald wrote not about small-town conformity, as Lewis did, but about the modern urban life that was its antithesis. Fitzgerald glamorized, criticized, and in many ways embodied the giddy nightlife and status seeking of the Jazz Age. Born in St. Paul, Minnesota, into a family of modest means, he grew up admiring and emulating the wealthy. He married flamboyant flapper Zelda Sayre, daughter of a prominent Alabama judge, and together they embodied the dizzy, indulgent, free-spirited life of the decade. But Fitzgerald's novels, including *This Side of Paradise* (1920), *The Beautiful and the Damned* (1922), and *The Great Gatsby* (1925), criticized the era's obsessions with success, glamour, consumerism, advertising, and status. The Fitzgeralds, along with other writers who were critical of American superficiality and conformity, moved to Paris. Eventually, the life Fitzgerald both lived and criticized caught up with him. By the end of the decade, he—like the nation—was broken by his excesses. In 1931, he came home to Baltimore an alcoholic; Zelda was diagnosed with schizophrenia and spent the rest of her life in and out of mental institutions.

During their years in Paris, the Fitzgeralds often joined other expatriate writers at the salon of Gertrude Stein, a prolific author of novels, plays, operas, poems, and biographies. Born in 1874 to German Jewish parents in Pennsylvania, in 1903 she moved to France, where she remained for the rest of her life, looking back to America for her subject matter. In Paris she met another American, Alice B. Toklas, who became her lifetime partner. Their openly lesbian relationship gave Stein material for her writing, including *The Autobiography of Alice B. Toklas* (1933). In the 1920s, she dubbed the writers who gathered at her salon the **Lost Generation** for their alienation from mainstream American society.

DOCUMENT

Carter, " 'These Wild Young People' by One of Them"

The Granger Collection, New York

■ Gertrude Stein (right) and Alice B. Toklas walk their poodle, Basket II, in a French village in 1944.

POVERTY AMID PLENTY

Most Americans in the 1920s were neither investing in Florida real estate nor frequenting Gertrude Stein's Paris salon. Even so, they were not immune to the desires and dreams that the consumer economy sparked. The middle class and the more prosperous members of the working class enjoyed many of the comforts, amusements, and appliances that the booming economy made available; the poor struggled just to make ends meet. Throughout the 1920s, the nation's poorest people continued to be the most mobile, moving in search of jobs, security, and a place they could settle and call home. Henry Crews, son of a white Georgia sharecropper, longed for "that single house where you were born, where you lived out your childhood . . . your anchor in the world." But he never had such a home. Like that of many other hardworking sharecroppers and factory workers, his family moved frequently in search of a better life, a dream that often proved elusive.

If Zelda Sayre Fitzgerald embodied the Jazz Age, Myrtle Terry Lawrence embodied the experience of the sharecropper. Born in Alabama in 1893, she began chopping and hoeing cotton at age six. She spent two weeks in school in the first grade, which was the full extent of her formal education. She married Ben Lawrence when they were both thirteen years old and had her first child at fourteen. With her husband, she worked in the cotton fields for nearly three decades, eventually becoming a major organizer of black and white sharecroppers in the Southern Tenant Farmers' Union (STFU), which fought for the rights of landless farmers.

Myrtle Lawrence, a tough-talking, tobacco-chewing sharecropper, was hardly a southern belle. She took pride in vigorous outdoor work, which she preferred to housework. As her daughter-in-law recalled, "She wasn't no housekeeper. Bless her heart." Myrtle Lawrence's refusal to be bullied propelled her in the 1930s to leadership in the STFU.

Sharecropping required hard work and careful planning to carve out a meager life, but many did so with pride. Ed Brown, a young black sharecropper, worked on six different plantations, moving about in search of better conditions or to escape from debt or threats of violence. To improve their circumstances, Ed took odd jobs to earn extra money, while his wife Willie Mae took care of the children, picked cotton, took in laundry, and as Ed noted with appreciation, kept "things . . . lookin very pretty."

Life was a struggle for southern sharecroppers, black and white. African Americans faced the most difficult jobs and the added insults of racism. Blacks continued to move north in large numbers in search of improved opportunities. However, immigrants had a better chance of moving into semiskilled jobs, while blacks were relegated to unskilled jobs. Many ended up in domestic service, where they worked long hours for low pay. They tried to avoid live-in work, where they had little freedom from the watchful gaze of employers and barely any time with their own families. If they returned to the South, they faced work in the fields or factories for long hours under miserable conditions or in coal mining, logging, and sawmilling, where dangerous working conditions killed thousands of laborers.

Latinos joined African Americans at the bottom of the socioeconomic ladder in the Southwest and Midwest, working in jobs that offered almost no opportunity to save money or acquire property. Immigrants from Asia also faced difficulty finding stable jobs with decent pay and working conditions. Many ended up in domestic service. A young Japanese woman went to work for a family in Oakland, California. "I had to bring the coal up, all the time I went up and down," she later recalled. "Then I had to wash diapers. Me, I grew up on a farm, so I never had to do that. When I came to America, I didn't know

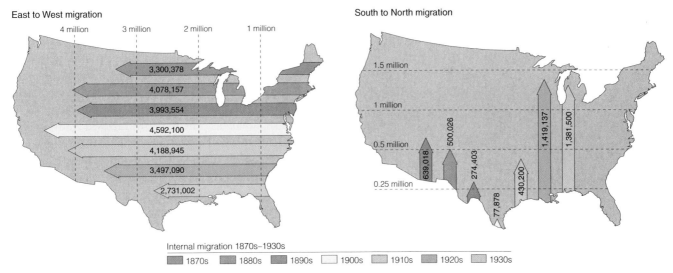

East to West migration

4 million   3 million   2 million   1 million

3,300,378
4,078,157
3,993,554
4,592,100
4,188,945
3,497,090
2,731,002

South to North migration

1.5 million
1 million
0.5 million
0.25 million

639,018
77,878
500,026
274,403
430,200
1,419,137
1,381,500

Internal migration 1870s–1930s
1870s 1880s 1890s 1900s 1910s 1920s 1930s

■ **MAP 21.2 Americans on the Move, 1870s–1930s**
Between the 1870s and the 1930s, millions of Americans moved around the country, mostly from east to west, but also from south to north.

anything. So I just had to cry." For many domestic workers, loss of a job also meant loss of housing, creating constant mobility. Nevertheless, the poor maintained strong ties of kinship and community and helped each other survive under difficult conditions.

Industrial workers struggled throughout the decade, especially in a political climate hostile to unions. With the crushing of labor radicalism in the Red Scare after World War I, union organizing and strikes declined. But workers continued to protest low wages and poor working conditions. In March 1929, young women textile workers in Elizabethton, a small town nestled in the Blue Ridge Mountains of eastern Tennessee, closed down the American Glanzstoff plant in protest against low wages, petty rules, and arrogant employers. Soon, the protest spread to textile mills across the region. At Glanzstoff, the strikers returned to work when the company promised better pay and agreed not to discriminate against union members. But the employers broke their promises, so the women struck again. The governor sent in the National Guard, armed with machine guns. More than 1,000 people were arrested in confrontations with the troops.

The strikers were young women mostly in their teens and early twenties. They combined labor militance with an air of playfulness. On the picket lines, they expressed their autonomy and independence, but they also found opportunities to flirt and carouse beyond the watchful eyes of parents. Although the strike was ultimately crushed and many of the participants were blacklisted, few expressed regrets. Bessie Edens knew she would not get her job back, but she "didn't care whether they took me back or not. I didn't! If I'd starved I wouldn't of cared, because I knew what I was a'doing when I helped to pull it. And I've never regretted it in any way. . . . And it did help the people, and it's helped the town and the country."

THE STOCK MARKET CRASH

Rural poverty and the plight of workers were the undercurrents of the superficial prosperity of the 1920s. The symbolic end of the Jazz Age arrived on "Black Tuesday," October 29, 1929, when the inflated and overextended stock market came crashing down. In one day, the value of stocks fell $14 billion. By end of the year, stock prices were down 50 percent; by 1932, they had dropped another 30 percent. In three years, $74 billion of the nation's wealth had vanished. The effect on the economy was catastrophic. Industrial production fell by half. More than 100,000 businesses went bankrupt. Banks failed at an alarming rate: more than

2,000 closed in 1931 alone. Unemployment rose to staggering levels, reaching 25 percent by 1932 and rarely dropping below 17 percent throughout the 1930s.

In keeping with the social policies that had prevailed throughout the 1920s, relief efforts were slim. No federal relief or welfare, no unemployment insurance, no Social Security, no job programs existed to help those who had lost their jobs, their savings, and their homes. Although many wealthy people lost their fortunes, which had been built on speculative investments, the poor suffered the most. People who lost their homes and farms moved into makeshift shelters in shantytowns, which they nicknamed **Hoovervilles** to mock the ineffectual efforts of President Herbert Hoover to respond to their plight.

The causes of the stock market crash and the decade-long economic depression that followed were complex and varied. Stock prices had risen dramatically, especially at the end of the 1920s. Speculators had been purchasing stocks on 10 percent margins, meaning they put down only 10 percent of the cost and borrowed the rest from brokers and banks. The popularity of installment buying in the consumer goods market had devastating effects when applied in this manner to the stock market. Investors expected to get rich quickly by selling their stocks at a higher price and paying back the loans from their huge profits. This system worked for a few years, encouraging investors with limited funds to make risky investments in the hope of gaining large fortunes. When the price of stocks spiraled out of control, far beyond their actual value, creditors demanded repayment of their loans, and investors were unable to pay their debts.

The collapse of the stock market alone would not necessarily have caused such a severe and prolonged depression. Poor decision making by financial and political leaders exacerbated underlying weaknesses in the economy. The Federal Reserve curtailed the amount of money in circulation and raised interest rates, making it more difficult for people to get loans and pay off their debts. These policies had profound worldwide implications and contributed to an international crisis. Banks in Germany and Austria, for example, depended on loans from the United States, and many went bankrupt, causing a ripple effect across Europe. The Hawley-Smoot Tariff of 1930 also contributed to the downward spiral. Although industrialists had convinced the Republican-controlled Congress that the tariff would protect American commodities from competition from cheaper foreign goods, they were wrong. Foreign governments retaliated by raising their own tariffs to keep out American goods. These monetary and trade policies backfired, and the economic crisis spread throughout the western industrial world.

WATCH

"Prosperity of the 1920s and the Great Depression"

Within the United States, the unequal distribution of wealth exacerbated the effects of the economic downturn. Throughout the decade, the nation may have looked prosperous, but most of the wealth was concentrated in the hands of a small number of people. The gap between the rich and the poor widened during the 1920s, in part because of Coolidge administration policies that lowered taxes on the wealthy. The majority of the population lost purchasing power, resulting in the decline of consumer-oriented industries as the market for their products shrank. Although the wealthy spent money extravagantly, they spent a smaller percentage of their money on consumer goods than wage earners. If average Americans had been able to buy more cars, household appliances, and other products, those industries might have survived, and the economy might have recovered more quickly. Political leaders, and the business-oriented public policies they had promoted throughout the decade, left the country ill prepared to address the crisis and meet the needs of families deprived of their means of livelihood.

Conclusion

The 1920s witnessed the decline of the reform spirit that had prevailed in the Progressive Era, the rise of conservative political leadership, and an economy spinning out of control. On the surface, the country looked prosperous. Cities grew, an urban culture flourished, automobiles and other trappings of consumer culture proliferated. But beneath the visible affluence was the hidden poverty that prevailed throughout the decade. National leaders promoted business interests and paid little attention to social welfare, the environment, or the need to regulate the economy.

Reactionary impulses led to immigration restriction, the Supreme Court's validation of compulsory sterilization laws, persecution of outsiders, and a revival of the Ku Klux Klan. Radicals of all sorts faced a repressive political environment that curtailed union activism and political dissent. After achieving the right to vote, the women's movement fragmented. The movement for black economic empowerment persisted, especially under the leadership of black nationalist Marcus Garvey. But hostility to minorities continued. The Scopes trial illustrated tensions between new scientific theories and traditional religious beliefs. By the end of the 1920s, it was clear that Prohibition was a dismal failure and that the federal government was ill equipped to enforce it.

Although political reform withered, cultural vitality flowered. Hollywood emerged as a major industry, and the Jazz Age reflected the widespread appeal of African American music. A black arts movement flourished, centered in Harlem, and writers of the Lost Generation—disenchanted with the status quo—gathered in Greenwich Village or moved to France. Across the country, a youth culture challenged the gender and sexual mores of the past. Consumer culture expanded as increasing numbers of families purchased cars, radios, and new fashions.

Few who were involved in the private preoccupations of the decade could have foreseen the disaster ahead. When the stock market crashed, President Hoover tried to address the crisis by extending the political philosophy that had prevailed throughout the decade: private enterprise would bring the economy back to health. But Hoover and the nation soon discovered that in the Great Depression, the old formulas would no longer work.

CHRONOLOGY: 1920–1929

1920	Harding elected president.
	Nineteenth Amendment (women's suffrage) ratified.
1921	Sheppard-Towner Act provides nurses for maternal and infant care.
1922	Five-Power Naval Treaty.
1923	Equal Rights Amendment proposed.
1924	Coolidge elected president.
	Johnson-Reid Act limits immigration.
	Portable radio introduced.
1925	Scopes trial, Dayton, Tennessee.
	F. Scott Fitzgerald, *The Great Gatsby*.
1926	Gertrude Ederle is first woman to swim across English Channel.
1927	Charles Lindbergh flies nonstop from New York to Paris.
	Al Jolson stars in *The Jazz Singer*, first talking movie.
	Sacco and Vanzetti executed.
	Buck v. Bell upholds compulsory sterilization laws.
1928	Hoover elected president.
	Tamiami Trail across Florida Everglades completed.
1929	Stock market crash.

For Review

1. How did the U.S. presidents of the 1920s use the power of the presidency?

2. What were some of the Progressive political impulses that stayed alive in the 1920s, despite the prevailing conservatism of the decade?

3. How did outsiders to the American mainstream create the most American forms of popular culture: jazz and Hollywood movies?

4. Why is the decade known as the "Jazz Age"? What was "roaring" about the "roaring twenties"?

5. What was the Scopes trial about, and why was it important?

6. What was the impact of the *Buck v. Bell* Supreme Court decision?

7. Who was left out of the consumer culture and prosperity of the 1920s?

8. What were some of the causes of the 1929 stock market crash?

Created Equal Online

For more *Created Equal* resources, including suggestions for sites to visit and further reading, go to **MyHistoryLab.com.**

Part Eight

From Depression and War to World Power, 1929–1953

The Great Depression and World War II tested Americans' faith in their federal government to a degree unmatched in the nation's history. Economic collapse in the 1930s and the threat of German and Japanese aggression from 1941 to 1945 presented challenges beyond the reach of ordinary citizens, local communities, and businesses acting alone. The federal government began to take more responsibility for economic and social well-being at home and for the defense and spread of American values around the world.

The Great Depression resulted in a fundamental reordering of American politics. President Franklin Delano Roosevelt (FDR), who took office in 1933, believed that the federal government must assume an active role in banking, agriculture, and social welfare. He sponsored a large number of federal initiatives, known collectively as the New Deal. The New Deal aimed to put people back to work, restore faith in American businesses, boost purchasing power among consumers, and cushion the effects of economic downturns on industrial workers.

The effects of the New Deal were uneven. Many workers, including domestic servants, agricultural laborers, and part-time and seasonal employees, did not qualify for Social Security and other benefits. In the South, government policies that discouraged landowners from planting crops led to the displacement of many black and white sharecropping families. On the other hand, employees of many large companies won higher wages and improved job security as a result of militant labor protests. African American civil rights activists, local communist organizations such as urban Unemployed Councils, and southern sharecroppers' and tenants' unions gave voice to the groups hit hardest by the Depression.

The New Deal did not end the Depression. On the morning of December 7, 1941, the Japanese conducted a surprise air attack on the U.S. Pacific naval fleet stationed in Pearl Harbor, Hawaii. Americans reacted with shock and outrage to what the president called this "day of infamy." The U.S. entry into World War II put large numbers of Americans back to work, many of them in the expanding defense industries.

The conflict brought Americans together in shared hardship, sacrifice, and national purpose. At the same time, the war placed strains on the social fabric. All over the country, family members separated from one another to fight or to search for work. In the Midwest, blacks and whites competed for scarce wartime resources, such as housing. On the West Coast, more than 100,000 Japanese immigrants and U.S. citizens of Japanese descent were forced into internment camps.

Elected to an unprecedented fourth term in 1944, Roosevelt proved to be a commanding leader during wartime as well as economic depression. In the last stages of the war, the president met several times with his British and Soviet counterparts, Winston Churchill and Josef Stalin, to plan for the postwar reconstruction of Europe and Asia. Roosevelt's death in April 1945 catapulted Vice President Harry S. Truman into the presidency. After Germany surrendered, the new president authorized the dropping of atomic bombs on the Japanese cities of Hiroshima and Nagasaki, effectively ending the war in the Pacific. Together, the two bombs killed 120,000 Japanese civilians and wounded at least 130,000 more. The Atomic Age ushered in a new chapter in the history of human warfare.

Together with its allies, the United States emerged victorious from the war, but unlike its allies, America had escaped extensive physical destruction. The Soviet Union, an ally in the war against Germany and Japan, emerged as America's greatest postwar enemy. The development of weapons of mass destruction introduced a new and profound threat to humanity as well as to the natural environment. To secure its supremacy in world affairs, the United States helped form the North Atlantic Treaty Organization (NATO). For the first time, Americans were part of a multination peacetime alliance, one that required them to defend a member of the alliance even if they themselves were not attacked

World War II also profoundly altered life in the United States. The perceived communist threat led some Americans to suspect domestic groups of internal subversion: African Americans agitating for their civil rights, labor leaders attempting to organize southern factories, and leftists who expressed support for communism in general and the Soviet Union in particular. Supported by government contracts, the defense industry became an integral part of the nation's economy.

Recovering quickly from the disruptions of war, young couples produced the baby boom, a generation that shaped American culture and society in significant ways. In the new and growing suburbs, many (predominantly white) Americans achieved their dream of home ownership, and businesses found plenty of room to expand in new industrial parks. Yet, not all Americans shared in this newfound prosperity and security, and not all were willing to forgo their rights to free speech and free assembly in the struggle against communism.

Chapter 22

Hardship and Hope: The Great Depression of the 1930s

■ Will Rogers, left, is shown here with William Harrison Hays, one of many powerful political leaders with whom Rogers socialized.

In 1934, Will Rogers commented on the causes of the Great Depression during his weekly radio broadcast. He noted that it was "not the working classes that brought on the economic crisis, it was the big boys that thought the financial drunk was going to last forever, and overbought, overmerged and overcapitalized." As a result, the "difference between our rich and poor grows greater every year. . . . Our rich are getting richer all the time. . . . There was not a millionaire in the country whose fortune did not come from the labor of others. We need to arrange it so that a man that wants work can get work, and give him a more equal division of the wealth the country produces."

Rogers was a plainspoken critic of the nation's rich and powerful; he was also a Cherokee, a comedian, a movie star, a journalist, and an adviser to President Franklin Delano Roosevelt (FDR). Rogers articulated a new vision of American national identity that took shape in the 1930s. In contrast to an earlier notion of the United States as an Anglo-Saxon country into which newcomers might assimilate, this new Americanism included ethnic minorities, particularly those of European immigrant background. The Great Depression tarnished the status of the nation's business elite and opened up the political process to party realignments and new leaders. The popular culture expressed and reflected this new Americanism; Will Rogers was its most prominent voice. When the *Wall Street Journal* and the *New York Times* condemned him for his criticism of corporate elites, Rogers responded with a humorous assault on the nation's Anglo-Saxon leaders and their myths:

> I have a different slant on things, for my ancestors did not come over on the Mayflower. They met the boat. . . . I hope my Cherokee blood is not making me prejudiced, I want to be broad minded, but I am sure it was only the extreme generosity of the Indians that allowed the Pilgrims to land anywhere. Suppose we reverse the case. Do you reckon the Pilgrims would have ever let the Indians land? Yeah, what a chance, what a chance. The Pilgrims wouldn't even allow the Indians to live after the Indians went to the trouble of letting them land, of course, but they'd always pray. . . . You've never in your life . . . seen a picture of one of the old Pilgrims praying when he didn't have a gun right by the side of him. That was to see that he got what he was praying for.

Born in 1879 in Oolagah, in Indian Territory (present-day Oklahoma), Rogers got his start as a rope-twirling cowboy on the vaudeville circuit. He worked his way through Wild West shows, demonstrating his impressive riding and roping skills, even though he found the spectacles demeaning to Native Americans, who were always defeated in the shows' mock battles. In the 1920s, Rogers worked as an entertainer in Hollywood, where his Cherokee identity shaped both his humor and his social criticism.

In the 1930s, the Great Depression gave rise to a cultural and political upheaval that helped propel Rogers to stardom and political influence. President Franklin Roosevelt coveted his support, and Rogers obliged by promoting the New Deal, the president's program for economic recovery. However, Rogers also pushed the president to the left by advocating such measures as taxing the rich and redistributing wealth. In 1932, Oklahoma nominated Rogers for president as the state's favorite son; three years later, California Democratic leaders urged him to run for the Senate. But in 1935, before any of these possibilities could come to fruition, Rogers died in a plane crash.

The response to Rogers's death illustrates his stature as a national leader and spokesperson for a new multicultural America. Congress adjourned in his memory, President Roosevelt sent a well-publicized letter to Rogers's family, the governor of California proclaimed a day of mourning, flags flew at half-staff, bells rang in Rogers's honor in more than 100 cities, and nearly 100,000 people filed by his coffin at Forest Lawn Cemetery in Los Angeles. Radio stations across the country broadcast his memorial service from the Hollywood Bowl, presided over by a Protestant minister and a Catholic priest, while a Jewish cantor sang a Hebrew mourning chant. Across town, Mexican American citizen groups placed a wreath on Olvera Street that read "*Nosotros Lamentamos la Muerte de Will Rogers*" (We Mourn the Death of Will Rogers). In the predominantly black Los Angeles community of Watts, an African American fraternal group joined black performers from Rogers's films in a parade to honor the Cherokee movie star. Back in his hometown of Claremore, Oklahoma, the Cherokee performed a death dance in memory of their fallen kinsman.

This massive national grieving reveals not only Rogers's popularity, but also the culture of 1930s America. The economic crisis unleashed changes in society that opened the door for a politically radical Cherokee to become one of the most popular figures of the decade. Millions of Americans experienced poverty—many for the first time. The shared experience of loss and suffering permeated the country.

Franklin Roosevelt drew a new political coalition into the Democratic party that elected him to the presidency four times. It included native born and foreign born, working class and middle class, Anglo-Saxons and ethnic minorities, and people of color. The Depression gave Roosevelt the opportunity to forge a strong national government and to promote a more representative democracy. His inclusiveness efforts brought citizens of recent immigrant background into the political mainstream but stopped short of the color line. Nevertheless, African American voters abandoned the Republican party to vote for FDR.

The **New Deal,** a package of remedies put together by Franklin Roosevelt to address the problems of the Depression, provided relief to many Americans in need but did not eradicate poverty or end the Depression. Yet, as American families from every region of the country drew around their radios to hear the president's fireside chats, as they made heroes of Will Rogers and other outsider celebrities, and as they held onto their faith in the nation's promise in spite of its worst economic crisis, they helped forge a more inclusive nation.

The Great Depression

■ *What caused the Great Depression, and how did it affect ordinary Americans?*

The Great Depression, part of a global economic crisis, defined the 1930s in the United States. It shaped American culture, the political life of the nation, the public policies that resulted, and the cultural expressions that reflected the spirit of the people during a time of national crisis. Its effects permeated the lives of Americans from the mansions of the wealthy to the shanties of the poor and from the boardrooms to the bedrooms. The Depression drove thousands of farmers from the drought-stricken southern Great Plains to California. But the story is not simply one of despair and hardship. It is also one of strong communities, resourcefulness, and hope.

CAUSES OF THE CRISIS

The Great Depression of the 1930s was the worst economic depression in the nation's history. But it was neither the first nor the last. **Capitalism,** the system of private enterprise that forms the basis of the American economy, has cycles of ups and downs. Under capitalism, the free market operates with minimal interference from the government. In the United States, prior to the 1930s, the government stepped in to regulate the economy primarily to protect economic competition. Progressive Era reforms prevented corporations from establishing monopolies, so that competition could flourish. In the free market economy, consumers would determine which companies would succeed, based on the quality of their products and services. Because the government did not determine the levels of industrial or agricultural productivity, and did not set the prices, the economy was subject to changing circumstances that led to times of prosperity and times of recession or, in the case of severe economic downturns, depression. The circumstances that affected the up-and-down cycles of the economy included international economic trends as well as the workings of capitalism itself.

Communism and socialism are economic systems with greater levels of government regulation. Communist countries have state-directed economies in which the government owns and operates farms and factories, sets prices, and pays all workers' wages. There is no free market and no competition among businesses. In socialist states, governments own and operate certain industries and services, such as electricity and other utilities, or health care systems. Socialist countries also provide citizens with certain welfare benefits such as medical care, relief from poverty, income for the unemployed, and

In the Shadow of the American Dream

In her 1937 photograph "At the Time of the Louisville Flood," Margaret Bourke White depicts the painful irony of poverty in the midst of affluence. Here, hungry Americans stand in a breadline in front of a billboard proclaiming American prosperity. The billboard, depicting a family on a drive through the country, celebrates American consumer culture and leisure. The breadline shows deprivation in the midst of the Depression.

QUESTIONS

1. What does the photograph suggest about class and racial divisions in Depression-era America?

2. What do the details in the photograph—including clothing, possessions, and landscape—reveal about American dreams and realities in the 1930s?

old-age insurance. A number of capitalist countries offer these kinds of benefits to their citizens under a system known as welfare capitalism.

Before the 1930s, the United States provided none of these **welfare state** benefits. Without any policies that would serve as a safety net for workers who lost their jobs, many wage-earners and their families fell into poverty during times of economic downturn. In the Great Depression of the 1930s, the economic crisis was so severe that one-quarter of the nation's workers, nearly 14 million people, lost their jobs, leaving them and their families—40 million people in all—without any income or security. Many of these people had never known poverty before. Among the newly poor were thousands of middle-class Americans who now faced the loss of their homes and savings. For working-class and poor Americans, the impact of the Depression was devastating because they had little economic security to begin with.

The Great Depression in North America and Western Europe

The Wider World

The Great Depression was a global economic catastrophe, as shown in this graph, which illustrates unemployment rates and declines in industrial production among selected North American and western European countries with economic structures similar to that of the United States. No industrial nation – with the exception of the Soviet Union with its centralized economy – was spared the ravages of the crisis.

Although the Depression was global in scope, it did not affect every country to the same extent. The United States was hit the hardest by the economic crisis, both in terms of industrial production and unemployment. The American economy was the most overextended and suffered the most dramatic effects of the 1929 stock market crash. The impact on Germany was almost as severe. The German economy remained weak after its defeat in World War I and was further weakened by repaying large sums owed to the United States. In some countries, the impact on industrial production was less severe, but unemployment reached high levels nonetheless.

Most nations responded to the Great Depression by increasing the central government's role in the economy. Some, including the United States and Great Britain, moved toward greater social welfare measures. Others, especially Germany, moved toward greater investment in the military. How each nation experienced and responded to the Depression foreshadowed in some measure its role in World War II.

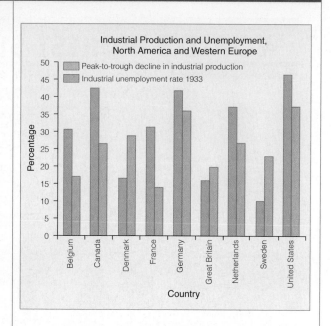

QUESTIONS

1. Which countries had the greatest decline in industrial production?

2. Which countries had relatively small declines in industrial production, but high unemployment rates? What might account for those discrepancies?

The Great Depression was a global economic catastrophe. Of the major world powers, only the Soviet Union—as a communist society, with state-directed labor, agriculture, and industry—was immune to the collapse of the capitalist system after 1929. In fact, the Soviet economy grew throughout the 1930s, and its relative health led many people in troubled capitalist systems to look to communism as an alternative. Socialism also gained many converts across Europe. The powerful nations of the world all moved toward greater government intervention in their economies. England, France, and the United States moved toward deficit spending to help stimulate the economy and instituted relief programs. Italy, Germany, and Japan also increased government intervention in the economy, but they used different strategies to address the crisis, particularly military spending. These varied responses to the Depression contributed to the conflicts and alliances that would eventually culminate in World War II.

Within the United States, the business values that had prevailed throughout the 1920s were now suspect. Business practices in every area of the economy, from finance to factories to agriculture, contributed to the disaster. For many Americans, the Great Depression really began in the 1920s. Food production and distribution stumbled along weakly throughout the 1920s, creating widespread rural poverty. Large corporations bought up smaller companies, putting many independent shops and manufacturers out of business. During the 1920s, 1,200 big corporations absorbed more than 6,000 independent businesses. By 1929,

200 corporations controlled nearly half of all industry, which limited competition and made it difficult for new, smaller businesses to flourish.

Although the 1920s economy looked healthy on the surface, prosperity rested on an unsound foundation. Many people obtained consumer goods on credit, so when people lost their jobs, they could not pay their debts. Throughout the decade, the gap between the rich and poor increased. By 1929, the top 1 percent of Americans earned 14.7 percent of the nation's income, while the poorest 40 percent shared 12.5 percent. Nearly 80 percent of the nation's families had no savings. Americans with high annual incomes of $10,000 or more—2.3 percent of the people—held two-thirds of all savings. As Will Rogers and many other social critics would later point out, the concentration of wealth among the richest Americans during the 1920s contributed to the persistence of the crisis in the 1930s.

International factors also played a role in the economic collapse. American overseas loans soared in the 1920s, reaching $900 million by 1924 and $1.25 billion by 1928. Germany was a large borrower, for example. Following its defeat in World War I, Germany had been required to make large reparation payments to France and other countries. The United States provided loans to Germany to help the country make its payments. When the stock market crashed, foreign economies like that of Germany also weakened and could not repay their debts. To make matters worse, the United States had established high tariffs to keep foreign goods out of the country so that Americans would buy only American-made goods. In turn, other countries established their own tariff barriers. As a result, American exports fell $1.5 billion between 1929 and 1933. Over the same four years, the gross national product (GNP) fell by $12 billion.

> *Although the 1920s economy looked healthy on the surface, prosperity rested on an unsound foundation.*

SURVIVING HARD TIMES

In human terms, the Depression dealt a devastating blow to large numbers of Americans: crushing poverty, hunger, humiliation, and loss of dignity and self-worth. Many felt a profound shame that they could no longer earn a living and support their families. The few jobs available often went to the young, strong, well fed, and well groomed. In 1934, an Oklahoma woman poured out her heart in a letter to President Roosevelt: "The unemployed have been so long without food-clothes-shoes-medical care-dental care etc—we look pretty bad—so when we ask for a job we dont' get it. And we look and feel a little worse each day—when we ask for food they call us bums—it isent our fault...no we are not bums." Yet the shabby appearance of the jobless helped neither their self-respect nor their work prospects. In another letter to the president, an unemployed worker from Oregon explained the difficult choices: "We do not dare to use even a little soap when it will pay for an extra egg [or] a few more carrots for our children." These letters were among thousands of requests for help sent to FDR.

Families provided the first line of defense against disaster, especially in the early days of the crisis. Many families adapted to hard times by abandoning time-honored gender roles. As men lost jobs, women went to work. More than 6 million single women held jobs during the Depression. Married women also took jobs to support their families, often providing the only source of income if husbands were out of work. These women faced hostility from many who believed that working wives took jobs from unemployed men. But the jobs women held, as secretaries, nurses, and waitresses, were defined as "women's work"— occupations that had no impact on male employment at the time. These jobs paid lower wages than most jobs held by men. A white woman earned, on average, 61 percent of a white man's wages; a black woman earned a mere 23 percent. Still, the jobs women filled provided at least a little much-needed income.

Sons and daughters also went to work, taking on the responsibilities of adulthood. Marriage rates plummeted as young people helped support their families in the face of economic hardship. Many parents struggled to provide for their families under difficult conditions, sometimes risking their health and safety to do so. Erminia Pablita Ruiz Mercer remembered when her father was injured while working in the beet fields in 1933. "He didn't want to live if he couldn't support his family," so he risked experimental back surgery and died on the operating table. Young Erminia then dropped out of school to work as "a doughnut girl" to support her mother and sisters.

ENDURING DISCRIMINATION

For many poor families, hard times were nothing new. As one African American noted, "The Negro was born in depression. It only became official when it hit the white man." Throughout the 1930s, black Americans suffered the impact of economic hard times disproportionately. By 1932, black unemployment reached 50 percent. Unemployed white workers began seeking the jobs that were usually held by black workers, even though they would have shunned such work during prosperous times. With local white authorities in charge of relief, impoverished southern blacks had few places to turn for assistance. African Americans also faced increasing violence; the number of lynchings increased from eight in 1932 to twenty in 1935.

Many poor people joined the growing ranks of **hobos,** riding the rails from town to town, looking for work. But poverty did not erase racial hierarchies or sexual codes, especially for nine young African Americans who came to be known as the "Scottsboro Boys." On March 25, 1931, the youths, ranging in age from thirteen to twenty-one, were taken from a train in Paint Rock, Alabama, after a fight with a group of white men. Two white women, also on the train, accused the nine of rape. Narrowly avoiding a lynching, the youths were taken to jail in Scottsboro, where they began a long ordeal. Within two weeks, an all-white jury convicted them of rape, and they were sentenced to death. The communist-backed International Labor Defense (ILD) took up the case and appealed it to the Alabama Supreme Court. The ILD also organized protests and rallies across the country, calling for justice for the Scottsboro Boys. In spite of the ILD efforts, the Alabama Supreme Court upheld the convictions, but in November 1932 the U.S. Supreme Court ordered a new trial on the grounds that the defendants did not get a fair trial.

The first defendant to be retried was quickly convicted again and sentenced to death. At this point, the case became a major rallying point for civil rights activists, liberals, and radicals. Support for the young men came from all over the world, including the British Parliament and the Communist party. In 1935, the U.S. Supreme Court reversed the second set of convictions on the grounds that excluding blacks from the jury denied the defendants due process. Yet in the next two years, five of the defendants were again tried and found guilty. Although none of the Scottsboro Boys was executed, they all spent long years in prison. Eventually, the charges against the youngest four were dropped. Although all appeals failed and the five remaining prisoners were never cleared of the crime, several were paroled, and the last of the nine was released from prison in 1950. In 1976, the repentant former segregationist governor of Alabama, George Wallace, pardoned one of the nine, Clarence Norris.

> *Racial discrimination intensified the suffering of African Americans during the Depression.*

Racial discrimination intensified the suffering of African Americans during the Depression. By 1935, 90 percent of employed black women worked as either domestics or agricultural laborers. As these jobs became scarce, black women's labor-force participation fell from 42 percent to 38 percent over the decade.

Mexican American families could barely survive on the low wages paid to Mexican laborers. According to a 1933 study, working children's earnings constituted more than one-third of their families' total income. The work was often grueling. Julia Luna Mount

■ The Scottsboro Boys, pictured here surrounded by the National Guard, were sentenced to death on unsubstantiated accusations that they raped two white women on a railroad car in 1931. Although none was executed, they spent years in prison and became the focus of an international effort to gain their release.

recalled her first day at a Los Angeles cannery: "I didn't have money for gloves so I peeled chilies all day long by hand. After work, my hands were red, swollen, and I was on fire! On the streetcar going home, I could hardly hold on my hands hurt so much." Young Julia was lucky—her father saw her suffering and did not make her return to the cannery. But Carmen Bernal Escobar's father could not afford to be soft-hearted about work: "My father was a busboy and to keep the family going . . . in order to bring in a little more money . . . my mother, my grandmother, my mother's brother, my sister and I all worked together" at the cannery.

Those with cannery work, hard as it was, were among the fortunate. Many more Mexicans were deported. Most were children born in the United States. In a pattern that continued throughout the century, the United States opened or closed its doors to Mexican immigrants depending on the need for their labor. They were deported during the Depression when unemployment was high, then recruited again during the labor shortage of World War II. In the 1930s, Mexicans who applied for relief were offered assistance only if they agreed to return to Mexico. But deportation brought more sorrows. In Ciudad Juarez, 2,000 repatriates lived in a large open corral without resources or shelter; dozens died from disease.

THE DUST BOWL

White families from the nation's heartland also suffered extreme deprivation. Severe drought exacerbated the difficulties of farmers across Oklahoma, Texas, Kansas, Colorado, and New Mexico, an area that came to be known as the **Dust Bowl.** Farmers had used the land mainly for grazing until high grain prices during World War I enticed them to plow under millions of acres of natural grasslands to plant wheat. Plowing removed root systems from the soil, and years of little rainfall caused the land to dry up. By the middle of the decade, high winds picked up the loose topsoil, creating dust storms across the open plains. The worst storm occurred on April 14, 1935, when winds up to 70 miles per hour carried clouds of dust that turned the sky black, suffocated livestock, and lodged in people's homes, clothes, hair, and lungs. The ecological disaster drove 60 percent of the population out of the region.

Migrant farm families fleeing the Dust Bowl came to symbolize the suffering wrought by the Depression. The photographs of Dorothea Lange, the songs of Woody Guthrie, and the writings of John Steinbeck all immortalized their plight. Steinbeck's Pulitzer prize–winning novel *The Grapes of Wrath* (1939) and its film version have remained classics of American popular art. Writing in *The Nation* in 1936, Steinbeck described the Dust Bowl migrants streaming into California:

> Poverty-stricken after the destruction of their farms, their last reserves used up in making the trip, they have arrived so beaten and destitute that they have been willing at first to work under any conditions and for any wages offered. . . . They are not drawn from a peon class, but have either owned small farms or been farm hands in the early American sense, in which the "hand" is a member of the employing family. They have one fixed idea, and that is to acquire land and settle on it. . . . They are not easily intimidated. They are courageous, intelligent, and resourceful. Having gone through the horrors of the drought and with immense effort having escaped from it, they cannot be herded, attacked, starved, or frightened.

Thousands of **Okies,** as the Dust Bowl migrants came to be known, piled belongings on their cars and made their way to California in hopes of starting over. There they joined Mexican migrant farm workers, African American laborers, and others down on their luck hoping for work.

■ An Oklahoma farmer and his sons try to find shelter from the storm of dust that blew across the plains in 1935. Severe drought after years of excessive plowing created dry loose topsoil that was picked up by high winds. More than half of the residents of the Dust Bowl moved out of the area as a result of the devastation.

Arthur Rothstein, 1936. The Library of Congress

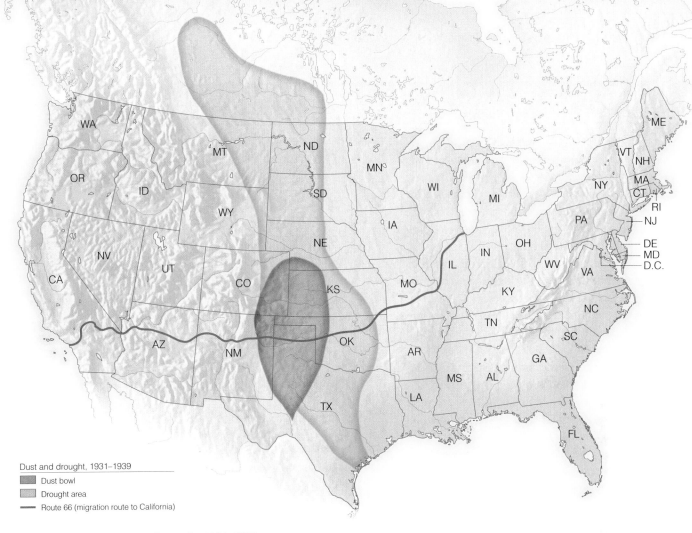

Dust and drought, 1931–1939

- ■ Dust bowl
- Drought area
- —— Route 66 (migration route to California)

■ **MAP 22.1 Dust and Drought, 1931–1939**

Drought cut a giant swath across the middle of America during the years of the Great Depression. The hardest hit region was the Dust Bowl area of Oklahoma, Texas, New Mexico, Colorado, and Kansas. Many people fled the afflicted areas, abandoning farms, piling their belongings on their cars, and driving along Route 66 to California.

Presidential Responses to the Depression

■ *How did Presidents Hoover and Roosevelt respond to the Great Depression?*

Until the collapse of the economy, President Herbert Hoover had earned wide admiration for his political achievements. Although he seemed the perfect embodiment of the spirit of the prosperous 1920s, his ideas about politics and economics were ill suited to the crisis of the 1930s. Dissatisfaction with Hoover's response to the Depression gave Franklin Delano Roosevelt a landslide victory in the 1932 presidential election. Promising to take action to ease the nation's suffering, the optimistic and pragmatic Roosevelt seemed to embody hope for an end to the crisis. First Lady Eleanor Roosevelt became one of FDR's most trusted advisers. She and other liberal activists helped shape FDR's response to the crisis.

HERBERT HOOVER: FAILED EFFORTS

Hoover's first major political achievement came in Europe during World War I, when he headed the Commission for Relief in Belgium. There he organized a massive effort funded by private and government contributions that fed more than 9 million people for nearly five

Songs of the Great Depression

Interpreting History

Popular songs expressed the spirit, sorrows, and longings of Depression-era Americans. According to folk-music historian Alan Lomax, the twelve-year-old daughter of a striking Harlan County, Kentucky, mineworker wrote "Which Side Are You On?" in 1937. The song became a popular anthem for labor militancy.

Woody Guthrie (1912–1967) wrote more than a thousand songs about the struggles of common people and the dispossessed. In 1931, when the Okemah, Oklahoma, boomtown period was over, Guthrie left his home for the Texas panhandle town of Pampa, where in 1933 he married the sister of a musician friend. After the 1935 Great Dust Storm, due to the lack of work and driven by a search for a better life, Woody headed west along with the mass migration of "dust bowl refugees." Moneyless and hungry, he hitchhiked, rode freight trains, and even walked to California, developing a love for traveling on the "open road"—a practice he would often repeat. His song "Union Maid" expresses the hopes and spirit of union workers, and "So Long, It's Been Good to Know Yuh" captures the sorrows of Dust Bowl migrants.

Bettmann/CORBIS

■ Woody Guthrie, singer and songwriter, immortalized the spirit of ordinary Americans during the struggles of the Great Depression. His songs became anthems of the era and remain classics of American folk music.

WHICH SIDE ARE YOU ON?

By Florence Reece (sung to the tune of an old English song, "Jack Munro")

Come all of you good workers
Good news to you I'll tell
Of how the good old union
Has come in here to dwell.

Chorus

Which side are you on,
Tell me, which side are you on?

My daddy was a miner,
He's now in the air an' sun,
Stick with him, brother miners,
Until this battle's won.
They say in Harlan County
There are no neutrals there
You'll either be a union man,
Or a thug for J. H. Blair.
O gentlemen, can you stand it,
O tell me if you can,
Will you be a lousy scab,
Or will you be a man?
Don't scab for the bosses,
Don't listen to their lies,

years. Later, he became the U.S. food administrator and headed the American Relief Administration. He earned praise as a visionary Progressive for his ability to mobilize volunteer efforts and to find efficient ways to meet people's needs. President Warren G. Harding then appointed him secretary of commerce.

It is no surprise that the popular Republican won the presidency in 1928. But even Hoover worried about "the exaggerated idea the people have conceived of me. They have a conviction that I am a sort of superman, that no problem is beyond my capacity. . . . If some unprecedented calamity should come upon the nation . . . I would be sacrificed to the

Us poor folks haven't got a chance,
Unless we organize.

UNION MAID

By Woody Guthrie (first verse and chorus)

There once was a union maid
Who never was afraid
Of goons and ginks and company finks
And the deputy sheriffs who made the raids;
She went to the union hall
When a meeting it was called
And when the company boys came 'round
She always stood her ground.

Chorus

Oh, you can't scare me.
I'm sticking to the union, (3 times)
Oh, you can't scare me.
I'm sticking to the union, (2 times)
Till the day I die.

"SO LONG, IT'S BEEN GOOD TO KNOW YUH (DUSTY OLD DUST)"

By Woody Guthrie (selected verses and chorus)

I've sung this song, but I'll sing it again,
Of the place that I lived on the wild, windy plains,
In the month called April, the county called Gray
And here's what all of the people there say:

Chorus

So long, it's been good to know ye; (3 times)
This dusty old dust is a-getting my home,
And I've got to be drifting along.

A dust storm hit, and it hit like thunder;

It dustedus over, and it covered us under;
Blocked out the traffic and blocked out the sun.
Straight for home all the people did run.

The sweethearts sat in the dark and they sparked,

They hugged and kissed in that dusty old dark,
They sighed and cried, hugged and kissed
Instead of marriage, they talked like this:
Honey, so long, it's been good to know ye . . .

Now, the telephone rang, and it jumped off the wall;

That was the preacher a-making his call.
He said, "Kind friend, this may be the end;
You've got your last chance of salvation of sin."

The churches was jammed, and the churches was packed,

And that dusty old dust storm blowed so black;
The preacher could not read a word of his text,
And he folded his specs and he took up collection, said:
So long, it's been good to know ye.

QUESTIONS

1. *What makes the songs emblematic of the era in which they were written?*

2. *How are issues of class addressed in these songs?*

unreasoning disappointment of a people who expected too much." The unprecedented calamity arrived, and Hoover's predictions were correct.

Had prosperity continued, Hoover might have left a legacy of presidential leadership to match his earlier achievements as a Progressive administrator of food relief in Europe. Declaring that "excessive fortunes are a menace to true liberty," he favored steeply graduated inheritance and income taxes on the wealthy, with no tax burden on the poor. He believed that society had a responsibility to care for those in need and that the prosperous should bear much of the burden. After the stock market crash, Hoover increased spending for public works—programs in which the government created jobs for people who needed employment—to the unprecedented sum of $700 million. He established the Reconstruction Finance Corporation to make government credit available to banks and other financial institutions. Seeking to restore confidence in the economy, he strove for a balanced budget by raising taxes and cutting spending—a strategy that underestimated the depth of the Depression and made the situation worse.

As the Depression set in and brought widespread misery, Hoover fully expected that charitable organizations would step in and provide assistance to the poor. He believed that government relief to the needy had demoralizing effects on people. In 1931, he pledged that if voluntary and local efforts were unable "to prevent hunger and suffering in my country, I will ask the aid of every resource of the Federal Government." But he had "faith in the American people that such a day [would] never come." Even when it was clear that the crisis was far beyond the help of charitable groups, Hoover remained strongly opposed to direct relief for the poor. Private giving did increase to record levels; unfortunately, it was not sufficient.

Hoover believed that giving people the means to make a living was better than offering them direct relief. Thus, for example, he approved a grant of $45 million to feed livestock during the 1930 drought but rejected a proposed grant of $25 million to feed farmers and their families. His logic was consistent: livestock provided farmers with the means to make a living so they could feed their families. But this philosophy offered little comfort to farmers who watched their families starve as their hogs lapped up food provided by the government.

Hoover's popularity reached its lowest ebb in 1932. A group of World War I veterans in Portland, Oregon, organized a march on Washington, D.C., called the Bonus March. The veterans were due to receive a bonus of $1,000 each in 1945. The group had asked to have their bonuses early, in 1932, to help ease their suffering during the Depression. Hoover refused. More than 20,000 veterans traveled to Washington to petition Congress. The House passed a bill to pay the bonus immediately, but the Senate refused to follow suit. The

IMAGE

Bonus Expeditionary
Force March on
Washington

■ This photo, taken in Washington, D.C., on July 28, 1932, shows the Bonus Army's temporary city on fire. Americans were appalled by the callousness of President Hoover, who stood by as the U.S. Army attacked the peacefully protesting veterans with tanks and tear gas. The Capitol looms in the background.

The National Archives

determined veterans set up a tent city and settled in with their families. On the last day of the congressional session, when Hoover again refused to meet with the protesters, the veterans began to leave. But some did not depart quickly enough, and a police officer began shooting at the unarmed demonstrators, killing one person.

Army Chief of Staff Douglas MacArthur stepped in and escalated the violence. His troops used tear gas and bayonets to prod the veterans and their families to vacate the area, then set fire to the tent city. The attack injured more than 100 people and killed one baby. The image of federal troops assaulting a group of peaceful veterans stunned the public. Although MacArthur had ordered the brutality, the public directed its outrage against Hoover. As most people saw it, Hoover had heartlessly spurned the veterans' legitimate request. By the time of the 1932 election, Hoover had lost most of his public support.

FRANKLIN DELANO ROOSEVELT: THE PRAGMATIST

In contrast to Hoover, Franklin Delano Roosevelt was born into a family of wealth and privilege whose ancestors included European aristocrats and passengers on the *Mayflower*. Pampered as a child, at age fourteen he went to Groton, then the nation's most exclusive boarding school; from there he attended Harvard College and Columbia Law School. In 1905, during his first year at Columbia, he married a distant cousin, Eleanor Roosevelt, the niece of President Theodore Roosevelt.

Franklin Roosevelt was elected to the New York State Senate in 1911, and in 1913 he became assistant secretary of the navy. He ran unsuccessfully as the Democratic vice presidential nominee in 1920. His political plans derailed suddenly in 1921 when he was stricken with polio. The painful and incapacitating illness threw the normally ebullient Roosevelt into despair. He had always assumed that he would control his own destiny. Now he could no longer use his legs. Formerly athletic, Roosevelt depended on braces, crutches, and a wheelchair to move around. But his upbringing had given him extraordinary reserves of self-confidence and optimism, and these qualities helped to sustain him in the face of his paralysis.

FDR's bout with polio and subsequent paralysis did nothing to dampen his political ambitions, although he as well as journalists and photographers took pains to hide his disability in photographs and newsreels. He became governor of New York in 1928, following the same career path as Theodore Roosevelt. But, unlike his Republican cousin, Franklin was a Democrat. In the 1932 presidential campaign, FDR made few specific proposals, but he

Franklin Delano Roosevelt Presidential Library

■ In this 1941 photograph, FDR is pictured with his dog Fala and Ruthie Bie, a friend's granddaughter, in Hyde Park, New York. This is one of only two known photographs of Roosevelt in his wheelchair. Careful to project an image of strength, vitality, and optimism, FDR avoided photos that would call attention to his physical disability. Yet many Americans found inspiration and hope knowing that their president, like the nation, could triumph over adversity.

TABLE 22.1			
The Election of 1932			
Candidate	**Political Party**	**Popular Vote (%)**	**Electoral Vote**
Franklin D. Roosevelt	Democratic	57.4	472
Herbert Hoover	Republican	39.7	59
Norman Thomas	Socialist	2.2	–

promised the American people a "New Deal." Although Hoover was intensely unpopular, supporters within the Republican party defended his record and supported his efforts to balance the budget. There were others on the ballot, notably socialist Norman Thomas and communist William Z. Foster. Polls showed that 5 percent of the electorate favored Thomas, but in the end only half of those, fewer than 1 million voters, actually marked their ballots for Thomas, and a much smaller number for Foster. Many voters on the left cast their ballots for Roosevelt, fearing that a vote for Thomas might throw the election to Hoover. FDR won a landslide victory, the largest electoral margin since 1864.

Like Theodore Roosevelt before him, FDR was committed to strengthening the federal government. But Franklin was less interested in protecting and preserving old-stock Anglo-Saxon Americans from the cultural and demographic impact of immigration than his Republican cousin had been. Lawmakers in the 1920s had closed off immigration, silenced dissenters, deported foreign radicals, and suppressed labor insurgency. In contrast, FDR's strategy was one of inclusion rather than exclusion; he welcomed the newcomers into his vision of America and cultivated their allegiance. Immigrants from southern and eastern Europe were among FDR's most ardent supporters. Millions of them became naturalized citizens and voted for the first time in the 1930s, overwhelmingly as Democrats.

ELEANOR ROOSEVELT: ACTIVIST AND FIRST LADY

FDR's pragmatism prevented him from extending his vision of inclusiveness to people of color. He feared he would lose the support of southern Democrats if he advocated racial justice. His wife, Eleanor, had no such qualms. As an advocate for civil rights and a political activist in her own right, she transformed the role of first lady from official hostess to influential presidential adviser with a major public presence. Eleanor Roosevelt was widely considered the most powerful woman in American politics until her death at age seventy-eight in 1962.

Like Franklin, Eleanor came from a sheltered, upper-class background. But her early life, unlike his, was filled with sadness. Both her parents died when she was a young child, and at age ten she went to live with her grandmother, who left her in the care of a harsh governess. The young woman began to flourish when she went abroad to study. The rigorous education developed her strengths and confidence, which would serve her well throughout her life.

Eleanor bore six children in ten years. But she and Franklin had a partnership that was more political than sexual. Upon her discovery in 1918 that Franklin was having an affair with her secretary, Lucy Mercer, Eleanor moved into a separate house on the Roosevelt estate. The two remained married, developing a strong bond of friendship and a deep political alliance.

A powerful advocate for civil rights, social justice, women's equality, and international cooperation, Eleanor Roosevelt was largely responsible for many of the most humane programs of the

Bettmann/CORBIS

■ African American contralto Marian Anderson sings on the steps of the Lincoln Memorial on April 9, 1939. Eleanor Roosevelt arranged the concert after the DAR refused to allow Anderson to sing in Constitution Hall. The event attracted a live audience of 75,000, while millions more listened on the radio.

New Deal. She spoke out publicly on a wide range of issues and prodded FDR to adopt her positions. Although FDR was reluctant to support an antilynching bill in Congress for fear of alienating southern white voters, the first lady campaigned vigorously against lynching. When the Daughters of the American Revolution (DAR) denied the African American opera star Marian Anderson the right to perform at Constitution Hall in Washington, D.C., Eleanor Roosevelt promptly resigned from the DAR in protest and arranged for Anderson to perform at the Lincoln Memorial on Easter Sunday 1939, where a huge audience stood in the cold to hear her sing.

After FDR died in 1945, Eleanor Roosevelt remained politically active. She was a major force in the adoption of the United Nations' Declaration of Human Rights in 1948, and she remained involved in Democratic politics throughout the 1950s. In 1962, President John F. Kennedy appointed her chair of the President's Commission on the Status of Women, which issued a report that identified widespread discrimination and helped to launch the feminist movement of the 1960s and 1970s.

"NOTHING TO FEAR BUT FEAR ITSELF"

When FDR took office, the influence of Eleanor Roosevelt and his other liberal advisers was not yet evident. What was clear, however, was the new president's ability to reassure a troubled nation. In his inaugural address, Roosevelt endeavored to ease the nation's anxieties with reassuring words: "Let me assert my firm belief that the only thing we have to fear is fear itself—nameless, unreasoning, unjustified terror which paralyzes needed efforts to convert retreat into advance." Roosevelt launched his advance immediately. Panic had prompted many Americans to pull out their bank savings, causing many banks to fail. To stop the run on banks, FDR called Congress into a special session and announced a "bank holiday," temporarily closing all the nation's banks. He could have nationalized the banking system, a move toward socialism that would likely have received widespread support. But Roosevelt favored government regulation, not government ownership. He proposed the Emergency Banking Bill, providing government support for private banks. Congress passed the bill instantly, to the applause of the bankers who helped draft it.

LISTEN

Franklin D. Roosevelt, First Inaugural Address (1933)

In the first of his "fireside chats" to millions of radio listeners, whom he addressed as "my friends," Roosevelt assured citizens that the banks that reopened were sound. He used the medium of radio skillfully to explain his policies and to communicate comforting and reassuring messages that reached people in the intimate setting of their homes. FDR urged Americans to join with him in an effort to rebuild trust:

DOCUMENT

Franklin Roosevelt, Fireside Chat (September 6, 1936)

> There is an element in the readjustment of our financial system more important than currency, more important than gold, and that is the confidence of the people themselves. Confidence and courage are the essentials of success in carrying out our plan. . . . We have provided the machinery to restore our financial system; and it is up to you to support and make it work. It is your problem, my friends, your problem no less than it is mine. Together we cannot fail.

The next day, bank deposits exceeded withdrawals as a result of the confidence he inspired. Will Rogers spoke for many when he said, "My bank opened today. Instead of being there to draw my little dab out, I didn't even go to town. Shows you I heard Roosevelt on the radio." Mildred Goldstein from Joliet, Illinois, was among thousands who wrote to FDR in response to his "fireside chats." She explained what prompted her letter:

> You are the first President to come into our homes; to make us feel you are working for us; to let us know what you are doing. Until last night, to me, the President of the United States was merely a legend. A picture to look at. A newspaper item. But you are real. I know your voice; what you are trying to do. Give radio credit. But to you goes the greater credit for your courage to use it as you have.

The New Deal

▮ *What was the New Deal, and how did it develop over time?*

The New Deal drew on Progressive Era reform impulses to extend the reach of the federal government to solve social problems. It provided assistance to many Americans suffering the effects of the Great Depression and established the welfare state that would last half a century. Based on pragmatism, experimentation, and shrewd political calculation, FDR's efforts to address the Depression began with a flurry of activity in the first 100 days of his administration and developed into a more progressive agenda by 1935, often called the **Second New Deal.** The New Deal countered the cyclical nature of capitalism and offered a safety net for industrial workers. It legitimized labor unions and established a system of regulation and cooperation between industry and labor. It also supported massive building projects from dams to bridges, altering the nation's landscape. Although Roosevelt faced critics from the left and the right of the political spectrum, his New Deal policies won him a resounding reelection in 1936. Many New Deal programs failed, but those that succeeded created the foundation of the modern American state. The broad-based reform effort, however, did not end the Depression or eradicate poverty.

THE FIRST HUNDRED DAYS

FDR understood that the people wanted "action, and action now," and so he acted quickly and pragmatically. His approach was largely experimental, rather than driven by an overarching philosophy. As one of his first acts, he encouraged Congress to repeal Prohibition. In 1933 the states quickly ratified the Twenty-First Amendment, repealing the Eighteenth. Repeal of Prohibition helped the economy by providing additional tax revenues from liquor sales, since they were once again legal, and a market for farmers' corn and wheat, which were used in the production of liquor.

Roosevelt appointed a cabinet composed of a number of liberals, including Henry A. Wallace of Iowa as secretary of agriculture, Harold L. Ickes of Illinois as secretary of the interior, and Frances Perkins of New York as secretary of labor—the first woman ever appointed to the cabinet. In addition to his cabinet, FDR appointed several academics, known as the Brain Trust, to serve as advisers.

One of FDR's most pressing challenges was to prop up prices for producers while keeping them low enough for consumers. Poverty in the midst of plenty was one of the Depression's cruelest ironies. Because farmers could no longer afford to transport their goods to market, food rotted while millions of people went hungry. FDR took action by developing the Farm Relief Act, which included the Farm Mortgage Act that lowered mortgage rates for farmers to help them keep their farms. Also included was the Agricultural Adjustment Act (AAA). In a highly controversial provision of the AAA, the government sought to prop up farm prices by limiting supply. That is, it paid farmers to destroy livestock and take acreage out of production. Many Americans recoiled at the systematic slaughter of 6 million piglets and the plowing under of 10 million acres of cotton. This policy boosted profits for larger farms but did little to alleviate the problems of smaller, poorer farmers. Sharecroppers and tenant farmers fared even worse.

On farms and in cities, most Americans in need desperately wanted to work and provide for their families. They considered government relief a sign of failure and a source of deep shame and humiliation. Many citizens searched for ways to preserve their pride. One woman wrote to Eleanor Roosevelt asking to borrow money in order to avoid charity:

> *Please* Mrs. Roosevelt, I do not want charity, only a chance from someone who will trust me. . . . I am sending you two of my dearest possessions to keep as security, a ring my

husband gave me before we were married, and a ring my mother used to wear. . . . If you will consider buying the baby clothes, please keep [the rings] until I send you the money you spent. It is very hard to face bearing a baby we cannot afford to have, and the fact that it is due to arrive soon, and still there is no money for the hospital or clothing, does not make it any easier. I have decided to stay home, keeping my 7 year old daughter from school to help with the smaller children when my husband has work. . . . The 7 year old one is a good will-ing little worker and somehow we must manage—but without charity.

Like this letter writer, most Americans valued self-sufficiency. But the Depression caused such widespread suffering, the government had to step in. In May 1933, Congress passed legislation creating the Federal Emergency Relief Administration (FERA), which provided $500 million in grants to the states for aid to the needy. Roosevelt placed Harry Hopkins in charge. Hopkins, an energetic and brash young reformer, disbursed $2 million during his first two hours on the job. He then persuaded Roosevelt to launch a tem-porary job program, the Civil Works Administration (CWA). The CWA provided government-sponsored jobs for more than 4 million workers. But the program came under fire from conservatives, and FDR ended it a few months later.

> *Most Americans valued self-sufficiency. But the Depression caused such widespread suffering, the government had to step in.*

That same year, Roosevelt combined his interest in conservation with his goal of provid-ing work for unemployed young men. The Civilian Conservation Corps (CCC) operated under the control of the U.S. Army. CCC workers lived in camps, wore uniforms, and con-formed to military discipline. They planted millions of trees, dug canals and ditches, built more than 30,000 wilderness shelters, stocked rivers and lakes with nearly 1 billion fish, and preserved historic sites. Their work revived depleted forests and provided flood control. By 1935, the CCC had employed more than 500,000 young men and kept them, in FDR's words, "off the city street corners."

Another measure that linked natural resources to the recovery effort was the Tennessee Valley Authority (TVA), an experiment in government-owned utilities that brought power to rural areas along the Tennessee River in seven states in western Appalachia—among the poorest areas in the nation. This far-reaching government-owned project offered a radical alternative to American private-enterprise capitalism. Under the TVA, the government built five dams, improved twenty others, and constructed power plants; it produced and sold electricity to the valley's farmers and facilitated the development of industry in the region. The TVA also boosted local economies by selling fertilizer and electricity, providing flood control, and improving river navigation. Business conservatives and southern Democrats in Congress opposed the plan because it used government money to provide jobs and electricity to rural African Americans in the Tennessee Valley. The TVA became one of the largest and cheapest suppliers of power in the nation. Years later, President Dwight D. Eisenhower condemned the TVA as a New Deal example of "creeping socialism," but it was one of Roosevelt's most successful and enduring projects.

MAP

The Tennessee Valley
Authority

The National Industrial Recovery Act (NIRA), passed by Congress in 1933, became the centerpiece of the first New Deal. The NIRA established the National Recovery Administration (NRA) to oversee the regulation of the economy. In his second fireside chat, Roosevelt called the NRA "a partnership in planning" between business and government. The NRA enabled businesses in each sector of the economy to form trade associations and set their own standards for production, prices, and wages. But in return, businesses had to agree to sanction labor unions. Section 7(a) of the NIRA guaranteed collective bargaining rights to workers, sparking new hope for union organizers.

FDR's first hundred days also included the creation of the Home Owners' Loan Corporation, providing refinancing of home mortgages at low rates. Because the plan helped stem the tide of foreclosures and also guaranteed the repayment of loans, it pleased home-owners, banks, and real-estate interests. It helped gain for FDR the support of a large segment of the middle class.

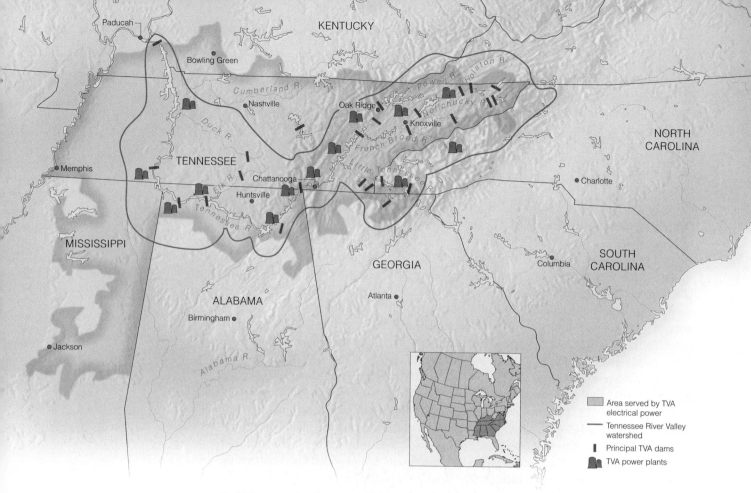

MAP 22.2 Areas Served by the Tennessee Valley Authority

The Tennessee Valley Authority (TVA) brought electricity to a large area in western Appalachia, one of the poorest regions in the country. The government-owned project strengthened the economy and improved living conditions in the area.

Legend:
- Area served by TVA electrical power
- Tennessee River Valley watershed
- Principal TVA dams
- TVA power plants

While the NIRA supported workers and the Home Owners' Loan Corporation helped protect the assets of the middle class, the 1934 Indian Reorganization Act addressed the needs of impoverished Indians. The act resulted from the efforts of John Collier, whom Roosevelt appointed as commissioner of Indian affairs. Collier opposed the policy of land allotment that resulted from the 1887 Dawes Act. Under allotment, Native American land holdings had dwindled from 130 million acres to 49 million acres—much of it desert. Collier rejected the assumption that Indians' survival depended on their assimilation into white culture. He altered the government boarding schools' curriculum to include bicultural and bilingual education and eliminated military dress and discipline.

The Indian Reorganization Act recognized the autonomy of Indian tribes, ended the allotment program, and appropriated funds to help Indians add to their land holdings. It also provided for job and professional training programs as well as a system of agricultural and industrial credit. In keeping with Collier's goal of Indian self-government, each tribe decided whether to accept the terms of the Indian Reorganization Act. In the end, 181 tribes voted to accept the law, while 77 opted out of it.

The Navajo were among the tribes that rejected the Indian Reorganization Act. Many Navajo perceived Collier as yet another heavy-handed government agent. This tension heightened during an environmental conflict over Navajo herding rights. Convinced that the Navajo were herding far more sheep and goats than the fragile desert ecosystem could support, Collier proposed a plan by which the federal government would purchase 400,000 head

■ On October 28, 1935, Commissioner of Indian Affairs John Collier stands with a group of Flathead Indian chiefs as Secretary of the Interior Harold L. Ickes signs the first constitution providing for Indian self-rule. Franklin Roosevelt appointed Collier to bring the New Deal to Native Americans.

of Navajo livestock. Although Collier had been more receptive to Indian concerns than almost any other federal authority who preceded him, he could not reconcile the conflicting interests of tribal autonomy, environmentalism, and development.

MONUMENTAL PROJECTS TRANSFORMING THE LANDSCAPE

Conflicts pitting development against environmental concerns emerged not only on tribal lands but all over the country. The New Deal years gave rise to huge construction projects that altered the landscape and affected the natural environment. Skyscrapers, bridges, dams, and monuments built during the 1930s symbolized human and technological triumph in the midst of hardship. They provided jobs, sources of energy, and inspiration for many—but they also cost the lives of many workers, the natural contours of the land, and in some cases the homes and livelihoods of people living in their path.

In addition to the dams built as part of the TVA, gigantic new dams provided electricity and irrigation in the arid West. Construction on Hoover Dam on the Colorado River 30 miles from Las Vegas began in 1931. Working in the desert heat that sometimes reached 143 degrees, laborers built the colossal dam in four years. Heat prostration and accidents claimed several lives. The huge Grand Coulee Dam piled 12 million cubic yards of concrete across the Columbia River in Washington State. Higher than Niagara Falls, standing 46 stories high and 12 city blocks long, it provided jobs to thousands of workers—77 of them died during its construction. The dam provided electricity to much of the Northwest and irrigation for over half a million acres of land in the Columbia basin. In 1941, the Bonneville Power Administration hired folk singer Woody Guthrie to compose music to celebrate the dam's completion. Among the 26 songs Guthrie wrote was "Roll On Columbia," later designated the official state song. While some rejoiced, others saw the dam as a tragedy. Members of the Arrow Lake Tribe (now part of the Colville Confederated Tribes) whose village, homes, and livelihood were destroyed when the river basin flooded, held a "ceremony of tears" commemorating the loss of the salmon and their habitat which had been the source of the tribe's economy.

NOVEMBER 23, 1936   **10** CENTS

REG. U.S. PAT. OFF.

© 2000 COPYRIGHT RENEWED – TIME INC.

Margaret Bourke-White/Getty Images

■ The gigantic concrete walls of the Fort Peck Dam adorned the cover of the first issue of *Life* magazine in this photograph by Margaret Bourke-White. The dam, authorized by FDR in 1933, employed over 11,000 workers. Located in northeast Montana, it is the highest of six major dams along the Missouri River. At 21,206 feet in length and over 250 feet in height, it is the largest hydraulically filled dam in the United States, and it creates Fort Peck Lake, the fifth largest man-made lake in the United States.

The Golden Gate Bridge, another Depression-era project, spanned the entrance to San Francisco Bay. In spite of hard times, voters in the six counties surrounding the bridge approved a $35 million bonding bill to pay for it. The project was the first to employ a dramatic safety device: a huge net slung under the bridge. It saved the lives of nineteen workers who fell during construction, but it gave way when a platform broke off, plunging eleven men to their deaths. When the bridge opened in 1937, 32,000 vehicles and 19,000 pedestrians passed over the picturesque engineering marvel on the first day.

Monumental architecture also soared skyward in the nation's cities. In 1930, construction began on the Empire State Building in New York City, the tallest building in the world up to that time. Other grandiose buildings altered the Manhattan skyline, including the dazzling and ornate Rockefeller Center, which opened its doors in 1937.

Farther west in South Dakota's Black Hills, a determined sculptor named Gutzon Borglum blasted tons of granite from 5,725-foot Mount Rushmore to carve out the portraits of four U.S. presidents—Washington, Jefferson, Lincoln, and Theodore Roosevelt. The project gained funding from Congress during the New Deal and reached completion in 1941. The site remains a major tourist destination to this day.

PROTEST AND PRESSURE FROM THE LEFT AND THE RIGHT

New Deal projects and programs did not please everyone. Challenges came from all directions. In spite of FDR's efforts to help businesses survive and remain profitable during the Great Depression, many business leaders continued to oppose the New Deal, charging that FDR was a dictator and that his program amounted to socialism. At the same time, FDR faced criticism from the left. Closest to home was First Lady Eleanor Roosevelt, who continued to press for racial equality and other social justice measures. Many others agreed that Roosevelt's policies did not go far enough to ease the suffering caused by the economic crisis. Some thought that New Deal policies aimed at bolstering capitalism were ill-advised, and that capitalism itself was the problem. Disenchantment with capitalism drew many Americans to the cause of socialism and swelled the ranks of the small Communist party.

The Communist party drew its inspiration from the Soviet Union and, during the 1930s, developed a strategy known as the Popular Front to build alliances with sympathetic American liberals. Not all liberals belonged to the Popular Front, but many people with progressive political leanings shared with the socialists and the Communist party a commitment to economic justice, unemployment relief, civil rights, and union organizing. Those left out of most New Deal programs, including many African Americans in the South, were drawn to the Communist party. Birmingham, Alabama, provides one example. The Depression hit Birmingham early and hard. By 1928, unemployment had reached 18 percent. Many impoverished black steelworkers, along with farm laborers in the surrounding countryside, joined the "invisible army" of the Communist party. Together, they fought for better working conditions and racial justice. One young black coal miner, Angelo Herndon, recalled the dangers of organizing and the need for secrecy: "With our few pennies that we collected we ground out leaflets on an old rickety mimeograph machine, which we kept concealed in the home of one of our workers. We were obliged to work very quietly, like the Abolitionists in the South during the Civil War, behind drawn shades and locked doors."

> The "Radio Priest" called for a redistribution of wealth and attacked Wall Street, international bankers, and the evils of capitalism.

Although most African Americans supported FDR and the Democratic party during the Depression, between 3,000 and 4,000 members of the black community of Birmingham, Alabama, joined the Communist party and related organizations. Nationally, the actual membership of the party remained small—it peaked at 100,000 during World War II, when the United States and the Soviet Union were allies—but its influence increased during the Depression.

By 1934 and 1935, much of the pressure on Roosevelt came from workers, whose hopes that the NIRA would guarantee collective bargaining rights were dashed by the intransigence of employers. The 1920s had taken a toll on labor unions. Membership had declined from a high of 5 million in 1920 to 2 million by 1933. But workers continued to strike for improved wages and working conditions. In 1934, nearly 1.5 million workers participated in 1,800 strikes. Often, unemployed laborers joined picket lines, refusing to work as strikebreakers.

In addition to the communists, socialists, labor unions, and grassroots organizations that sprang up all over the country, a number of individuals proposed alternatives to Roosevelt's program and gained large followings. The most influential of these were Dr. Francis Townsend, Father Charles E. Coughlin, and Senator Huey P. Long. In 1934, Townsend, a retired physician and health commissioner from Long Beach, California, introduced an idea for a pension plan that sparked a nationwide grassroots movement. Townsend proposed a 2 percent national sales tax that would fund a pension of $200 a month for Americans over age sixty. The **Townsend Plan** became hugely popular, especially among elderly Americans. In 1936, a national survey indicated that half of all Americans favored the plan. Though the plan was never implemented, the groundswell of support that it generated probably hastened the development and passage of the old-age insurance system contained in the 1935 Social Security Act.

Coughlin also inspired a huge following. A Catholic priest from Canada, he served as pastor of a small church outside Detroit, Michigan. He began to broadcast his sermons on the radio, using his magnetic personality to address political as well as religious issues. Soon he became a media phenomenon, broadcasting through 26 radio stations to an audience estimated at 40 million. The "Radio Priest" called for a redistribution of wealth and attacked Wall Street, international bankers, and the evils of capitalism. When a Minnesota radio station polled listeners to see whether they wanted to hear Coughlin's program, 137,000 said yes. Only 400 said no.

Initially, Coughlin strongly supported Franklin Roosevelt and the New Deal. But he soon grew impatient with what he considered the slow pace of New Deal reforms. In 1934, Coughlin launched his own political party, the National Union for Social Justice, which he

Coughlin, "A Third Party"

used to challenge Roosevelt's leadership. The activist priest promoted a populist message that was hostile to both capitalism and communism. He told his radio listeners, "I call upon every one of you who is weary of drinking the bitter vinegar of sordid capitalism and upon every-one who is fearsome of being nailed to the cross of communism to join this Union which, if it is to succeed, must rise above the concept of an audience and become a living, vibrant, united, active organization, superior to politics and politicians in principle, and independent of them in power." Soon, his message turned from social justice populism to right-wing bigotry. His virulent anti-Semitism and admiration for the fascist regimes of Adolf Hitler in Germany and Benito Mussolini in Italy drove away many of his followers. By 1940, Coughlin had ceased broadcasting and abandoned all political activities, under orders of the Catholic Church.

Huey P. Long was among the most powerful, and colorful, politicians of the era. He rose from modest origins to become a lawyer and a public service commissioner. In 1928, Long won the governorship of Louisiana. His progressive leadership inspired tremendous loyalty, especially among poor workers and farmers. He did more for the underprivileged people of Louisiana than any other governor. He expanded the state's infrastructure; developed social services; built roads, hospitals, and schools; and changed the tax code to place a greater burden on corporations and the wealthy. He proved unique among southern politicians in that his public statements were free of racial slurs. But he also trampled the democratic process. His ambition had no bounds, and he used any means to accumulate power. Through his tremendous popular appeal, Long developed a huge power base and eventually gained control of Louisiana's legislature, courts, state bureaucracies, and even local governments.

In 1932, Long resigned the governorship and won election to the U.S. Senate. Soon, he gained a national following. Initially he supported FDR, but by 1933 he had broken with the president and forged his own political movement based on his Share-Our-Wealth Plan. Giving voice to the resentments many Americans felt toward "wealthy plutocrats," Long advocated a radical redistribution of the nation's wealth. He called for new taxes on the wealthy and proposed to use the funds to guarantee a minimum annual income of $2,500 for all those in need. As he put it, "How many men ever went to a barbecue and would let one man take off the table what was intended for nine-tenths of the people to eat? The only way you'll ever be able to feed the balance of the people is to make that man come back and bring back some of the grub he ain't got no business with." Long's plainspoken radicalism won the hearts of his followers, including Will Rogers, who publicly urged FDR to back Long's proposals. However, many of his congressional colleagues considered him an agitator. Such skepticism did little to limit Long's ambition, and by 1935 he was planning to challenge FDR in the next presidential election. But he never had the chance. In September 1935, the son-in-law of one of his vanquished political opponents assassinated him.

Other challenges took the form of viable third parties, especially at the state level. In Wisconsin, the legacy of Progressive senator Robert M. La Follette was alive and well, particularly in the political popularity of his two sons, Senator Bob and Governor Phil. In 1934, the brothers formed the Wisconsin Progressive party, which supported the New Deal but pulled it strongly to the left.

Meanwhile in neighboring Minnesota, a coalition of workers and farmers formed the Minnesota Farmer-Labor party. In 1930, populist Floyd Olson became the nation's first Farmer-Labor governor. At the party's 1934 convention, Olson made his position clear: "I am not a liberal. I enjoy working on a common basis with liberals for their platforms, etc., but I am not a liberal. I am what I want to be—I am a radical. I am a radical in the sense that I want a definite change in the system, I am not satisfied with tinkering, I am not satisfied with patching, I am not satisfied with hanging a laurel wreath upon burglars and thieves and pirates and calling them code authorities or something else." Olson considered the possibility of a third-party bid for the presidency in 1936, but his plans never reached fruition. He contracted cancer and died in August 1936 at the age of forty-four.

On the West Coast, discontented voters mounted a similar challenge to party-politics-as-usual. Some Democrats persuaded Upton Sinclair, a veteran socialist and author of the 1906 muckraking novel *The Jungle,* to run for governor on their ticket in 1934. Sinclair ran on his End Poverty in California (EPIC) plan, which would have let the state take over idle land and factories and permit unemployed laborers to use them for their own needs. Sinclair won the 1934 California Democratic primary with an overwhelming majority. But Democratic party regulars, including FDR, refused to support his candidacy. Without the support of his own party, and facing opposition from wealthy Republicans who spared no expense to defeat him, Sinclair lost the election. Nevertheless, Sinclair's tremendous popularity signaled to Roosevelt that if he hoped to retain the support of his constituents, he would need to move significantly to the left.

THE SECOND NEW DEAL

By 1935, Roosevelt began to respond selectively to his critics from the left. Although Eleanor Roosevelt continued to promote civil rights, the president depended on southern white voters to be reelected and to get his New Deal measures through Congress. So he was careful not to alienate southern Democrats by cultivating African American voters in the North. However, he did reach out to industrial workers. In the spring of 1935, Congress passed the National Labor Relations Act, also known as the Wagner Act, which strengthened and guaranteed collective bargaining and gave a huge boost to labor unions.

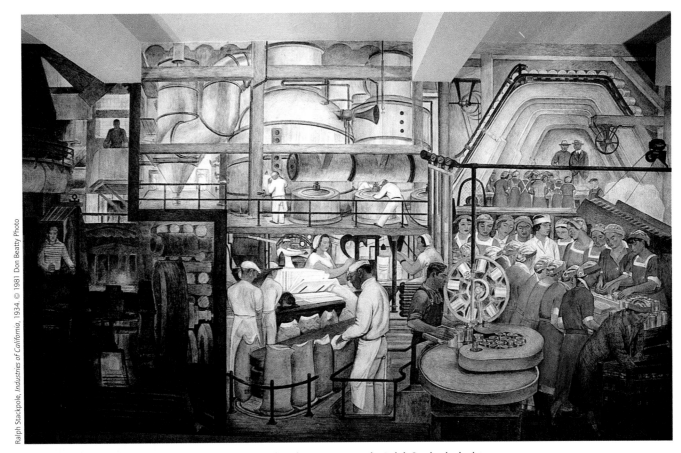

Ralph Stackpole, *Industries of California*, 1934. © 1981 Don Beatty Photo

■ In the mural *Industries of California*, on San Francisco's Coit Tower, WPA artist Ralph Stackpole depicts the city's diverse workforce. Across the country, government-funded artists created works of public art that portrayed life in local communities.

TABLE 22.2		
Key New Deal Legislation, 1933–1938		
Year	**Act or Agency**	**Key Provisions**
1933	Emergency Banking Act	Reopened banks under government supervision
	Civilian Conservation Corps (CCC)	Employed young men in reforestation, flood control, road construction, and soil erosion control projects
	Federal Emergency Relief Act (FERA)	Provided federal funds for state and local relief efforts
	Agricultural Adjustment Act (AAA)	Granted farmers direct payments for reducing crop production; funds for payment provided by a processing tax, later declared unconstitutional
	Farm Mortgage Act	Provided funds to refinance farm mortgages
	Tennessee Valley Authority (TVA)	Constructed dams and power projects and developed the economy of a seven-state area in the Tennessee River Valley
	Home Owners' Loan Corporation	Provided funds for refinancing home mortgages of nonfarm homeowners
	National Industrial Recovery Act (NIRA)	Established a series of fair competition codes; created National Recovery Administration (NRA) to write, coordinate, and implement these codes; NIRA's Section 7(a) guaranteed labor's right to organize (act later declared unconstitutional)
	Public Works Administration (PWA)	Sought to increase employment and business activity by funding road construction, building construction, and other projects
	Federal Deposit Insurance Corporation (FDIC)	Insured individual bank deposits
	Civil Works Administration (CWA)	Provided federal jobs for the unemployed
1934	Securities and Exchange Act	Created Securities and Exchange Commission (SEC) to regulate trading practices in stocks and bonds according to federal laws
	Indian Reorganization Act	Restored ownership of tribal lands to Native Americans; provided funds for job training and a system of agricultural and industrial credit
	Federal Housing Administration (FHA)	Insured loans provided by banks for the building and repair of houses
1935	Works Progress Administration (WPA)	Employed more than 8 million people to repair roads, build bridges, and work on other projects
	National Youth Administration (NYA)	WPA program that provided job training for unemployed youths and part-time jobs for students in need
	Federal One	WPA program that provided financial assistance for writers, artists, musicians, and actors
	National Labor Relations Act (Wagner Act)	Recognized the right of employees to join labor unions and to bargain collectively, reinstating the provisions of NIRA's Section 7(a); created the National Labor Relations Board (NLRB) to enforce laws against unfair labor practices
	Social Security Act	Created a system of social insurance that included unemployment compensation and old-age survivors' insurance; paid for by a joint tax on employers and employees
1938	Fair Labor Standards Act	Established a minimum wage of 25 cents an hour and a standard work week of 44 hours for businesses engaged in interstate commerce

Also in 1935, Congress passed the Social Security Act, perhaps the most important and far-reaching of all New Deal programs. The act established a system of old-age pensions, unemployment insurance, and welfare benefits for dependent children and the disabled. The framework of the Social Security Administration shaped the welfare system for the remainder of the century. The welfare system, extensive as it was, did not reach all Americans and left out many of the most needy. Social Security, the most widespread of the programs, was designed primarily to provide unemployment insurance and retirement income for male wage-earners, based on a percentage of the wages they earned while in the workforce. Social Security provided an important safety net for large numbers of workers and the elderly, but it did not cover domestic employees, seasonal or part-time workers, agricultural laborers, or housewives. The other major welfare program, Aid to Families with Dependent Children (AFDC), was designed specifically for poor people. AFDC made matching funds available to states to provide relief for the needy, mostly dependent women and children with no means of support. Unlike Social Security, which was provided to many retired workers regardless of their circumstances, AFDC relief programs, which came to be known as "welfare," were administered according to need.

The architects of this welfare system included top New Deal advisers, many of them women who had been active reformers, such as Eleanor Roosevelt. These advocates hoped to protect women and children from the destitution that almost certainly resulted if a male bread-winner lost his job, deserted his family, or died. The system presumed that a man ordinarily earned a **family wage** that let him support his wife and children and that women were neces-sarily economically dependent on men. Thus, a deeply entrenched gender system prevailed through the 1930s. As a result, while some male breadwinners received benefits like Social Security, impoverished women and children received public charity. These payments were usually meager, designed to support a woman and her children until she could remarry — but not enough to lift them out of poverty.

Because there were no nationally established guidelines on how to distribute welfare funds, states could determine who received assistance. The Social Security Act did little to assist African Americans, especially in the South, where black women were deliberately excluded by local author-ities who preferred to maintain a pool of cheap African American labor rather than provide relief for black families.

In 1935, Congress allocated the huge sum of nearly $5 billion for the Emergency Relief Appropriation. Roosevelt used a significant portion of the money to expand his public works program. By executive order he established the Works Progress Administration (WPA), which pro-vided millions of jobs for the unem-ployed. The project mandated that WPA jobs would make a contribu-tion to public life and would not compete with private business. The jobs included building streets, high-ways, bridges, and public buildings; restoring forests; clearing slums; and extending electricity to rural areas. The WPA National Youth Administration gave work to nearly 1 million students.

The wages paid to WPA workers proved pitifully low. And like most other New Deal programs, the WPA left out the most needy. It provided work only to those already on the relief roles, and just one person per

The Library of Congress

■ Dorothea Lange took photographs for the Farm Security Administration (FSA) documenting the lives of Depression-era migrants. This 1939 photo, "Mother and Children on the Road, Tulelake, Siskiyou County, California," is one of Lange's many portraits of impoverished families.

**WPA Project at
Tonawanda
Reservation**

family could hold a WPA job. This policy ruled out most women as well as older children. It also neglected the vast majority of the unemployed who were not on relief. A 1937 letter to Harry Hopkins from the Workers' Council of Colored People in Raleigh, North Carolina, pointed to the failure of the WPA to provide jobs for black women. The writer explained that the wages paid to domestic and farm laborers were so low that, even if they worked fourteen-hour days, they could not pay their rent.

The most effective WPA program was Federal One, which provided financial support for writers, musicians, artists, and actors. The Federal Theater Project, under the direction of Hallie Flanagan, former head of Vassar College's Experimental Theater, became an arena for experimental community-based theater. The Federal Theater Project included sixteen black theater units. Their most notable production was an all-black version of *Macbeth* set in Haiti and staged in Harlem. Federal One supported thousands of artists and brought the arts to a wide public audience through government-funded murals on public buildings, community-theater productions, local orchestras, and the like. By the late 1930s, the program came under political attack for supporting artists who expressed leftist sensibilities, and Congress cut off its funding. In 1943, the WPA was dissolved.

The New Deal did not reach everyone. Programs were geared toward full-time industrial workers, most of whom were white men. Domestic workers, Mexican migrant laborers, black and white sharecroppers, Chinese and Japanese truck farmers—all were among those ineligible for Social Security, minimum wages and maximum hours, unemployment insurance, and other New Deal benefits. But the New Deal established the national welfare state and provided assistance and security to millions of working people along with disabled, dependent, and elderly Americans. Such sweeping programs also solidified Roosevelt's popularity among the poor, workers, and much of the middle class.

FDR'S SECOND TERM

In the 1936 campaign, FDR claimed that the election was a battle between "the millions who never had a chance" and "organized money." Lashing out at "economic royalists" and their "entrenched greed," Roosevelt boasted that the "forces of selfishness and of lust for power" had united against him: "They are unanimous in their *hate* for me—*and I welcome their hatred*." His strategy paid off. Roosevelt won the election by a landslide of more than 60 percent of the popular vote. Six million more voters cast ballots than had done so in 1932, and 5 million of those new votes went to Roosevelt. His strongest support came from the lower ends of the socioeconomic scale. The 1936 election also swept Democrats into Congress, giving them a decisive majority in both the House and the Senate.

With such a powerful mandate, Roosevelt was well positioned to promote a new legislative program. As his first major effort, he took on the Supreme Court. Dominated by conservative justices, the Court had invalidated some major legislation of Roosevelt's first term, including the AAA and the NIRA. Roosevelt feared that the justices would unravel the New Deal by striking down its progressive elements. To shift the balance of power on the Court, he proposed a measure that would let the president appoint one new justice for every one on the Court who had at least ten years of service and who did not retire within six months after turning seventy.

Emboldened by his landslide victory, FDR believed that he could persuade Congress and the nation to go along with any plan he put forward, but he was mistaken. Many viewed his "court packing" plan as a threat to the fundamental separation of powers and feared that it would set a dangerous precedent. Some

TABLE 22.3			
The Election of 1936			
Candidate	**Political Party**	**Popular Vote (%)**	**Electoral Vote**
Franklin D. Roosevelt	Democratic	60.8	523
Alfred M. Landon	Republican	36.5	8
William Levine	Union	1.9	—

considered it an affront to the more aged justices, such as the respected liberal Louis Brandeis, a man in his eighties. Powerful Republicans in Congress forged an alliance with conservative Democrats, mostly from the South, to defeat the plan. This informal alliance dominated Congress for the following two decades. The Court blunder cost Roosevelt considerable political capital and empowered his opponents. In the end, his plan proved unnecessary anyway. The Court did not undercut the New Deal. Within the next few years, retirements allowed Roosevelt to appoint several new justices who tipped the balance in his favor.

A New Political Culture

◼ *How did the Depression and the New Deal change the way Americans of different backgrounds thought of themselves and their fellow citizens?*

FDR continued to face strong opposition from conservatives on the right and from radicals, communists, and socialists on the left. But his political fortunes benefited from the emergence of a new and more inclusive national culture. This new Americanism emanated from the working class and found expression in the labor movement, popular culture, and the political coalition that came together in the Democratic party. These nationalizing forces cut across lines of class and region and occasionally challenged hierarchies of gender and race, creating a more inclusive national culture.

THE LABOR MOVEMENT

The labor insurgency that erupted during the early years of the New Deal demonstrated the need for a new national labor movement. The American Federation of Labor (AFL), restricted to skilled workers, left out most of the nation's less-skilled industrial laborers. John L. Lewis of the United Mine Workers (UMW) and Sidney Hillman of the Amalgamated Clothing Workers of America were among several union leaders from a number of industries—including mining, steel, rubber, and automobile—who left the AFL to form a new and more broad-based labor organization, the Congress of Industrial Organizations (CIO). Hillman and others argued that higher wages were good for the economy because workers would then be able to purchase consumer products, benefiting industry as well as workers. Lewis and Hillman played key roles in the CIO's growth into a national force, but the impetus came from the workers themselves.

The CIO's first major action came in 1936 in Akron, Ohio, where workers in the rubber industry organized a **sit-down strike,** a new strategy whereby laborers stopped work and simply sat, shutting down production and occupying plants so that strikebreakers could not enter and take their jobs. Sit-down strikes became a prominent labor tactic during 1936 when 48 strikes broke out across the nation. The numbers shot up the following year to about 500 strikes that lasted more than one day. March 1937 alone witnessed 170 sit-down strikes that affected about 170,000 workers. Striking workers expressed their enthusiasm for the tactic in song:

> When they tie the can to a union man, sit down! Sit down!
>
> When they give him the sack, they'll take him back, sit down! Sit down!
> When the speed-up comes, just twiddle your thumbs, sit down! Sit down!
> When the boss won't talk, don't take a walk, sit down! Sit down!

The most powerful demonstration of workers' discontent came in the automobile industry, where speed-ups of the assembly line drove workers to rebellion. Charlie Chaplin's poignant film *Modern Times* (1936) expressed workers' frustration at being treated as little more than cogs in machines. "Where you used to be a man," lamented one auto worker, "now you are less than their cheapest tool." In 1936, a spontaneous strike erupted against General Motors in Atlanta; it soon spread to Kansas City, Missouri; Cleveland, Ohio; and the main plants at Flint, Michigan. Two weeks into the strike, workers clashed with police. Frank Murphy, Michigan's pro-labor governor, refused to use National Guard troops against the strikers, and Roosevelt declined to send in federal troops. John L. Lewis negotiated on behalf of the workers, who demanded recognition of their union.

Women as well as men participated actively in the Flint strike. Twenty-three-year-old Genora Johnson Dollinger, wife of a striker and mother of two young sons, organized 500 women into the Women's Emergency Brigade, made up primarily of strikers' wives, sisters, and girlfriends. Wearing red berets and armbands, they ran soup kitchens and first-aid stations. They also entered the fray when necessary, as when they broke plant windows so that the company could not use tear gas effectively against the strikers inside. Dollinger arranged a children's picket line as well, in which her two-year-old carried a sign that read, "My daddy strikes for us little tykes." Reflecting on the Women's Emergency Brigade after the strike, Dollinger wrote, "It's a measure of the strength of those women of the Red Berets that they could perform so courageously in an atmosphere that was often hostile to them. We organized on our own without the benefit of professional leadership, and yet, we played a role, second to none, in the birth of a union and in changing working families' lives forever."

The sit-down strike at Flint lasted forty-four days and forced General Motors to recognize the United Auto Workers (UAW), which was a CIO union. The strike scored a clear victory for the workers and boosted the CIO's stature as a national union of industrial workers. Membership in the UAW quadrupled in the next year. Bowing to the formidable power of the national union in the wake of the UAW success, U.S. Steel surrendered to the CIO even without a strike, ending its policy of hiring nonunion workers and signing an agreement with the Steel Workers' Organizing Committee. The CIO brought together workers from all over the country. Most of its member unions were open to racial and ethnic minorities and women.

■ Some strikes became violent, as did this one in 1934 when police battled striking teamsters armed with pipes on the streets of Minneapolis.

National Archives

The labor movement became one of the most promising avenues for racial minorities to assert their claims for equal rights. Along with southern African Americans who joined unions, Mexican laborers in California also organized on their own behalf. They faced not only persistent exploitation in fields and factories but also the constant threat of deportation. During the Depression, approximately one-third of the Mexican population in the United States—more than half a million people—was deported to Mexico, even though the majority were native-born American citizens. Some of those who remained formed unions and struck for better pay and working conditions. During 1933, agricultural workers mounted thirty-seven major strikes in California alone. They scored a number of successes; more than half of the conflicts led to wage increases.

> The labor movement became one of the most promising avenues for racial minorities to assert their claims for equal rights.

Dorothy Ray was only sixteen years old when she began organizing Mexican workers at the grassroots level in California. She found it particularly rewarding to witness "the diminishing of bigotry . . . watching all those Okies and Arkies...all their lives they'd been on a little farm in Oklahoma; probably they had never seen a Black or a Mexicano. And you'd watch in the process of a strike how those white workers soon saw that those white cops were their enemies and that the Black and Chicano workers were their brothers." Another successful effort at multiracial organizing occurred in the Arkansas delta in 1934. The Southern Tenant Farmers' Union (STFU) brought together black and white tenants and sharecroppers to fight for better working conditions.

THE NEW DEAL COALITION

FDR's support of labor unions brought workers of all ethnic and racial backgrounds solidly into the Democratic fold. They joined a coalition that included voters who had never before belonged to the same party, particularly northern blacks and southern whites. Although African Americans in the South were disenfranchised, blacks in the North had voted Republican for sixty years, loyal to the party of Lincoln. In a dramatic shift, black voters in northern cities overwhelmingly backed FDR in 1936 and remained in the Democratic party for the rest of the century.

FDR continued to cater to powerful southern congressmen and southern white voters. Nevertheless, he made some gestures on behalf of African Americans and put civil rights measures on the liberal agenda for the first time since Reconstruction. In May 1935, FDR issued Executive Order 7046, banning discrimination in WPA projects. By the late 1930s, 15 to 20 percent of those with WPA jobs were black. Although the pay was meager—$12 a week—it was double what many blacks had been able to earn previously. In spite of FDR's lukewarm support for civil rights, African Americans in the North benefited from New Deal programs. As one black preacher exhorted his congregation prior to the 1936 election, "Let Jesus lead you and Roosevelt feed you."

Other racial and ethnic minorities also joined the New Deal coalition. In 1939, Latinos organized their first national civil rights assembly, El Congreso de Pueblos de Habla Española—the Spanish-Speaking People's Congress, which opened with a congratulatory telegram from Eleanor Roosevelt. Immigrants from Europe and their children also became loyal Democratic voters.

In spite of this diverse coalition, many Americans remained bitterly opposed to FDR. On the left, socialists and communists criticized the New Deal for patching up capitalism rather than transforming the economic system. On the right, conservative business leaders despised Roosevelt for the constraints he placed on business and the intrusion of the government into the economy. Critics from the political right considered the New Deal akin to communism. In 1938, Congress created the House Un-American Activities Committee (HUAC), chaired by Martin Dies of Texas. Formed ostensibly to investigate American fascists and Nazis in the United States, the committee instead pursued liberal and leftist groups throughout World War II and the Cold War.

A NEW AMERICANISM

The New Deal coalition reflected not only Roosevelt's popularity but also a new and more inclusive American identity. An expanding mass culture fostered this sensibility, spread largely through the national media. It is no accident that Franklin Roosevelt found his way into the homes and hearts of Americans through his fireside chats over the radio; his mastery of that technology made him the first media-savvy president. During the 1930s, 70 percent of all households owned a radio—more than owned a telephone. The motion-picture industry also expanded into small towns across the country.

Movie plots portrayed the triumph of common people over the rich and powerful and celebrated love across class and ethnic lines. Even gangsters appeared as sympathetic characters whose illegal activities seemed somehow justified by the corrupt system they tried to thwart. Although racial stereotypes persisted in motion pictures throughout the decade, notable exceptions, such as Will Rogers's films, featured strong minority characters who outwitted their more powerful foes.

Popular movies also challenged traditional gender and class hierarchies. Female stars, such as Katharine Hepburn, Rosalind Russell, Bette Davis, and Mae West, portrayed independent women. For example, the 1931 film *Front Page* was remade at the end of the decade. In the original version the hero, Hildy Johnson, was a man—but in the remake, entitled *His Girl Friday,* Hildy became a woman. The strong-willed reporter, played by Rosalind Russell, divorces her work-obsessed boss, played by Cary Grant, and then competes with him on the job. Kicking off her high heels to race barefoot down a street, she rescues a man thought to be a communist from a threatening lynch mob.

New sports celebrities also embodied the nation's diversity. Baseball star Joe DiMaggio, son of an Italian immigrant fisherman, became a national hero. African American boxer Joe Louis, the "Brown Bomber" who was born into a sharecropper family in Alabama, became heavyweight champion of the world at age twenty-three. In 1938, when Louis fought German boxer Max Schmeling at Yankee Stadium, the fight attracted 70,000 fans and grossed more than $1 million. When the black fighter knocked out Schmeling in the first round, he seemed to strike a blow for America against Hitler's Nazi Germany.

A number of women also became heroes in the 1930s for their daring exploits, personal courage, and physical prowess. Athletes like tennis champion Helen Wills and Olympic track star and brilliant golfer "Babe" (Mildred) Didrikson (later Zaharias) greatly expanded the popularity of women's sports. Renowned aviator Amelia Earhart, the first woman to fly solo across the Atlantic, devoted her life to advancing both feminism and commercial aviation. When her plane disappeared during an attempted around-the-world flight in 1937, many of her admirers were so

SHE LEARNED ABOUT MEN FROM HIM!

CARY GRANT
ROSALIND RUSSELL
in
HOWARD HAWKS'
"HIS GIRL FRIDAY"
with
RALPH BELLAMY
GENE LOCKHART
Based on a play by
BEN HECHT
CHARLES MacARTHUR
Screen play by
CHARLES LEDERER
Directed by
HOWARD HAWKS
A COLUMBIA PICTURE

Photofest

■ This poster for the movie *His Girl Friday* shows the strong heroine (Rosalind Russell) and her ex-husband and boss (Cary Grant). Although the two reconcile and remarry in the end, there is no indication that the feisty reporter will become a full-time homemaker.

convinced of her invincibility that they refused to believe she had died. Even today, people still speculate about her fate.

One of the most beloved celebrities of the decade was a horse: the unlikely champion Seabiscuit. The little Thoroughbred overcame a crippling injury and beat the odds to win major national races, becoming a symbol of hope for Depression-weary Americans.

Conclusion

The Great Depression of the 1930s was the nation's worst economic crisis. When Franklin Delano Roosevelt became president, he put into place a wide range of programs aimed at solving the crisis and providing relief to suffering Americans. His New Deal created a welfare state that established the principle of government responsibility for the well-being of vulnerable citizens. Before the New Deal, people suffered the fluctuations of the market economy with no recourse beyond the assistance of kin, communities, and charities. Older Americans who

National Air and Space Museum, Smithsonian Institution (SI A-A45874)

■ Amelia Earhart was the first woman to fly solo across the Atlantic. The legendary aviator gave preliminary flying lessons to her friend Eleanor Roosevelt. FDR convinced his wife not to take up flying, but the first lady always regretted her decision.

could no longer work had no government-guaranteed pensions and often faced poverty in old age. Bank failures could wipe away life savings. Unemployment could mean starvation for a worker's family. The New Deal provided Social Security for the elderly, unemployment compensation for workers who had lost their jobs, minimum hours and wages, and economic aid to women and children who had no means of support. It also established national banking and business regulations, as well as the right of workers to unionize and engage in collective bargaining. Labor unions grew and flourished under the New Deal. Government protections offered many Americans an unprecedented level of economic security.

The Roosevelt administration addressed many of the nation's problems and used the federal government in innovative ways to intervene in the economy and to mitigate some of the misfortunes caused by the Depression. Most New Deal policies protected factory workers in large companies. The safety net did not extend to many of the neediest Americans, including Mexican American migrant workers, African American and white sharecroppers, seasonal agricultural laborers, or domestic workers. Although the national government extended its reach considerably, at the local level many persistent problems remained entrenched. FDR was reluctant to press for antilynching legislation for fear of alienating southern congressmen who still retained enormous power. FDR faced critics from the left as well as the right. Although his conservative opponents accused him of socialist leanings, the New Deal actually rescued and shored up capitalism.

The Depression caused widespread suffering, but it also gave rise to a new national culture. Farm families uprooted from the Dust Bowl found themselves in similar circumstances with Mexican agricultural workers and unemployed African Americans. A spirit of cooperation born of crisis strengthened communities. The popular culture reflected a new multicultural Americanism that elevated former outsiders like the Cherokee Will Rogers to national stardom. Immigrants and their children became part of mainstream America.

In spite of the new multicultural spirit, the cruel fate of the Scottsboro Boys and the failure to enact antilynching legislation illustrate the persistence of institutionalized racism. But civil rights activists continued to work for social justice, with support from communists, radicals, and First Lady Eleanor Roosevelt. Although the New Deal reinforced women's economic dependence on men, the popular culture featured strong women who challenged traditional gender roles.

The New Deal was the Roosevelt administration's response to a global economic crisis. With the exception of the communist Soviet Union, which had already abandoned capitalism, all industrialized nations responded to the Depression by increasing the role of the state in the economy. Italy, Germany, and Japan moved to fascism and nearly total state direction of the economy, while Britain and France established welfare states that would become more fully developed after World War II. The United States' system of social welfare was not as extensive and inclusive as those that emerged in some western European democracies. But it was part of a larger trend toward government intervention in the economy and greater protections for citizens.

Within the United States, the New Deal neither reached nor satisfied everyone. Some groups thought that it went too far; others believed it did not go far enough. But it eased some of the harshest effects of the economic crisis and established a national safety net that included several programs which have endured to this day. What the New Deal did *not* do was end the Depression. It would take another global crisis, World War II, to create full employment and revive the economy — and bring with it more hardship and hope.

For Review

1. What were the most profound effects of the Great Depression on national institutions and American citizens?

2. In what ways did Eleanor Roosevelt use her position as first lady?

3. How did Franklin Roosevelt use radio to communicate with the American people?

4. What pressures did Roosevelt encounter from the left and the right of the political spectrum?

5. In what ways did labor unions develop and change during the New Deal, and how did Americans of different backgrounds mobilize as workers?

6. What was the New Deal coalition?

Created Equal **Online**

For more *Created Equal* resources, including suggestions for sites to visit and further reading, go to **MyHistoryLab.com.**

Chapter 23

Global Conflict: World War II, 1937–1945

■ Franz Steiner just after his release from Dachau. After starving the prisoners, the Nazis fed them boiled potatoes to fatten them up before they were released, so their emaciated bodies would not be visible to the outside world. Later in the war, the Nazis no longer made any effort to keep up appearances.

In 1938, Franz Steiner was a young man with a newly minted law degree when he was rounded up by the Nazis and taken from his home in Vienna, Austria, to the Dachau concentration camp. There he was imprisoned to provide slave labor for the Germans. His life had been pleasant up to that time. A talented artist and musician, he was well-educated and spoke several languages. But then everything changed.

In 1938, Dachau was not yet a death camp, but imprisoned Jews who were weak or ill perished nonetheless. Under the brutal conditions—sleeping on cold, straw-covered floors and lacking adequate shoes, clothes, or food—many died. Some could get out if they could prove that they would leave the country immediately. Franz was lucky: he was relatively healthy, and he had a sponsor in the United States, a family friend who agreed to take him in. But the quota of Jews allowed to enter the United States was already filled for the year.

In spite of the horror unfolding in Europe, American officials granted few exceptions to the immigration restrictions put into place in the 1920s.

With the doors to the United States closed, Franz secured a ticket on a French ship bound for Shanghai, China, an open city that required no entry visa. After three months in Dachau, Franz was released. His parents assured him that the Nazis would leave them alone, since they were too old and frail to work. Reluctantly, Franz departed, leaving his parents in Austria.

In Shanghai, Franz settled with thousands of other Jews who had fled the Nazis and now lived alongside the local Chinese. Like many Jewish families in Europe at the time, Franz's relatives were rapidly scattering all over the world. On August 11, 1940, he wrote that his uncle "fled from France went to Brazil and from there to Argentina. Hope he arrived in good shape." Still optimistic that his parents would survive in Vienna, he noted, "Parents write regularly." But he worried about his younger brother, twenty-year-old Hans, who had escaped from Austria on a boat with friends.

After a year in Shanghai, Franz was finally allowed to enter the United States. By April 1941, he had settled in San Francisco, changed his name to Frank, and taken a job with an electric lighting company. But he remained worried about his parents and his brother. He wrote in his diary, "My parents asked for an affidavit" to get out of Austria. "Hans is in Yugoslavia, hope he will survive it."

But Hans did not survive it. The Germans finally caught up with Hans and his friends and shot them all, dumping them in a makeshift grave. Frank did not learn of his brother's fate until after the war. Meanwhile, Frank continued to correspond with his parents in Vienna. The last letter he sent to his parents was returned to him unopened, stamped by the Nazis with the fiction that they had "emigrated" to Auschwitz. Frank never heard from them again. Along with millions of others, they died in a death camp as part of Hitler's "Final Solution" to rid Europe of Jews.

After three years in the United States, Frank married an American woman and became a citizen. Half a century later, he retired comfortably in San Diego, surrounded by his art and still performing at the piano. He donated the last letter he wrote to his parents—still unopened—to the Yad Vashem Holocaust Memorial Museum in Israel.

Frank Steiner's story is one small piece of the global saga of disruption, dislocation, loss, suffering, death, and survival during World War II. The war affected countries and peoples all over the globe. The conflict demanded human and technological resources on an unprecedented scale and left massive destruction in its wake. The huge scale of destruction was unlike that of any previous war. At least 55 million soldiers and civilians died. In the **Holocaust,** Nazi Germany's campaign of genocide, 6 million European Jews—like Frank Steiner's parents and brother— perished along with thousands of Romani (Gypsies), Poles, mentally and physically disabled people, homosexuals, and others deemed "racially inferior."

The war also had a tremendous impact on people under colonial rule. Germany's bombardment of England and occupation of France, Holland, and Belgium weakened these countries' hold over their vast colonies. Japan's defeat of the American, British, Dutch, and French forces in Southeast Asia from 1940 to 1942 shocked the Western powers. Japan's brutal occupation of neighboring nations, as well as the momentum for independence generated by the war, set in motion a postwar wave of decolonization in Asia and Africa.

The war also transformed the United States into a political and military superpower. The United States was the only major combatant that did not suffer massive destruction on its home territory. It had two powerful advantages: an ocean barrier on its east and west coasts, plus tremendous natural resources that could provide the materials needed for modern warfare, such as steel and oil. In order to minimize American casualties, President Franklin Delano

Roosevelt (FDR) pursued a strategy to make the United States the "arsenal of democracy," providing armaments and supplies to the other Allied powers so that their armies would do most of the fighting. Although the Soviet Union carried the largest burden of fighting and suffered the highest losses, millions of Americans also fought, and hundreds of thousands died in the conflict.

Military service had a leveling effect on social relations, as soldiers came together from all classes and ethnic groups. The vast majority of the troops—more than 85 percent—were white men from a wide variety of backgrounds. Although soldiers of color usually fought in segregated units, their battlefield successes and sacrifices gave them a sense of belonging to the nation and fueled postwar movements for equality and civil rights.

Americans fought and died to stop Germany's aggression in Europe and Japan's belligerence in Asia. The United States also fought in the name of freedom against racism and tyranny. Yet the United States withheld that freedom from many who most needed it: Jewish refugees seeking safety in the United States, Japanese American citizens forced into relocation camps, and soldiers of color who fought in segregated units to preserve the very freedoms they were denied at home.

No bombs dropped on the American mainland, yet the war reached into every aspect of national and personal life. Families scattered and regrouped; women entered previously all-male realms of work and military service; couples came together and split apart. Although wartime brought prosperity, the rationing of essential goods and the scarcity of consumer products brought nearly all Americans into the war effort. As soldiers and war industry workers moved around the country, local and regional sensibilities gave way to a stronger national identity. Factories stopped making consumer items and instead turned out war machines. Scientists developed new weapons of mass destruction. Cities burgeoned as workers flooded into the lucrative war industries. The U.S. military and defense establishment expanded to the formidable scale it would maintain during and after the war. World War II changed life within America and transformed the United States into the most powerful nation in the world.

The United States Enters the War

■ *Why were most Americans initially opposed to entering the war, and what changed their minds?*

During the 1930s, the rise of **fascism** and militarism in Italy, Germany, and Japan created a terrible dilemma for Americans. Disillusioned by World War I and preoccupied with the hardships of the Great Depression, they disagreed strongly with one another about how to respond to overt aggression in Africa, Europe, and Asia. The ensuing debate became a turning point in the nation's relationship with the outside world.

Initially, most Americans opposed involvement in the war. But after December 7, 1941, support for entering the war became nearly unanimous. The Japanese attack on Pearl Harbor, Hawaii, shocked the nation and catapulted the United States into the war. Congress responded immediately by declaring war, unleashing a military mobilization that sent millions of Americans overseas to fight. Domestic policies interned Japanese nationals and American citizens of Japanese descent, monitored foreign nationals, and set off migrations within the United States and across its borders in response to the demand for labor in war industries. Mobilizing for World War II gave rise to a unity of purpose that lasted throughout the war and into the postwar era.

FASCIST AGGRESSION IN EUROPE AND ASIA

In Italy, Spain, and Germany, where weak economies and high unemployment created political unrest, fascist leaders rose to power with strong popular support. These new leaders promised economic recovery through strengthening the military and national expansion. They also encouraged intense nationalist sentiments, urging people to identify strongly with the state. Fascist party leader Benito Mussolini had held power in Italy since 1921, suppressing dissident voices and imposing one-party rule. According to Mussolini,

> Fascism combats the whole complex system of democratic ideology, and repudiates it.... Fascism denies that the majority, by the simple fact that it is a majority, can direct human society.... it affirms the immutable, beneficial, and fruitful inequality of mankind, which can never be permanently leveled through the mere operation of a mechanical process such as universal suffrage.... For Fascism, the growth of empire, that is to say the expansion of the nation, is an essential manifestation of vitality, and its opposite a sign of decadence. Peoples which are rising, or rising again after a period of decadence, are always imperialist; and renunciation is a sign of decay and of death.

By the early 1930s, fascism had gained strength in Germany and Spain as well. The term *fascist* has since been applied to the various right-wing dictatorships that arose during the period between the two world wars. Fascist governments were antidemocratic, antiparliamentary, and frequently anti-semitic and hostile to other racial minorities and outsiders. Appealing to nationalistic and often racist sentiments, these governments generally ruled by police surveillance, coercion, and terror.

Germany emerged as the most powerful fascist state in Europe. After Germany's defeat in World War I and the severe economic depression that Germany experienced in the 1920s, Adolf Hitler's National Socialist (Nazi) party won broad support in the weakened country. On January 30, 1933, Hitler became chancellor of Germany. Extolling fanatical nationalism and the racial superiority of "Aryan" Germans, Hitler blamed Jews for Germany's problems. He began a campaign of terror against Jews, homosexuals, suspected communists, and anyone else he saw as promoting "un-German" ideas. Hitler vowed to unite all German-speaking peoples into a new empire, the "Third Reich."

> *In Italy, Spain, and Germany, where weak economies and high unemployment created political unrest, fascist leaders rose to power with strong popular support.*

The fascist governments forged alliances to increase their power and launched campaigns of aggression and expansion. As conflict increased in Europe, hostilities spread into Africa as well. In 1935, Italy invaded the independent African nation of Ethiopia. The following year, Nazi troops seized the Rhineland, in the western region of Germany, in violation of the Versailles agreement, which would soon be followed by a sweep across western Europe. Hitler and Mussolini signed the **Axis** pact, and Japan forged an alliance with Germany. Soon after that, civil war erupted in Spain. Hitler and Mussolini extended aid to the fascist General Francisco Franco, who was trying to overthrow Spain's republican government.

Although Spanish republicans appealed to antifascist governments for help in the fight against Franco, only the Soviet Union came to their assistance. The United States maintained an official policy of neutrality. American Catholics and State Department conservatives believed that the anticommunist Franco would promote social stability. But many on the left, including large numbers of writers and intellectuals, championed the beleaguered Spanish government and denounced the fascists. Cadres of Americans sympathetic to the republican cause, including the Abraham Lincoln Brigade, joined Soviet-organized international forces to fight against Franco.

In Germany, anti-Semitic fervor reached a frenzy on the evening of November 7, 1938. In a spasm of violence known as *Kristallnacht* (Night of the Broken Glass), Hitler launched a massive assault against Jews throughout Germany. For three days, German mobs attacked synagogues and Jewish homes and businesses. Thirty-five Jews were killed and thousands arrested. The rioters destroyed 7,500 shops and 119 synagogues. The Nazi reign of terror against the Jews continued throughout the war, culminating in death camps and genocide.

By 1940, Hitler was sweeping through Europe, invading Denmark, Norway, Holland, Belgium, Luxembourg, and then France.

As persecution of the Jews intensified in the spring and summer of 1938, Hitler annexed Austria to the Third Reich and then demanded the Sudetenland—the German-speaking area of Czechoslovakia bordering Germany and Austria. This area had become part of the newly formed Czechoslovakia in the breakup of the Austro-Hungarian Empire after World War I. The Sudetenland was key to Hitler's goal of uniting all German-speaking Europe into the Third Reich. Soviet leader Josef Stalin offered to join France and Britain to keep Hitler out of the Sudetenland and halt his aggression. But the leaders of France and Britain rebuffed Stalin's suggestion. In September 1938—with no representatives from Czechoslovakia present—British and French leaders met with Hitler in Munich and agreed to let him have the Sudetenland in return for his promise that he would seek no more territory.

Shortly thereafter, Stalin, fearing that the anticommunist leaders of France and Britain were trying to redirect Hitler's aggression toward the Soviet Union, signed a nonaggression pact with Hitler. Eventually, Hitler broke all his promises. Throughout the war and after, the Munich meeting became the symbol of "appeasement," a warning that compromise with the enemy leads only to disaster.

IMAGE

Hitler and Mussolini
in Munich, 1940

In the next few years, the fascist states expanded their power and territory. In 1939, with the help of the Soviet Union and in violation of the Munich agreement, Germany invaded Poland, which fell quickly. At that point, Britain and France declared war on Germany. That same year, Madrid finally fell to Franco's forces. Britain, France, and the United States recognized Franco as victor of the Spanish Civil War. The Soviet Union sent troops into Finland, gaining Finnish territory in 1940.

By 1940, Hitler was sweeping through Europe, invading Denmark, Norway, Holland, Belgium, Luxembourg, and then France. In just six weeks, the Nazis had seized most of western Europe. Hitler then turned his forces on Great Britain. In the summer and fall of 1940, German raids on British air bases nearly destroyed the British Royal Air Force (RAF). Hitler then ordered the bombing of London and other English cities, attacking civilians day and night in what came to be called the Battle of Britain.

In the Far East in the 1930s, events had taken an equally alarming turn. Nationalistic militarists gained control of the Japanese government in Tokyo and began a course of expansion. In 1931–1932, Japanese troops occupied the large Chinese province of Manchuria, installed a puppet government, and gave the province a Japanese name: Manchukuo. Five years later, the Japanese launched a full-scale war against China. The United States extended aid to China and discontinued trade with Japan. In 1940, Japan joined Germany and Italy in the Axis alliance and invaded the French colony of Indochina. Kazuko Kuramoto remembered the nationalist propaganda she learned as a Japanese child raised in Manchuria:

> I was born into a society of Japanese supremacy and grew up believing in Japan's "divine" mission to save Asia from the "evil" hands of Western imperialism.... "You are Japan's only future, a glorious future," adults around us used to say. We believed it with passion.... I joined the Red Cross Nurse Corps to help my country win the war.... "Asia for the Asians!"

Japan's efforts to rid Asia of white Western imperialism inspired some Asians to view Japan as a model of strength. But it was also a cynical ploy of the Japanese leaders, who sought to conquer all of Asia and considered other Asian peoples racially inferior to the Japanese. The Japanese treated the people in the countries they occupied with extreme brutality.

THE GREAT DEBATE OVER INTERVENTION

In spite of the events unfolding in Europe and Asia, during the mid-1930s the overwhelming majority of Americans still opposed intervention in foreign conflicts. Congress passed the Neutrality Acts of 1935, 1936, and 1937, outlawing arms sales or loans to nations at war and forbidding Americans from traveling on the ships of belligerent powers. In 1937, a Gallup poll indicated that 70 percent of Americans believed that the United States should have stayed out of World War I. A peace movement spread across college campuses. Students marched with banners bearing slogans such as "Scholarships, not Battleships." In a "peace strike" in the spring of 1936, half a million students boycotted classes and attended antiwar events. Nevertheless, President Roosevelt and others believed that the United States would be unable to remain aloof from the mounting international crises.

When Japan invaded China in 1937, FDR refused to comply with the provisions of the latest Neutrality Act, on the technicality that neither combatant had officially declared war. By creatively interpreting the law, he was able to offer loans to the embattled Chinese. Roosevelt felt strongly that the United States should actively help resist the Axis powers. In 1940, he told the nation, "Frankly and definitely there is danger ahead—danger against which we must prepare. But we well know that we cannot escape danger, or the fear of danger, by crawling into bed and pulling the covers over our heads."

U.S. citizens still remained bitterly divided over the question of whether to get involved in the conflict. Those who agreed with Roosevelt believed that the nation should take any action "short of war" to help defeat the aggressors in Europe. By sending supplies, the United States could become the "arsenal of democracy" to fight fascism without sending troops and risking American lives. But opponents to this idea spanned the political spectrum. They included moral or religious pacifists, peace activists of the Communist and Labor parties, and anti-semites who supported Hitler. The pro-Nazi German American Bund, an organization that supported Germany, complained about Roosevelt's "Jew Deal"—a reference to Jews among FDR's advisers.

The largest organization to oppose Roosevelt's effort was the America First Committee. With 450 chapters, the group claimed several hundred thousand members. Centered largely in the Midwest, the America Firsters included some active Nazi supporters. Conservative businesspeople also took part. Others, long opposed to Roosevelt and the New Deal, feared that war would give additional power to the already strong federal government. The group's most visible spokesperson was famed aviator Charles Lindbergh, whose anti-semitism fueled his staunch opposition to any involvement in the conflict. Although Lindbergh's position antagonized many who once admired him, he also attracted followers.

Despite intense nonintervention sentiments, public opinion began to shift. Many Americans were shocked

OURS...to fight for

Freedom of Speech

Freedom of Worship

Freedom from Want

Freedom from Fear

Norman Rockwell, *Four Freedoms*, War Bond Poster, printed by permission of the Norman Rockwell Agency, © 1943. The Norman Rockwell Family Entities

■ Early in 1941, Roosevelt stressed the need to protect the "Four Freedoms": freedom of speech, freedom of religion, freedom from want, and freedom from fear of armed aggression. For many Americans, the Four Freedoms translated into intensely personal terms. Norman Rockwell captured this personal dimension in his depiction of the "Four Freedoms" that adorned the cover of the *Saturday Evening Post*. These images were reproduced widely throughout the war to inspire the purchase of war bonds and came to symbolize the democratic values for which the nation was fighting.

when Hitler swiftly conquered much of Europe. News reports of the German occupation of France and the intense bombardment of England in the Battle of Britain bolstered FDR's efforts to take action. The president pledged his support for England against the Nazis, and a few months later Congress approved the Lend-Lease agreement to lend rather than sell military equipment to the Allied countries.

TABLE 23.1			
The Election of 1940			
Candidate	**Political Party**	**Popular Vote (%)**	**Electoral Vote**
Franklin D. Roosevelt	Democratic	54.8	449
Wendell L. Willkie	Republican	44.8	82

When Hitler broke his promise to Stalin and attacked the Soviet Union in June 1941, FDR extended Lend-Lease to the Soviets. During the summer, FDR and British Prime Minister Winston Churchill met on a ship off the coast of Newfoundland to develop a joint declaration known as the Atlantic Charter. The two leaders announced that the United States and Britain sought no new territories. Furthermore, they recognized the right of all peoples to choose their own form of government and to approve any territorial changes that might affect them. The charter called for international free trade and navigation as well.

DOCUMENT

Lindbergh, Radio Address

The charter articulated the **Allies'** war aims, but it also had profound implications for colonial rule around the world. Realizing the possible cost of losing British colonies, Churchill retreated from the global implications of the charter. The declaration, he claimed, applied primarily to European nations under Nazi rule. Roosevelt walked a fine line between contradicting Churchill and supporting the idea of empire. However, the words of the charter—along with the Allies' condemnation of racism and territorial expansion by Germany and Japan—emboldened anticolonial activists around the world. Within fifteen years after the end of World War II, 800 million previously colonized people won their independence, and forty new nations formed.

As the United States inched closer to entry into the conflict, FDR still faced political and economic troubles at home. Although Allied munitions orders had already stimulated the economy, as late as 1939, 9.4 million Americans—17.2 percent of the labor force—remained jobless. In the 1940 presidential election, Roosevelt defeated Republican challenger Wendell Wilkie. FDR began an unprecedented third term as war loomed and economic hardship at home persisted. But Japan's surprise attack on Pearl Harbor in 1941 would end both the neutrality debate and the economic depression.

THE ATTACK ON PEARL HARBOR

For nearly a decade, tensions had been mounting between the United States and Japan as American leaders tried to contain Japan's expansion in Asia. Roosevelt hoped that a strong U.S. military presence in the Pacific would persuade Japan's premier, General Hideki Tojo, to avoid a confrontation with the United States. When Japan continued its aggression in Asia, FDR froze Japanese assets in the United States, putting trade with Japan under presidential control. This move, he hoped, would bring Japan to the bargaining table. Instead, on November 25, 1941, the Japanese dispatched aircraft carriers toward Hawaii and sent troops to the border of Malaya in Southeast Asia.

Although U.S. intelligence sources had broken the codes with which the Japanese encrypted messages about their war plans, they did not realize that the Japanese intended to strike Hawaii. One memo indicating that the Japanese were heading toward Pearl Harbor lay buried under a pile of intelligence reports. As a result, American military officials failed to warn the U.S. forces stationed in Pearl Harbor. At 7:55 a.m. on December 7, Japanese planes swooped over Pearl Harbor and bombed the naval base. The assault caught the American forces completely off guard and destroyed most of the

■ On December 7, 1941, the Japanese launched a surprise attack on the U.S. naval base at Pearl Harbor, Hawaii. The attack brought the United States immediately into World War II and was the only time that the war came to American soil.

AP/Wide World Photos

U.S. Pacific fleet. Only a few aircraft carriers that were out at sea survived. Two hours after the attack on Pearl Harbor, the Japanese also struck the main U.S. base at Clark Field in the Philippines, destroying half of the U.S. Air Force in the Far East.

The Japanese attack on Pearl Harbor shocked the nation and catapulted the United States immediately into World War II. President Roosevelt somberly told millions of Americans gathered around their radios that the day of the attack would "live in infamy." Most former doubters now joined the war effort.

For some, war mobilization came immediately. Sixteen-year-old John Garcia watched flames rising at Pearl Harbor from his house four miles away. The young Hawaiian reached the scene in time to witness the second round of bombings. "I spent the rest of the day swimming inside the harbor, along with some other Hawaiians. I brought out I don't know how many bodies, and how many were alive and how many dead.... We worked around the clock for three days."

In less than two hours, the Japanese had wrecked 188 planes—most of the American aircraft on the island—and sunk 19 ships, including 8 battleships, 3 destroyers, and 3 cruisers. American aircraft carriers were not in port at the time of the attack, which meant that the Japanese failed to destroy some of the most powerful naval vessels that would be used in the Pacific war.

When the smoke cleared, 2,323 American service personnel were dead. Congress immediately declared war against Japan. Representative Jeannette Rankin from Montana cast the only dissenting vote. (The first woman elected to Congress and a lifelong pacifist, Rankin had also voted against the United States' entry into World War I.) Three days later, Germany and Italy declared war against the United States.

The Limits of Racial Tolerance

Envisioning History

(Both photos) Dr. Seuss Collection, Mandeville Special Collections Library, University of California, San Diego (June 11, 1942)

These two political cartoons by Dr. Seuss, known for his whimsical children's books and progressive political ideas, demonstrate that even among liberal activists, racial tolerance during World War II did not extend to Japanese Americans. Dr. Seuss drew dozens of cartoons that criticized anti-Semitic and anti-black prejudices, but he also promoted the idea that Japanese American citizens were disloyal and dangerous. The "5th Column" refers to the assumption that Japanese Americans were working on behalf of the enemy while living within the United States. Stereotyped images such as these contributed to anti-Japanese sentiment that ultimately resulted in the relocation of Japanese Americans from the West Coast into internment camps.

QUESTIONS

1. What are the characteristics Seuss ascribes to the Japanese Americans in the top cartoon, and what does the location indicate?

2. What do the details in the drawing in the bottom cartoon suggest about Seuss's ideas regarding race relations during the war?

3. What do these cartoons reveal about Dr. Seuss's attitudes toward Japanese Americans and African Americans during World War II?

4. Why would a liberal antiracist like Dr. Seuss portray Japanese Americans in such a negative, stereotyped manner?

JAPANESE AMERICAN RELOCATION

The assault on Pearl Harbor sparked widespread rumors along the U.S. West Coast that Japanese and Japanese Americans living there planned to sabotage the war effort. Powerful farming interests eager to eradicate Japanese American competition pushed for an evacuation. General John L. DeWitt, chief of the Western Defense Command, argued that people of Japanese ancestry posed a particular threat: "The Japanese race is an enemy race and while many second and third generation Japanese born on United States soil, possessed of United States citizenship, have become 'Americanized,' the racial strains are undiluted.... It therefore follows that along the vital Pacific Coast over 112,000 potential enemies, of Japanese extraction, are at large today."

Not everyone agreed that Japanese Americans should be removed from the West Coast. U.S. Attorney General Francis Biddle protested that there was "no reason" for a mass relocation. J. Edgar Hoover, director of the FBI, also opposed the plan, arguing that DeWitt's suggestion reflected "hysteria and lack of judgment." Nevertheless, the Roosevelt administration gave in to the pressure, with the support of California Attorney General Earl Warren. In February 1942, Roosevelt signed Executive Order 9066, which suspended the civil rights of American citizens of Japanese descent. The order authorized the removal of 110,000 Japanese and Japanese Americans from the West Coast. Of those, 70,000 were **Nisei,** native-born American citizens. Families received at most a week's notice to evacuate their homes and move to prison-like camps surrounded by barbed wire and guarded by armed soldiers. There were ten such camps, most of them located in arid, desolate spots in seven western states. At the camps, internees lived in makeshift wooden barracks, where entire families crowded into one room.

Not all Japanese Americans were evacuated. General Delos Emmons, the military governor of Hawaii, insisted that removing the Japanese from those islands would cripple the economy, as well as the defense of Oahu. In Hawaii, Japanese and Japanese Americans made up more than 90 percent of the skilled workers and agricultural laborers needed to rebuild and sustain the island. In their defense, Emmons proclaimed, "There have been no known acts of sabotage committed in Hawaii." Business leaders concurred, hoping to retain their labor force. But the Japanese living on the West Coast lacked the broad support that those in Hawaii enjoyed.

The experience of internment proved so devastating that, after the war, 5,766 *Nisei* renounced their American citizenship. One of those was World War I veteran Joseph Y. Kurihara, who recalled, "It was really cruel and harsh. To pack and evacuate in 48 hours

National Archives

■ The family pictured here was among thousands of loyal citizens of Japanese ancestry removed from their homes on the West Coast and relocated to internment camps. Here, the Hirano family, George, Hisa, and Yasbei (left to right), pose at the Colorado River Relocation Center in Poston, Arizona. Hisa holds a photo of her son, an American soldier, who is off fighting the war.

■ Internment camps during World War II

■ **MAP 23.1 The Internment of Japanese Americans During World War II**

After the Japanese attack on Pearl Harbor, President Franklin Delano Roosevelt signed an order authorizing the removal of people of Japanese descent from the West Coast. These Japanese Americans were relocated to internment camps built in arid and isolated areas in the West as well as in two locations in Arkansas.

was an impossibility. Seeing mothers completely bewildered with children crying from want and peddlers taking advantage and offering prices next to robbery made me feel like murdering those responsible." Kurihara emigrated to Japan—a country he had never seen.

While the internment experience alienated many Japanese Americans, fully 33,000 joined the armed services—including 1,200 who enlisted from the internment camps—and proved their patriotism on the battlefield. In the Pacific, their knowledge of the Japanese language proved critical in translating intercepted Japanese military documents. General Charles Willoughby, chief of intelligence in the Pacific, estimated that Japanese American military contributions shortened the war by two years. They also served ably in Europe, suffering huge casualties. The Japanese Americans of the 442nd Regiment lost one-fourth of their soldiers in battles in North Africa and Italy. They suffered another 800 casualties rescuing the Texan "Lost Battalion," 211 men surrounded by German troops in the Vosges Mountains of France. As one Texan recalled, "We were never so glad to see anyone as those fighting Japanese Americans." The 442nd Regiment won 18,143 individual decorations for distinguished service. Welcoming them home in 1946, President Harry Truman declared, "You fought not only the enemy, you fought prejudice—and you won."

Nevertheless, the U.S. government would take its time acknowledging that the internment had been a grave injustice. The Supreme Court upheld the constitutionality of the policy, and Roosevelt would not rescind the evacuation order until after his reelection in 1944. The camps finally closed in 1945. All told, Japanese Americans lost property valued at $500 million. Not until 1968 would the government reimburse former internees for some of their losses. And not until 1983 would a Special Commission on Wartime Relocation and Internment of Civilians concede that because of "race prejudice, war hysteria and a failure of political leadership," the U.S. government had committed "a grave injustice" to more than 110,000 people of Japanese ancestry. In 1988, Congress enacted legislation awarding restitution payments of $20,000 each to 60,000 surviving internees—a small gesture for Americans whose only "crime" was their Japanese ancestry.

FOREIGN NATIONALS IN THE UNITED STATES

Although Japanese Americans were the only U.S. citizens interned solely on the basis of their ancestry, German and Italian nationals living in the United States were also subject to new regulations, and in some cases relocation and incarceration. The Smith Act of 1940 required all foreign-born residents to be registered and fingerprinted, and it broadened the grounds for deportation. In 1942, all enemy aliens (citizens of countries at war with the United States) were required to be fingerprinted and photographed and to carry registration cards at all times. On the West Coast, they were subject to travel restrictions, curfews, and in certain designated areas, relocation.

Naturalization was a concrete way for newcomers to clarify their status and their loyalty.

Six hundred thousand Italians and 314,000 Germans living in the United States were subject to these requirements. Several thousand who belonged to organizations that were considered sympathetic to the German or Italian government were arrested and given hearings to determine if they posed a security risk. Several hundred were deemed potentially dangerous and interned for the duration of the war. Approximately 10,000 Italian nationals were forced to relocate from their homes on the West Coast. A few hundred German and Italian immigrants who were naturalized U.S. citizens were also relocated from designated coastal areas.

Some enemy aliens went to extreme lengths to prove their patriotism during wartime. Italian-born Annunziata Bongiorno took to her bed until her son, an American citizen and a conscientious objector, enlisted to restore the family's honor. Wartime conditions also prompted large numbers of immigrants to become American citizens. Between 1941 and 1945, more immigrants became naturalized citizens than in any previous five-year period. More than 112,000 were naturalized during their service in the armed forces. But the vast majority of those naturalized—1,539,000—were civilians. For the first time, the majority were women. The largest numbers came from countries that were embroiled in the war: the British Empire, Italy, Germany, Poland, and the Soviet Union. Naturalization was a concrete way for newcomers to clarify their status and their loyalty.

WARTIME MIGRATIONS

Even before the United States officially entered World War II, the conflict had begun to change the face of the nation. The sleepy town of Richmond, California, perched near the north end of San Francisco Bay, underwent a profound transformation when the nation stepped up war production. The town's mostly white population of 23,000 ballooned to 120,000 after industrialist Henry Kaiser constructed four shipyards there. The yards employed over 150,000 workers, more than one-fourth of them African American. Most were young, married migrants from the South, and there were slightly more women than men. They came to Richmond attracted by the better pay and benefits, along with the opportunity for greater freedom than they had known in the Jim Crow South.

Margaret Starks, daughter of southern tenant farmers, moved to Richmond. She established a blues club, edited a black newspaper, and played an active role in the National Association for the Advancement of Colored People (NAACP). Her club became a center for African American cultural and political life. Thus, black migrants not only established their own community institutions but also transformed the life of the city. This same process unfolded all over the country, bringing black culture into cities and creating a diverse urban landscape.

Many cities, however, were ill equipped to handle the influx of migrants. An estimated 60,000 African Americans moved into Chicago, for example, causing an enormous housing crisis. Many newcomers lacked privacy as they crowded into basements and rooms rented from total strangers. Huge numbers of whites also moved north, many leaving hardscrabble farms, and hoping to prosper in booming war industries.

Wartime also saw new migration from abroad and a reversal of earlier immigration policies. Because of the alliance with China in the war against Japan, in 1943 Congress repealed the Chinese Exclusion Act, and migrants from China became eligible for citizenship for the first time. Few Chinese actually arrived, however, and most immigration restrictions remained in force. The most significant wartime migration came from Mexico. In 1942, Mexico joined the Allies and provided an air force squadron trained in the United States that fought in the Pacific. An executive agreement between the United States and Mexico created the **bracero** program, which stipulated that the migrants were to be hired on short-term contracts and treated fairly. Under the *bracero* program, 300,000 Mexicans, mostly agricultural workers, came to the United States to labor in rural areas such as California's San Joaquin Valley, taking the place of "Okies" who migrated to cities for defense work. By the mid-1960s, nearly 5 million Mexicans had migrated north under the program.

> *Wartime also saw new migration from abroad and a reversal of earlier immigration policies.*

Total War

■ *What were the major differences for the United States between the war in Europe and the war in the Pacific?*

World War II consisted of two wars, one centered in Europe and the other in the Pacific. Combatants in both conflicts engaged in **total war**—attacks on civilian as well as military targets. The advantageous geographic position of the United States enabled it to wage total war without attacks on its own cities.

In Europe, Hitler unleashed the Holocaust, his plan to destroy European Jewry. The Germans swept across Europe, breaking treaties and occupying countries in an effort to establish a German-speaking Third Reich. In Asia, Japan colonized many of its neighboring countries in an effort to dominate and occupy all of Asia.

THE HOLOCAUST

European Jews faced the worst of the war's ravages. Hitler's war aims included conquering all of Europe and destroying European Jewry. Throughout the war, Nazi anti-Jewish policies escalated from persecution and officially sanctioned violence to imprisonment in concentration camps, slave labor, and ultimately Hitler's "Final Solution," genocide. Nazis developed increasingly efficient means of killing Jews. Some Jewish men, women, and children perished by firing squads in mass executions. Others died of disease and malnutrition in concentration camps or at the hands of Nazi doctors in gruesome medical experiments. In the infamous Nazi death camps, guards herded prisoners into "shower rooms" that were actually gas chambers.

Nazi Murder Mills

American officials knew of the Nazi persecution of the Jews but did little about it. Throughout the 1930s, American Jewish groups pressured the Roosevelt administration to ease immigration laws to allow Jewish refugees to enter the country. But the United States continued to enforce the immigration restrictions passed in 1924, which were based on national origin, and raised the legal quotas only slightly. Those laws allowed only a small number of Jews to enter the country.

In 1938, Roosevelt organized an international conference on the refugee crisis in Evian, Switzerland, with thirty-two nations attending. But no nation agreed to accept large numbers

■ **MAP 23.2 Nazi Concentration and Extermination Camps**
Under Hitler, the Nazis established dozens of concentration camps where Jews and others whom the Nazis deemed "undesirable" were imprisoned. In addition to these sites, there were hundreds of slave labor camps attached to factories across Germany where Jews were forced to work for Nazi enterprises. After Hitler began his genocidal "Final Solution," six camps became sites of systematic mass murder, with efficient killing operations, including gas chambers disguised as shower rooms.

of refugees, so the conference had little practical impact. In 1939, a pro-Nazi rally in New York City drew 20,000. That same year, congressional leaders defeated the Wagner-Rogers bill, which would have amended immigration quotas to allow the entry of 20,000 Jewish children.

When the Nazis began their policy of extermination in 1941, they tried to keep it a secret. But Dr. Gerhard Riegner, the World Jewish Congress representative in Geneva, Switzerland, learned about the Holocaust from a German source and informed American diplomats. U.S. State Department officials heard reports of the Holocaust but decided to keep the information quiet. Despite official silence, Rabbi Stephen S. Wise, a prominent American Jewish leader, heard the news and held a press conference in November 1942. But the American press, preoccupied with military events and reluctant to publish stories of atrocities without official verification, gave the Holocaust little coverage. Meanwhile, despite reports of Nazi genocide, the U.S. government turned away boatloads of Jewish refugees, sending them back to Germany to their deaths.

Nazi persecution of the Jews raised American sensitivity to the issue of racism but did little to diminish anti-semitism within the United States. In fact, American hostility toward Jews reached new heights during World War II. In a 1942 survey of American voters, 51 percent agreed that Jews "have too much power in the United States." At the height of Nazi genocide against the Jews in 1944, when asked to identify the greatest "menace" to the nation, 24 percent of Americans polled listed Jews.

In Europe, American military strategists knew of the existence and location of Nazi death camps, but they decided not to try to bomb the camps or the railroad lines leading to them. Some Europeans under Nazi domination, however, risked their lives to rescue and shelter Jews. While the United States stood by, smaller nations took action. For example, Denmark defied the Nazis even though occupied by them—taking a far greater risk than anything the United States might have done—and managed to save nearly all Danish Jews. Shanghai, China, became home to more Jewish refugees than any other city in the world. And the tiny Dominican Republic took in more European Jews than any other country in the Western Hemisphere.

THE WAR IN EUROPE

When the United States finally entered the war after the attack on Pearl Harbor in 1941, the leaders of the Allied Powers, including the United States, Britain, and the Soviet Union, had to develop a strategy to defeat Germany. But the Allies did not always agree on how to conduct the war, and relations between the United States and the Soviet Union remained strained. Unable to fully overcome the hostility and suspicion that had

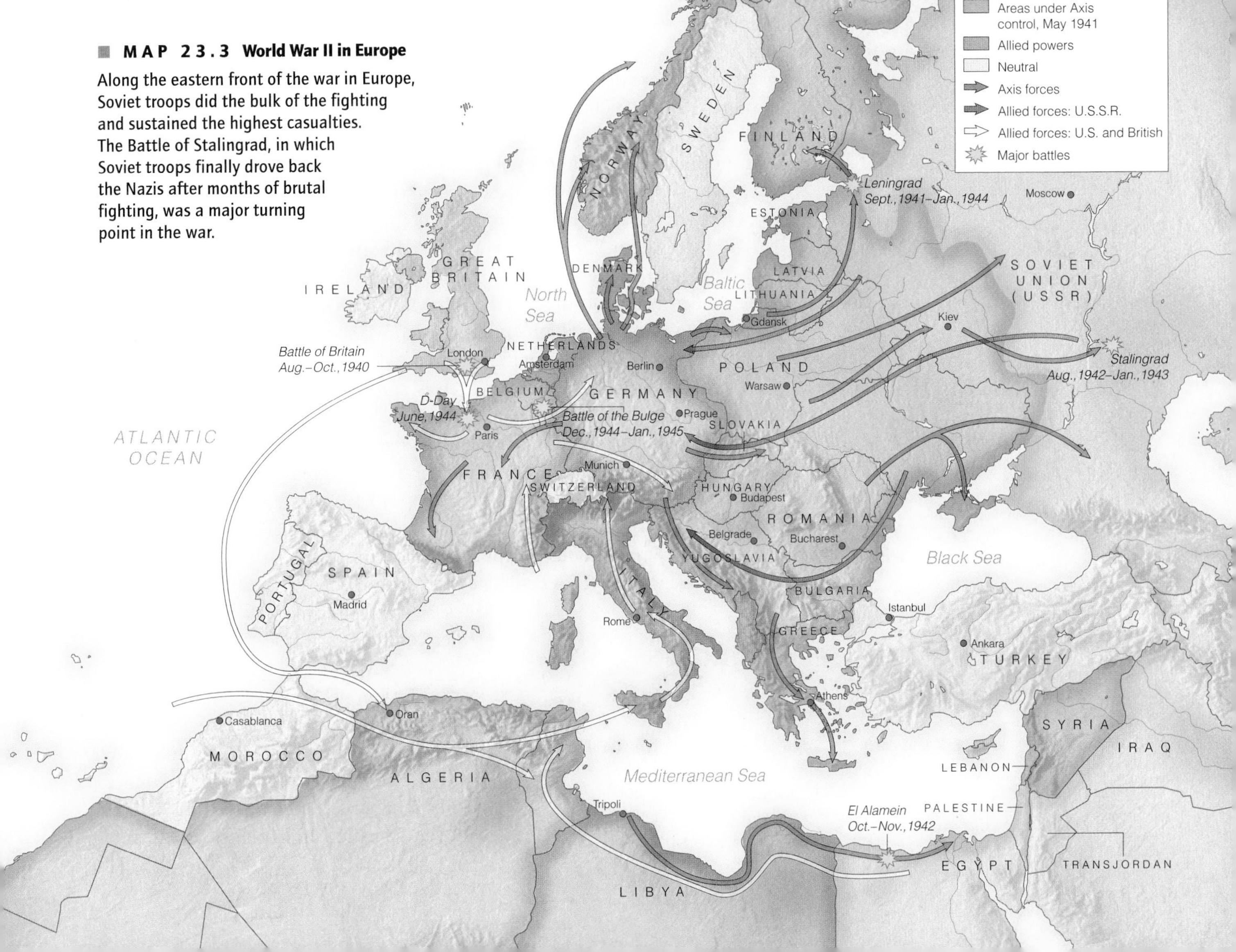

■ **MAP 23.3 World War II in Europe**

Along the eastern front of the war in Europe, Soviet troops did the bulk of the fighting and sustained the highest casualties. The Battle of Stalingrad, in which Soviet troops finally drove back the Nazis after months of brutal fighting, was a major turning point in the war.

World War II in Europe

- Axis powers
- Areas under Axis control, May 1941
- Allied powers
- Neutral
- Axis forces
- Allied forces: U.S.S.R.
- Allied forces: U.S. and British
- Major battles

World War II in Europe

marked their earlier encounters, leaders of both countries fought the war with postwar power considerations in mind.

Like the United States at Pearl Harbor, the Soviet Union suffered a shocking blow when the Nazis launched a surprise invasion in June 1941 in violation of the nonaggression pact Hitler had signed with Stalin in 1938. The Soviets suffered huge losses as 200 German divisions advanced across eastern Europe and into the Soviet Union toward Moscow. With the full might of the German forces now concentrated on the front lines against the Russians in eastern Europe, Soviet premier Joseph Stalin urged the United States to open a second front in western Europe to divert the Germans toward the west and relieve pressure on the Soviet Union. In May 1942, Roosevelt assured Stalin that the United States would support an Allied invasion across the English Channel into France. But British Prime Minister Winston Churchill persuaded FDR to delay that dangerous maneuver and instead launch an invasion of French North Africa, which was controlled by the German occupation forces in Vichy, France.

While the Allies turned their attention to North Africa, the Soviets managed single-handedly to force the German army into retreat at Stalingrad, where fierce fighting lasted from August 1942 to January 1943. The Battle of Stalingrad was a major turning point in the war and stopped German aggression on the eastern front. Axis soldiers in North Africa surrendered in May 1943. The following summer, Allied forces overran the island of Sicily and moved into southern Italy. Italians overthrew Mussolini and opened communication with General Dwight D. Eisenhower, commander of the Allied forces in Europe. By 1944, the Allied forces reached Rome.

The long-awaited Allied invasion across the English Channel finally began on June 6, 1944, code named D-Day. At dawn, in the largest amphibious landing in history, more than 4,000 Allied ships descended on the French beaches in Normandy. As the troops splashed onto shore, they met a barrage of German fire. Many thousands died on the beach that day. Over the next ten days, more than 1 million soldiers landed in Normandy, along with 50,000 vehicles and more than 100,000 tons of supplies, opening the way for an advance into Nazi-occupied France.

As the war continued to rage, Roosevelt prepared for the November election. Much of the 1944 campaign swirled around Roosevelt's suitability for reelection: whether he should serve an unprecedented fourth term, and whether his health would hold up—the sixty-two-year-old president suffered from heart disease and high blood pressure. Democratic party regulars believed that Vice President Henry A. Wallace was too liberal, so they persuaded FDR to drop him from the ticket and replace him with Senator Harry S. Truman from Missouri. The Republicans chose Thomas E. Dewey, governor of New York, to run against FDR. Democrats campaigned on the slogan "Don't change horses in midstream," and the electorate apparently agreed. Roosevelt won the election and continued his wartime leadership.

In the months after D-Day, the Allies liberated Paris and went on to defeat the Germans in Belgium at the Battle of the Bulge, sending them into full retreat. The Allied armies then crossed the Rhine River and headed for Berlin. Eisenhower stopped his troops at the Elbe River to let Soviet troops take Berlin. Eisenhower hoped that giving the Soviets the final triumph would ease postwar relations with the Soviet Union—but he also wanted to save American lives. Huge numbers of Soviet troops died in the siege of Berlin, but the war in Europe was nearly over. With the Soviets approaching his bunker in April 1945, Hitler committed suicide. Germany surrendered at Reims, France, on May 7, 1945—V-E (Victory in Europe) Day.

FDR did not live to see Germany defeated. On April 12, 1945, he died suddenly of a cerebral hemorrhage. As a stunned nation mourned, Truman took the oath of office as the nation's thirty-third president.

TABLE 23.2			
The Election of 1944			
Candidate	**Political Party**	**Popular Vote (%)**	**Electoral Vote**
Franklin D. Roosevelt	Democratic	53.5	432
Thomas E. Dewey	Republican	46.0	99

■ **MAP 23.4 World War II in the Pacific**
During World War II, the Japanese occupied vast territories in Asia and the Pacific. The Battle of Midway in 1942 was the first major victory for the United States in the Pacific and helped turn the tide of the war in favor of the Allies.

THE WAR IN THE PACIFIC

World War II in the Pacific

As the conflict in Europe came to an end, the war in the Pacific still raged. Following the attack on Pearl Harbor, Japan continued its conquests in the Pacific. In April 1942, General Douglas MacArthur, driven from the Philippines to Australia, left 12,000 American and 64,000 Filipino soldiers to surrender on the Bataan peninsula and the island of Corregidor. On the infamous "Bataan Death March" to the prison at Camp O'Donnell, the Japanese beat, tortured, and shot the sick and starving troops. As many as 10,000 died on the march.

Now in control of Indochina, Thailand, the Philippines, and the chain of islands from Sumatra to Guadalcanal, Japan's military leaders planned to destroy what remained of the U.S. fleet. But MacArthur marshaled his forces and achieved a major victory in the Battle of the Coral Sea in May 1942. U.S. intelligence sources discovered that the Japanese were planning a massive assault on Midway Island, a naval base key to Hawaii's defense. Under the command of Admiral Chester Nimitz, the United States launched a surprise air strike on

June 4, 1942, sinking four Japanese carriers, destroying 322 planes, and virtually eliminating Japanese offensive capabilities. Two months later, Nimitz's forces landed at Guadalcanal in the Solomon Islands, subduing the Japanese in five months of brutal fighting. Having seized the offensive, U.S. troops continued toward Japan. MacArthur's forces took New Guinea, and by February 1944, Nimitz secured the Marshall Islands and the Marianas.

At about the same time that Allied forces in Europe were landing in Normandy, the United States invaded Saipan, a Japanese-controlled island that protected Japan's territory. In a savage air battle on June 19, the Americans shot down 346 Japanese planes and lost 50 of their own. The attack killed 22,000 Japanese civilians—two-thirds of the island's population. The United States suffered 14,000 casualties. The grueling battle secured for the United States a strategic base for launching bombing raids on Tokyo. The bloody war in the Pacific continued, with critical Allied victories on the islands of Iwo Jima and Okinawa in the spring of 1945.

Crucial to these victories were the sensitive radio communications of a special U.S. Marine unit of Navajo "code talkers." Keith Little was one of the young Navajo men who volunteered for military service upon hearing that the Japanese had attacked Pearl Harbor. Little and 400 other Navajo became part of a special unit that developed an intricate code, based on the Navajo language, to transmit top-secret information without risk of decoding by the Japanese. Ironically, many of these men had been educated in government boarding schools that forbade them to speak their native language. Now that same government called upon them to use their language to help win the war. The Navajo language was particularly well suited to code because very few people besides Navajo knew it. In a process code named "Magic," the all-Navajo 382nd Platoon of the U.S. Marine Corps encoded and decoded sensitive military information almost instantly and flawlessly. In two days on the Pacific island of Iwo Jima, six code talkers transmitted more than 800 messages, working around the clock, without a single error. Signal Officer Major Howard Conner recalled, "Without the Navajos the Marines would never have taken Iwo Jima."

Meanwhile, fighting continued in China, where the struggle against Japanese aggression grew complicated because China was also engaged in a civil war. Initially, the Chinese Nationalists appeared to have the largest military forces to resist the Japanese, so Roosevelt declared support for Jiang Jieshi (Chiang Kai-shek), the corrupt and unpopular Nationalist leader. Jiang continued to demand Allied support as a growing communist movement, led by Mao Zedong (Mao Tse-tung), challenged the Japanese and gained support among Chinese peasants. Although the Nationalists failed to stop the Japanese, Roosevelt continued to back Jiang's ineffective leadership, rather than supporting the Chinese communists, setting the stage for political tensions that persisted after the war.

The war in the Pacific was particularly vicious. Racism on both sides fueled acts of extreme brutality. Japan's leaders believed that their racial superiority gave them a divine mission to conquer Asia. The Japanese tortured prisoners of war and civilians in their conquered

The National Archives

■ Associated Press photographer Joe Rosenthal took this photo, "Old Glory Goes Up on Mt. Suribachi, Iwo Jima," and won a Pulitzer Prize for it in 1945. Although controversy surrounded the photo (some witnesses claimed it was staged with a larger flag after the original flag had been planted), it became an icon of American determination and unity in World War II.

lands. They tested biological weapons and conducted medical experiments on live subjects. Japanese troops forced Chinese and Korean women into sexual slavery, euphemistically calling them "comfort women."

Racial hostility also promoted American battlefield savagery. U.S. troops in the Pacific often killed Japanese combatants instead of taking prisoners and desecrated the enemy dead with disrespect equal to that meted out by the Japanese on the bodies of their foes. On the home front, American cultural images and popular sentiments vilified the Japanese not only as a hated enemy but also as a monstrous race. War correspondent Ernie Pyle explained that "in Europe we felt that our enemies, horrible and deadly as they were, were still people. But…the Japanese were looked upon as something subhuman and repulsive, the way some people feel about cockroaches or mice." Respectable magazines such as *Science Digest* ran articles titled "Why Americans Hate Japs More Than Nazis."

■ Navajo "code talkers" operate a portable radio in the Pacific combat zone in 1943.

As American troops closed in on Japan, Roosevelt approved a plan to firebomb Japanese cities. The Allies had already bombed German cities, destroying much of Hamburg and Dresden and killing thousands of civilians. To persuade Americans to accept the bombing strategy with its inevitable civilian casualties, government censors lifted the ban on stories of Japanese treatment of American war prisoners. Reports of atrocities, as well as virulently racist images of the Japanese, flooded the media. On March 9 and 10, 1945, bombing raids led by General Curtis LeMay leveled sixteen square miles of Tokyo—one-fourth of the city—and left 185,000 dead or wounded. LeMay's bombers then turned to other cities. Firebombs reportedly killed more civilians than Japanese soldiers who died in battle.

The Home Front

■ *In what ways did World War II alter life for the Americans who remained at home?*

As bloody battles raged across Europe and Asia, wartime mobilization brought Americans from all regions and backgrounds together in shared service and sacrifice. Industries as well as citizens dedicated themselves to the war effort. Automobile manufacturers stopped making cars and instead turned out tanks, jeeps, and other military vehicles. Citizens made do with government-rationed basic staples, including certain foods and materials such as gasoline. As able-bodied men left their jobs to fight the war, new work opportunities opened up for women as well as for disabled Americans.

Cities and centers of war production brought together young women and men who found new opportunities for work as well as for social and sexual experimentation. Gay men and lesbians discovered newly visible communities in both military and civilian life. Although class, gender, and racial injustices persisted, the war offered new sources of pride and patriotism for women and people of color and raised expectations that they would achieve full inclusion in the American promise.

Many Americans hoped that the liberal spirit of the New Deal would endure during the war; others were eager for an end to what they perceived as Depression-era class conflict and hostility to business interests. To some extent, both sides got their wish. Full employment, the increasing strength of unions, and high taxes on the wealthy pleased New Deal liberals. Profit guarantees, freedom from antitrust actions, no-strike pledges, and low-cost imported labor gratified pro-business conservatives. Congress dismantled some of the New Deal's most successful agencies, including the Civilian Conservation Corps (CCC), the Works

Projects Administration (WPA), and the National Youth Administration. Full employment during wartime made these job programs unnecessary.

PROPAGANDA AND BUILDING MORALE

Like all other major powers involved in the conflict, the United States mounted a propaganda drive to promote support for the war effort. FDR created the Office of War Information (OWI) in 1942 to coordinate morale-boosting and censorship initiatives. Working in partnership with the motion picture industry and other media outlets, the OWI sponsored movies, radio programs, publications, and posters. These productions portrayed the war as a crusade to preserve the "American way of life" and encouraged American women and men to work in war industries, enlist in the armed forces, and purchase war bonds. The biggest box office hit of the war years was a government-sponsored war propaganda film, *This Is the Army*, starring Ronald Reagan. Many film stars, including Reagan, served their military duty by performing in productions and movies to promote the war effort.

The call for unity stifled the expression of class conflict that had prevailed during the Depression. Eric Johnston, head of the Motion Picture Producers' Association and FDR's business adviser, insisted that Hollywood remove class conflict from its films: "We'll have no more *Grapes of Wrath*, we'll have no more *Tobacco Roads*, we'll have no more films that deal with the seamy side of American life. We'll have no more films that treat the banker as a villain."

Maintaining the morale of the fighting men was critical to sustaining the war effort. Officials tried to ease the hardships of combat by providing cigarettes and beer, entertainment by and for the troops, and live performances by Hollywood celebrities such as Bob Hope and Ginger Rogers. Promises of the good life waiting at home—especially images of cozy houses, warm hearths, and alluring women—reminded the men overseas why they were fighting. "Pinups"—photos of sexy but wholesome-looking women—adorned the walls of barracks, suggesting the joys that would follow victory.

Under government sponsorship, all the major radio networks aired a series of programs in 1942 to mobilize support for the war. One highly acclaimed segment, "To the Young," included this conversation:

YOUNG MALE VOICE: "That's one of the things this war's about."
YOUNG FEMALE VOICE: "About us?"
YOUNG MALE VOICE: "About *all* young people like us. About love and gettin' hitched, and havin' a home and some kids, and breathin' fresh air out in the suburbs...about livin' an' workin' *decent*, like free people."

The enemy drew on the same images in their efforts to persuade American soldiers to surrender. One lurid piece of propaganda that the Japanese scattered among the American troops in the Pacific pictured a young Caucasian man and woman locked in a passionate kiss under the moonlight. The leaflet read:

That unforgettable embrace under the beautiful moon with the warmth of HER shapely body nestled against yours; that blood-tingling kiss; that over-powering sense of passion that

■ Sailors relax in the Aircraft Repair Unit (ARU-145) during their free time at Guadalcanal. The walls above their cots are decorated with "pinups" of young women in alluring poses, reminding the men of the pleasures that await them after the war.

sweeps over you—these and many other pleasant memories you'll be able to relive again if you'll throw down your arms, surrender and prepare to get out of this hell-hole.

Inside the card was the grim alternative: the same young man's bloody body with the warning: "but if you continue to resist—Then, under the beautiful tropical moon, only death awaits you. Bullet-holes in your guts—agonizing death! You have the two alternatives. Take your choice."

Within the United States, government censors made sure that no photographs showing badly wounded soldiers or mutilated bodies reached the public. The censors also removed any images that might elicit sympathy for the enemy, such as pictures of injured or frightened enemy soldiers suffering at the hands of American soldiers. Photographs that appeared in the American media generally sanitized the horror of war, depicting noble American soldiers and a shadowy, faceless enemy. Rarely, if ever, did those on the home front see the true extent of the war's destructiveness and brutality. When men returned home severely traumatized by what they had seen, even their trauma was censored. As just one example, for more than three decades, the army suppressed John Huston's *Let There Be Light*, a film documentary of World War II veterans in a psychiatric hospital suffering from post-traumatic stress disorder.

> *Within the United States, government censors made sure that no photographs showing badly wounded soldiers or mutilated bodies reached the public.*

HOME FRONT WORKERS, ROSIE THE RIVETER, AND VICTORY GIRLS

Wartime opened up new possibilities for jobs, income, and labor organizing, for women as well as for men, and for new groups of workers. Disabled workers entered jobs previously considered beyond their abilities, fulfilling their tasks with skill and competence. For example, deaf people streamed into Akron, Ohio, to work in the tire factories that became defense plants, making more money than they ever made before.

Along with new employment opportunities, workers' earnings rose nearly 70 percent. Income doubled for farmers and then doubled again. Labor union membership grew 50 percent, reaching an all-time high by the end of the war. In spite of no-strike pledges, strikes pressured the aircraft industry in Detroit and elsewhere. A major strike of the United Mine Workers Union erupted in 1943. Congress responded with the Smith-Connally Act of 1943, which gave the president power to seize plants or mines wherever strikes interrupted war production.

Women and people of color joined unions in unprecedented numbers. Some organized unions of their own. Energetic labor organizers like Luisa Moreno and Dorothy Ray Healy organized Mexican and Russian Jewish workers at the California Sanitary Canning Company into a powerful CIO cannery union that achieved wage increases and union recognition. Unions with white male leadership, however, admitted women and people of color reluctantly and tolerated them only during the war emergency. Some unions required women to quit their jobs after the war.

Nevertheless, World War II ushered in dramatic changes for American women. Wartime scarcities led to increased domestic labor as homemakers made do with rationed goods, mended clothing, collected and saved scraps and metals, and planted "victory gardens" to help feed their families. Employment opportunities for women also increased. As a result of the combined incentives of patriotism and good wages, women streamed into the paid labor force. Many women took "men's jobs" while the men went off to fight.

Rosie the Riveter became the heroic symbol of the woman war worker. Pictures of attractive "Rosies" building planes or constructing ships graced magazine covers and posters. Future Hollywood star Marilyn Monroe first gained attention when her photograph appeared in *Yank*, a magazine for soldiers. The magazine pictured her not as the sex goddess she later became, but as a typical Rosie the Riveter, clad in overalls, working at her job in a defense plant.

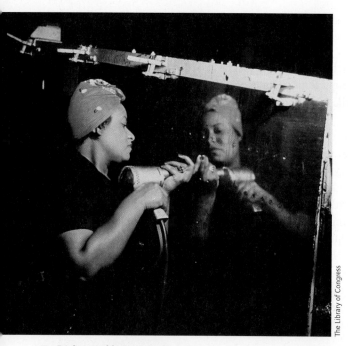

The Library of Congress

■ During World War II, Rosie the Riveter became an icon of the working woman doing a "man's job" in the war production industries. The Rosie pictured here riveting was one of thousands who enjoyed the excitement and high wages of wartime work.

Until 1943, black women were barred from work in defense industries. Poet Maya Angelou recalled that African Americans had to fight for the jobs they wanted. She became the first black streetcar conductor in San Francisco during the war, but not without a struggle. She made herself a promise that "made my veins stand out, and my mouth tighten into a prune: I WOULD HAVE THE JOB. I WOULD BE A CONDUCTORETTE AND SLING A FULL MONEY CHANGER FROM MY BELT. I WOULD." And she did.

For the first time, married women joined the paid labor force in droves and public opinion supported them. During the Great Depression, 80 percent of Americans had objected to the idea of wives working outside the home; by 1942, only 13 percent still objected. However, mothers of young children found very little help. In 1943, the federal government finally responded to the needs of working mothers by funding day care centers. More than 3,000 centers enrolled 130,000 children. Still, the program served only a small proportion of working mothers. Most women relied on family members to care for their children. A Women's Bureau survey in 1944 found that 16 percent of mothers working in war industries had no child care arrangements. Meager to begin with and conceived as an emergency measure, government funding for child care would end after the war.

Before the war, most jobs for women were low-paying, nonunion positions that paid an average of $24.50 a week. Wartime manufacturing jobs paid almost twice that—$40.35 a week. During the conflict, 300,000 women worked in the aircraft industry alone. Almira Bondelid recalled that when her husband went overseas, "I decided to stay in San Diego and went to work in a dime store. That was a terrible place to work, and as soon as I could I got a job at Convair [an aircraft manufacturer]. . . . I worked in the tool department as a draftsman, and by the time I left there two years later I was designing long drill jigs for parts of the wing and hull of B-24s."

New opportunities for women also opened up in the armed services. All sectors of the armed forces had dwindled in the years between the two wars and needed to gain size and strength. Along with the 10 million men age 21 to 35 drafted into the armed services and the 6 million who enlisted, 100,000 women volunteered for the Navy WAVES (Women Accepted for Voluntary Emergency Service) and 140,00 for the Women's Army Auxiliary Corps (WAAC). In 1943, the WAAC became the Women's Army Corps (WAC), dropping "Auxiliary" from the name.

Most female enlistees and war workers enjoyed their work and wanted to continue after the war. The extra pay, independence, camaraderie, and satisfaction that their jobs provided had opened their eyes to new possibilities. Although most of the well-paying positions for women disappeared after the war as the returning veterans reclaimed their jobs, women did not disappear from the paid labor force. The numbers of employed women continued to rise in the postwar years. Edith Speert, like many others, was never again content as a full-time housewife and mother. Edith's husband, Victor, was sent overseas in 1944. During the eighteen months of their separation, they penned 1,300 letters to each other, sometimes two or three times a day. The letters revealed the love and affection they felt for one another, but Edith did not hesitate to tell Victor how she had changed. In a letter from Cleveland, dated November 9, 1945, she wrote:

Sweetie, I want to make sure I make myself clear about how I've changed. I want you to know *now* that you are not married to a girl that's interested solely in a home—I shall definitely have to work all my life—I get emotional satisfaction out of working; and I don't doubt that many a night you will cook the supper while I'm at a meeting. Also, dearest—I shall never wash and iron—there are laundries for that! Do you think you'll be able to bear living with me? . . . I love you, Edith

Despite the shifting priorities of women, the war reversed the declining marriage and fertility rates of the 1930s. Between 1941 and 1945, the birthrate climbed from 19.4 to 24.5 per 1,000 population. The reversal stemmed, in part, from economic prosperity as well as the possibility of draft deferments for married men in the early war years. However, the desire to solidify relationships and establish connections to the future during a time of great uncertainty perhaps served as the more powerful motivation. Thus, a curious paradox marked the war years: a widespread disruption of domestic life accompanied by a rush into marriage and parenthood.

At the same time that the war prompted family formation, wartime upheaval sent the sexual order topsy-turvy. For many young women, moving to a new city or taking a wartime job opened up new possibilities for independence, excitement, and sexual adventure. One young worker recalled:

> Chicago was just humming, no matter where I went. The bars were jammed . . . you could pick up anyone you wanted to. . . . There were servicemen of all varieties roaming the streets all the time. There was never, never a shortage of young, healthy bucks. . . . We never thought of getting tired. Two, three hours of sleep was normal. . . . I'd go down to the office every morning half dead, but with a smile on my face, and report for work.

Some young women, known as "victory girls," believed that it was an act of patriotism to have a fling with a man in uniform before he went overseas. The independence of these women raised fears of female sexuality as a dangerous, ungoverned force. The worry extended beyond the traditional concern about prostitutes and "loose women" to include "good girls" whose sexual standards might relax during wartime. Public health campaigns warned enlisted men that victory girls would have their fun with a soldier and then leave him with a venereal disease, incapable of fighting for his country.

> *At the same time that the war prompted family formation, wartime upheaval sent the sexual order topsy-turvy.*

Wartime also intensified concerns about homosexuality. Urban centers and the military provided new opportunities for gay men and lesbians to form relationships and build communities. Although the military officially banned homosexuals, many served by keeping their orientation secret. If discovered, gay men faced severe punishment, including confinement in cages called "queer stockades" or in psychiatric wards. Lesbians faced similar sanctions, although the women's corps, in an effort to assure the civilian world of their recruits' femininity, often looked the other way.

RACIAL TENSIONS AT HOME AND THE "DOUBLE V" CAMPAIGN

Nazi policies against the Jews discredited racial and ethnic prejudice, forcing Americans to confront the reality of racism in their own country. Anthropologist Ruth Benedict, in her 1943 book *The Races of Mankind*, urged the United States to "clean its own house" and "stand unashamed before Nazis and condemn, without confusion, their doctrines of a Master Race." Swedish sociologist Gunnar Myrdal's *American Dilemma: The Negro Problem and Modern Democracy* called on the nation to live up to its democratic promise: "The great reason for hope is that this country has a national experience of uniting racial and cultural diversities and a national theory, if not a consistent practice, of freedom and equality for all." Americans of color responded to the call for unity and demonstrated their patriotism; in return, they expected full inclusion in the democracy. There would be no return to the old racial order. As black leader W. E. B. Du Bois noted, World War II was a "War for Racial Equality" and a struggle for "democracy not only for white folks but for yellow, brown, and black."

Nevertheless, throughout the war years racial tensions within the United States persisted. Black workers, who were excluded from the best-paying jobs in the defense industries, mobilized

■ African American pilots, known as the Tuskegee Airmen, served in the U.S. Army air force. Here members of the Mustang fighter group listen to a mission briefing in Italy in September 1944.

DOCUMENT

Randolph, "Why Should We March"

against discrimination on the job. Their most powerful advocate was African American civil rights leader A. Philip Randolph, who had organized the overwhelmingly black Brotherhood of Sleeping Car Porters and won the union a contract with the railroads in 1937. At the beginning of American involvement in the war in 1941, Randolph pressured FDR to ban discrimination in defense industries. He threatened to organize a massive march on Washington if Roosevelt did not respond. Roosevelt issued Executive Order 8802, which created the Fair Employment Practices Commission (FEPC) to ensure that blacks and women received the same pay as white men for doing the same job. The FEPC narrowed pay gaps somewhat, but it did not solve the problem. The American Federation of Labor, which included the highest-paid workers, still refused to accept blacks as members and fought with the FEPC over the equal-pay policy.

Sometimes the presence of racial minorities in previously all-white work settings led to hostilities. White men who labored on the home front resented the women and people of color who were filling "men's jobs." They also resented the soldiers who earned praise for their heroic military manhood. Many worried about losing their jobs to returning veterans as well as their privileged status as white men.

For example, Montana's copper workers asked the federal government to issue them special certificates equating their wartime contribution with that of soldiers. The government denied their request and in 1942 sent a regiment of black miners from the South to help fill the labor shortage in Montana's copper mines. White miners—many of whom had immigrant parents and had only just begun to enjoy full inclusion in white America—were now being told that black men were their equals. The white miners refused to work next to black men and walked out of the mines en masse.

In Detroit in 1943, white workers at the Packard auto plant walked off the job when three black employees were promoted. With increasing numbers of black Southerners arriving to work in the city's war industries, overcrowding strained the boundaries of traditionally segregated neighborhoods. White residents at a new housing complex attacked black newcomers attempting to move in. The violence escalated into several days of rioting, resulting in 34 deaths and 1,800 arrests.

In Los Angeles, the death of a Mexican American youth, José Díaz, at a gravel pit called Sleepy Lagoon sparked sensational news coverage and whipped up anti-Mexican fervor. Although police never determined the cause of Díaz's injuries, they filed first-degree murder charges against twenty-two Mexican Americans from the neighborhood. The jury found the young men guilty, but an appeals court overturned the convictions. Nevertheless, hostility continued to mount against Mexican American youths, particularly *pachucos* who sported zoot suits, distinctive attire with flared pants, long coats, and wide-brimmed hats. Pachucos wore the zoot suit as an expression of ethnic pride and rebelliousness as well as incipient political consciousness. Young Mexican American men and women flaunted their distinctive clothing and enjoyed the sense of unity it inspired. Some zoot-suiters would later become active in the Chicano movement of the 1960s—including the future leader of the United Farm Workers, César Chávez. Chávez remembered that it took "a lot of guts to wear those pants, and we had to be rebellious to do it, because the police and a few of the older people would harass us."

In spite of discrimination at home, people of color responded enthusiastically to the war effort.

For eight days in June 1943, scores of soldiers hunted zoot-suiters in Los Angeles bars, theaters, dance halls, and even in their homes, pulling off their clothes and beating them. Soon the attacks expanded to all Mexican Americans, and then to African Americans as well, some of whom also wore the zoot-suit style. The Los Angeles police sided with the rioters. They stood by during the beatings and then arrested the naked and bleeding youths and charged them with disturbing the peace. In spite of the fact that 500,000 Latinos fought in the war, the rioting raged until the War Department made the entire city of Los Angeles off limits to military personnel. Only a handful of soldiers, but more than 600 Mexican Americans, were arrested. President Roosevelt worried that the zoot-suit violence might strain relations with Mexico. He therefore allocated federal funds for job training and educational improvements for Spanish-speaking Americans.

In spite of discrimination at home, people of color responded enthusiastically to the war effort. The numbers of blacks in the U.S. Army soared from 5,000 in 1940 to 700,000 by 1944, with an additional 187,000 in the U.S. Navy, Coast Guard, and Marine Corps. Four thousand black women joined the WACs. Almost all soldiers fought in segregated units, despite protests by the NAACP that "a Jim Crow army cannot fight for a free world." Nearly 1 million blacks also joined the industrial labor force during the war. African Americans fought for the "Double V"—victory over fascism abroad and racial discrimination at home. Wartime experiences and sacrifices would inspire African Americans, along with Mexican Americans and other citizens, to mobilize for civil rights after the war.

Like Keith Little and his boarding-school buddies who became Navajo code talkers, American Indians all over the country declared their willingness to fight for the cause. The Iroquois League announced: "It is the unanimous sentiment among the Indian people that the atrocities of the Axis nations are violently repulsive to all sense of righteousness of our people. This merciless slaughter of mankind upon the part of those enemies of free peoples can no longer be tolerated." The Cheyenne agreed, vowing to defeat an "unholy triangle" determined to "conquer and enslave the bodies, minds and souls of all free people." The Navajo tribal council reflected this widespread sentiment: "There exists no purer concentration of Americanism than among the First Americans."

Fully 25,000 Indians, including 800 women, served in the military during the war. By 1945, nearly one-third of all able-bodied Indian men between eighteen and fifty years old had served. Five percent of them were killed or wounded in action. Native Americans enlisted at a higher rate than the general population, prompting the *Saturday Evening Post* to editorialize, "We would not need the Selective Service if all volunteered like the Indians."

Zelda Webb Anderson, "You Just Met One Who Does Not Know How to Cook"

Interpreting History

Zelda Webb Anderson became one of the first black women to enter military service during World War II. She served as an officer in the Women's Army Auxiliary Corps (WAACS), renamed the Women's Army Corps (WAC) in 1943. After the war she earned a doctorate in education at the University of California, Berkeley. Her forty-two-year career in education included a stint teaching at the University of East Africa in Dar-es-Salaam, Tanzania. She related her wartime experiences to the University of Nevada Oral History Program in 1995.

I reported for duty in January 1942.... This was so exciting to me. We had black officers, and our basic training was the same as for men. They would simply tell us, "You wanted to be in a man's army, so now you got to do what the men do." We learned military courtesy, history, how to shoot an M-1, go on bivouac, bathe in a teacup of water, eat hardtack rations....

Zelda Webb Anderson

Courtesy, Zelda Webb Anderson and University of Nevada Oral History Project

Every evening troops of male soldiers would march by our barracks en route to the mess hall. I told the commanding officer that we would like to have some shades at the windows. "Oh, no. You wanted to be in the man's army. Fine—you have to do what the men do." I told all the girls, "Listen, they won't give us any shades. So I want you to get right in front of the windows buck naked." The next day we had shades at all the windows....

They pulled me out of basic training the third week and sent me to officer training in Des Moines. All of the instructors were white, but white and black officers were being trained in the same facility, in the same classes, and we slept in the same barracks. After OCS I was assigned to a laundry unit.

A black enlisted WAAC could either be in the laundry unit or she could be in the hospital unit. In the laundry unit, if she had a

In addition to those who enlisted, half of all able-bodied Native American men not in the service and one-fifth of women left reservations for war industry jobs. At the beginning of the war, men on reservations earned a median annual income of $500, less than one-fourth the national average. One-third of all Indian men living off reservations were unemployed. Worse, the average life expectancy for Native Americans in 1940 was just thirty-five years, but sixty-four years for the population at large. Like others who found new opportunities during the conflict, Indians hoped that the economic progress they made would be permanent. But the boom would end for them when the war ended. Fewer than 10 percent of Native Americans who relocated to cities found long-term employment after the war.

The End of the War

■ *What alternatives were available for ending the war in Europe and in the Pacific, and why did the United States choose the strategies it employed to end the war?*

Unity at home was fragile as Americans worked together—sometimes uneasily—on behalf of the war effort. A large group devoted their efforts to the Manhattan Project, the building of an atomic bomb. In addition, the unity of the Allies abroad was fragile. The college degree, she could work at the front counter.... If she had less than that, then she did the laundry—very demeaning. And in the hospital unit they let her wash walls, empty basins, wash windows—all that menial work....

I was assigned to duty at Fort Breckenridge, Kentucky. The post commander's name was Colonel Throckmorton. In a pronounced southern accent he told me, "You're going over to that colored WAC company, and you're going to be the mess officer."

I said, "Sir, I have not had any mess training."

"All you nigras know how to cook."

I said, "You just met one who does not know how to cook; but if you send me to Fort Eustis, Virginia, for training I will come back and be the best mess officer you have on this post."

"I ain't sending you to no school, and you're going over there to be a mess officer." When I about-faced, I kept on going. I didn't even salute him....

[Much later, after developing a more cordial relationship with Colonel Throckmorton,] I told him that segregation has not allowed white people to know black people: "We know you very intimately, but you don't know how we think, how we react, and so you just try to push your stuff on us, not giving a damn about how we feel about this. And then when we rebel, or you meet somebody like me, who decides that you can't do this to me, then you think I'm cantankerous; you think I'm an agitator. I'm just trying to give you an education...."

I lived out the rest of my days very happy in the Army. If I had succumbed to the treatment that they had given other blacks before, and not spoken up for myself, my morale would have been down.... In this life, you've got to speak up for yourself. You can't go around shuffling your feet with your head hung down acting apologetic. If you see something you want, you must go after it. One day somebody will recognize it, and it's a victory for you, especially when it's somebody who has denigrated you because of your race....

Our country has not solved all of its problems. You have to live democracy before you can preach democracy. I've got four granddaughters, and I don't want them put in a position where they don't have equal opportunities, equal chances, and then they have to fight the same old battles that I fought again.

QUESTIONS

1. *Why do you think Anderson, as a woman and an African American, would choose to enlist in the U.S. Army during World War II?*

2. *According to Anderson, in what ways did the segregation of the armed forces distort white officers' views of blacks?*

United States and the Soviet Union were unable to fully overcome their mutual distrust, in spite of the need to defeat a common enemy. As the war drew to a close, Allied leaders maneuvered for advantage in the postwar era. Tensions simmering below the surface affected the course of the war as well as the final victory.

THE MANHATTAN PROJECT

This distrust was nowhere more apparent than in the development and use of the atomic bomb. The Manhattan Project, the secret project created to develop nuclear weapons, unfolded in sites across the country and employed thousands of people—yielding the weapon that would mark the end of the war in the Pacific and commence the unsettling years of the Atomic Age.

The secret project to develop the bomb was underway for years before the war ended. In 1939, scientists in Berlin achieved atomic fission by splitting the uranium atom, making it possible to release the tremendous energy stored in the atom. Albert Einstein, the German Jewish physicist who came to the United States after Hitler came to power in 1933, had warned Roosevelt that the Germans might be developing an atomic weapon. Einstein urged the United States to establish a small research program to keep pace. In 1942, Roosevelt authorized the Manhattan Project, the research program to develop nuclear weapons based at a top-secret laboratory in Los Alamos, New Mexico, and carried out in sites across the

DOCUMENT
Einstein, Letter to President Roosevelt

Casualties of World War II

The Wider World

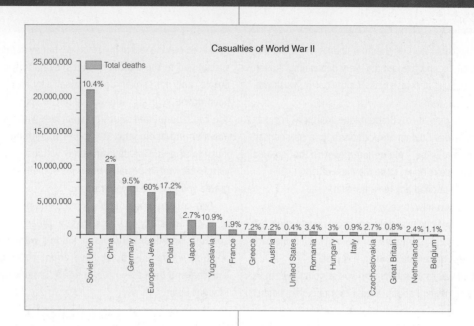

This graph compares the numbers of deaths of different ethnic and national groups in World War II. Among the warring nations, the Soviet Union lost the most people, in terms of actual numbers as well as percentages. Sixty percent of European Jews died in the Holocaust, making their loss the highest relative to the prewar population.

QUESTIONS

1. Which countries lost the most in terms of actual numbers of deaths, and which ones had the highest losses in terms of the proportion of the population?

2. How did the United States fare compared to other countries involved in the war?

country. The building of the bomb was the work of 125,000 people and cost nearly $2 billion. The first test of the device took place on July 16, 1945, at Alamogordo, New Mexico.

PLANNING FOR THE POSTWAR ERA

While the Manhattan Project was underway, Allied leaders met several times to plan for the postwar era. Roosevelt hoped to ensure American dominance and to limit Soviet power. At a conference in Teheran, Iran, in 1943 Roosevelt insisted that the eastern European states of Poland, Latvia, Lithuania, and Estonia should be independent after the war. As the war wound down, Churchill, Stalin, and Roosevelt met again at Yalta, in Ukraine, in February 1945. They agreed to demand Germany's unconditional surrender and to divide the conquered nation into four zones to be occupied by Britain, the Soviet Union, the United States, and France.

It became obvious at Yalta that separate spheres of influence would prevail after the war, and that the Soviet Union would control much of eastern Europe. Poland was a source of contention. Although Stalin nominally agreed to allow free elections in eastern Europe, he intended to make sure that the countries bordering the Soviet Union would be under his control. He also pledged to enter the war against Japan and received assurances that the Soviet Union would regain the lands lost to Japan in the 1904–1905 Russo-Japanese War. These concessions were deeply disturbing to anticommunists in the United States, who feared that the Soviet Union would have too much power in the postwar world. Later, many would claim that Roosevelt "sold out" the United States to the Soviet Union at Yalta.

■ Eight American presidents elected consecutively following World War II were veterans of that war. Pictured in wartime service, from top left, are: Dwight D. Eisenhower, John F. Kennedy, Lyndon Johnson, Richard Nixon, Gerald Ford, Jimmy Carter, Ronald Reagan, and George H. W. Bush.

In July 1945, the newly sworn-in American president, Harry Truman, joined Stalin and Churchill (replaced by Clement Attlee after Churchill's election loss) at Potsdam, near Berlin. The three leaders issued a statement demanding "unconditional surrender" from Japan while privately agreeing to let Japan retain its emperor. The rest of the conference focused on postwar Europe. At Potsdam, Truman learned of the successful test of the atomic bomb. With the new weapon in his hands, he now knew that Soviet assistance would not be needed to end the war in the Pacific, and he determined to prevent the Soviet Union from gaining a foothold in postwar Japan.

VICTORY IN EUROPE AND THE PACIFIC

As the war ended in Europe, Allied troops liberated the Nazi concentration camps. At that moment, the world finally learned the extent of Hitler's "Final Solution." Among the soldiers who first entered the camps were a number of Japanese Americans. Ichiro Imamura described the sight at Dachau: "When the gates swung open, we got our first good look at the prisoners.... They were like skeletons—all skin and bones.... They were sick, starving and dying." Some of the survivors saw the Japanese American soldiers and feared that they were Japanese allies of the Germans. A *Nisei* soldier reassured them, "I am an American soldier, and you are free."

As the victors carved up Hitler's Third Reich, the war in the Pacific continued. The United States persisted in demanding "unconditional surrender" and vowed to continue to

The National Archives

■ Slave laborers rest in the Buchenwald concentration camp near Jena, Germany. These inmates were among those who were still alive when troops of the 80th Division entered the camp on April 16, 1945. At labor camps such as this one, and death camps such as Auschwitz, 6 million Jews, along with thousands of Romani (Gypsies), Poles, mentally and physically handicapped people, and homosexuals, died in the Holocaust.

blockade Japan's ports, firebomb its cities, and possibly launch an invasion if the Japanese refused to surrender. A land invasion would have resulted in thousands of American casualties. In addition to concerns about casualties Truman also worried about the postwar balance of power in Asia if the Soviet Union were to join the invasion.

The atomic bomb offered Truman an alternative means to end the war. He would avoid an invasion of Japan, and he would make sure that the Soviet Union would have no role in the occupation of Japan after the war. He also wanted to send a message to Stalin that the United States would be the dominant power in the postwar world. But Truman's advisers did not all agree about whether or how the new weapon should be deployed. Some argued against using the bomb and favored responding to Japanese peace overtures. They believed that the Japanese would be willing to surrender if they knew that the emperor would not be executed.

Even the scientists who had developed the bomb disagreed about the wisdom of using it. Some urged a demonstration in a remote, unpopulated area that would impress the Japanese but would not cause loss of life. General George C. Marshall and other military leaders argued in favor of dropping the bomb on military or industrial targets, with ample warning ahead of time to enable civilians to leave target areas. But others agreed with Truman that dropping the bomb on a major city, without warning, would be the only way to persuade the Japanese to surrender unconditionally. Given the death and destruction already inflicted on Japanese cities by firebombing, the atomic bomb seemed to some an escalation of current strategy.

Hundreds of thousands of civilians had already perished in the war as the bombing of civilian targets became commonplace. The Japanese bombed civilians in Nanjing, China; the Germans did the same in Guernica, Spain. Allied bombing raids nearly demolished the German cities of Berlin and Dresden and the Japanese capital of Tokyo. One night of conventional bombing in Tokyo in March 1945 killed as many civilians as the atomic bomb dropped on Hiroshima. With its huge air force, the United States became the greatest bombing power during the war. But the atomic bombs took civilian casualties to a new level, not only because of the enormous death toll wrought by a single bomb but also because of the deadly radioactive fallout that lingered. Conventional bombing raids did not create fallout to harm survivors, their descendants, or the environment. But the effects of radiation were not yet known when Truman made his decision to use the new weapon.

When the first bomb exploded over Hiroshima on August 6, 1945, and the second on Nagasaki two days later, the horrifying destructiveness of nuclear weapons became apparent. More than 100,000 Japanese civilians died as a result of these attacks, and the two cities were destroyed. Even though the American public saw few images of the carnage on the ground, the huge mushroom cloud and the descriptions of cities leveled and people instantly incinerated shocked the nation and the world. In addition to the immediate devastation wreaked by the bomb, deadly radioactive fallout remained in the atmosphere, causing illness and death for months and even years after the attack.

On August 14, 1945—V-J (Victory in Japan) Day—the Japanese agreed to surrender; the official ceremony of surrender took place on September 2. Many people breathed a sigh of relief that the war was finally over. But others believed firmly that the Japanese would have

■ Two days after the atomic bombing of Hiroshima, Americans dropped another atomic bomb on the ancient city of Nagasaki, pictured here after the attack. Critics argued that Japan was about to surrender and that the destruction of a second city was unnecessary. But military strategists insisted that the second attack was necessary to end the war.

surrendered without the dropping of the bombs, especially if they knew that the victors would allow the emperor to remain. Many who supported the use of the bomb questioned the decision to drop it on cities and believed that the second bomb, dropped on Nagasaki, was unnecessary. Doubts and controversies over the use of the weapon, and the nuclear arms race that it sparked, have continued to this day.

Conclusion ■

The Japanese attack on Pearl Harbor on December 7, 1941, put an end to the debate over whether the United States should enter World War II. FDR immediately declared war, and within days Americans were fighting against fascist regimes in Europe and the Pacific. Millions of American men and women joined the military and served overseas.

The war changed life for Americans in profound ways. Although wartime forged a sense of unity as the nation came together to fight against fascism, it also highlighted fissures within American society. The government evacuated 110,000 Japanese Americans from their homes on the West Coast and interned them in detention camps. Members of minority groups usually fought in segregated units, while racial tensions and conflicts erupted at home, even as the country fought against a racist foe. Women joined the paid labor force and the armed services in unprecedented numbers, while at the same time official and cultural messages reminded them that their primary service to the nation was as wives and mothers.

The booming wartime economy put an end to the Great Depression and brought full employment. African Americans from the rural South, Mexican American agricultural laborers, Japanese Americans from internment camps, and American Indians from impoverished reservations joined thousands of other men and women who migrated to industrial centers to work in war-related industries, or they entered the armed forces. Many who faced discrimination at home served heroically overseas, including the African American Tuskegee Airmen, the Navajo code talkers, and the highly decorated Japanese American troops who fought in Europe. The war sparked a campaign for the Double V: victory over fascism abroad and racism at home.

In the end, World War II left massive devastation in its wake all across the globe. The Holocaust destroyed most of European Jewry. The waging of "total war" killed millions of civilians as well as soldiers and caused devastation across the world. The United States dropped two atomic bombs on Japanese cities, ending the war in the Pacific and ushering in the Atomic Age.

The United States was the only country involved in the war that emerged from it stronger than before the conflict began. Although more than 400,000 Americans died in the conflict, American casualties were far below those suffered by other countries. At the end of the war, the United States was the most powerful nation in the world.

But the war's conclusion did not lead to the era of peace Americans expected. European colonial empires staggered on the brink of collapse. Only the United States and the Soviet Union remained as major military powers, shifting the international balance of power from a multipolar to a bipolar system. Tensions that simmered during the war between the United States and the Soviet Union would explode into the Cold War within a few years after the war's end. For the next half-century, the fallout from World War II, as well as the power struggle between the United States and the Soviet Union, would shape political relationships across the globe.

For Review

1. What was the immediate impact of the Japanese attack on Pearl Harbor?

2. How did Americans mobilize for war within the United States?

3. What is "total war" and how was it manifested in World War II?

4. How did the war affect Americans, especially women and minorities?

5. What was the Manhattan Project and why was it created?

6. What persuaded Truman to drop atomic bombs on Hiroshima and Nagasaki?

7. How did the relationship between the United States and the Soviet Union unfold and develop during the war?

Created Equal Online

For more *Created Equal* resources, including suggestions for sites to visit and further reading, go to **MyHistoryLab.com**.

Chapter 24

Cold War and Hot War, 1945–1953

■ Soviet and American troops meet in central Germany in May 1945.

At 11:30 A.M. on April 25, 1945, U.S. Army private Joseph Polowsky glimpsed what looked like the future. The young Chicago native was riding in the lead jeep of an American force along the Elbe River in central Germany when he spotted Russian soldiers on the far side, their medals glistening in the morning sun. Elated, he and five of his comrades found a small boat and paddled across to the eastern bank. Using Polowsky's knowledge of German to communicate, the American soldiers embraced their Soviet allies with laughs and tears. The Russians produced bottles of vodka, and toasts, pledges, singing, and dancing followed. After years of pressing Germany from east and west, the Allies had finally linked up in the heart of Hitler's empire. A reporter wrote of the scene, "You get the feeling of exuberance, a great new world opening up."

Despite his conservative Republican background, Polowsky spent much of the rest of his life advocating American-Russian friendship. He could not forget the transforming experience of that April day along the Elbe and the hopes it engendered for a peaceful future. However, what followed the Allied victory turned out to be not a "great new world" of international peace and brotherhood, but the **Cold War** of U.S.-Soviet hostility that lasted for more than four decades. The opposing ideologies—**communism** and capitalist democracy—joined with conflicting national interests to produce this heavily armed standoff. The American effort to contain the expansion of communist influence entailed a radical reorientation of American involvement abroad in peacetime, including the nation's first peacetime military alliance, the North Atlantic Treaty Organization (NATO). At times the Cold War turned into a hot war of actual shooting, most importantly in the Korean War of 1950–1953 and the Vietnam War in the following decade.

In some ways, the Cold War encouraged efforts at social reform. America's new leading role in world affairs brought its domestic life into the spotlight of world attention. Racial discrimination and violence at home embarrassed American leaders as they spoke of leading the anticommunist "free world" abroad.

But in other ways, the Cold War constrained efforts to bring American life more fully into line with its democratic and egalitarian promise. Rising tensions with communist movements and governments overseas stimulated anxieties about possible subversion within the nation's own borders. Anticommunist fervor put unions on the defensive and encouraged women to shun the workplace in favor of family life and parenting, particularly in the nation's growing suburbs. This second Red Scare—the first had followed World War I in 1919—reached flood tide by 1950 with the rise to prominence of Senator Joseph McCarthy. The young Republican from Wisconsin made a career of blaming supposedly disloyal Americans at home for setbacks to U.S. goals abroad in places such as China and Korea. He left a bitter legacy that long outlasted his political demise in 1954.

The Uncertainties of Victory

■ *How were the world and the United States different at the end of World War II than they had been at the beginning?*

It was five o'clock in the afternoon when the Senate recessed on April 12, 1945. The vice president walked through the Capitol building to the private office of his old friend and mentor, Sam Rayburn of Texas, the House majority leader. He had just mixed himself a cocktail when an aide told him that he was to call the White House immediately. Picking up the phone, he was instructed to come to the White House right away. "Jesus Christ and General Jackson," he said as he put down the receiver, his face suddenly pale. Within fifteen minutes, Harry Truman was being ushered into the private quarters at 1600 Pennsylvania Avenue. Eleanor Roosevelt greeted him with the somber news: "Harry, the president is dead." Stunned, he finally said, "Is there anything I can do for you?" She replied, "Is there anything *we* can do for *you*? For you are the one in trouble now."

Franklin Roosevelt was dead; it was almost unimaginable. Elected four times to the presidency, he had dominated American politics like no figure before or since. Just as the unprecedented destruction of World War II was finally ending, the leadership of the nation passed into new and less tested hands. Peace brought an array of uncertainties and immediate needs. The victors had to reconstruct a world that had been damaged, physically and psychologically, almost beyond recognition. Spared the destruction visited elsewhere, the United States faced the different challenge of demobilizing its military forces and reconverting to a peacetime economy. Intense conflicts along the color line and in the workplace revealed real differences among Americans about the shape of the democracy they had fought to defend.

GLOBAL DESTRUCTION

World War II wrought death on a scale that defies comprehension: 60 million human beings lost their lives. From England in the west to the islands of New Guinea in the east, from the

Ed Clark/Getty Images

■ Franklin D. Roosevelt's death at his vacation home in Warm Springs, Georgia, stunned a nation and a world that had not known another U.S. president for thirteen years. Navy bandsman Graham Jackson was one of Roosevelt's favorite musicians. As the procession began to transport the president's body north for burial in Hyde Park, New York, Jackson captured the grief of millions of Americans as he played the sweet, slow strains of "Going Home."

Baltic Sea in the north to the Sahara Desert in the south, much of Europe and Asia was left in ruins. Soviet and American power had finally crushed the Axis, with Berlin now a "city of the dead" and Japan's urban landscape devastated by firebombing and nuclear attacks. Many of the victors were only marginally better off.

Only one of the major combatants emerged from the war in better shape than at the beginning. With no fighting on their soil after the initial Japanese attack on Pearl Harbor, American civilians spent the war years in safety. Orders for war materials ended the Great Depression in the United States and created full employment as factories worked overtime to supply the Allied armies. The American people, one official remarked in 1945, "are in the pleasant predicament of having to learn to live 50 percent better than they have ever lived before." Many Americans suffered terribly in the war, of course; 400,000 died, leaving behind desolate families, and millions of veterans returned with traumas that colored the remainder of their lives. But such casualties paled in comparison to those of other belligerent nations. With just 6 percent of the world's population and 50 percent of its wealth, the United States enjoyed a position of staggering economic advantage.

Americans' overriding fear was that the end of the fighting might return the country to the state it had faced when the war began: economic depression. The nation's awesome industrial productivity depended on government spending, which was now to be cut back sharply. International trade might pick up much of the slack, but the war had destroyed most of the purchasing power of U.S. trading partners in Europe and Asia. Rising tensions between the two primary victors—the United States and the Soviet Union—hampered the process of postwar reconstruction. President Truman showed his frustration with the Soviet military occupation of eastern Europe by lecturing Soviet diplomats and abruptly cutting off Lend-Lease aid to the USSR. Soviet dictator Joseph Stalin feared America's new global military might, manifested in its monopoly of the atomic bomb, and was determined to secure his European border against future invasion from the West.

VACUUMS OF POWER

World War II altered the world's ideological and physical landscape. Japan and Germany, the centers of prewar power in Asia and continental Europe, were now vacuums waiting to be filled and reshaped by their conquerors. In addition to defeating two nations, the Allies had also discredited the ideas on which those governments had been built: fascism and **militarism.** These were the ideas of the extreme political right: the glorification of the racially defined state and its aggressive military expansion. Fascism's murderous character tarred those who had collaborated with the Axis during the war, primarily conservatives in countries such as France who preferred fascism to socialism.

Into many of the postwar vacuums of power flowed a newly prominent worldwide political left. Socialists, communists, and other radicals espoused communal rather than individualistic values. The Red Army's primary role in defeating the German troops who had overrun Europe evoked admiration for the Soviet Union among antifascists everywhere. The occupying Soviet forces installed communist governments in eastern Europe by force (sometimes called "Red Army socialism"), and Socialist and Communist parties rose sharply in popularity in France, Italy, Belgium, and

■ **MAP 24.1 Occupation of Germany and Austria, 1946–1949**

By the end of World War II, U.S. and British forces had liberated western Europe and Soviet forces controlled eastern Europe. In central Europe, the Allies jointly occupied Germany and Austria.

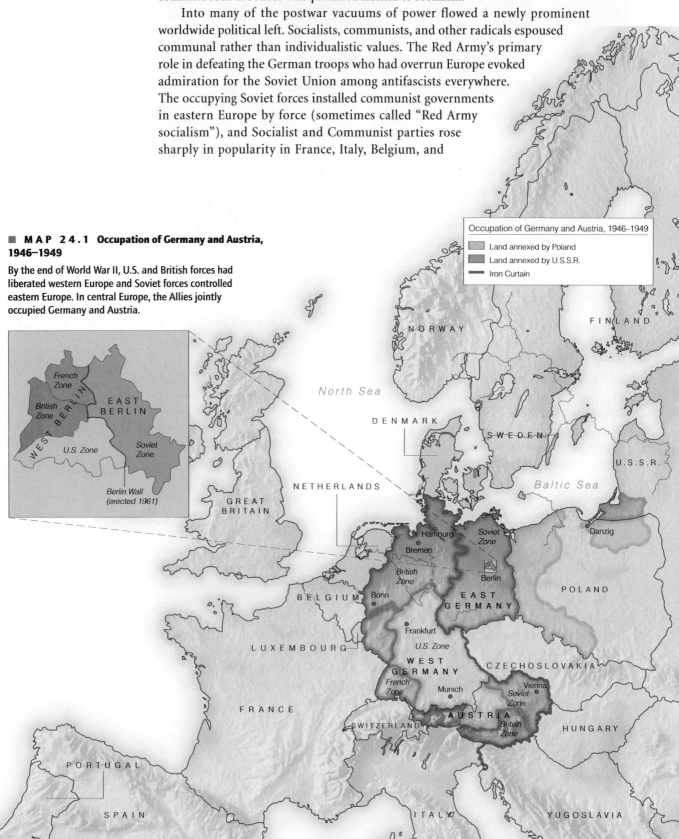

Scandinavia. The nominally socialist Labor party took power in Great Britain, defeating war leader Winston Churchill and his Conservative party at the polls. Europeans across the continent established welfare states to provide a minimum standard of living for all their citizens.

This turn to the left encompassed most of the globe. Africans began organizing for eventual independence from European rule, and Asians launched the final phase of their anticolonial struggle for liberation. Indonesia fought its way free from the Dutch, and India gained its freedom from Britain. In French Indochina, Ho Chi Minh quoted from Thomas Jefferson's Declaration of Independence as he announced the creation of an independent Vietnam. (Truman ignored Vietnam's appeal for American recognition, just as Wilson had done twenty-six years earlier at the Versailles peace conference after World War I; see Chapter 20). Masters of much of the world a few years earlier, the European colonial powers fought desperately to hold onto the last pieces of their dwindling empires. The Allies established the new United Nations (UN) in San Francisco in April 1945, just days after Truman succeeded FDR in office. Eventually housed in New York, the UN embodied hopes for a more peaceful and democratic world. Its General Assembly gave all nations an equal voice and vote in deliberations, and its small Security Council—responsible for guiding any UN military actions—gave a permanent seat and veto power to five nations: the United States, the USSR, Britain, France, and China. The 1948 UN Human Rights Charter helped put practitioners of colonialism and racial discrimination on the defensive by declaring worldwide support for the principles of national self-determination and equal treatment for all peoples.

Masters of much of the world a few years earlier, the European colonial powers fought desperately to hold onto the last pieces of their dwindling empires.

POSTWAR TRANSITION TO PEACETIME LIFE

The fundamental task for Americans at home was to reconvert from a wartime society back to a peacetime one. They were especially eager to bring home the 12 million men in uniform serving abroad. Eager to resume their civilian life, the returning servicemen walked off ships' gangplanks into a country in transition. Factories were trying to convert from producing war materials to making consumer products. Wartime rationing was lifted on goods such as sugar and gasoline, and the 35-mph speed limit was withdrawn. But as orders for war materials dried up, taking jobs with them, wartime inflation ("too many dollars chasing too few goods") persisted. Housing remained especially scarce. In the richest country in the world, one-third of the citizens still lived in poverty, with neither running water nor flush toilets.

To ease the transition home, Congress had passed the Servicemen's Readjustment Act of 1944 (the GI Bill) to extend crucial financial aid to veterans. It provided low-cost mortgages that helped create an explosion in home ownership. It created Veterans Administration hospitals to provide lifetime medical care. And it paid tuition and stipends for colleges and vocational training, making higher education broadly available for the first time. The 2 percent of veterans who were women also made use of these benefits. In the postwar era, when American politics generally became more conservative—shifting away from the New Deal reform spirit and toward an anticommunist emphasis—the GI Bill was the one area in which the United States expanded its own welfare state. The $14.5 billion spent on veterans over the next decade marked a public investment that helped propel millions of families into an expanding middle class.

The postwar transition presented particular challenges to American women. Millions of them had gone to work outside the home during the war and found economic independence in doing so. Now they faced powerful pressures to leave the workforce and return to a domestic life of old and new families. Many women accepted this return to the domestic sphere, content to focus on marriage and family life. But millions felt varying degrees of resentment over their loss of hard-earned compensation and self-esteem. "War jobs have uncovered unsuspected abilities in American women," one argued. "Why lose all these abilities?"

The Most Populous Urban Areas

The Wider World

In the imperial age at the dawn of the twentieth century, the most powerful nations had the most populous cities. Economic and military might correlated closely with dense urban centers of industry and finance. London, the capital of the world's largest empire, had 6.5 million residents in 1900. After the two World Wars, the United States had replaced Great Britain as the most powerful nation, and New York was home to 7.8 million people in 1950. In the second half of the twentieth century, however, population growth slowed in the industrialized nations while accelerating in much of Asia, Africa, and Latin America.

1900	1950	2000	2015 (projected)
1. *London*	*New York*	*Tokyo*	*Tokyo*
2. *New York*	*Tokyo*	Mexico City	Bombay (Mumbai)
3. *Paris*	*London*	*New York*	Mexico City
4. *Berlin*	Shanghai	São Paulo	São Paulo
5. *Chicago*	*Paris*	Bombay (Mumbai)	*New York*

Italicized cities are in the industrialized regions of the world: North America, Europe, and Japan.

Source: United Nations, Department of Economic and Social Affairs, Population Division, http://www.un.org/esa/population/publications/WUP2005/2005wup.htm; About: Geography, http://geography.about.com/library/weekly/aa011201f.htm.

QUESTIONS

1. In 1950, New York replaced London as the economic hub of the capitalist world—the most important center for banking, finance, and corporate headquarters. How might this position of American's largest city have helped shape the goals and policies of U.S. leaders in the early Cold War?

2. How do these rankings reflect changes in Europe's position in the world across the twentieth century?

CHALLENGING RACIAL DISCRIMINATION

African Americans faced a similar problem. After finding new opportunities in industrial employment during the war, they were laid off afterward in favor of returning white veterans. Like women, blacks were expected by others to retreat into deference. Black veterans spearheaded the resistance to this notion. They had fought in disproportionate numbers for their country and for the cause of defeating the world's most murderous racists, the Nazis. They then returned to a nation still deeply segregated, by law in the South and by practice elsewhere. Like Native American, Latino American, and Asian American veterans, they were determined to be full citizens in the country for which they had spilled their blood. "I went into the Army a nigger," one black soldier said about typical white views of him, but "I'm coming out a man."

African American efforts to overcome discrimination met fierce white resistance in 1946 and 1947. In the South, where most black Americans still lived, a wave of beatings and lynchings greeted black veterans in uniform and their attempts to register to vote. White Northerners also used violence to preserve the segregated character of neighborhoods in Chicago, Detroit, and other cities. They destroyed the property and threatened the lives of blacks who dared to move to previously all-white blocks, effectively confining African Americans to impoverished areas. Sometimes local authorities encouraged such extralegal use of force. The police chief of Cicero, Illinois, was indicted for conspiracy to incite a riot in 1951 after several thousand white residents destroyed an all-white apartment building to prevent African American veteran Harvey E. Clark and his family from moving in.

The retreat of European colonialism and American competition with the Soviet Union nonetheless encouraged many white Americans to acknowledge the contradiction between leading the "free world" and limiting the freedoms of Americans of color. A series of Supreme Court decisions validated the long-term strategy of the National Association for the Advancement of Colored People (NAACP) for contesting segregation in the courts. Court rulings outlawed segregation in voting primaries (*Smith v. Allwright*, 1944), interstate transportation (*Morgan v. Virginia*, 1946), contracts for house sales (*Shelley v.*

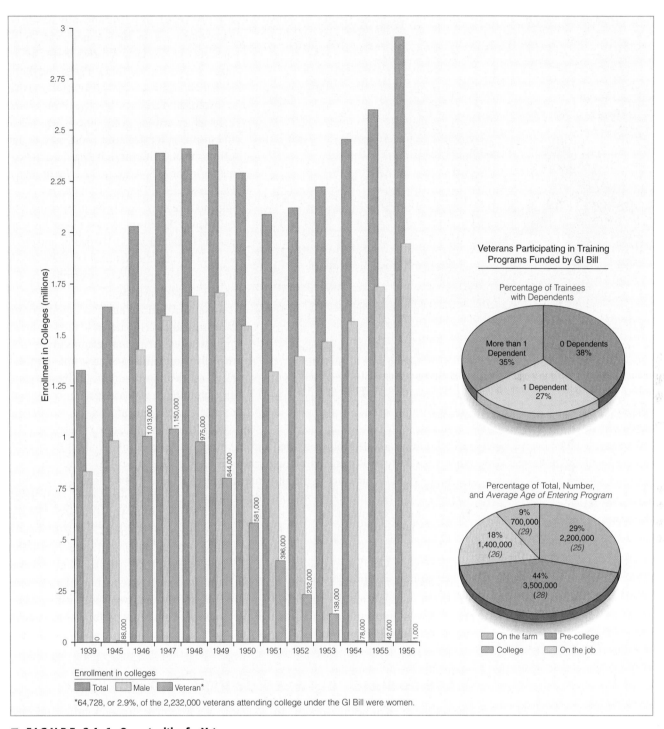

Enrollment in colleges
■ Total ☐ Male ■ Veteran*

*64,728, or 2.9%, of the 2,232,000 veterans attending college under the GI Bill were women.

■ **FIGURE 24.1 Opportunities for Veterans**

The number of Americans attending college increased sharply after World War II. In the early postwar years, federal government spending through the 1944 GI Bill gave veterans unprecedented opportunities for access to education and other job training programs.

Kraemer, 1948), and graduate schools (*Sweatt v. Painter* and *McLaurin v. Oklahoma*, 1950). The California Supreme Court overturned a state law banning interracial marriage *(Pérez v. Sharp*, 1948), pointing the way toward the elimination two decades later of similar laws in other states in the U.S. Supreme Court's *Loving v. Virginia* decision (1967).

Popular culture moved in the same direction of breaking down racial barriers. *Billboard* magazine in 1949 changed the category of "race music" to "rhythm and blues" as white record producers and radio disc jockeys such as Alan Freed began to bring the early rock 'n' roll of

The first person of color to play modern major league baseball, Jackie Robinson starred for the Brooklyn Dodgers from 1947 to 1956, helping them win six National League pennants and one world championship. His success opened the way for other black players to follow, eventually bringing the demise of the old professional Negro Leagues. Robinson credited Dodgers general manager Branch Rickey for his willingness to break the color line in the nation's favorite game.

Ray Howard/AP Wide World Photos

African American musicians to mainstream white audiences. By 1955, young white musicians such as Bill Haley and Elvis Presley joined black stars such as Chuck Berry and Little Richard in creating a wildly popular sound that transcended racial categories. Professional baseball erased its color line when Jackie Robinson, a former four-sport star at the University of California, Los Angeles, and lieutenant in the U.S. Army, joined the Brooklyn Dodgers in 1947. Despite vicious verbal taunting and threats of bodily harm by some fans and players, Robinson refused to lose his temper and remained a model of dignity and excellence as he won the National League's Rookie of the Year honors. Two years later he won the Most Valuable Player award.

Native Americans and Mexican Americans faced similar discrimination in the Southwest and elsewhere. With war veterans in the fore, they also organized to contest unfair education and election practices. "If we are good enough to fight, why aren't we good enough to vote?" asked returning Navajo soldiers in New Mexico and Arizona, where the state constitutions prohibited Indian residents from voting until successfully challenged in 1948. When the family of Private Felix Longoria, who died in combat in the Philippines, was denied the right to bury him in the all-white cemetery in Three Rivers, Texas, a new Latino veterans' organization called American GI Forum publicized the injustice. A young Texas senator named Lyndon Johnson, destined eventually for the White House, stepped in and arranged a burial with full military honors in prestigious Arlington National Cemetery instead. The League of United Latin American Citizens (LULAC) followed a strategy similar to that of the NAACP regarding educational discrimination, leading to the Ninth Circuit Court's decision in *Mendez v. Westminster* (1947) outlawing segregated schools for Mexican Americans in California. In parallel fashion, indigenous Alaskans organized in the Alaska Native Brotherhood successfully lobbied the territorial legislature in Juneau to pass an antidiscrimination law in 1945.

CLASS CONFLICT BETWEEN OWNERS AND WORKERS

Like people of color, white workers also sought to improve their situation in the uncertain aftermath of World War II. In many ways, 1946 seemed like 1919. A world war had just ended, in which corporations had made handsome profits. American workers had enjoyed nearly full employment and improving wages and had joined unions in large numbers. In 1946, one-third of the workforce held a union card, the largest portion ever. But the end of war-related orders led to job cuts and the loss of overtime wages, and by the spring of 1946, 1.8 million workers were out on strike.

Mirroring World War I, the conclusion of hostilities in 1945 revealed rising tensions between the United States and the Soviet Union. The spread of leftist revolutions abroad amplified fears of communist influence in American unions, especially because a few of the most effective Congress of Industrial Organizations (CIO) organizers were Communist party members or at least sympathetic to an emphasis on class conflict between owners and workers. As in

1919, a Red Scare began to develop, egged on by a business community that used the supposed threat of the tiny U.S. Communist party to weaken the much larger and less radical union movement. In contrast to the end of World War I, however, federal law guaranteed the right of workers to bargain collectively, and the strikes of 1946 resulted in some negotiated wage increases.

The tide turned against unions as anticommunism intensified. President Truman, long considered a friend to organized labor, helped crush major strikes by railroad workers and coal miners in 1946 when he saw them as threatening the nation's economy. The CIO's Operation Dixie to organize southern workers of all colors failed, defeated by the skillful appeals of local businesses to white supremacist sentiment among the working class. The Republican party claimed a sweeping victory in the 1946 congressional elections, taking control of both the House and the Senate in a stark rejection of Truman's leadership. Republicans and conservative Democrats then passed the Taft-Hartley Act in 1947 over the president's veto, weakening unions by prohibiting secondary boycotts (against the products of a company whose workers were on strike) and requiring union officials to swear anticommunist oaths. Two years later, an increasingly conservative CIO expelled eleven unions that still had leftist and communist leadership. At the same time, the expanding U.S. economy after 1947 pulled many skilled workers up into the middle class and gave them a larger stake in the status quo.

The Quest for Security

■ *How did the meaning of "security" change for the United States after 1945?*

On February 21, 1947, a British official in Washington informed the U.S. government that Britain could no longer provide financial assistance to the anticommunist governments of Greece and Turkey. This information marked a watershed in modern world history. Long the greatest imperial power and the dominant outside force in the Middle East, Britain was beginning a slow retreat. Left in its wake were vacuums of power, particularly in the Middle East, South Asia, and Africa. President Truman and his advisers believed that either Soviet or American influence would flow into these regions. The Truman administration formulated a policy to contain communism in the eastern Mediterranean that it quickly expanded to encompass the entire noncommunist world. Powerful new nuclear weapons supported this policy and increased anxieties about the nation's security.

REDEFINING NATIONAL SECURITY

U.S. policymakers had ended World War II with one primary goal. They were determined to revive the global capitalist economy that had nearly dissolved in the Great Depression of the 1930s and had then been battered by the war. American prosperity and freedom, they believed, depended on a world system of free trade because Americans simply could not consume all the products of their efficient farms and factories. If they could not sell the surplus abroad, the United States would slide back into a

Time & Life Pictures/Getty Images

TWENTY CENTS MAY 15, 1950

TIME
THE WEEKLY NEWSMAGAZINE

WORLD & FRIEND
Love that piaster, that lira, that tickey, and that American way of life.

$6.00 A YEAR (REG. U. S. PAT. OFF.) VOL. LV NO. 20

■ The cover of *Time* magazine on May 15, 1950, suggested the growing worldwide popularity of Coca-Cola, a quintessential American product. Not only did the United States have vast military and political influence in the early Cold War, but its powerful economy also exported American goods and values around the world. The international diffusion of American popular culture—movies, clothes, food, and music—helped shape world history in the twentieth century, particularly after 1945.

Members of NATO (1949)
Members of Warsaw Pact (1955)
Nonaligned counties
($) Participants in the Marshall Plan, 1947–1952
Year first atomic device was tested
by that country

ICELAND

NORWAY
Oslo

SWEDEN
Stockholm

FINLAND
Helsinki

Baltic
Sea

U.S.S.R.
1949

IRELAND
Dublin

DENMARK
Copenhagen

U.S loan of $3.5 billion, 1946

1952
GREAT
BRITAIN
London

NETHERLANDS
Amsterdam

Berlin blockade,
1948–1949

Berlin

Warsaw

POLAND

ATLANTIC
OCEAN

Brussels
BELGIUM
Bonn

EAST
GERMANY

WEST
GERMANY
Joined NATO, 1955

Prague
CZECHOSLOVAKIA

Communist coup, 1948
U.S.S.R. invasion, 1968

Anti-communist revolution
failed, 1956

Paris

LUX.

Withdrew forces from NATO, 1966

FRANCE

1960

SWITZ.
Zones of occupation ended, 1955

AUSTRIA
Vienna

HUNGARY
Budapest

ROMANIA

Black
Sea

Belgrade

Bucharest

Lisbon

PORTUGAL
Madrid

SPAIN

Joined NATO, 1982

YUGOSLAVIA
Tito–Stalin Schism, 1948

BULGARIA
Sofia

Rome

ITALY

GREECE
Athens

TURKEY
Ankara

ALBANIA
Withdrew from Warsaw Pact, 1968

Truman Doctrine, 1947
joined NATO, 1952

■ **MAP 24.2 Europe Divided by the Cold War**

For centuries Europe had controlled much of the rest of the world. After 1945, the Soviet Union occupied the eastern half of the continent and Americans wielded dominant influence in the western half. This division of Europe into communist and noncommunist blocs lasted until the end of the Cold War in 1989.

depression. The 1930s had shown that closed economic doors led to despair, poverty, and aggression, as in Germany and Japan. "We can't go through the thirties again," President Truman emphasized to his aides. He and other political leaders hoped for a world with greater liberty and more democracy. But Dean Acheson, the powerful undersecretary (1945–1947) and then secretary of state (1949–1953), emphasized that U.S. foreign policy was not primarily concerned with "a lot of abstract notions." Instead, the emphasis with each country was on "what you do—these business transactions."

"National security" was expanding to mean something very different from simply defending the nation's territory against invasion. For the disproportionately powerful United States, national security after 1945 came to be identified with the creation and preservation of a free-trading capitalist world order. American national security was seen to be at stake almost everywhere around the globe.

The primary threat to that security came from the Soviet Union. The Red Army's occupation of eastern Europe was part of the problem, as it symbolized the Soviets' military prowess. Even more troubling to the Truman administration was the political influence of the USSR in a world turning leftward. The real danger lay in Soviet encouragement, by example and assistance, of revolutions that rejected market economies and individualist ethics. Demoralized by the war's destruction and by grim postwar economic conditions, western Europeans and others seemed to be considering the paths of socialism and communism. "Hopeless and hungry people," Acheson warned, "often resort to desperate measures."

CONFLICT WITH THE SOVIET UNION

The antifascist alliance of the Soviet Union and the United States dissolved rapidly as their conflicting interests reemerged after the defeat of Germany. Long skeptical of the capitalist world it wanted to replace, the Soviet government viewed expansive U.S. interests as evidence of "striving for world supremacy." Yet Moscow was just as clearly expanding its own sphere of national security, with Soviet troops remaining in areas they had occupied during the war: Manchuria, northern Korea, Iran, and especially eastern and central Europe. These forward military positions, combined with Moscow's rhetoric of encouraging revolution abroad, increased American anxieties about rising communist movements in Asia and Europe. Each side spoke of the other's goal as "world domination."

Contrasting experiences in World War II amplified historical and ideological differences. Whereas the war brought the United States out of the 1930s global capitalist depression (which the Soviets had avoided), it brought the USSR into a depression caused by the invading Germans' destruction of the western portion of the country. With a decimated population, a battered economy, and minimal air and naval forces, the postwar Soviet Union remained a regional power based on its army. The United States was the only truly global power, with a vast naval armada and air force projecting military might to every continent, undergirded by the most productive economy in world history.

The two nations' visions of the postwar world order reflected these relative positions. Americans sought an open world for the free flow of goods and most ideas, and proved willing to tolerate and even embrace dictatorial governments as long as they were anti-communist and open to foreign trade and investment. Meanwhile, the Soviets called for a more traditional division of the world into separate spheres of influence for the great powers. The horrific experience of near national extinction at the hands of the Nazis ensured that Stalin would not budge on issues of fundamental Soviet security.

Conflicts over specific areas liberated from the Nazis hastened the onset of the Cold War in the first eighteen months after the end of World War II. Whereas the Soviets wanted reparations and a deindustrialized Germany that could never threaten it again, the United States considered a rebuilt industrial German state crucial for a healthy, integrated western European economy. Britain and France had gone to war in defense of an independent Poland, but for Stalin control of Poland was not negotiable because it had been "the corridor for attack on Russia." Moscow and Washington also clashed over Iran, on Russia's southern border, where the Soviets briefly encouraged a leftist uprising in the northern part of the oil-rich country to counteract British and American influence in the capital city of Tehran. U.S. policymakers worried about Soviet requests to Turkey for greater control of the Bosporus and Dardanelles, the straits leading out of the Black Sea into the Mediterranean. When the British announced in February 1947 their imminent withdrawal from Greece, where leftists and monarchists were fighting a fierce civil war, the Truman administration believed it was time to respond decisively.

THE POLICY OF CONTAINMENT

Diplomat George Kennan best articulated the policy of **containment** in an influential telegram sent from his post at the U.S. embassy in Moscow in February 1946. Kennan explained Soviet hostility as a result of traditional Russian insecurity overlaid with newer Marxist justifications. He called for "the adroit and vigilant application of counterforce" against all Soviet efforts at expanding their influence. One month later, on March 5, 1946, former British prime minister Winston Churchill warned that a Russian "iron curtain" had descended across Europe from the Baltic Sea in the north to the Adriatic Sea in the south, imprisoning all those to the east of it. "The reins of world leadership are fast slipping from Britain's competent but now very weak hands," the U.S. State Department argued. "These reins will be picked up either by the United States or by Russia."

Picking up those reins meant a fundamental reorientation for the United States. No longer just the dominant force in the Western Hemisphere, it would have to maintain its wartime projection of military forces around the globe—permanently. To do so would require huge expenditures that Congress had to approve and public support for an unprecedented international role. In an address to Congress on March 12, 1947, asking for $400 million in aid for Greece and Turkey, the president simplified the world system into two "ways of life," those of "free peoples" and those of "terror and oppression" under communist rule. All nations must choose between them, he declared, and the United States must support "free peoples who are resisting attempted subjugation by armed minorities or outside pressures."

DOCUMENT
The Marshall Plan

The **Truman Doctrine,** as it became known, exaggerated a real problem in order to win public support for a new international role for the United States. It funded the governments of Turkey and Greece but it framed the new policy broadly, opening the path to supporting anticommunist regimes and opposing revolutions around the world for decades to come. The most important immediate step was the reconstruction of a vibrant, reintegrated western European economy. The United States provided $13 billion between 1948 and 1952 to fund the European Recovery Program, commonly known as the **Marshall Plan** for its chief architect, Secretary of State George Marshall (1947–1949). His assistant, Dean Acheson, reminded Americans doubtful about such expenditures that western Europe's recovery was "chiefly a matter of national self-interest" for the United States, for European markets were crucial for American economic health.

Ensuring western European security against the Red Army also entailed the first U.S. military alliance in peacetime. The victors of World War II divided a defeated Germany into separate zones of occupation, based on wartime agreements that reflected their respective military positions. The Allies also shared occupation of the capital city of Berlin, although it was deep in the Soviet-controlled eastern sector of the country, in the expectation that a reunified, de-Nazified Germany would be governed from there someday. The British, French, and American decision in March 1948 to create a unified state out of the western sectors of Germany led a few months later to a year-long Soviet blockade of western access to Berlin and fears of a general war. The joint U.S.-British "Operation Vittles" airlifted tons of food to the isolated residents of West Berlin, preserving that city as a capitalist island in a communist country. The creation of NATO in 1949 made the American military commitment to Europe permanent. The point of NATO for western Europe, its British first secretary general said, was to "keep the Americans in, the Russians out, and the Germans down."

The onset of the Cold War determined the fate of the defeated powers of World War II. The Truman administration was determined to "push ahead with the reconstruction of those two great workshops of Europe and Asia—Germany and Japan." This agenda replaced initial concerns about rooting out Nazism and punishing war criminals, as at the Nuremberg trials of surviving Nazi leaders in 1945–1946. A similar story unfolded in Japan. The American occupation under General Douglas MacArthur initially (1945–1947) emphasized democratization

■ Harry Truman grew up on a farm in western Missouri and in Independence, a suburb of Kansas City. After serving as a captain in the U.S. Army during World War I, he returned home and rose through the ranks of the local Democratic party. Truman was elected to the U.S. Senate in 1934 and to the vice presidency in 1944; he became president after Franklin Roosevelt's death in April 1945. Known for his straightforwardness and sometimes bluntly honest speech, Truman always considered himself a man of the people. He served almost two full terms in the White House.

of Japanese society, including building labor unions, weakening corporate monopolies, ensuring women's political rights, and punishing war criminals. But rising U.S. tensions with the Soviets and the imminent victory of the Communist forces in China's civil war prompted American officials to shift course by 1948. Henceforth, they focused on rebuilding as quickly as possible Japan's industrial economy as the hub of capitalist Asia and reduced efforts at social reforms that might slow that process.

COLONIALISM AND THE COLD WAR

Most of the world's nonwhite majority still lived under European colonial control, and for them the struggle for national independence and racial equality was the great issue of the late 1940s and 1950s. In this north–south conflict of **colonialism,** as opposed to the east–west conflict of the Cold War, the United States held an awkward position. Its primary NATO partners included the greatest colonial powers: Britain, France, Belgium, the Netherlands, and Portugal. Racial segregation in the United States further undercut American leadership of the "free world."

With European rule in Asia and Africa on the way out, the Truman administration sought a gradual transfer of colonial rule into the hands of local pro-West elites. Violent revolutions—in the spirit of 1776—were to be avoided. The U.S. grant of official independence to the Philippines in 1946, though masking significant continued American influence, was offered as a model, as was the British departure from India a year later. However, the importance of Europe for America meant supporting even those imperialists who did not leave peacefully, such as the French digging in against communist-led revolutionaries in Vietnam (part of French Indochina).

UNION OF SOVIET SOCIALIST REPUBLICS

ALEUTIAN ISLANDS
(U.S.)

MONGOLIA

AFGHANISTAN

TIBET
(to China 1950)

CHINA

NORTH
KOREA
(1948)

PAKISTAN
(1947)

SOUTH
KOREA
(1948)

JAPAN
(U.S. Administration,
1945–1952)

PACIFIC
OCEAN

LAOS
(1953)

Okinawa
(U.S. Administration until 1972)

Midway Island

INDIA
(1947)

BURMA
(1948)

TAIWAN (1949)

Wake Island

BANGLADESH
(1971)

VIETNAM
(1954)

PHILIPPINE
ISLANDS
(1946)

PACIFIC TRUST
ISLANDS

INDIAN
OCEAN

THAILAND

KAMPUCHEA
(CAMBODIA, 1953)

MALAYSIA
(1957–1963)

SRI LANKA
(1946)

Singapore
(1965)

PAPUA
NEW
GUINEA
(1975)

SOLOMON
ISLANDS
(1978)

INDONESIA
(1949)

AUSTRALIA

Countries gaining independence after WWII
(date of independence)

Communist bloc

Allied with United States

Countries gaining independence after WWII
that also have bilateral defense treaties with U.S.

Countries gaining independence after WWII
that are also a part of the Communist bloc

■ **MAP 24.3 Asia After World War II**

The weakening of Western colonial powers in the war with Japan paved the way for national independence across Asia after 1945. Some of these newly independent nations chose a capitalist form of society and others a communist form. The new East-West tensions of the Cold War complicated the longer North-South struggle for freedom from colonial control.

The British withdrawal from Palestine in 1948 created a peculiar dilemma for the United States. Jewish settlers—primarily from Europe and often survivors of the Holocaust—proclaimed the new state of Israel against the wishes of the Arab majority. Secretary of State Marshall and others urged Truman not to recognize Israel to avoid imperiling U.S. relations with the Arab oil-producing states. The president sympathized with the Jewish desire for a homeland, however, and understood the importance of American Jews as constituents of the Democratic party in the 1940s. His decision to recognize Israel, which most Middle Easterners viewed as a new colonial state, set the United States on a course of enduring friendship with that nation and enduring conflict with Israel's Arab neighbors and the Palestinians.

Events in the Middle East struck closer to home for some Americans. Not all Jewish Americans were Zionists, but many fervently supported the new nation of Israel. Some joined the thousands of World War II veterans from around the world who volunteered in the Israeli military forces. West Point-trained Colonel David Marcus, former commandant of the U.S. Army Ranger school, lost his life in the fighting around Jerusalem in 1948, where he commanded four Israeli brigades and planned strategy crucial for Israel's military success. Americans of Arab descent experienced the events of that year very differently. For the hundreds of thousands of Palestinians who lost their lands, houses, and livelihoods as a result of the Israeli-Arab fighting, the Israeli War of Independence was a disaster. Most wound up in refugee camps in the region, but some found their way to the United States. Edward Said grew up in a Christian Palestinian family in Jerusalem, but his family fled to Cairo during the UN partition of the territory in 1947. Said's father held American citizenship, however, and Said eventually came to the United States, where he attended the Mt. Hermon School in Massachusetts, Princeton University, and Harvard University. He became a prominent scholar of comparative literature at Columbia University and served as one of the most articulate defenders of the rights of the Palestinian people until his death in 2003.

THE IMPACT OF NUCLEAR WEAPONS

While policymakers wrestled with issues of national security, scientists in the 1940s dramatically increased Americans' sense of personal security by introducing the use of antibiotics. "Miracle drugs" such as penicillin cured common bacterial infections that had previously been debilitating or fatal. Antibiotics suggested a future of personal health and longevity unimaginable to previous generations. What science gave with one hand, it threatened to take away with the other, however. The use of atomic weapons on Japan foreshadowed a future of utter insecurity in which instantaneous destruction of entire nations could occur without warning.

WATCH

Duck and Cover

Bettmann/CORBIS

■ Soldiers watch as "Dog," a 21-kiloton nuclear device, is dropped from a bomber at the Nevada Test Site at Yucca Flat, northwest of Las Vegas, in November 1951. U.S. atomic specialists tested nuclear weapons first in the Marshall Islands of the western Pacific Ocean, especially the Bikini atoll, beginning in 1946, and then in Nevada beginning in January 1951. Residents downwind from the test sites suffered various deleterious health effects from radiation exposure, including elevated cancer rates.

Even without being used again in war after 1945, nuclear weapons altered the American environment. Weapon tests with such code names as "Dirty Harry" released vast quantities of radiation into the atmosphere. The Atomic Energy Commission assured those near the mushroom clouds, "Fallout does not constitute a serious hazard." But local cancer rates spiked upward for Bikini Islanders in the Pacific, where the first tests occurred, and then for farmers and ranchers in Utah and Nevada, when tests began sixty-five miles northwest of Las Vegas in 1951.

Related dangers stalked other parts of the "nuclear West." Navajo Indians mining uranium in the Four Corners region (where Utah, Colorado, Arizona, and New Mexico meet) paid dearly for their intensive exposure to the poisonous material, as did thousands of workers involved in nuclear weapon production. Weapon assembly plants in Hanford, Washington, and Rocky Flats, Colorado, leaked radioactivity into the groundwater. In combination with the nuclear power industry, atomic weapon development resulted in an enormous supply of radioactive waste—deadly for 10,000 more years—that the U.S. government still does not know how to dispose of safely.

The government offered reassurances about the safety of the atom, and the Atomic Energy Commission covered up evidence of radioactivity's ill effects. But many Americans were anxious about this destructive new power that loomed over their lives, especially as the Soviet-American arms race intensified. Science fiction stories painted frightening pictures of a future devastated by nuclear war. Movies such as *The Blob* and *The Attack of the Crab Monsters* portrayed a world haunted by exposure to radiation. *Them!* featured mutant ants the size of buses crawling out of a New Mexico atomic test site. Concerns about a nuclear world escalated with the successful 1952 test of an American hydrogen bomb, a thousand times more powerful than the device that destroyed Hiroshima. Always suspicious of centralized power, Americans worried that one person in the Oval Office or the Kremlin could almost instantaneously obliterate entire continents.

American Security and Asia

■ *Why was Asia particularly important to the United States during the early postwar period?*

Japan did not conquer independent nations in its sweep southward at the start of World War II. Tokyo's army defeated imperial powers: the French in Indochina, the Dutch in Indonesia, the British in Singapore and Malaya, and the Americans in the Philippines. In a single swoop, Japanese soldiers demonstrated the absurdity of white supremacy and cleared the way for the end of colonialism in Asia.

Japan's retreat in 1945 left vacuums of power throughout the region. Into them flowed two contenders: the returning but gravely weakened European imperialists, and Asian nationalists such as Ho Chi Minh in Vietnam. Americans were not passive observers of this struggle as they sought to establish a new free-trading order in the region. As communist forces fought a civil war in China, the U.S. government bulked up its military and intelligence capacities and went to war in Korea.

THE CHINESE CIVIL WAR

Despite frequent discrimination against Chinese immigrants in the United States, Americans had long felt a special connection to China. Half of the thousands of Christian missionaries sent abroad by American churches in the early twentieth century had been posted there. Entrepreneurs eyed the Chinese market, home to one-fifth of the world's potential consumers. Selling cigarettes to the Chinese brought tobacco baron James B. Duke much of his wealth, which he then used to endow the university in North Carolina that bears his name. During

The Unity of Communists?

China Stock

Were all communists conspiring against the United States and its interests? This was a critical question for American policymakers as they shaped U.S. relations with the rest of the world after World War II. In this photograph, the new Chinese leader Mao Zedong (left) helps Soviet ruler Josef Stalin celebrate his birthday on December 21, 1949. Two months later, the two men signed a mutual defense treaty. But Stalin and Mao turned out to be bitter competitors rather than friends, and the alliance between their countries frayed badly and then dissolved over the next two decades.

QUESTIONS

1. What do Mao's and Stalin's expressions and postures in this photograph seem to suggest? Which pairs of American political leaders might show up in a similar photograph?

2. Which kinds of conflicts might explain the two men's coolness toward each other: conflicts of personality, of ideology, or of national interest?

3. What difference might it have made for U.S. policymakers to perceive communists as not all united?

World War II, Chinese resistance to Japan's invasion occupied millions of Tokyo's soldiers who would otherwise have been shooting at American GIs. The close U.S. alliance with the government of Jiang Jieshi seemed to confirm American hopes that Asia's largest nation would follow a pro-American path. Republican senator Kenneth Wherry of Nebraska declared that the United States would "lift Shanghai up and up, ever up, until it looks just like Kansas City."

However, many Chinese wanted Shanghai to look just like itself—or perhaps like Moscow. The partisans of the Chinese Communist party (CCP) under Mao

NSC-68

Interpreting History

Bettmann/CORBIS

■ Workers at the Douglas Aircraft Company's Santa Monica factory assemble Nike guided missiles for the U.S. Army in 1955. Large military contracts proliferated during the Cold War and stimulated the growth of Sunbelt states like California.

acquisition of nuclear weapons, President Truman ordered his National Security Council on January 31, 1950, to conduct "a reexamination of our objectives in peace and war and of the effect of these objectives on our strategic plans." The resulting study, known as NSC-68, called for a military buildup to counter Soviet expansionism. Some specialists on the USSR, such as George Kennan, questioned NSC-68's accuracy regarding Soviet intentions and successes. But the subsequent North Korean invasion of South Korea seemed to confirm the idea of "international communism" on the march.

From NSC-68: U.S. Objectives and Programs for National Security (April 14, 1950)

Concerned about the trend of international events in the wake of the Communist revolution in China and the Soviet Union's

The Soviet Union, unlike previous aspirants to hegemony, is animated by a new fanatic faith, antithetical to our own,

Zedong's leadership fought more effectively against the Japanese than Jiang's soldiers had. Japan's withdrawal in 1945 initiated four years of civil warfare between the Communists and Jiang's anticommunist Nationalists. Younger American diplomats and journalists in China, many of them missionaries' children who had grown up there, argued that the CCP was more popular than the corrupt Nationalist regime and was independent of the USSR. Rejecting the advice of these "China hands," the Truman administration provided $3 billion in aid to Jiang. The logic of the Truman Doctrine required containment of communism everywhere. Nevertheless, the policy failed in China. Americans watched in frustration as the CCP defeated the Nationalists, who retreated to the island of Taiwan. On October 1, 1949, Mao announced the establishment of the People's Republic of China (PRC).

This was the first communist government created without the presence of Soviet troops. Might the rest of Asia also choose communism? Profound suspicions on both sides prevented any Sino-American accommodation. The U.S. government refused to recognize the People's Republic, just as it had done with the USSR in 1917. Faced with U.S. hostility and sharing a common ideology with the Soviet Union, Mao papered over historic Chinese–Russian tensions and signed a mutual defense pact with Moscow in February 1950. For American policymakers, the so-called loss of China increased the importance of building capitalist societies in the rest of Asia, particularly Japan and—fatefully—South Korea and seeks to impose its absolute authority over the rest of the world....

Any substantial further extension of the area under the domination of the Kremlin would raise the possibility that no coalition adequate to confront the Kremlin with greater strength could be assembled. It is in this context that this Republic and its citizens in the ascendancy of their strength stand in their deepest peril.

The issues that face us are momentous, involving the fulfillment or destruction not only of this Republic but of civilization itself.... The assault on free institutions is world-wide now, and in the context of the present polarization of power a defeat of free institutions anywhere is a defeat everywhere....

Our policy and actions must be such as to foster a fundamental change in the nature of the Soviet system.... In a shrinking world, which now faces the threat of atomic warfare, it is not an adequate objective merely to seek to check the Kremlin design, for the absence of order among nations is becoming less and less tolerable....

The integrity of our system will not be jeopardized by any measures, covert or overt, violent or non-violent, which serve the purposes of frustrating the Kremlin design, nor does the necessity for conducting ourselves so as to affirm our values in actions as well as words forbid such measures....

The total economic strength of the U.S.S.R. compares with that of the U.S. as roughly one to four.... The military budget of the United States represents 6 to 7 percent of its gross national product (as against 13.8 percent for the Soviet Union). . . . This difference in emphasis between the two economies means that the readiness of the free world to support a war effort is tending to decline relative to that of the Soviet Union.

It is true that the United States armed forces are now stronger than ever before in other times of apparent peace; it is also true that there exists a sharp disparity between our actual military strength and our commitments.... It is clear that our military strength is becoming dangerously inadequate....

In summary, we must... [engage in] a rapid and sustained build-up of the political, economic, and military strength of the free world.

QUESTIONS

1. *What is the precise problem that the United States faces, according to NSC-68?*

2. *How does NSC-68's analysis of the Soviet threat in 1950 compare with American understanding today of the threat from Islamist terrorist organizations such as al Qaeda?*

and Vietnam. China's revolution also became a major issue in American politics. "Who lost China?" Republicans demanded rhetorically and effectively, presuming that it had once been America's to lose.

No one in the United States cared more about events in China than citizens and residents of Chinese descent. The FBI suspected of espionage any Chinese Americans who had sympathies toward the new Communist government in Beijing, and many lost their jobs. Most Chinese students and professors visiting in the United States when the communists took power did not want to go home. Meanwhile, Chinese immigrants who had already worked for years to improve their status in America shared the broad post-1945 desire to build comfortable material lives. Upwardly mobile young families moved to the suburbs, aided by the 1948 Supreme Court decision banning racial restrictions on real estate sales. William Chew's grandfather had worked on the transcontinental railroad; his father served in World War I and then became a cannery superintendent; and Chew himself became an engineer, with children who also succeeded him in the professions. Chew and his family made the difficult choice to leave the urban Chinese community in which he had grown up: "I longed to mow a green lawn and wax my car on weekends; to take my children to Sunday school and have backyard bar-b-ques with our neighbors and friends." In 1940, twenty-eight cities had had Chinatowns. By 1955, that number had fallen to sixteen.

THE CREATION OF THE NATIONAL SECURITY STATE

A week before Mao's announcement that China had become a communist country, President Truman shared some equally grim news with the American public: the Soviet Union had detonated its first nuclear device. The United States had lost the atomic monopoly that for four years assured Americans of their unique position of military strength. Truman asked his advisers for a full reevaluation of the nation's foreign policy.

The result was the top-secret National Security Council document 68, or **NSC-68,** which articulated the logic of what became the **national security state:** a government focused on the imperatives of military power, global involvement, and radically increased defense spending. NSC-68 argued that there was no longer any such thing as peacetime. The United States had entered an era of permanent crisis because of the expansion of communism and the hostile intentions of the Soviet Union. America's worldwide interests meant that it must oppose revolutions or radical change anywhere on the globe. NSC-68 went beyond the containment policy of the Truman Doctrine to call for fostering "a fundamental change in the nature of the Soviet system." This armed struggle necessitated secrecy and centralization of power in the hands of the federal government.

The National Security Act of 1947 and its 1949 amendments created the institutions of the new national security state. The Central Intelligence Agency (CIA) organized spying and covert operations, the Department of Defense unified the separate branches of the military, and the National Security Council (NSC) coordinated foreign policy information for the president. NSC-68 called for permanent military expenditures at a level of war readiness; it argued that this policy would stimulate rather than bankrupt the U.S. economy. Scores of communities became dependent on military spending—a kind of military welfare state. NSC-68's call for secrecy encouraged government deception of the public in the interest of "national security," with a consequent decline in democratic input into the nation's foreign relations.

America's new global military power included large U.S. military installations around the world, even in peacetime. American soldiers occupied Japan and western Germany, and U.S. military bases remain in those nations even today. Locals were often amazed by GIs' physical health, abundant provisions, and casual style. One young Japanese woman recalled the shock of seeing men chewing gum in public, something "unthinkable for a well-brought-up person to do." Yet "the Japanese people liked the American soldiers. Instantly. They were young boys, healthy, smiling all the time, very friendly." She also recalled American efforts to democratize Japanese society. "Almost all the old rules disappeared" as schools changed overnight. "We could talk back to teachers. We could discuss things." And "they made no distinction between boys and girls," as women gained political equality with men under the American occupation.

Many German and Austrian women married American soldiers. One woman from Vienna recalled how she and her friends were "fascinated by these young men; they seemed so carefree, happy, and well-fed." The GIs' casual manner—such as walking with their hands in their pockets—intrigued young Germans. American soldiers also brought with them American products that proved very popular abroad, especially jazz music (and soon rock 'n' roll) and Hollywood movies.

Sfc. Al Chang/Defense Visual Information Center (Department of Defense), HD-SN-99-03118

■ Near Haktong-ni, Korea, on August 28, 1950, an Army corpsman fills out casualty tags, while one American soldier comforts another who has just seen his buddy killed in action. Men who fought together on the front lines in Korea, as in other wars, experienced physical and psychological traumas unparalleled in civilian life. They often developed strong friendships with each other but sometimes had difficulty making the transition back to peacetime routines at home.

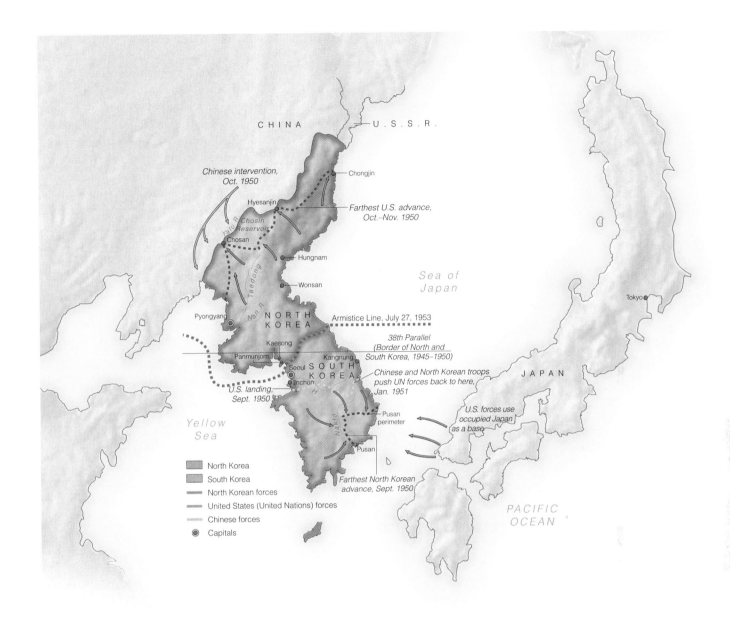

■ **MAP 24.4 The Korean War, 1950–1953**

The strategic location of the Korean peninsula enhanced the importance of what had originally been a civil conflict among Koreans. Korea's close proximity to China, the Soviet Union, and U.S.-occupied Japan made the outcome of that conflict very important to all of the great powers. The Americans and Chinese carried on the bulk of the fighting against each other in the full-scale war that unfolded in 1950.

AT WAR IN KOREA

Two months after NSC-68 arrived on the president's desk and four months after Senator McCarthy began his attacks on the Democratic administration, troops from communist North Korea poured across the 38th parallel into South Korea on June 25, 1950. The alarmist recommendations of NSC-68 now seemed fully justified to U.S. policymakers. The origins of the conflict on the Korean peninsula were more complicated than they appeared at first glance, however, and the United States was deeply involved.

Korea had been colonized by Japan since 1910. After Japan's defeat in 1945, Soviet and U.S. forces each occupied half of the peninsula. In the north, the Soviets installed a dictatorial Communist regime under Kim Il Sung, who had fought with the Chinese

The Korean War, 1950–1953

The National Archives

■ Korean refugees carry what they can of their worldly goods through heavy snow near Kangnung, on the east coast just south of the 38th parallel, on January 8, 1951. Wild swings in fortune in the Korean War contributed to the devastation wrought on the peninsula's civilians who were caught in the fighting, sometimes more than once. First North Korean troops conquered almost all of South Korea, except the Pusan perimeter; then U.S. and UN troops pushed all the way to the Chinese border in the north. At that point, Chinese forces entered the war and hurled the Americans back far south of the 38th parallel. Finally, U.S. and UN troops fought their way back to just north of the 38th, where the cease-fire in 1953 drew the new border between the two Koreas.

Communists in their common struggle against Japan. In the south, the Americans established an authoritarian capitalist regime led by Syngman Rhee, who had taken classes at Princeton University with Woodrow Wilson and had lived in the United States most of the previous four decades. The 38th parallel was an arbitrary dividing line for a nation that had been unified for 1,300 years, and both governments sought to reunite Korea under their control. Border skirmishes intensified after the Soviets and Americans withdrew in 1948, and leftist rebellions continued across much of the south. The CIA acknowledged that Rhee was "unpopular among many—if not a majority— of non-Communist Koreans." Some 100,000 Koreans lost their lives in the fighting between 1945 and 1950.

U.S. forces arrived in late June 1950, just in time to prevent the South Korean army from being driven off the peninsula, and then slowly pushed the North Koreans backward toward the 38th parallel in hard fighting. Truman received UN approval for this "police action," along with a small number of troops from several other nations.

Americans assumed the North Korean invasion had been orchestrated by Moscow as part of a plan of worldwide communist aggression. The Truman administration considered defense of South Korea crucial to demonstrate the credibility of U.S. power. The U.S. government took preemptive actions against possible aggression elsewhere. It sent the 7th Fleet to defend Taiwan, which it had previously assumed China would eventually conquer and reabsorb; it increased assistance to anticommunist forces in the Philippines and Vietnam; and it rearmed West Germany as part of NATO. The U.S. annual military budget grew from $13 billion in 1950 before the war to $50 billion in 1953, setting a pattern for vast military expenditures ever since.

General Douglas MacArthur's brilliantly executed landing of fresh U.S. troops at the port of Inchon behind North Korean lines on September 15, 1950, created a turning point in the war. North Korean forces abandoned the South's capital city of Seoul, fleeing northward to avoid being caught between two American armies advancing from different directions. South Korea was retaken; containment had succeeded. Should American commanders now shift to rolling back communism by proceeding north of the 38th parallel? The opportunity was irresistible, despite Truman's determination to keep this a limited war. MacArthur ignored signals that the Chinese would not allow U.S. soldiers to come all the way to their border at the Yalu River—the equivalent for Americans of having the Soviet Army arrive at the Rio Grande. On November 27, 200,000 Chinese soldiers struck hard, driving American soldiers south of the 38th parallel again in the longest retreat in U.S. history, some 300 miles.

MacArthur wanted to take this "entirely new war" directly to the Chinese, using conventional or even nuclear bombing campaigns against the People's Republic. However, Joint Chiefs of Staff chair General Omar Bradley called this idea "the wrong war, at the wrong place, at the wrong time, and with the wrong enemy." MacArthur's growing insubordination forced Truman to fire the popular general in April 1951 because the president had no desire to start a larger war that would draw in the USSR. The bloody fighting in Korea stalemated that spring close to the original dividing line, where the front remained as the two sides negotiated for two years before signing a cease-fire in July 1953. All the while, the U.S. Air Force used its supremacy in the skies to rain down extraordinary destruction on the North. "We burned down *every* town in North Korea," boasted General Curtis LeMay. American deaths totaled 37,000, and China lost nearly a million soldiers. Three million Koreans on both sides died—10 percent of the population of the peninsula—and another 5 million became refugees. Containment succeeded at enormous cost, and the Korean peninsula is still divided and heavily armed today.

> The fighting in Korea enabled Senator McCarthy and the Red Scare to dominate political life in the United States.

The Korean War shaped subsequent American politics and society in critical ways. The stalemate frustrated those who agreed with General MacArthur that there was "no substitute for victory." But the ominous threat of nuclear weapons meant that wars had to be limited. The fighting in Korea enabled Senator McCarthy and the Red Scare to dominate political life in the United States. The results were sometimes absurd, with the Democratic authors of the containment policy and the national security state being red-baited as "soft on communism." The Republican party rode such charges to electoral victory in November 1952. (They also benefited from evidence of petty corruption among some Truman administration officials, such as the president's appointment secretary accepting bribes.) Republican presidential nominee General Dwight Eisenhower was perhaps the most popular American alive because of his leadership of the Allied victory in Europe in World War II, and he swept into the White House over Democrat Adlai Stevenson, the governor of Illinois.

A Cold War Society

Which were the most important changes in Americans' lives in the early Cold War era?

Expanding economic opportunities and narrowing political freedoms characterized American society in the first decade of the Cold War. Anticommunist repression pushed dissident views to the margins of the nation's political life. Americans largely accepted this new conformity for two reasons: their desire to support their government during international crises, especially the Korean War, and a consumer cornucopia that surrounded them with attractive material goods. A generation that had survived the Great Depression embraced the culture of consumption and convenience that emerged after World War II. Factories that had produced jeeps, tanks, and weaponry turned to manufacturing cars and appliances; men who had learned to build roads and barracks for the military now began to erect suburban housing with equal speed. Americans moved to the suburbs, and to the South and the West.

By 1947, the United States was launching into an era of extraordinary economic expansion that continued for twenty-five years. Since Ben Franklin's time, Americans had been known for thrift in their pursuit of wealth, but after 1945 the long-cherished principle of delaying gratification declined steeply. "Buy now, pay later," General Motors urged, as it offered an installment plan to customers. Diner's Club introduced the first credit card in 1950. In a formulation breathtaking for its distance from Puritan and immigrant traditions of saving for the future, writer William Whyte observed that "thrift is now un-American."

FAMILY LIVES

Many white Americans embraced the opportunity to move to the suburbs after World War II. Seeking larger homes and yards and quieter neighborhoods, they flocked to new developments such as Levittown outside New York City on Long Island. In their first three hours of

Charles Rotkin/CORBIS

■ A new cloverleaf intersection on a freeway arches across the northern New Jersey suburbs in 1949. Multilane, limited-access highways became common after World War II. A new word, "smog" (neither smoke nor fog), emerged to describe the urban pollution caused by trucks and commuter vehicles.

IMAGE

Levittown

business in 1949, Levittown's developers sold 1,400 houses. In 1944, construction had begun on just 114,000 new houses; in 1950, the number jumped to 1.7 million. Suburbs did not welcome all, however. Even as federal courts struck down segregation laws in some spheres of American life, the Veterans Administration and the Federal Housing Administration agencies were encouraging residential separation by race. Private banks did the same, and the contracts that developers such as Alfred and William Levitt signed with homebuyers prohibited resale to nonwhites. Other government policies, including highway construction and tax benefits for homeowners, promoted the growth of suburbs at the cost of cities. A third epoch in American residential history began by 1970 when more Americans resided in suburbs than cities, parallel to the 1920 shift from a rural majority to an urban one.

Suburban life encouraged a sharpening of gender roles among the growing middle class. Men commuted to work while women were expected to find fulfillment in marriage and motherhood, including a nearly full-time job of unpaid housework. Most women did so while either feeling isolated in their homes or finding community with other women in their neighborhoods and churches. "We married what we wanted to be," one female college graduate recalled. "If we wanted to be a lawyer or a doctor we married one." An enormous amount depended on a woman's choice of a husband, including class status and lifelong material well-being. Despite this partial retreat from wartime employment, however, fully one-third of American women continued to work for pay outside the home. The economic circumstances of most black women offered them little choice, and most wound up doing double housework: their own and that of families employing them as domestics. Middle-class women tended to view their paid work as a job rather than a career, a way to increase the family income if they did not have small children at home. Quotas in graduate schools and sex-segregated employment limited the number of female professionals.

> *From 1946 to 1964, women giving birth at a younger age to more children created the demographic bulge known as the baby boom.*

After a lengthy decline during the 1930s, marriage and birth rates picked up during the war and then accelerated sharply after 1945. From 1946 to 1964, women giving birth at a younger age to more children created the demographic bulge known as the baby boom. Large families reinforced the domestic focus of most women, putting the work of child-rearing at the center of their lives. Fatherhood became increasingly a badge of masculinity, with Father's Day emerging as a significant holiday for the first time. Family physician Benjamin Spock published *Baby and Child Care* (1946), a runaway best-seller that helped shift the emphasis in American parenting from strictness to greater nurturance.

Strong feelings about pregnancy hinged on the marital status of the expectant mother. Married mothers were celebrated, but unmarried ones were rebuked. Despite the greater freedom of the war years, the sexual double standard remained in place, with women's virtue linked directly to virginity in a way that men's was not. Birth control devices such as the diaphragm were legal only for married women and only in certain states. Women seeking to terminate unwanted pregnancies had to consider illegal abortions, the only kind available before 1970; millions did so, including one-fifth of all married women and a majority of single women who became pregnant. Two studies of American sexual behavior by Dr. Alfred Kinsey of Indiana University revealed that Americans often did not practice what they preached. The Kinsey reports of 1948 and 1953 shocked the public with their revelation of widespread premarital and extramarital sexual intercourse as well as homosexual liaisons.

THE GROWTH OF THE SOUTH AND THE WEST

Before World War II, American cultural, industrial, and financial power had always been centered in the urban North, but federal expenditures during the war began to change this pattern. The U.S. Army built most of its training bases in the South, where land close to the coasts was thinly populated and inexpensive. Military bases and defense industries sprang up along the West Coast to project power into the Pacific against Japan. The San Francisco Bay area sprawled with shipyards and sailors, and southern California became the center of the nation's aircraft industry. U.S. troops built the Alcan (Alaska-Canada) Highway, and millions of GIs passed through Hawaii en route to the Pacific battlefront. Fighting against the Japanese to defend Pearl Harbor and the Aleutian Islands brought the once distant territories of Hawaii and Alaska more into Americans' consciousness, setting them on the path to statehood in 1959.

The **Sunbelt** of the South, the Southwest, and California grew rapidly after the war, whereas older Rustbelt cities of the Northeast and Midwest such as Buffalo and Detroit began to lose manufacturing jobs and population. Like the 440,000 people who moved to Los Angeles during the war, postwar migrants to California and Arizona appreciated the weather and the economic opportunities. Military spending underwrote half the jobs in California during the first decade of the Cold War. Migrants from south of the border, meanwhile, found work primarily in California's booming agricultural sector. The U.S. government continued to use the *bracero* program as an exception to immigration laws for Mexicans willing to do arduous labor in the hot fields of California and the Southwest, thus encouraging the large influx of Mexicans into the area.

MAP

Population Shifts, 1940–1950

Two industries particularly stimulated the growth of the Sunbelt: cars and air conditioning. Automobiles helped shape the economies of western states, where new cities were built out of sprawling suburbs, and governments erected highways rather than railroads, subways, or other forms of public transportation. New car sales shot up from 70,000 in 1945 to 7.9 million in 1955. Inexpensive gasoline, refined from the abundant crude oil of Texas and Oklahoma, powered this fleet. Automobile exhaust pipes replaced industrial smokestacks as the primary source of air pollution, which by the 1960s shrouded Los Angeles—the "city of angels"—in smog. Air conditioning also became widely available after World War II and contributed to the breakdown of the South's regional distinctiveness. From Miami and Atlanta to Houston and Washington, D.C., the new Sunbelt depended on the indoor comfort brought by controlling summertime heat and humidity.

HARRY TRUMAN AND THE LIMITS OF LIBERAL REFORM

On the political front, the onset of the Cold War narrowed the range of American political discourse. In seeking to consolidate the New Deal legacy, President Truman found himself boxed in by conservative Republican opponents. Allied governments in western Europe had embraced the idea that access to health care was a right of every citizen in a modern democratic state. But when Truman proposed a system of national health care, conservatives quashed his proposal in Congress, pushed by an American Medical Association lobbying campaign that denounced the idea as a "monstrosity of Bolshevik bureaucracy."

Perhaps the most blatant omission of the New Deal was protection against racial discrimination. Now, as the Cold War intensified, the fact that millions of Americans still lacked basic civil rights guarantees was a glaring contradiction amid rhetoric about ensuring rights and liberties throughout the "free world." In 1947, the President's Committee on Civil Rights called for a strong federal commitment to racial equality. Truman campaigned for reelection in 1948 on a platform of support for civil rights that was unprecedented in the White House; he made the first presidential address ever to the NAACP. That summer he ordered the desegregation of the armed forces and the federal civil service.

African American voters in Chicago, Cleveland, and other northern cities played a key role in swing states; their solid support lifted Truman to a narrow and surprising victory over the heavily favored Republican candidate, New York governor Thomas Dewey. Truman's reelection was all the more impressive because of the fracturing of the Democratic party. Alienated by the civil rights plank, white Southerners walked out of the Democratic convention and ran South Carolina governor Strom Thurmond as an independent candidate. The "Dixiecrats" won four states in the Deep South, foreshadowing the abandonment by white Southerners of the party of their parents in the 1960s. From the opposite side of the party, many liberals jumped ship for Henry Wallace, Roosevelt's former vice president, running as the Progressive party candidate. Truman won as a man of the moderately liberal center, fierce against communism, usually supportive of the rights of organized labor, and opposed to discrimination.

TABLE 24.1			
The Election of 1948			
Candidate	**Political Party**	**Popular Vote (%)**	**Electoral Vote**
Harry S. Truman	Democratic	49.5	304
Thomas E. Dewey	Republican	45.1	189
J. Strom Thurmond	State-Rights Democratic	2.4	38
Henry A. Wallace	Progressive	2.4	—

COLD WAR POLITICS AT HOME

Anticommunism turned out to be an inadequate shield for liberals and moderates in the partisan warfare pervading American politics in the late 1940s and early 1950s. In a pattern that became known as **McCarthyism,** mostly Republican conservatives blamed liberal Democrats in the administration for communist successes abroad—especially in China and Korea. Using a tactic called "red-baiting," conservatives accused liberals of sympathizing with and even spying for the Soviet Union. The hunt for domestic subversives to explain international setbacks was grounded in the reality of a handful of actual Soviet spies, most notably Julius Rosenberg (executed for treason in 1953 along with his apparently

TABLE 24.2			
The Election of 1952			
Candidate	**Political Party**	**Popular Vote (%)**	**Election Vote**
Dwight D. Eisenhower	Republican	55.1	442
Adlai E. Stevenson	Democratic	44.4	89

innocent wife Ethel) and nuclear scientist Klaus Fuchs. But this second Red Scare expressed primarily the frustration of being unable to translate vast U.S. power into greater control of world events. And it served, above all, to cast suspicion on the patriotism of liberals at home.

Despite his general support for civil liberties, Truman helped set the tone for pursuing suspected traitors. In an unsuccessful effort to fortify his right flank against Republican attacks, he established a federal employee loyalty program in March 1947 as the domestic equivalent of the Truman Doctrine. Attorney General Tom Clark drew up a list of supposedly subversive organizations that the FBI and state committees on "un-American activities" then hounded. In a case with sobering implications for free speech, federal courts in 1949 convicted the leaders of the U.S. Communist party of promoting the overthrow of the U.S. government. Words alone, the courts ruled, could be treasonable—the same logic as the wartime Sedition Act of 1918 (see Chapter 20). Conservative congressional Democrats pushed through the Internal Security Act of 1950 to require Communist party members to register with the government and allow emergency incarceration of suspected subversives. Calling it "a long step toward totalitarianism," Truman vetoed the measure, but Congress overrode the veto by a huge margin.

Republicans reaped the benefits of the Red Scare. Most Americans who had sympathized in any way with the Soviet Union in the Depression years were by the late 1940s merely liberal Democrats, but the House Un-American Activities Committee (HUAC) zeroed in on their earlier records. Investigating Hollywood, the television industry, and universities as well as the executive branch of the U.S. government, HUAC destroyed the careers of prominent figures and average Americans.

The era found its name in the previously obscure junior senator from Wisconsin, Republican Joseph McCarthy. With a single speech in Wheeling, West Virginia, on February 9, 1950, the genial but ambitious politician soared to prominence. "I have here in my hand a list of 205" Communist party members working in the State Department, he declared. Over the next four years, the numbers and names changed as McCarthy stayed one step ahead of the evidence while intimidating witnesses before his Senate subcommittee. In reality, one reporter joked, McCarthy "couldn't find a Communist in Red Square" in Moscow. He talked about communists, but his show was about Democrats. As the war in Korea raged, he mercilessly red-baited the Truman administration. But after the Republican electoral victory in 1952, his excesses lost their partisan utility. With the end of the war in Korea and his ill-advised attacks on the U.S. Army itself as supposedly infiltrated by communists (the Army-McCarthy hearings), he was at last censured by his Senate colleagues in 1954 and died an early, alcohol-related death in 1957.

DOCUMENT

McCarthy, Wheeling, West Virginia Speech

WHO IS A LOYAL AMERICAN?

The Cold War politics of inclusion and exclusion established a new profile for loyal Americans. Private familial and material concerns were expected to replace public interest in social reform. "No man who owns his own house and lot can be a Communist," real estate developer William Levitt declared. "He has too much to do." He also had a wife, presumably, in an era when anticommunists launched a withering assault on homosexuals as "perverts" and threats to the nation's security. Church membership climbed in tandem with condemnations of "godless Communism," and Congress added the words "under

■ From 1951 to 1953, Mexican American miners went on strike against the Empire Zinc Mining Company in Silver City, New Mexico. Women took on major roles in this labor action, which inspired a famous movie, *Salt of the Earth*. Defiant in the face of police and company shotguns and billy clubs, Elvira Molano (center) served as co-chair of the union negotiating committee and became known as "the most arrested woman" during the strike.

Courtesy, Los Mineros Collection, Chicano Research Collection, Arizona State University Libraries

God" to the Pledge of Allegiance. Warning that "God is giving us a desperate choice, a choice of either revival or judgment," revivalist preacher Billy Graham launched his first evangelical crusade in Los Angeles in 1949, en route to becoming the nation's foremost religious figure. Discrimination against Roman Catholics and Jews, though still evident, declined as Catholics such as McCarthy proved intensely anticommunist and as pictures and stories emerged to reveal the horrors of the Nazi Holocaust against the Jews. More inclusive references to the "Judeo-Christian tradition" became common.

American leadership of the global anticommunist cause strengthened the struggle for racial equality at home, within certain limits. The NAACP and most African Americans took an anticommunist position in accord with Truman, in return for his support of civil rights. They downplayed their concern for colonial independence in Africa and Asia to support NATO. The American GI Forum (Latino veterans) and the Japanese American Citizen League also worked within the confines of Cold War politics to end discrimination. However, more radical black leaders such as scholar W. E. B. Du Bois and actor and singer Paul Robeson refused to make any such accommodation to anticommunism. Offended by the hypocrisy of segregation in the land of liberty, they insisted on full freedom everywhere in the "free world." The government responded by restricting their travel and diminishing their livelihoods. In a move right out of the Soviet playbook, Robeson's name was erased from the list of football All-Americans for 1917 and 1918 (he had starred for Rutgers University), leaving only ten men on those teams.

For impoverished Native Americans, the government seemed to give with one hand and take away with the other. In 1946, Truman established the Indian Claims Commission to consider payment for lands taken and treaties broken. But gestures toward compensation led to policies of termination. Developers seeking access to Indian lands joined reformers troubled by reservation poverty in urging Congress—with limited success—to terminate the special status Indian tribes had held with the federal government since its founding. Dillon S. Myer, who had overseen internment camps for Japanese Americans during World War II, became director of the Bureau of Indian Affairs in 1950. He closed reservation schools, withdrew support for traditional cultural activities, and launched an urban relocation program, all intended to move Native Americans into the mainstream and get the government "out of the Indian business."

Immigrants also received mixed messages. The McCarran-Walter Act (1952) ended the long-standing ban on allowing people of Asian descent not born in the United States to become U.S. citizens. But it preserved the discriminatory 1924 system of "national origins" for allocating numbers of immigrants from different countries. The bill also strengthened the attorney general's authority to deport aliens who were suspected of subversive intentions. Like Guatemalan-born leftist Luisa Moreno, a successful labor organizer in California who was deported in 1950, immigrants learned that their welcome depended on their politics. The powerful 1953 film *Salt of the Earth*—with its pro-union, pro-socialist, pro-feminist, and pro-Latino sympathies—was condemned as subversive and rarely screened until the 1970s.

Conclusion

McCarthyism at home and the war in Korea ensured a generation of hostility between the United States and China. It tied the People's Republic more closely to the USSR, strengthening the common belief that international communism was a unified movement. The United States committed itself to defending Taiwan from recapture by the Beijing government. The firing of the "China hands" deprived the State Department of the bulk of its Asian expertise, smoothing the path to an ill-informed war in Vietnam. The Korean War also jump-started the moribund Japanese economy as American dollars poured into Japan, where the U.S. war effort was based. Japanese conservatives called it "a gift from the gods."

Frustrations with the course of war in Korea affirmed the inward focus of American society in the 1950s. Despite the organizing efforts of political activists such as civil rights workers, most citizens seemed to look increasingly to their personal and familial lives for satisfaction and meaning. From the powerful U.S. economy flowed an unprecedented river of consumer goods, including the new artificial materials—plastic, vinyl, nylon, polyester, Styrofoam—that have pervaded and polluted American life ever since. As peace came to Korea and U.S. soldiers returned from across the Pacific, Americans sought the good life at home.

CHRONOLOGY: 1945–1953

1945	Harry S. Truman becomes president upon death of Roosevelt.
	Atomic bombs dropped on Hiroshima and Nagasaki.
	V-E Day (May 7); V-J Day (August 14).
	United Nations created.
1946	*Morgan v. West Virginia* outlaws segregation in interstate transportation.
	Winston Churchill gives "Iron Curtain" speech, Fulton, Missouri.
1947	Jackie Robinson joins Brooklyn Dodgers.
	Taft-Hartley Act limits labor union activities.
	Truman Doctrine of containing communism announced.
1948	New Mexico and Arizona grant Indians right to vote.
	Modern state of Israel founded.
	U. S. armed services desegregated.
1949	Billy Graham launches his first evangelical crusade in Los Angeles.
	Establishment of People's Republic of China.
	USSR acquires nuclear weapons.
1950	Sen. Joseph McCarthy accuses State Department of harboring communists.
	North Korean troops invade South Korea.
1951	Ethel and Julius Rosenberg convicted of treason.
1952	Dwight Eisenhower elected president.
1953	Korean War ends.

For Review

1. Which were the most important causes of the Cold War?

2. Why did average Americans seem to focus on their personal lives rather than on politics after the end of World War II?

3. As president of the United States, what did Harry Truman seem to stand for and believe in, and what compromises did he make?

4. How were the Cold War and the struggle for decolonization related to each other?

5. In which ways did family life change for Americans in the late 1940s and early 1950s?

6. How were McCarthyism and the Korean War connected?

The Cold War at Full Tide, 1953–1979

During the third quarter of the twentieth century, the Cold War cast a long shadow over the United States and the rest of the world. Tensions mounted at home and abroad as the United States and the Soviet Union vied for power among the world's nations. In poor Third World countries, insurgents attempted to throw off the yoke of colonialism and play the two superpowers against each other. The United States used a variety of strategies to counter Soviet influence in Latin America, Africa, the Middle East, and Southeast Asia, including military force in Korea and Vietnam, white-knuckle diplomacy in Cuba, extensive aid to non-aligned countries, and covert operations worldwide.

Soviet advances in science and technology spurred the U.S. government to sponsor bold new domestic initiatives in the areas of public education and space exploration. The Cold War even helped shape a post–World War II domestic ideal: a nuclear family living in a house in the suburbs, with a breadwinner father and a full-time homemaker mother. Many Americans believed that their prosperous, consumer-oriented economy, with its emphasis on individualism and personal choice, was a key weapon in the fight against communism.

In a feverish arms race, both the United States and the USSR rushed to stockpile weapons of mass destruction. Constant innovations in the technology of nuclear weaponry (such as intercontinental ballistic missiles) made the bombers used in World War II obsolete. The hydrogen bomb, tested successfully for the first time in 1953, dwarfed the power of the atomic bomb that had leveled Hiroshima. Nevertheless, citizens who criticized the arms buildup risked being branded unpatriotic. More than ever before, domestic policy was intertwined with foreign policy.

The rise of multinational corporations meant that large, impersonal institutions, whether government or private, were shaping American life. Middle-level managers—men in "grey flannel suits"—represented the corporate ethos of loyalty to the company above all else. At the same time, many Americans sought to work within their local communities for social and political change. In the South, African American men and women launched a dramatic assault on the system of legal segregation known as "Jim Crow." Working at the grassroots level, these activists boycotted buses, marched, sat in at lunch counters, and went to jail. Their efforts provoked the courts and Congress to act, culminating in the Civil Rights Acts of 1964 and 1965. For the first time in American history, the federal government assumed responsibility for eliminating discrimination in the workplace and guaranteeing all citizens the right to vote.

Other groups also organized and entered the political arena. Indians, disabled Americans, California farm workers, and gay men and lesbians all formed organizations to counter discrimination and advance their civil rights. The women's movement affected all aspects of American society, enabling women to play a greater role in the political and economic life of the country. A new environmentalist movement secured legislation protecting wilderness areas and endangered species and ensuring that Americans had clean air to breathe and clean water to drink.

Lyndon B. Johnson assumed the presidency after the assassination of John F. Kennedy in 1963. Johnson hoped to revitalize the New Deal legacy by expanding social welfare programs. His program, called the Great Society, sought to address seemingly intractable problems such as poverty, lack of health care for the elderly, and the deterioration of inner-city neighborhoods. But Johnson also expanded the U.S. military presence in Vietnam, an effort that cost an increasing number of American lives. Even constant bombing proved futile to stem the civil war that pitted Americans and anticommunist Vietnamese against the National Liberation Front of South Vietnam and their comrades in the north. Johnson's successor, Richard M. Nixon, also found himself mired in a war that was becoming increasingly unpopular among Americans.

Protests against the war in the late 1960s and early 1970s highlighted an emerging youth culture. The baby boom generation, born in the two decades after World War II, embraced sexual freedom and new forms of music (such as rock 'n' roll) in an apparent attempt to defy their parents and "the Establishment" in general. Many Americans felt betrayed by both Johnson and Nixon, believing that tens of thousands of American soldiers had died in vain in Vietnam. The Watergate break-in at Democratic headquarters, leading eventually to Nixon's resignation, contributed to a growing, widespread disenchantment with government authority.

By the late 1970s, developments abroad had greatly complicated Cold War politics. Middle Eastern oil-producing nations imposed an oil embargo on the United States, highlighting U.S. dependence on fossil fuels. Islamic fundamentalists were beginning to retaliate violently against the spread of American influence and culture in Muslim countries. And at home, a conservative backlash emerged to counter the expansion of the welfare state, the heightened visibility of the feminist movement, and widening civil rights protests.

Chapter 25

Domestic Dreams and Atomic Nightmares, 1953–1963

AP/Wide World Photos

Vice President Richard M. Nixon and Soviet Premier Nikita Khrushchev touring the 1959 American National Exhibition in Moscow.

In 1959, Vice President Richard M. Nixon traveled to Moscow in the Soviet Union to visit the American National Exhibition, a showcase of American consumer goods and leisure equipment. The main attraction of the exhibition was a full-size, six-room, ranch-style house. In a lengthy and often heated debate with Soviet Premier Nikita Khrushchev at the opening of the exhibition, Nixon extolled the virtues of the American way of life while his opponent promoted the communist system. The two leaders did not discuss missiles, bombs, or even modes of government. Rather, they argued over the relative merits of American and Soviet washing machines, televisions, and electric ranges in what came to be known as the "Kitchen Debate," one of the most noted verbal sparring matches of the century.

The model home, filled with labor-saving devices and presumably available to Americans of all classes, offered tangible proof, Nixon claimed, of the superiority of free enterprise over communism. He proclaimed that the home adorned with a wide array of consumer goods represented the essence of American freedom:"To us, diversity, the right to choose, . . . is the most important thing. We don't have one decision made at the top by one government official. . . . We have many different manufacturers and many different kinds of washing machines so that the housewives have a choice. . . . Would it not be better to compete in the relative merits of washing machines than in the strength of rockets?"

Nixon's focus on household appliances was not accidental. After all, arguments over the strength of rockets would only point out the vulnerability of the United States in the event of a nuclear war between the superpowers. Debates over consumer goods provided a reassuring vision of the good life available in the Atomic Age.

Nixon called attention to a built-in, panel-controlled washing machine. "In America," he said, "these [washing machines] are designed to make things easier for our women." Khrushchev countered Nixon's boast of comfortable American housewives by expressing pride in productive Soviet female workers. The Soviets, he claimed, did not share that "capitalist attitude toward women."

According to American journalists, Nixon's knock-out punch in his verbal bout with the Soviet premier was his articulation of the American postwar domestic dream: successful bread-winners supporting attractive homemakers in well-appointed, comfortable homes. Sharing Nixon's sentiments about politics, consumerism, and gender, most reporters hailed the vice president's trip as a major triumph. The American National Exhibition in Moscow seemed to demonstrate the superiority of the American way of life.

Nixon's emphasis on the home and family during the Kitchen Debate reflected the central concerns of postwar Americans. In spite of deep divisions in American society, in certain ways Americans behaved with remarkable conformity. This is nowhere more evident than in the overwhelming embrace of the nuclear family. The GI Bill, with its provisions for home mortgage loans, enabled veterans of modest means to purchase homes. Although residential segregation prevailed throughout the postwar era, limiting most suburban developments to prosperous white middle- and working-class families, many veterans of color were able to buy their first homes. The "American way of life" embodied in the suburban nuclear family, as a cultural ideal if not a universal reality, motivated countless postwar Americans to strive for it, to live by its codes, and—for Americans of color—to demand it.

Scientific discoveries in the 1950s also inaugurated the modern era of exploration beyond Earth's atmosphere, fueled by the space race between the United States and the Soviet Union. The National Aeronautics and Space Administration (NASA), established in 1958, sent the first American into space in 1961. But science also brought pesticides, smog, and other pollutants. Americans at the time rarely considered the environmental effects of consumer goods, cars, petrochemicals, or nuclear power.

Nor did most Americans consider that the visible prosperity hid considerable poverty within the nation. The economy expanded rapidly during the 1950s and 1960s, spreading the affluent life to millions of Americans. At the same time, 40 to 50 million Americans remained poor, unable to enjoy the material advantages of the celebrated American way of life.

Nevertheless, the decade from 1953 to 1963 was a time of expansive optimism about the future. The **baby boom,** as the dramatic rise in the nation's birthrate came to be known, demonstrated widespread faith in the future for American children. Americans of all backgrounds and economic levels pushed the birthrate up. It was also an era of growth for U.S. influence abroad, the domestic economy, consumer culture, and television. Suburbs, highways, and shopping malls expanded to meet the needs of increasing numbers of families with young children. The nation itself expanded with the addition of Hawaii and Alaska as states.

It was also a decade of anxiety and challenges to the status quo. In the international arena, fears of war continued. Eisenhower had brought an end to the Korean War without a decisive victory. Tensions with the Soviet Union prevailed, along with new fears about communist China. Domestic anticommunism put a damper on political protest. Nevertheless, the continuing nuclear arms race prompted an antinuclear movement promoted largely by housewives. And persistent racial discrimination led to increasing civil rights activism.

People in the civil rights movement and emerging youth and counter cultures expressed dissatisfaction with prevailing racial, gender, and sexual codes. Americans worried about the perils of the Atomic Age as the nuclear arsenals of both superpowers continued to grow. Science fiction films about alien invaders reflected concerns about foreign dangers. The Soviet Union's 1957 launching of *Sputnik*, the first artificial satellite to orbit Earth, alarmed Americans and forced the nation to confront the possibility of Soviet technological superiority. Eisenhower's presidency fostered stability and business growth at home, Cold War aims abroad, and the escalation of the nuclear arms race. Cold War tensions erupted in the Kennedy era, first in the failed attempt to invade Cuba at the Bay of Pigs, and much more ominously in the Cuban missile crisis, which brought the United States and the Soviet Union to the brink of nuclear war. The United States appeared to be at the height of its strength and power, yet at the same time, more vulnerable than ever before.

Cold War, Warm Hearth

■ *In what ways did the suburban family home promote Cold War ideology?*

In the midst of the uncertainties of the postwar era, family fever swept the nation and affected all Americans. These years witnessed an unprecedented rush into marriage and childbearing, unlike anything before or since. The baby boom that began during and immediately after World War II accelerated in the 1950s, along with rising rates of marriage, declining age at marriage, and lower divorce rates following an immediate postwar peak. Americans of all racial, ethnic, and religious groups, of all socioeconomic classes and educational levels, brought the marriage rate up and the divorce rate down. Popular television shows such as *The Honeymooners*, featuring working-class couples, and *Leave It to Beaver*, depicting middle-class families, placed the consumer-oriented home at the center of attention. So did mainstream *Life* magazine and the glossy African American *Ebony*. Women embraced as well as chafed against the new domestic ideal. Prosperity stimulated unprecedented consumer spending as Americans of all backgrounds struggled to achieve the American Dream.

CONSUMER SPENDING AND THE SUBURBAN IDEAL

Since the end of World War II, the American economy had been growing by leaps and bounds. The gross national product (GNP) hit a record high of $482.7 billion by the end of the 1950s and continued to grow in the 1960s with rising productivity and low unemployment. Big business as well as big government contributed to the economic growth. Large industrial corporations generated jobs and productivity, while the federal government invested in social welfare, scientific research, space exploration, and a national highway system. Development of military and commercial technology expanded, and the defense industry generated increasing exports as well as domestic economic growth.

This dramatic economic expansion generated a huge increase in spending power. Between 1947 and 1961, the number of families rose 28 percent, national income increased

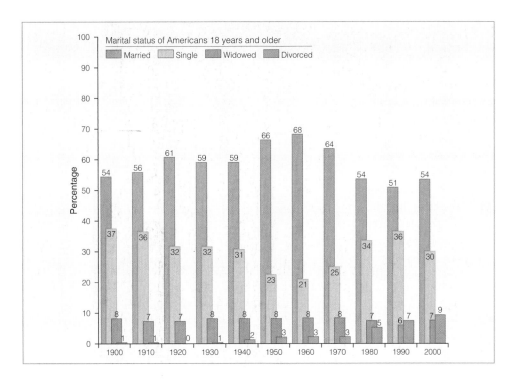

■ **FIGURE 25.1 Marital Status of the U.S. Adult Population, 1900–2000**

Following World War II, Americans married in record numbers. The high rate of marriage corresponded with a relatively low divorce rate. Beginning in the 1970s, the marriage rate plummeted and the divorce rate rose dramatically.

more than 60 percent, and the number of Americans with money to spend beyond basic necessities doubled. Rather than putting this money aside for a rainy day, Americans were inclined to spend it. Investing in one's home, along with the trappings that would enhance family life, seemed the best way to plan for a secure future.

Between 1950 and 1970, the suburban population more than doubled, from 36 million to 74 million. Fully 20 percent of the population remained poor during this prosperous time. But most families of ample as well as modest means exhibited a great deal of conformity in their consumer behavior, reflecting widely shared beliefs about the good life. They poured their money into homes, domestic appliances, televisions, automobiles, and family vacations. As prosperity spread throughout the 1950s, expenditures for food and clothing increased modestly, and spending on household appliances, recreation, automobiles, and televisions more than doubled. Homeowners moved into more than 1 million new suburban houses each year.

Nuclear families who settled in the suburbs provided the foundation for new types of community life and leisure pursuits, sometimes at the expense of older ones grounded in ethnic neighborhoods and kinship networks. Family-oriented amusement parks such as Disneyland in Anaheim, California, which opened in 1955, catered to middle-class tastes, in contrast to older venues such as Coney Island, known for their thrill rides, class and ethnic mixing, and erotic environments. Religious affiliation rose to an all-time high as Americans built and joined suburban churches and synagogues, complete with youth programs and summer camps. Families shared leisure time gathered around television sets or piled into cars for outings to local drive-in theaters and weekend excursions. In 1949, fewer than 1 million American homes had a television. Within the next four years, the number soared to 20 million.

These suburban families were more prosperous and healthier than ever before. Dreaded childhood diseases were nearly eliminated by advances in science and medicine, especially vaccines. Dr. Jonas Salk became an international hero when he developed the vaccine against polio. In 1952, he gave the vaccine to himself, his wife, and their three children, thereby easing public fears about the dangers of vaccination.

The Distribution of Wealth

The Wider World

After World War II, the countries devastated by the war experienced dramatic economic growth. Postwar economic growth advanced even more quickly in the United States, which had not experienced wartime destruction. The countries of Europe and Japan recovered more slowly with the help of investment by the United States.

By 1960, the United States was by far the wealthiest nation among the major World War II belligerents. This chart, comparing average per capita income, demonstrates that by 1960, on average, Americans were far wealthier than citizens of other industrialized countries. However, the statistics do not show inequalities of wealth, which persisted everywhere.

QUESTIONS

1. What accounts for the high per capita income of the United States in 1960?

2. What might explain the relative affluence of the United Kingdom and Canada compared to the other countries included in the chart?

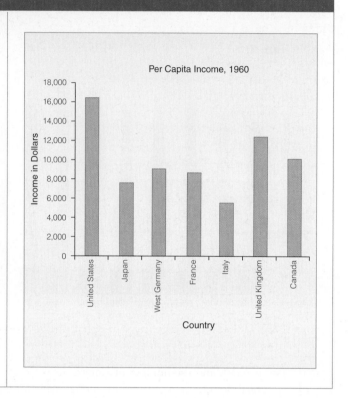

Per Capita Income, 1960

The house and commodity boom had tremendous propaganda value during the Cold War, as Nixon demonstrated in the Kitchen Debate. Although they may have been unwitting soldiers, consumers who marched off to the nation's shopping centers to equip their new homes joined the ranks of Americans taking part in the Cold War. As early as 1947, newscaster and noted cold warrior George Putnam described shopping centers as "concrete expressions of the practical idealism that built America . . . plenty of free parking for all those cars that we capitalists seem to acquire. Who can help but contrast [them] with what you'd find under communism?"

The Cold War made a profound contribution to suburban sprawl. In 1951, the *Bulletin of the Atomic Scientists* devoted an issue to "defense through decentralization" that argued in favor of depopulating the urban core to avoid a concentration of residences or industries in a potential target area for a nuclear attack. Joining this effort was the American Road Builders' Association, a lobbying group second only in power and wealth to the munitions industry. In 1956, Congress passed the Interstate Highway Act, which provided $100 billion to cover 90 percent of the cost for 41,000 miles of national highways. When President Dwight D. Eisenhower signed the bill into law, he stated one of the major reasons for the new highway system: "[In] case of atomic attack on our key cities, the road net must permit quick evacuation of target areas."

The Highway Act had its greatest impact on business and transportation, however. As the largest public works project the nation had ever mounted, this centrally planned transportation system was a boon to the auto, trucking, oil, concrete, and tire industries. In addition, it contributed to the national pastime of family road vacations and tourism. Cheap gas also fueled America's car culture. Cars gave Americans increased mobility and enabled suburban dwellers to drive to work in the cities. But reliance on the automobile doomed the nation's passenger train system and led to the decline of public transportation. Cars also contributed to suburban sprawl, air pollution, and traffic jams.

Few worried about these consequences at the time, however. Many people believed that residential expansion into the suburbs provided protection against labor unrest, which might lead to class warfare. According to the Cold War ethos, class conflict within the United States would weaken the nation and harm its image abroad, bolstering the Soviet Union and making the United States vulnerable to communism. In the suburbs, working-class and middle-class Americans could pursue the American dream of individualism and upward mobility through private life, rather than collective action at work.

The worst-case scenario was communist infiltration within the United States and the defeat of the United States in the Cold War. Pentagon strategists and foreign policy experts feared that the Soviet Union might gain the military might to allow its territorial expansion and, eventually, world domination. But observers also worried about other internal dangers: racial strife, emancipated women, class conflict, and familial disruption. To alleviate these fears, Americans turned to the family as a bastion of safety in an insecure world. Most postwar Americans longed for security after years of economic depression and war and saw family stability as the best bulwark against the new dangers of the Cold War.

RACE, CLASS, AND DOMESTICITY

Many Americans think of the 1950s as a golden era of economic prosperity and happy families nestled in comfortable suburban homes. Large numbers of Americans achieved this lifestyle, but it was not available to everyone. The government subsidized suburban developments and restricted who could live in them. After World War II, the nation faced a severe housing shortage. The federal government gave developers financial subsidies to build affordable single-family homes and offered Federal Housing Authority (FHA) loans and income tax deductions to homebuyers. These benefits enabled white working-class and middle-class families to purchase houses. Second- and third-generation European immigrants moved out of their neighborhoods in the cities and into the suburbs.

In many suburbs, contracts for the sale of houses included restrictions that excluded Jews and prevented racial minorities from purchasing homes in white neighborhoods. Gradually, these restrictions began to lift. But it remained

Park Forest, Illinois, 1953. Courtesy, Sandra Weiner. Photo by Dan Weiner.

■ Commuters, mostly men, left their suburban homes each morning to go to jobs in the cities, returning home at night. Suburbs served as "bedroom communities," inhabited mostly by women and children during the day.

difficult for people of color to move to the suburbs. Despite the expansion of the black and Latino middle class and the increase in home ownership among racial minorities, most suburban developments excluded nonwhites. The FHA and lending banks maintained policies known as **red lining,** which designated certain neighborhoods off limits to racial minorities. They refused mortgage loans to people of color wishing to buy houses in redlined areas, even if the prospective buyers could afford the purchase price, because they feared that property values would decline in racially mixed neighborhoods. Although racial minorities remained concentrated in urban and rural areas, some did move to the suburbs, usually into segregated communities.

For Americans of color, suburban home ownership offered inclusion in the postwar American dream. In her powerful 1959 play *A Raisin in the Sun*, African American playwright Lorraine Hansberry articulated with great eloquence the importance of a home in

> *Although intended to revitalize cities, urban renewal actually accelerated the decay of inner cities and worsened conditions for the urban poor.*

the suburbs, not to assimilate into white America but to live as a black family with dignity and pride. Asian Americans also had good reason to celebrate home and family life. With the end of the exclusion of Chinese immigrants during World War II, wives and war brides began to enter the country, helping build thriving family-oriented communities. After the disruptions and anguish of internment, Japanese Americans were eager to put their families and lives back together. Mexican Americans and Mexican immigrants, including *braceros*, established flourishing communities in the Southwest. Puerto Ricans migrated to New York and other eastern cities, where they could earn four times the average wage on the island.

Racial segregation did not prevail everywhere. For example, in Shaker Heights, Ohio, a suburb of Cleveland, white residents made a conscious decision, as a community, to integrate their neighborhood. Drawing on postwar liberal ideals of civil rights and racial integration, they welcomed black homeowners. They succeeded in this effort by emphasizing class similarity over racial difference. White residents encouraged other white families to move into Shaker Heights, pointing out that their prosperous black neighbors were "just like us." The City of Claremont, California, established an interracial housing cooperative of Mexican and African American residents along with white married college students at the edge of the Arbol Verde barrio, a Mexican American neighborhood. Desegregation experiments such as these established harmonious, racially integrated communities at a time when residential segregation was the norm across the country.

White attitudes toward racial integration began to shift, but only slightly. In the late 1950s, 60 percent of whites outside the South said they would stay in their homes if a black family moved next door, but only 45 percent said they would remain in the neighborhood if large numbers of people of color moved in. In 1964, demonstrating their belief in property rights over civil rights, 89 percent of those polled in the North and 96 percent in the South believed that "an owner of property should not have to sell to a Negro if he doesn't want to." Disapproval of racial integration was strongest in the most intimate realm of life: the family. During the 1950s, most white Americans—92 percent in the North and 99 percent in the South—approved of laws banning marriage between whites and nonwhites. As late as the mid-1960s, more than half of northern whites and more than three-fourths of southern whites still opposed interracial marriage.

As residents and businesses migrated to the suburbs, slum housing and vacant factories remained in the central cities. With declining tax bases, city governments had few resources to rebuild and revitalize urban neighborhoods. The Housing Acts of 1949 and 1954, promising a "decent home and suitable living environment for every American family," granted funds to municipalities for urban renewal. However, few of those federal dollars provided low-income housing. Mayors, bankers, and real estate interests used the money to bulldoze slums and build gleaming office towers, civic centers, and apartment complexes for affluent citizens, leaving the poor to fend for themselves in the remaining dilapidated corners of the cities.

Although intended to revitalize cities, urban renewal actually accelerated the decay of inner cities and worsened conditions for the urban poor. Federally funded projects

Russell Lee/ The Library of Congress

■ At a time when many corporations and professions excluded African Americans, many black entrepreneurs opened their own establishments to serve their own communities. This black-owned dress shop in Chicago catered to middle-class African American women.

often disrupted and destroyed ethnic communities. In St. Paul, Minnesota, the construction of U.S. Highway 94, while enabling suburbanites to commute to the city, obliterated the thriving urban African American neighborhood of Rondo. In Los Angeles, the Dodgers' stadium built in Chávez Ravine offered baseball fans and their families access to the national pastime, but it destroyed the historically rooted Mexican American neighborhood in its path. The $5 million project displaced 7,500 people and demolished 900 homes.

Along with the urban poor, rural Americans reaped few benefits of postwar affluence. Many rural residents had no electricity or running water during the 1950s and therefore had no TV sets or washing machines. Much of rural America, especially in the South, remained poor. The 1950s marked the greatest out-migration from the South as the mechanization of farms—particularly the mechanical cotton picker—reduced the number of workers on the land. More than one-fourth of the population left Kentucky and West Virginia, where unemployment in some areas reached 80 percent.

This underclass of millions of Americans living in poverty was largely hidden from view. In 1962, Michael Harrington's exposé *The Other America* shocked the nation with its portrait of poverty in the midst of prosperity. But in the 1950s, the American media were more preoccupied with the small number of communists in the nation than the vast numbers of impoverished citizens. Most Americans were putting their efforts into achieving the suburban ideal and conforming to its familial expectations.

WOMEN: BACK TO THE FUTURE

The nuclear family ideal of the 1950s included a full-time wife and mother and a breadwinner husband. This vision of domesticity contrasted with the expanded opportunities and experiences for women during World War II. It also masked a major postwar trend: the proportion of women who fit the mold of full-time homemaker was rapidly shrinking.

The National Archives

■ After World War II, women were forced out of most of the high-paying skilled jobs that they had occupied during wartime to make room for the returning men. The jobs available to women were mostly "pink-collar" jobs in the service industry. Here, women operate rolling food carts that enabled a New Jersey factory to feed its workers lunch in a mere twenty minutes.

Although most American women married, had children, and carried the lion's share of responsibility for housework and child-rearing, increasing numbers of married women also held jobs outside the home. The employment of married women began to rise during World War II and kept rising after the war, even though most of the well-paying and highly skilled jobs returned to men at the war's end.

For the majority of white working-class and middle-class women, the end of the war closed off a number of opportunities for occupational training, professional education, and careers. Often a woman's best chance to secure a decent standard of living was to marry a competent breadwinner. But the pressures on blue-collar as well as white-collar men to earn enough money for the trappings of middle-class affluence strained their ability to provide. Married women took jobs to help pay the bills. College-educated women often worked in clerical positions as secretaries or clerks, but these jobs did not make use of their knowledge and skills. Working-class women found work in the "pink collar" service sector in jobs such as waitress and hairdresser—with low pay and few chances for advancement. For most Mexican women, pink-collar work was an improvement over migrant farm labor or factory work. African American women also found these jobs preferable to domestic work in white middle-class homes.

Many women worked part-time while their children were at school, as they considered themselves homemakers, not wage-earners. With few other opportunities for creative work, women embraced their domestic roles and turned homemaking into a profession. Many fulfilled their role with pride and satisfaction and extended their energies and talents into their communities, where they made important contributions as volunteers in local parent-teacher associations (PTAs) and other **civic organizations.** Most postwar mothers finished childbearing by the time they were thirty and had many years ahead of them when their child-rearing responsibilities ended. Some expanded part-time employment into full-time occupations when their children left the nest. Others felt bored and frustrated and drowned their sorrow with alcohol or tranquilizers. In 1963, author Betty Friedan described the constraints facing women as the "problem that has no name" in her feminist manifesto *The Feminine Mystique.*

Despite the powerful cultural expectation that women's primary responsibilities were to care for their homes and families, many single and married women followed alternative paths. Women pursued careers in a wide range of fields, including the arts, business, and politics. Harvard Medical School admitted its first female students in 1945, although the medical profession remained heavily male dominated.

Some women managed to buck the prevailing gender role with ease; others found it difficult. Minnesota Democrat Coya Knudson, a member of the U.S. House of Representatives, paid a heavy price for her political ideals. While she was in Washington, D.C., working to pass legislation for such causes as college scholarships and school lunches, her husband – a notorious and abusive drunkard who never supported his wife's public service – told *Life* magazine that his wife had abandoned her domestic responsibilities to dally in the male world of politics. The article, titled "Coya Come Home," cast aspersions on Knudson's morals and suggested that she neglected her family. She subsequently lost her seat in Congress to a Republican challenger who used "Coya Come Home" as a campaign slogan. Knudson returned to her loveless marriage and dutifully stayed with her husband until his death in 1969. She remained a respected member of her community, although she never ran for office again.

Education was one avenue available to women, as students as well as teachers. But higher education did not fully open its doors to women. Because few women gained access to graduate and professional schools and most well-paying jobs were reserved for men, college degrees for white women did not necessarily open up career opportunities or greatly improve their job and earning prospects. By 1956, one-fourth of white female students married while still in college. Many of these women dropped out of school to take jobs in order to support their husbands through college. But the situation was quite different for black women. Like their mothers and grandmothers, most black women had to work to help support their families. Even in the prosperous postwar years, few black families could survive on the meager earnings of a single breadwinner. Young black women knew that a college degree could mean the difference between working as a maid for a white family and working as a secretary, teacher, or nurse. Although relatively few in number, more than 90 percent of black women who entered college completed their degrees.

Black women also aspired to the role of homemaker, but for very different reasons than white women. Although poverty still plagued large numbers of black citizens, the black middle class expanded during the 1950s. Postwar prosperity enabled some African Americans, for the first time, to strive for family life in which the earnings of men were adequate to allow women to stay home with their own children rather than tending to the houses and children of white families. Celebrating that possibility in 1947, *Ebony* magazine proclaimed: "Goodbye Mammy, Hello Mom." World War II "took Negro mothers out of white kitchens, put them in factories and shipyards. When it was all over, they went back to kitchens—but this time their own. . . . And so today in thousands of Negro homes, the Negro mother has come home, come home perhaps for the first time since 1619 when the first Negro families landed at Jamestown, Virginia." For a black woman, domesticity

Washington Post. Reprinted by permission of the D.C. Public Library

■ On November 1, 1961, 50,000 women in communities across the country took to the streets to protest nuclear testing. Under the sponsorship of Women Strike for Peace, these demonstrators used their authority as mothers, and brought along their children, to highlight their stake in the future.

Rachel Carson, *Silent Spring*

In 1962, Silent Spring, *Rachel Carson's eloquent exposé of the chemical industry's deadly impact on the health of the planet, landed on the best-seller list, where it stayed for months. The book, which eventually sold 1.5 million copies and remains in print today, galvanized the environmental movement of the 1960s and 1970s. Carson called the chemical industry "a child of the Second World War" and creator of "elixirs of death." She reported that annual pesticide production increased from 124 million pounds in 1947 to 637 million pounds by 1960. Twenty years later it had reached 2.4 billion pounds. "In the course of developing agents of chemical warfare," she noted, "some of the chemicals created in the laboratory were found to be lethal to insects. The discovery did not come by chance: insects were widely used to test chemicals as agents of death for man."*

Alfred Eisenstaedt/Getty Images

■ Environmentalist Rachel Carson, author of *Silent Spring*.

It took hundreds of millions of years to produce the life that now inhabits the earth—eons of time in which that developing and evolving and diversifying life reached a state of adjustment and balance with its surroundings. The environment, rigorously shaping and directing the life it supported, contained elements that were hostile as well as supporting. Certain rocks gave out dangerous radiation; even within the light of the sun, from which all life draws its energy, there were short-wave radiations with power to injure. Given time—time not in years but in millennia—life adjusts, and a balance has been reached. For time is the essential ingredient; but in the modern world there is no time.

meant "freedom and independence in her own home." It is no wonder that in the early 1960s, women of color bristled when white feminists such as Betty Friedan called upon women to break free from the "chains" of domesticity.

MOBILIZING FOR PEACE AND THE ENVIRONMENT

Some women did not wait for the new feminist movement to make their voices heard. Marine biologist Rachel Carson was one such woman. She wrote several books and articles, including her 1951 best-seller *The Sea Around Us*. Carson became increasingly concerned about the impact of manufactured chemicals on the environment, especially the insecticide DDT, which had been poisoning the earth since World War II. Her 1962 book *Silent Spring* brought attention to the worldwide problem of pesticide poisoning and helped launch the environmental movement that has flourished ever since.

Women also led the movement to stop the testing and proliferation of nuclear weapons. On November 1, 1961, 50,000 suburban women in more than 60 communities staged a protest, Women Strike for Peace (WSP). Participants lobbied government officials to "End the Arms Race—Not the Human Race." The strikers were mostly educated, middle-class mothers; 61 percent did not work outside the home. WSP leaders were part of a small group of feminists who had worked on behalf of women's rights throughout the 1940s and 1950s. According to *Newsweek* magazine, the strikers "were perfectly ordinary looking women. . . . They looked like the women you would see driving ranch wagons, or shopping at the village market, or attending PTA meetings. . . . Many [were] wheeling baby buggies or strollers." Within a year their numbers grew to several hundred thousand. The FBI kept the group under surveillance, and in 1962 the leaders were called before the House Un-American Activities

The rapidity of change and the speed with which new situations are created follow the impetuous and heedless pace of man rather than the deliberate pace of nature. Radiation is no longer merely the background radiation of rocks, the bombardment of cosmic rays, the ultraviolet of the sun that have existed before there was any life on earth; radiation is now the unnatural creation of man's tampering with the atom. The chemicals to which life is asked to make its adjustment are no longer merely the calcium and silica and copper and all the rest of the minerals washed out of the rocks and carried in rivers to the sea; they are the synthetic creations of man's inventive mind, brewed in his laboratories, and having no counterparts in nature.

To adjust to these chemicals would require time on the scale that is nature's; it would require not merely the years of a man's life but the life of generations. And even this, were it by some miracle possible, would be futile, for the new chemicals come from our laboratories in an endless stream; almost five hundred annually find their way into actual use in the United States alone. The figure is staggering and its implications are not easily grasped—500 new chemicals to which the bodies of men and animals are required somehow to adapt each year, chemicals totally outside the limits of biologic experience.

Among them are many that are used in man's war against nature. Since the mid-1940s over 200 basic chemicals have been created for use in killing insects, weeds, rodents, and other organisms described in the modern vernacular as "pests"; and they are sold under several thousand different brand names.

These sprays, dusts, and aerosols are now applied almost universally to farms, gardens, forests, and homes—nonselective chemicals that have the power to kill every insect, the "good" and the "bad," to still the song of the birds and the leaping of fish in the streams, to coat the leaves with a deadly film, and to linger on in the soil—all this though the intended target may be only a few weeds or insects. Can anyone believe it is possible to lay down such a barrage of poisons on the surface of the earth without making it unfit for all life? They should not be called "insecticides" but "biocides."

QUESTIONS

1. *What connection does Carson make between time and the environment?*

2. *Why does Carson believe insecticides should be called biocides?*

Committee (HUAC). Under questioning, these women spoke as mothers, claiming that saving American children from nuclear extinction was the essence of "Americanism." They brought their babies to the hearings and refused to be intimidated by their congressional inquisitors as supporters cheered and threw flowers from the gallery. These women carried the banner of motherhood into political activism, much as their nineteenth-century predecessors had done.

Decades later, the antinuclear protesters would be vindicated—unfortunately too late for many people exposed to radiation during the early years of the Cold War. At the time, the real dangers of nuclear testing had not yet come to light. But in the 1980s and 1990s, declassified top-secret documents confirmed that people living in the path of fallout from nuclear test sites, as well as military personnel working at or near the sites during the 1940s and 1950s, suffered disproportionately from cancer and other illnesses caused by radioactivity.

The Civil Rights Movement

■ *What were the major goals of the civil rights movement in the 1950s?*

Persistent racial discrimination proved to be the nation's worst embarrassment throughout the Cold War. Black leaders and federal officials understood that the national government needed to promote civil rights at home to save face abroad. The Soviet Union and other communist countries pointed to American race relations as an indication of the hypocrisy and failure of the American promise of freedom for all. Yet national leaders paid only lip service to racial justice and failed to provide the strong support necessary to defeat "Jim Crow," the system of racial segregation in the South. Jim Crow was a legal, or *de jure*,

■ **MAP 25.1 The Nuclear Landscape**

The production and testing of nuclear weapons affected many regions across the country, especially in the West and South. Sites established during World War II remained active during the Cold War, as the nuclear arms race accelerated. The sites included testing grounds, uranium mining areas, laboratories, and plants where weapons were manufactured.

set of institutions that prevailed throughout the South. Although the nation's leaders acknowledged the need to address Southern segregation, they did nothing to address the unofficial, or *de facto*, segregation that prevailed throughout the rest of the country.

Nevertheless, at the grassroots level, racial minorities continued to work for equal rights. For example, Mexican Americans in the Southwest continued to press for desegregation of schools, residential neighborhoods, and public facilities through organizations such as the middle-class League of United Latin American Citizens (LULAC) and the Asociación Nacional México-Americana (ANMA), a civil rights organization that emerged out of the labor movement. Slow progress was made before 1963, when the power of the civil rights movement—and the violence of southern white opposition—finally compelled the federal government to take action.

BROWN V. BOARD OF EDUCATION

DOCUMENT

Brown v. Board of Education of Topeka, Kansas

The first major success in the struggle to dismantle the Jim Crow system in the South came in the 1954 Supreme Court decision in *Brown v. Board of Education*. Civil rights strategists decided to pursue their cause in the courts rather than through Congress. They knew that southern Democrats in Congress, who held disproportionate power through their seniority and control of major committees, would block any civil rights legislation that came before the House or Senate.

They believed that they had a better chance of success through the courts.

Initially, civil rights attorneys worked within the system of segregation. The *Plessy v. Ferguson* decision in 1896 justified Jim Crow laws on the principle of providing "separate but equal" facilities. The civil rights attorneys argued that southern school systems violated the segregation laws because the separate, racially segregated schools were far from equal. In Clarendon County, South Carolina, for example, public funds provided $179 per white child but $43 per black child. Soon the lawyers shifted their strategy to claim that "separate" was inherently unequal and began the push to overturn *Plessy v. Ferguson*. Leading the charge was Thurgood Marshall, general counsel of the NAACP and a graduate of Howard University Law School.

The NAACP lawyers filed suit against the Topeka, Kansas, Board of Education, on behalf of Linda Brown, a black child in a segregated school. The case reached the U.S. Supreme Court, where NAACP general counsel Thurgood Marshall argued that separate facilities, by definition, denied African Americans their equal rights as citizens. A key argument in the case was the psychological effect of the stigma of segregation on black children. Psychologist Kenneth Clark, testifying as an expert witness, gave evidence showing that black children educated in segregated schools developed a negative self-image and responded more positively to white dolls than to black dolls. Although this argument was persuasive with the Court and helped to bring about school desegregation, some black leaders at the time objected to the use of that psychological argument. Those critics of the strategy argued that black children did not need to interact with white children in order to gain self-esteem and pointed to the positive influence of black teachers who believed in their students' capabilities. They claimed that low self-esteem among black children resulted from widespread discrimination against black Americans, not simply black students' lack of interaction with white students.

In 1953, during the three-year period that the Supreme Court had the *Brown* case before it, President Eisenhower appointed Earl Warren as chief justice. Warren had been state attorney general and then governor of California during World War II and had approved the internment of Japanese Americans—a decision he later deeply regretted. He now used his political and legal skills to strike a blow for justice. He knew that such a critical case needed a unanimous decision to win broad political support. One by one, he persuaded his Supreme Court colleagues of the importance of striking down segregation. On May 17, 1954, Warren delivered the historic unanimous ruling: "To separate [black children] from others of similar age and qualifications solely because of their race generates a feeling of inferiority as to their status in the community that may affect their hearts and minds in a way unlikely ever to be undone. . . . We conclude that in the field of public education the doctrine of 'separate but equal' has no place. Separate educational facilities are inherently unequal."

Ed Clark/Getty Images

■ Children in segregated schools studied in wretched physical conditions but benefited from dedicated African American teachers. The Supreme Court struck down school segregation in the landmark 1954 case *Brown v. Board of Education*, arguing in its unanimous decision that separate facilities were inherently unequal.

WHITE RESISTANCE, BLACK PERSISTENCE

Winning the *Brown* case was a great triumph, but it was only the first step. Desegregation would be meaningful only when it was enforced, and that was another matter entirely. At first, there seemed to be some cause for optimism. In Hoxie, Arkansas, for example, the all-white-male school board agreed to integrate the schools, believing it was the right thing to do. Integration happened easily and without incident. Black and white children got along well and their families—long accustomed to living side by side in this small southern town—had almost no problems with their children attending integrated schools. But when the national media showcased Hoxie's successful integration, segregationists from Little Rock came to the town and mobilized some of the white residents to fight against integration. The resulting turmoil led to the resegregation of Hoxie's schools.

In the face of the kind of organized resistance that destroyed integration efforts in places like Hoxie, local officials were reluctant to implement the *Brown* decision. The national government did little to enforce integration. Even the Supreme Court delayed its decision on implementation for a full year and then simply called for the process to begin "with all deliberate speed" but specified no timetable. Political leaders did not come forward to work on the task, leaving sympathetic educators and eager black Americans with no support.

President Eisenhower expressed neither "approbation nor disapproval" of the *Brown* decision. Instead of calling for immediate desegregation, he said, "I don't think you can change the hearts of men with laws or decisions." Eisenhower remarked that "the Supreme Court decisions set back progress in the South at least fifteen years. . . . The fellow who tries to tell me that you can do these things by force is just plain nuts."

In 1955, the year after *Brown v. Board of Education,* white Mississippians murdered fourteen-year-old Emmett Till for allegedly whistling at a white woman. The boy had come from Chicago to Mississippi, where he was visiting relatives. His mutilated body was found in the Tallahatchie River. Although Till's killers later confessed to the murder, an all-white jury found them not guilty. Eisenhower remained silent about Till's murder and the travesty of justice, even when E. Frederic Morrow, his one black adviser, beseeched him to condemn the lynching.

Eisenhower's hands-off policy emboldened southern segregationists to resist the Supreme Court's desegregation decision. When it became clear that the federal government would do nothing to enforce the ruling, white resistance spread across the South. State legislatures passed resolutions vowing to protect segregation, and most southern members of Congress signed the 1956 "Southern Manifesto" promising to oppose federal desegregation efforts.

A crisis at Central High School in Little Rock, Arkansas, finally forced Eisenhower to act. Under a federal district court's order to desegregate, school officials were prepared to comply and had carefully mobilized community support. But Arkansas Governor Orville Faubus, facing reelection, decided to play the race card. Using Central High's integration plan as his target, he created a crisis by instructing state National Guard troops to maintain "order" by blocking the entry of black students into the school.

■ Teacher Marjorie Beach with an integrated kindergarten class in Washington, D.C., as the school year began in September 1954 following the Supreme Court's ruling in *Brown v. Board of Education* the previous spring.

© Bettmann/CORBIS

■ **MAP 25.2** **Major Events of the Civil Rights Movement, 1953–1963**

Most of the major events of the early stages of the black freedom struggle took place in the South. Black south-erners formed the backbone of the movement, but the grassroots protest movement drew participants from all regions of the country, all racial and ethnic groups, cities and rural areas, churches and universities, old and young, lawyers and sharecroppers.

Eisenhower initially refused to intervene in the crisis. Hoping for a compromise, he met with Faubus, who agreed to allow the school to integrate peacefully. But Faubus broke his word, withdrew the National Guard troops, and left Little Rock, leaving the black students unprotected. On September 23, 1957, as nine black students attempted to enter Central High, a huge crowd of angry whites surrounded them. With international news cameras broadcasting pictures of the shrieking and menacing mob, Eisenhower took action to stop the embarrassing fracas. Furious at Faubus for his insubordination, Eisenhower denounced the "disgraceful occurrence," federalized the Arkansas National Guard, and sent 1,000 para-troopers to Little Rock. Unwilling to "acquiesce in anarchy and the dissolution of the union," Eisenhower acted to maintain federal authority. Although the Little Rock Nine, as the coura-geous students came to be called, finally gained entry to Central High, Governor Faubus closed the schools in Little Rock for the entire next year. Out of 712 school districts that had desegregated after the *Brown* decision, only 49 remained desegregated by the end of Eisenhower's term. Most of the others reverted to segregation.

BOYCOTTS AND SIT-INS

Schools were not the only segregated institutions in the South. Under Jim Crow laws, black passengers were required to sit in the back section of buses, leaving the front of the bus for whites. If the "white" section at the front of the bus filled up, black passengers were required to give up their seats in the rear for white passengers. On December 1, 1955, Rosa Parks and the black community of Montgomery, Alabama, were ready to take on the system. Parks, who worked as a seamstress, was a widely respected leader in Montgomery's black commu-nity, active in her church, and secretary of the local NAACP. On her way home from work that day, sitting in the first row of the "colored" section of the bus when the front of the bus filled with passengers, she refused to move when a white man demanded her seat. Parks was arrested, and black Montgomery sprang into action.

Literally overnight, the Montgomery bus boycott was born. E. D. Nixon, president of the Alabama NAACP and the head of the local chapter of the Brotherhood of Sleeping Car Porters, and Jo Ann Robinson, the leader of the local Women's Political Council (a black alternative to the segregated League of Women Voters), mobilized the boycott. They gathered with fifty community representatives that night at the Dexter Avenue Baptist Church to plan strategy. They mobilized other black churches to spread the word to their congregations on Sunday, and black-owned taxi companies geared up to take the place of buses. By Monday, all of black Montgomery had heard the news of the boycott. The buses that day were empty of black riders. For 381 days, more than 90 percent of Montgomery's black citizens sacrificed their comfort and convenience for the sake of their rights and dignity. As one elderly black woman replied when a white reporter offered her a ride as she walked to work, "No, my feets is tired but my soul is rested."

> *For 381 days, more than 90 percent of Montgomery's black citizens sacrificed their comfort and convenience for the sake of their rights.*

Martin Luther King Jr., pastor of the Dexter Avenue Baptist Church, was a newcomer to Montgomery when the bus boycott began. He embraced the opportunity to become the leader of the boycott and, eventually, the most powerful spokesperson for the civil rights movement. His stirring and impassioned words inspired thousands of black citizens to join the cause. As he told the 5,000 listeners who gathered in his church on the first night of the boycott, "If you will protest courageously and yet with dignity and Christian love, in the history books that are written in future generations, historians will have to pause and say, 'there lived a great people—a black people—who injected a new meaning and dignity into the veins of civilization.' This is our challenge and our overwhelming responsibility."

The bus boycott ended a year later when the Supreme Court ruled that Montgomery's buses must integrate. The momentum generated by the boycott galvanized the civil rights movement. King and other leaders formed the Southern Christian Leadership Conference (SCLC), which united black ministers across the South in the cause of civil rights. The boycott tactic spread to other southern cities. As boycotts continued, a new strategy emerged: the **sit-in.**

On February 1, 1960, four African American students at North Carolina Agricultural and Technical College in Greensboro, inspired by the example of the bus boycott, entered the local Woolworth store and sat down at the lunch counter. When they were told, "We do not serve Negroes," they refused to leave, forcing the staff at Woolworth's to physically remove the nonviolent protesters. Undaunted, the students returned to the lunch counter the next day with twenty-three classmates. By the end of the week, more than a thousand students joined the protest. By this time, white gangs had gathered, waving Confederate flags and menacing the black undergraduates. But the students responded by waving American flags. An expression of their patriotism as well as their political shrewdness, the flag identified the protestors not as subversives acting against social order but as citizens claiming the values and identity of the nation.

In May 1961, members of the Congress of Racial Equality (CORE) organized the Freedom Rides, in which black and white civil rights workers attempted to ride two interstate buses from Washington, D.C., to New Orleans in an effort to challenge segregation at facilities used in interstate travel. Their journey began peacefully, but when they reached Rock Hill, South Carolina, a group of whites beat John Lewis, one of the young black riders, for entering a whites-only rest room. In Anniston, Alabama, a mob slashed the tires of one of the buses, threw a fire bomb through a window, and pummeled the riders with fists and pipes. After the brutal beatings, reinforcements from the Student Nonviolent Coordinating Committee (SNCC) arrived to continue the Freedom Rides. They persevered, facing beatings along the way until they reached Jackson, Mississippi, where they were immediately arrested and jailed for violating local Jim Crow laws. By August, 300 additional protesters had been locked in the jail, all refusing bail. The spirit and strength of the civil rights workers inspired many others to join them in the movement. They came from all over the South as well as the North, white as well as black, giving up comfort and safety, risking—and in some cases sacrificing—their lives. Many of those who survived remained active in the movement and dedicated their lives to political change. John Lewis, for example, survived being beaten on the Freedom Rides to continue civil rights work with Martin Luther King Jr. and was later elected to Congress from Georgia.

The Eisenhower Years

■ *How was Eisenhower's foreign policy advanced through covert operations and cultural diplomacy?*

Dwight D. Eisenhower, elected president in 1952, chose not to provide strong support for the civil rights movement. A respected and widely admired World War II general, Eisenhower could have used his leadership to bolster the cause. His reluctance to do so allowed southern segregationists to block implementation of the *Brown* decision and opened the way for violent resistance to the civil rights movement. His presidency was notable largely for moderation and maintaining the status quo, with very few major new initiatives and a style of leadership that rested more on his personal stature than his actions. Ike, as he was known, presided over the nation during a time of great prosperity, and his policies encouraged business expansion. However, the former general did try to stem the defense buildup. Eisenhower tried to fight the Cold War in a fiscally responsible manner. In his farewell address at the end of his second term as president, Eisenhower warned the nation against the growing power of the **military-industrial complex**, the term he coined to describe the armed forces and the politically powerful defense industries that supplied arms and equipment to them.

THE MIDDLE OF THE ROAD

Born in Texas, raised in Kansas, and educated at the U.S. Military Academy at West Point, Eisenhower became a career soldier who served as the supreme commander of the Allied forces in western Europe during World War II. Eisenhower planned and carried out the daring Allied invasion at Normandy on D-Day. As early as 1948, both the Democrats and the Republicans courted Eisenhower as a presidential candidate. But he resisted, believing that military leaders should not get involved in politics; indeed, he had never even registered to vote. In 1952, however, when he was president of Columbia University, he changed his mind and accepted the Republican nomination, choosing California Senator Richard M. Nixon—known as a dogged anticommunist crusader—as his running mate. The Democrats nominated Illinois Governor Adlai E. Stevenson. The cerebral Stevenson, dubbed an "egghead" by the press, was no match for the former general, whose supporters donned campaign buttons boasting "I Like Ike." The popular Eisenhower won the election with the largest landslide up to that time and was reelected by an even wider margin in 1956.

As president, Eisenhower pursued a path down the middle of the road. His pro-business legislative agenda and appointments pleased conservatives, and he gratified liberals by extending many of the policies of the welfare state enacted during the New Deal. He agreed to the expansion of Social Security and unemployment compensation and an increase in the minimum wage. He also made concerted efforts to reduce defense spending, believing that continued massive military expenditures would hinder the nation's economic growth. In December 1953, Eisenhower announced the New Look, a streamlined military that relied less on expensive conventional ground forces and more on air power and advanced nuclear capabilities.

TABLE 25.1			
The Election of 1956			
Candidate	**Political Party**	**Popular Vote (%)**	**Electoral Vote**
Dwight D. Eisenhower	Republican	57.6	457
Adlai E. Stevenson	Democratic	42.1	73

■ American popular culture reflected the playful part of the Cold War, poking fun at the competition between the superpowers. Here a customer in an Atlanta, Georgia, restaurant eagerly anticipates her first bite of a "Sputnikburger," complete with a large satellite olive pierced with three toothpicks for antennae, and topped with a miniature cocktail hotdog.

DOCUMENT

National Defense
Education Act

Eisenhower's plans to reduce defense spending derailed on October 4, 1957, when the Soviet Union launched *Sputnik*, the first artificial Earth satellite. Although *Sputnik* could not be seen with the naked eye—it was only 22 inches in diameter and weighed only 184 pounds—it emitted a beeping noise that was broadcast by commercial radio stations in the United States, making its presence very real and causing near hysteria among the public. The Soviet's launching of *Sputnik II* a month later seemed to confirm widespread fears that the United States was behind in the space race and, more significantly, in the arms race. Eisenhower's popularity in the polls suddenly dropped 22 points.

Acquiescing to his critics, the president allotted increased funds for military, scientific, and educational spending. NASA, which developed the program of space exploration, was one result of this increase. But Eisenhower believed that "the most critical problem of all" was the lack of American scientists and engineers. He led the federal government to subsidize additional science and math training for both teachers and students. He also called for an improvement in overall education so that the next generation would be "equipped to live in the age of intercontinental ballistic missiles." On September 2, 1958, Eisenhower signed Public Law 85–864, also known as the National Defense Education Act (NDEA), which authorized more than $1 billion in education spending.

Throughout his presidency, Eisenhower maintained a hands-off policy toward big business. His secretary of defense, former head of General Motors Charles Wilson, made the memorable comment that "what's good for General Motors business is good for America." But not everyone agreed. Eisenhower's pro-business policies had a harmful impact on the nation's environment. Eisenhower promoted the passage of the Submerged Land Act, which removed from federal jurisdiction more than $40 billion worth of oil-rich offshore lands. Under the control of state governments, oil companies could—and did—gain access to them. The *New York Times* called the act "one of the greatest and surely the most unjustified give-away program" in the nation's history. The administration's willingness to allow businesses to expand with little regulation, and with virtually no concern for the environment, contributed to increasing pollution of the air, water, and land during the 1950s and helped spark the environmental movement of the 1960s and 1970s.

EISENHOWER'S FOREIGN POLICY

The New Look, Eisenhower's plan for a streamlined defense establishment, contained military spending and shifted American military priorities from reliance on conventional weapons to nuclear deterrence and covert operations. An experienced military leader, Eisenhower understood the risks involved in warfare. Shortly after taking office, he ended the Korean War with a truce rather than escalating the conflict in pursuit of victory.

During Eisenhower's presidency, the United States and the Soviet Union both solidified their separate alliances. The North Atlantic Treaty Organization (NATO), formed in 1949, increased American influence in western Europe. The twelve NATO nations agreed that an attack on any

The Family Fallout Shelter

In the early years of the Atomic Age, homeowners were encouraged to provide protection for their families in case of a nuclear attack. Official government pamphlets, construction companies, and popular journals offered advice on how best to prepare for a possible nuclear war. In 1961, *Life* magazine featured the Carlson family posing in their own fallout shelter. The article accompanying this photograph of the Carlsons emphasizes family togetherness as well as individual responsibilities based on age and gender. The tone of the article is upbeat and cheerful, and the shelter itself is stocked with games and supplies to make the family's confinement in the shelter as comfortable and enjoyable as possible.

The Cuban missile crisis sparked a rash of shelter building, but relatively few Americans actually constructed shelters. This type of protection was available only to those with single-family houses and either yards or basements with space to construct them. In addition, questions about effectiveness, cost, and the world into which surviving citizens would emerge after an attack discouraged most Americans from investing in private shelters. Nevertheless, the family fallout shelter and the civil defense drills in schools

Time & Life Pictures/Getty Images

Envisioning History

that accompanied the onset of the Atomic Age became eerie icons of the era.

QUESTIONS

1. According to the photograph and the text, what were the expected roles for men and women in the Atomic Age?

2. What do the demeanor, expressions, and positions of the family members in this photograph suggest about the psychological impact of the Atomic Age?

one of them would be considered an attack on all, and they maintained a force to defend the West against a possible Soviet invasion. NATO expanded in 1952 to include Greece and Turkey, and West Germany joined in 1955. The Soviet Union formed a similar alliance, the Warsaw Pact, with the countries of eastern Europe. Confrontations between the United States and the Soviet Union over the fate of Europe gave way to more subtle maneuvers regarding the Third World—a term originally referring to non-aligned nations in the Middle East, Africa, Asia, and Latin America.

After Joseph Stalin died in 1953, Nikita Khrushchev became the new leader of the Soviet Union and called for peaceful coexistence with the United States. To limit military expenditures and improve relations, the superpowers arranged high-level summit meetings. In 1955, delegates from the United States, the Soviet Union, Britain, and France met in Geneva. Although the meeting achieved little of substance, it set a tone of cooperation. In 1959, Khrushchev came to the United States, met with Eisenhower, and toured the country. Despite the Soviet downing of an American U-2 spy plane in 1960 and the capture of American pilot Gary Powers, the superpowers began to discuss arms limitation. Both countries agreed to limit aboveground testing of nuclear weapons in light of the health and environmental risks such tests posed.

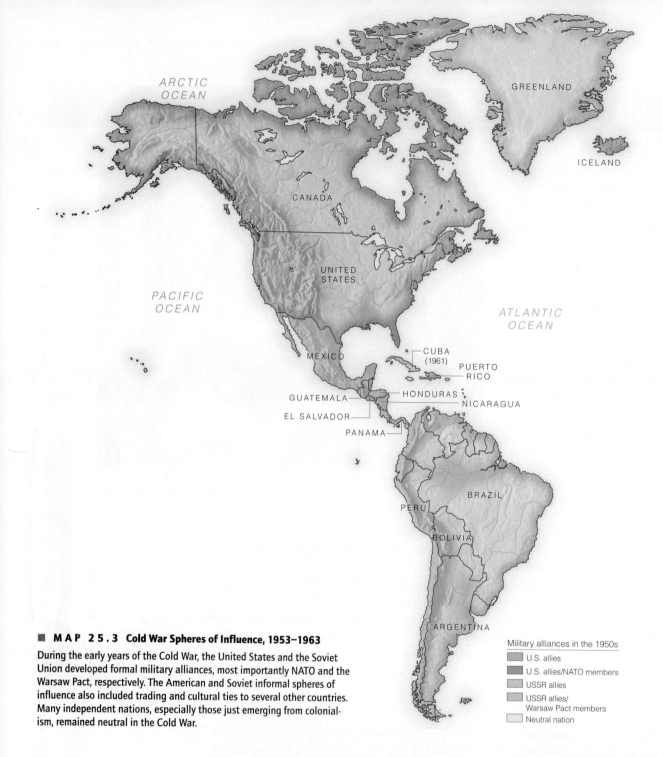

■ MAP 25.3 Cold War Spheres of Influence, 1953–1963
During the early years of the Cold War, the United States and the Soviet
Union developed formal military alliances, most importantly NATO and the
Warsaw Pact, respectively. The American and Soviet informal spheres of
influence also included trading and cultural ties to several other countries.
Many independent nations, especially those just emerging from colonial-
ism, remained neutral in the Cold War.

Military alliances in the 1950s
- U.S. allies
- U.S. allies/NATO members
- USSR allies
- USSR allies/Warsaw Pact members
- Neutral nation

As the United States and the Soviet Union worked toward greater cooperation, they
faced challenges from within their separate "spheres of influence" and vied for the loyalty of
newly independent states in the Third World. In 1956, the Soviet Union faced armed uprisings in Poland and Hungary, two "satellite" nations chafing under Soviet domination. In
Poland, rebels resisting Moscow's control took to the streets, demanding that the Soviet
Union recognize Wladyslaw Gomulka, who had been an opponent of Stalin, as the leader of
Poland. After three days of fighting, the Soviet Union capitulated to the rebels' demand. In
Hungary, maverick communist Imre Nagy took power and pledged to create a multiparty
democracy. As revolution spread across Hungary, Soviet troops brutally crushed the rebel-
lion, killing Nagy and thousands of other Hungarians.

While the United States and the Soviet Union competed with each other to gain influence in Third World countries, leaders from those countries came together to discuss ways to
achieve self-determination. In April 1955, in Bandung, Indonesia, representatives from

twenty-nine nations—primarily from Asia, Africa, and the Middle East—met in what President Sukarno of Indonesia called "the first international conference of colored peoples in the history of mankind." Nearly all the participants came from countries that had previously been colonized by western European countries. Most were former colonies of Britain, France, Belgium, Holland, or Portugal. Although they shared no specific political ideology, the conference carried an implicit condemnation of Western powers and a commitment to eliminating the vestiges of colonialism and racial discrimination worldwide. Suspicious of the motives of the participants and worried about the outcome, Eisenhower sent no greeting to the gathering and tried to ignore or sabotage it. However, Adam Clayton Powell, one of three black members of the U.S. Congress, attended the conference as a "journalist," providing an unofficial U.S. presence.

The Eisenhower administration continued to distrust countries that maintained neutrality in the Cold War, fearing that those not aligned with the United States might turn to communism and become allies of the Soviet Union. In 1956, Secretary of State John Foster Dulles declared that neutrality "is an immoral and shortsighted conception." Anticommunism became the guiding principle behind nearly all U.S. foreign policy, taking precedence over other American ideals, such as support for democratically elected governments and national self-determination. Acting on its anticommunist priority, the United States helped overthrow democratically elected leaders and prop up corrupt and often brutal dictatorships.

The Central Intelligence Agency (CIA) was a major player in this drama, with 15,000 agents working around the world by the end of the 1950s. Congress established the CIA in 1947 to gather strategic intelligence from foreign countries and to engage in covert political activity. Through

Anticommunism became the guiding principle behind nearly all U.S. foreign policy, taking precedence over other American ideals.

covert operations in 1953, the CIA helped overthrow the elected government in Iran—which had seized control of Western-owned oil fields in the country—and restore the dictatorship of Shah Reza Pahlavi, whose unpopular Western-leaning regime would be overthrown by Islamic fundamentalists in 1979. In 1954, the CIA helped overthrow the elected government of Jacobo Arbenz in Guatemala. U.S. officials considered Arbenz a communist because he sought to nationalize and redistribute large tracts of land, much of it owned by the Boston-based United Fruit Company. Eisenhower also supported unpopular anticommunist dictators in Peru and Venezuela. In 1958, Latin Americans expressed their displeasure when Vice President Richard M. Nixon, on a goodwill tour of South America, faced angry protesters wherever he went. Nixon was nearly killed in Caracas, Venezuela, when demonstrators attacked his motorcade.

In 1959, revolutionary leader Fidel Castro overthrew Cuba's U.S.-friendly dictator Fulgencio Batista. Castro established a regime in Cuba based on socialist principles. His government took control of foreign-owned companies, including many owned by Americans. Castro's socialist policies alarmed U.S. officials and investors in Cuba. Eisenhower's hostility encouraged Castro to forge an alliance with the Soviet Union. The CIA then launched a plot to overthrow Castro, which would culminate in an ill-fated invasion in 1961. In 1960–1961, the CIA also helped orchestrate the overthrow and assassination of charismatic left-leaning Patrice Lumumba, the first minister of the Republic of the Congo in Africa, soon after its independence from Belgium.

U.S. policymakers, with their anticommunist preoccupations, and people in Third World countries, with their campaigns against colonialism and racism, had little interest in each other's priorities. A case in point was Egypt, where in 1952 Gamal Abdul Nasser overthrew the corrupt monarchy of King Farouk and established a government neutral in the Cold War. In 1954, Nasser declared himself prime minister of the new government and accepted aid from both the United States and the Soviet Union. When Nasser engaged in trade with Soviet-bloc countries and extended diplomatic recognition to communist China, the United States canceled loans that were to support the building of the huge Aswan Dam, a major development project for the Egyptian economy. In response, Nasser nationalized the British-controlled Suez Canal in 1956, arguing that canal tolls would provide alternative funding for the dam. The British government, with the help of France and Israel, launched an attack against Egypt to regain control of the canal.

Although he distrusted Nasser, Eisenhower strongly criticized Britain for its effort to retain its imperial position in the Middle East. To avoid further antagonizing Nasser and other Third World leaders, Eisenhower denounced Britain's Suez attack and threatened economic sanctions, forcing the British to back down. Although leaders in Africa and Asia applauded Eisenhower's actions, the episode weakened U.S. relations with Nasser, who forged ties with the Soviet Union. Eisenhower now feared that "Nasserism" might spread throughout the Middle East.

In the spring of 1957, Congress approved the Eisenhower Doctrine, a pledge to defend Middle Eastern countries "against overt armed aggression from any nation controlled by international communism." However, U.S. policymakers rarely distinguished between nationalist movements and designs by "international communism," which they defined as Soviet aggression. Because American leaders believed that struggles for national self-determination in Third World countries were inspired and supported by the Soviet Union, they used the Eisenhower Doctrine to provide justification for U.S. military intervention to support pro-Western governments. When leaders in Lebanon and Jordan appeared friendly to Nasser, Eisenhower stepped in, sending 14,000 U.S. marines to Lebanon and setting up an anti-Nasser government there. Britain intervened in Jordan, restoring King Hussein to the throne.

CULTURAL DIPLOMACY

In addition to power politics and military interventions, American foreign policy during the early Cold War era promoted cultural relationships. Initiatives geared toward promoting international friendship and a positive view of the United States, especially in the developing world, were part of American "cultural diplomacy." Cultural diplomacy included programs developed by agencies and individuals to provide assistance to Third World countries and peoples.

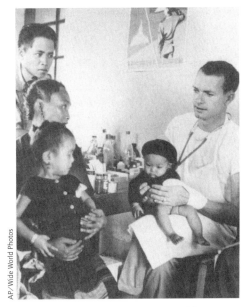

Dr. Tom Dooley is pictured here providing medical care to Laotian children. Known as the "jungle doctor," he represented American expertise and benevolence, as well as fervent anticommunism, during the early years of the Cold War.

One of the earliest and most successful individuals to promote American cultural diplomacy was Dr. Tom Dooley, known as the "jungle doctor." A native of St. Louis and a devout Catholic, Dooley joined the U.S. Navy medical corps during World War II and remained in the navy reserves until 1950. After earning his medical degree, he moved to Southeast Asia, where he set up clinics to provide medical care for impoverished villagers. He quickly became a major celebrity. In a 1960 Gallup poll, Dooley was among the ten most admired Americans. President Dwight D. Eisenhower said of Dooley, "Few, if any, men have equaled [Dooley's] exhibition of courage, self-sacrifice, faith in his God and his readiness to serve his fellow man." When Dooley died of cancer in 1961 at the age of thirty-four, he was honored by Congress and posthumously awarded the U.S. Navy's Legion of Merit. His legacy helped inspire John F. Kennedy's creation of the Peace Corps.

Dooley's life personifies the complex legacy of U.S. cultural diplomacy during the early years of the Cold War. Although he was a practicing Catholic, he rejected the role of the religious missionary—a role largely discredited in the anticolonial post–World War II years as tied to racist and imperialist designs. Rather, Dooley promoted modernization and development, embracing an internationalist vision that was grounded in respect and appreciation for the local culture and customs of the people with whom he lived. Dooley was the model for the protagonist of the best-selling novel *The Ugly American*, written by Far East correspondent William Lederer and political theorist Eugene Burdick, both navy veterans. *The Ugly American* was a scathing attack on American diplomats working in Asia who had disdain for Asian people and who never bothered to learn the language, history, or cultures of the countries where they were stationed. In contrast to the arrogant diplomats, the character modeled on Dooley was sensitive to the people and well loved. As a result, he was the most effective ambassador for the nation, in contrast to the official diplomats who often fostered dislike for Americans.

Dooley's zeal to help the people of Southeast Asia went far beyond medical care. A passionate anticommunist, in 1956 he assisted the Central Intelligence Agency (CIA) and the U.S. Navy in leading the exodus of 900,000 Catholic refugees from newly created communist North Vietnam to South Vietnam, where the United States backed a noncommunist dictatorship under Ngo Dinh Diem. He recounted that experience in a best-selling book, *Deliver Us from Evil*, and wrote two other books that chronicled his activities at the clinics he founded in the villages and jungles of Laos. His books praised Diem's regime in South Vietnam and promoted the cause of anticommunism in Southeast Asia. He portrayed himself as a peaceful crusader against communism who spread American values in Southeast Asia and opposed imperialism. The CIA supported Dooley's efforts and helped publicize his cultural diplomacy.

Dooley's work in Southeast Asia provided essential medical care to people in need and also served American interests in the early years of the Cold War. But his decision to live and work in the remote villages of Laos was not based simply on self-sacrifice. As a homosexual, Dooley would have had a difficult life within the United States in the 1950s. Anticommunist crusaders purged homosexuals from government employment, and gay men and lesbians faced harassment, ostracism, and often the loss of their jobs. Dooley escaped the intense homophobia of his home country by creating communal living situations with other men in remote areas of Laos, far from public view. There he could keep his sexual orientation private. If he had remained in the United States, the anticommunists whose political passions he shared would have purged him from their ranks.

OUTSIDERS AND OPPOSITION

The 1950s often are remembered as a time of political and cultural complacency among white Americans, with most of the opposition to the nation's institutions emanating from people of color. There is a good deal of truth to this picture. But some young whites, in the South as well as North, joined in the struggle for civil rights; their numbers increased in the 1960s. Others were drawn to the music and dance of black America, especially the fusion of rhythm-and-blues with country-and-western, which took the form of early rock 'n' roll. Distinct forms of protest also emerged from within the white middle class: the rebellion of the Beats who rejected staid conformity, the stirrings of discontent among women, and the antinuclear and environmental movements. The arts also reflected a rejection of mainstream values, as Jackson Pollock and other abstract expressionist painters challenged the artistic conventions of the time and shifted the center of the art world from Paris to New York. Even the sexual revolution of the 1960s had its roots in widespread defiance of the rigid sexual codes of the 1950s.

One clue that all was not tranquil in America was the widespread panic that the nation's young were out of control. Adult authorities worried about an epidemic of juvenile delinquency, blaming everything from parents to comic books. New celebrities such as movie stars Marlon Brando and James Dean portrayed misunderstood youth in rebellion against a corrupt and uncaring adult world. In the classic youth movie *Rebel Without A Cause*, Dean plays a good-hearted but angry young man who suffers from a domineering mother and a wimpish apron-clad father who refuses to stand up to her. When asked, "What are you rebelling against, Johnny?" Brando's tough-guy character in *The Wild One* answers, "I dunno; what've you got?" In these films, and in J. D. Salinger's novel *Catcher in the Rye*, young women and men strain against the authority and expectations of their parents and the adult world, dreaming of freedom and personal fulfillment.

Sexual mores were rigid in the 1950s—and widely violated. Single young women who became pregnant faced disgrace and ostracism unless they married quickly, which many did. Abortion, which had been

Rudolph Burckhardt/Sygma/CORBIS

■ Jackson Pollock shocked the art world when he began dripping paint on large canvases. Abstract expressionist painters like Pollock celebrated their break from conventional forms and representations. National leaders embraced abstract expressionism as symbolic of American artistic freedom, and thousands of Americans hung reproductions of abstract art on the walls of their suburban homes.

illegal since the late nineteenth century but tacitly accepted until after World War II, became increasingly difficult to obtain, with hospitals placing new restrictions on legal therapeutic abortions. Illegal abortionists who had long practiced without interference faced increasing harassment, forcing the practice underground, where it became much more dangerous. A double standard encouraged men to pursue sexual conquest as a mark of manhood and virility but tarnished the reputation of women who engaged in sexual intercourse prior to marriage. Nevertheless, young men and women frequently violated those rigid sexual mores. When the oral contraceptive pill, which came on the market in 1960, provided relatively safe and effective birth control, it was hailed initially as a boon to family planning. But the pill also eased fears of pregnancy for single women and helped to usher in the sexual revolution of the 1960s.

In many ways, the youth of the 1950s were already undermining the constraints that toppled in the next decade. Nowhere is this development more obvious than in the explosion of rock 'n' roll, with its roots in African American rhythm-and-blues, its raw sexuality, and its jubilant rebelliousness. Chuck Berry's hit "School Days" expressed youthful restlessness, and Little Richard's "Long Tall Sally" and "Rip It Up" exulted in sensual pleasure. Bill Haley and his Comets invited youngsters to "Rock Around the Clock."

Photofest

■ In *The Wild One* (1954), Marlon Brando portrayed a young man angry at the world. The young actor from Omaha, Nebraska, had already earned acclaim on Broadway. Two decades later he won an Oscar playing the title role in *The Godfather* (1972).

Rock 'n' roll emerged out of the fusion of musical traditions. Artists from many ethnic backgrounds experimented with a variety of forms. Jewish songwriters Jerry Leiber and Mike Stoller wrote dozens of songs for black artists, including "Hound Dog" for black blues singer Willie Mae Thornton, later recorded by white Southerner Elvis Presley. The first Mexican American rock 'n' roll star, Ritchie Valens, sang romantic ballads such as "Donna" along with jazzed-up versions of Mexican folk songs like "La Bamba." Rosie and the Originals—an all-girl band led by Mexican American Rosie Mendez—sang rock 'n' roll hits such as "Angel Baby."

Performances as well as lyrics carried erotic power. Chuck Berry pumped his electric guitar and shimmied across the stage, Little Richard danced on top of the piano and tore off his shirt, and James Brown begged "Please, please, please," while collapsing on the floor. Elvis Presley thrust his hips in his trademark style, sending young audiences into a frenzy. Criticism of his sexually charged gyrations persuaded producers to show him only above the waist during his appearance on Ed Sullivan's TV show. Rock 'n' roll music and dancing added powerful elements of sexuality and rebellion to the youth culture of the 1950s. Many of those impulses found political expression in the 1960s.

Youth were not the only ones rebelling; men, too, were in revolt. According to widely read sociological tracts of the time, including William Whyte's *The Organization Man*, C. Wright Mills's *White Collar*, and David Riesman's *The Lonely Crowd*, middle-class men were trapped in boring, routinized jobs, groomed to be "outer-directed" at the expense of their inner lives, and saddled with the overwhelming burden of providing for ever growing families with insatiable consumer desires.

A few highly visible American men provided alternative visions. Hugh Hefner built his Playboy empire by offering men the trappings of the "good life" without its burdensome responsibilities. The Playboy ethic encouraged men to enjoy the sexual pleasures of attractive women without the chains of marriage and to pursue the rewards of consumerism in well-appointed "bachelor flats" rather than appliance-laden homes. *Playboy*

Social Welfare History Archives, University of Minnesota Libraries, American Social Health Association Records, box 179

■ Since sex was rarely discussed in most middle-class families, many parents relied on schools to provide elementary sex education, and a generation of suburban children learned the facts of life from nervous teachers and a variety of simplified texts.

magazine celebrated this lifestyle, epitomized in the airbrushed photographs of nearly nude, young, female "bunnies" who seemed to promise sex without commitment.

Beat poets, writers, and artists offered a very different type of escape. In their literary works, such as Allen Ginsberg's poem *Howl* and Jack Kerouac's epic *On the Road*, and in their highly publicized lives, the Beats celebrated freedom from conformity, eccentric artistic expression, playful obscenity, experimentation with drugs, open homosexuality, and male bonding. While eschewing the sort of luxurious consumerism Hefner extolled, the Beats shared with the Playboy ethic a vision of male rebellion against conformity and responsibility. The mainstream men who indulged in these fantasies were more likely to enjoy them vicariously than to bolt from the breadwinner role. The dads who were honored on the new consumer holiday of Father's Day far outnumbered the freewheeling Beats and bachelors.

The Kennedy Era

■ *How did Kennedy's foreign and domestic policies differ from those of Eisenhower?*

Embodying both the spirit of youth and rugged masculinity was Eisenhower's successor, John Fitzgerald Kennedy, the first American president born in the twentieth century and the first Roman Catholic president. In his inaugural address, Kennedy claimed that "the torch has been passed to a new generation." It was a fitting metaphor for a young man who had been reared to compete and to win, whether the contest was athletic, intellectual, or political. But at the time of his election, it was not clear that a new generation had grabbed the torch. The young candidate was largely the creation of his father, Joseph, whose forebears had emigrated from Ireland during the 1840s. Joseph Kennedy rose to power and wealth as a financier, Hollywood executive, and ambassador to England. Ambitious and demanding, the elder Kennedy was known for his ruthlessness in business and politics and for his blatant philandering. He groomed his oldest son, Joseph P. Kennedy Jr., for greatness, specifically for the presidency. But when young Joe was killed in World War II, the father's ambitions settled on the next in line, John.

John F. Kennedy became a hero during World War II, winning military honors for rescuing his crewmates on his patrol boat, PT-109, when it was rammed by a Japanese destroyer. The rescue left him with a painful back impairment and exacerbated the symptoms of Addison's disease, which plagued him all his life and necessitated daily cortisone injections. His father coached him to bear up under the pain, hide his infirmity, and project an image of health and vitality. "Vigor" was a word Kennedy used often and an aura he projected, inspiring a national craze for physical fitness that survives to this day. Young JFK also emulated his father's brash sexual promiscuity, even after his marriage to Jacqueline Bouvier in 1953.

In 1946, Kennedy won election to the House of Representatives, and in 1952 he defeated the incumbent Republican Henry Cabot Lodge to become the Democratic senator from Massachusetts. JFK's father financed all of his political campaigns, and in 1960 the elder Kennedy bankrolled and masterminded JFK's narrowly successful run for the White House. Kennedy selected as his running mate the powerful Senate majority leader, Lyndon B. Johnson

WATCH

Kennedy–Nixon Debate

of Texas, whom he had battled for the nomination. Concerned that his Catholicism would be a liability in the campaign, Kennedy spoke publicly about his faith, explaining that his religious beliefs would not interfere with his ability to do the job.

Just before the election, with the help of his brother Robert—whom he later appointed attorney general—Kennedy arranged to have Martin Luther King Jr. released from prison in Georgia, where hostile authorities had sentenced him to six months in jail for a minor traffic violation. This intervention secured the African American vote for Kennedy and the support of other minorities. Mexican Americans formed "Viva Kennedy" clubs throughout the Southwest. Voters of color helped Kennedy defeat his Republican foe, Eisenhower's vice president, Richard Nixon, by a slim margin.

TABLE 25.2			
The Election of 1960			
Candidate	**Political Party**	**Popular Vote (%)**	**Electoral Vote**
John F. Kennedy	Democratic	49.9	303
Richard M. Nixon	Republican	49.6	219

KENNEDY'S DOMESTIC POLICY

With such a thin margin of victory, Kennedy lacked a popular mandate for change. But he quickly established himself as an eloquent leader. In his inaugural address, the new president inspired the nation with his memorable words, "And so, my fellow Americans, ask not what your country can do for you; ask what you can do for your country." Focusing his address on foreign policy, he declared: "Let every nation know . . . that we shall pay any price, bear any burden, meet any hardship, support any friend, oppose any foe to assure the survival and the success of liberty." In his first two years, he sought mainly to avoid division at home and to wage the Cold War forcefully abroad. He believed that prosperity was the best way to spread the fruits of affluence, rather than government programs that would promote a redistribution of wealth. Accordingly, he supported corporate tax cuts to stimulate the economy, which grew at a rate of 5 percent each year from 1961 to 1966.

Although Democrats held strong majorities in both houses, powerful southern conservatives often teamed up with Republicans to form a functional majority in Congress to defeat reform legislation. Kennedy knew that it would be futile to champion the cause of civil rights in the face of that alliance. But he did support issues important to his working-class constituents and proposed a number of legislative initiatives, including increasing the minimum wage, health care for the aged, larger Social Security benefits, and the creation of the Department of Housing and Urban Development (HUD).

When the steel industry challenged Kennedy's authority and threatened his economic policy by announcing a major price increase shortly after he had helped negotiate a new contract with the steel union that would have kept prices stable, he mobilized all the power of his administration to force the steel magnates to back down. Kennedy also demonstrated strong leadership in the space program, presiding over the first manned space flight and declaring that the United States would land a man on the moon by the end of the 1960s.

DOCUMENT

John F. Kennedy, Space Program Speech

KENNEDY'S FOREIGN POLICY

Kennedy was the first U.S. president to understand and recognize the legitimacy of movements for national self-determination in the Third World. In 1957, while still in the Senate, he gave a speech calling on the French to grant independence to Algeria, which was still under French rule. As president, he endeavored to support movements to end colonial rule while at the same time containing the spread of communism. His efforts earned him a great deal of goodwill among Africans and other non-Europeans. But if nationalist movements appeared friendly to the Soviet Union, Kennedy worked against them. He sharply increased military spending and nuclear arms buildup as a show of strength and preparedness against possible Soviet aggression.

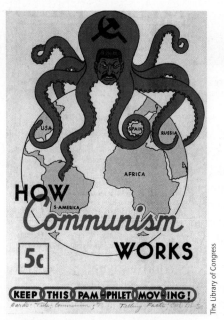

The Library of Congress

■ Anticommunist pamphlet published by the Catholic Library Service.

One of Kennedy's most popular initiatives was the creation of the Peace Corps, a program that sent Americans, especially young people, to nations around the world to work on development projects. In 1961, Kennedy signed the Charter of Punta del Este with several Latin American countries, establishing the Organization of American States (OAS) and the Alliance for Progress, a program designed to prevent the spread of anti-Americanism and communist insurgencies in Latin America. The alliance offered $20 billion in loans to OAS countries for democratic development initiatives.

Kennedy continued the strategies of Truman and Eisenhower to fight communism in South Vietnam by supporting the corrupt regime of Ngo Dinh Diem. But the National Liberation Front (NLF), founded in 1960 and supported by Ho Chi Minh's communist regime in North Vietnam, gained the upper hand in its struggle against Diem. In response, Kennedy increased the number of military advisers in South Vietnam from 800 to 17,000. By 1963, it was obvious that Diem's brutal regime was about to fall to the NLF, and Kennedy allowed U.S. military advisers and diplomats to encourage Diem's overthrow.

Kennedy also faced a crisis brewing in Cuba. Fidel Castro's revolution initially represented the sort of democratic insurgency that Kennedy wanted to support. But Castro's socialism turned the United States against him, and he established close ties with the Soviet Union. Kennedy now saw the strategically located island as a major threat where "communist influence . . . festers some 90 miles off the coast of Florida." During the Eisenhower administration, the CIA began planning an invasion of Cuba with the help of Cuban exiles in Florida. Kennedy's national security advisers persuaded Kennedy to allow the invasion to proceed.

On April 17, 1961, U.S.-backed and -trained anticommunist forces, most of them Cuban exiles, landed at the Bahía de Cochinas (Bay of Pigs) on the southern coast of Cuba. Castro expected the invasion—his agents in Florida had infiltrated the Cuban exiles—so his well-prepared troops quickly surrounded and captured the invaders. No domestic uprising against Castro occurred to support the invasion. Kennedy quickly realized that his only chance of success would be to call in the military with large-scale air support. Unwilling to take that step, Kennedy pulled back in humiliating defeat, telling his adviser Clark Clifford, "I have made a tragic mistake." Nevertheless, the president continued to support covert efforts that tried but failed to destabilize Cuba and assassinate Castro.

Another crisis soon erupted in Berlin. Located 200 miles deep in East Germany, with only two highways connecting it to West Germany, West Berlin was a showcase of Western material superiority and an espionage center for the Western powers. In June 1961, Khrushchev threatened to end the Western presence in Berlin and unite the city with the rest of East Germany. His plan was motivated in part to stop the steady stream of East Germans into West Berlin. Kennedy refused to relinquish West Berlin. On August 13, 1961, the East German government constructed a wall to separate East and West Berlin. Guards patrolled the wall with orders to shoot anyone who tried to cross, and many who tried lost their lives. Two years later, Kennedy stood in front of the wall and pledged to defend the West Berliners, making his memorable statement of solidarity, "*Ich bin ein Berliner*" ("I am a Berliner").

The most serious foreign policy crisis of Kennedy's presidency came in 1962, when the Soviet Union, at Castro's invitation, began to install intermediate-range nuclear missiles in Cuba. Kennedy's close advisers presented a series of options for actions that could be taken in response. The most dramatic and dangerous would be a full-scale military invasion of the island, which would topple Castro but would surely prompt military retaliation by the Soviet Union. Another option was a more limited military intervention, an air strike to destroy the missiles before they became operational. Others proposed a blockade of Cuban ports to prevent the missiles from entering. Another possibility was to negotiate secretly with Castro, Soviet leaders, or both. Kennedy decided against behind-the-scenes negotiations as well as the drastic move of military intervention and instead established a "quarantine" around the island to block Soviet ships from reaching Cuba, hoping that the Soviet Union would back down and withdraw the missiles. A quarantine, unlike a blockade, was not considered an act of war; nevertheless, Kennedy put the Strategic Air Command on full alert for possible nuclear war.

The Cuban Missile Crisis

It was a risky move. On national television, Kennedy warned the Soviet Union to remove the missiles or face the military might of the United States: "We will not prematurely or unnecessarily risk the costs of worldwide nuclear war in which even the fruits of victory would be ashes in our mouth, but neither will we shrink from that risk at any time it must be faced." Khrushchev accused Kennedy of bringing the two nations to the brink of nuclear war. For the next five days, tensions mounted as Russian ships hovered in the water beyond the quarantine zone. Finally Khrushchev proposed an agreement, offering to remove the missiles if the United States would agree not to invade Cuba. Kennedy also privately promised to remove missiles in Turkey as soon as the crisis was over. The two leaders managed to diffuse the crisis, but they were both sobered by the experience of having come to the brink of nuclear war. They soon established a telephone "hotline" linking the White House and the Kremlin for quicker communication in any future crisis. In 1963, the two leaders signed a nuclear test ban treaty.

1963: A YEAR OF TURNING POINTS

The test ban treaty was one of several markers of change in 1963. That same year, the President's Commission on the Status of Women, which Kennedy had appointed under the leadership of Eleanor Roosevelt, published a report that documented widespread discrimination against women in jobs, pay, education, and the professions. In response to the findings, Kennedy issued a presidential order requiring the civil service to hire people "without regard to sex" and supported passage of the Equal Pay Act of 1963. The commission's report, along with the publication the same year of Betty Friedan's call to arms, *The Feminine Mystique*, provided fuel for the feminist movement that burst across the nation in the next few years.

Also in 1963, in Birmingham, Alabama, Martin Luther King Jr. led a silent and peaceful march through the city. Chief of Police Bull Connor unleashed the police, who blasted the demonstrators with fire hoses and attacked them with police dogs. Four black children were later killed when segregationists bombed an African American church. The Kennedy administration responded by bringing the full force of its authority to bear on the officials in Birmingham. But the crisis intensified. Alabama's segregationist governor, George Wallace, refused to admit two black students to the University of Alabama, threatening to stand in the doorway to block their entrance.

Finally, on June 10, 1963, Kennedy federalized the Alabama National Guard and for the first time went before the American people to declare himself forcefully on the side of the civil rights protesters and to propose a civil rights bill. The violence in the South had raised "a moral issue," he declared, "as old as Scriptures and...as clear as the Constitution." A few months later, on August 28, more than 250,000 people gathered at the nation's capital in front of the Lincoln Memorial for the culmination of the March on Washington, a huge demonstration for jobs as well as freedom, where Martin Luther King Jr. delivered his inspiring "I Have a Dream" speech.

Civil Rights March on Washington

In the fall of 1963, a confident Kennedy began planning his reelection campaign for the next year. To mobilize support, he visited Texas. "Here we are in Dallas," he said on November 22, 1963, "and it looks like everything in Texas is going to be fine for us." Within an hour of uttering those optimistic words, the president lay dying of an assassin's bullet.

In the days following President Kennedy's assassination, as shock and grief spread across the nation, a bizarre series of events confounded efforts to bring the assassin to justice. Police arrested Lee Harvey Oswald, who had previously lived in the Soviet Union

CHRONOLOGY: 1953–1963

1953	CIA engineers coup in Iran, restores shah to power.
1954	*Brown v. Board of Education* outlaws school segregation.
1955	Polio vaccine approved for use.
	Disneyland opens in Anaheim, California.
	Montgomery, Alabama, bus boycott begins.
1956	Interstate Highway Act.
1957	Central High School in Little Rock, Arkansas, integrated.
	USSR launches satellite *Sputnik*.
1958	National Defense Education Act.
1959	Nixon–Khrushchev Kitchen Debate.
	Cuban Revolution.
1960	Oral contraceptive pill comes on the market.
	Beginning of lunch counter sit-ins (Greensboro, North Carolina).
1961	Bay of Pigs invasion of Cuba.
	Berlin Wall constructed.
1962	Rachel Carson, *Silent Spring*.
	Cuban missile crisis.
1963	Lyndon B. Johnson becomes president after assassination of John F. Kennedy.
	Equal Pay Act of 1963.
	Betty Friedan, *The Feminine Mystique*.

and who had loose ties to organized crime. Oswald claimed that he was innocent. But before he could be brought to trial, Oswald himself was murdered. Jack Ruby, a nightclub owner who also had links to organized crime, shot Oswald while he was in the custody of the Dallas police—an event witnessed by millions on live television. Ruby later died in prison. The newly sworn-in president, Lyndon B. Johnson, appointed a commission to investigate the assassination under the leadership of Supreme Court Chief Justice Earl Warren. The Warren Commission eventually issued a report concluding that Oswald and Ruby had both acted alone. The commission findings created a heated controversy. Many people at the time and since believed that there was evidence of a conspiracy. In 1978, a panel of the House of Representatives suggested that Kennedy may have been the victim of a plot, possibly involving the Mafia. Conspiracy theories continue to circulate to this day, finding expression in dozens of books, articles, and motion pictures.

At the time, however, the nation simply mourned. Americans were stunned, horrified, and grief-stricken at the murder of the young and widely admired president. Coming at a time of peace and prosperity when optimism prevailed throughout the nation, the Kennedy assassination began a slow but persistent trend toward national disillusionment, increasing during the Johnson administration as racial problems persisted and the war in Vietnam escalated, and reaching tragic depths with the assassinations of Martin Luther King Jr., African American leader Malcolm X, and senator and presidential candidate Robert Kennedy later in the decade.

Conclusion

During the years between the election of Dwight D. Eisenhower and the assassination of John F. Kennedy, the nation experienced unprecedented prosperity as increasing numbers of Americans moved into middle-class suburbs and enjoyed the fruits of a rapidly expanding consumer economy. Men and women rushed into marriage and childbearing, creating the baby boom and a powerful domestic ideology resting on distinct gender roles for women and men. At the same time, the Cold War set the tone for foreign policy as well as domestic life, fostering fears of nuclear war, intense anticommunism, and pressures to conform to mainstream political and cultural values.

Beneath the apparently tranquil surface, anxiety and discontent simmered. Some Americans began to resist the limitations and exclusions of the widely touted "American way of life." African Americans in the South demanded their rightful place as full citizens, challenging the Jim Crow system and accelerating the civil rights movement through nonviolent protests, boycotts, and sit-ins. Young people created a vibrant youth culture to the pulsating rhythms of rock 'n' roll. Beatniks, peace activists, and environmentalists expressed incipient political and cultural dissent.

President Dwight D. Eisenhower personified the politically moderate side of the 1950s. He promoted business interests but worried about the growth of the "military-industrial complex" and reluctantly supported the civil rights movement. John F. Kennedy's election in 1960 ushered in a new era of Cold War militance, tempered by caution in the face of the Cuban missile crisis. He also actively supported the civil rights movement at home and anticolonialism abroad. Kennedy inspired many young Americans to become involved in politics. His assassination in 1963 traumatized the nation. But by that time the rumblings of vast social change had already begun and would explode in the years ahead, pushed along by a divisive war in Vietnam.

For Review

1. Who had access to the postwar suburban ideal? Who was excluded, and why?

2. What were the expected gender roles of the 1950s, and how were they challenged?

3. What strategies did civil rights activists develop and use? How effective were they? What resistance did they encounter?

4. Why is the decade of the 1950s considered a time of conformity?

5. How did Eisenhower steer a path down the "middle of the road"?

6. Who rebelled against the status quo in the 1950s, and why?

7. What marked Kennedy as a new type of president?

8. Why was 1963 a turning point?

Created Equal Online

For more *Created Equal* resources, including suggestions for sites to visit and further reading, go to **MyHistoryLab.com**.

Chapter 26

The Vietnam War and Social Conflict, 1964–1971

■ A native of New York City, Bob Moses graduated from Hamilton College in upstate New York and did graduate work at Harvard University. He was inspired by the sit-in movement that began in 1960 in the American South and soon moved south to join SNCC.

The soft-spoken black man with the strange northern accent first showed up in small-town McComb, Mississippi, in the summer of 1961. Robert Parris Moses had come on a mission of democracy. An organizer for the new Student Nonviolent Coordinating Committee (SNCC), he was there to encourage impoverished African Americans to register to vote. Over the next four years in the Deep South, Bob Moses paid a price for his commitments. Local police imprisoned him, and white supremacists beat him severely and murdered dozens of his fellow activists in the black freedom movement. But Moses remained committed to nonviolence and racial integration. His quiet courage became legendary in the movement. One summer night in 1962, he returned to a deserted SNCC office in Greenwood, Mississippi, that had just been ransacked by a white mob. Three other SNCC workers had barely escaped with their lives.

Moses simply looked around, made up a bed in the corner of the devastated main room, and went to sleep. He refused to be intimidated.

During the 1960s, an extraordinary number of idealistic young people became involved in public life in an effort to make real their nation's promises of freedom, justice, and equality. The civil rights movement inspired the social movements that followed: for ending the war, for preserving the environment, and for securing the rights of women, Latinos, Indians, and gay men and lesbians. But organizing for change inevitably brought activists up against fierce resistance from what they called "the establishment." Disillusionment and radicalization often followed. Public life became deeply contentious by 1968 as young radicals challenged more conservative citizens on issues of race, war, and gender.

The escalating American war in Southeast Asia loomed over all. Lyndon Johnson brought the nation to its apex of liberal reform with his extensive Great Society legislation. However, the high-flying hopes of Democratic liberals crashed to earth with the destructive war that the Johnson administration waged against seasoned communist revolutionaries in far-off Vietnam. Out of the wreckage of 1968 emerged a Republican president, Richard Nixon, and a growing conservative backlash against the social changes advocated by people of color, the counterculture, the antiwar movement, and the rising tide of women's liberation.

Lyndon Johnson and the Apex of Liberalism

■ *What did Johnson hope to achieve with his Great Society programs?*

Wealth provided the foundation on which the **Great Society** was built. American economic expansion after World War II had created history's richest nation by 1960. From 1961 to 1966, the economy accelerated at an annual growth rate of more than 5 percent with very low inflation, stimulated by large tax cuts and extensive military spending. The 41 percent increase in per capita income during the 1960s was not evenly distributed, however. Economist Paul Samuelson explained in 1970, "If we made an income pyramid out of a child's blocks, with each layer portraying $1000 of income, the peak would be far higher than the Eiffel Tower, but almost all of us would be within a yard of the ground." And the distribution of wealth (stocks and real estate) was far more skewed than that of income. The president and the Congress believed that economic expansion would continue indefinitely and the nation could therefore afford government policies to improve the welfare of less affluent Americans. In the same years, the Supreme Court expanded individual liberties in important ways.

THE NEW PRESIDENT

Lyndon Baines Johnson was one of the most remarkable American characters of the twentieth century. Journalist David Halberstam called him "a man of stunning force, drive and intelligence, and of equally stunning insecurity"—both a giant among political leaders and a bully with those who worked for him. Johnson grew up in a family struggling to stay out of poverty in the Texas hill country west of Austin. He entered Democratic politics early as an avid supporter of Franklin Roosevelt and the New Deal, aided by the business savvy and loyalty of his wife, Lady Bird Johnson, who grew wealthy through ownership of TV and radio stations. As

■ Lyndon Johnson took the presidential oath of office on board Air Force One, returning to Washington from Dallas, where John Kennedy had just been assassinated on November 22, 1963. His wife, Lady Bird, is on his right, and Jacqueline Kennedy, still in blood-stained clothes, stands on his left. Johnson adroitly channeled the public outpouring of grief for the murdered young president into support for their shared legislative goals.

First Lady, she became widely known for her leadership in highway beautification. Lyndon Johnson rose like a rocket through Congress to become perhaps the most powerful Senate majority leader ever (1954–1960) and then vice president (1961–1963). Kennedy's assassination catapulted him into the Oval Office as the nation's first Texan president.

Like his home state, Johnson was physically big and at times intimidating. His earthy humor and homely style contrasted sharply with Kennedy's telegenic sophistication. Eastern elites cringed at the idea of Johnson as Kennedy's successor in the White House; the fact that Kennedy was killed in Texas did not help. But Johnson retained Kennedy's cabinet and advisers and used the memory of the fallen young president to rally support for his administration. Johnson turned out to be the more liberal of the two men, in part because as a young man, Johnson taught in a rural Mexican American school, and this experience had given him a firsthand understanding of poverty and discrimination that his predecessor lacked. Johnson's focus was different, too. He retained Kennedy's anticommunist commitments abroad, but his heart remained at home. "I don't want to be the President who built empires, or sought grandeur, or extended dominion," he told the nation. He wanted to perfect American society: to enhance American security by refashioning the central nation of the "free world" into a model for all others.

First he had to win reelection. Less than a year remained until voters went to the polls in 1964. The Republicans nominated right-wing Senator Barry Goldwater of Arizona, a sign of the party's sharp swing away from its moderate northeastern elements toward its conservative western and southern constituencies. Conservative organizers such as the Young Americans for Freedom thought that Republican leaders such as Dwight Eisenhower and Richard Nixon were too much like Democrats. Goldwater instead believed in unrestricted markets and a

TABLE 26.1			
The Election of 1964			
Candidate	**Political Party**	**Popular Vote (%)**	**Electoral Vote**
Lyndon B. Johnson	Democratic	61.1	486
Barry M. Goldwater	Republican	38.5	52

minimal role for the federal government in every aspect of American life except the military. He spoke casually about using nuclear weapons against communists abroad. Goldwater declared that "extremism in the defense of liberty is no vice," but Johnson zeroed in on that extremism and swept to the largest electoral majority of any president (61 percent). Voters also chose the most liberal Congress since the Great Depression. Few realized then that Goldwater, not Johnson, was the better indicator of where American politics would soon be heading.

THE GREAT SOCIETY: FIGHTING POVERTY AND DISCRIMINATION

DOCUMENT

Johnson, "The War on Poverty"

In pursuit of what he called the Great Society, Johnson first declared a "War on Poverty." No citizen in the richest nation on earth should live in squalor, he believed. The president's sensitivity to this issue, despite his personal rise to wealth, fit with a growing national concern, stimulated in part by political activist Michael Harrington's widely read book *The Other America* (1962). The poor were everywhere, from decaying inner cities to rural areas such as Appalachia. More than one out of five Americans lived below the conservatively estimated official poverty line ($3,022 for a nonfarm family of four in 1960), and 70 percent of them were white.

The president and a large congressional majority passed several measures to alleviate poverty. They sharply increased the availability of money and food stamps through the Aid to Families with Dependent Children ("welfare") program, and they raised Social Security payments to older Americans. Several programs focused on improving educational opportunities as an avenue out of poverty: Head Start offered preschool education and meals for youngsters, the Elementary and Secondary Education Act sent federal funds to the least affluent school districts, and an expanded system of student loans facilitated access to college. The Job Corps provided employment training, and Volunteers in Service to America (VISTA) served as a domestic Peace Corps, funneling people with education and skills into poor communities to serve as teachers and providers of other social services.

How well did these programs work? Americans have debated this question ever since. Some defended the programs as reducing the number of people living in poverty and giving educational and employment opportunities to many previously deprived of such chances. Critics on the right believed that the programs instead encouraged dependence on government and thus actually worsened the problem. Critics on the left argued that the programs did not go far enough in attacking the root causes of poverty and were never sufficiently funded because of the Vietnam War. Three conclusions seem clear about the War on Poverty. First, it did not eliminate poverty. Second, it did help reduce the number of poor people by one-third between 1960 and 1969 (from 22 percent to 14 percent). Third, the elderly benefited most from the higher payment schedules put into place by the War on Poverty, as the share of Americans over age sixty-five in the poor population dropped from 40 percent in 1959 to 16 percent by 1974.

No barrier to opportunity in the early 1960s was higher than the color bar. Both opportunist and idealist, Johnson as president shed his segregationist voting record (necessary for election in Texas before 1960) and became the most vocal proponent of racial equality ever to occupy the Oval Office. Two factors facilitated his change in position. One, blatant inequalities for American citizens weakened the United States in its competition with the Soviets and Chinese for the loyalty of the nonwhite Third World majority. Two, the African American freedom struggle in the South had reached a boiling point. Black frustration was mounting over white brutality and the seeming indifference or even hostility of the national government. The persistence of local organizers across the South, such as Bob Moses, forced the U.S. government to move.

The Civil Rights Act of 1964 fulfilled the implicit promise of the *Brown v. Board of Education* decision a decade earlier. The 1964 act made desegregation the law of the land as it

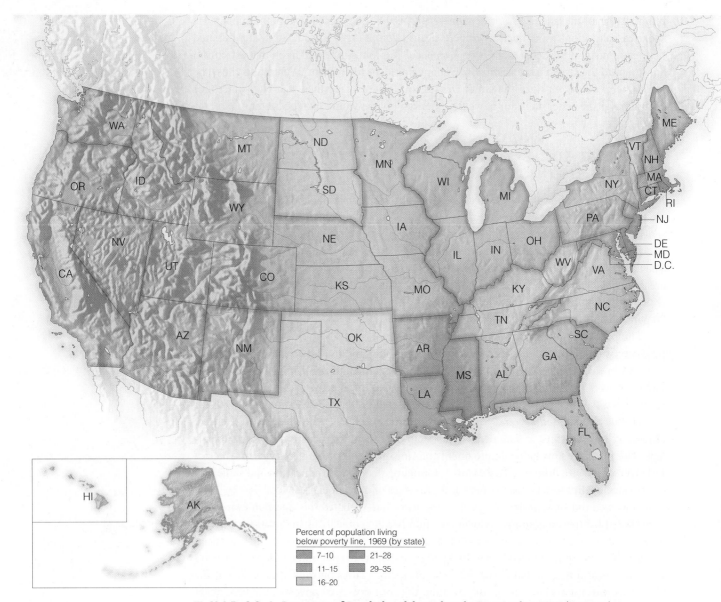

Percent of population living
below poverty line, 1969 (by state)

- 7–10
- 11–15
- 16–20
- 21–28
- 29–35

■ **MAP 26.1 Percentage of Population Living Below the Poverty Line, 1969 (By State)**
The United States in the 1960s was a nation of unprecedented wealth and comfort. Yet millions of Americans still lived in poverty. Prodded by other reformers, President Johnson sought to reduce the number of impoverished citizens through the Great Society programs. The southeastern and south-central states had the highest poverty rates, a legacy of slavery and limited industrialization.

outlawed discrimination in employment and in public facilities such as restaurants, theaters, and hotels. The Civil Rights Act also included women as a minority group. When Alabama police beat peaceful marchers on the Edmund Pettis Bridge outside Selma on March 7, 1965, horrifying most national television viewers, Johnson seized the opportunity to push the Voting Rights Act through Congress. This legislation provided federal voting registrars in states that refused the ballot to African Americans. The single most important legislation of the twentieth century for bringing political democracy to the South, the Voting Rights Act increased the percentage of blacks voting in Mississippi from 7 percent to 60 percent in two years. Black electoral power began to bring unprecedented change to Dixie's political and racial landscape. Also in 1965, a new Immigration Act eliminated the discriminatory national-origins system, with most immigrants thereafter arriving from Asia and Latin America rather than Europe.

MAP

**Impact of the Voting
Rights Act of 1965**

THE GREAT SOCIETY: IMPROVING THE QUALITY OF LIFE

Johnson's vision of the Great Society extended to the broader quality of life in the United States. Health care was perhaps the most fundamental issue for citizens' sense of personal security. After 1965, the new Medicare system paid for the medical needs of Americans over sixty-five, and Medicaid underwrote health care services for the poor. Rising concern about the quality of corporate products led to new federal efforts to protect citizens as consumers. In 1964, when more than half of adults smoked tobacco, the surgeon general issued the first government report linking smoking to cancer. A year later, consumer advocate Ralph Nader used research studies to show that Chevrolet's sporty new Corvair was "unsafe at any speed." Despite industry resistance, higher federal standards for automotive safety followed. Public pressure also led to the establishment of new requirements for publishing the nutritional values of packaged food. The federally funded Public Broadcasting System (PBS) was established to provide television programs that were more educational than the fare tied to advertising on the three corporate networks (NBC, CBS, and ABC). In fact, most Great Society measures targeted all Americans rather than just the disadvantaged.

Nothing more directly threatened the quality of American life than the degradation of the natural environment. The costs of the unrestrained and much-heralded economic growth since World War II showed up in the nation's air, water, and land. The leaded gasoline that fueled the booming auto industry created smog; industrial effluents polluted lakes and rivers; petrochemical wastes poisoned the ground. Biologist Garrett Hardin called these developments "the tragedy of the commons," wherein the pursuit of narrow individual self-interest leads to the despoiling of the common environment. For example, the very low price of gasoline in the United States compared with that of other industrialized nations did not (and still does not) recoup any of the vast environmental costs of its use. The products of science that had contributed so much to the creation of wealth were turning out to have hidden costs, and a new wave of citizen action to protect the environment began to build.

Growing public awareness prompted the Clean Air Act (1963) and the Clean Waters Act (1966), which set federal guidelines for reducing smog and preserving public drinking sources from bacterial pollution. Even the long dam-building tradition in the American West faced new questions. A quarter century after Hoover Dam blocked the Colorado River, engineers completed the Glen Canyon Dam (1963) upstream at the Arizona-Utah border, drowning one of the nation's most spectacular canyons under the new Lake Powell. Demands for the dam's removal began immediately and helped spur passage of the Wild and Scenic Rivers Act in 1968. Meanwhile, Congress passed the Wilderness Act in 1964, setting aside 9 million acres of undeveloped public lands (almost all west of the Mississippi River) as a place "where man is a visitor who does not remain." In a nation growing more urban and more crowded, most Americans began to accept the idea that what little wilderness remained should be preserved. By the year 2000, the wilderness system incorporated 95 million acres of roadless areas.

THE LIBERAL WARREN COURT

The government's judicial branch responded to pressures for reform more swiftly than did the executive and legislative branches. Dwight Eisenhower did not expect liberal leadership from Earl Warren when he named him chief justice of the U.S. Supreme Court in 1953. As California's attorney general, Warren had helped implement the internment of Japanese Americans during World War II, but he later came to regret that policy. The Warren Court produced the unanimous 1954 school desegregation case *Brown v. Board of Education* (see Chapter 25) and steadily expanded the constitutional definition of individual rights. This shift in interpreting the law reached even those deemed to have lost many of their rights: prisoners. *Gideon v. Wainwright* (1963) established the right of indigent prisoners to legal counsel, and *Escobedo v. Illinois* (1964) confirmed the right to counsel during interrogation, a critical hindrance to the use of torture. After *Miranda v. Arizona* (1966), police were required to inform anyone they arrested of their rights to remain silent and to speak to a lawyer. Reading captured suspects their "Miranda rights" became a touchstone scene for a whole generation of television police shows.

One individual right that had often been limited was the importance of each citizen's vote. As populations grew in certain areas more than others, legislative districts within states often came to be unequal in size. In *Baker v. Carr* (1962), the Court found that the reapportionment of states' legislative districts after each ten-year census was an issue for courts as well as legislatures to decide. In *Reynolds v. Sims* (1964), the Court required that such reapportionment weight each vote equally ("one man, one vote"). These decisions helped fast-growing urban areas capture political might proportional to their populations within a state. Urban areas gained power compared to slow-growing rural areas.

The Warren Court bolstered other rights of individuals against potentially coercive community pressures. Decisions in 1962 and 1963 strictly limited the practice of requiring prayers in public schools. In 1963, the Court narrowed standards for the definition of "obscenity," allowing freer expression in the arts but also in pornography. *Griswold v. Connecticut* (1965)

> The Warren Court bolstered the rights of individuals against potentially coercive community pressures.

established the use of contraceptive devices by married people as a matter of private choice protected by the Constitution. In 1967, the Court heard the case of Mildred Jeter, a black woman, and Richard Loving, a white man, Virginians who had evaded their state's ban on interracial marriage by traveling to Washington, D.C., for their wedding and then returning home to Virginia to live. In the aptly titled *Loving v. Virginia*, the Court declared marriage one of the "basic civil rights of men" and overturned the laws of the last sixteen states restricting interracial unions. Also in 1967, President Johnson appointed the esteemed chief NAACP legal counsel Thurgood Marshall—who had mounted the successful argument in *Brown v. Board of Education* thirteen years earlier—as the first black Supreme Court justice.

The Supreme Court's interpreting of the Constitution to expand individual rights disturbed many conservative Americans. They saw the Court as another arm of an intrusive national government that was extending its control over matters previously left to local communities and the states. For them, the goal of integration did not justify the busing of schoolchildren. Rising crime rates worried them more than police brutality. Many Roman Catholics were troubled by the legalization of contraceptives. Incensed by the ban on requiring school prayer, Protestant fundamentalists sought redress through political involvement, which they had previously shunned, initiating a grassroots religious conservative movement that helped bring Ronald Reagan to power in 1980. The Warren Court served as a lightning rod for traditionalists' distress at changes in Americans' private behavior. In the contest between local and national authorities ongoing since the Articles of Confederation of the 1780s, the 1960s represented a high-water mark of Washington's influence in the lives of individual citizens.

Into War in Vietnam

■ *Why did the United States go to war in Vietnam, and why did it not win the war?*

The 1960s also marked the culmination of the U.S. government's efforts to control revolutionary political and social change abroad. The Truman Doctrine's logic of containing communism spanned the entire globe, but few imagined that the United States would overreach itself, tragically, in Vietnam. Johnson's accomplishments at home were forever overshadowed by the war he sent Americans to fight in the quiet rice paddies and beautiful highland forests of Southeast Asia. The Vietnam War of 1965–1973 might be better named the "American War": it reflected the beliefs and commitments of Cold Warriors in Washington more than the realities of life on the ground in Southeast Asia. An aggressive U.S. anticommunist policy abroad collided with leftist revolutionaries throughout the Third World, and it was ill fortune for the Vietnamese that this collision struck them hardest of all.

Military Expenditures in 1966

The U.S.-Soviet competition at the heart of the Cold War (1946–1989), for all its fierceness, was never a very even struggle, as the table here shows. Communist revolutions in such countries as China (1949) seemed to indicate growing Soviet international influence, but the United States and its democratic capitalist allies remained far more economically powerful. The robust character of late twentieth-century capitalism enabled the United States and its allies to build larger and more effective military systems than their communist opponents—and they could do so without diminishing their high material standards of living.

Country	Total ($ billion)	Per capita ($)	Percentage of GNP
United States	68.0	346	9.2
Soviet Union	30.0	129	8.9
China	6.5	8	10.0
United Kingdom	6.1	120	6.4
France	4.5	91	4.4
West Germany	4.3	76	3.6

Source: U.S. Census Bureau, http://www2.census.gov/prod2/statcomp/documents/1968–13.pdf, Fig. 1257.

QUESTIONS

1. What do these statistics suggest about the relative strengths of these nations?

2. How are military power and economic power related to each other?

3. What other important forms of power can nations wield?

The Wider World

"They were just in the intersection when our convertible rolled up," recalled former Stanford University student body president and draft resistance organizer David Harris.

THE VIETNAMESE REVOLUTION AND THE UNITED STATES

Americans viewed the conflict in Vietnam as part of a broader struggle between communist and noncommunist nations. It did not start out that way, however. It began as one of many efforts to end European colonialism. Vietnamese nationalists, varying in ideologies but led by Ho Chi Minh and the Indochinese Communist party, had sought since the 1930s to liberate their country from French colonial rule. Japanese advances during World War II put the Vietminh (Vietnamese nationalists) on the same side as the Americans, and Ho worked closely with the U.S. Office of Strategic Services (OSS), precursor to the Central Intelligence Agency (CIA).

After the defeat of Germany and Japan, the French wanted to regain control of their colonies in Africa and Asia, including Vietnam. Their British friends provided troop transport ships for French soldiers, and the United States provided most of the funds to support France in its war against the Vietminh (1946–1954). Cold War priorities won out: a weakened France had to be bolstered as the linchpin of a reintegrated, anticommunist western Europe, while the Vietminh were led by Communist party members. But the Vietnamese defeated the much more heavily armed French, capped by the climactic victory at the battle of Dien Bien Phu in May 1954, which surprised most Western observers. Two months later, the Geneva Accords divided the country temporarily at the 17th parallel until national elections could be held within two years to reunify Vietnam. Like the 38th parallel in Korea (see Chapter 24), the 17th parallel was an arbitrary latitude on the map used to divide peoples who did not want to be separated. Ho's forces solidified their control of the north, the French pulled out entirely, and the Eisenhower administration made a fateful decision to intervene directly to preserve the southern part of Vietnam from communism. The United States created a new government led by the Roman Catholic, anticommunist Ngo Dinh Diem in a new country called "South Vietnam." "This is our offspring," Senator John Kennedy observed of the rulers in the capital city of Saigon, but most Americans still knew nothing about South Vietnam.

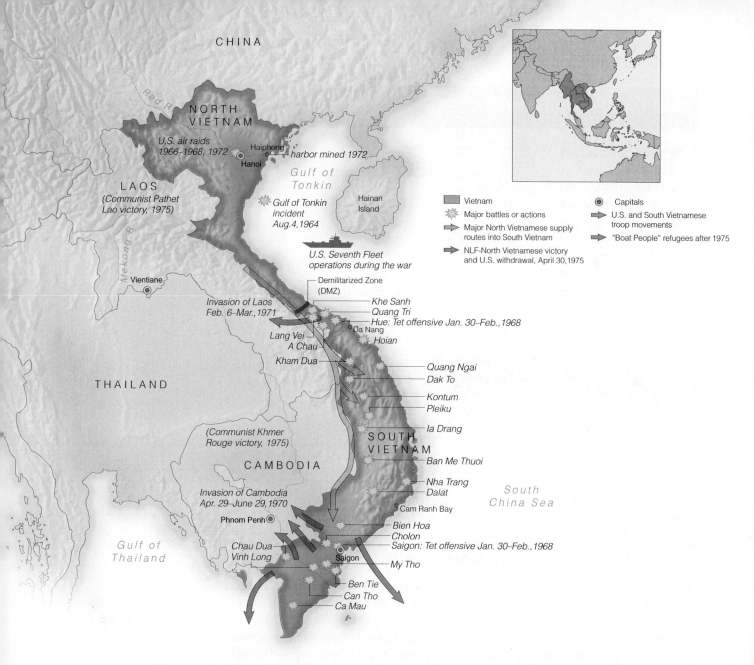

MAP 26.2 The American War in Vietnam

Before U.S. combat troops entered Vietnam in 1965, few Americans knew where this Southeast Asian country was. Vietnam's geography and place names quickly became familiar in the United States as hundreds of thousands of young Americans served there and some 58,000 died there. Vietnam's elongated shape, its borders with Cambodia and Laos, and its proximity to China all affected the course of the fighting for Americans between 1965 and 1973.

The Vietnamese revolution was only half over, however. The French colonialists withdrew, but the Saigon regime did not hold elections. In North Vietnam, the sometimes brutal internal revolution for the creation of a socialist society proceeded with an extensive program of land redistribution. In South Vietnam, Diem ruled for eight years with increasing repression of communists and other dissenters. U.S. funding kept him in power. Southern members of the old Vietminh began a sabotage campaign against the Saigon government and formed the National Liberation Front (NLF) in 1960, with the support of the government of North Vietnam in Hanoi. Diem and his American supporters called them Viet Cong or VC, roughly equivalent to the derogatory American term *Commies*. As the struggle to overthrow Diem intensified in the early 1960s, President Kennedy increased the number of

U.S. military personnel from the 800 under Eisenhower to 16,000. They made little difference, however, as the unpopular Saigon government continued to lose ground to the NLF guerrillas. Just three weeks before Kennedy's murder, several of Diem's own generals assassinated him with the tacit support of U.S. officials in South Vietnam and Washington.

JOHNSON'S WAR

Lyndon Johnson inherited his predecessors' commitment to preserving a noncommunist South Vietnam. Bolstered by Kennedy's hawkish advisers, especially Secretary of Defense Robert McNamara (1961–1968), he believed that American credibility was at stake. But Johnson faced a swiftly deteriorating military situation. The NLF, which the administration portrayed as merely a tool of North Vietnam, was winning the political war for the South, taking control of the countryside from the demoralized Army of the Republic of Vietnam (ARVN). Faced with the choice of escalating U.S. involvement to prevent an NLF victory or withdrawing entirely from the country, Johnson escalated.

> *Faced with the choice of escalating U.S. involvement or withdrawing entirely from the country, Johnson escalated.*

How he did so was crucially important. There was neither a national debate nor a congressional vote to declare war. Johnson did not want to distract Congress from his Great Society agenda, nor did he want to provoke the Soviet Union or China. But he believed he had to preserve a noncommunist South Vietnam or else face a debilitating backlash from Republicans, who would skewer him as McCarthy had done to Truman over the "loss" of China fifteen years earlier. So the president used deception, describing offensive American actions as defensive and opening up a credibility gap between a committed government and a skeptical public. When the war did not go well, this credibility gap widened steadily until it finally drove Johnson not to run for reelection in 1968.

In August 1964, North Vietnamese ships in the Gulf of Tonkin fired on the U.S. destroyer *Maddox*, which was aiding South Vietnamese sabotage operations against the North. The president portrayed the incident as one of unprovoked communist aggression, and Congress expressed almost unanimous support through its Gulf of Tonkin Resolution. With this substitute for a declaration of war, Johnson ordered American planes to begin bombing North Vietnam, and the first American combat troops splashed ashore at Da Nang in South Vietnam on March 8, 1965. In July, the administration made the key decision to add 100,000 more soldiers, with more to follow as necessary.

The president also offered a piece of the Great Society to his opponents in Vietnam if they would halt their struggle. He promised a vast economic development program for the Mekong River delta "on a scale even to dwarf our" Tennessee Valley Authority. Like most of his compatriots, the president assumed that foreign peoples fundamentally wanted to be like Americans. Johnson and his advisers tended to believe that, in the words of a U.S. officer in the film *Full Metal Jacket* (1987), "Inside every Vietnamese there is an American trying to get out."

DOCUMENT

Johnson, The Tonkin Gulf Resolution Message

The carrot of American-style economic development was accompanied by the stick of U.S. military force. American strategy had two goals: to limit the war so as not to draw in neighboring China (to avoid a repeat of the Korean War), and to force the NLF and North Vietnam to give up their struggle to reunify the country under Hanoi's control. The problem was the political nature of the guerrilla war in the South: a contest for the loyalty of the population, in which NLF operatives mingled easily with the citizenry. This kind of war made the enemy difficult to find, as had often been true for the British in fighting the American revolutionaries in the 1770s. Because guerrillas were like fish swimming in the sea of citizens who supported them, in Chinese leader Mao Zedong's formulation, U.S. commanders decided to drain the sea. The "strategic hamlet" program uprooted rural peasants and concentrated them in fortified towns, creating "free fire zones" in their wake where anything that moved was a target. The U.S. Air Force pounded the South as well as the North, dropping more bombs on this ancient land (smaller than either Germany or Japan) than had been used in all theaters on all sides in World War II.

These tactics destabilized and traumatized society in South Vietnam as one-fourth of the population became refugees. The American war urbanized the South by force: from 85 percent rural in 1965, it became 65 percent urban by 1974. The strategy of attrition wielded by General William Westmoreland, the commander of U.S. forces in Vietnam, also alienated the citizenry of the South. Lacking a clear military front in a guerrilla conflict, U.S. commanders used body counts of enemy dead as a primary method of demonstrating progress in the war. This strategy created great pressure on officers to produce bodies. In a war where Americans had difficulty distinguishing the enemy from noncombatants, a new rule became increasingly standard: "If it's dead and Vietnamese, it's VC."

AMERICANS IN SOUTHEAST ASIA

Given America's wealth, size, and superior weaponry, most U.S. soldiers who went to Vietnam in 1965–1966 had no doubt they would win the war. Their confidence reflected generations of American successes on battlefields across Europe and the Pacific Ocean. As emissaries from a culture that valued material wealth and technological sophistication, they tended to dismiss Vietnamese people as primitive and weak. They typically looked down on Asians. Very few knew anything about Vietnamese history or culture, and almost none spoke the Vietnamese language. This war, unlike World War II of their parents' generation, had no D-Day on the beaches of France as in 1944, with a staging across the narrow channel in familiar England.

Initial U.S. optimism reflected a grave underestimation of the NLF and the North Vietnamese.

Although a small number of Americans worked closely with their South Vietnamese allies, most GIs encountered Vietnamese in subservient roles as laundry workers, prostitutes, waitresses, and bartenders. Blinkered by anticommunism and far removed from their own revolutionary roots, Americans from the top brass to the lowest "grunts" marched into a country they did not understand but assumed they could control.

President Johnson spoke of the conflict as a case of one sovereign nation—North Vietnam—invading another one—South Vietnam. However, few Vietnamese saw the war in those terms. The United States, dismissing the failure of the French before them, had intervened not so much in an international war as in an ongoing revolution that aimed to reunify the country. Few Vietnamese, whatever their opinions of communism, viewed the corrupt Saigon regime as legitimate or democratic. After all, it was kept in place by foreigners, whereas the North was ruled by people who had expelled the French foreigners. Even the U.S. embassy admitted privately that "if any elected assembly sits in Saigon, it will be on the phone negotiating with Hanoi within one week." One U.S. sergeant concluded that "anticommunism is a lousy substitute for democracy."

Initial U.S. optimism reflected a grave underestimation of the NLF and the North Vietnamese. From President Johnson down to soldiers on patrol in the jungle, Americans assumed that communists did not have popular support and that the inferior weaponry of communist forces could not withstand the firepower of the world's strongest military, which dominated the air and the surrounding sea. These assumptions were fatal miscalculations. Ho Chi Minh was an extremely popular leader, and intervention from the other side of the world only strengthened his position. As the war expanded, NLF recruiting in the south snowballed, and the people of North Vietnam remained loyal to their authoritarian government. Communist forces proved willing to endure profound hardship and sacrifices to prevail, some even living underground in the labyrinthine tunnels of Cu Chi to avoid U.S. bombs. Their morale was much higher than that of the ARVN.

Who were the 3 million Americans who went to Vietnam? The initial forces contained experienced soldiers, but as the war escalated this professional army was diluted with hundreds of thousands of young draftees. Student deferments protected more comfortable Americans, so GIs were predominantly those who lacked money and education. Although 70 percent were white men, black, Hispanic, and Native American enlistees shipped out in

© Jules Feiffer

■ Cartoonist Jules Feiffer suggested in 1966 some of the ongoing confusion of many Americans about Asia and its many nations and peoples, and why the United States was involved in a war in Vietnam. Anti-Asian prejudice had long contributed to problems in U.S.-Asian relations. President Johnson claimed that the United States was protecting the lives and interests of South Vietnamese against both North Vietnam and China.

disproportionate numbers. It became a teenage army, filled with eighteen-year-olds whose main aim, one ABC correspondent reported, "was to become nineteen." In sharp contrast to the motives of the NLF and the North Vietnamese army, few of these young men (along with 10,000 women who volunteered as nurses) were in Vietnam to win the war regardless of the cost or duration. They had only to survive twelve months before returning home to the safety of a peacetime society.

North Vietnamese regular army units came south to match the growing number of U.S. forces, and they occasionally engaged the Americans in large set battles, as at Ia Drang valley in the fall of 1965. U.S. troops fought well in such firefights, making devastating use of their superior weapons and air power. However, the bulk of the fighting consisted of smaller engagements with deceptive enemies on their home turf who faded in and out of the civilian population with ease. Ambushes and unexpected death haunted Americans on patrol, and relentless heat and humidity wore them down.

American soldiers felt mounting frustration and rage over the nature of the war that they were ordered to fight. Lacking a clear battlefront and an understandable strategy for winning the war, they were commanded simply to kill the often mysterious enemy. Yet distinguishing civilians from combatants in a popular guerrilla war was not always easy, especially when so many civilians evidently supported the NLF and so few Americans spoke Vietnamese. "How can you tell the enemy?" one GI asked. "They all look the same." The U.S. ally, the ARVN, was riddled with NLF infiltrators and rarely fought effectively. Realizing that few of the people they were supposed to be defending actually wanted them there but under orders to produce enemy bodies, many U.S. troops on the ground began to slide toward a racial war against all Vietnamese. "You can't have a feeling of remorse for these people," said one marine. "I mean, like I say, they are an enemy until proven innocent."

Many GIs resisted this logic, sometimes showing real kindness to Vietnamese civilians. But atrocities on both sides inevitably followed from this kind of war. The worst came in the village of My Lai on March 16, 1968, where 105 soldiers from Charlie Company—enraged by the recent deaths of several comrades in ambushes—slaughtered, often after torturing or raping, more than 400 Vietnamese women, children, and old men. The U.S. Army covered up the massacre for a year and a half, and eventually found only Lieutenant William Calley, the leader of Charlie Company's First Platoon, guilty of murdering Vietnamese civilians. He was paroled after four years of house arrest.

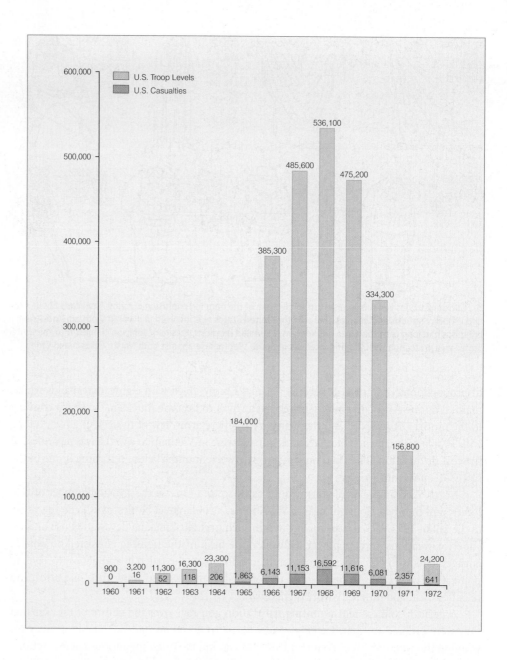

FIGURE 26.1 U.S. Troops and Deaths in Vietnam (as of December 31 of each year)

1968: THE TURNING POINT

In late 1967 the public face of the war effort remained upbeat. General Westmoreland declared that he could now see "some light at the end of the tunnel." But other prominent members of the administration, including Secretary of Defense McNamara, were beginning to express doubts privately to the president. Any remaining hopes of an imminent victory were crushed by the startling Tet Offensive (named for the Vietnamese New Year) that began on January 30, 1968. NLF insurgents and North Vietnamese troops attacked U.S. strongholds throughout South Vietnam. They even occupied the courtyard of the U.S. embassy for six hours. This risky tactic paid off for the communists with enormous political gains, despite military losses. U.S. troops killed thousands of their enemy as they ended and then reversed the advances of Tet. But the blow to American public confidence in Johnson and his military commanders proved irreversible. Far from being on the verge of defeat, as the administration had been claiming, the communists had shown that they could mount simultaneous attacks around the country. Revered television newscaster

Walter Cronkite announced that "we are mired in stalemate" in Vietnam. Westmoreland requested 200,000 more troops.

The Tet Offensive coincided with two other crises in early 1968 to convince American political and business elites that U.S. international commitments had become larger than the nation could afford. First, a week before Tet began, the North Korean navy seized the U.S. intelligence ship *Pueblo* in the Sea of Japan and temporarily imprisoned its crew. U.S. commanders were left scrambling to find enough forces to respond effectively without weakening American commitments in Europe and elsewhere. Second, a British financial collapse devalued the pound and caused the London government to announce its imminent withdrawal from its historic positions east of the Suez Canal, placing new military burdens on the United States in the Middle East. These events reduced international confidence in the U.S. economy, causing a currency crisis in March 1968 as holders of dollars traded them in for gold. The chair of the Federal Reserve Board warned Wall Street leaders of "either an uncontrollable recession or an uncontrollable inflation" as fears rose of another 1929 stock market crash. Financial leaders added their powerful voices to those of other dismayed Americans demanding a deescalation of the war.

The political career of Lyndon Johnson was a final casualty of these events. His support on the left withered as the antiwar and **black power** movements expanded. Meanwhile, his more centrist supporters were joining the backlash against civil rights, urban violence, and antiwar protesters, peeling off to the Republican party. On March 12, antiwar challenger Senator Eugene McCarthy of Minnesota nearly defeated the incumbent president in the New Hampshire Democratic primary. Johnson's vulnerability was clear. Senator Robert Kennedy of New York joined the race two weeks later. In a televised speech on March 31 that caught the divided nation by surprise, Johnson announced an end to U.S. escalations in the war, the start of negotiations in Paris with North Vietnam, and an end to his own career: "I shall not seek, and I will not accept, the nomination of my party for another term as your President."

Ngo Vinh Long Collection

■ A North Vietnamese militia fighter named Kim Lai escorts an American pilot whom she captured after his plane crashed over the North. American GIs often were struck by the diminutive size of the average Vietnamese in comparison to the average American. Bigger, better equipped, and much better armed than their opponents, most U.S. soldiers and officers before 1968 went into the field in Vietnam certain that they would be victorious.

"The Movement"

■ *What did the protest movements of the 1960s have in common?*

While national leaders were defending what they called the "frontiers of freedom" abroad, young Americans in the mid- and late 1960s organized to expand what they considered the frontiers of freedom at home. Television for the first time tied the country together in a common culture whose shared images were transmitted simultaneously around the nation. The expanding war in Vietnam radicalized people who had initially been optimistic about reforming American society. Black power, the New Left, the counterculture, women's liberation, and other movements often had quite divergent goals. But participants overlapped extensively and activists spoke of "the Movement" as if it were a unified phenomenon. At the heart of the youth movements of the decade lay a common quest for authenticity—a rejection of hypocrisy and a distrust of traditional authorities—that fused cultural and political protest. Few American households remained untouched.

FROM CIVIL RIGHTS TO BLACK POWER

The black freedom struggle in the South that broke into the national consciousness so dramatically in the early 1960s inspired other activists. By 1966, however, the civil rights movement fractured as it confronted the limits of its success. It had achieved the goals of ending legal discrimination and putting southern African Americans in the voting booth, but it had not brought about a colorblind society. Racial prejudice among many white conservatives remained virulent, and white liberals, such as those in the Kennedy and Johnson administrations, revealed themselves as not always trustworthy allies. Expecting only hostility from conservatives, civil rights workers were more disillusioned with what they saw as liberal betrayals.

The Justice Department and the Federal Bureau of Investigation (FBI) did little to restrain the violence of the Ku Klux Klan until white organizers Michael Schwerner and Andrew Goodman and black co-worker James Chaney were murdered in the summer of 1964. Two months later, at the national Democratic party convention in Atlantic City, New Jersey, Johnson crushed the effort of the biracial Mississippi Freedom Democratic party (MFDP) to replace the state's regular, all-white Democratic delegates. The president was determined to avoid further alienating white southern voters as he pursued a huge victory in the November elections. Former sharecropper and MFDP organizer Fannie Lou Hamer, who had suffered permanent damage when beaten by Mississippi police for her efforts to register black voters, expressed the anger of African Americans at this defense of segregation by the president and his party. To a national television audience, Hamer declared, "If the Freedom Democratic Party is not seated now, I question America. Is this America? The land of the free and the home of the brave?" Even the thousand white volunteers from northern and western colleges who courageously went to Mississippi for the 1964 "Freedom Summer" wound up unintentionally alienating many younger black organizers. The confident style and skills of volunteers from Yale, Stanford, and other elite universities highlighted anew the tendency of even well-intentioned whites to try to take over and manage African Americans' lives.

For centuries, the black freedom struggle had woven together elements of racial separatism with elements of integration into the larger American culture. For many younger African Americans, the pendulum now swung toward a need for greater independence from the white majority. They took inspiration from Malcolm X, the fiery and eloquent minister of the Nation of Islam (Black Muslims), who until his murder in 1965 captivated listeners with denunciations of white perfidy and demands for black self-respect. After winning the heavyweight boxing title in 1964, Cassius Clay announced that he was a Black Muslim and was changing his name to Muhammad Ali. After fielding hostile questions from journalists at the news conference, Ali declared, "I don't have to be what you want me to be." In 1966, SNCC members began to speak of the need for "black power" rather than for the integrated "beloved community" they had initially sought in 1960.

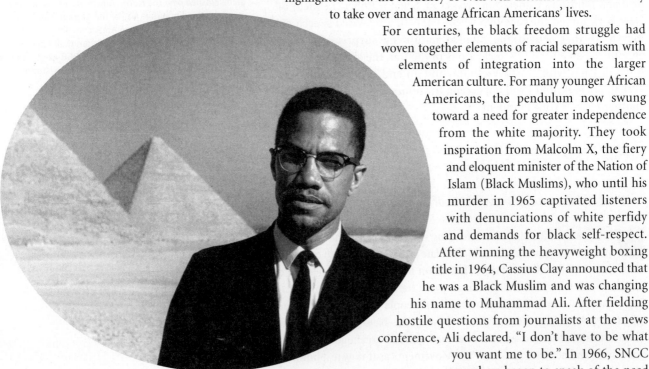

■ A leading spokesperson for the Black Muslims, Malcolm X converted to orthodox Islam and softened his antiwhite rhetoric in the two years before his murder in 1965. Like SNCC's Bob Moses, Malcolm increasingly identified with the Third World. Here he is shown in Egypt on a 1964 pilgrimage to Mecca, Saudi Arabia.

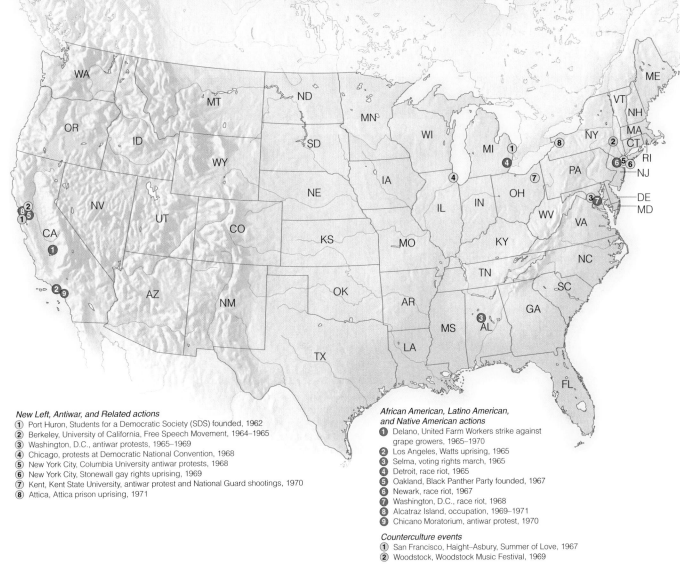

New Left, Antiwar, and Related actions
1. Port Huron, Students for a Democratic Society (SDS) founded, 1962
2. Berkeley, University of California, Free Speech Movement, 1964–1965
3. Washington, D.C., antiwar protests, 1965–1969
4. Chicago, protests at Democratic National Convention, 1968
5. New York City, Columbia University antiwar protests, 1968
6. New York City, Stonewall gay rights uprising, 1969
7. Kent, Kent State University, antiwar protest and National Guard shootings, 1970
8. Attica, Attica prison uprising, 1971

African American, Latino American, and Native American actions
1. Delano, United Farm Workers strike against grape growers, 1965–1970
2. Los Angeles, Watts uprising, 1965
3. Selma, voting rights march, 1965
4. Detroit, race riot, 1965
5. Oakland, Black Panther Party founded, 1967
6. Newark, race riot, 1967
7. Washington, D.C., race riot, 1968
8. Alcatraz Island, occupation, 1969–1971
9. Chicano Moratorium, antiwar protest, 1970

Counterculture events
1. San Francisco, Haight–Asbury, Summer of Love, 1967
2. Woodstock, Woodstock Music Festival, 1969

■ **M A P 2 6 . 3   Major Social and Political Protests, 1962–1971**
While not the first decade to witness dramatic public protests, the 1960s did become synonymous with large groups of citizens—especially young ones—demanding changes in public policies that they perceived as unjust. Foremost among these groups were civil rights workers, antiwar activists, women's rights supporters, and counterculture youth. Students emerged as important agents of change in the 1960s.

The issue of violence loomed large in the shift from civil rights to black power. The Black Panther party formed in Oakland, California, in response to police brutality. The heavily armed Panthers engaged in several shootouts with police and were eventually decimated by an FBI campaign against them. White Americans were shocked by the uprisings and riots that swept through black urban communities during the summers of 1964 to 1968. Triggered by the actions of white police, the riots expressed the fierce frustrations of impoverished people whose lives remained largely untouched by the achievements of the civil rights struggle. The most destructive outbreaks occurred in the Watts district of Los Angeles in 1965 and in Detroit and Newark in 1967. The violence in Watts killed 34 people, wounded 1,000, and destroyed $45 million of property. Ninety people died and 4,000 were injured across the country in the 1967 riots, most of them African Americans killed by police as fires and looting spread through African American neighborhoods. "Our nation is moving toward two societies, one black, one white—separate and unequal," the National Advisory Commission on Civil Disorders announced in its 1968 report.

Black power thrived primarily as a cultural movement that promoted pride in African American and African history and life. The slogan "black is beautiful" captured this spirit: long degraded by their white compatriots as inferior, black Americans in the late 1960s and

Martin Luther King Jr. and the Vietnam War

Interpreting History

Most Americans approved of the war in Vietnam until at least 1968. Appreciative of Lyndon Johnson's commitment to reduce poverty and end racial discrimination at home, African Americans generally supported the president's policies in Southeast Asia. However, younger, more radical civil rights workers were among those who opposed the first insertion of U.S. combat troops in 1965. Within two years, the nation's most prominent black leader, Martin Luther King Jr., decided that he could no longer keep quiet about his growing unease with the American war effort. A storm of criticism greeted his public denunciation of the war, most of it suggesting that he should limit himself to domestic civil rights work. But King no longer believed that events at home and abroad could be separated. The

Time & Life Pictures/Getty Images

■ His birthday now a national holiday, Martin Luther King Jr. has become widely accepted as a heroic figure in the American past. But in the last few years of his life, King's increasingly sharp criticisms of injustice in American society disturbed many fellow citizens.

following excerpt is from his speech at Riverside Church, New York City, April 4, 1967.

A few years ago there was a shining moment in that struggle [against poverty and discrimination]. It seemed as if there was a real promise of hope for the poor—both black and white—through the Poverty Program. There were experiments, hopes, new beginnings. Then came the build-up in Vietnam and I watched the program broken and eviscerated as if it were some idle political plaything of a society gone mad on war. . . . I was increasingly compelled to see the war as an enemy of the poor and to attack it as such. . . .

We were taking the black young men who had been crippled by our

1970s reversed this equation to celebrate their cultural heritage. This could be as basic as a hairstyle, the natural Afro replacing hair straightened to look like European American hair. At universities, new departments of African American studies fostered the exploration of black history. Unlearning habits of public deference to whites, most African Americans began referring to themselves as "black" rather than "Negro."

Cultural black power mixed with a different kind of political black power by the late 1960s: the election of black officials. Although militant black power advocates garnered the most media attention, most African Americans supported Lyndon Johnson and used the Voting Rights Act to pursue their goals in the realm of electoral politics. In 1966, Carl Stokes of Cleveland was elected the first black mayor of a major American city. African Americans won local offices across the South, and in 1972 Andrew Young of Georgia and Barbara Jordan of Texas became the first black U.S. representatives elected from the South since Reconstruction.

THE NEW LEFT AND THE STRUGGLE AGAINST THE WAR

The black struggle for equality inspired many white students. In the summer of 1962, a group of young liberal college activists met at a labor union summer camp in Michigan. The Students for a Democratic Society (SDS) wrote a charter that became known as the Port Huron Statement. It called for a rejuvenation of American politics and society to replace the complacency that they saw pervading the country. Racial bigotry and poverty particularly troubled these optimistic young reformers, along with the overarching threat of nuclear destruction (highlighted anew by the missile crisis in Cuba a few months later). They hoped society and sending them 8,000 miles away to guarantee liberties in Southeast Asia which they had not found in Southwest Georgia and East Harlem. So we have been repeatedly faced with the cruel irony of watching Negro and white boys on TV screens as they kill and die together for a nation that has been unable to seat them together in the same schools. . . .

As I have walked among the desperate, rejected and angry young men [in the ghettos of the North the last three summers] I have told them that Molotov cocktails and rifles would not solve their problems. I have tried to offer them my deepest compassion while maintaining my convictions that social change comes most meaningfully through non-violent action. But they asked—and rightly so—what about Vietnam? They asked if our own nation wasn't using massive doses of violence to solve its problems, to bring about the changes it wanted. Their questions hit home, and I knew that I would never again raise my voice against the violence of the oppressed in the ghettos without having first spoken clearly to the greatest purveyor of violence in the world today—my own government. . . .

[Our troops in Vietnam] must know after a short period there that none of the things we claim to be fighting for [such as freedom, justice, and peace] are really involved. Before long they must know that their government has sent them into a struggle among Vietnamese, and the more sophisticated surely realize that we are on the side of the wealthy and the secure while we create a hell for the poor.

QUESTIONS

1. *How does King believe that the U.S. war in Vietnam is related to problems at home in American society?*

2. *What might have been the more negative and positive racial aspects of the Vietnam War?*

3. *What precisely does King believe to be wrong with the U.S. war in Vietnam?*

Source: Bruce J. Schulman, Lyndon B. Johnson and American Liberalism (Boston: Bedford, 1995), 208–212.

to become a kind of "white SNCC," promoting participatory democracy to redeem the promise of Cold War America.

SDS served as the central organization of the New Left. Communism was simply not important to these activists. Nor was conservatism, which was then at its nadir. They focused instead on the behavior of the liberals who ran the U.S. government from 1961 to 1968. They developed a critique of "corporate liberalism" as promoting the interests of the wealthy and the business community far more than providing for the needs of the disadvantaged. From this perspective, communism was a false threat and anticommunism a distraction from the real problems of the nation, especially as the war in Vietnam expanded.

After 1965, SDS's initially broad reform agenda narrowed to stopping the Vietnam War. Protests about other issues also disrupted college campuses, such as the Free Speech Movement at Berkeley in 1964–1965; this successful effort to eliminate restrictions on students' lives set a precedent for campus activists elsewhere. But the escalation of the war moved draft-age opponents to focus on ending it. "Hell no, we won't go!" became their slogan. SDS members organized the first major antiwar protest outside the White House on April 17, 1965, bringing their organization into alliance with the small group of religious and secular pacifists already working against the war. Then mainstream Democrats began abandoning Johnson over the war as it grew. The president had alienated the powerful chair of the Senate Foreign Relations Committee, J. William Fulbright of Arkansas, by issuing misleading reports during the brief U.S. military intervention in the Dominican Republic in April 1965 to defeat a left-leaning but not communist coup attempt. Fulbright then held televised hearings on the American war in Southeast Asia in January 1966, raising grave doubts about its wisdom. Draft resistance increased as young men moved to Canada, as did SNCC's Bob Moses, or went to jail, as did boxing champion Muhammad Ali. "Man, I ain't got no quarrel with the Vietcong," the boxer explained.

"Protests Against the Vietnam War"

Antiwar protesters followed the same trajectory of radicalization as black power advocates. Their dismay turned to rage as the Johnson administration continued to expand a war that was destroying much of Vietnam while killing tens of thousands of American soldiers and many more Vietnamese for no reason its opponents considered legitimate. Having long admired Castro's revolution in Cuba, SDS began cheering for Ho Chi Minh and imagining itself as "the NLF behind Lyndon Johnson's lines." In combination with or in support of black militants, white radicals took over buildings on university campuses in 1968–1969: Columbia, Cornell, Harvard, San Francisco State, and many others. SDS ultimately broke apart in the confusion and exhilaration of its growing demand for revolution against the larger systemic enemies, imperialism and capitalism, not just corporate liberalism. Such fantasies of violence, as well as real bombings by a splinter group called the Weather Underground, alienated most Americans, including most peaceful antiwar protesters. But radical rage could not be understood apart from the ongoing destruction of Vietnam by a government acting in the name of all Americans.

CULTURAL REBELLION AND THE COUNTERCULTURE

While the New Left moved from wanting to reform American society to wanting to overthrow it, the counterculture sought to create an alternative society. Called "hippies" by those who disliked them, these young people were alienated by the materialism, competition, and conformity of American life in the Cold War. Like utopian idealists in previous centuries, they envisioned an America free from hypocrisy and artificiality. They tried to live out alternative values of gentleness, tolerance, and inclusivity. Sporting headbands, long hair, and beads, many identified with traditional Native Americans, who had repeatedly challenged the greed and deceptions of white culture from the time of Metacom and Popé in the seventeenth century. In place of junk foods, they promoted health foods; in place of profit-seeking businesses, they established co-ops. Referring to themselves as "freaks" for not fitting into "straight" society, they pursued what they saw as an authentic life. "Do your own thing" was the common slogan.

■ African American students march out of the student union at Cornell University in April 1969 after occupying the building during the annual Parents' Weekend on campus. With the support of radical white students such as those in SDS and some faculty, the black Ivy Leaguers were protesting racial discrimination, racial threats, and a recent cross-burning on campus, and they demanded the creation of a black studies program. The weapons in the picture went unused, but their presence on university grounds symbolized the extreme divisiveness and anger in American society between 1968 and 1970.

Division of Rare & Manuscript Collections. Cornell University Library

In reaction against the conformity of mainstream society, members of the counterculture explored the limitations of consciousness to expand their self-knowledge. They went beyond the nicotine and alcohol that were the common stimulants of their parents' culture to experiment with such mind-altering drugs as marijuana, peyote, hashish, LSD, and cocaine. Spirituality was an important path into consciousness for many in the counterculture. Religious traditions associated with Asia, particularly Buddhism, gained numerous adherents, as did spiritual customs and practices of traditional Native Americans. Others rediscovered the "authentic" Jesus obscured by the institutional structures of the formal Christian church (earning themselves the nickname "Jesus freaks"). Music served as the most common coin of the countercultural realm, from the political folk sound of Joan Baez and Bob Dylan to the broadly popular Beatles and the more distinctly countercultural rock 'n' roll of the Grateful Dead and Jefferson Airplane.

Andy Warhol was the most famous producer of Pop Art, a new artistic style that developed in the late 1950s and 1960s. Pop Art emphasized realistic renditions of everyday objects common in mass culture, in self-conscious contrast to more elitist traditions of art. This 1968 painting is part of Warhol's most well-known series of Pop Art pieces.

QUESTIONS

1. Why might Warhol have chosen Campbell's soup as a subject for painting?

2. What kinds of associations or symbolism might canned soup have had in American culture in the 1960s?

Envisioning History

By its nature, the counterculture had no clear membership. Millions of American youth dabbled in it to varying extents, smoking marijuana and listening to rock 'n' roll. A much smaller, more committed group pursued the building of communities—communes—that might coexist with the quest for unrestrained individual expression. These young people were centered in the Haight-Ashbury neighborhood of San Francisco until the 1967 Summer of Love. Counterculture youth gathered at the Woodstock music festival in upstate New York in August 1969, and they established 3,500 rural communes from Vermont to New Mexico by 1970. With the nation at war against communists in Southeast Asia, critics pointed to communes at home as subversive of the nuclear family and of American capitalist values.

Older Americans experienced the counterculture largely as spectacle. The mainstream media emphasized the alternative aspects of the hippie lifestyle in its coverage. Viewers were varyingly disgusted by, attracted to, and titillated by the hair, clothing, nudity, and blurred gender distinctions. Celebrating the counterculture and its rock 'n' roll sound, the musical show *Hair* took Broadway by storm in 1968. Meanwhile, entrepreneurs realized that they could market the anti-materialist counterculture profitably. Young Americans eagerly bought up records, clothing, jewelry, and natural foods, unintentionally revealing how consumer values pervaded American life.

One of the most visible changes of the 1960s was often called the sexual revolution. Changes in Americans' sexual behavior in the 1960s reflected in part the counterculture's goal of living an authentic, honest life in which words matched actions. The sexual revolution removed some of the penalties for the premarital and extramarital sex that had previously been fairly common but unacknowledged. The appearance of the birth control pill in 1960 underpinned the shift to more open sexual relationships by freeing women from the fear of pregnancy. Attitudes toward

Campus Crusade for Christ, International

■ The search by many young people in the 1960s counterculture for greater consciousness led them to a spiritual path. These young evangelists held a Campus Crusade for Christ rally at the University of Texas at Austin in 1969. The emphasis of evangelical Christians on the person of Jesus rather than on a particular denominational tradition attracted many converts. The sandals, long hair, and gentleness associated with Jesus made a particularly good fit with the style and values of the "hippies," although most evangelicals appeared traditionally clean-cut and held conservative political views.

abortion also became more tolerant. New York passed the first state law legalizing some abortions in 1970, and three years later the Supreme Court established a woman's constitutional right to abortion in the landmark case of *Roe v. Wade*. For American women, the sexual revolution proved a double-edged sword. It legitimated female sexuality and helped remove the old stereotyping of women as either "madonna" (virginal until married) or "whore" (lustful and degraded). But it also created pressures from men, especially within the counterculture, for women to have sex with many partners lest they be cast as "uptight" and unliberated.

WOMEN'S LIBERATION

The movement for women's liberation arose in the late 1960s as a way to resist these kinds of limitations and expectations. Women's liberation built on developments earlier in the decade. In 1963, writer Betty Friedan, a former labor journalist and then homemaker, published *The Feminine Mystique,* a widely read book that captured the frustrations of many women who had accepted the role of suburban homemaker after World War II. Friedan condemned the middle-class home as a "comfortable concentration camp" for women that limited their growth as individuals with the often monotonous routines of housework and child-rearing. Friedan and other liberal feminists founded the National Organization for Women (NOW) in 1966 to lobby against sexual discrimination in the public sphere in such areas as employment, wages, education, and jury duty. These challenges had radical

DOCUMENT

National Organization for Women, Statement of Purpose

implications for women's and men's earnings and thus for responsibilities within families, but NOW did not yet focus on issues inside the private sphere of the home.

The shift to the view that "the personal is political" came from younger, mostly white women who had been active in the civil rights and antiwar struggles. Inspired by the courage and successes of the protest movements in which they figured prominently, these female activists had also learned that traditional gender roles restricted them even in organizations dedicated to participatory democracy. Ironically, radical men could be as patronizing and disrespectful of women's abilities as mainstream men. Younger feminists in 1967 and 1968 began to organize themselves to promote their own liberation from the shackles of traditional gender roles. They agreed with NOW's challenge to discrimination in the public sphere, but they focused even more on the personal politics of women's daily lives, on issues such as parenting, child care, housework, and abortion. Feminism should liberate men as well as women, they believed, for men also had the contours of their lives unnecessarily constrained by gendered expectations.

Many Americans discovered the women's liberation movement when a hundred activists picketed the 1968 Miss America Pageant in Atlantic City, New Jersey. The young feminists were protesting the promotion of physical appearance and charm as the primary measures of women's worth. They crowned a live sheep "Miss America" and paraded it along the boardwalk, making fun of the way contestants—like all women—"are appraised and judged like animals at a county fair." They objected to "the tyranny of beauty" and the extensive expectations of how women should present themselves for male approval. One protester sprayed Toni Home Permanent hair spray at the booth of a pageant sponsor, only to be charged with disorderly conduct and "emanating a noxious odor"—an irony that underlined the activists' point. Other feminists set up a "Freedom Trash Can" into which they threw items they considered unnatural sources of discomfort and exploitation: high-heeled shoes, girdles, hair curlers, bras, and copies of *Playboy* and *Cosmopolitan*. There was talk of burning the contents of the "Freedom Trash Can," an event that did not happen but that the media helped turn into a myth of "bra-burning" militant feminists.

The new wave of feminism that washed through American culture at the end of the 1960s triggered fierce debates about the nature of gender. Was there a uniquely feminine way of knowing, seeing, and acting, or were women in essence the same as men, distinguishable ultimately by their individuality? Was womanhood biologically or only culturally constructed? Feminists disagreed sharply in their answers. Other differences inevitably divided a broad movement that addressed the lives of 51 percent of the entire American people. For example, NOW did not support gay rights until 1973, whereas many radical feminists believed lesbianism to be critical for women's full independence and autonomy. Women of color often found hierarchies of race and class more significant than those of sex; to them, as to many white working-class women, Friedan's statement that she wanted "something more than my husband and my children and my house" seemed the distant complaint of a woman of the leisure class. One's sex alone did not define one's entire identity.

However, diversity within the feminist movement did not hide a common commitment to expanding women's possibilities. One critical aspect was the need to unlearn niceness and passivity, just as black power advocates sought to unlearn deference. White men would no longer be the sole proprietors of

Bettmann/CORBIS

■ The new wave of organizing for women's rights that emerged in the late 1960s had many faces. Some protests against sex discrimination and disrespect for women were angry and others were gentle, as in this 1970 scene. "Raising consciousness" was a central strategy of the movement, as women and men became more aware of the gendered assumptions that had long governed—and channeled—their lives and their thoughts.

assertiveness; grown women would no longer be "girls" nor grown black men "boys." The women's movement that emerged out of the 1960s permanently transformed women's lives and gender relations in American society, in areas ranging from job and educational opportunities, sexual harassment, and gender-neutral language to family roles, sexual relations, reproductive rights, and athletic facilities.

THE MANY FRONTS OF LIBERATION

Like the women's movement, the Chicano, pan-Indian, and gay liberation movements of the late 1960s were grounded in older organizing efforts within those communities. The struggles for "brown power," "red power," and "gay power" also reflected the newer influence of black power and its determination to take pride in what the dominant American society had denigrated for so long. Activists on college campuses successfully pressured administrations to establish interdisciplinary ethnic studies programs, such as the first Chicano studies program at California State University at Los Angeles in 1968. Ethnic cultural identity went hand in hand with the pursuit of political and economic integration into mainstream American life.

The most prominent push to organize Latinos was the effort led by Cesar Chávez and Dolores Huerta to build a farm workers' union in California and the Southwest. These primarily Mexican American migrant workers harvested most of the hand-picked produce that

■ Cesar Chávez led a march during the United Farm Workers strike—*huelga*—against large grape growers in Delano, in California's central valley, in 1966. The UFW effort, in which women such as UFW Vice President Dolores Huerta (a mother of 11) figured prominently, included not only union organizing but also building a broader network of community institutions to improve the lives of Mexican American laborers. The Roman Catholic faith and pacifism of Chávez and others in the movement deeply impressed many non-Chicanos who supported the strike, such as Senator Robert F. Kennedy.

Americans ate, but their hard work under severe conditions failed to lift them out of poverty. National consumer support for boycotts of table grapes and iceberg lettuce helped win recognition for the United Farm Workers (UFW) union and better pay by 1970, despite efforts by conservative leaders such as President Richard Nixon and California governor Ronald Reagan to encourage grape consumption in support of large growers. Younger Mexican Americans organized to oppose the discrimination against them that remained common across the Southwest, especially in schools. They looked with pride on their Mexican heritage, even appropriating the formerly pejorative term *Chicano*. In March 1968, 10,000 youngsters walked out of their East Los Angeles schools to demand curriculum revisions that would include Latino history, recruitment of more Mexican American teachers, and an end to tracking Chicanos into vocational education classes. Two years later, 20,000 people attended the Chicano Moratorium in East Los Angeles to protest the U.S. war in Vietnam.

Puerto Ricans, the largest Spanish-speaking ethnic group located primarily on the East Coast, experienced a similar growth in militancy and nationalist sentiment during the late 1960s. By the 1960s, more than a million natives of the Caribbean island had moved to the East Coast, many to the New York City area. The majority came after World War II, and 47,000 served in the Vietnam War. Immigrant schoolteacher Antonia Pantoia founded the youth organization ASPIRA, which provided the educational springboard for two generations of Latino political and community leaders. Despite being the only Latino immigrants already holding American citizenship when they arrived, Puerto Ricans experienced similar patterns of both discrimination and opportunity as Mexican Americans. Younger Puerto Ricans formed the Young Lords in 1969 as a more militant and nationalist alternative to established Puerto Rican community organizations, one that combined pride in Puerto Rican identity and the Spanish language with leftist politics and opposition to the Vietnam War.

The most destitute of Americans, Indians also sought to reinvigorate their communities. On the Northwest coast, they staged "fish-ins" in the mid-1960s to assert treaty rights. In 1968, urban activists in Minneapolis formed the American Indian Movement (AIM). On November 20, 1969, just days after the largest antiwar march in Washington, seventy-eight Native Americans seized the island of Alcatraz in San Francisco Bay "in the name of all American Indians by right of discovery." For a year and a half, they used their occupation of the former federal prison site to publicize grievances about anti-Indian prejudice and to promote a new pan-Indian identity that reached across traditional tribal divisions. In 1973, armed members of AIM occupied buildings for two months at Wounded Knee near Pine Ridge, South Dakota, site of the infamous 1890 U.S. Army massacre of unarmed Sioux. AIM sought to bring down the conservative tribal government of the Oglala reservation, but the failure of that effort led to internal dissent and FBI harassment that eventually dissolved the organization. Tribal governments sought "red power" in their own quieter way. They asserted greater tribal control of reservation schools across the country. They also regained sovereignty over some lands previously lost, such as Blue Lake in northern New Mexico, which the Taos Indians reacquired.

> *Mexican Americans organized to oppose the discrimination against them that remained common across the Southwest.*

Although they lacked a unifying ethnic identity, gay men and lesbians also found opportunities to construct coalitions in the more open atmosphere of the late 1960s. Building on earlier community organizing by older homosexuals in New York, San Francisco, and Los Angeles, more militant youth began to express openly their anger at the homophobic prejudice and violence prevalent in American society. The demand for tolerance and respect reached the headlines when gay patrons of the Stonewall Bar in New York fought back fiercely against a typically forceful police raid on June 27, 1969. Activists of the new Gay Liberation Front emphasized the importance of "coming out of the closet": proudly acknowledging one's sexual orientation as legitimate and decent. Like "black is beautiful," this tactic represented an effort to recast the terms of one's identity apart from an ongoing tradition of prejudice. The American Psychiatric Association listed homosexuality as a mental disorder until 1973.

Michael Evans/New York Times

■ The first gay pride parade was a daring and hasty political protest by some 200 men and women, who walked for an hour up the Avenue of the Americas in New York City in 1970. They were taking a public stand against widespread discrimination and violence against homosexuals. Such discrimination and violence did not disappear over the next three decades, but the movement for gay rights dramatically altered the visibility and mainstream acceptance of gays and lesbians in the United States. By 1999, the gay pride parade had become a six-hour party sponsored by the likes of Budweiser beer and United Airlines and attended by First Lady Hillary Rodham Clinton and the Republican mayor of New York, Rudolph Giuliani.

The Conservative Response

■ *What motivated the conservative revival of the late 1960s and early 1970s?*

The majority of Americans had mixed feelings about the protests that roiled the nation. They were impressed by the courage of many who stood up against discrimination, and by 1968 they wanted to find a way out of the war in Southeast Asia. But they were alienated by the style and values of others who loudly demanded change in American society. Moderate and conservative citizens and generations of recent European immigrants resented what they saw as a lack of appreciation for the nation's virtues and successes. Powerful backlashes developed against the counterculture, antiwar radicals, and changes in race and gender relations. The political and social upheavals of 1968 opened the door to a Republican return to the White House, and Richard Nixon slipped through.

BACKLASHES

The backlash first developed in response to the increasing assertiveness of people of color. European Americans in every part of the United States had long been accustomed to deference from nonwhites and racial segregation, either by law in the South or by custom elsewhere. Like most white Americans, conservatives resented what they considered blacks' ingratitude at the civil rights measures enacted by the federal government, including black power's condemnation of whites as "crackers" and "honkies." Urban riots and escalating rates of violent crime, along with the Supreme Court's expansion of the rights of the accused, deepened their anger. They associated crime with urban African Americans, for although whites were still the majority of criminals, blacks (like any other population with less money) were disproportionately represented in prisons. Many in the white working class feared that desegregating schools and neighborhoods would lead to a decline in their property values. While keeping darker-skinned Americans economically and socially subordinated, most whites still expected them to want to emulate mainstream white American society. They were troubled by the militancy of Chicanos in the Southwest, Puerto Ricans in the Northeast, Indians on reservations and in cities, and African Americans almost everywhere.

Asian Americans were perceived as less volubly angry than other Americans of color. Conservatives appreciated this, dubbing them a "model minority"—one that worked hard, succeeded academically and in other ways, and did not "complain." In fact, many young Americans of Japanese, Chinese, and Filipino ancestry were also involved in antiwar and antiracist organizing in the late 1960s. But it was true that the 1965 Immigration Act allowed the Chinese American and Filipino American populations to nearly double by the end of the decade, as new arrivals brought with them traditional immigrant ethics of hard work and a focus on achieving material success. These new immigrants joined an important group of earlier refugees from China's communist revolution, who were often very well educated and fairly affluent when they arrived. A prominent example was Shanghai-born An Wang, who was earning a Ph.D. in physics at Harvard University when the communist revolution at home prevented him from returning. Wang's innovative work on computer memory led him to found Wang Laboratories in 1961, and he became, for a time, one of America's richest people and a major philanthropist.

The broad conservative backlash of the late 1960s was not only about race. It also represented a defense of traditional hierarchies against the cultural rebellions of the 1960s. Proud of their lives and values, conservatives rejected a whole array of challenges to American society. Raised to believe in respecting one's elders, they resented

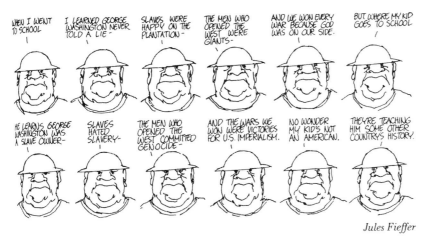

Jules Fieffer

■ Cartoonist Jules Fieffer portrayed the generation gap that separated many younger Americans from many older ones by the early 1970s. Movements for black and Native American civil rights and against the U.S. war in Vietnam led to a profound shift in how many citizens, especially younger ones, understood their nation and its politics. A new generation of historians began to cast serious doubts on many long-accepted truisms about the American past.

the disrespect of many youth, who warned, "Don't trust anyone over thirty." A generation that had fought and sacrificed in the "good war" against the Nazis found the absence of patriotism among many protesters unfathomable. The United States remained one of the most religious of industrialized societies, and conservative churchgoers emphasized obedience to authorities. They feared the effects of illegal drugs on their children. They resented being told that their assumptions about the roles and behavior of men and women, on which they had built their daily lives, were wrong. They did not want to argue about the behavior of the U.S. government; "America: Love It or Leave It" became a favorite bumper sticker.

The backlash against the social changes of the 1960s contained elements of class antagonism as well. Working-class whites resented both the often affluent campus rebels and the black and Latino poor targeted by some Great Society programs. They believed that their values of hard work, restraint, and respectability were increasingly unappreciated and even mocked. Politicians seized on these feelings of working-class alienation for political gain. Republican leaders from Goldwater to Nixon to Reagan gave voice to these resentments and drew votes away from Democratic blue-collar strongholds. Democratic governor George Wallace of Alabama also became a spokesperson for the anger of many "forgotten" whites on both sides of the Mason-Dixon line. Even television gave voice to the backlash in the likable character of Archie Bunker on *All in the Family*, a wildly popular program from its first airing in 1971.

THE TURMOIL OF 1968 AT HOME

The traumas of 1968 brought the conservative backlash to the critical stage. First came the Tet Offensive in Vietnam, creating fears that the war might become an interminable quagmire. Conservatives, like most other Americans, found it incredible that the mighty United States could not vanquish so small an enemy. Then, on April 4, just five days after President Johnson announced his retirement plans, a gunman named James Earl Ray assassinated Martin Luther King Jr. in Memphis, where he had gone to support a strike by sanitation workers. King had become more openly radical in his final years, opposing the war and working on class-based organizing of poor people. But he remained the nation's leading apostle of nonviolence, and his murder evoked despair among millions of citizens, especially African Americans. Police battled rioters and arsonists in black neighborhoods of 130 cities across the nation, with 46 people dying in the clashes. National Guard troops ringed the White House as smoke from hundreds of fires rose over Washington, D.C. Large parts of the nation's capital looked like a war zone.

Summer brought more shocking news. Charismatic Senator Robert Kennedy's entry into the presidential campaign inspired renewed hopes among Democratic liberals. On the night of his victory in the June 5 California primary, Kennedy was shot by a deranged gunman, Sirhan Sirhan, and died the next morning. Americans were stunned by this second murder of a Kennedy. Vice President Hubert Humphrey seemed assured of the nomination at the Democratic convention in Chicago in August, despite his association with Johnson's war policies. Some 10,000 antiwar activists, including hundreds of FBI *agents provocateurs* (spies seeking to provoke violence), showed up to engage in protests outside the convention. Chicago's Democratic mayor Richard Daley unleashed thousands of police on protesters, bystanders, and photographers in an orgy of beatings that subsequent investigations called a police riot. Ninety million Americans watched on television as a deeply divided Democratic party appeared helpless before the violence.

Into the vacuum of public anger and alienation that accompanied the liberals' self-destruction in Chicago stepped two men. The spread of the conservative backlash from 1964 to 1968 gave George Wallace a wider constituency for his right-wing populist message of hostility to liberals, blacks, and federal officials. With the national Democratic party committed to racial integration, the former Alabama governor ran for president as an independent candidate and won 13.5 percent of the popular vote in November. Republican candidate Richard Nixon, fresh from a unified convention in Miami, campaigned as the candidate of "law and order" and promised that he had a secret plan to end the war in Vietnam. His contacts with the South

TABLE 26.2			
The Election of 1968			
Candidate	**Political Party**	**Popular Vote (%)**	**Electoral Vote**
Richard M. Nixon	Republican	43.4	301
Hubert H. Humphrey	Democratic	42.7	191
George Wallace	American Independent	13.5	46

Vietnamese government helped ensure that no last-minute breakthrough in the Paris peace talks would boost Humphrey's popularity, and the former vice president squeezed past the current one by less than 1 percent of the popular vote.

THE NIXON ADMINISTRATION

A lonely, aloof man of great tenacity and ambition, Nixon had worked hard to remake his public image for 1968. Widely viewed as a somewhat unscrupulous partisan since his early career in Congress, he had refashioned himself as a statesman with a broad vision for reducing international tensions between the great powers. Foreign policy fascinated Nixon, and unlike Johnson, he found domestic governance utterly dull—a matter of "building outhouses in Peoria." He won the Republican presidential nomination primarily because he bridged the gap between the party's conservative Sunbelt wing and its moderate eastern wing. He sounded like a conservative in the campaign against Humphrey, but once in the White House he governed as the most liberal Republican since Theodore Roosevelt, pressed by a Congress still controlled by Democrats.

Nowhere was this clearer than on issues related to natural resources. Much had happened to the environment since the Republican Roosevelt's conservation efforts, none of it for the better. A powerful movement was building to protect natural resources and human health from the effects of air and water pollution. Biologist Paul Ehrlich's best-selling *The Population Bomb* (1968) warned of the dire consequences of the globe's runaway growth in human population. In 1969, the government banned the carcinogenic pesticide DDT, its original usefulness against mosquito-born malaria in World War II now almost forgotten in light of its broadly toxic effects on wildlife and aquatic ecosystems. That same year a huge oil spill off Santa Barbara fouled 200 miles of pristine California beaches, and the Cuyahoga River in Cleveland, its surface coated with waste and oil, caught fire and burned for days. *Apollo 8* astronauts brought home unprecedented pictures of the earth that seemed to dramatize the vulnerability of the small blue-green planet as it hung alone in space. Environmentalists around the country proclaimed April 22, 1970, as "Earth Day."

> *Foreign policy fascinated Nixon, and unlike Johnson, he found domestic governance utterly dull.*

Congress responded with legislation that mandated the careful management of the nation's natural resources. The Environmental Protection Agency was established in 1970. Amendments to the Clean Air (1970) and Clean Water (1972) acts tightened restrictions on harmful emissions from cars and factories. The Endangered Species Act (1973) created for the first time the legal right of nonhuman animals to survive, a major step toward viewing the quality of human life as inextricable from the earth's broader ecology. Nixon did not take the lead in promoting environmental laws, about which he personally cared little. He told business supporters that "in a flat choice between smoke and jobs, we're for jobs." But the president recognized the bipartisan popularity of actions to limit ecological damage, and he followed Congress's lead.

What Nixon did care deeply about at home was politics, not policy. Antiwar demonstrations reached their height during Nixon's first two years in the White House (1969–1970). He and Vice President Spiro Agnew loathed the protesters, whom they saw as weakening the nation. The two men pursued what Agnew called "positive polarization": campaigning to further divide the respectable "silent majority," as the president labeled his supporters, from voluble liberal Democrats in Congress and radical activists on the streets, whom they associated with permissiveness and lawlessness. In this broad cultural battle for political supremacy, the president appealed to conservative white southern and northern ethnic Democrats. His "Southern strategy" centered on opposing the use of court-ordered busing to desegregate public schools. He nominated two very conservative Southerners to the Supreme Court, only to see the Senate vote both of them down.

Early in his administration, Nixon began wielding the power of the federal government to harass his political opponents. Johnson had used the FBI, the CIA, and military intelligence agencies to infiltrate and thin the ranks of antiwar demonstrators and nonwhite nationalists. Nixon continued those illegal operations, agreeing with his predecessor that radical activists constituted a threat to national security. Nixon went beyond other presidents in assembling an "enemies list" that included prominent elements of the political mainstream, especially liberals, the press, and his Democratic opponents. The president was particularly concerned about controlling secret information. The Pentagon Papers were a classified Defense Department history of U.S. actions in Vietnam revealing that the government had been deceiving the American public about the course of the war. When disillusioned former Pentagon official Daniel Ellsberg leaked the study to the *New York Times* for publication in 1971, Nixon was enraged. The White House created a team of covert operatives nicknamed the "plumbers" to "plug leaks" by whatever means necessary, including breaking into the office of Ellsberg's psychiatrist in search of information they might use to discredit him publicly. The Supreme Court rejected the Justice Department's argument against allowing the publication of the Pentagon Papers.

■ On July 20, 1969, astronauts Neil Armstrong and Edwin "Buzz" Aldrin put the first footprints on the moon. The U.S. flag they planted epitomized the sense of national accomplishment in space, even as divisions wracked American society at home. The actual flag here was made of rigid material because no lunar breeze existed to make the flag wave.

Courtesy, National Aeronautics and Space Administration

ESCALATING AND DEESCALATING IN VIETNAM

Nixon recognized that in Vietnam the Truman Doctrine (see Chapter 24) had been stretched to the breaking point. The United States simply could not afford to send its troops everywhere abroad to contain the expansion of communism. The president and his national security adviser, Henry Kissinger, had ambitious plans for shifting the relationships of the great powers to America's advantage. To deal with China and the Soviet Union, they first had to reduce the vast U.S. engagement in the small country of Vietnam, which had grown wildly out of proportion to U.S. interests there. Under the Nixon Doctrine, the United States would provide military hardware rather than U.S. soldiers to allied governments, which would have to do their own fighting against leftist insurgencies. In South Vietnam, this doctrine required "Vietnamization," or withdrawing American troops so ARVN could shoulder the bulk of the war.

The key to a successful withdrawal from Vietnam for Nixon was to preserve U.S. "credibility." The perception of power could be as important as its actual exercise, and the president wanted other nations, both friend and foe, to continue to respect and fear American military might. There was no immediate pullout but a gradual process that lasted for four years (1969–1973), during which almost half of the total U.S. casualties in Vietnam occurred. To avoid a humiliating collapse of the Saigon regime as soon as Americans left, Nixon did his utmost to weaken the communist forces during the slow withdrawal. The administration escalated in order to deescalate. The president ordered the secret bombing and invasion of neighboring Cambodia and Laos, an intensified aerial assault on North Vietnam, and the mining of Haiphong Harbor near Hanoi. Enormous protests rocked the United States after the announcement of the Cambodian invasion on April 30, 1970. A strike by hundreds of thousands of students disrupted classes on more than 700 college campuses. National Guard troops killed four students at a demonstration at Kent State University in Ohio and two at Jackson State College in Mississippi, deepening the sense of national division.

Kent State Demonstrations

A majority of Americans now opposed the nation's war effort, a level of dissent unprecedented in U.S. history. Most telling of all was the criticism of some veterans returning from Vietnam. Although most stayed quiet about their traumatic experiences, some organized the Vietnam Veterans Against the War and even held public hearings into atrocities—war crimes—they and others had committed. These dissenters, including a young officer and future U.S. senator named John Kerry, were extremely hard for prowar Americans to discredit. The morale of American soldiers still in Vietnam plummeted as the steady withdrawal of their comrades made clear that they were no longer expected to win the war. Drug abuse and racial conflict increased sharply among GIs. Even "fragging" (killing one's own officers) escalated before the peace accords were signed in Paris and the United States evacuated its last combat troops in 1973.

Conclusion

Between 1964 and 1971, young, nonwhite, and female Americans laid claim to greater equality. The ratification of the Twenty-Sixth Amendment in 1971 reduced the voting age from twenty-one to eighteen, in acknowledgment of the sacrifices of young people sent to fight in Vietnam. In large numbers, women challenged and overcame traditional limits on their personal and work lives. Racial discrimination and segregation were outlawed. Immigration law for the first time welcomed new Americans equally, regardless of nation of origin or color of skin.

These years also witnessed striking disjunctures. The nation accomplished humanity's age-old dream of walking on the surface of the moon when Neil Armstrong stepped out of the *Apollo 11* spacecraft on July 20, 1969, while at home the country sometimes appeared to be coming apart at the seams. Poverty rates dropped to their lowest point ever, yet violence seemed to pervade the land. The slaughter of forty-three people (mostly African Americans) by white state police retaking the Attica prison in upstate New York after an inmate insurrection in 1971 was one of the single most deadly confrontations between Americans since the Civil War.

The Vietnam War ended the Cold War consensus about the nation's duty to oppose communism abroad. The loss of this cornerstone of public purpose disoriented many citizens. The deceptive manner in which Johnson and Nixon waged the war eroded Americans' faith in their public officials. American life also grew more informal as the egalitarian style of the various social movements of the 1960s spread into the broader culture. But the removal of some of the most blatant distinctions of race and gender did not

CHRONOLOGY: 1964–1971

1964	Gulf of Tonkin Resolution (supporting Johnson on Vietnam).
	Civil Rights Act of 1964 (employment).
	Wilderness Act.
1965	Voting Rights Act of 1965
	Griswold v. Connecticut legalizes birth control for married couples.
	Watts (Los Angeles) uprising.
1966	Clean Water Act.
	National Organization for Women (NOW) founded.
1967	Thurgood Marshall appointed first African American to U.S. Supreme Court.
	Riots in Detroit, Michigan, and Newark, New Jersey.
	Tet offensive (by Communist forces in Vietnam).
1968	My Lai massacre.
	Martin Luther King Jr. assassinated.
	Richard Nixon elected president.
1969	Huge antiwar protests in Washington, D.C.
	Stonewall raid, New York City.
	Astronauts Neil Armstrong and Buzz Aldrin walk on the moon.
1970	United States invades Cambodia (expanding war in Vietnam).
	National Guard troops kill four students, Kent State University in Ohio.
1971	Pentagon Papers published.

extend to differences of class. In the watershed cases of *San Antonio Independent School District v. Rodriguez* (1973) and *Milliken v. Bradley* (1974), the Supreme Court, led by Chief Justice Warren Burger, affirmed the autonomy of local school districts. Wealthier districts did not have to share financing with poorer ones, nor did they have to share students by means of busing. The Court ruled that there was no constitutional right to an education of equal quality. The ladder of social mobility remained slippery in a nation whose neighborhoods were still stratified between the affluent and the poor.

For Review

1. What did Lyndon Johnson think was wrong with American society, and how did he try to fix it?

2. How successful were Johnson's Great Society programs?

3. How was the U.S. war in Vietnam connected to the Great Society?

4. What were the most important reasons for the U.S. failure in Vietnam?

5. In which ways and how closely were the various protest movements of the 1960s related to each other?

6. How central were race relations to the conservative backlash that appeared in the late 1960s?

7. How persuasive is it to view the politics of the 1960s as divided into three camps: establishment liberals, radical protesters, and conservatives?

Created Equal Online

For more *Created Equal* resources, including suggestions for sites to visit and further reading, go to **MyHistoryLab.com.**

Chapter 27

Reconsidering National Priorities, 1972–1979

■ Emily Howell Warner, the first woman hired as a pilot by a scheduled U.S. carrier.

ABC television news anchor Howard K. Smith began his coverage of a women's rights march in New York City in 1970 by quoting with approval the words of Vice President Spiro Agnew: "Three things have been difficult to tame. The ocean, fools, and women. We may soon be able to tame the ocean, but fools and women will take a little longer." Condescension toward women pervaded American society, and few men even noticed it. The political upheavals of the 1960s had barely touched the relationships between most women and men by the start of the new decade. But all this changed as the 1970s unfolded.

The spread of ideas about women's liberation in the 1970s transformed the personal lives of almost every American, female and male alike. **Feminism** challenged the most basic and intimate assumptions about relationships, family, work, and power. It also sharply expanded women's opportunities. For example, Emily Howell Warner was born in 1939 and grew up in Colorado, wanting to be a flight attendant. Friends suggested she try flying lessons instead. On a regular commercial flight one day, a flight attendant took her up to see the cockpit. She was fascinated by "all those dials and switches" and knew she wanted to fly. After years of hard work and training, in 1973 Warner became the first woman hired as a pilot by a scheduled U.S. carrier, Frontier Airlines. At first she felt uncertain where she fit in: women were part of the flight attendant group and men were part of the pilot group, leaving her to eat alone on some layover trips. But her professionalism and respect for fellow workers soon earned her acceptance everywhere. Within three years, she was the first female promoted to captain, and in 1986 Warner commanded the first all-female flight crew on a commercial flight.

Feminism joined with other developments of the decade to force Americans to reexamine much that they had taken for granted. Elected on the promise to end the war in Southeast Asia "with honor," President Nixon escalated the fighting before eventually withdrawing U.S. forces from Vietnam. At the same time, he repaired relations with both China and the Soviet Union as those two communist powers drew apart. Americans thus suffered their first clear defeat in war while also seeing the Cold War splinter. Scandal in the White House then forced the first resignation of a U.S. president and deepened public distrust of political authorities. American economic growth—the foundation of the country's power—stumbled because of spending on the Vietnam War and oil shortages. High-paying manufacturing jobs declined as factories began to move overseas in pursuit of cheaper labor, and skilled blue-collar workers saw their status as middle-class Americans start to slip. Unemployment grew sharply. A growing environmental movement raised disturbing questions about whether an expanding economy and exploitation of natural resources should continue to top the country's list of priorities.

The nation celebrated its 200th birthday in 1976 amid these uncertainties. That year, one-term Georgia governor Jimmy Carter won election to the White House by promising to restore honesty and trust to the federal government. In his first two years in office, Carter shifted the nation's foreign-policy focus away from fighting communism toward building warmer relations with the Third World. He saw Americans' dependence on imported oil as a primary national security problem and implored citizens to scale back their lavish consumption of fossil fuels. But his presidency eventually foundered on persistent economic stagnation and inflation at home, upheavals abroad, and Carter's own limitations as chief executive.

Journalist Tom Wolfe famously dubbed the 1970s the "Me Decade." The label did have some merit: many Americans turned away from the public sphere after the exhilarating but divisive politics of the 1960s and pursued self-exploration and self-fulfillment instead. Crime, divorce, premarital and extramarital sex, and drug use all increased while the nation's economic health and international status declined. But the 1970s also witnessed a rethinking of long-standing assumptions: about how democracy should work at home, what role the nation should play in international affairs, how people ought to treat the environment, and how men and women should relate to each other. The decade offered a window of opportunity for Americans to reimagine their values and priorities for the future.

Twin Shocks: Détente and Watergate

■ *How did détente and the Watergate scandal affect U.S. foreign relations and American politics?*

Richard Nixon had long been the nation's leading anticommunist. No one had more fiercely opposed leftists at home and communists in China and the Soviet Union. However, the president was more a savvy political opportunist than an ideologue. He and his national security adviser, Henry Kissinger, saw a chance to use mounting Chinese-Soviet tensions to the advantage of the United States as they withdrew American armed forces from Vietnam.

At the same time that Nixon manipulated the Cold War abroad, the Republican president initiated a campaign of illegal actions at home to weaken his political opponents in the Democratic party. This strategy backfired in the Watergate scandal, which drove him from office in 1974. Having undercut the logic of anticommunism abroad by warming relations with communist leaders in Beijing and Moscow, Nixon eroded the bipartisan consensus at home that had long supported the Cold War.

TRIANGULAR DIPLOMACY

Nixon and Kissinger prided themselves on their "realpolitik" approach to foreign policy: their pragmatic assessment of other powers' security needs, regardless of ideology, and their collaboration with those powers on issues of common concern. In 1969, China and the USSR gave Nixon and Kissinger an ideal opportunity to exercise their realpolitik skills. That year, tensions that had been building between the two communist states erupted in brief skirmishing between Chinese and Soviet troops on their shared border. For two decades, Americans had seen the communist bloc as impenetrable. But Nixon realized he could play China and the USSR against each other, and he seized the chance. That is, he saw a way to make not only Chinese leader Mao Zedong but also Soviet leader Leonid Brezhnev into another "Tito," an independent communist with ties to the West, like Premier Josef Tito of Yugoslavia. Nixon thus envisioned a "triangular diplomacy" that he hoped would divide the communist world.

> *Nixon realized he could play China and the USSR against each other, and he seized the chance.*

The president and Kissinger, a former Harvard professor with an intriguing German accent, also shared a commitment to secrecy. Any fundamental revision of the nation's foreign policy, they believed, could happen only if they concentrated all decision-making in the White House. They set out to keep Congress, the press, and even their own State Department in the dark. Diplomatic innovation thus went hand in hand with an unprecedented extension of the secretive national security state.

In February 1972, after a secret foray by Kissinger to Beijing, Nixon stunned Americans and the world by announcing that he would be the first U.S. president to visit China. The Soviets and the Vietnamese expressed dismay at the news, and liberal Democrats at home could only gape, speechless, at their opponent's diplomatic coup: how could Nixon, a dyed-in-the-wool anticommunist, go to China? But that was precisely the point: as Democratic party insider Clark Clifford explained, Nixon was "the first president since the [Second World] War who didn't have to worry about Richard Nixon" attacking him for being "soft" on communism.

As it turned out, Nixon's visit brought a host of benefits. Live television coverage showed Nixon toasting Mao while a Chinese military band played "America the Beautiful" and "Home on the Range." Americans' impression of the People's Republic as a grim, forbidding land began to give way to a renewed interest in China as an exotic but intriguing place. Cultural exchanges soon proliferated: first ping-pong teams, then legions of students. U.S. businesses also cast a covetous eye at the immense China market. Trade between the two nations rose dramatically over the next three decades.

Nixon and Kissinger now constructed the other leg of their diplomatic triangle. As they anticipated, the Soviets had taken alarm at the warming of relations between their two greatest rivals. They signaled their concern to Washington and suggested that the United States include them in the new arrangements. The Russians and the Americans both wanted to reduce the costliness of maintaining enormous nuclear arsenals, and each side saw lucrative trading possibilities with the other. Nixon flew to Moscow for a summit meeting with Brezhnev in May 1972 that initiated a policy of **détente** (relaxation of tensions). A trade pact quickly followed. The two superpowers also agreed to limit offensive nuclear weapons (the Strategic Arms Limitations Treaty, or SALT I) and to ban antiballistic missile defense systems (the ABM treaty).

The National Archives

■ President Nixon met the premier of the People's Republic of China, Mao Zedong, in Beijing on February 29, 1972. The U.S. government had shunned China since its communist revolution in 1949. Richard Nixon's amiable visit there stunned observers and altered the dynamics of the Cold War.

Like the Soviet leaders, Nixon and Kissinger sought to preserve the existing international balance of power. Deal making with China and the USSR constituted one step in this process. In another, the two men sought to stifle socialist revolutions in Third World nations by bolstering pro-American allies there. For instance, the duo feared that the democratic election of socialist Salvador Allende in Chile in 1970 would lead to "another Cuba." A socialist leader might nationalize the investments of U.S. corporations in Chile and perhaps challenge Washington's capitalist dominance in the Western Hemisphere. Determined to block these possibilities, the CIA secretly funded a right-wing military coup in Chile in September 1973. Allende died in the assault on the presidential palace, and the rebel forces murdered thousands of his supporters and established a brutal military dictatorship under General Augusto Pinochet. "I don't see why we need to stand by and watch a country go Communist because of the irresponsibility of its own people," Kissinger explained privately.

There was little danger of such voter "irresponsibility" in South Africa, a nation that would not see democratic elections for another two decades. Still, the Nixon administration backed the white minority regime there, despite worldwide criticism of the government's policies of total racial segregation, or apartheid. Nixon's "southern strategy" of appealing to segregationist whites at home during the 1968 election campaign thus had an international parallel. He sought to preserve a pro-American order in South Africa, the southern tip of a continent rife with political instability.

Nixon and Kissinger reached beyond Latin America and Africa. They also bolstered the autocratic regime of Shah Reza Pahlavi of Iran. They sold him unlimited arms in return for Iranian oil shipments and political support in the strategic Middle East, where the United States had few allies. The president could not know it at the time, but preserving the shah's oppressive rule carried a high price—one that the United States would begin to pay before the 1970s were over.

SCANDAL IN THE WHITE HOUSE

Meanwhile, on the domestic front, Washington police caught agents of Nixon's reelection campaign breaking into the Democratic National Committee headquarters in the **Watergate** hotel and office complex on June 17, 1972. The burglars' goal was to put in place secretive listening devices, or "bugs." Later, the White House tried to cover up its connections to the crime.

Ironically, the Republicans hardly needed to resort to illegal actions to hold onto the White House in 1972. The New Deal coalition that had kept the Democrats as the majority party since the 1930s was fast unraveling. White Southerners and many ethnic European Northerners were abandoning the party amid its increasing identification with black civil rights, feminism, and cultural liberalism. Middle- and upper-middle-class liberal activists had helped nominate Senator George McGovern of South Dakota, a former World War II pilot and college professor, as the Democratic presidential candidate, primarily on the basis of his principled and long-standing opposition to the war in Vietnam. Playing upon voter anxiety about cultural changes, the Republicans tarred McGovern's supporters with favoring "the 3 A's": acid (the drug LSD), abortion, and amnesty for draft evaders. McGovern's campaign never overcame that image of radicalism, and in November Nixon won 61 percent of the popular vote. He also swept the electoral votes of every state but one. Bumper stickers reading "Don't blame me, I'm from Massachusetts" proliferated as the Watergate scandal deepened.

TABLE 27.1			
The Election of 1972			
Candidate	**Political Party**	**Popular Vote(%)**	**Electoral Vote**
Richard M. Nixon	Republican	60.7	520
George S. McGovern	Democratic	31.5	17

The Watergate break-in had been only one part of the administration's broader campaign against Nixon's political opponents. The president had compiled a lengthy and secret "enemies list." And in May 1969, Nixon and Kissinger had established the first in a long series of wiretaps without court warrants on their own staffs and on reporters. They were determined to discover the source of a newspaper story that had mentioned secret American bombing of neutral Cambodia. Several wartime presidents in the past had successfully silenced dissenters, but Nixon overreached still further. The president ultimately poisoned the very heart of American politics by his clandestine use of the government's powerful executive branch to undermine the mainstream opposition party and others who seemed to challenge his policies.

The president and his aides regularly discussed "how we can use the available federal machinery to screw our political enemies," in the words of White House counsel John Dean. They persuaded the FBI and the CIA to monitor and harass antiwar activists and pushed the Internal Revenue Service to investigate prominent Democrats. They extorted large contributions to the Republican party from corporate executives by making it clear that federal agencies would otherwise impede the pursuit of their business interests. The *New York Times*'s publication of the classified Pentagon Papers in 1971 stiffened the resolve of the Committee to Reelect the President (CREEP) to stop any further leaks. The committee assembled a group of undercover operatives (the "plumbers") to stop leaks and engineer "dirty tricks" against the Democrats. Their activities included smearing the reputation of one leading presidential candidate, Senator Edmund Muskie of Maine, and sowing dissent and distrust among Democratic voters.

After the bungled Watergate break-in, the president directed the cover-up from the beginning, then lied about it to the public. He also used the CIA to hinder the FBI's investigation into the matter. He approved payments of hush money to the burglars to keep them quiet about their ties to the White House. Nixon's abuse of power escalated as he pressured his subordinates to perjure themselves in court. For most of a year, the cover-up held, and Nixon won reelection in 1972.

Richard Nixon, "I am not a crook"

But the persistent investigations by *Washington Post* journalists Bob Woodward and Carl Bernstein kept the heat on. In early 1973, the administration began to crack due to a grand jury probe in the federal court of Judge John Sirica. The president's men lost confidence that the cover-up would hold and began looking for ways to save their own skins. Convicted Watergate burglar James McCord wrote Judge Sirica that the White House had indeed been involved in the break-in. White House counsel Dean and former Attorney General John Mitchell refused Nixon's requests to absorb full blame and become scapegoats. Congress initiated its own televised investigations that mesmerized a national audience. The Senate Watergate committee, chaired by eloquent conservative North Carolina Democrat Sam Ervin, methodically exposed with growing bipartisan support the criminal actions in the White House. The key issue, as framed by Republican committee member Howard Baker of Tennessee, became "What did the president know, and when did he know it?"

On July 16, 1973, White House aide Alexander Butterfield told the Ervin committee that a built-in recorder taped all conversations in the Oval Office. Almost certainly, these tapes would provide answers to questions about the president's role. Both Congress and Justice Department special prosecutor Archibald Cox subpoenaed the White House tapes, but Nixon refused to hand them over. Instead, he fired Cox on October 20 in what

On August 9, 1974, Richard Nixon became the only U.S. president to resign from office. As he left by helicopter one last time from the south lawn of the White House, he offered a defiant victory gesture rather than a presidential salute (inset). Vice President Gerald Ford, with his wife, Betty, then walked back to the White House to be sworn in as the nation's 38th president.

DOCUMENT

Committee's Conclusion on Impeachment

became known as the Saturday Night Massacre. Outraged, Congress initiated impeachment proceedings against the president. In the spring of 1974, the House Judiciary Committee passed bills of impeachment for his specific abuses of power. Before the full House could vote to impeach him and the Senate decide on his guilt or innocence, the Supreme Court ruled that the White House had to turn over the subpoenaed tapes. The content of the tapes revealed the extent of the president's involvement in the cover-up and his personal crudeness, vindictiveness, and ethnic and racial prejudices. Facing a certain guilty verdict, Nixon resigned on August 9, 1974, less than halfway through his second term.

THE NATION AFTER WATERGATE

Never before had a U.S. president resigned from office. Many citizens celebrated the outcome of the Watergate investigations as evidence of democracy's resilience and power to uncover criminal activity in the White House and bring down a corrupt president. But the affair also discredited political institutions Americans had long respected. If you can't trust the president, U.S. citizens lamented, whom *can* you trust? Indeed, the Nixon administration proved quite corrupt. A whole raft of senior officials, including the president's closest aides, H. R. Haldeman and John Ehrlichman, went to prison. Even Vice President Spiro Agnew had been forced to resign amid the Watergate investigations when a Maryland jury found him guilty of tax evasion dating back to his years as governor there. The actions of Nixon and those who served him permanently tarnished the reputation of politicians, and some citizens responded by disengaging from the political process. The percentage of eligible voters actually casting ballots sank from 61 percent in 1968 to 53 percent in 1980, diminishing the practice of democracy: rule by the people.

Since 1945, the executive branch had grown increasingly powerful during the international crises of the Cold War, but Nixon's fall crippled the "imperial presidency." After Watergate, Congress began to reclaim its constitutional responsibilities in international affairs. As the bicentennial of American independence approached, citizens' suspicion of corruption in high places recalled the Whiggish attitudes of the country's revolutionary leaders two centuries before. Most immediately, Congress swung strongly to the Democrats in the 1974 elections, slowing the Republicans' rise to the status of majority party.

The man who replaced Nixon in the White House faced a daunting situation. Gerald Ford, longtime Republican member of Congress from Grand Rapids, Michigan, and House minority leader, had been tapped by Nixon to replace Agnew as vice president. Well liked by members of both parties, Ford seemed to embody the antidote to the extreme styles of both Nixon and Agnew. To restore decency and trust in the government, Ford saw his role as healing what he called "the wounds of the past." Within a month, he granted a "full, free, and absolute pardon" to Nixon for any crimes he may have committed as president, precluding any trial and punishment within a court of law. However, most Americans believed that Nixon should have faced justice for his actions, as had the people who carried out his orders. Ford's approval ratings plummeted overnight from 72 percent to 49 percent and never fully recovered.

If Ford inherited the fallout from Watergate at home, abroad he inherited the pending defeat in Vietnam. Few Americans wanted to dwell on the meaning of the disastrous U.S. involvement in Southeast Asia. Military veterans returned to a nation determined to ignore or demean their sacrifices, and they quickly learned to keep their combat-induced traumas to themselves. When Saigon finally fell to the combined invasion of National Liberation Front

Hubert Van Es/Bettmann/CORBIS

■ The last U.S. combat troops left Vietnam in 1973. Forces of the National Liberation Front and North Vietnam swept into the capital of South Vietnam, Saigon, on April 30, 1975. Here, one day earlier, a U.S. Marine helicopter on the roof of the U.S. embassy loads Americans and a few Vietnamese allies onto one of the last flights out.

■ Many South Vietnamese fled the communist victory in their country in 1975, including this woman and her family crossing the Mekong River. Refugees undertook extremely perilous journeys by boat to other Southeast Asian nations, and half a million eventually made their way to the United States.

and North Vietnamese fighters on April 30, 1975, Americans watched the televised images with both bitterness and relief. Two weeks later, Cambodian communist forces briefly seized the U.S. container ship *Mayaguez*, provoking Ford to demonstrate that the United States was still ready and willing to flex its military muscle. But forty-one U.S. soldiers died in the rescue mission to save thirty-nine sailors whom, it turned out, Cambodia had already released. Ford and Kissinger, continuing as the new president's secretary of state, pursued détente with the Soviets at summit meetings in Vladivostock (1974) and Helsinki (1975). At the same time, they supported anticommunist forces in various Third World conflicts, such as the civil war that erupted in Angola after that country achieved its independence in 1975.

Discovering the Limits of the U.S. Economy

■ *How did economic changes affect the way Americans felt about their country?*

Defeat in Vietnam and corruption in the White House were soon joined by grim economic news. Generation after generation of Americans had watched their incomes rise, and most children expected to be wealthier than their parents had been. Since World War II had pulled the U.S. economy out of the Great Depression, median family income had doubled. Most Americans saw themselves as citizens of the world's richest country and prized the status that came with this privilege. But by 1973, the famous American standard of living began to decline. The three pillars of postwar prosperity—cheap energy, rising wages, and low inflation—simultaneously crumbled. The costs of the Vietnam War struck home at the same time that an oil embargo spawned by conflict in the Middle East gripped the country. Moreover, a widening environmental movement raised questions about the pursuit of endless economic growth on a planet that more and more people realized had limited natural resources. For the first time since the 1930s, Americans started to doubt what the economic future had in store for them.

THE END OF THE LONG BOOM

Stagnation and inflation typically do not strike an economy at the same time. With stagnation, prices and wages stay level or even decline; with inflation, prices rise and jobs often multiply. During the 1970s, however, a terrible new economic scourge dubbed "stagflation" hit the United States. For the first time, employment and wages stagnated while prices climbed. What explained this phenomenon? Spending on the Vietnam War and on Great Society programs had pulled prices upward. The government had never raised enough taxes to cover the cost of the war, so it paid the bills by simply printing more dollars—a sure-fire way to create inflation. In 1971, annual inflation stood at 4.3 percent, more than twice the pre-Vietnam rate; three years later it reached 11 percent, and by 1980 it topped out at 13.5 percent.

These figures devastated Americans' sense of economic security. Average real wages (income adjusted for inflation) dropped by 2 percent a year from 1973 to the 1990s. Unemployment rose to 9 percent in 1975, driven in part by continued automation of the workplace. Only the continued flow of women into the workforce, seen by most families as an economic necessity, kept the majority of U.S. families afloat financially. The portion of citizens living in poverty, which had dropped sharply through the 1960s to 11 percent in 1973, rose again, hitting 15 percent by 1982. The gap between rich and poor began widening.

> For the first time since the 1930s, Americans started to doubt what the economic future had in store for them.

So ended the long boom of economic growth that had buoyed American life from 1945 to 1973. But perhaps the most telling evidence of the weakening economy came with the drop in the growth of productivity: output per worker-hour had risen at an annual average of more than 3 percent during the postwar boom. From 1974 to 1992, it rose at less than half that rate.

This decline stemmed in part from competition from abroad, particularly West Germany and Japan. With U.S. assistance (and without the military expenditures that so burdened the United States), those countries had finally rebuilt their economies after World War II and boasted new, more efficient industrial facilities. Imported cars, for example, grew from just 8 percent of the U.S. market in 1970 to 22 percent in 1979 as Hondas, Toyotas, Volkswagens, and Mercedes streamed onto American highways. And the trade surplus that had long symbolized global U.S. economic superiority evaporated in 1971. That year, U.S. imports overtook exports for the first time in the twentieth century. Worried international investors traded in dollars for gold, forcing Nixon to end the twenty-seven-year-old Bretton Woods monetary system that had linked all other currencies to the dollar at fixed exchange rates. Freed from the fixed rate of $35 per ounce of gold, the value of the dollar dropped like a stone; by the end of the decade, it took $800 to buy an ounce of gold.

In this competitive environment, the *Wall Street Journal* reported, American companies "seek places where labor, land, electricity, and taxes are cheap." Corporations found those places in the American South and Southwest, regions characterized by few labor unions, low wage rates, minimal taxes, and negligible local government regulations. Many more such places were in neighboring Mexico, where U.S. companies established *maquiladoras* as early as 1965. These assembly plants, often just a few hundred yards across the Mexican-U.S. border, allowed corporations to hire primarily female workers at low wages and avoid strict U.S. environmental, labor, and safety laws. "The worst drawback of maquiladora work is all the damage we do to our health" by working with toxic chemicals and solvents, one employee reported. The wages, cheap by U.S. standards, were nonetheless higher than elsewhere in Mexico and drew laborers from central Mexico north to the border region. The long-term decline of the U.S. Rustbelt—the series of urban industrial centers strung across the American Northeast and Midwest—accelerated in the 1970s.

Stanley J.Forman, *The Soiling of Old Glory*, Pulitzer Prize 1976

■ White resistance to school busing in Boston sometimes turned violent in the mid-1970s. On April 5, 1976, white high school students from South Boston and Charlestown met with a city council member who supported their boycott of classes. Outside City Hall, they chanced upon lawyer Theodore Landsmark and assaulted him. Photographer Stanley J. Forman won the Pulitzer Prize for this photo.

High unemployment and shrinking real wages contributed to rising anti-immigrant sentiment. Two white autoworkers in Detroit in 1982 got into an altercation in a bar with Vincent Chin, a Chinese American (and son of a World War II veteran) whom they called a "Jap." Angered that Japanese auto sales were undercutting jobs in Detroit, they made Chin a scapegoat for their rage, chasing him down the street and beating him to death with a baseball bat. At the same time, Vietnamese refugees who had fled the communist victory in their homeland in 1975 to make a life as shrimp fishers on the Gulf Coast of Texas found their equipment sabotaged by some white competitors.

From Texas to California, Latinos also suffered violence at the hands of both officials and private citizens. For example, three members of the Ku Klux Klan abducted a Latino hitchhiker outside San Diego and delivered him to the U.S. Immigration Service for deportation to Mexico, even though he was an American citizen. Twelve poor Mexican American women brought suit against a Los Angeles medical center for sterilizing them while they were giving birth. In *Madrigal v. Quilligan* (1978), a federal court found that the unwanted sterilizations had resulted from miscommunication rather than malice. But public pressure resulting from the case helped persuade the hospital to stop encouraging Latinas to give up the ability to have more children.

Black Americans also faced an increasing backlash against hard-won civil rights gains. While court-ordered busing to integrate schools in segregated neighborhoods proceeded slowly but peacefully in the South, northern urban whites dug in their heels. In Boston, violence erupted in the school hallways and the streets from 1975 to 1978 as economically vulnerable working-class whites harassed African Americans attending schools in white ethnic neighborhoods of South Boston, and blacks defended themselves.

THE OIL EMBARGO

Nothing revealed Americans' newfound economic vulnerability more than the 1973–1974 boycott initiated by the Oil Producing and Exporting Countries (OPEC). The United States and the Soviet Union, along with Mexico and Venezuela, retained large oil reserves. But the largest producers were the Arab countries around the Persian Gulf, especially Saudi Arabia. These nations had resented the creation of Israel in 1948 and the resulting displacement of the Palestinians. Hostility intensified with the events of 1967. That year, Israel seized control of the West Bank of the Jordan River, the Gaza Strip, and the Golan Heights. Six years later, Egypt and Syria struck back, attacking and threatening to overrun Israel.

At this point, the United States intervened. Nixon instructed the Pentagon to "send everything that will fly" to the Israelis—a massive resupply of weapons, combined with intelligence on Arab troop movements. "We will not let Israel go down the tubes," the president declared. The tide of battle turned. Henry Kissinger then shuttled between Tel Aviv

U.S. Dependence on Petroleum Imports

Global warming results from the burning of fossil fuels like petroleum, and the United States uses more fossil fuels than any other nation. Abundant natural resources, particularly coal and oil, long encouraged Americans' sense of national strength and autonomy. After World War II, however, the United States switched from exporting to importing petroleum. Dependence on imported oil has grown dramatically ever since, as Americans have built a vibrant economy and culture that hinge on access to relatively inexpensive oil.

QUESTIONS

1. What does this graph suggest about Americans' lifestyle choices and their attitudes toward conservation?

2. How does dependence on imported oil help determine U.S. foreign policy?

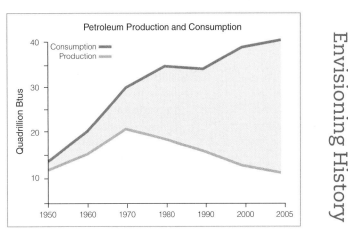

Source: Energy Information Administration, U.S. Department of Energy, Annual Energy Review 2005.

Envisioning History

and Cairo to negotiate a ceasefire. His diplomatic skills won him the Nobel peace prize and laid the groundwork for a warming of U.S. relations with Egypt (the most populous Arab nation, though not an oil producer).

However, the other Arab states expressed outrage at this demonstration of America's close links with the Israelis, and Kissinger's being Jewish only underlined the point. The U.S. commitment to Israel had never been clearer, and Arabs of all political persuasions were determined to voice their displeasure. In October 1973, the OPEC nations initiated an embargo on selling oil to the United States and to western European nations that had supported Israel in the war. Never before in peacetime had foreign policy affected Americans so directly. Oil supplies dwindled, and prices at gas pumps skyrocketed to four times their previous levels. Even when OPEC lifted the embargo after five months, it kept prices high by limiting production.

Steeper energy costs powerfully accelerated inflation. Decades of easy access to cheap gasoline came to a sudden halt. As American drivers formed long lines at the pump, President Ford urged them to drive at lower speeds to conserve gas. Americans confronted new and sobering limits on their mobility.

THE ENVIRONMENTAL MOVEMENT

The oil embargo encouraged many U.S. citizens to rethink the nation's cavalier use of natural resources. Environmental consciousness spread rapidly in the 1970s as evidence revealed the impact of industrial growth on the quality of life in the United States. Environmental organizations such as the Sierra Club, the National Wildlife Federation, and the Audubon Society saw their memberships soar. For the first time, the media began to examine the daunting range of environmental problems plaguing the United States and the rest of the world: acid rain, groundwater contamination, smog, rainforest destruction, oil spills, nuclear waste disposal, species extinction, ozone depletion, and global warming. A growing interest in ecology—human interaction with the wider web of life—expanded the efforts of older conservationists to preserve parklands. Residents of an urbanized mass society began to contemplate the wider consequences of small private acts such as watering the lawn, flushing the toilet, or leaving the lights on.

A new generation of Americans, unable to remember Depression scarcities and wartime rationing, was wasteful, sometimes extravagantly so. U.S. soldiers had expressed surprise when displaced Vietnamese civilians built shelters out of the aluminum cans the troops threw away so casually. Home to only 6 percent of the global population, the United States consumed as much as a third of the world's energy from nonrenewable fossil fuels such as oil and coal. Polluted air hung over the largest U.S. cities. The first evidence of global warming began to appear in the 1970s. Scientists also noticed the rapid thinning of the ozone layer in the earth's atmosphere in 1973. They attributed the problem in part to the widespread use of aerosol spray cans—especially by Americans, the world's wealthiest people. The production of inexpensive plastics from oil had also soared since World War II. Styrofoam cups and plastic containers littered the roadsides. Disposable diapers and other nonbiodegradable products accumulated in landfills in what became known as the throwaway culture.

Environmentalists argued that the idea of unlimited consumption of natural resources was fundamentally irresponsible, both to future human generations and to other species. They urged Congress and the Environmental Protection Agency (EPA) to require fuel-efficient engines from carmakers and to promote renewable energy sources such as water, solar, and wind power. Citizen groups such as the Clamshell Alliance in New England and the Abalone Alliance in California protested the construction of new nuclear power plants. These operations, they pointed out, had no reliable method in place for disposing of nuclear waste. What if the public were exposed to radiation? Their warnings had merit: cancer rates began to rise in populations that had close contact with radioactive materials from the early Cold War years forward, such as communities near the Hanford nuclear facility in south central Washington state and towns downwind from the Atomic Test Site in Nevada. One Utah mother who lost a daughter to cancer felt "disappointed and hurt" by the "horrific neglect and indifference" of a government that would permit such contamination and then deny that there was any danger. "We were used. We were conned," another woman testified to Congress about government secrecy regarding the impact of radiation. "They knew and they didn't tell us."

> Environmentalists argued that the idea of unlimited consumption of natural resources was fundamentally irresponsible.

A broad critique of the chemical industry's impact on public health also emerged in the 1970s. As it turned out, pesticides worked their way up the food chain into people's bodies. Some artificial sweeteners proved carcinogenic, and the lead that manufacturers had added to gasoline and house paint for generations caused brain damage. Long-standing industrial dumping of toxic chemicals made headlines. In 1975, investigations revealed that tons of cancer-causing polychlorinated biphenyls (PCBs) from General Electric plants lined the bottom of the Hudson River north of New York City. Four years later, the EPA announced that the nation had 32,000 to 50,000 major sites containing hazardous waste.

The crisis at Love Canal in New York helped bring the issue of toxic waste home to Americans. The Hooker Chemical Company had buried tons of poisonous waste in a dry canal in the town of Niagara Falls between 1947 and 1952 and then covered it over with dirt. The company gave the land to the town, which promptly built a school on it. A middle-class neighborhood soon grew up around the site. But the ground smelled odd and oozed mysterious substances. Sometimes it even caught on fire for no apparent reason. By the 1970s, local rates of cancer and other severe illnesses had soared. The chemical and industrial plant workers who lived in the neighborhood began to suspect that their quiet loyalty to their employers was no longer worth the risk to the health of their families. Persistent activism by community members, led by housewife and mother Lois Gibbs and publicized by reporter Michael Brown, finally overcame local, state, and company officials' efforts to keep the contents of the buried canal secret. In August 1978, New York governor Hugh Carey at last agreed to buy out the entire neighborhood, seal it off, and move residents elsewhere. The Love Canal debacle accelerated American workers' loss of faith in the corporations and governments they had once trusted. "There are ticking time bombs all over," an EPA official concluded. "We just don't know how many potential Love Canals there are."

Discovering the limits of the U.S. economy so soon after the Vietnam War and the Watergate scandal spawned a crisis of confidence. Some Americans resented the idea of limits: on how much gas they could buy, how much the economy could grow, how much influence the United States could have abroad. At the same time, others began to embrace the idea of creating a healthier lifestyle that focused less on material consumption. Cigarette smoking started to decline. Organic food sales picked up. Exercise, especially running, became an increasingly common activity for middle-class adults. The wildly successful Nike athletic shoe company was established in 1972; co-founder Bill Bowerman, the University of Oregon track coach, poured urethane rubber over a waffle iron to create the first waffle-sole running shoe. Entrants in the New York City Marathon ballooned from 126 in 1970 to 10,000 by 1978. Interest in outdoor recreation—hiking, camping, and bicycling—grew exponentially. Recycling also started its climb from a fringe activity to common practice in a few parts of the country. The government began to get the message, too. Federal agencies banned the use of hazardous products such as the pesticide DDT and the artificial sweetener sodium cyclamate in the original Gatorade formula. And in January 1974, Congress reduced the national speed limit to 55 miles per hour to conserve fuel.

> *In January 1974, Congress reduced the national speed limit to 55 miles per hour to conserve fuel.*

Reshuffling Politics

■ *Which were the most significant political reforms of the 1970s?*

The skepticism toward authority and tradition spawned by the counterculture, the Vietnam War, and the Watergate scandal spread through American culture in the 1970s. The use of illegal drugs, especially marijuana, was widespread. Casual sexual relationships proliferated in a decade when contraceptive pills had become widely available and the AIDS virus had not yet been identified. Popular and critically acclaimed films featured tales of malfeasance in high places. *All the President's Men* (1976) told the story of the Nixon administration's Watergate crimes. *Apocalypse Now* (1979) revealed the madness of the American war in Vietnam. *Three Days of the Condor* (1975) portrayed the CIA as a rogue agency beyond democratic control. *Chinatown* (1975) suggested the vast corruption marring the early twentieth-century growth of Los Angeles. *Blazing Saddles* (1974) hilariously spoofed the heroic westerns that had long served as the staple of American moviegoers' diet. And *One Flew Over the Cuckoo's Nest* (1975) used novelist Ken Kesey's story of an insane asylum to imply that those in charge were more dangerous than the inmates. In this atmosphere, Congress began to reassert its authority against the "imperial presidency," and in 1976 voters put an obscure, devout Georgia peanut farmer and former one-term governor in the White House.

CONGRESSIONAL POWER REASSERTED

The double shock of defeat in Vietnam and the Watergate scandal reawakened a Congress that had grown accustomed to deferring to the White House in foreign affairs. Tellingly, Congress had never formally declared war on North Korea or North Vietnam, although such declaration is its constitutional duty. Angered by the illegalities and deception in both the Johnson and Nixon administrations, Congress passed the War Powers Act in 1973 to limit the president's capacity to wage undeclared wars. The bill required the chief executive to obtain explicit congressional approval for keeping U.S. troops in an overseas conflict longer than ninety days.

Congress did not limit its muscle-flexing to keeping Americans out of conflicts with Third World leftists. It also promoted human rights within the communist bloc, cutting against the grain of Secretary of State Kissinger's realpolitik approach to Moscow. The Jackson-Vanik Amendment of 1974 sought to make the Soviet Union pay for its repression of Jewish dissidents by linking détente directly to human rights, much to Kissinger's dismay. To acquire most-favored-nation trading status with the United States, Moscow would have to let Jews emigrate.

With encouragement from voters and journalists, Congress also uncovered its eyes and began to investigate the covert side of American foreign policy that had gathered momentum since 1945. After Watergate popped the cork on the bottled-up secret abuses of the executive branch, other troubling news spilled out about the nation's intelligence agencies. Dissident former CIA agents such as Philip Agee began revealing "dirty tricks" that the agency had long used. And *New York Times* investigative reporter Seymour Hersh, author of the My Lai massacre exposé a few years earlier, uncovered the CIA's Operation Chaos. This program of illegal domestic espionage against antiwar dissidents paralleled FBI abuses such as the Cointelpro campaigns to defame Martin Luther King Jr. and destroy the Black Panthers and the American Indian Movement. Congressional committees led by Otis Pike of New York in the House and Frank Church of Idaho in the Senate initiated their own investigations of the national security state's tactics. Their documentation of CIA involvement in assassination attempts against foreign leaders such as Fidel Castro of Cuba and Patrice Lumumba of the Congo suggested that U.S. government agencies would secretly go to any lengths to prevail in the Cold War.

These revelations stirred fierce controversy among those who took an interest in national and international politics. Many citizens decried what their government had done in their names and without their knowledge. However, officials claimed that the extreme conditions of the Cold War and the duplicity of the Soviets necessitated secrecy. Convinced that information gathered by the Church and Pike committees threatened to

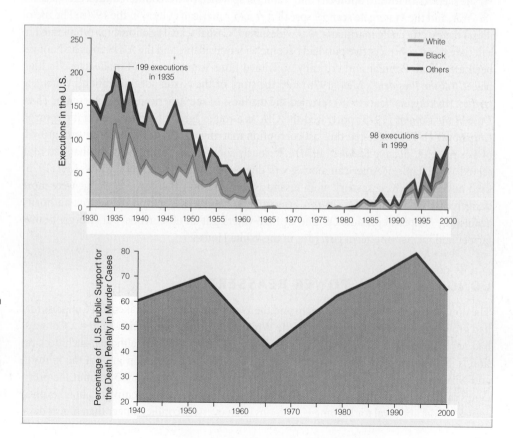

■ **FIGURE 27.1 The Death Penalty: Practices and Opinions**

The use of the death penalty distinguished the United States from most other industrialized nations, which had banned it. In 1972, the Supreme Court struck down existing capital punishment statutes as "arbitrary and capricious." Four years later, the Court upheld rewritten state and federal laws that provided clearer guidance for the imposition of the death penalty.

undermine public trust in U.S. foreign policy officials, congressional leaders stopped official publication of the Pike report (although the *Village Voice* published a leaked copy). Nonetheless, in combination with the Freedom of Information Act of 1966—which required the public release of most federal documents after twenty-five years—these congressional reports created a paper trail that altered Americans' perceptions of what their government did abroad.

At the core of this controversy were two burning questions. How transparent could a democratic society and its government afford to be when they also had global interests to protect? And when democratic openness and imperial self-interest conflicted, which should win out?

JIMMY CARTER: "I WILL NEVER LIE TO YOU"

In the backwash of Watergate, two presidential candidates—both outsiders to national politics—became advocates for opposing sides in the debate about power and openness in 1976. Former California governor Ronald Reagan made a strong run at the Republican nomination, falling just short at the Kansas City convention as incumbent Gerald Ford held on to head the GOP ticket. Reagan articulated conservative Americans' anger at seeing U.S. autonomy and power abroad hemmed in. He opposed détente with the Soviets, supported anticommunists everywhere, and warned against a treaty that would return control of the Panama Canal to the Panamanians. Ford found himself burdened by the faltering economy, weakened by Reagan's criticisms from the right, and hampered by widespread resentment of his pardon for Nixon. He struggled back from a 33-point deficit in opinion polls to fall just short with 49 percent of the votes in the general election. The hopes of moderate Republicans faded as the party moved to the right after 1976.

Ford Campaign Ad: Feeling Good About America

Jimmy Carter was the winner. The former Georgia governor had worked relentlessly to gain the Democratic nomination after starting out as the choice of just 4 percent of primary voters. He based his candidacy on moral uplift. Contrasting himself to the Nixon administration, he told audiences, "I will never lie to you." Instead, Carter promised openness, accountability, and a government "as good and decent as the American people." He pledged to heal a nation exhausted by conflict. The emphasis on morality came naturally to the born-again Christian who taught Sunday school, the first president to hail from the Deep South in more than a century. His open faith and cultural conservatism won him support from less liberal Democrats whom the McGovern campaign had alienated in 1972.

Carter was also a Naval Academy graduate, a former nuclear engineer, and a successful peanut farmer and businessperson. Yet the unusual green color of his campaign buttons and posters conveyed a subtle conservationist message, and liberals appreciated his attention to issues of poverty. Moreover, his support for civil rights during his governorship in Georgia had made him a symbol for a pragmatic new generation of white and black southerners. In sum, Americans were not completely sure who their new president really was. Carter kept his diminutive first name: Jimmy, not James nor even Jim. He wore denim, and he carried his own bags. At his inaugural parade, he and his wife Rosalynn chose to walk down Pennsylvania Avenue rather than ride in a limousine.

The new president entered the White House at a time of unusual resistance to executive authority. He encountered an assertive and suspicious Congress. He served an alienated and isolationist public that had given him a slim victory with no clear mandate. He had to grapple with an alert and skeptical media that had dropped most

TABLE 27.2			
The Election of 1976			
Candidate	**Political Party**	**Popular Vote(%)**	**Electoral Vote**
Jimmy Carter	Democratic	50.0	297
Gerald R. Ford	Republican	47.9	241

The Church Committee and CIA Covert Operations

Interpreting History

In 1975–1976 the U.S. Senate Select Committee to Study Governmental Operations with Respect to Intelligence Activities engaged in the first comprehensive review by Congress of the actions of the Central Intelligence Agency. Under the leadership of Frank Church (D-Idaho), the committee investigated both intelligence gathering ("spying") and covert operations, the secret side of American foreign policy during the Cold War. One of the most controversial issues that the Church committee examined was evidence of the CIA's attempted use of assassination as a means of dealing with key figures in Cuba, the Congo, the Dominican Republic, South Vietnam, and Chile.

Alleged Assassination Plots Involving Foreign Leaders (Interim Report, November 20, 1975)

The Committee has received evidence that ranking Government officials discussed, and may have authorized, the establishment with the CIA of a generalized assassination capability....

The evidence establishes that the United States was implicated in several assassination plots.... Our inquiry also reveals serious problems with respect to United States involvement in coups directed against foreign governments....

Once methods of coercion and violence are chosen, the probability of loss of life is always present. There is, however, a significant difference between a coldblooded, targeted, intentional

Bettmann/CORBIS

■ A star baseball pitcher who may once have turned down an offer to play professional baseball in the United States, Fidel Castro led a leftist, anti-American revolution in Cuba in 1959. U.S. hostility and Castro's evolving politics led him to declare Cuba a communist state in 1961. The CIA tried unsuccessfully to arrange for Castro's assassination.

vestiges of its traditional deference to the Oval Office. And he faced an economy still mired in stagflation as unemployment and prices kept rising and interest rates reached 21 percent.

Politics and ideology also hamstrung the new president, limiting his ability to lead his own party in governing the nation. The New Deal coalition of the working class, people of color, and liberals had been unraveling for more than a decade. Carter had campaigned almost as an independent and developed few ties to the main Democratic constituencies. Thus he enjoyed little loyalty from his own party. The Georgian was also the first Democratic president since the 1930s who did not fully subscribe to the New Deal principle of government regulation of the economy. As a social moderate but an economic conservative, Carter had a strong desire to balance the federal budget. This vision placed him closer to the Republicans than to many in his own party. A businessperson, he also considered fiscal responsibility a primary virtue. Powerful liberal Democrats in Congress, by contrast, remained committed to government spending on programs such as Social Security and welfare, which Carter supported with less enthusiasm.

Carter's tendency to take moralistic stands did not mesh well with the horse-trading style of compromise that characterized Congress. The president and his aides tried to govern as outsiders to the federal government. They viewed insiders as selfish and narrow minded. They failed to cultivate relationships with Democratic leaders in Congress such as powerful killing of an individual foreign leader and other forms of intervening in the affairs of foreign nations....

Non-attribution to the United States for covert operations was the original and principal purpose of the so-called doctrine of "plausible denial."

Evidence before the Committee clearly demonstrates that this concept, designed to protect the United States and its operatives from the consequences of disclosures, has been expanded to mask decisions of the President and his senior staff members....

"Plausible denial" can also lead to the use of euphemism and circumlocution, which are designed to allow the President and other senior officials to deny knowledge of an operation should it be disclosed....

It is possible that there was a failure of communication between policymakers and the agency personnel who were experienced in secret, and often violent, action. Although policymakers testified that assassination was not intended by such words as "get rid of Castro," some of their subordinates in the Agency testified that they perceived that assassination was desired and that they should proceed without troubling their superiors....

Running throughout the cases considered in this report was the expectation of American officials that they could control the actions of dissident groups which they were supporting in foreign countries. Events demonstrated that the United States had no such power. This point is graphically demonstrated by cables exchanged shortly before the coup in Vietnam. Ambassador Lodge cabled Washington on October 30, 1963, that he was unable to halt a coup; a cable from William Bundy in response stated that "we cannot accept conclusion that we have no power to delay or discourage a coup." The coup took place three days later....

Officials of the CIA made use of persons associated with the criminal underworld in attempting to achieve the assassination of Fidel Castro. These underworld figures were relied upon because it was believed that they had expertise and contacts that were not available to law-abiding citizens....

It may well be ourselves that we injure most if we adopt tactics "more ruthless than the enemy."

QUESTIONS

1. *What are the dangers to the United States of using assassination as a tool of U.S. foreign policy? Is the use of assassination compatible with the practice of democracy? How might it affect American society at home, as well as the way other nations perceive the United States?*

2. *Did the attacks of September 11, 2001, change the way Americans view the possible use by their government of assassination and other covert operations abroad? Should the attacks have altered Americans' attitudes about these issues?*

House Speaker Thomas ("Tip") O'Neill of Massachusetts. Meanwhile, seasoned legislators of both parties looked down on the new administration as inexperienced and naive. With suspicion and condescension flowing in both directions between the White House and Capitol Hill, one senior Democratic member of Congress complained that Carter's popularity with the legislature was so low that he "couldn't get the Pledge of Allegiance through Congress" if he needed to.

RISE OF A PEACEMAKER

Carter's idealism proved more effective, at least during his first two years, in refashioning U.S. foreign policy. The president started the national healing process with his first official act in office: he granted a "full, complete, and unconditional pardon" to those who had evaded the draft during the Vietnam War. He also tried to replace indiscriminate anti-communism with the promotion of human rights as the main theme in international affairs. "We are now free of that inordinate fear of Communism which once led us to embrace any dictator who joined us in that fear," he told an audience at Notre Dame University.

All presidents since 1945 had loudly supported human rights in the Soviet bloc. Carter defended dissidents in authoritarian countries friendly to the United States as well.

Jimmy Carter Presidential Library

▓ After his inauguration as president, Jimmy Carter got down to work in the Oval Office. Serious, conscientious, and extremely hard working, Carter immersed himself in many of the details of his administration's policies. The image of him sequestered and industrious at his desk came to symbolize, for many, both the strengths and weaknesses of his presidency.

His commitment to ending racial discrimination at home and his promotion of human rights abroad led to his administration's strong support for an end to white minority rule in southern Africa, including the establishment of Zimbabwe out of the old white-ruled Rhodesia in 1980. In a highly symbolic move, Carter appointed black civil rights leader and fellow Georgian Andrew Young as UN ambassador and point man on Africa policy.

Upon taking office, Carter fired the director of the CIA, George H. W. Bush. In the wake of the congressional investigations of the CIA, he reined in the agency's covert operations. Carter wanted to shift Americans' attention away from East–West Cold War tensions. Instead, he encouraged the public to acknowledge the burgeoning problems between industrialized nations of the Northern Hemisphere and mostly poor countries of the Southern Hemisphere. The president made control over the Panama Canal a test case for this reorientation. The canal symbolized U.S. dominance of the hemisphere and served as a focus of resentment among many Latin Americans. Since 1903, the United States had ruled the ten-mile-wide Canal Zone as its own colony. Acknowledging this colonialist past, Carter signed treaties on September 7, 1977, to return sovereignty of the canal to Panama.

Defenders of U.S. control of the canal, led by prominent Republican Ronald Reagan, fought the treaties fiercely. They saw them as irresponsibly giving away an American asset. "We built it, we paid for it, and we're going to keep it," Reagan insisted. But other prominent conservatives, including Henry Kissinger and movie star John Wayne, acknowledged the symbolic importance of the canal for strengthening U.S. relations with Latin America. They supported the president. Carter threw all his political weight into the campaign, and the Senate approved the treaties by a thin margin in the spring of 1978.

The Carter administration's other great diplomatic achievement came with the Camp David accords, an agreement between Egypt's president Anwar Sadat and Israel's prime minister Menachem Begin. The Arab–Israeli conflict had remained one of the most intractable problems in modern diplomacy, yet Carter had unusual credibility in tackling the issue. His concern as a Christian for the "Holy Land" claimed by both Jewish Israelis and mostly Muslim Palestinians gave him sympathy for both sides. Sadat himself created an opening for diplomacy in 1977 by becoming the first Arab leader to visit Israel. Carter then took action. He invited Sadat and Begin to Camp David, the presidential retreat in rural western Maryland. There his persistence, plus promises of American aid to all parties, kept the marathon negotiations on track. In March 1979, the Egyptian and Israeli leaders signed two accords: Egypt became the first Arab state to grant official recognition to Israel. In turn, Israel agreed to withdraw its troops from the Sinai peninsula and apparently to stop building additional settlements on the Palestinian West Bank of the Jordan River. The framework for peace implied eventual autonomy for the Palestinians in the West Bank and the Gaza strip.

Though promising, the Camp David accords failed to bring peace to the Middle East. Israeli settlements in the West Bank continued to proliferate, and anti-Israeli terrorism by Palestinians persisted. But Carter had persuaded two major players in the region to take a big step back from open hostility. The world rightly proclaimed him a peacemaker.

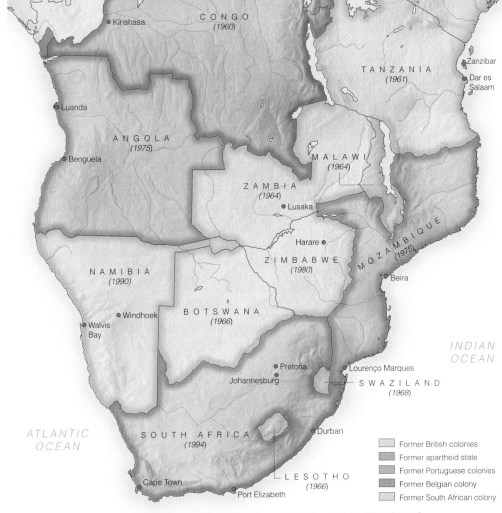

■ **MAP 27.1** **The Gradual Liberation of Southern Africa from White Minority Rule**
The Carter administration supported the ending of white minority rule in southern Africa. The last redoubts of "white supremacy" included Rhodesia, which became Zimbabwe in 1980, and South Africa, which granted independence to Namibia in 1990 and ended apartheid in 1994.

Legend:
- Former British colonies
- Former apartheid state
- Former Portuguese colonies
- Former Belgian colony
- Former South African colony

THE WAR ON WASTE

Within three months of taking office, Carter called for the "moral equivalent of war" to meet the deepening national energy crisis. The OPEC oil embargo of 1973 and his own thoughtfulness allowed the president to understand better than his immediate predecessors that the country's dependence on imported oil put Americans at the mercy of other oil-producing nations. He exhorted his fellow citizens to stop being "the most wasteful nation on Earth." Conserve energy, he implored them. Switch off lights and turn down thermostats.

The administration created the Department of Energy and granted tax incentives to promote development of alternative sources such as solar energy. The EPA required U.S. automakers to meet stricter fuel efficiency standards for their engines. High prices encouraged a renewed search for domestic sources of oil. In 1977 workers completed the 800-mile-long, 48-inch-wide Trans-Alaska Pipeline System. The system linked the state's northern oil fields at Prudhoe Bay on the Arctic Ocean with a tanker terminal in Valdez, on Alaska's southern coast on the Pacific Ocean. With new oil now flowing freely, Carter worked with Congress to pass the 1980 Alaska National Interest Lands Conservation Act. This legislation created the single largest addition ever to the nation's wilderness system, 47 million acres, and the new Wrangell–St. Elias National Park.

The most controversial power alternative came in the form of nuclear energy. Obtained by harnessing the force of splitting atoms, nuclear energy seemed to promise unlimited pollution-free power. But it entailed the use of a deadly radioactive fuel,

The Wider World

Conservative Religious Resurgence in the 1970s

1977 Judaism	1979 Catholicism	1979 Protestantism	1979 Islam
Likud party wins election in Israel, supported by conservative religious Jews and committed to expanding Jewish settlements in Palestinian territory.	Polish archbishop becomes Pope John Paul II, initiating a revival in Roman Catholic Church that helped weaken communist rule in eastern Europe.	Conservative political group Moral Majority founded by evangelical minister Jerry Falwell, helping to organize the watershed conservative victory in the 1980 U.S. elections.	Revolution in Iran creates first modern Islamist government, encouraging Islamist revolutionaries elsewhere.

One of the most striking features of the late 1970s was the political resurgence of conservative elements in all of the three major monotheistic religions. Both in the United States and abroad, many Christians, Jews, and Muslims organized to promote the influence of a fundamentalist form of their faith traditions on their political systems. While some religious people disagreed with the conservatives and instead emphasized social justice efforts, the organizing of religious conservatives in the 1970s and 1980s reshaped the political landscape of the United States and the Middle East. Rather than merely a coincidence, this broad turn to the religious right suggests disillusionment with the more secular and more socialist aspects of post-World War II societies.

These simultaneous changes within the three great monotheistic religions suggest something more than mere coincidence.

QUESTIONS

1. Which worldwide economic, cultural, or political changes may have contributed to this wave of conservative religious resurgence?

2. How might a global perspective on religious change affect how we understand specific developments within American religion?

---

uranium. In March 1979, the partial meltdown of the nuclear core of the Three Mile Island reactor in Pennsylvania leaked radiation and forced a major evacuation. Nevertheless, existing nuclear power plants continued to generate 11 percent of the nation's electricity in 1979, a figure that climbed to 22 percent by 1992 as other plants under construction came on line. However, because of negative public opinion and the high cost per unit of nuclear power, no new plants ordered by utility companies after 1974 were ever completed.

In 1979, a revolution in Iran cut off the United States from the world's second-largest oil producer. The event initiated a new round of energy price increases, escalated inflation, and further intensified public anxieties. In an unusual display of frankness for a country's leader, President Carter acknowledged that the nation seemed adrift. He gathered an array of advisers at Camp David for extended reflection on how the nation might set a new direction for itself. He emerged to give a major speech on July 15, 1979. In it, he linked America's energy problems to a broader national "crisis of confidence." "In a nation that was proud of hard work, strong families, close-knit communities and our faith in God," he explained, "too many of us now tend to worship self-indulgence and consumption."

Carter and the "Crisis of Confidence"

But Carter proved more effective at identifying the problem of America's insatiable appetite for energy than he was at offering a remedy. His call for sacrifice and unity made for courageous but ultimately self-defeating politics in a society accustomed to unrestrained consumption. Other politicians, such as Ronald Reagan, moved swiftly to smooth Americans' ruffled feathers with a cheerful message: U.S. citizens were fine just as they were. As one supporter of the oil and gas industry claimed, "This country did not conserve its way to greatness. It produced its way to greatness."

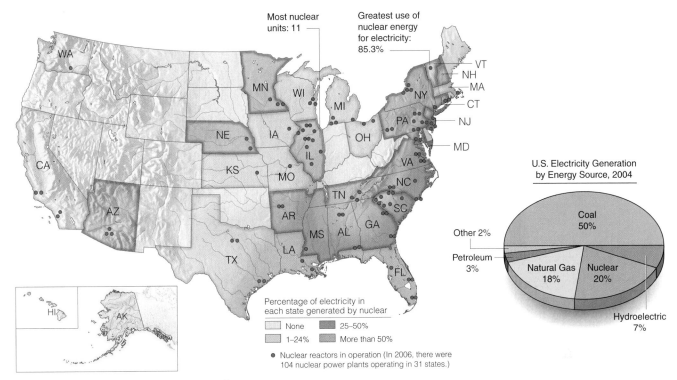

■ **MAP 27.2** **Building Nuclear Power Plants**

Between 1969 and 1980, all of the nation's 104 commercial nuclear power reactors either came on line (56) or were in the process of being planned or built (48). The United States has roughly one-quarter of the 434 commercial nuclear power reactors in the world. Despite nuclear energy's important role in U.S. electricity production, there is still no system in place for the permanent disposal of radioactive waste.

Pressing for Equality

■ *How successful were feminists in their struggle for gender equality?*

ood morning, boys and girls!" This standard classroom greeting reveals the central place of gender in how Americans identify people from a young age. Few people consider the phrase offensive, even though they probably would protest if a teacher addressed class members as "blacks and whites" or "tall people and short people." Should one's sex (a biological characteristic) or gender (the social assumptions associated with sex) constitute the fundamental dividing line among human beings? The spread of feminism through U.S. society from the 1970s onward raised this question.

THE MEANINGS OF WOMEN'S LIBERATION

In a decade marked by hard rethinking of major issues, feminists provided one of the most profound challenges of all. Few American households avoided at least some reconsideration of the roles of men and women. Just as the nation reimagined its foreign policy in less assertive terms and with greater concern for human rights, feminists called for equality between the sexes while honoring their differences. This call resonated with a growing number of Americans. The women's movement cast a spotlight on the need for justice in both the private sphere of personal relationships and the public sphere of the workplace and the law.

Between 1968 and 1973, some 500 new feminist publications cropped up in the United States. Gloria Steinem's *Ms.* magazine became the most prominent, selling out

John S. Zeedick/AP/Wide World

■ The cooling towers of the Three Mile Island nuclear power plant loom over the Susquehanna River just south of Harrisburg, Pennsylvania. On March 28, 1979, a mechanical malfunction combined with human error to create a partial meltdown of the reactor's nuclear core.

the 250,000 copies of its first issue in January 1972 within eight days. Its then revolutionary name symbolized women's desire not to have their marital status revealed through the title of "Miss" or "Mrs." After all, the title "Mr." said nothing about a man's marital status, so why should not a woman's title be similarly neutral? Thousands of consciousness-raising meetings also made women aware that their own experiences with discrimination were part of a broader pattern of injustice toward women.

The millions of American women who found their lives changing in the 1970s did not agree on all issues. Women of color aligned themselves more closely with the nationalist movements of their brothers than with mainstream feminism, which many deemed maternalistic and ignorant of their needs as poor and minority women. Working-class women of all colors often focused on issues common to all workers, including wages, workplace conditions, and union representation. Community organizers such as Lois Gibbs of Love Canal zeroed in on neighborhoods and families. Feminists differed among themselves on such issues as pornography: some found it inherently exploitive of women, while others considered it primarily a matter of free expression.

However, all women shared certain concerns. Even as many female Americans remained wary of the label *feminist*—fearing associations with anger, militancy, and dislike of men—they nonetheless tended to agree with feminist positions on issues from equal pay for equal work to abortion rights and more egalitarian distribution of household chores within families.

The women's movement also sought to unmask the violence constraining all women's lives: sexual harassment, domestic abuse, and rape. Many men were sympathetic, but not all. A "Take Back the Night" march of 300 undergraduates at the University of California, Davis, in 1982 protested the threat of male violence against women. When the marchers reached "fraternity row," they encountered graphic hostility: young men hung out of windows shouting obscenities; a driver backed his car directly into the crowd; a young man urinated on several marchers while others "mooned" them; some men threatened to rape the female marchers later. University disciplinary action against the perpetrators could not mask the reality that a peaceful march for a rape-free society apparently still threatened some men. Even a woman's home was not safe at times. Until the mid-1970s, a husband could force himself sexually on his wife and not be considered a rapist by the law.

NEW OPPORTUNITIES IN EDUCATION, THE WORKPLACE, AND FAMILY LIFE

In the 1970s, educated women gained access to a host of new opportunities in the workplace. Young women in college, unlike their mothers, expected to choose and develop a career after graduation even more than they anticipated getting married. The number of women entering graduate and professional schools soared. The percentage of female students in law school shot up from 5 percent to 40 percent between 1970 and 1980. In addition, most single-sex private colleges and universities, such as Yale and Vassar, went coeducational. Many dormitories housed both men and women, allowing young people from the middle and upper classes to live in close proximity for the first time.

A similar process unfolded in the workplace. Employment in the United States, formerly divided into "men's" and "women's" work, saw a blurring of those lines. Help-wanted advertisements stopped categorizing jobs as male and female, and women joined the ranks of police officers and construction workers. The post-1950 pattern of women flocking into the paid workforce passed a milestone in 1980. That year, more than half of women with children under six years old had paying jobs outside the home. However, most of these jobs were lower-wage service positions that offered neither union support nor much upward mobility. In Texas, for example, for every dollar European American males earned, Latino men earned 60 cents, European American women earned 55 cents, Asian American women earned 54 cents, black women earned 44 cents, and Latina women earned 40 cents. Women fared better in the professions; the percentage of female lawyers and Ph.D.s tripled in the 1970s, and that of female physicians doubled.

Despite these gains, professional women still averaged only 73 percent of the pay of their male colleagues. They also encountered stubborn traditional gender expectations. Late in the decade, one New York City judge ordered a female attorney—dressed in a tailored designer pantsuit and silk blouse—to leave his courtroom and not return unless she showed up in a skirted suit that demonstrated "proper respect" for the court.

Not surprisingly, family life also changed shape in these years. In the 1950s, more than 70 percent of American families with children had a father who worked outside the home and a mother who stayed at home. By 1980, only 15 percent of families were configured that way. Yet society's growing acceptance of mothers in the workforce did not necessarily mean that these women enjoyed a lighter domestic load. Most working mothers still had primary responsibility for parenting. For example, President Nixon vetoed a 1970 bill to establish a federally funded day care system. Such a program, he declared, "would lead to the Sovietization of American children." Although many fathers accommodated their wives' work lives, working mothers continued to bear the brunt of the "second shift": child-rearing and housework in addition to a full-time paid job.

Minnesota Historical Society (Neg. #94451)

■ A scientist with a Ph.D. from the University of Minnesota, in 1934 Jeannette Piccard became the first woman to reach the stratosphere, piloting a balloon to a height of 57,000 feet. In a second career much later in life, Piccard joined the ministry of the Episcopal Church. In 1974, she and ten other women were ordained as Episcopal priests in Philadelphia, setting off a two-year controversy within the national church about the legitimacy of the ordinations in a previously all-male clergy. In 1976, the General Convention of the Episcopal Church voted to change church law and ordain both women and men. Here Piccard gives an invocation in the U.S. House of Representatives in Washington in 1977.

Changing roles brought new marital stresses, and divorce rates climbed in this decade. In 1970, one-third as many divorces as marriages occurred annually; in 1980, the figure was one-half. No-fault divorce laws, beginning with California's in 1970, eased the process and the stigma attached to divorce, although its emotional impact on adults and children remained hard to measure. Men benefited financially when marriages split up. Their average living standard rose sharply, whereas that of women and their children plummeted. Children living with both parents had a 1-in-19 chance of growing up poor. The likelihood rose to 1 in 10 for children living with just a father; for those living with just a mother, the odds reached 1 in 3.

EQUALITY UNDER THE LAW

Paralleling the logic of the black civil rights movement, the modern women's movement pressured lawmakers to eliminate the legal underpinnings of sex-based discrimination. Title IX of the Educational Amendments of 1972 required schools to spend comparable amounts on women's and men's sports programs. This critical step symbolized women's shift away from spectatorship and cheerleading to the female athleticism that helped define American popular culture by the end of the twentieth century. Mia Hamm and her teammates on the wildly popular U.S. women's soccer team that won the 1999 world championship represented the first generation of women to grow up with strong institutional support for girls' sports.

Pat Summitt's extraordinary success as a college women's basketball coach demonstrates the impact of the change in federal law. Raised on a farm in rural Tennessee, Summitt starred as a player in college and on the U.S. Olympic team. With Title IX newly in place, the twenty-two-year-old became the part-time head coach of an obscure University of Tennessee women's team in 1974. Thirty years later, she had become the most successful women's basketball coach in college history, with over 850 victories and 6 national titles. More than 12,000 fans now pour into Knoxville's Thompson-Boling Arena for home games. Summitt's annual salary approaches $1 million, and she has become one of the most recognizable faces in the state of Tennessee—and, indeed, in college sports. Summitt recognizes that her contribution to the rise of women's athleticism in the United States hinged on the support the university chose to give her: "I can't say enough about what U. of T. did when Title IX was passed."

After languishing for decades among failed proposals in Congress, the proposed Equal Rights Amendment to the Constitution finally rode to an overwhelming victory among senators and representatives in 1972. The legislature then sent it to the states for possible ratification by 1980. Simple in its language, the ERA declared "Equality of rights under law shall not be denied or abridged by the United States or by any State on account of sex."

On January 22, 1973, in the landmark case of *Roe v. Wade*, the Supreme Court ruled (by a 7–2 vote) that constitutional privacy rights were "broad enough to encompass a woman's decision whether

■ Congress passed Title IX of the Educational Amendments of 1972, denying federal funds to schools that did not provide equal money to women's and men's sports programs. A New Jersey court ruled in 1973 that the nation's largest youth baseball program must admit girls, and these Hoboken youngsters became the first girls to play Little League.

or not to terminate her pregnancy" in its first six months. This decision established women's constitutional right to determine the course of their own pregnancies. Feminists had pointed out that the question was never *whether* women would have abortions but *how*: they would have them either in the offices of skilled physicians or at the hands of illegal and often dangerous practitioners.

DOCUMENT

Roe v. Wade

BACKLASH

Even as the majority of Americans accepted the fundamental tenets of feminism, some fiercely defended existing gender roles. The mainstream media often painted women's rights activists as angry man-haters. Indeed, the media seized the opportunity to associate feminism with "bra-burning," a titillating way to blend women's rights with the sexual revolution and thus downplay the serious issues that women were raising. One Chicana worker involved in a strike against the Farah slacks company in Texas responded, "I don't believe in burning your bra, but I do believe in having our rights."

The women's movement posed a challenge to traditional ideas about masculinity. Men wondered what equality for women really meant and how it might change their intimate and professional relationships with women. Should men still open doors for women? Should they begin to do half (or more) of housework and parenting? Should they not comment on a female colleague's appearance?

Women's growing economic independence and educational opportunities often altered the dynamics of power in male–female relationships. Many men from all classes and ethnicities, feeling defensive about assumptions and behaviors that were increasingly labeled sexist, resisted these changes. One Latino graduate student at Stanford University resolved never to date "college girls." "When I want a real woman, I go to the barrio in East San Jose and pick up a high school girl." Many men also found the increasingly open acknowledgment of lesbianism threatening because it implied their potential irrelevance to women. The challenge to machismo took the form of public spectacle in 1973. That year, women's tennis champion Billie Jean King (age twenty-nine) agreed to play former Wimbledon champion Bobby Riggs (fifty-five) in a nationally televised "Battle of the Sexes" in the Houston Astrodome. More than 45 million Americans watched King crush her self-proclaimed "male chauvinist pig" opponent in straight sets.

That men would have mixed feelings about women's liberation surprised no one. But some of the stiffest resistance came from women who had built their identities on motherhood and homemaking and now strongly defended that tradition. Led by Illinois lawyer and mother Phyllis Schlafly, antifeminists sought to uphold an established family structure that they believed divorce, gay rights, abortion, and day care would destroy. In their view, femininity meant service to one's family. "Feminists praise self-centeredness," Schlafly declared, "and call it liberation." In addition to defending their own choices, female antifeminists also worried about the impact of dual-career families on children.

Opponents of women's liberation made two major legislative gains in the late 1970s. First, Congress passed the Hyde Amendment in 1976, which forbade the use of Medicaid funds for abortions. In practice, the amendment limited access to abortion to those women who could afford to pay for it themselves. Second, Schlafly's Stop-ERA campaign helped defeat the Equal Rights Amendment by limiting its ratification to only thirty-five of the required thirty-eight states. Schlafly claimed that the amendment would "destroy the family, foster homosexuality, and hurt women." ERA opponents condemned "unisex toilets" and the drafting of women into combat that they believed the amendment would bring. In these women's views, the ERA would also draw out the worst in men, letting husbands opt out of supporting their wives and freeing divorced men from paying alimony. Antifeminists resented the disrespect for motherhood that they felt from some feminists. Still, they agreed with feminists that tens of millions of American women were just one man removed from welfare. At the heart of the controversy, the two sides differed on the best way to protect women's interests. Should women's economic independence be enhanced, or should men be tied more tightly to their families?

Though discouraging for some, the narrow defeat of the ERA could not mask feminism's growing influence throughout American culture. The "first woman" stories that began showing up in the media during the 1970s marked the entrance of women into previously all-male roles. Like physicians, lawyers, and other figures of cultural authority, religious leaders now increasingly consisted of women, including the first Lutheran pastor (1970), the first Jewish rabbi (1972), and the first Episcopal priest (1974). In 1981, Sandra Day O'Connor became the first female Supreme Court justice. And mainstream organizations such as churches and municipalities ran feminist-created community institutions, including rape crisis centers, women's health clinics, and battered women's shelters. In 1978, the National Weather Service began using male as well as female names for hurricanes. By the 1980s, the movement had made major inroads into gender discrimination, although subtle forms of it remained. Younger women, confident that their fair treatment under the law was secure, began shying away from the term *feminism* and its lingering associations with rejection of men.

INTEGRATION AND GROUP IDENTITY

In 1978, a divided U.S. Supreme Court handed down a ruling on the contentious policy of **affirmative action**. The justices decided by a 5–4 vote in the *Bakke* case that strict racial quotas were unconstitutional, but that universities could consider race as one of several factors in determining a candidate's qualifications for admission. The Court, like the American public, was wrestling with the broader 1970s problem of how to reform American society in ways that would preserve its historic strengths while removing the ills that the previous decade's political activism had laid bare.

A central problem was the tension between the ideal of color-blind integration and new expressions of pride in distinctive racial and ethnic identities. In 1973, armed American Indian Movement activists for two months occupied buildings in Wounded Knee, South Dakota—site of the infamous 1890 U.S. Army massacre of defenseless Sioux—to promote a pan-Indian nationalist consciousness. In 1977, ABC's enormously popular eight-part television miniseries *Roots* dramatized the human pathos contained in the long saga of African American slavery. Many white ethnic Americans in these years leavened their long-standing cultural assimilation with renewed attention to their own roots in particular European countries, especially Ireland and Italy.

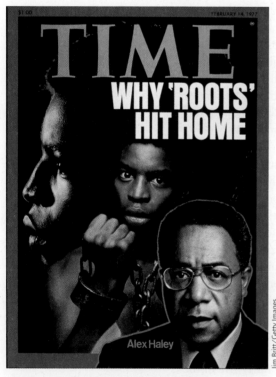

Jim Britt/Getty Images

■ The 1977 miniseries version of Alex Haley's Roots captured the largest television audience ever to that time. The powerful drama about Haley's ancestors offered tens of millions of Americans an intimate and sympathetic understanding of the story of black slavery and survival. Roots also represented the post-1960s emphasis on preserving and respecting group histories and identities rather than emphasizing only individual success and assimilation into the mainstream.

Conclusion

Americans' self-confidence and pride as a nation had been deeply shaken by the combination of the Vietnam War, the Watergate scandal, and the economic downturn after 1973. Disillusioned by the corruptions of public life, many citizens turned inward and heeded the advice of Robert J. Ringer in his 1977 best-seller *Looking Out for Number One*. But others found motivation in the decade's events—especially the revelation that presidents, corporate executives, and other authorities had lied to them. They learned what earlier Americans had discovered in the 1760s and 1770s about imperious British officials and the corrupting effects of managing a global empire. Like the revolutionaries of George Washington's generation, they sought to strengthen representative government. They pressed Congress to investigate the executive branch, and they elected an unusual outsider as president in 1976. Historians in this decade began to write more skeptically about those in power and more sympathetically about average Americans whom the history books had long ignored. The resurgence of conservatism in the 1980s recast many public policies, but it could not erase the vision of gender equality, environmental responsibility, and egalitarian governance that had taken hold among many citizens.

For Review

1. Which were the most important changes in American life in the 1970s?

2. What was the relationship between economic weakness and political and social reform?

3. What did Richard Nixon do in the Watergate affair, and why did he resign from the presidency?

4. How successful was Jimmy Carter as a leader?

5. Why did environmental issues emerge as key national concerns in the 1970s?

6. What did feminism mean, and what impact did it have in the United States?

Created Equal Online

For more *Created Equal* resources, including suggestions on sites to visit and books to read, go to **MyHistoryLab.com.**

CHRONOLOGY: 1972–1979

1972	Watergate break-in.
	Nixon visits China.
	Founding of *Ms.* magazine.
1973	*Roe v. Wade* legalizes abortion.
	American Indian Movement members occupy Wounded Knee.
	Endangered Species Act.
	OPEC oil embargo.
	American troops withdraw from Vietnam.
1974	Nixon resigns presidency; Gerald R. Ford becomes president.
1975	Vietnam reunified under communist rule.
	Congressional investigations of CIA covert operations.
1976	Hyde Amendment prohibits use of Medicaid funds for abortions.
1977	Carter issues general amnesty for draft evaders.
	Trans-Alaska Pipeline system completed.
	ABC airs miniseries *Roots*, based on book by Alex Haley.
1978	Bakke Supreme Court decision.
1979	Camp David peace accords.
	Partial meltdown of nuclear core at Three Mile Island nuclear plant.
	Iranian revolution.

Part Ten

Global Connections, 1979–2007

After the uncertainties and reforms of the 1970s, many Americans sought reassurance about their country's direction. In the 1980s, President Ronald Reagan left his imprint on both domestic and foreign affairs. Reagan gave voice to conservatives, including those who favored a federal retreat from social welfare programs. Bolstered by the Moral Majority and other fundamentalist Christian groups, conservatives engaged in the so-called culture wars with liberals. Conservatives disapproved of feminists, black power advocates, gay rights activists, and environmentalists. Reagan and Congress implemented policies that shrank the federal government's commitment to social welfare programs. Reagan also reinvigorated Cold War rhetoric—he denounced the Soviet Union as an "evil empire"—and pushed military spending to unprecedented levels. Yet Reagan welcomed the initiatives of Soviet leader Mikhail Gorbachev, who sought to ease tensions with the West.

Unable to meet the basic needs of its own people and bogged down in an unwinnable war in Afghanistan, the Soviet Union disintegrated in 1991. Simultaneously, the United States embarked on a remarkable period of economic growth and expansion. President Bill Clinton favored free trade policies, such as the North American Free Trade Agreement (NAFTA), which he and others hoped would knit the world's nations together in pursuit of political and economic progress.

Nevertheless, domestic and foreign conflicts thwarted much of this hopeful vision. At home, the AIDS epidemic and drug addiction claimed many lives. Clashes among African Americans, Latinos, and Korean Americans in Los Angeles in 1992; the bombing of an Oklahoma City federal building by domestic antigovernment terrorists in 1995; attacks on abortion clinics; and a series of shootings by high school students revealed persistent faultlines in American society. Backed by the Supreme Court, a number of state and local governments passed anti-immigrant and anti–affirmative action laws. The culture wars were hot and, in some cases, deadly.

The most violent assaults on the United States came from forces outside as well as within it. The Middle East had become a tinderbox of fears and resentments. In Iran, Islamic militants overthrew the U.S.-backed shah in 1979. Throughout the region, many Islamic fundamentalists expressed their resentment over the military and political presence of the United States in Israel and Saudi Arabia. During the 1991 Gulf War, the United States successfully reversed Iraq's seizure of oil fields in Kuwait. Yet U.S. attempts to protect its economic and political interests in the Middle East continued to outrage Islamic militants.

By the end of the 1990s, some Americans were able to focus inward and enjoy prosperity. The stock market was booming. Cheap gas prices encouraged affluent Americans to purchase huge sport utility vehicles with little regard for their environmental impact. However, ten years of high employment masked the hidden effects of a transformed economy, one characterized by a decline in labor union membership and the rise of an ill-paid service sector. A substantial proportion of Americans lived from paycheck to paycheck.

On September 11, 2001, Americans were forced to confront their own vulnerabilities. Anti-U.S. terrorists sponsored by Al Qaeda, a radical Islamist group, hijacked commercial airliners and flew them into the Twin Towers of the World Trade Center in New York City and into the Pentagon outside Washington, D.C. Some 3,000 people were killed. Within a month, anthrax-laced letters caused death and havoc in the offices where they were delivered and the postal centers that processed them, heightening pervasive fear and insecurity among Americans.

The events of September 11 highlighted grim realities: certain foreign groups despised such cherished American values as democracy, liberalism, and consumerism. Moreover, U.S. foreign policies in the Middle East fanned the fires of anti-Western extremism. Terrorists were becoming more successful in enlisting people who were willing to die in attacks on the United States and more resourceful in using modern technology in those attacks. These terrorists were stateless, freed from the political tasks of protecting their own citizens, monitoring national borders, or dealing with internal dissidents.

In 2002, these realities prompted the United States to invade Afghanistan and displace the ruling Taliban, hosts to Al Qaeda's training network. The following year, the United States invaded Iraq in what the Bush administration called a preemptive attack on a dangerous, destabilizing regime—the dictatorship of Saddam Hussein. At home, issues related to war, terrorism, and civil liberties became increasingly divisive among Americans.

Chapter 28

The Cold War Returns— and Ends, 1979–1991

Reagan National Library

CHAPTER OUTLINE

- Anticommunism Revived

- Republican Rule at Home

- Cultural Conflict

- The End of the Cold War

■ As president, Ronald Reagan loved spending time outdoors at his ranch near Santa Barbara, California.

On July 16, 1979, just west of Albuquerque, New Mexico, a dam holding wastewater and residue from a uranium mine broke. Some 94 million gallons of radioactive water—with "a terrible odor and a dark chocolatey color," as one witness discribed it— flooded into the Rio Puerco and on to the Rio Grande. The Church Rock dam failure was one of the largest releases of radioactive poisons on American soil besides the official nuclear bomb tests. The environmental disaster made local residents, mostly Native Americans, wary of government and industry assurances about the safety of uranium.

Not far from Church Rock, the Anaconda Copper Company operated the nation's largest uranium mine, producing the fuel for nuclear power. The mine closed in the early 1980s. At public hearings in 1986 concerning the future of the mine and its small mountain of poisonous tailings, Anaconda's scientists argued that the mine did not threaten human health in the area. Thus, they said, the tailing piles and the polluted ponds did not need to be cleaned up. Herman García, a Laguna Indian who lived in the adjoining village of Paguate, listened carefully but remained unconvinced. "We lost five people from cancer" last year in tiny Paguate alone, he explained. "I'm no expert," he concluded, but "I'd like for some of these experts to go out there and swim in those ponds. Then when I see them swim, then maybe I feel more secure."

The Native American West and the nuclear West have overlapped to a remarkable extent ever since participants in the Manhattan Project began building the first atomic bomb in 1942. Repeatedly, the U.S. government constructed major nuclear sites in the West on lands surrounded by Indian settlements. These included the laboratories of Los Alamos, New Mexico; bomb factories and nuclear waste dumps in Hanford, Washington; the Nevada Test Site for atomic weapons north of Las Vegas; and uranium mines in the Black Hills of South Dakota. Some of this overlap resulted from geological coincidence: almost 90 percent of the nation's uranium lay on or adjacent to Indian lands. Some of it stemmed from politics. The sparse populations of Pueblo, Western Shoshone, and Yakima lacked the political clout to prevent their lands from becoming what the National Academy of Science called "national sacrifice areas."

In the 1980s, nuclear weapons and waste sparked controversy in the United States. President Ronald Reagan, himself a westerner, expanded the nation's nuclear arsenal, and his administration publicly discussed fighting and winning a nuclear war against the Soviet Union. An accident in 1986 at the Chernobyl nuclear power plant outside the Soviet city of Kiev only heightened public concerns. The disaster killed more than 100 people and irradiated hundreds of thousands more. Frightened by rising U.S.-Soviet tensions, citizens in western Europe and the United States organized an international movement to freeze further development of nuclear weapons.

In 1979, two international incidents raised questions about U.S. military effectiveness. A revolution in Iran led to the taking of American hostages and a dramatic rejection of American cultural values, and the Soviet Union sent troops into Afghanistan to prop up a Soviet-allied but weakening government. Angered, Americans put tough-talking Republicans in the White House for twelve years. These leaders' emphasis on military might challenged the Soviet leadership, while changes in eastern Europe and the USSR brought an end to the Cold War and the breakup of the Soviet Union.

The Reagan administration also avidly promoted free markets. Its policies produced great wealth at the top of the socioeconomic ladder, increasing the distance between the daily experiences of the rich and the poor. These policies also catalyzed bitter struggles over natural resources, particularly those on western public lands.

Finally, the newly organized religious right clashed with liberal opponents over such issues as abortion and homosexuality. In these years, Christian fundamentalists and their allies sought to reverse cultural liberties that had emerged since the late 1960s.

Anticommunism Revived

Why did Cold War tensions increase after 1979?

We're going down!" cried U.S. political officer Elizabeth Swift on the phone to the State Department. These were her last words as a crowd of young Iranians poured into the U.S. embassy in Tehran on the morning of November 4, 1979, and cut telephone lines. In a

■ **MAP 28.1 Trouble Spots in the Middle East, 1979–1993**

Oil production around the Persian Gulf and the close American relationship with Israel made political instability in the Middle East a central concern of the U.S. government. American leaders particularly feared the spread
of either Soviet influence or Islamist revolution, both of which opposed American cultural values and U.S.
strategic interests.

move that shocked Americans, Islamic militants seized fifty-two embassy personnel and held
them for over a year.

In the late 1970s, revolutionaries of a different political bent—socialist and leftist—took
the offensive against authoritarian regimes in Central America. Indeed, the Third World
seemed to be turning away from U.S. leadership in the wake of the American defeat in
Vietnam. To make matters worse, the Soviet Union stepped up its support for leftists abroad.
In December 1979, the Red Army invaded Afghanistan. Fed up with these humiliating events
overseas and with relentless inflation at home, American voters elected Ronald Reagan as
president—the most conservative chief executive since Calvin Coolidge. Reagan promised to
resurrect the Cold War, and he delivered.

IRAN AND AFGHANISTAN

In January 1979, the Iranian people overthrew the longtime authoritarian government of Shah
Reza Pahlavi. Under the shah's rule, the nation's enormous oil wealth had flowed into the hands
of a small elite. Meanwhile, the impoverished majority of devout Shi'a Muslims grew increasingly resentful of the shah's closeness with his American allies. His secret police had detained
50,000 political prisoners; in the shah's time, his critics said, "only the cemeteries prospered."
The revolution found its leader in the austere religious figure Ruhollah Khomeini, who shouldered aside more moderate opposition groups. Returning from exile in Iraq and then Paris,
Khomeini created a popular **theocracy** grounded in a strict interpretation of Islamic law.

For the United States, connections with both Iran and Saudi Arabia since the 1940s had formed the two pillars of American policy toward the oil-rich Persian Gulf. Indeed, the CIA had engineered the 1953 coup that overthrew the short-lived Iranian nationalist government of Muhammad Mussadiq and restored the then-young shah to power (see Chapter 25). American officials maintained close ties with the shah thereafter.

The drop in Iran's oil production that accompanied the 1979 revolution unleashed the United States' second oil shock of the 1970s. By that time, the nation depended on imports for 43 percent of its oil. American gas prices soared by 60 percent amid shortages, sending another wave of inflation rolling through the U.S. economy.

Hunted by the rebels, the shah took his money and fled Iran. Several months later, the Carter administration let him fly to New York to seek treatment for cancer. Enraged that the United States harbored their nation's most wanted criminal, Iranians demanded the shah's extradition to Tehran to stand trial. Washington refused. Within a month, militants stormed the U.S. embassy—"that nest of spies," Khomeini called it, referring to the CIA's presence in Iran.

The hostages' captors paraded them before television cameras to force Washington to return the shah. Carter refused to give in, but he focused the rest of his presidency on engineering the hostages' release. He thus had little energy and few resources to devote to his campaign for reelection. ABC television created the news show *Nightline* to provide daily reports on the crisis. In April 1980, Carter finally approved a military rescue effort. But mechanical failures forced the mission to abort, and the collision of two helicopters during the attempt killed several U.S. soldiers. Secretary of State Cyrus Vance resigned in protest against the attempted use of force. He was the first State Department head to quit over a matter of principle since William Jennings Bryan resigned in 1915 to express his desire to stay out of World War I (see Chapter 20). Americans' frustration deepened, and their resentment of anti-American radicals in the Third World intensified. Not until after the shah's death in 1980 did the two governments finally negotiate the hostages' release.

At its root, what did the Iranian challenge mean for American power? Khomeini and his followers despised the values they associated with modern U.S. culture: secularism, materialism, gender equality, alcohol consumption, and sexual titillation. They sought to export the cleansing power of a puritanical version of the Islamic faith throughout the Middle East and beyond. Indeed, the revolutionaries condemned the atheistic Soviets just as fiercely as they did the materialistic Americans. Khomeini applauded all movements that sought "to gain liberation from the superpowers of the left and the right." U.S. policymakers had feared that instability in Iran might lead to a communist takeover of that country. Instead, the creation of the world's first revolutionary Islamic state in 1979 presented an entirely different challenge to American interests overseas.

Just seven weeks after the seizure of hostages in Tehran, the first of 110,000 Russian troops rolled south across the USSR's border into neighboring Afghanistan. Their goal: to stabilize the pro-Soviet government there against anti-communist Islamic guerrilla fighters. Moscow had resolved to prevent the spread of **Islamist** revolution into the heavily Muslim southern regions of the USSR.

But few Americans saw this invasion as a defensive operation. Rather, they feared a push toward vulnerable Iran as Red Army troops marched beyond eastern Europe for the first time in more than thirty years. The Carter administration halted most trade with the Soviets and withdrew the nuclear Strategic Arms Limitation Treaty (SALT II) from Senate consideration. In addition, the president organized a western boycott of the 1980 Olympics in Moscow and increased military spending. The "Carter Doctrine" proclaimed the U.S. commitment to preserve the status quo in the Persian Gulf region, even if it meant the use of military force. And the CIA began funding the Afghan guerrillas. Détente was dead; containment was back. Next came efforts to roll back the Soviets.

Bettmann/CORBIS

■ Ruhollah Khomeini led the 1979 revolution in Iran that established the modern world's first Islamic theocratic state. The events in Iran encouraged Islamist revolutionaries across the Middle East, Asia, and North Africa. For Americans, the closest analogy was the Bolshevik revolution of 1917 in Russia, which provided a model for other communist revolutions abroad.

THE CONSERVATIVE VICTORY OF 1980

By mid-1980, Carter's public approval rating had dropped to the lowest level of any preceding modern president. Interest rates surpassed 20 percent, and inflation reached 13.5 percent. Even the president acknowledged a "crisis stage." With their dollars no longer buying what they used to, Americans wondered what the future would bring. For many voters, Carter's inability to free the hostages in Tehran or reverse the Soviet occupation of Afghanistan symbolized the limitations of his presidency. Even his own party threatened to abandon him, as the vigorous challenge in the Democratic primaries by liberal Senator Edward Kennedy of Massachusetts revealed.

Onto this stage strode Ronald Reagan. Long considered too conservative to win the presidency, the former California governor projected the confidence and strength that many Americans wanted, even if they did not share all of his views. The sixty-nine-year-old one-time actor sailed through the Republican primaries. For his main tactic, he appealed to nostalgia, particularly among whites, for a rosier past—a time of rising wages and U.S. military might. While Carter spoke of learning to live within limits, Reagan insisted that "we are too great a nation to limit ourselves to small dreams."

Reagan's electoral victory in 1980 symbolized the meshing of politics and entertainment. An actor on the ultimate stage, he understood the presidency as a matter of public performance even more than substantive policies. With little interest in the actual process of governing, he gave his advisers minimal guidance. He focused his own efforts on promoting an idealized version of America to the public. He deeply believed in this version, even when his stories about it occasionally derived from film plots. For example, he claimed to have filmed the liberation of Nazi death camps in Europe in World War II, when in fact he did not leave the United States during the war. Nevertheless, with his sunny disposition and ease before the camera, Reagan projected the image of an attractive, competent leader.

The media loved Reagan. Indeed, his presidency fit with the new emphasis on constant entertainment, as cable television, VCRs (1976), ESPN (1979), MTV (1981), and CDs (1983) swept the culture. Daily newspaper readership plummeted from 73 percent to 50 percent during the 1980s. Equally telling, the average length of an uninterrupted "sound bite" on the evening news dropped from 42 seconds in 1968 to fewer than 10 seconds in 1988. Anything longer, the networks believed, would bore viewers. And no one projected simplicity with greater warmth or sincerity than Reagan. Even his fiercest opponents admired his irrepressible good humor when, after being shot by would-be assassin John Hinkley in 1981, the president surveyed the surgeons standing around his operating table and quipped, "I hope you're all Republicans."

Yet the 1980 election was about more than just Reagan's likable personality. It revealed the nation's renewed interest in conservative ideas. Republicans won control of the Senate for the first time since 1952, managing to defeat several of the chamber's most respected liberal Democratic members. Several basic values united the party: an unhindered private sector and entrepreneurial initiative to create affluence, plus free markets and individual responsibility to solve the nation's social problems. Republicans, like most Democrats, also believed that the United States had a moral obligation to preserve world order and halt further expansion of communist influence. Reagan proclaimed that "government was the problem, not the solution." The United States' key European allies also moved to the right in the 1980s, especially Great Britain under the leadership of Margaret Thatcher.

Reagan Presidential Ad: A Bear in the Woods

TABLE 28.1			
The Election of 1980			
Candidate	**Political Party**	**Popular Vote (%)**	**Electoral Vote**
Ronald Reagan	Republican	50.7	489
Jimmy Carter	Democratic	41.0	49
John B. Anderson	Independent	6.6	–

RENEWING THE COLD WAR

"Sometimes in our administration," Reagan once joked, "the right hand doesn't know what the far-right hand is doing." But all hands in the White House agreed on the importance of restoring confidence in the nation's engagements abroad, particularly in the Third World. In the 1970s, leftist insurgencies in Asia, Africa, and Latin America—especially Vietnam, Cambodia, Angola, Ethiopia, El Salvador, and Nicaragua—had suggested the retreat of U.S. power. Equally troubling to many, when the U.S. government did assert its power, it often seemed to support antidemocratic or racist governments—as long as they were anticommunist and open to foreign investment. Never much concerned with foreign affairs in the best of times, most Americans now felt disillusioned.

Reagan "Evil Empire" Speech

Reagan set out to heal the public's bruised pride. Reagan blamed the Soviet Union for "all the unrest that is going on." He rejected the 1970s policy of détente that had emerged during the Nixon administration and had taken further shape under Ford and Carter. Often, Reagan spoke as though the Chinese–Soviet split had never happened—as though all communists were still united. His was "a kind of 1952 world," one aide recalled. "He sees the world in black and white terms." Pointing to the Soviet occupation of Afghanistan and its 1983 shoot-down of a Korean Air Lines civilian jet that had strayed into Soviet airspace, the president denounced the USSR as "an evil empire." His pronouncement echoed the language of the wildly popular film *Star Wars* (1977), which cast the plucky heroes—like Americans and their allies—as righteous rebels against a malignant imperial power. Americans, Reagan vowed, must overcome their post-1973 "Vietnam syndrome" and stand ready once again to use force abroad.

The Reagan administration backed up the president's words by launching the largest peacetime military buildup in American history. The Pentagon's budget increased 40 percent between 1980 and 1984. The new president also revived covert operations. He gave CIA director William Casey the green light to provide secret assistance to anticommunist governments and insurgencies throughout the Third World, despite their sometimes questionable human rights records.

However, the administration's aggressive rhetoric about rolling back communism masked an unwillingness to put U.S. soldiers in harm's way abroad. The one exception came during the civil war in Lebanon in 1983. U.S. forces initially deployed as peacekeepers there began siding with the Israeli-backed Christian government troops against Syrian-supported Muslim rebels. Within weeks, a Muslim suicide bomber—one of the first of many to come in the Middle East—drove a truck full of explosives into the American barracks at the Beirut airport, killing 241 marines. The administration quietly backed off from mediating further Middle East conflicts. It covered its retreat with an invasion two days later of the tiny Caribbean island of Grenada. There, thousands of U.S. troops quickly overthrew a Marxist government and a small contingent of Cuban supporters.

In Central America, extreme inequalities between landowning elites and vast peasant majorities had fueled leftist insurgencies against the authoritarian governments of El Salvador, Guatemala, and Nicaragua. Moreover, some small assistance from Cuba and the Soviet Union had found its way to the rebels. Reagan passionately opposed these insurgents. He authorized the CIA to work hand in hand with the regimes, even though they used death squads to torture and murder dissidents and sometimes slaughtered whole villages and towns to wipe out possible resistance.

In Nicaragua, the Sandinista rebels had managed to overthrow the pro-American dictatorship of Antonio Somoza in 1979. The Sandinistas set about building a more egalitarian and socialistic state while still preserving 60 percent of this nation's wealth in private hands. Carter had adopted a wait-and-see attitude. But after Reagan took office in 1981, the CIA created the counterrevolutionary "Contras," recruited primarily from Somoza's brutal former National Guard. The Contras waged an undeclared war on the new government in

Reagan, Support for the Contras

CENTRAL AMERICAN EYE CHART

P
OV
ERTY
HUNGER
INJUSTICE
CORRUPTION
REVOLUTION

DEMOCRATS

Sacramento Bee

'C - O - uh - M - M - uh - U - uh - N - uh - I - S - M!'

The Sacramento Bee/Courtesy of the California State Library

■ Critics of Reagan's policies toward Central America believed that he ignored the indigenous problems encouraging revolutions there, blaming instead the USSR and Cuba. The cartoon suggests that the Democratic party took a different view than the president. Many Democrats in the Congress did, and they were responsible for limiting Reagan's promotion of the Nicaraguan Contras. But many other Democrats went along with the popular president in defending the Contras and supporting right-wing regimes in the region.

the Nicaraguan capital of Managua. By 1987, 40,000 Nicaraguans had died in the fighting, most of them civilians. Reagan called the Contras "freedom fighters" and declared them "the moral equal of our Founding Fathers."

By contrast, several European and Latin American allies considered the Contras an illegitimate force of terrorists. A large coalition of church and university groups in the United States agreed. They organized fact-finding visits to Nicaragua and lobbying trips to Washington. Christian activists formed the "Sanctuary" movement to aid refugees from the right-wing dictatorships in Central America that sympathized with the Contras. The Pentagon, for its part, had no interest in sending troops to fight a popular government abroad. The opposition finally prevailed; Congress passed the Boland Amendments of 1982 and 1984 to restrict U.S. assistance to the Contras.

The plight of refugees fleeing the civil wars in Central America exposed the politicized thinking that had shaped U.S. immigration policies for decades. Officials distinguished between "political" refugees and "economic" refugees. Political refugees, they felt, had a well-founded fear of persecution. Economic refugees were supposedly looking only for better economic opportunities. The Reagan administration used this distinction to justify supporting certain foreign governments while opposing others. For example, the U.S. government had warmly welcomed and financially assisted people fleeing communist regimes, such as Hungary in the 1950s and Cuba since the 1960s. Likewise, Nicaraguan immigrants were treated well because their choice to leave Nicaragua provided ammunition in the propaganda war against the Sandinistas. However, Salvadorans and Guatemalans, deemed economic refugees, were turned away. In 1984, U.S. officials admitted only 328 Salvadorans into the country while refusing 13,045—a ratio opposite that for Nicaraguans.

These policies encouraged the emergence of militantly anticommunist expatriate communities in the United States. Such groups then lobbied to sustain U.S. hostility toward leftist regimes in their homelands. The anti-Castro Cuban community in Miami offered the most dramatic example. Immigrants who left Vietnam and Cambodia after the communist victories there in 1975 brought a similar perspective.

Republican Rule at Home

■ *What did the Reagan administration want to change about American society?*

While reasserting U.S. power abroad, Reagan also aimed to reorient domestic policies toward the free market. A young women named Lori, for example, was what the president called a "welfare cheat." Writer Barbara Ehrenreich told the story of a neighbor in New York City representative of welfare recipients: a single white mother with one child. Lori had been married for two years to a man who beat her and once chased her around the house with a gun. Welfare had made it possible for her to leave him, a move she described as like being born again, "as a human being this time." Lori sometimes earned close to $100 a week from cleaning houses and waiting tables—not enough to support herself and her daughter, but a useful supplement to the small government payments. She chose not to report this to the welfare office, spending it instead on little things deemed inessential by welfare regulations: deodorant, hand lotion, and an occasional commercial haircut.

Lori's story helps illuminate some of the major trends of the 1980s. Inflation finally eased and the stock market perked up. Congress and the White House slashed taxes. However, annual budget deficits and the national debt (the accumulation of previous deficits) soon soared as tax revenues decreased and military spending increased. The administration shrank government programs for the poor and portrayed welfare recipients like Lori as lazy and irresponsible. Washington was unsympathetic to concerns over the environment and opened public lands in the West to new commercial uses. By the 1990s, the gap between rich and poor widened noticeably and the vaunted American middle class worried about its declining economic security.

> *Annual budget deficits and the national debt soared as tax revenues decreased and military spending increased.*

"REAGANOMICS"

Taxes played a crucial role in the Reagan administration's efforts to reduce government involvement in the economy. Compared with America's closest allies in Europe, U.S. tax rates were already low because of the country's smaller welfare provisions. But a tax revolt had begun brewing in the 1970s, exemplified by California's Proposition 13 (1978), which cut property taxes by more than half. In 1981, Reagan proposed a new tax law to lower federal income tax rates by 25 percent over three years. Congress passed the legislation, and the top individual rate—paid only by the wealthiest Americans—dropped from 70 percent to 28 percent. Congress also cut taxes on corporations, capital gains, and inheritances, further benefiting the most affluent Americans.

While taxes shrank, federal spending on the military soared. The Pentagon bolstered its conventional and nuclear arsenals and gave service personnel a morale-boosting salary increase. After 1983, billions of dollars poured from the U.S. Treasury into the president's proposed Strategic Defense Initiative (SDI) for a national missile defense system. The funds for the weapons buildup could come from only one source: social programs at home. However, most domestic spending went to popular programs, such as Social Security and Medicare, which primarily benefited the middle class. Leaving those in place, Reagan instead reduced funding for welfare programs, including food stamps, school lunches, job training, and low-income housing. His administration derided impoverished single mothers as "welfare queens." The welfare state, the administration contended, was encouraging dependence and stifling individual responsibility.

The assault on welfare had links to racial issues as well. Reagan portrayed welfare recipients—most of whom were white and lived in rural areas—as primarily urban and African American. The president had made a blunt appeal to white southern voters in 1980. He had campaigned in Philadelphia, Mississippi, a tiny town but a national symbol of antiblack violence since three civil rights workers had been murdered nearby in 1964. There, Reagan spoke of his support for "states' rights"—the same language that those who supported the killers had used. The Reagan administration also opposed any form of affirmative action, calling instead for the "colorblind" application of law. The president and his supporters argued that prejudice no longer had any significant effect on the decisions that employers and others made. Ironically, Reagan's own Justice Department demonstrated the opposite: it sought unsuccessfully to win tax-free status for Bob Jones University in Greenville, South Carolina, and other schools and colleges that discriminated against people of color.

Reducing welfare spending did not close the budgetary gaps that lower taxes and higher military outlays had opened. "Supply-side" economists had promised that tax cuts would encourage investment and thereby generate wealth and eventually more tax revenues, even with lowered rates. But Reagan's own vice president and former challenger in the Republican primaries, George H. W. Bush, had dismissed these assumptions as "voodoo economics." Bush's perspective had merit. To close the budget gaps, the government instead resorted to borrowing money. Formerly the world's largest creditor nation, the United States became its largest debtor nation. Between 1981 and 1989, the national debt ballooned to almost $3 trillion. Moreover, during the twelve years of Republican rule ending in 1993, annual budget deficits jumped from $59 billion to $300 billion. Paying the interest on the new debt pushed interest rates higher and siphoned off funds that could have been used instead for productive purposes.

Despite these problems, "Reaganomics" did help the national economy recover somewhat from the traumas of the 1970s. The tight money policies of the Federal Reserve Board after 1979 eventually tamed inflation, which dropped from 13.5 percent in 1980 to 3 percent in 1983. The Fed's high interest rates also choked off the nation's cash flow and provoked a severe recession in 1981–1982, with unemployment reaching above 10 percent. However, the economy revived again in 1983 and was growing at a robust annual rate of 6.8 percent by 1984.

In that year, rising confidence in the economy helped Reagan crush his opponent, Carter's former vice president, Walter Mondale. Even the novelty of placing a woman, Geraldine Ferraro, on a major ticket as the vice presidential candidate could not bolster the Democratic challenge. Reagan, now seventy-three and limiting his campaign appearances to well-orchestrated photo opportunities, won reelection handily and continued his economic course. After several years of excellent returns on Wall Street, the stock market crash of October 1987 caught investors by surprise. Nevertheless, it did not provoke a broader economic downturn, as the 1929 crash had done.

TABLE 28.2

The Election of 1984

Candidate	Political Party	Popular Vote (%)	Electoral Vote
Ronald Reagan	Republican	59.0	525
Walter Mondale	Democratic	41.0	13

THE ENVIRONMENT CONTESTED

The 1980 election marked the sharpest turn ever in American environmental policy. The new administration reversed two decades of growing bipartisan consensus on the need for greater protection of the environment. Reagan instead supported corporations' demands for fewer environmental regulations and easier access to natural resources on public lands. The president ridiculed the idea of preserving wilderness for its own sake. He even claimed that "trees cause more pollution than automobiles do."

A coalition of powerful western land users and politicians known as the "Sagebrush Rebellion" had an ally in the White House. Emboldened, they launched a quest to turn federal lands over to the states and open them to commercial use. These lands, most of them in the West, were administered by the U.S. Forest Service and the Bureau of Land Management (BLM). They had ended up in federal hands primarily because successive waves of settlers had deemed them undesirable. They included snowy mountains in the Rockies and Sierras and vast deserts in the Great Basin of Nevada and Utah. By the 1980s, different groups desired them for two mutually exclusive purposes: corporations and ranchers wanted to harvest timber and minerals from them and use them for grazing, and environmentalists and outdoor enthusiasts sought to designate them for recreational and scenic use.

■ **MAP 28.2 Federally Owned Lands in the West (As a Percentage of a State's Total Lands)**
The vast majority of federal public lands lie in the states west of the Mississippi River. In the 1980s, those lands were at the center of a dispute between citizens who saw them as national treasures and others, mostly local businesspeople and ranchers, who wanted the lands sold to individuals or transferred to states that would open them to easier exploitation.

The officials Reagan appointed to oversee these lands and assume responsibility for protecting them had little respect for the agencies they ran. Critics described the situation as "foxes guarding the chicken house." The officials openly disdained environmentalists, including those in the moderate wing of the Republican party. Anne Gorsuch at the Environmental Protection Agency (EPA), Robert Burford at the BLM, and John Crowell in charge of the Forest Service rewrote regulations to favor private enterprise. They sold grazing, logging, and mining rights on public lands at prices far below market value, despite their stated commitment to market economics.

Gorsuch, Burford, and Crowell were moderates in comparison to James Watt, the new secretary of the interior who controlled national parks and wildlife refuges. A native of Wheatland, Wyoming, Watt had worked as a lawyer in Denver for a private foundation dedicated to helping businesses gain access to public lands. An ideologue, he declared that only two kinds of people lived in the United States: "liberals and Americans." Watt was also a Christian fundamentalist who believed that the end of time was very near. In his Senate confirmation hearings, he suggested that the nation had little need for long-term public land management because Christ would soon be returning and the known world would pass

■ James Watt, Reagan's first secretary of the interior, became one of the most polarizing figures in a polarized decade. He made clear that he considered environmentalists his opponents as he worked to promote the interests of mining and timbering companies as well as ranchers. The Department of the Interior manages the national parks, monuments, and wildlife refuges, as well as the Bureau of Land Management's extensive lands (national forests fall under the Department of Agriculture's jurisdiction).

away—an interpretation of stewardship that not even all fundamentalists shared, much less the broader American public. Watt's abrasive personal style eventually alienated even the White House, and he resigned in 1983.

The administration's reversal of federal environmental policies alarmed a wide range of citizens and stimulated a backlash. Membership in environmental organizations soared, in such traditional groups as the Sierra Club and the Audubon Society as well as in more radical ones such as Greenpeace. Most Americans wanted to breathe cleaner air, drink safe water,

and make recreational use of national forests, national parks, and BLM lands. In much of the rural West, jobs in the recreation industry now outnumbered those in the logging, mining, and ranching businesses. The public also took alarm at the 1986 Chernobyl nuclear accident in the USSR. Three years later, concerns intensified when the oil tanker *Exxon Valdez* ran aground in Prince William Sound in Alaska, coating 1,000 miles of pristine coastline with crude oil.

THE AFFLUENCE GAP

As the Reagan administration eased corporate access to the nation's natural resources, the disparity between rich and poor expanded further. Whereas most Americans' real wages (wages after inflation is factored in) declined, the professional classes fared well, and the wealthiest citizens gained enormously. For example, the salary of an average corporate chief executive officer was 40 times greater than that of a typical factory worker in 1980; by 1989, it was 93 times greater. By 1989, the top 1 percent of American families possessed more assets than the bottom 90 percent—a ratio typical of Third World nations.

A series of corporate mergers and consolidations further enriched well-off Americans, as did financial speculation and manipulation on Wall Street. *Business Week* wrote of a "casino economy" in which insider trading and leveraged buyouts (business takeovers financed by debt) created paper wealth rather than actual products. Defenders of the aggressive new tactics on Wall Street argued that those taking great risks deserved great rewards and that new wealth trickled down to the broader American citizenry. "Greed is all

The Mall of America

After Minnesota's professional football and baseball teams, the Vikings and the Twins, moved from suburban Bloomington to downtown Minneapolis in 1982, developers began constructing the Mall of America in the space left behind. The largest retail and entertainment complex in the nation opened in 1992. With more than 500 stores, a roller coaster, and a walk-through aquarium, the Mall of America represented the apex of the suburban mall shopping experience that gradually replaced most downtown urban shopping after World War II. Automobiles were crucial, and the Mall of America had over 12,000 parking spaces. This vast consumer enterprise epitomized the material acquisitiveness at the center of 1980s popular culture.

QUESTIONS

1. Malls represent a fully climate-controlled indoor environment. Which features visible in this photograph nonetheless demonstrate a desire to make shoppers feel connected to the outdoors? Why might the architects have designed the mall in this fashion?

2. How might the feeling and experience of shopping in this setting compare with the feeling and experience of shopping in a traditional downtown area?

3. To what extent did privately owned malls become the new community gathering places for Americans, replacing older public spaces?

right," fabulously wealthy financier and corporate takeover specialist Ivan Boesky assured the 1986 graduating class of the business school of the University of California at Berkeley. "I want you to know that. I think greed is healthy. You can be greedy and still feel good about yourself." Six months later, however, Boesky began a three-year prison term for illegal insider trading.

The explosion of wealth at the top fueled an emerging culture of extravagance, reminiscent of similar trends in the late nineteenth century and in the 1920s. Newly identified "yuppies" (young urban professionals) embodied the drive for material acquisition, in contrast to the anticonsumerist inclinations of the late 1960s and early 1970s. Jerry Rubin, a member of the anarchist "yippies" in the 1960s, once dropped dollar bills onto the floor of the New York Stock Exchange—which traders scurried madly to grab—to dramatize and mock the stock market's pursuit of profit. By the 1980s, however, Rubin was working as an investment banker. Ronald and Nancy Reagan were older but shared similar values. They relished lavish amenities like those made popular on the television shows *Dynasty*, *Dallas*, and *Lifestyles of the Rich and Famous*.

As the affluence gap widened, the broad middle class watched its job security slip. Early in the decade, the recession had prompted factory shutdowns and mass layoffs. More than a

■ Wealthy Americans have had varying attitudes about how to deal with their good fortune. The newly rich of the 1980s seemed eager to display their wealth publicly. Here New York real estate tycoon Donald Trump and his wife Ivana posed with part of the large domestic staff that catered to their daily needs. Observers noted the expanding gap between wealthy and poor in this decade; homelessness increased sharply while millionaires grew in number.

DOCUMENT

Reagan, The Air
Traffic Controllers
Strike

million industrial jobs disappeared in 1982 alone. Manufacturers' decisions to keep moving plants abroad for cheaper labor only worsened the situation. Although the 1980s saw the creation of 20 million new jobs, most of these were in the nonunionized service sector and offered low pay and few benefits. In his first year in office, Reagan broke a strike by the nation's 12,000 air traffic controllers by firing the protesting public employees and hiring permanent replacements. By 1990, 8 million Americans had tried the unskilled work available at McDonald's fast-food restaurants. "To work at McDonald's you don't need a face, you don't need a brain," one of them recalled. "You need to have two hands and two legs and move 'em as fast as you can. That's the whole system. I wouldn't go back there for anything."

The poorest Americans did not fare well in the 1980s. The bottom tenth saw their already meager incomes decline by another 10 percent. In 1986, a full-time worker at minimum wage earned $6,700 per year— almost $4,000 short of the poverty level for a family of four. Homelessness worsened in cities as the government cut funding for welfare and institutional care for the mentally ill while housing costs rose. More than 1 million people lived on the streets, one-fifth of them still employed. One out of eight children went hungry and 20 percent lived in poverty, including 50 percent of black children.

These Americans received minimal sympathy from the nation's political leaders. By contrast, Congress and the White House provided large federal subsidies to "needy" businesses such as the Chrysler Corporation. The collapse of the savings and loan (S&L) industry provides the most striking example. Deregulation in the late 1970s had reduced oversight of the formerly sedate financial practices of S&Ls by federal regulators. But S&Ls remained insured by the U.S. government. As a result, some S&L executives, such as Charles Keating, engaged in rampant speculation and fraud. A decline in real estate prices bankrupted 600 shaky S&Ls by 1991, leaving taxpayers with a bill for nearly $500 billion. Federal Deposit Insurance Corporation chair William Seidman described the U.S. government as "a full partner in a nationwide casino."

Despite Reagan's record, 40 percent of union household members and 50 percent of all blue-collar workers cast their ballots for this staunch opponent of unions. Why? Part of the explanation lies in the decline of working-class voting during the 1970s. Disillusioned with a political process they saw as corrupt, numerous workers neglected to go to the polls on voting day. Many of those who did vote decided that the Democratic party had become increasingly co-opted by cultural liberalism and no longer spoke for the working class. Reagan's charisma and appeal to patriotism also attracted many citizens who might once have voted for their economic interests instead. Finally, white Americans increasingly defined their political loyalties on the basis of social and cultural issues—such as opposition to abortion, homosexuality, and affirmative action—rather than economic interests. Conservative Christians, in particular, strongly supported the Republican cause.

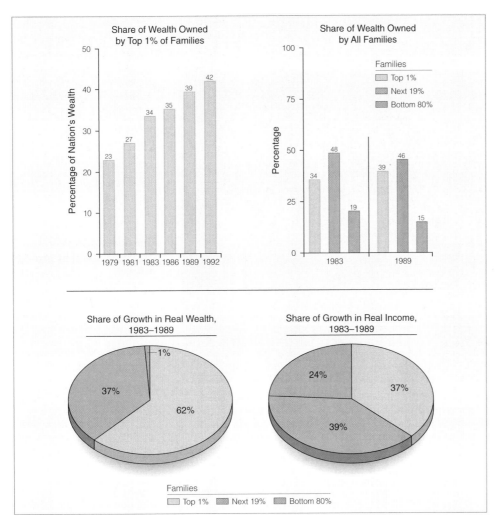

■ **FIGURE 28.1 Unequal Distribution of Wealth and Income**

The 1980s were excellent years for wealthy Americans. The "trickle-down" effect touted by some Reagan administration officials—predicting that greater wealth accumulation among the rich would trickle down to the less affluent—had little impact.

Cultural Conflict

■ *Which cultural issues did Americans most seem to disagree about?*

One of the nation's foremost religious figures, Reverend Pat Robertson controlled the Christian Broadcasting Network and ran unsuccessfully for the 1988 Republican presidential nomination. Like other social conservatives of this era, he promoted "family values" and traditional gender roles. Robertson went so far as to declare that feminism "encourages women to leave their husbands, kill their children [and] practice witchcraft." In contrast, author Susan Faludi wrote the 1991 best-seller *Backlash* about opposition to the women's movement. She became an important critic of gender roles in American society and how they limit people's life experiences and possibilities. In contrast to Robertson, Faludi concluded, "All women are feminists. It's just a matter of time and encouragement."

As Robertson and Faludi demonstrate, Americans embroiled themselves throughout the 1980s in a contentious debate about values. Their society had changed in the previous generation in ways that some citizens disdained but others applauded. Americans argued primarily about issues that had come to the fore during the social movements of the 1960s and 1970s: sexuality, gender roles, the place of religion in public life, and multiculturalism. These often bitter "culture wars" dominated talk shows and newspaper editorial pages throughout much of the last two decades of the twentieth century.

Religion and Politics in the 1980s

Interpreting History

William E. Savro/*New York Times*, Nov. 11, 1980

■ Before he became involved in politics, Jerry Falwell had already made a name for himself as a prominent preacher in his hometown of Lynchburg, Virginia, as the senior minister of the large Thomas Road Baptist Church and the founder of Liberty University. His organization, the Moral Majority, became the most well-known conservative evangelical Christian organization of the 1980s.

I n 1979, Baptist minister Jerry Falwell founded the Moral Majority in Lynchburg, Virginia. The organization represented the growing engagement of conservative evangelical Christians in American politics, and Falwell emerged as the most prominent figure of the new religious right. However, not all Christians were

conservative. Robert McAfee Brown, a Presbyterian minister and theologian, represented more liberal elements of the church that understood both the Bible and the problems of American society differently than Falwell.

The Goals of the Moral Majority (1980) by Jerry Falwell

We must reverse the trend America finds herself in today. Young people . . . have learned to disrespect the family as God established it. They have been educated in a public-school system that is permeated with secular humanism. They have been taught that the Bible is just another book of literature. They have been taught that there are no absolutes in our world today. . . . These same young people have been reared under the influence of a government that has taught them socialism and welfarism. . . .

I personally feel that the home and the family are still held in reverence by the vast majority of the American public. I believe

THE RISE OF THE RELIGIOUS RIGHT

Some of the Americans most troubled by the state of American society were conservative white Protestants. Disproportionately from the South, they had long avoided political involvement and sought to keep church and state separate. They had particularly distrusted Roman Catholicism and state aid for religious education that would include parochial schools. But anti-Catholicism declined sharply among these conservative Christians after the Supreme Court banned organized school prayer in 1962 and legalized abortion in 1973. Increasingly, conservative white Protestants saw secularism as their real enemy and conservative Catholics as allies.

Together these groups criticized the post-1960s shift in mainstream values away from respect for traditional authorities—the church, political leaders, and the military—and toward freer sexual expression and general self-indulgence. What the nation needed, they believed, was a return to reverence for God. The growth of Christian fundamentalism paralleled rising religious fundamentalism around the globe, whether among Jews in Israel, Hindus in India, or Muslims in Iran and the Arab Middle there is still a vast number of Americans who love their country, are patriotic, and are willing to sacrifice for her. I remember that time when it was positive to be patriotic. . . . I remember as a boy . . . when the band struck up "The Stars and Stripes Forever," we stood and goose pimples would run all over me. . . .

It is now time to take a stand on certain moral issues. . . . We must stand against the Equal Rights Amendment, the feminist revolution, and the homosexual revolution. . . .

Americans have been silent much too long. We have stood by and watched as American power and influence have been systematically weakened in every sphere of the world. . . .

The hope of reversing the trends of decay in our republic now lies with the Christian public in America. We cannot expect help from the liberals. They certainly are not going to call our nation back to righteousness and neither are the pornographers, the smut peddlers, and those who are corrupting our youth.

The Politics of the Bible (1982) by Robert McAfee Brown

In Christian terms, and I think in terms with which all Jews could also agree, my real complaint about the Moral Majority's intrusion of the Bible into American politics, is that they are not biblical enough. . . .

The Moral Majority's biblically inspired political agenda involves a very selective, very partial, and therefore very distorted use of the Bible. They have isolated a set of concerns that they say get to the heart of what is wrong with America—homosexuality, abortion, and pornography. . . .

Take the issue of homosexuality. If one turns to the scriptures as a whole, to try to come up with their central concerns, homosexuality is going to be very low on such a list even if indeed it makes the list at all. There are perhaps seven very ambiguous verses in the whole biblical canon that even allude to it. . . . [But there are] hundreds and hundreds of places where the scriptures are dealing over and over again with questions of social justice, the tendency of the rich to exploit the poor, the need for all of us to have a commitment to the hungry, . . . [and] the dangers of national idolatry, that is to say, making the nation into God, accepting uncritically whatever we have to do as a nation against other nations. . . .

When one looks over the agenda of the Moral Majority there is absolutely no mention of such things. . . . We seem to be living in two different worlds, reading two different books.

QUESTIONS

1. *Which specific issues in American society most trouble Jerry Falwell? What specifically about "liberals" does he seem most unhappy about?*

2. *What does Robert McAfee Brown find most unpersuasive about Jerry Falwell's use of the Bible to understand American society and its problems?*

3. *Which of these two interpretations do you find most compelling, and why?*

Source: Irwin Unger and Robert R. Tomes, *American Issues,* 2nd ed. (Prentice-Hall, 1999), vol. 2, pp. 362–364, 375–377.

East. For all their differences, religious people in these cultures shared a common quest: preserving spiritual purity and cultural traditions in an increasingly secular, integrated world.

Conservative Christians were not a fringe group. As many as 45 million Americans—20 percent of the population—identified themselves as fundamentalist Christians in 1980. In combination with a similar number of Catholics, they represented a vast potential force in American politics. And their ranks were growing, while membership in the more liberal mainline Protestant denominations, such as the Presbyterians and Episcopalians, declined steadily after the 1960s. Rather than emphasizing theological doctrine, these groups focused on individuals' emotional connection with a forgiving God. They built church schools, Bible colleges, and publishing houses to reinforce their message. Evangelism on secular college campuses expanded through such organizations as Intervarsity and Campus Crusade for Christ. Hal Lindsey's apocalyptic story about the second coming of Christ, *The Late Great Planet Earth,* sold more than 10 million copies in the 1970s.

Conservative Christians mobilized in the 1980 campaign to support Reagan's candidacy. Critics noted that Reagan himself attended church only occasionally and seemed an indifferent father. They contrasted the divorced candidate with his born-again, Sunday-school-teaching opponent, Jimmy Carter. But Reagan's conservative views on abortion and gay rights and his support for school prayer resonated with fundamentalists. They flocked to the Republican party and to new conservative religious organizations, such as the Moral Majority, founded in 1979 in Lynchburg, Virginia, by Reverend Jerry Falwell. More than 60 million people each week watched—and many sent money to—"televangelists," including Falwell, Robertson, and Jim Bakker.

> In its quest for profits, unrestrained capitalism had no inherent respect for tradition.

Suffusing the GOP with a distinctly southern, grassroots flavor, the religious right also highlighted a major faultline in the modern Republican party: the tension between social conservatives, who emphasized community and tradition, and free marketeers, who promoted entrepreneurial capitalism. In its quest for profits, unrestrained capitalism had no inherent respect for tradition. Indeed, it could bring unwelcome changes, as Rustbelt industrial workers had discovered when their employers moved south and overseas. Marrying Jesus to the market proved difficult. Should the state play a minimal role in the economy and society, as free-market libertarians believed, or should it monitor and restrain personal behavior, as social conservatives implied?

Reagan managed to keep the two wings of the party together, often referring to his "11th commandment" to "speak no ill of another Republican." But tensions persisted. When Falwell called on "all good Christians" to oppose the 1981 Supreme Court nomination of Arizona's conservative Sandra Day O'Connor on the grounds that she was insufficiently hostile to abortion, Arizona senator and party elder Barry Goldwater—a staunch proponent of small government and personal privacy—retorted that "every good Christian ought to kick Jerry Falwell right in the ass."

Gender and sexuality issues particularly aroused the ire of religious conservatives. They blamed feminism for weakening male authority in the family and for increasing divorce rates. A growing anti-abortion movement gained national visibility by 1980. During the 1970s, twenty-two states repealed their sodomy laws, reflecting a slowly increasing acceptance of gays and lesbians. But the religious right, which viewed homosexuality as immoral, fiercely resisted this trend. Dismayed by the prevalence of casual sexual relationships in the 1970s, church conservatives urged abstinence on young Americans.

The heyday of the sexual revolution ended in the early 1980s, when researchers identified the human immunodeficiency virus (HIV), which causes acquired immunodeficiency syndrome (AIDS). The deadly epidemic spread swiftly through the gay male communities of San Francisco and New York as a result of unprotected sex. Many fundamentalists viewed AIDS as a divine punishment for homosexual activity. "The poor homosexuals," Reagan aide Pat Buchanan wrote. "They have declared war on nature and now nature is exacting an awful retribution." The Reagan administration refused to help mobilize a campaign against the new plague. AIDS continued to spread during the 1990s and beyond, among gays and heterosexuals, both in the United States and abroad—especially in such places as China, southern Africa, and Russia. New drugs slowed the onset of actual AIDS in many HIV-infected Americans while scientists continued the frustrating quest for a cure.

Yet another epidemic swept through the United States during the 1980s, striking impoverished urban neighborhoods especially hard. The culprit was crack cocaine. Powerfully addictive, it contributed to gang violence and record homicide rates in several cities. Drug-related convictions skyrocketed, stimulating a boom in prison building, a doubling of the nation's inmate population, and new police special weapons and tactics (SWAT) teams to deal with heavily armed drug operators.

This effort tended to ignore the deeper forces behind drug dealing, which included persistent poverty and a consumer culture obsessed with immediate gratification. Dealing crack offered a rare avenue to wealth in the poorest communities. On the wall of one Detroit crack house, a dealer posted this notice for employees: "[With] hard work and dedication we will all be rich within 12 months." Yet for all the mayhem they caused, crack and other illicit drugs were responsible for the deaths of 5,000 Americans each year, a small number compared to the 500,000 American lives lost each year to alcohol and tobacco. Clearly, addiction to legal as well as illegal substances remained a pervasive problem.

DISSENTERS PUSH BACK

The liberal and radical reform energies that had percolated in the late 1960s and early 1970s did not evaporate entirely in the conservative 1980s. Nuclear threats engaged activists from both the peace and environmental movements. The accidents at Three Mile Island (1979) and Chernobyl (1986) intensified public anxieties about the dangers of nuclear energy. Nuclear weapons were even deadlier: after all, their very purpose was to wreak destruction on a scale that would create what scientists called "nuclear winter," a depopulated planet shrouded in radioactivity. The sharp increases in both Soviet and U.S. nuclear arsenals alarmed residents in those countries and across Europe, where many of the missiles were located. Americans and others who remembered Hiroshima expressed shock when Reagan administration officials spoke of winning a nuclear war and the president wrongly claimed that commanders could recall submarine-based missiles after firing them. The broad-based nuclear freeze movement that emerged in the United States and western Europe in the early 1980s instead encouraged arms control negotiations that would bear fruit a few years later.

Racial justice remained a primary concern for Americans of color and liberal and leftist activists, particularly in light of the Republican administration's opposition to affirmative action. Determined to honor the foremost leader of the civil rights movement, antiracists convinced Congress in 1983 to designate Martin Luther King Jr.'s birthday a national holiday. By 1985, a robust antiapartheid movement—inspired by South African church leader and Nobel peace prize winner Desmond Tutu—successfully campaigned to reduce U.S. investments in racially segregated South Africa. Perhaps the most prominent face of left-leaning politics in the decade was that of Reverend Jesse Jackson, a former aide to Martin Luther King Jr. Jackson sought the Democratic nomination for president in 1984 and 1988, winning a handful of primaries in 1988 with his multiracial Rainbow Coalition. Jackson's candidacy encouraged several million African Americans to register to vote for the first time.

Eric Draper/AP/Wide World

■ While immigrants brought their own distinctive cultures to the United States, American popular culture spread abroad. The broadcast of National Basketball Association (NBA) games in dozens of other countries helped basketball become the world's second most popular game (after soccer). Personable stars like Earvin "Magic" Johnson of the Los Angeles Lakers and particularly Michael Jordan of the Chicago Bulls became popular icons around the world.

Gay rights advocates also raised their voices in the 1980s. Faced with the twin scourges of AIDS and homophobic violence, homosexuals and their heterosexual supporters lobbied for the inclusion of sexual orientation as a category of discrimination in civil rights laws. Others took to the streets, organized by the militant organization AIDS Coalition to Unleash Power (ACT-UP). In October 1987, nearly half a million Americans marched in Washington in support of gay rights. A few widely admired figures, such as tennis champion Martina Navratilova, publicly acknowledged their homosexuality, helping others to view this sexual orientation as acceptable rather than deviant. By the end of the 1980s, the record was mixed. Gays and lesbians remained the only Americans against whom tens of millions of their fellow citizens openly believed it acceptable to discriminate, but the rights of homosexuals, nonetheless, had much wider support than ever before.

Sexual harassment did not exist in the United States until the 1980s—at least not legally. "Boys will be boys," the saying went about adult men. But what some men called flirting, many women found offensive, and by the late 1970s feminists had begun challenging the legality of such behavior. Legal scholar Catherine MacKinnon identified two forms of sexual harassment: one when sexual submission to a supervisor becomes a condition of employment, and a second when behavior toward a woman in the workplace creates a hostile environment that interferes with her work. MacKinnon helped represent Mechelle Vinson of Washington, D.C., who sued Meritor Savings Bank and the vice president who had hired Vinson and promoted her for four years while maintaining a sexual relationship with her. When Vinson tried to end the relationship, the vice president raped her and the bank eventually fired her. In the landmark case of *Meritor Savings Bank v. Vinson* (1986), the U.S. Supreme Court unanimously found the bank and its vice president guilty of sexual harassment in both its forms. The Court agreed with an earlier appeals court that "sexual harassment which creates a hostile or offensive environment for members of one sex is every bit the arbitrary barrier to sexual equality at the workplace that racial harassment is to racial equality."

THE NEW IMMIGRANTS

For two decades after the restrictive immigration law of 1924, the flow of newcomers from abroad slowed to a trickle. The trickle became a stream again after World War II, and then legislation in 1965 opened the gates even wider. As a result, a wave of new immigrants, 3.5 million in the 1960s and 4.5 million in the 1970s, hit the United States. The 1980s set the record as 6 million people entered the country legally, along with a similar number without documentation.

These newcomers brought an unprecedented cultural and ethnic diversity. Communist rule in eastern Europe and prosperity in western Europe had reduced the emigration from that continent; only 10 percent of the most recent arrivals in the United States were Europeans. Forty percent came instead from Asia—particularly China, the Philippines, and South Korea—and 50 percent from Latin America and the Caribbean, particularly Mexico. From 1965 to 1995, 7 million Latinos and 5 million Asians moved to the United States. Mexicans had been journeying north in smaller numbers since that country's 1910 revolution. But between 1970 and 1990, the Mexican American population of the southwestern states tripled, and the Asian American population of the western states increased sixfold.

> *A wave of new immigrants, 3.5 million in the 1960s and 4.5 million in the 1970s, hit the United States. The 1980s set the record as 6 million people entered the country legally.*

The new immigrants came for the same reasons their predecessors had. Many were fleeing political and religious persecution in their home countries, but most sought new economic opportunity. A small number, primarily from South Korea and Hong Kong, arrived with some assets that helped them get started in business. However, most came with few resources and took what work they could find in garment sweatshops, on farms, as domestic servants and janitors, and as gardeners. They willingly endured profound hardship to build better lives for their families. They also rekindled the nation's long-standing cultural diversity, especially in Sunbelt cities from Miami, Florida, to San Diego, California.

Global Immigration in the 1980s

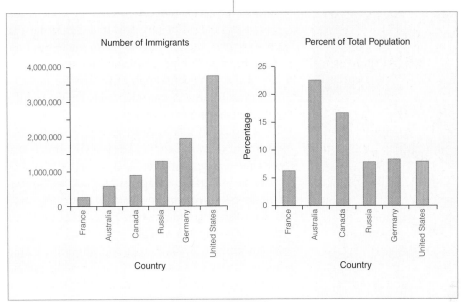

Source: Migration Policy Institute, http://www.migrationinformation.org.

The Wider World

The United States is peopled primarily by immigrants and the descendants of immigrants. This is as true of areas such as the Dakotas, with their older waves of European immigrants, as it is of California, Florida, and Texas, with their more recent influx of people from Latin America and Asia. Americans often discuss immigration as though issues related to it were unique to their country. In fact, immigration is a global phenomenon, and the United States has both similarities to and differences from other nations. One striking feature of American life is the very large *number* of people who move here from other countries; as a *percentage* of the already large population of the United States, these immigrants are also significant, but less so than in some other nations, as these bar graphs show.

QUESTIONS

1. What factors might make the United States, Canada, and Australia popular destinations for migrants from elsewhere?

2. Why during these particular years did Germany and Russia have so many immigrants, especially from eastern Europe and areas of the former Soviet Union?

3. How might the information in these graphs help Americans rethink their assumptions about the nation's uniqueness?

In 1981, citizens of San Antonio elected Henry Cisneros as the first Mexican American mayor of a major city. In Los Angeles, one-third of residents were foreign born by 1990.

Most Americans had foreign-born ancestors who had come to the United States with the same dreams that motivated the newest arrivals. Still, the non-European origins of the latest immigrants troubled some white citizens. Conservatives, in particular, worried about the growing diversity of American society and feared a decline of the Eurocentric culture they had grown up with. They were also anxious that poor immigrants might drain taxpayers' dollars by winding up on welfare. The Immigration and Naturalization Service (INS) stepped up patrols of the 2,000-mile U.S. border with Mexico to limit the rising number of undocumented Mexican workers heading north. By the early 1990s, the INS was apprehending and expelling 1.7 million undocumented workers every year. The desperate efforts of migrants to elude Border Patrol officers and cross into the United States led to deaths from thirst and exposure in the deserts that stretched across much of the region. A sign on one California freeway near the border showed the silhouette of a fleeing family as a warning to drivers to watch for pedestrians.

■ Young Mexican American women participate in a Cinco de Mayo celebration in Houston, Texas.

Despite the distaste that some Americans of European heritage felt for the new immigrants, the Latin American and especially Asian origins of the recent arrivals mirrored the rising economic significance of the Pacific Rim countries to the United States. In 1979, U.S. trade across the Pacific surpassed trade across the Atlantic for the first time. By 1996, the value of American trade with Asia was more than twice that with Europe. And Latin Americans, particularly Mexicans, provided a convenient supply of workers for the U.S. economy. They were available when companies needed them, and they could be shut out when that need evaporated.

In the early 1980s, Americans worried that Japan's economy, the world's second largest, was growing much faster than that of the United States. Bitter bumper stickers reflected competitive anxieties and old racial antagonisms, such as "Toyota—By the Same People Who Brought You Pearl Harbor." But Americans in this decade also began to consume large quantities of sushi (to go with the new popularity of Thai restaurants, along with the nation's 35,000 Chinese restaurants), and millions of American children began to enjoy creative Japanese cartoons and electronic games such as Nintendo's Super Mario (1985). Other aspects of Asian cultures spread widely in American society, including martial arts traditions from across East Asia and Chinese traditional medicine such as herbal remedies and acupuncture. The warming of U.S. relations with the People's Republic of China allowed thousands of Chinese intellectuals to visit the United States, dovetailing with an existing tradition of Chinese American academic success. With its one-child family policies to prevent population growth, China became the largest source of international adoptions for American parents. Immigration doubled the total number of Asian Americans in the 1980s, which reached almost 7 million by the end of the decade.

The End of the Cold War

■ *After forty-five years, why did the Cold War end?*

"My fellow Americans, I'm pleased to tell you today that I've signed legislation that will outlaw Russia forever. We begin bombing in five minutes." Ronald Reagan, in 1984, thought he was telling a joke at a microphone that was not turned on. He was wrong. Indeed, after three years of the president's military buildup and confrontational rhetoric toward the Soviet Union ("the focus of evil in the world")—including talk of fighting and winning a nuclear war—many Americans found his attempted humor disturbing. However, by the end of his presidency four years later, a stunning reversal had occurred. Reagan had traveled to Moscow, embraced Soviet leader Mikhail Gorbachev in front of Lenin's tomb, and announced that the Soviets had changed.

For Americans, the greatest surprise of the 1980s came with this warming of U.S.-Soviet relations after 1985. Few had imagined such a scenario during Reagan's first two years in office, when his administration became the first in four decades not to collaborate on nuclear arms control with the USSR. But in the Soviet Union, the rise to power of Communist party reformer Gorbachev permanently changed the face of international politics. The American president finally agreed to work toward the common goal of reducing tensions between the two superpowers.

At the same time, the Reagan administration stumbled at home when a scandal involving Iran and the Nicaraguan counterrevolutionaries (Contras) came to light in 1986. The disaster revealed a secret foreign policy apparatus and a president out of touch with the daily governance process. Dramatic events in Europe then unfolded independently of the administrations of Reagan or George H. W. Bush, his successor in the White House. In 1989, eastern Europeans tore down the Berlin Wall and ended Soviet rule in their countries. Two years later, the Soviet Union unraveled into its separate components, Russia being the largest. The end of the Cold War enabled Bush to focus on the Middle East, where an international force under his leadership drove Iraq out of occupied Kuwait and reestablished the status quo in that oil-rich region.

> *Reagan's primary role in ending the Cold War was to support Gorbachev's quest for change within the Soviet Union.*

FROM COLD WAR TO DÉTENTE

In the 1980s, internal Soviet politics finally ended the Cold War. Gorbachev and other reformers, like many Americans in the 1960s, boldly questioned orthodox thinking. They could see that the vast military expenditures of the 1960s and 1970s had devastated the Soviet economy. By the 1980s, the USSR's state-run economy was creaking to a halt. It simply could not provide the consumer products that Soviet citizens had learned about from the world beyond their borders. Gorbachev warned of the danger of Russia becoming merely "an Upper Volta with missiles"—an impoverished nation that had squandered its wealth to build a nuclear arsenal.

As the 1980s unfolded, events further weakened the authority of the Soviet government. The USSR's occupation of Afghanistan became a quagmire resembling the United States' disastrous involvement in Vietnam, and the last Soviet troops finally withdrew in 1989. Initial Soviet efforts to cover up the nuclear accident at Chernobyl in 1986 only worsened matters, revealing the costs of corrupt communist rule. Nationalist movements for independence in the Baltic states, the Caucasus region, and central Asia gathered momentum. In his six years in power (1985–1991), Gorbachev tried to preserve the Soviet system by reforming it through *glasnost* (greater political liberty) and *perestroika* (economic restructuring allowing some private enterprise). However, his government proved unable to control the forces for change that it had helped unleash.

Reagan's primary role in ending the Cold War was to support Gorbachev's quest for change within the Soviet Union. To that end, Reagan moved from confrontational rhetoric to pursuing a policy of détente. Gorbachev became head of the Soviet Communist party in 1985, at the start of Reagan's second term. The American president had already built up the U.S. military and was now thinking about his place in history. He wanted to leave office having earned a reputation as a peacemaker.

Beneath Reagan's strident rhetoric about national military strength ran a streak of radical idealism, including a desire to eliminate the threat of nuclear warfare. This desire prompted him to launch the Strategic Defense Initiative. He expected the United States eventually to share the technology with the Soviets. Despite his Cold War posturing during his first term, the U.S. president had been troubled by the 1983 television drama *The Day After* and its sobering images of the aftermath of a nuclear war on American soil. The Soviet downing of a Korean Air Lines civilian jet that fall reminded him and others of the tragic costs of making mistakes with weapons.

Once he felt convinced that Gorbachev was serious about internal reform and rapprochement with the United States, Reagan took action. At a summit conference in Reykjavik, Iceland, in 1986, the two leaders came within a whisker of agreeing to eliminate nearly all of their nations' nuclear arsenals. The next year, they signed the more limited but still symbolically important Intermediate Nuclear Force (INF) treaty. The agreement removed short-range and intermediate-range missiles from Europe and enabled each side to conduct on-site verification of the other side's compliance. The INF treaty marked the first actual reduction in the total number of nuclear weapons stored in the two nations' arsenals.

THE IRAN-CONTRA SCANDAL

Failures elsewhere offset Reagan's success with the Russians. His administration suffered its worst damage when it tried through illegal means to solve two foreign policy challenges with one stroke. Its main strategy consisted of linking a problem in the Middle East with one in Central America.

Revolutionary fervor intensified in the Middle East after the 1979 Iranian revolution, and hostage-taking and terrorism—the "poor man's nuclear bomb"—proliferated. In 1981, U.S. warplanes shot down two Libyan fighter jets when the jets tried to restrict American pilots' movements over the Mediterranean Sea. In 1986, Americans bombed the Libyan capital of Tripoli in retaliation for apparent Libyan involvement in the killing of two U.S.

soldiers in Germany. Things took an even nastier turn in 1988 when an American warship in the Persian Gulf killed 290 civilians by shooting down an Iranian airliner, apparently by mistake. In revenge, pro-Iranian Libyan agents exploded a bomb on Pan Am Flight 109 over Lockerbie, Scotland, before the end of the year, killing 11 on the ground and 259 aboard the plane, including 35 students from Syracuse University.

Islamist revolutionaries also threatened moderate Arab leaders and assassinated Egyptian president Anwar Sadat in 1981. Lebanon became the center of a radical anti-Israeli campaign to seize Americans as hostages, especially after the United States' 1983 engagement against Muslim forces in the civil war there. Despite his 1980 campaign promise never to negotiate with terrorists, Reagan approved the illegal sale of U.S. arms to Iran in return for the freeing of a handful of hostages held by pro-Iranian radicals in Lebanon.

Events were heating up in Central America as well. The CIA-created Contras failed to overturn the new Sandinista government in Nicaragua. Even though the Contras lacked public support in Nicaragua and the United States, the president and his advisers were determined to keep them afloat. But they had a problem: how to fund the effort. Most Americans did not share Reagan's enthusiasm for the Contras and feared greater U.S. military involvement in Central America. Beginning in 1982, Congress passed the Boland Amendments, restricting aid to the Nicaraguan counter-revolutionaries. These restrictions culminated in a 1984 ban on helping them "directly or indirectly" beyond a token dose of humanitarian assistance. Faced with their chief's expressed desire to shore up the Contra cause, the president's men found an alternative solution.

The National Security Council (NSC) established a secret operation run by staff member Lieutenant Colonel Oliver North. Free from public or congressional oversight, North worked closely with CIA director William Casey. North and his colleagues solicited funds for the Contras from wealthy, conservative Americans and from sympathetic foreign governments, including Saudi Arabia and Taiwan. Then North hit on what he called the "neat idea" of "using the Ayatollah Khomeini's money to support the Nicaraguan freedom fighters." Iran desperately needed weapons for its war against neighboring Iraq (1980–1988), so North and his colleagues started diverting profits to the Contras from new sales of U.S. Army property to Tehran. One operative joked about the "Contra-bution," although some of the funds wound up in the private accounts of North and others involved in the diversion.

■ Lieutenant Colonel Oliver North of the National Security Council became the public face of the Iran-Contra scandal. North displayed his medals from the Vietnam War in testimony before Congress, but his smug version of patriotism and his admitted deceitfulness alienated many members of Congress.

Fred Ward/Stock Photo

The NSC's action was illegal: it sold U.S. government property without authorization from the Pentagon, and it broke U.S. laws banning aid to the Contras. When news of the operation finally leaked out in November 1986, it shocked the nation. Details emerged from separate investigations by a presidential commission, a Justice Department independent prosecutor, and a congressional committee.

North's televised testimony before Congress made him a hero to some. He criticized Congress for its failure to support the president's policies in Central America, and he painted his own actions as patriotic. Others thought him a scoundrel. After all, he had run a private foreign policy that subverted the legislature's constitutional responsibilities and then had shredded documents that detailed his role. He later admitted, "I tried to avoid telling outright lies [before Congress], but I certainly wasn't telling the truth." His celebrity status among conservatives almost won him a victory as the Republican candidate for the U.S. Senate from Virginia in 1992.

What did the president know, and when did he know it? The old Watergate question about Richard Nixon came to the fore again. Reagan called North a "national hero" but claimed ignorance of any illegal activities, including the diversion of funds from Iranian arms sales to the Nicaraguan rebels. When some of Reagan's aides testified that he had approved negotiating with terrorists for the release of hostages, the president denied it. Questioned by investigators, the president said he could not remember details about his decisions and policies. This possibility gained credence a few years later when the public learned of his affliction with Alzheimer's disease.

But in early 1987, 90 percent of Americans did not believe Reagan was telling all he knew. People could not decide which scenario was worse: that Reagan knew about the Iran-Contra deal and approved it, or that he did not know what his own administration was doing in his name. Reagan's job approval ratings dropped from 67 percent to 46 percent. The first round of memoirs by former aides also appeared in the final years of his administration, revealing an isolated president out of touch with the government he nominally headed. For example, the former actor breezily admitted that he was happiest when "each morning I get a piece of paper that tells me what I do all day long." News that an astrologer—hired by First Lady Nancy Reagan—had helped set the president's schedule for years did not help either. Nonetheless, Reagan held onto much of his personal popularity to the end of his term. In the phrase of Representative Pat Schroeder of Colorado, he was the "Teflon president" to whom no bad news could stick.

A GLOBAL POLICE?

Although George H. W. Bush had made his career in the Texas oil business and then in that state's Republican party, his roots lay in the party's moderate northeastern elite. His father, Prescott Bush, had been a U.S. senator from Connecticut, and he himself ran the CIA in 1975–1976. After losing in the 1980 party primaries, Bush agreed to run as Reagan's vice presidential candidate. He then moved to the political right throughout the 1980s.

When Bush's turn at the presidency finally came in 1988, he ran a bruising campaign that made a caricature of his Democratic opponent, Governor Michael Dukakis of Massachusetts. Bush skewered his opponent as a liberal and a "card-carrying member" of the American Civil Liberties Union, an organization dedicated to defending the Bill of Rights. Senator Joseph McCarthy had used this same phrase to describe members of the American Communist party four decades earlier. Thus, Bush implied that liberals were subversives.

TABLE 28.3			
The Election of 1988			
Candidate	**Political Party**	**Popular Vote (%)**	**Electoral Vote**
George H. W. Bush	Republican	53.4	426
Michael S. Dukakis	Democratic	45.6	111

Bush also accused Dukakis of coddling criminals. His campaign ads focused on Willie Horton, a black man convicted of murder. While on parole from a Massachusetts prison during Dukakis's governorship, Horton raped a white woman and killed her husband. Republicans appealed to whites' anxieties about race, sex, and safety. "If I can make Willie Horton a household name," Bush's campaign strategist Lee Atwater promised, "we'll win the election." He succeeded on both fronts.

As president, however, Bush proved cautious. Hemmed in by a Democratic-controlled Congress, he had what his chief of staff called a "limited agenda" at home. His most enduring domestic action came with his 1991 appointment of archconservative Clarence Thomas, an African American lawyer from Georgia, to fill the seat of retiring Supreme Court justice Thurgood Marshall. Only forty-three years old and with little experience as a judge, Thomas was chosen because of his conservative views and his race. The Senate narrowly confirmed him, 52–48, after contentious hearings in which a former aide, Anita Hill, accused Thomas of sexual harassment.

> The president feared that too much change too fast might create unrest across Russia and eastern Europe.

"I much prefer foreign affairs," the president once confided in his diary. He proceeded just as carefully in this realm as he did with domestic policy. Some of the most dramatic events of the twentieth century unfolded during his presidency. Poles, Czechs, and Hungarians—encouraged by Gorbachev's promise not to intervene militarily in other Warsaw Pact nations—peacefully overthrew their communist rulers in 1989. East Germans did the same. The Berlin Wall—the twenty-eight-year-old symbol of Cold War tensions—finally toppled on November 8. Three months later, Nelson Mandela walked out of the South African prison where he had been held for twenty-seven years. The white supremacist government there agreed to hold the first elections in which all South Africans could vote. The Baltic states of Lithuania, Latvia, and Estonia seceded from the USSR in 1990 and 1991. Rather than rejoicing at the shrinking of Soviet power, Bush urged Soviet citizens to move cautiously. The president feared that too much change too fast might create unrest across Russia and eastern Europe. But after a failed coup attempt by Communist hard-liners in August 1991, the Soviet Union broke into its sixteen constituent states. Russian president Boris Yeltsin replaced Gorbachev as the major figure in Moscow.

The Bush administration acted more boldly in its own hemisphere. In Panama, under the brutal leadership of Manuel Noriega, tensions grew between the Panamanian Defense Forces (PDF) and U.S. soldiers based in the Canal Zone. Bush and Noriega had known each other since the mid-1970s, when each had headed his country's intelligence agency. They had worked together in the early 1980s when Noriega provided logistical support for the Contras' war in nearby Nicaragua. But the Panamanian dictator had since parted ways with the Americans and had deepened his lucrative role as an intermediary in smuggling Colombian cocaine into the United States. Meanwhile, the crack cocaine epidemic tightened its grip in poor American neighborhoods. Rising popular concern about crack-related violence increased Americans' willingness to take action against Noriega. When the dictator overturned Panamanian election results that went against him and further confrontations erupted between American and Panamanian soldiers, Bush decided to step in.

In December 1989, 24,000 U.S. troops invaded the small Central American nation. They crushed the PDF, and thousands of civilians died in the crossfire. Noriega took refuge in the home of the Vatican emissary in Panama City. U.S. commanders applied psychological pressure. Knowing Noriega's distaste for rock 'n' roll music, they set up enormous speakers and floodlights outside the residence. At a deafening volume, they blared such songs as Linda Ronstadt's "You're No Good" and Sonny Curtis's "I Fought the Law (and the Law Won)." Noriega eventually surrendered and was brought to Miami, where he was convicted of drug trafficking and imprisoned.

Developments in the Middle East provoked the most important move of the George H. W. Bush administration: the initiation of the Persian Gulf War of 1991. After the Iranian revolution, Iraq and Iran had clashed over disputed border territories. The Reagan administration had provided weapons to both sides at different points. The president wanted neither combatant to win a decisive victory that would destabilize the area. With two-thirds of the world's known oil reserves in the states surrounding the Persian Gulf, the U.S. government especially dreaded seeing control of the region's oil prices and supplies shift from conservative Saudi Arabia to revolutionary Iran.

Iraq ended the eight-year war in a strong position in 1988, and two years later it invaded tiny, neighboring, oil-rich Kuwait, annexing it as Iraq's "nineteenth province." With Americans and their Japanese and European allies dependent on Middle Eastern oil, Bush declared the invasion unacceptable. He rushed more than 200,000 troops to Saudi Arabia in "Operation Desert Shield" to discourage further aggression by Iraqi leader Saddam Hussein. At the same time, the United Nations slapped economic sanctions on Iraq.

■ **MAP 28.3   The Soviet Bloc Dissolves**

No change in world politics since World War II was greater than the collapse of the Soviet Union and its satellite states in eastern Europe. Eastern European countries soon sought membership in NATO, and post-communist Russia built closer relations with the United States and western Europe. The transition from socialist to capitalist economies was difficult, however, and many poorer citizens found daily life little easier than it had been before.

The Soviet Union and the Communist bloc in Eastern Europe dissolve

Former Union of Soviet Socialist Republics (USSR), dissolved 1991

Eastern European countries that overturned Communist rule, 1989–1990

Robert Trippett/Sipa Press

■ In the 1970s, antifeminists defeated the Equal Rights Amendment in part by opposing the idea of American women in combat. Attitudes about women had changed enough by 1991 that thousands of female service personnel participated in the Persian Gulf War with no public outcry. In Bethesda, Maryland, one soldier says goodbye to her family before shipping out to the Persian Gulf in September 1990.

Bush's Early Response in the Persian Gulf War

Within three months, Bush shifted his attention to liberating Kuwait. He doubled the number of U.S. troops in the region to 430,000. He also gained the support of the UN, which demanded Iraqi withdrawal by January 15, 1991. The U.S. Congress backed him as well, voting to support any actions necessary to drive Iraq out of Kuwait. Bush went on the offensive because he faced a shrinking window of opportunity. He had wide international support, including troops from several European and Arab nations, but growing clashes in Jerusalem between Israelis and Palestinians threatened to break up this alliance by rekindling Arab anger at Israel.

On January 16, 1991, U.S.-led coalition forces began five and a half weeks of bombing against Iraq. Then, on February 25, coalition forces poured across the border from Saudi Arabia in "Operation Desert Storm." The offensive freed Kuwait and sent Iraqi troops in headlong retreat toward Baghdad. The Iraqis burned oil wells as they fell back, blanketing the battlefield in smoke. Four days later, Bush halted the U.S. advance, having restored Kuwaiti sovereignty. Saddam Hussein remained in power and later crushed uprisings by Iraqi dissidents. The politics of coalition warfare helped prohibit further U.S. action, for no Arabs wanted Americans ruling Iraq.

What did the Gulf War reveal? It showed Bush at his most successful, managing an international coalition few would have thought possible a few years earlier. The war's outcome seemed to validate two strategic lessons that U.S. commanders had learned

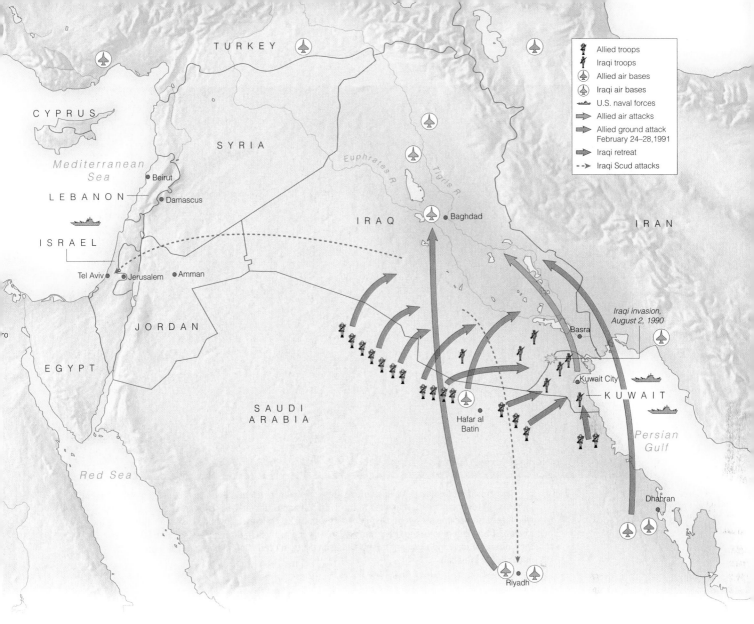

■ MAP 28.4 The Persian Gulf War

Rarely had U.S. strategic and economic interests been so openly the motivation for war. Oil brought American soldiers to defend Saudi Arabia and drive Iraqi troops out of Kuwait. But many Arab states supported the U.S.-led coalition because they opposed Iraqi President Saddam Hussein's occupation of Kuwait.

Map legend:
- Allied troops
- Iraqi troops
- Allied air bases
- Iraqi air bases
- U.S. naval forces
- Allied air attacks
- Allied ground attack February 24–28, 1991
- Iraqi retreat
- Iraqi Scud attacks

during the Vietnam War. The first was the importance of preserving absolute control of the media. During the Persian Gulf conflict, the Pentagon kept journalists away from most of the action to limit the images that Americans saw of the fighting. The public viewed endless videos of "smart" bombs hitting their targets in Baghdad but none of the tens of thousands of Iraqi soldiers being killed during their retreat from Kuwait. The second lesson, advocated by General Colin Powell, the African American chair of the Joint Chiefs of Staff who emerged from the war as a national hero, was to marshal overwhelmingly superior forces before going into battle, thus ensuring the success of the operation.

Some 35,000 American women in the volunteer armed forces served in the war, mostly in rear support positions but also as pilots flying reconnaissance and search and rescue missions. Fifteen died, and enemy forces captured two others. Even though many of these female service personnel in the war had small children, their assignments close to the line of fire generated little public outcry. American women could now be warriors.

■ Here President George H. W. Bush greets General Colin Powell at a press conference regarding Iraq's invasion of Kuwait in 1990, which led to the 1991 Persian Gulf War. Unlike his son George W. Bush, who later also became president, George H. W. Bush had traveled widely and was deeply interested in foreign affairs before entering the White House. The senior Bush had served as U.S. ambassador to the United Nations and as chief of the U.S. liaison office in China before becoming vice president under Ronald Reagan.

Time & Life Pictures/Getty Images

The 1991 Persian Gulf War raised the question of whether the U.S. military had become a mercenary force, with allies chipping in more than seven times what Washington spent to fund U.S. soldiers. "Why should I fight?" one wealthy Kuwaiti sitting out the war in comfort in Cairo asked. "We can pay other countries to fight for us." The conflict seemed to demonstrate a U.S. willingness to act as a global police force in the post–Cold War era. But the war also stimulated the further growth of anti-Americanism among Islamist revolutionaries, including Saudi-born Osama bin Laden; they considered it a sacrilege for non-Muslim American soldiers to operate bases in Saudi Arabia, home to Mecca, Islam's holiest site. Finally, the war foreshadowed Bush's defiant claim at a 1992 international environmental conference that, when it came to oil, "the American lifestyle is not negotiable."

MAP

The Middle East in the 1980s and 1990s

Conclusion

The Republican era of Ronald Reagan and George H. W. Bush reshaped American relations with the rest of the world, as well as politics and economics in the United States. Both sets of changes hinged on the elevation of individualism and market forces above communal values and government planning. At home, the Republican ascendancy successfully challenged five decades of New Deal assumptions about government's role in economic regulation and its responsibilities toward the poor. A booming stock market underwrote a culture increasingly focused on the individual acquisition of wealth. Popular television shows of the 1980s such as *Dynasty* reflected a widespread admiration for affluence and conspicuous consumption.

The collective dreams represented by the Soviet experiment evaporated into history in these years, leaving capitalism unchallenged as a system of economic organization across most of the globe. U.S. military power stepped into the vacuum left by the Soviet demise, most visibly in the 1991 Persian Gulf War. But that military revival came at the cost of vast deficit spending and a sharp recession in 1991–1992, which paved the way for Bill Clinton's victory over George H. W. Bush in the 1992 presidential campaign.

For Review

1. How did the Islamist revolution in Iran fit in the global politics of the renewed Cold War after 1979?

2. Why did American voters elect Reagan twice to the presidency? Were they pleased with the results of his eight years in the White House?

3. What meanings did "conservative" have in the 1980s?

4. How were Republican foreign policies and domestic policies related to each other in this era?

5. To what extent was the political engagement of a religious group—the Christian Right—a new phenomenon in American life?

6. How significant was the Persian Gulf War of 1991, and why?

Created Equal Online

For more *Created Equal* resources, including suggestions for sites to visit and further reading, go to **MyHistoryLab.com**.

CHRONOLOGY: 1979–1991

1979	Iranian revolution; militants take American hostages.
	Soviet Union invades Afghanistan.
1980	Ronald Reagan elected president.
1981	Iran releases American hostages.
	United States funds Contras to try to overthrow new leftist Nicaraguan government.
1983	HIV identified as virus that causes AIDS.
	241 U.S. marines killed in bombing of Beirut barracks.
1984	Reagan reelected president.
1986	Chernobyl nuclear power plant disaster (Ukraine).
	Iran-Contra scandal revealed.
1987	Intermediate Nuclear Force Treaty.
	Stock market crash.
1988	Libyan terrorist bomb downs Pan Am Flight 103 over Lockerbie, Scotland.
	George H. W. Bush elected president.
1989	Oil tanker *Exxon Valdez* runs aground off Alaska coast.
	Berlin Wall falls.
	United States invades Panama to seize Manuel Noriega.
1990	Iraq invades and occupies Kuwait.
1991	Persian Gulf War against Iraq.
	Soviet Union dissolves into Russia and other component states.

Chapter 29

New Fault Lines at Home and Abroad, 1991–2000

CHAPTER OUTLINE

- The Economy: Global and Domestic

- Tolerance and Its Limits

- The Clinton Years

- The Contested Election of 2000

■ Jack Welch (right), former chief executive officer of General Electric, dines with global media executive Rupert Murdoch.

Jack Welch retired as chief executive officer of General Electric in 2000. The previous year, his income had been $123 million, mostly in stock and stock options. When he left the company, he was granted the use of a Manhattan apartment for the rest of his life, including food, wine, and laundry services. He was also given access to corporate jets and other benefits worth more than $2 million per year. Welch's enormous income and retirement package reflected the upward redistribution of wealth that occurred throughout the 1990s. A very small number of people, most of them corporate executives like Jack Welch, became extremely wealthy while the majority of Americans saw their real income decline.

As the gap between the wealthy and the poor grew, so did the U.S. economy, which expanded throughout the 1990s. Increasing numbers of Americans invested in the soaring stock market, many for the first time. The crime rate declined. Moreover, the strong economy also emboldened consumers to buy and use products and resources, such as huge gas-guzzling sport utility vehicles, with little concern for the environmental impact. As the new millennium dawned, the economy began to falter. The stock market fell, and there were signs of an impending recession.

The 2000 U.S. Census revealed a number of striking changes in the nation's population during the 1990s. Among the most dramatic was the growth in the Latino population, from 22.4 million to 35.3 million, making the number of Latinos—most of them Mexican American—nearly equal to that of African Americans. Immigrants from Asia and Latin America also added increasing linguistic diversity, fueling controversies over bilingual education and "English-only" political initiatives.

In national politics, the rifts between liberals and conservatives that had opened up in the 1960s persisted. Struggles over cultural issues such as abortion and gay rights polarized the political climate. Throughout most of the 1990s, one party controlled the White House while the other controlled the Congress. A Democratic Congress during the Republican administration of George H. W. Bush passed the 1990 Americans with Disabilities Act, requiring reasonable accommodation for disabled persons in employment and access to public places. The Clean Air Act, passed in the same year, reduced smokestack and auto emissions. New legislation also increased funding for Head Start and boosted the minimum wage. The Twenty-seventh Amendment to the Constitution, ratified in 1992, prohibited midterm congressional pay raises.

In 1992, Democrats took back the White House, but in 1994 Republicans swept into control of Congress with a conservative agenda, hemming in President Bill Clinton, a Democrat of liberal social inclinations who, nonetheless, presided over the final destruction of the Aid to Families with Dependent Children (AFDC) program, the central feature of the national welfare system since the New Deal of the 1930s.

Throughout the decade, racial hostilities flared, intensified by such events as the beating by police of African American motorist Rodney King and the murder trial of media celebrity O. J. Simpson. Anti-immigrant sentiments increased in response to recent immigration from Asia, Latin America, and especially Mexico. Nevertheless, studies showed that Americans had become more accepting of people whose racial or national backgrounds were different from their own. Americans' faith in political leadership, at low ebb since Watergate, sank even farther as Republicans doggedly pursued Clinton's unseemly sexual behavior, leading to his impeachment by the House of Representatives, although he was acquitted by the Senate and remained in office.

Money continued to pour into politics, even as voters called for campaign finance reform. Third-party candidates tapped widespread eagerness for a new type of politics. A Supreme Court dominated by conservatives nevertheless upheld liberal decisions, including abortion rights, gender equality, and the rights of gays and lesbians. In 2000, however, the Supreme Court decided one of the closest and most divisive elections in the nation's history, handing the White House to the Republican candidate who had lost the popular vote, George W. Bush, son of the former president.

Internationally, Cold War power struggles gave way to other issues: regional and civil wars, ethnic strife, the environment and global warming, trade and labor relations, and terrorism. Domestically, concerns of environmentalists ranged from the protection of a single tree to climate change affecting the entire planet. The labor movement turned much of its attention to service workers and the global economy, addressing such issues as the export of jobs, known as **outsourcing,** and the existence of sweatshops at home and abroad. In spite of the booming economy, many Americans were unhealthy and lacked adequate health care.

The post–Cold War era raised new questions about the role of the United States in the world. Americans no longer looked to Russia as a threat but to new international foes, especially terrorist networks operating outside the authority of particular countries. Within the nation, episodes of domestic terrorism, such as the bombing of a federal building in Oklahoma City and a series of school shootings by children, made Americans feel that dangers lurked within their previously safe havens.

The Economy: Global and Domestic

◼ *How did the expanding economy affect those at the top and bottom of the income ladder?*

After the sharp recession of 1991–1992, by nearly all measures, the economy expanded in the 1990s. The stock market boomed, unemployment declined, and most Americans appeared to be better off financially at the end of the decade than at the beginning. But the overall growth of the economy did not benefit everyone, and many actually lost ground—especially those who lost manufacturing jobs, nonunionized workers who toiled for low wages under grim working conditions, and the nation's most vulnerable workers: poor single mothers, new immigrants, and unskilled people of color.

THE POST–COLD WAR ECONOMY

The end of the Cold War had a profound effect on the nation's economy. The demise of the Soviet Union put a final end to the arms race against a superpower foe and made cutting the defense budget politically acceptable. But the closing of defense-related plants in southern California, once the center of the nation's Cold War defense contracts that absorbed nearly a fifth of all federal defense dollars, devastated the regional economy. By the mid-1990s, half the workers in the southern California aerospace industry had been laid off, part of a national trend that resulted in the loss of more than half a million jobs. Many workers lost not only their jobs but also their homes, their economic security, and their sense of community. Louis Rodriguez, president of the International Federation of Professional and Technical Engineers Local 174, explained how he felt when his Long Beach, California, shipyard closed: "The shipyard has been a second family to me. When I get out of here, I will have lost my family."

While defense industries shrank, the technology sector of the economy expanded, opening up new opportunities for young computer experts and entrepreneurs and generating fortunes for corporate executives. At the same time, mergers of giant multinational companies concentrated wealth and power in an ever smaller number of ever larger corporations.

◼ Casino Sandia on the Sandia Pueblo in New Mexico. Many Native American communities across the country built gambling facilities on tribal lands. Although casinos brought needed income, they remained controversial.

In the last three years of the decade, corporate mergers totaled $5 trillion. Media giants America Online and Time-Warner merged in 2000. In 2001, Nestlé bought Ralston-Purina for $10 billion. Many of the largest mergers crossed national boundaries, as when the German automobile maker Daimler-Benz absorbed the American Chrysler. American companies were the largest target of global buyouts. In 1999 alone, foreigners paid $233 billion to buy American companies.

While corporations expanded, so did efforts to control their power. Microsoft initially lost an antitrust suit that ordered the computer software giant to be split into two companies. Microsoft appealed the ruling in 2001, and ultimately the Justice Department settled the suit with minor sanctions against the company. The controversial settlement generated opposition. Nine states that participated

in the original suit refused to endorse the agreement, and calls for tougher penalties continued. In several states, civil suits against huge tobacco companies limited cigarette advertising and marketing and levied fines on tobacco companies totaling in the billions.

Across the country, innovative business ventures proliferated. The 1988 Indian Gaming Regulatory Act enabled Indian entrepreneurs to build lucrative Las Vegas–style casinos on tribal lands, bringing new jobs and an estimated $4 billion a year to formerly impoverished communities. The Mashantucket Pequot east of Hartford, Connecticut, opened Foxwoods in 1992, and it quickly became the largest casino in the Western Hemisphere. The Oneida followed suit a few years later with the Turning Stone casino near Utica, New York. In Arizona, casinos brought in $830 million a year. Some Indian casinos failed, however, and gambling always took a largely hidden toll in the losses of already poor local residents. Indian communities remained divided over the wisdom of trying to profit from America's growing inclination to take risks in hopes of winning big. Jose Lucero of New Mexico's Santa Clara tribe near Santa Fe feared that rebuilding Indian life around gambling was "like a leisure virus—we're trading our souls for money [when] we are supposed to be stewards of this land."

However, the advantages for the tribes were substantial. The Oneida tribe of Wisconsin, for example, used the profits from its 2,000-slot-machine complex outside Green Bay for an electronic components factory, an industrial park, a printing firm, a bank, a hotel, and four convenience stores. Tribal government outlays increased from $40 million to $250 million over the decade, providing subsidized housing, health care, student counseling, a new day care center, and a new elementary school built in the shape of a turtle, a sacred creature in Oneida mythology. The money also helped revive the Oneida language, with a new written form and a CD of ancestral tales told by tribal elders. The tribe also spent $11 million in 1995 recovering property it once owned, bringing it into the tax-free zone of the reservation. In addition to this communal spending, the tribe paid out $225 a year to all its members. By comparison, the tiny band of Minnesota Shakopee, just south of Minneapolis and St. Paul, used much of the profits from its bustling casino to provide annual bonuses of $400,000 to each member.

THE WIDENING GAP BETWEEN RICH AND POOR

Some policy experts believed that promoting business and expanding the wealthiest class would stimulate the economy, create jobs, and boost consumer spending. Others disagreed. In the mid-1990s, two liberal economists noted, "The tide of economic growth no longer lifts all boats. We see the recent period as one in which the large yachts, moored in the safe harbors, rose with the tide, while the small boats ran aground. The notion that we can 'grow our way out' of the economic problems facing so many families is now obsolete." In the last decade of the century, the bottom 60 percent of the population saw their real income decline, even as the economy boomed. Accumulated wealth—property and investments—was an even better measure of security and influence, and the top 1 percent of Americans owned more wealth than the bottom 90 percent combined. Microsoft chair Bill Gates alone was wealthier than the bottom 45 percent of all U.S. households together. A century earlier, famed capitalist J. P. Morgan insisted that no corporate chieftain should earn more than 20 times what his workers were paid, but by 1980 a typical chief executive of a large U.S. company took home 40 times the earnings of an average factory worker; by 1990 the ratio had grown to 85 times, and by 2000 it reached 531 times. An average CEO earned more in one workday than the average worker earned in a year.

Although one-third of the nation's African Americans were part of the middle class, black families had fewer assets and resources, making their hold on middle-class status more precarious than that of their white peers. The poorest African Americans were concentrated in low-paying jobs, lacking the quality health care and education that would make social and economic mobility possible. Full-time employment did not necessarily mean an escape from poverty. Among fully employed black heads of households without a high school education, 40 percent of the women and 25 percent of the men did not earn enough

How Much Do the World's CEOs Make Compared to Workers?

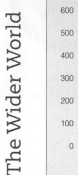

The Wider World

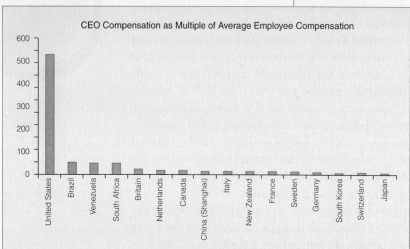

CEO Compensation as Multiple of Average Employee Compensation

Germany, and South Korea, and those with a high standard of living, such as Switzerland and Sweden, are among those countries with the smallest gap between executive and worker pay. Developing countries with weak economies and low standards of living tended to be at the higher end of the scale, although none comes close to the gap within the United States.

In the 1990s, one indication of the increasing gap between the rich and poor was the skyrocketing pay of American CEOs compared to the average corporate employee. This graph shows that the gap between top executives and workers in the United States was vastly greater than that of other nations—nearly ten times greater than its closest rival, Brazil. The graph also shows that nations with robust and expanding economies, such as Japan,

QUESTIONS

1. What does the graph indicate about the relationship between relatively healthy economies and the executive/ worker pay gap?

2. What does the huge gap between corporate executive and worker pay in the United States suggest about the health of the American economy and the economic well-being of average working Americans?

to achieve economic self-sufficiency. Almost 50 percent of all black children lived in households below the poverty line, compared to 16 percent of white children. The rate of unemployment was more than twice as high for blacks as for whites.

Recent immigrants from Asia, Africa, and Latin America joined African Americans in jobs at the bottom of the economy. Despite the controversy over illegal immigration, a quarter of a million undocumented workers toiled in the fields of agribusiness. At the same time, 2 percent of able-bodied citizens were in jail, nearly half of them black, because of the arrest and incarceration policies of the **war on drugs** that hit minority communities particularly hard. Prisoners were often required to work while incarcerated. Convicts provided data entry, packed golf balls, and filled a wide array of jobs for less than minimum wage, and most of their earnings went back to the government. These and other workers at the bottom of the labor force gained little or nothing from the economic boom of the 1990s.

SERVICE WORKERS AND LABOR UNIONS

While globalization continued to erode the power of most labor unions, low-wage workers in the service industries and certain sectors of the meat industry had one advantage over laborers working for multinational corporations: their jobs could not be exported. Many service workers organized successfully for better wages and working conditions. In 2000, for example, striking janitors of Service Employees International Union Local 1877 in Los Angeles marched eight miles past cheering crowds to the upscale business center of Century City. A few weeks later, the janitors had achieved a wage increase of 26 percent, raising their hourly pay from less than $8 to more than $10. This was a tremendous triumph for a union whose

Undocumented immigrants, 1995

1,000,000 – 2,000,000   24,000 – 100,000

500,000 – 1,000,000   Less than 24,000

100,000 – 500,000

■ **MAP 29.1 States with Large Numbers of Undocumented Immigrants, 1995**

In the 1990s, fully 77 percent of all undocumented immigrants entered the country legally, with visas in hand. During the 1990s, the total proportion of the foreign born in the United States, including those with and without legal status, increased from 9 to 11 percent, still less than the 15 percent in 1900. Immigrants paid $133 billion dollars annually in local, state, and federal taxes, and generated an annual contribution to the American economy in the range of $25 to $30 billion.

membership was 98 percent immigrant: 80 percent Central Americans, more than half women, and all of them poor.

Other service workers also won improved contracts. Unionized hotel workers in San Francisco negotiated a five-year contract that increased pay for the lowest-paid workers, room cleaners and dishwashers, by 25 percent, from $12 to $15 an hour. In Las Vegas, African American hotel worker Hattie Canty, who helped organize 40,000 employees of large casino hotels, said of her efforts, "It has not been a picnic for me, but I don't think I'd like to go on a picnic every day. I have enjoyed the struggle. I'm not the only Hattie. There's lots of Hatties out there." Yatta Staples went out on the picket line in front of the Minneapolis hotel where she worked as a waitress, telling reporters, "I'll stay here as long as it takes." In the summer of 1997, 185,000 Teamsters went on strike against United Parcel Service and won an improved contract with higher wages and benefits for part-time as well as full-time workers.

Strikes did little to benefit nonunionized workers, especially undocumented immigrants, and sweatshop laborers both inside and outside the United States. There were some attempts to improve working conditions for those most exploited by the global economy. In April 1997, representatives from clothing manufacturers, human rights groups, and labor organizations drafted an agreement that tried to improve conditions for garment workers around the world. Companies that agreed to the voluntary pact would limit workweeks to sixty hours, with a maximum of twelve hours of overtime. The companies had to pay "at least the minimum wage required by local law or the prevailing industry wage, whichever is higher." The pact forbade employment of children under age fifteen and contained policies protecting workers from harassment and unsafe working environments. Even full compliance with such minimal standards would leave workers in the global garment industry

■ Sweatshops like this one in the 1990s resemble those of a century earlier. Immigrant women labor in garment factories, working long hours in difficult conditions for meager wages.

subject to much longer hours, lower wages, and worse working conditions than legally permitted in the United States. Critics also raised questions about how enforceable such voluntary standards would be. Nevertheless, the pact at least called attention to widespread exploitation in the global economy.

INDUSTRY VERSUS THE ENVIRONMENT

The global economy affected not only the human condition but also the natural world. Environmental activists mobilized in response, with new forms of civil disobedience. Julia Butterfly Hill was one such activist. On a cold December night in 1997, the twenty-three-year-old environmentalist climbed onto a small platform that had been constructed 180 feet above ground in a giant redwood tree in Humboldt County, California. She remained there for two years, trespassing on the property of the Pacific Lumber Company, which was threatening to cut down the 1,000-year-old tree as part of its logging operations.

Tree sitting was a strategy Earth First! activists developed to protest the destruction of the trees. Julia Hill took a forest name—Butterfly—and pledged that her "feet would not touch the ground" until the tree was safe from destruction. For two years, Hill endured rain and hail storms, ninety-mile-per-hour winds, bone-chilling cold, and harassment from the logging company. Finally, the president of Pacific Lumber, John Campbell, agreed never to cut down the tree or other trees in a 2.9-acre buffer zone, and Hill agreed to come down. For her civil disobedience, she paid a $50,000 fine, contributed by supporters, which the court designated to Humboldt State University for forestry research. Although her success was modest in terms of saving endangered forests, her actions raised environmental awareness across the globe and called attention to the impact of economic expansion on the natural world.

■ Julia "Butterfly" Hill in the giant redwood tree where she lived for two years.

Tolerance and Its Limits

◼ *In what ways did Americans demonstrate increasing tolerance for those different from themselves?*

Racial discrimination had eased over the course of the twentieth century, but persistent inequalities of power and economic opportunity continued to disadvantage Americans of color, who remained disproportionately poor, in prison, and on welfare. The economic downturn of the early 1990s widened the chasm between affluent white and poor nonwhite Americans. Highly publicized incidents of police brutality directed against racial minorities generated protests and, occasionally, violence. Nevertheless, there were signs that Americans were becoming more tolerant of one another and more willing to accept and even appreciate their diversity.

THE LOS ANGELES RIOTS: "WE CAN ALL GET ALONG"

Shortly after midnight on March 3, 1991, police pulled over Rodney King, an African American motorist, after a high-speed chase on a Los Angeles freeway. The four officers dragged the unarmed black man from his car and kicked and beat him with their batons for fifteen minutes. The beating left King with a fractured cheekbone, broken bones at the base of his skull, and a broken leg. A bystander recorded the beating on videotape, which was broadcast repeatedly on national television, sparking outrage among Americans of all races.

At the highly publicized trial in April 1992, defense lawyers for the police officers argued that King, who was clearly cowering on the videotape, was resisting arrest and that the police responded appropriately. The jury of ten whites, one Asian, and one Latino acquitted the officers. The acquittal ignited five days of rioting in the African American community of South Central Los Angeles, leaving fifty-eight people dead and $1 billion in property destroyed. Community leaders called for calm; even Rodney King implored the public: "We can all get along. We've just got to." Months later, a federal court in Los Angeles convicted two of the officers involved in the beating of violating King's civil rights—too late to avert the violence that erupted after the initial verdict.

Of the 58 people who died in the violence, twenty-six were black, eighteen were Latino, ten were white, and two were Asian. Of the 4,000 businesses that were destroyed, most belonged to Latinos and Koreans. Perpetrators of the violence, as well as the victims, came from all racial groups. Antonia Hernandez, president of the Mexican American Legal Defense and Educational Fund, noted, "The hardest part is rebuilding the spirit of the city—what holds us together as Angelinos. It's the rebuilding of trust. . . . It's connecting communities that have never been connected." Several community groups came together in an effort to ease tensions, including the Japanese American Citizens League, Chinese for Affirmative Action, and the Asian Pacific Legal Center. "I think that much of the cause of the race relations problem comes down to economics—who has jobs, who has businesses, where is the money going," said Los Angeles City Council member Michael Woo. Jimmy Franco, director of the League of United Latin American Citizens, concurred: "These areas are the poorest areas of

◼ In the aftermath of the violent uprising that followed the acquittal of police officers in the beating of motorist Rodney King, Koreans and African Americans in Los Angeles express their solidarity, hoping to heal the wounds and divisions that tore apart their city.

Vermont Civil Union Law

On April 26, 2000, Vermont became the first state to grant legal recognition to same-sex couples, affording them all the legal protections, privileges, and responsibilities of married couples. The law unleashed a storm of controversy and raised questions about the legal status in other states of civil unions contracted in Vermont. Nevertheless, in the first year after its enactment, 2,479 same-sex couples forged civil unions in Vermont, 478 of them among Vermonters and the rest from other states. Two-thirds were lesbian unions. Several states began to consider similar bills, but others moved to prohibit such unions. Nebraska amended its state constitution to outlaw same-sex marriage and civil unions. On the national level, conservative lawmakers endeavored to introduce a constitutional amendment that would ban civil unions and restrict marriage to heterosexual couples. Among other provisions, the Vermont Civil Union Law stipulated the following:

(1) Civil marriage under Vermont's marriage statutes consists of a union between a man and a woman. . . .

■ Kathleen Peterson and Carolyn Conrad exchange vows in front of Justice of the Peace T. Hunter Wilson. The ceremony in Brattleboro, Vermont, on July 1, 2000, marked the first legal union under Vermont's civil union law. Vermont was the first state to provide recognition and legal status to gay and lesbian couples.

Jim Bourg/REUTERS

(2) Vermont's history as an independent republic and as a state is one of equal treatment and respect for all Vermonters. . . .

(3) The state's interest in civil marriage is to encourage close and caring families, and to protect all family members

the city. If it weren't Rodney King, it would have been something else. It just took something like this to set off the anger."

VALUES IN CONFLICT

Many citizens worried that the bonds holding Americans together might be fraying. Although white men continued to control nearly all the major economic and political institutions in the nation, a 1993 poll found that a majority of white men believed that their advantage in terms of jobs and income, along with their influence over American culture, was declining. In 1991, former University of Colorado football coach Bill McCartney formed the Promise Keepers, a conservative Christian group dedicated to restoring the traditional privileges and responsibilities of husbands and fathers in the home. The Promise Keepers held evangelical revivals that drew tens of thousands of mostly working-class white and some black men to rallies across the country. They believed that men should be good providers for their families, strong role models for their children, and committed spouses.

Other groups and initiatives appeared that appealed to men across the political spectrum: the National Fatherhood Initiative, Father to Father (launched by Vice President Al Gore in 1995), the Fatherhood Project, the Institute for Responsible Fatherhood and Family Revitalization, and Fathers' Education Network. African American men also felt the need to bolster manhood from the economic and social consequences of abandonment and divorce, focusing on those who have been especially at risk.

(4) Legal recognition of civil marriage by the state is the primary and, in a number of instances, the exclusive source of numerous benefits, responsibilities and protections under the laws of the state for married persons and their children.

(5) Based on the state's tradition of equality under the law and strong families, for at least 25 years, Vermont Probate Courts have qualified gay and lesbian individuals as adoptive parents.

(6) Vermont was one of the first states to adopt comprehensive legislation prohibiting discrimination on the basis of sexual orientation. . . .

(7) The state has a strong interest in promoting stable and lasting families, including families based upon a same-sex couple.

(8) Without the legal protections, benefits and responsibilities associated with civil marriage, same-sex couples suffer numerous obstacles and hardships.

(9) Despite longstanding social and economic discrimination, many gay and lesbian Vermonters have formed lasting, committed, caring and faithful relationships with persons of their same sex. These couples live together, participate in their communities together, and some raise children and care for family members together, just as do couples who are married under Vermont law.

(10) While a system of civil unions does not bestow the status of civil marriage, it does satisfy the requirements of the Common Benefits Clause. Changes in the way significant legal relationships are established under the constitution should be approached carefully, combining respect for the community and cultural institutions most affected with a commitment to the constitutional rights involved. Granting benefits and protections to same-sex couples through a system of civil unions will provide due respect for tradition and long-standing social institutions, and will permit adjustment as unanticipated consequences or unmet needs arise.

(11) The constitutional principle of equality embodied in the Common Benefits Clause is compatible with the freedom of religious belief and worship guaranteed in Chapter I, Article 3rd of the state constitution. Extending the benefits and protections of marriage to same-sex couples through a system of civil unions preserves the fundamental constitutional right of each of the multitude of religious faiths in Vermont to choose freely and without state interference to whom to grant the religious status, sacrament or blessing of marriage under the rules, practices or traditions of such faith.

QUESTIONS

1. *What political principles and values provided the foundation for Vermont's civil union law?*

2. *In what ways does the Vermont civil union law distinguish between civil marriages and civil unions?*

and fatherhood. Efforts geared specifically toward African American men included MAD DADS (Men Against Destruction—Defending Against Drugs and Social Disorder) and the 1995 Million Man March, organized by Nation of Islam Reverend Louis Farrakhan, which drew hundreds of thousands of black men to demonstrate their solidarity at a rally in Washington, D.C.

At the same time, gay men and lesbians mobilized to gain acceptance and legitimacy for the families that they formed. Although a 1994 poll showed that 52 percent of respondents "claimed to consider gay lifestyle acceptable," 64 percent were opposed to legalizing gay marriage or allowing gay couples to adopt children. In response to fears that gay unions would undermine traditional marriage, Congress passed the Defense of Marriage Act in 1996, which defined marriage as a union between a man and a woman. In 2000, Vermont became the first state to grant legal status to civil unions between same-sex couples.

Values also collided around the rights and traditions of American Indians as tribal communities came into conflict with non-Indian environmentalists, sports enthusiasts, and scientists. In the upper Midwest, treaties with the government in 1837 and 1842 granted the Chippewa hunting, fishing, and gathering rights in the territories ceded to the United States. Federal courts consistently upheld these treaties, which include rights to take up to half of the fish and game allowed by state conservation requirements and to use methods such as spear fishing that are illegal for non-Indians. In the 1980s and 1990s, non-Indians challenged these policies and accosted Native Americans in fishing boats with rocks and insults.

Mary Ann Chastain/AP/Wide World Photos

■ Two protesters dressed as monkeys imprisoned in cages take part in a demonstration against Procter and Gamble's use of animals in product testing. An animal-rights group, People for the Ethical Treatment of Animals (PETA), staged the protest on January 23, 1998, in front of Procter and Gamble's manufacturing facility in Greenville, South Carolina.

Native American cultural practices also clashed with environmentalist sensibilities over religious practices involving the gathering and sacrificing of golden eaglets. The Department of the Interior, weighing laws protecting Indian religious freedoms against those protecting national parks and wildlife, allowed the Hopi to gather up to forty young eagles a year. The Hopi usually took about fifteen birds for a ceremony that culminated in their sacrifice. The Interior Department's policy was consistent with long-standing treaties as well as recent law, including the American Indian Religious Freedom Act of 1978. But many environmentalists agreed with the news columnist who wrote, "When native peoples, no matter how badly abused by us in the past, seek to perpetrate equally senseless barbarities on helpless creatures, we should stand on principle and use our awesome power to stop, not to enable them." Animal rights activists raised similar arguments against mainstream institutions, including scientific laboratories that used animals for research, and the meat industry, which engaged in inhumane practices.

COURTROOM DRAMAS: CLARENCE THOMAS AND O. J. SIMPSON

Two of the most controversial legal clashes of the decade centered on accusations against successful black men and exposed deep chasms along lines of class and gender as well as race. The first of these episodes was the 1991 Senate hearing to confirm the appointment of conservative Judge Clarence Thomas to the U.S. Supreme Court. President George H. W. Bush nominated Thomas to replace the retiring liberal Justice Thurgood Marshall. Both jurists were black but otherwise had little in common; they occupied opposite ends of the political and judicial spectrum. Although Bush claimed that Thomas was the "best man for the job," the American Bar Association gave him the lowest rating of any justice confirmed in the previous three decades. Many people became skeptical during the confirmation hearings when Thomas claimed that he had not formed any opinion on the highly charged issue of abortion. But when University of Oklahoma law professor Anita Hill accused Thomas of sexual harassment when she worked for him at the Equal Opportunity Employment Commission in the early 1980s, the question of Thomas's professional qualifications faded to the background and the hearings focused exclusively on Hill's accusations.

In live televised hearings, the African American law professor testified that Thomas had made crude and lurid remarks to her as well as unwanted sexual overtures. Several of the all-white-male panel of senators questioned Hill's credibility, wondering why she continued to work for Thomas after the alleged harassment. Thomas drew on the long history of black men being falsely accused of sexual aggression to counter the charge of sexual harassment, accusing his

Democratic opponents of conducting a "high-tech lynching." In the end, Thomas was confirmed. But Hill's testimony, and what appeared to her supporters as the insensitive behavior of the senators, brought the issue of sexual harassment to a high level of national consciousness. The hearings also highlighted the fact that Congress was overwhelmingly white and male, motivating female candidates and their supporters to alter that reality the following year. As a result of the 1992 elections, the number of female senators tripled from two to six, including the first black female senator, Carol Moseley Braun, Democrat from Illinois. The number of congresswomen rose from twenty-eight to forty-seven.

In 1994, television viewers were again riveted by a media spectacle, this time a sensational murder case in Los Angeles. The victims were the white ex-wife of black celebrity O. J. Simpson, former football star and film actor, and her male friend. Simpson's blood was found at the scene, hair and other forensic and DNA evidence linked him to the crime, he had no reliable alibi, and a motive was evident in his pattern of jealous rage and brutality against the murdered woman. No other suspects in the case were ever identified. But Simpson's team of lawyers unearthed evidence that before the Simpson case, white police detective Mark Fuhrman had boasted of planting evidence and had made racist comments. The mostly black and female jury was sympathetic to the possibility that Fuhrman had framed Simpson. In Los Angeles, in the wake of the Rodney King beatings, African Americans had ample reason to distrust the police.

Finally, in early October 1996, after a trial that lasted nearly a year, it took the jury only two hours to acquit Simpson of all charges. Pundits focused on the racial divide: blacks were more inclined to believe Simpson was innocent, and whites more likely to consider him guilty. Simpson was later convicted in a wrongful death civil suit (with lower standards for conviction than a criminal case), which found him responsible for the deaths and ordered him to pay damages. Simpson managed to shelter his assets, however, so the families of the victims never received any monetary compensation.

THE CHANGING FACE OF DIVERSITY

These highly charged events illuminated racial tensions, but there was also evidence that Americans were accepting the nation's diversity and adopting a more inclusive vision. Immigrants represented 10 percent of the population, the highest proportion of foreign-born residents since the 1930s. The numbers of Asians and Pacific Islanders increased by 45.9 percent, with those of Chinese ancestry forming the largest group, followed by those with origins in the Philippines. The Latino population grew by nearly 60 percent. Among the nation's Latinos, nearly two-thirds were of Mexican ancestry.

Not everyone celebrated these developments. In California, with one-third of the nation's Latino population, voters responded with Proposition 187 to deny public education and most other public social services to undocumented immigrants, and Proposition 227 to end bilingual education. Large numbers of Latino voters opposed these measures. In subsequent elections, many young Latinos and new citizens marshaled their political power and voted for the first time. In Los Angeles during the 1990s, Latinos became the largest single ethnic group. By 2000, whites no longer constituted a majority of California's multiethnic population, dropping from 57 percent in 1990 to 47 percent in 2000.

By 2000, whites no longer constituted a majority of California's multiethnic population, dropping from 57 percent in 1990 to 47 percent in 2000.

At the same time, politics and ideas based on distinct and rigid racial lines gave way to a growing recognition of intermixing. Artists actively explored this phenomenon. In her widely acclaimed one-woman play *Twilight, Los Angeles*, mixed-race dramatist Anna Deveare Smith explored the uprising in South Central Los Angeles by interviewing and then performing the perspectives of a wide range of white, black, Asian, Latino, male, female, young, and old people who were involved in the conflict. By transforming herself on stage into each of those people, she suggested that we, as a

Jack Smith/AP/Wide World

■ Golf superstar Tiger Woods celebrates his triumph at the U.S. Amateur Championships in North Plains, Oregon, August 25, 1996. Woods, the son of an African American father and a Thai mother, was one of several mixed-race celebrities in the 1990s.

society, were all of those people as well. In his 1996 film *Lone Star*, John Sayles examined a Texas border town where white, black, Latino, and Indian peoples were all interconnected in their lives, communities, and families. From cross-racial love to debates over the local school's history curriculum, the film explored in microcosm the challenges and rewards of an inclusive American identity.

In the world of sports, young golfer Tiger Woods, son of a black Vietnam veteran father and a Thai mother, became the reigning superstar of the sport most closely identified with the world of the white elite. Pop star Prince was one of many artists who crafted a persona that highlighted both racial and gender ambiguity. On job and college application forms, a growing number of mixed-race Americans refused to be identified as belonging to one particular racial group. Reflecting this development, the U.S. Census of 2000 allowed people to check more than one box to indicate their identity group.

The Clinton Years

■ *What was the impact of the "Republican revolution" during Clinton's presidency?*

In many ways, William Jefferson Clinton reflected the changes in American culture. He was the first American president born after World War II. His father died three months before he was born; his mother remarried when he was four years old. Raised in Arkansas in a working-class family, he was an outstanding student and musician. He considered becoming a professional saxophone player, but in the 1960s he met President John F. Kennedy, who inspired him to enter public life. Clinton attended Georgetown University and studied at Oxford University in England as a Rhodes scholar. Like many college students of his generation, he opposed the Vietnam War and avoided the draft. He attended Yale Law School, where he met Hillary Rodham from Illinois, whom he married in 1975.

In 1978, at the age of thirty-three, Clinton was elected governor of Arkansas. After one term, he was defeated in his bid for reelection, but he reclaimed his job as governor four years later by defining himself as a centrist New Democrat. When he ran for president in 1992, Clinton received the support of the Democratic Leadership Council, a group of **New Democrats** who shifted the national party to the right of its previous New Deal liberal position.

WATCH

Clinton Presidential Campaign Ad (1992)

Clinton was a brilliant campaigner and a charismatic leader with a disarming personal style that contributed to his victory over the incumbent George H. W. Bush. The sluggish economy also helped Clinton win the election. Throughout his presidency, despite political failures and scandals, Clinton achieved consistently high presidential job performance ratings in national polls. He also benefitted from the recovery of the economy during his administration. But accusations of corruption and sexual impropriety plagued him throughout his two terms. Ultimately, during his second term as president, his dishonesty about an affair with a young White House intern led to his impeachment by the House of Representatives. Although he was acquitted by the Senate and retained his office, the incident cast a cloud over his presidency.

The Clinton years were marked by relative peace and prosperity, but several incidents of domestic and international terrorism, as well as violent crimes committed by children, raised anxieties among Americans. And as scientific discoveries like the human genome project held out the promise of health and longevity, Americans continued to cause themselves harm from unhealthy consumption of food, drugs, and weapons.

THE 1992 ELECTION

In 1992, the incumbent president, George H. W. Bush, faced an uphill battle. The recession of 1991–1992 hit white-collar as well as blue-collar workers as unemployment climbed above 8 percent. During twelve years of Republican presidents, the national debt had more than quadrupled to $4.4 trillion. The Republican party platform, reflecting pressures from the right wing of the party, attacked permissiveness in American society, opposed abortion and gay rights, and called for a smaller government. The Democrats nominated the forty-six-year-old Bill Clinton, who selected as his running mate Al Gore, senator from Tennessee. A wild-card in the election was the Reform party candidacy of H. Ross Perot, a Texas billionaire who financed his own campaign and used the national media to tap into voter discontent with the two major parties.

Much of the campaign reflected the culture wars, pitting what many saw as the socially permissive legacy of the 1960s against conservative efforts to restore traditional "family values" to American public life. Many Americans worried that the prevalence of single-parent families, the high rate of divorce, and the pervasiveness of sex and violence in the popular culture all reflected a decline in moral standards and an erosion of American society. In May 1992, Vice President Dan Quayle delivered a speech criticizing the popular television show *Murphy Brown*, whose unmarried title character had given birth to a child. But Republicans were not the only critics of popular culture. Al Gore's wife, Tipper, for example, had long been an advocate of parental advisories and ratings of popular music.

Clinton won the election by a comfortable margin, but Perot garnered 19 percent of the popular vote, the largest showing for a third-party candidate since Theodore Roosevelt ran on the Progressive party ticket in 1912. Clinton began his term with a solidly Democratic House and Senate, which included a new infusion of women, along with the nation's first senator of American Indian descent, Ben Nighthorse Campbell, a Republican from Colorado. Saying that he wanted his advisers to "look like America," Clinton appointed two Latinos, three blacks, and three women to the fourteen-member cabinet.

TABLE 29.1			
The Election of 1992			
Candidate	**Political Party**	**Popular Vote (%)**	**Electoral Vote**
William J. Clinton	Democratic	43.1	370
George H. W. Bush	Republican	37.4	168
H. Ross Perot	Independent	18.8	—

CLINTON'S DOMESTIC AGENDA AND THE "REPUBLICAN REVOLUTION"

Clinton ran into trouble early in his administration when he tried to fulfill his campaign promise to allow gays and lesbians to serve openly in the military. Top military officials, already unhappy with having a new commander in chief who had avoided military service during the Vietnam War, vehemently opposed lifting the ban against gays. Ultimately, Clinton compromised and established a new policy of **don't ask, don't tell,** which allowed homosexuals to serve as long as they did not make their sexual orientation known.

Clinton's effort to reform the health care system was also unsuccessful. With rising health care costs and millions of uninsured citizens, Clinton's campaign promises to provide national health insurance and reduce the cost of health care had wide public support but fierce opposition from the medical establishment and the pharmaceutical and insurance industries. Clinton appointed his wife, Hillary Rodham Clinton, an attorney

DOCUMENT

Clinton Healthcare Reform Proposals

Adam Nadel/AP/Wide World Photos

■ The 1995–1996 government budget impasse resulted in shutdowns of many public facilities and services. Here tourists are turned away from the Statue of Liberty.

and longtime advocate on behalf of children and families, to head a task force to develop a plan. But the task force, deliberating behind closed doors, failed to come up with a workable strategy acceptable to all sides. After a year of hearings and no action in Congress on the complicated task-force proposal, the Clintons abandoned the effort.

Clinton achieved a major success when he pushed through Congress a budget that raised taxes on the wealthiest Americans, cut spending to reduce the deficit, and expanded tax credits for low-income families. In the next three years, the economy markedly improved. Other legislative successes included passage of the "motor voter" act, which allowed eligible voters to register when applying for drivers' licenses, and the Family and Medical Leave Act, which required employers to grant unpaid medical leave for up to twelve weeks. Clinton appointed two relatively liberal Supreme Court justices, Ruth Bader Ginsburg in 1993 and Stephen Breyer in 1994.

The 1994 congressional elections dealt a devastating blow to Clinton's legislative agenda. In the midst of the campaign, about 300 Republican congressional candidates, under the leadership of Speaker of the House Newt Gingrich, stood on the Capitol steps and endorsed a "Contract with America," calling for **welfare reform,** a balanced budget, more prisons and longer sentences, increased defense spending, an end to legal abortion, and other conservative measures. Only 39 percent of the electorate voted, and a whisker-thin majority of those voted Republican. Nevertheless, the Republicans declared a "Republican revolution" as they took control of both the House and Senate for the first time in forty years and pushed Congress to the right of center.

The new Congress passed a large tax cut and a tough anticrime bill, increased military spending, and reduced federal regulatory power over the environment. Clinton used his veto power to limit the Republican agenda, but he also undercut the conservative momentum by taking on some of their issues as his own, such as **free trade** and welfare reform. The "Republican revolution" did not last long. In 1995 and again in 1996, Congress forced a shutdown of the federal government rather than agree to Clinton's proposed budget, leading to widespread frustration and anger as Democrats and Republicans blamed each other for the stalemate. Support for the "Contract with America" wore thin, and the public was quickly disenchanted with the gridlock in Washington. In his 1996 State of the Union address, Clinton announced that the "era of big government is over," and he signed the Welfare Reform Act, abolishing the sixty-year-old program Aid to Families with Dependent Children (AFDC).

Clinton won reelection easily in 1996, defeating seventy-three-year-old Senate Majority Leader Bob Dole of Kansas. Republicans lost some seats but stayed in control of both houses of Congress. The 1996 campaign was more expensive than any preceding elections, with Democrats spending $250 million and Republicans $400 million. Billionaire H. Ross Perot ran again, although his showing at the polls was much weaker than 1992. Public opinion polls showed a growing concern over the vast amounts of money poured into elections, but campaign finance reform remained a difficult issue for lawmakers, whose own success at the polls depended on large financial contributions.

THE IMPEACHMENT CRISIS

Clinton's personal behavior left him vulnerable to political enemies, who took full advantage of every opportunity to discredit him. In 1993, the Clintons were investigated for possible complicity in a failed Arkansas investment scheme known as Whitewater. Although a few of the Clintons' close associates were found guilty of conspiracy, tax evasion, and mail fraud in the deal, four years of persistent investigation cleared the Clintons of any wrongdoing. Nevertheless, the Whitewater scandal activated the Office of the Independent Counsel, an independent investigative unit put into place during the Nixon administration to investigate the Watergate break-in. The independent counsel, former judge Kenneth Starr, with the help of the congressional Republicans, pursued Clinton throughout his two terms and nearly brought down his presidency. In the end, however, it was not Clinton's financial dealings but rather his sexual behavior that led to his impeachment.

TABLE 29.2			
The Election of 1996			
Candidate	**Political Party**	**Popular Vote (%)**	**Electoral Vote**
William J. Clinton	Democratic	49.24	379
Robert Dole	Republican	40.71	159
H. Ross Perot	Reform	8.4	—

Clinton's sexual behavior became an issue well before he entered the White House. During the 1992 campaign, Gennifer Flowers, a former nightclub singer, told a tabloid that she and Clinton had had an affair when he was governor. Early in his presidency, Paula Jones, a former Arkansas state employee, filed a sexual harassment suit against Clinton, claiming that he had propositioned her when he was governor of Arkansas. Eventually, the case was dismissed, but it came back to haunt him later.

In 1998, Kenneth Starr reported to the House Judiciary Committee that he had evidence that Clinton had an extramarital affair with a young White House intern, Monica Lewinsky. Starr claimed that Clinton had broken the law in an effort to cover up the affair. Lewinsky and Clinton had both been called to testify in the Paula Jones case, and both denied having had a sexual relationship. Starr claimed that Clinton had lied under oath and had instructed his close adviser and friend, Vernon Jordan, to find Lewinsky a job to keep her quiet. Starr charged Clinton with perjury, witness tampering, and obstruction of justice. As proof of the affair, Starr produced twenty hours of taped phone conversations recorded by Lewinsky's co-worker and confidante Linda Tripp. Clinton vehemently denied the charges, but Lewinsky had saved a dress with a stain containing the president's DNA, providing the investigation with the "smoking gun" it needed.

As Starr and congressional Republicans pressed the investigation with relentless determination, the media saturated the nation and the world with sordid and graphic details of the president's sexual encounters with the young intern. Polls showed that Americans disapproved of Clinton's personal behavior, but they did not want him removed from office. With the economy booming, Clinton garnered high job performance ratings, rising to 79 percent at the height of the scandal. Negative sentiment against Kenneth Starr and congressional Republicans mounted as the investigation dragged on for four years at a cost to taxpayers of $40 million.

DOCUMENT

Articles of
Impeachment Against
Clinton (1999)

Public opinion notwithstanding, the House of Representatives impeached—that is, brought charges against—Clinton on December 19, 1998, accusing him of perjury and obstruction of justice, based on Clinton's false testimony in the Paula Jones case. Removal from office requires two steps: the House of Representatives brings formal charges known as "articles of impeachment," and the Senate tries the impeached official on these articles. A two-thirds vote of the Senate is required for conviction. The vote in the House of Representatives fell strictly along party lines. The bill of impeachment was then sent to the Senate, where the majority of senators determined that Clinton's misdeeds did not meet the standard for "high crimes and misdemeanors" required to remove a president from office. The Senate thus acquitted him.

TRADE, PEACEMAKING, AND MILITARY INTERVENTION

Stymied in Congress by Republican opposition, the president turned his attention increasingly to foreign policy. In 1993, with the president's strong encouragement, Congress approved the North American Free Trade Agreement (NAFTA), eliminating tariffs and trade barriers among the United States, Mexico, and Canada and thus creating the largest free trade zone in the world. In 1994, Congress approved the General Agreement on Tariffs and Trade (GATT), which reduced tariffs on thousands of goods and phased out import quotas imposed by the United States and other industrialized nations. Supporters argued that these measures would increase global competition and improve the U.S. economy. Businesses would benefit from the easing of trade barriers, and consumers would have access to lower-priced goods.

NAFTA and GATT barely passed Congress. Clinton faced strong opposition from liberal Democrats in industrial areas and from labor unions, who feared that these measures would result in jobs going abroad, declining American wages, and a relaxation of environmental controls over companies moving outside U.S. borders. In the first few years of NAFTA and GATT, these fears seemed justified. Some jobs went abroad, and threats of moving gave employers a negotiating edge over workers. In Mexico, the impact of NAFTA was even worse. The peso collapsed as money and goods flowed across the border, and the average wages for workers fell from $1.45 to $.78 per hour.

Equally controversial were Clinton's efforts to grant China **most-favored-nation** status, which would designate China as a full trading partner with the United States.

Human rights activists argued that China's dismal record of violent suppression and imprisonment of political dissenters should preclude favorable trading terms. But with an eye to China's huge potential market for American goods and favorable site for U.S.-owned factories, Congress approved Clinton's proposal.

Despite this new alliance with a former foe, Cold War politics did not entirely disappear from foreign policy. The tiny communist nation of Cuba, suffering severe economic hardship since the collapse of its benefactor, the Soviet Union, remained off limits to U.S. trade and tourism. Cuban Americans in southern Florida, who had fled Cuba after Fidel Castro's successful revolution, blocked any efforts to ease relations between the two countries. Democrats as well as Republicans were reluctant to alienate these voters; their numbers and political clout in the most populous part of the nation's fourth largest state gave them considerable power.

Relations between the United States and Cuba were strained anew in November 1999 when a small boat carrying a group of Cubans trying to escape to Florida capsized, drowning everyone aboard except a six-year-old boy, Elian Gonzales, who was found floating on an inner tube off the coast of Florida. Elian's relatives in Miami argued that the boy should stay in the United States, where he could grow up in a democratic society—a goal his mother died trying to achieve. However, his father wanted him back in Cuba, and a court decided that the boy should be returned to his remaining parent. After months of intense media coverage in both countries and futile efforts at negotiation, U.S. government agents stormed the small house where Elian was staying and seized the boy, who eventually returned to Cuba with his father.

■ Activists protest at the opening of the meeting of the World Trade Organization (WTO) in Seattle, Washington, on November 1, 1999. During the four days of the meeting, demonstrators took to the streets in opposition to the organization's environmental and labor policies.

Reuters New Media Inc./CORBIS

While tensions with Cuba continued, most of Clinton's diplomatic efforts focused on peacekeeping and peacemaking. Clinton endeavored to ease hostilities in some of the world's most conflict-ridden areas. Northern Ireland had been fraught with violence for thirty years. Irish Catholic nationalists wanted to break ties with England and join the Republic of Ireland; Protestants loyal to Great Britain wanted to remain part of the United Kingdom. The United States, with political and diplomatic connections to London as well as strong ties to the Irish, wanted to help resolve the crisis. Clinton made several trips to Ireland to promote peace. He appointed former Senator George Mitchell of Maine as negotiator, who spent months working on a settlement. Despite dissent and violence by extremists on both sides, by the time Clinton left office, an agreement had been reached that established a shared coalition government.

In the Middle East, Clinton brought Yasser Arafat, leader of the Palestine Liberation Organization (PLO), and Yitzak Rabin, Israeli prime minister, to Washington for talks that led to an historic 1993 handshake and pledges to pursue a peace agreement. As in Northern Ireland, those efforts were hampered by violent extremists on both sides. Rabin was assassinated by a fanatical right-wing Israeli, leading to the election of a hawkish new prime minister, Benjamin Netanyahu. The peace process fell apart for several years until negotiations finally resumed in the late 1990s. But just when an agreement seemed to be within reach, large-scale violence between Palestinians and Israelis erupted again in the summer of 2000. Clinton left office with no agreement in sight.

In the final weeks of Clinton's presidency in 2000, he made a historic visit to Vietnam—the first by an American president since the war. Because Clinton had protested against the war decades earlier, his visit held great symbolic power, and his administration was the first to reopen formal relations with the Vietnamese government. Although the United States lost the war, westernization had taken hold in Vietnam, with investment beginning to flow in from Europe, the United States, and Japan, as well as American popular culture and technology. Cheering crowds welcomed the president of the superpower that Vietnam had defeated twenty-five years earlier.

The legacy of the war in Vietnam and the end of the Cold War raised new questions about how and when to use American military force. Most of the overseas crises during

Richard Vogel/AP/Wide World Photos

■ Bill Clinton was the first American president to visit Vietnam since 1969. He is pictured here during his historic visit on November 17, 2000, walking with Vietnamese President Tran Duc Luong (left) as they passed Vietnamese soldiers during official welcoming ceremonies.

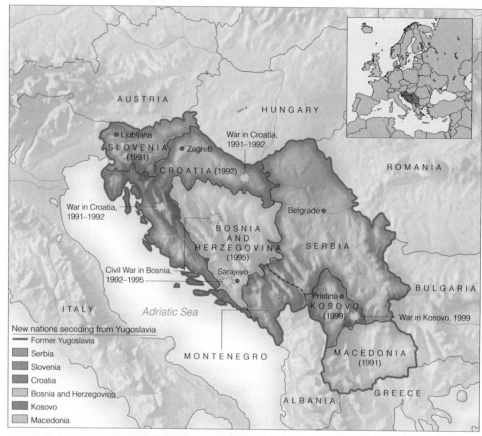

■ **MAP 29.2 The Breakup of the Former Yugoslavia**

Created in 1919 as a multiethnic nation, Yugoslavia split apart in 1991–1992. After Slovenia and Croatia gained their independence swiftly, Bosnia deteriorated into fierce ethnic fighting dominated by Serb atrocities and encouraged by the Serbian government of Slobodan Milosevic. A brief U.S. bombing campaign in 1995 finally brought the Serbs to peace negotiations. Similar ethnic fighting in the province of Kosovo in 1999 led to another U.S. bombing campaign and Kosovo's quasi-independence under NATO guidance. In 2006, Montenegro's citizens voted narrowly to establish their full independence from Serbia.

Clinton's presidency stemmed from problems of national disintegration, ethnic conflict, and humanitarian disasters resulting from political chaos and civil wars.

In 1992, President Bush had sent U.S. marines to Somalia in east Africa as part of a UN effort to provide famine relief and to restore peace in the war-torn nation. After Clinton took office, Somali warlord Mohammed Farah Aidid killed fifty Pakistani UN peacekeepers. The U.S. forces then mobilized against Aidid, shifting the peacekeeping mission to military engagement. As part of the effort to hunt down Aidid, U.S. soldiers killed hundreds of Somali citizens, creating intense anti-American sentiment among the population. Amid that hostile atmosphere, in September 1993, Aidid's forces killed eighteen American soldiers in a firefight and dragged the body of one victim through the streets. The outraged American public viewed the grim spectacle on TV, and the experience left Clinton with no clear guidelines on humanitarian intervention abroad. Largely as a result of the disaster in Somalia, when ethnic conflict led to genocide in Rwanda in central Africa in 1994, the United States and other western nations refused to intervene.

Ethnic conflict was also the cause of trouble in the Balkans. From 1945 to 1980, Marshal Josip Broz Tito ruled over a unified communist Yugoslavia, maintaining stability by suppressing ethnic rivalries. But after Tito's death in 1980 and the end of the Cold War in 1989, ethnic nationalism pulled Yugoslavia apart, with Slovenia and Croatia breaking away in 1991–1992. The region erupted in bloody conflicts. After sustained Serbian attacks on Muslims in Bosnia between 1992 and 1995, Clinton reluctantly agreed to air strikes against the Serbs, leading to the 1995 Dayton Accords, which brought an end to the war. When Serbian president Slobodan Milosevic embarked on a murderous campaign to drive the majority Muslim ethnic Albanians out of Serbia's southern province of Kosovo, Clinton finally ordered air strikes that forced the Serbs to retreat. Milosevic was voted out of office in 2000. The following year, Serbian authorities arrested Milosevic and turned him over to the War Crimes Tribunal in The Hague, which had indicted Milosevic for crimes against humanity.

DOCUMENT

The Balkan Proximity
Peace Talks
Agreement

TERRORISM AND DANGER AT HOME AND ABROAD

While the Clinton administration endeavored to carve out a new role for the United States in the post–Cold War world, several international terrorist attacks against the United States killed hundreds of people in the 1990s and highlighted the strength of extremist groups whose members were deeply hostile to the United States and its interventions around the world.

International terrorism proved to be one of the most difficult issues to confront. In June 1996, a truck bomb killed nineteen U.S. airmen in Dhahran, Saudi Arabia. Two years later, bombs exploded at two U.S. embassies in east Africa, killing 224 people in Nairobi, Kenya, and Dar es Salaam, Tanzania. Four men were convicted of conspiracy in the terrorist attacks. They were identified as followers of Islamist militant Osama bin Laden, one of the guerrillas who had been funded by the CIA in the 1980s to resist the Soviet invasion of Afghanistan. Bin Laden, originally from Saudi Arabia, was living in Afghanistan under the protection of the fundamentalist Taliban regime. He was known to be the leader of the Al Qaeda terrorist network operating in several countries throughout the Middle East. On October 12, 2000, a small boat pulled up next to the destroyer USS *Cole* in Yemen's port of Aden. A bomb exploded and ripped a hole in the destroyer, killing seventeen Americans and wounding thirty-nine others. Two suicide bombers carried out the attack. U.S. officials believed that they, too, were associated with Osama bin Laden.

> *International terrorism proved to be one of the most difficult issues to confront.*

Islamist radicals also struck in New York City. On February 26, 1993, a bomb exploded in the parking garage underneath the World Trade Center, the skyscrapers dominating the New York skyline in Lower Manhattan. Six people were killed and more than a thousand were injured. Eight years later, the same twin towers were attacked again, with far more devastating consequences.

Not all terrorists came from abroad. On the morning of April 19, 1995, a two-ton homemade bomb exploded at the Alfred P. Murrah Federal Building in Oklahoma City. The huge building crumbled, killing 168 people, including 19 children. The attack was the worst act of terrorism in the nation's history to that date. Initial news reports speculated that the terrorists were Arabs, but it turned out that the attack was carried out by American citizens with a hatred for the government. Timothy McVeigh, a veteran of the 1991 Persian Gulf War, and his accomplice, Terry Nichols, were found guilty of the bombing.

Antigovernment individuals and groups had long operated within the United States, and during the 1990s their activities—as well as FBI efforts to curtail them—intensified. Investigations throughout the decade uncovered networks of antigovernment militias, tax resisters, and white supremacist groups, many of them heavily armed and isolated in remote rural areas. Some antigovernment extremists acted alone, like former mathematics professor Theodore Kaczynski, known as the "Unabomber," who for two decades sent bombs through the mail, killing three people and injuring twenty-nine. His demand to have his antigovernment manifesto published in major national newspapers led to his identification and arrest.

The FBI tried to prevent these extremists from causing harm, but some of their efforts went awry. In 1992, during a standoff in Idaho, an FBI agent shot and killed the wife and son of Randall Weaver, a former Green Beret and antigovernment militia supporter who had failed to appear for trial on weapons charges. The following year in Waco, Texas, the FBI stormed the heavily armed compound of an antigovernment religious sect known as the Branch Davidians. The leader of the group, David Koresh, had barricaded the compound. The FBI, acting on reports of abuse of members, particularly women and children, tried to force Koresh and his group out of the building. But a fire broke out, killing eighty men, women, and children inside. The FBI came under intense criticism for its aggressive tactics in these cases. For antigovernment extremists, these actions prompted revenge. The Oklahoma City bombing apparently was intended in part as retaliation for the FBI assault against the Branch Davidians precisely two years earlier. Timothy McVeigh was sentenced to death for the Oklahoma City bombing. The execution by lethal injection took place on June 11, 2001.

The McVeigh case revived a debate about the death penalty, particularly in light of recent evidence of many botched legal defenses in capital cases. Opponents pointed to the preponderance of convicts of color on death row, representation by incompetent attorneys, and the execution of mentally retarded offenders, to argue that the death penalty should be abolished. The governor of Illinois declared a moratorium on executions when a study revealed that many death row inmates were cleared of charges as a result of new DNA evidence. Public opinion began to shift, but the majority—including the U.S. presidents from both parties throughout the decade—continued to support the death penalty.

Joe Marquette/AP/Wide World

■ Abortion remained one of the most controversial political issues throughout the 1990s. Here abortion rights advocate Inga Coulter of Harrisburg, Pennsylvania, and antiabortion crusader Elizabeth McGee of Washington, D.C., take opposing sides in a demonstration outside the Supreme Court building on December 8, 1993.

The Oklahoma City bombing was the worst but not the only example of domestic terrorist attacks. After the Supreme Court's 1973 decision in *Roe* v. *Wade* legalized abortion, antiabortion activists worked to have the decision reversed. Most antiabortion protesters were peaceful and law-abiding. But a small militant fringe of antiabortion crusaders switched their targets of protest from elected officials to abortion providers and turned to violence. In 1993, half of all abortion clinics reported hostile actions, including death threats, fires, bombs, invasions, blockades, and shootings. In 1993 and 1994, vigilantes shot and killed one abortion provider, tried to kill another, and shot employees at two clinics in Brookline, Massachusetts.

The violence spurred Congress to pass the Freedom of Access to Clinic Entrances Act in 1994, making it a federal crime to block access to clinics. But ultimately, the intimidation and violence were effective. Although abortion remained legal, the procedure became increasing difficult to obtain. Few medical residency programs in obstetrics and gynecology routinely taught the procedure, and considering the dangers posed by antiabortion terrorists, few physicians were willing to perform abortions. By the end of the decade, there were no abortion providers in 86 percent of largely rural counties in the country. Abortions continued to be available in cities, mostly in specialized abortion clinics. Between 1990 and 1997, the number of abortions declined by 17.4 percent. But the political battles continued. After years of controversy and debate, the French abortion pill RU-486 received FDA approval for use in the United States, making it possible for individual doctors to prescribe the pill and for women to avoid surgery.

WEAPONS AND HEALTH

In spite of episodes of domestic terrorism, violent crime declined throughout the decade, especially crimes committed by youths. But a spate of school shootings in which children murdered other children sparked national soul searching and finger pointing as Americans wondered whom and what to blame. The murderers were mostly white middle-class boys who appeared to be "normal kids." The worst of these shootings occurred on April 20, 1999, at Columbine High School in a suburb of Denver, Colorado, where two boys opened fire and killed twelve of their schoolmates and a teacher before killing themselves.

The common factors in all of these killings were that the children used guns and that they got the weapons easily, often from their own homes. **Gun control** advocates noted that the easy access to firearms in the United States was unique among Western industrial nations. In 1992, 367 people were killed by handguns in Great Britain, Sweden, Switzerland, Japan, Australia, and Canada combined. The total population of those countries equaled that of the United States, where in that same year, handguns killed 13,220 people. Public opinion polls showed that most Americans favored gun control, but the powerful gun lobby and the National Rifle Association argued that the Second Amendment to the Constitution guaranteed individuals the unlimited right to bear arms. Congress enacted the Brady Bill, a gun control measure named for James Brady, the White House press secretary who was gravely wounded in the 1981 assassination attempt on President Ronald W. Reagan. The bill required a waiting period for handgun purchases and banned assault rifles. Nevertheless, access to firearms remained easy. In the 2000 election, only two states, Oregon and Colorado, where two of the worst school shootings occurred, voted to establish some controls on the purchase of guns.

Americans in the 1990s also harmed themselves in less violent ways. Despite the nation's near obsession with fitness, both the wealthy and the poor suffered from a number of afflictions. Eating disorders plagued millions of Americans. Among the affluent, anorexia nervosa (self-starvation) and bulimia (frequent binging and purging) affected an estimated 5 million Americans, especially young women, who were influenced in part by a fashion fad that glamorized emaciated bodies. Men also strove for a fashionable body, sometimes with the aid of drugs to enhance athletic performance or muscle buildup. In 2000, the Mayo Clinic reported a 30 percent annual increase in eating disorders, mostly among young women, but in a growing number of men as well. The opposite problem plagued the lower end of the economic ladder, where obesity increased dramatically, especially among children. With popular fast-food chains offering "supersized" high-fat meals, the proportion of overweight children jumped from 5 percent in 1964 to 20 percent in 2000.

Illegal drugs, including marijuana, cocaine, and heroin, remained popular in spite of official efforts to curb the trade. However, illegal drugs represented only one dimension of Americans' desire to solve their problems through the use of chemical substances. Some mind-altering drugs, such as Prozac and other antidepressants, were legal and available by prescription. While these medications proved very effective in treating

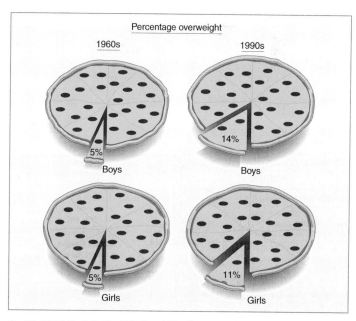

■ **FIGURE 29.1 Childhood Obesity Rates for Boys and Girls Age 6–17, 1960s and 1990s**

During the last half-century, obesity rates among children in the United States rose dramatically, especially in the 1990s. Childhood obesity is associated with a wide range of medical problems that can affect the health of overweight children throughout their lives. In the 1960s, boys and girls were equally likely to be more than 20 percent overweight. But by the 1990s, obesity had become more prevalent among boys.

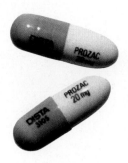

mental illness, some mental health experts worried that these drugs were being overprescribed, especially for children, as life's normal ups and downs were increasingly diagnosed as maladies such as depression and attention deficit disorder. Aging **baby boomers** also boosted the profits of pharmaceutical companies. Women turned to hormone replacement therapies to offset the effects of menopause. Skyrocketing sales of Viagra, a drug for treating male impotence, reflected middle-aged men's concerns about waning sexual potency.

Medical developments brought new cures and new worries. Antibiotics were so widely prescribed that forms of drug-resistant bacteria began to proliferate. Tuberculosis appeared in new deadly forms that did not respond to treatment with available antibiotics. In 1997, researchers in Scotland cloned a sheep, raising hopes that cloning could lead to new medical breakthroughs and fears that human cloning might be next. In 2000, scientists charted the entire human genome, or genetic code, offering the possibility of finding causes and cures for genetically linked diseases. As the century came to an end, scientific breakthroughs gave rise to new hopes as well as new questions.

The Contested Election of 2000

■ *What flaws in the American electoral system did the 2000 election reveal?*

The first presidential election of the new millennium was the most bitterly contested in more than a century. The Democratic candidate won the national popular vote, but with ballot counts incomplete in the key state of Florida, the Supreme Court ultimately declared the Republican candidate the victor. The election exposed defects in the election process, from faulty ballots and voting machines to the role of the media, and raised serious questions about the value of the electoral college. The election also revealed that flaws in the system disfranchised large numbers of poor and minority voters. But in the end, the transfer of power took place smoothly, and the nation accepted the outcome.

THE CAMPAIGN, THE VOTE, AND THE COURTS

The Democrats nominated Vice President Al Gore, who hoped to benefit from Clinton's high approval rating and the healthy economy. The Republicans nominated George W. Bush, governor of Texas and son of the former president. Bush chose as his running mate Dick Cheney, who had been the elder Bush's secretary of defense. Gore chose Senator Joe Lieberman from Connecticut as his running mate, the first Jew to run on a presidential ticket.

Only half of the nation's eligible voters turned out to vote. Even before all the polls had closed, the national media began to report the results. Early in the evening, they declared that Florida, a key state with 25 electoral votes, had gone to Gore. But soon after that announcement, they changed their projection and put Florida back into the "undecided" group of states. It became clear that whoever took Florida, where Bush's brother Jeb Bush was governor, would win the election. By the next day, Gore had won the national popular vote by half a million votes, but Bush was ahead in Florida. Bush's lead was so narrow that it triggered an automatic recount.

■ In Palm Beach, Florida, voters received this confusing "butterfly ballot." Thousands of voters in the predominantly Democratic county accidentally voted for Reform candidate Pat Buchanan instead of Democrat Al Gore. With only a few hundred votes separating Bush and Gore in Florida, it is quite possible that the butterfly ballot may have cost Gore the election.

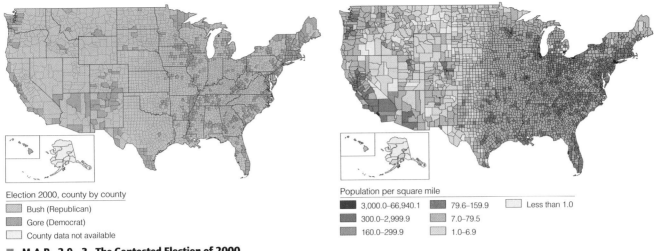

Election 2000, county by county
- ▨ Bush (Republican)
- ▨ Gore (Democrat)
- ☐ County data not available

Population per square mile
- ⬛ 3,000.0–66,940.1
- ▨ 300.0–2,999.9
- ▨ 160.0–299.9
- ▨ 79.6–159.9
- ▨ 7.0–79.5
- ▨ 1.0–6.9
- ☐ Less than 1.0

■ **M A P 2 9 . 3 The Contested Election of 2000**

The 2000 election was so close and so fraught with problems that it was ultimately decided by a 5–4 vote of the Supreme Court. As these maps show, Democratic votes were concentrated in the densely populated urban areas and Republican votes in the sparsely populated rural areas.

With all eyes on Florida, a number of serious irregularities surfaced. Voters in Palm Beach County had been given a confusing "butterfly" ballot, resulting in more than 20,000 mismarked ballots. In other counties, registered voters had been turned away at the polls because of inaccurate and incomplete voter registration lists. Some voter lists inaccurately listed eligible voters as felons. Most of these disfranchised voters were African American, who usually voted Democratic. In several largely minority counties, old voting machines that used a punch-card ballot system had failed to count thousands of ballots.

For weeks after the election, the outcome was still unknown. Democrats insisted that because Bush's lead had narrowed to a few hundred votes, tallied by inaccurate voting machines, ballots in four Florida counties should be recounted by hand. Republicans pointed out that it would be unfair to recount votes in only four heavily Democratic counties, especially with no standard way of determining voter intent on punch-card ballots with ambiguous marks on them. Florida's secretary of state, Katherine Harris, a Republican who headed Florida's campaign for George W. Bush, refused to extend the deadline to allow the recounts to take place and declared Bush the winner by 537 votes out of 6 million cast statewide.

Gore contested the results, and the Florida Supreme Court ordered that the recount proceed. Bush then appealed to the U.S. Supreme Court to reverse the decision of the Florida Supreme Court. After thirty-six days of partial vote counting and court battles, a U.S. Supreme Court ruling stopped further vote counting in Florida, effectively giving the presidency to Bush in a sharply divided 5–4 decision, with the most conservative judges voting in favor of Bush. The four dissenting judges issued a stinging rebuke of their five colleagues responsible for the decision. In his dissenting opinion, Justice Stephen Breyer wrote that the majority ruling "can only lend confidence to the most cynical appraisal of the work of judges throughout the land."

THE AFTERMATH

What became clear in the months after the election were the widespread flaws in the election system in Florida and elsewhere. Across the country, outdated voting machines yielded inaccurate vote counts,

TABLE 29.3			
The Election of 2000			
Candidate	**Political Party**	**Popular Vote (%)**	**Electoral Vote**
George W. Bush	Republican	47.88	271
Al Gore	Democratic	48.39	266[a]
Ralph Nader	Green	2.7	–
[a] One District of Columbia Gore elector abstained.			

The Great American Voting Machine

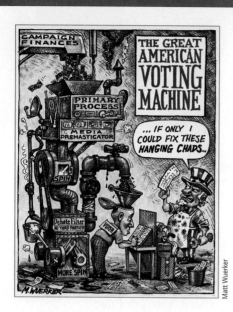

Matt Wuerker

The 2000 election exposed many problems in the voting process. This political cartoon suggests that the controversial Florida ballots and methods of counting them were only the final symptoms of an electoral system that was flawed at many levels. The reference to "hanging chads" concerns the bits of paper that did not totally separate from thousands of punch-card ballots, confounding the vote count.

QUESTIONS

1. What does this cartoon suggest about problems with the American electoral process, not just the voting system?

2. What is the cartoon's point about how voters choose their elected officials?

and long lines at polling places prevented voters from casting ballots. Low-income and minority voters were more likely to be disfranchised because they lived in precincts with faulty voting machines or overcrowded polling places. The U.S. Civil Rights Commission estimated that, in Florida, black voters were nine times more likely than white voters to have had their votes rejected.

In addition to those whose votes did not count, many others were prevented from voting altogether. In Florida, "suspected felons" were removed from voter registration lists without being informed and without the opportunity to demonstrate that they were law-abiding citizens eligible to vote. An estimated 15 percent of the list was inaccurate, and more than half of those voters were African American. According to the U.S. Civil Rights Commission, "Perhaps the most dramatic undercount in Florida's election was the nonexistent ballots of countless unknown eligible voters, who were turned away, or wrongfully purged from the voter registration rolls . . . and were prevented from exercising the franchise." As a result, hundreds of African American citizens with no criminal record arrived at the polls, only to discover that they had been disfranchised. An investigation by scholars of constitutional law concluded that the disfranchisement of African American voters in Florida constituted a violation of the 1965 Voting Rights Act. They determined that if those African American voters had been able to cast ballots, they would have provided more than the 537 votes Gore needed to win.

The election also renewed a national debate over the value of the electoral college. Opponents argued that Gore was the rightful winner because he won a majority of the popular vote. Advocates claimed that the electoral college protected the interests of less populous states and that Bush was fairly elected because he won the majority of states. Congress and state legislatures began discussions of various forms of electoral reform, but abolishing the electoral college was not among them. Representatives of small states would likely block any such measures.

Policymakers and media moguls also debated the role of the media in reporting election returns. Some argued for a blackout on early returns until all polls across the country were closed, to avoid the possibility that early results might influence voters who had not yet voted. Others proposed that only official results be announced, to avoid the problem of erroneous reporting that occurred on election night 2000. But media representatives countered that a free press should be able to report the news as it happens, although they agreed on the need to ensure accuracy.

LEGACIES OF ELECTION 2000

In addition to the unprecedented Supreme Court decision, the 2000 election was remarkable in other ways. For the first time, a first lady was elected to public office: Hillary Rodham Clinton became a Democratic senator from New York. In another Senate race, a deceased candidate was elected. Mel Carnahan, Democratic governor of Missouri, had run against Republican incumbent senator John Ashcroft. But Carnahan died in a plane crash a few weeks before the election, too late to have his name removed from the ballot. The acting governor pledged to appoint Carnahan's widow if he won the election, and she picked up the campaign. Carnahan was elected and his widow went to the Senate. (The defeated candidate, John Ashcroft, became George W. Bush's first attorney general.)

Third-party politics also critically influenced the outcome of the presidential election. Several third-party candidates had achieved national visibility during the 1990s and won elections at the state and local levels, including professional wrestler Jesse Ventura, elected governor of Minnesota in 1998 on the Reform party ticket. In 2000, Ralph Nader wreaked havoc for the Democrats with his Green party candidacy for president. Although Nader gained fewer than 3 percent of the votes, his candidacy drew off some of the left-leaning elements of the Democratic party—enough votes to cost Al Gore the election.

The election results left the Congress almost evenly divided, with a thin Republican majority in the House and a 50–50 split in the Senate. Within a year, Senator James M. Jeffords from Vermont bolted the Republican party and became an independent, giving the Democrats a majority in the Senate. The closely divided Congress began to take up issues raised by the contested election, including various measures to improve the voting process, and campaign finance reform.

President George W. Bush immediately began to reverse several Clinton-era policies, including a number of environmental protections. His first big legislative success was the passage of a major tax cut. During his first year in office, the economy went from boom to bust and headed into a recession. The robust stock market of the 1990s wilted in early 2001. Nevertheless, as the new millennium dawned, the United States remained the wealthiest and most powerful nation in the world. Bush retreated from international treaties on issues ranging from global warming to nuclear test ban agreements, and he revived the Reagan-era proposal for a nuclear missile shield. But the place of the nation in the global community was yet to be defined. Soon, monumental events shattered the nation's sense of security and prompted Bush to engage in the world in unprecedented ways.

Conclusion

In the 1990s, new economic, political, and cultural fault lines appeared in the United States. A widening gap between the rich and the poor left the majority of Americans losing ground economically while a very small elite became extremely wealthy. Union membership reached a new

CHRONOLOGY: 1991–2000	
1991	Los Angeles police beat and arrest Rodney King.
1992	South Central Los Angeles riots follow acquittal of police in Rodney King case.
	FBI shootout at Ruby Ridge, Idaho.
1993	FBI storms compound of the Branch Davidian cult in Waco, Texas.
	Congress approves North American Free Trade Agreement (NAFTA).
	Arab–Israeli peace talks.
	18 American soldiers die in Somalia; United States withdraws.
1994	House leadership announces "Contract with America."
	O. J. Simpson murder trial.
1995	Truck bomb destroys federal building in Oklahoma City.
	U.S. intervenes against Serbs in war in Bosnia.
	Dayton peace accords signed.
1996	Welfare Reform Act.
1998	Lewinsky–Clinton affair revealed.
	Clinton impeached by House of Representatives.
1999	Senate acquits Clinton.
	Dow Jones passes 10,000.
	U.S. bombing campaign frees province of Kosovo from Serbian rule.
	Elian Gonzales affair.
2000	Supreme Court decides contested election; George W. Bush becomes president.

low, although service workers successfully struck for better pay and working conditions. Americans demonstrated increasing tolerance for people who looked and acted differently from themselves. Polls showed declining levels of racial, ethnic, and religious hostility and greater acceptance of homosexuality, single parenthood, and family arrangements that deviated from the nuclear family model. But episodes of racial discrimination—by police, courts, and voting officials—continued. Politics remained an arena in which culture wars flared over abortion, gun control, and welfare reform. A Democratic president faced impeachment by his Republican foes in Congress while maintaining high approval ratings from the public.

The role of the nation in the world shifted, and a half-century of political certainties evaporated. The end of the Cold War meant that the United States had to develop a new international mission. The struggle against the Soviet Union and the communist foe had come to an end. Russia was America's friend; China was a trading partner. But conflicts around the globe, many of them grounded in ancient ethnic and religious hostilities, posed challenges for the world's most powerful nation. The United States focused on markets and trade, the nation's supply of oil, the need for political order to maintain international stability, and the danger of **rogue nations** developing nuclear arms. President Clinton promoted peace initiatives in Northern Ireland and the Middle East, although conflicts in those regions persisted.

At the dawn of the new century, several crises challenged Americans' sense of security. A deeply flawed presidential election revealed profound problems in the nation's voting systems. A sharp and sudden downturn in the economy shattered the optimism many middle-class people felt during the booming Clinton years and forced many of the working poor into desperate circumstances. Already reeling from these disturbing developments, the nation was soon shaken to its core by a terrorist attack that forced a new reckoning at home and abroad.

For Review

1. What contributed to the increasing gap between the rich and poor during the 1990s?

2. What were the effects of immigration and outsourcing on the American economy and workers?

3. What was the impact of corporate mergers on American companies?

4. What new fault lines appeared within American society during the 1990s, and what old ones seemed to ease?

5. What were the most serious threats facing the nation and its citizens in the post-Cold War era?

6. How did Clinton respond to domestic and foreign challenges during his presidency?

7. What problems led to the contested election of 2000?

Created Equal Online
For more *Created Equal* resources, including suggestions for sites to visit and further reading, go to **MyHistoryLab.com.**

Chapter 30

A Global Nation in the New Millennium

■ Smoke rises from the crash of United Airlines Flight 93 near Shanksville, Pennsylvania. For almost all Americans, the hijackings and destruction of September 11, 2001, came indeed out of a clear blue sky. Anti-American actions of the previous decade by Islamist terrorists had created little anxiety in a powerful nation that had imagined itself safe from major attack.

Val McClatchey

CHAPTER OUTLINE

- **George W. Bush and War in the Middle East**

- **The American Place in a Global Economy**

- **The Stewardship of Natural Resources**

- **The Expansion of American Popular Culture Abroad**

- **Identity in Contemporary America**

At the beginning of the third millennium C.E., the United States was more closely connected than ever to the rest of the world. The processes of globalization—increasing trade, communication, travel, and migration—linked the nation to a world often torn by ethnic and religious strife. That strife from abroad impinged on Americans in a shocking new way on September 11, 2001. On a sunny Tuesday morning, nineteen hijackers—four of them trained as pilots—seized control simultaneously of four large commercial jets and turned them into suicidal missiles. At 8:48 a.m., one flew into the 110-story north tower of New York City's World Trade Center, igniting an enormous fireball. Fifteen minutes later, the second plane flew into the south tower. In less than two hours, both towers collapsed, killing the thousands of people still inside. Among the dead were hundreds of firefighters, police officers, and other rescue workers who had raced into the towers to evacuate the occupants. The third plane flew into the Pentagon. The fourth was also being directed toward Washington, apparently to destroy the White House or the Capitol Building, until it crashed in a field seventy-five miles southeast of Pittsburgh.

The carefully coordinated assaults killed almost 3,000 people, destroyed the two tallest buildings in the country's largest city, and left a gaping hole in the headquarters of the nation's military command. Not since the Japanese assault on Pearl Harbor sixty years earlier had the United States experienced a devastating attack on its own soil. During the intervening half-century of the Cold War, the Soviet Union and other communist forces had never attempted direct aggression against the American homeland. Who was responsible for the most horrific act of terrorism against civilians in U.S. history?

The nineteen perpetrators were self-styled holy warriors of a secretive, extremist Islamist organization known as Al Qaeda, organized by wealthy, charismatic Saudi Arabian expatriate Osama bin Laden. Al Qaeda worked out of Afghanistan, hosted by the repressive Islamic government of the Taliban, which rose to power in 1996 out of the chaos that followed the withdrawal of the Soviet army in 1989. The rage of bin Laden and other Islamist terrorists against the United States had been building throughout the 1990s, fueled by the presence of "infidel" American troops in Saudi Arabia since the 1991 Persian Gulf War, by American support for Israel, and by the rapid spread of secular American popular culture around the globe. At odds with moderate Islamic mainstream thought throughout the world, bin Laden announced in 1998: "To kill Americans and their allies is an individual duty of every Muslim who is able."

At the heart of American society remained a common assumption, that the United States is a democratic country. The events on United Airlines Flight 93, one of the four doomed planes on September 11, 2001, revealed the tenacity of the belief in majority rule. After the hijackers seized control and herded the passengers into the rear of the cabin, a dozen passengers and crew members were able to communicate by phone with people on the ground. They learned that two other planes had already crashed into the World Trade Center towers in New York City, and they realized that these hijackers—unlike previous ones who sought concrete gains and an escape—planned only destruction for them all. Face to face with imminent death and the certainty that many others would perish if they failed to act, the passengers discussed what to do. They made a plan to rush the hijackers, led by several large, athletic passengers, including Mark Bingham, a prominent gay businessperson and rugby player from San Francisco. Should they proceed? Quintessential Americans, they took a vote. GTE Airfone operator Lisa Jefferson heard the rest: "Are you guys ready?" asked Todd Beamer, a tall father of two from Cranbury, New Jersey. Screams and a sustained scuffle followed before the line went dead. The plane, headed for the heart of Washington, crashed in an unpopulated part of western Pennsylvania with no casualties on the ground.

The September 11 attacks both jolted the country's political course and highlighted anew certain continuing themes in American society and politics. Just seven months in the Oval Office when the planes struck the twin towers in New York, George W. Bush did more to shape the U.S. response than any other individual. The president chose to invade Afghanistan and Iraq as part of a global "war on terror." The September 11 attacks and their aftermath also underlined how intertwined were the U.S. economy and the global economy, and how access to key natural resources such as oil determined much of daily life and the country's foreign policy. The attacks and their aftermath demonstrated, too, how widely American popular culture had spread around the globe, and how culturally diverse American society had become. The United States, still a nation of immigrants and their descendants, embodied the new global era.

George W. Bush and War in the Middle East

■ *What were the Bush administration's priorities, and how were they affected by the attacks on September 11, 2001?*

The attacks of September 11, 2001, constituted perhaps the most significant event in American life since Japan's surrender in 1945. People remember where they were when they first learned what had happened, and they recall vividly the terrible televised images of destruction. As citizens of the sole remaining superpower after the collapse of the Soviet Union, Americans had grown accustomed to unprecedented global power and influence during the 1990s. They had no great power rival. For most of those ten years, they had experienced rapid economic growth as well. The nation, it seemed, was wealthy and secure.

The events of September 11 changed all that. The economy, already sliding into recession, accelerated its downward course. Just seven months in office, the administration of President George W. Bush responded by leading the nation into a "war on terror" abroad and at home. Within two years, U.S.-led efforts succeeded in overthrowing the governments of Afghanistan and Iraq. Complicated, long-term military occupations ensued, with U.S. forces continuing to engage in bloody battles against insurgents in both countries. International opinion about the United States turned sharply negative, especially due to the war in Iraq. In an effort to prevent further terrorist attacks at home, Congress passed the "USA Patriot Act," granting greater powers to the executive branch of the federal government. Authorities detained hundreds of immigrants, primarily young men of Middle Eastern descent. These policies then faced the test of public approval in the 2004 and 2006 elections.

> *President George W. Bush responded by leading the nation into a "war on terror" abroad and at home.*

THE PRESIDENT AND THE "WAR ON TERROR"

George W. Bush did not have an auspicious record of achievement before his election as governor of Texas in 1994 and as president of the United States six years later. He grew up primarily in Midland, Texas, the grandson of a U.S. senator from Connecticut and the eldest son of a wealthy oilman, diplomat, and eventual U.S. president, George H. W. Bush. "W.," as he was sometimes called to distinguish him from his father, attended the elite Phillips Academy in Andover, Massachusetts, and he earned degrees from Yale and Harvard Business School, though his modest academic achievements hinted at the benefits of unofficial forms of affirmative action for the scions of wealthy and powerful families. His sociability and charisma earned him many friends. He avoided going to Vietnam when he was of draft age by serving in the Air National Guard, though he apparently failed to show up for much of a year of that service in 1972.

After a mixed career in business and a strong taste for the partying life, Bush gave up drinking at age forty and became a devout, conservative Christian. This ambitious and now more serious man made his way up in Republican political circles, benefiting from family connections as well as a warm, "regular guy" personality that appealed to many working-class Americans. Before his presidency, Bush had travelled to few places other than Mexico. "I'm not going to play like a person who has spent hours involved with foreign policy," he admitted during the 2000 campaign. Once president, he took a unilateralist and almost isolationist stance, to the dismay of close U.S. allies. The United States rejected or withdrew from international agreements limiting global warming, weapons testing, and war crime prosecutions.

DOCUMENT

George W. Bush, National Security Strategy

The events of September 11 stunned all Americans and gave the president a new focus. Finding and destroying Al Qaeda and its allies was now "the purpose of this administration," Bush told his cabinet. Four weeks after the attacks on New York and Washington, U.S. planes initiated the "war on terror" by bombing Taliban and Al Qaeda positions in Afghanistan. By October 19, U.S. special operations forces were working on the ground with anti-Taliban Afghan insurgents. Several European nations provided troops and other military assistance. By December, the Taliban had been driven from power throughout the country, and U.S. and allied forces had killed and captured hundreds of Taliban and Al Qaeda fighters. Many of the prisoners were transferred to the U.S. naval base at Guantanamo Bay, Cuba, to be held indefinitely and interrogated as enemy combatants. Despite continued pursuit and a reward of $25 million, the United States was not able to find Osama bin Laden, who was assumed to be hiding in the remote, snowy mountains of the Pakistan-Afghanistan border region.

SECURITY AND POLITICS AT HOME

The war on Islamist terrorism was not only a foreign affair. Just as the onset of the Cold War in the late 1940s had incorporated a hunt for domestic traitors, the war on terrorism in the early 2000s included a search for potential Al Qaeda sympathizers at home. Like the Cold War, the war on terrorism was framed as a long-term struggle against a maniacal, evil enemy who would not be easily defeated. Also as in the Cold War, American leaders announced that some civil liberties would have to be curtailed in order to protect the nation. The USA Patriot Act of October 2001 increased the U.S. Justice Department's range of options for spying on and detaining citizens and noncitizens suspected of pro-terrorist activities. Determined to prevent another major terrorist attack, Attorney General John Ashcroft oversaw the arrest of hundreds of undocumented immigrants and their imprisonment in what the Justice Department later admitted were often unduly harsh conditions—not unlike Guantanamo, observers noted. Congress created the vast new Department of Homeland Security (DHS) in an effort to better coordinate intelligence, police, and military authorities for defending the nation from future attacks.

> *Bush's conservatism did not include conserving natural resources.*

Beyond terrorism, George W. Bush sought to move the nation in the direction of what he called "compassionate conservatism." One conservative activist noted that the new administration turned out to be "more Reaganite than the Reagan administration." In the economic realm, this meant promoting the private sector and reducing federal spending on social programs for the poor. It meant reducing the government's role in regulating health and safety issues in the workplace. And it meant pushing large tax cuts through Congress in 2001 and 2003 to the disproportionate benefit of the wealthiest 1 percent of Americans. The number of poor Americans grew 17% from 2001 to 2004, and the share of national income going to corporate profits rather than to wages and salaries reached its highest level since 1950. The budget surpluses of Bill Clinton's last years disappeared, as the Bush administration ran enormous annual deficits by retaining the tax cuts while sharply increasing military spending. Under Bush, the nation built the largest deficit in its history.

Bush's conservatism did not include conserving natural resources. Bush and Vice President Dick Cheney, former oil executives, were strongly supported by corporate interests, particularly in the energy business, that sought easier access to public resources. The administration promoted oil drilling offshore and in the Arctic National Wildlife Refuge, encouraged mining and timber clear-cutting across western federal lands, and refused to regulate carbon dioxide emissions despite powerful evidence of global warming. The administration also loosened federal regulations on industrial air pollution, on water pollution by the coal industry, and on arsenic levels in drinking water. It eased off Clinton-era efforts to enforce an array of environmental standards. Northeastern moderate Republicans, such as Representative Sherwood Boehlert of New York and Senator Lincoln Chafee of Rhode Island, found themselves increasingly isolated in a party now far distant from its conservationist heritage in Theodore Roosevelt's presidency.

Sexual issues remained flashpoints of political controversy. Explicit and suggestive sexuality pervaded popular culture, including two-thirds of television shows, causing particular concern among parents of young children. So did the revelation in 2002 of years of child sexual abuse by Roman Catholic priests involving more than 4,000 children and the

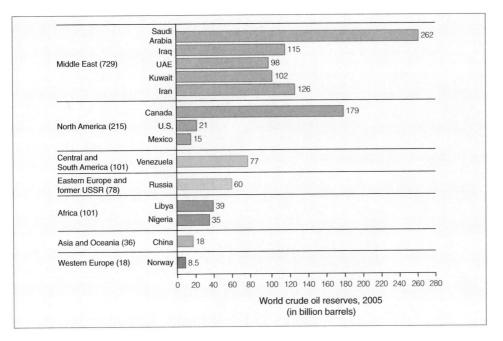

■ **FIGURE 30.1**   **World Crude Oil Reserves, 2005**

Source: U.S. Department of Energy, Energy Information Administration.

failure of the church authorities in many cases to punish offending clergy. At the same time, Americans were increasingly accepting of homosexual couples. In *Lawrence v. Texas* (2003), the U.S. Supreme Court overturned state laws banning private homosexual behavior between consenting adults. That same year, the Episcopal church elected its first openly gay bishop, Gene Robinson of New Hampshire. In 2004, Massachusetts legalized same-sex marriage. Wal-Mart, the nation's largest private employer, expanded its antidiscrimination policy to include gay and lesbian workers. One-third of the nation's largest companies now offered employees in same-sex marriages or committed relationships the same benefits and supports, such as health care insurance, that they offered employees with traditional families. President Bush opposed same-sex marriage on the grounds that marriage between a man and a woman was "one of the most fundamental, enduring institutions of our civilization." Marriage and family remained social institutions in transition, for better or worse: only 56 percent of adults were now married, compared with 75 percent thirty years earlier. Fewer than half of American households consisted of married couples and fewer than half of them included children.

INTO WAR IN IRAQ

President Bush's most momentous decision was to invade and occupy Iraq in the spring of 2003. This was a very different proposition from the attack on Afghanistan. The effort to destroy Al Qaeda and its Taliban hosts in Afghanistan had widespread support in the United States and across much of the world. By contrast, invading a sovereign nation that had not attacked or even threatened the United States divided Americans and alienated most of the rest of the world. The United Nations refused to support the invasion. America's western European allies were dismayed. Among America's major allies, only the British government of Prime Minister Tony Blair provided enthusiastic political support and a significant number of troops. Given this lack of support, why did the Bush administration invade Iraq?

The "War on Terror"

host, the Islamist Taliban regime in Afghanistan. Beyond overthrowing the Taliban, opinions were divided in the United States and among American allies abroad over what else to do. Capturing or killing Al Qaeda leader Osama bin Laden seemed the likeliest endeavor, but this proved more difficult than imagined. Bin Laden remained at large, reported to be in western Pakistan.

President Bush and his advisers instead chose to intervene decisively in the Middle East in order to reshape regional politics and, they hoped, reduce the attractiveness of anti-American, anti-Israeli Islamist revolution for young Muslims. The decision to invade and occupy Iraq reflected a bold and sweeping view of American capabilities to improve the political landscape of Muslim societies burdened with authoritarian rulers. President Bush outlined this approach

he terrorist attacks of September 11, 2001, inevitably demanded a response by the U.S. government. The Bush administration had widespread bipartisan and international support for a retaliatory assault on Al Qaeda and its

Some observers pointed to personal reasons. Bush would be "finishing" the Persian Gulf War of 1991, when his father oversaw the liberation of Kuwait from Saddam Hussein's invading Iraqi forces but did not send troops to Baghdad to overthrow Saddam. Bush would also be avenging Saddam's effort to assassinate the elder Bush on a visit to Kuwait in 1993. Other observers emphasized the centrality of Iraq's oil reserves, the largest in the world after those of Saudi Arabia, Canada, and Iran. "If the Gulf produced kumquats, would we be doing this?" asked one administration official rhetorically. The president himself claimed two primary reasons for the invasion: that Saddam possessed "weapons of mass destruction"—chemical, biological, or nuclear—and could attack the United States or its allies "on any given day," and that Iraq had ties to Al Qaeda "and was equally as bad, equally as evil and equally as destructive." Secretary of Defense Donald Rumsfeld cited "bulletproof" evidence of direct Iraq–Al Qaeda links. But after U.S. forces occupied Iraq, these two official reasons for the war were placed in doubt. U.S. troops found no weapons of mass destruction (though Saddam had indeed used chemical weapons on dissident Iraqi civilians fifteen years earlier), and Secretary of State Colin Powell admitted there was no "smoking gun" proof of a link between Al Qaeda's religious *in his graduation address to the United States Military Academy in West Point, New York, on June 1, 2002.*

America has no empire to extend or utopia to establish. We wish for others only what we wish for ourselves—safety from violence, the rewards of liberty, and the hope for a better life.

In defending the peace, we face a threat with no precedent. Enemies in the past needed great armies and great industrial capabilities to endanger the American people and our nation. The attacks of September the 11th required a few hundred thousand dollars in the hands of a few dozen evil and deluded men. . . .

For much of the last century, America's defense relied on the Cold War doctrines of deterrence and containment. In some cases, those strategies still apply. But new threats also require new thinking. Deterrence—the promise of massive retaliation against nations—means nothing against shadowy terrorist networks with no nation or citizens to defend. Containment is not possible when unbalanced dictators with weapons of mass destruction can deliver those weapons on missiles or secretly provide them to terrorist allies.

We cannot defend America and our friends by hoping for the best. We cannot put our faith in the word of tyrants, who solemnly sign non-proliferation treaties, and then systemically [sic] break them. If we wait for threats to fully materialize, we will have waited too long. . . .

The war on terror will not be won on the defensive. We must take the battle to the enemy, disrupt his plans, and confront the worst threats before they emerge. In the world we have entered, the only path to safety is the path of action. And this nation will act. . . .

Because the war on terror will require resolve and patience, it will also require firm moral purpose. In this way our struggle is similar to the Cold War. Now, as then, our enemies are totalitarians, holding a creed of power with no place for human dignity. Now, as then, they seek to impose a joyless conformity, to control every life and all of life.

Some worry that it is somehow undiplomatic or impolite to speak the language of right and wrong. I disagree. Different circumstances require different methods, but not different moralities. Moral truth is the same in every culture, in every time, and in every place. Targeting innocent civilians for murder is always and everywhere wrong. Brutality against women is always and everywhere wrong. There can be no neutrality between justice and cruelty, between the innocent and the guilty. We are in a conflict between good and evil, and America will call evil by its name. By confronting evil and lawless regimes, we do not create a problem, we reveal a problem. And we will lead the world in opposing it.

QUESTIONS

1. *Who is Bush targeting in this proposed "war on terror"?*

2. *How does this speech compare to previous calls to arms, such as Woodrow Wilson's call to join World War I (Chapter 20), Franklin Roosevelt's call to join World War II (Chapter 23), and Harry Truman's call to oppose the Soviet Union (Chapter 24)?*

Source: http://www.whitehouse.gov/news/releases/2002/06/print/20020601-3.html.

zealots and Saddam's fiercely secular dictatorship. The bipartisan reports of both the 9/11 Commission and the Senate Intelligence Committee in 2004 found that the primary reasons the president and his advisers gave for invading Iraq were not true.

A deeper reason for the U.S. invasion of Iraq appeared to be the administration's view of September 11 as an opportunity to preemptively reshape the Middle East into a region less hostile to the United States and Israel. Secretary of Defense Donald Rumsfeld declared that terrorist attacks on New York and Washington created "the kind of opportunities that World War II offered to refashion the world." A liberated Iraq, right in the center of the Middle East, might have a "demonstration effect" of pro-American capitalist democracy that would turn the rest of the region away from authoritarianism and Islamist revolution. Bush spoke of the overthrow of Saddam as "a watershed event in the global democratic revolution." This statement represented a highly optimistic view of how Americans might bring change to the Middle East, part of a new U.S. strategic doctrine emphasizing preemptive action against the nation's enemies. "We must take the battle to the enemy" in the war on terrorism, Bush declared in 2002, "and confront the worst threats before they emerge." Terrorism was now "a permanent condition," and indeed

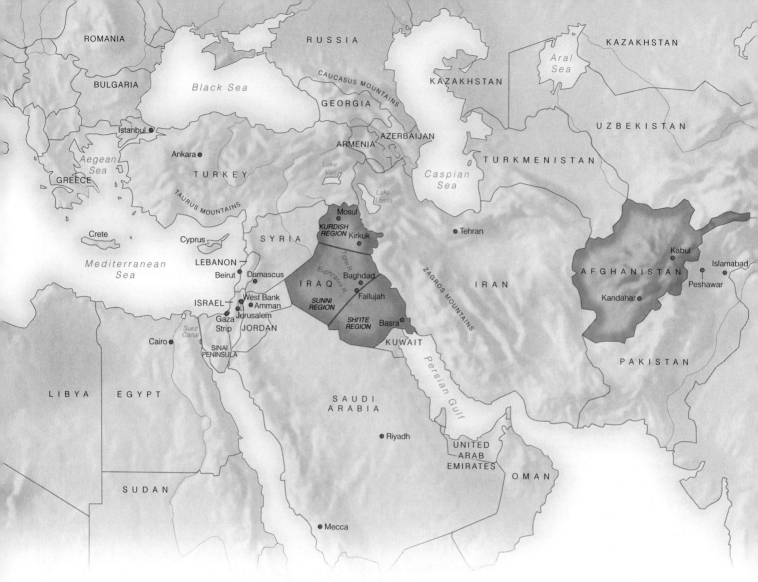

■ **MAP 30.1 Iraq and Afghanistan**

The U.S. occupation of Iraq that began in 2003 placed more than 100,000 American soldiers in the center of the volatile Middle East. A multisided insurgency against those forces grew in strength, with Iraq increasingly divided ethnically into three parts, dominated respectively by Kurds in the north, Sunnis in the center, and Shi'a in the south. By 2007, civil war between Sunnis and Shi'a had convinced a majority of Americans that the United States should withdraw its troops from a situation growing only more perilous.

Islamist terrorists continued to unleash attacks in nations as varied as Indonesia, Kenya, Turkey, Saudi Arabia, Spain, Israel, and the United Kingdom. The most powerful nation in the world therefore had to go on the offensive, the president announced, a prospect that startled most other countries and contributed to a building wave of anti-American sentiment. This feeling grew particularly strong in Muslim nations, where Bush was believed to be targeting all Muslims rather than just terrorists.

The U.S.-led offensive in Iraq that began on March 19, 2003, was a successful military action. Some 200,000 U.S. and British troops, with a few other allied forces, overran Saddam's defenses and occupied the nation of 25 million people within four weeks. The rapid military victory and the presence of so many U.S. troops initially stunned neighboring Iran and Syria into reducing aid to anti-Israeli terrorist groups. Most Iraqis celebrated their liberation from Saddam's brutal regime, and many seemed to welcome the American soldiers. Seven months later, U.S. soldiers captured Saddam himself.

■ Nothing undercut the U.S. effort to extend its influence in the Middle East more than the photographs that emerged in the spring of 2004 of U.S. troops abusing Iraqi detainees at Abu Ghraib prison outside Baghdad. Here, two of these photographs are displayed on a street in neighboring Iran. The Abu Ghraib scandal dismayed America's allies, enraged Muslims everywhere, and almost certainly enhanced Al Qaeda recruiting. One Iraqi American observed that the Bush administration had "done a good job of occupying the land of Iraq, but a horrible job of occupying the hearts of the Iraqi people."

But military occupations rarely age well, especially without sufficient troops for the task. To minimize political costs at home, Secretary of Defense Rumsfeld refused the army chief of staff's recommendation to use at least twice as many troops in order to ensure civil order and allow a new government to work. Instead, widespread looting ravaged Baghdad, and essential services and personal security deteriorated in the aftermath of the old government's defeat. "Baghdad," one gasoline station owner observed, "is like the Wild West now." Saddam loyalists, Iraqi nationalists of various stripes, and arriving foreign Islamist revolutionaries initiated a multisided insurgency against the American occupiers. The number of U.S. and Iraqi deaths shot upward. The U.S. invasion of Iraq seemed to be increasing rather than reducing the threat of terrorism to Americans and others. Indeed, some observers suggested that Osama bin Laden might be pleased to have so many U.S. troops trying to control an unhappy Muslim population for the stimulus it provided to recruiting anti-American **jihadists.** Sunnis and Shi'a also faced off against each other in what began to look like civil war.

The Bush administration turned over official sovereignty to a new Iraqi government on June 28, 2004, with 130,000 U.S. troops remaining in the country in an effort to provide security against insurgents. "We don't do empire," insisted Secretary of Defense Rumsfeld. But two months earlier, photographs and eyewitness reports were made public of U.S. troops abusing, torturing, and sexually humiliating Iraqi detainees at the Abu Ghraib prison outside Baghdad. After a week's delay, the president finally apologized. For most Middle Easterners and for Muslims around the world, however, this was compelling evidence that Bush's rhetoric about liberating Iraq was merely a cover for what they saw as fundamental American disdain for Muslims.

THE ELECTION OF 2004 AND THE SECOND BUSH ADMINISTRATION

President Bush entered his campaign for reelection with solid support in his own party but mixed reviews from others. Many nations considered the U.S. attack on Iraq to be unjustified and unwise. Western Europeans resented Bush's lack of interest in their concerns, making him probably the least-popular American president ever in Europe. Less than three years after the attacks of September 11, 2001, Americans still tended to support him on foreign policy matters. But many voters were troubled by the growing insurgency in Iraq and by a still-weak economy, and the president's approval ratings remained below 50 percent.

> Katrina was the nation's third major crisis during Bush's presidency, after the September 11 attacks and the invasion of Iraq.

The Democratic Party hoped to exploit Bush's vulnerability by nominating Senator John Kerry of Massachusetts, a decorated Vietnam War hero with a moderately liberal legislative record. Democratic party activists hoped to blunt the appeal of the president's "war on terror" and emphasis on patriotism by nominating a man whose courage under fire in Vietnam contrasted with Bush's safe spot in the Texas National Guard during that war. It did not quite work. The president prevailed in a narrow popular-vote victory. The electoral college outcome of 2004 hinged on Ohio, where a difference of 136,000 votes put Bush over the top.

Two issues predominated in the minds of the majority of voters. One was the struggle against Islamist revolutionaries, which many tended to see as the same as the war in Iraq and on which they trusted Bush's leadership more than Kerry's. The second was what voters described as "moral values," a sense that Bush—even if they sometimes did not agree with his specific policy choices—had personal integrity, a quality they were less sure of with Kerry's nuanced views of complicated policy issues. Christian conservatives were particularly important in getting Republican voters to the polls, passing initiatives in eleven states to ban same-sex marriage and winning four new seats in the Senate and four in the House to give the president a larger majority in Congress. Nonetheless, Bush's gain of 3 percentage points over his popular vote total in 2000 marked the smallest increase for an incumbent president since 1900.

After the election, the president's political fortunes mostly declined. The situation in Iraq continued to deteriorate, as deepening ethnic and religious divisions undermined efforts to reconstruct a stable society. American public support for the war edged downward. At home, Bush appointed two new conservative justices in 2005 to the Supreme Court, Chief Justice John Roberts and Associate Justice Samuel Alito. But an ethics scandal brought down the once-powerful House majority leader, Republican Tom DeLay of Texas. Two other Republican congressmen resigned because of financial and sexual scandals and another pleaded guilty to accepting bribes. Public confidence in the Republican-run Congress dimmed.

On August 29, 2005, Hurricane Katrina flooded New Orleans, causing at least 700 deaths and a massive evacuation of nearly the entire city—the worst American flood since the 1920s. The city and state government responses were utterly inadequate, and the federal government's failure was even worse. Only the National Weather Service did its job well, precisely predicting the power of the storm. During the days it took for relief workers and troops to rescue people and restore order, Americans and the world watched in disbelief as television cameras showed ongoing scenes of extraordinary human misery. The city's disproportionately black poor suffered most of all.

Katrina was the nation's third major crisis during Bush's presidency, after the September 11 attacks and the invasion of Iraq, and the administration was fiercely criticized from all sides for its performance. Even the $2 billion reconstruction effort went poorly. Republican Senator Susan Collins of Maine called the scale of waste and fraud "breathtaking." Evacuees headed to

TABLE 30.1			
The Election of 2004			
Candidate	**Political Party**	**Popular Vote (%)**	**Electoral Vote**
George W. Bush	Republican	50.8	286
John Kerry	Democratic	48.3	251
Ralph Nader	Green	<1	–

other cities in the region, particularly Houston, as part of the largest diaspora since the 1930s Dust Bowl, cutting in half the city's 450,000 pre-Katrina population.

Meanwhile, the war in Iraq dragged on. Insurgent attacks—snipers, suicide bombers, roadside bombs, and car bombs—averaged 100 per day a year after the invasion. By early 2007, over 3,000 U.S. soldiers and at least 500,000 Iraqis had died. "The planning for peace," noted Republican Senator Richard Lugar, "was much less developed than the planning for war."

A civil war now ravaged Iraq, gradually replacing most of the initial insurgency against U.S. forces. The Kurds in the north held onto their territory while the two largest Muslim groups—the majority Shi'a and minority Sunnis—battled for control in the rest of the country. In the first three months of 2006, gunmen executed at least 3,800 residents of Baghdad alone. Ethnic violence promoted ethnic separation as mixed neighborhoods realigned along Shi'a–Sunni lines. Educated Iraqi professionals and their families fled the country in droves, eliminating the very middle class that Americans had assumed would lead a post-Saddam Iraq. For their part, U.S. troops—unable to speak Arabic and untutored in Iraqi culture—became increasingly disillusioned with their uncertain and hazardous mission. "I don't like any of these people," Sergeant Jim Graham admitted. "And I don't want them getting close to me or my soldiers." In November 2006, the U.S. Central Command released a chart showing the country closing in on "chaos." Whatever opportunity had existed to create a stable, successful Iraq appeared lost.

> A substantial majority of Americans, including growing numbers of conservatives, now opposed the president's war policies.

A substantial majority of Americans, including growing numbers of conservatives, now opposed the president's war policies. In November 2006, voters elected a Democratic majority in both the House and the Senate. Under pressure, controversial Secretary of Defense Rumsfeld, a key architect of the war, resigned the next day. Certain results of the war were clear. Violence in Iraq was spiraling out of control. The Middle East was less stable rather than more, with Iranian influence growing and even the U.S.-allied government of Saudi Arabia planning to build an electrified fence along its border with Iraq to keep out the trauma next door. In Afghanistan, the Taliban reemerged and provoked bloodier fighting with U.S. and NATO forces in 2006 than at any time since its overthrow in 2001. Richard Clarke, Bush's former chief counterterrorism official, declared that the invasion of Iraq "has greatly undermined the war on terrorism." Anti-American sentiment around the world remained much higher in 2007 than it had been in 2001. Meanwhile, the U.S. military developed shortages of personnel and equipment, and the National Guard was stretched thinner than ever before. One of six veterans returning home from Iraq suffered serious psychological effects. A February 2007 *Washington Post* investigation of the famous Army medical center Walter Reed Hospital revealed shabby and negligent rehabilitation treatment of injured Iraq veterans. The costs of the war continued to rise, as did U.S. deficits. In March 2007, President Bush's public approval rating reached a new low of 29 percent, one of the lowest of any president in fifty years.

The American Place in a Global Economy

How did globalization affect Americans' lives?

While the president navigated difficult political waters, ordinary Americans struggled to find their place in a changing world economy. Mollie Brown James, for example, grew up in a small Virginia town west of Richmond. In 1950, at age nineteen, she moved to Paterson, New Jersey, joining the broad river of black Southerners who sought better economic opportunities and greater personal freedom in the North. She took a job in 1955 with the Universal Manufacturing Company in Paterson, with decent wages and benefits, unlike what had been available to her in Virginia. She stayed with Universal for thirty-four years. With union-negotiated wages, overtime pay, and company-paid health insurance, she

Elizabeth Dalziel/AP/Wide World Photos

■ The U.S.-Mexico border divides a great deal of wealth from stark poverty. Here a shack in Ciudad Juarez contrasts with El Paso in the background. But the border region from Texas to California is also a vibrant economy where the languages and cultures of the two countries mix in fascinating ways.

helped pull her family into the middle-class world of owning their own home and car and saving for retirement. But the peace of mind that came from a secure job vanished in 1989 when Universal closed the Paterson plant and moved its manufacturing operations to Matamoros, Mexico, just across the Rio Grande River from Brownsville, Texas.

James's job did not disappear. It moved and was inherited by twenty-year-old Balbina Duque Granados. She, too, had grown up in a small town located in an agricultural area, in the Mexican province of San Luis Potosí, and she, too, had moved 400 miles north to find better-paying work in a booming manufacturing city. She was thrilled to land the difficult, repetitive job—her "answered prayer"—at a *maquiladora,* one of the foreign-owned assembly plants along Mexico's border with the United States that wed First World engineering with Third World working conditions. Her employer was also satisfied, paying her $.65 an hour to do what James had been paid $7.91 an hour for. But Granados's job was no more secure than James's had been. The beginnings of successful worker organizing in Matamoros encouraged the company to shift many of its operations sixty miles upriver to Reynosa, where the union movement was weaker. A journalist asked whether she would move there if her job did. "And what if they were to move again?" she replied. "Maybe to Juarez or Tijuana? What then? Do I have to chase my job all over the world?"

THE LOGIC AND TECHNOLOGY OF GLOBALIZATION

Like many other workers in the United States and abroad, Mollie James and Balbina Duque Granados learned firsthand the relentlessly international logic of the economic system known as capitalism. Those who have capital—extra money—invest it in corporations, whose purpose is to produce a profit for their shareholders. A corporation's profitability depends on keeping costs—labor and materials—down and expanding into new markets. Those markets are not limited by nationality; a business tries to sell not just to Americans but to customers wherever they might be found. Capitalists tend to be internationalists.

The technological innovations facilitating the integration of the U.S. economy into the world economy in the late 1900s were not so much a new force as an acceleration of an older trend. Just as the telegraph and telephone had helped create a nation unified by rapid communication, the spread of personal computers and the Internet linked Americans even more closely to other nations. In the 1920s, the head of General Electric, Owen Young, spoke of his ambition to "obliterate the eastern, western, northern and southern boundaries of the United States," for "the sphere of our activities is the world."

At the start of the twenty-first century, engineering breakthroughs sped up the process of globalization. The integration of computers into every aspect of commerce and private life increased the efficiency with which businesses could operate. Retailers, for example, could monitor their inventory much more closely and eliminate unnecessary expenses. Computers boosted American productivity (the amount of work performed by a person in a given time period), which had declined between 1973 and 1996. Since the 1980s, the spread of cable television and DVD players provided constant entertainment, and Cable News Network (CNN) offered a standardized package of world news available twenty-four hours a day around the globe. Atlanta-based CNN was so international in its aims that its founder, Ted Turner, banned the word *foreign* from its broadcasts.

Americans were also speeding up their daily routines in the new millennium. The desire for immediate gratification and efficiency that had nurtured fast food and microwave ovens encouraged the spread of cell phones, beepers, personal digital assistants, overnight package delivery, and constant news headlines scrolling across TV screens. Computers processed more information faster on ever smaller silicon chips. Cell phones proliferated among businesspeople, students, and commuters. As prices dropped, cell phones even reached into poorer areas. Increased international air travel helped tourism compete with oil as the world's largest industry. The spread of the Internet—especially such popular sites as You Tube and MySpace—and the use of e-mail and instant messaging epitomized the shift toward instant global communication. Just as the Berlin Wall had long symbolized the divided world of the Cold War, the Internet became the emblem of the post–Cold War era of an increasingly unified global economy.

FREE TRADE AND THE GLOBAL ASSEMBLY LINE

The ideology of free trade underpinned the tighter meshing of Americans' lives with the world economy. Free trade meant the reduction of tariffs, or taxes on imported and exported goods. Nations that supported free trade had industries that were eager to expand and were strong enough to compete successfully in a global market; nations with less competitive industries used tariffs to protect those industries from less expensive and higher-quality imports. As a new nation in the late 1700s and 1800s, the United States had enacted high tariffs to protect its domestic producers, while England, the world's leading economic power at the time, had sought to reduce tariffs and increase trade with America. When the United States emerged after World War II as the new leading economic nation and U.S. manufacturers and farmers looked increasingly to foreign markets, U.S. tariff rates plummeted. From averages of 30–50 percent before 1945, they dropped to 5 percent by 1990. In 1965, the sum of all exports and imports amounted to 10 percent of the U.S. gross national product (GNP); by 1990, it had surpassed 25 percent and continued to climb.

Advocates of free trade argued that global markets unhindered by national tariffs benefited consumers everywhere by giving them access to the best goods at the lowest prices. America's NAFTA treaty with Canada and Mexico reflected this belief (see Chapter 29), as did the European Union with its newly unified currency, the euro. In the United States, by the start of the new millennium, most leaders of both major political parties, corporate executives, bankers, and most other elites supported free trade.

But others objected to this internationalist economic ideology. Environmentalists and labor unions led the forces opposing unregulated globalization of the U.S. economy. Environmentalists warned of the pollution costs to the world's environment of U.S. factories relocating to poorer and less regulated nations, such as Mexico and China. Labor organizers

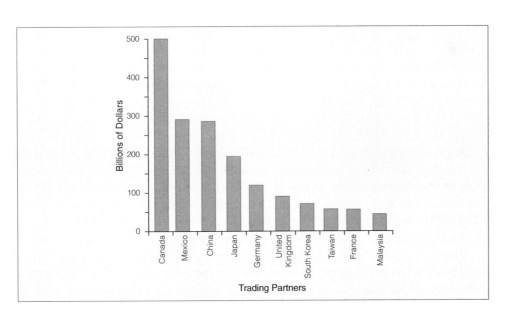

■ **FIGURE 30.2 Top Ten U.S. Trading Partners, 2005 (Total Value of Imports and Exports in Billions of Dollars)**

Americans do the most business with Canada and Mexico, followed by east Asia and then western Europe. U.S. economic vitality has always depended to some extent on foreign trade, but that dependence grew steadily in the past generation.

decried the flight of American jobs as manufacturers sought less expensive and more compliant—often desperate—workers abroad. Human rights activists spotlighted the grim working conditions in many overseas plants, including the prevalence of child labor. In 1999, in Seattle, and in 2001, in Genoa, Italy, thousands of antiglobalization protesters disrupted meetings of the World Trade Organization and of the leaders of the largest industrialized nations.

A "race to the bottom" for labor and environmental standards resulted from the development of a global assembly line. With capital able to move swiftly around the world and take its factories with it, nations and localities felt that they had little choice but to compete in offering multinational corporations the most advantageous terms possible. Such terms meant minimal government regulation, little protection for workers, nonexistent pollution standards, and even local subsidies in place of corporate taxes. Just as industries in the 1890s had formed national trusts to evade state regulations on commerce, the multinational corporations of a century later escaped the reach of national governments. This trend also represented an extension of the same logic that created the American Sunbelt over the previous half-century, when businesses from the Northeast and Midwest relocated to states with lower wage rates, fewer unions, weaker environmental standards, and minimal taxes. Corporate income taxes, which had been dropping since the 1950s, shrank by another third between 1986 and 2000. The *maquiladoras* on the Mexican border were part of a broader pattern of the corporate search for efficiency and profit, as companies, like Mollie James's Universal Manufacturing Company and RCA, took their production lines first to the American South and then abroad.

> Was the new Boeing 777, manufactured piece by piece in twelve different countries, an "American" airplane?

As a result, corporations and their products became less identifiable by nationality. Boeing Aircraft had long been the largest employer in the Seattle area, but was the new Boeing 777, manufactured piece by piece in twelve different countries, an "American" airplane? Japanese companies also moved many manufacturing plants overseas, including to the United States, to be closer to important markets. Was a Toyota made by American workers in Georgetown, Kentucky, a "foreign" car? A worker sewing the "American" company label on a trendy piece of clothing might be in Malaysia or Taiwan. Or she might be a Mexican American working in a southern California garment factory—and have a sister across the border in Mexico sewing for the same company at still lower wages. In an age of globalization and international commerce, insistence on purity of product lineage—"Buy American" campaigns—no longer made sense.

WHO BENEFITS FROM GLOBALIZATION?

The increasing globalization of the U.S. economy at the end of the twentieth century created enormous wealth while sharpening class inequalities. The stock market skyrocketed. The Dow Jones average of the value of 30 top companies' stocks rose steadily from 500 in 1956, to 1,000 in 1972, and to 3,000 in 1991. Then it quadrupled in value in just fifteen years, surpassing 12,000 in 2006. Wealthy Americans who owned the bulk of corporate stock reaped the most gain, but middle- and even working-class Americans with retirement funds invested in the market also benefited handsomely. The process of globalization and the steady expansion of the U.S. economy after 1992 also encouraged a growing belief among Americans, especially affluent ones, that markets alone offered the best solution to social problems. But markets and their strict dependence on the profit motive proved unable to preserve the quality of the environment, to pull the 37 million officially poor Americans above the poverty line ($19,200 for a family of four in 2004), or to preserve the security of the vast middle class that had stabilized American politics since World War II. Inequalities within the United States reflected growing global inequality as 20 percent of the world's people (mostly in Europe and North America) consumed 86 percent of its goods and services.

American consumers enjoyed many of the fruits of the more integrated world economy. At least in industries not dominated by monopolies, the corporate quest for lower production costs, along with fierce international competition and technological innovation, reduced prices of many goods and services. Computers, airline travel, and gasoline were all significantly less expensive in real dollars (adjusted for inflation) than they had been a generation earlier. Competition abounded in the robust retail sector of the U.S. economy, including catalog and Internet shopping. Wal-Mart represented the epitome of how the globalized economy could benefit consumers. By 2000, the discount store that Sam Walton had opened in Arkansas in 1962 surpassed General Motors as the largest American company, responsible for 6 percent of all U.S. retail sales. Wal-Mart's success resulted from relentlessly cutting costs through sharp management, using cheaper imported goods and employing a nonunion workforce, and passing its savings along to customers in the form of lower prices. In towns across the United States, Wal-Mart put smaller local competitors out of business, and its efficiency became the standard to which other large retailers aspired. Wal-Mart's growth made it Mexico's largest private employer and Latin America's largest retailer by 2007.

The benefits that Americans experienced as consumers in the global economy were offset by their declining status as workers. As manufacturers moved to the Sunbelt and then overseas, high-wage, unionized jobs providing health insurance and pension benefits disappeared. Average real wages declined for more than two decades after 1973, and union membership shrank from one-third of the workforce in the early 1950s to one-tenth in 2000. Family incomes were maintained or increased only by the addition of second and third wage earners,

"Meritocracy worked for my grandfather, it worked for my father, and it's working for me."

■ An important tension in American history is the conflict between the ideal of equal opportunity for all and the reality of inherited wealth and privilege. The unsuccessful efforts of the Bush administration to eliminate the federal estate tax, which affected the inheritances of less than 1 percent of U.S. citizens, represented the latest round in the debate about the relationship between political democracy and inherited economic inequality. In a pure meritocracy, all citizens would be rewarded for their personal achievements rather than those of their parents or ancestors.

especially women. Americans spent more than they earned. The average household had thirteen credit cards and carried $8,500 in debt on them, in addition to owing car and home mortgage payments. In 2005, the average personal savings rate dropped below zero, the first time since the Great Depression that Americans spent more than they made.

Already wider in the United States than in any other industrialized nation, the distance between rich and poor continued to grow, whittling away at Americans' self-image as a middle-class society. The share of the national income going to the richest 1 percent nearly doubled in the last quarter of the twentieth century, while the share going to the bottom 80 percent shrank. Three million Americans lived in gated communities in extremely affluent suburbs, while one of five American children grew up in poverty and 21 million citizens sought emergency food assistance each year. One of the nation's leading newspapers unknowingly captured this disparity with two articles a few pages apart, headlined "As Closets Bulge, Americans' Taste in Gifts Often Turns Toward the Taste Buds" and "Food Drives Find Cupboard Is Nearly Bare."

The political system, which helps determine how wealth and opportunity are distributed in a society, seemed to offer little respite from the widening gap between haves and have-nots. The fraction of eligible citizens who made the effort to vote in presidential elections declined to just over half in 2004 and in off-year congressional elections to just over a third, with the likelihood of voting closely correlated to a person's affluence. The fierce partisanship, personal attacks, and culture of scandal that dominated American politics alienated many.

Citizens were also disillusioned by the blatant manner in which money came to dominate the political process. With the average cost of a successful Senate campaign at $7.5 million and a House campaign approaching $1 million, few but the wealthy could campaign for Congress.

> *Elected members of Congress spent inordinate amounts of time raising money from wealthy donors.*

Almost half of the representatives first elected in 2002 were millionaires. Elected members of Congress spent inordinate amounts of time raising money from wealthy donors. Democratic Senator Richard Durbin of Illinois admitted that the system of fund-raising is corrupting: "It forces you into compromising yourself." Republican Senator John McCain of Arizona called campaign financing "an elaborate influence-peddling scheme in which both parties conspire to stay in office by selling the country to the highest bidder." For average Americans, exclusive fundraising dinners that sometimes reaped more than $30 million signaled a kind of political access they could not hope to match. The ability of business to outspend labor 15 to 1 in contributing to campaigns helped ensure minimal publicity to any discussions of the gulf between rich and poor.

The Stewardship of Natural Resources

■ *What are the most important ways in which the environment is changing, and how might these affect American society?*

No issue in the early twenty-first century was more global or more significant than the environment. Winds and waters do not respect political boundaries, nor do the materials borne on them. The condition of the natural environment affects all living creatures, yet the prevailing calculus of the market and private ownership does not apportion responsibility for its care. The free market system has no mechanism for offsetting, or even measuring, the costs of depleted natural resources. A generation ago, biologist Garrett Hardin warned of "the tragedy of the commons": that individuals' incentives to preserve the quality of their own property do not carry over to resources held in common. Litter is an obvious example, and air, water, and ground pollution are the more serious cases. Global warming—or climate change—is the issue looming over all others.

American culture has long celebrated human domination of the natural world and the benefits it brings, especially the growth in productivity that permitted living standards to rise dramatically across decades and centuries. At the same time, the rise of environmentalism and ecological understanding since 1960 offered a different way of imagining people's place on the earth.

ECOLOGICAL TRANSFORMATIONS

Ecosystems are always dynamic, and changes in weather and Native American land use had reshaped the North American environment long before the followers of Christopher Columbus arrived on the continent. But European settlement and industrialization altered the face of the land in ways that would dumbfound a time traveler from the 1500s. Even a visitor from 1900 would be astonished by the intensity of human development of the land: vast cities with their sprawling suburbs and roads and highways everywhere. The key factor was population growth. Just as the number of people in the world quadrupled from 1.5 billion to 6 billion during the twentieth century, the population of the United States quadrupled from 75 million in 1900 to 300 million by 2006. Immigration and natural reproduction accounted for much of this, as did the much longer average lifespan ushered in by antibiotics and antiviral vaccines.

The most dramatic changes in the land in the twentieth century resulted from the exploitation of wood, minerals, and water, particularly in the majority of the country lying west of the Mississippi River. Commercial logging eliminated all but 3 percent of the old-growth forests of the fifty states. The clear-cuts scarring the mountainsides and hillsides of the Pacific Northwest and Alaska told the tale, as did the erosion caused by the overgrazing by cattle of public lands managed by the Interior Department's Bureau of Land Management

Ogallala Aquifer

■ **MAP 30.2** **Water Sources in the American West**

Rapid population growth has put great pressure on the limited water sources of the arid interior West. The water in the region's major rivers is fully allocated, and pumping is fast depleting underground reserves, such as the Ogallala Aquifer below the Plains states. Access to water will help determine the course of future growth in the western half of the country.

in Utah, New Mexico, and other western states. The Mining Act of 1872 still granted to private corporations the rights to such valuable minerals as gold and copper on public land for the remarkable nineteenth-century price of $2.50 per acre. Mining companies took full advantage of the opportunity, resulting in rock and chemical wastes piled in vast slagheaps and dumped in toxic holding ponds from Arizona to Montana. In the arid but increasingly populated western states, water was the most critical resource for population growth. The U.S. Army Corps of Engineers and the Bureau of Reclamation built huge dams from the 1930s to the 1980s, providing irrigation, flood control, and hydropower but also destroying wild rivers and causing silt to begin filling up the reservoirs. Increasing diversions of the Rio Grande left that now misnamed river so dry that, by 2001, it failed to reach the Gulf of Mexico, trickling to a halt fifty feet short. Groundwater pumping for agricultural irrigation in the plains states and on the eastern slope of the Rocky Mountains was draining the vast underground Ogallala Aquifer at a rate that will empty it within a few more decades.

American prosperity came at a price. The prodigious growth of the U.S. economy depended on the consumption of ever-increasing amounts of energy, most of it from coal, oil, and natural gas. Though making up less than 5 percent of the world's population, Americans accounted for a quarter of the globe's energy consumption. They depended on other countries to provide much of it for them: in the early 2000s, the United States imported 29 percent of its total energy needs and 60 percent of its oil, primarily from Saudi Arabia, Venezuela, Canada, and Mexico. Fossil fuels, such as coal and oil, could not be renewed; once burned, they were gone, and the world had a finite supply of such fuels. Americans were constructing a lifestyle that was unsustainable in the long run. And the need for imported oil helped shape

A nighttime photograph taken from a satellite above the south Pacific Ocean reveals the use of electricity in North America. Only Alaska and some parts of the inland western states (Nevada, Idaho, eastern Oregon) appear mostly unlit. The growth of the Sunbelt states of the South and West after 1970 was dramatic, but the bulk of the U.S. population remained east of the Mississippi River, especially in the Northeast and Midwest. The demand for electrical power even with most citizens in bed was enormous.

Courtesy, National Aeronautics and Space Administration

U.S. foreign policy decisionmaking regarding Iraq and other resource-rich nations.

POLLUTION

The world's growing population was consuming five times as much fossil fuel in the early 2000s as in 1950, helping stimulate a steady rise in the earth's average temperatures. Americans caused 25 percent of carbon dioxide emissions, the largest contribution to the foremost environmental problem, global warming. The release of large amounts of carbon dioxide from burning coal, oil, and other fossil fuels helps trap extra heat within the earth's atmosphere—the greenhouse effect—and melt ice in high-altitude and polar regions. In the summer of 2000, startled scientists found open water at the North Pole, a sight humans had never before seen. Greenhouse gases also contribute to a thinning of the ozone layer of the atmosphere, which enables more of the sun's ultraviolet rays to reach the earth's surface and causes skin cancer rates to soar.

In the early twenty-first century, industrial manufacturing still figured importantly in the human assault on the air and the atmosphere, but the internal combustion engine had long since surpassed coal burning as the leading cause of pollution. The United States produced and used more cars and trucks than any other nation. The automobile and its symbolism of convenience and personal freedom defined much of American culture. With minimal public transportation outside a handful of major cities, Americans were deeply committed to a car-dependent lifestyle. As a price, they quietly accepted an annual death toll of more than 40,000 people from accidents on the road, two-thirds the number each year of all U.S. deaths in the Vietnam War. The highway infrastructure strained under the pressure of a 60 percent rise in the number of licensed drivers from 1970 to 2000 but only a 6 percent growth in total miles of roads. Negotiating traffic jams was a standard part of the daily lives of the majority of Americans who lived in the suburbs created by urban sprawl, especially around such cities as Los Angeles and Atlanta. Smog increasingly obscured the once sublime spectacular vistas of Arizona's Grand Canyon. Thousands of cars daily jammed Yosemite National Park in the Sierra Nevada mountains of California, making it an almost urban setting with air quality on the verge of violating federal standards. Yet park managers' efforts to limit automobile access to the valley were repeatedly defeated by popular opposition.

Daily life in the United States came to depend in countless ways on the use of synthetic chemicals, production of which was hundreds of times greater than it had been before World War II. Many chemicals were crucial components of Americans' comfortable modern lives. But more than 50,000 known toxic waste dumps in the United States leached poisonous chemicals and heavy metals into the soil and water, such as the polychlorinated biphenyls that lined the bottom of the Hudson River north of Albany and the arsenic and cadmium that clogged the Milltown Dam on Montana's scenic Clark Fork River six miles upstream from Missoula. Cancer rates among Americans grew sharply in the twentieth century, partly because people lived significantly longer lives (giving more time for cancers to appear) and partly because they were exposed to a much larger array of carcinogenic materials in the environment.

No synthetic product was more pervasive in the United States than plastic, a post-1945 product made from petroleum. Its prevalence and extraordinary durability helped it become a major factor in loading up the nation's landfills. The most deadly and durable pollutants, though, remained the radioactive wastes created by six decades of nuclear development. No one knew yet how to dispose safely of millions of tons of materials impregnated with plutonium and other human-made radioactive elements, 30 percent of it casually poured into dirt or stored in flimsy containers prone to leakage. The chain of nuclear poison arched across the American West—from the bomb factory at Hanford in south-central Washington through the weapons testing site in southwestern Nevada—then eastward to the uranium-processing plants in Paducah, Kentucky, and Barnwell, South Carolina. The U.S. nuclear weapon complex of some 3,000 sites put its often fatal touch on the lives of millions of Americans: uranium miners, military workers, soldiers used to observe test explosions at close range, and citizens living downwind from the Nevada Test Site in Nevada and Utah. The National Academy of Sciences concluded in 2000 that many of these sites would be permanent national sacrifice zones, toxic to humans for at least tens of thousands of years.

ENVIRONMENTALISM AND ITS LIMITATIONS

The ideas of most Americans about how to manage natural resources changed in the twentieth century. Environmental consciousness blossomed since the 1960s, rediscovering a tradition that linked eighteenth-century naturalist William Bartram with nineteenth-century transcendentalist Henry David Thoreau and twentieth-century conservationists of both major political parties. Awareness of humans' connections with their broader ecological context led to significant reforms, such as the banning of carcinogenic pesticides and leaded gasoline, the cleaning up of polluted water in the Great Lakes, and the introduction of catalytic converters to reduce harmful emissions from automobile exhaust pipes and factory smokestacks. Recycling became common, and some dams were destroyed, freeing long-constricted rivers, such as the Penobscot in Maine.

Yet issues of public land management and pollution control remained among the most controversial problems in American public life in the new millennium. Since 1980, the Republican party supported the exploitation of natural resources to produce wealth and raise standards of living, departing at least in tone from the party's earlier conservationist bent. Meanwhile, the Democratic party became associated with environmental protection. This contrast was dramatically displayed in January 2001 when President Clinton rushed to provide new protections to a swath of federal lands in the West before his term ended, while president-elect George W. Bush was appointing as secretary of the interior Colorado attorney Gale Norton, who strongly opposed such protections. Both Bush and his vice president, Dick Cheney, had extensive experience in the energy industry, and their administration promoted new oil and gas drilling in wilderness locations that included Alaska's Arctic National Wildlife Refuge.

Beyond partisan differences and the broad tendency of even the most well-known corporate polluters to pose as friendly to the environment, the relationship of Americans to their natural environment continued to be paradoxical. By large majorities in public opinion polls, they supported strong antipollution laws and the preservation of public lands from economic development. But in their daily lives, Americans consumed natural resources, particularly gasoline, electricity, and water, at a rate unmatched by other societies. Measures that had reduced some of the nation's energy consumption since the 1970s were soon reversed: Congress revoked the national 55-mph speed limit in 1995, and ever larger cars, trucks, and especially sport utility vehicles steadily reduced the average gas mileage of passenger vehicles.

While scientists and some utilities urged a reduction in the nation's expanding use of fossil fuels, Vice President Cheney dismissed conservation as merely "a sign of personal virtue" rather than a basis for a sound energy policy. For his part, President Bush acknowledged in 2006 that "America is addicted to oil." Regarding water, many residents across the arid Southwest, most of them newcomers, remained determined to recreate the green lawns they had left behind in the East and Midwest. When an investigator for the Las Vegas city

AP/Wide World

■ In 2005, Hurricane Katrina blew in from the Gulf of Mexico and devastated the southern coast of Mississippi and Louisiana. The city of New Orleans, built below sea level and dependent on a system of dikes and levees to protect it from the waters of Lake Pontchartrain and the Mississippi River, experienced massive flooding. At least 700 people—most of them poor—died in the initial flooding and the deprivation of the days that followed.

water district confronted one resident about his wasteful sprinkler, the man responded, "Man, with all these new rules, you people are trying to turn this place into a desert."

The Expansion of American Popular Culture Abroad

■ *Why is American culture attractive to many peoples elsewhere?*

Just as the U.S. economy and American environmental problems could not be separated from the outside world, the nation's cultural life grew more closely tied to that of other nations at the dawn of the new millennium. During the Cold War, from the 1940s through the 1980s, American foreign relations hinged on problems of national security and the projection of military might abroad. The dissolution of the Soviet Union in 1991 and the retreat of communism ended the bipolar division of the world and left the United States the sole remaining superpower. By the early 2000s, American popular culture rather than armed strength had emerged as the leading edge of U.S. influence around the world.

Over the first half of the twentieth century, the United States slowly replaced Great Britain as the dominant force in international affairs. The economic and military aspects of this shift of influence were clear by the end of World War II, and its cultural elements soon followed. American power extended the preeminence of English as the global language of commerce and diplomacy, and ambitious and privileged youth from beyond Europe aimed no longer for an education at England's Oxford and Cambridge but rather at prestigious U.S. universities. American culture had become less regionally distinctive and more nationally homogeneous in the twentieth century because of improvements in transportation and communication. By the beginning of the twenty-first century, this same process of homogenization of popular consumer culture was at work on a worldwide scale. American themes and products stood out in an increasingly global popular culture, although they were resisted by some abroad who preferred more local identities and traditions, often rooted in ethnicity or religious conviction.

A CULTURE OF DIVERSITY AND ENTERTAINMENT

Known for its informality and diversity, American culture proved powerfully attractive to peoples all over the world, partly because racial and ethnic diversity was more pronounced in the United States than in any other major power. African Americans, Latino Americans, and Asian Americans all figured prominently in the popular realms of sports, music, and films. Television was the leading medium for this culture of entertainment, beaming CNN, MTV, ESPN, and "reality" shows around the world. From jazz to rock 'n' roll to rap, American popular music spread across the globe, as did American jeans and sneakers, symbols of informality and comfort. Hollywood's movies dominated cinemas and DVD players everywhere, providing 85 percent of films screened in Europe.

The idea of individual choice pervaded American culture, backed by constitutional guarantees of freedom of expression. Freedom to choose included matters of religion, politics, and other weighty areas, which had long made the United States a beacon of liberty to people oppressed for their beliefs. But freedom of choice came increasingly by the new millennium to refer to consumer goods. The United States was the largest market in the world, and its citizens had unparalleled choices of what to buy. In 1960, Americans already had 3,000 shopping centers and four square feet of retail space per person. By 2000, those numbers had soared to 40,000 and nineteen, respectively, for their children and grandchildren. The premium placed on acquiring material goods seemed to many foreign observers the primary American value.

Advertising grew in prominence as the central link between popular culture and the selling of products. Sports became steadily more commercialized. Postseason college football games began in 1985 to include the names of their corporate sponsors, creating such events as the Chick-Fil-A Peach Bowl and the Weed Eater Independence Bowl. By the early 2000s, newspapers ranked bowl games—once hallowed for their own traditions—by the simple criterion of how much money

THE FINAL MERGER

■ In recent years, the process of globalization has tied the world more closely together than ever before. Increasing trade, tourism, and communication encouraged the mixing of different cultures. American popular culture has been a powerful influence around the globe, including American music, fast food, television, clothing, and movies. Mickey Mouse's ears famously symbolized the Disney Company, American television and films, and their worldwide prominence in popular entertainment.

sponsors paid to participating teams. In the 1990s and 2000s, "hoops" joined baseball as a popular U.S. export. National Basketball Association (NBA) games were telecast to more than 190 countries in forty-one languages. Sports also brought foreigners to the United States as professional baseball and basketball teams recruited Latin American, European, African, and Asian athletes.

U.S. INFLUENCE ABROAD SINCE THE COLD WAR

Cultural influences flowed both ways for Americans, with immigrants in particular bringing with them traditions and perspectives that refreshed the cultural mix of life in the United States. Japanese comics, Thai cuisine, Cuban salsa music, and soccer helped shape daily routines for many Americans. But increased trade and communication since the end of the Cold War above all enabled the further spread of American popular culture. American-accented English straddled the globe, the language of international commerce and of 80 percent of postings on the World Wide Web. The informality and individualism of the Internet made it seem quintessentially American in style even as it became the most important global disseminator of information and disinformation. The U.S. dollar remained one of the world's two primary trading currencies, along with the euro, and the dollar became the de facto and even the de jure currency of several other nations. Mickey Mouse's empire expanded to EuroDisney outside Paris and to Tokyo Disneyland. American studies became a major field of scholarship at universities around the world.

America's most popular eatery served 50 million customers a day at its 32,000 franchises across the globe. McDonald's Golden Arches appeared everywhere, from Japan and France to Russia and China. Even Mecca in Saudi Arabia, Islam's holiest site and the destination of millions of Muslim pilgrims, had a McDonald's. The company generated half of its revenues from non-U.S. operations.

America's cultural influence went beyond material interests. American religious missionaries worked in poor countries around the world, combining their spiritual mission with a commitment to improving daily life in concrete ways involving health care, education, and agriculture. Pentecostalists gained millions of converts in Latin America since the 1970s, and mainstream denominations, such as Lutherans, Episcopalians, and Roman Catholics, saw their numbers rise sharply in Africa. The most fully homegrown American religion was especially active in proselytizing abroad—the Church of Jesus Christ of Latter Day Saints (Mormons), headquartered in Salt Lake City, had more than 5 million members in the United States and another 5 million worldwide.

Another channel for American influence abroad is the U.S. military. The United States has retained its military superiority, with a defense budget larger than that of the next ten biggest military powers combined. When provoked, as by the September 11 attacks, American forces can wield extraordinary power and quickly

Hasan Hamali/AP/Wide World

■ The spread of American fast-food chains around the globe suggested that American culture may be a more powerful influence abroad than U.S. military might. The end of the Cold War led to McDonald's restaurants proliferating in downtown Moscow and Beijing, the capital cities of America's greatest opponents since World War II. Seventy-one McDonald's restaurants have opened in Saudi Arabia since 1993.

Capital Punishment, Abolition and Use

The European democracies are among the 123 nations that have abolished the death penalty, which Europeans tend to view as a barbaric punishment from the past.

Abolition of the Death Penalty

Selected Countries	Year
Italy	1944
West Germany	1949
United Kingdom	1969
Canada	1976
Spain	1978
France	1981
Australia	1985
South Africa	1995

Of the 73 nations that still use the death penalty, the United States is by far the largest and most important liberal democracy. Most other nations using the death penalty are in Asia, the Middle East, and Africa.

In the United States, the federal system means that most executions are carried out by individual states, mostly in the South. Of the 1,037 people executed since the Supreme Court reinstated the death penalty in 1976, more than one-third have been in Texas. After Texas, Virginia, Oklahoma, Missouri,

Countries with Most Executions, 2005

Country	Number of Executions
China	1,770[a]
Iran	94
Saudi Arabia	86
United States	60
Pakistan	31

[a] Known executions—the actual total may be much larger.

and Florida have the most executions. Twelve states—mostly in New England and the upper Midwest—have abolished the death penalty.

QUESTIONS

1. Why do you think European nations have eliminated capital punishment?

2. Why do you think most U.S. states and many non-European nations still allow the death penalty?

3. What do these statistics suggest about American cultural values in comparison to the rest of the world?

Source: Data from Franklin E. Zimring, *The Contradictions of American Capital Punishment.* (New York: Oxford University Press, 2003), 23; Death Penalty Information Center, http://www.deathpenaltyinfo.org.

The Wider World

reshape the histories of other nations, as demonstrated in Afghanistan and Iraq. But occupying other nations and charting the long-term future of other societies has proved difficult. Instead, the expansion of American culture abroad seems a safer and more effective way to influence other nations.

RESISTANCE TO AMERICAN POPULAR CULTURE

Like Christian, Jewish, and Hindu fundamentalists, all of whom grew prominent in the final decades of the twentieth century, Muslim fundamentalists rejected the radical egalitarianism and the unbridled pursuit of pleasure—especially the sexual titillation—so prevalent in American popular culture. The relative equality of women and the lack of respect for traditional social and religious hierarchies seemed to them emblems of American decadence, as the Islamic rulers of Afghanistan—the Taliban—demonstrated in the 1990s in their brutal repression of women's rights. Osama bin Laden and his followers resented U.S. policies of supporting Israel and certain oil-producing Arab nations, but they also fiercely condemned the secular, egalitarian character of American society, which they considered anti-Islamic. During the 1991 Persian Gulf War, Saudi Arabian officials tried to isolate U.S. troops from Saudi citizens, fearing the effects of contact with such diverse forces as female soldiers, bawdiness, Christianity, and American music and television.

The demise of communist regimes in Russia and eastern Europe opened the gates to a flood of western influences and brought the opportunities and inequalities of a suddenly privatized economy. State-provided safety nets disappeared, class differences widened, women's economic status declined, and the old Communist parties regained some popularity among voters scared by the instabilities of American-style capitalism. Western Europeans also remained ambivalent about the spread of American values and lifestyles. Although many of them, especially among the young, found American culture attractive and learned English in record numbers, traditionalists who were proud of their own national culture took a dim view of such innovations as fast food.

> *A world more tightly integrated in economic ways was at the same time divided by ethnic conflicts.*

Other nations sometimes found the U.S. government overbearing and resented its unparalleled military power. Rapidly modernizing China, the world's most populous country, was a growing rival to the United States in Asia, even as the two nations became major trading partners. In April 2001, a U.S. surveillance plane collided over the South China Sea with a Chinese fighter jet that had been following it. The Chinese pilot died, but the American plane managed to crash-land safely at a Chinese military airport on Hainan Island. China detained the crew of twenty-four men and women for ten days. Public and congressional anger in the United States paralleled the outrage in China, but the two governments, mindful of their growing economic interdependence, resolved the crisis after a brief standoff. Americans were surprised by the intensity of anti-American nationalism within Chinese society.

Two opposing trends characterized world affairs. One consisted of the unifying forces of economic internationalism and globalization, carrying with them a tide of American-dominated cultural styles. The other was made up of the resisting forces of political and ethnic nationalism, as well as religious revolutionaries such as the anti-Israeli Hamas and Hezbollah. A world more tightly integrated in economic ways was at the same time divided by ethnic conflicts, revealed in wars in the Caucasus region on Russia's southern border, the Darfur region of western Sudan, and Iraq. As people around the world felt themselves increasingly sucked into the vortex of a powerful global economy that they could not control, many responded by renewing their allegiances to older, more local traditions. Ethnic, religious, and national identities often offered more meaningful alternatives to a purely economic identity as consumers. "I don't find foreign countries foreign," Gillette Corporation chair Alfred M. Zeien said, and many people in other nations felt the same way about the United States. But for others, as the terrorist attacks of September 11, 2001, made all too clear, American life seemed fundamentally alien and increasingly threatening.

Identity in Contemporary America

■ *What are the most important kinds of identity in the United States?*

The 2000 U.S. Census revealed a society in the midst of change. Americans have long been known as a particularly restless and mobile people, and one out of five changed residences every year. The post-1965 wave of immigrants continued to rise (and foreign adoptions rose dramatically), bringing in millions of new Americans of Asian heritage. Latino Americans surpassed African Americans as the nation's largest minority. This latest surge in immigration boosted the number of Roman Catholics and Buddhists as American society remained by far the most openly religious—still primarily Protestant—of the industrialized nations. Geographically, Americans lived farther south and west than earlier generations; none of the twenty fastest-growing states were in the Northeast or Midwest.

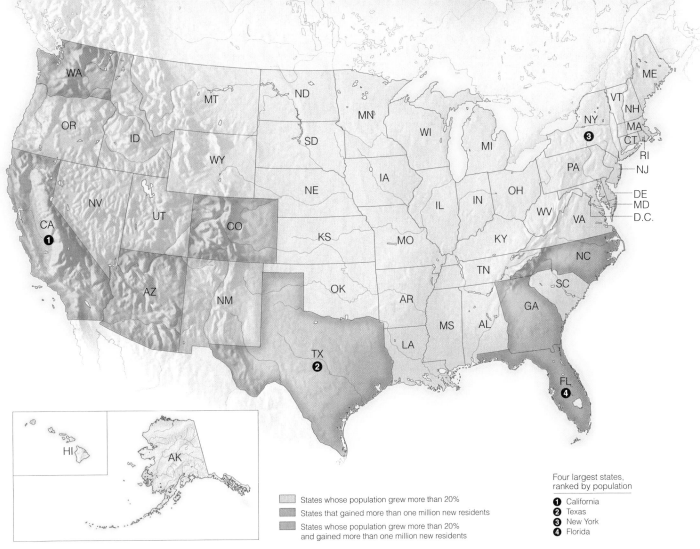

States whose population grew more than 20%

States that gained more than one million new residents

States whose population grew more than 20% and gained more than one million new residents

Four largest states, ranked by population

❶ California
❷ Texas
❸ New York
❹ Florida

■ **MAP 30.3 State Population Growth, 1990–2000**
The population of the United States continued to shift slowly out of the long-urbanized Northeast to the Sunbelt of the South and West. Los Angeles replaced Chicago as the nation's second largest city, after New York. Retirees and workers alike preferred sunnier, warmer climates.

Americans were older than they used to be: life expectancy rose to 77 from 45 years in 1900. More than half lived in suburbs. Average household size dropped by 50 percent over the twentieth century. Whereas in 1900 just 6 percent of married women worked outside the home, 61 percent did so by 2000, including 64 percent of those with children under age six. The "family wage" that so many men earned in the mid-twentieth century was disappearing, helping bring in its wake changes in gender roles as women became crucial breadwinners as well as homemakers and child-raisers.

NEGOTIATING MULTIPLE IDENTITIES

Americans derived their sense of identity from myriad sources, including nationality, work, socioeconomic status, religion, race, ethnicity, family, gender, region, and sexual orientation. Since the struggles for equality that emerged dramatically in the 1960s, individual identities and group identities have often been in tension. The achievement of legal equality and the outlawing of explicit discrimination did not immediately change deeply embedded patterns of exclusionary behavior. The policy of affirmative action had developed as a preference in hiring or admission for members of an underrepresented group who were roughly comparable to others in qualifications. It aimed to balance some of the effects of an existing but little-noticed bias that favored white Americans and men, such as when colleges used lower admission standards for children of alumni or when powerful white men tended to hire other white men.

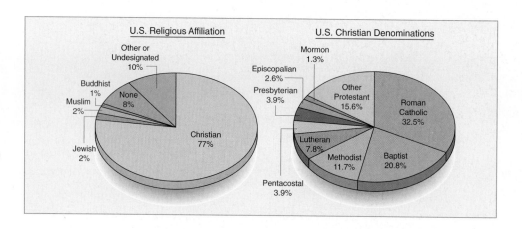

■ **FIGURE 30.3** Self-Described Religious Affiliation in the United States, 2000

The most noticeable change during the last 30 years in American religious life has been the growth of evangelical and fundamentalist Protestant congregations and the shrinking of mainline Protestant denominations.

Opponents of affirmative action called it "reverse discrimination" and argued that race and sex should no longer be criteria for success in a colorblind society that promoted individual achievement. By 2000, these opponents had succeeded in eliminating affirmative action from the admission process of the large state university systems of Texas and California. Supporters of the policy—including several large corporations and many high-ranking military officers—observed that employers and others were not colorblind yet, so that a group remedy, such as affirmative action, remained essential for the advancement of more than a token few from groups that had faced discrimination in the past. In 2003, the Supreme Court decided that the University of Michigan Law School could continue to use race as one of its considerations for admission, though it could not use a specific racial quota. This confirmed the Court's 1978 *Bakke* decision (see Chapter 27).

Ideas about racial identity remained at the heart of the controversy over affirmative action. Those who used the term *race* to group people according to skin color and other visible features, such as eye shape, commonly assumed that race had an important biological meaning as a way of distinguishing one human population from another. However, biologists noted that the genetic differences between races are miniscule compared with differences between individuals of the same race. They suggested that categorizing people by skin color made as much sense as organizing library books by the size and color of their covers rather than their internal contents. Indeed, the racial category "white" had changed over time to encompass such formerly excluded groups as Irish Americans and Jewish Americans. Despite its lack of scientific basis, the use of race as a primary marker of identity long served to preserve a higher status for Americans of European heritage. One could be mostly "white" yet still be "black," thanks to the one-drop tradition regarding African heritage (that any observable percentage of African "blood" defined a person as black). Thus, a white woman could have a black child in the United States, for example, but a black woman could not have a white child.

The U.S. government's decision in the 2000 census to allow citizens to identify themselves as belonging to more than one racial group reflected the complications and occasional absurdities of racial categorization.

SOCIAL CHANGE AND ABIDING DISCRIMINATION

One of the most striking changes in American society over the past five decades has been the desegregation of public life. Latinos and Asians became much more numerous in the United States. Twenty-eight Latinos—six of them women—were elected to the U.S. Congress in 2006. African Americans emerged from the enforced separation of Jim Crow into greater prominence. Roughly one-third of blacks were middle-class, and thousands won election to local, state, and national political offices. Black Americans became central in the nation's cultural life in music, literature, theater, and sports. By 2001, even a new

Where is the West?

Envisioning History

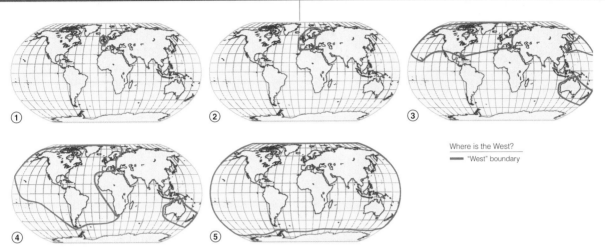

Where is the West?
— "West" boundary

■ **MAP 30.4** 1: The West as England.   2: The West as medieval European Christendom.   3: The West as the Cold War Atlantic alliance (NATO) plus European settler colonies and usually Japan.   4: The contemporary cultural West (emphasizing language, religion, and "high culture"), including Latin America, areas of concentrated European settlement in South Africa, and sometimes the Philippines.   5: The perhaps future West of globalization?

These five maps suggest how the meaning of the "West" has changed over time. The maps use different criteria to determine what is part of the West and what is not part of the West. Most of the maps also reflect a primarily American view of the world.

QUESTIONS

1. What are the most important criteria used in these maps to determine what is "Western"?

2. What are the implications of understanding the "West" in each of these ways?

3. How might the changing character of the "West" alter the way we understand other broad identities, such as being "white" or being "Muslim"?

4. How might China view Map 5?

Source: Adapted from Martin W. Lewis and Karën E. Wigen, *The Myth of Continents: A Critique of Metageography* (Berkeley: University of California Press, 1997), 50–51.

president from the Republican party—known since 1964 for its lack of support from black voters—appointed two African Americans to run the nation's foreign relations: Secretary of State Colin Powell and National Security Advisor (and later secretary of state) Condoleezza Rice. Workplaces were racially integrated to an extent that would have been hard to imagine in 1950, and interracial marriages rose steeply in the final decades of the twentieth century.

The lives of women in the United States also changed dramatically during the last half of the twentieth century. Most worked outside the home, from jobs in the service and manufacturing sectors to careers in the professions and politics. In 2000, women made up one-third of the students in the nation's medical schools and one-half in law schools. Their presence in leading political positions ranged from local officials to more than a dozen U.S. senators, two U.S. Supreme Court justices, a U.S. attorney general, and two U.S. secretaries of state. The passage of Title IX in 1972, prohibiting gender discrimination in school programs that received federal money, created a tidal wave of social change for American girls. In 1971, one in twenty-seven girls played high school sports; by 1998, the ratio was one in three. Sports programs and teams for girls comparable to those for boys nourished a new generation of American women for whom athletic competition and achievement were the norm rather than the exception.

■ Born and raised in Alabama, Condolezza Rice became a political scientist and a specialist in Russian affairs at Stanford University. She served on the National Security Council during the George H. W. Bush administration and returned to Stanford as provost of the university during the 1990s. A key foreign policy adviser for George W. Bush since his first presidential campaign, and a close family friend of the Bushes, Rice served as national security adviser and then succeeded Colin Powell as secretary of state in 2005.

Anti-homosexual attitudes persisted as one of the nation's fiercest prejudices but nonetheless declined in mainstream American society during the last thirty years. Gay men and lesbians became more open and prominent in such public venues as television and politics, helping millions of other Americans shed some of the homophobia they had unknowingly learned during childhood. During the 2004 election campaign, many Americans learned that Mary Cheney, daughter of conservative Vice President Dick Cheney, was a lesbian. In 2006, when Mary Cheney and her partner of fifteen years announced that Mary was pregnant, her parents said they were pleased.

These improvements for the majority of Americans who were not heterosexual white men jostled against abiding forms of discrimination and inequality. Violence and the threat of violence against homosexuals, people of color, and particularly women (primarily domestic violence at the hands of husbands and lovers) remained very real, but most prejudices found more subtle avenues of expression. Working women continued to average less than three-quarters the wages of working men. Many employers, police officers, store owners, bank loan officers, and others in positions of authority treated African Americans and Latino Americans with greater suspicion than they did other citizens, a practice that became known as racial profiling. Poverty and unemployment disproportionately affected black communities and families. Given the powerful legacy of the past, white individuals on average possessed ten times more real wealth (much of it inherited) than their African American counterparts. Residential neighborhoods and public schools remained largely segregated by race, and the deeply symbolic Confederate flag still occupied a place of public honor in several southern states. Popular black comedian Chris Rock reminded mostly white audiences of the enduring but unstated advantage of being white in the United States: "Ain't no white man here willing to trade places with me—and I'm rich!"

Native Americans shared this combination of improving status and continuing discrimination. Their numbers were reviving, from a mere 250,000 in 1900 to 2 million in 2000. A series of federal court decisions in the 1970s and 1980s strengthened Indians' "unique and limited" sovereignty over the tribal reservations, which constituted 2 percent of U.S. land. Starting with the Iroquois of upstate New York in 1970, several eastern Indian nations sued state and federal governments for the return of parts of lands that had been illegally seized from them in the past, or for compensation. From Florida to Maine, these nations won a combination of small portions of public land and millions of dollars in compensation in cases from the 1970s through the 1990s. Beginning in the 1990s, casino revenues brought much-needed resources to a number of Indian nations. At the same time, the process of assimilation continued as a majority of Indians lived in urban areas and were married to non-Indians. Reservations suffered from severe unemployment rates and remained some of the poorest communities in the country, dependent on federal assistance for food and other basic necessities. Anti-Indian sentiments continued to surface in states as diverse as Montana, Wisconsin, Arizona, and New York.

STILL AN IMMIGRANT SOCIETY

Economic opportunity and individual liberty still lured millions of people from other nations to the United States at the start of the new millennium. About a million now came legally each year, and another 300,000 entered without official papers. For the first time since the 1930s, one in nine Americans had been born abroad; in New York City the ratio was one in four. In 2004, 15 percent came from Europe, 33 percent arrived from Asia, and 43 percent from Latin America and the Caribbean. Like Italy in 1900, Mexico in 2000 became the most important single source of new Americans. The demographic transition of California in 2000 from a white majority to a more diverse ethnic and racial mix like that of Hawaii symbolized the nation's shift to the South and West, even as the aspirations and work habits of the newcomers remained very much the same as those of their European predecessors.

■ The diversity of contemporary American society is particularly evident in public places, such as this rush-hour subway car.

Only the hardiest and most motivated people made the difficult, emotionally wrenching, and often dangerous move to the United States. Many fled political persecution in countries such as Guatemala, Haiti, Vietnam, and Cuba. In contrast to the left-leaning and often socialist attitudes of immigrants in 1900, political refugees in 2000 were sometimes fierce anticommunists who helped pressure the U.S. government to take an even harder line toward regimes in Havana and Hanoi. Most immigrants came to stay, but some worked to save money and return home to their families, carrying with them not only money, but also bits of American culture. Other people flowed outward too, as American students and tourists traveled all over the globe. Some Americans worked abroad, usually for U.S.-based multinationals such as oil companies, to earn better wages and then return home. Others served in the military, worked for aid agencies and church groups, or joined in the resurgence of the Peace Corps.

Despite increasing contacts overseas, Americans responded to the wave of newcomers with an ambivalence common in previous periods of high immigration. Many in the working class feared competition from highly motivated laborers accustomed to much lower wages. Many elites worried whether cultural diversity might weaken national unity. Conservative political leaders promoted new restrictions and stronger border patrols. Some members of Congress ridiculed the idea of there being value in traveling abroad by boasting that they did not even have passports. In 1998, the Republican House majority leader, Dick Armey of Texas, announced: "I've been to Europe once; I don't have to go again." Such disdain for other cultures among some American political leaders dismayed U.S. allies overseas.

Most Americans got used to having more immigrants around. Americans cheered for the one in four major league baseball players who were born in Latin America or had parents from there, and they became accustomed to the high number of Asian Americans in college classrooms. They also cheered for baseball players from Japan and heard more Spanish on college walkways. Many churches worked to help new arrivals adjust to life in the United States. Nearly all-white Iowa even began an immigrant recruitment drive to sustain a vibrant state economy that lacked sufficient workers. Mexico opened a consulate in Omaha to serve the needs of its immigrants in the northern Plains states. Above all, American employers depended on immigrant workers to keep the nation's powerful economy afloat—to pick its fruits and vegetables, tend its young children, construct its new buildings, and work in its factories.

Conclusion

What held Americans together as they moved into the twenty-first century was a common loyalty to a set of ideas about economic opportunities and individual liberties. Unlike such nations as Germany and Israel, where citizenship was extended automatically only to people of a certain ethnicity, the United States awarded citizenship to all those who were born within its borders, regardless of ethnicity or race. Those born elsewhere became citizens on the basis not of their past lineage but of their future commitments— of their newly sworn loyalty to the U.S. Constitution, with its guarantees of freedom and its responsibilities of citizenship. In a vast society of multiple political and cultural beliefs, the scope of specific freedoms and the nature of individual responsibilities inevitably remained matters of ongoing tension and conflict. Nonetheless, the United States continued to address most of its problems through an orderly legal system, in contrast to the ethnic and religious strife marking so many of the world's nations.

Americans will face some basic challenges in the near future. Will the currently increasing inequality in American society—in terms of income, wealth, and power— weaken the bonds that hold the nation together? Policies regarding taxes, Social Security, health care, and welfare will help determine if most Americans will continue to see themselves as middle-class members of a mostly middle-class society. The process of globalization will not make this any easier. The tighter integration of the U.S. economy and the world economy has thus far helped create great wealth, but that wealth is distributed very unevenly among Americans. Who has how much wealth and influence will remain a crucial determinant of the nation's future. In addition, the graying of the baby boom generation—8,000 of them reaching age sixty each day, and still more retiring—will exacerbate pressures on the health care system, along with the growing number of Americans without health insurance. So will the sharp rise in obesity, with the average American now twenty-five pounds heavier than in 1960. Huge government deficits will restrict options for managing these problems.

Another challenge will be the use and distribution of natural resources. As national and world populations continue to increase, so will the demand for oil, water, and timber. How will crowding and greater competition affect the quality of American life? How long can American society remain centered on the automobile and its emphasis on individual mobility? Behind all environmental issues looms the largest issue of all: climate change and how it may reshape societies around the globe.

The expansion of American influence abroad will continue to create problems as well as benefits for Americans. U.S. military, economic, political, and cultural leadership is clear. But the enormous reservoir of goodwill toward the United States that was evident around the world through most of the twentieth century has been draining rapidly in recent years. Ongoing U.S. military operations in Afghanistan and Iraq have convinced millions of peoples in those regions and elsewhere that the United States is an aggressive nation bent on dominating the world and humbling Islamic nations in particular. The torturing of detainees devastated America's reputation for fair play. Islamist terrorism appears to be growing, and the proliferation of nuclear technology makes this a particularly disturbing prospect. Whether the United States will gain more than it loses by its military engagements abroad remains an open question. And the U.S. relationship with China will be crucial to the shape of international affairs in the coming decades.

And finally, how well will Americans respond to the greater complexity of their society as their ranks come to include larger numbers of immigrants, non-Christians, people of color, people who are openly homosexual, and others not previously considered mainstream? By 2050, census projecters foresee a majority of citizens of non-European descent. In comparison to most other cultures, American society has been unusually inclusive of people of diverse backgrounds and beliefs. Whether it will continue to be so will determine, as much as any other factor, the future of the United States.

For Review

1. How successful has George W. Bush been as president, and in what ways?

2. Was the U.S. invasion of Iraq in 2003 related to the terrorist attacks of September 11, 2001? Why or why not?

3. To what extent is "globalization" the same thing as "Americanization"?

4. Why has the United States faced resistance and even hostility from many people and governments in the Middle East and elsewhere?

5. To what extent has discrimination been reduced and equal opportunity increased in the United States?

6. How do recent immigrants compare with previous immigrants in American history?

CHRONOLOGY: 2001–PRESENT

2001	Democrats gain control of Senate after James Jeffords leaves Republican party.
	Al Qaeda terrorists attack World Trade Center and Pentagon.
	U.S. forces attack Afghanistan and overthrow Taliban regime.
2002	Republicans regain control of Senate.
2003	Space shuttle *Columbia* disintegrates as it reenters Earth's atmosphere.
	U.S. and allied forces invade and occupy Iraq.
	U.S. forces capture Saddam Hussein.
	Supreme Court legalizes gay sexual conduct in *Lawrence v. Texas*.
2004	George W. Bush reelected president.
	Republicans increase their majority in Senate.
2005	Hurricane Katrina devastates New Orleans.
	John Roberts becomes Chief Justice of Supreme Court and Samuel Alito becomes Associate Justice.
2006	Democrats gain majorities in both the House and Senate.
	3000th U.S. military fatality in Iraq.
2007	130,000–160,000 U.S. troops still serving in Iraq.

Created Equal **Online**

For more *Created Equal* resources, including suggestions for sites to visit and further reading, go to **MyHistoryLab.com.**

The Declaration of Independence

The Articles of Confederation

The Constitution of the
United States of America

Amendments to the Constitution

Presidential Elections

In Congress, July 4, 1776

The Unanimous Declaration of the Thirteen United States of America

When, in the course of human events, it becomes necessary for one people to dissolve the political bonds which have connected them with another, and to assume, among the powers of the earth, the separate and equal station to which the laws of nature and of nature's God entitle them, a decent respect to the opinions of mankind requires that they should declare the causes which impel them to the separation.

We hold these truths to be self-evident: That all men are created equal; that they are endowed by their Creator with certain unalienable rights; that among these are life, liberty, and the pursuit of happiness; that, to secure these rights, governments are instituted among men, deriving their just powers from the consent of the governed; that whenever any form of government becomes destructive of these ends, it is the right of the people to alter or to abolish it, and to institute new government, laying its foundation on such principles, and organizing its powers in such form, as to them shall seem most likely to effect their safety and happiness. Prudence, indeed, will dictate that governments long established should not be changed for light and transient causes; and accordingly all experience hath shown that mankind are more disposed to suffer, while evils are sufferable, than to right themselves by abolishing the forms to which they are accustomed. But when a long train of abuses and usurpations, pursuing invariably the same object, evinces a design to reduce them under absolute despotism, it is their right, it is their duty, to throw off such government, and to provide new guards for their future security. Such has been the patient sufferance of these colonies; and such is now the necessity which constrains them to alter their former systems of government. The history of the present King of Great Britain is a history of repeated injuries and usurpations, all having in direct object the establishment of an absolute tyranny over these states. To prove this, let facts be submitted to a candid world.

He has refused his assent to laws, the most wholesome and necessary for the public good.

He has forbidden his governors to pass laws of immediate and pressing importance, unless suspended in their operation till his assent should be obtained; and, when so suspended, he has utterly neglected to attend to them.

He has refused to pass other laws for the accommodation of large districts of people, unless those people would relinquish the right of representation in the legislature, a right inestimable to them, and formidable to tyrants only.

He has called together legislative bodies at places unusual, uncomfortable, and distant from the depository of their public records, for the sole purpose of fatiguing them into compliance with his measures.

He has dissolved representative houses repeatedly, for opposing, with manly firmness, his invasions on the rights of the people.

He has refused for a long time, after such dissolutions, to cause others to be elected; whereby the legislative powers, incapable of annihilation, have returned to the people at large for their exercise; the state remaining, in the mean time, exposed to all the dangers of invasions from without and convulsions within.

He has endeavored to prevent the population of these states; for that purpose obstructing the laws for naturalization of foreigners; refusing to pass others to encourage their migration hither, and raising the conditions of new appropriations of lands.

He has obstructed the administration of justice, by refusing his assent to laws for establishing judiciary powers.

He has made judges dependent on his will alone, for the tenure of their offices, and the amount and payment of their salaries.

He has erected a multitude of new offices, and sent hither swarms of officers to harass our people and eat out their substance.

He has kept among us, in times of peace, standing armies, without the consent of our legislatures.

He has affected to render the military independent of, and superior to, the civil power.

He has combined with others to subject us to a jurisdiction foreign to our constitution, and unacknowledged by our laws, giving his assent to their acts of pretended legislation:

For quartering large bodies of armed troops among us;

For protecting them, by a mock trial, from punishment for any murder which they should commit on the inhabitants of these states;

For cutting off our trade with all parts of the world;

For imposing taxes on us without our consent;

For depriving us, in many cases, of the benefits of trial by jury;

For transporting us beyond seas, to be tried for pretended offenses;

For abolishing the free system of English laws in a neighboring province, establishing therein an arbitrary government, and enlarging its boundaries, so as to render it at once an example and fit instrument for introducing the same absolute rule into these colonies;

For taking away our charters, abolishing our most valuable laws, and altering fundamentally the forms of our governments;

For suspending our own legislatures, and declaring themselves invested with power to legislate for us in all cases whatsoever.

He has abdicated government here, by declaring us out of his protection and waging war against us.

He has plundered our seas, ravaged our coasts, burned our towns, and destroyed the lives of our people.

He is at this time transporting large armies of foreign mercenaries to complete the works of death, desolation, and tyranny already begun with circumstances of cruelty and perfidy scarcely paralleled in the most barbarous ages, and totally unworthy the head of a civilized nation.

He has constrained our fellow-citizens, taken captive on the high seas, to bear arms against their country, to become the executioners of their friends and brethren, or to fall themselves by their hands.

He has excited domestic insurrection among us, and has endeavored to bring on the inhabitants of our frontiers the merciless Indian savages, whose known rule of warfare is an undistinguished destruction of all ages, sexes, and conditions.

In every stage of these oppressions we have petitioned for redress in the most humble terms; our repeated petitions have been answered only by repeated injury. A prince, whose character is thus marked by every act which may define a tyrant, is unfit to be the ruler of a free people.

Nor have we been wanting in our attentions to our British brethren. We have warned them, from time to time, of attempts by their legislature to extend an unwarrantable jurisdiction over us. We have reminded them of the circumstances of our emigration and settlement here. We have appealed to their native justice and magnanimity; and we have conjured them, by the ties of our common kindred, to disavow these usurpations, which would inevitably interrupt our connections and correspondence. They, too, have been deaf to the voice of justice and of consanguinity. We must, therefore, acquiesce in the necessity which denounces our separation, and hold them, as we hold the rest of mankind, enemies in war, in peace friends.

We, therefore, the representatives of the United States of America, in General Congress assembled, appealing to the Supreme Judge of the world for the rectitude of our intentions, do, in the name and by the authority of the good people of these colonies, solemnly publish and declare, that these United Colonies are, and of right ought to be, FREE AND INDEPENDENT STATES; that they are absolved from all allegiance to the British crown, and that all political connection between them and the state of Great Britain is, and ought to be, totally dissolved; and that, as free and independent states, they have full power to levy war, conclude peace, contract alliances, establish commerce, and do all other acts and things which independent states may of right do. And for the support of this declaration, with a firm reliance on the protection of Divine Providence, we mutually pledge to each other our lives, our fortunes, and our sacred honor.

JOHN HANCOCK

New Hampshire
Josiah Bartlett
William Whipple
Matthew Thornton

Massachusetts
John Adams
Samuel Adams
Robert Treat Paine
Elbridge Gerry

New York
William Floyd
Philip Livingston
Francis Lewis
Lewis Morris

Rhode Island
Stephen Hopkins
William Ellery

New Jersey
Richard Stockton
John Witherspoon
Francis Hopkinson
John Hart
Abraham Clark

Pennsylvania
Robert Morris
Benjamin Rush
Benjamin Franklin
John Morton
George Clymer
James Smith
George Taylor
James Wilson
George Ross

Delaware
Caeser Rodney
George Read
Thomas McKean

Maryland
Samuel Chase
William Paca
Thomas Stone
Charles Carroll of Carrollton

North Carolina
William Hooper
Joseph Hewes
John Penn

Virginia
George Wythe
Richard Henry Lee
Thomas Jefferson
Benjamin Harrison
Thomas Nelson, Jr.
Francis Lightfoot Lee
Carter Braxton

South Carolina
Edward Rutledge
Thomas Heyward, Jr.
Thomas Lynch, Jr.
Arthur Middleton

Connecticut
Roger Sherman
Samuel Huntington
William Williams
Oliver Wolcott

Georgia
Button Gwinnett
Lyman Hall
George Walton

Between the States of New Hampshire, Massachusetts Bay, Rhode Island and Providence Plantations, Connecticut, New York, New Jersey, Pennsylvania, Delaware, Maryland, Virginia, North Carolina, South Carolina, Georgia

Article 1

The stile of this confederacy shall be "The United States of America."

Article 2

Each State retains its sovereignty, freedom and independence, and every power, jurisdiction, and right, which is not by this confederation expressly delegated to the United States, in Congress assembled.

Article 3

The said states hereby severally enter into a firm league of friendship with each other for their common defence, the security of their liberties and their mutual and general welfare; binding themselves to assist each other against all force offered to, or attacks made upon them, or any of them, on account of religion, sovereignty, trade, or any other pretence whatever.

Article 4

The better to secure and perpetuate mutual friendship and intercourse among the people of the different states in this union, the free inhabitants of each of these states, paupers, vagabonds, and fugitives from justice excepted, shall be entitled to all privileges and immunities of free citizens in the several states; and the people of each State shall have free ingress and regress to and from any other State, and shall enjoy therein all the privileges of trade and commerce, subject to the same duties, impositions, and restrictions, as the inhabitants thereof respectively; provided, that such restrictions shall not extend so far as to prevent the removal of property, imported into any State, to any other State of which the owner is an inhabitant; provided also, that no imposition, duties, or restriction, shall be laid by any State on the property of the United States, or either of them.

If any person guilty of, or charged with treason, felony, or other high misdemeanor in any State, shall flee from justice and be found in any of the United States, he shall, upon demand of the governor or executive power of the State from which he fled, be delivered up and removed to the State having jurisdiction of his offence.

Full faith and credit shall be given in each of these states to the records, acts, and judicial proceedings of the courts and magistrates of every other State.

Article 5

For the more convenient management of the general interests of the United States, delegates shall be annually appointed, in such manner as the legislature of each State shall direct, to meet in Congress, on the 1st Monday in November in every year, with a power reserved to each State to recall its delegates, or any of them, at any time within the year, and to send others in their stead for the remainder of the year.

No State shall be represented in Congress by less than two, nor by more than seven members; and no person shall be capable of being a delegate for more than three years in any term of six years; nor shall any person, being a delegate, be capable of holding any office under the United States, for which he, or any other for his benefit, receives any salary, fees, or emolument of any kind.

Each State shall maintain its own delegates in a meeting of the states, and while they act as members of the committee of the states.

In determining questions in the United States, in Congress assembled, each State shall have one vote.

Freedom of speech and debate in Congress shall not be impeached or questioned in any court or place out of Congress: and the members of Congress shall be protected in their persons from arrests and imprisonments, during the time of their going to and from, and attendance on Congress, except for treason, felony, or breach of the peace.

Article 6

No State, without the consent of the United States, in Congress assembled, shall send any embassy to, or receive any embassy from, or enter into any conference, agreement, alliance, or treaty with any king, prince, or state; nor shall any person, holding any office of profit or trust under the United States, or any of them, accept of any present, emolument, office or title, of any kind whatever, from any king, prince, or foreign state; nor shall the United States, in Congress assembled, or any of them, grant any title of nobility.

No two or more states shall enter into any treaty, confederation, or alliance, whatever, between them, without the consent of the United States, in Congress assembled, specifying accurately the purposes for which the same is to be entered into, and how long it shall continue.

No State shall lay any imposts or duties which may interfere with any stipulations in treaties entered into by the United States, in Congress assembled, with any king, prince, or state, in pursuance of any treaties already proposed by Congress to the courts of France and Spain.

No vessels of war shall be kept up in time of peace by any State, except such number only as shall be deemed necessary by the United States, in Congress assembled, for the defence of such State or its trade; nor shall any body of forces be kept up by any State, in time of peace, except such number only as, in the judgment of the United States, in Congress assembled, shall be deemed requisite to garrison the forts necessary for the defence of such State; but every State shall always keep up a well regulated and disciplined militia, sufficiently armed and accoutred, and shall provide, and constantly have ready for use, in public stores, a due number of field pieces and tents, and a proper quantity of arms, ammunition and camp equipage.

No State shall engage in any war without the consent of the United States, in Congress assembled, unless such State be actually invaded by enemies, or shall have received certain advice of a resolution being formed by some nation of Indians to invade such State, and the danger is so imminent as not to admit of a delay till the United States, in Congress assembled, can be consulted; nor shall any State grant commissions to any ships or vessels of war, nor letters of marque or reprisal, except it be after a declaration of war by the United States, in Congress assembled, and then only against the kingdom or state, and the subjects thereof, against which war has been so declared, and under such regulations as shall be established by the United States, in Congress assembled, unless such States be infested by pirates, in which case vessels of war may be fitted out for that occasion, and kept so long as the danger shall continue, or until the United States, in Congress assembled, shall determine otherwise.

Article 7

When land forces are raised by any State for the common defence, all officers of or under the rank of colonel, shall be appointed by the legislature of each State respectively, by whom such forces shall be raised, or in such manner as such State shall direct; and all vacancies shall be filled up by the State which first made the appointment.

Article 8

All charges of war and all other expences, that shall be incurred for the common defence or general welfare, and allowed by the United States, in Congress assembled, shall be defrayed out of a common treasury, which shall be supplied by the several states, in proportion to the value of all land within each State, granted to or surveyed for any person, as such land and the buildings and improvements thereon shall be estimated according to such mode as the United States, in Congress assembled, shall, from time to time, direct and appoint.

The taxes for paying that proportion shall be laid and levied by the authority and direction of the legislatures of the several states, within the time agreed upon by the United States, in Congress assembled.

Article 9

The United States, in Congress assembled, shall have the sole and exclusive right and power of determining on peace and war, except in the cases mentioned in the 6th article; of sending and receiving ambassadors; entering into treaties and alliances, provided that no treaty of commerce shall be made, whereby the legislative power of the respective states shall be restrained from imposing such imposts and duties on foreigners as their own people are subjected to, or from prohibiting the exportation or importation of any species of goods or commodities whatsoever; of establishing rules for deciding, in all cases, what captures on land or water shall be legal, and in what manner prizes, taken by land or naval forces in the service of the United States, shall be divided or appropriated; of granting letters of marque and reprisal in times of peace; appointing courts for the trial of piracies and felonies committed on the high seas, and establishing courts for receiving and determining, finally, appeals in all cases of captures; provided, that no member of Congress shall be appointed a judge of any of the said courts.

The United States, in Congress assembled, shall also be the last resort on appeal in all disputes and differences now subsisting, or that hereafter may arise between two or more states concerning boundary, jurisdiction or any other cause whatever; which authority shall always be exercised in the manner following: whenever the legislative or executive authority, or lawful agent of any State, in controversy with another, shall present a petition to Congress, stating the matter in question, and praying for a hearing, notice thereof shall be given, by order of Congress, to the legislative or executive authority of the other State in controversy, and a day assigned for the appearance of the parties by their lawful agents, who shall then be directed to appoint, by joint consent, commissioners or judges to constitute a court for hearing and determining the matter in question; but, if they cannot agree, Congress shall name three persons out of each of the United States, and from the list of such persons each party shall alternately strike out one, in the petitioners beginning, until the number shall be reduced to thirteen; and from that number not less than seven, nor more than nine names, as Congress shall direct, shall, in the presence of Congress, be drawn out by lot; and the persons whose names shall be drawn, or any five of them, shall be commissioners or judges to hear and finally determine the controversy, so always as a major part of the judges who shall hear the cause shall agree in the determination; and if either party shall neglect to attend at the day appointed, without shewing reasons which Congress shall judge sufficient, or, being present, shall refuse to strike, the Congress shall proceed to nominate three persons out of each State, and the secretary of Congress shall strike in behalf of such party absent or refusing; and the judgment and sentence of the court to be appointed, in the manner before prescribed, shall be final and conclusive; and if any of the parties shall refuse to submit to the authority of such court, or to appear or defend their claim or cause, the court shall nevertheless proceed to pronounce sentence or judgment, which shall, in like manner, be final and decisive, the judgment or sentence and other proceedings being, in either case, transmitted to Congress, and lodged among the acts of Congress for the security of the parties concerned: provided, that every commissioner, before he sits in judgment, shall take an oath, to be administered by one of the judges of the supreme or superior court of the State where the cause shall be tried, "well and truly to hear and determine the matter in question, according to the best of his judgment, without favour, affection, or hope of reward": provided, also, that no State shall be deprived of territory for the benefit of the United States.

All controversies concerning the private right of soil, claimed under different grants of two or more states, whose jurisdictions, as they may respect such lands and the states which passed such grants, are adjusted, the said grants, or either of them, being at the same time claimed to have originated antecedent to such settlement of jurisdiction, shall, on the petition of either party to the Congress of the United States, be finally determined, as near as may be, in the same manner as is before prescribed for deciding disputes respecting territorial jurisdiction between different states.

The United States, in Congress assembled, shall also have the sole and exclusive right and power of regulating the alloy and value of coin struck by their own authority, or by that of the respective states; fixing the standard of weights and measures throughout the United States; regulating the trade and managing all affairs with the Indians not members of any of the states; provided that the legislative right of any State within its own limits be not infringed or violated; establishing and regulating post offices from one State to another throughout all the United States, and exacting such postage on the papers passing through the same as may be requisite to defray the expences of the said office; appointing all officers of the land forces in the service of the United States, excepting regimental officers; appointing all the officers of the naval forces, and commissioning all officers whatever in the service of the United States; making rules for the government and regulation of the said land and naval forces, and directing their operations.

The United States, in Congress assembled, shall have authority to appoint a committee to sit in the recess of Congress, to be denominated "a Committee of the States," and to consist of one delegate from each State, and to appoint such other committees and civil officers as may be necessary for managing the general affairs of the United States, under their direction; to appoint one of their number to preside; provided that no person be allowed to serve in the office of president more than one year in any term of three years; to ascertain the necessary sums of money to be raised for the service of the United States, and to appropriate and apply the same for defraying the public expences; to borrow money or emit bills on the credit of the United States, transmitting, every half year, to the respective states, an account of the sums of money so borrowed or emitted; to build and equip a navy; to agree upon the number of land forces, and to make requisitions from each State for its quota, in proportion to the number of white inhabitants in such State; which requisitions shall be binding; and, thereupon, the legislature of each State shall appoint the regimental officers, raise the men, and cloathe, arm, and equip them in a soldier-like manner, at the expence of the United States; and the officers and men so cloathed, armed, and equipped, shall march to the place appointed and within the time agreed on by the United States, in Congress assembled; but if the United States, in Congress assembled, shall, on consideration of circumstances, judge proper that any State should not raise men, or should raise a smaller number than its quota, and that any other State should raise a greater number of men than the quota thereof, such extra number shall be raised, officered, cloathed, armed, and equipped in the same manner as the quota of such State, unless the legislature of such State shall judge that such extra number cannot be safely spared out of the same, in which case they shall raise, officer, cloathe, arm, and equip as many of such extra number as they judge can be safely spared. And the officers and men so cloathed, armed, and equipped, shall march to the place appointed and within the time agreed on by the United States, in Congress assembled.

The United States, in Congress assembled, shall never engage in a war, nor grant letters of marque and reprisal in time of peace, nor enter into any treaties or alliances, nor coin money, nor regulate the value thereof, nor ascertain the sums and expences necessary for the defence and welfare of the United States, or any of them: nor emit bills, nor borrow money on the credit of the United States, nor appropriate money, nor agree upon the number of vessels of war to be built or purchased, or the number of land or sea forces to be raised, nor appoint a commander in chief of the army or navy, unless nine states assent to the same; nor shall a question on any other point, except for adjourning from day to day, be determined, unless by the votes of a majority of the United States, in Congress assembled.

The Congress of the United States shall have power to adjourn to any time within the year, and to any place within the United States, so that no period of adjournment be for a longer duration than the space of six months, and shall publish the journal of their proceedings monthly, except such parts thereof, relating to treaties, alliances or military operations, as, in their judgment, require secrecy; and the yeas and nays of the delegates of each State on any question shall be entered on the journal, when it is desired by any delegate; and the delegates of a State, or any of them, at his, or their request, shall be furnished with a transcript of the said journal, except such parts as are above excepted, to lay before the legislatures of the several states.

Article 10

The committee of the states, or any nine of them, shall be authorized to execute, in the recess of Congress, such of the powers of Congress as the United States, in Congress assembled, by the consent of nine states, shall, from time to time, think expedient to vest them with; provided, that no power be delegated to the said committee for the exercise of which, by the articles of confederation, the voice of nine states, in the Congress of the United States assembled, is requisite.

Article 11

Canada acceding to this confederation, and joining in the measures of the United States, shall be admitted into and entitled to all the advantages of this union; but no other colony shall be admitted into the same, unless such admission be agreed to by nine states.

Article 12

All bills of credit emitted, monies borrowed and debts contracted by, or under the authority of Congress before the assembling of the United States, in pursuance of the present confederation, shall be deemed and considered as a charge against the United States, for payment and satisfaction whereof the said United States and the public faith are hereby solemnly pledged.

Article 13

Every State shall abide by the determinations of the United States, in Congress assembled, on all questions which, by this confederation, are submitted to them. And the articles of this confederation shall be inviolably observed by every State, and the union shall be perpetual; nor shall any alteration at any time hereafter be made in any of them, unless such alteration be agreed to in a Congress of the United States, and be afterwards confirmed by the legislatures of every State.

These articles shall be proposed to the legislatures of all the United States, to be considered, and if approved of by them, they are advised to authorize their delegates to ratify the same in the Congress of the United States; which being done, the same shall become conclusive.

The Constitution of the United States of America

Preamble

We the People of the United States, in Order to form a more perfect Union, establish Justice, insure domestic Tranquility, provide for the common defence, promote the general Welfare, and secure the Blessings of Liberty to ourselves and our Posterity, do ordain and establish this Constitution for the United States of America.

Article I

Section 1

All legislative Powers herein granted shall be vested in a Congress of the United States, which shall consist of a Senate and House of Representatives.

Section 2

The House of Representatives shall be composed of Members chosen every second Year by the People of the several States, and the Electors in each State shall have the Qualifications requisite for Electors of the most numerous Branch of the State Legislature.

No Person shall be a Representative who shall not have attained to the Age of twenty five Years, and been seven Years a Citizen of the United States, and who shall not, when elected, be an inhabitant of that State in which he shall be chosen.

Representatives and direct Taxes shall be apportioned among the several States which may be included within this Union, according to their respective Numbers, *which shall be determined by adding to the whole Number of free Persons, including those bound to Service for a Term of Years, and excluding Indians not taxed, three fifths of all other Persons.** The actual Enumeration shall be made within three Years after the first Meeting of the Congress of the United States, and within every subsequent Term of ten Years, in such Manner as they shall by Law direct. The Number of Representatives shall not exceed one for every thirty Thousand, but each State shall have at Least one Representative; *and until such enumeration shall be made, the State of New Hampshire shall be entitled to chuse three, Massachusetts eight, Rhode-Island and Providence Plantations one, Connecticut five, New York six, New Jersey four, Pennsylvania eight, Delaware one, Maryland six, Virginia ten, North Carolina five, South Carolina five, and Georgia three.*

When vacancies happen in the Representation from any State, the Executive Authority thereof shall issue Writs of Election to fill such Vacancies.

The House of Representatives shall chuse their Speaker and other Officers; and shall have the sole Power of Impeachment.

Section 3

The Senate of the United States shall be composed of two Senators from each State, *chosen by the Legislature thereof,* for six Years; and each Senator shall have one Vote.

Immediately after they shall be assembled in Consequence of the first Election, they shall be divided as equally as may be into three Classes. The Seats of the Senators of the first Class shall be vacated at the Expiration of the second Year, of the second Class at the Expiration of the fourth Year, and of the third Class at the Expiration of the sixth Year so that one third may be chosen every second Year; *and if Vacancies happen by Resignation, or otherwise, during the Recess of the Legislature of any state, the Executive thereof may make temporary Appointments until the next Meeting of the Legislature, which shall then fill such Vacancies.*

No Person shall be a Senator who shall not have attained to the Age of thirty Years, and been nine Years a Citizen of the United States, and who shall not, when elected, be an Inhabitant of that State for which he shall be chosen.

The Vice President of the United States shall be President of the Senate, but shall have no Vote, unless they be equally divided.

The Senate shall chuse their other Officers, and also a President *pro tempore,* in the Absence of the Vice President, or when he shall exercise the Office of President of the United States.

The Senate shall have the sole Power to try all Impeachments. When sitting for that Purpose, they shall be on Oath or Affirmation. When the President of the United States is tried the Chief Justice shall preside: And no Person shall be convicted without the Concurrence of two thirds of the Members present.

Judgment in Cases of Impeachment shall not extend further than to removal from Office, and disqualification to hold and enjoy any Office of honor, Trust or Profit under the United States: but the Party convicted shall nevertheless be liable and subject to Indictment, Trial, Judgment and Punishment, according to Law.

Section 4

The Times, Places and Manner of holding Elections for Senators and Representatives, shall be prescribed in each State by the Legislature thereof; but the Congress may at any time by Law make or alter such Regulations, except as to the Places of chusing Senators.

The Congress shall assemble at least once in every Year, *and such Meeting shall be on the first Monday in December, unless they shall by Law appoint a different Day.*

Section 5

Each House shall be the Judge of the Elections, Returns and Qualifications of its own Members, and a Majority of each shall constitute a Quorum to do Business; but a smaller Number may adjourn from day to day, and may be authorized to compel the Attendance of absent Members, in such Manner, and under such Penalties as each House may provide.

Each House may determine the Rules of its Proceedings, punish its Members for disorderly Behaviour, and, with the Concurrence of two thirds, expel a Member.

Each House shall keep a Journal of its Proceedings, and from time to time publish the same, excepting such Parts as may in their Judgment require Secrecy; and the Yeas and Nays of the Members of either House on any question shall, at the Desire of one fifth of those Present, be entered on the Journal.

---

*Passages no longer in effect are printed in italic type.

Neither House, during the Session of Congress, shall, without the Consent of the other, adjourn for more than three days, nor to any other Place than that in which the two Houses shall be sitting.

Section 6

The Senators and Representatives shall receive a Compensation for their Services, to be ascertained by Law, and paid out of the Treasury of the United States. They shall in all Cases, except Treason, Felony and Breach of the Peace, be privileged from Arrest during their Attendance at the Session of their respective Houses, and in going to and returning from the same; and for any Speech or Debate in either House, they shall not be questioned in any other Place.

No Senator or Representative shall, during the Time for which he was elected, be appointed to any civil Office under the Authority of the United States, which shall have been created, or the Emoluments whereof shall have been encreased during such time, and no Person holding any Office under the United States, shall be a Member of either House during his Continuance in Office.

Section 7

All Bills for raising Revenue shall originate in the House of Representatives; but the Senate may propose or concur with Amendments as on other Bills.

Every Bill which shall have passed the House of Representatives and the Senate, shall, before it become a Law, be presented to the President of the United States; If he approve he shall sign it, but if not he shall return it, with his Objections to the House in which it shall have originated, who shall enter the Objections at large on their Journal, and proceed to reconsider it. If after such Reconsideration two thirds of that House shall agree to pass the Bill, it shall be sent, together with the Objections, to the other House, by which it shall likewise be reconsidered, and if approved by two thirds of that House, it shall become a Law. But in all such Cases the Votes of both Houses shall be determined by yeas and Nays, and the Names of the Persons voting for and against the Bill shall be entered on the Journal of each House respectively. If any Bill shall not be returned by the President within ten Days (Sundays excepted) after it shall have been presented to him, the Same shall be a Law, in like Manner as if he had signed it, unless the Congress by their Adjournment prevent its Return, in which Case it shall not be a Law.

Every Order, Resolution, or Vote to which the Concurrence of the Senate and House of Representatives may be necessary (except on a question of Adjournment) shall be presented to the President of the United States; and before the Same shall take Effect, shall be approved by him, or being disapproved by him, shall be repassed by two thirds of the Senate and House of Representatives, according to the Rules and Limitations prescribed in the Case of a Bill.

Section 8

The Congress shall have Power To lay and collect Taxes, Duties, Imposts and Excises, to pay the Debts and provide for the common Defence and general Welfare of the United States; but all Duties, Imposts and Excises shall be uniform throughout the United States;

To borrow Money on the credit of the United States;

To regulate Commerce with foreign Nations, and among the several States, and with the Indian Tribes;

To establish an uniform Rule of Naturalization, and uniform Laws on the subject of Bankruptcies throughout the United States;

To coin Money, regulate the Value thereof, and of foreign Coin, and fix the Standard of Weights and Measures;

To provide for the Punishment of counterfeiting the Securities and current Coin of the United States;

To establish Post Offices and post Roads;

To promote the Progress of Science and useful Arts, by securing for limited Times to Authors and Inventors the exclusive Right to their respective Writings and Discoveries;

To constitute Tribunals inferior to the supreme Court;

To define and punish Piracies and Felonies committed on the high Seas, and Offences against the Law of Nations;

To declare War, grant Letters of Marque and Reprisal, and make Rules concerning Captures on Land and Water;

To raise and support Armies, but no Appropriation of Money to that Use shall be for a longer Term than two Years;

To provide and maintain a Navy;

To make Rules for the Government and Regulation of the land and naval Forces;

To provide for calling forth the Militia to execute the Laws of the Union, suppress Insurrections and repel Invasions;

To provide for organizing, arming, and disciplining, the Militia, and for governing such Part of them as may be employed in the Service of the United States, reserving to the States respectively, the Appointment of the Officers, and the Authority of training the Militia according to the discipline prescribed by Congress;

To exercise exclusive Legislation in all Cases whatsoever, over such District (not exceeding ten Miles square) as may, by Cession of particular States, and the Acceptance of Congress, become the Seat of the Government of the United States, and to exercise like Authority over all Places purchased by the Consent of the Legislature of the State in which the Same shall be, for the Erection of Forts, Magazines, Arsenals, dock-Yards, and other needful Buildings;—And

To make all Laws which shall be necessary and proper for carrying into Execution the foregoing Powers, and all other Powers vested by this Constitution in the Government of the United States, or in any Department of Officer thereof.

Section 9

The Migration or Importation of such Persons as any of the States now existing shall think proper to admit, shall not be prohibited by the Congress prior to the Year one thousand eight hundred and eight, but a Tax or duty may be imposed on such Importation, not exceeding ten dollars for each Person.

The Privilege of the Writ of Habeas Corpus shall not be suspended, unless when in Cases of Rebellion or Invasion the public Safety may require it.

No Bill of Attainder or ex post facto Law shall be passed.

No Capitation, or other direct, Tax shall be laid, unless in Proportion to the Census or Enumeration herein before directed to be taken.

No Tax or Duty shall be laid on Articles exported from any State.

No Preference shall be given by any Regulation of Commerce or Revenue to the Ports of one State over those of another: nor shall Vessels bound to, or from, one State, be obliged to enter, clear, or pay Duties in another.

No Money shall be drawn from the Treasury, but in Consequence of Appropriations made by Law; and a regular Statement and Account of the Receipts and Expenditures of all public Money shall be published from time to time.

No Title of Nobility shall be granted by the United States: And no Person holding any Office of Profit or Trust under them, shall, without the Consent of the Congress, accept of any present, Emolument, Office, or Title, of any kind whatever, from any King, Prince, or foreign State.

Section 10

No State shall enter into any Treaty, Alliance, or Confederation; grant Letters of Marque and Reprisal; coin Money; emit Bills of Credit; make any Thing but gold and silver Coin a Tender in Payment of Debts; pass any Bill of Attainder, ex post facto Law, or Law impairing the obligation of Contracts, or grant any Title of Nobility.

No State shall, without the Consent of the Congress, lay any Imposts or Duties on Imports or Exports, except what may be absolutely necessary for executing its inspection Laws: and the net Produce of all Duties and Imposts, laid by any State on Imports or Exports, shall be for the Use of the Treasury of the United States; and all such Laws shall be subject to the Revision and Controul of the Congress.

No State shall, without the Consent of Congress, lay any Duty of Tonnage, keep Troops, or Ships of War in time of Peace, enter into any Agreement or Compact with another State, or with a foreign Power, or engage in War, unless actually invaded, or in such imminent Danger as will not admit of delay.

Article II

Section 1

The executive Power shall be vested in a President of the United States of America. He shall hold his Office during the Term of four Years, and, together with the Vice President, chosen for the same Term, be elected, as follows:

Each State shall appoint, in such Manner as the Legislature thereof may direct, a Number of Electors, equal to the whole Number of Senators and Representatives to which the State may be entitled in the Congress: but no Senator or Representative, or Person holding an Office of Trust or Profit under the United States, shall be appointed an Elector.

The Electors shall meet in their respective States, and vote by Ballot for two Persons, of whom one at least shall not be an Inhabitant of the same State with themselves. And they shall make a List of all the Persons voted for, and of the Number of Votes for each;

which List they shall sign and certify, and transmit sealed to the Seat of the Government of the United States, directed to the President of the Senate. The President of the Senate shall, in the Presence of the Senate and House of Representatives, open all the Certificates, and the Votes shall then be counted. The Person having the greatest Number of Votes shall be the President, if such Number be a Majority of the whole number of Electors appointed; and if there be more than one who have such Majority, and have an equal Number of Votes, then the House of Representatives shall immediately chuse by Ballot one of them for President; and if no Person have a Majority, then from the five highest on the List the said House shall in like Manner chuse the President. But in chusing the President, the Votes shall be taken by States, the Representation from each State having one Vote; A quorum for this Purpose shall consist of a Member or Members from two thirds of the States, and a Majority of all the States shall be necessary to a Choice. In every Case, after the Choice of the President, the Person having the greatest Number of Votes of the Electors shall be the Vice President. But if there should remain two or more who have equal Votes, the Senate shall chuse from them by Ballot the Vice President.

The Congress may determine the time of chusing the Electors, and the Day on which they shall give their Votes; which Day shall be the same throughout the United States.

No person except a natural born Citizen, or a *Citizen of the United States, at the time of the Adoption of this Constitution,* shall be eligible to the Office of President; neither shall any Person be eligible to that Office who shall not have attained to the Age of thirty five Years, and been fourteen Years a Resident within the United States.

In Case of the Removal of the President from Office, or of his Death, Resignation, or Inability to discharge the Powers and Duties of the said Office, the Same shall devolve on the Vice President, and the Congress may by Law provide for the Case of Removal, Death, Resignation or Inability, both of the President and Vice President, declaring what Officer shall then act as President, and such Officer shall act accordingly, until the Disability be removed, or a President shall be elected.

The President shall, at stated Times, receive for his Services, a Compensation, which shall neither be encreased nor diminished during the Period for which he shall have been elected, and he shall not receive within that period any other Emolument from the United States, or any of them.

Before he enter on the Execution of his Office, he shall take the following Oath or Affirmation:—"I do solemnly swear (or affirm) that I will faithfully execute the Office of President of the United States, and will to the best of my Ability, preserve, protect and defend the Constitution of the United States."

Section 2

The President shall be Commander in Chief of the Army and Navy of the United States, and of the Militia of the several States, when called into the actual Service of the United States; he may require the Opinion, in writing, of the principal Officer in each of the executive Departments, upon any Subject relating to the Duties of their respective Offices, and he shall have Power to grant Reprieves and Pardons for Offences against the United States, except in Cases of Impeachment.

He shall have Power, by and with the Advice and Consent of the Senate, to make Treaties, provided two thirds of the Senators present concur; and he shall nominate, and by and with the Advice and Consent of the Senate, shall appoint Ambassadors, other public Ministers and Consuls, Judges of the supreme Court, and all other Officers of the United States, whose Appointments are not herein otherwise provided for, and which shall be established by Law: but the Congress may by Law vest the Appointment of such inferior Officers, as they think proper in the President alone, in the Courts of Law, or in the Heads of Departments.

The President shall have Power to fill up all Vacancies that may happen during the Recess of the Senate, by granting Commissions which shall expire at the End of their next Session.

Section 3

He shall from time to time give to the Congress Information of the State of the Union, and recommend to their Consideration such Measures as he shall judge necessary and expedient; he may, on extraordinary Occasions, convene both Houses, or either of them, and in Case of disagreement between them, with Respect to the Time of Adjournment, he may adjourn them to such Time as he shall think proper; he shall receive Ambassadors and other public Ministers; he shall take Care that the Laws be faithfully executed, and shall Commission all the officers of the United States.

Section 4

The President, Vice President and all civil Officers of the United States, shall be removed from Office on Impeachment for, and Conviction of, Treason, Bribery or other high Crimes and Misdemeanors.

Article III

Section 1

The judicial Power of the United States, shall be vested in one supreme Court, and in such inferior Courts as the Congress may from time to time ordain and establish. The Judges, both of the supreme and inferior Courts, shall hold their offices during good Behaviour, and shall, at stated Times, receive for their Services, a Compensation, which shall not be diminished during their Continuance in Office.

Section 2

The judicial Power shall extend to all Cases, in Law and Equity, arising under this Constitution, the Laws of the United States, and Treaties made, or which shall be made, under their Authority;—to all Cases affecting Ambassadors, other public Ministers and Consuls;—to all Cases of admiralty and maritime Jurisdiction;—to Controversies to which the United States shall be a Party;—to Controversies between two or more States;—between a State and Citizens of another State;—*between Citizens of different States;*—between Citizens of the same State claiming Lands under Grants of different States, and between a State, or the Citizens thereof, and foreign States, Citizens or Subjects.

In all Cases affecting Ambassadors, other public Ministers and Consuls, and those in which a State shall be Party, the supreme Court shall have original Jurisdiction. In all the other Cases before mentioned, the supreme Court shall have appellate Jurisdiction, both as to Law and Fact, with such Exceptions, and under such Regulations as the Congress shall make.

The Trial of all Crimes, except in Cases of Impeachment, shall be by Jury; and such Trial shall be held in the State where the said Crimes shall have been committed, but when not committed within any State, the Trial shall be at such Place or Places as the Congress may by Law have directed.

Section 3

Treason against the United States, shall consist only in levying War against them, or in adhering to their Enemies, giving them Aid and Comfort. No person shall be convicted of Treason unless on the Testimony of two Witnesses to the same overt Act, or on Confession in open Court.

The Congress shall have Power to declare the Punishment of Treason, but no Attainder of Treason shall work Corruption of Blood, or Forfeiture except during the Life of the Person attainted.

Article IV

Section 1

Full Faith and Credit shall be given in each State to the public Acts, Records, and judicial Proceedings of every other State. And the Congress may by general Laws prescribe the Manner in which such Acts, Records and Proceedings shall be proved, and the Effect thereof.

Section 2

The Citizens of each State shall be entitled to all Privileges and Immunities of Citizens in the several States.

A Person charged in any State with Treason, Felony, or other Crime, who shall flee from Justice, and be found in another State, shall on Demand of the executive Authority of the State from which he fled, be delivered up, to be removed to the State having Jurisdiction of the Crime.

No Person held to Service or Labour in one State, under the Laws thereof, escaping into another, shall, in Consequence of any Law or Regulation therein, be discharged from such Service or Labour, but shall be delivered up on Claim of the Party to whom such Service or Labour may be due.

Section 3

New States may be admitted by the Congress into this Union; but no new State shall be formed or erected within the Jurisdiction of any other State; nor any State be formed by the Junction of two or more States, or Parts of States, without the Consent of the Legislatures of the States concerned as well as of the Congress.

The Congress shall have Power to dispose of and make all needful Rules and Regulations respecting the Territory or other Property belonging to the United States; and nothing in this Constitution shall be so construed as to Prejudice any Claims of the United States, or of any particular States.

Section 4

The United States shall guarantee to every State in this Union a Republican Form of Government, and shall protect each of them against Invasion; and on Application of the Legislature, or of the Executive (when the Legislature cannot be convened) against domestic violence.

Article V

The Congress, whenever two thirds of both Houses shall deem it necessary, shall propose Amendments to this Constitution, or, on the Application of the Legislatures of two thirds of the several States, shall call a Convention for proposing Amendments, which, in either Case, shall be valid to all Intents and Purposes, as Part of this Constitution, when ratified by the Legislatures of three fourths of the several States, or by Conventions in three fourths thereof, as the one or the other Mode of Ratification may be proposed by the Congress; Provided *that no Amendment which may be made prior to the Year One thousand eight hundred and eight shall in any Manner affect the first and fourth Clauses in the Ninth Section of the first Article*; and that no State, without its Consent, shall be deprived of its equal Suffrage in the Senate.

Article VI

All Debts contracted and Engagements entered into, before the Adoption of this Constitution, shall be as valid against the United States under this Constitution, as under the Confederation.

This Constitution, and Laws of the United States which shall be made in Pursuance thereof; and all Treaties made, or which shall be made, under the Authority of the United States, shall be the supreme Law of the Land; and the Judges in every State shall be bound thereby, any Thing in the Constitution or Laws of any State to the Contrary notwithstanding.

The Senators and Representatives before mentioned, and the Members of the several State Legislatures, and all executive and Judicial Officers, both of the United States and of the several States, shall be bound by Oath or Affirmation, to support this Constitution; but no religious Test shall ever be required as a Qualification to any Office of public Trust under the United States.

Article VII

The Ratification of the Conventions of nine States, shall be sufficient for the Establishment of this Constitution between the States so ratifying the Same.

Done in Convention by the Unanimous Consent of the States present the Seventeenth Day of September in the Year of our Lord one thousand seven hundred and Eighty seven and of the Independence of the United States of America the Twelfth[†] IN WITNESS whereof We have hereunto subscribed our Names,

George Washington
President and Deputy from Virginia

Delaware
George Read
Gunning Bedford, Jr.
John Dickinson
Richard Bassett
Jacob Broom

Maryland
James McHenry
Daniel of St. Thomas Jenifer
Daniel Carroll

Virginia
John Blair
James Madison, Jr.

North Carolina
William Blount
Richard Dobbs Spraight
Hugh Williamson

South Carolina
John Rutledge
Charles Cotesworth Pinckney
Charles Pinckney
Pierce Butler

Georgia
William Few
Abraham Baldwin

New Hampshire
John Langdon
Nicholas Gilman

Massachusetts
Nathaniel Gorham
Rufus King

Connecticut
William Samuel Johnson
Roger Sherman

New York
Alexander Hamilton

New Jersey
William Livingston
David Brearley
William Paterson
Jonathan Dayton

Pennsylvania
Benjamin Franklin
Thomas Mifflin
Robert Morris
George Clymer
Thomas FitzSimons
Jared Ingersoll
James Wilson
Gouverneur Morris

[†]The Constitution was submitted on September 17, 1787, by the Constitutional Convention, was ratified by conventions of the several states at various dates up to May 29, 1790, and became effective on March 4, 1789.

Amendment I

Congress shall make no law respecting an establishment of religion, or prohibiting the free exercise thereof; or abridging the freedom of speech, or of the press; or the right of the people peaceably to assemble, and to petition the Government for a redress of grievances.

Amendment II

A well regulated Militia being necessary to the security of a free State, the right of the people to keep and bear Arms, shall not be infringed.

Amendment III

No Soldier shall, in time of peace be quartered in any house, without the consent of the Owner, nor in time of war, but in a manner to be prescribed by law.

Amendment IV

The right of the people to be secure in their persons, houses, papers, and effects, against unreasonable searches and seizures, shall not be violated, and no Warrants shall issue, but upon probable cause, supported by Oath or affirmation, and particularly describing the place to be searched, and the persons or things to be seized.

Amendment V

No person shall be held to answer for a capital, or otherwise infamous crime, unless on a presentment or indictment of a Grand Jury, except in cases arising in the land or naval forces, or in the Militia, when in actual service in time of War or public danger; nor shall any person be subject for the same offense to be twice put in jeopardy of life or limb; nor shall be compelled in any criminal case to be a witness against himself, nor be deprived of life, liberty, or property, without due process of law; nor shall private property be taken for public use, without just compensation.

Amendment VI

In all criminal prosecutions, the accused shall enjoy the right to a speedy and public trial, by an impartial jury of the State and district wherein the crime shall have been committed, which district shall have been previously ascertained by law, and to be informed of the nature and cause of the accusation; to be confronted with the witnesses against him; to have compulsory process for obtaining witnesses in his favor, and to have the Assistance of Counsel for his defence.

Amendment VII

In Suits at common law, where the value in controversy shall exceed twenty dollars, the right of trial by jury shall be preserved, and no fact tried by a jury, shall be otherwise re-examined in any Court of the United States, than according to the rules of the common law.

Amendment VIII

Excessive bail shall not be required, nor excessive fines imposed, nor cruel and unusual punishments inflicted.

Amendment IX

The enumeration in the Constitution, of certain rights, shall not be construed to deny or disparage others retained by the people.

Amendment X*

The powers not delegated to the United States by the Constitution, nor prohibited by it to the States, are reserved to the States respectively, or to the people.

Amendment XI
[Adopted 1798]

The Judicial power of the United States shall not be construed to extend to any suit in law or equity, commenced or prosecuted against one of the United States by Citizens of another State, or by Citizens or Subjects of any Foreign State.

Amendment XII
[Adopted 1804]

The Electors shall meet in their respective states, and vote by ballot for President and Vice President, one of whom, at least, shall not be an inhabitant of the same state with themselves; they shall name in their ballots the person voted for as President, and in distinct ballots the person voted for as Vice President, and they shall make distinct lists of all persons voted for as President, and of all persons voted for as Vice President, and of the number of votes for each, which lists they shall sign and certify, and transmit sealed to the seat of the government of the United States, directed to the President of the Senate;—The President of the Senate shall, in the presence of the Senate and House of Representatives, open all the certificates and the votes shall then be counted;—The person having the greatest number of votes for President, shall be the President, if such number be a majority of the whole number of Electors appointed; and if no person have such majority, then from the persons having the highest numbers not exceeding three on the list of those voted for as President, the House of Representatives shall choose immediately, by ballot, the President. But in choosing the President, the votes shall be taken by states, the representation from each state having one vote; a quorum for this purpose shall consist of a member or members from two-thirds of the states, and a majority of all the states shall be necessary to a choice. And if the House of Representatives shall not choose a President whenever the right of choice shall devolve upon them, before *the fourth day of March* next following, then the Vice President shall act as President, as in the case of the death or other constitutional disability of the President.—The person having

*The first ten amendments (the Bill of Rights) were ratified and their adoption was certified on December 15, 1791.

the greatest number of votes as Vice President, shall be the Vice President, if such number be a majority of the whole number of Electors appointed, and if no person have a majority, then from the two highest numbers on the list, the Senate shall choose the Vice President; a quorum for the purpose shall consist of two-thirds of the whole number of Senators, and a majority of the whole number shall be necessary to a choice. But no person constitutionally ineligible to the office of President shall be eligible to that of Vice President of the United States.

Amendment XIII
[Adopted 1865]

Section 1

Neither slavery nor involuntary servitude, except as a punishment for crime whereof the party shall have been duly convicted, shall exist within the United States, or any place subject to their jurisdiction.

Section 2

Congress shall have power to enforce this article by appropriate legislation.

Amendment XIV
[Adopted 1868]

Section 1

All persons born or naturalized in the United States, and subject to the jurisdiction thereof, are citizens of the United States and of the State wherein they reside. No State shall make or enforce any law which shall abridge the privileges or immunities of citizens of the United States; nor shall any State deprive any person of life, liberty, or property, without due process of law; nor deny to any person within its jurisdiction the equal protection of the laws.

Section 2

Representatives shall be apportioned among the several States according to their respective numbers, counting the whole number of persons in each State, excluding Indians not taxed. But when the right to vote at any election for the choice of electors for President and Vice President of the United States, Representatives in Congress, the Executive and Judicial officers of a State, or the members of the Legislature thereof, is denied to any of the male inhabitants of such State, being twenty-one years of age, and citizens of the United States, or in any way abridged, except for participation in rebellion, or other crime, the basis of representation therein shall be reduced in the proportion which the number of such male citizens shall bear to the whole number of male citizens twenty-one years of age in such State.

Section 3

No person shall be a Senator or Representative in Congress, or elector of President and Vice President, or hold any office, civil or military, under the United States, or under any State, who, having previously taken an oath, as a member of Congress, or as an officer of the United States, or as a member of any State legislature, or as an executive or judicial officer of any State, to support the Constitution of the United States, shall have engaged in insurrection or rebellion against the same, or given aid or comfort to the enemies thereof. But Congress may by a vote of two-thirds of each House, remove such disability.

Section 4

The validity of the public debt of the United States, authorized by law, including debts incurred for payment of pensions and bounties for services in suppressing insurrection or rebellion, shall not be questioned. But neither the United States nor any State shall assume or pay any debt or obligation incurred in aid of insurrection or rebellion against the United States, or any claim for the loss or emancipation of any slave; but all such debts, obligations and claims shall be held illegal and void.

Section 5

The Congress shall have power to enforce, by appropriate legislation, the provisions of this article.

Amendment XV
[Adopted 1870]

Section 1

The right of citizens of the United States to vote shall not be denied or abridged by the United States or by any State on account of race, color, or previous condition of servitude.

Section 2

The Congress shall have power to enforce this article by appropriate legislation.

Amendment XVI
[Adopted 1913]

The Congress shall have power to lay and collect taxes on incomes, from whatever source derived, without apportionment among the several States, and without regard to any census or enumeration.

Amendment XVII
[Adopted 1913]

The Senate of the United States shall be composed of two Senators from each State, elected by the people thereof, for six years; and each Senator shall have one vote. The electors in each State shall have the qualifications requisite for electors of the most numerous branch of the State legislatures.

When vacancies happen in the representation of any State in the Senate, the executive authority of such State shall issue writs of election to fill such vacancies: *Provided,* That the legislature of any State may empower the executive thereof to make temporary appointments until the people fill the vacancies by election as the legislature may direct.

This amendment shall not be so construed as to affect the election or term of any Senator chosen before it becomes valid as part of the Constitution.

Amendment XVIII
[Adopted 1919, repealed 1933]

Section 1

After one year from the ratification of this article the manufacture, sale, or transportation of intoxicating liquors within, the importation thereof into, or the exportation thereof from the United States and all territory subject to the jurisdiction thereof for beverage purposes is hereby prohibited.

Section 2

The Congress and the several States shall have concurrent power to enforce this article by appropriate legislation.

Section 3

This article shall be inoperative unless it shall have been ratified as an amendment to the Constitution by the legislatures of the several States, as provided in the Constitution, within seven years from the date of the submission hereof to the States by the Congress.

Amendment XIX
[Adopted 1920]

The right of citizens of the United States to vote shall not be denied or abridged by the United States or by any State on account of sex.

Congress shall have power to enforce this article by appropriate legislation.

Amendment XX
[Adopted 1933]

Section 1

The terms of the President and Vice President shall end at noon on the 20th day of January, and the terms of Senators and Representatives at noon on the 3d day of January, of the years in which such terms would have ended if this article had not been ratified and the terms of their successors shall then begin.

Section 2

The Congress shall assemble at least once in every year, and such meeting shall begin at noon on the 3d day of January, unless they shall by law appoint a different day.

Section 3

If, at the time fixed for the beginning of the term of the President, the President elect shall have died, the Vice President elect shall become President. If a President shall not have been chosen before the time fixed for the beginning of his term, or if the President elect shall have failed to qualify, then the Vice President elect shall act as President until a President shall have qualified; and the Congress may by law provide for the case wherein neither a President elect nor a Vice President elect shall have qualified, declaring who shall then act as President, or the manner in which one who is to act shall be selected, and such person shall act accordingly until a President or Vice President shall have qualified.

Section 4

The Congress may by law provide for the case of the death of any of the persons from whom the House of Representatives may choose a President whenever the right of choice shall have devolved upon them, and for the case of the death of any of the persons from whom the Senate may choose a Vice President whenever the right of choice shall have devolved upon them.

Section 5

Sections 1 and 2 shall take effect on the 15th day of October following the ratification of this article.

Section 6

This article shall be inoperative unless it shall have been ratified as an amendment to the Constitution by the legislatures of three fourths of the several States within seven years from the date of its submission.

Amendment XXI
[Adopted 1933]

Section 1

The eighteenth article of amendment to the Constitution of the United States is hereby repealed.

Section 2

The transportation or importation into any State, Territory, or possession of the United States for delivery or use therein of intoxicating liquors in violation of the laws thereof, is hereby prohibited.

Section 3

This article shall be inoperative unless it shall have been ratified as an amendment to the Constitution by conventions in the several States, as provided in the Constitution, within seven years from the date of the submission hereof to the States by the Congress.

Amendment XXII
[Adopted 1951]

Section 1

No person shall be elected to the office of the President more than twice, and no person who has held the office of President, or acted as President, for more than two years of a term to which some other person was elected President shall be elected to the office of the President more than once. But this Article shall not apply to any person holding the office of President when this Article was proposed by the Congress, and shall not prevent any person who may be holding the office of President, or acting as President, during the term within which this Article becomes operative from holding the office of President or acting as President during the remainder of such term.

Section 2

This article shall be inoperative unless it shall have been ratified as an amendment to the Constitution by the legislatures of three-fourths of the several States within seven years from the date of its submission to the States by the Congress.

Amendment XXIII
[Adopted 1961]

Section 1

The District constituting the seat of Government of the United States shall appoint in such manner as the Congress shall direct:

A number of electors of President and Vice President equal to the whole number of Senators and Representatives in Congress to which the District would be entitled if it were a State, but in no event more than the least populous State; they shall be in addition to those appointed by the States, but they shall be considered, for the purposes of the election of President and Vice President, to be electors appointed by a State; and they shall meet in the District and perform such duties as provided by the twelfth article of amendment.

Section 2

The Congress shall have power to enforce this article by appropriate legislation.

Amendment XXIV
[Adopted 1964]

Section 1

The right of citizens of the United States to vote in any primary or other election for President or Vice President, for electors for President or Vice President, or for Senator or Representative in Congress, shall not be denied or abridged by the United States or any state by reason of failure to pay any poll tax or other tax.

Section 2

The Congress shall have the power to enforce this article by appropriate legislation.

Amendment XXV
[Adopted 1967]

Section 1

In case of the removal of the President from office or his death or resignation, the Vice President shall become President.

Section 2

Whenever there is a vacancy in the office of the Vice President, the President shall nominate a Vice President who shall take the office upon confirmation by a majority vote of both houses of Congress.

Section 3

Whenever the President transmits to the President pro tempore of the Senate and the Speaker of the House of Representatives his written declaration that he is unable to discharge the powers and duties of his office, and until he transmits to them a written declaration to the contrary, such powers and duties shall be discharged by the Vice President as Acting President.

Section 4

Whenever the Vice President and a majority of either the principal officers of the executive departments or of such other body as Congress may by law provide, transmit to the President pro tempore of the Senate and the Speaker of the House of Representatives their written declaration that the President is unable to discharge the powers and duties of his office, the Vice President shall immediately assume the powers and duties of the office as Acting President.

Thereafter, when the President transmits to the President pro tempore of the Senate and the Speaker of the House of Representatives his written declaration that no inability exists, he shall resume the powers and duties of his office unless the Vice President and a majority of either the principal officers of the executive department or of such other body as Congress may by law provide, transmit within four days to the President pro tempore of the Senate and the Speaker of the House of Representatives their written declaration that the President is unable to discharge the powers and duties of his office. Thereupon Congress shall decide the issue, assembling within 48 hours for that purpose if not in session. If the Congress, within 21 days after receipt of the latter written declaration, or, if Congress is not in session, within 21 days after Congress is required to assemble, determines by two-thirds vote of both houses that the President is unable to discharge the powers and duties of his office, the Vice President shall continue to discharge the same as Acting President; otherwise, the President shall resume the powers and duties of his office.

Amendment XXVI
[Adopted 1971]

Section 1

The right of citizens of the United States, who are 18 years of age or older, to vote shall not be denied or abridged by the United States or any state on account of age.

Section 2

The Congress shall have the power to enforce this article by appropriate legislation.

Amendment XXVII
[Adopted 1992]

No law, varying the compensation for the services of the Senators and Representatives shall take effect, until an election of Representatives shall have intervened.

Year	Candidates	Parties	Popular Vote	Electoral Vote	Voter Participation
1789	George Washington		*	69	
	John Adams			34	
	Others			35	
1792	George Washington		*	132	
	John Adams			77	
	George Clinton			50	
	Others			5	
1796	John Adams	Federalist	*	71	
	Thomas Jefferson	Democratic-Republican		68	
	Thomas Pinckney	Federalist		59	
	Aaron Burr	Dem.-Rep.		30	
	Others			48	
1800	Thomas Jefferson	Dem.-Rep.	*	73	
	Aaron Burr	Dem.-Rep.		73	
	John Adams	Federalist		65	
	C. C. Pinckney	Federalist		64	
	John Jay	Federalist		1	
1804	Thomas Jefferson	Dem.-Rep.	*	162	
	C. C. Pinckney	Federalist		14	
1808	James Madison	Dem.-Rep.	*	122	
	C. C. Pinckney	Federalist		47	
	George Clinton	Dem.-Rep.		6	
1812	James Madison	Dem.-Rep.	*	128	
	De Witt Clinton	Federalist		89	
1816	James Monroe	Dem.-Rep.	*	183	
	Rufus King	Federalist		34	
1820	James Monroe	Dem.-Rep.	*	231	
	John Quincy Adams	Dem.-Rep.		1	
1824	John Quincy Adams	Dem.-Rep.	108,740 (30.5%)	84	26.9%
	Andrew Jackson	Dem.-Rep.	153,544 (43.1%)	99	
	William H. Crawford	Dem.-Rep.	46,618 (13.1%)	41	
	Henry Clay	Dem.-Rep.	47,136 (13.2%)	37	
1828	Andrew Jackson	Democratic	647,286 (56.0%)	178	57.6%
	John Quincy Adams	National Republican	508,064 (44.0%)	83	
1832	Andrew Jackson	Democratic	687,502 (55.0%)	219	55.4%
	Henry Clay	National Republican	530,189 (42.4%)	49	
	John Floyd	Independent		11	
	William Wirt	Anti-Mason	33,108 (2.6%)	7	
1836	Martin Van Buren	Democratic	765,483 (50.9%)	170	57.8%
	William Henry Harrison	Whig		73	
	Hugh L. White	Whig	739,795 (49.1%)	26	
	Daniel Webster	Whig		14	
	W. P. Magnum	Independent		11	
1840	William Henry Harrison	Whig	1,274,624 (53.1%)	234	80.2%
	Martin Van Buren	Democratic	1,127,781 (46.9%)	60	
	J. G. Birney	Liberty	7,069	—	
1844	James K. Polk	Democratic	1,338,464 (49.6%)	170	78.9%
	Henry Clay	Whig	1,300,097 (48.1%)	105	
	J. G. Birney	Liberty	62,300 (2.3%)	—	
1848	Zachary Taylor	Whig	1,360,967 (47.4%)	163	72.7%
	Lewis Cass	Democratic	1,222,342 (42.5%)	127	
	Martin Van Buren	Free-Soil	291,263 (10.1%)	—	

*Electors selected by state legislatures.

Year	Candidates	Parties	Popular Vote	Electoral Vote	Voter Participation
1852	Franklin Pierce	Democratic	1,601,117 (50.9%)	254	69.6%
	Winfield Scott	Whig	1,385,453 (44.1%)	42	
	John P. Hale	Free-Soil	155,825 (5.0%)	—	
1856	James Buchanan	Democratic	1,832,955 (45.3%)	174	78.9%
	John C. Frémont	Republican	1,339,932 (33.1%)	114	
	Millard Fillmore	American	871,731 (21.6%)	8	
1860	Abraham Lincoln	Republican	1,865,593 (39.8%)	180	81.2%
	Stephen A. Douglas	Democratic	1,382,713 (29.5%)	12	
	John C. Breckinridge	Democratic	848,356 (18.1%)	72	
	John Bell	Union	592,906 (12.6%)	39	
1864	Abraham Lincoln	Republican	2,213,655 (55.0%)	212[*]	73.8%
	George B. McClellan	Democratic	1,805,237 (45.0%)	21	
1868	Ulysses S. Grant	Republican	3,012,833 (52.7%)	214	78.1%
	Horatio Seymour	Democratic	2,703,249 (47.3%)	80	
1872	Ulysses S. Grant	Republican	3,597,132 (55.6%)	286	71.3%
	Horace Greeley	Dem.; Liberal Republican	2,834,125 (43.9%)	66[†]	
1876	Rutherford B. Hayes [‡]	Republican	4,036,298 (48.0%)	185	81.8%
	Samuel J. Tilden	Democratic	4,300,590 (51.0%)	184	
1880	James A. Garfield	Republican	4,454,416 (48.5%)	214	79.4%
	Winfield S. Hancock	Democratic	4,444,952 (48.1%)	155	
1884	Grover Cleveland	Democratic	4,874,986 (48.5%)	219	77.5%
	James G. Blaine	Republican	4,851,981 (48.2%)	182	
1888	Benjamin Harrison	Republican	5,439,853 (47.9%)	233	79.3%
	Grover Cleveland	Democratic	5,540,309 (48.6%)	168	
1892	Grover Cleveland	Democratic	5,556,918 (46.1%)	277	74.7%
	Benjamin Harrison	Republican	5,176,108 (43.0%)	145	
	James B. Weaver	People's	1,041,028 (8.5%)	22	
1896	William McKinley	Republican	7,104,779 (51.1%)	271	79.3%
	William Jennings Bryan	Democratic People's	6,502,925 (47.7%)	176	
1900	William McKinley	Republican	7,207,923 (51.7%)	292	73.2%
	William Jennings Bryan	Dem.-Populist	6,358,133 (45.5%)	155	
1904	Theodore Roosevelt	Republican	7,623,486 (57.9%)	336	65.2%
	Alton B. Parker	Democratic	5,077,911 (37.6%)	140	
	Eugene V. Debs	Socialist	402,283 (3.0%)	—	
1908	William H. Taft	Republican	7,678,908 (51.6%)	321	65.4%
	William Jennings Bryan	Democratic	6,409,104 (43.1%)	162	
	Eugene V. Debs	Socialist	420,793 (2.8%)	—	
1912	Woodrow Wilson	Democratic	6,293,454 (41.9%)	435	58.8%
	Theodore Roosevelt	Progressive	4,119,538 (27.4%)	88	
	William H. Taft	Republican	3,484,980 (23.2%)	8	
	Eugene V. Debs	Socialist	900,672 (6.0%)	—	
1916	Woodrow Wilson	Democratic	9,129,606 (49.4%)	277	61.6%
	Charles E. Hughes	Republican	8,538,221 (46.2%)	254	
	A. L. Benson	Socialist	585,113 (3.2%)	—	
1920	Warren G. Harding	Republican	16,152,200 (60.4%)	404	49.2%
	James M. Cox	Democratic	9,147,353 (34.2%)	127	
	Eugene V. Debs	Socialist	919,799 (3.4%)	—	
1924	Calvin Coolidge	Republican	15,725,016 (54.0%)	382	48.9%
	John W. Davis	Democratic	8,386,503 (28.8%)	136	
	Robert M. La Follette	Progressive	4,822,856 (16.6%)	13	
1928	Herbert Hoover	Republican	21,391,381 (58.2%)	444	56.9%
	Alfred E. Smith	Democratic	15,016,443 (40.9%)	87	
	Norman Thomas	Socialist	267,835 (0.7%)	—	

[*]Eleven secessionist states did not participate.
[†]Greeley died before the electoral college met. His electoral votes were divided among the four minor candidates.
[‡]Contested result settled by special election.

Year	Candidates	Parties	Popular Vote	Electoral Vote	Voter Participation
1932	Franklin D. Roosevelt	Democratic	22,821,857 (57.4%)	472	56.9%
	Herbert Hoover	Republican	15,761,841 (39.7%)	59	
	Norman Thomas	Socialist	881,951 (2.2%)	—	
1936	Franklin D. Roosevelt	Democratic	27,751,597 (60.8%)	523	61.0%
	Alfred M. Landon	Republican	16,679,583 (36.5%)	8	
	William Lemke	Union	882,479 (1.9%)	—	
1940	Franklin D. Roosevelt	Democratic	27,244,160 (54.8%)	449	62.5%
	Wendell L. Willkie	Republican	22,305,198 (44.8%)	82	
1944	Franklin D. Roosevelt	Democratic	25,602,504 (53.5%)	432	55.9%
	Thomas E. Dewey	Republican	22,006,285 (46.0%)	99	
1948	Harry S Truman	Democratic	24,105,695 (49.5%)	304	53.0%
	Thomas E. Dewey	Republican	21,969,170 (45.1%)	189	
	J. Strom Thurmond	State-Rights Democratic	1,169,021 (2.4%)	38	
	Henry A. Wallace	Progressive	1,156,103 (2.4%)	—	
1952	Dwight D. Eisenhower	Republican	33,936,252 (55.1%)	442	63.3%
	Adlai E. Stevenson	Democratic	27,314,992 (44.4%)	89	
1956	Dwight D. Eisenhower	Republican	35,575,420 (57.6%)	457	60.6%
	Adlai E. Stevenson	Democratic	26,033,066 (42.1%)	73	
	Other	—	—	1	
1960	John F. Kennedy	Democratic	34,227,096 (49.9%)	303	62.8%
	Richard M. Nixon	Republican	34,108,546 (49.6%)	219	
	Other	—	—	15	
1964	Lyndon B. Johnson	Democratic	43,126,506 (61.1%)	486	61.7%
	Barry M. Goldwater	Republican	27,176,799 (38.5%)	52	
1968	Richard M. Nixon	Republican	31,770,237 (43.4%)	301	60.6%
	Hubert H. Humphrey	Democratic	31,270,533 (42.7%)	191	
	George Wallace	American Indep.	9,906,141 (13.5%)	46	
1972	Richard M. Nixon	Republican	47,169,911 (60.7%)	520	55.2%
	George S. McGovern	Democratic	29,170,383 (37.5%)	17	
	Other	—	—	1	
1976	Jimmy Carter	Democratic	40,828,587 (50.0%)	297	53.5%
	Gerald R. Ford	Republican	39,147,613 (47.9%)	241	
	Other	—	1,575,459 (2.1%)	—	
1980	Ronald Reagan	Republican	43,901,812 (50.7%)	489	52.6%
	Jimmy Carter	Democratic	35,483,820 (41.0%)	49	
	John B. Anderson	Independent	5,719,722 (6.6%)	—	
	Ed Clark	Libertarian	921,188 (1.1%)	—	
1984	Ronald Reagan	Republican	54,455,075 (59.0%)	525	53.3%
	Walter Mondale	Democratic	37,577,185 (41.0%)	13	
1988	George H. W. Bush	Republican	48,886,000 (53.4%)	426	57.4%
	Michael S. Dukakis	Democratic	41,809,000 (45.6%)	111	
1992	William J. Clinton	Democratic	43,728,375 (43%)	370	55.0%
	George H. W. Bush	Republican	38,167,416 (38%)	168	
	H. Ross Perot	Independent	19,237,247 (19%)	—	
1996	William J. Clinton	Democratic	45,590,703 (50%)	379	48.8%
	Robert Dole	Republican	37,816,307 (41%)	159	
	H. Ross Perot	Reform	7,866,284 (8.4%)	—	
2000	George W. Bush	Republican	50,456,167 (47.88%)	271	51.2%
	Al Gore	Democratic	50,996,064 (48.39%)	266*	
	Ralph Nader	Green	2,864,810 (2.72%)	—	
	Other	—	834,774 (1%)	—	
2004	George W. Bush	Republican	60,934,251 (50.8%)	286	55.3%
	John F. Kerry	Democratic	57,765,291 (48.3%)	251	
	Ralph Nader	Independent	463,653 (<1%)	0	

*One District of Columbia Gore elector abstained.

affirmative action   Policies designed to improve the educational and employment opportunities of historically underrepresented groups such as women and African Americans. *p. 864*

Alien and Sedition Acts   Laws enacted by the Federalist-dominated Congress in 1798 to limit the speech of their critics and to make it more difficult for immigrants to become citizens. *p. 270*

Allies   Members of an alliance, such as the military coalition led by the United States, the Soviet Union, and Great Britain during World War II. *p. 719*

almshouse   A privately financed home for the poor; a poorhouse. *p. 153*

American Federation of Labor (AFL)   A union of skilled craft workers organized by Samuel Gompers, in 1886; advocated higher wages and better working conditions and focused its organizing efforts primarily on skilled white men. *p. 546*

anarchists   Persons who reject all forms of government as inherently oppressive and undesirable. *p. 545*

Archaic period   The second long stage of North American habitation, covering about 7,000 years, from roughly 8000 to 1000 BCE (or from 10,000 to 3,000 years ago). During this period, inhabitants adapted to diverse local environments, gathering plants and hunting smaller animals than during the previous Paleo-Indian period. *p. 7*

archipelago   A group of islands, such as the Hawaiian archipelago. *p. 14*

asiento   A contract negotiated by the Spanish crown (between 1595 and 1789) with other European powers such as Portugal, France, England, and the Netherlands to provide a fixed number of slaves annually to Spain's American colonies for a set payment. *p. 106*

Axis   A political alignment or alliance, such as the military coalition between Germany, Italy, and Japan during World War II. *p. 716*

Babel   A city described in the Bible where constructing a tower was made impossible by the confusion of varied languages. This term from Chapter 11 of the Book of Genesis is used to describe any scene of clamor and confusion. *p. 138*

baby boom   The period of increased U.S. childbirths from roughly the early 1940s to the early 1960s. *p. 920*

barracoon   An enclosure or barrack used for the confinement of slaves before their forced deportation from the African coast. *p. 116*

Bill of Rights   A set of amendments assuring basic rights, proposed by James Madison to help ensure acceptance of the newly drafted Constitution, and based on suggestions from the states. Ten of the twelve items passed by Congress were ratified by the states in 1791; these first ten amendments to the Constitution became known as the Bill of Rights. *p. 260*

Black Codes   Legislation passed by southern state lawmakers in 1865 to reassert white control over blacks by limiting their freedom of movement, political rights, and economic opportunity. *p. 462*

black power   The slogan used by young black nationalists in the mid- and late 1960s. *p. 821*

"bloody shirt"   A partisan rallying cry used to stir up or revive sectional or party animosity after the American Civil War; for example, post–Civil War Republicans "waved the bloody shirt," associating some Democrats with a treasonous acceptance of secession during the war, while opponents had spilled their blood for the Union. *p. 517*

Boston marriages   Unions of two women based on long-term emotional bonds in which the women live together as if married to each other. *p. 618*

braceros   Mexican nationals working in the United States in low-wage jobs as part of a temporary work program between 1942 and 1964. (The *bracero* program was established by an executive agreement between the presidents of Mexico and the United States, providing Mexican agricultural labor in the Southwest and the Pacific Northwest.) *p. 725*

Bull Moosers   Supporters of Theodore Roosevelt in the 1912 presidential election when he broke from the Republican party and ran as a third-party candidate on the ticket of the Progressive (or Bull Moose) party. *p. 596*

burgess   A representative elected to the popular branch of the colonial legislature in either Virginia or Maryland. *p. 56*

Cajuns   The Louisiana word for French-speaking people Acadians (from Nova Scotia) who were forced to move south in 1755 during the French and Indian War. Many of these refugees eventually settled in French Louisiana, where they have had a lasting impact on the culture. *p. 146*

capitalism   The now almost worldwide economic system of private ownership of property and profit-seeking corporations. *p. 682*

carpetbaggers   A negative term applied by Southerners to Northerners who moved to the South after the Civil War to pursue political or economic opportunities. *p. 463*

Central Powers   A World War I alliance of Germany, Austria-Hungary, Italy, and the Ottoman Empire (Italy withdrew in 1915). *p. 623*

checks and balances   The rules controlling interactions among the executive, legislative, and judicial branches of government, making up a novel system designed to prevent any single branch from overreaching its powers, as set forth in the Constitution in 1787. *p. 254*

Chinese Exclusion Act   Congressional legislation passed in 1882 to bar most Chinese workers from entering the United States. *p. 501*

civic organizations   Membership organizations that exist to further the public life and welfare of a community. *p. 784*

Civil Rights Act of 1875 Congressional legislation that guaranteed black people access to public accommodations and transportation; the Supreme Court declared the measure unconstitutional in 1883. *p. 487*

civil service reform Measures designed to eliminate the spoils system in government hiring, in favor of maintaining professional standards in public service. *p. 520*

coffle A procession or train of enslaved prisoners, bound together for travel (from the Arabic word for "caravan"). *p. 116*

Cold War The conflict and competition between the United States and the Soviet Union (and their respective allies) that emerged after 1945 and lasted until 1989. *p. 745*

colonialism The centuries-old system of mostly European nations controlling and governing peoples and lands outside of Europe. *p. 757*

Columbian exchange The two-way interchange of plants, animals, microbes, and people that occurred once Christopher Columbus established regular contact by sea between Europe and the New World. *p. 21*

comfort women Women, mostly Chinese and Korean, forced into sexual slavery by Japanese troops during World War II. *p. 731*

common school system Tax-supported public education to provide elementary schooling free to young children. *p. 380*

communism A totalitarian form of government, grounded in the theories of German philosopher Karl Marx and the practices of V. I. Lenin in Russia, that eliminated private ownership of property in supposed pursuit of complete human equality; the system of government also featured a centrally directed economy and the absolute rule of a small group of leaders. *p. 745*

Compromise of 1850 Congressional legislation that provided that California would enter the Union as a free state that year, and that New Mexico and Utah would eventually submit the slavery question to their voters. As part of this compromise, the federal government abolished the slave trade in Washington, D.C. *p. 395*

Confederate States of America The would-be new nation formed in February 1861 by seven southern states—South Carolina, Mississippi, Florida, Alabama, Georgia, Louisiana, and Texas—in a bid for independence from the United States of America. By late spring 1861, the Confederacy also included Virginia, Arkansas, Tennessee, and North Carolina. *p. 425*

consumer economy an economic system in which most people work for wages, which they use to purchase manufactured goods and foodstuffs. *p. 651*

containment During the Cold War, the U.S. policy of trying to halt the expansion of Soviet and communist influences. *p. 756*

coverture French term for the dependent legal status of a woman during marriage. Under English law, the male family head received legal rights, and his wife lost independent status, becoming, in legal terms, a *femme covert*. *p. 85*

czar The monarch (king) of Russia before the 1917 revolution. *p. 624*

Dawes Act Congressional legislation (formally the Dawes Severalty Act) passed in 1887, eliminating common ownership of Indian tribal lands in favor of a system of private property. The law hastened the decrease in the number of Indian-held acres, from 138 million acres in 1887 to 78 million thirteen years later. *p. 521*

Democratic-Republicans The political party that emerged after the Revolution to oppose the Federalists' support for a strong central government; favored states' rights and the agrarian way of life. Thomas Jefferson, a leader of the Democratic-Republicans, was elected president in 1800. *p. 264*

Democrats Members of the Democratic party, a political party descended from the Democratic-Republican party of the early national period and formed under the leadership of Andrew Jackson, who assumed the presidency in 1829. The party favored local and state (rather than federal) control of economic issues, but beginning in the 1930s, under the leadership of President Franklin D. Roosevelt, the party advocated more robust federal intervention in social welfare as well as economic development. *p. 340*

détente The lessening of military or diplomatic tensions, as between the United States and the Soviet Union. *p. 841*

diaspora The dispersion of a population abroad, whether forced or voluntary. The term is often applied to Jewish settlement outside the eastern Mediterranean region and to the spread of Africans across the Americas due to the Atlantic slave trade. *p. 134*

don't ask, don't tell A policy established by the Clinton administration allowing gays and lesbians to serve in the military so long as they do not disclose their sexual orientation. *p. 911*

Dred Scott V. Sanford The 1857 case in which the Supreme Court held that residence on free soil did not render a slave a free person, for black people, enslaved and free, had (in the words of the court) "no rights which the white man was bound to respect." *p. 417*

Dust Bowl The plains regions of Oklahoma, Texas, Colorado, and New Mexico affected by severe drought in the 1930s. *p. 687*

Edmonds Act Congressional legislation passed in 1882 and aimed at Utah Mormons; it outlawed polygamy, stripped polygamists of the right to vote, and provided for a five-member commission to oversee Utah's elections. *p. 520*

electoral college An intricate system in which each state appoints electors, equal in number to its representation in Congress, to elect the president and vice president. The electoral college is a provision of the Constitution (Article II, Section 1) because the framers were unwilling to approve the direct election of president and vice president. *p. 255*

emancipation National or state-sponsored program to free slaves. *p. 437*

Embargo Act of 1807 A law passed by Congress, at the urging of President Thomas Jefferson, to halt the shipment of U.S. goods to Europe in response to British military and naval aggression. *p. 302*

encomienda The Spanish *encomienda* system, imposed in Spain's American empire, requiring Indian communities to supply labor or pay tribute to a local colonial overlord (identified as an *encomendero*). *p. 44*

Entente The alliance of Britain, France, and Russia, later joined by Italy and the United States, during World War I. *p. 622*

Era of Good Feeling A term used by historians to describe the presidency of James Monroe (1816–1820), when partisan tensions eased among voters and their political leaders. *p. 311*

Erie Canal Waterway linking the New York cities of Troy and Albany, on the Hudson River, with Buffalo, on the eastern tip of Lake Erie; in the 1820s, the opening of the Erie Canal revolutionized trading between the Midwest and East Coast and established New York City as the most important financial center in the United States. *p. 332*

established churches Religious denominations that receive special favors, financial or otherwise, from state governments. *p. 282*

family wage A level of income sufficient for an individual worker, usually a man, to support a spouse and family through a single salary. *p. 705*

fascism A form of right-wing dictatorship exalting nation and race above the individual. *p. 715*

Federalists A coalition of nationalist leaders who favored creating a stronger central government to replace the Articles of Confederation in the late 1780s; the strongest essays endorsing their proposed new Constitution were entitled *The Federalist Papers.* *p. 257*

feminism The belief that women and men are of equal value and that gender roles are, to a considerable degree, created by society rather than being simply natural. *p. 839*

flappers Young women in the 1910s and 1920s who rebelled against the gender conventions of the era with respect to fashion and behavior. *p. 651*

flotilla Any sizeable fleet of ships, or, more specifically, a naval term for a unit consisting of two or more squadrons of small warships. *p. 164*

free trade International economic relations characterized by multinational investment and a reduction or elimination of tariffs. *p. 912*

free labor ideology The ideas, represented most forcefully by the antebellum Republican party, that workers should profit from their own labor and that slavery is wrong. *p. 401*

Freedmen's Bureau Federal agency created by Congress in March 1865 and disbanded in 1869. Its purposes were to provide relief for Southerners who had remained loyal to the Union during the Civil War, to support black elementary schools, and to oversee annual labor contracts between landowners and field hands. *p. 460*

Fugitive Slave Act of 1850 Congressional legislation that required local and federal law enforcement agents to retrieve runaways no matter where they sought refuge in the United States. *p. 410*

globalization The process of integration—economic, but also cultural—of different parts of the world into a more unified system of trade and communication. *p. 17*

Grange An organization founded by Oliver H. Kelly in 1867 to represent the interests of farmers by pressing for agricultural cooperatives, an end to railroad freight discrimination against small farmers, and other initiatives. Its full name was National Grange of Patrons of Husbandry. *p. 485*

Great Awakening The interdenominational Christian revival that swept Britain's North American colonies between the 1730s and the 1750s, inspired at first by the preaching of Jonathan Edwards and George Whitefield. *p. 155*

Great Migration The movement of African Americans out of the South to northern cities, particularly during World War I. *p. 635*

Great Society In the 1960s, President Lyndon Johnson's programs for reducing poverty, discrimination, and pollution, and for improving health care, education, and consumer protection. *p. 809*

guerrilla war A conflict fought not on the basis of conventional warfare but by mobilizing small groups of fighters who attack and harass superior forces. *p. 366*

gun control The legal regulation of firearms. *p. 919*

Haymarket bombing A labor protest held in Chicago's Haymarket Square that erupted in violence on May 4, 1886. A bomb blast killed eight people, including several policemen, and the incident marked the decline of the Knights of Labor, associated in the minds of many Americans with violent labor protest. *p. 545*

headright System in which English colonial governments granted a fixed amount of land, usually fifty acres, to any head of household for every family member or hired hand that person brought into the colony. Sometimes fewer acres were granted for women and children on the grounds that they would clear and plant less land. *p. 56*

hobo Migrant worker or poor and homeless vagrant who traveled on trains from location to location, usually in search of employment. *p. 686*

Holocaust The name given to the Nazi genocide against the Jews during World War II. Six million Jews were murdered. *p. 714*

Homestead Act Legislation passed in 1862 that granted 160 acres of land free to each settler who lived on and made improvements to government land for five years. *p. 437*

Hoovervilles   Shantytowns, named for President Hoover and occupied largely by people who lost their homes and farms during the Great Depression. *p. 676*

horticultural   Pertaining to the art and science of growing fruits, vegetables, and ornamental plants. *p. 8*

Iberian   Relating to Europe's Iberian Peninsula, the location of Spain and Portugal. *p. 16*

imperialism   The policy of extending a nation's authority by territorial acquistion (through negotiation or conquest) or by the establishment of political or economic control over other nations. *p. 558*

indenture   A document binding one person to work for another for a given period of time. Indentured servants received food, shelter, and clothing, plus "freedom dues" when their terms of service ended to help them get started independently. *p. 108*

Interstate Commerce Act   Congressional legislation passed in 1887 mandating that railroads charge all shippers the same freight rates and refrain from giving rebates to their largest customers; established the Interstate Commerce Commission to enforce the new legislation and oversee and stabilize the U.S. railroad industry. *p. 521*

Iroquois League   A Native American confederacy, located in central New York, originally composed of the Cayuga, Mohawk, Oneida, Onondaga, and Seneca Indians and later including the Tuscarora. *p. 49*

Islamist   Pertaining to an ideology promoting the creation of governments based on a fundamentalist interpretation of Islamic law. *p. 871*

isthmus   A narrow strip of land connecting two larger land areas (such as the isthmus of Panama). *p. 25*

jihadist   A Muslim engaged in what is seen as holy war in behalf of Islam. *p. 933*

Jim Crow   The name given to the set of legal institutions that ensured the segregation of nonwhite people in the South. *p. 532*

juke joint   A small, inexpensive establishment where patrons could eat and drink or dance to music from a jukebox. *Juke* is a word of West African origin popularized by African Americans in the Sea Islands of South Carolina. *p. 651*

kachina   An Indian religious system, inspired by Mesoamerican traditions, and present in the American Southwest for more than 800 years; the kachina cult used masks for group performances associated with rain, curing, fertility, warfare, and the ancestors. Among many Pueblo and Hopi Indians, this tradition was epitomized by kachina (or katsina) dolls. *p. 44*

Kansas-Nebraska Act   Congressional legislation passed in 1854 that divided Nebraska Territory into two states, Kansas and Nebraska, whose respective voters would decide for themselves whether to allow slavery. A compromise brokered by Senator Stephen Douglas of Illinois, this act angered abolitionists because it repealed the Compromise of 1820, which had banned slavery north of the Missouri Compromise line of 36°30'. *p. 408*

Kentucky and Virginia Resolutions   Resolutions issued by two state legislatures in 1798 in response to the Alien and Sedition Acts passed by Congress; proclaimed that individual states had the right to declare such measures "void and of no force." *p. 271*

Knights of Labor   A secret order founded in 1869 to organize productive people, regardless of their race, religion, sex, ethnicity, or regional affiliation; blended a critique of the late nineteenth-century wage system with the belief in dignity and a call for collective action, especially among workers. Its high point came in 1886 with the organizing of unions, including some that were biracial, throughout the country. *p. 525*

laissez-faire   A belief in little or no government interference in the economy. *p. 517*

League of Nations   International organization founded in 1919 as a forum to resolve conflicts between nations. It was replaced by the United Nations in 1945. *p. 645*

Lecompton Constitution   A Kansas state constitution drawn up by proslavery advocates in 1857; sought to nullify the doctrine of popular sovereignty in the state, decreeing that even if voters rejected slavery, any slaves already in the state would remain enslaved under the force of law. *p. 417*

Lewis and Clark Expedition   A "corps of discovery" commissioned by President Thomas Jefferson in 1804 to explore the newly acquired Louisiana Territory. Led by Meriwether Lewis and William Clark and lasting twenty-eight months, the party reported on an array of subjects, including the cultural practices of western Indians and the natural features of the land, but failed to find a water route that would connect the Pacific Northwest to eastern markets. *p. 298*

manifest destiny   The idea, first promoted in the 1840s, that the United States had a God-given right to expand its territory; used to justify territorial growth, expansion of economic markets, and conquest. *p. 384*

manumission   A formal emancipation from slavery; the act (by an individual owner or government authority) of granting freedom to an enslaved person or persons. *p. 127*

Marbury v. Madison   An 1803 Supreme Court decision establishing the right of the judiciary to declare acts of both the executive and legislative branches unconstitutional. *p. 292*

market revolution   The combined effects of transportation innovation, technological change, and economic growth, especially during the first half of the nineteenth century. *p. 317*

Marshall Plan   U.S. economic assistance to western Europe for rebuilding after World War II, 1948–1952. *p. 756*

McCarthyism   The political campaign led by Senator Joseph McCarthy (R-Wisconsin) to blame liberals at home for setbacks to U.S. interests abroad, due to what he considered liberals' sympathies with communism. *p. 770*

mercantilism   A commercial policy that sought to achieve economic self-sufficiency and a favorable balance of trade (often by planting colonies) in order to promote a country's prosperity, strength, and independence in the seventeenth and eighteenth centuries. *p. 72*

Mesoamerica   The transitional region between North and South America, composed of Mexico and Central America. *p. 8*

mestizo   A person of mixed European and American Indian ancestry. *p. 79*

Mexican Cession   Territory ceded by Mexico to the United States as a result of the 1848 Treaty of Guadalupe Hidalgo; the 530,000 square miles constituted almost half of the territory of Mexico. *p. 395*

middle ground   The geographical region occupied by diverse cultural groups engaged in trade. *p. 276*

middle passage   For European slave ships, the middle passage was the second of three legs in the triangular round-trip voyage from Europe to Africa to America and back to Europe. For enslaved Africans, the middle passage came to mean not only the transatlantic journey itself, but the entire process of removal from an African homeland and ultimate sale to an American master. *p.114*

militarism   A policy of aggressive military preparedness that exalts the use of force as a solution to international problems. *p. 748*

military-industrial complex   The term used by President Dwight D. Eisenhower to describe the military arms industry. *p. 793*

monetary policy   Government policies designed to affect the national economy through bank lending policies, interest rates, and control of the amount of money in circulation. *p. 265*

Monroe Doctrine   Policy announced by President James Monroe in 1823 that the era of European colonization of the Americas had ceased; warned foreign powers, especially Russia, Spain, and Britain, that the United States would not allow them to intervene in the Western Hemisphere. *p. 338*

Morrill Act   Legislation passed by Republican Congress in 1862 to create a system of agricultural (land-grant) public colleges. *p. 437*

most-favored-nation status   A designation allowing countries to export their products to the United States with tariffs no greater than those levied against most other nations. *p. 914*

mulatto   A person of mixed European and African ancestry; the first-generation offspring of a Caucasian and a Negroid parent. *p. 79*

National Labor Union   An alliance of craft unions founded in 1866 to represent the interests of workers, including the eight-hour day and arbitration of industrial disputes. *p. 459*

National Republicans   A political party, led by John Adams in the 1820s, that favored a greater federal role in funding internal improvements and public education; forerunner of the Whigs, formed in opposition to President Andrew Jackson. *p. 338*

national security state   The reorientation of the U.S. government and its budget after 1945 toward a primary focus on military and intelligence capabilities. *p. 764*

National Trades Union   Organization formed in 1834 to help workers gain greater political influence. *p. 375*

nativists   American citizens born in the United States who oppose further immigration, especially from anywhere outside northwestern Europe. *p. 378*

New Deal   Programs President Franklin Delano Roosevelt put together to address the problems of the Great Depression and to provide relief to Americans in need; during his campaign for president, he promised the nation a "new deal." *p. 682*

New Democrats   Members of the Democratic party, many of them organized in the Democratic Leadership Council, who espouse center to center-right policies. *p. 910*

Nisei   Japanese Americans born in the United States of Japanese immigrant parents. *p. 722*

NSC-68   The 1950 directive of the National Security Council that called for rolling back, rather than merely containing, Soviet and communist influences. *p. 764*

nullification   The doctrine that a state has the right to ignore or nullify certain federal laws with which it disagrees. *p. 342*

Okies   Migrants from Oklahoma who left the state during the Dust Bowl period in search of work. *p. 688*

Oregon Trail   A 2,000-mile-long trail used by people from the Midwest to establish new homesteads in the Oregon Territory following the Panic of 1837. *p. 370*

outsourcing   The export of jobs to countries where the cost of labor is cheaper. *p. 899*

pachucos   Young Mexican American men who expressed attitudes of youthful rebellion in the 1940s. Many wore the Zoot Suit, also fashionable among urban African Americans. *p. 737*

Pacific Railroad Act   Legislation that granted to the Union Pacific and the Central Pacific railroads cash subsidies and a 400-foot right of way along the Platte River route of the Oregon Trail. *p. 437*

Paleo-Indians   The earliest human inhabitants of North America, who first migrated to the continent from Siberia more than 15,000 years ago; faced with a warming climate and the disappearance of many large game animals roughly 10,000 years ago (8000 BCE), they learned to hunt smaller animals and adapted to varied local conditions during the Archaic Period (to c. 1000 BCE). *p. 6*

Panic of 1837   Economic crisis and depression caused by a combination of overspeculation—in bridges, canals, and turnpikes—and a large failure of grain crops in the West. *p. 375*

Pendleton Act   Congressional legislation passed in 1883; established a merit system for federal job applicants and created the Civil Service Commission, which administered competitive examinations to candidates in certain job classifications. *p. 520*

pest house   In colonial times, a shelter to quarantine those possibly infected with contagious diseases (such as new-comers arriving in American ports from Africa or Europe) to prevent the spread of shipborne pestilence. *p. 122*

planned obsolescence   A concept whereby producers intend for their products to eventually become obsolete or outdated and require replacement, thus perpetuating a cycle of production and consumption. *p. 665*

Plessy v. Ferguson   The 1896 case in which the Supreme Court decided that states could segregate public accommodations by race. *p. 562*

pocket veto   An indirect veto of a legislative bill made when an executive (such as a president or governor) simply leaves the bill unsigned, so that it dies after the adjournment of the legislature. *p. 460*

political machine   A group that effectively exercises control over a political party, usually at the local level and organized around precincts and patronage. *p. 653*

popular sovereignty   The idea that residents of a state should be able to make decisions on crucial issues, such as whether or not to legalize slavery. *p. 410*

Populists   Agrarian reformers who formed the Populist, or People's party, a major (third) political party that emerged mostly in the Midwest and South in the late 1880s to address the needs of workers and farmers in opposition to government monetary policies and big business. The party faltered after its presidential candidate, William Jennings Bryan, lost in the 1896 election. *p. 537*

presidio   A military garrison in an area under Spanish control. *p. 173*

privateer   A ship (or a crew member) licensed to harass enemy shipping in wartime. *p. 95*

producer economy   An economic system dominated by individuals who are self-producers of manufactured goods and foodstuffs rather than employees working for wages. *p. 651*

Progressivism   A notion of political reform central to the "Progressive Era" (the first two decades of the twentieth century), when urban reformers with a faith in progress sought to address local and national social problems through political and civic means. *p. 591*

quitrent   A fixed rent paid annually by a tenant to a proprietor or landowner. *p. 86*

race suicide   A fear articulated by Theodore Roosevelt and others that the low birthrate of Anglo-Saxon Americans, along with the high birthrate of immigrants from southern and eastern Europe and elsewhere, would result in a population in which "inferior" peoples would outnumber the "American racial stock." *p. 615*

Real Whigs   Radical theorists in eighteenth-century England who stressed that power corrupts and criticized mainstream Whig views of "balanced" government; their calls for vigilance and virtue among citizens won favor in the American colonies. *p. 183*

Reconstruction era   The twelve years after the Civil War when the U.S. government took steps to integrate the eleven states of the Confederacy back into the Union. *p. 459*

redemption system   An eighteenth-century arrangement in which potential migrants in Europe signed up with an agent who agreed to pay for their Atlantic passage. Reaching America, the newcomer signed a pact to work for several years for an employer. In exchange for much-needed labor, the employer agreed to pay back the shipper, "redeeming" the original loan that had been made to the immigrant "redemptioner." *p. 144*

red lining   A business practice in which lending institutions deny credit to racial or ethnic minorities who live in poor neighborhoods. *p. 782*

Red Scare   Post–World War I repression of socialists, communists, and other left-wing radicals ("Reds"). *p. 648*

regressive tax   A tax that decreases in rate as the base increases, so that someone with a large holding pays a relatively small amount. A fixed tax of $100 is regressive, since persons with $1,000 or $1 million shoulder very different relative burdens. This is the opposite of a progressive tax, where those with less pay at a lower rate. *p. 185*

Regulators   In the 1760s, owners of small farms in North Carolina's Piedmont, lacking adequate political representation in the colony, banded together to protect their interests, oppose unjust taxes, and "regulate" their common affairs. *p. 185*

Republican mother   A wife and mother whose primary role is caring for and socializing future citizens (her children); an ideal favored by some elites after the American Revolution. *p. 285*

Republican party   Founded in 1854, this political party began as a coalition of Northerners who opposed the extension of slavery into the western territories. *p. 413*

rescate   In the colonial Southwest, the organized process of tribute in which Spaniards paid a ransom to Indians for the release of captives that one tribe had taken from another. The ransomed Indians often became Christians working as servants in Spanish households. Some captives were Hispanic settlers captured in raids. *p. 140*

Restoration   Period beginning in 1660, when Charles II became king, restoring the British monarchy after the brief experiment of the Puritan Commonwealth, until the end of the Stuart family dynasty in 1688. *p. 83*

rogue nations   A label used by the U.S. government to refer to nations it considers hostile, unpredictable, and potentially dangerous. *p. 924*

Rosie the Riveter   A heroic symbol of women workers on the homefront during World War II. *p. 733*

sachem   Algonquin Indian term for a Native American leader or chief. *p. 88*

scalawag   A negative term applied by southern Democrats after the Civil War to any white Southerner who allied with the Republican party. *p. 463*

Second Great Awakening A series of Protestant religious revivals that began in the 1790s and continued through the 1820s. Prominent revivalists such as Charles Grandison Finney sought to link the life of the spirit with political action and reform efforts. *p. 353*

Second New Deal The agenda of policies and programs initiated by President Franklin Delano Roosevelt beginning in 1935 that was intended to strengthen the lot of American workers while simultaneously preserving the capitalist system. *p. 696*

sectionalism Intense political conflict between North and South in the nineteenth-century United States. *p. 311*

separation of powers The constitutional doctrine upholding the independence of each of the three branches of the federal government: executive (president), legislative (Congress), and judicial (Supreme Court). *p. 254*

Sherman Anti-Trust Act Congressional legislation passed in 1890 outlawing trusts and large business combinations. *p. 522*

sit-down strike A strategy employed by workers agitating for better wages and working conditions in which they stop working and simply sit down, thus ceasing production and preventing strikebreakers from entering a facility to assume their jobs. *p. 707*

sit-in A form of civil disobedience in which activists sit down somewhere in violation of law or policy in order to challenge discriminatory practices or laws. The tactic originated during labor struggles in the 1930s and was used effectively in the civil rights movement in 1960. *p. 792*

Social Darwinism A late nineteenth-century variation on the theories of British naturalist Charles Darwin, promoting the idea that only the "fittest" individuals will, or deserve to, survive (i.e., the idea that society operates on principles of evolutionary biology). *p. 522*

Social Gospel A reform movement around the end of the twentieth century that stressed the responsibility of religious organizations to remedy a wide range of social ills related to urban life. *p. 551*

social stratification The schematic arrangement of a population into a ranking of horizontal of social layers (strata), or an identifiable hierarchy of classes within a society. *p. 11*

socialism A form of government in which the means of production are owned collectively and managed by the state. *p. 542*

Sons of Liberty Secret societies of American colonists that successfully resisted Parliament's 1765 Stamp Act; their agitations continued over the ensuing decade. *p. 180*

speakeasies Establishments where alcohol was illegally sold during the Prohibition era. *p. 654*

suffrage The right to vote. *p. 254*

Sunbelt The band of states from the Southeast to the Southwest that experienced rapid economic and population growth during and after World War II. *p. 769*

tariff A government tax on imported goods. *p. 265*

Tejanos Spanish-speaking residents of the Mexican state of Texas. Today many Mexican Americans in Texas refer to themselves as Tejanos as a point of cultural and state pride. *p. 335*

temperance A social movement embracing either total opposition to alcohol consumption or support for its moderate use. *p. 240*

tenant farmer A farmer who pays a landowner for use of the land in cash or with a share of the crop. In the South, tenant farmers often owned their own mules (for plowing), in contrast to sharecroppers, who did not. *p. 400*

Texians The name used by Euro-Americans who lived in the Mexican state of Texas. *p. 335*

theocracy A government by officials who are regarded as divinely guided. *p. 870*

three-fifths clause The policy asserted in Article I, section 2, of the U.S. Constitution that in apportioning representatives and direct taxes among the states according to population, each slave would count as "three fifths of all other Persons." Section 2 of the Fourteenth Amendment (1868) did away with the three-fifths clause. *p. 256*

tithe A levy or donation (generally a tenth part) given to provide support, usually for a church. *p. 31*

total war The attacking of both military and civilian targets. *p. 725*

Townsend Plan A proposal by Dr. Francis Townsend in 1934 for a 2 percent national sales tax that would fund a guaranteed pension of $200 per month for Americans older than age 60. *p. 701*

Trail of Tears The name Cherokee Indians gave to their forced removal from the Southeast to the West in 1838 and 1839 as part of the federal government's Indian removal policy. During the journey, U.S. troops destroyed the material basis of Cherokee culture and separated many families; over 4,000 Indians died. *p. 367*

Treaty of Ghent Peace treaty signed by the United States and Great Britain in 1815, ending the War of 1812. *p. 310*

trickle-down economics An economic concept whereby the government aids the wealthiest strata as well as large corporations in the belief that the benefits of this aid will "trickle down" to the middle and lower classes. *p. 659*

Truman Doctrine President Truman's policy of containment, articulated in a March 1947 speech. *p. 756*

trusts A combination of firms or corporations created for the purpose of reducing competition and controlling prices throughout an industry. *p. 500*

Underground Railroad A secret network of abolitionists developed during the antebellum period to help slaves escape and find refuge, many in the North or in Canada. *p. 410*

unicameral legislature A legislative body that has only one chamber, or house. *p. 86*

utopian Relating to communities organized to strive for ideal social and political conditions; utopians intend that their communities should serve as a model to the larger society. *p. 382*

Victorianism   Middle-class, chiefly Protestant, ideology popular during the reign of Britain's Queen Victoria (1837–1901). Victorians professed social values such as self-control, sexual restraint, and personal ambition. *p. 356*

war hawks   Politicians who favor specific forms of military action as a tool of U.S. foreign policy. *p. 303*

War of 1812   A military and naval conflict that pitted U.S. forces against the British and their Indian allies. The end of the war eliminated the post-Revolutionary British threat to U.S. sovereignty. *p. 305*

war on drugs   The global campaign spearheaded by the federal government to eliminate the production of illegal drugs and their importation into the United States, and its domestic counterpart in which drug violations are treated harshly by the legal and criminal justice system. *p. 902*

Watergate   The Washington, D.C., hotel-office complex where agents of President Nixon's reelection campaign broke into Democratic party headquarters in 1972; Nixon helped cover up the break-in, and the subsequent political scandal was called "Watergate." *p. 842*

welfare reform   The legislative campaign in the 1960s through the 1990s to abolish Aid to Families with Dependent Children in favor of a program that sets limits on the amount of time a poor family can receive government aid (culminating in the Temporary Aid to Needy Families Act of 1996). *p. 912*

welfare state   A nation in which the government provides a "safety net" of entitlements and benefits for citizens unable to economically provide for themselves. *p. 683*

Whigs   A national political party formed in 1834 in opposition to the presidency of Andrew Jackson and his policy of expanding the power of the president. The Whigs favored congressional funding for internal improvements and other forms of federal support for economic development. *p. 344*

Whiskey Rebellion   Protest in 1794 by western Pennsylvania farmers and grain distillers who objected to a high federal tax on the whiskey they produced. *p. 268*

Wobblies   Members of the Industrial Workers of the World (IWW), a radical labor union formed in 1905. *p. 611*

yellow journalism   Newspaper articles, images, and editorials that exploit, distort, or exaggerate the news in order to inflame public opinion. *p. 579*

Part Opener 1
Page 2: Laurie Platt Winfrey, Inc.

Chapter 1
Page 8: Lee Boltin Picture Library
Page 17: (Top) © Charles E. Rotkin/CORBIS
Page 17: (Bottom) Museum of the History of Science, Oxford, Oxfordshire, UK/Bridgeman Art Library
Page 18: Topkapi Serail-Museum/AKG Photo
Page 36: Courtesy of Map Collection, Yale University Library
Page 38: (Top) © Charles E. Ratkin/CORBIS
Page 38: (Center) Courtesy Map Collection, Yale University Library
Page 38: (Bottom) Lee Boltin Picture Library

Chapter 2
Page 39: Leonard Harris/Stock, Boston, Inc.
Page 41: Courtesy of the John Carter Brown Library at Brown University
Page 50: Harry Engels/Photo Researchers, Inc.
Page 67: The Granger Collection, New York
Page 68: (Top) The Granger Collection, New York
Page 68: (Bottom) Leonard Harris/Stock, Boston, Inc.

Chapter 3
Page 72: Réunion des Musées Nationaux/Art Resource, NY
Page 75: Courtesy Texas A & M University, Nautical Archaeology
Page 76: (Bottom) Thaw Collection, Fenimore Art Museum, Cooperstown, NY
Page 76: William L. Clements Library, University of Michigan
Page 99: (Bottom) © Copyright theTrustees of the British Museum
Page 100: Thaw Collection, Fenimore Art Museum, Cooperstown, NY

Part Opener 2
Page 102: The Menil Collection, Houston

Chapter 4
Page 104: Voyage Pittoresque dans le Bresil, Rugendas plate 10, 2nd part. The Newberry Library, Chicago
Page 106: (Top) © Copyright the Trustees of the British Museum (1982,1-12.1)
Page 109: Albert and Shirley Small Special Collections Library, University of Virginia
Page 110: Chicago Historical Society, ICHi-x.1354
Page 124: (Bottom) Museum Volkenkunde, Leiden, The Netherlands (360-5696)
Page 134: (Top) Voyage Pittoresque dans le Bresil, Rugendas plate 10, 2nd part. The Newberry Library, Chicago
Page 134: (Bottom) Chicago Historical Society, ICHi-x.1354

Chapter 5
Page 139: (Bottom) Charm, c. 1870, Potawatomi, Founders Society Purchase. Photograph ©1992 The Detroit Institute of Arts (81.614)
Page 153: © Science Museum Pictorial/Science & Society Picture Library, London
Page 154: Gustavus Hesselius, "Tishcohan," 1735. Courtesy of the Historical Society of Pennsylvania (HSP) Collection, Atwater Kent Museum of Philadelphia.
Page 158: Attributed to Mary Leverett Denison Rogers, "Harvard Hall." Courtesy of the Massachusetts Historical Society, MHS #427
Page 163: © Pat & Chuck Blackeley
Page 166: (Top) Gustavus Hesselius, "Tishcohan," 1735. Courtesy of the Historical Society of Pennsylvania (HSP) Collection, Atwater Kent Museum of Philadelphia (1834.1).

Chapter 6
Page 167: Courtesy, American Antiquarian Society
Page 169: Hunterian Museum and Art Gallery, University of Glasgow
Page 182: Peabody Essex Museum. Photograph by Mark Sexton
Page 196: (Top) Peabody Essex Museum. Photograph by Mark Sexton
Page 196: (Bottom) Courtesy, American Antiquarian Society

Chapter 7
Page 203: Henry Gray, "The Morning After the Attack on Sullivan's Island, June 1776." Gibbes Museum of Art/Carolina Art Association, 1907.002.0001
Page 207: The Library of Congress
Page 213: Collection of the Museum of Early Southern Decorative Arts, Old Salem Museum and Gardens (Acc. #3119)
Page 218: The Library of Congress
Page 230: Chicago Historical Society, ICHi-x.1937.36
Page 232: (Top) "Old Salem Inc.; Collection of the Museum of Early Southern Decorative Arts" (Acc. #3119)
Page 232: (Bottom) The Library of Congress

Chapter 8
Page 233: CORBIS
Page 238: Courtesy of the American Numismatic Society
Page 250: Anchorage Museum of History and Art (4.81.68.9)
Page 256: Susan Anne Livingston Ridley Sedgwick, "Elizabeth 'Mumbet' Freeman," 1842. Courtesy of the Massachusetts Historical Society (MHS image #0028)
Page 260: Abby Aldrich Rockefeller Folk Art Museum, Williamsburg, VA, Colonial Williamsburg Foundation, (Acc. #1935.301.4 [slide 1989-173])
Page 261: (Top) Courtesy of the American Numismatic Society
Page 261: (Bottom) Abby Aldrich Rockefeller Folk Art Museum, Williamsburg, VA, Colonial Williamsburg Foundation, (Acc. #1935.301.4 [slide 1989-173])

Chapter 9
Page 262: Courtesy of Florida Stage. Photograph by Susan Lerner.
Page 267: (Top) Paul Rocheleau Photography
Page 267: (Bottom) The National Archives
Page 276: Gilbert Stuart, "Joseph Brant," 1786. Fenimore Art Museum, Cooperstown, New York (N-199.61). Photo by Richard Walker
Page 293: (Top) The National Archives
Page 293: (Bottom) Gilbert Stuart, "Joseph Brant," 1786. Fenimore Art Museum, Cooperstown, New York (N-199.61). Photo by Richard Walker

Part Opener 4
Page 296: Smithsonian Institution, American Art Museum/Art Resource, NY

Chapter 10
Page 302: Courtesy, JPMorgan Chase Archives (NEG #1077-26-1)
Page 307: The Library of Congress
Page 314: (Bottom) Museum of Spanish Colonial Art, Collections of the Spanish Colonial Arts Society, Inc., Santa Fe, NM. Bequest of Alan and Ann Vedder. Photograph by Jack Parsons
Page 315: The Granger Collection, New York
Page 325: William Clark, "Eulachon (T. Pacificus)," 1806, Voorhis Journal #2. William Clark Papers, Missouri Historical Society Archives

Part Opener 8

0678 Joe Jones, "We Demand," 1934. Gift of Sidney Freedman, 1948. The Butler Institute of American Art, Youngstown, Ohio (948-0-110)

Chapter 22

Page 680: The Library of Congress
Page 696: Collection of David J. and Janice L. Frent
Page 707: Kobal Collection/United Artists
Page 710: Photofest
Page 712: (Top) Collection of David J. and Janice L. Frent
Page 712: (Bottom) Kobal Collection/United Artists

Chapter 23

Page 723: Gift of Mr. and Mrs. Jim Kawaminami, Japanese American National Museum. Photo by Norman Sugimoto
Page 731: The National Archives
Page 734: (Bottom) The National Archives
Page 744: (Top) Gift of Mr. and Mrs. Jim Kawaminami, Japanese American National Museum. Photo by Norman Sugimoto
Page 744: (Bottom) Harry S. Truman Presidential Library

Chapter 24

Page 745: The National Archives
Page 756: (Top) Joseph Sohm; ChromoSohm Inc./CORBIS
Page 756: (Bottom) Cathy Crawford/CORBIS
Page 757: Harry S. Truman Presidential Library
Page 760: Photofest
Page 761: ChinaStock
Page 773: (Top) Cathy Crawford/CORBIS
Page 773: (Bottom) Joseph Sohm; ChromoSohm Inc./CORBIS

Part Opener 9

Page 774: Ernest Crichlow, "By the Gate," 1953. The Harmon and Harriet Kelley Foundation for the Arts.

Chapter 25

Page 779: Library of Congress
Page 793: Collection of David J. and Janice L. Frent
Page 806: (Top) The Library of Congress
Page 806: (Bottom) The Library of Congress

Chapter 26

Page 813: Collection of David J. and Janice L. Frent
Page 822: John Launois/Stock Photo

Page 826: (Bottom) The Library of Congress
Page 827: © Copyright The Andy Warhol Foundation for the Visual Arts/ARS, NY/Art Resource, NY
Page 837: (Top) Collection of David J. and Janice L. Frent
Page 837: (Bottom) Courtesy, National Aeronautics and Space Administration

Chapter 27

Page 839: Courtesy of Emily Warner and Colorado Womens' Hall of Fame
Page 841: Collection of David J. and Janice L. Frent
Page 853: (left) Collection of David J. and Janice L. Frent
Page 853: (right) Collection of David J. and Janice L. Frent
Page 860: John S. Zeedick/AP/Wide World
Page 865: (Top) Collection of David J. and Janice L. Frent
Page 865: (Bottom) Time & Life Pictures/Getty Images

Part Opener 10

Page 866: Nam June Paik, "Global Encoder," 1994. Courtesy of Nam June Paik and Carl Solway Gallery, Cincinnati, Ohio. Photo by Tom Allison and Chris Gomien

Chapter 28

Page 873: Photofest
Page 878: (Bottom) Vladimir Sichov/Sipa Press
Page 879: Superstock
Page 880: Ted Thai/Sygma/CORBIS
Page 897: (Top) Bettmann/CORBIS
Page 897: (Bottom) Photofest

Chapter 29

Page 898: OutlineLive/CORBIS
Page 901: W. Cody/CORBIS
Page 904: (Bottom) Walker Shaun/SIPA Press
Page 920: (Top) James Keyser/Getty Images
0923 Amy E. Conn/AP/Wide World Photos

Chapter 30

Page 930: Time & Life Pictures/Getty Images
Page 952: AP/Wide World
Page 953: Getty Images
Page 954: Stockphoto
Page 955: Time & Life Pictures/Getty Images